The Palgrave Handbook of Management History

Bradley Bowden • Jeffrey Muldoon •
Anthony M. Gould • Adela J. McMurray
Editors

The Palgrave Handbook of Management History

Volume 1

With 65 Figures and 6 Tables

Editors
Bradley Bowden
Griffith University
Nathan, QLD, Australia

Jeffrey Muldoon
Emporia State University
Emporia, KS, USA

Anthony M. Gould
Département des relations industrielles
Université Laval
Québec, QC, Canada

Adela J. McMurray
School of Management
RMIT University
Melbourne, VIC, Australia

ISBN 978-3-319-62113-5   ISBN 978-3-319-62114-2 (eBook)
ISBN 978-3-319-62115-9 (print and electronic bundle)
https://doi.org/10.1007/978-3-319-62114-2

© Springer Nature Switzerland AG 2020
This work is subject to copyright. All rights are reserved by the Publisher, whether the whole or part of the
material is concerned, specifically the rights of translation, reprinting, reuse of illustrations, recitation,
broadcasting, reproduction on microfilms or in any other physical way, and transmission or information
storage and retrieval, electronic adaptation, computer software, or by similar or dissimilar methodology
now known or hereafter developed.
The use of general descriptive names, registered names, trademarks, service marks, etc. in this publication
does not imply, even in the absence of a specific statement, that such names are exempt from the relevant
protective laws and regulations and therefore free for general use.
The publisher, the authors, and the editors are safe to assume that the advice and information in this book
are believed to be true and accurate at the date of publication. Neither the publisher nor the authors or the
editors give a warranty, expressed or implied, with respect to the material contained herein or for any errors
or omissions that may have been made. The publisher remains neutral with regard to jurisdictional claims
in published maps and institutional affiliations.

This Palgrave Macmillan imprint is published by the registered company Springer Nature Switzerland AG.
The registered company address is: Gewerbestrasse 11, 6330 Cham, Switzerland

This book is dedicated to the founding figures of management history:
- *Sidney Pollard (1925–1998)*
- *Dan Wren (1932–)*
- *Art Bedeian (1946–)*

As management historians, we stand on the shoulders of giants.

Preface

The *Palgrave Handbook of Management History* is going to press in a time of crisis as the effects of the Coronavirus and its aftermath cause the most profound economic, social, and managerial challenge since World War II. For a management historian who has a profound faith in the extraordinary resilience and strength of liberal, democratic free-market societies, this crisis brings to the fore the most fundamental issues of management – how do societies innovate, create value and wealth, provide sustainable employment, and raise the living standards of the ordinary citizen? In recent times, these issues – which have remained *the* fundamental challenges of *every* society – have taken second place behind concerns as to the environment, inequality, and the detrimental effects of globalization. As we move forward out of this crisis, these secondary problems still deserve attention, most particularly those relating to the detrimental effects of globalization, a process of economic integration that has stripped too many societies of their painfully constructed manufacturing capabilities, managerial expertise, labor skills, and employment opportunities. However, as we move forward, we need to remind ourselves of the gains that have been made across the decades and centuries rather than sink into a misinformed state of despair. On almost every front, the world is better placed to handle economic, social, and medical crises than what it was even 30 years ago. On every front, gains have been extraordinary. Poverty has been curtailed in every region on the planet. Literacy and education have increased massively. The supportive structures of the state in terms of welfare programs, medical advances, and educational experiences now provide a far more significant safety net than that which existed 30 or 40 years ago. In the USA, for example, in 2019 the *percentage* of Gross Domestic Product spent on social support services (e.g., education, health, welfare, etc.) was double what it was in 1960 and 50% higher than what it was in 1990 (OECD 2019). In absolute terms, the gains have been even more significant, given the massive increases in the American economy's overall capacity.

In considering the problems and possibilities before us, we need to remind ourselves how management has become one of the central institutions of modern civilisation. Whereas once the world of business was dominated by the activities of small-scale, family-owned enterprises, today the bulk of the goods and services produced within market economies are generated by corporate entities, each staffed by a bevy of managers and associated professionals (e.g., accountants, human resource staff, marketing and information technology personnel, etc.). Yes, it is true that small-scale entrepreneurs and start-ups still generate much of a modern economy's innovative drive, inventing new technologies and more efficient work practices. It is also true that small firms have similar managerial problems to large ones: they need to marshal resources effectively, motivate staff, and sell into competitive markets. Increasingly, however, innovation is only economically meaningful to the extent that new ideas are taken up by corporate behemoths and transformed into goods and services produced *en masse*. Numerically as well as economically, small-scale entrepreneurs find themselves overshadowed by an ever-growing class of professional managers. An Organisation for Economic Co-operation and Development (OECD) survey, for example, estimated that in 2014 only 15.8% of OECD labor force participants were self-employed. In 26 of the 37 OECD countries, moreover, self-employment declined between 2000 and 2014, often by significant margins (Peetz 2019: 163–164). In the case of the USA, labor force statistics suggest that only 10% of the workfroce were self-employed in 2014 (Desilver 2019). By contrast, the most recent US labor force statistics indicate that 11.38% of the workforce, some 14.8 million people, were employed in "management occupations." If we extend our estimates to include those in associated "business and financial occupations" the figure grows to 22 million, or 14.8% of the labor force (United States Bureau of Labor Statistics 2020).

The extraordinary rise of management as a profession and a discipline confronts us with fundamental questions that are central to the modern experience. What is management and in what ways do modern forms of management – as found in democratic market societies – differ from those found in both pre-industrial and totalitarian societies, if indeed there is a difference at all? Is the advance of modern forms of management a positive or negative historical phenomenon? Do the forms of management that emerged in the North Atlantic littoral during the eighteenth and nineteenth centuries have a universal application? Has there been a convergence or a divergence of global managerial practices across the last 50–100 years? It is to these questions that the *Palgrave Handbook of Management History* speaks.

In both the opening chapter (1, "Management History in the Modern World") and the introductory section of the *Handbook* (What is Management and Management History), we begin our exploration of these questions with a consideration of the deep divides that now characterize management history, a battle that has seen understandings of management itself become contested terrain. In reflecting upon current divisions within the discipline in our opening section, my Co-Editor, Jeffrey Muldoon (Chap. 5, "Conflicting Visions: A Recap About the Debates Within Management History"), makes a noteworthy point that I can only but endorse:

> My perception is that the field is very different from the one I entered into about 10 years ago. In some ways, the field is worse. Although the Journal of Management History remains a well-regarded journal, we no longer see history articles published in higher-level journals such as the Journal of Management. Although we have new perceptions, the clarity and precision that I believe characterized the field during the period of ascendancy and domination by the University of Oklahoma (Dan Wren) and the Louisiana State University ascendancy is increasingly gone. Yet, at the same time, we also have witnessed increased debates that are furthering the field. No matter one's perspective, these current debates about

traditional history versus the new postmodernist history can only benefit the field, as it moves us beyond single studies with little connection to each other to rigorous debates that may advance the discipline. Although I am a critic of much of the new history, I am respectful of the talents of the postmodernist side, their intellectual contributions, and mostly, because it is inspiring debate.

As I observe in the *Handbook*'s introductory Chap. 1, "Management History in the Modern World: An Overview," the contested field of management history today witnesses three different understandings of not only management but also its historical evolution. Long dominant is the tradition to which Muldoon is a proud exponent, one historically associated with the Management History Division of the Academy of Management in general and Dan Wren (University of Oklahoma) and Art Bedeian (Louisiana State University) in particular. Unabashed enthusiasts for free market capitalism, this US tradition has been primarily concerned with the ideas that have shaped management and how management has dealt with human problems of alienation and disengagement even as it pursued greater efficiencies. Existing alongside this American tradition is another school of thought of equally long standing, one associated with the Austrian-born English management historian Sidney Pollard – a tradition to which I subscribe. Although the differences between the American and Pollardian traditions are modest in the broad scheme of things, Pollard differed from his US counterparts in placing greater emphasis on the rupture that occurred in managerial practices with the Industrial Revolution. In Pollard's opinion, any resemblance between pre-industrial and modern forms of management – as they exist in market economies – are more apparent than real. As Pollard (1965: 7) explained it, modern managers are "unlike the builders of the pyramids" in that they have to "not only show absolute results in terms of certain products of their efforts, but to relate them to costs, and sell them competitively." Long ascendant, both the American and Pollardian traditions of management history are now under challenge from a new "critical" or "postmodernist" tradition that perceives management in universally hostile terms, as a source of oppression and degradation. As Roy Jacques and Gabrielle Durepos (2015: 101) expressed it in the *Routledge Companion to Management and Organizational History*, management "emerges from several major forces related to American industrialization beginning in the 1870s and largely completed by 1920"; changes initially associated with "an American 'Reign of Terror'" during the late nineteenth century, a time when capitalism and management "effectively silences the fight that was going on between labour and employers for authority within the factory." The problem with "management history," Jacques and Durepos (2015: 102) continue, is that "stories" about worker experiences from outside management "disciplines" (i.e., labor history, sociology, etc.) have typically been ignored by management history – a point that has undoubted merit.

In essence, the first half of the *Palgrave Handbook of Management History* is largely theoretical in purpose, as we explore both the debates that currently define the field *and* the historical origin of the concepts and understandings that underpin these debates. It is with these debates that we begin the *Handbook* with our first section,

What is Management and Management History? Edited by Jeffrey Muldoon, this section begins with a discussion as to the nature of management and concludes with Muldoon's Chap. 5, "Conflicting Visions: a Recap About the Debates Within Management History."

Although the first half of the *Handbook* is largely theoretical in nature, we would be negligent in our duties if we failed to locate current debates and understandings within a long-term perspective. This explanation necessarily entails two interrelated but distinct undertakings. One involves an exploration of the deep intellectual and organizational roots of management in the human experience. The other is an examination of the rupture that I believe occurred in managerial and work practices during the closing decades of the eighteenth century and the opening decades of the nineteenth century in the economies located around the North Atlantic littoral. It is to this issue that we turn in the *Handbook's* second part: Work, Management, and Economic Organization in the Pre-modern World. In doing so, this part emphasizes rather than downplays the transformation that occurred during the Industrial Revolution. In terms of transport, for example, the tonnage of a single modern bulk freighter easily surpasses that put to sea by the *combined* fleets of Genoa and Venice in the thirteenth century – fleets whose size and complexity were among the wonders of the late medieval world. In such circumstances, long-distance maritime trade was largely restricted to luxury items of high value (silks, spices, dyed woolen cloth, etc.) and durable necessities (grain, timber, wine). On land, transport problems were even more apparent. Only items of considerable value would bear the cost of transport that exceeded ten miles or more, an outcome that restricted the great bulk of pre-industrial production to strictly local needs. In turn, the gearing of production to local wants curtailed the need for innovation. Everywhere in the pre-modern world, a lack of smelted metal – which only became a common commodity from the 1780s – resulted in "capital" goods lacking in durability. In the absence of durable capital goods, productivity remained low. Across the globe, every society found itself bound within a Malthusian trap, a world in which temporary gains in population and output invariably hit what appeared an unbreakable resource ceiling. Even in England, the most dynamic European society, per capita living standards in the early 1700s were little different to those experienced in the early 1300s (Phelps Brown and Hopkins 1956). The Industrial Revolution thus heralded more than a new age of managerial endeavor. It also marked the dawn of a new era in the human experience, one where material plenty rather than privation became the lived experience of the typical citizen.

Both the Industrial Revolution and the revolution in ideas that preceded it (the European Enlightenment) entailed new ways in looking at the world, a transformation associated with not only new intellectual concepts but also new intellectual disciplines: most notably economics and management. Accordingly, in the third part of the *Handbook* (The Foundations of Knowledge and Management: An Introduction), Kaylee Boccalatte and I explore the epistemological and economic understandings that came to define the modern world. In doing so, we also investigate the oppositional currents – some grounded in socialism and Marxism and others in English Romanticism and German and Italian philosophic idealism – that emerged in contradiction to these dominant understandings. Following on from this, my fellow Editor, Jeffrey Muldoon, examines how the discipline of management emerged in the century and a half prior to World War II in a section entitled The Classic Age of Management Thought: Mid-nineteenth Century Until 1939. In this part, Muldoon investigates, among other things, the intellectual and practical contributions of Frederick Taylor, Henry Ford, Elton Mayo, Kurt Lewin, and those associated with Britain's Tavistock School, contributions that remain seminal not only to the managerial endeavors of the modern world but also to the disciplines of management, management history and organizational psychology. In the Handbook's fifth section, Postmodernism, I conclude the first half of the *Palgrave Handbook of Management History* by returning to the debates that currently divide management history through an exploration of the lives, ideas, and intellectual influence of the three most significant postmodernist thinkers: Jacques Derrida, Michel Foucault, and Hayden White. In considering the ideas of these three philosophers as well as postmodernism more generally, it is argued (Chap. 27, "Postmodernism: An Introduction" by Bowden) that "In the final analysis ... the fundamental differences between post-modernist and non-postmodernist historians revolves more around different understandings of freedom rather than different epistemologies." As disciples of Friedrich Nietzsche, Martin Heidegger, or Benedetto Croce, leading postmodernist philosophers have advocated a complete freedom of individual will and being. In considering this call for absolute freedom, I echo Albert Camus's (1951/1978: 296–297) belief that absolute freedom is always tyrannical, just as absolute virtue is always homicidal.

In the second volume of the *Palgrave Handbook of Management History,* we move from a consideration of the theoretical principles and debates that have both underpinned and divided management history to an estimation of how management has developed since World War II and how managerial practices have manifested themselves in various geographical locations. In the first section of this half of the Handbook, entitled Management in the Age of Prosperity, 1940s to 1980, Kevin Tennent has brought together seven chapters, penned by nine authors, covering themes such as Keynesianism, Peter Drucker, Michael Porter, Alfred Chandler, industrial relations, the rise of marketing and organizational psychology, as well as British management more generally. In summing up the transformation that occurred between 1945 and 1980, Tennent (Chap. 32, "Management in the Age of Prosperity, c. 1940–1990: Section Introduction") makes the pertinent point that these years represented a,

> ... third era of globalization, with an increasing emphasis on cross border trade in intermediate products and horizontal FDI with the expansion of multinational enterprises across borders, in the capitalist world at least. This impetus created new opportunities for managers and the overarching ideology of managerialism based around the planning and coordination of economic activity by dispassionate administrators, people who were ideally separated from the ownership of capital.

The post-1945 transformation in managerial ideas and practices is continued in Anthony Gould's section, Management in an Age of Crisis, which brings together seven single-authored chapters. In introducing this section, Gould (Chap. 40,

"Introduction: Public Policy Failure, the Demise of Experts, and the Dawn of a New Era") speaks to the central dilemmas of the modern world, observing how

> The story of the 45th U.S President's political ascendancy embodies the paradox of the last 50 years. Experts have let down the public... they have often been wrong ... Wallowing in the intellectual debris of post-industrialism, more experts used more theory and logic to misread who was to be the President of the United States in 2016 ... the decimated middle-class and those worse-off ... were fed-up with the experts, and not without justification. A new and dystopic era had emerged. It was post-neoliberalism – post-industrialism.

In the final two sections of the *Palgrave Handbook of Management History,* we turn our attention towards a consideration of how management has manifested itself geographically. In doing so, the question that we have constantly before us is the following: are we witnessing at a national or a regional level a continued application of Western models of management that largely emerged from the Anglosphere, or are we now witnessing something fundamentally different in Asia, Africa, Latin America, and Continental Europe? In short, has there been a convergence or divergence of managerial practices? To answer this fundamental question our pen-ultimate section – Different Experiences: Europe, Africa, and the Middle East – examines the history of management in Africa (four chapters), the Middle East (one chapter), and Europe (chapters on France, Denmark, and the Orthodox East, i.e., Byzantium and Russia). In summary, this section points to the following conclusion: that in Africa and the Middle East, a Western model of capitalism and management has prevailed within the formal economy, as it has continued to do in Western Europe. By contrast, the historical experiences of Byzantium and Russia – each of which acted as the militarized eastern sentinels of European culture – proved infertile soil for Western models of capitalism and management. In our final section, we continue this geographical exploration through a consideration of the experiences of India, China (two chapters), Latin America, Australia, and New Zealand as well as Asia more generally. In doing so, we are led towards similar conclusions to that found in our penultimate section, namely that a Western model of capitalism and management has largely prevailed. The key exception to this rule, we suggest, has been China. As Elly Leung's (Chaps. 59, "The Making of a Docile Working Class in Pre-reform China," and 60, "Governmentality and the Chinese Workers in China's Contemporary Thought Management System") two chapters indicate, in China a new system of social and workplace despotism has emerged, a system of oppression based upon a fusion of traditional confucian beliefs and an updated variation of Mao Zedong's model of Marxism. Achieving extraordinary economic successes in the closing decades of the twentieth century and the opening decades of the twenty-first century, the long-term viability of this peculiar Chinese system of management now appears questionable. As mass uprisings in Hong Kong have indicated, Western models of freedom are hardly alien to modern Chinese aspiration. Such outcomes point to the fact that the Western model of management has been successful in large part because it has been associated with individual freedom. As Sidney Pollard (1965: 6–7) observed in *The Genesis of Modern Management,* "the absence of legal enforcement of unfree work was not only one of the marked characteristics of the new capitalism, but one of its seminal ideas, underlying its ultimate power to create a more civilized society."

In exploring the genesis and history of management the *Palgrave Handbook of Management History* owes a debt to many people, most particularly to the 27 authors who have contributed to our 63 chapters. A special debt is owed to our Section Editors, most particularly Kevin Tennent (University of York, UK), Anthony Gould (Laval University, Quebec), and Jeffrey Muldoon (Emporia State University, USA). As friends, collaborators, fellow authors, and editors, they have carried an often-heavy burden over the last 2 years. I would also like to acknowledge the efforts of Adela McMurray in initiating this project and in helping us through the project's initial travails. Finally, I would like to extend a special thanks to the staff of Palgrave's London office. In doing so, I – as well as all the editors and authors involved in this project – am particularly in the debt of Ruth Lefreve. Without her efforts and encouragement, this work would not have been possible.

Brisbane
March 2020

Bradley Bowden

References

Camus A (1951/1978) The rebel(trans: Bower A). Alfred A Knopf, New York

Desilver D (2019) Ten facts about American workers. Pew Research Centre, Washington DC. https://www.pewresearch.org/fact-tank/2019/08/29/facts-about-american-workers/

Jacques R, Durepos G (2015) A history of management histories: does the story of our past and the way we tell it matter. In: McLaren PG, Mills AJ, Weatherbee TG (eds) The Routledge companion to management and organizational history. Routledge, London/New York, pp 96–111

Organisation for Economic Co-operation and Development (2019) Social expenditure update 2019: Public social spending is high in many OECD countries. Organisation for Economic Co-operation and Development, Paris. http://www.oecd.org/els/soc/OECD2019-Social-Expenditure-Update.pdf

Peetz D (2019) The realities and futures of work. Australian National University Press, Canberra

Phelps Brown EH, Hopkins SV (1956) Seven centuries of the prices of consumables, compared with builders' wage rates. Economica 23(92):296–314

Pollard S (1965) The genesis of modern management: a study of the Industrial Revolution in Great Britain. Edward Arnold, London

United States Bureau of Labor Statistics (2020) Economic news release, Table 3 – union affiliation of employed wage and salary workers by occupation and industry. United States Bureau of Labor Statistics, Washington DC. https://www.bls.gov/news.release/union2.t03.htm

Contents

Volume 1

Part I Introduction **1**

1 Management History in the Modern World: An Overview 3
Bradley Bowden

Part II What Is Management and Management History? **23**

2 What Is Management? 25
Bradley Bowden

3 Debates Within Management History 45
Jeffrey Muldoon

4 Methodologies Within Management History 67
Jeffrey Muldoon

**5 Conflicting Visions: A Recap About the Debates Within
Management History** 87
Jeffrey Muldoon

**Part III Work, Management, and Economic Organization in
the Pre-modern World** **111**

6 The Pre-modern World and Management: An Introduction 113
Bradley Bowden

7 Management in Antiquity: Part 1 – The Binds of Geography 131
Bradley Bowden

**8 Management in Antiquity: Part 2 – Success and Failure in the
Hellenic and Roman Worlds** 153
Bradley Bowden

9 From Feudalism to Modernity, Part I: Management, Technology, and Work, AD 450–1750 ... 183
Bradley Bowden

10 From Feudalism to Modernity, Part 2: The Revolution in Ideas, AD 450–1750 ... 215
Bradley Bowden

11 The Origins of Robust Supply Chain Management and Logistics in the Caribbean: Spanish Silver and Gold in the New World (1492–1700) ... 245
Oliver W. Aho and Robert A. Lloyd

12 Transformation: The First Global Economy, 1750–1914 ... 271
Bradley Bowden

Part IV The Foundations of Knowledge and Management: An Introduction ... **307**

13 The Foundations of Knowledge and Management: An Introduction ... 309
Bradley Bowden and Kaylee Boccalatte

14 Intellectual Enlightenment: The Epistemological Foundations of Business Endeavor ... 321
Bradley Bowden

15 Economic Foundations: Adam Smith and the Classical School of Economics ... 345
Bradley Bowden

16 Neo-Classical Thought: Alfred Marshall and Utilitarianism ... 367
Kaylee Boccalatte

17 Foundations: The Roots of Idealist and Romantic Opposition to Capitalism and Management ... 387
Bradley Bowden

18 The Marxist Opposition to Capitalism and Business ... 411
Kaylee Boccalatte

19 Conflicting Understandings of the Industrial Revolution and Its Consequences: The Founding Figures of British Management History ... 435
Bradley Bowden

Contents

xvii

Part V The Classic Age of Management Thought (Mid-Nineteenth Century Until 1939) **473**

20 Certain Victory, Uncertain Time: The Limitations of Nineteenth-Century Management Thought 475
Jeffrey Muldoon

21 Taylor Made Management 499
Jeffrey Muldoon

22 Henry Ford and His Legacy: An American Prometheus 521
Jeffrey Muldoon

23 Spontaneity Is the Spice of Management: Elton Mayo's Hunt for Cooperation 545
Jeffrey Muldoon

24 Organizational Psychology and the Rise of Human Resource Management 565
Jeffrey Muldoon

25 To the Tavistock Institute: British Management in the Early Twentieth Century 593
Jeffrey Muldoon

26 Kurt Lewin: Organizational Change 615
Jeffrey Muldoon

Part VI Postmodernism **633**

27 Postmodernism: An Introduction 635
Bradley Bowden

28 The Intellectual Origins of Postmodernism 645
Bradley Bowden

29 Paul-Michel Foucault: Prophet and Paradox 671
Bradley Bowden

30 Jacques Derrida: Cosmopolitan Critic 699
Bradley Bowden

31 Hayden White and His Influence 723
Bradley Bowden

xviii   Contents

Volume 2

Part VII Management in the Age of Prosperity (1940s to 1980) 747

32 Management in the Age of Prosperity, c. 1940–1990: Section Introduction 749
Kevin D. Tennent

33 Keynesianism: Origins, Principles, and Keynes's Debate with Hayek 755
Kaylee Boccalatte and Bradley Bowden

34 The Age of Strategy: From Drucker and Design to Planning and Porter 781
Kevin D. Tennent

35 Chandler and the Visible Hand of Management 801
Kevin D. Tennent

36 Industrial Relations in the "Golden Age" in the UK and the USA, 1945 1980 823
Jim Phillips

37 The Rise of Marketing 841
Alex G. Gillett and Kevin D. Tennent

38 Organizational Psychology's Golden Age, 1940–1970 859
Alice White

39 British Management 1950–1980 873
John Quail

Part VIII Management in an Age of Crisis 887

40 Introduction: Public Policy Failure, the Demise of Experts, and the Dawn of a New Era 889
Anthony M. Gould

41 Labor and Employment Practices: The Rise and Fall of the New Managerialism 913
John Godard

42 A Return to the Good Old Days: Populism, Fake News, Yellow Journalism, and the Unparalleled Virtue of Business People 935
Mark Balnaves

43 Why did the Great Recession Fail to Produce a *New* New Deal in the USA? 951
Jon D. Wisman

Contents

xix

44 Trade Union Decline and Transformation: Where to for Employment Relations? 971
Bradley Bowden

45 The New Executive: Interconnected Yet Isolated and Uninformed – Leadership Challenges in the Digital Pandemic Epoch 1011
Kathleen Marshall Park

46 Conclusion: Management Theory in Crisis 1047
Jean-Etienne Joullié

Part IX Different Experiences: Europe, Africa, and the Middle East **1071**

47 Different Experiences: Europe, Africa, and the Middle East – An Introduction 1073
Bradley Bowden

48 Management in the Middle East 1081
Anthony M. Gould

49 Work and Society in the Orthodox East: Byzantium and Russia, AD 450–1861 1105
Bradley Bowden

50 Changing Corporate Governance in France in the Late Twentieth Century 1141
Peter Wirtz

51 Flexicurity: The Danish Model 1163
Jørgen Burchardt

52 Pre-colonial Africa: Diversity in Organization and Management of Economy and Society 1185
Grietjie Verhoef

53 Africa and the Firm: Management in Africa Through a Century of Contestation 1207
Grietjie Verhoef

54 Managing Africa's Strongest Economy: The History of Management in South Africa, 1920–2018 1239
Grietjie Verhoef

55 Why Entrepreneurship Failed to Emerge in "Developing Countries": The Case of Colonial Africa (1952–1972) 1269
Michele Akoorie, Jonathan M. Scott, Paresha Sinha, and Jenny Gibb

Part X Different Experiences: Asia, Latin America, and the Pacific **1287**

56 Introduction: Management Heterogeneity in Asia 1289
Anthony M. Gould

57 The Perfect Natural Experiment: Asia and the Convergence Debate 1317
Anthony M. Gould

58 Indian Management (?): A Modernization Experiment 1331
Nimruji Jammulamadaka

59 The Making of a Docile Working Class in Pre-reform China 1351
Elly Leung

60 Governmentality and the Chinese Workers in China's Contemporary Thought Management System 1367
Elly Leung

61 In Search of the Traces of the History of Management in Latin America, 1870–2020 1387
Carlos Dávila

62 Think Big and Privatize Every Thing That Moves: The Impact of Political Reform on the Practice of Management in New Zealand 1411
Andrew Cardow and William Wilson

63 Management in Australia – The Case of Australia's Wealthiest Valley: The Hunter 1431
Bradley Bowden

Index 1465

About the Editors

Professor Bradley Bowden is an Australian academic and management historian. He is currently Editor-in-Chief of the *Journal of Management History* and Co-Editor in the Palgrave Macmillan Debates in Business History Series. He has twice won the Academy of Management's John F Mee Award for Outstanding Contribution to Management History. Between 2016 and 2017, he also served as Chair of the Management History Division of the Academy of Management.

Professor Jeffrey Muldoon is Associate Professor and Baehr Distinguished Professor at Emporia State University. His research interests include management history (with special emphasis on the Hawthorne studies and the career of George Homans), social exchange, entrepreneurship, and leadership. His research has appeared in such journals as *Stress and Health*, *Leadership and Organization Development Journal*, *Personnel Review*, *Career Development International*, and the *Journal of Management History*. His research in history had won the Best Student Paper at the Academy of Management in 2009 and the Most Outstanding Paper Award for the *Journal of Management History* in 2013 for his paper on The Hawthorne Legacy. Professor Muldoon is on numerous editorial boards, including Associate Editor of *Journal of Management History*. He also won the John F Mee award.

Professor Anthony M. Gould is *Professeur titulaire* (full professor) of Employment Relations at Laval University, Canada, and Chief Editor of *Relations industrielles/Industrial Relations*, the oldest journal of its kind in the world. Concurrently, he is a Visiting Research Professor at Griffith University in Brisbane, Australia, and sits on the International Advisory Committee of Macquarie University's Centre for Workforce Futures in Sydney, Australia, and the International Advisory Committee for the University of NSW Business School's *Economic and Labour Relations Review* also in Sydney. Professor Gould has served on the editorial committees of well-known scholarly journals including the highly respected *Journal of Management History*, a role for which he was awarded *Emerald Publishing*'s Best Reviewer Prize in 2017. With aide and encouragement from talented and generous colleagues, since 2010 Professor Gould has authored more than 20 peer-reviewed articles (often with others) concerning labor and economic history, industrial sociology, management strategy, and research methods. This *corpus* is published mostly in elite scholarly journals (as measured by *impact factor* and *Cite-Score, etc.*) and has been cited multiple times.

Professor Gould has held professional jobs in six countries while maintaining consulting and governance-based relationships with individuals and institutions in the Middle East and Asia. Prior to entering academia in 2007, he was a Senior Executive in large government agencies in Australia and the UK.

Professor Adela J. McMurray has extensive research experience in public and private sectors and has published over 280 refereed publications. Her research is internationally recognized and she is the recipient of four Australian Research Council grants, two Cooperative Research Centre grants, and various other competitive grants totaling over $5 million. Professor McMurray is Associate Editor of the *Journal of Management History*, has chaired the USA Academy of Management's International Theme Committee, and is a member of the Management History Division and a number of editorial advisory boards. She is the recipient of national and international awards for best research papers, teaching, and supervision excellence.

Contributors

Oliver W. Aho Department of Economics, Management, and Project Management, Western Carolina University, Cullowhee, NC, USA

Michele Akoorie ICL Graduate Business School, Auckland, New Zealand

Mark Balnaves Gulf University for Science and Technology, Kuwait City, Kuwait University of Newcastle, Newcastle, NSW, Australia

Kaylee Boccalatte James Cook University, Douglas, QLD, Australia

Bradley Bowden Griffith Business School, Griffith University, Nathan, QLD, Australia

Jørgen Burchardt Museum Vestfyn, Assens, Denmark

Andrew Cardow School of Management, Massey University, Albany, New Zealand

Carlos Dávila School of Management, Universidad de los Andes, Bogotá, Colombia

Jenny Gibb School of Management and Marketing, University of Waikato, Hamilton, New Zealand

Alex G. Gillett The York Management School, University of York, York, UK

John Godard University of Manitoba, Winnipeg, MB, Canada

Anthony M. Gould Département des relations industrielles, Université Laval, Québec, QC, Canada

Nimruji Jammulamadaka Indian Institute of Management Calcutta, Kolkata, India

Jean-Etienne Joullié Gulf University for Science and Technology, Hawally, Kuwait
Université Laval, Québec, QC, Canada

Elly Leung Business School, University of Western Australia, Perth, WA, Australia

Robert A. Lloyd Fort Hays State University, Hays, KS, USA

Jeffrey Muldoon Emporia State University, Emporia, KS, USA

Kathleen Marshall Park Department of Administrative Sciences, Metropolitan College, Boston University, Boston, MA, USA

MIT Sloan School of Management, Cambridge, MA, USA

Jim Phillips Economic and Social History, University of Glasgow, Glasgow, UK

John Quail York Management School, University of York, York, UK

Jonathan M. Scott School of Management and Marketing, University of Waikato Tauranga CBD Campus, Tauranga, New Zealand

Paresha Sinha School of Management and Marketing, University of Waikato, Hamilton, New Zealand

Kevin D. Tennent The York Management School, University of York, York, UK

Grietjie Verhoef College of Business and Economics, University of Johannesburg, Johannesburg, South Africa

College of Global Business, Monash University, Melbourne, VIC, Australia

Alice White Wellcome Trust, London, UK

William Wilson School of Economics and Finance, Massey University, Albany, New Zealand

Peter Wirtz IAE Lyon School of Management, Magellan Research Center, University of Lyon, Lyon, France

Jon D. Wisman Professor of Economics, American University, Washington, DC, USA

Part I
Introduction

Management History in the Modern World: An Overview

1

Bradley Bowden

Contents

Introduction: What Is Management History? 4
A Note on the Meaning and Nature of Management 13
Cross-References 20
References 20

Abstract

Management history as a discipline is different from business and economic history in that it is primarily concerned with the supply side of the economic equation, with the nature of work, the ideas that guide it, and the economic wealth that is produced as a result of managerial oversight and endeavor. In terms of theoretical perspectives, management history embraces three main intellectual frameworks. The most significant of these has been associated with the founding figures of the Management History Division of the (American) Academy of Management, most particularly Claude George, Dan Wren, Ronald Greenwood, and Arthur (Art) Bedeian. Unabashed enthusiasts for free market capitalism, this US tradition is most concerned with the intellectual history of management, and the ideas that shaped managerial practice. By contrast, a different British tradition of management history associated with Sidney Pollard has been more directly focused on managerial practices, arguing that "modern management" is fundamentally different from earlier iterations found in pre-industrial societies. More recently, a critical or postmodernist tradition has gained influence in management history, an intellectual perspective that views management in largely negative terms. In this introductory chapter, we evaluate the strengths and weaknesses of these three management history perspectives.

B. Bowden (✉)
Griffith Business School, Griffith University, Nathan, QLD, Australia
e-mail: b.bowden@griffith.edu.au

© The Author(s), under exclusive licence to Springer Nature Switzerland AG 2020
B. Bowden et al. (eds.), *The Palgrave Handbook of Management History*,
https://doi.org/10.1007/978-3-319-62114-2_117

Keywords

Management history · Wren · Bedeian · Pollard · Postmodernism · Foucault · Hayden White · Critical management

Introduction: What Is Management History?

Producing the *Palgrave Handbook of Management History* has been a massive undertaking. Involving some 63 chapters, it explores both the ideas and experiences of management *and* the ways in which these ideas and experiences have shaped the world around them across the ages. Its approach is broad and encompassing, covering every issue that a person interested in a management-related theme would want to have include: whether that interest relates to economics, classical management thought, Marxist and postmodernist critiques of management, management practices in antiquity, the emergence of cost accounting, employment relations, the current crisis of wealth creation, or managerial practices in South America, France, Russia, India, China, or New Zealand or a range of other societies. In covering these broad areas of management's past, the *Palgrave Handbook* primarily speaks to the present, to understanding *both* the debt that we owe to the past *and* the unique features that management brings to modern democratic societies that distinguish us *from* the past.

Before advancing further, we must first ask ourselves a number of key questions. What is management history? How does it differ from business history or even economic history?

As a continuous intellectual discipline, both the origins and the continuing beating heart of management history are primarily located within the Management History Division of the (American) Academy of Management (AOM), a division I had the honor of chairing in 2016–2017. Significantly, when the AOM decided to adopt a divisional structure in 1971, the MHD was one of the ten foundational divisions. Claude George from the University of North Carolina not only chaired the MHD's inaugural meeting; he also acted as the Division's Chair for the first 3 years of its existence (Greenwood 2015). In a book first published a few years before the MHD's formation, *The History of Management Thought*, George (1968/1972: vii) declared that the purpose of management history was one of providing "a framework for understanding the development of management thought," thereby helping "to unify the broad field of management for scholars and practitioners alike." What George was clearly most interested in was an *intellectual* history of management, most particularly in the United States, and the ways in which (largely American) managerial concepts and philosophies shaped managerial practice. In an article published in 1987, "Management History: Issues and Ideas for Teaching and Research," Dan Wren – another founding member of the MHD who served as Chair in 1975 – spelt out broader objectives for management history. A figure whom my co-editor, Jeffrey Muldoon, describes in his detailed chapter on this topic, ▶ Chap. 5, "Conflicting Visions: A Recap About the Debates Within Management History," as a historian who has "occupied the commanding heights of the

1 Management History in the Modern World: An Overview

field," Wren (1987: 341) continued to associate management history with "the history of ideas or concepts." However, he also argued in favor of the study of institutions, the "business firm," and "organizational life cycles" (Wren 1987: 341). In doing so, Wren (1987: 342) also asked: "Managing today is different from that of last year, the last decade, or what date we choose. But *how* different?" [emphasis in original].

Implicit in Wren's question is the concept of a fundamental rupture in the history of management, a rupture that distinguishes the management of "today" from that of yesteryear. Strangely, however, Wren and his famed co-authors – most particularly Ronald Greenwood and Arthur (Art) Bedeian – continued to take an ambivalent position on this key issue. In their book, *Management Innovators: The People and Ideas That Have Shaped Modern Business*, Wren and Greenwood (1998: 6) stated that "Management is an ancient practice; it had its place (and still does) in governmental, religious, military, and other types of early organization." Wren and Greenwood (1998: 6), however, then immediately go on to state that "none of these [earlier institutions] grew to the scale and scope of the modern business enterprise, which needs to not only to adapt [to] ever-changing economic, social, and political forces but also to do this in a profitable fashion." Elsewhere, Wren and Greenwood (1998: 6) declare their book to be "the story of American business enterprise," a study that traces how American inventors and innovators changed "the way we live," creating "entirely new industries" within a "competitive environment." Implicit in these principles is not only a belief in American "exceptionalism" but also the understanding that management history differs from business history in that it pays special heed to people and their ideas. In other words, the key driver of managerial and societal change is not economics, or technology, but rather the innovative individual who transforms previous concepts and/or practices. Similar themes characterize Wren and Bedeian's *The Evolution of Management Thought*, a work that is without doubt the most influential study yet undertaken in management history. Originally a sole-authored work by Wren, with subsequent editions being co-authored with Bedeian (it is currently in its seventh edition with an eighth in the pipeline), this study continues to depict management as an "ancient" craft that can be traced back to the ancient Sumerians and Egyptians (Wren and Bedeian 1972/2017: 20). At the same time, however, it draws an implicit distinction between past and modern managerial practices, Wren and Bedeian (1972/2017: 3) opening the first chapter of their book with the following statement:

> The practice of management is ancient, but the formal study of management, based on an evolving body of knowledge is relatively new. Rarely, if ever, in human history has an activity emerged as fast as management and proven so indispensable so quickly.

In the same paragraph, Wren and Bedeian (1972/2017: 3) also hark back to the theme of George's (1968/1972) earlier work, declaring "the evolution" of management "thought" to be their "primary focus." In pursuing this theme, Wren and Bedeian – like George, Wren and Greenwood – are clearly guided by an underlying belief in American "exceptionalism," largely confining their study to American thinkers, practitioners, and experiences. Wren and Bedeian also differ from the "critical studies" that now dominate much of the field in management and organizational studies in being unabashed enthusiasts for free market capitalism.

Wren and Bedeian have profoundly influenced understandings of management history not only through their research but also through their teaching. Between the two of them, they helped train a generation of management historians – including my co-editor, Jeffrey Muldoon – as they turned the University of Oklahoma (Wren) and Louisiana State University (Bedeian) into bastions for management history scholarship. From these bastions, Wren and Bedeian acted as mentors, colleagues, and intellectual leaders for US management history, a tradition that placed ideas and intellectual history at the center of study. Accordingly, if one talked to an executive member of the MHD at the AOM's Annual Meeting prior to say 2010, one could almost be assured that one was speaking to a colleague of Wren or Bedeian, if not one of their former students.

Long dominant, the Wren-Greenwood-Bedeian school of management history was not, however, the only intellectual tradition within management history in the 1960s and 1970s. In Britain, a different tradition emerged through the work of Sidney Pollard (1958, 1963, 1965), a Jewish-Austrian refugee from fascism who spent most of his career at the University of Sheffield. As I discuss at depth in a subsequent chapter – "Conflicting Understandings of the Industrial Revolution and its Consequences: The Founding Figures of British Management History" – Pollard differed from George, Wren, Greenwood, and Bedeian not only in terms of his intellectual background but also in relation to the debates with which he engaged. Whereas George, Wren, Greenwood, and Bedeian were first and foremost students of management, Pollard was an economic historian whose research conclusions turned him into a management historian. Like Arnold Toynbee (1884/1894), John Nef (1932a, 1932b, 1934, 1937, 1943, 1950/1963), and John Clapham (1926/1967, 1932/1967, 1938/1951) before him, the most important questions in human existence for Pollard related to the transformative rupture that we know as the Industrial Revolution, a transformation that produced an industrial civilization unlike any before it.

Whereas the works of George, Wren, Greenwood, and Bedeian were informed by an implicit belief in American "exceptionalism," Pollard's work was informed by underlying assumptions as to British "exceptionalism." Unlike Wren, Greenwood, and Bedeian, Pollard was also unequivocal in drawing – as the title of his major book, *The Genesis of Modern Management: A Study of the Industrial Revolution in Great Britain*, suggests – a sharp distinction between pre-modern and modern forms of management. In Pollard's (1965: 6–7) estimation, modern managers in democratic, market economies differ from those found in both pre-modern and totalitarian societies in having the following characteristics: they deal with a free and mobile workforce, they need to possess an acute understanding of costs, they sell into a competitive market economy, they oversee capital-intensive forms of production, and they need to constantly innovate. Above all, Pollard associated the Industrial Revolution – and the industrial civilization that it spawned – with the transformation of managers into a new professionalized social class, creating wealth as a paid

1 Management History in the Modern World: An Overview 7

occupation that typically owns few of the productive assets it oversees. As to the nature of the Industrial Revolution, Pollard argued it was first and foremost a "managerial revolution" rather than a "technological revolution" and that modern management was both the creation and the creator of the Industrial Revolution. For the hallmark of the Industrial Revolution, Pollard (1965: 102) argued, was not so much technological change as,

> ... improvements in organization ...involving better layout of factory space, division of labour, design of the product with the process of production in mind, interchangeability of parts, control of raw material stocking and supply.

As a management historian, Pollard differed from his American counterparts in being more concerned about managerial *practices* than managerial *ideas*. Despite such differences, however, Pollard shared more common ground with his US counterparts than he did with either his fellow economic historians or the emerging leaders of business history such as Alfred D Chandler. Like Wren, Greenwood, and Bedeian, Pollard believed that "modern management" as manifest in liberal, market economies is a progressive social force. Nowhere, Pollard argued, was this more evident than in its relationship with a new class of legally free wage laborers, a workforce that had to be not only recruited and managed but also motivated. As Pollard (1965: 6–7) explained it, "the absence of legal enforcement of unfree work was not only one of the market characteristics" of the new managerial form of capitalism. It was also "one of its most seminal ideas, underlying its ultimate power to create a more civilized society." As a management historian – rather than a business or economic historian – Pollard was also more concerned about the *supply* side of the economic equation than the demand side. This differentiated his ideas from those of Chandler (1965, 1977, 1990) and subsequent business historians, who place greater emphasis on the ways in which the railroads and steam-powered shipping created new mass consumer markets after 1830. For Pollard, the most important driver "from the side of demand" was not the consumer, but rather the supply-side needs of other industries. Consequently, for Pollard (1958: 217) the key event in the Industrial Revolution, around which everything else turned, was "the emergence of an engineering industry," capable of creating and maintaining "the new equipment and the motors or engines needed by the first industries to be mechanised." From this central and indispensable core, Pollard (1958: 217) identified a ripple effect that fuelled industrial take-off as the engineering industry fostered increased coal and iron production, improved transport, and enhanced managerial and employee skills. In other words, in the Pollardian strand of management history, "modern management" is primarily worthy of its study because of its capacity to *create* wealth rather than because of the consumer demand that benefits from that wealth.

In recent decades, traditional forms of management history – be they those informed by the American tradition of George, Wren, Greenwood, and Bedeian or the Britain tradition founded by Pollard – have come under sustained attack from postmodernist-informed "critical management studies." In their *A New History of*

Management, for example, Cummings et al. (2017: 35, 41) declared their intention to write a "Foucauldian"-inspired "counter-history," directed toward "overturning" our "assumptions of how management studies came into being . . . [and] what 'good' it seeks to serve." Elsewhere, in a study entitled, "A History of Management Histories," Jacques and Durepos (2015: 97) similarly condemn, "Management histories that . . .have a scientist slant and appear timeless, universal, linear, progressive . . .These histories portray our current condition as an unquestioned and uncontested outcome of our past."

The new "critical perspectives" owe a clear debt to French philosophers such as Jacques Derrida (1967a/1976, 1967b/2001), Jean-Francois Lyotard (1979/1986, 1988/1991), Michel Foucault (1966/1994, 1969/1972, 1975/1991, 1976/1978), and Bruno Latour (1991/1993). In the view of Lyotard (1979/1986: 51), for example, modern capitalism and its associated systems of management was an inherently "dehumanizing process," a system of rigorously enforced inhumanity undertaken in the name of "efficiency and development" (Lyotard 1988/1991: 67, 6). Lyotard's postmodernist colleague, Michel Foucault, painted an even darker picture of "the development of capitalism," associating it with new systems of "micro-power" that entailed "infinitesimal surveillances, permanent controls, extremely meticulous orderings of space" (Foucault 1976/1978: 140, 145). For Derrida as well, the modern industrial civilization produced by the West was a retrograde endeavor. As Derrida (1993/2006: 106) expressed it in a lecture given in 1993, "never have violence, inequality, exclusion, famine, and thus economic oppression affected so many human being in the history of earth and humanity."

If we are to sum up the three main theoretical frameworks within management history – the George-Wren-Greenwood-Bedeian tradition, the Pollardian perspective, and the new critical or postmodernist viewpoint – we can ascertain areas of both agreement and difference. Implicit if not explicit in all three perspectives is the belief that nineteenth-century industrialization represented a fundamental break with the past, creating new systems of management and profoundly different economic and social relationship both within the workplace and without. Despite the hostility of the "critical" perspective to industrial capitalism, modern forms of management, and "ethnocentrism" (Derrida 1967a/1976: 3; Whittle and Wilson 2015), all three traditions are also Eurocentric in terms of the primary focus of their research and the methodologies that they use to study the past. Both the George-Wren-Greenwood-Bedeian and Pollardian traditions are positivist in methodological orientation, believing that the primary task of the historian entails the reconstruction of a reasonably accurate understanding of the past. Art Bedeian (1996: 312), for example, in summing up what he believed to be the guiding principles for any researcher, declared, "that truth is to be sought in an independent and rational manner." The idea that one can come to an "objective" assessment of the past, based upon rational and dispassionate criteria is, of course, an anathema to the postmodernist management historian. In articulating an alternative perspective in an article entitled "Research Strategies for Organizational History," Rowlinson et al. (2014: 253, 257) dismiss the positivist claim that there is an objective truth "that exists independently and prior to being discovered and told by the historian," arguing instead in favor of the view that

1 Management History in the Modern World: An Overview

there is a "fictive" element in any historical account. In a similar vein, Durepos (2015: 162) rejects the view that "management and organizational history" can be built upon "truth claims, objective history, fixed meanings." Instead of giving a primacy to "objectivity" and "truth," Durepos (2015: 161) recommends a deliberate "destabilizing" of the "dominant narratives" of the past. Cummings et al. (2017: 333) also declare that the purpose of their *A New History of Management* is one of "unsettling" established "orthodoxies" in ways that "lead to new thinking and liberating actions."

Although the postmodernist approach to methodology makes it the declared foe of positivism, it nevertheless remains the case that postmodernist frameworks are as much a product of the intellectual traditions of Western Europe as any other. As I discuss in ▶ Chap. 17, "Foundations: The Roots of Idealist and Romantic Opposition to Capitalism and Management," postmodernism is the intellectual offspring of German idealist philosophy, a school of thought that always paid greater heed to individual consciousness than the circumstances of the material world. Among the German idealist thinkers, postmodernism in all its hues owes a particular debt to Friedrich Nietzsche, who argued that history – whether accurate or otherwise – is only useful to the extent that it inspires action and that "Ultimately the point is to what *end* a lie is told" (Nietzsche 1895/1990: 127). Rather than being directly inspired by Nietzsche and German idealism, however, most of today's postmodernist and "amodernist" management historians (Michael Rowlinson, John Hassard, Stephanie Decker, Gabrielle Durepos, Albert Mills) obtain their guiding principles through the mediating intellectual prisms of Foucault and the American postmodernist, the late Hayden White. Like Nietzsche, Hayden White (1973: 371) declared that historical writing should create an "illusionary world, outside the original world of pure power relationships," a world "in which the weak" forge a different image of both past and future so as to challenge "the authority" of the "strong." In other words, historical accuracy is of little value in and of itself. Instead, management history – like all forms of history – only obtains meaning through its capacity to inspire the weak and the oppressed into active resistance against established authority.

If the critical or postmodernist perspective differs from the older traditions in management history in terms of methodology, it also differs in the issues to which it primarily speaks. Whereas both the George-Wren-Greenwood-Bedeian and Pollardian traditions were primarily concerned with the "supply side" of the economic equation – with modern management's unprecedented capacity to create wealth – the critical perspective is, as Mollan (2019: 513) recently observed, preoccupied with "postmodernist concerns with power and its distribution," an orientation that prioritizes "inequality and discrimination in work, pay, and advancement based on gender, ethnicity, race, or sexuality." A preoccupation with the distribution of wealth, rather than its creation, is of course hardly confined to Marxist and postmodernists. Along with worries as to climate change, concerns as to social, racial, and gender inequality increasingly dominate academic disciplines in management, business, and the social sciences more generally. In his hugely influential *Capital in the Twenty-First Century*, Thomas Picketty (2013/2014: 15), for example, had a chapter heading entitled: "Putting the Distributional Question Back at the Heart of Economic Analysis." Elsewhere, Picketty (2013/2014: 257, 259) declares that "half the population" of Western Europe "own virtually nothing" and that for "millions of people, 'wealth' amounts to little more than a few weeks' wages in a checking account."

In many ways the growing concern with *distribution* of wealth, and a corresponding decline in the traditional interest of management historians with wealth creation, is paradoxical. In most advanced and developing economies, per capita income levels are at historic highs. In comparison with past societies, comparatively few people are employed in low-paid, menial jobs. In the United States in 2018, for example, 43.5% of the workforce were employed in managerial and professional jobs. Only 22.7% worked in low-paid retail, hospitality, or service jobs. All the rest worked in comparatively well-paid jobs in manufacturing, construction, mining, protective services, and private-sector administration (United States Department of Labor 2019). The percentage of national gross domestic product (GDP) allocated to public social expenditure is also approaching record highs in most OECD countries, averaging slightly more than 20% of GDP. In the United States, where public social expenditure is close to the OECD average, the amount expended in 2018, measured as a share of GDP, is more than double that spent in 1960. In 2018, expenditures were also approximately 50% higher than they were in 1990 (OECD 2019). Similarly, although no one would deny that discrimination on the base of race, ethnicity, and religion still occurs, it is nevertheless the case that discrimination because of gender, race, or sexual orientation is illegal in virtually every advanced economy. Female workforce participation is – in virtually every society – at or close to historic highs.

The comparative disinterest with wealth creation in modern academia points, it is arguable, to the comparative success of past managerial endeavors. For countless generations a matter of overriding concern, wealth creation (i.e., production, logistics, entrepreneurship, productivity, etc.), now appears a secondary issue. While happily conceding that issues relating to inequality deserve the attention of management historians, it is nevertheless also the case that a declining interest in wealth creation has arguably contributed to management history's inability to contribute in a meaningful way to recent debates in economic history as to when, why, and how the wealth-producing capacities – and associated living standards – of Northwestern Europe diverged from those found elsewhere. The product of the so-called "convergence/divergence" debate (i.e., when did the economic capacities of advanced European societies diverge and converge with those located elsewhere in the globe), this emerging literature (Allen 2003; Allen et al. 2011; Broadberry and Gupta 2006; Parthasarathi 1998; Pomeranz 2000; Li and Zanden 2012; van Zanden 2002; van Bavel and van Zanden 2004) is highly significant for management history for two main reasons. First, it points to the great difficulty that pre-industrial societies experience in trying to escape from what Allen (2003: 406) describes as "the Malthusian trap," in which a growing population eventually confronts an apparently immutable productive ceiling. The result is a vicious historical cycle of diminished per capita wealth, famine, disease, population collapse, and an eventual demographic recovery that ends up confronting the same immutable ceiling. The classic example of this is found in the experiences of Western Europe between the thirteenth and seventeenth centuries. As Fig. 1 indicates – which draws on the so-called Phelps Brown-Hopkins (1956) wage-price index for skilled building workers in southern England between 1264 and 1650 – a collapse in population in the mid-fourteenth century caused by the Black Death resulted in a massive spike in living standards as the survivors opted to farm only the most fertile land. As population recovered, however, living standards collapsed. Accordingly, in the mid-seventeenth century, the real wage of a skilled English worker was little better than that enjoyed by their counterpart in the thirteenth century.

The obvious conclusion that one is forced to draw from Fig. 1 is that the many managerial and technological advances obtained by management during antiquity, the High Middle Ages, the Renaissance, and the Reformation – printing, blast furnaces, windmills, compasses, new foods from the Americas, double-entry book-keeping, bills of exchange, and merchant banking – were incapable of freeing Western Europe from the "Malthusian trap" in which it found itself. By comparison, Fig. 2, which draws on research by Broadberry and Gupta (2006) into real wages in Europe, India and East Asia between 1500 and 1800 allows for very different conclusions. In tracing the "grain wage" of unskilled workers in a variety of locations – including southern England, Milan and Florence (considered together), and India – Broadberry and Gupta's (2006) research indicates that living standards c.1600 were much the same whether you lived in England, Florence, Vienna, Valencia, or northern or western India [note: a grain wage measures the kilograms of wheat a person could buy if they spent all their wage on wheat or a calorific equivalent in rye, barley, or rice]. Everywhere, societies appeared stuck in a classic Malthusian trap as population grew faster than available resources. In Europe, the possession of a colonial empire – although it enriched a comparatively small number

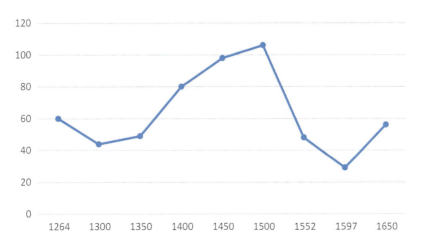

Fig. 1 Real wage of skilled building worker in Southern England, 1264–1650 (1447 = 100) (Source: Phelps Brown and Hopkins: "Seven centuries of ... builders' wage rates," Appendix B)

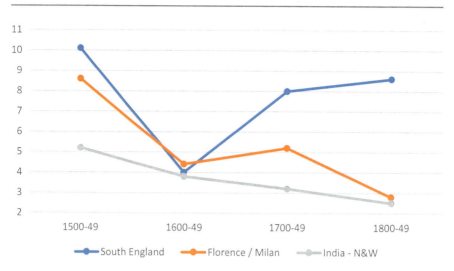

Fig. 2 Real wages (in kg of wheat) of unskilled building laborers, 1500–1549 to 1800–1849: Southern England, Florence/Milan, and Northern and Western India (Source: Broadberry and Gupta, Early Great Modern Divergence, Tables 2, 6)

of fortunate individuals – did little to guarantee improved overall circumstances. In Madrid and Valencia, for example, Broadberry and Gupta (2006: 6) calculate that the typical unskilled worker was poorer in 1700–1740 than they had been in 1500–1549, when the riches of Mexico and the Andes were still in the initial stages of Spanish exploitation. Palma and Reis's (2019) recent study of Portuguese circumstances also indicates that Portugal also gained no fundamental economic or managerial benefit from its colonial empire. As Palma and Reis (2019: 478) record, "Over the long run, there was no per capita growth: by 1850 per capita incomes were not different from what they had been in the early 1530s." By 1700–1749, however, the economic trajectory of England experienced a dramatic change, real wages moving sharply upward even as those elsewhere continued to decline, a trend that was to become even more pronounced in the nineteenth century.

What caused English (and, to a lesser degree, Dutch) circumstances to diverge so fundamentally from that found elsewhere? This is arguably *the* most important question in not only management history but also in the whole human experience. By understanding the answer to this question, we gain insight not only into the role of management in historical change but also as to the circumstances that underpin economic dynamism, entrepreneurship, managerial endeavor, improved real wages, and social cohesion in our own world. In many ways, this book series the *Palgrave Handbook of Management History* can be construed as an attempt to understand not only the answer to the question of why England followed a different trajectory from other societies – leading to what the economic historian John Nef (1950/1963) described as a fundamentally new "industrial civilization" – but also the *consequences* that ensued from the managerial and technological revolutions of the eighteenth and nineteenth centuries. Inevitably, those who lived within the confines of the new transformed global economy experienced a wide-range of experiences. As we shall ascertain, things looked very different from the point of view of the worker in the Bengal jute-mill, where traditional Indian values remained strong, than they appeared in New World societies such as Australia, South Africa, and New Zealand. The maturation of the new managerial and industrial order also produced – as we shall explore – not only new understandings of management but also new social tensions, economic crises, and transformative successes and failures. Only by looking at all of the complexities that produced the modern world, and the similarities and variations within it, can we fully comprehend the full story of management history.

A Note on the Meaning and Nature of Management

In the opening chapter of the *Palgrave Handbook of Management History,* ▶ Chap. 2, "What Is Management?," I explore in some depth the nature and meaning of management – and the different forms that it has assumed in pre-modern societies, modern totalitarian regimes, and modern liberal democracies. It is nevertheless useful at this point to consider how the main theoretical perspectives in management history – the George-Wren-Greenwood-Bedeian tradition, the Pollardian framework, and the critical or postmodernist perspective – each understand the term "management" and how these understandings differ from the standard textbook definition (i.e., management is "planning, organizing, leading and controlling"), a definition whose broad scope allows virtually any system of organized work to be considered under managerial direction.

In the introduction to their book, *Management Innovators*, Wren and Greenwood differentiated "ancient management" from management as found in advanced capitalist societies, associating the latter with three unique characteristics. First, Wren and Greenwood (1998: 6) argued modern forms of management are distinguishable by the "scale and scope" of their operations, the scale of the firm's activities demanding the formation of the "modern business enterprise." Second, the enterprise needs "to adapt" to "ever-changing economic, social, and political forces." Finally, the enterprise needs to operate "in a profitable fashion." Clearly, this is a tighter and more restrictive definition than the classic textbook fashion. By associating "management" with the "modern business enterprise," however, it not only differentiates modern "management" from pre-modern management, it also technically excludes modern small-scale activities undertaken by the self-employed and the small family business.

A more useful definition and discussion is found in *The Evolution of Management Thought*, where Wren and Bedeian (1972/2017: 3) begin their first chapter by stating: "For a broad working definition, management may be viewed as the activity whose purpose is to achieve desired results through the efficient allocation and utilization of human and material resources." Significantly, Wren and Bedeian (1972/2017: 3–10) then proceed to distinguish various forms of management – which they broadly group into three categories (traditional, command, and market) – according to various attributes: cultural, economic, social, political, human, technological, and organizational. Unlike economists and Marxists, who tend to see new forms of technology as the key driver of innovation and change, Wren and Bedeian (1972/2017: 7) relegate technology to a secondary role behind managerial innovation and organization, declaring technology to be "a means to an end that can produce beneficial as well as detrimental results." Wren and Bedeian also draw a clear distinction between "tradition-bound" managerial activities from those undertaken according to what they refer to as the "market method." In 'tradition-bound' societies, Wren and Bedeian (1972/2017: 5, 7) argue, management suffers from a lack of "innovation," offering their citizens "little incentive to seek new knowledge, to explore, or to experiment." If, in Wren and Bedeian's (1972/2017: 5–6) view, "modern societies" result from a combination of "tradition-bound" approaches, centralized "command" systems, and "the market method," it is nevertheless clearly the latter approach that is held to be superior. In Wren and Bedeian's (1972/2017: 6) estimation, the "market method" is more than a system of market exchanges. Rather it is recognized "as an economic philosophy," a set of principles that creates "the need for a formal body of management thought" and which "opens the way to the competitive use of resources."

Although the Wren-Bedeian formulation provides us with a far more sophisticated definition that the standard textbook description (i.e., planning, organizing, leading, controlling), it nevertheless suffers from some arguable flaws, most particularly when it comes to distinguishing managerial activity in pre-modern market economies from that found in industrialized capitalist societies. If we turn our mind, for example, to Renaissance Italy and the thriving commercial metropolis of Venice, we can clearly perceive a society characterized not only by managerial activities but also an economy operating according to the "market method." "The island city at the end of the fifteenth century was," Jacob Burckhardt (1867/1878: 51) famously observed, "the jewel-basket of the world," the place "where the business of the world is transacted." Of the Venetian businessperson, the great Belgium historian, Henri Pirenne (1925/1952: 86), declared that "No scruple had any weight with the Venetians. Their religion was the religion of business men." In the early fourteenth century, the Venetian arsenal or shipbuilding yard was also the most extensive manufacturing facility in Europe, covering some 32 acres at the entrance way to the Grand Canal (Nef 1950/1963: 65). Venice was also the birthplace of the commercial bank "cheque" and of double-entry bookkeeping, Luca Pacioli (1494/1994: 4) declaring that the double-entry system described by him to be the one "used in Venice." Yet, for all of its notable achievements, the Venetian economy little resembled a modern market economy. In terms of both production and exchange, Venice's merchants catered for a tiny elite market, excelling as they did in the production of expensive textiles and glassware. Writing of the situation that prevailed in the thirteenth century, Pirenne (1936: 161) observed that "the tonnage of a single [early] twentieth-century ship" was equal in tonnage "to that of the whole Venetian or Genoese fleet." Because the demand for its manufactured products among gullible Italian, German, and French aristocrats far exceeded demand, Venetian merchants had little need to concern themselves with costs. Even if a Venetian merchant was driven to seek efficiencies in production, any such move would have been stymied by the various craft guilds, institutions that North and Thomas (1973: 57) accurately refer to as "early-day monopolists." Despite the appearances conveyed by the activities at the arsenal, capital intensity in Venetian production was low. Moreover, those capital goods that did exist (warehouses, spinning wheels, weaving frames, ships) were – given the European-wide shortage of iron and steel – invariably made of wood. In the absence of artificial forms of energy (i.e., peat, coal, oil, gas, etc.), Venetian society also placed insatiable demands on forest reserves for domestic cooking and heating, for the charcoal used in iron making, and for the firing of bricks and glass. As Venetian society, and that of Renaissance Italy more generally, hit a Malthusian resource ceiling, all available sources of wood were felled. In Genoa, Venice's great commercial rival, the price of wood used in shipbuilding rose 12-fold between the late fifteenth century and the late sixteenth century (Cipolla 1981: 246). Similar price rises would have been experienced in Venice. In consequence, for all its apparent managerial and commercial dynamism, Venice proved no more capable of break-ing through the apparently immutable Malthusian ceiling than any other Italian society, experiencing the same general decline in living standards that character-ized Milan and Florence (see Fig. 2).

If the Wren-Bedeian definition of management – for all of its obvious benefits when compared to the standard textbook delineation – remains ambivalent as to the differences between pre-modern and modern forms of management within market economies, when we turn our attention to the critical or postmodernist tradition, we ascertain distinctions that are both clearer and more problematic.

Arguably, the most determined attempt to define both the origins and meaning of the concept of "management" within the critical or postmodernist tradition is found in Jacques and Durepos's study, "A History of Management Histories." Dismissing "the bland impressions" associated with the "Wren and Bedeian" formulation, Jacques and Durepos (2015: 101) argue that "management did not just happen." Instead, drawing on a mid-nineteenth century book by Freeman Hunt (*Work and Wealth: Maxims for Merchants and Men of Business*), Jacques and Durepos (2015: 97) describe "the history of management knowledge as a crawl out of the primordial ooze." In their view, "management" – unlike various pre-modern forms of workplace supervision – is *not* an activity inherent to all societies. Rather, Jacques and Durepos (2015: 101) somehow conclude, "What is now called management emerges from several major forces related to American industrialization beginning in the 1870s and [was] largely complete by 1920." In other words, in attempting to define "management," Jacques and Durepos advocate a form of reverse American "excep-tionalism," whereby US management and business is declared the global leader in ignominy rather than innovation.

To prove their point that "management" is a fundamentally new concept in the human experience, Jacques and Durepos (2015: 100) point to the fact that the term is not used in a number of nineteenth-century texts, ignoring the research by Muldoon and Marin (2012) that point to the concept entering the English lexicon in the late sixteenth century. In Jacques and Durepos's estimation, it is also not industrial capitalism per se that is the principal source of oppression, as it was for Marx and Engels (1848/1953: 61) who declared in 1848 in their *Communist Manifesto* that "proletarians have nothing to lose but their chains" and "a world to win." Nor, presumably, is it factory mechanization per se, a process that was obvious in England by 1770, a century before the date that Jacques and Durepos associate with the emergence of "management." Instead, Jacques and Durepos (2015: 101) contend that the inauguration of new systems of management in the United States after 1870 was central to an employer conspiracy to silence "the fight that was going on between labour and employers for authority within the factory." Whereas, previously, Jacques and Durepos (2015: 101) claim, employers had instituted "an American 'Reign of Terror'" against workers, the post-1870 systems of management enveloped workers in a "narrative of [employer] legitimation," a discourse that emphasized education, rationality, fairness, and employee welfare rather than overt oppression and violence. Implicit in the Jacques-Durepos definition of management is the assumption – common to critical/postmodernist scholars – that culture is of overriding importance in the workplace, as it is everywhere else. If one holds to this view, then it does not require a physical revolution to break the power of capitalism and management. Rather we can follow the advice of Nietzsche (1886/1989: 31, 27), who declared that through acts of will it is always possible to break the "invisible spell" of societal mores, or of Foucault (1966/1994: xx), who similarly believed that we can break free of the "fundamental codes" of "culture" through acts of will.

Superficially attractive, the Jacques-Durepos argument that the concept of management was a post-1870 American invention does not survive cursory examination. In the pages of Leo Tolstoy's *Anna Karenina*, for example, an aristocratic concern as to efficient estate management pervades almost every chapter, the central character noting how a neighbor "engaged a German expert from Moscow and paid him 500 roubles to investigate the management of their property, and found that they were losing 3000 roubles a year on farming" (1876/1978: 357). Similarly, in Ivan Turgenev's *Fathers and Sons*, written when serfdom was still the central institution in Russian society, the same concern with more efficient forms of management is once more evident, one of the central characters (Bazarov) complaining to his friend:

> I've seen your father's entire establishment . . . The cattle are poor, the horses, run-down. The buildings are in bad shape and the workers look like confirmed loafers . . . And the good little peasants are taking your father for all he's worth. (Turgenev 1862/2009: 34)

If we go even further back in time to the first surviving textbook on farm management, or indeed on any form of management, Cato the Elder's (160 BC/1913: 34) *De Agricultura*, we read the following advice directed to estate managers or overseers:

He should strive to be expert in all kinds of work, and . . . often lend a hand. By doing so, he will better understand the point of view of his hands . . . First up in the morning, he should be the last to bed at night.

The Jacques-Durepos argument that late nineteenth-century American managers were the first to locate supervisory practices within a cultural context – one that emphasized fairness and worker welfare while simultaneously advancing employer interests – is also without merit. In Tolstoy's (1876/1978: 363) *Anna Karenina*, for example, we read how the lead character (Levin) observes that Russian farm management was only successful when it interested "labourers in the success of the work," appealing to peasants "not as abstract man power" but rather as Russians with peculiar national instincts and values. If we look to the British Industrial Revolution of the late eighteenth and nineteenth centuries, it is also evident that cultural concerns were at the forefront of management thinking as managers sought to implement new systems of wealth creation. As the noted English labor historian E. P. Thompson (1967) observed in an article entitled "Time, Work-discipline, and Industrial Capitalism," the precondition for the success of industrial capitalism rested on management's capacity to instill a sense of "time discipline" among workers. Whereas pre-industrial forms of work are largely individualistic, it making little difference exactly when a weaver or farmer starts work, industrial capitalism is collectivist in its work methods. Typically, a factory will not operate, and a plane will not fly, unless all workers are present at their designated time. In instilling this sense of "time discipline," Thompson (1963/1968: 451) – a lifelong socialist – believed that management was profoundly altering society for the better, noting how between 1760 and 1830 "The 'average' English working man became more disciplined, more subject to the productive tempo of the 'clock', more reserved and methodical, less violent." In early industrial Britain, Robert Owen was also hardly unique in establishing a model village community, New Lanark, for his workforce: a community in which Owen provided his workers with houses, shops, sporting facilities, and churches. Far from being rarities, Pollard (1965: 200) observed that "A list of large works providing their own attached cottage estates or a controlling share of them reads like a roll-call of the giants of the industrial revolution."

In considering the distinction between pre-modern and modern forms of management, assuming that there are in fact profound differences, we can ascertain that on this point both the Wren-Bedeian and the Jacques-Durepos definitions of management are found wanting. Jacques and Durepos solve the difficulty of delineating pre-modern forms of management from modern manifestations by a simple sleight of hand: they deny the existence of management prior to its supposed initiation in post-1870 America. Wren and Bedeian, by contrast, thoughtfully draw important distinctions between "tradition-bound" managerial systems and those that are underpinned by "market" methods, without differentiating how "market-focused" managerial systems have marked differences depending on whether or not they are part of a modern industrial society. In comparison, Pollard, in his most notable study, *The Genesis of Modern Management*, placed the distinction between "modern management" and earlier expressions at the forefront of his work. As noted earlier,

Pollard (1965: 6–7) associated "modern management" with six unique characteristics which he argued were either partially or fully absent in earlier iterations of managerial practice: they deal with a free and mobile workforce, they need to possess an acute understanding of costs, they sell into a competitive market economy, they oversee capital-intensive forms of production, they need to constantly innovate, and they have attributes in terms of training and responsibilities that differentiate them from entrepreneurs on one side and the workplace supervisor on the other.

One of the factors that caused Pollard to argue for such a tight definition of "modern management" is found in the fact that he focused his research on a restricted managerial experience, the Industrial Revolution in Great Britain between 1760 and 1830, a period that he associated with a total transformation in the human condition. This narrow focus was, however, arguably a cause of weakness as well as strength. The dates chosen by Pollard for the Industrial Revolution (i.e., 1760 to 1830) correspond to the accession of George III and the death of George IV rather than to any profound technological or managerial change. As such they follow the convention established by Arnold Toynbee (1884/1894) in his posthumously published, *Lectures on the Industrial Revolution of the eighteenth century in England*. In attempting to compress the transformative managerial experience into an arbitrarily demarked 60 period, Pollard was required to understate both earlier and subsequent achievements. Thus, on the one hand, Pollard (1965: 156) argued that the period between 1760 and 1830 was unique in possessing a new class of professional managers, a cohort that he described as "one of the most dynamic social groups of their age, responsible for initiating many of its decisive changes." On the other hand, Pollard (1965: 127) correctly pointed to the fact that the growing number of factories in post-1760 Britain was fortunate in being able to draw on the large class of professional managers that already existed in the English coal industry. As Pollard well realized, his recognition of the importance of the coal industry to British managerial and industrial advancement brought him into conflict with the earlier work of the American economic historian, John Nef, who argued that the expansion of English coal production was seminal to what he claimed was an earlier "industrial revolution" in England between 1540 and 1640. Assuming immense size, and utilizing a level of capital intensity unknown elsewhere, the British coal industry by the 1630s was producing some two million tons of product per year, at a time "when the rest of the world combined," as Nef (1950/1963: 14) recorded, "probably produced less than one-fifth as much."

If Pollard paid insufficient heed to managerial advances prior to 1760, he even more obviously understated the developments that occurred after 1830, most particularly in transport, where steam-powered railroads and iron-hulled ships created a mass global market for the first time. "At once effect and cause," the English historian John Clapham (1926/1967: 425) noted, "railway development coincided with a development of metallurgy and mining quite without precedent." In every field of metal production, engineering, and mining, the needs of the railroads drove large-scale increases in production. In 1847–1848 alone, British railroads placed orders for 400,000 tons of iron running rails (Clapham 1926/1967: 428).

1 Management History in the Modern World: An Overview 19

Locomotives and rolling stock also placed huge demands on iron smelters, as did a booming export trade. As most readers would be aware, Clapham's highlighting of the railroad "revolution" of the 1840s was one subsequently taken up by Chandler (1977: 79–80), who argued that not only were the railroads "the pioneers in the management of modern business enterprise"; they were also "essential to high-volume production and distribution – the hallmark of the large modern manufacturing or marketing enterprises."

One thing that is apparent if we look across the three main intellectual traditions within management history – the George-Wren-Greenwood-Bedeian tradition, the Pollardian perspective, and the critical or postmodernist theoretical framework – is that none of them utilizes the common textbook definition (i.e., planning, organizing, leading, controlling). Implicit or explicit in all three management history traditions is the viewpoint that what Pollard called "modern management," and Wren and Bedeian referred to as the "market method," is of comparatively recent origin. It is also true, however, that as a comparatively recent societal institution, "modern" management builds on earlier experiences and achievements, in terms of not only organizational skills and practices but also technology, language, culture, legal frameworks, urban and rural infrastructure, financial practices, and the like. Accordingly, in perusing the *Palgrave Handbook of Management History*, the reader needs to have constantly in the back of their minds the following question: How did a particular historical practice or intellectual approach contribute to the development of management, *and* how are such practices and approaches different from the experiences and intellectual premises of management in modern, liberal democratic societies?

In the two and a half years that I have been involved in the compilation and writing of the *Palgrave Handbook of Management History*, it was perhaps inevitable that my own ideas as to the defining characteristics of "modern" management would undergo amendment and modification. Although my ideas on management history remain essentially Pollardian, I nevertheless believed that Pollard erred in two principal ways. First, as this preceding discussion suggests, Pollard understated managerial achievements both before and after the British Industrial Revolution of 1760 to 1830. In doing so, he arguably paid too much attention to managerial achievements in manufacturing and insufficient heed to managerial gains in agriculture, mining, finance, and transport. Second, I believe that Pollard – as with most other management historians – understated the extent to which modern management and modern industrial society are both energy-intensive and metal-intensive. Given the modern concerns with global warming and climate change, the association of modern management with these attributes would appear obvious. However, I believe most of us underestimate the extent to which modern societies rely on both artificial forms of energy and smelted metals. As previously noted, in a pre-industrial society, there is typically only one source of energy for heating, cooking, the firing of bricks and glass, the processing of alcoholic spirits, food processing, etc. – wood. Prior to the eighteenth century, wood was also required for charcoal in the forging or casting of iron, a production attribute that severely restricted the production and use of iron. In the absence of iron, capital intensity was more or less impossible. Where metal was used in manufacture or agriculture, it was typically only applied on the cutting or working surfaces. The low level of metal usage that characterized pre-modern societies can be ascertained from the fact that between 1700 and 1710 the production of cast iron in Great Britain amounted to a miniscule 24,000 tons per year. Much of this production, moreover, would have been consumed by the military for use as cannon, muskets, iron cannon balls, and the like. A century later, by comparison, Britain's cast iron production amounted to more than ten times this amount. In 1837, more than a million tons was smelted – a 400-fold increase on early eighteenth-century output (Riden 1977). For the first time in the human experience, a hardened smelted metal had become a common rather than a rare commodity. This revolution in iron production – made possible due to changes in smelting techniques that allowed for the substitution of coal-derived coke in lieu of wood-derived wood – not only fundamentally altered the nature of management, heralding capital-intensive production methods in manufacturing, agriculture, and transport. It also allowed society to break out of the Malthusian trap which had previously restricted the economic and social possibilities of *every* society in the human experience.

Cross-References

▶ Certain Victory, Uncertain Time: The Limitations of Nineteenth-Century Management Thought
▶ Conflicting Visions: A Recap About the Debates Within Management History
▶ Foundations: The Roots of Idealist and Romantic Opposition to Capitalism and Management
▶ What Is Management?

References

Allen RC (2003) Progress and poverty in early modern Europe. Econ Hist Rev 56(3):403–443
Allen RC, Bassino J-P, Ma D, Moll-Murata C, van Zanden JL (2011) Wages, prices, and living standards in China, 1738-1925: in comparison with Europe, Japan, and India. Econ Hist Rev 64 (1):8–38
Bedeian AG (1996) Thoughts on the making and remaking of the management discipline. J Manag Inq 5(4):311–313
Broadberry S, Gupta B (2006) The early modern great divergence: wages, prices and economic development in Europe and Asia, 1500–1800. Econ Hist Rev 49(1):2–31
Burckhardt J (1867/1878) The civilization of the renaissance in Italy, 2nd edn. The Modern Library, New York
Cato the Elder (160 BC/1913) De agricultura. In: A Virginian Farmer (ed.) Roman farm management: the treatises of Cato and Varro. Macmillan, New York, pp 19–50
Chandler AD Jr (1965) The railroads: pioneers in modern corporate management. Bus Hist 39 (1):16–40
Chandler AD Jr (1977) The visible hand: the managerial revolution in American business. Belknap Press, Cambridge
Chandler AD Jr (1990) Scale and scope: the dynamics of industrial capitalism. Belknap Press, Cambridge
Cipolla CM (1981) Before the industrial revolution: European society and economy, 1000–1700, 2nd edn. Cambridge University Press, Cambridge

Clapham JH (1926/1967) Economic history of modern Britain: the early railway age 1820–1850. Cambridge University Press, Cambridge

Clapham JH (1932/1967) Economic history of modern Britain: free trade and steel 1850–1886. Cambridge University Press, Cambridge

Clapham JH (1938/1951) Economic history of modern Britain: machines and national rivalries 1887–1914. Cambridge University Press, Cambridge

Cummings S, Bridgman T, Hassard J, Rowlinson M (2017) A new history of management. Cambridge University Press, Cambridge

Derrida J (1967a) Of grammatology. John Hopkins University Press, Baltimore

Derrida J (1967b) Writing and difference. Routledge and Kegan Paul, London/New York

Derrida J (1993/2006) Spectres of Marx: the state of the debt, the work of mourning and the new international. Routledge Classics, New York/London

Durepos (2015) ANTi-history: toward amodern histories. In: McLaren PG, Mills AJ, Weatherbee TG (eds) The Routledge companion to management and organizational history. Routledge, London/New York, pp 153–180

Foucault M (1966/1994) The order of things: an archaeology of the human sciences. Vintage Books, New York

Foucault M (1969/1972) The archaeology of knowledge. Pantheon Books, New York

Foucault M (1975/1991) Discipline and punish: the birth of the prison. Vintage Books, New York

Foucault M (1976/1978) The history of sexuality – an introduction. Pantheon Books, New York

George (1968/1972) The history of management thought. Englewood Cliffs, New York

Greenwood R (2015) A first look at the first 30 years of the first division: The management history division. In: Bowden B, Lamond D (eds) Management history: Its global past and present. Information Age Publishing, Charlotte

Hunt F (1857) Work and wealth: maxims for merchants and men of business. Stringer & Townsend, New York

Jacques R, Durepos G (2015) A history of management histories: does the story of our past and the way we tell it matter. In: McLaren PG, Mills AJ, Weatherbee TG (eds) The Routledge companion to management and organizational history. Routledge, London/New York, pp 96–111

Latour B (1991/1993) We have never been modern. Harvard University Press, Cambridge

Li B, van Zanden JL (2012) Before the great divergence? Comparing the Yangzi delta and the Netherlands at the beginning of the nineteenth century. J Econ Hist 72(4):956–989

Lyotard J-F (1979/1986) The postmodern condition: A report on knowledge. Manchester University Press, Manchester

Lyotard J-F (1988/1991) The inhuman. Stanford University Press, Stanford

Marx K, Engels F (1848/1953) The communist manifesto. In: Marx K, Engels F (eds) Selected works, vol 1. Foreign languages Publishing House, Moscow, pp 21–61

Mollan S (2019) Phenomenal differences: varieties of historical interpretation in management and organization studies. Qual Res Org Manage Int J 14(4):495–515

Nef JU (1932a) The rise of the British coal industry, vol 1. Frank Cass and Co., London

Nef JU (1932b) The rise of the British coal industry, vol 2. Frank Cass and Co., London

Nef JU (1934) Prices and industrial capitalism in Germany, France and England 1540-160. Econ Hist Rev 7(2):155–185

Nef JU (1937) The progress of technology and the growth of large-scale industry in Great Britain 1540-160. Econ Hist Rev 5(1):3–34

Nef JU (1941) The responsibility of economic historians. J Econ Hist 1(1):1–8

Nef JU (1943) The industrial revolution reconsidered. J Econ Hist 3(1):1–31

Nef JU (1950/1963) War and human progress: an essay on the rise of industrial civilization. Norton & Company, New York

Nietzsche F (1886/1989) Beyond good and evil: prelude to a philosophy of the future. Vintage Books, New York

Nietzsche F (1895/1990) The anti-christ. In: Nietzsche F (ed) Twilight of the idols/The anti-christ. (trans: Hollingdale RJ). Penguin Classics, London, pp 127–222

North DC, Thomas RP (1973) The rise of the Western world: A new economic history. Cambridge University Press, London

Organisation for Economic Co-operation and Development (2019) Social expenditure update 2019: Public social spending is high in many OECD countries. Organisation for Economic Co-operation and Development, Paris. http://www.oecd.org/els/soc/OECD2019-Social-Expenditure-Update.pdf

Pacioli L (1494/1994) Accounting books and records: the *summa de arithmetica, geometria, proportioni et proportionalita*. Pacioli Society, Seattle

Palma N, Reis J (2019) From convergence to divergence: Portuguese economic growth 1527-1850. Econ Hist Rev 79(2):477–506

Parthasarathi P (1998) Rethinking wages and competitiveness in the eighteenth century: Britain and South India. Past Present 158(1):79–109

Phelps Brown EH, Hopkins SV (1956) Seven centuries of the prices of consumables, compared with builders' wage rates. Economica 23(92):296–314

Picketty T (2013/2014) Capital in the twenty-first century. Belknap Press, Cambridge

Pirenne H (1925/1952) Medieval cities: their origins and the revival of trade. Princeton University Press, Princeton

Pirenne H (1936) Economic and social history of medieval Europe. Routledge & Kegan Paul, London

Pollard S (1958) Investment, consumption and the industrial revolution. Econ Hist Rev 11 (2):215–226

Pollard S (1963) Factory discipline in the industrial revolution. Econ Hist Rev 16(2):254–271

Pollard S (1965) The genesis of modern management: A study of the industrial revolution in Great Britain. Edward Arnold, London

Pomeranz K (2000) The great divergence: China, Europe, and the making of the modern world economy. Princeton University Press, Princeton

Riden P (1977) The output of the British iron industry before 1870. Econ Hist Rev 30(3):442–459

Rowlinson M, Hassard J, Decker S (2014) Research strategies for organizational history: A dialogue between historical theory and organization theory. Acad Manag Rev 39(2):250–274

Thompson EP (1963/1968) The making of the English working class, 2nd edn. Penguin, Harmondsworth

Thompson EP (1967) Time, work-discipline, and industrial capitalism. Past Present 38(1):56–97

Tolstoy L (1876/1978) Anna Karenina. Penguin Classics, London

Toynbee A (1884/1894) Lectures on the industrial revolution of the 18th century in England. Longman, Green and Co., London

Turgenev I (1862/2009) Fathers and children: Norton critical edition. W.W. Norton and Co., New York. [Note: in the interests of political correctness, recent editions have abandoned the original title, Father and sons]

United States Bureau of Labor Statistics (2019) Economic news release, 18 Jan 2019: table 3 – union affiliation of employed wage and salary workers by occupation and industry. United States Bureau of Labor Statistics, Washington DC. https://www.bls.gov/news.release/union2.t03.htm

van Bavel JP, van Zanden JL (2004) The jump-start of the Holland economy during the late-medieval crisis, c.1350-c.1500. Econ Hist Rev 58(3):6503–6532

van Zanden JL (2002) The 'revolt of the early modernists' and the 'first modern economy': an assessment. Econ Hist Rev 55(4):619–641

White H (1973) Metahistory: the historical imagination in nineteenth-century Europe. John Hopkins University Press, Baltimore

Whittle A, Wilson J (2015) Ethnomethodology and the production of history: studying "history-in-action". Bus Hist Rev 57(1):41–63

Wren DA (1987) Management history: issues and ideas for teaching and research. J Manag 13 (2):339–350

Wren DA, Bedeian AG (1972/2017) The Evolution of Management Thought. Wiley, New York

Wren DA, Greenwood RG (1998) Management innovators: The people and ideas that have shaped modern business. Oxford University Press, New York

Part II

What Is Management and Management History?

What Is Management?

2

Bradley Bowden

Contents

Introduction 26
Foundations 30
Different Paths 38
Conclusion 41
References 43

Abstract

A ubiquitous feature of the modern world, management is also one of its more poorly understand institutions. Commonly, as evidenced in management textbooks, "management" is associated with four functions: planning, organizing, leading, and controlling. This section argues that this narrow view is in grievous error, encompassing as it does systems of work based on slavery and totalitarian control. Accordingly, we need to extend our definition to include five other characteristics. First, management – if it is properly fulfilling its functions – is attentive to costs, including the value it places on labor. Second, management involves maximizing "competitive advantage" built on firm and labor specialization. Third, output is directed toward competitive mass markets, markets that help sustain production based on specialization. Fourth, management can only properly function when it is supported by legal frameworks that guarantee contracts and protect property and individual rights. Finally, modern management is unlike that found in preindustrial societies based on hereditary privilege – and that found in totalitarian regimes – in that it deals with free labor vested with a genuine capacity for choose in deciding on both an occupation and an employer.

B. Bowden (✉)
Griffith Business School, Griffith University, Nathan, QLD, Australia
e-mail: b.bowden@griffith.edu.au

© The Author(s), under exclusive licence to Springer Nature Switzerland AG 2020
B. Bowden et al. (eds.), *The Palgrave Handbook of Management History*,
https://doi.org/10.1007/978-3-319-62114-2_4

Keywords

Braudel · Coal · Communism · Chandler · China · Drucker · Engels · Entrepreneurship · Foucault · Kant · Keynes · Locke · Hobbes · Hume · Adam Smith · Marx · Pollard · Postmodernism · Protestantism · Rousseau · Voltaire · Weber

Introduction

Management, as a discipline and an occupation, has become a ubiquitous feature of the modern world. Among college and university students, business administration and management is now the most commonly studied degree (Stockwell 2014; Creighton 2017: 1, 4). Even if we do not aspire to be a manager, or have a managerial role thrust upon us, the institutions and mores of management pervade almost every aspect of our lives. For those of us who work, a manager allocates the tasks that we perform and assesses our performance. If we have a gripe in terms of the service we or a family member experience at a school, hospital, or restaurant, we seek out the relevant manager, believing this person to be the one ultimately responsible for the service that caused our complaint. Managers are also held accountable for the ultimate success or failure of a business; an accountability that reflects Peter Drucker's (1963: 13) maxim in his classic study, *The Practice of Management*, that "the quality and performance of its managers is the only effective advantage an enterprise in a competitive economy can have." Evidence of the benefit of modern entrepreneurial and managerial performance is found in the comparative abundance that today surrounds even the world's developing economies. According to World Bank (2017) estimates, the percentage of the world's population experiencing extreme poverty fell from 42.2% to 10.7% between 1981 and 2013. Almost everywhere, the advance of modern industrialized economies has opened up unprecedented opportunities. In most Western societies, a female is more likely to complete a university degree than a male. In the developing world, literacy and attendance at school – rather than a life of toil – are now the norm for the vast majority of adolescents. As Antonio Guterres (2017: 23), the United Nation's Secretary-General, observed in his annual report in 2017, even in sub-Saharan Africa – historically a laggard – 80% of children were regularly attending school by 2015.

Despite its central placement in our lives, many assumptions about "management" do not survive elementary scrutiny. In the first instance, we need to ask ourselves: "What, if anything, is novel and revolutionary about modern management when compared to that found in earlier societies, where those overseeing economic activities had to engage in the same core tasks – planning, organizing, leading, and controlling – that today's textbooks identify as the universal characteristic of management?" (see, e.g., Bartol et al. 2005: 5). This is a fundamental question which typically receives confused or contradictory answers. In Morgen Witzel's (2012: 7) *A History of Management*, for example, we are told that management did "emerge" as a "discipline" in the nineteenth century. However, we are also told that most preindustrial societies boasted successful examples of "management," an outcome that leaves us none the wiser as to modern management's unique characteristics. Similar confusion is evident in the use of terms closely associated with management such as "entrepreneurship" and "capitalism." Murphy et al. (2006: 12, 16), for example, ascribe the massive expansion in per capita wealth that occurred throughout the world after 1800 to "the advent of entrepreneurship," only to then point to the "success of entrepreneurship in ancient and medieval times." Again, we are left none the wiser as to the transformative nature of modern management and entrepreneurship.

Attribution of modern management's distinctive character to its association with "capitalism" is also unconvincing. In their *Communist Manifesto*, Karl Marx and Frederick Engels (1848/1951: 37) praised capitalism for having created "during its rule of scarce 100 years...more massive and more colossal productive forces than have all preceding generations together." The problem with this assertion is that "capitalism" existed for centuries before the Industrial Revolution. As Fernand Braudel (1946/1975a: 319) demonstrated in *The Mediterranean and the Mediterranean World in the Age of Philip II*, by the sixteenth century, "commercial capitalism" – characterized by sophisticated finance and banking systems, domination of long-distance trade routes and control of luxury goods' markets – clearly existed in an "already modern and indisputably effective form." In carrying out their financial and commercial tasks, sixteenth-century capitalists clearly needed "managers" as much as any modern firm. If association with "capitalism" cannot by itself explain the transformative capacities of modern management so it is also the case that management's successes during the Industrial Revolution cannot be ascribed simply to technological innovations. In the early stages of the Industrial Revolution, when economic expansion was particularly pronounced, the availability of steam-powered machines was modest. In Britain's textile industry, the first to experience large-scale mechanization, initial technological advance was confined to spinning. Even in 1835, steam-powered weaving looms were – as Sidney Pollard (1965: 37) observed – "relatively rare," leaving "large weaving sheds full of hand looms."

In examining the distinguishing characteristics of modern management, we also need to consider not only how it differs from the forms of work oversight found in preindustrial societies but also how management in democratic societies (the United States, the Eurozone, the United Kingdom, Australia, Japan, etc.) is like and different to that found in undemocratic societies where government-imposed controls restrict the free movement of labor (i.e., the People's Republic of China, North Korea, etc.). For in his seminal text, *The Genesis of Modern Management*, Pollard (1965: 6) remarked that "the absence of legal enforcement of unfree work was not only one of the marked characteristics" of the new industrial societies that emerged in Western Europe and North America in the early nineteenth century; it was also "one of its most seminal ideas, underlying its ultimate power to create a more civilized society." During the epoch of the Industrial Revolution, there were, however, broad swathes of the industrializing world where various forms of unfree labor (i.e., the slave plantations of the Americas and the Russian estates worked with serfs) not only prevailed but actually grew in size and importance due to the demands of increasingly urbanized societies for cotton, sugar, grains, and tobacco. In the twentieth century, as well, use of various forms of unfree or semi-free labor continued to play important roles in a number of major economies (i.e., Nazi Germany, the Soviet Union). Now many of the problems of managers experienced by managers using various forms of unfree labor are comparable to those experienced by managers in democratic societies. Resource inputs need to be garnered. Production processes need to be planned, organized, and monitored. We can, nevertheless, understand that managers operating with unfree workforces are in a fundamentally different situation to that of a manager in a democratic society with a free labor force. For not only can labor choose to vacate their jobs in the latter situation, it is also the case that democracies place significant constraints on the exercise of managerial authority (i.e., restrictions on child employment, minimum wages, hours of work, etc.).

If there is confusion as to the unique and transformative features of modern management, it is also evident that management's very legitimacy as an occupation and intellectual discipline has been placed under constant question. Indeed, since the dawn of the Industrial Revolution, there has always been a body of opinion that regarded new forms of work and management with ill-disguised hostility. Believing that an embrace of science and material progress must have a deleterious effect on the human spirit, the French political philosopher, Jean-Jacques Rousseau (1763/1979: 118, 157, 176), observed in his classic study, *Emile*, that, "By dint of gathering machines around" us – machines that are increasingly "ingenious" – our senses become ever "cruder." In contrast, Rousseau believed, the noble "Canadian savage," living in the wilds of North America, "does not make a movement, not a step, without having beforehand envisaged the consequences. Thus, the more his body is exercised, the more his mind is enlightened: his strength and reason grow together." In the 1970s this emphasis on the degrading effects of modern work and management found new expression in the critiques of "labor process" theorists. As Harry Braverman (1974: 120–121), the dominant influence in this genre explained in a work subtitled *The Degradation of Work in the Twentieth Century*, "Modern management," having "come into being" with the "scientific management" of Frederick Taylor, worked to reduce individuals "to the level of general and undifferentiated labor power." More recently, the growing body of postmodernists have viewed the occupation and discipline of management through an even darker lens; a core component of what Michel Foucault (1980: 100, 102) described as a "disciplinary society" in which new forms of "governmentality" subject individuals to constant scrutiny. Echoing such themes, Miller and O'Leary declared in a 1987 study that management-related disciplines such as accounting were part of "a vast project of standardisation and normalisation of the lives of individuals" both "within the enterprise and outside it." In 2017, in their *A New History of Management*, a collection of Foucauldian postmodernists – Stephen Cummings et al. (2017: xii, 315) – argued in favor of "alternative management histories" in which management is transformed into a "liberalizing" social force, as if this is *not* the role that it has historically fulfilled over the last two centuries.

In exploring both the nature of modern management and the intellectual debates that its increasingly central placement in society has engendered, this opening section of this *Handbook* will argue three main points. First, this study stands in the tradition of J.H. Clapham (1930/1967), Pollard (1965), and Alfred Chandler (1977) in believing that modern management – as found in modern, market-based democracies – differs fundamentally from both earlier, preindustrial systems of management and that found in totalitarian and semi-totalitarian societies where respect for private property, individual rights, and the free movement of labor are not entrenched norms. In terms of economic performance, as Pollard (1965: 6–7) accurately observed, the system of management that first emerged in Britain's factories between 1760 and 1830 profoundly differed from that found in previous epochs in that they not only had to sell their goods at a "profit" but also "to relate them to costs and sell them competitively." Unlike "managers" from the preindustrial era, who had neither the inclination nor the means to understand their production costs – and who in the case of public works programs such as the construction of the pyramids were intent on production regardless of cost – Britain's factory managers faced unprecedented problems in estimating costs (and hence profits). Selling into new mass markets that were opened up by both the comparative cheapness of factory products and the extension of revolutionary new forms of internal communication (i.e., canals and railroads), managers faced challenges on many fronts. Logistics chains for raw materials (i.e., cotton) and foodstuffs were long and complex, often being intercontinental in scope. Increasingly, production and transport expenses were associated not with traditional variable costs (predominately wages) but rather with fixed capital charges (machinery, transport equipment, physical premises, etc.). In confronting such tasks, the managers of the Industrial Revolution were entering into virgin territory. As Pollard (1965: 215) notes in relation to the new managerial task of cost accounting, "there was no tradition, no body of doctrine, no literature worthy of the name."

If, we suggest, an understanding of costs is one thing that differentiates the "modern" manager from their preindustrial counterpart, another is found in the fact that the former typically operates within mass markets, markets that shape not only the conditions of sale but also the very nature of production. For, as Adam Smith (1776/1999: 121) observed in *The Wealth of Nations*, "When the market is very small, no person can have any encouragement to dedicate himself entirely to one employment." Without a capacity to specialize, individuals and firms have a limited capacity to exploit their peculiar competitive advantage through the "division of labor" that Smith (1776/1999: 109) accurately identified with, "The greatest improvement in the productive powers of labor." Without firm specialization, there can also hardly be a global system of trade based upon nations exploiting their particular "competitive advantage" (i.e., Australia's vast plains and benign climate made it a preeminent wool producer). In *The Visible Hand*, Alfred Chandler (1977: 8, 76–82) claimed that the creation of mass markets and the consequent "managerial revolution" was preeminently an American phenomenon, a product of railroad expansion and the advent of telegraphic communication. In truth, it was the completion of Britain's canal system that created the world's first internal mass market. From 1761, when the completion of the Bridgewater Canal brought cheap coal supplies to the budding industrial center of Manchester, an ever growing network of canals crisscrossed England and the Scottish lowlands. In developing its canal system in the latter half of the eighteenth century, Britain was, moreover, merely exploiting the historical advantages that it obtained from not only being an island and a maritime power but also in having coastal access to plentiful coal supplies. Whereas in other European nations in 1800, the lack of readily available supplies of coal for heating and cooking still caused near insurmountable barriers to urban expansion, Britain's system of waterborne transportation allowed it to break these bonds.

Whereas what this study considers to be "modern management" is distinguished in part by mass markets and production systems where managers can trace and control their costs, it is also argued that a third fundamental characteristic is that it operates within a society that respects private property and individual rights, both within the workplace and without. The importance of such protections and rights was notably highlighted by Thomas Hobbes in his *Leviathan* in 1651. Without protection from arbitrary interference in their business and personal affairs, Hobbes (1651/2002: 62) observed, "industry" must inevitably be curtailed; and without industry life was invariably "solitary, poor, nasty, brutish, and short." Subsequently, in his *Two Treatises on Government*, John Locke (1680/1823: 202) extended this association of economic success and protection from arbitrary authority so as to include the formulation that legal frameworks had to be based on the "consent of the people" through their elected representatives; representatives who would act "as the fence to their properties." It is around such freedoms and protections that the whole intellectual and social fabric of modern management has been built; a social and economic tradition that holds true a set of fundamental principles: that private property is sacrosanct, that governments should foster education and protect freedom of expression, that economic success is built on innovation and individual endeavor, and that all established doctrine – religious and political – should be subject to critical scrutiny. The post-1760 process of industrialization, associated with increased national and firm specialization within a global market, can thus be seen as comprising not one but multiple managerial models, in which only one – associated with market economies that respect private property and individual rights while allowing free movement of capital and labor – has proven an enduring success.

Foundations

If we accept that "management" as it exists in Western societies is not an age-old phenomenon that exists wherever humans come together for an economic purpose but is instead a fundamentally modern construct, then the inevitable question becomes, "Why did modern systems of management associated with industrial capitalism first emerge in Britain in the decades either side of 1800?"

Despite the vast amount of research undertaken in economic and business history, there is no ready answer to the above question. For his part, Max Weber (1922/1927: 367) famously identified the advance of capitalism – and its associated systems of managerial organization – with the emergence of a "Protestant" and, more particularly, Calvinist "ethic," an ethic which not only placed value on the pursuit of wealth as "a God-given task" but which also excused a "ruthless exploitation" of workers in the pursuit of "eternal salvation." Although there is some merit in Weber's argument, we should nevertheless be wary of drawing a direct correlation between Protestantism/Calvinism and the "new capitalism." Whereas there were, no doubt, many nineteenth-century factory owners who took inspiration from their Calvinist faith, the same could be said of Protestant slave owners in the American South. More recently, Niall Ferguson (2011: 39), in his *Civilization: The West and the Rest*, suggests that Western economic and business success was a product of European political fragmentation. Devoid of any controlling center, it was, Ferguson suggests, Europe's divisions – rather than its shared commonalities – that opened the door to innovation and endeavor. What is left hanging by this explanation is why the Industrial Revolution and its associated managerial advances were in the first instance a product of the English-speaking world of the North Atlantic rather the Dutch-speaking Lowlands of continental Europe; a continental area associated not only with even higher levels of fragmentation but also longer traditions of international finance and trade. In seeking explanations for this latter quandary, Lars Magnusson (2009: 23), in his *Nation, State and the Industrial Revolution: The Visible Hand*, suggests that the Netherlands lost out to Britain because of its weaker state structures, a weakness that made it the ultimate loser given the "logic of violence" that characterized the late eighteenth century's history of trade wars and military confrontations. By this criterion, however, one would expect France to have at least rivaled Britain in the industrial stakes given that it was its arguable superior when it came to eighteenth-century violence and warfare. The years associated with the inauguration of the Industrial Revolution (1760–1790) were also years in which Britain, having won the Seven Years' War (1756–1763), suffered a period of comparative military weakness, a weakness that saw it not only temporarily lose its naval supremacy but also permanently forego control of its North American colonies south of the St Lawrence seaway.

Although there are no agreed answers as to the reasons behind the managerial and industrial revolutions of the eighteenth and nineteenth centuries, a number of factors nevertheless present themselves in explanation. First and foremost, although management as we understand it is a modern construct, it nevertheless draws of deep historical roots, roots that are located in legal and political domains as well as commercial realms. As Fernand Braudel (1982: 22) observed in his *Civilization and Capitalism*, the industrial capitalism of the nineteenth century built on traditions of "commercial capitalism" that were already well-established by the sixteenth century. Rather than being associated with a simple "market economy," Braudel (1946/1975a: 451) concluded that by 1500 European commercial capitalism occupied the upper echelons of an economic hierarchy, wherein the great banking and trading families controlled the highly profitable long-distant trade in luxury goods (spices, silks, dyes, and finished cloth). In the process they became masters of a suite of financial and commercial tools – bills of exchange, share-ownership, double-entry booking, long-term financial credit – without which the managerial and entrepreneurial practices of the Industrial Revolution would have been inconceivable. Similarly, without the development of long-term credit and banking the new centralized states that emerged during the fifteenth century in England, France, and above all Spain – which were built around dynastic monarchies but which increasingly employed professionalized bureaucracies – would also have been impossible. As Max Weber (1922/1978: 956–957) makes clear, these emergent state systems were utterly dependent upon a new type of bourgeoisie – financially literate and numerate in accounting – that was also capable to applying new principles of bureaucratic organization to the collection of taxes, the administer of justice, and the waging of wars. Initially a feature of the absolutist states that dominated the European landscape during the Century of Enlightenment (1680–1789), bureaucratic principles – which Weber (1922/1978: 973) believed owed their "technical superiority" to their reduction of organizational "friction and of material and personal costs" – also became a characteristic feature of large capitalist enterprises. As Weber (1922/1978: 681) also accurately observes, modern management and industrial capitalism would also have been impossible without an agreed system of legal, enforceable contracts, a legal system enforced more by accepted business mores than judicial prescription. "In an increasingly expanding market," Weber (1922/1978: 669) explained, "those who have market interests constitute the most important group. Their influence predominates in determining which legal transactions the law should regulate by means of power-granting norms."

Whereas the experiences garnered in long-distance commerce and in the administration of Europe's growing civil bureaucracies provided the managers who came of age in the Industrial Revolution with a wealth of technical skills upon which they could draw, it was the European Enlightenment that provided the wellsprings for critical inquiry and scientific innovation. In outlining the core principles of the Enlightenment in his *Critique of Pure Reason*, Immanuel Kant (1787/2007: 593) declared that there was no authority or issue that was "so sacred" that it should not be subject to "searching examination." The dictates of religion, the rule of kings, and the constitution of organizations and cities, none were to be spared. In England, David Hume (1739/1893: 287), a founder of British empiricism, similarly declared in his *Treatise on Human Nature* "that in the case of enormous tyranny and oppression, 'tis lawful to take up arms even against the supreme power, and that as government is a mere human invention for mutual advantage and security, it no longer imposes any obligation...when once it ceases to have that tendency." It was this willingness to expose every aspect of the human condition to scrutiny, rather than a commonality of answers, that makes the European Enlightenment the continuing foundation of our intellectual understandings. Even Michel Foucault (1984: 32), the preeminent influence in postmodernist thinking, in an article entitled "What is Enlightenment?," conceded that "modern philosophy is the philosophy that is attempting to answer" the same question/s as that "raised so imprudently two centuries ago." Although declaring he was neither "'for' nor 'against' the Enlightenment" – and the path of scientific and material progress that it heralded – Foucault (1984: 42–43) nevertheless conceded "that as an enterprise for linking the progress of truth and the history of liberty in a bond of direct relation, it [the Enlightenment] formulated a philosophical question that remains for us to consider." Without the traditions of critical inquiry that the Enlightenment fostered, the adaptability and problem-solving capacity that have characterized management since the late eighteenth century would have been improbable. For as Harbison and Myers (1959: 22) once observed, "the most complicated organization to manage is the sizeable industrial establishment. Here technical know-how, marketing ability, financial and administrative skills are all required."

The Enlightenment emphasis on science, critical inquiry, and innovation found its most obvious expression in the spread of new steam-powered technologies. First employed in the Durham coal industry in 1715 to pump water from the region's ever-deepening mine shafts, the size and complexity of the early Newcomen engines suggested that this novelty was of limited application. By 1800, however, the invention of more compact, high-pressure Bolton and Watt and – more particularly – Trevithick engines allowed steam power to displace water-powered Arkwright machines in Britain's textile districts. As steam power became entrenched in textile manufacture, productivity soared as output increasingly reflected the growing importance of fixed capital. Whereas in 1800 it is estimated that there was on average £10 of fixed capital for every textile worker, by 1830 there was on average £100 of plant and equipment per worker. As productivity and capital intensity soared, a series of profound changes occurred in the nature of work. In terms of employee numbers, workplaces assumed unprecedented size. In 1816, when Robert Owen was implementing his private model of "welfare capitalism," his New Lanark mill employed 1600 workers. By the 1830s, Manchester alone boasted seven mills with more than a 1000 factory hands. Another 76 Manchester mills provided work for more than 500 hands (Pollard 1965: 92–93).

Managerial emphasis on capital intensity and productivity also transformed the *type* of worker that textile mills and other factories employed. Initially employers had scoured the orphanages and poor houses for children to staff their mills, having found that adults were reluctant to subject themselves to the discipline that factory life entailed. By 1850, however, as Hugh Cunningham (2011: 68) observes, management was "seeing the advantages in an intensive rather than an extensive use of labour. . .In this kind of environment children were more of a hindrance than a help." Rather than seeking cheap labor, managers instead sought out literate, skilled workers. As a result the demand for child labor plummeted. By 1851, only 30% of English and Welsh children worked. Of those who did, only 15.4% of males and 24.1% of females were found in factories. Not only was a majority spared childhood work for the first time in human history, children were also increasingly excused the premature death rate that had long appeared an essential condition of human existence. As a result, 40% of the English population was under 15 years of age by 1851 (Kirby 2011: 122–124). The fact that paid labor was, as a result of mechanization, less associated with physical strength also provided unprecedented opportunities for women. As the labor historian, E.P. Thompson (1963: 452–453) noted in *The Making of the English Working Class*, the "abundant opportunities for female employment. . .gave women the status of wage-earners." Among the laboring population, for the first time, the "spinster," "the widow," and "the unmarried mother" had the opportunity to free themselves from reliance on male relatives and/or the parish poorhouse. Increasingly, factory work was also associated with high wages and a life of modest comfort. As Frederick Engels (1892/1951: 376), Karl Marx's long-term colleague and patron, recorded in reflecting upon the changes that had occurred to the employment of skilled workers over the course of the latter half of the nineteenth century, "That their condition has remarkably improved since 1848 there can be no doubt…they have succeed in enforcing for themselves a relatively comfortable position, and they accept it as final."

If an emphasis on science and innovation, inspired by Enlightenment traditions of critical inquiry, transformed the nature of work, it was also the case that the initiation of the Industrial Revolution in Britain reflected the presence of certain material prerequisites. The first of these was foodstuffs as the growth of large urban populations placed unprecedented demands on local agriculture. Significantly, in the open decades of the seventeenth century, England was unusual in that – as a result of the so-called enclosure movement in which common and waste land was fenced and used for large-scale commercial farming – its agriculture sector was far more productive than any other European society. In visiting England during the 1720s and in writing home about his experiences there, the French philosopher, Voltaire (1726/2002: 33), was astounded by the progressive state of English farming, observing that, "The feet of the peasants" were "not bruised by wooden shoes; they eat white bread." Whereas other Western European societies, most particularly France, struggled to avoid famine, Britain in 1750 was a net wheat exporter (Deane and Habakkuk 1963: 69). In the eighteenth and early nineteenth centuries, Britain – like the other industrializing societies of Western Europe – could also draw if necessary on grain, timber, and flax from the east Baltic littoral (Poland, Lithuania, Latvia, and Estonia); a process associated with the enserfment of a once largely independent peasantry in Eastern Europe as vast commercialized landed estates became the norm. As the nineteenth century progressed, however, it was only the foodstuffs (most particularly wheat) of the New World that made continued industrialization and urbanization possible. Effectively, with cheaper seaborne transport costs due to larger, steam-powered ships, the agricultural capacity of the United States, Canada, Argentina, South Africa, Australia, and New Zealand was annexed for the use of the industrialized districts of the North Atlantic. This proved a great boon for both capital and labor, lowering input costs and reducing the cost of living for industrial workers. It was, however, as O'Rourke (1997) observed in an article entitled "The European Grain Invasion," an unmitigated disaster for European landholders as the price differential between North American and British grain receipts fell to virtually nothing, an outcome that meant that an acre of wheat-growing land in England had no more productive value than an acre of farmland in Minnesota or Illinois.

Although Britain had an agricultural advantage over its European rivals during the eighteenth century, this in itself cannot explain why the United Kingdom was the industrial pioneer given that other Western European nations could also access imported foodstuffs with comparative ease. Rather, Britain's advantage lay in overcoming an even more difficult obstacle to urban and industrial expansion: access to energy. Historically,

European societies – as with those in other parts in Eurasia and Africa – had relied on wood for heating and cooking, as well as for the charcoal that was an essential ingredient in steelmaking. But as forests were depleted, only Britain was able to quickly draw on a cheap, readily available substitute: the coal deposits of the Tyne and Wear valleys. In London, as in other British seaports, seaborne coal became "a commodity only less indispensable" for existence "than bread itself" (Nef 1932: 103). As Nef (1932: 103) noted, "There was no parallel on the Continent for the remarkable growth in coal mining which occurred in Britain." By the early eighteenth century, Nef continued (1932: 322), the "entire production of the rest of the world did not perhaps amount to much more than a sixth of that of Great Britain." Whereas in the first half of the seventeenth century the economic advantage provided by cheap "sea coals" was largely restricted to coastal ports, in the latter half of the century, the extension of canals also provided benefit to the industrializing centers of the English Midlands (Manchester, Birmingham, Leeds, etc.). The scale of this benefit can be ascertained by the load a horse could pull. If pulling a wagon – on a good, macadamized road – it is estimated that a horse could transport two tons at most. By comparison, it is estimated (Deane and Habakkuk 1963: 72) that the same horse could pull 50 tons when the load was placed in a canal barge, a result that caused the price of coal in Manchester to plummet by more than 75% when the Bridgewater Canal was opened in 1761.

Underestimation of the importance of waterborne transport – most particularly for coal but also for the transport of other inputs (cotton, grains, steel) as well as finished goods – has caused some erstwhile management historians to make gross historical errors. Notable evidence of this is found in *A New History of Management*, where it is asserted (Cummings et al. 2017: 61) that when Adam Smith wrote *The Wealth of Nations* (i.e., 1776)

> ...industrialism was as far away as the iPad from the first automobile. Rail travel was 100 years in the future. Smith's own examples describe how transporting goods from London to Edinburgh took 6 week for the return trip in a 'broad-wheeled wagon.'

Leaving aside the fact that in 1776 the first British passenger railroad (the Stockton and Darlington, opened 1825) was less than 50 years away – rather than a 100 – the underlying presumptions of Cummings and co. display ignorance as to the material preconditions for industrial takeoff. For if, as Cummings et al. assert, British communications were in fact dependent upon the "broad-wheeled wagon," then the Industrial Revolution would have been impossible for a host of reasons. There could have been no mass markets, forcing producers to restrict their output – as they historically done – to local needs. In the absence of a substantial market, labor specialization would have been severely restricted. Resource inputs, where available, would have remained – as they historically had – prohibitively expensive. Urban communities, forced to rely – as they historically had – on local sources of fuel, would have remained small and scattered. The fact that the Industrial Revolution did proceed reflects the fact that the constraints imposed by the speed of the "broad-wheeled wagon" were overcome through a combination of sea transport, canal barges, and tramways.

Britain's canals and seaborne coal trade provided not only many of the material preconditions for the post-1750 managerial and industrial revolutions, they also provided key organizational underpinnings. Nef (1932: 322), in particular, has made a forceful case that Britain's northern coalfields "provided a fertile field for the growth of capitalistic forms of industrial organization." In terms of business organization, the inherently speculative nature of coal mining (i.e., one can never know the extent of any particular seam) created complex systems of share-ownership and interlocking directorships. The need to coordinate production, shipping, and sales provided experience in dealing with long-distance logistics and supply chains. The size of coal mining workforces, which could see more than a 100 engaged in a particular pit, also forced employers and managers to become expert in industrial relations, an expertise that was reflected in the formation of long-lived "vends" (cartels) directed toward the control of both wages and prices. The solid, compact colliers that hauled coal along Britain's coastal sea routes also provided the backbone for Britain's merchant fleet and, through this, its naval supremacy. It was also a converted collier, the *Endeavour*, captained by a Whitby seafarer (James Cook) who had learned his trade shipping Durham's coal, which brought the first Europeans to the Australian east coast, thereby setting in train a series of events that led to British settlement in the Antipodes.

As the growth of commerce and industry from the sixteenth century created new classes of entrepreneurs, financiers, and traders who obtained their wealth and property away from the land and agriculture, so there also grew demands for political representation and freedom from the arbitrary rule of kings and aristocrats. In addition to systems of "protections" for property, individual rights, and expression, the growth of Western industrial capitalism also hinged on what Weber (1922/1978: 668) referred to as a system of legal "privilege" that gave force to individual "autonomy," whereby the actions of individuals and groups were both protected and enforced by law. Thus, unlike the situation that prevailed in preindustrial societies – and which still prevails in undemocratic societies – the scope for individual and group action in democratic, market-based economies is not primarily determined by hereditary privilege or by entrenched rights for privileged groups (i.e., the Chinese Communist party and its functionaries). Rather, as Weber (1922/1978: 669) concluded, it is primarily "contractual" in nature.

In the new industrial capitalism that emerged after 1750, the legal and economic relationship between master and servant proved particularly problematic, both within the workplace and without. Whereas historically the gulf between employer and employee had been slight – with much of a society's output coming from the household economy – in post-1750 industrializing economies, the size of workforces in manufacturing, mining, and, subsequently, the railroads confronted managers with new problems in relation to recruitment, supervision, motivation, and employee involvement. Governments were also forced to redefine the relationships that they had with their citizens, extending legal protections to embrace conditions of workplace employment. First evidenced in the British *Factory Act 1833* – which both restricted the employment of children and created the world's first professional factory inspectorate – the state's protective framework was gradually extended to embrace adult employment, a minimum wage, hours of work, and bargaining rights. Although the initial factory laws were inspired by abhorrence at many of the worst features of the Industrial Revolution (child labor, long hours, lack of sanitation, high injury rates), they also reflected the *philosophic* appreciation that employees have rights and interests that are separate to those of the employer for whom they work. As the early twentieth-century management theorist, Chester Barnard (1938: 88, 93), recognized, "Strictly speaking" organizational objectives have "no meaning for the individual." Instead, most individuals only find work a positive experience when "the benefits it confers" exceed job "burdens." Organizational "efficiency," therefore, was correlated with a business's "capacity to offer inducements in sufficient quantity to maintain the equilibrium of the system."

With the destruction of long-established handicraft industries due to the steady advance of mechanization, large-scale unemployment and underemployment existed alongside serious labor shortages. A shortage of coal miners, and of skilled metal workers capable of building and maintaining the new industrial machinery, provided the most severe bottlenecks. The task of overcoming such labor problems extended well beyond the factory gates. In the slums of London, Liverpool, and Manchester, the concentrations of poorly paid workers provided not just breeding grounds for disease but also a population that was dissatisfied both industrially and politically. Significantly, solution to the social and industrial problems that the Industrial Revolution created in Britain during the first half of the nineteenth century came as much from within the new urban working class itself as from the state. In church "Sunday schools," workers taught themselves and their children how to read. Religious education, most particularly that associated with the non-Conformist sects (Methodists, Presbyterians, Baptists), also emphasized values of sobriety, self-improvement, and discipline that equipped their members for material success. At a time when social security was nonexistent, membership of friendly and mutual societies not only provided protection from sickness and injury, they also opened up the possibility of home ownership. Church and friendly society membership also trained workers in managing budgets, conducting meetings, public speaking, and organizing (Thompson 1963: 456–458). Although authorities long feared the revolutionary currents evident among industrial workers, in truth, as the Sidney Webb and Beatrice Webb (1920: 201) observed, by the 1840s most union leaders accepted the economic logic of capitalism. Far from opposing material progress, they sought instead to enhance their members' contribution to economic growth by fostering craft skills and improving workplace conditions. While the female franchise was not obtained in Britain until the twentieth century, working class demands saw a gradual extension of male voting rights through the Reform Bills of 1832, 1867, and 1884. By the latter date, universal male franchise was established as a permanent reality.

As British society, both within the workplace and without, reflected the informed participation of an increasingly literate and education workforce, so it was that the benefits of industrial capitalism were extended in a host of areas: improved civic services, free education, improved health facilities, old age pensions, and the like. By the closing decades of the nineteenth century, even the most vocal critics of industrializing capitalism were conceding the positive transformations that had occurred. In reflecting upon the Britain of 1892 and that which he described in 1844 in his *Condition of the Working-Class in England*, Frederick Engels (1892/1951: 370–371) admitted that, "the most crying abuses. . .have either disappeared or have been made less conspicuous. Drainage has been introduced or improved, wide avenues have been opened out. . .England has thus outgrown the juvenile state of capitalist exploitation described by me."

Given the dark images that the Industrial Revolution tends to conjure up – Satanic mills, child labor, urban slums, exploitation – it is easy to overlook the fundamentally progressive and transformative role that management played at this critical moment in human history. That people suffered during the Industrial Revolution is regrettable but is in itself hardly newsworthy. As Braudel (1946/1975b: 725) observed, throughout history the "price of progress" was "social oppression. Only the poor gained nothing, could hope for nothing." This was as true of Confucian China as it was of ancient Egypt. The economic world forged through the Industrial Revolution – in Britain in the first instance – differed in creating a workforce and a society in which the poor were notable beneficiaries. In workplaces where employees were entrusted with increasingly expensive machines, literacy and education became the new norm. Whereas at the dawn of the Industrial Revolution the agricultural and town laborer was mute when it came to politics, the economic and social order that emerged during the Industrial Revolution thrived on the active participation of its members, both as employees and citizens. Yes, the new managerial order that gave effect to the Industrial Revolution was based on competition, the pursuit of self-interest, and private property. Yes, social and income inequality were to remain its necessary hallmarks, John Maynard Keynes (1936/1973: 379) conceding "that there is social and psychological justification for significant inequalities. . .There are valuable activities which require the motive of money-making." What nevertheless made it such an enduring success was the benefits that it conferred on the "servants, laborers, and workmen of different kinds" who, as Adam Smith (1776/1999: 78–79) accurately noted, "make up the greater part of every great political society." For, Smith (1776/1999: 78–79) continued, "No society can surely be flourishing and happy, of which the far greater part of the members are poor and miserable. . .what improves the circumstances of the greater part can never be regarded as an inconveniency of the whole."

Different Paths

If the system of "management" that emerged in conjunction with the "Industrial Revolution" differed in virtually every way from that which had characterized early systems of "management" – concerned as it was with managing capital intensive factories and mines; with accurately tracing its internal costs; with recruiting and overseeing workers who were literate, skilled and active political citizens; with the direction of its output toward competitive mass markets – we should nevertheless *not* conclude that this model of management was a universal attribute of all industrializing and modernizing societies. As we have noted above, the urbanization of Western Europe – which was associated with the retreat of feudalism, social diversification, and an expansion of political rights – was initially dependent upon grain from the Baltic and Eastern Europe, a process associated in Eastern Europe with the growth of landed estates and the reduction a hitherto largely independent peasantry to a condition of serfdom. With the opening up of the New World to European settlement, a similar process was replicated on a larger and more sinister scale. For while the growing of grains (most particularly wheat) was well-suited to the efforts of the sturdy, yeomen farmers who became the popular backbone of the North American democracies in the United States and Canada, the production of coffee, sugar, tobacco,, and cotton fueled a massive expansion in global slavery during the eighteenth and early nineteenth centuries. Even in those places in which it was grown in the Old World (Egypt, Algeria, Spain, Madeira), the growing of cotton and more particularly sugar was typically associated with large-scale plantations and workforces ground into the dirt by back-breaking work and poverty. For, as Braudel (1946/1975a: 155) noted, plantation economies associated with sugar growing – and subsequently cotton, tobacco, and coffee – represented highly specialized forms of agriculture that (prior to the twentieth century) were seldom found alongside either subsistence agriculture or family-based farming. Given that agricultural workforces cannot be sustained by sugar, coffee, tobacco, or cotton – and that these commodities attracted higher returns than grains – plantation owners had to import food for their workers in addition to exporting their produce, typically to distant markets. Such requirements, when combined the needs for fixed investments in milling equipment and plantation barracks, made New World plantations the preserve of commercially oriented ventures that were beyond the means of the ordinary settler of European ancestry.

With profit maximization their goal, and the sustenance of their workforces their principal costs, slavery proved to be the lifeblood of the New World plantations. Significantly, its progress advanced hand-in-glove with the managerial and economic advances in its British heartland. Prior to 1750, Hugh Thomas (1997: 318) estimates in his massive tome on the Atlantic slave trade, some 85% of British textile exports were shipped to West Africa where they were exchanged for slaves; slaves who were then shipped to the Americas to grow cotton and sugar. Ships then completed their great triangular oceanic route by returning to their home port loaded with plantation produce. In many cases, Thomas (1997: 540–541) reveals, the same merchants boasted ownership of British textile mills, slave ships, and slave-worked plantations. British ships also carried slaves for other nations, Thomas (1997: 264) estimating that in the decade between 1740 and 1750 British ships carried over 200,000 slaves, far more than any other nation. Nor was it the case that slavery's role diminished as the eighteenth century progressed. Instead, with Eli Whitney's discovery of the cotton gin in 1793 removing a major obstacle to supply, slavery in the southern states of the United States experienced expansion as American cotton exports rose 25-fold between 1792 and 1820. Within the British Empire itself, the slave population grew by more than a quarter between 1790 and 1806, causing the

British abolitionist, William Wilberforce, to bemoan the fact that slavery was being "more fondly nourished than before...fattened with fuller meals of misery and murder" (cited Thomas 1997: 540–541).

The global experiences that gave rise to the modern world – a world characterized by integrated markets, labor and capital specialization, capitalism, and the steady advance of democracy and civic rights in the industrializing districts on either side of the North Atlantic – indicate that the dynamic that drove the Industrial Revolution produced not one model of management and work but several. For if we think about the management of a slave plantation in the Americas in the early decades of the nineteenth century, it is evident that it was as much a part of the global system of firm specialization and market exchanges as a textile mill in Lancashire. If it survived for any length of time, we can also assume that its owners and managers operated their plantation on rational, bureaucratic principles, paying attention to their internal costs as well as to changes in market demand for their produce. Despite such shared commonalities, we can nevertheless also understand that the managerial model on which a slave plantation in the Americas, or a Russian landed estate worked with serfs, was not only profoundly different to one based on free labor, it was also – in the medium to long-term – incompatible with it. For managers, a reliance on slavery leads to an inevitable productivity trap. Whereas, as we noted above, the amount of fixed capital associated with the average British textile worker rose tenfold between 1800 and 1830, such advances were not possible with workforces that were not literate, skilled, and motivated. In terms of the relationships between governments and citizens, the forms of legal protections and contractual arrangements that rapidly became the norm in industrializing states (protective factory acts, sanitation laws, minimum hours, collective bargaining through trade unions) were also incompatible with systems of unfree labor (serfdom, slavery, etc.). Economies based on unfree labor also denied themselves the social cohesion, dynamism, and innovation that were to be found in societies such as late nineteenth-century Britain where, as noted above, even Engels was forced to concede that "the most crying abuses" had largely disappeared.

If we disqualify – as this study does – the managerial systems associated with Russian serfdom and New World slavery from inclusion within the ranks of "modern management," then we must logically also exclude those societies in today's world that are also characterized by large-scale use of unfree or partially free labor. Prominent among this latter category in the current global economy is the People's Republic of China. As a report commissioned for the World Trade Organization, undertaken by the International Trade Union Confederation (ITUC 2010: 1), reveals, China has never ratified four core International Labor Organization standards relating to forced labor and child labor. According to the ITUC report, "forced labor" is still a common feature of China's "commercial enterprises." China is also characterized by "the worst forms of child labor," often undertaken under "forced conditions." Under the Chinese "hukou" (household registration) system, the ITUC (2010: 9–10) report also notes, Chinese workers are legally denied freedom of movement. Those working in cities in breach of their registration – a group estimated to comprise 35% of China's urban workforce (130 million people) in 2010 – suffer from what the ITUC refers to as, "Institutionalized discrimination." "Many employers," the ITUC (2010: 14) concluded, "withheld employees' payments until the contract's expiration," a condition that the ITUC believes places workers in circumstances akin to de facto "forced labor." "Trafficking in human beings" the ITUC (2010: 15) also found to be "a serious problem" with the Chinese government impeding the work of nongovernmental agencies who seek to mitigate both the extent and the effects of human trafficking.

The lesson of history over the last two centuries is that societies that deny their citizens not only free movement of capital and labor but also individual freedom of expression have ultimately proved economic as well as political failures. And while the People's Republic of China may prove an exception to this rule, the author very much doubts it. For where a society has in the past relied to a significant extent on unfree or partially free labor – labor denied opportunities for freedom of movement and unprotected by enforceable contracts and laws that guarantee it an income regarded by a worker's peers as fair and just – this has resulted in one of two outcomes: either the abolition from within of that part of the economy characterized by unfree labor, as occurred with the abolition of slavery in the British Empire and the United States in 1834 and 1865, respectively, and with the ending of Russian serfdom in 1861, or total internal collapse (as occurred in the Soviet Union in 1991).

In the final analysis, therefore, systems of management cannot be understood apart from the societies that they do so much to shape. The system of management that emerged in association with the Industrial Revolution has prospered in large part because it has been associated with individual freedom, respect for private property, free labor forces, the regulation of business and employment through an agreed system of contracts and laws, and last, but not least, political democracy. Unsurprisingly, societies demarked by such characteristics have also proven their worth through a record of innovation that has fueled increased productivity and economic advance. That this managerial model has endured, while others have not, speaks volumes.

Conclusion

In his *Practice of Management*, Peter Drucker (1963: 17), one of the most thoughtful as well as long-lived management thinkers of the twentieth century, lamented the fact that, "Despite its critical importance. . .management is the least known and the least understood of our basic institutions." If we are to talk about "management" and "management history," therefore, we need to define with some care what we mean by the term "management." It will certainly not suffice to define management – as text books are wont to do – as involving the coordination of four functions: planning, organizing, leading, and controlling. For if we accept this definition, as many have, this is little to differentiate the job of a manager employed on a current construction project in Sydney, London, or New York from the overseers who spent their working day building the pyramids of ancient Egypt or China's Great Wall. Nor is there much to distinguish the modern construction manager from their counterparts in Stalinist Russia who were also responsible for notable engineering feats (the Dnieper hydro-electric dams, the White Sea canal, the Moscow subway system, the Moscow-Volga Waterway). In all cases, after all, planning has/had to occur. Labor has/had to be recruited and kept on task. Deadlines met and achieved within available resources. Despite such similarities, one nevertheless makes the gravest of grave errors in confusing management as it has existed in democratic societies since the Industrial Revolution with that found in either preindustrial or modern totalitarian societies; societies in which coercion of the unfree or semi-free was seminal to the obtainment of economic objectives. In describing, for example, the systems of work and management involved in building the Moscow-Volga Waterway – an engineering marvel that permanently protected Moscow from transport-induced shortages – Schlogel (2008/2012: 286) recounts how:

> The commandants of the individual sectors competed with one another to increase productivity, i.e., to exploit slave labour...Many prisoners, exhausted by the work, fell into the concrete foundations and were buried in them; many terminally sick workers were buried alive because hospital beds had to be kept free for those still capable of work.

If we are to differentiate "modern management" as found in industrialized, democratic societies from other historical forms of task completion, it is evident that we must look beyond the standard textbook definition. In summary, "modern management" can be differentiated by five characteristics. First it is attentive to its costs, both in terms of its expenditures on materials and – more importantly – on the value it places on labor. Yes, efficiency and productivity necessarily depend on maximizing outputs per unit of labor. But this is obtained by increasing the outputs through the use of fixed capital, effective organization, and innovation: not by devaluing the price of labor. Second, modern management is based on establishing its unique competitive advantage, an advantage that comes through firm and labor specialization. A third factor, closely connected with the second, is the direction of output – whether in the form of goods or services – toward mass markets and a system of free exchange; for only mass markets can sustain production units based on specialization. The fourth prerequisite for modern systems of management is associated with legal frameworks that sanction negotiated contracts of exchange and employment while also protecting private property and individual rights. Finally, modern management is built on the free movement of capital and labor, on the right of individuals to choose whether they wish to work for themselves or on behalf of another party for hire and reward. If we are to extend our definition, then, from "management" to "management history," then the latter is not a general history of work throughout the ages. Rather, it must be an account of the emergence of the particular *type* of management – associated with the above characteristics – and of its fundamentally progressive role in human advance over the last 270 years.

References

Barnard CI (1938) The functions of the executive. Harvard University Press, Cambridge, MA

Bartol K, Tein M, Mathews G, Martin D (2005) Management: a Pacific rim focus, 4th edn. McGraw-Hill, North Sydney

Braudel F (1946/1975a) The Mediterranean and the Mediterranean world in the age of Philip II, vol. 1. Torch Books, New York

Braudel F (1946/1975b) The Mediterranean and the Mediterranean world in the age of Philip II, vol. 2. Torch Books, New York

Braudel F (1982) Civilization and capitalism: The wheels of commerce. Harper & Row, 1982

Braverman H (1974) Labor and monopoly capital: the degradation of work in the twentieth century. Monthly Review Press, New York

Chandler AD Jr (1977) The visible hand: the managerial revolution in American business. Belknap Press, Cambridge, MA

Clapham JH (1930/1967) An economic history of modern Britain: The early railway age, 1820–1850. Cambridge University Press, Cambridge

Creighton A (2017) Unis falling to deliver for business. Australian

Cummings S, Bridgman T, Hassard J, Rowlinson M (2017) A new history of management. Cambridge University Press, Cambridge

Cunningham H (2011) Child labour's global past 1650–2000. In: Lieten K, van Nederveen ME (eds) Child labour's global past, 1650–2000. Peter Lang, Bern, pp 61–74

Deane P, Habakkuk HJ (1963) The take-off in Britain. In: Rostow WW (ed) The economics of take-off into sustained growth. Macmillan, London, pp 63–82

Drucker P (1963) The practice of management. Pan Books, London

Engels F (1892/1951) Preface of the 1892 edition: the condition of the working-class in England in 1844. In: Marx K, Engels F (eds) Selected works, vol. 2. Foreign Languages Publishing House, Moscow, pp. 368–380

Ferguson N (2011) Civilization: the West and the rest. Penguin Books, London

Foucault M (1980) Governmentality. In: Foucault M (trans: Gordon C, Marshall L, Mepham J, Soper K) Power/knowledge: selected interviews and other writings. Pantheon Books, New York, pp 1972–1977

Foucault M (1984) What is enlightenment? In: Rabinov P (ed) The Foucault reader. Penguin, London

Guterres A (2017) Report of the secretary-general on the work of the organization, 2017. United Nations, New York

Harbison F, Myers CA (1959) Management in the industrial world: an international analysis. McGraw-Hill, New York

Hobbes T (1651/2002) Leviathan. Broadway Press, Peterborough

Hume D (1739/1893) A treatise on human nature, vol. 3. Clarendon Press, Oxford

International Trade Union Confederation (2010) Internationally recognised core labour standards in the People's Republic of China: report for the WTO council review of the trade policies of the People's Republic of China, 12 May. https://www.ituc-csi.org/IMG/pdf/Chinal_Final-2.pdf. Accessed 12 Jan 2018

Kant I (1787/2007) Critique of pure reason. Penguin Classics, London

Keynes JM (1936/1973) The general theory of employment, interest and money. MacMillan, London

Kirby P (2011) The transition to working life in eighteenth and nineteenth-century England and Wales. In: Lieten K, van Nederveen ME (eds) Child labour's global past, 1650–2000. Peter Lang, Bern, pp 119–136

Locke J (1680/1823) Two treatise on government. McMaster Archive of the History of Economic Thought, Toronto. http://www.yorku.ca/comninel/courses/3025pdf/Locke.pdf. Accessed 9 Jan 2018

Magnusson L (2009) Nation, state and the industrial revolution: the visible hand. Routledge, London

Marx K, Engels F (1848/1951) The communist manifesto. In: Marx K, Engels F (eds) Selected works, vol. 1. Foreign Languages Publishing House, Moscow, pp. 32–61

Miller P, O'Leary T (1987) Accounting and the construction of the governable person. Acc Organ Soc 12(3):235–265

Murphy P, Liao L, Welsch H (2006) A conceptual history of entrepreneurial thought. J Manag Hist 12(1):12–35

Nef JU (1932) The rise of the British coal industry, vol 2. Frank Cass & Co., London

O'Rourke K (1997) The European grain invasion, 1870–1913. J Econ Hist 57(4):775–801

Pollard S (1965) The genesis of modern management: a study of the industrial revolution in Great Britain. Edward Arnold, London

Rousseau JJ (1763/1979) Emile, or treatise on education. Penguin Classics, London

Schlogel M (2008/2012) Moscow 1937. Polity Press, Cambridge

Smith A (1776/1999) An inquiry into the nature and causes of the wealth of nations. Penguin Classics, London

Stockwell C (2014) Same as it ever was: top ten most common college majors. USA Today College. http://college.usatoday.com/2014/10/26/same-as-it-ever-was-top-10-most-popular-college-majors/. Accessed 7 Dec 2018

Thomas H (1997) The slave trade: the history of the Atlantic slave trade 1440–1870. Picador, London

Thompson EP (1963) The making of the English working class. Penguin, London

Voltaire (1726/2002) Letters on England. Pennsylvania State University Electronic Series Publication, Hazlcton

Webb S, Webb B (1920) The history of trade unionism, 1666–1920. Longmans, Green & Co., London

Weber M (1922/1927) General economic history. The Free Press, Glencoe

Weber M (1922/1978) Economy and society, vol. 2. University of California Press, Berkeley

Witzel M (2012) A history of management thought. Routledge, Abington

World Bank (2017) On-line database: indicators – agricultural and rural development. https://data.worldbank.org/indicator/SI.POV.DDAY?end=2016&start=1981&view=chart. Accessed 8 Nov 2017

Debates Within Management History

3

Jeffrey Muldoon

Contents

Introduction 46
Context 46
Slavery 51
Taylor: Wizard or Weasel? 55
Mayo's Many Problems 56
Taylor and Mayo: Friends or Foes? 58
Who Are Management Thinkers? 60
The Prime Mover 62
Conclusion 63
References 64

Abstract

The purpose of this chapter is to examine the various debates within management history. Although these debates touch upon epistemology and method, they are not the focus of the chapter. Rather, the chapter focuses on various debates about context, slavery, Taylor, Mayo, the prime movers, and identification of management thinkers. I recap the events, offer explanations, and attempt to develop further research queries.

Keywords

Historical context · Slavery · Taylor · Mayo

J. Muldoon (✉)
Emporia State University, Emporia, KS, USA
e-mail: jmuldoon@emporia.edu

© The Author(s), under exclusive licence to Springer Nature Switzerland AG 2020
B. Bowden et al. (eds.), *The Palgrave Handbook of Management History*,
https://doi.org/10.1007/978-3-319-62114-2_6

45

Introduction

In addition to debates about history, namely, its method assumptions and other macro issues, there are issues regarding smaller-scale problems, such as the role of Taylorism and the benefits of the Hawthorne studies. The previous chapter was informed by such debates, as different schools of thought have different traditions and levels of understanding over these issues. For example, Marxist and critical studies scholars have vastly different perceptions of the Hawthorne studies than do more mainstream historians. Likewise, some scholars view Henry Ford as a hero; others view him as a tyrant. Of course, these debates have been ongoing since the beginning of management as an academic discipline. There is little difference in the shape, discourse, or even criticisms of various management concepts that have not already been mentioned. For example, as I (Muldoon 2012) demonstrated in articles on Hawthorne criticisms, the same criticisms mentioned today (originality, lack of theory, design, and worker manipulation) are the same of yesteryear.

Yet, these debates enliven and enrich the profession. They force us to ask important questions and use different sources to determine the past as it was. For example, the work on the Hawthorne studies and originality forced scholars to ask such questions as what made the Hawthorne studies distinct over it competitors. Do we have a political bias in our profession? Are our political biases different than those in other professions? These questions demonstrate the newness of the profession and the lack of an overriding paradigm. Thus, they demonstrate the limits of the field. More precisely, they demonstrate the real and seemingly insurmountable divides that exist within the field.

That being said, there is good and bad history – regardless of the source, political bias, or worldview. The purpose of this chapter is to delve into these debates so as to either repeat the debate, answer the debate, change the terms of the debate, or spur more debate. The first section is on the role of context, especially how that context is related to various political debates and movements that intersect with management. The second section is on the question of what role should slavery have in management thought. The third section and fourth section are a recap of the debate on Taylor and Mayo. The fifth section of the paper is on the question of who are management thinkers. The final section is on prime movers.

Context

Recently scholars have been extending the boundaries of management thought by considering the questions related to the context in which various studies have occurred (e.g., Hassard 2012). I have found this work very interesting and well done. But more work is needed on this issue, especially since scholars do not consider all issues regarding particular time periods. We need to consider the social, economic, academic, and political context more deeply within which management has been developed. This would enable scholars to view why certain theories developed and other theories declined. However, there is a word of caution – to truly understand the context of the periods in which management thought developed, we need to immerse ourselves in that time period (Bailyn 2015 for a perspective of a true past master).

One issue that has been generally ignored is the academic context. The university after the Second World War was vastly different from the one before the war (Homans 1984; Schlesinger 2000). However, I believe scholars treat it as a constant. The period after the war was one of growth, government and corporate funding, and increased enrollments (Steinmetz 2007). These changes made major differences in how management was developed. For instance, Foster et al. (2014b) point out that the Hawthorne studies did not receive attention in the textbook press until after the war. While I agree with this finding, it ignores the academic context in which the studies occurred. American universities did not hire young faculty due to a lack of funding during the Depression – even Harvard (Homans 1984). Second, both the Depression and the War limited the amount of journal possible due to money issues, as well as the amount of books. There were only a handful of journals in sociology before the war. Third, the problems of labor after the war are ignored – making additional ways of dealing with labor needed. Fourth, both sociology, management, and psychology were changing in different ways – becoming more scientific and less of an advocacy.

Scholars have been attempting to attach management thought to a wide variety of political and social contexts (e.g., Cummings et al. 2017). One of those contexts has been the Progressive Era in the United States. While some work has been done in this area (including this book series), more work is needed. Historians tend to downplay management in their works on the Progressive Era, but I imagine that the same process that led to psychology and sociology being formed played a role in transforming management, namely, the transformation of knowledge that allowed scholars to recognize government intervention, private property, and the difference between the individual and the group (Kloppenberg 1986).

However, an admonishment to scholars, when writing about the Progressive Era, scholars should be aware of the complexities of the period. There were so many types of progressivism and such rigorous debate that treating as progressivism one cohesive movement would be difficult to do (Filene 1970). Cummings et al. did not do so – conflating the efficiency movement with conservation, when it was far more comprehensive (Muldoon 2019). The efficiency movement is such a large, international movement that both John Rockefeller and Vladimir Lenin were both members. One particular issue is that the Progressive Era was less about restraining markets and more than opening them up (McCormick 1981). What drove Progressives was the idea that business corrupted politics and that we should have government regulation to prevent that from occurring. In addition, businessmen were as important to the reform movement as other experts (Wiebe 1962). This was not the case in Great Britain, where political and intellectual leaders believed management needed to get its house in order (Searle 1971). One important point is that it would be wrong to assume that the United States was a free market system. It had both a welfare state (Skocpol 1992) and a significant degree of economic regulation, but on the state level, rather than federal (McCormick 1981).

Scholars are attempting to get a handle on the New Deal and its impact on management thought. Mills and his coauthors (2014, 2015, 2017) have demonstrated the importance of the New Deal for organizational behavior and management. This is somewhat ironic because many of the postmodernists dislike artificial labels and the New Deal is an artificial label since it had no coherent thought pattern (Brinkley 1995). I would similarly state that one of the problematic issues with Wren and Bedeian (2018) is that they do not denote enough attention to the New Deal as they should, which I regard as a limitation in their work.

A word of caution when considering the New Deal: People need to pay close attention to the phase of the New Deal because it was so complex. We must understand the complexities of it, since it is wrapped myth. Many scholars believe the New Deal to be Keynesian or antibusiness; it was both and neither. It depends on the phase of the New Deal. The first New Deal enjoyed the backing of big business (Schlesinger 1959, 1960). The first New Deal's origin was from associationism, the attempt of big business to avoid price competition by creating voluntary cartels (Gordon 1992). The first New Deal's major accomplishment, the National Recovery Administration, had its basis in the Swope Plan, the brainchild of the CEO of General Electric (Schlesinger 1958, 1959; Kennedy 1999). Notably, the Du Ponts supported Roosevelt because they believed the repeal of prohibition and the restoration of the alcohol tax would lead to a reduction of the corporate tax rate (Gordon 1992). It was not until the Second New Deal, and the 1936 election, that FDR took an adverse position to entrenched privilege. Some of the most ardent business opponents of FDR had originally been his supporters.

In terms of Keynesian economics, the picture is even more complex. In fact, one of the first major criticisms of the New Deal was James McGregor Burns, who argued that the New Deal needed more Keynesianism and that its limitations were due to a lack of government spending. Scholars have noted that Roosevelt and Keynes did not admire or even understand each other. In fact, Roosevelt ran in 1932 as a deficit hawk (Kennedy 1999). In 1937, Roosevelt actually sported balanced budgets, which may have caused another recession. One of Amity Shales (2007) points was that both conservative economists (Irving Fisher) and liberal economists (Keynes) had major issues with the New Deal. Of course, identifying a coherent theme in the New Deal is nearly impossible because the body of domestic programs and legislation was so diverse in its intellectual underpinnings, political support, and emotional appeals that no one could make consistent sense of it all (Brinkley 1995). Some of the New Dealers, such as Adolf Berle and Felix Frankfurter, hated each other less out of personality, but more on different views of the world.

Even so, there were crucial distinctions to be made in the rhetoric, versus the practice, of the New Deal administration in the late 1930s. As the historian Alan Brinkley (1995) noted, many liberals made distinctions between tyrannical businessmen, such as a Henry Ford, and enlightened businessmen, such as Henry Kaiser. After the events in 1937 and 1938, many New Dealers wished to use the state to promote competition and protect consumer rights. Even during the most radical programmatic changes, New Dealers were uninterested in breaking up large monopolies despite the presence of various exponents of Brandeis and Frankfurter, such as Benjamin Cohen and Thomas Corcoran (Schwartz 1994; Brinkley 1995). The New Deal's position on monopolies was one of ambivalence. The New Deal settled into two categories: (1) the "broker state," whereby the government would settle between various groups (Hawley 1966), and (2) the compensatory state, whereby the government would use fiscal methods to address issues in the economy but largely leave untouched the inner workings of capitalism (Brinkley 1995). The compensatory state used Keynesian policies to balance countercyclical shifts in the economy or used government funds to build infrastructure in the South and West to create new markets (Schwartz 1994). The New Deal was as pro-business as it was antibusiness.

What can we suggest in terms of new research from the points raised? Firstly, more research is needed on the political thought and activities of managers who played a crucial role in shaping the role of the state. Kim Phillips-Fein (2010) has written an excellent book on how business leaders led a revolt against big government. However, scholars should pay attention to the roles that business leaders took in enlarging the government and rent-seeking behaviors (Krueger 1974; Olson 1982). Henry Kaiser might not have been as successful in business without government backing (Schwarz 1994). Much of what scholars blame on the problems of the market are often rent-seeking behaviors that business leaders have pursued. Secondly, corporate involvement in the state would indicate that management has always had a deep concern, with social responsibility and promoting work as a means of solving social problems. One of the ideas that lead to the National Recovery Plan was the Swope Plan, which was the brainchild of Gerald Swope, President of General Electric (Kennedy 1999). John Hassard (2012) makes a similar point about Hawthorne works and welfare capitalism. However, this observation should be tempered with the fact that managers at the time had different social concerns than they do now and that concepts, such as welfare capitalism, are mentioned in traditional works of management history.

Greater attention needs to be spent on the Second World War. Simply put, the issue facing industrial nations, and especially the United States in 1945, was, to paraphrase Carl Becker, not who would rule abroad, but who would rule at home. The war greatly changed British, American, Japanese, Russian, and French social systems. The change of these social systems had to change management thought. Due to their losses in the War, the Japanese, French, and the Germans were able to reimage what management could be. For example, we know the Japanese embraced quality management after the War. But greater attention should be played on this issue. Likewise, the prestige of the Soviet state had never been higher than it was after the war. The British, though they won the war, lost an Empire and deferential social system and gained a welfare state and an American presence in their affairs. In part, the decline of British power was one of the reasons why the research of Joan Woodward was funded (Garrity et al. 2018).

The net result saw big business gain prestige in a manner unseen since the 1920s (Blum 1976; Brinkley 1995). The new war agencies were populated by big business men, such as Donald Nelson, William Knudsen, and Charles Wilson, thereby cultivating the relationship between big business and the government. The public's attitude toward big business radically changed during the War (Blum 1976). Many people believed it was the production capacity of the United States that caused the defeat of the Axis (Kennedy 1999). A number of businessmen had entered government service during the War and had become the famous "dollar a year men" (i.e., businesspeople who worked for government for a purely nominal sum). The prestige of big business even reached the hallowed halls of academia. Columbia's Allan Nevins, the eminent business historian, would comment to his classes that without big business, he would have two Gestapo men looking over him while he lectured (Jumonville 1999).

One of the arguments behind why Mayo's version became the dominant viewpoint was that businessmen believed that it would allow them the right to manage (Bruce and Nyland 2011). As I mentioned in my Hawthorne chapter, one of the reasons why human relations got noticed after the war was dealing with the aftermath of an unsteady labor situation. The willingness of managers to use different methods in dealing with labor, such as human relations, may have had to do with the prestige they gained during the war. In addition, liberal attitudes toward big business were tempered. Liberals also began to see voters as consumers, which changed their attitude toward corporate size. Consumers and liberals now recognized the benefits of economics of scale. Scholars should consider these issues as well in their analyses. As Peter Drucker wrote, managers and union leaders needed to search for ways to promote trust. Rather than using contracts (such as collective bargaining) or regulation, both sides needed to find ways to promote trust on a spontaneous basis. In addition, from a marketing and strategic standpoint, big business reorganized society through advertising. It weakened the citizen consumer concerned with social responsibility (Cohen 2003). This probably had a huge influence on how workers and the public viewed management.

One issue that scholars have ignored is the role of the Cold War in shaping management. Mills and coauthors (Kelley et al. 2006; Foster et al. 2014a) have argued that management historians have ignored the contributions of management thinkers, such as Frances Perkins, and concepts such as the New Deal. I find this comment curious, namely, because Franklin Roosevelt remained a popular figure in the Post-War Era (Leuchtenburg 1993). In addition, neither the Republicans nor their conservative allies sought to overturn various aspects of the New Deal, such as Social Security, Keynesianism, or farm payments (Patterson 1997). In fact, the Republican, Eisenhower, began one of the most massive public projects in history – the interstate road system. The 1950s were noted for their consensus, not their radicalism nor conservatism (Pells 1985). Even Ronald Reagan did not wish to overturn the New Deal, maintaining popular memories of it. Finally, if the Cold War were as intellectually constraining as Schrecker and others make it out to be, then how come we had a New Left?

Yet, the Cold War presumably did play a role in management. For example, what role did Americans have in transporting American management concepts to its allies? We have some notion of this since quality production was brought to Japan through American thinkers. A second reason – did the Soviets reject American concepts of management, or did they embrace them? Wren and Bedeian have an excellent article on Taylor and Leninism (2004), but future work is needed on the Stalin and post-Stalin period. A third important question should be – did the Cold War provide legitimacy to managers or did it limit it? The answer would depend upon which time period within the Cold War. The image of operations management took a hit during the Vietnam War, especially with the loss of respect of Robert McNamara and his methods of management. Did this limit operations management from gaining momentum? Did the emergence of Silicon Valley and its rejuvenation of the US economy aid in the Cold War? Did it create an increased emphasis on entrepreneurship in the profession?

One major issue that needs to be discussed is the role of the Cold War in distorting the ethics and morals of managers. Derek Leebaert (2002) wrote an important work in recognizing the true cost of the Cold War while at the same time as praising the righteousness of fighting communism. The cost to America was an increased level of unethical misconduct. The modern paper shredder, long a symbol of shredding unwarranted documents by business, has its genesis in the government. Likewise, would corporate espionage have been as common if there were not as many espionage and counterespionage agents out there? In addition, we know that affirmative action came into being due to government dictating policy in its contracting companies. In addition, the United States took on civil rights issues due to Soviet criticism. Due to both the War and Cold War, many companies entered into contracts with the US government – what other policies did the government enforce due to the Cold War?

One last question of context – why the United States? This previous section reveals a deep US bias. Indeed, of the top management thinkers in history, most have worked in the United States or were United States citizens. While the United States has dominated other sciences, I do not think that any other field comes with the dominance of the United States than management. Management did play a key role in establishing the United States as a global military and economic power – but what other factors lead to the United States becoming such a hotbed of management. In my chapters on Taylor, nineteenth-century management, and British management, I provide some answers – namely, knowledge transformation, number of engineers, number of universities, and a style based on production. One additional answer could be that of the three major conflicts of the twentieth century (the world wars and Cold War), and the United States emerged the winner of each. Scholars should consider this issue as well.

Slavery

Slavery has long plagued the human race. This practice, a holdover from the ancient world, continues to plague humanity even into the modern world despite the best efforts for its eradication. Wren and Bedeian (2018) do not consider the impact of slavery on management thought, an oversight that has been criticized. A principle issue is that slavery is not free labor. Despite the attempts of Marxian and critical scholars to argue that free labor is wage slavery, there is a vast difference between the two concepts. However, there are also questions whether American slaveholders produced works of management thought. Mostly, they borrowed concepts from ancient Rome and Greece – which Wren and Bedeian do cover.

One of Wren and Bedeian's most prominent critics, Bill Cooke (2003), whose paper on slavery has influenced many scholars, has works in critical management and postmodernism. The major implication of Cooke's work is that management is a flawed approach because much of the conceptualization of management is racism. Therefore, management and business historians, such as Chandler, Wren, and Bedeian, have overlooked the role of slavery and management's racist origins to ensure the legitimacy of management. Presumably, although Cooke does not write this, if management could accept its' racist and elitist past, perhaps we could build a management that is more receptive to social responsibility.

Cooke bases his argument on several facts. Firstly, he points out that slavery was big business. The economy of the South, if a separate nation, would have been, based on Fogel's work, the world's fourth largest economy. Secondly, Cooke demonstrates that Southern slavery barons were highly committed to extracting every penny they could from their slaves. Cooke notes that Jefferson sounded and acted like an efficiency expert. Thirdly, he notes that the South was industrializing, embracing some of the elements of modernism. Fourthly, Cooke, drawing on Richards (2000), argues that the South was the most politically powerful part of the United States, connected to the North's capitalistic structure. Fifthly, he notes that Taylor's racism, "notwithstanding his abolitionist parents," was such that he had the same racist views toward workers that a slave master would direct toward a slave. Cooke argues:

> First, for management to be modern, it has to take place within the capitalist system. Slavery is excluded from capitalism explicitly by Chandler with his assertion of ancientness, and his claims for a lack of separation of ownership and control in particular, and tacitly by Burnham and Braverman with their specification of wage labour as a defining feature. Second, for management to be management, the activities carried out in its name have to be of a certain level of sophistication – for Chandler, beyond the apparently simple harnessing of enslaved people's seasonally varying labour, for Burnham and Braverman in order to achieve wage labourers' submission to capitalist relations and processes of production. Third there has to be a group of people carrying out these management activities who have a distinctive identity as managers.

Cooke concludes that the slaveholding class was one based on capitalism, their viewpoints, and techniques mirrored those of modern business owners.

Cooke's opinions have found favorable reception among scholars and little written criticism. Although there is truth in what he writes, he makes several mistakes and ignores the crucial issues between the North and South, such that one could possibly call Cooke a "Civil War denialist." He completely glosses over the concept of free labor, the major underpinning of the Republican Party. That is not to say that the Republican Party consisted of abolitionists, but they viewed free labor as being morally, economically, and socially better than slave labor or other types of pre-modern labor models (such as indentured servitude) (McPherson 1988). The fear that slavery would spread into the territories and lower the status of free labor was the proximate cause of the American Civil War (Potter 1976). In fact, free labor was one of the crucial concepts that lead to the development of the American working class (Foner 1970). The free labor movement did recognize that laborers (even African Americans) should have some rights that could not be taken from them. I would suggest that critics read Allen Guelzo's (2008) and Harry Jaffa's (1959) work on the Lincoln-Douglas debates of 1858 or, even better, read the words of Lincoln himself, when he stated that slaves should enjoy the benefits of their labor.

Secondly, the lack of free labor caused the slaveholding South to develop moral arguments and other methods to gain slave acquiesce and self-serving reasons as to why they held slaves. Their major ideology was paternalism, an idea developed by Eugene Genovese (1976), considered one of the best historians on American slavery. Paternalism was a myth propagated by the slaveholding classes to justify, defend, and then advocate for slavery – not just for African Americans but for whites as well. Slave masters had the responsibility for clothing, sheltering, feeding, and protecting their slaves. Slaveholders also took a strong interest in the reproductive activities of their slaves and attempted to control their religion. In turn, these behaviors (which were self-serving) led slaveholders to believe that they were morally superior to Northerners because, due to paternalism, they were not exploiting their slaves. Their attention to slavery allowed them to devote their time and effort to classical work. In fact, rather than leaving contributions to management, they sought legitimation from classical works of the Greeks and Romans. The Southern view was that slavery was honorable. I imagine a scholar calling a Southerner the economic equivalent of a Northern mill owner would get that scholar, at minimum, a severe beating.

Thirdly, rather than being integrated into Northern political culture, the South was, slowly but surely, losing control of the political process (McPherson 1988). They had lost the House and Presidency in 1860. The territories acquired by the Mexican American War were probably more likely to be settled by the North, due to the population boom. Likewise, Northern Men of Southern principles, like James Buchanan, were absolutely hated in the North. The connection between the Northern Democracy and the Southern Democracy was shattered over the Kansas crisis. Even a reliable pro-Southern senator, such as Stephen A. Douglas, was unacceptable due to his unwillingness to endorse the Lecompton Constitution of Kansas. Cotton Whigs, Northern businessmen who did business with the South and favored concil-iation, were becoming ardent republicans.

Fourthly, Cooke overstates the numbers gathered by Fogel (1989). As Oscar Handlin noted, quantifying the slaveholding economy is difficult, since not only did slaveholders have a different perspective on economics, but the numbers were, at best, incomplete. This is the reason why Fogel's work received a poor reception among historians. Rather than suggesting a big business, half of Southern slaves lived on farms rather than on plantations and that only a quarter of Southern slaves lived on plantations with more than 50 slaves. In fact, Northerners were outstripping the South as many fortunes were produced by industrialization. Another particular issue is that Fogel and Engerman (1974) get facts wrong. For example, they vastly overstate the railroad connections in the South. Namely, they only considered one part of the railroad connection – when square feet and population are considered, the South had only half of the railroad capacity of the North. They also overstate production as well (McPherson 1988).

Fifthly, many abolitionists had a strong dislike of immigrants, especially those who were Catholic, suggesting that they were not very enlightened. The fusion of the various anti-slavery movements may have stumbled on the nativism of some of the groups, including the American (Know Nothing) Party. One of the major undertakings that early Republican leaders, such as Lincoln and William Henry Seward, did was to build bridges to all anti-slavery elements and limit nativism. Nevertheless, Taylor's racist opinions were not uncommon during the Progressive Era. In fact, many Progressives, such as Taylor, had similar attitudes toward immigrants and believed in concepts such as Social Darwinism and eugenics.

Finally, Cooke ignores the crucial and key differences between pre-modern and modern management. While the South did participate in a market economy, they could not be considered capitalistic, because their labor relationships were not market driven. They were driven by the paternalistic myths that were propagated by the slave owners. Slaves were not treated as individual workers who engaged in market relationships. They were treated like they were cattle – their sexual relationships, religion, social relationships, and living conditions were under the control of slave owners. They had no legal rights – slaves were not citizens; they could not legally sue. Slave owners could, under certain conditions, even kill their slaves without fear of penalty. Under all conditions, slave owners could brutally whip and even rape slaves. The only concept similar to this type of abuse was the conditions of Russian serfs. The system was so oppressive that the only way they could rebel was through covert means. Their conditions, material and otherwise, were vastly inferior to industrial workers in the North. Each of these conditions should be considered pre-modern.

To summarize, Cooke's approach ignores crucial economic and political distinctions between the North and South. Simply put, the South was based on a classical system. Southern plantation owners were trained in the classics and viewed themselves as the successors to Rome and Ancient Greece. They did not view issues the same as the North – the idea of a theory of management would have been alien to them. As Marx and Eugene Genovese have noted, the slaveholding South was a pre-modern society. Management was a modern idea embraced by the North – which changed its political culture from 1815 onward embracing commerce, industry, advancement, and innovation. The North was exemplified in the person of Abraham Lincoln, who was a lawyer, the prime profession of the industrializing north. While the North did not have comprehensive management theories, several of its thinkers, such as Lincoln, did consider the issue of labor and ownership. Some of these concepts were proto-Marxism, liberalism in the nineteenth-century sense, or Christian charity. Nevertheless, business interests in the North did not view the South as a similar economic system. Many Northern businessmen were abolitionists. Taylor and other reformers were related to and descendants of some of the pre-Civil War reformers. To deny these differences is to deny the Civil War.

Mostly, it is difficult, if not impossible, to overestimate the vast differences between the North and the South. This is reflected in the different working conditions between the two regions. As Lincoln himself wrote about labor conditions in the North, "I am glad to know that there is a system of labor where the laborer can strike if he wants to! I would to God that such a system prevailed all over the world." He noted, in terms of the rights, slaves "in some respects she (a slave woman) certainly is not my equal; but in her natural right to eat the bread she earns with her own hands without asking leave of any me else, she is my equal, and the equal of all others." The right of free workers for the fruits of their labor and their right to protect those fruits were something that was part and parcel of modernity. The basic division between slavery and free labor, and free labor's victory, meant that a new system of management would have to emerge.

Taylor: Wizard or Weasel?

Frederick Winslow Taylor has had a long career of being both admired and hated, praised and denounced, and honored and pilloried. For most management historians, Taylor has a strong reputation as a genius who saved the world; for other historians, Taylor is a mountebank who passed guesses as scientific fact. Arthur Bedeian summed it up best – Taylor: Wizard or Weasel? There seems to be little in the way between those two points, as scholars line up behind either one or the other of those two categories. Of course, it does beg the question – could he be both or neither? In fact, as was once said about another great figure, Taylor is such a large figure that he has contradictions and inconsistencies simply accrued to him. The literature reveals these divisions.

The chapter on Taylorism recaps some of the debate, so I will not repeat myself here. I suggest that Taylor, much like the Hawthorne studies, has a different legacy in management, sociology, or psychology. During his lifetime, Taylor was attacked and denounced as an exploiter of labor and a mountebank who dehumanized workers. If one were to review the work of Charlie Chaplin, Henry Cabot Lodge, and John Dos Passos, the image of the chained worker is one that is clearly seen. Their work could be seen as pre-modern, preferring a simpler, slower pace of labor. Lodge claimed that Taylorism violated concepts of the Renaissance. However, at the same time, when we review the work of Harold Lloyd and Lyndall Urwick, we see a person leading a charge that would transform the world into modernity. Peter Drucker goes forward, arguing that Taylor's contribution was America's greatest contribution to the world and was the guarantor of the Allied victory in World War II.

The first real salvo of the battle over Taylorism was launched by John Hoagland (1955), who argued that Taylor did not add anything new and that his work was derivative of others, especially Charles Babbage. Hoagland was actually booed for mentioning these criticisms at the Academy of Management. But things got really serious when Charles Wrege and Perroni (1974) started writing about Taylor. A talented archival historian, Wrege pursued Taylor with a ferocity of Javert chancing down Jean Valjean. Wrege was, in some ways, a model historian, who would have crossed an ocean to verify a comma. Wrege made two arguments. Firstly, Taylor lied or, at best, exaggerated his experiments. His depiction of Schmidt was a false one; Schmidt was hard working and industrious, a worker who built his own home. Secondly, more discouraging, was that Taylor committed plagiarism. While scholars have had issues with Wrege, his works have been widely read and cited. I found him to overstate and lack nuance, but I admired his diligence and effort.

There have been several rebuttals. One from Edwin Locke (1982) was widely cited and highly influential. Locke's point was interesting – Taylor got the major issues correct. In fact, Locke points out that Taylorism could be seen as a forerunner of goal-setting and modern occupational testing and training. Chris Nyland (1998) has made several important and lasting contributions in tracing the relationship between Taylorism and Progressivism/Liberalism. In fact, Rexford Tugwell, a member of the Brains Trust, was a real admirer and sought to plan the economy in a Taylorite fashion. Others, such as Wagner-Tsukamoto (2007, 2008), have pointed out the strengths and weaknesses of Taylorism. The strength was that it attempted to eliminate conflict between management and the worker through a mutual gains strategy and proper incentives. Wagner-Tsukamoto, however, did note that Taylorism had a limited approach in that he assumed that managers would behave well.

Taylorism itself has a complicated past. Firstly, Taylorism could be seen as an attempt, by businessmen, to rationalize work, similar to the process of rationalizing other aspects of life, including home, education, and social. Secondly, Taylorism also could be seen as an attempt by management to destroy worker culture and deprive them of the opportunity to express themselves. Scholars should review works by Herbert Gutman and David Montgomery to understand how worker culture expressed attitudes toward work. Thirdly, Taylorism could be viewed as either part of the Enlightenment or Progressivism. Fourthly, scholars have written about the dehumanizing aspects of Taylorism – many critics, especially those in Great Britain, did not feel that Taylorism was ethical, to use a loaded term.

I feel the next era of research for Taylorism should be in two distinct categories. The first one is exposited by Cummings, Bridgman, Hassard, and Rowlinson in their work, *A New Management History*. I have expressed my opinions about the issues and merits of that work, both in the *Journal of Management History* and in this Palgrave series, but Cummings et al. do raise an interesting point – what was the relationship between Taylorism and the larger efficiency movement? The efficiency movement had a very large tent – both Lenin and Rockefellers were members of it. I would state the examining the relationship between the two movements would be interesting. I would also urge scholars to examine Taylorism through the lens of social networks and innovation theory to explain how this breakthrough happened. My speculation was that Taylor really did an expert job at promoting and developing a cadre of disciples.

Mayo's Many Problems

Elton Mayo and the Hawthorne studies have had a most unusual career in management history. I think that no other work has inspired so much research or provoked as much anger in scholars. There have been heated comments written over the years regarding Mayo, the results, interpretations, writings of the study, and design. It seems that every scholar brings their own biases toward the studies as they see what they want to see. This does not mean that they are wrong – the thing about Hawthorne is that the studies are so broad, so imprecise, that we could read what we wish, even to the point of viewing the political biases of the Hawthorne researchers and critics. Most commenters viewed Mayo and his group as conservative and protectors of the status quo; others attacked Mayo for being vaguely radical; and some, in the case of Daniel Bell, attacked him for being both. Mayo certainly had an interesting career, especially since the aims of the Harvard Group, rather than being radical, were limited in their purpose.

There are several crucial issues that make the Hawthorne Studies and Mayo complicated. The first one is the myth that he discovered human relationships at work. Of course, there are other scholars that could be seen as developing or focusing on human relationships – including Whiting Williams, Henry Denison, and Stanley Mathewson. In fact, the British experience with human relations reveals that they had recognized a social side to the enterprise well before Mayo did – John Child states that 10 years prior to the Hawthorne studies, we see something similar in British management thought. In fact, as Wren and Bedeian (2018) point out, we can see Mayo's ideas in Taylor's. Locke (1982) goes further and states that Taylor recognized group influence. John Hassard (2012) argues that Western Electric had a well-developed human relations program as part of their welfare capitalism initiatives. The Hawthorne studies seem to have discovered nothing new.

There is much merit in these opinions. However, there are subtle differences between the various forms of human relations. Firstly, there was a difference between welfare capitalism and Mayo's writings. This is true due to the fact that welfare capitalism was all but dead by 1933 (Kennedy 1999). Secondly, did management thinkers have access to the materials that a modern scholar would have? Although many people wrote about human relations, the number of journals was limited, and concerns about social aspects about industrial relations did not emerge until later. Finally, we need to consider more the circumstances in which Mayo and his associates worked – carrying the concept of human relations up until the present.

Likewise, there are tremendous debates about the facts and findings of the Hawthorne studies. There is little agreement about the findings of the study. In fact, one commentator called the studies scientifically worthless (Carey 1967). Parsons (1974), Carey (1967), and Argyle (1953) have each published a well-known article about the issues of the study. Morgan Witzel has argued that the studies could not be replicated; Homans argued that there was plenty of replication. Some saw the studies having better controls; others saw them as being more qualitative, a pilot study for more substantial research. Writer Wilbert Moore (1947) viewed the studies as having poor or little theory (Child 1969); British observers admired that Mayo provided a vocabulary through which theory could be developed. Shifting through the various opinions will take time and energy. Perhaps one solution may be tracking the expertise of the critics.

Much vitriol has been directed toward Mayo – who has been under attack over the years. Many scholars have argued that Mayo's political views were fascistic; others have attacked him over his lack of credentials; others have attacked him for being a poor scientist and more of an advocate. Henry Landsberger (1958) offered a defense of the Hawthorne studies that reasoned that *Management and the Worker* was scientifically sound, but Mayo's advocacy was in error. In addition, scholars have found that Mayo was not a real medical doctor but someone who faked his academic credentials. It has also came out that Mayo had strong ties to businesses that funded his research. Others, especially those who were his students and associates, have noted his brilliance, insight, and vision. One particular issue is that Mayo acted in a manner different to the ways in which other academics act – both modern and contemporary.

A major problem with the Hawthorne studies and Mayo is that the historians have lost the context of the studies. I have written about the context in several articles. However, another potential contextual issue is that Mayo had the pulse on what academics and others wished. A potential explanation for why Mayo and the studies have gained such attention was that they were examining something very important – what causes spontaneous cooperation. Spontaneous cooperation is the concept that people freely exchange, without discussing beforehand, the benefits each party will entail. Another way to look at it, Mayo and his group were researching what causes trust in a society. Taylor assumed that trust could come from science. However, he failed to note that workers had little reason to trust management. In fact, they should feel the opposite. Likewise, Mayo was interested in what structures exist in society to promote trust as humanity moved pre-modern concepts to modern concepts. Society switching from a premarket subsistence-based mode of production to a modern one based on the market created social problems. Mayo sought to understand what created trust. Mayo ignored the structures that existed that promoted trust – but his fascination with trust marks a major part of modern management.

Perhaps one particular solution to these problems is for historians to ask questions like: Why did Mayo's version of human relations become the standard? Why did Mayo gain the level of recognition that eluded other scholars and commentators such as Williams? Did Mayo's Harvard connections play a role? What were the aspects of Hawthorne that have allowed it to be criticized? I have started answering some of these questions with my research. The important issue of the Hawthorne studies was not what happened in Cicero but how people were inspired by the studies. Future research should examine Mayo's connections to younger scholars, who would refine and develop his work.

Taylor and Mayo: Friends or Foes?

Taylor and Mayo have had an interesting coexistence together. If nothing else, no two men in the literature have been as cited and misunderstood as these men. The popular literature focuses on the fact that Mayo saved workers from the throes of autocratic scientific management by allowing them freedom to develop social relationships at work (Muldoon 2012). Thus, it would appear that these two scholars are foes. Apparently, the Taylor society did not hold Mayo in high regard (Bruce 2015). Some critics of Taylor, such as the journalist Stuart Chase, argued that Mayo's ideas would trump Taylor, due to the social costs of Taylorism. It seemed natural that these two concepts would be placed in competition against each other, like a matched pair.

Yet, Taylor recognized the need for relationships, and Roethlisberger (1948) had kind things to say about Taylorism and viewed human relations as an extension of Taylorism. Mayo (1945: 69–70) recognized three persistent challenges in industrial civilization as the following (Cooper 1962):

1. The application of science and technical skill to some material good or product.
2. The systematic ordering of operations.
3. The organization of teamwork - that is of sustained cooperation.

Taylor would have also likely recognized these challenges. However, Taylor's focus was more on the first two issues, with less emphasis on the second. Taylor dealt with the issue of the organization of teamwork through the education of the workforce and higher pay. The difference between Taylor's and Mayo's perspectives was regarding pay as a motivator. The primary assumption of Taylor was that of the rationality of a worker, namely, the drive for self-improvement. He made an assumption that a psychologist would not have made.

Mayo ignored the first two issues listed above and developed an approach to analyze teamwork. Mayo's assumption that the workers were irrational precluded the fact that workers could ever totally buy into a system based on science. Even if such a system existed, it could not consider every single contingency. Taylor overestimated the ability of planners to plan. Only through a system that encouraged "spontaneous collaboration" could workers achieve "sustained cooperation." Mayo was unclear what the system was but pointed out that social skills on the part of management were a necessity when working with groups, although he did not elaborate on what those specific social skills were (Mayo 1945; Mayo and Lombard 1944). Yet Mayo lacked an overall structure to provide an answer to both. That answer would come from Peter Blau (1964) and George Homans (1961). Therefore, what Mayo sought was to extend Taylorism to handle the organization of spontaneous cooperation. In fact, modern high-performance work systems combine the factors of both Mayo and Taylor.

Scholars have written extensively about the relationship between these two very different and interesting men. Given the level of writing, it is not surprising that this theme has been exhausted and is no longer worthy of consideration. In fact, Dan Wren wrote to me that the two are so different that there is little benefit in comparing them. The typical response – one forwarded by Stuart Chase – was that human relations replaced scientific management. This point was raised by some of Mayo's associates, such as William Foote Whyte. However, while there is some merit to each statement, a better point might be what limitation of Taylorism did human relations touch upon? The biggest issue was that despite the success of Taylorism and rationalization of work, trust between management and labor remained low. Peter Drucker (1946) noted that human relations had the potential to address the issue of trust.

Who Are Management Thinkers?

This is one of the most difficult questions that management historians have had to answer over the years. Given that modern management is a combination of engineering, sociology, psychology, anthropology, and economics with little overlap at times between those schools of thought, it has been difficult to determine who is or who is not a management thinker. For example, Milton Friedman is considered one of the great economists of the twentieth century, but he has written, mostly as a public intellectual, about shareholder rights and corporate social responsibility. Abraham Maslow, Job Adams, B.F. Skinner, and many other psychologists have made contributions to management thought without gracing a business school. The question becomes even more difficult for consultants and actual managers. How much consideration should we give popularizers such as Tom Peters and other consultants? Is Jack Welch or Sheryl Sandberg a management thinker? Should we give attention to a popularizer as much as someone who produces original work? How do we determine influence?

Compounding this question are the attitudes brought into consideration by the new management historians who point out the social embeddedness of these questions. If history is subjective and based on power, then we could consider new thinkers that have been ignored? To them, management is too male, too white, too beholden to power, and too capitalistic. There are several examples of this new trend. Bridgeman et al. (2017) urge researchers to consider Theodore Roosevelt, Louis Brandeis, and Gifford Pinchot as management scholars. Kristen Williams and Albert G. Mills have argued that scholars should consider Frances Perkins as well. Other scholars have argued that we should consider Charles Clinton Spalding and Mary Van Kleeck. The point of this research is expressed by Williams and Mills (2017): "we directly challenge the assumption that history is unchangeable and push for new and evolved thoughts and interpretations. Therefore, this is an exercise in rethinking the discipline, the concepts and practices and the players (visible and invisible); and discovering new insights into the notion and construction of MOS and associated histories." This is an apt viewpoint.

However, there are several issues about these claims. Firstly, the concept that management thinkers have been sexist and racist limiting the influence of certain thinkers is not a deep or original concept. To state otherwise is history by wish and, as scholars, that is something we should not do. Secondly, the influence of a person's thought can be determined through contextual, textual, and citation analysis. We could see, as with traditional management history, a progression from the work of Taylor to Mayo to Carnegie and beyond. It is probable that Taylor had a deep impact on management thought. It is not probable that Theodore Roosevelt, who failed at business, had a direct impact on management thought. Of course, Progressives, New

Dealers, and their conservative critics did have an impact – but that impact may have been indirect. Thirdly, although looking at history from the viewpoint of the disadvantaged has its benefits, our commitment to history should, and must, outweigh our commitment to justice – whatever that may be.

Furthermore, traditional historians have sought to unearth figures in history, such as Whiting Williams, whom Wren wrote a very good biography about. Bedeian and Greenwood have written about several figures that history has ignored or not provided adequate context. The purpose of this history is to force us to analyze why a particular thinker or model came to dominate the field or became the prime mover as I stated in the last section. Yet, contrary to the *New Management History*, we consider that conservative thinkers, who came to management from fields, are ignored. One of them is George Homans, the father of social exchange theory (SET). SET is one of the most researched and important theories in management influencing fields such as motivation, leadership, performance, personality, justice, and attitudes. Yet, Homans does not receive the recognition that is his due. Homans should have been assigned to play a major role in management history, ranking with such men as Barnard, Mayo, and Simon. Yet, in Wren and Bedeian's (2009) classic work on management thought, Homans does not receive credit for his contribution to SET; his name is only mentioned for his work in the *Human Group* (1950) and his contribution to the Hawthorne studies. Also, George (1968) does not mention Homans at all. The lack of reference to Homans' work in the literature is somewhat incongruent with what scholars thought about Homans during his lifetime. For example, William Foote Whyte, in *Organizational Behavior: Theory and Application*, argues that Homans made the following contributions to management: event-process analysis, exchange, and distributive justice (Whyte 1969). That is to say nothing about his contributions to industrial sociology (Appold 2006; Miller and Form 1951) or his defense of the Hawthorne studies (Muldoon 2012, 2017).

Why does Homans not receive more mention in the annals of management history? For one, Homans, despite writing on industrial sociology and management, was a sociologist who mostly dealt with theory. Homans' inability to gain a position in the Harvard Business School and his subsequent departure to the sociology department consigned him to a career as a theorist (Muldoon et al. 2013). Had Homans worked with Fritz Roethlisberger and other leading lights in the business school, his contributions would have been clearer. Since Homans wrote more on general phenomena rather than on management, it makes sense that his contributions to management thought would not have been as clear as works of other researchers. It would appear that the common definition of managerial thinkers is a narrow one – for better or worse. We should consider other thinkers and approaches to revise and develop our historical understanding.

I have written on this issue in several papers. Several of my colleagues have written on similar subjects. I find this debate to be interesting and a worthwhile debate. Some of the answers to these questions should be gathered through citation and contextual analyses. Other answers could be attained through a careful reading of previous accounts of management such as early works recapping industrial sociology and organizational behavior. I would suggest that a very fruitful variation would be to textbooks from the 1930s onward for forgotten figures and debates. I would also suggest gathering information about secondary sources would.

About the question of who are management thinkers in terms of the practitioner versus academic becomes all the more complicated. There is a deep divide between practitioner and academic management. This divide is getting worse despite the efforts of Jeffrey Pfeffer (1998), whose attempts to address the situation have gone unheeded. From what I could tell, actual managers find most academics to be banal and unrealistic. Academics believe that managers make decisions on heuristics. This divide has been written about quite a bit in the literature, but why the divide exists has not been discussed. Morgan Witzel (2011) does spend time on it, but I believe more work is warranted. I believe that one of the major factors was money; when universities became the primary form of support, interest shifted into a more academic fashion. Pfeffer, despite his focus on applied research, has also argued that management is a low paradigm field and we lose prestige because of it. This is the same issue raised by sociologists during the 1940s when they compared themselves to economics. It seems that we view issues from a perspective of academic politics rather than applicability to business.

The Prime Mover

As I mentioned in the previous chapter about myths, another one of our ongoing debates (and a fruitless one in my opinion) is the search for the original or prime mover. The one particular area of this research has been on Mayo's work, especially his notion of the influence of groups on work. We have learned in the last 40 or so years that Taylor understood groups (Locke 1982), that Whiting Williams and Henry Denison anticipated the Hawthorne studies, and that the Taylor Society had similar attitudes to work arrangements. I have deep respect for these scholars and their work, but this hunt for the prime mover reminds me what J. Franklin Jameson once wrote about the same hunt for the prime mover in history:

> Friday was spent at our tiresome history meeting, where a fellow read a paper on the origin of the military system of England, which he traced back nearly to when our ancestors chattered in the tree-tops. He couldn't quite, because, as I suggested to him, standing armies were impossible among those who held on to branches by their tails.

I sometimes feel this way when I read an article about some forgotten thinker.

This concept is not unusual to management history. As Pitirim Sorokin once wrote regarding social science, we often have a "Columbus Syndrome" in that we consistently rediscover new concepts again and again. In fact, the idea of multiple discoveries is not unusual either. The famous Bayes' theorem, now one of the major concepts in statistics, may not have been developed by the good Reverend Bayes but by someone else. John Maynard Keynes was foreshadowed by William Trufant Foster and Waddill Catchings, two American economists. Milton Friedman noted that economists at the University of Chicago had produced proto-Keynesian work before the Great Depression, and he argues, as a result of this discovery, that the Chicago economists were not impressed with Keynesian economics. There was work performed on what we now call social exchange theory, which was developed, in part, in the nineteenth century, and some of the work Bronwislow Malinowski and Radcliffe-Brown anticipated it.

This theme is so common that there is a name for it – Stigler's conjecture (also referred to as "Stigler's law of eponymy") developed by the University of Chicago economist George Stigler and his statistician son Stephen. Stiglers' work started as a scholarly joke on the work of the great sociologist Robert K. Merton, who proposed a similar concept called the "Matthew effect." The "Matthew effect" states "this pattern of recognition, skewed in favor of the established scientist, appears principally (i) in cases of collaboration and (ii) in cases of independent multiple discoveries made by scientists of distinctly different rank." One of the examples of the "Matthew effect" was stated by Dan Wren (2005), who argued that the Harvard connection benefited Mayo, which could be an example of the Matthew effect.

However, my work (which was noted in Wren and Bedeian) found that there were other factors that allowed the Hawthorne studies to become the major contribution. There are other factors that could lead to one study dominating over another. According to George Stigler (1988:35), "an important way, if not the most important way, in which one influences a field is through one's students." Having followers makes a major difference. Mayo produced several highly influential students; Taylor prepared a generation of followers; and Barnard directly influenced Herbert Simon, who, along with Richard Cyert and James G. March, launched a new school. A second major consideration is the time and place in which the work was performed. Certain topics tend to be trendy at certain times; original works that go against it have a strike against it. A third point is how well someone sells the discovery. This was a talent that Elton Mayo had.

A better question to ask, rather than hunting for original concepts and stating myths, is to better understand the past. That is not to say that tracking down forgotten scholars and thinkers is not worthwhile. It is! However, I believe we have misused this information and have not used it to spur important research questions. Why did one particular version dominate over another? What were the contextual factors? Did one research study have different merits as compared to another? Did the scientist have a better social network? These are questions that warrant further study in the field.

Conclusion

I have found much interest in recapping the ongoing debates and arguments in the field of management history. I hope the reader found it interesting as well. The purpose of these debates is to advance the field. We have gone a long way from the days when we blindly accepted certain narratives about the field. We have dug deeper, researched further, and, in the process, challenged some of the basic concepts of our field. We are also starting to expand past the Taylor/Mayo axis and consider other management thinkers, especially those who are more recent, forgotten about, or were never considered. In doing so, I hope my field could enjoy the gift of professional maturity.

Besides some of the fault lines mentioned in this chapter, I would also suggest the following areas of debate, namely, a broader understanding of the shift from the classical education offered in the West to one more driven by occupational concerns. Did this shift play a role in the creation of management as a distinct field? In what ways will in-depth citation and contextual analysis further uncover previous concepts that have been ignored? Another question would be to track the convergence and divergence between management thought and its allied fields of economics, sociology, and psychology. A particularly interesting point would be the comparison of management with economics, especially since management assumes that there are rules for riches. Hopefully, by tracking these developments, we could have a greater grasp on management thought.

References

Appold SJ (2006) Elements and identity: Homans as an industrial sociologist. In: Trevino AJ (ed) George Homans: history, theory and methods. Paradigm, Boulder

Argyle M (1953) The relay assembly test room in retrospect. Occup Psychol 27(1):98–103

Bailyn B (2015) Sometimes an art: nine essays on history. Knopf, New York

Blau P (1964) Exchange and power in social life. Wiley, New York

Blum JM (1976) V was for victory. Harcourt Brace Jovanovich, Boston

Brinkley A (1995) The end of reform. Knopf, New York

Bruce K (2015) Activist manager: the enduring contribution of Henry S. Dennison to management and organization studies. J Manag Hist 21(2):143–171

Bruce K, Nyland C (2011) Elton Mayo and the deification of human relations. Organ Stud 32 (3):383–405. https://doi.org/10.1177/0170840610397478

Carey A (1967) The Hawthorne studies as radical criticism. Am Sociol Rev 32:403–416

Child J (1969) British management thought: a critical analysis. George Allen & Unwin, London

Cohen L (2003) A Consumers' republic: the politics of mass consumption in postwar America. Vintage Books, New York

Cooke B (2003) The denial of slavery in management studies. J Manag Stud 40(8):1895–1918

Cummings S, Bridgman T, Hassard J, Rowlinson M (2017) A new history of management. Cambridge University Press, Cambridge

Drucker PF (1946) For industrial peace. Harper's Weekly 193:385–395

Filene PG (1970) An obituary for "the progressive movement". Am Q 22(1):20–34

Fogel RW (1989) Without consent or contract: the rise and fall of American slavery. Norton, New York

Fogel RW, Engerman SL (1974) Time on the cross: evidence and methods, 2 vols. Little, Brown and Company, Boston

Foner E (1970) Free soil, free labor, free men: the ideology of the republican party before the civil war. Oxford University Press, New York

Foster J, Helms Mills J, Mills AJ (2014a) Shades of red: cold war influences on Canadian and US business textbooks. J Manag Educ 38(5):642–671

Foster J, Mills AJ, Weatherbee T (2014b) History, field definition and management studies: the case of the New Deal. J Manag Hist 20(2):179–199

Garrity C, Liguori EW, Muldoon J (2018) Woodward's aegis: a critical biography of Joan Woodward. J Manag Hist 24(4):457–475

Genovese E (1976) Roll, Jordan, roll: the world the slaves made. Vintage Books, New York

George CS (1968) The history of management thought. Prentice Hall, Englewood Cliffs

Gordon C (1992) New deals: business, labor, and politics in America, 1920–1935. Cambridge University Press, Cambridge

Guelzo AC (2008) Lincoln and Douglas: the debates that defined America. Simon & Schuster, New York

Jaffa HV (1959) Crisis of the house divided: an interpretation of the issues in the Lincoln-Douglas debates. University of Chicago Press, Chicago

Hassard JS (2012) Rethinking the Hawthorne studies: the Western electric research in its social, political and historical context. Hum Relat 65(11):1431–1461

Hawley E (1966) The new deal and the problem of monopoly: a study in economic ambivalence. Princeton University Press, Princeton

Hoagland JH (1955) Management before Frederick Taylor. In: Academy of management proceedings, vol 1955, no. 1. Academy of Management, Briarcliff Manor, pp 15–24

Homans GC (1984) Coming to my senses: the autobiography of a social scientist. Transaction Books, New Brunswick

Jumonville N (1999) Henry Steele Commager: midcentury liberalism and the history of the present. The University of North Carolina Press, Chapel Hill

Kelley ES, Mills AJ, Cooke B (2006) Management as a cold war phenomenon? Hum Relat 59 (5):603–610

Kennedy DM (1999) Freedom from fear: the American people in depression and war, 1929–1945, vol. 9. Oxford University Press

Kloppenberg JT (1986) Uncertain victory: social democracy and progressivism in European and American thought, 1870–1920. Oxford University Press, New York

Krueger A (1974) The political economy of the rent-seeking society. Am Econ Rev 64(3):291–303

Landsberger HA (1958) Hawthorne revisited: management and the worker: its critics and developments in human relations in industry. Cornell University Press, Ithaca

Leebaert D (2002) The fifty-year wound: how America's cold war victory shapes our world. Little, Brown, Boston

Leuchtenburg WE (1993) In the shadow of F.D.R.: from Harry Truman to Bill Clinton, Rev edn. Cornell University Press, Ithaca

Locke EA (1982) The ideas of Frederick W. Taylor: an evaluation. Acad Manag Rev 7(1):14–24

Mayo E (1945) The social problems of an industrial civilization. Harvard University Press, Cambridge

Mayo E, Lombard G (1944) Teamwork and labor turnover in the aircraft industry of southern California. Business research studies. Harvard Press, Cambridge

McPherson JM (2003) [1988]. Battle cry of freedom: the Civil War era. Oxford University Press, New York

McCormick RL (1981) The discovery that business corrupts politics: a reappraisal of the origins of progressivism. Am Hist Rev 86:247–274

Miller DC, Form WH (1951) Industrial sociology: an introduction to the sociology of work relations. New York, Harper and Brothers

Mills AJ, Weatherbee TG, Foster J, Helms Mills J (2015) The New Deal, history, and management & organization studies: lessons, insights and reflections. In: Genoe McLaren P, Mills AJ, Weatherbee TG (eds) Routledge companion to management & organizational history. Routledge, London, pp 265–284

Moore WE (1947) Current issues in industrial sociology. Am Sociol Rev 12(6):651–657

Muldoon J (2012) The Hawthorne legacy: a reassessment of the impact of the Hawthorne studies on management scholarship, 1930–1958. J Manag Hist 18(1):105–119

Muldoon J (2017) The Hawthorne studies: an analysis of critical perspectives, 1936–1958. J Manag Hist 23(1):74–94

Muldoon J (2019) Stubborn things: evidence, postmodernism and the craft of history. J Manag Hist 25(1):125–136

Muldoon J, Liguori EW, Bendickson J (2013) Sailing away: the influences on and motivations of George Caspar Homans. J Manag Hist 19(2):148–166

Nyland C (1998) Taylorism and the mutual-gains strategy. Ind Relat J Econ Soc 37(4):519–542

Olson M (1982) The rise and decline of Nations: economic growth, stagflation, and social rigidities. Yale University Press, New Haven

Parsons HM (1974) What happened at Hawthorne?: New evidence suggests the Hawthorne effect resulted from operant reinforcement contingencies. Science 183(4128):922–932

Patterson JT (1997) Grand expectations. Oxford University Press, New York

Pells RH (1985) The liberal mind in a conservative age: American intellectuals in the 1940s and 1950s. Harper & Row, New York

Phillips-Fein K (2010) Invisible hands: the businessmen's crusade against the New Deal. W. W. Norton & Company, New York

Potter DM (1976) The impending crisis, 1848–1861. Harper and Row, New York

Roethlisberger FJ (1948) Human relations: rare, medium, or well-done? Harv Bus Rev 26(1):89–107

Schlesinger AM (1958) Crisis of the old order, vol 1. Houghton Mifflin, Boston

Schlesinger AM (1959) The coming of the new deal, vol. II. Houghton Mifflin, Boston

Schlesinger AM (1960) The politics of upheaval, vol. III. Houghton Mifflin, Boston

Schlesinger AMJ (2000) A life in the twentieth century. Houghton Mifflin, Boston

Schwarz JA (1994) The new dealers. Knopf, New York

Searle GR (1971) The quest for national efficiency: a study in British politics and political thought, 1899–1914. Berkeley/Los Angeles: University of California Press

Shales A (2007) The forgotten man: a new history of the great depression. HarperCollins, New York

Skocpol T (1992) Protecting soldiers and mothers: the political origins of social policy in the United States. Harvard University Press, Cambridge, MA

Steinmetz G (2007) American Sociology before and after World War II: the (temporary) settling of a disciplinary field. In: Calhoun C (ed) Sociology in America. University of Chicago Press, Chicago

Stigler GJ (1988) Memoirs of an unregulated economist. Basic Books, New York

Wagner-Tsukamoto S (2007) An institutional economic reconstruction of scientific management: on the lost theoretical logic of Taylorism. Acad Manag Rev 32(1):105–117

Wagner-Tsukamoto S (2008) Scientific management revisited: did Taylorism fail because of a too positive image of human nature? J Manag Hist 14(4):348–372

Whyte WF (1969) Organizational behavior: theory and application. RD Irwin

Wiebe RH (1962) Businessmen and reform: a study of the Progressive movement. Harvard University Press, Cambridge, MA

Williams KS, Mills AJ (2017) Frances Perkins: gender, context and history in the neglect of a management theorist. J Manag Hist 23(1):32–50

Wrege CD, Perroni AG (1974) Taylor's pig-tale: a historical analysis of Frederick W. Taylor's pig-iron experiments. Acad Manag J 17(1):6–27

Wren DA (2005) The history of management thought, 5th ed. Wiley, Hoboken

Wren DA, Bedeian AG (2004) The Taylorization of Lenin: rhetoric or reality? Int J Soc Econ 31(3):287–299

Wren DA, Bedeian AG (2009) The evolution of management thought, 6th edn. Wiley, New York

Wren DA, Bedeian AG (2018) The history of management thought, 7th edn. Wiley, Hoboken

Methodologies Within Management History

4

Jeffrey Muldoon

Contents

Introduction 67
The Importance of Facts and Sources 68
Creativity and the Historian 75
Context 77
Theory and Quantification 81
To Be a Potter 83
Cross-References 84
References 84

Abstract

The purpose of this chapter is to discuss some of the methods currently used in management history. It addresses some of the major issues currently in the field: quantification, theory, creativity, facts, and sources, and those figures which have managed to lose ground. This chapter builds on previous chapters focused on the various debates within the field of management history. I also discuss some of the various contributions of management historians.

Keywords

History · Methods · Creativity · Theory

J. Muldoon (✉)
Emporia State University, Emporia, KS, USA
e-mail: jmuldoon@emporia.edu

© The Author(s), under exclusive licence to Springer Nature Switzerland AG 2020
B. Bowden et al. (eds.), *The Palgrave Handbook of Management History*,
https://doi.org/10.1007/978-3-319-62114-2_7

Introduction

When George Homans (1984) decided to become a sociologist, he asked his mentor, Lawrence J. Henderson, on what courses should he take. Henderson provided Homans with several different suggestions, but the one, perhaps most interesting, was that Homans should study history, since it was the one social science with a clear method. Since this statement, the development of social sciences has continued. History has come to be regarded more as an art, rather than a science. The historical method, so crucial to becoming a historian, is considered so basic and unimportant that many historians, especially those who study field such as management history, have little training in the methods and terminology of history. Put more simply, too often doctoral programs ignore management history in favor of other courses.

It is with this in mind that I have written this chapter. I would like to discuss the role and types of sources; the use of theory and social sciences; issues with quantification; and issues with context. I also discuss the importance of time periods and the difference between historical fact and interpretation. One of the difficult issues is that we often talk about invented traditions, without understanding the difference between historical fact and interpretation. A tradition is, by definition, fictive, since it is an interpretation. There is also a section discussing the role of creativity and management history. The purpose of this section is to discuss how management historians can be creative. The concluding section includes a discussion of an excellent American history, David Potter.

The Importance of Facts and Sources

History is the remembered past (Lukacs 1968). We must use evidence to determine the remembered past based on probability and detective work. One of the issues I find most troubling about the postmodernist history is that it disdains facts in favor of interpretations that are usually to the whim of the historian. I would like to define these terms briefly. A fact is something that is true and is based on the preponderance of evidence. That is to say, it is more likely than not that something occurred (Bogue 1983). An example of a fact is that Elton Mayo was born in 1880. This is a simple fact, but facts can be more complicated. For example, we could provide facts on how Henry Ford's policies led to changes in manufacturing.

This is not to say that evidence is completely true and whole and that we were completely objective in our analysis. But history must have some moorings on evidence. We cannot document history by wish; it must be grounded in evidence. This is my issue with postmodernism. Postmodernism is skeptical and, indeed, sometimes outrightly hostile to most forms of historical evidence (Appleby et al. 1994). Its proponents note that official documents are flawed sources of evidence because they either do not consider all relevant factors or because individuals in power seek to control the record. Similarly, oral history and memoirs are flawed since memories are social creations. Within organizations, according to postmodernists, it is only the constructed memories of the powerful that endure. Other types of evidence, such as demographics, are deliberately ignored in that reference to such sources mitigates historical explanations built around power and oppression, which postmodernists regard as the real drivers of history (cite).

That different people take different sides should not be surprising. The importance of history means that there will be consistent argument, debate, and conflict over facts and, more importantly, their relationship with each other. Historians play an important role – they are the ones who develop narratives that inform countries and professions. It is for this reason that George Orwell made Winston Smith a historian (Bailyn 1994). Smith was not an independent historian; his history was dictated by the state.

Modern researchers do not have this level of coercion, despite the pressures they face. Rather the historical record is a field of intense debate. However, factual evidence can serve as a bridge, a template to test whether our assumptions and theories are correct. Evidence emerges from a wide variety of sources. Each source – whether it is oral history, official documents, or autobiographies – has a limitation. According to Salevouris and Furay (2015, p. 14): "History is not 'what happened in the past'; rather, it is the act of select analyzing, and writing about the past. It is something that is done, that is constructed, rather than an inert body of data that lies scattered through the archives." However, different sources can lead to more accurate histories. Based on these sources, historical facts and interpretations emerge.

Sources are crucial to the historian – they are for historians what experiments and surveys are to scientists of various types. There are three types of sources in history. The basic source is primary source material. Primary sources are evidence from those who witnessed, participated, or commented on the period during which we study (Salevouris and Furay 2015). They could consist of corporate and government records; private papers of important (or even non-important) figures; and autobiographies, diaries, and oral histories of participants; they could consist of newspapers and other accounts. Secondary sources are often derived from primary sources. They are interpretations and arguments that historians have developed from primary sources. A third type of source, tertiary, would be textbooks or history books, which are based on secondary sources. An example of this would be the Oxford History of the United States (Salevouris and Furay 2015).

There has been an argument thrown around in certain circles that primary sources are better than secondary and tertiary sources. This is not true, in my opinion. Firstly, the explicit differences between a primary, secondary, or tertiary source are unclear. Rather than being placed in rigid categories, there is great fluidity between them. For example, a biography, considered by most historians to be a secondary source, could be a primary source, depending upon the questions being asked. In his work on Lincoln's memory, Merrill Peterson (1994) uses what would be considered secondary sources as primary sources. Secondly, secondary and tertiary sources help scholars develop research questions to better understand primary documents. Thirdly, secondary and tertiary sources enable scholars to understand the past, the different uses of languages, how people lived, and other pertinent issues. Secondary and tertiary sources can be considered a Berlitz book.

Yet, facts alone are not enough to create history. Knowing when Elton Mayo was born does not really matter. What matters is the relation of facts to each other as Lytton Strachey once wrote. The relationship between facts allows for historical construction to occur. These historical constructions lead to the development of historical interpretations. A historical interpretation is the "process through which we describe, analyze, evaluate, and create an explanation of past events" (Slatta, https://faculty.chass.ncsu.edu/slatta/hi216/hist_interp.htm), and this process is based on historical evidence. That Mayo is *the* father of human relations is an example of historical interpretation. There is a fictive element to this, in that it is constructed (Lukacs 1968). This opinion may be true or false, but there must be evidence behind it. There is considerable evidence to support this position; just as there is considerable evidence to oppose this opinion. Given that other scholars can also lay claim to this title, it makes more sense to state that Elton Mayo was *a* (rather than *the*) father of human relations. As Salevouris and Furay (2015) write: "all good history is interpretation."

Interpretations can range from who is the father/mother of a field to the importance of a study of figure and to larger issues, such as naming a time period. History without time is merely a collection of facts. Although snapshot versions of history have value, they are limited because they do not track evolution and development. Take a history of Australia written for the bicentennial (i.e., 1988) of the founding of the Australian nation. There is a considerable amount of detail, but unless someone knew the history of Australia, then such a history is limited (Bailyn 2015). There is little understanding of how and why Australia emerged. Time explains how events and individuals interact. If we are to state that history is a narrative, facts are the characters, interpretations are the narrative, and then time periods are the setting.

Compounding this is the confusion of myths versus history. In scholarly professions, we often use myth to provide a sense of legitimacy. Management has sought – over the years – to seek legitimacy through several different methods, the use of theory building, the scientific method, and practical application (Pfeffer 1993). As a new field, we have status anxiety and envy toward other more established fields (Steinmetz 2005). This is a common trend throughout other, more established, fields as well. Economics has envy of physics and sociology has an envy of economics (Steinmetz 2005). In fact, scholars such as Jeffrey Pfeffer (1993) have bemoaned the lack of a clear paradigm in the field of management, noting that we are losing ground to other business fields. Therefore, we tend to stress certain figures and events. But myths based on facts often go much further than facts would allow.

Yet, there is considerable argument over "invented traditions (please see Weatherburn 2019)." Since a tradition is, by definition, an interpretation invented by individuals in the field, perhaps it is the reason why managers start the process of management with Frederick Winslow Taylor, rather than such flawed figures as Henry Ford, whose violent anti-union policies and anti-Semitism made him a compromised figure (Lacey 1986). Perhaps, had Ford died in 1918 soon after his electoral defeat when he was compared to Moses, we would have used him as a model. Yet, we also focus on Taylor for reasons that were historical as well, namely, that Taylor appeared at the right time and place for management to emerge as a distinct field. A check of how Taylor inspires thinkers is clear. Similarly, while there were other efforts to understand social man, the Hawthorne studies were the study that inspired scholars to reexamine the field to consider the role of social motivation in terms of economic motivation, i.e., to what extent does an economic benefit shape human behavior. Likewise, checking a listing of citation numbers would reveal what contemporaries believed about the Hawthorne studies and how it inspired thinkers of his own time (Muldoon 2012). It is important to note, therefore, that the complexities of history usually do not lead to ready reduction.

To debunk myths, management historians often create straw men. Wrege and Perroni argued (p. 26) that scholars should "think to look at the idol early enough in the game to discover that it had feet of clay before it was hoisted onto a pedestal." I am curious as to how we answer the question in management: who do we idealize? One of the favorite targets of critics has been the Hawthorne studies. Firstly, scholars have, for the last several years, pointed out that the Hawthorne studies were poor methodologically, that they proved nothing, and that Mayo had a biased viewpoint (Gabor 2000). Secondly, we have also been told that Mayo did not discover "social man" and that its discovery had been researched many years before. These concepts were not alien to the people who wrote at the time the studies gained fame (Muldoon 2012). In addition, the argument that welfare capitalism and human relations were similar concepts is something that is objectively false. If anything, welfare capitalism encouraged worker revolt by reducing all relationships to economic exchanges. By contrast, human relations attempted to solve the underlying alienation of workers that caused revolt (Cohen 1990). As historians look at the Hawthorne studies, the key question should be: why did the Hawthorne studies gain prominence (rather than whether this or that aspect of the project was methodologically valid)? An explanation could be that other ways of dealing with worker revolt were exhausted and managers needed new techniques (see chapter on Mayo).

Compounding our problems as historians is the fact that our interpretations change from one period to the next. I agree with Williams and Mills (2017) that we have, at times, neglected the contributions of certain management thinkers of the past. Williams and Mills selected, as an example of this viewpoint, the work of Frances Perkins, who was President Roosevelt's Secretary of Labor. There are several reasons that Williams and Mills gave for Perkins deletion from the historical record. The points include anticommunism, attacks from her colleagues in the New Deal, and administrative studies focusing on major undertakings like the Tennessee Valley Authority. Therefore, Frances Perkins did not receive credit for some of her ideas, including important concepts like the triple bottom line.

While I believe that this was a strong article, I am not convinced that the historical record is wrong. Namely, they do not demonstrate, in any way, that Perkins' work influenced management *thinkers*, even if, as Labor Secretary, she influenced management *practice*. Certainly, Perkins played a key role in the development of an important body of government *policy*. Much of this body of policy was, however, later overturned by conservatives in Congress. In addition, most business leaders were opposed to the New Deal by 1935, and, given the connection between business research and big business, it would make sense for management scholars to ignore certain thinkers and focus on others. Therefore, there is a degree of subjectivity. Although Perkins *advocated* ideas like the triple bottom line, Williams and Mills (2017) do not demonstrate that she really *developed* the concept. To demonstrate that she was an early developer of the triple bottom line, they would need to conduct a citation analysis.

Another important area of management history research has focused on Elton Mayo's work, especially his notion that social groups have a profound influence on work. However, we have learned in the last 40 or so years that Taylor also understood groups (Locke 1982), that Whiting Williams and Henry Denison anticipated the Hawthorne studies, and that the Taylor Society had similar attitudes to work arrangements. Of course, I am not sure people were aware of the research of others; nor did they really believe that Mayo was original. Even if there is evidence that ideas relating to social groups were in circulation prior to Mayo, I would still find this hunt for the prime mover problematic. As Pitirim Sorokin (1956) once wrote regarding social science, we often have a "Columbus Syndrome" in that we consistently rediscover new concepts again and again. In fact, the idea of multiple discoveries is not unusual either. The famous Bayes Theorem, now one of the major concepts in statistics, may not have been developed by the Good Reverend Bayes but by someone else. John Maynard Keynes was foreshadowed by William Trufant Foster and Waddill Catchings, two American economists. Milton and Rose Friedman (1998) noted that economists at the University of Chicago had produced proto-Keynesian work before the Great Depression, and he argues, as a result of this "discovery," that the Chicago economists were not impressed with Keynesian economics. Similarly, what we now call social exchange theory had a "prehistory," in which some of the ideas that characterized it were first floated in the nineteenth century. Some of the work of Malinowski and Radcliffe-Brown also anticipated this body of theory. But does this lessen in any way the originality or significance of the intellectual currents associated with social exchange theory in the twentieth century? I would say not.

This theme – the search for prime movers – is so common that there is a name for it, Stigler's conjecture (also referred to as Stigler's law of eponymy), developed by the University of Chicago economist George Stigler and his statistician son, Stephen. The Stiglers' work started as a scholarly joke on the work of the great sociologist Robert K. Merton, who proposed a similar concept called the "Matthew Effect." The "Matthew Effect" states "this pattern of recognition, skewed in favor of the established scientist, appears principally (i) in cases of collaboration and (ii) in cases of independent multiple discoveries made by scientists of distinctly different rank." One of the examples of the "Matthew Effect" was stated by the noted management historian, Dan Wren (2005), who argued that the Harvard connection benefited Mayo over would-be theoreticians from lower-ranked institutions. Certainly, such outcomes – favoring the senior scholar from the better known institution – would be an example of the Matthew Effect. Yet there are other explanations as to why certain ideas capture the imagination of their time. Looking at time periods, and contextual cues, is beneficial to understanding our judgments of fact, i.e., why certain interpretations and theories are accepted as valid.

4 Methodologies Within Management History 73

This leads to my next point. If one was to look for a single work that has defined "traditional" or "mainstream" management history, it would be *The Evolution of Management Thought*. Currently in its seventh edition, this work was originally the creation of Dan Wren (University of Oklahoma) with latter editions being updated, revised, and expanded in collaboration with Wren's colleague, Arthur (Art) Bedeian (Louisiana State University). For Wren and Bedeian (2018), management is seen in overwhelmingly positive terms, driving a process of both intellectual enlightenment and economic and political liberation. The influence of Wren and Bedeian's ideas is found not only in their publications but also in their leadership roles within the (American) Academy of Management (AOM) and as PhD supervisors and intellectual mentors. For a generation, Wren, Bedeian, their colleagues, and their former students dominated management history within the United States. Both Wren and Bedeian were foundation members of the AOM's Management History Division (MHD) in 1971. Subsequently, Wren served as the Division's Chair in 1975 with Bedeian becoming Chair in 1977 (Greenwood 2015). Writing of Wren's influence, Jack Duncan, the past President of the (United States) Southern Management Association, wrote in 2003 that, "management scholars generally agree that Dan Wren is the most distinguished management historian of the current generation. Most scholars, I believe, would consider Dan of equal status to business historians such as Alfred Chandler" (cited Novicivic et al. 2015, p. 18). In the last decade, however, Wren's approach has come under attack from postmodernist-inclined "critical management historians."

One of the major criticisms of Wren's approach has come from Novicevic et al. (2015). The argument provided is that Wren and traditional management scholars "developed their web of shared beliefs about the history of management thought not only objectively but also relationally through their socialization in their academic communities." One of the primary concerns that they express was the use of time periods to describe the evolution of history, Novicevic et al. (2015, p. 23) complaining how Wren reconstructs history by describing a connection in time between events, not only between the past and the present but also "between management's present and future." In short, they complain that we err when we use the historical past to guide the future.

In their critique, Novicevic and his co-authors argue for a "decentering" and a reimagining of management history that frees the future from the dictates of the past. In doing so, they remove history of its most potent and salient force – time. Yes, it is true that there is a fictive element to time periods. They are merely interpretations that historians use to make sense of a series of events. One question is – if we eliminate time periods – how can we organize history? This would be akin to eliminating chapters in a book, stages in a play, or yards on a football field. Time periods make history understandable and approachable. This is part of the fictive element that I refer to above. Time periods are interpretations based upon facts. We construct concepts, such as eras, to make history understandable and coherent. To suggest this does not make one a postmodernist – in fact, traditional history understood this concept all too well (see Lukacs 1968). These types of interpretations are what we use to make sense of the world. Without time periods, we would have historical snap shots. Basically, we would change history from being a moving picture (with time going forward) to a series of unrelated snap shots, with little understanding of how and why we move from one period to the next.

Then how do we determine what to name the time period? There are two general methods. The first general method is to name the time period after the major ruler or figure that best fits the generation. In the United States, we would talk about the Age of Jackson, named after the President Andrew Jackson, whose characteristics were a symbol of the age. In many ways, Jackson's policies defined his generation, in that it led to clear lines of both policy and social organization and behavior. However, scholars have generally abandoned naming periods after Presidents and kings, although there are exceptions (we still talk about a Victorian age). The concept of naming time periods after a reigning figure declined due to the decline of biography. The second general approach is naming the time period after political, economic, and military movements. We still talk about the New Deal era. We now talk about the Jacksonian period as the market revolution.

For management, talking about time periods still makes a great deal of sense. We know that management goes through fads and fashions – suggesting that certain issues are important at certain times. Personality was once considered to be a dead construct; now it is one of the most important constructs in the literature. We have now moved past the Big Five (Openness, Conscientiousness, Extraversion, Agreeableness, Neuroticism) to research other constructs. There were management thinkers who scientifically studied management before Taylor and human relations before Mayo. Yet both Taylor and Mayo seem to fit their eras – although I would not speak of an Age of Taylor or Mayo. The reason why time periods work is due to the concept of generations (Mannheim 1952). Arguments within generations arise due to the different sociohistorical experiences that a generation has. Some young people in the 1960s became leftists and others conservatives. Both rejected New Deal liberalism (Klatch 1999). Another reason why management is based on time periods would be that management is a response to socioeconomic conditions. For example, one reason why human relations became so accepted was that some viewed it as a solution to the labor problems that emerged during the Great Depression and Second World War. To write history without time periods would cause more issues than it would solve.

Let's take human relations as a time period. Firstly, we could see the genesis of human relations in the scientific management era. In fact, if we could, we could see human relations well before the scientific management era. Some critics of Elton Mayo noted that he was basically writing arguments like the Gospel of Luke, as assertions of divinely inspired fact (Roethlisberger 1960). For example, Whiting Williams wrote several books and articles that predated Mayo's work. Taylor recognized the importance of groups. One of the notable contributions has been that of Christopher Nyland, who wrote about the policies of the Taylor Society. Therefore, the roots of human relations movement could be seen well before Mayo even started writing on industrial relationships.

If the human relations movement had a "prehistory," this does not change the fact that the movement really began with the work of Mayo, Mary Parker Follett, and

4 Methodologies Within Management History

Chester Barnard. There are several crucial explanations for this outcome. Firstly, the concept of Taylorism had a very negative reputation in many circles. This had less to do with Taylor's ideas or the ideas of his associates and more to do with how individuals perceived them. Remember, Taylor promised a mental revolution but wrought rebellion. Secondly, the decline of welfare capitalism, which was ending by the 1920s and ended in the 1930s, meant that new techniques were needed to develop connections with workers. The incredibly high levels of violence and strikes of the 1930s and 1940s provided important reasons to search for methods to produce trust. Accordingly, we are justified talking about a certain time period, the "human relations era."

Creativity and the Historian

Creativity is an extremely important part of the historian's craft as it is how the field progresses. Creative historians stretch the field by asking new questions, uncovering new sources, or through the reinterpretation of existing sources. According to Bernard Bailyn (2015, p. 81), who has written about creative historians, a creative historian is someone that shifted the direction of "historical inquiry" through "substantive and enduring discovery." The list of historians that have won Pulitzer Prizes contains many individuals who would fit the definition of a creative historian.

What are some of the examples of creative historians? Bailyn lists several notable ones. His list is personal and reflects his eclectic taste and experiences. The first historian that he would list as a creative historian would be the American Perry Miller, who was a professor to Bailyn, Edmund S. Morgan, and Arthur M. Schlesinger, Jr., among others. Miller primarily wrote about Puritans, their beliefs, and their ongoing relevance to the American mind (Middlekauff 1969). What made Miller's work so important was that he expanded history. Previously, when scholars considered the Puritans, their criticisms were similar to those of the seventeenth century: that Puritans were boring, enemies against pleasure and nature, and overly pedantic (Middlekauff 1969). The statement that summarized prevailing thought about the Puritans came from H.L. Mencken, who wrote that the Puritans had a "haunting fear that somewhere, someone might be happy" (in Middlekauff 1969, p. 171). Yet, Miller, noting the richness of ideas through previously under-researched sermons, argued the ongoing relevance of Puritan thought to American intellectual life. His discovery of the deep connections between Puritans and the Church of England demonstrated the underlying uniformity in religious persuasion that was born from their experiences in England. Yet, this uniformity would die in the next age, as it witnessed the growth of multiple religious experiences. In other words, the Puritans expressed beliefs that were initially common but became unique because they held on them whereas others let them go. This was a notable and deep discovery that transformed the field.

A second historian that Bailyn considered to be a creative historian was Charles McLean Andrews, who was a historian attached to Yale University (Johnson 1986). Andrews' great achievement was to place the Colonial period of America in an

Atlantic context, through stressing connections between Colonial America and the British Empire. The previous generation of American historians had grappled with the question of how democracy emerged in America (Bailyn 2015). The first approach was the one provided by Henry Baxter Adams, which stated that democracy and American politics could trace its roots to Anglo-Saxon village institutions. The "germs" (Baxter's phrase) eventually took place in America, building a democratic nation. Frederick Jackson Turner disagreed with this approach. He argued that American democracy was the experience of the American frontier. Turner (1920, p. 293) wrote that "American democracy was born of no theorist's dream; it was not carried in the Susan Constant to Virginia, nor in the Mayflower to Plymouth. It came out of the American forest, and it gained new strength each time it touched a new frontier." By contrast, Andrews argued, based on little used archives, that the British Empire had a deep connection to American democracy (Bailyn 2015). Therefore, colonial America could not be understood without careful consideration of the British Empire. When Bailyn and others examined the pamphlets at the time of the American revolution, they noted various references to the travails of British revolutionaries.

Which management historians could be considered creative? Again, the most creative historian, as well as the best, has been Dan Wren, who developed the standard approach by developing a narrative of the evolution of management thought. Wren has the equivalent prestige to Alfred Chandler, the famed business historian (Novićević et al. 2015). The reason is that Wren largely created the structure of management history. The previous works tracing the development of management thought, such as Whyte (1969) or George (1972), merely provided a brief overview of the concepts or gave biographical data. What Wren did, and did successfully in my opinion, is to create a synthesis of management thought, tracing its evolution from one period to the next. Wren (1987) also rediscovered an important, but forgotten, figure, Whiting Williams, whose work on human relationships predated those of Elton Mayo. This discovery encouraged me to examine why the Hawthorne studies became prominent. Another creative management historian could be Charles Wrege, whose work was not in synthesis, but discovery. His work on both the Hawthorne studies and Taylor, based on years of research, has greatly influenced subsequent historians.

This leads me to one final point. Mills and Novicevic (2019) took issue with my review of the *New Management History* (co-authored by Stephen Cummings, Todd Bridgman, John Hassard, and Michael Rowlinson) which I pointed out that the authors wished to supplant Wren and Bedeian from their perch. When they called their work *A New History*, basically, it is res ipsa loquitur, the thing speaks for itself. Given that their interpretations, worldview, and motivations are different than Wren's, it should be obvious that they wish to supplant or start the process of supplanting the standard history of the field. There is nothing wrong with this. We should seek to build on the foundations of excellent scholars of the past. My problem was over interpretation not ambition. Unlike Bowden, who challenged their postmodern assumptions, I merely pointed out some of their points lacked nuance and an understanding of the broader historical literature. This is a common criticism that could be directed at any history or historian. However, I do respect that they are stretching the field, forcing us to consider new approaches. Scholars, such as Rowlinson and other like-minded postmodernists, can be creative as well. They are forcing us to consider our roots.

Context

One of the most important aspects of history is to consider the social, economic, political, and intellectual context of the time in which we study. To do so is extremely important because the past is radically different than the present (Bailyn 2015). Context helps to give a better understanding to primary sources. For example, there has been a recent debate among Lincoln scholars over the sexuality of Abraham Lincoln. This is an important debate, because the Lincoln heritage is a rich and distinct one. As David Donald (1956) noted, politicians often try "to get right with Mr. Lincoln." In this case, history serves as a common framework, a useful myth to rally society (Peterson 1994). In scholarly professions, we often use myth to provide a sense of legitimacy. Accordingly, there have been attempts by several scholars and activists to enlist Abraham Lincoln as a gay man. Yet, the evidence for such a conclusion is sparse. The fact that Lincoln shared a bed with a man for a period is inconsequential. In fact, many of the lawyers who traveled the legal circuits shared beds. The one exception to this rule was Judge David Davis, owing less to his role as a judge and more to his obese size. Likewise, as Doris Kearns Goodwin pointed, strong intimate relationships between males were common at the time. A better understanding of the context of Lincoln's society and time would have prevented a line of inquiry that is based more conjecture than historical fact. It is also interesting to note there are very few works on James Buchanan's sexuality, for whom there is much more evidence of homosexuality than Lincoln. Of course, Lincoln was the far superior President.

How do we learn about the context of the past? We immerse ourselves in both primary and secondary sources. We attempt to make an understanding of the types of language used and other cultural aspects of the past. The past is a very different place, and the great historian can detect importance from seemingly obscure events. As Salevouris and Furay (p. 67) write, "The past is a foreign country; they do things differently there." One of the most important works of history has been the work of Robert Darnton (1984), whose work on a massacre of cats in the eighteenth century reveals how different the past is compared to the present. Using the anthropology of Clifford Geertz, Darnton reconstructed a massacre of cats, which to Darnton was a symbolic action. The cats were murdered by a group of disaffected workers (this could be considered one of the first examples of counterproductive work behavior), who were upset with their master and mistress and murdered the cats as a form of a joke. Further, humor was found in the fact that the massacre implied that the master was a cuckold. This is a barbaric act by modern standards. The fact that we have a hard time understanding it is suggestive of just how remote the past is compared to the present. Yet, Darnton, by combing through primary and secondary sources, could uncover the reason why this occurred: it was simply a form of worker protest.

One issue to note is the common abuse of "the Whig interpretation" of history. Coined many years ago by Herbert Butterfield (1931), the "Whig interpretation" is a tendency to lump the progressive forces of history as the good guys against the forces of darkness. This is typical in history; many historians, especially those of the liberal stripe, view the world as advancing toward progressive values and beliefs. In doing so, they strip history of its nuance and complexity. As both Butterfield and Bailyn (2015) pointed out, Martin Luther and other Protestant leaders were was as intolerant as the Pope against whom they protested. The concept of freedom developed during the seventeenth century only bares a distant relationship of freedom today. Put simply, we try to find those in the past that have our values and grade them accordingly, which makes history less interesting and relevant.

We have this same tendency in management history. Let me state clearly that management has been a great blessing to society. And the people who have benefited most from management are the average worker, an outcome that (Bowden 2018) is contrary to the expectations of those scholars who have a leftist bent. This is not to say that the workers of the past were wrong to oppose Taylorism or Fordism. Take Taylorism as an example. Taylorism encroached onto worker freedom in their search for higher wages. The workers of the time had little reason to trust Taylor, a middle-class reformer and someone who received his wages from the owners. Furthermore, Taylor's rhetoric was deeply upsetting and even hateful. His writings have whole passages dedicated to the racial and intellectual inferiority of whole ethnic classes. True, as some of his defenders point out, these values were common at the time. However, we must also understand that a man who writes such horrible things about workers would have a problem convincing them to buy into his theory.

One of the most difficult issues in history is dealing with the losers. It has been difficult for Americans to write about the Loyalists, those Americans who continued to support Britain during the Revolutionary War (Bailyn 2015). Most writers of American history painted the Loyalists as traitors, fools, and morally bankrupt. Yet, many of the Loyalists, men such as Thomas Hutchinson, were loyal to the Crown and the British system and were sober in thought and deed and did not believe that the Crown's activities gave the right of rebellion. In fact, the problem of justifying the rebellion required American ministers to spend a tremendous amount of time searching the Bible for justification. The Loyalists often had a clearer understanding of the real relationship between Britain and American than did the rebels. In fact, given the special relationship between American and Britain, we have moved toward something closer to the Loyalist version than the rebels. Hutchinson may have finally won over Thomas Jefferson, who hated Great Britain.

Who are the losers in management thought? Well it depends upon who is writing. As mentioned above, the workers who opposed Taylorism have been, at times, denounced as fools. However, they had important reasons to reject Taylorism, including, but not limited to, taking away many of the privileges labor had, in exchange for higher wages. Of course, we also assume, because we are modern individuals driven by the market, that wages matter. However, in traditional peasant culture, wages did not matter as much. As we later learned, based on Hawthorne studies, and Equity Theory, pay does have social dimensions and social implications. In short, the connection between pay and worker behavior is more complex than Taylor though.

Another area where historians sometimes have issues is in judging the winners. We can see an example of this in the Hawthorne studies. In writing about the Hawthorne studies, some critics, both contemporary and historical, view the Hawthorne studies as a means for management to regain the right to manage (Harris 1982). For instance, Bruce and Nyland (2011, p. 401) wrote, "Mayo provided the business community with a sound body of intellectual prize-fighters who would support them when they launched their post-New Deal campaign to win back the right to manage that they believed had been challenged during this era." True, management lost power during the War over issues such as production and pricing, but, as stated above, it was going to gain back that power; even liberals realized government intervention in the economy did not work – all one had to do to recognize it was to read an edition of the *New Republic* (Brinkley 1995). Even then, big business played a major role in securing government contracts, revealing a complicated picture of the state. Roosevelt himself stated that Dr. New Deal was retired. Conversely, many executives entered into government service. It was also the case that large parts of the American public had a skeptical and even hostile view toward unionism. As the question of labor's participation in production decisions was debated, many labor leaders – men such as United Automobile Workers President Walter Reuther – stood against labor's participation in decision-making at both the firm and workplace levels (Lichenstein 1989, 1982; Patterson 1997). Accordingly, the ability of labor to make fundamental changes to the nature of capitalism is a greatly overstated argument. How could big business regain the right to manage when it never lost it? Labor's position of ascendency in the country had never been secure and was by no means secure in 1946 (Lichenstein 1989; Patterson 1997). Indeed, it would appear management had all the means to regain prestige and power even without the Hawthorne studies. During the war, it seemed to many that the effects of unionized labor were causing more problems than benefits. In 1944, there were 4956 labor stoppages alone. In 1945, there were 4750, and in 1946, there were 4985. Most of these strikes were wildcat strikes, which means that they occurred against the wishes of the unions to which the striking workers belonged. In fact, some contemporaries saw the Hawthorne studies (Chase 1946; Drucker 1946) as a means to lower the amount of discord in society. To dismiss someone like Stuart Chase as a management shill would be misrepresentative, considering he was a man of the left. His work appeared in the left-wing publication, the *Nation*, which opposed the Cold War. Conversely, conservative magazines would not publish his works.

Not only does history happen within context, historians also write in the context in which they live. If we trace the books and articles published by major presses and journals, we would notice that the amount of certain topics rise and decline. For example, of the great books published on Abraham Lincoln, in a biography written by Benjamin Thomas, there is no recognition of Frederick Douglass, the preeminent

African American abolitionist. Yet, there is today a vast literature on the relationship between Lincoln and the various abolitionists, including Douglas, a literature that traces a deep and complicated relationship. This shift reflects the fact that historians now write with a different strain of historical thought in mind than that of the 1950s. A thematic study of the *Journal of Management History* (Schwarz 2015) would find a great increase in papers of women and minorities in management. Old topics, such as the Hawthorne studies, reflected a single article published in 2010–2014. This reflects a change in management history.

When I was at Gettysburg College many years ago, we read two differing frameworks of the Reconstruction (i.e., the Unionist occupation of the United States South during the late 1860s and early 1870s), written by two different authors. The first was written by Hillary Herbert (1912) who was highly critical of Reconstruction policies, many of which sought to give African Americans the same civil rights as other Americans. The second was written by Kenneth Stampp (1965) who was favorable to Reconstruction and wished that Reconstruction had worked. Herbert had fought in the Civil War on the Southern side, was from South Carolina, and had opposed racial integration. Stampp was a Northerner from Wisconsin, who came from a family with strong progressive tendencies. He also wrote during the 1960s, which some have called the Second Reconstruction. The lesson was, when reading history, consider the historian. I never read history the same way again. However, scholars have been aware of this type of technique for years. In management history we have similar lines of debates. Hanlon, who is a radical historian, views worker's refusal to work and rebellion as pushing management forward. Other scholars view workers' rebellion with a less favorable view.

Interpretations can change how we view facts. One of the great American historians on slavery was U.B. Phillips, who was Southerner, located at Yale University. Phillips was the most influential and thorough historian regarding the Southern plantation system in the first half of the twentieth century (Hofstadter 1944). Phillips was a great historian, but he was a deep racist, whose attitudes to African Americans were, if not hostile, deeply patronizing and paternalistic. Phillips' contention was that slavery was an economic blight but an acceptable method of racial control. Phillips also noted that slaves were treated well. Again, Kenneth Stampp (1956) overturned this observation by arguing the reverse: that slavery was an economically efficient system but a deep and cruel social system. Rather than viewing slaves as docile and lazy, Stampp argued that they actively resisted. Stampp's position would be validated as historians of slavery gathered evidence from different sources.

There is a myriad of examples about the problems of contextual analysis. To do it properly, we need to conduct thorough analysis of citations and texts to recreate social networks. This work must be done through evidence. This is a painstaking process but one that could lead to a better understanding of the past. As I have written before, the reason why I respect Bernard Bailyn as a historian is that he looked at old evidence with a new eye and, in the process, discovered new pathways that scholars had previously been unaware of. This should be the goal. I feel too often that the new management history wishes to tear down canon because they

Theory and Quantification

There has been a call, in recent years, to use theory to make management history better and to gain more respect in the field. When I entered the field a little over 12 years ago, theory was the mania of the profession; I see little reason to believe it has changed. Our top journals often reject papers because they lack theory or do not make enough of a theoretical contribution, a phrase that is often used but one I find puzzling. Theory is a term that is often used to describe concepts and other phenomena. Whether these concepts and phenomena are theoretical, I am not sure. Often, we call something theory, but it does not fit what a scientist would call a theory. In fact, much of what we call theory, such as Talcott Parsons's work, would fail this distinction. This point is not an idiosyncratic one, as both Sutton and Staw could not define a theory, merely what it is not. Even under their definition theories, such as the covering law approach, would not fit Sutton and Staw's definition of theory (DiMaggio 1995).

I find this embrace to be slightly ironic. It is not because many of the critical theorists are poor theorists. The opposite is true; many of them are excellent theorists. One of them, Roy Suddaby, has been named an outstanding reviewer in our preeminent journal, the Academy of Management Review. The embrace is ironic because they are doing what they claim others do – namely, shaping their narrative and worldview to those who are in power. At present, people who wish to build theory are in power in the academic profession. Naturally, those scholars who wish to gain admittance to the higher levels of the academy will, in turn, shape their work to reflect a scholarly bent. This drive has been repeated in several academic fields, including sociology and economics, two fields with a close connection to management.

Yet, I would caution future management historians in their embrace of theory. I believe that theory is a generalizable approach that approximates the real world. It ignores complexities that the real world has. Many historians, especially those who pay close attention to primary material, are often skeptical that theory or laws would apply to history (Salevouris and Forney 2015). Despite the attempts over the years to make history a science, it remains completely a craft and an art. History also cannot be falsified and therefore does not fit what a scientist would state what a theory should be.

This hunt for theory development reminds me of the experiences of George Homans (1984), the father of social exchange theory, one of the most important theories in social sciences in general and management, in particular. Homans had unusual training for a student of sociology; he took no classes in sociology, and his principal professors were Lawrence Henderson, a medical doctor, and Elton Mayo, a psychologist. Henderson felt that the one social science with defined boundaries was history, and Henderson encouraged Homans to conduct research there. This is the reason why Homans's first scholarly book focused on English villages in the Middle Ages. It was a topic that could be safely considered historic. Yet, Homans moved passed this to type of research – and even studies about industry – to theory, because to gain prestige, he needed to be a theorist.

History and the social sciences have had an unusual association. Richard Hofstadter, a Columbia-based historian, wrote a series of books that used concepts and theories from sociology, including the work of his Columbia colleague, Robert Merton. Over the years, we have witnessed many works that have combined both history and social sciences, such as psychology, sociology, and economics. The reception of these works has been mixed, to say the least (Handlin 1979; Peterson 1994). For example, there were several works published on Abraham Lincoln that argued that Lincoln commenced the Civil War due to his poor relationship with his father. Basically, the America created by George Washington served as a proxy for Lincoln's father. These and other works based on psychology have, with good reason, been highly controversial. Yet, psychology has helped to revive biography, which has lost prestige due to the Annales and Marxist schools (Garraty 1960).

Likewise, works that use quantitative techniques also have a problematic place in management history. Much of the controversy has been devoted to the field of cliometrics, which was developed in the 1950s to the 1970s by economists, such as Robert Fogel. The principle work on this issue was by Fogel and his co-author Stanley Engerman, *Time on the Cross*. This work argued that slavery was highly profitable; that slavery was highly efficient; and that slaves were only marginally economically exploited. In fact, the authors argued that slaves were treated better under slavery than they were afterward. These were stunning observations that upended generations of thought on slavery.

Needless to say, the book was highly controversial. Both scholars were attacked as racists, even though they wrote the book to destroy myths that were propagated against African Americans for years. Fogel was married to an African American woman. Fogel would win the Noble Prize. The book itself would win the Bancroft Prize, one of the top awards in history. Yet, its reputation in historical circles has not been high. The book launched a whole cottage industry of attack. Scholars, such as Oscar Handlin and James McPherson, noted that both Fogel and Engerman made numerous mistakes in calculation. Herbert Gutman criticized not only the erroneous calculations but also the failure of Fogel and Engerman to consider social aspects such as lynching and whipping. Arguably, however, the most damning critique was that made by Haskell (1975), who observed:

> Fogel and Engerman should have known from the beginning that any comparison of regional efficiency in the antebellum period was fraught with breathtaking difficulties. The basis for their comparison, a rather controversial economist's tool known as the "geometric index of total factor productivity," gives results whose interpretation is debatable in even the most conventional applications. The index is essentially nothing more than a ratio of output to input: it ranks as most efficient that region, or other economic entity, which achieves the highest output with the lowest inputs of capital, labor, and land. The fatal limitation of the index, given the uses to which Fogel and Engerman wished to put it, is that it measures output in market value, rather than physical units (contrary to the impression given in

volume one of *Time on the Cross*). There is no escaping this limitation, for one cannot aggregate a total output composed of bales of cotton, bushels of peas, pounds of pork, etc., without reducing everything to dollar value.

Although Fogel and Engerman did respond to their critics, the conversations between the economists and historians were not fruitful. Simply put, using quantification is important, but unless you understand the nuance of the time period, you will have a difficult time using those numbers. However, quantification is important and necessary for historians, especially those of us who study management and business.

To Be a Potter

I would like to conclude this chapter with a discussion of an American historian who exhibited some of the best characteristics that a historian should possess. His name was David M. Potter, who was a professor at Yale and then Stanford, where he served as Coe Professor of History. He was a student of U.B. Phillips, who, given their shared Southern heritage, would suggest that his ideas would be not too dissimilar to that of his mentor. But, unlike Phillips, he was able to transcend the limitations of his heritage and, in the process, made a substantial contribution to American historiography. His most significant contribution was his work on the Secession crisis, which is the period from Lincoln's election until the battle of Fort Sumter in April 1861. This is a very controversial period of American history, when the Civil War really started. Potter's book was published in 1942 and has been reprinted several times since then. No less an observer than Sir Dennis Brogan (1969) called the work the second most original dissertation and one of the most durable contributions of an American historians. This durability has endured despite the opening of the Lincoln papers and the publication of many other books on the Civil War and antebellum America.

It was on the basis of this contribution that won Potter his professorship at Yale. What was truly remarkable about Potter was that he was able to transcend his background as a Southerner and to write as someone that could look beyond his sectionalist background. Not only did Potter cover the Succession crisis, he also explored the ideas and passions that drove the crisis. It covered not just the political maneuverings but also the passions and ideas of the general public. He also developed a portrait of Lincoln as he was, an untried but talented politician, struggling with a new minted party and an uncertain mandate. He also describes with nuance and understanding the contradictions between the liberal and conservative wings of the Republican Party and how this division played a role in the crisis. He also wrote intelligently and ingeniously on Lincoln's decision to prevent the Crittenden Compromise – which would have curtailed the need for succession by entrenching slavery in United States law – from passing through Congress.

The reason why I mention Potter's work is that in management we are something at a crossroads. The recent economic stagnation and the market crash of 2008 have damaged management. Increasingly, there are scholars who are questioning the various foundations of the field; there are scholars attempting to defend those foundations. I must confess that I have played a role in this debate. Debates such as these are good for the field. History is a series of arguments. These arguments must be based on evidence. To examine the evidence in a dispassionate way, to rise above our biases, to base arguments on limited evidence, requires that we demonstrate some of the sound judgment that Potter possessed.

Cross-References

▶ Debates Within Management History
▶ What Is Management?

References

Appleby JO, Hunt L, Jacob M (1994) Telling the truth about history. W. W. Norton, New York
Bailyn B (2015) Sometimes an art. Knopf, New York
Batiz-Lazo B (2019) What is new in "a new history of management"? J Manag Hist 25(1):114–124
Bailyn B (1994) On the teaching and writing of history. Montgomery Endowment, Dartmouth College, Hanover
Bogue AG (1983) Historians and radical republicans: a meaning for today. J Am Hist 70(1):7–34
Bowden B (2018) Work, Wealth, and Postmodernism: The Intellectual Conflict at the Heart of Business Endeavour. Palgrave Macmillan. London, United Kingdom
Brinkley A (1995) The End of Reform. New York, NY: Knopf
Brinkley A (1998) Liberalism and its discontents. Harvard University Press, Cambridge, MA
Brogan D (1969) David M. Potter. In: Cunliffe M, Winks RW (eds) Pastmasters: some essays on American historians. pp 316–344, New York: Harper & Row
Bruce K, Nyland C (2011) Elton Mayo and the deification of human relations. Organ Stud 32 (3):383–405. https://doi.org/10.1177/0170840610397478
Burnier D (2008a) Frances Perkins' disappearance from American public administration: a genealogy of marginalization. Adm Theory Praxis 30(4):398–423
Burnier D (2008b) Erased history: Frances Perkins and the emergence of care-centred public administration. Adm Soc 40(4):403–422
Butterfield H (1931) The Whig Interpretation of History, London: G. Bell
Chase S (1946) Calling all social scientists. Nation Mag 162:538
Cohen L (1990) Making a new deal: industrial workers in Chicago, 1919–1939. Cambridge University Press, New York
Cummings S, Bridgman T, Hassard J, Rowlinson M (2017) A new history of management. Cambridge University Press, Cambridge
Darnton R (1984) The great cat massacre and other episodes in French cultural history. Basic Books, New York
DiMaggio PJ (1995) Comments on "what theory is not". Adm Sci Q 40(3):391–397
Donald D (1956) Lincoln reconsidered. Knopf, New York
Drucker PF (1946) For industrial peace. Harper's Wkly 193:385–395
Foster J, Mills AJ, Weatherbee TG (2014) History, field definition and management studies: the case of the new deal. J Manag Hist 20(2):179–199
Friedman M, Friedman R (1998) Two lucky people: memoirs. Chicago University Press, Chicago

4 Methodologies Within Management History

Gabor A (2000) The capitalist philosophers: the geniuses of modern business – their lives, times, and ideas. Random House, New York

Garraty JA (1960) The art of biography. Knopf

George CS (1972) The History of Management Thought, 2nd ed., Prentice Hall, Englewood Cliffs, NJ

Greenwood RA (2015) A First Look at the First 30 Years of the First Division: The Management History Division. HCBE

Handlin O (1979) Truth in History. Cambridge, MA: Harvard University Press

Harris HJ (1982) The right to manage: industrial relations policies of American business in the 1940s. University of Wisconsin Press, Madison

Haskell TL (October 2, 1975) The true and tragical history of 'Time on the Cross'. The New York Review of Books. Retrieved 17 Oct 2019

Herbert HA (1912) The abolition crusade and its consequences; four periods of American history. Scribner's Sons, New York

Hofstadter R (1944) UB Phillips and the plantation legend. J Negro Hist 29(2):109–124

Homans GC (1984) Coming to my senses: the autobiography of a social scientist. Transaction Books, New Brunswick

https://faculty.chass.ncsu.edu/slatta/hi216/hist_interp.htm

Johnson RR (1986) Charles McLean Andrews and the invention of American colonial history, William Mary Q, Third series, 43(4):520–541

Klatch RE (1999) A generation divided: the new left, the new right, and the 1960s. University of California Press, Berkeley

Lacey R (1986) Ford: the men and the machine. Little, Brown, Boston

Lichenstein NA (1982) The Most Dangerous Man in Detroit: Walter Reuther and the Fate of American Labor. New York, NY: Basic Books

Lichtenstein NA (1982) Labor's war at home: the Cio in world war ii (labor in crisis). Cambridge University Press, Cambridge

Lichtenstein N (1989) From corporatism to collective bargaining: organized labor and the eclipse of social democracy in the postwar era. The rise and fall of the New Deal Order, 1980, 122–152

Locke EA (1982) The ideas of Frederick W. Taylor: an evaluation. Acad Manag Rev 7(1):14–24

Lukacs J (1968) Historical consciousness; or, the remembered past. Harper & Row, New York

Mannheim K (1952) The problem of generations. In: Kecskemetied P (ed) Essays on the sociology of knowledge by Karl Mannheim. Routledge & Kegan Paul, New York

Middlekauff R (1969) Perry Miller. In: Cunliffe M, Winks RW (eds) Pastmasters. pp 167–190

Mills AJ, Novicevic MM (2019) Management and organizational history: a research overview. Routledge

Muldoon J (2012) The Hawthorne legacy: a reassessment of the impact of the Hawthorne studies on management scholarship, 1930–1958. J Manag Hist 18:105–119

Muldoon J (2019) Stubborn things: evidence, postmodernism and the craft of history. J Manag Hist 25(1):125–136

Novicevic MM, Jones J, Carrahar S (2015) Decentering Wren's evolution of management thought. In: McLaren PG, Mills AJ, Weatherbee TG (eds) The Routledge companion to management and organizational history. Routledge, London, pp 11–30

Patterson JT (1997) Grand expectations. Oxford University Press, New York

Peterson MD (1994) Lincoln in American memory. Oxford University Press, New York

Pfeffer J (1993) Barriers to the advance of organizational science: paradigm development as a dependent variable. Acad Manag Rev 18(4):599–620

Roethlisberger FT (1960) "Foreword" to a paperback edition of Elton Mayo's The human problems of an industrial civilization. Viking Press, New York

Salevouris MJ with Furay C (2015) The methods and skills of history: a practical guide. Wiley Blackwell, Malden

Schwarz C (2015) A review of management history from 2010–2014 utilizing a thematic analysis approach. J Manag Hist 21(4):494–504

Sorokin P (1956) Fads and foibles in modern sociology and related sciences. Regnery, Chicago

Stampp KM (1956) The Peculiar institution: slavery in the Ante-Bellum South. Knopf, New York

Stampp K (1965) The era of reconstruction, 1865–1877. Knopf, New York

Steinmetz G (2005) The genealogy of a positivist haunting: comparing prewar and postwar U.S. sociology. Boundary 2(32):107–133

Turner FJ (1920) The significance of the frontier in American history. In: The frontier in American history. Holt, New York, p 293

Weatherburn M (2019) Human relations' invented traditions: sociotechnical research and worker motivation at the interwar Rowntree Cocoa Works. Hum Relat. https://doi.org/10.1177/0018726719846647

Whyte WF (1969) Organizational behavior: theory and application. RD Irwin, Homewood

Williams K, Mills A (2017) Frances Perkins: gender, context and history in the neglect of a management theorist. Journal of Management History, Vol. 23 No. 1, pp. 32–50

Wren DA (1987) The white collar hobo. Ames, IO: Iowa State University Press

Wren DA (2005) The History of Management Thought, 5th ed., John Wiley and Sons, Hoboken, NJ

Wren DA, Bedeian AG (2018) The history of management thought, 7th edn. Wiley, Hoboken

Conflicting Visions: A Recap About the Debates Within Management History

5

Jeffrey Muldoon

Contents

Introduction	88
Traditional History	89
A New History	91
A New History of Management	94
ANTi-History	98
Other Histories	99
Myths	103
Conclusion	105
Cross-References	107
References	107

Abstract

The purpose of this chapter is to recap the various debates about management history by considering the roles of traditional history, postmodernism, radical history, and ANTi-history. I also track the development of various myths and discuss the competing strengths and weaknesses of the various models. My purpose is to provide a discussion of the models – not to offer judgment but a reasoned appraisal for the purpose of edification and debate.

Keywords

Traditional history · Postmodernism · Management history · Radical history

---

I would like to acknowledge Emerald Publishers who consented to allow me to reproduce this section and the one in postmodernism. It appeared in a slight different form in as Muldoon 2019.

J. Muldoon (✉)
Emporia State University, Emporia, KS, USA
e-mail: jmuldoon@emporia.edu

© The Author(s), under exclusive licence to Springer Nature Switzerland AG 2020
B. Bowden et al. (eds.), *The Palgrave Handbook of Management History*,
https://doi.org/10.1007/978-3-319-62114-2_5

Introduction

I begin, mea maxima culpa, by stating that I did not write this chapter as a detached scholar but rather as an active participant and curious observer on some of the ongoing methodological and epistemological issues in the field. As such, I cannot claim to be comprehensive nor unbiased. What I can do is to provide the observations of a young but published scholar, one who has been involved in several debates about the field (Muldoon 2019). My perception is that the field is very different from the one I entered into about 10 years ago. In some ways, the field is worse. Although the *Journal of Management History* remains a well-regarded journal, we no longer see history articles published in higher-level journals such as the *Journal of Management*. Although we have new perceptions, the clarity and precision that I believe characterized the field during the period of ascendancy and domination by the University of Oklahoma (Dan Wren) and the Louisiana State University ascendancy is increasingly gone. Yet, at the same time, we also have witnessed increased debates that are furthering the field.

No matter one's perspective, these current debates about traditional history versus the new postmodernist history can only benefit the field, as it moves us beyond single studies with little connection to each other to rigorous debates that may advance the discipline. Although I am a critic of much of the new history, I am respectful of the talents of the postmodernist side, their intellectual contributions, and mostly, because it is inspiring debate. As a younger scholar, there is much to learn about their steadfastness in questioning ongoing nostrums. That Rowlinson's (2015) initial paper on the Historic Turn, which was rejected by the Academy of Management, provides hope to any scholar who has had a good paper rejected. Like it or not, Rowlinson's work is something that a management historian has to come to grips with. The hope I have is that we can provide sufficient attention to the field of management history, increasing the prestige of what is currently one of the smallest divisions in the academy of management.

Management and organizational research and historical analysis have a curious history. Joseph Litterer, whose work on the standardization of business was one of the first works of management history published, abandoned his research to become a traditional organizational behaviorist. Twenty or so years later, Arthur Bedeian did not quite abandon history, but he moved his research line from a purely historical approach to one that embraced traditional empirical research and theory building. In fact, during one seminar at Louisiana State, Bedeian stated that scholars seeking a future in management history had gloomy prospects. Of his contemporaries, he noted only Charles Wrege and Daniel Wren were able to make a career as a management historian. Yet, it was also true that many scholars, such as Alfred Chandler, George Homans, and Peter Drucker produced, at one point or another, historical research. Unfortunately, the "management" and "organizational studies" fields have moved into a more purely "scientific approach," one that often ignores history. A number of prodigious management historians, such as Milorad Novicevic and John Humphreys, have a successful publication record in other areas of management. In fact, some of their management history has contributed to theory building elsewhere (e.g., Novicevic et al. 2017).

Management history as a disciplinary field arguably started in 1972 when Daniel Wren (1972) published the first substantial work of management history. Previously, Claude George's (1968) work focused on merely recounting dates, works, and figures. Wren's attempted to provide a framework on the evolution of management thought – one that explained how figures from ancient history up to the past have influenced the field. Subsequently, Wren occupied the commanding heights of the field. Management scholars often felt the need to either contradict this analysis or, alternatively, use his framework as a basis of their own research. In fact in my first two published papers, I took exception to several parts of his work and wrote papers that were a respectful rebuttal (Muldoon 2012) but nevertheless a rebuttal. Yet, there has been an influential and growing movement that has challenged his work – often noting that he placed management history in an iron box, ignoring some figures at the expense of others and ignoring topics (such as slavery) that could cause embarrassment to management (Novicevic et al. 2015; Cummings et al. 2017).

I regard this critical movement as a mixed bag. Firstly, for the field of management history to grow, we need different voices. The voice of one person, no matter how sober and well-informed, cannot and should not speak for the voice of entire history of the field. I appreciate some of the different voices and approaches. Revision and argument are not antithetical to history. In fact both are necessary for the field to grow and expand. Therefore, revisionism is not a specific brand of history but how history is developed. Yet, and this part I decry, we often unfairly and unnecessarily attack the works of great previous historians. I write this chapter to provide an overview of the debate between traditional histories versus the new history. I talk about how this debate informs the following topics: an overview of traditional history, the challengers, and the role of myth.

Traditional History

Management history started largely with the work of Daniel Wren (1972) and his friends and colleagues, Ronald Greenwood, Charles Wrege, and Arthur Bedeian. Wren and his colleagues' work was grounded in empiricism and provided the traditional narrative of management history – with a progression of scholars starting in ancient times to the era of Frederick Winslow Taylor that created management thought. Wren was especially important in developing this approach, as his work on management thought has enhanced his reputation to the point where he is considered the "Alfred Chandler" of management history (Novicevic et al. 2015). Wren's work was the first to take management's history seriously. Unlike Claude George (1968), Wren provided not just a description but also a background and context for his work. The purpose was to provide the reader with the "gift of professional maturity" so that scholars can understand where we came from, where we are going, and the perils and promise of the field (Bedeian 2004). Wren and Bedeian also viewed the work of the past as the foundation on which current management thought is built, thereby providing assurances for those in the present that "progress in scholarship is a multigenerational endeavor" (Wren and Bedeian 2018, pg. xix).

Contrary to the criticisms sometimes made against him, Wren's history as embodied in *The Evolution of Management Thought* (now in its 7th edition) is consistently changing from one edition to the next. The method that Wren and (later Bedeian) provided was one based around examining scholarly works to produce a narrative. Although unstated, the primary method employed by Wren and Bedeian is probability based on the preponderance of evidence (Bogue 1983). Necessarily, both methods require consistent revision and review of the historical record in the light of new scholarship. As a craft, historians carefully weigh the evidence based on the historical record. Interpretations change as evidence changes – much as it would in Bayesian statistics. The individual historian may be prone to error – but the hope is that the review process and the community of scholars can correct errors and promote more accurate histories. The net process of management history over the last 50 years is an impressive body of evidence.

In essence, Wren and Bedeian sought to understand how various theories in management have emerged by capturing their chronological relationship in the belief that this approach best captures the "zeitgeist" that "compose the people and time" who form management thought. Wren and Bedeian therefore use time as a boundary for writing a compelling history that demonstrates the development of management thought. This is revealed by their selection of the term evolution – suggesting not Darwin, but a development of the field. The term evolution implies two distinct things. Firstly, evolution implies a development over time. It is that way they track development from one time to the next. Second, it implies things get better. These assumptions and methods have been challenged by those associated with the so-called Historic Turn in management thought.

One of the salient elements of Wren and Bedeian's work is the concept that they divide management history into four chronological periods – which are the (1) the early period, (2) the scientific management era, (3) the social person era, and (4) the modern era. They use these four simple but elegant domains to track the transformation of management, demonstrating how management has unfolded since the ancient Egyptians and Sumerians. One of the implications of their research is that management moves through fads and that one generation leaves a general framework through which other generations emerge. The basis of this type of research, as noted by Novecivic, Logan, and Carraher, is that:

1. Chronological studies proposing periodization in the evolution of management thought
2. Studies aimed at ensuring that management's knowledge base does not contain any myths or misinterpretation from the past
3. Studies uncovering examples from the past to serve as benchmarks for the future
4. Studies aimed at reevaluating the past against our current knowledge base to identify management fads and fashions

Up until recently, scholars adopted this type of framework, relatively uncritically. In fact, in one of the reviews of my Hawthorne paper (2012), a reviewer complained that I was being too critical of Wren's perspective. My own perspective was that Wren's work was so good that it should serve as an inspiration for criticism, either because there was a gap in his study or because there was a quibble with his interpretation. I felt that Wren's work was the Bible of management thought in the same way Viteles work has been for motivation and industrial/organizational psychology (Mills 2012). I have recommended this book to colleagues, doctoral students, and even practitioners who wish to understand management. There is no topic of management thought that I do not want to read Wren's opinion, as I have found it sober and well-informed. I am also in complete agreement with him that history runs through periods as it usually is the experience of generations that produced and interpret historical events.

A New History

Despite the commanding heights that Wren's work has long occupied, there has been a group of scholars who have criticized not just the findings of Wren and Bedeian but also the philosophical underpinnings of it – namely, the use of time periods. Critics of this type of format argue that they are artificial constructs imposed upon history by historians, with little regard or understanding of the nuances of the past. For example, one of the contemporary criticisms is that there were recognized systems for systematic or if not scientific management long before Taylor. Starting with Bill Cooke, scholars have demonstrated that slavery, especially in the United States, could be viewed as a massive management enterprise – one that combined elements of human capital, profit, and strategy – well before Taylor. Therefore, what Wren and Bedeian did was to impose a heuristic and, indeed, random structure on the past that did not adequately reflect it. In fact, what they did was to ignore negative events that would damage management's legitimacy.

One of the major criticisms of Wren's approach has come from Novecivic et al. (2015). The argument provided is that Wren and traditional management scholars "developed their web of shared beliefs about the history of management thought not only objectively but also relationally through their socialization in their academic communities." As a correction, Novecivic and his coauthors have argued for a more eclectic approach to conceptualizing the history of management thought. This approach has been echoed by other scholars who have sought to include those have previously been excluded from the construction of the dominant historical narratives. Notable among these are those associated with the growing body of postmodernist thought.

Novecivic and his coauthors have extended their criticisms by arguing that approaches such as those pursued by Wren and Bedeian ignore the polarized views that often develop in history. For example, they note that different scholars have varying viewpoints of Taylorism – observing how "Taylorism has been both recognized as the legitimate object of theorizing (Wagner-Tsukamoto 2008) and denied as a myth (Wrege and Greenwood 1991)." Yet, Wren ignores these viewpoints, positing instead the view that Taylorism was a valid undertaking to promote both social harmony and management's own legitimacy. Novecivic et al. also draw upon Bevir's (2003) framework, which holds that we are constrained in developing meaningful interpretations of the past. Moreover, it is suggested those interpretations that do emerge and become part of the accepted field are often the result of subjective experience. Bevir also argues that we often use theory to provide a grossly simplified account of the past that ignores the inherent complexity of history. Seen from this perspective, Wren's assumption that his work is based upon positivist factual claims is nothing than subjective thought.

According to the critique of Novecivic and his coauthors the framework that Wren produced is, therefore, nothing more than an organizing structure that is "fictive" and useful only as a narrative device. Rather than being an objective outcome of history, it is in fact subjective. As Novecivic et al. write:

> Wren has had the capacity to change the webs of shared beliefs about management history that he inherited. In particular, we claim that Wren changed the way in which the history of management thought is now commonly viewed and taught by introducing the analytical framework of social, political, and economic factors that influenced historical change in management practices. We argue that in his book Wren depicts this historical change through the meanings that we uncover from his framework-based conceptualization and narration of the history of management thought.

That Wren's framework became dominant, Novecivic and his coauthors suggest, primarily reflected not its intellectual strengths but rather its spread and adoption through socialization – a salient point in that Novecivic and Carraher were students of Wren. The implication that what Wren produced was not real. Instead, it was but one socially constructed reality, created through Wren's synthesis. Similarly, attempts to develop a "normal history" (to use a Kuhnian phrase) – such as that created by Wren – require a foundation. The past only becomes historical if it consists of events that could have been made only at the time. Wren uses an interdependent viewpoint that consists of both historical and his own judgment.

My take is very different. Although history has been studied for thousands of years, it did not assume its modern form until the time of the mid-nineteenth-century German historian and philosopher, Leopold Von Ranke. Ranke, influenced by the Germanic idealistic tradition, sought to understand the past "as it essentially was." The basis of this research was empirical approach that used critical treatment of unused, original resources. These new historians eliminated the use of the will of God to explain historical outcomes (unlike the mid-ninetieth-century American historian Frances Parkman, who believed that God enabled Wolfe to beat de Montcalm). The ideal historian was someone that would cross an ocean to verify a comma. Therefore, the path that Ranke set historians on was evidence-based analysis that sought to reconstruct the past based on judgment calls. Factual analysis was the key. Despite arguments from postmodernists, there was, even here, an understanding that the past was separate from history. History is based on judgment

5 Conflicting Visions: A Recap About the Debates Within Management History

calls based on the concept of probability. It is possible that Abraham Lincoln was not elected President in 1860 – but it is not probable. There are such things as facts, and not all interpretations are equal – a point even postmodernists recognize.

Let's take the facts of Taylorism. Was Taylorism a myth or legitimate? Those are two different viewpoints by two sets of historians. How could we reconcile them? Well, it does not mean that those two viewpoints are equal validity. For example, as I will note later, Wrege was an excellent empirical historian, who often lacked judgment and failed to see the big picture. To be sure, Wrege did advance the field, but his principle motivation was to debunk Taylor and other historical figures. He did not continue and ask why Taylorism was so esteemed, even if it was built on flawed foundations. Yet, Wrege and Greenwood (especially Greenwood) did believe that Taylorism had benefits even if the man was a jerk. To this day, we continue to use Taylorite concepts of testing, measuring, and theorizing about work. Taylor imagined a new world of plenty produced by management, a new world that has come about. But at the same time, Taylor was also elitist, a liar, a braggart, and a narcissist. Wrege was right, but he did not go far enough. Likewise, Wagner-Tsukamoto (2007, 2008) recognized the limitations of Taylorism while conceding its underlying excellence. The separation into two camps ignores nuance.

The historian must make judgment calls – those judgment calls must be based on evidence; they must consider alternate evidence, and those must be based on the preponderance of the evidence. Furthermore, there is no such thing as "normal history." The field itself is fraught with contentious arguments about interpretations. History is argument without end – there are no all-powerful covering laws in history. Instead, economic, social, and psychological forces combine to move human beings in differing ways at differing times. In fact, the way to get published in history is very different than science. Whereas scientists are bound by normal science (only theory shifts can rescue them), historians are geared toward finding new evidence, to alter the given historical record. Applied to Wren, he consistently updates his work to consider new evidence.

That being said, the one criticism of Wren is that he has kept his superstructure. However, I could not find of any reason why he would have to abandon it. For example, during the scientific management era, management thinkers talked about issues related to scientific management. Likewise, during the human relations era, management thinkers sought to research and understand social relationships at work. That is not to say that scholars did not research social relationships during the scientific management or scientific management during the human relations era. Rather one field was dominant during the time. The use of time is exceptionally important to historical research and narrative. Without such, history would not make much sense or provide little value. Should we, for example, stop referring to America in the period from 1848 to 1877 as the Civil War era? Yes, it is true that many other things happened in these years besides the prospect or reality of civil war. But it was the threat of Civil War and, subsequently, the profound effects of actual armed conflict that did more than anything else to shape the lived experience during these years. Eras take form by major events, social, political, economic, or military.

A New History of Management

The fundamental divide that has opened between traditional forms of management history and advocated by the supporters of the so-called Historic Turn has become even more pronounced with the publication of *NHM*, a work co-authored in 2017 by Cummings, Bridgman, Hassard, and Rowlinson. Claiming that their work provides the basis "for a new, deeper history of management," Cummings et al. (2017, p. 33, xii) declare that the work of "pioneers," such as Wren, is outmoded and unfit for use in "our times." Explicitly framing their study within "a Foucauldian" perspective, Cummings et al. (2017, p. 41) declare that their aim is to write a "counter-history" that no longer accepts "conventional truths." In doing so, they argue several radical positions: that Adam Smith was not a believer in free markets; that Frederick Taylor was no fan of the "efficiency" movement that adopted his name; that the Hawthorne studies were poor scholarship and a detriment to the field; and that Weber was not concerned with bureaucracy.

The postmodernist move into management history is a comparatively recent development. While there were antecedents to this movement, it really started in 2004, with the publication of Clark and Rowlinson's paper calling for a Historic Turn in management research. According to Clark and Rowlinson (2004, pg. 331), the Historic Turn "is an increasing call for an historical perspective in organisation studies ... the 'historic turn' that has transformed the way other branches of the social sciences and humanities 'go about their business.'" This statement was not controversial that scholars over the years, including Wren and Bedeian, have called upon historical awareness and method in the profession. What was controversial was Clark and Rowlinson's call for this Historic Turn to be based upon "such as the 'discursive turn', deconstruction and post-modernism. Within history itself this transformation is associated with hermeneutics, the 'linguistic turn', and the revival of narrative.... (pg. 331)." Their declared social purpose was also different from that of people such as Wren and Bedeian in that it sought to find new foundations of management history, seeking to make the profession less supportive of management and more supportive of radical ideas.

This broadly postmodernist approach to history has challenged the dominant empiricist model as expressed by Wren and Bedeian. As Novecivic et al. (Novicevic et al. 2015, p. 13) accurately observed in a chapter published within *The Routledge Companion to Management and Organizational History*, "a significant number of management historians" now reject the idea that management history can be written on the basis of "positivist factual truth-claims." Elsewhere in the same volume, Munslow (2015, p. 136) declared that "meanings are fictively construed. There are no lessons in the past." Although such "critical management" perspectives draw on multiple sources – most particularly Michel Foucault, Hayden White, the "amodernist" French theorist, and Bruno Latour – their influence within management history has grown exponentially since 2004 when Clark and Rowlinson published, in Business History, their call for a "Historic Turn" in organizational studies. Admittedly, as Bowden (2018, p. 204, 212) notes, there is a "disingenuous" character to much of the literature that the call for an "Historic Turn" has spawned in that it frequently uses Foucauldian and postmodernist frameworks without acknowledging their source. The original Clark and Rowlinson (2004) article, for example, only mentions Foucault on two occasions and postmodernism on three – despite being couched in what we are clearly Foucauldian ideas. While the movement is inchoate (and contradictory – see Bowden 2018), there is, nevertheless, a deep and resounding skepticism of the empirical history that Wren and Bedeian have published.

The postmodernist approach has its focus on power and, as Richard Evans (1997) expressed it, the ability of those in power to create sustaining narratives that maintain the current power relationships. As Evans has noted, this approach has some of its roots in the New Labor history, where scholars have attempted to provide a voice for the voiceless and attempt to reconstruct as past that had been lost. Yet, E.P. Thompson and Herbert Gutman were empiricists, who used many different techniques to cobble together a forgotten past. However, postmodernists – even those who are not completely devoted it – are skeptical of historical fact. Advocating what they refer to as ANTi-history, amodernists Durepos and Mills (2012, pg. 5) argue that all knowledge is inherently subjective and that research should be primarily informed not by empirical discoveries of past realities but by considerations "as to who benefits from a specific interpretation of the past." A similar opinion is expressed by Hassard, Rowlinson, and Decker (Rowlinson et al. 2014, p. 257) in an article entitled "Research Strategies for Organizational History," where it is declared that there is a "fictive" component in all historical writing. Seen from this perspective, it is power – and the uses and abuses of power – that is decisive in shaping and distorting the nature of evidence, be it in the cause of the oppressed or the oppressors. Postmodernism is skeptical and indeed, sometimes outrightly hostile to most forms of historical evidence (Appleby et al. 2004). Its proponents note that official documents are flawed sources of evidence because they either do not consider all relevant factors or because those individuals in power seek to control the record. Similarly, oral history and memoir are flawed due to the fact that memories are social creations. Within organizations, therefore, it is only the constructed memories of the powerful that endure. Other types of evidence, such as demographics, etc., are deliberately ignored in that reference to such sources mitigates historical explanations built around power and oppression, which postmodernists regard as the real drivers of history. Time periods are also considered artificial constructs that detract attention from the immediacy of power and oppression. In short, there is no evidence, no way of getting to the past, which does not reflect the manipulated social creations of one or more power interests. Accordingly, the narratives that historians create as an intellectual framework are mere fictions that typically support the dominant framework and are examples of power.

These postmodernist ideas *do* have a deep benefit to the profession in that they force us to consider both our methodological roots in a deeper way and the foundations of the field. For example, in Cummings et al.'s (2017) book on management history, it is argued that management historians willfully ignore the contributions of figures such as Louis Brandeis and Theodore Roosevelt and their commitment to liberalism, focusing instead on the production efficiency of

Frederick Winslow Taylor. Elsewhere, Cummings et al. argue that Adam Smith was not a neoliberal icon but rather a believer in the welfare state; that the use of the term laissez-faire in association with Smith is a misuse; that Max Weber was not primarily focused on bureaucracy; that management ignores its deep relationship to chattel slavery; and that historians (most likely Wren) have cherry-picked the evidence to provide legitimacy to the field of management.

At its best, therefore, the postmodernist approach forces the traditional scholar to focus on questions and issues that we have ignored. One of the particular strengths of postmodernist research in management is that it forces us to puncture many of the myths that surround our profession such as the sanctity of the scientific method and the peer review process. The myth goes that management scholars hypothesize based on theory, collect data, analyze data, and then provide a write-up. This is often not the case. Hypothesizing after the results are known is more common than we care to admit; we cannot even define one of key terms, theory; and the peer review process probably rewrites manuscripts more than we are prone to admit. We also tend to believe that methodological problems only exist when they appear to be a myth or a gross overstatement; we perform statistical analysis when none of our survey methods are random; we often do not test the theory as intended. This is to say nothing about the lack of common definitions on basic terms such as job satisfaction and strategy.

Yet, despite the above strengths, postmodernism turn is rife with problems. One of the issues that the new management history does not solve and, indeed, exhibits the same sin is how management history is taught to students. To really make the past alive, to make it relevant to the business student, is one of the most difficult aspects of education. I believe that despite the changes they make to history, they do not bridge this issue. Indeed, their embrace of postmodernism would appear to be anathema to the business student who prefers empiricism. From my observation, undergraduate business students typically want facts and practical application. They do not want long debates on the issue of subjectivity and power. Instead, the vast majority appreciate the essential role that management plays in both the individual business and the economy at large, matching supply with demand and instigating the efficiencies that engenders increased wealth from fewer resource inputs. Accordingly, it is not only a matter of the obscurantist postmodernist writing style annoying the typical undergraduate and frustrating the master's student with concepts that are difficult to relate to practical problems. It is also the case that postmodernism seeks to actually destabilizing management as a concept. Although some may concur with such a "deconstructionist" action, I take an opposite position, agreeing with Bowden (2018) that "modernism" (i.e., our modern industrial society built around free enterprise) and management (i.e., the mechanisms for maximizing the potential of free market societies) need to be defended as both sources of wealth and freedom.

Another problem is that there is really nothing new or original within postmodernism. Rather, it is a simply more radical reiteration of the relativism practiced by Carl Becker and Charles Beard, two past Presidents of the American Historical Association, during the 1930s. As with today's postmodernist, these two historians "mocked the notion that the facts speak for themselves" and dismissed the "objective reconstruction of the past" as "a vacuous ideal" (Novick 1988, p. 293). Theses relativists from the 1930s also resembled today's postmodernist in arguing that the constraining influence of wealthy donors limited the objectivity of history; that activist practitioners dominated the field in the interests for the status quo; and that the field was dominated by Anglo-Saxon Protestants who left little place for the "professional historians of recent immigrant background, none [for those] of working-class origin, and hardly any [for those] who were not Protestant" (Novick 1988: 61; 68–69).

Looking back, it is not surprising that relativism would come to dominate after the First World War as God died in the mud in Flanders Field. Much like the post-Civil War generation, this generation found all Gods dead and that there were no absolutes and little to die for. *Goodbye to all That* was the mantra for those that survived the war. It is not surprising that postmodernists such as Foucault would reject both Marxism and capitalism and in the process adopt a largely nihilist philosophy. The post-Cold War world has become the age of fracture, where shared meanings and viewpoints are falling apart, where structures no longer seem to hold, and where – despite the best attempts of society – racism and sexism remain constant and permanent (Appleby et al. 2004). There are no sunny uplands. A "postmodern" view is also found in the work of Thomas Kuhn, who suggests that science is driven by social factors and not scientific facts (Appleby et al. 2004). A "Kuhnian" view can thus be seen throughout the postmodernist literature in that historical narratives are socially constructed.

Another problem with the new management history is that it ignores the most salient force of history: time. One particular question if we eliminate time periods, how can we organize history? This would be akin to eliminating chapters in a book, stages in a play, or yards on a football field. Time periods make history understandable and approachable. Likewise, whereas from a certain (generally accepted) perspective, we perceive two boxers in the ring as two separate entities, an alternate reality, using quantum mechanics, suggests that the boxing match is merely a single concept, as they are merely two sets of molecules colliding in a vast empty vacuum. Of course, if we say that they are the same, and that Ali and Frazier were the same entity, we would be laughed at any sports bar or pub. One way to consider is whether the First World War and the Second World War existed in a meaningful sense. From one perspective they are the same – featuring a revisionist Germanic state – seeking to overturn the old imperial world of Europe with a new imperial world. Therefore, from this perspective, the Kaiser was merely the dress rehearsal for Hitler. Of course, there was a vast difference between the Kaiser and Hitler. Ignoring the difference between the two wars is to say nothing of the relative rise and decline of powers such as Great Britain, the United States, France, and Russia/Soviet Union. Despite the artificial nature of time periods, they are useful and accurate devices to describe the past.

The largest problem with postmodernism is that it can lead to the denial of known facts. Gordon Wood, winner of the Pulitzer and Bancroft prizes, one of the great historians of his generation, and the top historian of the early American Republic, has stated that a postmodernist would have a difficult time stating that a Holocaust denier is wrong, because one historical opinion is as valid as the next (Wood 2008).

Wood's argument is thus similar to that of George Orwell, when he points to the fallacy of an insistent belief that $2 + 2 = 5$. Rather than leading to a broadening of approach, such arguments merely result in error. As Appleby et al. write, "Postmodernism renders problematic the belief in progress, the modern periodization of history, and the individual as knower and doer." History becomes nothing more than another measure of control. Worse still, since history is subjective, we can change history to suit our needs since there is no "reality," only our poor ability to describe it. Hence that is the reason why Taylor is now socially responsible.

ANTi-History

ANTi-history is one of the most ambitious attempts by management historians and historians in general to develop a framework to describe how history is made (Duperos and Mills 2012). Their ambitions are justified in many ways. I have a real appreciation for it – even if I feel that take their arguments too far. ANTi-history argues that knowledge is the product of actors and networks, whose actions determine how people see the world. Therefore, since history is a product of actor networks, it is necessarily subjective. Accordingly, written history is nothing more than a story that supports the needs of the actor networks. This line of argument suggests that as the actor network changes, therefore, history changes – making the past immutable and history subjective. Consequently, there is little in the way of facts and evidence. Instead, what we have are merely the mental images and justifications of those in the network.

Duperos and Mills have written a very interesting and useful framework. Unlike other postmodernists they address some of the key problems with postmodernism by positing that history is necessarily subjective and that the historical record is a fusion of the authors network – a network which includes archivists, other historians, and the public. In addition, the historian has within their network the actual historical figures who impact upon the historical record on the basis of their actions. For instance, in their chapter on the removal of German emigres from an airline that Pan Am had control over, Durepos and Mills correctly demonstrate that historical actors *can* transform the narrative to fit their political needs. I believe this framework has great utility for use in certain types of archives, most particularly corporate archives. In fact, I believe that the approach advocated by Durepos and Mills is a necessary and essential one for those examining the inner workings of how corporations save records.

Yet, despite its strengths I do have two issues with the ANTi-history. Firstly, I find the level of cynicism to be extremely high. I would not say that Duperos and Mills have a conspiratorial view of the world, but it is close. Namely, I would dispute their view that archivists can influence the historical record in a negative fashion. My experience of archivists is that they wish to maintain the historical record as it was – the warts and all. Perhaps, my experience is shaped by dealings with government or academic archivists (rather than corporate). But I believe that it would be a gross dereliction of their responsibility and professional ethics for any archivist to manipulate the archival record. And I doubt that any significant number resort to such unethical behavior. Secondly, I believe that the handling of certain issues by Durepos and Mills – such as the removal of Germans from Pan American's subsidiary – does not fully consider the historical record. I could buy into the fact that Juan Trippe would act opportunistically by removing the pilots to maintain control. Yet, I believe there is a shade of gray: American military leaders were concerned, even during the 1920s and 1930s, with the rebirth of German might. Given how closely aligned air industry was to the military (and how closely Trippe worked with the government), he would have acquiesced (one suspects) to the viewpoint of the American government and military.

Perhaps more troubling is that historians have been using this type of framework (i.e., one that gives primary to actor networks and interests) for years. When I was an undergraduate at Gettysburg College many years ago, we read two differing frameworks of the Reconstruction written by two different authors. The first was written by a Hilary Herbert that was highly critical regarding many Reconstruction policies; the second was written by Kenneth Stampp that was favorable and wished that Reconstruction had worked. Herbert had fought in the Civil War on the Southern side, was from South Carolina, and had opposed racial integration. Stampp was a Northerner from Wisconsin, who came from a family with strong progressive tendencies. He also wrote during the 1960s, which some have called the Second Reconstruction. The lesson was when reading history, consider the historian. I never read history the same way again. However, scholars have been aware of this type of technique for years. But, Durepos and Mills do provide a theoretical framework.

But even more troubling is that there are times when the actor network theory does not hold. In fact, there are numerous times when people go against their network (Lukacs 2011). One particular example would be the experience of Ronald Radosh (2001). Radosh was what is known as a "red diaper" baby, meaning that his parents were members of the Communist Party of the United States. Party members were devoted to the party: they lived together, worked together, and socialized together. They also had articles of faith. These articles of faith could not be questioned. To be a communist meant that your life's values were determined by Moscow. One of those articles was that the Rosenbergs, the atomic spies, were innocent of the charges brought against them. Radosh's memoir recounts how this fact was pounded into him as a young man. But Radosh rebelled: he abandoned the party and became a member of the New Left. When Radosh started writing the major study on the Rosenbergs (with Joyce Milton), Radosh came to the conclusion that they were guilty. Radosh wrote this knowing that it would completely lead to him being ostracized in the academy. How would ANTi-history explain this? There was little in Radosh's network that would suggest either his level of honesty or his willingness to break with previous beliefs. However, these are mostly quibbling. I think this framework could be used to describe how traditions emerge.

Other Histories

Two additional histories I would like to discuss are Gerard Hanlon's *The Dark Side of Management* and Morgen Witzel's *A History of Management Thought*. Hanlon's (2015) book is written from a critical even Marxist perspective and builds on

Reinhard Bendix's work, *Work and Authority in Industry*. Like Bendix, Hanlon proposes that management thought is highly ideological and contentious in nature. But Hanlon goes further in that he argues that the central purpose of management is to alter social relationships so as to shift money from one class to another. Management is not about wealth creation, efficiency, or effectiveness. Rather it is a "political endeavor" whose purpose is to modify social relationships so that market-based solutions, competitiveness, self-care, and individualism run paramount. Hanlon also argues that management is necessitated by labor's refusal to bend to capitalists, necessitating managerial action to circumvent or undermine this refusal. It is from this perspective that Hanlon contemplates the policies and understandings of Taylor, Mayo, and Ford. This is an interesting perspective and one that I am sure will gain great esteem in management critical studies.

Let me state that I disagree with Hanlon's framework. That being said, he does such an artful job that I could see and understand his perspective. For example, I agree with him that concepts related to market wages, utilitarian work values, monetary incentives, and individualism were not originally part of the typical worker's perspective. It took political and social movements (one of which management is one) to bring workers to the perspective of modernity. I also agree that we should consider worker perspectives more fully when we write about various management interventions. I would also agree that management is a form of social control – something that management scholars are often not unware or, if they are aware, something that they prefer not to be aware of. I also believe that he has some apt things to say about the relationship between Taylorism and Mayoism: in that Mayoism could be seen as an extension of the former.

I find, however, his arguments to be unconvincing. In large part this is because Hanlon views every action taken by a manager with a degree of hostility. It has long been noted that managers were often racist and unwilling to hire African Americans. Henry Ford did that – he seemed to be unbiased in hiring even if he did primarily hire African Americans to dangerous jobs. Yet Hanlon seems critical of this, noting that Ford hired immigrants and African Americans due to the fact that native-born Americans were generally reluctant to work on Ford's assembly lines. In addition, Hanlon is selective in his use of evidence. He cites with approval Bell's and Moore's criticisms of the Hawthorne studies, but he never cites or discusses whether or not those criticisms were fair or not. It is difficult to see, in reading Mayo's writings, a justification for Hanlon's view that Mayo was really adjusting "man to machine." What Mayo was more likely trying to do was to discover what managers could do, besides contracts and government action, to promote spontaneous cooperation and reduce the amount of labor upheaval at the time. Likewise, it is difficult to envision how worker resistance leads to wealth. Anyone familiar with the work on counterproductive work behavior would understand how false that statement is and that worker resistance leads to exceptionally high costs to business. In addition, it is a facile argument that management is blind to the dark side of management – there are a consistent series of books, articles, and other materials about management shortcomings.

5 Conflicting Visions: A Recap About the Debates Within Management History   101

Lastly, Hanlon is critical of two aspects of management. The first is management's claims to scientific objectivity, and the second is the claim that management promotes hierarchy. In terms of management's claims to scientific evidence, it is true that Taylor's work, although it had the residue of science, was not as scientific as he claimed. Likewise, scholars have noted for years the problems of the Hawthorne studies. Yet, research is driven by empirically testing theory, measurement, and evidence-based research. Although, there are quibbles regarding management research (we could be much better on replication), we do try to use scientific methods in gathering research. If anything, management scholars are aware of the vast complexity of research – hence the strong field of contingency management. Likewise, I am baffled by the claim that management is based on and promotes hierarchy. Yes it does, but I could not think of a society, except for maybe some ninetieth-century utopian societies, where there was not a hierarchy. In fact, modern management probably is a better hierarchy since there are systems that promote meritocracy. I am not sure if Hanlon promotes a romantic view of the past or the future in that there are no power differences.

Morgen Witzel is the author of *A History of Management Thought*, a work which, I believe, provides the best survey of management thought outside of Wren and Bedeian. Witzel is in many ways a bit of an outliner. He is more of management consultant and practitioner than he is an academic, although he is a fellow at the University of Exeter. I find Witzel's work to be an interesting addition because he asks the question that I have been wondering for a long time – when did management move from an applied science to one based on theory building, data mining, and nonpractical results? Witzel has proposed that beginning in the 1890s, when management started to emerge, the new profession of management was desirous of the professional respect enjoyed by law, medicine, or accountancy. This societal respect has, however, not happened. It has not emerged. Instead, management finds itself disrespected, without honor. Even some of its best thinkers, such as Jeff Pfeffer, decry the lack of respect of management in the field of social science. Witzel argues that part of the problem is that management is ignorant of its past, it does not cite seminal articles of the past, or, if we do, we do not read them.

Witzel also proposes that management started to lose its way during the 1940s when the Carnegie School (i.e., a school of management thought identified with academics from the Carnegie Mellon University in Pittsburg) emerged to challenge classical management. What is notable is that the Carnegie School provided one of the first, sustained attempts at theory development by academics for academics. While Elton Mayo was a member of the Harvard Business School, he addressed actual managers more than he did in academics. His associate Fritz Roethlisberger was similar, although he had more of a foot in academia. George Homans, another of Mayo's students, moved over to sociology, where he developed theory. Yet, Carnegie was firmly entrenched in academia and taught business, as William Starbuck noted, as one would teach physics. Despite all the praise that Herbert Simon, Richard Cyert, and James March gained, however, there is also some justification in the criticism that they started us down the road of abstruseness.

I like Witzel's approach as he writes like someone who is heavily engrossed in the field in terms of both research and practitioners, unlike Wren and Bedeian, who write in a more scholarly way. I disagree with Witzel. I believe we do not cite historical arguments, because it would reveal that the emperor has no clothes – most of what we research today is impractical or similar concepts restated. Modern management is more precise and scientific, but have we, in any way, advanced the tools that manager's actually use? Would someone who is a manager notice a real difference between self-determination theory and two-factor theory? Likewise what would a manager say about some of the insights that we have produced? For example, one suspects that most managers would say that the supposed theoretical insight that resources are a source of competitive advantage is something that is self-evidently obvious. Similarly, would a practicing manager care about the various amounts of vocabulary/theory building and item analysis that we do? I am not sure a manager would be impressed by this. Nicholas Butler's famous statement rings true: "An expert is one who knows more and more about less and less until he knows absolutely everything about nothing." Significantly, those management thinkers, like Michael Porter, Tom Peters, and Peter Drucker, who have attempted to move past and offer applied evidence, are often attacked.

I do have a couple of quibbles with Witzel's framework. Firstly, he does not cite many articles from the *Journal of Management History* and other academic journals. For instance, if he wrote about John Hassard's work on the Hawthorne studies, he might have a differing perspective. Likewise, his perspective on certain issues would change if he read more about the contextual history in which management occurred. For example, was the Progressive Era more about constraining markets or about setting them free? Probably it was both, depending on what vision of progressivism someone adhered to. Likewise, while he mentions the importance of the Second World War on management, he fails to sufficiently reflect upon the esteem which wartime managers were able to garner. If he did, he would note that management's current low status was not always apparent. Likewise, he overstates the amount that Henry Ford borrowed from scientific management. Indeed, some Taylorites did not believe that Ford used scientific management at all. In fact, given that Ford did not read much, it makes sense that he may developed something similar on his own. Lastly, I believe that Witzel protests too much about management's status. Again, who are we less prestigious compared to? Management academics typically make more than economists, sociologists, and psychologists. Although we are not as highly compensated as accountants, the demand for accounting has exploded over the years due to the regulatory environment. Accounting research is also difficult to undertake. Likewise, the demand for operations management has waxed and waned. Although management as a discipline maybe on the downside, new challenges are always emerging to provide opportunities for those scholars who are intent on solving them.

Myths

We consistently hear the term myth regarding management history. We hear about the myths of Taylorism and Hawthorne studies. In fact, some scholars concede that both myth and historical reality can often contend with each other. Mainstream history is characterized by a similar dichotomy. Our memory of Lincoln is often very different from what actually occurred. One particular reason is that we use Lincoln as a perspective to determine an answer to the question: What is America? What America should be? What should we as a society to be based on the ideals of Lincoln? As David Donald (Donald 1956) has noted, politicians often try to get right with Mr. Lincoln. In this case, history serves as a common framework, a useful myth to rally society (Peterson 1994). In scholarly professions, we often use myth as a means to provide us with a sense of legitimacy. Management has sought – over the years – to seek legitimacy through several different methods, the use of theory building, the scientific method, and practical application to provide us with a sense of legitimacy (Pfeffer 1993). As a new field, we have status anxiety and envy toward other more established fields. This is a common trend throughout science. Economics has envy of physics and sociology as an envy of economics (Steinmetz 2005). In fact, scholars such as Jeffrey Pfeffer (1993) have bemoaned the lack of a clear paradigm in the field of management, noting that we are losing ground to other business fields.

We have also used myths to provide legitimacy as well. Perhaps, it is the reason why managers start the process of management with Frederick Winslow Taylor, rather than such flawed figures as Henry Ford, whose violent anti-union policies and anti-Semitism made him a comprised figure (Lacey 1986). Perhaps, had Ford died in 1918, soon after his electoral defeat, when he was compared to Moses, we would have used him as a model. Yet, we also focused on Taylor for reasons that were historical as well. Namely, that Taylor appeared at the right time and place for management to emerge as a distinct field. A check of how Taylor inspire thinkers is clear. While there were other efforts to understand social man, the Hawthorne studies were the study that inspired scholars to reexamine the field to consider the role of social motivation in terms of economic motivation. Likewise, checking a listing of citation numbers would reveal what contemporaries believed about the Hawthorne studies and how it inspired thinkers (Muldoon 2012). It is important to note, therefore, that the complexities of history usually do not lead to a ready reduction.

To debunk myths, management historians often create strawmen. Wrege and Perroni argued (pg. 26) that scholars should "think to look at the idol early enough in the game to discover that it had feet of clay before it was hoisted onto a pedestal." I am curious as to how we answer the question in management: who do we idealize? One of the favorite targets has been the Hawthorne studies. Firstly, scholars have, for the last several years, pointed out that the Hawthorne studies were poor methodologically, that they proved nothing, and that Mayo had a biased viewpoint (Gabor 2000; Hassard 2012). Secondly, we have also been told that that the Mayo did not discover "social man" and that its discovery had been researched many years before.

These concepts were not therefore alien to people who wrote at the time the studies gained fame. In addition, the argument that welfare capitalism and human relations were similar concepts is something that is objectively false (Wren and Bedeian 2018). If anything, welfare capitalism encouraged worker revolt – which human relations attempted to solve. The question should be: why did the Hawthorne studies gain prominence?

Of particular impact on the field has been the work of Charles Wrege. Wrege is the one historian that postmodernists and traditional historians can all say a good work about. There are many positive things that could be said about his work and him as an individual. He was never too busy to help younger scholars and never too satisfied to just accept established facts. As a historian, Wrege was an empiricist who would be willing to cross an ocean to verify a comma. Postmodernists respect him because he challenged norms. Wrege was, in some aspects, a model scholar. In other ways, he was not. Wrege spent too much time trying to gather truth that he saw the world in black and white and in the process produced, in my opinion, non-judicious history. Wrege was so driven to criticism that he not only lost sight of the forest, but of the trees as well, focusing on branches. I am not sure if Wrege was the one that introduced the practice of calling history myth or the ongoing hunt for originality – but he certainly contributed to these trends in the field.

Wrege's work on Taylor exhibits this sin. Whenever there is an issue with Taylor's account, Wrege automatically denounces Taylor as a scoundrel. For example, Wrege and Stoka call Taylor a plagiarist, but they overplay their hand. Morris Cooke did write some of the *Fundamentals of Scientific Management*. But it was based on a speech that Taylor gave. So it was Taylor's ideas, with Cooke as a contributor or to use a phrase, a ghost author. Taylor also published his book with Cooke's knowledge and consent, even offering to provide royalties to Cooke. Hough and White point out that it was Taylor's ideas and published under Taylor's name. Taylor was the author in the "true sense" in that he assumed responsibility and was published using his authority. Taylor was not publishing an academic paper but was relaying a story using memory devices that make a connection with previous knowledge. Martha Banta makes a note that Taylor's stories served as a way of passing the principles of scientific management through a narrative device. They were a selling point – not a scientific paper.

Often times scholars point out that there is no Kuhnian paradigm in management history, noting that scholars have had different takes on issues related to Taylor (Novicevic et al. 2015). Some view it as a myth; others view it as a good viewpoint. Of course, neither history nor science ever reaches a consensus on many issues. Despite the protective powers and validity of intelligence testing, there are still scholars that challenge the conventional viewpoint. Likewise, despite the evidence, there are still people who believe that the earth is flat. In fact, scholars often impose consensus on other scholars through control of journals and funding in the field. Yet, even if there is a consensus, there can still be divergent voices.

The question of originality has been an ongoing issue since at least the time of Hoagland (1955), whose article pointed out that Taylor's work had been preceded by Charles Babbage. We are also pointed to the fact that there were many antecedents to the work of Fayol and others over the centuries. One of the most recent tendencies has been to try to find origins of concepts – even among those long forgotten figures who were not management thinkers. While this searching for intellectual roots has long been the domain of traditional scholars, the postmodernists have taken this issue to the extreme. If we believe that history is completely fictive, then we can cut history to fit any fashion we desire. Meaning that we can select historical figures that fit what we regard as modern values, distorting the historical record. This would exactly the thing that Winston Smith did in Orwell's *1984* when he changed history by distorting the war records of Oceania and eliminating unpersons.

Conclusion

At present we are at the crossroads in management history. The dominance of the LSU-Oklahoma is ending. Both Wren and Bedeian have retired from teaching, meaning that there are no new students. The postmodernist school, with bases in Europe and Canada, seems to becoming more and more popular. What the postmodernist school is doing is ripping up many of the established nostrums, challenging many of the standards of traditional management history. In part it does this by noting that history goes beyond the great man model and by considering different voices. Of course, such postmodernist approaches have been tried in mainstream history – with disastrous consequences. As postmodernist influence has increased, so has the field of history in the United States (and elsewhere) witnessed a gradual decline of majors, interest, and relevance to modern life. Most academic history today is jargon-laden works of figures of little historical importance that has little relevance to ongoing debates in politics and the society at large. By contrast, the 1950s witnessed the likes of Arthur M. Schlesinger Jr., C. Vann Woodward, and Richard Hofstadter, each of whom provided works that informed the political culture of the 1950s. If we cannot understand the past, then why should we research it? If the figures of the past, with their brilliance and stupidity, nobility, and venality, have little to teach us, why study it? Winston Churchill, himself a great historian, always urged aspiring statesmen to study history so they could understand the present and the future. Churchill himself understood that his historical writings provided himself with a unique understanding of the present. For example, his writings on his great ancestor the Duke of Marlborough provided him with an understanding of two things. One, a person could be dead politically (as the Duke and Churchill were), and events could resurrect them. The second was that Marlborough's struggle against one would-be tyrant (Louis XIV) provided Churchill an understanding of Hitler that his contemporaries did not possess.

This is the crux of the matter – perhaps the one issue modernists and postmodernists can agree upon – that management needs to understand its past in order to improve its future. History teaches us that commonly agreed upon ideas – the best wisdom – are often wrong and that there are few Solomons out there. It also teaches us that history often repeats itself, especially in the social sciences, where common models wax and wane upon importance. If professional maturity is a gift, according to Bedeian, then it is treated like a pair of socks. We need to understand our field's past to understand its future. Yet, the inability of postmodernism to consider even basic facts damages the prospect for consideration.

At present, we are witnessing some contentious debates about management history. This is a good thing. It suggests that as a field we are growing, becoming mature, and perhaps gaining a greater degree of acceptance in the field. In many ways, management scholars do not study the past as much as they should. What they do learn is often inaccurate, simplistic, or an outright canard. Right now there is a dearth of management historical education in the United States, perhaps in other countries as well. When scholars do study, it is usually just Chap. 2 in principles of management textbook. Perhaps this is why we have so much of the "Columbus syndrome" in management in that we often rediscover what has been researched. The phrase old wine in new bottle is an apt description.

However, there are better and worse methods to research the past. Some such as postmodernism seem to offer some theoretical or reasoned approach. However, postmodernism is actually in decline in mainstream history and even literature. Would this approach gain increased respect in a field that is devoted to empiricism? I have serious doubts. In addition, this approach is dangerous in that we can play with facts to create narratives that support our own understanding of the past. In the *NHM*, we have learned that Taylorism was about conservation, a point that has been missed by a generation of historians, who have written extensively about the efficiency movement and scientific management. The *NHM* did so, because they wanted to make it seem that management has always been socially responsible. If they could make that change, what else could they do? History is not mad libs. We are constrained and bound by evidence. We cannot speculate or stretch the evidence to fit our world view. There is a reason why George Orwell made Winston Smith a historian of sorts.

Likewise, writing history without timeframes is difficult and perhaps even impossible. Timeframes do not emerge from the blue. Rather they emerge from a historians' consideration of events. Usually, these emerge with little difficulty. For example, if we were to write a world history, from 1945 until 1991, we would dub this period the Cold War, due to the confrontation between the Soviet Union and the United States. Likewise, in management history, we have clear lines, periods in which certain ideas are in fashion and others are not. That being said, one of the minor weaknesses of the Wren framework is that the current period is not as well developed. I believe examining Witzel's work would be beneficial, in that the obvious divided would be the separation between academics and practitioners.

Some scholars have urged that we adopt a Marxist perspective of management history. This type of approach would downplay biography and focus on structural and situational cues that are usually economic in nature. For example, a Marxist would analyze and argue that management is the result of various economic contingencies that have impacted society. The spread of the industrial revolution and the demand for coordination meant that managers were needed to handle the size of various corporate behemoths. While this analysis is correct, it does not explain

5 Conflicting Visions: A Recap About the Debates Within Management History

either the innovator or why nature of the discovery. For example, Taylor tended to focus on the most menial tasks with the dimmest of workers. "Schmidt," an ethnic and social stereotype created by Taylor, is not just a story device; it is also emblematic of a man with a deep bias against the lesser type. There are numerous disparaging remarks about Italians, Hungarians, and African Americans throughout his work. Taylor's heavy handiness prevented him from getting greater acceptance. Had he been more accepting and flexible person, his critics would have been lessened. Likewise, Mayo's inability to write for the academics, the lack of clarity in his thought, and his unwillingness to explain himself to his critics limited his appeal. Scholars in management history are focusing on critical biography and focusing on how factors influence scholars. A pure Marxian approach would have limited the appeal.

Cross-References

▶ Debates Within Management History
▶ What Is Management?

References

Appleby J, Hunt L, Jacob M (2004) Telling the truth about history. WW Norton & Company, New York
Bailyn B (2015) Sometimes an art: nine essays on history. Knopf, New York
Bedeian AG (2004) The gift of professional maturity. Acad Manag Learn Edu 3(1):92–98
Bogue AG (1983) Historians and radical republicans: a meaning for today. J Am Hist 70(1):7–34
Bowden B (2018) Work, wealth and postmodernism: the intellectual conflict at the heart of business Endeavour. Palgrave Macmillan, New York
Brinkley A (1995) The end of reform. Knopf, New York
Clark P, Rowlinson M (2004) The treatment of history in organisation studies: towards an 'historic turn'? Bus Hist 46(3):331–352
Coase RH (1977) The wealth of nations. Econ Inq 15(3):323–325
Cohen L (1990) Making a new deal: industrial workers in Chicago, 1919–1939. Cambridge University Press, New York
Commies RR (2001) A journey through the old left, the new left, and the leftover left. Encounter Books, San Francisco
Cooke B (2003) The denial of slavery in management studies. J Manag Stud 40(8):1895–1918
Cooper JM (1983) The warrior and the priest: Woodrow Wilson and Theodore Roosevelt. Harvard University Press, Cambridge, MA
Cummings S, Bridgman T, Hassard J, Rowlinson M (2017) A new history of management. Cambridge University Press, Cambridge
Donald D (1956) Lincoln Reconsidered. New York Knopf
Drucker PF (1979) Why management consultants? In: Zimet M, Greenwood RG (eds) The evolving science of management: the collected papers of Harold Smiddy and papers by others in his honor. American Management Associations, New York, pp 475–478
Durepos GA, Mills AJ (2012) Antihistory: theorizing the past, history, and historiography in management and organization studies. IAP, Charlotte
Evans RJ (1997) In defence of history. Granta Books, London

Filene PG (1970) An obituary for "the progressive movement". Am Q 22(1):20–34

Foner E (1970) Free soil, free labor, free men: the ideology of the republican party before the civil war. Oxford University Press, New York

Gabor A (2000) The capitalist philosophers. New York: Times Business

Genovese E (1976) Roll, Jordan, roll: the world the slaves made. Vintage Books, New York

George CS (1968) The history of management thought. Prentice Hall, Englewood Cliffs

Greenwood RG, Bolton AA, Greenwood BA (1983) Hawthorne a half century later: relay assembly participants remember. J Manag 9(2):217–231

Handlin O (1979) Truth in history. Harvard University Press, Cambridge, MA

Hanlon G (2015) The dark side of management: a secret history of management theory. Routledge, London

Hassard JS (2012) Rethinking the Hawthorne Studies: The Western Electric research in its social, political and historical context. Hum Relat 65(11):1431–1461

Hoagland JH (1955) Management before Frederick Taylor. In: Academy of management proceedings, vol 1955, no. 1. Academy of Management, Briarcliff Manor, NY, pp 15–24

Kloppenberg JT (1986) Uncertain victory: social democracy and progressivism in European and American thought, 1870–1920. Oxford University Press, New York

Kraines O (1960) Brandeis' philosophy of scientific management. West Polit Q 13(1):191–201

Lacey R (1986) Ford: The men and the machine Little, Brown, Boston

Link AS (1959) What happened to the progressive movement in the 1920's? Am Hist Rev 64(4):833–851

Lukacs J (2011) The future of history. Yale University Press, New Haven/London

McCormick RL (1981) The discovery that business corrupts politics: a reappraisal of the origins of progressivism. Am Hist Rev 86.247–274

McGerr M (2003) A fierce discontent: the rise and fall of the progressive movement in America 1870 to 1920. Oxford University Press, New York

Mills MJ (2012) The beginnings of industrial psychology: the life and work of Morris Viteles. Soc Ind Organ Psychol 49(3):39–44

Muldoon J (2012) The Hawthorne legacy: a reassessment of the impact of the Hawthorne studies on management scholarship, 1930–1958. J Manag Hist 18(1):105–119

Muldoon J (2017) The Hawthorne studies: an analysis of critical perspectives, 1936–1958. J Manag Hist 23(1):74–94

Muldoon J (2019) Stubborn things: evidence, postmodernism and the craft of history. J Manag Hist 25(1):125–136

Muldoon J, Marin DB (2012) John Florio and the introduction of management into the English vocabulary. J Manag Hist 18(2):129–136

Munslow A (2015) Managing the past. In: McLaren PG, Mills AJ, Weatherbee TG (eds) The Routledge companion to management and organizational history. Routledge, London, pp 129–142

Novicevic MM, Jones J, Carrahar S (2015) Decentering Wren's evolution of management thought. In: McLaren PG, Mills AJ, Weatherbee TG (eds) The Routledge companion to management and organizational history. Routledge, London, pp 11–30

Novicevic MM, Humphreys JH, Popoola IT, Poor S, Gigliotti R, Randolph-Seng B (2017) Collective leadership as institutional work: interpreting evidence from Mound Bayou. Leadership 13(5):590–614

Novick P (1988) That noble dream: the "objectivity question" and the American historical profession. Cambridge University Press, Cambridge, MA, pp 26–28

Organ DW (1988) Issues in organization and management series. Organizational citizenship behavior: the good soldier syndrome. Lexington Books/DC Heath and Com, Lexington

Peterson MD (1994) Lincoln in American Memory. New York Oxford

Pfeffer J (1993) Barriers to the advance of organizational science: Paradigm development as a dependent variable. Acad Manag Rev 18(4):599–620

Radosh R (2001) Commies: A Journey Through the Old Left, the New Left, and the Leftover Left. San Francisco: Encounter Books

Rosenbloom RS (1964) Men and machines: some 19th-century analyses of mechanization. Technol Cult 5(4):489–511

Rowlinson M (2015) Revisiting the historic turn: a personal reflection. Routledge, Abingdon, pp 70–80

Rowlinson M, Hassard J, Decker S (2014) Research strategies for organizational history: a dialogue between historical theory and organization theory. Acad Manag Rev 39(3):250–274

Searle GR. The quest for national efficiency: a study in british politics and political though George J. Stigler (1976) The successes and failures of Professor Smith. J Polit Econ 84(6):1199–1213

Skocpol T (1992) Protecting soldiers and mothers: the political origins of social policy in the United States. Harvard University Press, Cambridge, MA

Smith A (1965 [1776]) An inquiry into the nature and causes of the wealth of nations. Modern Library, New York

Smith JH (1998) The enduring legacy of Elton Mayo. Hum Relat 51(3):221–249

Snyder B (2017) The house of truth: a Washington political salon and the foundations of American liberalism. Oxford University Press, New York

Steinmetz G (2005) The Genealogy of a Positivist Haunting: Comparing Prewar and Postwar U.S. Sociology. Boundary 2(32):107–133

Viteles MS (1953) Motivation and morale in industry. W. W. Norton, New York

Wagner-Tsukamoto S (2007) An institutional economic reconstruction of scientific management: on the lost theoretical logic of Taylorism. Acad Manag Rev 32(1):105–117

Wagner-Tsukamoto S (2008) Scientific management revisited: did Taylorism fail because of a too positive image of human nature?. J Manag Hist 14(4):348–372

Witzel M (2016) A history of management thought. Routledge

Wood GS (2008) The purpose of the past: reflections on the uses of history. Penguin Press, New York

Wrege CD, Greenwood RG (1991) Frederick W. Taylor, the father of scientific management: myth and reality. Irwin Professional Pub, New York

Wren DA (1972) The Evolution of Management Thought. New York: The Ronald Press Company

Wren DA (1987) The white collar hobo. Iowa State University Press, Ames

Wren DA, Bedeian AG (2018) The history of management thought, 7th edn. Wiley, Hoboken

Part III

Work, Management, and Economic Organization in the Pre-modern World

The Pre-modern World and Management: An Introduction

Bradley Bowden

Contents

Introduction	114
The Poverty and Promise of the Past	118
The Structure of This Section	127
Cross-References	128
References	128

Abstract

In this introduction to our section on pre-modern management, the central question that is addressed is the following: were ancient and feudal managerial systems comparable to those found in modern, liberal-democratic societies? The answer to this question is "no." For although pre-modern forms of management were characterized by the attributes described in most textbooks (i.e., planning, organizing, leading, controlling), they lacked other characteristic features of "modern management." Pre-modern production was rarely directed toward competitive markets. Mass markets were even more uncommon. Instead, the tyranny of distance, and a reliance on either muscle power or wind in terms of transport, restricted most production to local markets. An absence of competitive markets meant that pre-modern managers were little concerned with costs. Pre-modern managers also differed from their modern counterparts in that they typically operated with few of the protections of both property and person that are the norm in today's democratic societies. In the past, unfree forms of labor were also commonplace. Due to a lack for smelted metals, pre-modern managers and producers also lacked durable capital equipment. This weakness manifested itself in both low levels of capital intensity and energy usage. Such failings, in all

B. Bowden (✉)
Griffith Business School, Griffith University, Nathan, QLD, Australia
e-mail: b.bowden@griffith.edu.au

© The Author(s), under exclusive licence to Springer Nature Switzerland AG 2020
B. Bowden et al. (eds.), *The Palgrave Handbook of Management History*,
https://doi.org/10.1007/978-3-319-62114-2_108

pre-modern societies, resulted in living standards inferior to those of our own. Nevertheless, for all its failings, "modern management" owes its success to the travails of past managers. In looking to the past, therefore, we need to both acknowledge our debt to bygone eras and recognize the advances built on past sacrifices.

Keywords

Pyramids · Management · Antiquity · Ancient technology · Medieval technology · Inequality · Climate change

---

Introduction

In addition to being the Editor of this *Palgrave Handbook of Management History,* I also have the privilege of being the Editor of the *Journal of Management History.* Recently, the journal published a thoughtful and well-written article by Chris Proctor and Mark Kozak-Holland, entitled *The Giza Pyramid: Learning from this Mega-project.* In this article, Proctor and Kozak-Holland (2019: 366) made the following point that I believe most people would share: "The construction of the Great Pyramid of Giza still stands as a testament to effective project management." Later they extend this praise of the managerial expertise of ancient Egypt to the economy more widely, noting how the Egyptians "managed projects for the diversion and construction of water, building canals and irrigation ditches, flood water basins, water supply tunnels, water purification and even sanitation systems."

Before endorsing the view that Ancient Egypt and the other societies of antiquity (Mesopotamia, Athens, Sparta, Rome, etc.) boasted managerial systems comparable to our own, however, let us first ask ourselves a number of basic questions. First, did the Ancient Egyptians produce – as modern managers do – for a competitive market economy? The answer to this question must be "no." For although the Ancient Egyptians, like peasant farmers everywhere, would have exchanged local produce at a "farmer's market," the prices charged in this market would have reflected little more than the seasonal balance between supply and demand. Food prices would have been dearest immediately before the harvest and cheapest immediately after it. Handicraft items (clothes, beer, basic tools, etc.) would have been made either at home or by a small number of "artisans," who would have charged according to custom-and-practice. Yes, there would have been some long-distance trade. However, we should not exaggerate the scale of these exchanges, given that Ancient Egypt always suffered from a chronic shortage of base metals (tin, copper, iron, etc.) that were neither available locally nor imported in significant volumes. Similarly, the famed construction projects of Ancient Egypt (the Pyramids, the great temples, etc.) reflected no market-driven need. These were, instead, state-funded (and tax-financed) endeavors. The same principle applies to the other great projects antiquity, such as the Athenian Pantheon and the Roman aqueducts.

6 The Pre-modern World and Management: An Introduction

The second question that we need to ask ourselves, which follows from the first, is: Were the Ancient Egyptians (and the other societies of antiquity) cost-efficient, marshalling resources to achieve production outcomes at the lowest possible cost? The answer to this question must also be "no." Vanity projects such as the Great Pyramids were built *regardless* of the cost. That costs *should* have factored in their thinking was evident even in antiquity, the Greek historian, Herodotus (c. 446 BC/ 1954: 179), left wondering as to:

> ... how much must have been spent ... on bread and clothing for the labourers during all those years the building was going on – not to mention the time it took ... to quarry and haul the stone, and to construct the underground chamber?

In Herodotus's opinion, the cost of the Great Pyramid must have been disproportionate to any benefit, Herodotus (c. 446 BC/1954: 178) concluding that its construction would have "brought the country into all sorts of misery." If for a rational Greek like Herodotus the construction of the Great Pyramids was an act of lunacy on a grand scale, it is nevertheless also true that the Greek and Roman understanding of costs never progressed beyond cash expenditures and measures of physical output. Perhaps the best insight into the thinking of arguably the most cost-obsessed producer of antiquity is found in Cato the Elder's *De Agricultura*, the oldest surviving text on farm management. In reflecting upon the operation of a slave-staffed *latifundia*, the basic unit of production in the western half of the Roman Empire, the most insightful observation in terms of cost-efficiency of Cato the Elder (c.160 BC/1913: 25) was found in his advice that *actual* farm output should be matched against *possible* output, given the number of days in which inclement weather restricted work. Beyond this, Cato's ideas on cost-efficiency involved curtailing cash expenditures to the bare bones, Cato (c. 160 BC/1913; 37) suggesting that slaves only be supplied with "a smock and a cloak every other year." There was little thought given to modern concepts such as capital depreciation, "good will," and the value of inventories. There were certainly none of the basic tools of modern cost management, such as double-entry bookkeeping.

A third question that demands our attention in comparing the managerial systems of Ancient Egypt, and those of antiquity more generally, with those that exist today in liberal, democratic societies is one relating to capital intensity, namely: did the societies of antiquity utilize labor-saving technologies in an economically significant way? Once more the answer must be "no." In addressing this question in relation to Ancient Egypt, I observe in the first chapter in this section, ► Chap. 7, "Management in Antiquity: Part 1 – The Binds of Geography," that "Even though Pharaonic Egypt's agricultural richness depended on its ability to channel water into irrigation ditches once the annual Nile flood had receded, there was little inventiveness shown in tackling this problem." Only under Hellenic kingdoms of the Ptolemies did the fields witness the use of high-capacity waterwheels and the "Archimedean" water screw. Prior to this Egypt relied on labor-intensive bucket and pulley systems to shift water from the Nile to the irrigation ditches (Wilson 2002). Even in the High Middle Ages (1100–1340), when the use of windmills and water mills became commonplace, we should not exaggerate the extent to which machine power replaced human and animal muscle power. To the extent that people had a choice of work in the feudal world, it typically involved, as Braudel (1986/1990: 676) noted, a choice "between equally backbreaking kinds of work." The low level of capital intensity in both antiquity and the feudal era reflects, in large part, a dearth of metals, most particularly cast iron. None of the societies of antiquity boasted a capacity to work cast iron. In medieval Europe, the great herald of economic progress – the village blacksmith – only appeared in the villages of northern France around 1200 (Cipolla 1981: 170). Consequently, a large part of the reason that the ancients showed so little interest in production costs is found in the fact that most of their tools and equipment – ships, plows, spinning wheels, weaving frames, and waterwheels – were made of wood. As a result, "capital" investments seldom lasted. Marine borers ate wooden ship's hulls. Spinning wheels and waterwheels broke, requiring constant repair and replacement. Often, business operators concluded that they were more trouble than they were worth, Cato the Elder advising his readers to avoid rural properties with many tools and much equipment. For, Cato the Elder (c. 160 BC/1913: 22) concluded, "When you find few tools, it is not an expensive farm to operate."

One of the distinctive features of modern management systems is that they deal with legally free workers, Sidney Pollard (1965: 6) observing that management's commitment to a legally free workforce during the Industrial Revolution was "one of its most seminal ideas, underlying its ultimate power to create a more civilised society." Is it also the case that in looking to the construction of the Great Pyramids, and the other economic activities of antiquity, we witness the mobilization of free labor forces? On this front, our answer must be more nuanced and equivocal than was the case with our first three questions. In antiquity, most of the population were legally free peasant farmers and self-employed artisans. Slavery was, however, commonplace in much of the Middle East. In late Republican and Imperial Rome, it became the norm, Appian (c.120/1913: 7) observing how in Italy "the race of slaves multiplied throughout the country, while the Italian people dwindled in numbers and strength, being oppressed by penury, taxes, and military service." Although we (rightly) associate Periclean Athens and classical Greece with democracy, slavery was also normalized in these societies. When, for example, the city-state of Mytilene rebelled against Athens during the Peloponnesian War, the great Athenian democracy initially voted to massacre "the entire adult male population . . . and to make slaves of the women and children." Subsequently overcome by compassion for the Mytilenians, who shared in Athens's commitment to democracy, the Athenians relented in their sentence, only massacring 1000 adult males (Thucydides, c.411 BC/1954: 212, 223). Similarly, when the city-state of Plataea – whose soldiers had fought to the death alongside the 300 Spartans at Thermopylae – sided with Athens, the Spartans killed its males and sold its women into slavery when the city fell into its hands (Thucydides, c.411 BC/1954: 235). Across the world of antiquity, as a general rule of thumb, the larger the project, the more likely it was that it would be undertaken by unfree labor of one sort or another. The Egyptian peasants who built the Great Pyramids may not have been slaves, but nor were they truly free,

6 The Pre-modern World and Management: An Introduction

gifted the ability to choose whether to work on the pyramid's construction or not. In Imperial Rome, the roads, the aqueducts, and the Colosseum were all slave-built. In marshalling this unfree workforce, no doubt, a level of ruthless "managerial efficiency" was typically displayed. Cato the Elder (c. 160 BC/1913: 25), for example, advised that a properly run farm should sell off as soon as possible "the surplus wine and corn, the old cattle, the worn out oxen ... [and] the old and sick slaves." Remunerative as such an approach may have appeared, is it one that has any resonance in modern management systems? I think not. Yes, it is true that modern businesses make staff redundant when there is no longer any economic need for their employment. However, this is very different to discarding one's slaves as if they were old wine or corn.

In looking at past management practices, there is a natural tendency to emphasize what we have in common with bygone systems of organization and work, rather than highlight the things that we possess but which they lacked. Among the things that the manager of early nineteenth-century Britain, Belgium, or the United States possessed, but which were totally absent in antiquity, we can include the following: cast iron, mechanical clocks, compasses, printed books and manuals, a largely literate workforce, steam power, and a host of mechanically powered machines. Also present in the Industrial Revolution (i.e., 1750–1830) were a range of legal protections and rights that either fully or partially absent in antiquity: protection of property from the arbitrary exertions of princely authority, freedom of expression, liberty of conscience, personal freedom to choose one's occupation, and employer. This is not to say that these technological, sociological, and legal attributes suddenly sprang, unannounced, from the soil in 1750. Rather, they represented the accretions of the centuries, a process of accumulation in which gains were sometimes sudden (i.e., the Gutenberg printing press of the 1450s, the first Newcomen steam engine in 1712), but more often the result of the reflection and/or tinkering by unknown artisans, peasants, and scholars. To the Mesopotamians of antiquity, we owe the foundations of Western principles of mathematics. To the people of the Middle East, we also owe the potter's wheel and wheeled transport. We are in debt to the Phoenicians when it comes to our traditions of phonetic writing. To classical Greece, and the Hellenistic kingdoms that emerged from Alexander's conquests, we derive geometry, philosophy, principles for logical deduction, medicine, and our understandings of democracy. To the Romans, we owe the understanding that economic and social relationships should be bound by legal principles that favor all citizens equally.

If we owe a debt to the past, it is nevertheless the case that we are not of the past. We are, instead, the people of a new modern and industrialized world that emerged from the pre-modern experience around 1750. Where the pre-modern world of management largely served local markets, the modern world of management tends the wants of national and global markets. Where the pre-modern manager had little need to worry about costs, the modern manager has every reason to concern themselves with expenses. Where the producer of antiquity and of the medieval era could typically marshal the resources of unfree and semi-free workforces, the modern manager can rarely avail themselves of such forms of labor.

The purpose of this section of this *Palgrave Handbook of Management History* is thus twofold. It cannot be content with merely acknowledging where we owe a debt to the past. It must also highlight where modern management differs from earlier systems of managerial endeavor and the reasons for this difference.

The Poverty and Promise of the Past

Writing of the working people of thirteenth- and fourteenth-century Europe, the economic historian, Carlo Cipolla (1981: 182), observed that they had "a mechanical outlook ... an irresistible taste for mechanical achievements." Until 25–30 years ago, this was still arguably the case in most Western societies. Most people worked on a farm, in a factory or a mine, or in warehousing and transport. People did things with their hands. Successful managers and entrepreneurs were admired in part because they were inventive, coming up with either a new technology or a way of using an old technology more efficiently. For most working-class being people, life was hard. Mass unemployment, deprivation, and even famine were the remembered experience of most families. Accordingly, what people primarily wanted from work was a system of management that promised both job security and increased material wealth. Farmers could understand that productivity and managerial efficiency were a good thing if it gave them more potatoes to sell at less cost. In a factory, most could also understand that increased productivity was a good thing in that it made an increase in pay more rather than less likely. Given that most people worked in private sector employment – where their jobs were exposed to market competition – few could afford to be blissfully ignorant as to the mechanics of management, production, and work.

A direct relationship not only to the world of production but also to what Adam Smith (1776/1999); Book III, Chap. III, para. I) called the "higgling of the market" is something that increasingly few possess. In the United States, where manufacturing reached its absolute peak in 1953 (17.2 million employees), an estimated 50.2% of the nonagricultural workforce being was engaged in industrial, mining, or transport occupations at this date. By late 2017, only 17.5% of the American workforce worked in such jobs (Bowden 2018: 281). Similar trends can be ascertained in most other Western societies. This is not to say, of course, that Western societies have abandoned the accoutrements of an industrial society: steel, aluminum, plastics, automobiles, computers, etc. Rather, they have largely outsourced the production of such needs to less prosperous societies. In terms of primary steel production, for example, the Chinese share of global production has hovered around the 90% mark over the last decade (Cunningham et al. 2019: 31). Understandably, such outcomes lead to the common delusion that – because the West no longer produces the steel it uses – we now live in a "postindustrial" or "postmodern" society, a world where the manufactured and energy-intensive underpinnings of an industrial society are important only to the extent that they add to climate change and environmental degradation.

6 The Pre-modern World and Management: An Introduction

A lack of understanding as to the hard-fought existence of past generations finds expression, I believe, in two things, both of which impair an understanding of management history. First, there is a tendency to romanticize the rural, pre-industrial past. This is a problem that I address at length in ▶ Chap. 17, "Foundations: The Roots of Idealist and Romantic Opposition to Capitalism and Management," where I observe that many now share the view of the English poet, William Wordsworth (1800/2009: 142, 144), that human existence finds "a better soil" in a "rustic life." To hold such ideas leads to the inevitable conclusion that the primary managerial concerns of past generations – in clearing the forests, in taming the rivers, and in furthering new industrial techniques – were historically retrograde activities. In truth, as Thomas Hobbes (1651/2002: 62) famously observed, a pre-industrial existence was "solitary, poor, nasty, brutish, and short." In a pre-industrial world, most people lived and died in filth. Indeed, such were the circumstances in which most people once lived that they are almost beyond imagining. A picture of what life was like for most is well-captured in Richard Hellie's (2006: 289–290) description of the typical peasant home in nineteenth-century Russia, in which he records how "The smoke was so dense that it left a line around the wall about shoulder height, where the bottom of the smoke cloud hung. The air was so toxic that it disinfected the hut to the extent that not even cockroaches could survive." In addition to the romanticization of the pre-industrial past, the popular understanding of antiquity suffers from what I think of as the "Hollywoodization" of the past and the tendency to extrapolate from the preserved ruins of places like Pompey. What most seem to overlook was that places like Pompey were holiday resorts for the rich and famous, a tiny prosperous elite within Roman society being. Their experience in no way resembled that of the ordinary person. The gulf in living standards that separates our modern industrial world from that of antiquity, or even seventeenth century Europe, is indicated in Fig. 1. This compares the annual "grain" or "wheat" wage of lower-class Romans (i.e., the bottom 22%), middle-class Romans (i.e., the middle 60%), and the typical English artisan from c.1688, with the circumstances of someone working on the US basic wage in 2019 ($10.35 per hour) for a standard 40-hour week. Although we return to this comparison in ▶ Chap. 7, "Management in Antiquity: Part 1 – The Binds of Geography," a brief word of explanation is nevertheless required here. In essence, a "grain wage" is calculated on what a certain historical income would buy if every cent obtained were spent on nothing other than wheat. Schiedel and Freisen (2009) calculated the figures for ancient Rome and seventeenth-century Europe. The US figures are calculated by the author and are based on current US wholesale wheat prices. As can be ascertained, a US citizen on the basic wage – a person most would regard as someone in dire circumstances – enjoys a level of material wealth infinitely superior to that of previous generations.

The gulf between modern managerial systems and those of the pre-modern era is also indicated in Fig. 1, which traces estimates of European population from Roman times to the mid-nineteenth century. As is self-evident, the pre-modern world boasted few people. Towns and cities were rare. Those that did exist were typically small affairs. Prior to the seventeenth century, even the countryside was home to

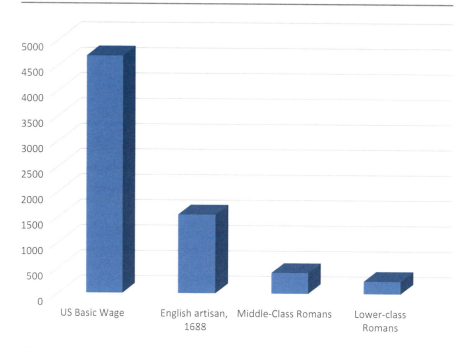

Fig. 1 Annual grain wage in kilograms. (Sources: Schiedel and Freisen, "The size of the economy and the distribution of income in the Roman Empire, p. 84; Bowden, Management in Antiquity, Part 1)

comparatively few people. As the French historian, Marc Bloch (1940/1962: 72), observed of medieval Europe, "The rural landscape ... bore few traces of human influence ... behind all social life there was a background of the primitive, of submission to uncontrollable forces, of unrelieved physical constraints." The less industrially developed the society, the more backward was the agricultural sector due to a shortage of metal tools and mechanical contrivances. A technologically undeveloped rural sector, in turn, required the work of a large number of farmers to support a comparatively small urban population. This tendency was evident not only in Europe but in other pre-modern societies as well. In nineteenth-century China, for example, it took the labor of 400 million peasants and small artisans to support a population of 7.5 million urban non-producers, i.e., scholars, bureaucrats, soldiers, etc. (Jones 1987: 4; Fig. 2).

If a lack of appreciation as to the economic gulf that separates our world from past societies can cause an underestimation of the difficulties confronted by earlier generations of administrators, overseers, and entrepreneurs, it is also the case that those largely devoid of the once-common "mechanical outlook" can easily overlook the managerial aspirations of bygone times. Among modern concerns about "carbon footprints" and global warming, I suspect that comparatively few readers would appreciate that coal is typically an essential ingredient in iron and steel production and that without steel there can be no bridges, hospitals, high-rise buildings, and

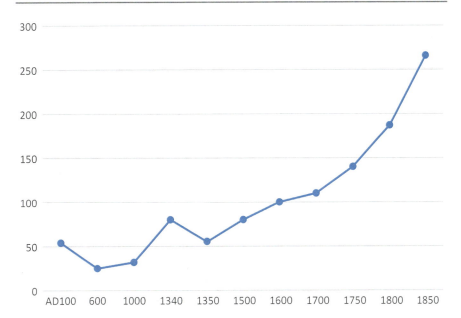

Fig. 2 Approximate Europe population, AD 100–1850∗. (Sources: de Ligt, Peasants, Citizens and Soldiers, pp. 6–8; Cipolla, Before the Industrial Revolution, p. 150; Braudel, Capitalism and Material Life, p.11) [∗Note: includes Russia]

factories. Yes, it is true that steel can be smelted by using large quantities of scrap-iron in lieu of coal. However, in developing societies such as China and India – as in pre-modern societies – this is rarely an option. It is this fact that does much to explain the enormous increase in world coal production and consumption during the last 30 years, even as many in the West decry problems of global warming, with global production rising from approximately 4,500 million tons in 1990 to over 7,500 million tons in 2018 (Cunningham et al. 2019: 31). It also does much to explain the obsession of past societies with base metals and mining, to the extent that we still describe civilizations and historical epochs in terms of their command of metals, i.e., Copper Age, Bronze Age, and Iron Age. For without an abundant supply of forged or smelted metal, it is impossible for a society to economically progress, given an absence or shortage of metal plows, axes, hoes, and the like. On this front, iron has a number of advantages over other alternatives. Although typically not as hard as bronze, it is easier and cheaper to produce. Iron ore is also more plentiful than copper and tin, the key ingredients in bronze. The problem with iron production stems from the fact that the smelting process requires the use of carbon-based material. Historically, pre-modern societies obtained this component from charcoal, i.e., burnt wood. As iron production increased, however, there can an inevitable point where the supply of wood wilted in the face of demand. In AD 1100, for example, it is estimated that China's per capita iron output exceeded the level that Europe obtained in 1700. By this stage, however, China's central rice region – the epicenter of iron production – had become "a great clear-felled zone" (Jones 1987: 4), an outcome that led to a collapse in Chinese iron production. Similarly, in England, where iron cannon and other iron goods dominated exports in the sixteenth century, the price of timber rose fivefold between 1570–1589 and 1630–1649 (Cipolla 1981: 2467). In short, difficulties in acquiring sufficient carbon-based material for smelting acted as an almost universal cap on iron production, a limitation that restrained the development and use of durable, metal-based capital goods and hence the possibility of economic and managerial progress.

Often in discussions of economics, culture, and management, there is a tendency to discuss the performance of Western Europe, and the so-called West, as a unitary bloc that – due to some supposed innate characteristic – came to dominate the world (see, e.g., Jones 1987; Huntington Huntington 1996/2003; North and Thomas 1973). As Niall Ferguson (2011: 4–5) expressed it in his book, *Civilization: The West and the Rest*:

> ... beginning in the late fifteenth century, the little states of Western Europe ... produced a civilization capable of not only conquering the great Oriental empires and subjugating Africa, the Americas and Australasia, but also of converting peoples all over the world to the Western way of life.

When we study the success and failure of ancient and medieval Europe being in terms of managerial success (i.e., a capacity to generate gains in productivity, per capita output, per capita income), however, the idea that there was a single "West," advancing in more or less unison, quickly becomes unsustainable. As Fig. 3

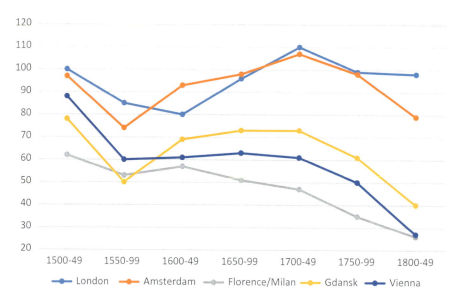

Fig. 3 Real consumption wage of unskilled European building workers, 1500–1549 to 1800–1849 (100 = London in 1500–1549). (Source: Palma and Reis, "From Convergence to Divergence," p. 500)

indicates, which traces the "real consumption wage" (i.e., the basket of goods and services a nominal wage will buy) of unskilled building workers in a number of Western and Central European cities – London, Amsterdam, Gdansk, Vienna, Florence, and Milan – two things are immediately apparent. The first is that during the seventeenth and eighteenth centuries, a marked divergence occurred between the circumstances that prevailed in England and the Netherlands, where comparative prosperity existed, and the situation in the other cities, where living standards steadily deteriorated. Significantly, the worst performers were Milan and Florence, cities associated with the glories of the Renaissance and a flourishing of cultural values that emphasized individualism and creativity. The second evident trend is that among the successful cities, even Amsterdam suffered a marked decline in living standards during the eighteenth century (Broadberry and Gupta 2006: 6). Evidence as to the declining circumstances of the Netherlands – a highly commercialized society that boasted the world's first stock market and Europe's most productive agricultural sector – is also indicated in Palma and Reis's (2019: 500) recent study, "From Convergence to Divergence," which points to a slow decline in the Netherlands's per capita output after 1650. The idea that by the eighteenth century, Europe – and most particularly Western Europe – had opened up a substantial gap in terms of living standards vis-à-vis the more prosperous regions of India, China, and Japan has also been shown to be a misnomer by recent research. As Allen et al. (2011: 30–31) note, "unskilled laborers in the major cities of China and Japan – poor as they were - had roughly the same standard of living as their counterparts in central and southern Europe for the greater part of the eighteenth century."

As management historians, we inevitably come to the key question in this section, if not the entire *Palgrave Handbook on Management History*, namely: what was it about England that caused it alone to break the technological and managerial bonds of the pre-modern world?

In search for an answer to this central question, it quickly becomes apparent that a society could excel in a number of managerial endeavors without a general transformation in managerial practices occurring across the whole economy. Indeed, the reverse is possible, i.e., progress in one area leading to developments that had an overall negative effect. The classical example of this is found in the experiences of Habsburg Spain during the sixteenth and seventeenth centuries. As Oliver Aho and Robert Lloyd note in ► Chap. 11, "The Origins of Robust Supply Chain Management and Logistics in the Caribbean: Spanish Silver and Gold in the New World (1492–1700)" of this section, *The Origins of Robust Supply Chain Management and Logistics in the Caribbean: Spanish Silver and Gold in the New World*, the exploration of the America's was primarily driven by "the search for metallic riches." The culmination of this search was found in the development and operation of the fabulously wealthy Potosi mine in Peru, a mine whose riches transformed monetary conditions in Europe under a cascade of silver. Of the "supply route the Spanish empire established during this time," Aho and Lloyd (► Chap. 11, "The Origins of Robust Supply Chain Management and Logistics in the Caribbean: Spanish Silver and Gold in the New World (1492–1700)") observe that it was "unlike any other seen in history," amounting to "the world's first supply chain that was maintained in consistent quantities over a substantial period of time (centuries) in an environment where the risks were unknown and extreme." Spanish expertise in the mining and transport of silver – a commodity of much value but of little use in the manufacture of capital goods – had two profoundly negative consequences. First, the flood of American silver led to the so-called Great Inflation as goods became more expensive expressed in terms of (now common) silver. Nowhere was this inflationary effect felt more severely than in Spain itself. Over the course of the sixteenth century, hitherto stable Spanish prices rose by 340%, an outcome that made Spanish-made goods prohibitively expensive vis-à-vis imports (North and Thomas 1973: 106). Despite the imposition of protective tariffs, the nascent Spanish manufacturing sector collapsed in the face of massive smuggling operations, an outcome that saw Spanish silver covertly traded for largely Dutch-made imports. Rather than growing richer from Potosi's wealth, the average Spaniard was reduced to penury, Spain's population falling by 25% across the course of the seventeenth century. Real wages collapsed (North and Thomas 1973: 104). The second problem that Spanish silver acerbated rather than mitigated was the indebtedness of the Spanish dynastic state. Every year, the bounty of the Spanish silver fleet was spent before it arrived, pledged as security against new loans. The Genoese, in particular, enriched themselves by acting as bankers to the Spanish crown. The scale of this business can be ascertained by the fact that in 1562, the Spanish crown – supported by the revenues of Castile, Aragon, Catalonia, Southern Italy, Milan, the Low Countries, and a vast influx of American silver – was spending over 25% of its annual budget on interest (North and Thomas 1973: 129).

Why was it that, as Fig. 3 indicates, the Netherlands and more particularly England followed a different managerial and economic trajectory to other European societies, avoiding the problems that beset Spain amid a bounty of unexpected wealth? Part of the explanation is found in what North and Thomas (1973: 1) referred to as "the establishment of institutional arrangements and property rights that create an incentive to channel individual economic efforts" into productive endeavors. Both England and the Netherlands were highly commercialized societies by the seventeenth century. Each boasted a stock market, well-established systems of merchant banking and marine insurance, and a capacity to draw on the accumulated savings of a large number of small-scale investors who had made their money in commerce, agriculture, or manufacturing. The Netherlands also pioneered large-scale deposit banking and the sale of perpetual annuities, whereby the lender received payment of interest in perpetuity rather than obtaining the return of their initial investment. As a result of such mechanisms, the interest rate charged in the Netherlands fell from 20% in 1500 to 3% in the seventeenth century (North and Thomas: 142). The Netherlands also benefited from the availability of peat, which could be used for both domestic cooking and heating and industrial purposes. By 1650, the Netherlands was burning prodigious quantities of peat, equivalent to 6,000 million kilocalories per year (Cipolla 1981: 273). This equated to the energy expended in 2 million human workdays. Among the industrial uses to which this energy was utilized were glassmaking, beer-making, and, above all, brickmaking. Although, as we noted in Fig. 2, English and Dutch real wages moved more or less in

6 The Pre-modern World and Management: An Introduction

125

tandem between 1500 and 1750, it is nevertheless the case that "the Netherlands was the more developed economy" during this period, boasting a per capita output some 10–20% higher than England's (van Zanden 2002: 631–632). By 1850, however, the value of per capita output in Holland – the most prosperous Dutch province – was 13.5% lower than it had been 200 years before (Palma and Reis 2019: 500).

What was it that caused the economy of the Netherlands to falter after 1750 while England continued to prosper? We can only conclude that the "institutional arrangements and property rights" that North and Thomas (1973) identified were *necessary* but not *sufficient* conditions for success. We can also conclude that an emphasis on individual initiative and entrepreneurship – both of which Dutch society possessed in spades – were also necessary rather than sufficient conditions. To this list, we can also add a highly productive agricultural sector and legal protections that restrained arbitrary behavior by the state, both of which were present in the Netherlands to a marked degree.

If we are to think of the key attributes of managerial success in addition to those commonly provided by textbooks (planning, organizing, leading, controlling) – namely, the direction of production toward competitive markets, an awareness of costs and a desire to reduce them, legal protections of person and property, and a legally free workforce – what was missing in the Netherlands? Two attributes, we suggest, were absent in the Netherlands, neither of which appear in the previous sentence but which we have nevertheless discussed previously: capital intensity based on durable metal machinery and tools and the direction of production toward not only a competitive market but one based on mass consumption. In terms of the former, the Dutch suffered almost insurmountable problems due to an absence of both iron and, more particularly, coal deposits. For although an exploitation of its peat deposits allowed the Dutch a capacity to transition to an energy-intensive economy, peat was more or less useless when it came to iron smelting. As other Western European societies stripped their forests bare in order to obtain the charcoal necessary for smelting, England alone came up with a cheaper and easily obtained alternative that spared further forest denudation, namely, coke, i.e., the high-carbon residue left when coal is slowly burnt. When English metallurgists worked out how to use coal-derived coke in iron smelting, the demand for coal soared to new heights. As Fig. 4 indicates, British coal production rose inexorably from 1750, underpinning what we think of as the Industrial Revolution. By 1790, almost 10 million tons was being mined annually. Over the next 30 years, this doubled to slightly more than 20 million tons. In the next 20 years, it doubled again (Pollard 1980). Increased coal production did more than underpin an expansion in iron and steel production. Whereas the growth of other European cities was constrained by a shortage of wood for cooking and heating, English cities grew exponentially. Providing a home to 70,000 people in 1500, by 1700 London was "the largest, busiest, and wealthiest metropolis in the world" (Cipolla 1981; 293). As England's mines became progressively deeper, eventually operating beneath the water table, ever more radical innovations were demanded. Accordingly, in 1712 the world's first steam engine – the so-called Newcomen engine – began pumping water from a pit in the English Midlands. As coal production soared so too did the production of iron and hence a

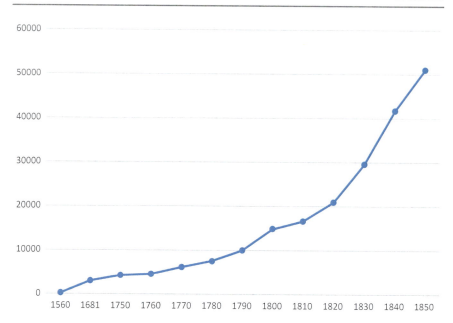

Fig. 4 British coal output, 1560–1850 (in thousands of tons). (Source: Pollard, "A New Estimate of British Coal Production," pp. 216, 229)

whole range of iron-based products: machinery, railroad locomotives, and iron-bottomed and steam-powered ships. By the mid-1860s, even though the tonnage of Britain's sailing ships still outnumbered that of the nation's iron-bottomed ships by more than five to one, it was the latter that carried most cargo (Clapham 1932/1967: 71). The surging demand for coal also indirectly contributed to the creation within England of the world's first mass market. In 1761, Britain's first canal (the Bridgewater Canal) was completed, linking Manchester to Lancashire's coalfields. By century's end a complex system of canals crisscrossed England's interior, allowing for the cheap importation of raw materials as well as ready access to urban consumer markets.

In returning to our original question as to whether or not ancient and feudal managerial systems were comparable to ours, the answer is "no." While both ancient and modern managerial systems were characterized by the classical textbook attributes (planning, organizing, leading, controlling), this section of this *Palgrave Handbook on Management History* nevertheless argues that "modern management" – as manifest in free-market, democratic societies – differs from pre-modern systems with regard to the following characteristics:

1. Production and services are directed toward competitive markets.
2. Production and services are directed toward mass markets.
3. Management is attentive to costs.
4. Management operates within a legal system that provides protection for both person and property.

6 The Pre-modern World and Management: An Introduction

5. Management operates within a system of institutional and economic arrangements that incentivize individual initiative and entrepreneurship.
6. Management works alongside a legally free workforce that must be motivated by management in order to achieve the most efficient outcomes.
7. Management utilizes high levels of capital intensity, associated with the use of durable metallic tools, implements, and machines.
8. Management exploits an energy-intensive production system, in which artificial forms of energy (coal, gas, wind, water, nuclear) are exploited to the full.

The Structure of This Section

This section is directed toward an understanding of the systems of management – and the ideas associated with those systems – that emerged in the Middle East, North Africa, and Western Europe from the time of the ancient Mesopotamians and Egyptians to the First World War (i.e., 1914). The circumstances that prevailed in the Balkans and Europe's Orthodox East, most particularly Russia, are dealt with separately in our section on European management.

In this section, four chapters deal with actual production and logistical management systems in the pre-modern era, namely:

- ► Chapter 7, "Management in Antiquity: Part 1 – The Binds of Geography"
- ► Chapter 8, "Management in Antiquity: Part 2 – Success and Failure in the Hellenic and Roman Worlds"
- ► Chapter 9, "From Feudalism to Modernity, Part I: Management, Technology, and Work, AD 450–1750"
- ► Chapter 11, "The Origins of Robust Supply Chain Management and Logistics in the Caribbean: Spanish Silver and Gold in the New World (1492–1700)"

A separate ► Chap. 10, "From Feudalism to Modernity, Part 2: The Revolution in Ideas, AD 450–1750" deals with the key intellectual underpinnings of managerial advance and regression between the fifth and seventeenth century, many of which were associated – both positively and negatively – with the Catholic Church and its Protestant rivals.

The final chapter in this section, *Transformation: The First Global Economy, 1750–1914*, looks at both the Industrial Revolution in Britain and the economic and managerial relationships that were established within the wider global economy. This final chapter, it should be noted, should be read and understood in conjunction with the chapters found in our sections on *Foundations of Modern Management* and *The Classical Age of Management Thought*, both of which deal with the key theoretical ideas associated with managerial and economic progress from the seventeenth century onward.

As readers will be aware, in this section all but one of the chapters is attributable to me. Where possible, most particular in the chapters dealing with antiquity and feudalism, I have attempted to use primary sources wherever possible (i.e.,

Thucydides, Livy, Polybius, Saint Augustine, Saint Thomas Aquinas, etc.). My ideas on management are *not* those found in the typical textbook as I draw a clear and definite distinction between both pre-modern and totalitarian forms of management and "modern management" as it is manifested in liberal, democratic societies. Atypical as my ideas of management are – which differ not only from that found in textbooks but also from the hostility expressed toward Western management by both Marxist and postmodernists of various ilk – they have no great claim to originality. My views on management are essentially those expressed by the great Austro-English historian, Sidney Pollard, as outlined in the opening pages of his classic study, *The Genesis of Modern Management*. My ideas differ from Pollard in only two regards, neither of them significant in greater scheme of things. First, I pay a greater heed to management's long historical heritage, a heritage that I am sure Pollard would also have willingly recognized. Second, I place a greater emphasis on the importance of capital intensity in the ascendancy of modern management, an emphasis that causes me to place a greater weight on metal production and energy usage. For whereas pre-modern societies were almost always economies of wood – with devastating effects for natural woodlands – modern economies are built around the harnessing of artificial forms of energy. Of these artificial forms of energy, carbon-based resources (coal, oil, gas) have always been – and remain – the most significant. For those concerned with climate change, this essential fact will no doubt be galling and unpleasant. However, essential fact it remains.

Cross-References

▶ Foundations: The Roots of Idealist and Romantic Opposition to Capitalism and Management
▶ From Feudalism to Modernity, Part I: Management, Technology, and Work, AD 450–1750
▶ Management in Antiquity: Part 1 – The Binds of Geography
▶ Management in Antiquity: Part 2 – Success and Failure in the Hellenic and Roman Worlds
▶ What Is Management?

References

Allen RC, Bassino J-P, Ma D, Moll-Murata C, van Zanden JL (2011) Wages, prices, and living standards in China, 1738–1925: in comparison with Europe, Japan, and India. Econ Hist Rev 64(1):8–38
Appian (c.AD120/1913) The civil wars: book 1, Loeb classical library. http://penelope.uchicago.edu/Thayer/E/Roman/Texts/Appian/Civil_Wars/1*.html. Accessed 7 Feb 2019
Bloch M (1940/1962) Feudal society, 2nd edn. Routledge & Kegan Paul, London
Bowden B (2018) Work, wealth and postmodernism: the intellectual conflict at the heart of business Endeavour. Palgrave Macmillan, Cham

6 The Pre-modern World and Management: An Introduction

Braudel F (1986/1990) The identity of France: people and production, vol 2, 2nd edn. Harper Torchbooks, New York

Broadberry S, Gupta B (2006) The early modern great divergence: wages, prices and economic development in Europe and Asia, 1500–1800. Econ Hist Rev 49(1):2–31

Cato the Elder (c. 160 BC/1913) De Agricultura. In: A Virginian Farmer (ed) Roman farm management: the treatises of Cato and Varro. Macmillan, New York, pp 19–50

Cipolla CM (1981) Before the industrial revolution: European society and economy, 1000–1700, 2nd edn. Cambridge University Press, Cambridge, UK

Clapham JH (1932/1967) Economic history of modern Britain: free trade and steel 1850–1886. Cambridge University Press, Cambridge, UK

Cunningham M, Van Uffelen L, Chambers M (2019) The changing global market for Australian coal. Reserve Bank of Australia Bulletin, Sept., 28–38

de Ligt L (2012) Peasants, citizens and soldiers: studies in the demographic history of Roman Italy, 225 BC and AD 100. Cambridge University Press, Cambridge, UK

Ferguson N (2011) Civilization: The West and the rest. Penguin, London

Hellie R (2006) The peasantry. In: Pirenne M (ed) The Cambridge history of Russia, vol 1. Cambridge University Press, Cambridge, UK, pp 286–297

Herodotus (c. 446 BC/1954) The histories. Penguin Classics, Harmondsworth

Hobbes T (1651/2002) Leviathan. Broadway Press, Peterborough

Huntington SP (1996/2003) The clash of civilizations and the remaking of world order. Simon & Schuster, New York

Jones EL (1987) The European miracle: environments, economies and geopolitics in the history of Europe and Asia, 2nd edn. Cambridge University Press, Cambridge, UK

North DC, Thomas RP (1973) The rise of the Western world: a new economic history. Cambridge University Press, London

Palma N, Reis J (2019) From convergence to divergence: Portuguese economic growth 1527–1850. J Econ Hist 79(2):477–506

Pollard S (1965) The genesis of modern management: a study of the industrial revolution in Great Britain. Edward Arnold, London

Pollard S (1980) A new estimate of British coal production, 1750–1850. Econ Hist Rev 33(2):212–235

Proctor C, Kozak-Holland M (2019) The Giza pyramid: learning from this megaproject. J Manag Hist 25(3):364–383

Schiedel W, Freisen SJ (2009) The size of the economy and the distribution of income in the Roman empire. J Roman Stud 99:61–91

Smith A (1776/1999) The wealth of nations. Penguin Classics, London

Thucydides (c.411 BC/1954) The history of the Peloponnesian war. Penguin Classics, Harmondsworth

van Zanden JL (2002) The 'revolt of the early modernists' and the 'first modern economy': an assessment. Econ Hist Rev 55(4):619–641

Wilson A (2002) Machines, power and the ancient economy. J Roman Stud 92:1–32

Wordsworth W (1800/2009) Preface of 1800. In: Owen WJB, Smyser JW (eds) Prose works of William Wordsworth, vol 1. Humanities e-Book http://ebookcentral.proquest.com/lib/griffith/detail.action?docID=3306065. Accessed 13 Nov 2018

Management in Antiquity: Part 1 – The Binds of Geography

7

Bradley Bowden

Contents

Introduction 132
Managerial and Economic Performance in Antiquity: Methods, Sources, and Difficulties ... 137
The Binds of Geography: Life Within the Civilized Frontier 140
The Binds of Geography: Life Beyond the Civilized Frontier 145
Conclusion 149
Cross-References 150
References 151

Abstract

In this first chapter on management in antiquity, we provide an overview of the different types of economic and managerial systems that existed in Europe and the Mediterranean Basin between 4000 BC and AD450. Within what we call the "civilized frontier" (Egypt, North Africa, the Middle East, the Mediterranean littoral, and Europe west of the Rhine), we can detect three types of economies: those based on irrigated agriculture (Mesopotamia and Egypt), dry-land wheat farming (southern Europe and the Middle Eastern hill-country) and maritime commerce (Greece, Phoenicia, Carthage). Beyond the "frontier" were societies constructed around either pastoral activity or subsistence agriculture. Despite their achievement, none of these societies proved capable of breaking the shackles imposed by geography and a preindustrial technological base. In all societies, the bulk of the population lived from the land. Even in Rome, the most sophisticated society of antiquity, living standards for all but a tiny elite were barely above subsistence. In no society can we see effective systems of management directed towards a competitive market economy. In the final analysis, the managerial record of antiquity is one of failure rather than enduring achievement.

B. Bowden (✉)
Griffith Business School, Griffith University, Nathan, QLD, Australia
e-mail: b.bowden@griffith.edu.au

© The Author(s), under exclusive licence to Springer Nature Switzerland AG 2020
B. Bowden et al. (eds.), *The Palgrave Handbook of Management History*,
https://doi.org/10.1007/978-3-319-62114-2_99

Keywords

Civilization · Rome · Greece · Technology · Germanic · Celtic · Arab · Medieval · Religion · Islam · Christianity · Transport · Technology · Slavery

Introduction

Intellectually and linguistically, the modern world owes an immeasurable debt to the societies that flourished in the Middle East, and across the Mediterranean basin, from around 4000 BC. To the Sumerians – who built an enduring civilization between 4000 and 2000 BC by draining the swamps and irrigating the deserts of lower Mesopotamia – we owe the foundations of Western principles of mathematics, as well as both the potter's wheel and wheeled transport. To the Phoenicians – a Canaanite-speaking people whose maritime culture, advancing from its original base in Lebanon and Palestine, bestrode the entire Mediterranean basin between 1500 BC and 300 BC – we owe our traditions of phonetic writing. From the Greek and Hellenistic societies that came to dominate the eastern Mediterranean, and the Latin culture which rose to dominate the entire Mediterranean world, we derive principles for geometry, architecture, philosophy, logical inquiry and deduction, medicine, and politics. Our modern political systems are also framed within the language of ancient Greece and Rome. From *demos*, the Greek term for people, and the political practices of Periclean Athens during the fifth century BC, we derive our original concepts of democracy. From *civis*, the Latin word for citizen, we derive not only our understandings of citizenship, premised on a legal system of rights and responsibilities, but also the very concept of civilization. For the ancient Greeks and Romans, as with us, the term "civilization" implied more than a people joined by a common system of culture, language, history, and belief. It implied a world built around city life, with all the shared benefits of literature, politics, education, and social interaction which were its inevitable handmaidens. As Richard Koerner (1941/1966: 8) remarked, "Urbanization was a fundamental principle of Roman policy." Behind the Roman armies that advanced into North Africa, Spain, the Balkans, Dacia (Romania), Gaul (France) and Britain came the accoutrements of urban life: permanent buildings, aqueducts, amphitheatres, administrators, crafts-people, merchants, money-lenders, and, perhaps most importantly, urban consumers. Although, as Braudel (1986/1990: 98) noted, the towns of the western half of the Empire "suffered enormously" from the Germanic invasions of the third century AD – and even worse depredations following the Germanic *Volkerwanderung* that began with a massed crossing of the frozen Rhine on the last day of 406 – the urbanized culture that Rome created survived even after the western Empire was militarily and politically destroyed. Significantly, this urbanized remnant – initially far stronger in the Greek-speaking Byzantine Empire that survived the fifth century invasions – provided a refuge for new patterns of religious belief as well as for traditions of literacy and learning. Although most towns of any size provided homes for a bevy of Jewish traders, craft workers, and Rabbinical scholars, it was proponents of the new

Christian faith that predominated. Mediated by Greek-speaking patriarchs in the eastern Mediterranean who laid the foundations for Greek and Russian Orthodoxy, and Latin-speaking theologians such as St Augustine and St Benedict in what came to be regarded as Western Christendom, the abbots and bishops of this new faith created powerful supranational institutions that permanently restricted the political and moral authority of dynastic rulers.

Given the intellectual, linguistic, and cultural debt that we owe to antiquity, it is hardly surprising that many trace the institutions and practices of modern business and managerial endeavor to antiquity. At first glance, the case for so doing appears overwhelming. As noted above, many of the intellectual and cultural underpinnings of our world are the legacy of antiquity. The Egyptian pyramids, and the architectural marvels of Periclean Athens and imperial Rome, remain a perpetual source of wonderment. Most first year management textbooks portray the tasks entailed in building antiquity's architectural marvels – tasks that entailed planning, organizing, leading and controlling – as evidence of management's ancient origins (see, for example, Bartol et al. 2005: 5). Similarly, in Morgan Witzel's (2012: 7) *A History of Management*, we are told that although management emerged as a "discipline" in the nineteenth century, most preindustrial societies boasted successful examples of "management." Even among the scholars of antiquity, there are more than a few who make the case that the Hellenistic and Roman world boasted most of the entrepreneurial and managerial attributes of modern industrial capitalism. Writing in the 1920s, Rostovtzeff argued that the Hellenistic states that emerged in the wake of Alexander the Great's conquests (336–323 BC) produced a flourishing "city-capitalism" associated with an "unprecedented" growth in "commerce, industry, and agriculture." Under the auspices of imperial Rome, Rostovtzeff continued, "a strong and numerous city-bourgeoisie" became "the leading force in the Empire" (Rostovtzeff and Fraser 1926/1957: xiv, 103). More recently, in a study entitled *The Roman Market Economy*, Peter Temin (2012: 2) has suggested that "markets knit the Roman economy together . . . ordinary Romans lived well . . . They lived well as a result of extensive markets, competitive advantage, and technological change." In the face of established opinion that water-mills only became common-place in the medieval era, both Lewis (1997) and Wilson (2002) contend that this Roman invention was widely adopted during antiquity, the latter claiming that its utilization represented a technological "break-through" (Wilson 2002: 11).

The claims as to the commercial, managerial, and technological achievement of antiquity falter when exposed to even cursory scrutiny. Although the smelting of metals – first of copper, then of bronze and iron – was a characteristic feature of Middle Eastern and European cultures from 3500 BC onwards, analysis of Greenland's ice cores indicates that the tonnage produced was miniscule until the years of the late Roman republic, when a spike in lead isotopes derived from the imperial silver-lead mines of southern Spain found their way to Greenland as atmospheric pollution. The spike in industrial smelting – which provided the coinage that was the life-blood of commercial exchange in a world devoid of paper money, bills of exchange and cheques – is also indicated by analysis of Spain's Rio Tinto mines, analysis that reveals some 6–16 million tons of silver and copper slag left as residue (Wilson 2002: 25–26. 29). This Roman mining and smelting achievement was, however, economically unsustainable. Not only did Roman mining efforts consume prodigious amounts of slave labor they were also only technically feasible in landscapes that allowed hydraulic sluicing to remove the initial layers of over-burden (Wilson 2002). By AD 180 the Spanish mines were abandoned, leading to a collapse in output, a debasement of the currency and a steady reversion to a barter economy during the late Empire. Indicative of the Empire's failing fortunes, the silver *denarius* that was the standard instrument of exchange across the Mediterra-nean world, comprised only 4% silver in AD270. A century and a half earlier the figure had been 97% (Wilson 2002: 27).

The inability of even the Roman economy, with its unprecedented resources, to sustain the coinage necessary for basic commerce points to more generalized failings. With limited access to metal goods, and the casting of iron remaining an unknown skill to the ancient world, achievements in manufacture and, more partic-ularly, agriculture were severely constrained. The population of Roman Italy during the reign of Augustus Caesar (28 BC – AD 14) probably amounted to no more than six million people, a total significantly less than that which today resides in Hong Kong (7.4 million). Of Italy's six million people, a third were probably slaves (Hopkins 1978: 68). Even where technological innovation was applied, it led to no generalized transformation. In the case of water-mills, Saller (2002: 265–266) estimates that even if this form of technology was commonplace – which he doubts – its effect on overall economic growth across the course of the Roman Empire would have amounted to "a rate less than 0.025% per year." Trapped within the confines of a preindustrial society, most members of the societies of antiquity lived in poverty and misery. In the case of imperial Rome, Schiedel and Freisen (2009: 84) estimate that at the height of empire somewhere between 65% and 82% of the population lived at or below subsistence level. In such circumstances, great displays of wealth – such as those evident in the holiday villas of the Roman elite at Pompeii – could only be achieved by extreme disparities in income, Schiedel and Freisen (2009: 76) concluding that the prosperous Roman elite amounted to as little as 1.2% of the total. Of the Roman villas that become the basis of Gallic production during the Late Empire, Braudel (1986/1990: 92) observes that they were "mon-strous" places, "a machine for enslaving and crushing human beings." Yes, it is true that the Roman aqueducts, sewers, and roads allowed for urban concentrations that were not equaled until the dawn of the modern era. But life for most, even in the great metropolis of Rome, was no bed of roses. Invariably, Rome's free-born lived in multistoried apartments (*insulae*) wherein exorbitant rents were extorted for jerry-built premises that were constantly in danger of collapse and fire. "Almost every-where," Carcopino (1940: 44) observed, "the higher you went in a building, the more breathless became the overcrowding." On the upper stories, "entire families were herded together" in an environment characterized by "dust, rubbish, and filth," circumstances in which "bugs ran riot" to such an extent that "bedding could be black with them." In such habitations, Rome's famed fountains and sewers were typically far distant, only the very wealthy enjoying private connections. Reflecting on such circumstances, Carcopino (1940: 40) correctly noted that, "The drainage

7 Management in Antiquity: Part 1 – The Binds of Geography 135

system of the [typically] Roman house is merely a myth begotten of the complacent imagination of modern times."

The fundamental problem with Roman society, as with the other societies of antiquity, is that it continually saw landed income as the only legitimate source of wealth; a situation that created a vicious circle in which any wealth that was created was ploughed back into low-productivity rural pursuits. In consequence, Rome not only remained devoid of the financial tools that characterized the European "commercial revolution" of the thirteenth century – bills of exchange, inter-bank transfers, cheques, double-entry book-keeping – its intellectual leaders also saw financial activity (lending, borrowing, etc.) as the domain of the morally bereft. Plutarch (c.AD100a/ 1993: 242), for example, in outlining the purpose for his essay, *Against Borrowing Money*, declared that he only wanted to show "what disgrace and indignity there is in the business." Such attitudes not only curtailed possibilities for entrepreneurial endeavor, they also restricted the growth of an urban middle-class sympathetic to new forms of wealth creation. Across the Empire as a whole, Schiedel and Freisen (2009: 84) estimate society's "middling" class at somewhere between 3.5% and 6.5% of the total. Modern managerial principles – which Pollard (1965: 6–7) associated with a capacity to motivate workers "without powers of compulsion" and an ability to relate output to costs and to sell "competitively" – were even more alien to the societies of antiquity. Even in Rome, arguably the most litigious society in the historical record, there was, as Hopkins (1978: 109) commented, "no tradition which legitimated the regular employment of free men." Accordingly, Roman society becoming increasingly bifurcated between the free (divided between a wealthy elite and an under-employed majority) and the enslaved.

In the world of antiquity, where entrepreneurial business pathways were more or less closed, there was only two sure ways of increasingly societal wealth: steal from others by force or enslave them (or, preferably, achieve both goals simultaneously). This fundamental fact of economic life was, arguably, better understood by the ancients themselves than by many modern commentators. The Athenian democracy of the fifth century BC, and its material achievements, would have been impossible without the slave-operated silver mines at Laurion and the tribute exacted from the Delian League. The latter, initially an anti-Persian maritime alliance, had by 454 BC been reduced to subject status, forced to pay the Athenian state 600 talents (1.56 tons) of silver per year (Thucydides, c.411 BC/ 1954: 132). In defending Athens need to go to war to defend its dominant position, Pericles accurately noted that Athenian prosperity rested on the fact that it had spent "more life and labor in warfare than any other state, thus winning the greatest power that has ever existed in history." The fact that the Athenian "empire is now like a tyranny," Pericles declared, was no reason to let it go, for to surrender it would bring the "state to ruin" (Thucydides, c.411 BC/ 1954: 161–62). Athens' vaunted war-making ability, with the accompanying benefits in land and treasure, paled into insignificance when compared with that of Rome. Writing in the first century AD, Livy observed that by 319 BC, Rome was "a nation ... in its eighth century of warfare." At this date another 700 years of warfare lay before the western half of Rome's empire, while the eastern half battled on for a further millennia. As Rome advanced it looted treasuries and temples, seized land, and enslaved people in their hundreds of thousands. "From the Second Punic War onwards," Howgego (1992: 4) observed, "Rome laid its hands by stages on the stored up wealth of the whole of the Mediterranean." The greatest cities of the Mediterranean basin – Carthage, Syracuse, Athens, Jerusalem – were sacked, the booty from Jerusalem's temple being used to build Rome's Coliseum. Plutarch (c.AD 100b/ 1999: 74) records that "so much money" was plundered from Macedonia in 167 BC "that the [Roman] people were exempt from taxes." Not until the third century AD were taxes on land, the principal source of regular income for the Roman state, reinstated. To compensate for the privileged position of Rome, the rest of the Empire was subject to land taxes that typically took a tenth of the annual harvest. In the case of Egypt, half the harvest was taken (Hopkins 1978: 16). The flows of goods, wealth, and slaves into the Italian heartland, therefore, depended in the first instance not on the "extensive markets" and "comparative advantage" of which Temin (2012: 2) speaks, but rather on militarily-enforced taxes. In summarizing the managerial and organizational consequences of such arrangements, Hokpins accurately remarked (1978: 17) that, "The considerable reliance on taxes levied on food helped the Roman state support a large superstructure with fairly simple economic institutions and only a small market sector."

If conquest and taxes directed great accumulations of wealth towards the Roman heartlands, the social consequences were uneven. Economically, the long-term consequences were retrograde. Ruined by the continual warfare that could take farmers and/or their sons away from their peasant farms for years at a time, the Roman rural yeomanry found themselves displaced by large *latifundia*: estates staffed by captured slave populations and their descendants. In reflecting upon this tendency, Appian (c.AD120/ 1913: 7) observed that:

> ... the ownership of slaves brought them [the rich] great gain from the multitude of their progeny, who increased because they were exempt from military service. Thus certain powerful men became extremely rich and the race of slaves multiplied throughout the country, while the Italian people dwindled in numbers and strength, being oppressed by penury.

Arguably the greatest failure of the Roman Empire, however, was that it remained at heart, a military tyranny. Its growth, survival, and eventual decline are all attributable, in the first instance, to the combat performance of its legions. Tacitus, arguably the greatest social commentator that Rome produced, was acutely aware of how Rome was perceived by the subjugated and by those beyond the frontier. Reflective of this understanding, he at one point places into the mouth of a supposed British highland chief a clarion call of resistance to Rome. In an address to his people, this chief is recorded as saying of the Romans: "Robbers of the world, having by their universal plunder exhausted the land, they rifle the deep . . .To robbery, slaughter, plunder, they give the lying name of empire; they make a solitude and call it peace." As Rome's economic and demographic strength ebbed away from the third century AD onwards, armed resistance from the disaffected was increasingly found within as well as without. Rome was thus, for all its grandeur, a society – like all others found in antiquity – trapped within the technological and organizational constraints of what remained a pre-industrial world. Only with its ruination were new forms of Western civilization – built around markets, entrepreneurship, commerce and the exploitation of carbon-based forms of energy – to emerge capable of breaking the shackles that bound the economies of antiquity.

In exploring the issue of management in antiquity – a substantial undertaking given the variety of societies and the length of the historical period that we are considering – this study will involve two distinct parts, or chapters. This chapter, Part 1, is therefore in part a prelude to Part 2, a chapter that primarily focuses on the Greek, Hellenic, and Roman experiences. In its focus, this Part or chapter, however, also addresses three topics that are arguably central to our understanding of antiquity. The first necessarily involves methodology and sources and how we judge the size of both populations and economies in antiquity. A difficult task, given the absence of most of the statistics to which modern economists and managers have become reliant (i.e., productivity, firm and economy-wide outputs, per capita income, etc.), but nevertheless an essential one. For if we are to venture opinions on the success or otherwise of economic and managerial endeavor in antiquity, we could hardly do this without some measures as to the economic wealth produced, and the living standards of the people whose toil produced that wealth. In the following two sections of this chapters, we will explore the economic and social diversity of the world of antiquity (i.e., the Middle East, Egypt and North Africa, the Mediterranean Basin, Gaul [France], Britain, and Germany). Although the societies of antiquity were, we argue, an interrelated whole, with even those societies beyond the "civilized frontier" trading with the more urbane cultures inside the frontier, each confronted different sorts of problems, problems largely determined by geography and the forms of economic activity which the land, and the technology of the time, allowed. It is only by understanding the diversity of antiquity, and how the various cultural and economic components related to each other, that we can comprehend the whole.

Managerial and Economic Performance in Antiquity: Methods, Sources, and Difficulties

The societies of antiquity were hierarchical in nature. This applies as much to democratic Athens as Pharaonic Egypt or imperial Rome. Yes, it is true that Athenian citizens made decisions relating to peace, war, and the investment of state funds through common consent. But it is also true that Athenian wealth, power, and leisure rested on a veritable army of slaves, amounting to some 30% of the total population. This makes it one of only five cultures in history that can truly be considered a "slave society," wherein slave numbers represented around a third of the total; the other four being Rome, the southern states of the United States of America prior to the Civil War, and nineteenth-century Brazil and Cuba (Hopkins 1978: 101). While slavery was atypical in most ancient societies built around subsistent peasant farming (i.e., Mesopotamia, Egypt, early republican Rome), the householder and his family in such cultures were invariably subject to state and religious taxes, forced labor on state projects, and military conscription. Hierarchical though ancient societies may have been, it is nevertheless wrong to think of them as having anything like a professional managerial class as we understand it, a class of people whose occupation is that of producing goods and/or services for sale as efficiently as possible so as to meet a consumer demand. The position closest to that of a "manager" was the "overseer" who supervised labor in mines, shipyards, construction projects and, in the case of Rome, in the commercially oriented but slave-operated *latifundia* that increasingly characterized agricultural in Roman Italy and the Empire's western provinces. Far from being autonomous agents, overseers were invariably little more than superior hands, a status clearly indicated in Cato the Elder's *De Agricultura*, the classic text on Rome farm management. In this, Cato (c.160 BC/ 1913: 34, 25) advises estate owners that they should make sure their overseers "often lend a hand" in the fields. If weather or other circumstances reduced working hours, then the overseer's task was to immediately "cut down" on "the slaves' rations." Even for the comparatively enlightened Pliny the Younger (c.90 AD/ 1963: 106), efficient estate management rested on having "a good type of slave" that enabled overseers to operate without resort to "chained slaves." On the *latifundia*, as with other forms of private business endeavor, it was not only the laborers and field hands who were slaves. Overseers, financial controllers, and the like also often fell into the same category, Rome acquiring tens of thousands of skilled, educated slaves with its conquest of the Hellenistic kingdoms of Greece, Egypt, and the Middle East during the late republic. Writing of Crassus, Rome's wealthiest citizen during the late republic, Plutarch (c.AD 100c/ 2005: 112) attributed his financial success in large part to his acquisition of slaves "of the highest quality – readers, secretaries, silver smiths, stewards." Such people were, Plutarch (c.AD 100c/ 2005: 112), continued, "the living tools for the management of a households." In the early Empire, even the centralized bureaucracies of the Roman state were headed by slaves. It was these people who were responsible for the day-to-day operation of empire, issuing instructions to provincial governors and imperial magistrates (Carcopino 1940: 62).

One of the consequences of the ancient world's operation without reference to modern understandings of management and economics is that we have few ways of reliably measuring performance. At the level of the private-sector business, the absence of anything resembling double-entry book-keeping curtail measurements of efficiency based on inputs and outputs. At a societal level, there is little agreement even as to the size of the population at any given point in time. For example, population estimates for Italy in 28 BC – a Roman census year at the transition point between republican and imperial rule – range from a high of 17 million (Lo Cascio and Malanima 2005) to a low of six million (Hopkins 1978; de Ligt 2012; Schiedel and Freisen 2009). In this debate, proponents of the higher estimate point to archaeological evidence, whereas advocates of the lower figure – which this study finds more credible – primarily rely on both likely agricultural output and the literary record (most particularly Livy's, *History of Rome from its Foundations* with its reports of Rome's census figures). Estimates in relation to investment are even more fraught, Wilson (2002: 6) observing that there are few figures "that a modern economist would want to use." In the case of Rome, Wilson (2002: 6) continues,

"We do not know ... gross national product, or *per capita* production figures ... at even a single moment in its history." Even where obtainable, income and expenditure figures from antiquity expressed in terms of historic currency – talents, drachmaes, tetradrachms, denarii, sesterces, etc. – also need to be treated with caution. For although the ancients universally eschewed paper money in favor of coinage, their currency – as much as our own – was subject to inflation and debasement.

In seeking to move beyond traditional sources of evidence, based on either archaeology or the literary record, economic historians have resorted to two principal methods. The first of these involves the selection of an early modern proxy, where we do have reasonably reliable figures, as a point of comparison. The most noted such effort is arguably that undertaken by Schiedel and Freisen (2009), who use "Golden Age" Netherlands (i.e., Netherlands in c.1600) as a point of comparison, observing that the Netherlands arguably reached the limits of what could be achieved by a preindustrial society in terms of per capita wealth. In comparison to the societies of antiquity, the Netherlands in the early seventeenth century enjoyed extremely high levels of commerce and trade, high levels of literacy and formal education, and plentiful sources of carbon-based energy derived from local peat bogs. On the basis of such attributes, Schiedel and Freisen (2009: 64) argue, with considerable justification, that its economic efforts must represent "an absolute ceiling" that even imperial Rome could not possibly have approached. Extrapolating from their figures – which suggest that the per capita gross domestic product (GDP) of the Netherlands in 1600 amounted to $2590 per year in current (i.e., 2018) US dollars, or approximately $7 day – we must logically conclude that the per capita output in imperial Rome was equivalent (at best) to no more than a couple of dollars per day, a level commensurate with the $1.90 per day income which the World Bank (2019a) currently regards as a measure of "extreme poverty."

A second means of estimating economic and managerial performance in antiquity involves the calculation of waged income and purchasing power through reference to a universal measure of wealth, namely wheat, a product which was, as Duncan-Jones (1978: 159) observed, "the basic foodstuff of subsistence diet in antiquity." In our modern world, our comparative wealth can be ascertained that we can produce the wheat necessary to sustain life at little cost. Or, to put it another way, even a basic modern income allows for the theoretic purchase of a considerable amount of wheat. In 2019, for example, the wholesale price at wheat traded hovered around US$215 per ton, or US$0.215 per kilogram. This means that someone on the federal minimum wage in the United States – which stood at US $10.35 in 2019 – could, if they worked a 40-hour week for 52 weeks of the year, have theoretically purchased 4682.52 kilograms of wheat over the course of a year. By comparison, Schiedel and Freisen (2009: 72) estimate that the per capita GDP of Rome at the peak of Empire, expressed in kilograms of wheat, was most probably in the range of 489 kilograms to 604 kilograms per year, i.e., a level somewhere between 10.4% and 12.9% of the current US minimum wage. Given that Rome was, however, like the other societies of antiquity, characterized by extreme income inequality, it is unlikely that such a bounty would have been enjoyed by a majority of the population. After estimating Roman income disparities, Schiedel and Freisen (2009: 84) calculate that 22% of the population within the Roman frontier would have received a per capita income that equated (on average) to 245.5 kilograms of wheat, a total equivalent to 5.2% of the current US minimum wage. The social stratum above them, representing 60% of the imperial population, are believed to have received a per capita income equivalent to 409 kilograms of wheat (8.7% of the US minimum wage). Considering the GDP of the Roman Empire as a whole, Schiedel and Freisen (2009: 62–63) calculate its GDP at the height of empire to be equivalent to 50 million tons of wheat. On current values, this equates to a GDP of approximately US $11 billion, a total roughly equivalent to that of the modern day Armenia or Nicaragua (World Bank 2019b).

Although we should treat the above estimates – and any attempt to convert historic calculations into modern day equivalents – with considerable caution, what is nevertheless clear is that even at the peak of its powers the Roman Empire's economy was a comparatively primitive affair. Devoid as it was of the technological and commercial innovations that were to transform the human condition during the Industrial Revolution, most members of Roman society lived a life sunk in poverty, misery, and illiteracy. As Jerome Carcopino (1940: 66) recorded, even in the city of Rome itself "the majority of what we should nowadays call the middle classes vegetated in semi-starvation within sight of the incredible opulence of a few thousand." If, however, the economic and managerial efforts of antiquity pale into insignificance when compared with the achievements of the modern world, it is also unfair to dismiss its achievements on the basis of such a comparison. For our own efforts are built, in part, on antiquity's legacy; a legacy built around their historic struggles to break out of the confines imposed by geography and nature. On this score, their legacy is thus found not only in the things that they achieved, but also in the efforts that ended in failure. It is certainly unwise to dismiss as futile the efforts for betterment undertaken by those cultures and civilizations that have preceded our own. It is to those efforts, and the geographical and technological constraints against which the struggled, that we now turn.

The Binds of Geography: Life Within the Civilized Frontier

Writing in what was arguably his greatest work, *The Mediterranean and the Mediterranean World in the Age of Philip II*, Fernand Braudel (1946a/1990: 773) concluded that "the fundamental reality of any civilization must be its geographical cradle." The view that cultures and civilizations are, first and foremost, a product of their geography is hardly novel. In Livy's (c.AD 14b/1960: 386) *History of Rome from its Foundations*, the city's dictator in its war against the Gauls in 386 BC is quoted as saying:

> Not without reason did gods and men choose this spot as the site of our City – the salubrious hills, the river to bring us produce from the inland regions and sea-borne commerce from abroad, the sea itself, near enough for convenience yet not so far as to being danger from foreign fleets, our situation in the very heart of Italy – all these advantages make it of all places in the world the best for a city destined to grow great

7 Management in Antiquity: Part 1 – The Binds of Geography

Similarly, Herodotus (c. 446 BC/ 1954: 133, 139), described by Cicero as "the Father of History," noted that the extraordinary agricultural wealth of Egypt rested on the Nile's "bottomless" springs and a "black and friable ... alluvial soil" totally unlike either the "reddish and sandy" soils of Libya or the "stone and clay" of Syria. The Greek historian, Polybius (c. 150 BC/ 1979: 283), also emphasized the importance of geography, attributing the food security and wealth of Greece to its maritime access to the Black Sea and its agricultural and pastoral hinterlands, observing that as "regards the necessities of life, there is no disputing the fact that the lands which surround the Pontus provide both cattle and slaves in the greatest quantities and the highest quality ... they also absorb the surplus produce of our own countries, namely olive oil and every kind of wine."

What is evident from the above quotations from Herodotus, Livy, and Polybius is the emphasis on geographic and economic diversity and, at least in the case of Livy and Polybius, on maritime trade and sea-borne commerce. It was this orientation towards the sea as a means of breaking the shackles imposed by the physical constraints of one's homeland that does so much to explain the intellectual and cultural dynamism of the Greeks, their Phoenician maritime rivals and, subsequently, Rome; the latter, admittedly, only embracing a maritime career when it became a military necessity in the First Punic War with Carthage (264 BC – 241 BC). Certainly by the second century BC, the Mediterranean basin and its hinterlands – including Spain and Gaul – represented what Braudel (1977: 81–82) referred to as a "world economy," an interconnected whole within which each part is inexplicable without reference to the totality. Reflective of this interconnectedness is Polybius's (c. 150 BC/ 1979: 285) observation that, with Rome's dominion of the eastern Mediterranean, "history" had become "an organic whole ... all events bear a relationship and contribute to a single end."

If the sea routes of the Mediterranean and Black Seas, and subsequently the North Sea, created an interconnected whole, it was nevertheless the case that a society's propensity for maritime adventure reflected its own landed resources. Least inclined to venture to sea were the civilizations based on the rich, irrigated river valleys of Mesopotamia and Egypt. The benefits of such environments – wherein irrigated cultivation required centralized bureaucracies skilled in writing, mathematics, astronomy and the harnessing of human labor – were obvious, Herodotus (c. 446 BC/ 1954: 158) declaring the Egyptians to be "much the most learned of any nation of which I have had experience." The disadvantages that accrued from such environments were, if less obvious, equally profound. Both lower Mesopotamia and Egypt lacked access – whether through home deposits or trade – to tin and iron, making them laggards in metallurgy. Moreover, the very fertility of the land and the abundant populations which it supported appears to have fostered a technological conservatism. Even though Pharaonic Egypt's agricultural richness depended on its ability to channel water into irrigation ditches once the annual Nile flood had receded, there was little inventiveness shown in tackling this problem. Only with the advent of the Hellenistic Greek kingdom of the Ptolemies (305 BC – 30 BC) were high-capacity water wheels and the "Archimedean" water-screw introduced. Prior to this, Egypt relied on labor intensive bucket and pulley methods

(Wilson 2002). This propensity to rely on labor intensive modes of work was most clearly demonstrated in the great vanity projects of the Pharaohs: the pyramids and underground mausoleums of the Valley of the Kings. Although the pyramids remain antiquity's most iconic relics, their construction was hardly an economically rational capital investment. The economic and social folly involved was self-evident to a logical Greek thinker such as Herodotus (c. 446 BC/ 1954: 178–180), who declared the construction of the great pyramids to be a "crime," a source of "the greatest misery" that reduced the Egyptian population into "abject slavery." The wealth of the Nile valley also proved in many ways to be as much curse as benefit, acting as a magnate for a succession of conquerors – Assyrians, Persians, Greeks, Romans, Arabs – each of whom sought to exploit its bounty for their own benefit. Under the Ptolemies, the Nile's irrigated farmlands became effectively the nationalized property of a Greek-speaking dynasty, a dynasty whose rule rested on Greek mercenaries and military settlements (Rostovtzeff and Fraser 1926/1957; Wilson 2002). This subject status was reinforced when Egypt came under the control of the Caesars from 30 BC onwards. Unlike Rome's other provinces, which remained nominally under the control of the Senate, Egypt became the personal property of the emperors. As noted earlier, imperial land taxes resulted in half the annual harvest being seized, a bounty that fed the Roman capital for 4 months of the year (Howgego 1992).

Whereas the bounty of Egyptian civilization was built upon irrigated farming, the economies of its eventual Greek and Roman conquerors were founded on dry-land farming of wheat, olives, and vineyards. For the small-scale peasant operations that engaged in such activities – in both classical Greece and early republican Rome – the returns were in most cases little above subsistence. In Rome, even the senatorial elite originally boasted only modest means. When in 458 BC, Livy (c.AD14b/1960: 213) records, a senatorial delegation approached Cincinnatus to ask him to serve as Dictator and lead Rome out of a military crisis, they found him "working in a little three-acre farm," his hands and face covered in "grimy sweat." Several centuries later, when another delegation approached Manius Curius, a senator who had served as Consul and led Rome to three military triumphs, they located him in a "little estate" that he worked "with his own hands, ... sitting by the fire and boiling turnips" (Plutarch, c.AD 100b/ 1999).

The comparative poverty of Rome's elite in the early republic – which caused Livy (c.AD14b/1960: 34) to declare that "nowhere" more than Rome "have thrift and plain living been for so long held in esteem" – reflected three basic facts about dry-land farming in antiquity. First, dry-land farming was invariably located in areas of thin soils. Most typically, it involved the farming of hillsides. Where they existed, river valleys and coastal plains were commonly malarial swamps. Their utilization required sustained levels of collective effort and investment that were beyond the resources of peasant-based communities. Even if not water-logged, the heavy soils of river bottoms were also typically impervious to the crude ploughs of antiquity (Braudel 1946b/1990). The second characteristic feature of dry-land farming was a dearth of livestock. This had a number of consequences. It made meat and dairy products a dietary rarity. Animal manure, which could have raised soil fertility, was also in short supply. Where animals were used in ploughing, there was an almost universal reliance on oxen rather than horse-power. Even when horses were used, the farmers of antiquity lacked the soft-leather collars that proved so effective in medieval Europe, collars that allowed medieval horses to do the work of four oxen (Parain, 1941/1966: 144). The third notable consequence of a reliance on dry-land farming, with its deficit of animal stock, was military. Chronically short of horses, Greek and Roman armies were built around infantry formations, rather than cavalry, an outcome that made their style of warfare far more plebeian than that which was to subsequently characterize the medieval world with its armored-clad knights.

If the economic deficiencies of dry-land farming are easily discerned, its benefits were, if less obvious, equally profound. First, free of the stultifying bureaucracies that characterized the civilizations of Mesopotamia and Egypt, dry-land farming communities were inherently more democratic. Increased wealth entailed increased responsibilities, most particularly in the military domain. In classical Greece and early republican Rome, the most respected and valued citizens were those who could afford the heavy helmets, shields, and body armor that allowed them to serve in the ranks of the Greek phalanxes and Roman legions. According to Livy (c.AD14b/1960: 82), in 550 BC Rome undertook a far-reaching restructure of its political order by means of an inaugural census, through which each adult male's contribution to "public service, in peace as well as in war, . . . could be in proportion to his means." The greater one's capacity to contribute to the state's defense, with all the military risks which that entailed, the greater was one's voting power in the popular assembly. The second, easily overlooked benefit of dry-land farming was a comparative abundance of leisure. Hopkins (1978: 24) observes that "most" Romans under the republic "were under-employed," their busy seasons corresponding with the planting and harvesting of their small grain crop. This left plenty of time for religious festivals, politics, and, above all, war-making. For in assessing the economics of Greece and Rome, it is easy to overlook the extent to which they were highly militarized and violent societies. When one reads Livy's (c.AD14b/1960) *History of Rome from its Foundations*, for example, there is a constant temptation to skip over the accounts of a seemingly endless list of wars, large and small. But it was this pattern of endless warfare that proved the decisive factor in the Roman economy, continually extending its reach and resources while undermining the sustainability of the small farmers upon which the state was originally built. Consequently, we read in Livy (c.AD14b/1960: 129–30) that, as early as 495 BC, an old army veteran could lament that:

> While I was on service . . . my crops were ruined by enemy raids, and my cottage was burnt. Everything I had was taken, including my cattle . . . I was expected to pay taxes, and fell, consequently, into debt. Interest on the borrowed money increased my burden; I lost the land which my father than grandfather had own . . . ruin spread like a disease.

The constrained opportunities offered by dry-land farming made the sea, along with landed warfare, one the few avenues through which the Mediterranean's peasant communities were able to break the bounds of their geographic homeland, be it through emigration, trade, or maritime warfare. Significantly, however, despite the ever beckoning presence of the Mediterranean, relatively few cultures ventured seaward. A number of factors explain this. Arguably the most important is the Mediterranean's comparative dearth of fish. Certainly its stocks, both in antiquity and in the medieval era, in no way rivaled those found in the cold-water fisheries of the Baltic and the North Sea (Braudel 1946b/1990). In the western Mediterranean, the wide expanses of the Tyrrhenian Sea effectively restricted maritime travel to the north-south corridors between Italy and Tunisia in the east and between Spain and North Africa in the west. Sudden and destructive storms, moreover, provided a constant threat to life and property even within sight of the coast. In the First Punic War (264 BC – 241 BC), for example, both of Rome's first two naval fleets were sent to the bottom as a result of storms, Polybius (c.150 BC/ 1979: 100) noting on the second such occasion that "the destruction being so complete that not even one of the wrecks could be salvaged." Piracy was a constant threat to not only shipping but also land-lubbers, Thucydides (c.411 BC/ 1954: 39) observing that "the ancient cities" of Greece were invariably "built at some distance from the sea" to protect themselves from this menace. In the face of such obstacles, it is therefore not surprising that in antiquity only three cultures built their fortunes on a voluntary embrace of the sea: the Phoenicians, the Greeks, and the Carthaginians.

By general consent it was the Phoenicians – a Canaanite-speaking people from what is now Lebanon and northern Israel – who acted as maritime pioneers (see, for example, Frankenstein 1977; Stieglitz 1990; Scott 2018). Driven to the seas by the aridity of the region's sandy coastal plains, as well as pressure from competing ethnic groups (most particularly the Hebrews and the Philistines), the Phoenicians pioneered a number of key commercial and maritime skills. Among the most important of these were phonetic writing, stellar navigation, sturdy mortise-and-tenon jointed keeled ships, brailed-rig sails that provided a limited capacity to take into the wind, and large ceramic amphorae that allowed for the transport of wine and olive oil (Scott 2018). While the political and commercial independence of the Phoenicians was curtailed by a series of Near Eastern empires (Assyrian, Babylonian, Persian), their Greek rivals maintained a precarious independence. In 480 BC, Athens – the largest of the Greek maritime states – famously asserted both its independence and naval supremacy in the eastern Mediterranean through a comprehensive victory over the Persian Empire, and a predominately Phoenician fleet, at the battle of Salamis. Such was city's naval domination in the ensuing decades that Pericles, the greatest of the Athenian democratic leaders, was able to boast that Athens "had more and better steersmen and sailors than all the rest of Hellas put together" (Thucydides, c.411 BC/ 1954: 39). Increasingly, however, Phoenician and Greek maritime activity was associated with emigration and colonization as people sought physical escape from the economic constraints of their homeland. By far the most successful of these immigrant societies were Greek-speaking Syracuse in Sicily and Punic-speaking Carthage in what is now Tunisia. In reflecting upon the Carthaginian naval domination of the western Mediterranean, Polybius (c. AD150 BC/ 1979: 345) recorded that "seamanship" was "their national calling and they occupy themselves with the sea more than any other people." Among other things, Carthaginian maritime capacity enabled this North African society to exploit previously untapped mineral resources in the western Mediterranean. Of particularly significance in this regard was Carthage's development of the silver mines of southern Spain, mines which were, following Carthage's defeat, to subsequently secure Rome's currency under the early Empire. Nevertheless, for all the success and sophistication of their maritime empires, Carthage, Athens, and the city-states of Phoenicia were all, in the end, destroyed utterly by the states that emerged from the landed hinterland. Tyre, the greatest of the Phoenician cities, was sacked and burned by Alexander the Great in 332 BC. Carthage was destroyed by Rome in 146 BC, its surviving citizens sold into slavery. Athens, defeated by Sparta in the Peloponnesian War, suffered a similar fate at the hands of Rome. Plutarch (c.AD100b/ 1999: 190), writing of the sack of Athens in 86 BC, recorded that, "There was no telling how many people were slaughtered; even now, people estimate the numbers by means of how much ground was covered with blood."

The comparative fates of the maritime powers of antiquity (Phoenicia, Athens, Carthage) and those most linked to Western supremacy in the early modern era (the Netherlands, Britain, and the United States) are instructive. In antiquity, the maritime powers all succumbed to entities who drew their strength from the land: Persia, Sparta, Macedonia, Rome. By contrast, control of the seas – and, subsequently, the air – has proved the foundation for modern economic and military supremacy. Where defeat, and a subsequent loss of supremacy occurred, it was to a rising maritime power. Dutch supremacy eventually gave war to that of Britain after four bitter wars (1652–1654, 1665–1667, 1672–1674, 1780–1784). The supplantation of British supremacy by the United States was, in turn, heralded by American success in the War of Independence. In the world wars of the twentieth century, the supremacy of the two great Anglo-Saxon powers, Britain and the United States, at sea and in the air, proved decisive. Arguably, American domination of the world's sea lanes, and the commercial prosperity that this delivered to the West, proved equally decisive in the Cold War contest against the Soviet Union.

The Binds of Geography: Life Beyond the Civilized Frontier

If the legions of Rome, based upon a peasant-soldier citizenry, eventually came to dominate the Mediterranean world, there nevertheless existed on the edges of this settled world another world, a world of pastoral nomads that acted at various times as prey and predator for more urbane communities. In North Africa, beyond the coastal ports and plains, extending into what Herodotus (c. 446 BC/ 1954: 332–336) referred to as the great "sand-belt," lived a nomadic people generally referred to as Numidian. In describing the land which they occupied, Polybius (c. 150 BC/ 1979: 429) claimed (perhaps optimistically) that "the total of horses, oxen, sheep and goats which inhabit the country is so immense that I doubt whether an equal number can be found in all the rest of the world." "The reason for this," Polybius (c. 150 BC/ 1979: 429) continued, was that "the African tribes make no use of cereals, but live among the flocks and herds." Sallust (c.40 BC/ 1963: 54), who served with Julius Caesar and was appointed governor of Numidia, recorded that the original native population "lived a nomadic life, roaming from place to place, bivouacking wherever they happened to be at nightfall." To the west of this Numidian population, Sallust (c.40 BC/Sallust 1963: 56) added, were "the Moors." To the south were "lands parched by the continual heat of the sun." Similar nomadic peoples, whose life revolved around horses and flocks of sheep and/or cattle, also occupied the Iranian plateau, the Arabian Peninsula, and, most significantly, the vast Eurasian steppes that stretch from modern-day Ukraine to Mongolia. Most commonly referred to in antiquity as "Scythians," Herodotus perhaps best summed up the classical view of these Eurasian nomads. On the one hand, Herodotus (c. 446 BC/ 1954: 286) dismissed the "Scythians" as "the most uncivilized nations in the world," a people without claim to "any of the arts of civilized life." On the other hand, he noted that these nomadic peoples, "accustomed, one and all, to fight on horseback with bows and arrows," were the most invincible of warriors when fighting on their grassy homelands (Herodotus, c. 446 BC/ 1954: 286).

In antiquity, the nomadic horsemen and camel-herders of North Africa, Arabia, the Iranian Plateau and the Eurasian steppe interacted with more settled societies that abutted them in three principal ways. First, they served as cavalry, mounted mercenaries, in the armies of whoever would hire them, most particularly of Carthage, the Hellenistic kingdoms, and Rome, a role in which they helped offset one of the chronic weaknesses of most armies of the ancient Mediterranean world, constructed as they were around peasant infantry. Second, they acted as raiders and, on occasion, conquerors, a threat which assumed an unprecedented dimension in the late fourth century AD, when the Huns – a Turkic people from the Mongolian steppes – pushed all before them as they moved westward towards the Roman frontier. Arguably, however, the most significant role of the nomadic horse-peoples who lived around the Mediterranean Basin was that of both conduit and barrier to the cultures who lived on the other side of their pasturelands. In antiquity, the lands and people who lay beyond the Sahara, and the steppes to the north of the Black Sea, remained shrouded in mystery and misunderstanding. Of the Ukrainian grasslands, Herodotus (c. 446 BC/ 1954: 276) recorded, "No one has any accurate information about what lies beyond the region … what lies beyond is mere hearsay." Only with the Arab conquests that began in the seventh century AD, and the conversion of the bulk of the nomadic horse people to Islam, was a semblance of cultural unity imposed on the regions which the nomads occupied, a unity that did much to enhance linkages between Europe, sub-Saharan Africa, the Indian sub-continent, and East Asia. Writing of the economic and cultural role of Islam between the seventh and fifteenth century, Braudel (1987/1993: 62) accurately noted that, "Trade-routes were its wealth … It alone … brought together the three great cultural zones of the Old World – the Far East, Europe and Black Africa. Nothing could pass between them without its consent or tacit acquiescence. It was their intermediary." Even without the intermediary role of Islam, a small but economically significant trade emerged between the Mediterranean and the Far East. The bulk of this trade, which tended to see Asian textiles, spices, and jewels exchanged for Greek or Roman silver, went via the Red Sea and India. Much smaller volumes went via the so-called "Silk Road," a route that connected the Roman and Chinese worlds via Syria, the Iranian plateau,

7 Management in Antiquity: Part 1 – The Binds of Geography

and the desert lands to the north of Tibet. Unfortunately for the Roman Empire its trade with India and the Far East was associated with what we would think of as a growing "foreign account deficit"; a deficit that saw a steady loss of silver and (to a lesser degree) gold coins to the eastern trade routes. When the Spanish silver mines closed in the late second century AD, these losses became insidious, contributing to rapid currency debasement (Howgego 1992; Wilson 2002).

If the ancients viewed the nomadic horse peoples who abutted their world with a mixture of disdain and fear, the same attitudes were even more manifest in relation to the Gallic and Germanic peoples to their north. Against these northern peoples Rome waged war for more than eight centuries. In the case of the Gauls, a series of early Celtic victories, which included the sacking of Rome in 390 BC, were followed by increasingly crushing defeats. With the surrender of Vercingetorix at Alesia in 52 BC, an independent Gallic existence in what is now France came to an end. With the defeat of Boudicca, and the massacre of her Iceni warriors in AD61, Britain too came under Roman sway. Unfortunately for Rome the Germanic tribes beyond the Rhine proved more resistant, the limits of empire delineated by Rome's disastrous defeat in the wilds of the Teutoburg forest in AD 9. Writing of this defeat, and the loss of three legions under the command of Varus (Varro), the Roman historian, Suetonius (c.AD130/Suetonius 1957: 62), recorded that it "nearly wrecked the Empire." So gravely did the emperor Augustus regard the defeat, Suetonius (c.AD130/Suetonius 1957: 62) continued that "he would often beat his head on a door, shouting: 'Quinetilius Varus, give me back my legions!'"

Greek and Roman contempt for the modes of Gallic and Germanic existence pervade the literary record. Writing of the Gauls whom Rome expelled from the Po Valley (Cisalpine Gaul), the Greek historian, Polybius (c. 150 BC/ 1979: 128–129) informed his readers in the second century BC that, "They lived in unwalled villages and had no knowledge of the refinements of civilization . . . they slept on straw and leaves." Of the lands to the west of the Rhine, Tacitus (c.AD98b/1942: 709) asked in his study, *Germany and its Tribes*, "who would leave Asia, or Africa, or Italy for Germany, with its wild country, its inclement skies, its sullen manners and aspect, unless indeed it was his home?" As to the Germanic lifestyle, Tacitus (c.AD98b/ 1942: 716–717) observed that:

> It is well known that the nations of Germany have no cities . . . They live scattered and apart, just as a spring, a meadow, or a wood has attracted them . . . No use is made by them of stone or tile . . . They are wont also to dig out subterranean caves, and pile on them great heaps of dung, as a shelter from the winter, . . . for by such places they mitigate the rigour of the cold.

The primitive nature of the Germanic condition, Tacitus (c.AD98b/1942: 711) continued, was also indicated by a dearth of metal goods, noting that, "Even iron is not plentiful with them." Tacitus (c.AD98b/1942: 711) also believed the Germans to be devoid of the work ethic that characterized more successful cultures, showing propensity for little other than warfare. Consequently, he concluded, they "lie buried in sloth," their "huge frames, fit only for a sudden exertion. They are less able to bear laborious work . . . Nay, they actually think it tame and stupid to acquire by the sweat of toil what they can win by their blood" (Tacitus, c.AD98b/1942: 710, 716).

There is little doubt that Greco-Roman depiction of the Gallic-Germanic "barbarians" to their north as uncouth savages was part fact, part exaggeration. In pre-Roman Gaul, so Braudel (1986/1990: 60–61) wrote in *The Identity of France*, Celtic metal craftwork revealed "extraordinary skill." The Gauls "were also," Braudel (1986/1990: 61) added, "weavers of both linen and wool, dyeing them in the bright colours they favoured . . . the [leather] wine-cask, a convenient substitute for the amphora, was a Celtic invention. They were the first people in Europe to manufacture soap." It is also evident that the cultural and technological gap between those within the western frontier of Empire and those who lived on the far side of the Rhine decreased over time. This was particularly so after the Germanic invasions of the third century AD, invasions which saw most of northern and eastern Gaul (France) fall under the control of the interlopers for an extended period. In the wake of these intrusions, the frontier between "civilized" and "barbarian" is best thought of as an area of transition, rather than an impermeable barrier. Within these vast "boundary regions," there occurred what the Marxist historian, Perry Anderson (1974: 110–111), describes as the "long symbiosis of Roman and Germanic social formations." In Gaul, rich and poor alike abandoned the unprotected cities for rural fortified villas. As taxes were increased across the Empire in a desperate search for military stability what was left of a free peasantry accepted, even in Italy, conditions akin to serfdom in order to gain the protection of a local lord (Stevens 1941/1966). On the Germanic side of the frontier, by contrast, economic life became increasingly monetarized. Culturally, as well, there was a narrowing of the gap that existed between those on either side of the frontier. By the time of the fifth-century Germanic *Volkerwanderung*, most of the German tribes shared the Christian faith of their Roman foes, albeit through adherence to an Arian creed that those who looked to Rome regarded as heretical. In consequence, when the Visigoths sacked Rome in 410 they showed, according to St Augustine (c.AD430/ 1945: 2), unexpected respect for "the churches of the apostles." "So far and no farther," St Augustine (c.AD430/ 1945: 2) added, "came the rage of the bloody enemy."

Although we should not exaggerate the backwardness of the Celtic and Germanic cultures of western Europe during antiquity nor should we understate it. If life for most of the inhabitants of Empire, even during the golden years of the first century AD, was eked out at the edge of subsistence, for those who lived in Gaul, Britain, and Germany, the circumstances of existence would have been even more precarious. The skilled metal-work to which Braudel referred would have been the preserve of a small craft elite, an elite working at the behest of a comparative handful of tribal chieftains. Certainly, northern Gaul and Britain remained the most backward corner of Rome's empire, Plutarch (c.AD100b 1999: 321) questioning the logic behind the conquest of Britain with the observation that, "there was nothing worth taking from people who lived such hard and impoverished lives." If we accept the argument (Hopkins 1978; Schiedel and Freisen 2009), as this author does, that the population of Roman Italy was around six million at the end of the first century BC, then it is difficult to believe – as Braudel (1986/1990: 83) suggests – that Gaul had "a minimum" of "8 or 9 million" at this time. A population total in the region of half that suggested by Braudel seems more likely. While Roman conquests unquestionably brought the Celtic and Germanic peoples of northern Europe into a permanent engagement with the Mediterranean world, they also entailed – as they did elsewhere – suffering and devastation. Of Julius Caesar's genocidal wars against the Gauls, Plutarch (c.AD100b/ 1999: 314) records that in "less than ten years ... he killed 1,000,000 and took the same number of prisoners." While in southern Gaul any depopulation was offset by the settlement of army veterans and immigrants from Italy – an outcome that contributed to the permanent "Latinization" of the region – the effects of urbanization and other positive attributes of Roman rule were far less pronounced in northern Gaul and Britain. Of these regions, Stevens (1941/1966: 118) writes, "town life hardly existed." If it is thus true, as Polybius (c.150 BC/ 1979: 285) noted, that incorporation into the Roman world made the peoples of western Europe and the Mediterranean Basin "an organic whole," peoples whose fate was to henceforth to be intimately interwoven, then it is also the case that geographic and nature continued to exert arguably even more powerful influences. Disparities, inequalities, and an unevenness of economic development remained antiquity's essential hallmarks.

Conclusion

In considering the world of antiquity, it is easy to become fixated on the achievements of the great urban centers of the Mediterranean Basin: Babylon, Tyre, Jerusalem, Athens, Corinth, Carthage, Rome. It was in these cities that the cultures of antiquity found their most vibrant expression in art, architecture, literature, politics, commerce, and trade. It is also to the citizens of these cities – Herodotus, Thucydides, Polybius, Livy, Plutarch – that we owe much of our understanding of the ancient world. We have to constantly remind ourselves, therefore, that this urbanized experience was an atypical one in antiquity. For an overwhelming majority, life involved a monotonous struggle to eke out a living from the land. One day was much like the next, life being dictated by the rising and setting of the sun and the changing of the seasons. This applied as much to the people whose lives appeared the freest, the nomadic horse-people and herders of Eurasian and North Africa plains and deserts, as to the Egyptian peasant wedded to their patch of soil. Even by comparison with the poorest peasant-farmer, the typical herder had few possessions. For each morning, the nomadic clan had to pack up their worldly possessions and move to new pastures. In summer these pastures were likely to be in cooler, mountainous regions, a fact that necessitated the constant crossing of streams, high-altitude passes, and areas of broken ground. In winter, even in North Africa, a return to lowland valleys exposed one to snow-blocked paths and raging torrents. Of the Celtic population of the Po Valley in the second century BC, a people who combined slash-and-cultivate agriculture with pastoral transhumance, Polybius (c.150 BC/ 1979: 128) noted that their only "possessions consisted of cattle and gold, since these were the only objects which they could easily take with them." For peasant farmers, the security of having the same roof over one's every night was offset by the fact that, as a member of a more organized society, one was exposed to the constant demands of one's political and social superiors: for taxes, religious tithes, forced labor, and military service. Often, even in good seasons, these demands could leave the famer and his family eking out a bare subsistence existence. In bad seasons, people starved. In short, life for most – as Thomas Hobbes (1651/2002: 62) expressed it, in summarizing the condition of pre-industrial existence more generally – was "poor, nasty, brutish, and short."

For all the architectural and intellectual achievement of antiquity, there was remarkably little progress in either manufacturing or, more particularly, agriculture. Even in classical Greece, as Meikle (2002: 242) observed, manufacturing was the preserve of "a relatively small number of craftsmen producing in workshops of very restricted scale." Under the Roman Empire outside Italy, it is probable that 90% of the population were still confined to agricultural and pastoral pursuits. Even in Italy itself, at the height of Empire, "power and wealth" was primarily dependent, as Hopkins (1978: 6) recorded, upon "the area and fertility of the land which each individual possessed." In these circumstances of low rural productivity and an artisanal manufacturing sector – which placed a firm ceiling on the possibilities for per capita increases in wealth – social and economic progress could only come by one means: through increased inequality, by the concentration of wealth in the hands of particular societies at the expense of others, and through the enrichment of the few at the expense of the many. Consequently, the architectural marvels of the Athenian Acropolis rested not on the natural wealth of Attica but rather the expropriated treasure of the so-called Delian League, Athens' subject maritime empire. Similarly, the atypical situation found in Italy under the Caesars, in which perhaps 30% of the population lived in towns and cities, reflected the fact that the Empire was able to call on the agricultural bounty of the whole Mediterranean Basin. Such dynamics meant, in short, that managerial endeavor in the ancient world was directed towards fundamentally different economic purposes to that found in modern, democratic societies. Whereas management has since the Industrial Revolution has *primarily* acted as a social institution for increasing societal wealth, in antiquity the main purpose of state bureaucrats, tax-collectors, and agricultural overseers was to ensure a *concentration* of wealth so as allow for both state-funded construction projects (i.e., pyramids, aqueducts, roads, canals, temples, etc.) and the personal extravagances of a few.

Cross-References

- ▶ Intellectual Enlightenment: The Epistemological Foundations of Business Endeavor
- ▶ Management in Antiquity: Part 2 – Success and Failure in the Hellenic and Roman Worlds
- ▶ What Is Management?

References

Anderson P (1974) Passages from antiquity to feudalism. New Left Books, London

Appian (c.AD120/1913) The civil wars: book 1. Loeb Classical Library. http://penelope.uchicago.edu/Thayer/E/Roman/Texts/Appian/Civil_Wars/1*.html. Accessed 7 Feb 2019

Bartol K, Tein M, Mathews G, Martin D (2005) Management: a pacific rim focus, 4th edn. McGraw-Hill, North Sydney

Braudel F (1946a/1990) The Mediterranean and the Mediterranean world in the age of Philip II, vol. 2. Harper Torchbooks, New York

Braudel F (1946b/1990) The Mediterranean and the Mediterranean world in the age of Philip II, vol. 1. Harper Torchbooks, New York

Braudel F (1977) Afterthoughts on material civilization and capitalism. John Hopkins University Press, Baltimore

Braudel F (1986/1990) The identity of France: people and production. Fontana Press, London

Braudel F (1987/1993) A history of civilizations. Penguin Books, Harmondsworth

Carcopino J (1940) Daily life in ancient Rome: the people and the city at the height of empire. Yale University Press, New Haven and London

Cato M (c.160 BC/1913) De agricultura. In: A Virginian farmer, Roman farm management: the treatises of Cato and Varro. Macmillan, New York, pp. 19–50

de Ligt L (2012) Peasants, citizens and soldiers: studies in the demographic history of Roman Italy, 225 BC and AD 100. Cambridge University Press, Cambridge

Duncan-Jones RP (1978) Two possible indices of the purchasing power of money in Greek and Roman antiquity. Publications de l'Ecole Francasie de Rome 37(1):159–168

Frankenstein S M (1977) The impact of Phoenician and Greek on the early iron age societies of southern Iberia and southwestern Germany. PhD thesis, University of London, London

Herodotus (c. 446 BC/1954) The histories. Penguin Classics, Harmondsworth

Hobbes T (1651/2002) Leviathan: the matter, form and power of commonwealth, ecclesiastic and civil. Broadway Press, Peterborough.

Hopkins K (1978) Conquerors and slaves. Cambridge University Press, Cambridge

Howgego C (1992) The supply and use of money in the Roman world 200 BC to AD 300. J Roman Stud 82:1–31

Koerner R (1941/1966) The settlement and colonization of Europe. In: Postan MM (ed) The Cambridge economic history of Europe, vol 1. Cambridge University Press, Cambridge, pp 1–91

Lewis MJT (1997) Millstone and hammer: the origins of water power. Hull University Press, Hull

Livy (c.AD14a/1960a) Rome and Italy: Books VI-X of the history of Rome from its foundations. Penguin Classics, Harmondsworth

Livy (c.AD14b/1960b) The early history of Rome: Books I-V of the history of Rome from its foundations. Penguin Classics, Harmondsworth

Lo Cascio E, Malanima P (2005) Cycles and stability: Italian population before the demographic transition (225 BC–AD1900). Rivistta di storia economica 21(3):5–40

Meikle S (2002) Modernism, economics and the ancient economy. In: Schiedel W, von Reden S (eds) The ancient economy. Routledge, New York, pp 233–250

Parain C (1941/1966) The evolution of agricultural techniques. In: M M Postan (ed) The Cambridge economic history of Europe, vol. 1. Cambridge University Press, pp. 125–179.

Pliny G (c.AD90/1963) Letter to Calvisius Rufus. In: G Pliny (ed) The letters of the Younger Pliny. Penguin Classics, Harmondsworth

Plutarch (c.AD100a/1993) Against borrowing money. In: Plutarch, Selected essays and dialogues: a new translation, Oxford University Press, Oxford, pp. 239–245

Plutarch (c.AD100b/1999) Roman lives. Oxford University Press, Oxford

Plutarch (c.AD100c/2005) Fall of the roman republic, rev. edn. Penguin Classics, London

Pollard S (1965) The genesis of modern management: A study of the Industrial Revolution in Great Britain. Edward Arnold, London

Polybius (c. 150 BC/1979) The rise of the Roman empire. Penguin Classics, London

Rostovtzeff M, Fraser PM (1926/1957) The social and economic history of the Roman Empire. Second edition. Clarendon Press, Oxford

Saller R (2002) Framing the debate over growth in the ancient economy. In: Schiedel W, von Reden S (eds) The ancient economy. Routledge, New York, pp 251–269

Sallust (c.40 BC/1963) The Jugurthine war. In: Sallust, The Jugurthine War/the conspiracy of Catiline. Penguin Books, Harmondsworth, pp 35–148

Schiedel W, Freisen SJ (2009) The size of the economy and the distribution of income in the Roman Empire. Roman Stud 99:61–91

Scott JC (2018) The Phoenicians and the formation of the Western world. Comp Civilizations Rev 78(4):24–40

St Augustine (c.AD430/1945) The city of god, vol 1. Everyman's Library, London

Stevens CE (1941/1966) Agriculture and rural life in the later Roman Empire. In: Postan MM (ed) The Cambridge economic history of Europe, vol 1. Cambridge University Press, Cambridge, pp 92–124

Stieglitz RR (1990) The geopolitics of the Phoenician littoral in the early iron age. Bull Am Sch Orient Res 279:9–12

Suetonius (c.AD130/1957) The twelve Caesars. Penguin Classics, Harmondsworth

Tacitus (c.AD98a/1942a) The life of Cnaeus Julius Agricola. In: Tacitus (ed: Hadas M) Complete works of Tacitus. The Modern Library, New York, pp 677–706

Tacitus (c.AD98b/1942b) Germany and its tribes. In: Tacitus (ed: Hadas M) Complete works of Tacitus. The Modern Library, New York, pp 709–732

Temin P (2012) The Roman market economy. Princeton University Press, Princeton

Thucydides (c.411 BC/1954) The history of the Peloponnesian war. Penguin Classics, Harmondsworth

Wilson A (2002) Machines, power and the ancient economy. J Roman Stud 92:1–32

Witzel M (2012) A history of management thought. Routledge, Abington

World Bank (2019a) Understanding poverty. https://www.worldbank.org/en/understanding-poverty. Accessed 10 Feb 2019

World Bank (2019b) GDP ranking, 2017. https://datacatalog.worldbank.org/dataset/gdp-ranking. Accessed 10 Feb 2019

Management in Antiquity: Part 2 – Success and Failure in the Hellenic and Roman Worlds

8

Bradley Bowden

Contents

Introduction	154
Breaking the Bonds of Geography: Success and Failure in the Hellenic Mediterranean	156
Breaking the Bonds of Geography: Success and Failure in the Roman Republic	162
The Failure of Empire	171
The Shattered Roman Legacy	174
Conclusion	177
Cross-References	179
References	179

Abstract

In this second chapter on management in antiquity, we focus on the managerial success and failure of Greece, the Hellenic world, and Rome. As in the first chapter, we argue that, in the final analysis, these societies were managerial failures. Greece and Rome proved only marginally more successful than ancient Egypt and Mesopotamia in breaking the bonds imposed by a preindustrial economy. Many of the basic technological attributes that characterized Medieval Europe – cast iron, crop rotation, the wheeled plough, windmills – were conspicuous by their absence. In Rome, notable achievements in construction (aqueducts, sewers, roads, concrete) were not matched by productivity-enhancing in either agriculture or manufacturing. In the western Roman Empire, the most significant economic development – which did temporarily improve rural per capita output – was the slave-operated latifundia, an institution founded in suffering and misery. As time went on, Rome failed to even maintain the mining output necessary to

---

B. Bowden (✉)
Griffith Business School, Griffith University, Nathan, QLD, Australia
e-mail: b.bowden@griffith.edu.au

© The Author(s), under exclusive licence to Springer Nature Switzerland AG 2020
B. Bowden et al. (eds.), *The Palgrave Handbook of Management History*,
https://doi.org/10.1007/978-3-319-62114-2_100

support its gold and silver coinage. By AD200, in consequence, Rome was sliding back into a barter-based economy. The key legacies of ancient Greece and Rome are thus not found in material achievements but rather in their intellectual insights; insights that emphasized such concepts as democracy, citizenship as a system of rights and responsibilities, representative government, organizational checks and balances, and equality before the law.

Keywords

Civilization · Rome · Greece · Technology · Germanic · Celtic · Arab · Medieval · Religion · Islam · Christianity · Transport · Technology · Slavery · Law · Cicero · Tacitus · Thucydides · Africa · Egypt · Gaul

Introduction

In Part 1 of our study of management in antiquity, we described how societies within what we referred to as the "civilized frontier" fell into three broad economic types; the river valley civilizations of Mesopotamia and Egypt where societal wealth was built around irrigated crops; cultures built around dry-land crop cultivation, most particularly of wheat (Greece, the Middle Eastern hill country, Italy, Spain, southern Gaul); and the societies whose wealth rested on maritime commerce and trade (Phoenicia, Carthage, Greece, and the Greek colonies of the western Mediterranean). Of these three types of societies, it was the latter which long appeared most likely to break out of the constraints imposed by geography and pre-industrial technology. For in the world of antiquity the creation of a civilization (i.e., societies characterized by cities and urbanized populations of priests, bureaucrats, traders, writers, etc.) could only come about by one of two means. Either one could concentrate the resources of one's own society by shifting wealth from the rural sector to the urban centers (a strategy pursued in Mesopotamia and Egypt) or one could draw on resources from other societies. Given the prohibitive cost of land transport, the latter strategy was most feasible if one controlled the sea lanes to one's homeland; a strategy that entailed either one becoming a significant naval power or the military occupation of the port cities from which others could disrupt one's maritime commerce. Despite the proximity of the civilizations of antiquity to the Mediterranean and Black Seas, it is at first glance surprising how few societies ventured down the maritime route. The great civilizations of Mesopotamia and Egypt remained perpetually land-locked, their water-borne activities being effectively confined to the Tigris, Euphrates, and Nile rivers. Other notable societies in antiquity – Assyria, Israel, the Hittites, the Celts – also never ventured to sea in an economically significant way. In the Old Testament, the only maritime adventure that is recorded involves Jonah being thrown overboard by terrified sailors caught "in a great storm," whereupon Jonah (c.300 BC/1985: 1541) is famously swallowed by "a great fish." The reason for the paucity of maritime cultures in the Mediterranean Basin reflected not only the risk entailed but also the investment of capital, labor, and time which naval and maritime life entailed. As the great Athenian leader, Pericles, is recorded as saying in 432 BC: "Seamanship, just like anything else, is an art. It is not something that can be picked up and studied on one's spare time; indeed, it allows no spare time for anything else" (Thucydides c.411 BC/1954: 121). When Rome, hitherto a distinctly land-locked power, fought Carthage for naval control of the western Mediterranean in the First Punic War (264 BC–241 BC), the financial costs were enormous. As Polybius (c.150 BC/1979: 109) recorded, "never before in the history of the world have two such immense forces been ranged against each other at sea." In the course of the war, the Carthaginians lost 500 quinqueremes, the five-decked warships that had become the key to naval victory. For the Romans, who only learnt the ropes of seamanship in the course of the conflict, the costs were even higher, the Latin-speaking power seeing 700 of its quinqueremes sent to the bottom (Polybius c.150 BC/1979: 109).

The naval dominance of the Greeks and Romans allowed each of these cultures to establish what Braudel (1977: 81–82) called a "world economy" within their realm of maritime and military influence, an economy in which the wealth of imperial peripheries were marshaled and directed towards the political and economic center. A maritime people almost from the outset the Greek world, even in the sixth century BC, stretched from the Black Sea's Crimean peninsula – where they traded olive oil and wine for grain and slaves – to Syracuse in Sicily, and Massilia (Marseilles) in southern Gaul (France). Long the dominant maritime force in the eastern Mediterranean, Greek cultural hegemony was extended to Egypt and the Middle Eastern hinterlands by the conquests of Alexander the Great in the fourth century, a cultural hegemony which was to last – despite Rome's annexations in the first century BC – until the Arab conquests. The incorporation of the Egypt, the Middle East, and the eastern Mediterranean under Rome's imperial rule thus resulted in a single *economic* zone, within which wealth was now directed towards Italy and Rome, but two *cultural* zones: a Greek-speaking East and a Latin-speaking West. Yes, it is true that the Romans themselves became Hellenized to a greater or lesser degree. Among educated Romans, an ignorance of Greek language and culture caused one to be regarded by one's social superiors as an uneducated gutter-snipe. Among the worst insults that Plutarch (c.AD100a/1999: 123) hurled in the direction of Gaius Marius – a general who reorganized the legions, thereby saving Italy from disaster at the hands of Germanic invaders – was the allegation that "he never learnt to read and write Greek and never spoke Greek on any important occasions." The Roman Empire, the final cultural and economic expression of the world of antiquity, thus preserved – and passed on to the modern world – two distinct philosophies and cultures, each of which encapsulated markedly different models for societal organization. Although mature Roman society bore a heavy Greek imprint, it always remained markedly different.

In many ways, Roman differences were socially and culturally liberating. Unlike the Greeks, who always perceived "citizenship" in terms of ethnicity and one's birthplace, the Romans came to embody a transnational view of "citizenship," something which could be conferred on any legally free individual who owed Rome allegiance: regardless of race or creed. By comparison with the ancient Greeks, Roman society also allowed women greater economic and social scope. Roman women could, unlike their Greek sisters, own large estates and lend money in their own right. They could, and did, mingle freely with men in important social events (see, for example, Gardner 1986/1991; Fraschetti 2001). Roman engineering skill with aqueducts and sewers overcame many of the sanitary problems that cursed Greek life, turning the multicity Olympic Games into a vast open cesspit. On the other hand, even by comparison with the highly militarized societies of classical Greece, Rome was a society geared towards war and its benefits, Plutarch (c.AD100b/1999: 74) recording that in the wake of the Roman conquest of Macedonia in 168 BC "the public treasury" was filled "with so much money that the people were exempt from taxes." Organized violence was, in short, the key to Roman success. If, in consequence, we owe much of our laws and political practices to Rome – representative government, equality before the law, citizenship open to all who pledge allegiance – in the field of management we owe the Romans precious little. Their one great economic innovation, which *did* raise rural productivity in the western Mediterranean basin, was the slave-operated *latifundia*, a place of enslavement, suffering, and misery. In consequence the positive legacies of Greece and Rome were primarily in the realm of ideas, in the words that they wrote and spoke, rather than their material achievements.

Breaking the Bonds of Geography: Success and Failure in the Hellenic Mediterranean

In a series of lectures given in London in May 1840, the English historian, Thomas Carlyle, argued that human achievement is primarily built upon ideas and human aspiration, rather than technology and economics. The key legacies of the past are thus intellectual, not material. Emphasizing his point, Carlyle (1840/2013: 92) observed of the legacy of ancient Greece:

> Greece, where is it? Desolate for thousands of years; away, vanished . . . Like a dream; like the dust of King Agamemnon! Greece was; Greece, except in the words it spoke, is not.

The view that the enduring legacy of classical Greece was one of intellectual attainment, "in the words it spoke," was clearly one sensed by the ancient Greeks themselves. In his *History of the Peloponnesian War*, Thucydides (c.411 BC/1954: 162) records the Athenian leader, Pericles, as saying that although "all things are born to decay," the achievements of Athens were such as to "be remembered for ever by posterity." The sense that the achievements of the Greeks were intellectual rather than material is also reflected in the assessment of economic historians. In tracing "the history of technology," Carlo Cipolla (1981: 167) noted that most share an appreciation that the "Greco-Roman world, while highly creative in other fields of human activity, remained . . . strangely inert in the technological field." An indicative assessment is that made by Scott Meikle (2002: 242), who argues that the Greek predilection for hoarding currency – often burying it in the ground for subsequent discovery by modern day treasure-seekers and fortunate Grecian home-renovators – was economically rational given that there was "no possibility of the productive investment of money ... and consequently there was virtually no lending for that purpose." "The bulk of production in the Greek world of the classical period," Meikle (2002: 242) also notes, "was done by free peasants at or near subsistence," a class of people not renowned for productive efficiency. In the highly militarized society of Sparta, the mundane tasks of commerce and manufacture were the preserve of noncitizens, an outcome that allowed Spartan adult males to devote all their time to warfare. Spartan agriculture rested on the enserfed *helots* of Messinia, a people who lived in dire circumstances. The most conservative of societies, the Spartan's constitution, according to Polybius (c.150 BC/1979: 344), also prohibited Spartans from using the gold and silver coinage of their neighbors. Instead, they are recorded as relying on "the exchange of their crops" and an "iron currency" made from Laconia's iron ore deposits. Of the Spartans and the other people of the Peloponnese, Pericles is cited as saying, "They are farmers ...they have no financial resources either as individuals or states" (Thucydides c.411 BC/1954: 120–121).

Across classical Greece, the war-time practice of devastating the olive trees and vineyards of one's opponents – crops whose replacements could take a decade or more to return to their former productivity – also acted as a constant curtailment to economic expansion. Meanwhile, the growth of commerce was curtailed by the absence of any system for tracing strings of debits and credits that could be settled through a final transfer at the end of a given period. The ready supply and apparent cheapness of slave labor also reduced the need for managerial or technological innovation. According to Duncan-Jones (1978: 162–163), a slave could be purchased in classical age Athens for a sum equivalent to a skilled craft worker's wage for 180 days. Seven centuries later, in the imperial Rome of the Emperor Diocletian, adult male slaves cost more than five times as much. Taken together, the obvious economic deficiencies of classical Greece – the absence of formalized credit arrangements, subsistence agriculture, a lack of technological innovation in either agriculture or manufacturing, and a propensity for internecine warfare – can only have had retrograde effect on the whole society. Unsurprisingly, by the middle of the second century BC, Polybius (c.150 BC/1979: 537) was reporting that the old Greek heartlands were suffering from "a general decrease of the population," a desertion of cities, and falling "agricultural production."

Although there is no doubting the intellectual dynamism of classical and Hellenistic Greece, its conceptual interests were typically only tangentially related to productive pursuits. Indeed, often the elitism of high Greek culture mitigated against symbiotic relationships between inquiry, theoretical science, and technological innovation. This tendency was arguably most evident in the work of Aristotle, whose ideas on science had a retarding effect on not only the world of antiquity but also medieval Europe. The essential problem with Aristotle's (c.330 BC/1941: 689–670, 712–713) philosophy of science is found in the clear distinction that he drew between "practical" and "empirical knowledge" on one hand (i.e., medicine, carpentry, etc.) and "natural science" and "theoretical knowledge" on the other. For Aristotle (c.330 BC/1941: 712, 860–861) "empirical knowledge" can never do more than provide a basis for "action". It cannot provide mechanisms for determining "truth," "theoretical knowledge," or "universal knowledge," terms which he used interchangeably. Conversely, "truth" and "natural science" – which Aristotle (c.330 BC/1941: 861) associated solely with theoretical physics, mathematics, and theology – can only involve understanding of the inner "essence" of things that "suffer no change," a category within which he fallaciously included "the heavenly bodies" (Aristotle c.330 BC/1941: 859).

If the economic deficiencies of the classical Greeks are evident to inquiry, we are left with the realization that there must have been strengths that offset these weaknesses, strengths that allowed the navies and armies of Greece and Macedonia to conquer the Eastern Mediterranean, creating a cultural dominance that was to endure in almost unchallenged fashion until the Arab conquests of the seventh century AD. The most obvious strength was organizational or political, expressed in a uniquely Greek combination of individual initiative and social cohesion. Unencumbered by the stultifying state bureaucracies of Mesopotamia and Egypt, the Greek emphasis on individual rights and social responsibilities found its most iconic expression in Pericles' funeral oration to Athens' fallen hoplite soldiers in 431 BC. In contrary to other societies, Pericles is recorded (Thucydides c.411 BC/1954: 147) as saying, "each single one of our citizens, in all the manifold aspects of life, is able to show himself the rightful lord and owner of his own person" (i.e., the society is premised on individual freedom). At the same, Pericles added, "this is a peculiarity of ours; we do not say that a man who takes no interest in politics is a man who minds his own business; we say that he has no business here at all" (i.e., citizenship involved pro-active social engagement). This combination of individual right and social responsibility found military expression in the peculiarly Greek phalanx, a formation that confronted its foes with a solid wall of shields (*hoplon*) and spears. Intact, the phalanx was near invincible. If it crumbled at a single point, then all were imperiled. As Cartledge (1977: 15–16) noted in emphasizing the importance of social cohesion in classical Greek warfare: "Warfare between masses of phalanxes (*phanges*) was not a graceful or imaginative affair, but required above all disciplined cohesion and unyielding physical and moral strength." The second Greek innovation with revolutionary combat potential was the trireme, a sleek warship with three decks of rowers tipped with an underwater bronze ram. According to Thucydides (c.411 BC/1954: 42), the trireme was a Corinthian invention, an invention that allowed it for a time an unmatched domination of "the sea routes," the city subsequently growing rich "from the revenues which came to it." It was, however, the Athenians who became the ultimate masters in the use of triremes. When a rich new seam of silver was discovered at Laurion the Athenian politician and subsequent naval commander, Themistocles, persuaded his fellow citizens to invest the windfall in the construction of 200 triremes. Upon this fleet the Persian invasion of Greece floundered at Salamis in 480 BC, a victory that heralded the golden age of Athenian maritime and cultural supremacy.

It says much for the militarized nature of the Greek city-states that their most obvious technical innovations related to warfare. Arguably, however, the greatest strength of the Greeks was that they became, far more so then their maritime rivals, the Phoenicians, a genuine "world-wide" civilization, a civilization that became part of the cultural heritage of the wider Mediterranean Basin and, ultimately, humanity as a whole. Although there is a popular tendency to think of "Greece" as classical age

Athens and Sparta, or as comprising merely the geographic area represented by the modern Greek republic, the Greek world was always much more than this. A maritime people from the outset, the Greek's historic "homelands" included Crete, the Aegean islands, and Ionia in modern day Turkey. Of the Greek city-state of Byzantine (modern day Istanbul), Polybius (c.150 BC/1979: 282) observed that its position "in relation to the sea affords greater advantages for its security and prosperity than that of any other city in our quarter of the world." As early as the seventh century BC, Greek colonies, trading posts, and city-states were well established in southern Italy, Sicily, Sardinia, Corsica, Spain, and southern Gaul (France). With the establishment of Massilia (modern day Marseilles), the Gallic hinterland was opened up to Greek commerce, a trade built around the exchange of Gallic grain and slaves for Greek wine and olive oil. From its dominating position on the Sicilian coast, the greatest of the western Greek city-states, Syracuse, competed with Carthage for maritime control of the east-west shipping trade.

If maritime prowess opened up the western Mediterranean to Greek commerce and culture, it was to the Macedonian phalanx, and the military skill of Alexander, that Greece initially owed its political, linguistic, and cultural domination of the East. Under Alexander's military successors the Hellenistic kingdoms of the Seleucids (Syria, Palestine, Mesopotamia) and the Ptolomies (Egypt) assumed a commercial and even intellectual significance that soon eclipsed the old city-states of the Greek homelands. The new Hellenistic cities – Antioch, Seleucia and, above all, Alexandria – soon boasted populations of between 100,000 and 200,000 people, totals that made them comparable in size to Athens at the height of its powers (Roberts 2007: 218–219; Van Wees 2011: 111–112). As was the case with subsequent Roman conquests, these Hellenistic cities benefited from the looting of treasuries during the Macedonian conquests, an outcome that stimulated commerce by releasing hoarded coinage back into circulation. But they also became centers for learning and scholarship. As Roberts (2007: 220) notes, Alexandria and Pergamon (in modern day Turkey) boasted "the two greatest libraries of the ancient world." It was Pergamon which introduced parchment as an alternative to less durable papyrus, an alternative that was to remain the principal writing material throughout the medieval era. It was Alexandria, however, that became the leading center for mathematics, science, and innovation. To Alexandria the world owes the geometry of Euclid. As noted in Part 1, it was also almost certainly to Alexandria that antiquity owed the high-capacity water-wheel and the "Archimedean" water-screw, inventions that were to transform water irrigation in the Near East (Wilson 2002: 7).

In reflecting on the rise and decline of cultures and civilizations, Braudel (1946/ 1990: 763) concluded that, "The mark of a living civilization is that it is capable of exporting itself, of spreading its culture to distant places." It is in this capacity to spread its wings – to move beyond what Braudel (1946/1990: 770) calls "its geographical cradle" – that we see the enduring legacy of Greece, a legacy evident in modern management as much as any other sphere. For when, as management historians, we think of the legacies of antiquity we need to distinguish between actual managerial achievements – which were generally slight in the case of Greece – and the heritage bestowed by not just the words they spoke but also by the values that their societies encapsulated, societies which, for all their diversity and division, emphasized rationality, inquiry, a respect for the individual worth of their fellow citizens, and a passionate engagement with the communities in which they lived. It is these latter qualities, rather than Greek and Macedonian military victories, that best explain the pervasive and enduring influence of Greek culture and language in the Middle East from the fourth century BC onwards. Yes, it is also true, that the Hellenistic kingdoms were no democracies, quickly adopting the absolutist behaviors of the emperors and pharaohs whom they had supplanted. Yes, it is true that in Israel and Egypt, two ancient cultures with a deep and abiding attachment to their unique forms of religious faith, the advance of Greek culture was met with revolt and armed resistance. In the Old Testament's passages on the Maccabees we therefore read how revolt was instigated when the Seleucid "king sent Gerontes the Athenian to force the Jews to violate their ancestral customs and live no longer by the laws of God, and to profane the Temple in Jerusalem and dedicate it to Olympian Zeus" (Maccabees 2 c.160 BC/1985: 727). In consequence, the Old Testament account continues:

> Judas, otherwise known as Maccabaeus, and his companions made their way secretly among the villages, rallying their fellow-countrymen; they recruited those who remained loyal to Judaism ... Making surprise attacks on towns and villages, he fired them ... and inflicted very heavy losses on the enemy (Maccabees 2 c.160 BC/1985: 731).

Successful as the Maccabean revolt was in re-establishing an independent Jewish state – a state that maintained its existence under the Hasmonean dynasty until the assertion of Roman rule after the death of Herod the Great – even it proved incapable of holding back the tide of Greek culture and language. In Israel's most densely settled district, the Galilee region, Greek inscriptions were appearing in synagogues by the first century BC. The major towns in the region – Tyre, Carmel, Ptolemais, Scythopolis – were Hellenic in culture and language. Among the large Jewish *diaspora* in Alexandria, Antioch, and the other major cities of the Near East, it is probable that most preferred Greek to Hebrew or Aramaic (Hengel 1969/1974; Hengel 1980; Feldman 1986). The presence of Greek documents among the Dead Sea Scrolls indicates, as Feldman (1986: 87) observed, "that knowledge of Greek had penetrated even the most fanatical religious groups." Almost certainly Jesus and his Apostles were at least partially fluent in Greek. Of the three original or Synoptic Gospels, those by Mark and Luke were originally written in Greek. Mathew's Gospel was quickly translated into this idiom, the lingua franca of the Near Eastern world (Wansbrough 1985).

The attractiveness of the Greek culture is not only indicated by its increasingly dominant placement in the Near East, a region where Greek ideas and beliefs had initially advanced at the point of the Macedonian *sarrisa*, the six meter pike which was the favored weapon of the Alexandrian phalanx. Its dynamism is also evident in the intellectual victories obtained in the world of its Roman military conquerors. In summing up the influence of Greek culture on Rome, and through the Romans on us, Gibbon (1776/1910: 39) observed in his *Decline and Fall of the Roman Empire* that:

> ... victorious Rome was herself subdued by the arts of Greece. Those immortal [Greek] writers who still command the admiration of modern Europe, soon became the favourite object of study and imitation in Italy and the western provinces ... it was almost impossible, in any province, to find a Roman subject of a liberal education, who was at once a stranger to the Greek and to the Latin language.

Plutarch, in his life of Cato the Elder, noted that even in the second century BC this fierce upholder of traditional Roman values was unusual in rejecting an embrace of Greek culture. "No one else in Rome had any objection to what was happening," Plutarch (c.100a/1999: 30) observed, "they were glad to see the younger generation acquiring some Greek culture." In dismissing as wholly spurious Cato's oft spoken belief "that Rome will be destroyed when it has become infected by Greek learning," Plutarch (c.100a/1999: 31) advised his readers – who lived at the peak of Empire some 250 years after Cato's death – that "we can see that this slander of his is hollow, since we live at a time when Rome is at the pinnacle of political success and has appropriated Greek learning and culture." As noted early, not only were the households of the Roman elite administered by predominately Greek slaves and freedmen, so too – up to and including the reign of Claudius – was the imperial bureaucracy. The imperial embrace of all things Greek is also clearly indicated in Suetonius' account of an aged Emperor Augustus's sojourn at the Isle of Capri; a community that was infamously associated with sexual debauchery under Augustus's successor, Tiberius. Free to give vent to his natural instincts, Augustus is described by Suetonius (c.139/1957: 105) as spending "a long time watching the gymnastic training of the many local *ephebi* – Greeks who had reached their nineteenth year but were not yet old enough to become full [Roman] citizens." Augustus also insisted of his household that, while at Capri, "the Romans should talk Greek and dress like the Greeks, and the Greeks should do the opposite." It is with the philosopher emperor, Marcus Aurelius, however, that imperial Rome arguably embraced Greek culture to the fullest. Beginning his philosophic *Meditations* with an acknowledgement of his debt to his "Greek training," Aurelius (c.AD 170/2006: 3) proceeds to set out principles for good government that are, in many of their features, consistent with the underlying ethos of Periclean Athens. We are thus informed that a political "commonwealth" should be "based on equality and freedom of speech" and respect for "the liberty of the subject" (Aurelius c.170/2006: 5); that the purpose of political union should always be directed towards "the benefit of our fellow citizens" (Aurelius c.AD 170/2006: 112); that "Justice is the best aim, as any failure is in fact a failure of justice" (Aurelius c.170/2006: 98).

If the Roman embrace of Greek culture was far-reaching, creating a synthesis to which the modern world owes a common debt in so many fields – architecture, drama, mathematics, philosophy, literature, medicine, rational inquiry, logic – the Romans were not Greek, any more than we are Roman. Rather than knitting into a single whole, the division between the Greek-speaking Eastern Mediterranean and the Latin-speaking western Empire become ever more pronounced over time, a division that was formalized in AD330 with the founding of a new imperial capital, Constantinople, on the site of the former city of Byzantine. A revealing difference between the two culture, Latin and Greek, is a Roman enthusiasm that the Greek world hardly ever embraced: gladiatorial games, battles fought to the death by slaves for public entertainment. In reflecting on the comparative rarity of gladiatorial amphitheaters in the Hellenistic east, and their conspicuous absence in the old Greek homelands, Carcopino (1940: 246) noted that "Greece itself fought tooth and nail against the contagion, and in Attica, at least, apparently succeeded." Although they were themselves members of violent, militarized societies, the Greeks found the Rome predilection and capacity for violence as too excessive for their taste. Arguably, it is this Grecian humanity, with its inherent respect for freedom and individual rights, which lies at the core of the continuing appeal of the ancient Greeks to the modern world.

Breaking the Bonds of Geography: Success and Failure in the Roman Republic

The enduring physical remnants of the Roman world, which stretch from Hadrian's Wall in a once remote northern corner to Britain to the marvels of Palmyra in the midst of the Syrian desert-lands, are seeming proof of Rome's past managerial and economic prowess. Of the Roman aqueducts, remarked Edward Gibbon (1776/1910: 48), an author whose account of Rome did much to shape popular understandings, "The boldness of the enterprise, the solidity of the execution, and the use to which they were subservient, rank the aqueducts among the noblest monuments of Roman genius and power." Under Roman rule, claimed Gibbon (1776/1910: 48–49), Italy was home to 1179 cities. "Gaul could boast of her twelve hundred cities." Thanks to the Roman skill at road building, Gibbon (1776/1910: 50) continued, "All these cities were connected with each other, and with the capital, by the public highways, which issuing from the Forum of Rome, traversed Italy, pervaded the provinces, and were terminated only by the frontier." Such was the construction of these roads, Gibbon (1776/1910: 51) accurately concluded, that their "firmness has not entirely yielded to the effort of fifteen centuries." In construction, the use of concrete was, as Mogetta (2015: 1) recently observed, "a quintessentially Roman achievement," its usage from the first century BC onwards allowing for new building styles, shorter project times, and a solidity of completed edifices. The mass production of fired bricks also provided Roman buildings with an enduring strength. In commerce, the introduction of a single currency outside of the imperial domain of Egypt (where coinage from elsewhere in the Empire was excluded) fostered trade and interchange. Even in Judea, an outpost of empire, Roman currency was all pervasive. When, in Luke's Gospel (c.AD65/1985, Book V: Chap. 20) Jesus asks of his inquisitors, "Show me a denarius. Whose portrait and title are on it?" he and his listeners know without looking what the answer will be: "Caesar's." Benefiting from the wealth of empire, Rome found itself at the center of a vast logistic web. "In the city and its suburbs," Carcopino (1940: 176) reflected, "the sheds of the warehouses (*horrea*) stretched out of sight."

While there is good reason to be impressed by Rome's technological and material achievements, there is even better reason for reminding ourselves of the things that it lacked, deficiencies that condemned the inhabitants of republic and Empire to life within a preindustrial society, with all the limitations and restrictions which that necessarily entailed. Unlike ancient Chinese societies, and those of Medieval Europe, Rome never developed the skill and capacity to cast iron, a short-coming that ensured a deficit of metal goods, most particularly in the agricultural sector. As noted in Part 1, Roman agriculture also lacked the soft leather collars that would have allowed for the efficient harnessing of horses as plough animals, an animal capable of four times the field work of Roman oxen. Roman horses, like those found elsewhere in antiquity, were also utilized without the benefit of either metal shoes or stirrups, deficiencies that severely limited their utility. In agriculture, the absence of the heavy, wheeled-plough that became standard in Medieval Europe made working the rich but heavy soils of Northern Europe's valley bottoms wellnigh impossible. A range of crops that became dietary staples in the medieval era – rye, oats, millet, hard durum wheat with its high protein content, rice, sugarcane, lemons, oranges – were other notable absentees (Ganshof and Verhulst 1941/1966). New World crops, such as the tomato and the potato, were also unknown. Although the Romans do appear to have invented the water-mill, the extent of its usage is much debated (for conflicting views, see Wilson 2002; Saller 2002). They certainly never invented the wind-mill, which was capable of operating a larger motor than the water-mills of either antiquity or Medieval Europe (Cipolla 1981: 174). The Roman world also operated without either mechanical clocks or magnetic compasses. On the maritime front, although the Romans emulated the Carthaginians in becoming masters of the quinquereme (five-decked) oared warship, their ship-building techniques differed in no significant way from those utilized by the Phoenicians and Greeks. Unlike medieval ship-wrights, who constructed a ship by first laying down its keel and ribbed frame before attaching the planking, their Greco-Roman predecessors did the reverse. Only when the planking was all laboriously assembled did the Greeks and Romans choose to install the internal frame. At sea the single-masted ships of antiquity had a limited capacity to tack into the wind; a failing that effectively restricted sea-borne travel to the direction of the prevailing trade winds. Even when winds where favorable the mariners of antiquity hugged to coast wherever possible. By comparison, the triple-masted caravel-type vessels pioneered by the Portuguese were to open the broad spaces of the Atlantic and Indian Oceans to European exploration and conquest (Cipolla 1981: 177–177).

Of all the absentees from the societies of republican and early imperial Rome, arguably the most significant was an item that even the medieval world took for granted: the "book," i.e., written material recorded and collated in "codex" rather than tablet or scroll fashion. Although the "codex" book – in which rectangular sheets of papyrus, parchment or paper are bound together and protected by a hard outer cover – appears to have been an invention of the late Roman republic its use only became commonplace during the Late Empire. Even then its systematic use was largely the preserve of religious groups, most particularly the various Christian sects, denominations who were to subsequently make the codex book the foundation of their intellectual authority. In comparison with scrolls, the benefits of codex books are manifest. Not only can they be used with greater ease than scrolls, they are also easier to preserve. Most significantly, they allow a complex series of interrelated texts to be gathered together in one place. Prior to the Christian adoption of codex forms of writing and compilation in the fourth century AD, for example, there was no conception of religious texts known as the "Bible," the "Old Testament," or the "New Testament." Rather there was simply a multitude of separate scripts, handed down from posterity without any agreed ordering or linkages. Reflecting on the common adoption of codex books around 400 AD, and their enthusiastic adoption by Christian scholars, Vessey (2007: xxxv) observes that "it held something of the promise of the Internet for users around the year 2000. It was a new technology of knowledge, a lively and liberating new medium of thought and exchange, with power to change worlds." It was a revolutionary and transformative power that the Roman world of Cicero, Julius Caser, and Augustus – to the extent to which it possessed this technology – chose to forgo.

The lack of technological innovation that characterized Roman society other than in fields related to engineering and construction (i.e., concrete, brick-making, roads, amphitheatres, aqueducts, and sewers) makes improbable the assessment of the economic historian, Mikhail Rostovtzeff, that even "in the early period of her history," Roman Italy "was not a poor country" (Rostovtzeff and Fraser 1926/1957: 9), a view echoed more recently by Peter Temin (2012: 2) who concluded that Romans "lived well as a result of extensive markets, comparative advantage, and technological change." Such conclusions run counter to not only logic, they are also at odds with most of the literary record from antiquity. Livy, in his *History of Rome from its Foundations*, for example, attributes early Roman success to thrift and a capacity to survive hard times. Of all of the societies with which Rome was acquainted, Livy (c.AD14a/1960a: 34) advised, "no country" was "free for so many generations from the vices of avarice and luxury" as Rome. "Indeed," Livy (c.AD14a/1960a: 34) continued, "poverty, with us, went hand in hand with content-ment." Of the Roman urban populace in the sixth century BC, Livy (c.AD14a/1960a: 105) declares them to be "a rabble of vagrants, mostly runaways and refugees" from nearby Etruscan cities. Even as Rome prospered the tradition that the society was foundered on poverty, thrift, and hard work remained deeply ingrained. Of Cato the Elder, typically held up as the firmest exponent of Roman values, Plutarch (c.100a/1999: 10) records that in the afternoons "he worked along-side his slaves, wearing in wintertime a labourer's toga and in the summertime no more than his underclothes; after work ... he sat down with his slaves, eating the same bread and drinking the same wine." By temperament, Romans were natural stoics, people willing to happily accept defeat and setback. It is thus hardly surpris-ing that the Roman world produced arguably the defining expression of Stoic philosophy in Seneca's *Letters from a Stoic*. For Seneca (c.AD70/1969: 48), as for the Romans as a whole, the ideal citizen was one "who refuses to allow anything that goes badly to affect him ... a mind that is 'invulnerable' and 'above all suffering'."

It is Rome's early poverty, and a common determination of the Roman citizenry to enrich themselves through war at their neighbor's expense, rather than any inherent riches, that are the best explanations for Rome's initial expansion. Rome was, Livy (c.AD14a/1960a: 54) observed, a society "founded by force of arms," a comment that at one and the same time acknowledged both its legendary creation at the hands of the Trojan hero, Aeneas, and the violence that accompanied its expansion. As early as the eighth century BC, Livy (c.AD14a/1960a: 56) records, Rome's neighbors "considered her not so much as a city as an armed camp in their midst threatening the general peace." The Greek historian, Polybius (c.150 BC/1979: 82), in his account of *The Rise of the Roman Empire*, emphasized a similar point, noting that, "in general the Romans rely upon force in all their undertakings." Of the economic logic of Roman warfare, Appian (c.AD120/1913: 7), a Greek historian from Alexandria, observed that as Rome "subdued" other peoples, it "used to seize a part of their lands and build towns there, or enrol colonists of their own to occupy those already existing." For, under the early Roman republic, access to the spoils of war provided financial windfalls for rich and poor alike. When an enemy was defeated some or all of its land was typically seized for Roman settlement. Often the defeated population was sold into slavery, the soldiery sharing in the resultant profits. Although the "treasury" of subject peoples was seized by the Roman state, rank-and-file soldiers retained the loot which they seized in the moment of victory. Even those not on active service benefited from military success, Livy (c.AD14a/1960a: 376) recording that in the wake of Rome's victory over the Etruscan city of Veii in 390 BC, the Senate granted "some three and a half acres of land from the estates of Veii to every plebeian – not the heads of the families only, but including in the number of recipients all free-born members of each household." Such a formula meant that a family of six was gifted 21 acres of land, a total that approximated the maximum area that was manageable for small-scale subsistence farming.

That Roman military expansion went hand-in-hand with the expropriation of the wealth of other societies, with evident benefits to both the Roman state and individual citizens, is clear. What is less clear is why Rome, initially little more than a collection of villages around Central Italy's Tiber river, was so much more successful in this task than its many enemies. It was in search of answers to this puzzle that Polybius (c.150 BC/1979: 41) directed his study of the republic in the second century BC, declaring in the book's introduction that:

> There can be surely nobody so petty or so apathetic in his outlook that he has no desire to discover by what means and under what system of government the Romans succeeded in less the fifty-three years in bringing under their rule almost the whole of the inhabited world, an achievement which is without parallel in human history.

By common consent, Rome's extraordinary success has been attributed to its unique system of constitutional checks and balances, a constitution which saw a Senate of aristocratic *patricians* oversee the state's executive officers (military leaders, magistrates, religious officials, etc.) while leaving the *plebeian* populace the capacity to veto senatorial actions, either through votes in the popular assembly or through the intervention of their political representatives, the "tribunes." In assessing this Roman system of checks and balances, Polybius (c.150 BC/1979: 317) concluded that, "it is impossible to find a better form of constitution that this." Certainly, the Roman capacity for internal political compromise ensured that, for centuries, the often severe stresses and strains of war were confronted without recourse to revolution,

Appian (c.AD120/1913: 7) accurately observing that until the late second century BC, "Internal discord did not ... bring them to blows ...The sword was never carried into the assembly." Another unique strength is found in the Roman willingness to extend citizenship to non-Romans on a large scale, a behavior which the Athenians, Spartans, and Corinthians of classical Greece would have regarded with incomprehension. Admittedly, the granting of citizenship appears to have originally acted as a form of forced population resettlement, a system whereby long-term Roman residents were relocated to conquered lands amidst their Latin enemies, passing on their way former enemies forced to settle in Rome. In describing this system's operation in 625 BC, Livy (c.AD14a/1960a: 71) records how, "Once again, thousands more Latins were given Roman citizenship and made to settle in the quarter [of Rome] where the Alter of Murcia stands." Once adopted as a principle for bringing former enemies within the Roman fold, however, citizenship was extended to an ever wider circle. Initially confined to Rome's Latin neighbors, and then to Italians, by the late Republic citizenship was being extended to supporters in the newly conquered provinces. Eventually, in AD212 under the Emperor Caracalla, citizenship was conferred on every legally free adult male resident within the Roman frontier. At this point, simply to live within the borders of Empire was sufficient qualification for the legal protection of citizenship, a protection extended without regard to ethnicity, race, or religion.

In modern representative democracies, the embrace of the Roman system of checks and balances is almost universal, not only in politics but also in business. In many democracies – Australia, the United States, France, Italy, to name a few – the "upper" parliamentary house, charged with oversight of both the executive and the elected popular assembly in the "lower" house, is given the nomenclature used in Rome: the Senate. Both houses are subject to popular scrutiny and, at regular intervals, re-election. Publicly listed businesses are subject to the same organizational principles. A board of directors, answerable to an annual vote of shareholders, oversees the executive officers who carry out the firm's day-to-day operations.

If in our modern world the acceptance of the constitutional principles of the Roman republic is almost unquestioned, in truth their Roman application – as is often typical with political compromises – merely covered over widening social and economic fissures, fissures which steadily undermined not only the constitution of the Roman republic but also the very social fabric upon which its success had been built. Whereas the armies of the early republic, the armies that defeated Hannibal and Carthage, were composed of a peasant soldiery fighting for their homelands, the ever increasing costs of war – and the growing availability of armies of slaves captured in war – eventually destroyed the precarious economics of small-scale farming. Yes, it is true, as we have previously observed, that the ordinary Roman citizen-soldier benefited from military victories. In addition to looted property, they regularly won the right to farm a few extra acres of land for themselves and their sons. It is also true that the mechanics of dry-land wheat cultivation allowed farmers and their sons a measure of seasonal leisure that could be devoted to warfare. But as the costs and duration of Rome's foreign wars became ever greater, the cost-benefit ratio increasingly worked against the small-scale citizen-farmer. As Keith Hopkins (1978: 4) has noted, "Over time, mass military service must have contributed to the impoverishment of many free Roman small-holders …Throughout the last two centuries BC there were commonly 100,000 Italians serving in the army, that is more than ten percent of the estimated adult male population." With the cost of war rising the Roman populace sought respite in a number of constitutional and legislative changes, each of which offered succor for a time. According to Livy (c.AD14a/1960a: 142), in 495 BC the popular assembly forced the Senate to accept the annual election of two "tribunes of the people," officials entrusted with the power of veto over judicial decisions and senatorial decree. At the same time, laws were passed making illegal the enslavement of citizens for unpaid debts. In 406 BC, soldiers were granted pay while on military service for the first time (Livy c.AD14a/1960a: 336). Under the tribunate of Gaius Gracchus (122–123 BC), a "dole" of grain was provided to Rome's urban poor at a subsidized price, a dole that was subsequently made free, becoming a unique feature of life in the capital (Appian c.AD120/1913: 21; Plutarch c.AD100a/1999: 104). None of these reforms, however, changed the economic and military dynamics of republican Rome. Indeed, some were soon regarded by the populace as having added to their plight. The payment of military wages while soldiers were away on ever longer campaigns forced, for example, the raising of a new tax. In pointing out the adverse effect of this impost, the tribunes cynically observed in 401 BC that, "the Senate's object in paying troops was simply to ruin by taxation those of the commons whom they failed to get butchered in the field" (Livy c.AD14a/1960a: 352).

At heart, republican Rome's very existence was founded on the implicit belief that a subsistence peasant economy could indefinitely sustain wars of foreign expansion. Inevitably, this implausible belief clashed with economic reality, triggering the series of conflicts that were to destroy the republic. According to the literary record (Plutarch c.AD100a/1999; Appian c.AD120/1913; Cassius Dio c.AD220/1914), the first of these crises was triggered in 134 BC when a young member of the senatorial class, Tiberius Gracchus, had cause to observe the economic state of the Italian countryside. As his brother, Gaius, recorded in a pamphlet cited by Plutarch (c.AD100a/1999: 89), "while Tiberius was travelling to Numantia through Etruria he saw the land had been abandoned, and how the only people framing or cultivating the land were slaves introduced from abroad." With the adult males in many peasant households away at war, "the rich," Appian (c.AD120/1913: 7) recorded, had been either seizing or buying up "their poor neighbors' allotments," allowing them to accumulate "vast tracts" which they operated "using slaves." Tiberius' solution to such problems was to return Rome to its peasant origins through a program of land redistribution. In advocating this program following his election as tribune in 133 BC, Tiberius is quoted as saying:

> The wild animals of our Italian countryside have their dens … Each of them a place of rest and refuge, but those who fight and die for Italy have nothing … Houseless and homeless they roam the land with their children and wives … These so-called masters of the world have not one clod of earth that they call their own.

The response of Rome's senatorial rich to Tiberius' program of land redistribution was public assassination. Tiberius and 300 of his supporters were beaten to death, their bodies thrown into the Tiber. When his brother, Gaius, attempted a similar reform program in 122–121 BC, he suffered a similar fate.

The fate of the Gracchi brothers reveals a fundamental fact about war and systems of representative democracy: the former has a tendency to destroy the latter. For, as Livy (c.AD14a/1960a: 54) noted in the early pages of his *History of Rome from its Foundations*, war has "no civilizing influence." A society that bases its relations with its neighbors on war and violence will, inevitably, become characterized by those same features in the conduct of its own internal affairs. In the case of Rome, the murder of the Gracchi heralded an era characterized by ever increasing levels of violence, resort to arms, and civil war; experiences which were to make the army the ultimate arbiter of political power in Rome. Of the Roman *plebeians*, Appian (c.AD120/1913: 27) observed that with the failure of the Gracchian reforms, they "lost everything," many reduced to perpetual reliance on the Roman "dole." In this reduced status, their only chance of betterment lay in full-time service in the legions which, under the so-called Marian reforms of the early first century BC, became the professional force of the modern popular imagination. When, between 91 BC and 88 BC, Rome's Italian allies rose in revolt due to the burdens imposed upon them, they were crushed by this newly professionalized force. Then, in 86 BC, the legions were for the first time unleashed against Rome itself as the architect of the army's professionalization, Gaius Marius, asserted his absolute authority. Of the resultant carnage, Plutarch (c.100a/1999: 164) records that, "Every street and every city was filled with people chasing and hunting down others . . . Headless bodies were tossed into the streets and trampled underfoot." When Marius' legions were evicted by those of Sulla another cycle of violence commenced. As Sulla addressed the Senate, his troops massacred 6000 opponents outside its doors. In the aftermath of this event, Plutarch (c.100a/1999: 208) cynically observes, "even the densest person in Rome came to understand that they had merely exchanged one monstrous tyranny for another."

Under Sulla's military successors – Pompey, Julius Caesar, Mark Anthony, Augustus – political violence and civil war became endemic. In the face of this new political reality, few were safe. Cicero, arguably the most articulate exponent of the Latin language that ever lived – and who declared in his study *On the Republic* that Roman success rested on "a moderation" in all things political (Cicero c.51 BC/2014: 76) – was butchered in 43 BC by supporters of Mark Anthony, his head and hands nailed to a platform in the Roman Forum. From this point onwards, it can be argued the Roman state existed to support the army, rather than the reverse applying. By the reign of Augustus, Hopkins (1978: 94, 29) estimates, almost half the imperial budget went on servicing the army. A further one-sixth of the budget went to the "dole" of grain (subsequently of bread) handed out to Rome's urban poor, a measure demanded both by their lack of access to gainful employment in a slave-dominated economy and their potentially explosive presence at the center of imperial power.

If it is Rome's slide into violence, civil war and, eventually, a permanent military dictatorship disguised behind the trappings of Empire, that has most fixated historians, this political transformation tends to detract attention from an equally significant economic and social transformation, a transformation which in the western half of the Empire saw peasant-based subsistence farming largely displaced by slave-operated estates, or *latifundia*. The economic dynamic that drove this transformation was vicious and self-reinforcing. Long-term military service undercut the viability of small-scale farms while, at the same time, bringing in armies of slaves to work the more commercially oriented *latifundia*. As Hopkins remarked of this dynamic, "Poor soldiers were engaged in capturing their own replacements."

There is no doubt that in the short to medium term, the slave-worked *latifundia* improved rural productivity, allowing a fewer number of farm workers to produce increased output. A number of factors contributed to this. First, unlike the chronically under-employed peasant farmers, who were busy only when their wheat was planted and harvested, the growing of a range of commercial crops (vineyards, olives, fruit orchards, vegetable gardens) allowed slave workforces to be deployed almost continually. Second, the importation of grain from the provinces allowed the *latifundia* to focus on higher value produce: meat, dairy produce, wine, and olives. Finally, large estates allowed for the application of rational economic principles directed towards profit-maximization. In outlining these principles, Cato the Elder (c.160 BC/1913: 25, 37) advised that on a well-run property "the old and sick slaves," "the old cattle" and "the worn out oxen" should be promptly sold off as they were "superfluous" to farm needs. Plutarch (c.AD100a/1999: 28–29), in his biography of Cato the Elder, also noted that, "A slave in Cato's house had to be either busy or asleep," and that any slip-shod work performances always resulted in a "beating" with "a leather strap."

Economically logical at the level of the individual *latifundia*, the managerial principles that Cato expounded mitigated against innovation and sustained gains in productivity. In the first instance, as Marc Bloch (1975: 6) noted, "The slave is a bad worker." Adam Smith, in *The Wealth of Nations* (1776: Book III, Chap. II, para. 10), made a similar point, declaring: "The experience of all ages and nations ... demonstrates that the work done by slaves, though it appears to cost only their maintenance, is in the end the dearest of any." The only motivation a slave has for working is the avoidance of punishment. Left unsupervised, many will do as little as possible. Once bought, a slave becomes perishable capital. In the ancient world, many had an unfortunate habit of dying before their purchase price could be recouped. The extensive use of slave labor also discouraged capital investment in machinery and the like, Cato (c.160 BC/1913: 22) informing the readers of his *De Agricultura* that a well-run farm was one in which "you find few tools," tools whose maintenance and replacement made a farm "expensive ...to operate." The displacement of peasant farmers also represented an attack on the manpower base of the legions who had advanced Rome's power. According to Hopkin's (1978: 68) estimates, the shift to slave-operated *latifundia* caused Italy's free rural population to fall from 4.1 to 2.9 million between 225 BC and 25 BC. As the pool of Italian recruits shrank, the legions were increasingly recruited from the provinces and, eventually, from the barbarian tribes from beyond the frontier.

Even in the short-to-medium term the ownership of slave-operated *latifundia* was no guarantee of capital gain. In the first century AD, for example, Pliny the Younger (c.AD90/1963: 106) informed a friend that he was considering purchasing an estate for "three million sesterces," adding: "It used at one time to be [worth] five million, but ... the general bad times have reduced the income from the land and brought down its value." Accordingly, Rome's senatorial elite sought to enrich themselves through a variety of often dubious speculative dealings. Of Cato the Elder, the most pious upholder of traditional Roman values, Plutarch (c.AD100a/1999: 29) observed that he "engaged in the most disreputable form of money-lending." He would also encourage his debtors to borrow more money so as to engage in risky shipping ventures, schemes in which Cato acted as a minor partner. If the venture succeeded, Cato gained all the profits, allowing his debtors to wipe away their accruals. If the venture failed, they were still in his debt. Cato also leant money to his more educated slaves so that "they could buy boys, train and educate them ... and then sell them a year later" at a profit to all concerned (Plutarch c.AD100a/1999: 29). Of Marcus Crassus, a political rival of Julius Caesar and the wealthiest Roman of his era, Plutarch (c.AD100b/2005: 112) recorded that, "public calamities were his principal source of revenue." Commanding gangs of slave fire-fighters, architects, and builders, Crassus "would buy up houses that were either on fire or near the scene of the fire," the panicked previous owners invariably letting "them go for next to nothing." If the fire was put out, Crassus achieved an immediate financial windfall. If they burnt down, he gained from ownership of a cheaply built replacement. Like Cato the Elder, Crassus was also a large-scale money-lender, his loans incurring a "heavy interest" charge after an initial interest-free period (Plutarch, cAD100b/2005: 113). For all Roman slave-owners, the common practice of allowing slaves to earn their own income, often through speculative ventures, so as to buy their own freedom was also financially remunerative. Not only did this practice act as a social safety-valve by offering slaves a way out of their condition, it also allowed owners to purchase new, younger slaves with the proceeds.

If the Roman elite indulged in an array of speculative practices, it is nevertheless the case that slaves and land remained the foundations of wealth in the late republic, circumstances that were to remain largely unchanged in imperial Rome. In the absence of high-productivity investment opportunities in manufacturing, the great bulk of wealth obtained from trade, money-lending, and real-estate speculation was eventually ploughed back into *latifundia*. Thus, when Pliny the Younger (c.AD90/ 1963: 106), in writing to his friend, Calvisius Rufus, informed him that although he had "some investments," it was nevertheless the case that "nearly all my capital is in land," he was articulating circumstances which were probably typical for someone of his economic standing. Indeed, rather than it being the case that the involvement of the Roman rich in money-lending added to the formation of a substantive financial sector, it arguably detracted from it. Most of the money lent by people such as Cato the Elder and Crassus would have been loaned to other members of the Roman elite, a practice that curtailed the need for formalized banking and credit. Pliny the Younger (c.AD90/1963: 106), for example, in outlining the means through which he could acquire the "three million sesterces" (an enormous sum) to buy a new estate, recorded that, "it will not be difficult to borrow. I can always have money from my mother-in-law." The problem with wealth obtained from speculative investments, moreover, is that one person's gain is typically another's loss. Similarly, where money was loaned for consumption rather than productive investments – as was often the case with elite money-lending in the late republic – there is little addition to productive wealth. The conspicuous wealth and success of someone like Crassus, therefore, typically came at the expense of members of the elite who found themselves sliding into debt. As Sallust (c.40 BC/1963: 184) recorded, late republican Rome was full of young senatorial aristocrats "who had squandered their inheritances in gambling-dens, pot-houses, and brothels." Growing desperate, in 68 BC a group of such individuals coalesced around a young senator called Catiline, who planned a revolutionary overthrow of the government and an abolition of debts. In outlining the need for revolution to his co-conspirators, Catiline is quoted as saying, "For us there is destitution at home and debts everywhere; misery now, and a still worse future to look forward to" (Sallust c.40 BC/1963: 190). Denounced by Cicero, Catiline, and his small army of supporters were crushed, fighting to the death to avoid capture. After the battle, Sallust (c.40 BC/1963: 233) records how members of Rome's elite came out to the battle-field and, "turning over the rebels' corpses, found friends, relatives, or men who had been their guests or their hosts." For all concerned, rich and poor alike, the financial and political dealings of the late Roman republic were not for the faint hearted.

The Failure of Empire

For management historians, the story of imperial Rome is best seen as one in which engineering and logistical prowess disguised underlying economic failure. Throughout the first century AD, and much of the second century AD, a number of bequests from the late republic tended to emphasize the former strength while masking the later. At the frontier the borders of Empire were more or less set, the loss of Varro's three legions in the Teutoburg forest in AD9 effectively ruling out a conquest of Germany. Under the empire only two significant additions were made to the imperial land mass, Britain and Dacia (Romania), both of which were of dubious economic and military value. Within the frontiers, the legions guaranteed acceptance (or at least acquiesce) of the *Pax Romana*. Only the Jewish population of Israel proved perpetually troublesome, rising in revolt in AD66–73 and AD132–AD136. With the bloody suppression of the latter revolt, a Jewish presence in Judea was effectively destroyed, not being re-established until the twentieth century. If internal peace allowed for an expansion of trade, interchange and urbanization these benefits were also fostered by the large store of currency – and gold and silver bullion – which the republican conquests had brought back into circulation. Under the imperial Caesars, only one major Mediterranean treasury remained to be looted: the Jewish Temple at Jerusalem. This oversight was redressed in AD70, when it too was duly sacked. As with the previous looting of Carthage, Athens, Syracuse, Corinth, and Alexandria, the pillaging of Jerusalem had a swift and profound monetary effect, Howgego (1992: 5) estimating that in the years after AD70 so much gold hit the market "that gold coin passed for half its usual value in terms of silver coin in Syria." Monetary stability was also guaranteed by Spain's silver mines, many of which had been inherited from Carthage. Roman conquests had also temporarily solved any labor problems, most particularly in the West. As noted previously, slaves comprised a third of Italy's population on the accession of Augustus (27 BC). The slave populations of Spain and southern Gaul (France) were probably of a similar magnitude. In Italy, the wealth of empire excused property owners from the land taxes that applied elsewhere, an amnesty that extended until the third century AD. Availability of slaves and avoidance of taxes underpinned the commercial success of the *latifundia*, Hopkins (1978: 106) noting that, "The new slave farms produced a surplus of marketable crops on land which had previously supported only peasants near the level of subsistence." An outflow of displaced Italian peasants, when combined with the settlement of army veterans at the end of their term of service, contributed to the Latinization of the western provinces, most particularly Gaul. Lyon, the Roman's Gallic capital, may have boasted a population of 100,000 by AD100, a population density only made possible by the provision of four water aqueducts (Braudel 1986/1990: 85–87).

The fundamental flaw in the Roman economic model is that it was premised on continuing military expansion. Once this stopped an existential crisis was inevitable. A predominately rural society, economic problems first manifested themselves on the agricultural front. By the early second century AD the commercial trade in slaves at the frontier – and a last mass influx of prisoners-of-war with the conquest of Dacia (Romania) – could no longer meet internal labor demand. This forced the *latifundia* to rely on domestically-bred slaves, a commodity which, as Jones (1956: 193) observed, "must in the nature of things be rather expensive articles." Although there remained much regional variation in slave prices, it is nevertheless evident that slave labor became increasingly scarce and expensive (Jones 1956; Duncan-Jones 1978; Anderson 1974). In consequence it is probable that agricultural output was already shrinking before the devastating Antoine Plague of AD165–AD180, a plague (almost certainly small-pox) associated with a mortality rate approaching 25 percent. As with the subsequent Black Death of the fourteenth century, the horrific toll of the Antoine Plague suggests a population that was already malnourished.

Problems on the labor supply front corresponded to growing monetary difficulties. As Anderson (1974: 82) remarked, the most significant effect of the Roman propensity to invest any spare capital in slave-operated *latifundia* was that it "tended to suffocate private commercial initiative and entrepreneurial initiative." Proof of this is particularly evident in mining, where there is little evidence of an active, private-sector engaged in large-scale exploration and development. Consequently, when long-worked Spanish mines were abandoned for various reasons at the end of the second century AD, there was – in the absence of any new treasuries to loot – a marked deficit of gold and silver. By AD250 the Roman denarius, once composed of almost pure silver, boasted a silver content of only 40 percent. Twenty years later the figure was four percent. This monetary crisis appears to have corresponded to a generalized collapse in mining output, analysis of Greenland's ice cores indicating a marked decrease in lead isotypes attributable to Roman atmospheric pollution from AD170 onwards (Wilson 2002).

Although historians will continue to debate the relationship between the steady collapse of the Roman economy and the invasions which temporarily drove in the frontiers in the early third century AD – i.e., were the invasions the cause of decline or merely a symptom of a degeneration already well underway? – what is clear is that by AD200 the Roman economy was increasingly incapable of supporting the army and state bureaucracy which held the keys to its future existence. Beset with unstable frontiers, a shrinking population and a diminished economic base, the imperial response was to increase the tax burden. Under the Emperor Diocletian, whose ascension to the imperial purple in AD286 stabilized the military situation, taxes were aligned to the land's estimated capacity. With the application of this formulae, the tax on property was by the fifth century some three times higher than what it had been under Augustus. Given the debasement of the currency, and the effective collapse of the monetary system, increased taxes were under Diocletian's *Cadastral Edict* of 301 largely set in kind (typically grain), changes that highlighted a generalized slide from a monetarized to a barter-based economy (Koerner 1941/1966: 26; Anderson 1974: 96). Under Diocletian's successor, the Emperor Constantine, another imperial edict forcibly tied landowners, and – more particularly – their tenants or *coloni* – to the land, an alteration that prefigured many of the features of what we think of as feudalism. Constantine's decree also made an array of urban crafts a hereditary obligation upon whose services the state had first call, a move that further stultified commerce and industry (Stevens 1941/1966: 115, 122).

As has proved the case in the modern world, the governmental attempt to salvage a grave financial crisis through increased taxation had negative long-term consequences. Across the empire what remained of a free peasantry did what they could to avoid the crippling new taxes. Some fled into the wilderness. Others, most particularly in Gaul, became rural bandits. More commonly, they willingly renounced their increasingly expensive freedom, placing both their families and their land under the control of powerful local landowners. In effect, the empire's peasantry consented to their own enserfment. For their part, the large landowners, finding such arrangements eminently satisfactory, also began transforming their slaves into tenants or sharecroppers, an arrangement that avoided the need for constant replenishment of their rural workforce through slave purchases. At the same time, imperial administrators were complicit in the widespread transfer of state-owned land into private hands, a measure designed to bring land that had lain fallow (due to a lack of workers) back into production. Even in Egypt, once an imperial preserve, virtually all agricultural land was in the hands of a few great landlords by the fifth century AD (Stevens 1941/1966: 121). Whereas in the late republic and early empire there were three principal forms of land ownership – small-scale peasant farms, slave-operated *latifundia,* and imperial property – by AD 400 there was effectively only one: the large landed estate worked by de facto serfs. In describing the experience of common humanity on these estates in the late fourth century, the Christian cleric, St John Chrysostom, recorded:

Who could be more oppressive than landlords? If you look at the way in which they treat their miserable tenants, you will find them more savage than barbarians. They lay intolerable and continual imposts upon men who are weakened with hunger and toil ... They use their bodies like asses and mules, or rather like stones, hardly letting them breathe (cited, Stevens 1941/1966: 123).

The Shattered Roman Legacy

In looking to the imperial Roman legacy, it is easy to perceive a continuum between the economy of the late Empire and that which characterized feudal Europe after the great Germanic *Volkerwanderung* that commenced at the end of AD406. There is certainly, in the case of Western Europe, much truth to such a conclusion. Yes, it is true, as Braudel (1986/1990: 98) observed of Roman Gaul, that it was "terribly wounded by the many barbarian raids, the looting, murder, rape, fire, manhunts, troop movements" that accompanied the final collapse of the western frontier. In Braudel's (1986/1990: 98) estimation, in northern and eastern France perhaps half the population perished as the result of these experiences, either directly or indirectly. However, in the highly Latinized areas of the western empire – Italy, Spain, southern France – the Germanic invaders had neither the capacity nor the interest in laying down a new social order. Rather, they were more intent in sharing the benefits of Rome's residual riches. In these areas, we *are* thus justified in seeing an essential continuum between the social and conditions of the late Empire and those which subsequently characterized Western feudalism. It is certainly wrong to perceive the old Latin elite as one rendered militarily and economically powerless by the Germanic invasions. Militarily, the vitality of the old elite, and their capacity to act in unison with the new Germanic populations, was indicated when in AD451 a combined Roman-Visigoth army inflicted a decisive defeat on the hordes of Attila the Hun at Châlons-sur-Marne in the French Champagne region.

If we can see a continuum between the social and economic patterns of the late empire and those of Western feudalism this is not the experience of North Africa, Egypt, the Balkans, and the Middle East. In these regions, profoundly different historical trajectories are evident, trajectories that were to shatter the unity of the Mediterranean world that had characterized Roman rule. In the Greek-speaking eastern sections of the empire, where slavery had never been as entrenched as it had been in the west, the eastern or Byzantine emperors made a determined effort to resurrect an independent and vibrant peasantry which could serve as the military backbone of revitalized armies. Under the reign of the Emperor Heraclius (AD610–641), these efforts involved the successful implantation of militarized peasant communities throughout the Byzantine Empire; communities granted land tenure, and excused from taxes, in exchange for military service. So buttressed, the eastern empire survived in its Balkan and Anatolian strongholds well into the second millennium AD, a Greek-speaking world characterized by a centralized bureaucratic state and an abiding commitment to its Orthodox Christian faith. By contrast, with the Arab conquests of the seventh century, the Middle East, Egypt, and North Africa were shorn from their previous interconnected relationship with Western Europe. For the next five centuries this Islamic world was, as Braudel (1987/1993: 73) observed, "the most brilliant civilization in the Old World." Although this new Islamic civilization acted as a trading partner to the Christian civilizations to its north and west, as well as an intermediary between Europe and the Far East, it also acted for almost a millennia as the West's greatest foe, engaged in an often deadly battle for dominance in the Mediterranean Basin.

The most significant, if most easily overlooked legacy, of Rome's failure is thus the shattering of a single Roman world and its replacement by three distinct, and often competing, cultural and economic entities: a politically fragmented and feudal Catholic Christendom in the West, a highly-centralized Byzantine civilization in eastern Europe and Anatolia, and an Islamic civilization in North Africa and the Middle East.

If a divided world is a legacy of Rome's failure, we are also stand in its debt in terms of a number of positive bequests. Arguably the most significant of these is urban life, the characteristic mode of existence in both the Greek and Roman worlds. Although cities and towns shrank in number and in population, they did not disappear. Nor did the interconnections between them perish, premises as they were on trade, the movement of people and the transmission of ideas. Indeed, in the politically fragmented conditions of Western Europe, urban centers were eventually to exert a cultural and economic autonomy far in excess of what had been possible under Rome. In all three of the civilizations that emerged from Rome's ruins, the towns and cities also found intellectual and economic sustenance from their association with the new religious faiths: Western Catholicism, Greek and Slavic Orthodoxy, and Islam. In each of these civilizations, the new religious institutions provided a permanent check on the authority of civil authority. In the West the defining exposition for this rival power is found in St Augustine's *The City of God,* a work in which St Augustine (c.430/1945: 1) argued that the "most glorious society" was the "city of God's faithful," a transnational society of believers. Admittedly, for many historians the transnational society to which St Augustine appealed is perceived as a negative rather than a positive development: a source of future bigotry, misogyny, and ill-spent wealth. Indeed, to Edward Gibbon (1776/ 1910: 430–431), in his *Decline and Fall of the Roman Empire*, Christianity was the principal cause of Rome's decline, a source of constant "error and corruption," and of intolerant bigotry, that destroyed "the religious harmony of the ancient world." In more recent times, the Marxist historian, Perry Anderson (1974: 91), has also attributed much of the blame for Rome's fall to Christianity, arguing that a "Christianization of the State" produced "a huge clerical bureaucracy" which the constrained resources of the imperial economy were incapable of supporting.

While it is difficult to accept Gibbons argument that Christianity was central to Rome's decline, given the deeply flawed structure of the Roman economy to which we have alluded, there is nevertheless a modicum of truth in the above allegations. One does not need to look far in the writings of the early church to find proof that the new faith saw women as occupying a subservient role, both inside and outside the family household. In St Paul's (c.AD61/1985: 1949) *Letter to the Colossians*, wives are instructed to "be subject to your husbands." Similarly, in this *First Letter to the*

Corinthians, Paul (c.AD57/1985: 1903) advised that "woman" was created "for the sake of man." This subservient role represented a retrograde step for women, given their legal rights under both the Roman republic and empire. As indicated in the letter of Pliny the Younger (c.AD90/1963: 106) which we cited earlier, within which Pliny indicated his intent to borrow three million sesterces from his mother-in-law, Roman women could hold substantial amounts of property in their own name. Roman women also had, as Mary Beard (2015: 307) accurately notes, "much greater independence" than was found in other ancient societies. Unlike women in classical Athens, who were expected to live their lives in household exclusion, Roman women dined with men, both before and after marriage. They also attended gladiatorial games and theatres, albeit in back row seats that were segregated from men. If the position of the relatively small cohort of urbanized, legally free women undoubtedly went backwards with Rome's decline, it is also true the various Christian denominations competed for increasingly scarce economic resources in the late empire. By the fifth century the western Catholic Church was, as Stevens (1941/1966: 122) recorded, "among the greatest" of "landlords," controlling vast swathes of countryside and armies of serfs; an outcome that was to become even more pronounced in Medieval Europe.

The fact that the Catholic Church became not only the holder of much property and wealth in the Late Empire, but also the principal institutionalized means through which the Roman legacy was transmitted to Medieval Europe (and thence to us), is indisputable. As such, the Church proved far less tolerant of intellectual diversity, rationality, and independent inquiry than either the Roman or Greek worlds of antiquity. By the fourteenth century, it had become arguably the greatest impediment to intellectual inquiry and the advance of knowledge. But it is also true that in Medieval Europe one was typically better off working land held by the Church, or one of its monastic orders, than if one was subject to a secular landlord. For, despite all their failings, the Church and its religious orders were, both in Eastern and Western Europe, virtually the sole representatives of literacy and learning in the post-Roman world. They acted as not only educators but also as the only form of social security, providing assistance to the widow, the sick, and the aged. It was to religious orders and Church scholars that we owe, moreover, the establishment of fundamentally new institutions for learning: universities. Female religious orders and monasteries also provided women in the post-Roman world with virtually their sole opportunity for an education, and a life outside the routines of marriage, birth, and child-raising. Although the Catholic Church was male-dominated, the scale and geographic reach of the female monastic movement should not be understated. As Graetzer and Rost (2015: 23) revealed in their extraordinary study of Catholic monasteries, we can identify 4606 monasteries that were established by the Catholic Church following the collapse of the western Empire. Of these, 1368 were female. Arguably, however, the most significant legacy which the Church transmitted to western Medieval Europe, albeit in a very different form, was the common sense of being part of a transnational community that bridged divisions of language and ethnicity. Under the Empire, one did not need to live in Rome or even Italy to be "Roman." Instead, being Roman implied sharing in a common culture based on laws, social norms, responsibilities, and allegiances. In the medieval world, this transnational identity – in part the bequest of Roman antiquity

8 Management in Antiquity: Part 2 – Success and Failure in the. . .   177

and in part a new creation – defined one as part of a new civilized identity: a "European." As Braudel (1987/1993: 315) observed of this new identity, in Medieval Europe a traveller, going about their business, "felt as much at home in Lübeck as in Paris, in London as in Bruges, in Cologne as in Burgos, Milan or Vince. Moral, religious and cultural values . . .were the same everywhere."

In considering Rome's legacy to the modern world, its intellectual bequests should not be understated. Our understandings of representative government, of organizational systems of checks and balances, and of the very concept of citizenship as a relationship based on legal rights and responsibilities – rather than, as the Greeks perceived it, as one rooted in geography and ethnicity – we owe to Rome. However, if we should not understate Rome's intellectual legacy, neither should we exaggerate its significance. In the final analysis, Rome was a failed civilization. Its failures were, overwhelmingly, managerial and economic. Its principal means of wealth creation was militarized theft, depriving other societies of not only their possessions but also their people. The Romans themselves well understood these facts, Tacitus (c.AD98/1942: 695) placing into the mouth of a British chieftain the following words: "Our goods and fortunes they [the Romans] collect for their tribute, our harvests for the granaries. Our very hands and bodies, under the lash and in the midst of insult, are worn down by the toil of clearing forests and morasses." A society based on such principles was never one that was going to be characterized by entrepreneurship, innovation, and the swift take-up of new technologies. In consequence, humanity's economic and social advance necessarily entailed Rome's ruination.

Conclusion

It is instructive that in his study of the *History of Civilizations* the great French social and economic historian, Fernand Braudel (1987/1993: 312), began his account of "the first European civilization" in the mid-fifth century AD, i.e., *after* the fall of the western Roman Empire. For Braudel (1987/1993: 313), "Feudalism built Europe," a society built around small-scale peasant farmers, working as share-croppers, tenants, or serfs. This was a world that was overwhelmingly rural in orientation, a society that literally dragged itself upwards from the ground, successfully redressing problems of agricultural productivity which confounded ancient Greece and Rome. For Braudel – concerned as he was with production, productivity, wealth creation, i.e., the issues which are central to management history – ancient Egypt, Greece, and Rome could be passed over with hardly a comment. For all the glory that was Greece, and the grandeur that was Rome, these were societies stuck in a doomed path. Seen from such perspective, the heavy wheeled-plough of Medieval Europe – which allowed Europe's peasantry to work the rich but heavy soils of the valley bottoms with comparative ease – was a greater achievement than the construction of the pyramids: the vainglorious project of the Egyptian pharaohs. There is some considerable merit in this approach. Few of the technological innovations upon which our modern industrial societies rest owe a debt to antiquity. Cast iron, mass-produced steel, magnetic compasses, windmills, artificial light and power, mechanical transport, paper, printing, vaccinations against disease, even the horse-stirrup, were unknown to the ancient world. Indeed, if Braudel can be faulted, it can be argued that his error rests not in his beginning the history of "European civilization" so late (i.e., in the AD450s), but in beginning it too early, i.e., with the history of European feudalism. For feudalism, one can argue, only proved marginally superior to antiquity in breaking out of the bounds imposed by a preindustrial existence. Certainly, modern management – understood, as Pollard (1965) perceived it, as a system of work that involves coordinating the employment of legally free individuals, whose efforts are directed towards the servicing of competitive markets – is no more a creation of feudalism than of antiquity. Rather, modern management is the child of the European Enlighten-ment, the product of rationality, science, and experimentation. Modern management, as most understand it, is also the product of free societies, of democracies, where the allocation of capital and labor cannot be achieved through mere decree. Its birthplace is thus found as much in the American and French Revolutions as in the Industrial Revolution of Great Britain. A seminal feature of these new forms of management – and of the new form of Western civilization which they helped create – is that, almost from the moment of it birth, it burst the bounds of its European cradle, becoming a truly global force. Far more than ancient Rome, it was based on national and regional specialization, and long-distance trade and commerce. No modern economy would survive for long without the benefits of long-distant trade in commodities, manufactured goods and services. Shanghai, Tokyo, Vancouver, and Sydney are in many ways the preeminent examples of this new world as much as London, Paris, and Amsterdam.

If one believes – as this author does – that the world of antiquity can tell us little about the efficacy of modern management practices, that all of its activities were doomed to end as dust, then this begs the obvious question: what, then, was this purpose of this endeavor, this account of management in antiquity? In part, the answer is a negative one, to emphasize the uniqueness of our modern world, a world whose prosperity does not primarily rest, as it did with ancient Rome, on slavery and the militarized theft of other societies' wealth. In itself, however, such a negative conclusion does a disservice to not only management history but also to scholarship and inquiry. As a management historian one is, arguably, more concerned with history, with the nature of the human condition, than with "management" narrowly defined. In looking to antiquity, and most particularly to ancient Greece and Rome, their great intellectual strength – a strength that every subsequent scholar has drawn on, to a greater or lesser degree – lay in their search for the true cause of things. As Plato (380 BC/2003: 277) observed in his *The Republic*, "Societies aren't made of sticks and stones." Instead, they are comprised of people "whose individual charac-ters, by turning the scale one way or another, determine the direction of the whole." To Plato – as to Thucydides, Livy, Plutarch, Cicero, Seneca, and the other scholars of antiquity who inform the modern intellectual tradition as much as that of antiquity – the foundations of knowledge are found in the commonalities of human responses to similar problems. For Livy (c.AD14a/1960a; c.AD14b/1960b), justification for his *History of Rome from its Foundation* was found in understanding the ways in which a society was molded though constant warfare. For Polybius (c.150 BC/1979: 41), his study into *The Rise of the Roman Empire* was guided by a search for the best "system of government." For Seneca, as for Romans more generally, the key to success was found within the individual psyche, in personal resilience. As Seneca (c.AD70/1969: 51) put it, "The supreme idea does not call for any external aids, it is home-grown, wholly self-developed." The enduring relevance of a study of antiquity, and most particularly the Greco-Roman world, is thus found in the questions which they asked, rather than necessarily the answers which they provided.

The relevance of classical studies is also found in the principles for historical inquiry which the ancients spelt out. If this author had to nominate the greatest historical work ever written, I would without hesitation nominate Thucydides' *History of the Peloponnesian War*. Like the greatest work of literature in the human experience, Homer's *The Iliad*, Thucydides' history is a human tragedy, a study of political overreach and vanity. As Thucydides (c.411 BC/1954: 48) lamented, "Never before had so many cities been captured and then devastated . . .; never had there been so many exiles; never such loss of live." In investigating the circumstances and, more importantly, the causes of this tragedy, Thucydides (c.411 BC/1954: 48) – unlike the postmodernist tradition in modern business schools, which sees all accounts as "fictive" (Rowlinson et al. 2014; Munslow 2015) – believed there was a "truth . . .to discover." The key to discovering this truth, Thucydides (c.411 BC/1954: 48) appreciated, is to look beyond the inevitable "partiality" of historical actors, a partiality that causes "different eye-witnesses to give different accounts of the same events." That the discovery of truth is no easy task, involving as it does the cross-checking of evidence "with as much thoroughness as possible," Thucydides (c.411 BC/1954: 48) well appreciated. But such difficulties, Thucydides (c.411 BC/1954: 48) believed, do not excuse inaccuracies in "factual reporting." Nor do they justify the view that all evidence is merely subjective, the expression of some particular power interests. For the job of the scholar, today just as much as in Thucydides' time, is to look beyond power interests – of which there were aplenty of Thucydides' day – to the nature of the human condition. This is the ultimate, and enduring, message of antiquity.

Cross-References

▶ Intellectual Enlightenment: The Epistemological Foundations of Business Endeavor
▶ Management in Antiquity: Part 1 – The Binds of Geography
▶ What Is Management?

References

Anderson P (1974) Passages from antiquity to feudalism. New Left Books, London
Appian (c.AD120/1913) The Civil Wars: Book 1, Loeb Classical Library, http://penelope.uchicago.edu/Thayer/E/Roman/Texts/Appian/Civil_Wars/1*.html. Accessed 7 Feb 2019
Aristotle (c.330a BCE/1941) Metaphysics. In: McKeon R (ed) The basic works of Aristotle. Random House, New York, pp 681–934
Aurelius M (c.AD 170/2006) Meditations. Penguin Classics, London

Beard M (2015) SPQR: a history of ancient Rome. Profile Books, London

Bloch M (1975) Slavery and Serfdom in the middle ages. University of California Press, Berkeley

Braudel F (1946/1990) The Mediterranean and the Mediterranean world in the age of Philip II, vol 2. Harper Torchbooks, New York

Braudel F (1977) Afterthoughts on material civilization and capitalism. John Hopkins University Press, Baltimore

Braudel F (1986/1990) The identity of France: people and production. Fontana Press, London

Braudel F (1987/1993) A history of civilizations. Penguin Books, Harmondsworth

Carcopino J (1940) Daily life in ancient Rome: the people and the city at the height of empire. Yale University Press, New Haven and London

Carlyle T (1840/2013) On heroes, hero-worship and the heroic in history. Yale University Press, New Haven

Cartledge P (1977) Hoplites and heroes: Sparta's contribution to the technique of ancient warfare. J Hell Stud 97:11–27

Cato M (c.160 BC/1913) De agricultura. In: Virginian Farmer A (ed) Roman farm management: the treatises of Cato and Varro. Macmillan, New York, pp 19–50

Cicero MT (c.51 BC/2014) On the republic. In: Cicero MT (ed) On the republic/on the laws. Cornell University Press, Ithaca

Cipolla CM (1981) Before the Industrial Revolution: European society and economy, 1000–1700, 2nd edn. Routledge, London

Dio C (c.AD220/1914) Roman history. 9 vols. William Heinemann, London

Duncan-Jones RP (1978) Two possible indices of the purchasing power of money in Greek and Roman antiquity. Publications de l'Ecole Francasie de Rome 37(1):159–168

Feldman LII (1986) How much Hellenism in Jewish Palestine? Hebr Union Coll Annu 57:83–111

Fraschetti A (ed) (2001) Roman women. University of Chicago Press, Chicago

Ganshof LF, Verhulst (1941/1966) Medieval agrarian society in its prime. In: Postan MM (ed) The Cambridge economic history of Europe, vol 1. Cambridge University Press, Cambridge, pp 340–659

Gardner JF (1986/1991) Women in Roman law and society. Indiana University Press, Bloomington and Indianapolis

Gibbon E (1776/1910) Decline and fall of the Roman Empire, vol 1. J.M. Dent & Sons, London

Graetzer G, Rost K (2015) Structural effects of sex-ratios and power distribution on the survival rates of female monasteries. Paper presented to the Academy of Management Annual Meeting, Vancouver, https://www.researchgate.net/publication/291365800_Structural_Effects_of_Sex-Ratios_and_Power_Distribution_on_the_Survival_Rates_of_Female_Monasteries. Accessed 19 Feb 2019

Hengel M (1969/1974) Judaism and Hellenism: studies in their encounter in Palestine during the early Hellenic period, 2 vols. Wipf & Stock Publishers, Eugene

Hengel M (1980) Jews, Greeks and barbarians: aspects of the Hellenization of Judaism in the pre-Christian period. Fortress Press, Philadelphia

Hopkins K (1978) Conquerors and slaves. Cambridge University Press, Cambridge

Howgego C (1992) The supply and use of money in the Roman world 200 BC to AD 300. J Roman Stud 82:1–31

Jonah (c.300BC/1985) The old testament. In: The new Jerusalem bible. Darton, Longman and Todd, London, pp 1541–1543

Jones AHM (1956) Slavery in the ancient world. Aust Econ Hist Rev 9(2):185–199

Koerner R (1941/1966) The settlement and colonization of Europe. In: Postan MM (ed) The Cambridge economic history of Europe, vol 1. Cambridge University Press, Cambridge, pp 1–91

Livy (c.AD14a/1960a) The early history of Rome: Books I–V of the history of Rome from its foundations. Penguin Classics, Harmondsworth

Livy (c.AD14b/1960b) Rome and Italy: Books VI–X of the history of Rome from its foundations. Penguin Classics, Harmondsworth

Luke (c.AD65/1985) The new testament: Luke's Gospel. In: The new Jerusalem bible. Darton, Longman and Todd, London, pp 1686–1733

Maccabees 2 (c.160 BC/1985) The old testament. In: The new Jerusalem bible. Darton, Longman and Todd, London, pp 718–746

Meikle S (2002) Modernism, economics and the ancient economy. In: Schiedel W, von Reden S (eds) The ancient economy. Routledge, New York, pp 233–250

Mogetta M (2015) A new date for concrete in Rome. J Roman Stud 105:1–40

Munslow A (2015) Managing the past. In: McLaren PG, Mills AJ, Weatherbee TG (eds) The Routledge companion to management and organizational history. Routledge, London and New York, pp 129–142

Plato (380 BC/2003) The republic. Penguin Classics, London

Pliny G (c.AD90/1963) Letter to Calvisius Rufus. In: Pliny G (ed) The letters of the Younger Pliny. Penguin Classics, Harmondsworth

Plutarch (c.AD100a/1999) Roman lives. Oxford University Press, Oxford.

Plutarch (c.AD100b/2005) Fall of the Roman Republic, revised edition. Penguin Classics, London

Pollard S (1965) The genesis of modern management: a study of the Industrial Revolution in Great Britain. Edward Arnold, London

Polybius (c.150 BC/1979) The rise of the Roman empire. Penguin Classics, London

Roberts JM (2007) The new Penguin history of the world, 5th edn. Penguin Books, London

Rostovtzeff M, Fraser PM (1926/1957) The social and economic history of the Roman Empire, 2nd edn. Clarendon Press, Oxford

Rowlinson M, Hassard J, Decker S (2014) Research histories for organizational history: a dialogue between historical theory and organization theory. Acad Manag Rev 39(3):250–274

Saller R (2002) Framing the debate over growth in the ancient economy. In: Schiedel W, von Reden S (eds) The ancient economy. Routledge, New York, pp 251–269

Sallust (c.40 BC/1963) The Jugurthine war. In: Sallust (ed) The Jugurthine war/the conspiracy of Catiline. Penguin Books, Harmondsworth, pp 35–148

Seneca (c.70AD/1969) Letter CVII. In: Seneca (ed) Letters from a stoic. Penguin Classics, Harmondsworth

Smith A (1776) An inquiry into the nature and causes of the wealth of nations. W. Strahan and T. Cadell, London

St Augustine (c.AD430/1945) The city of god, vol 1. Everyman's Library, London

St Paul (c.AD57/1985) First letter to the Corinthians. In: The new Jerusalem bible. Darton, Longman and Todd, London, pp 1891–1911

St Paul (c.AD61/1985) Letter to the Colossians. In: The new Jerusalem bible. Darton, Longman and Todd, London, pp 1945–1950

Stevens CE (1941/1966) Agriculture and rural life in the later Roman Empire. In: Postan MM (ed) The Cambridge economic history of Europe, vol 1. Cambridge University Press, Cambridge, pp 92–124

Suetonius (c.AD130/1957) The twelve Caesars. Penguin Classics, Harmondsworth

Tacitus (c.AD98/1942) The life of Cnaeus Julius Agricola. In: Tacitus (ed: Hadas M) Complete works of Tacitus. The Modern Library, New York, pp 677–706

Temin P (2012) The Roman market economy. Princeton University Press, Princeton

Thucydides (c.411 BC/1954) The history of the Peloponnesian war. Penguin Classics, Harmondsworth

Van Wees H (2011) Demetrius and draco: Athens' property classes and population in and before 317 BC. J Hellenic Stud 131:95–114

Vessey M (2007) Introduction. In: St Augustine (ed) Confessions. Barnes & Noble Classics, New York

Wansbrough H (1985) Introduction to the synoptic Gospels. The new Jerusalem bible. Darton, Longman and Todd, London, pp 1599–1608

Wilson A (2002) Machines, power and the ancient economy. J Roman Stud 92:1–32

From Feudalism to Modernity, Part I: Management, Technology, and Work, AD 450–1750

9

Bradley Bowden

Contents

Feudalism: An Historic Peculiarity	187
Medieval and Early Modern Europe: A Comparative Perspective	192
Medieval and Early Modern Life: The World of Production	196
Medieval and Early Modern Life: Commerce, Finance, and Trade	202
Conclusion	210
Cross-References	212
References	212

Abstract

In assessing managerial practices in the pre-modern world, one needs to maintain a sense of balance, to neither understate nor overstate the level of advancement. In looking at the achievements of Western and Southern Europe prior to 1750, for example, it is evident that many of the underpinnings of modern management were well established. Double-entry bookkeeping gave firms a better understanding of their costs, at least where they were desirous of such understandings. Mechanical clock allowed maritime officers the ability to calculate longitude, a feat that made oceanic commerce a feasible proposition. Mechanical printing opened the door to mass literacy. Despite such achievements, however, Western Europe had few of the attributes of "modern management" prior to 1750. There were no mass markets. In the early 1600s, the carrying capacity of Europe's entire maritime fleet (600,000–700,000 tons) was miniscule, equating to that of four modern "Capex" ships. In the absence of mass markets, there was little competition, allowing producers a capacity to charge high prices with little regard to costs. Capital intensity was low. Most "capital" equipment – ships, spinning wheels, weaving frames – was made of wood. Easily destroyed, such

---

B. Bowden (✉)
Griffith Business School, Griffith University, Nathan, QLD, Australia
e-mail: b.bowden@griffith.edu.au

© The Author(s), under exclusive licence to Springer Nature Switzerland AG 2020
B. Bowden et al. (eds.), *The Palgrave Handbook of Management History*,
https://doi.org/10.1007/978-3-319-62114-2_101

183

"investments" seldom endured. In the absence of a substantial stock of capital, the living standards of most were abysmal. Ultimately, only Britain proved capable of breaking the bonds of the pre-modern world. By exploiting its limitless reserves of coal, Britain turned a world of wood into a world of iron: a world of iron-ships, railways, mass markets, competition, and modern forms of management.

Keywords

Industrial Revolution · feudalism · energy · coal · European living standards · Asian living standards · real wages

The purpose of this chapter is to explore the extent to which modern management, with all its attendant material and social benefits, owes a debt to the feudal and early modern eras. Like many aspects of management history, the relationship between the experiences of these past epochs and the modern era (c.1750–) is complex. In the second chapter of this *Palgrave Handbook of Management History*, I (▶ Chap. 2, "What Is Management?") made the case that "modern management" is fundamentally different from that which exists in either pre-industrial or totalitarian societies in that it possesses five attributes which are either partially or totally absent in the latter: attention to costs, firm specialization, the gearing of production to mass markets, legal protection of property and individual liberty, and the free movement of capital and, more particularly, labor. In writing this chapter, I do not withdraw from this stance. It is nevertheless the case that modern management was, in the first instance, a product of the societies of Western Europe and North America. It is difficult to avoid the conclusion, therefore, that these societies possessed attributes that fostered the emergence of modern management. It is certainly the case that by the Middle Ages a form of commercial capitalism was enjoying a robust existence. For, by the thirteenth century, as North and Thomas (1973: 29) correctly observed, the Mediterranean had become "a gigantic highway for Italian merchant vessels." By the seventeenth century, the broad stretches of the Atlantic Ocean were also a Western highway; a highway plied by the fleets of Portugal, Spain, France, the Netherlands, and Britain. This flourishing of trade and commerce revolutionized not only the social structure of Europe but also its intellectual orientation. As the French philosopher, Voltaire (1734/2002: 36), observed, "A trading society ... grasps at every society."

If the transformative effects of commerce and trade in the medieval and early modern eras are indubitable, it is nevertheless important to remind ourselves of the abject poverty in which most Europeans lived prior to the Industrial Revolution. As Cipolla (1981: 31–32) recorded, "Peasants were always clothed in rags ...During epidemics of plague ... people waited for others to die to take their clothes." It is certainly the case that, when we shift our attention from the world of commerce to the lived work experiences of ordinary citizens, it is evident that even the most successful European societies were incapable of delivering sustained improvements in living standards. This failure is evidenced in the so-called Phelps Brown-Hopkins index, which traced the real wage of a skilled building worker from southern England between 1264 and 1954, measured against a basket of consumables. As is evident in Fig. 1 – which summarizes the results of this index for the period 1264 to 1880 (1447 representing 100 in the index) – it is evident that the only sustained improvement in living standards prior to the Industrial Revolution occurred between 1350 and 1500. Significantly, this improvement corresponded not to any gain in efficiency but rather to a demographic catastrophe induced by bubonic plague: the Black Death. For those who "benefited" from this catastrophe there was probably little in the way of rejoicing as the traumatized survivors rebuilt their lives among half-abandoned fields. Moreover, as the population regained its former strength an increased competition for scant resources drove living standards to unprecedented depths. According to Phelps Brown and Hopkins (1956: 306), the real wage of the skilled English building worker reached an all-time low in 1597, the year in which Shakespeare's *Midsummer Night's Dream* was first performed. Not until 1880 did the real wage of the skilled English building worker return to "the level enjoyed at the accession of Henry VIII" (i.e., 1510).

The inability of early modern societies to go beyond a seemingly fixed ceiling is also indicated in Fig. 2, which traces the per capita output of Holland, central and northern Italy, Portugal, and Spain between 1500 and 1750, measured in United States "international dollars," based on 1990 dollar values (i.e., so-called Geary-Khamis dollar). As is evident, these societies – each of which for a period stood at the cutting edge of European advancement – were, on a per capita basis, generally less prosperous in 1750 than previously (Palma and Reis 2019).

The fact that even Holland, the Netherland's most prosperous province, failed to break through a seemingly fixed economic ceiling leads us to the most fundamental question of this whole series, namely: Why was it that England, alone of all the

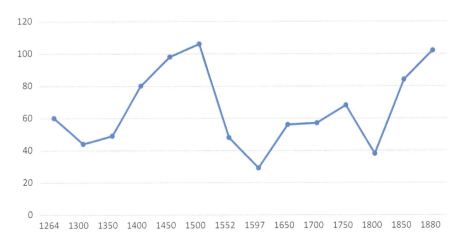

Fig. 1 Real wage of skilled building worker in southern England, 1264–1880 (1447 = 100). (Source: Phelps Brown and Hopkins: "Seven centuries of . . . builders' wage rates", Appendix B)

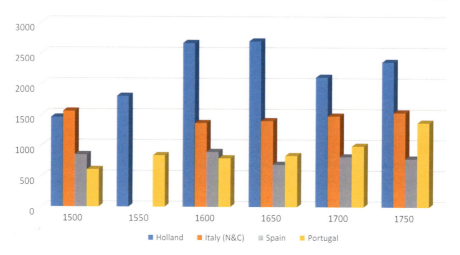

Fig. 2 Output per capita in US dollars (1990 value), 1500–1750 – Holland, northern and central Italy*, Portugal, and Spain*. (Source: Palma and Reis, "From Convergence to Divergence", Table 4. *Note: no figures for northern and central Italy or for Spain for 1550)

world's societies, led the way in forging a new chapter in human existence through the Industrial Revolution?

In searching for an answer to the above question – and explanation as to why it was that the economic progress of other European cities plateaued out after hitting an invisible ceiling – we are brought to a vital but easily overlooked fact: pre-industrial societies are almost always built on wood; wood used for housing, shipbuilding, smelting of ores, and – above all – domestic cooking and heating. In *every* advanced society, not only those of European extraction, there came a point in time where the supply of wood wilted in the face of insatiable demand. In China, it is estimated that in 1100 the per capita output of iron easily exceeded that subsequently obtained by Europe in 1700. But, by this stage, the Chinese southern rice region – the driver of increases in both population and iron output – had become "a great clear-felled zone," virtually devoid of trees (Jones 1987: 4). As Europe's material wealth advanced a similar assault on the native forests occurred, causing a marked spike in timber prices. In Genoa the price of lumber used for shipbuilding rose 12-fold between 1463–1468 and 1577–1578. An even graver crisis loomed in terms of charcoal, the wood-derived product which acted as a key ingredient in iron making. In England, the price of charcoal rose tenfold between the 1530s and the 1690s, eventually becoming all but unattainable (Cipolla 1981: 288). By the sixteenth century, the growing scarcity of charcoal – and the lack of an obvious substitute – confronted Europe with the same crisis that had previously halted Chinese industrial development.

The reason that England alone overcame the heating and smelting bottleneck that had confounded Chinese society is found in the fact that England alone had ready access to cheap supplies of easily transported coal. As early as the mid-1500s, the mines that abutted the Tyne and Wear rivers of Durham were producing 781,000 tons per year: a stupendous total by early modern standards. By the 1680s, annual coal production exceeded 3.1 million tons (Neff 1932a/1966: 19). In reflecting on this unprecedented production, the English historian, John Nuf 1932b/1966: 322), noted that by 1700, "The entire production of the rest of the world did not perhaps amount to much more than a sixth of that of Great Britain." Whereas the growth of other European cities was constrained by a shortage of wood for cooking and heating, English cities grew exponentially. The vast fleet of colliers that transported England's "sea coals" also provided the basis for English maritime prowess. As one seventeenth century contemporary remarked, the coal trade was the principal "nursery and school of [English] seamen" (cited, Cipolla 1981: 290). The English coal trade also acted as a "fertile ground" for new "capitalist forms of industrial organization" (Neff 1932b/1966: 322). As England's mines became progressively deeper, eventually operating beneath the water table, ever more radical innovations were demanded. Accordingly, in 1712 the world's first functional steam engine – the so-called Newcomen engine – began pumping water from a pit in the English Midlands. By 1750, this innovation was commonplace across the entire industry.

Inevitably, the European revolution in technology and managerial organization involved a transformation in the realm of ideas as much as in any other fields. In looking to the factors that both advanced and impeded technological and managerial progress in the medieval and early modern eras this *Palgrave Handbook of Management History* must, therefore, look not only to matters relating to production and exchange. We also need to examine the ferment of ideas that shaped improvement and regression. In this chapter, however, our attention will be largely restricted to the material elements of advance and regression. Discussion of the ideas that shaped the feudal and early modern worlds, be they religious or profane, is the focus of the subsequent chapter, *From Feudalism to Modernity, Part II: The Revolution of Ideas, AD 450 to 1750.*

Feudalism: An Historic Peculiarity

In looking for the roots of modern management, and hence the modern world, it is tempting to pass over the period between the fifth and fifteenth centuries as a long Dark Age, a millennium of stagnation and superstition. Yet, just as the modern era cannot be understood apart from the preceding early modern era (c.1500–1750), so the early modern period cannot be comprehended apart from the feudal epoch that preceded it. The moment we begin to examine "feudalism" as it existed in Western Europe between the tenth and fifteenth centuries, however, we are confronted with serious problems. For, as Bloch (1940/1962: xviii) observed in his classic study, *Feudal Society*, the use of the term feudalism "to designate a state of society" only gained traction during the eighteenth century. In its original form, the French term *féodal* simply referred to "that which concerns the fief," or *feodum*. It is also the case, as the British Marxist, Perry Anderson (1974: 154) noted, that feudalism "never existed in a 'pure state' anywhere in Europe." Indeed, many European societies never experienced the classic Western model of feudalism, in which power was distributed between princely states, feudal lords, commercial towns, and the Catholic Church. Even during the High Middle Ages (1100–1340), when the authority of the papacy was at its peak, there were, for example, many Europeans who worshipped in a mosque rather than a church. Until the late fifteenth century, much of Spain owed allegiance to Muslim emirs. Communities in Albania, Bosnia, and Kosovo permanently switched allegiance to Allah. Where Christian belief was maintained in Eastern Europe, the faithful typically looked to the Orthodox Patriarchs and Metropolitans of Constantinople or Moscow for direction instead of Rome. The cultural roots of these Orthodox societies owed much to the Greek-speaking Byzantine Empire; traditions that placed emphasis on communal solidarity and allegiance to the state to which one belonged. In Russia, this heritage produced, as Delanty (2019: 81) notes, "a distinct European inheritance" that caused it to experience "a different historical path to modernity from that in the West."

Given such complexities, how can one understand the term "feudalism," in ways that contribute to our understanding of management history?

Like many terms used to describe an historical experience, feudalism in the classic sense (i.e., as it existed in Western Europe c.1100) is perhaps best understood by delineating what it was not. First and foremost, we need to comprehend the fact that feudalism, as it existed in the High Middle Ages, was *not* based on the private landed wealth. On the contrary, as North and Thomas (1973: 63) accurately noted, "Feudal law did not recognize the concept of land ownership." For private property implies rights not only of ownership but also an ability to buy and sell at one's discretions. And the capacity to buy and sell implies the existence of a monetarized economy, something which was the very antithesis of feudal society. For feudalism involves, in essence, the replacement of *property* relationships – which can be expressed in monetary terms – with *personal* relationships. As such it bears passing resemblance to tribal kinship relationships. It differs from the latter, however, in that feudal relationships are based not on kinship but rather on the social obligations implied in the term *vassalage*. Under a vassalage relationship, occupancy of a given patch of land is not an inalienable right. Instead, it is something that has to be continually earned through service.

Rather than representing a "natural" form of social organization for an agricultural society, European feudalism is a historical peculiarity. It differs markedly from the societies of antiquity, which were characterized by a free peasantry (the classic Greek city-state, early republican Rome), slavery (Imperial Rome), or priestly bureaucracies (Mesopotamia, Pharaonic Egypt). What then explains the emergence of this historic peculiarity and its long hold on the European landscape and imagination? A good place to start is the system of serfdom as it existed in the late Roman Empire. In describing this system in ▶ Chap. 8, "Management in Antiquity: Part 2 – Success and Failure in the Hellenic and Roman Worlds," this author recorded that,

9 From Feudalism to Modernity, Part I: Management, Technology, and Work... 189

> Whereas in the late republic and early empire there were three principal forms of land ownership – small-scale peasant farms, slave-operated latifundia and imperial property – by AD 400 there was effectively only one: the large landed estate worked by de facto serfs.

What needs to be emphasized in relationship to the above circumstances is that what we are describing is *not* feudalism, even if it represents a step in that direction. For what we are dealing with in the late Roman Empire still represents a system of private ownership, governed by Roman law. The same finding applies, albeit with less force, to the situation that prevailed in the Merovingian kingdom (c. AD 450–751) that came to dominate Western Europe after the fall of the Western Roman Empire. The case for an essential continuum between the late Roman and Merovingian periods was made with particular vigor by the noted Belgium historian, Henri Pirenne. As Pirenne (1939: 116, 76) expressed it:

> ...the economic life of the Roman Empire was continued ... The great Gallo-Roman or Hispano-Roman or Italo-Roman estates survived ...The commercial activities of the Mediterranean continued with singular persistence.

In Pirenne's opinion it was not the Germanic invasions of the fifth century that destroyed the commercial and economic fabric of Roman life but rather the Muslim conquests of the seventh century. By closing the Mediterranean to European shipping, Pirenne argued, Islam destroyed the unity and cohesion of the Mediterranean world. In consequence, Pirenne (1939: 197) argued, "The urban life which had been maintained by the influence of commerce was obliterated ...It was the beginning of the Middle Ages" (Pirenne 1925/1952: 47).

Few, if any, historians would now support Pirenne's thesis that the fatal blow to the old Roman economy was delivered by the Islamic closure of the Mediterranean (see, for example, Davis 1970; North and Thomas 1973; Braudel 1986/1990). For at no point did the Mediterranean become an Islamic lake. Instead, Muslim fleets continued to face opposition from the Byzantine navy. Due to the latter's efforts, the Adriatic remained a Christian preserve, allowing trade between the emergent city-state of Venice, Constantinople, and the East. It would thus appear that Pirenne confused cause and effect. In other words, it was not the curtailment of Mediterranean commerce that caused the decline in monetary exchange, urbanization and a market economy. Rather, it was a collapsing economy that lay behind a collapse in Mediterranean commerce even before Islam arrived on the scene.

Although there is dispute among historians as to how Western Europe came to be feudal, it is nevertheless evident that, by the close of the Carolingian era (c. 780–900), Europe no longer bore much resemblance to the world of Roman antiquity. Everywhere, trade, commerce, and industry were a shadow of their former selves. Even in formerly prosperous areas, as Bloch (1940/1962: 60) noted in his classic study, "The most important towns had no more than a few thousand inhabitants," outside of which "spread forests, scrub and dunes – immense wildernesses." Despite the valiant efforts of the first Carolingian monarch, the Emperor Charlemagne (King of the Franks, 768–814) to establish a new silver currency, the denarii (dollar), monetarized exchanges became ever rarer. It was in this context of demographic and monetary collapse that feudalism took shape. As we have noted previously, the essence of feudalism involved the substitution of monetary and property relationships with personal relationships. Unable to pay the armored knights who had become the decisive factor in battlefield success, the Carolingian monarchs opted to give their military retainers the usage of a parcel of the royal estate in exchange for their services. The more powerful feudal lords, in turn, offered a share of this gifted estate to lesser knights in return for pledges of allegiance. Serfs, in providing labor and a share of their crop to their feudal lords, gained a modicum of military protection.

If we look to the core social and economic relationships that underpinned feudalism in the rural sector – where 90% of the population lived – it is evident that we are looking at a society of a primitive nature. Even in the best of times, people lived under threat of starvation. That this problem was well understood by the population of the time can be garnered from the fact that much of the population never married and reared families. If they did marry, they did so at a comparatively advanced age. In the English village of Croydon, for example, the average age at which women married in sixteenth and early seventeenth century was 27 (Cipolla 1981: 154). Among both men and women, a not insignificant share of the population escaped the burdens of family through life in a monastery. As Burckhardt (1867/1954: 349) observed, "Everybody has some cowled or frocked relative." For rich and poor alike, death was everywhere. Writing in 1762, at the dawn of the modern era, the French philosopher, Jean-Jacques Rousseau (1762/1979: 47) recorded, "Almost all of the first age is sickness and danger. Half the children perish before the first year."

Given the generalized poverty of Western feudalism, it is easy to perceive not only the society but its historical legacy in negative tones. This is the path taken by the Foucauldian-inclined Edward Said in his influential study, *Orientalism*. For Said (1978/2003: 71), the early feudal era was not only a time when "Europe was shut in on itself." It also marked the point when Europe first identified itself in opposition to the hostile (Muslim) "Other." By constantly defining itself against the "Other," Said (1978/2003: 12) argued, Europe set itself on a path of racial hostility to other cultures. Superficially, support for Said's view is easy to garner. For, at the intellectual core of most feudal societies was a deeply held religious faith, a sense of being part of the community of Christendom. As Greengrass (2014: xxvii) accurately observes: "Baptism was a universal rite of initiation." Yet, despite a long series of wars, most particularly the Crusades (1095–1291), the interactions between Christendom and the Muslim world were profound in their consequences. As we have previously noted, many European communities – most particularly in the Balkans – were themselves Muslim. Moreover, as Carlo Cipolla (1981: 180) accurately recorded, "Europe always proved extraordinarily receptive" to technologies and ideas derived from the East. Prominent among the technological innovations feudal Europe obtained from the East were the horse stirrup, the compass, paper, and gunpowder. Intellectually, the West borrowed "Arabic" numerals and new understandings in the fields of geometry, mathematic, and medicine.

The contrast between the inherent technological dynamism that characterized Western feudalism can be ascertained by the different ways in which Chinese,

European, and Middle Eastern societies approached mechanical printing. In China – the original home of both paper production and printing – the technique never became a platform for mass literacy, as Chinese printers remained wedded to hand-cut wooden presses. By contrast, in Europe by 1450 mechanical presses which boasted metal type were pulling 300 pages a day, an output that brought the printed page before a mass audience for the first time in human history (Cipolla 1981). Yet, despite constant trade between Europe and the East, the printing press was long regarded by the Muslim world, as de Bellaigue (2018: xv) notes in his study of *The Islamic Enlightenment*, "as an unwelcome and alien innovation." In the Ottoman Empire, long a major European power, the moveable-type printing press was only introduced in the 1840s (de Bellaigue, 2018: xxiv). The consequence of these divergent trends was profound. In the most significant Islamic societies of the early modern era – Turkey, Egypt, and Iran – only 3% were literate in 1800. By contrast, in England at this time 68% of males and 43% of females were literate (de Ballaigue 2018: xv). Even in Poland, an economic laggard in Europe, 21% of the adult population could read in 1800 (Allen 2003: 415).

The dynamic behind the technological prowess of Western feudalism is perhaps best summed up by Eric Jones (1987: 45) when he described feudal Europe as "a mutant civilization," a society that represented a receptive hybrid mix of cultures, ever open to practical innovations. Certainly, it is wrong to see feudalism simply from the perspective of the *fief* or manor. For Western feudalism was far more than a relationship between lord and serf. Instead it was characterized by division, fragmentation, and a diffusion of power. At every level of society the church acted not only as an alternative source of power to princely authority, it also served as a source of technical and organizational innovation. Writing of the Benedictine monasteries, Kieser (1987: 113) noted that they "attained more than their secular counterparts ... not only in management, production, and architectural methods, but also in agricultural skills." In a similar vein, Peter Wirtz (2017: 260) describes the ways in which the church "had a significant impact on the development of state structures in Europe, training bureaucrats and providing a model of dedicated service." The most radical element of Western feudalism, however, was its class of merchants, financiers, peddlers, and traders; a class of people who, in the otherwise closed world of the medieval fief, often seemed to appear from nowhere with goods and tales from distant lands. Whether this class of people only arrived on the scene in the tenth century (the Pirenne thesis) or was always present within feudalism is a matter of debate. What is nevertheless clear is that merchants and traders were a revolutionary force in Western feudalism precisely because they were perpetual outsiders. As Pirenne (1925/1952: 126–127) observed of merchants, traders, and wandering craft workers in his study, *Medieval Cities: Their Origins and the Revival of Trade*:

> They did not demand freedom; it was conceded to them because no one could prove that they did not already enjoy it ... In short, just as the agrarian civilization had made of the peasant a man whose normal state was servitude, trade made of the merchant a man whose normal condition was liberty.

If Western feudalism boasted evident strengths, we nevertheless need to be mindful of two things. First, its material successes were impressive only by comparison with what had come before. As we shall discuss in the ensuing sections, Western feudalism remained at heart an agricultural, pre-industrial society. To the extent that people had a choice of work in such a world it typically involved, as Braudel (1986/1990: 676) noted, a choice "between equally backbreaking kinds of work." The second thing we need to remind ourselves is that feudalism – at least in its Western European form – cannot be simply acquainted with serfdom. Rather, to restate our core argument in this regard, it represents a historical peculiarity; a society characterized by a high degree of mechanical innovation, and a diffusion of political and economic power. As such, Western feudalism was a fundamentally different society to that which existed in Eastern Europe – most particularly Russia – from the fifteenth century onward. For what we witness Eastern Europe is a process by which the aristocracy and the State enserfed a previously free peasantry so as to obtain the many accoutrements of Western society – clothes, furniture, wine, ships, and weapons – as well as the resources required to defend themselves from Western armies (i.e., state bureaucracies, professional armies, etc.). In doing so they not only ground their serfs into a state of abject poverty. They also cut the mass of their society off from interaction with a modernizing world, to their enduring detriment.

Medieval and Early Modern Europe: A Comparative Perspective

No society, can advance unless it feeds itself. And it is difficult for a society to feed itself unless it can constantly innovate. If it is insufficiently innovative, a society is almost inevitably exposed to a series of Malthusian cycles, in which population expansion is halted and reversed as the society hits a technologically and organizationally imposed ceiling. That this is exactly what happened to Europe in the feudal and early modern eras is suggested by Figs. 1 and 2. In the case of skilled building workers in southern England (Fig. 1), it is evident that a post-plague population revival between 1400 and 1500 induced a catastrophic fall in real wages in the sixteenth century. If we take a longer view and look at overall European population growth (including Russia) from the early feudal era (c.1000) to the mid-nineteenth century, as we do in Fig. 3, a more complex picture emerges. What is evident is that an initial period of demographic expansion, which saw Europe's population grow from around 32 million to 80 million in 1340 (a 150% gain), was sent into reverse by the famine and plagues of the 1340s, with a second period of population growth between 1350 and 1600 losing steam in the seventeenth century. Across the 410-year period between 1340 and 1700 – a period which saw the Renaissance, printing, increasing levels of urbanization, the discovery of the Americas – Europe's population grew by a mere 37.5% (from 80 million to 110 million). By contrast, in the 150-year period between 1700 and 1850, Europe's population soared by 142% as it numbers expanded from 110 million to 266 million (Cipolla 1981: 150; Braudel 1967/1974: 11). Looking across this 950-year span of European history, we can thus discern two periods of strong population growth (1000–1340 and 1700–1850),

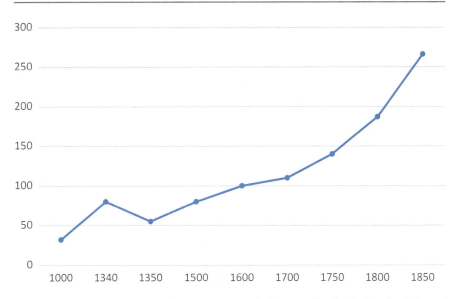

Fig. 3 Approximate Europe population, 1000–1850*. (Source: Cipolla, *Before the Industrial Revolution*, p. 150; Braudel, *Capitalism and Material Life,* p.11. *Note: includes Russia)

broken by a long period (1350–1700) of regression, stagnation, and modest growth. Such outcomes also suggest that the most significant advances were associated with (a) feudalism and (b) the process of modernization that ended in the Industrial Revolution.

In considering the feudal and early modern achievement, we need to also consider how well Europe performed in the basic task of feeding its population and in providing for their basic consumer needs, when compared to other advanced societies such as India and China. Such a comparison has particular need given the many claims for European exceptionalism (see, e.g., Jones 1987; Huntington 1996/2003; Ferguson 2008, 2011) and the recent literature on the so-called Great Divergence, which has seen Pomeranz (2000), Parthasarathi (1998), and others challenge long-held assumptions that European living standards were far superior to those of Asian societies even before the Industrial Revolution (see Jones 2017, for a summary of the "Great Divergence" debate).

Before considering the statistics that have emerged from the Great Divergence debate, it is necessary to discuss problems of measurement. In comparing the per capita performance of different societies, there are two principal measures: real wages and per capita gross domestic product (GDP). The former is intrinsically easier to calculate than the latter. All one has to do is put together a basic of consumables (typically food, clothing, fuel, and lighting) and then, by comparing nominal wages and prices, estimate how much of this basket a worker could purchase at different points in time. In Europe, estimations of real wages have been facilitated by the efforts of the International Scientific Committee on Price History. Established in 1929, and funded by the Rockefeller Foundation, this committee created an extensive European database, recording the real wage of building workers, both skilled and unskilled, between the thirteenth and twentieth centuries (see Cole and Crandall 1964, for a history of the Committee). Hence, when historians cite European statistics on real wages (i.e., the Phelps Brown-Hopkins index), they invariably draw on this committee's work. By comparison with estimations of real wages, calculation of historic GDP per capita is a more difficult proposition. Not only does it require an estimation of population, it also requires a value being placed on all the goods and services produced during a year, calculations which can never be more than "guesstimates."

In Fig. 4, drawing on Broadberry and Gupta (2006), we look at the "grain wage" – i.e., how many kilograms of wheat could a worker buy with their nominal wage – obtained by unskilled building laborers/laborers in three different regions between the first half of the sixteenth century and the first half of the nineteenth century: southern England, Florence/Milan, and India. Three things are immediately obvious. First, only southern England enjoyed a continuous advance in real wages between 1600–1649 and 1800–1849, suggesting that only England was capable of generating sufficient innovation to generate real wage increases for its workforce during this period. Second, it is clear that both Florence/Milan and India suffered an almost identical decline after 1650–1699. In each case, real wages in 1800–1849 were less than a third of those obtained in southern England. Finally, even in southern England – the most successful society – real wages were less at the end of our period than

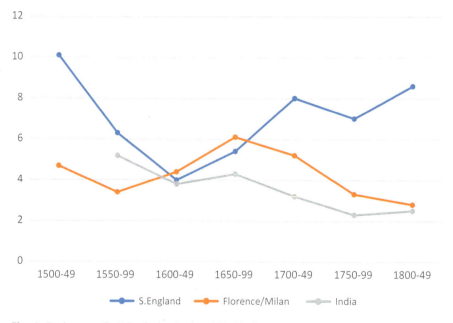

Fig. 4 Real wages (in KG of wheat) of unskilled building laborers, 1500–1549 to 1800–1849: southern England, Florence/Milan, and India. (Source: Broadberry and Bishnupriya, *Early Great Modern Divergence* Tables 2, 6. *Note: no Indian figures for 1500–49)

what they were at the beginning. It is difficult to escape the conclusion, therefore, that in all three regions were looking at comparatively backward systems of production. However, whereas England was at least going forwards economically, the other two regions were going backwards.

The findings by Broadberry and Gupta (2006), which point to a late divergence of living standards between even Europe's most advanced economies and those of Asia, are confirmed in a range of studies (see, e.g., van Zanden 2002; Allen 2003; Li and van Zanden 2012). For example, Allen et al. (2011: 30–31), in comparing eighteenth-century living standards in a range of cities in Europe, China, Japan, and India, found "that unskilled labourers in major cities of China and Japan – poor as they were – had roughly the same standard of living as their counterparts in central and southern Europe for the greater part of the eighteenth century." It "was only England and the Low Countries," Allen et al. (2011: 31) continue, that we witness European societies "that pulled ahead of the rest." That stagnation of living standards was the European norm is also indicated in Palma and Reis's (2019: 478) analysis of per capita income in Portugal between 1527 and 1850, where they observe that "Over the long run, there was no per capita growth: by 1850 per capita incomes were no different from what they had been in the early 1530s."

Given the fact that most European societies proved *incapable* of creating the conditions for transformative managerial endeavor, with even the per capita output of Holland going into reverse after 1650 (see Fig. 2), we keep coming back to the same question: what was it that allowed Britain alone to succeed where others failed? Significantly, the "Great Divergence" literature allows us to dismiss a number of (well-worn) arguments relating to culture and market institutions. The first of these arguments, i.e., managerial success is derived from culture, is most famously associated with Max Weber (1922/1927: 367), who identified the advance of capitalism and its systems of managerial organization with the emergence of a "Protestant" and, more particularly, Calvinist "ethic" (also see Weber 1905/2003). The problems with this argument, as exposed by recent research, are manifest. In the eighteenth century, real wages in Protestant Germany were little removed from those of Italy, India, and China (Allen et al. 2011). As late as 1800, the typical Berlin stonemason – with a wife and three children – spent 72.7% of his income on food. Almost half of his total income (44.2%) was spent on bread (Braudel 1967/1974: 90). In Holland, per capita growth was going backward by 1700. The North and Thomas (1970, 1973) argument that market institutions, which were by the 1600 highly developed in societies like the Netherlands, held the keys to success runs into similar problems.

Rather than being sufficient conditions for transformative managerial success, culture and market institutions – while indubitably important – appear merely necessary conditions. If we are to look for the decisive conditions for success, we suggest, we need to shift our vision from culture and institutions to the lived experiences of workers and managers in the fields of agriculture, manufacture, finance, and trade. In doing so, we can take away two key points from this section: that the key advances appear to have occurred in two widely separated periods, i.e., 1000 to 1340 and 1700 onward (see Fig. 3), and that from 1700 the economic

Medieval and Early Modern Life: The World of Production

If the most elementary requirement for a society's economic success is a capacity to feed one's self, and if it also the case that the first period of dramatic European population growth was associated with the feudal era (i.e., 1000 to 1340), this suggests that the place to start our search for the material conditions for European success is with an unlikely candidate: the medieval serf. And the achievements of the "typical" medieval serf can only be understood by comparing their practices with those of the small peasant farmer of antiquity, best exemplified (and recorded) in the lived experiences of republican Rome's soldier-farmer.

In Roman antiquity the iconic peasant experience is found in Livy's (c.AD 14/1960: 213) description of Cincinnatus, who was called from his "little three acre farm" to save Rome from yet another military crisis. Like his neighbors, Cincinnatus's farm was a self-contained unit that would have boasted, in addition to his three acres of continuous cropland, a farmhouse with a small garden for growing turnips, a few fruit trees, and, most probably, a couple of olive trees and a row or two of vines (Stevens 1941/1966: 94). To plow his fields, Cincinnatus would have used a variety of the swing plow. Suspended from a single wooden shaft, drawn by oxen, this plow amounted to little more than a curved, sharpened stick. Whether or (more likely) not this plow boasted a metal blade, it could do little more than scratch a shallow rut in thin soil (Fussell 1966: 177). Rich valley bottoms, such as those which prevailed in much of northern Europe, were beyond its capacity. A shortage of both iron and livestock in Roman antiquity also left farm laborers, even on the large *latifundia*, with little in the way of tools or animal power. In Rome, as elsewhere in antiquity, the tendency of wheat to rapidly strip nutriments from the soil also meant that half the farmland had to left fallow every season under the so-called two-field system.

The most obvious difference between the agricultural practices of Roman antiquity and those which prevailed in the feudal era involved, at least in northern Europe, the displacement of the "two-field" agriculture by the "three-field system." The advances evident in the "three-field system" are manifest. Under the three-field system, only a third of the farmland was left fallow, increasing the land under cultivation by 50%. Of the land farmed each season, half was sown with "corn" (typically a mix of wheat and rye). Planted in autumn (i.e., September–October), the crop was harvested in ensuing summer (i.e., July–August). In early spring (i.e., March), a second field was sown with *marsage* (i.e., peas, lentils, or clover), crops which restored soil nitrogen levels while giving the peasant and his beasts an additional source of food. Spring also witnessed the first plowings of the fallow as farmers sought to plow under weeds which, if left untended, would overgrow the sown crop (Braudel 1986/1990: 339–342). One of the benefits of secondary crops that acted as artificial pasture (i.e., clover, sainfoin, etc.) was that they allowed for an increase in livestock, most particularly horses and dairy cows. Although medieval cows were far smaller than modern varieties, typically producing only 500 liters of milk per year (Cipolla 1981: 126) – compared to the 10,000 liters expressed by modern cows – they nevertheless provided another source of calories and protein. Another obvious difference between the practices of antiquity and those of feudal Europe is found in the displacement of the swing plow by the heavy wheeled plow. Although wheeled plows could be drawn by either oxen or horses, they were – due to the introduction of shoulder harnesses – increasingly horse-drawn. Prior to the shoulder harness, introduced from the East in the ninth century, attempts to capture the horse's pulling power (which equated to that of four oxen) had been negated by neck harness, which tended to strangle the animal (Stevens 1941/1966: 143). Together, the horse and the heavy plow opened up the hitherto inaccessible soils of Europe's rich valley bottoms. Moreover, whereas the swing plow could do little more than create a shallow furrow, the heavy medieval plow could actually turn the soil over, burying weeds, and bringing nutriments to the surface. Increased levels of livestock also added to rural productivity by providing additional sources of manure. On a typical small plot, it is estimated that the serf and his family dug some 150 cartloads of manure into their fields each year (Braudel 1986/1990: 341). Collectively, the advance in medieval agriculture techniques contributed to a steady advance in grain yields. In France, these rose from 2.5 in the early Carolingian period to 4 or more during the High Middle Ages; an improvement which equated to a 60% gain in terms of rural productivity (Parain 1941/1966: 124).

One key but overlooked difference between the medieval serf and the peasant of Roman antiquity is that the former was a full-time professional. Indeed, the busy medieval schedule – sowing in autumn and spring, plowing of fallow in spring and summer, harvesting in late summer, and manuring of fields in every season – left time for little else. By comparison, the two-field system of antiquity left a comparative abundance of leisure; free time which the peasant soldiers of republican Rome invested in politics and war. Unlike the slaves employed on the Roman *latifundia*, the medieval serf also had reason to innovate. Yes, it is true that the medieval serf lacked both personal liberty and property rights. By custom and practice, however, peasant families were guaranteed a fixed share of their crop. Hence, a bigger crop added to household wealth. Over time, a number of factors worked to strengthen the peasant's hold on their plot; a tendency that further incentivized agricultural innovation. As a monetarized economy revived, feudal dues were increasingly commuted to a fixed monetary payment, effectively transforming the serf into a leaseholder. The demographic catastrophe induced by the Black Death (c.1347–1353) also strengthened the peasant's hand amid continent-wide labor shortages.

The importance of security of person and property in incentivizing rural productivity antiquity is best illustrated in the Dutch experience. A swampy and unattractive backwater in the tenth century, by the 1550s the Netherlands boasted Europe's most productive and commercialized agricultural sector. In many ways, as van Bavel and van Zanden (2004: 513) record, the Dutch experience between the eleventh and sixteenth centuries bears close resemblance with North America in the nineteenth century. A "frontier economy" with plentiful land and a shortage of labor in the eleventh century, Dutch farmers were attracted by promises of "almost absolute, exclusive property rights to the land they occupied" (van Bavel and van Zanden 2004: 504). Through constant experimentation the legally free Dutch farmers turned the "three-field" system of agriculture into one of continuous continuous cultivation as efficient forms of crop rotation avoiding the need for fallow. Initial labor shortages also caused high wages, forcing urban employers into high value-added activities (cloth manufacture, brewing, brickmaking). Meanwhile, the availability of peat fostered energy-intensive activities, most particularly glassmaking and brickmaking. Ready access to the sea facilitated an export trade. At the same time, the region's swamps and peat bogs necessitated investment in windmills to pump water from behind the dikes, further fostering technological innovation. When in the sixteenth century, the Netherlands began to suffer rural overpopulation the region avoided many of the problems experienced elsewhere. By 1550, half of the rural population of Holland – the most urbanized and populace Dutch province – was engaged in nonagricultural pursuits. Many found work in cloth weaving, fishing, and peat digging. Others moved into urban pursuits in manufacture, trade, and commerce. In consequence, 45% of Holland's population lived in towns and cities by the late sixteenth century (van Bavel and van Zanden 2004: 503).

In the Dutch experience, we witness an example of a society engaged in the early stages of industrial "takeoff," a process characterized – as the American economist, Walt Rostow (1963: 9) noted in a much acclaimed study – by the emergence of "new types of workers," "new technology," and "new and vigorous" forms of management. Yet, as Rostow also noted, not every society that experiences the early stages of "takeoff" makes the leap to full industrialization. The reason for this, Rostow (1963: 3) concluded, is found in the fact that initially dynamic industries often lose steam in the face of either demand or supply constraints, leading to "a more or less systematic path of deceleration." As Fig. 2 suggests, this appears to be exactly what happened to the Netherlands after 1600.

To better understand the factors that advanced and impeded innovation and transformative managerial practices, we need to extend our analysis from agriculture to manufacturing. In most accounts of medieval industry, it is textiles and clothing making which attracts most attention. At first glance, such an emphasis appears well justified. As Pirenne (1925/1952: 155) accurately recorded, "Cloth, more than any other manufactured product, was the basis of the commerce of the Middle Ages." In Florence in the mid-fourteenth century, there were, within a 60 kilometer radius of the city, as estimated 60,000 workers producing for the cloth trade (Braudel 1979/1982: 299). In 1680, in France's Languedoc region, there were 450,000 workers who supplemented their cottage income through spinning, weaving, or sewing (Braudel 1979/1982: 306). Parts of the cloth-making industry, most particularly fulling and dyeing, were also subject to mechanization as producers harnessed the power of water mills. Despite such attributes, however, we should not exaggerate the textile industry's technological and managerial advances. For, unlike the English cotton industry of the eighteenth and nineteenth centuries, which catered to a mass market, the medieval cloth trade served a small luxury custom. Production volumes were modest in the extreme. In the late thirteenth century, for example, Venice dominated the trade in high-quality cotton fabrics. Yet it processed only a miniscule 140 tons of raw cotton per year (Cipolla 1981: 209). In essence, the industry preyed on the gullibility of rich aristocrats, who paid inordinate sums so as to possess the latest Flemish or Italian fashion. Indeed, Eric Jones (1987: 86) declares the entire medieval trade in cloth to be a perfect example of Adam Smith's "bauble thesis"; a thesis which holds that the rich, by frittering away their money on "luxury and caprice," redistribute their wealth as if "they are led by an invisible hand" (Smith 1759/2017: 99). Such mechanisms are seldom capable of generating profound change. Innovation and advancement in the medieval and early modern textile industries was also much hindered by the craft guilds, which vigorously opposed new production techniques that could lead to either lower costs or unemployment. Where, as in Flanders, employers managed to circumvent the guilds, the resultant work practices proved to be neither enlightened nor sustainable. Writing of Flemish working conditions, Pirenne (1925/1952: 154) declared them to be "very miserable," producing "a brutish lower class, uneducated and discontented." The widespread outsourcing of work to the cottage sector – variously described as "proto-industrialization" or "putting-out" – also did little to foster managerial innovation or productivity. As Allen (2003: 408) observes, in the early modern era such practices were far more commonly associated with "economic stagnation" than advancement.

If we are looking for an industry central to European innovation and advancement, it is not textiles but iron making. For, as the American historian, Lewis Morgan (1878: 43), had reason to observe:

> The production of iron was the event of events in human experience, without a parallel, and without an equal ... Out of it came the metallic hammer and anvil, the axe and the chisel, the plough with the iron point, the iron sword; in fine, the basis of civilization.

Significantly, advances in iron and steelmaking in the feudal and early modern eras could not occur in isolation. Instead, innovation and increased production in this sector demanded linkages and advances in other industries, most particularly mining, transportation, and power generation, linkages which produced a cascading series of economic multipliers.

In the medieval era, the revolutionary effects antiquity of iron making first manifested themselves in an economically significant way in agriculture. The herald of an agricultural transformation was the medieval village blacksmith, a person who was a stranger to most rural communities prior to the twelfth century. In Picardy, part of France's agricultural heartland, few if any villages boasted a blacksmith in 1100. A century later a third of Picardy's villages had one, a development that prefigured the growing availability of a range of metal tools: heavy wheeled plows, hoes, axes, and knives (Cipolla 1981: 170). This proliferation of both blacksmiths and metal tools pointed to radical changes in smelting. Traditionally, European metallurgists – like their Indian and Asian counterparts – had smelted ore with the assistance of hand-operated bellows; a practice that gave the industry its small, cottage character. In the eleventh and twelfth century, however, iron makers in Western Germany and the Netherlands began connecting enormous bellows to large waterwheels (Braudel 1967/1974:279). By channeling the resultant blasts of heated air the new "blast furnaces" revolutionized production. The size of furnaces grew exponentially. European output increased from as little as 25,000 tons per year in 1400 to 100,000 tons per year in 1525 (Cipolla 1981: 216; Braudel 1967/1974; 282). The key role of water mills in transforming iron smelting was replicated in a range of industries: the grinding of grain, brewing, crushing ores, and pulping cloth rags into paper. In the English county of Surrey, there was by 1100 one water mill for every 35 families. By the fifteenth century, France boasted 70,000 water mills. Across Europe as a whole there were, by the late 1700s, half a million water mills in operation (Cipolla 1981: 97; Braudel 1986/1990: 145). Equally transformative was the wind-powered tower mill, an adaptation of a seventh-century Persian invention. Capable of operating away from fast-running streams, the windmill was also more powerful than its water-powered counterpart, generating up to 30 horsepower (Cipolla 1981: 173–174). In Holland, where the windmill became an iconic landmark, five new mills were being constructed each year by the late 1400s (van Bavel and van Zanden 2004: 520). In France there were an estimated 20,000 mills in operation by 1500, generating power equivalent to that of 600,000 horses (Braudel 1986/1990: 145). Such was the transformative effect of the new blast furnaces and new forms of power generation that (Braudel 1986/1990: 145) aptly describes the period between the twelfth and fifteenth centuries as Europe's "first industrial revolution."

If the harnessing of water and, subsequently, wind power allowed Europe to clear one set of technological hurdles, further advancement was curtailed by another: a shortage of wood for heating and smelting. The significance of this barrier cannot be overstated. For in our energy-intensive modern world – where many believe the environment is threatened by the contribution of carbon-based forms of energy (most particularly coal) to "climate change" – it is easy to overlook the destructive pressures which pre-industrial societies placed on forests and woodlands. As noted in the introduction to this chapter, wood was required for heating, cooking, and smelting as well as for construction and shipbuilding. The demands placed by urban centers on forest reserves were particularly prodigious, Paris requiring a ton of wood per person per year on the eve of the French Revolution (Braudel 1967/1974: 270–271). A partial solution to this problem was devised by the Dutch, who utilized locally sourced peat for domestic and industrial heating and firing. Peat, however, was no substitute for charcoal in iron smelting, a fact that made it nigh impossible for the Netherlands to assume leadership in this vital sector. Instead, leadership passed to England.

In large part, English inventiveness was driven by necessity. Lacking the copper need to make bronze cannon, England perfected the technique of making iron cannons. Although less durable than bronze, iron weapons were ideal for naval ships where guns were fired less frequently. Accordingly, by the late sixteenth century, the export of iron cannon was a lucrative English trade (Cipolla 1981:

289). This burgeoning business collapsed, however, as wood-derived charcoal became prohibitively expensive. Output from England's furnaces, which reached an unprecedented 75,000 tons in 1640, also fell away (Braudel 1967/1974: 253). The solution was found, as we have noted earlier, in a resource which England had in ready abundance: coal. Admittedly, even in England the practice of using coal-derived coke in iron and steelmaking in lieu of charcoal – a practice pioneered in 1627 – was initially slow to take hold. It nevertheless represented the breaking of a final technological barrier; a leap forward that totally and utterly transformed the nature of capital investment. For the fundamental problem with capital investment in pre-industrial societies is that only stone provided for durability, whether used in construction or road-building. Other investments seldom lasted for long. Wooden plows and weaving frames easily broke. Timber ships only lasted a few trips before their hulls were eaten away by marine borers. Horses and cows died prematurely. By contrast, although it took a century and a half of experimentation before British iron workers were to fully perfect the use of coke in lieu of charcoal, these ventures gradually opened up a new wold of managerial endeavor, a world built around iron rather than wood.

By the eighteenth century, the changed nature of capital investment was most evident in England, where a growing appetite for coal and iron advanced hand-in-hand with increasingly radical innovations. From the 1750s canals were constructed to provide inland towns with sought after supplies of coal, the first such system, the Bridgewater Canal – which linked Manchester to the Lancashire coal fields – opening for business in 1761. As coal demand surged, mines became ever deeper, necessitating the generalized adoption of the Newcomen steam engine so as to keep water levels in check.

If, by the 1700s, England had become the pace-setter in new technologies and work practices, we should not infer a lack of interest in things mechanical in the rest of Western Europe. On the contrary, European society – from the feudal era onward – always showed an almost obsessional interest in mechanical contrivances. This mechanical orientation, which was reflected in almost every area of endeavor, was arguably best demonstrated in a new approach to time. Previously, pre-industrial societies had always determined the time of day, and the passing of the seasons, by the location of the sun and moon. From the thirteenth century, however, there began a concerted move to measure time mechanically. Initially, there was little practical use for the resultant clocks. Rather, as Cipolla 1981: 182) observed, the people of feudal Europe "thought of measuring time in mechanical terms because they had developed a mechanical outlook." Eventually, however, European society found a use for the newly invented clock, just as it found use for a host of other inventions (the lateen sail, the compass, telescopes). For as European seafarers ventured out into the Atlantic and Indian Oceans the old navigational skills, acquired in the Mediterranean and North Seas, no longer applied. Even the North Star disappeared in the Southern Ocean. In this new maritime world, a calculation of longitude, and thus a determination of where one was in the vastness of the ocean, could only occur by reference to a set of tables that recorded time at different locations. And, without an accurate measurement of time, obtained from marine chronometers, such references were meaningless.

Despite all its technological achievements, Europe was in the 1700s still a largely pre-industrial society. The living conditions of the average peasant, building worker, or urban craftsman were little different from what they had been in the High Middle Ages. Yes, there were gains in agricultural productivity. But these tended to be swallowed up by increases in population. Of the 100–110 million people who inhabited Europe in 1700, only 3% to 4% regularly ate white wheaten bread. Most survived on coarse rye bread, oat or barley porridge, and boiled vegetables, washed down with cheap wine or low-strength beer (Braudel 1967/1974: 94). Commercial textile manufacture continued to be directed at a luxury market, leaving the bulk of the population in rags. The gains in agriculture and manufacturing were, in short, primarily found in capital equipment – and scientific and technical knowledge – rather than consumables. Nowhere were these latter advances more obvious that in shipping. By the sixteenth century, the single-masted ship of antiquity and the Norse longboat were distant memory. In their place were vessels that encapsulated European advancement, multi-mast affairs capable of tacking into the wind and armed with bronze or iron cannon. On observing such ships for the first time in 1517, one Chinese official reflected, with justifiable concern, "the westerns (sic) are extremely dangerous because of their artillery. No weapon ever made since memorial antiquity is superior to their cannon" (cited Cipolla 1981: 223).

Medieval and Early Modern Life: Commerce, Finance, and Trade

In the medieval and early modern eras, the gains made in the world of production were largely due to the efforts of a myriad of anonymous craft workers and farmers, tinkering away with modifications that seldom delivered much in the way of either recognition or financial fortune. If one wanted to advance one's wealth, one was better advised to enter the worlds of commerce, finance, and trade. In these worlds, across the entire time period we consider (i.e., AD 450–1750), the key dynamic was always the same: buy cheap and sell dear. And the key to buying cheap and selling dear was to enter the long-distance trade in commodities, obtaining cheaply at distant markets what could not be found locally.

Initially, in the early medieval era, the volume involved in long-distance trade was miniscule. Writing of the situation that prevailed in the 1200s, Pirenne (1936: 161) observed that "the tonnage of a single [early] twentieth-century ship" was equal in tonnage "to that of the whole Venetian or Genoese fleet." What made the activities of a comparative handful of entrepreneurs so significant during the twelfth and thirteenth centuries was a unique combination of risk and reward. Of these two factors it was, arguably, the former that was decisive in shaping revolutionary new accounting and financial practices. For in a well-ordered and well-policed society, a business-person can carry out their activities with little thought to robbery, murder, and mayhem. In the mind of the medieval merchant, however, such dangers were ever present. To transport luxury goods was dangerous enough. Even more hazardous was the prospect of returning home with a purse full of silver or gold. Not only did one face robbery from unknown assailants. There was also the possibility that some or all of one's money would be seized by some government official, acting at the direction of a princeling who was attempting to stem the flow of specie from their realm. How, in such circumstances, could a Venetian merchant exchange a shipment of spices or silk with a Parisian buyer and return home safely? The ingenious solution to this was the *instrumentum ex causa cambii*, or the "bill of exchange."

The operation of "bill of exchange" is brilliantly described in Luca Pacioli's famed study of accounting and mathematics, the *Summa de Arithmetica, Geometria, Proportioni et Proportionalita*.

If, for example, a Venetian merchant wished to purchase Flemish cloth from a Parisian merchant at the Champagne trade fair, he could deposit money (e.g., 200 Venetian ducats) with a Venetian bank or finance house. In return, he would receive, having paid the banker a commission, a "draft" payable in Paris in French livres. "To prevent misunderstanding," Pacioli (1494/1994: 56) recorded,

> ... such documentary credits, by custom, include specific written instructions ... details of the currency, the validity of the credit, whether partial shipments are allowed, detailed advice on commission, interest and other costs ... In other words, every what, why and how needed to support the transaction.

On obtaining the purchased cloth from his Parisian counterpart, the Venetian merchant would provide in exchange both his financial "draft" and a "duplicate receipt," obtained from his banker, which verified that the "draft" was backed by physical currency. On returning to Paris, the French merchant could then exchange this draft, having paid a commission to his banker, for local currency. Now, let us assume that our Venetian merchant has also sold the Parisian entrepreneur a shipment of spice for 200 Venetian ducats and obtained in return a "draft" (backed by a duplicate receipt) payable in Venice. On returning to Venice our merchant then presents this "draft" to his own banker, receiving in return his original 200 Venetian ducats, minus a commission (see Pacioli 1494/1994: 57). Under this system of financial exchange the need for physical currency is almost entirely eliminated. The Venetian merchant's original 200 ducat deposit provided, in effect, merely a backing for his international "draft"; a backing which could have been dispensed with if he had "credit" with his bank. For the Venetian and French bankers, each of whom benefited from commissions, the credits and debits in this international exchange have balanced out. Meanwhile, the Venetian and Parisian merchants have secured commodities which were scarce in their local markets, allowing them to sell locally for a handy profit. All that needed to occur at the end of this exchange process was a reconciliation of accounts between the various bankers. In the medieval and early modern worlds such "settlements" invariably occurred at one or other of the various trade "fairs" (Champagne, Piacenza, etc.). At these fairs the medieval bankers (or their representatives) typically arrived with "masses of bills of exchange" but little in the way of cash, the need for the latter being negated by the fact that credits and debits almost always "cancelled each other out" (Braudel 1979/1982: 90–91).

Although the "bill of exchange" was initially designed to overcome the dangers of long distance, it almost immediately gave rise to a host of new financial instruments. Often, rather than wait for payment on the date stipulated on their "draft" (e.g., 1 September), a merchant would sell his "bill of exchange" for a discount (e.g., 90% of its face value) in order to obtain cash sooner rather than later. Such "discounted bills" could then be sold or resold or used as a collateral for the purchase of goods or property. Because "bills of exchange" issued by well-known banks or financiers were easily traded, most merchants maintained deposit accounts with such reputable institutions. By the fifteenth century, the practice of issuing "checks" that drew on such deposits was commonplace. As Pacioli (1494/1994: 53) advised his readers, "Out of your deposits, individual payment by check (sic) may be made to anyone." The practice of conducting business through bank "credit" was also normalized, Pacioli (1494/1994: 1) noting that "Many without capital of their own whose credit was good have managed to finance large transactions using their credit." Typically, the interest rate charged in the medieval era for financing long-distance cargo shipments – the lifeblood of the emerging systems of commercial capitalism – was high. In Venice during its mercantile heyday, a charge of 20% was normal (Pirenne 1925/1952: 111). But, if interest rates and risks were high, so too were potential profits.

Long-distance trade and the new financial systems that were its lifeblood were also seminal to a revolutionary new system of accounting: double-entry booking. In describing the system as "used in Venice" in the fifteenth century, Pacioli (1494/1994: 4, 2) observed, "This double-entry system is really essential to merchants because, without making the entries systematically, they may not be able to control and manage their business. Without double-entry, businessmen would not sleep easily at night." The essence of the new double-entry system was the insight that: "The very day a debit is born, it has a twin credit. So it is quite natural for them always to go together" (Pacioli 1494/1994: 26). Without such understandings the modern business world would be inconceivable.

Even more revolutionary than the new system of double-entry booking was the generalization of a new commercial outlook, which underpinned not only new social relationships but also new bodies of commercial law. For the key to any capitalist system of commercial exchange is trust. The need for trust is most obvious at the level of individual exchange, Pacioli (1494/1994: 1) advising his readers that "In the business world nothing is considered more important than the word of a reputable businessman. Promissory notes are honoured and accepted based on a businessman's reputation." To enforce contracts a myriad of disciplinary procedures and regulations were established, first by the various merchant guilds and then, subsequently, by government. Of the situation that prevailed in late fifteenth century Europe, Pacioli (1494/1994: 53) advised that "A check (sic) is a formal legal document under federal law," by which he meant the legally enforceable procedures accepted "in Venice, Bruges, in Antwerp, Barcelona, and other places familiar to the world of commerce." Commercial relationships required, however, more than trust between merchants and bankers. They also required trust between the agents of the commercial world and government, assurances that were most vital in terms of liberty of person and security of property. It was this fundamental need which made this new commercial class – acquisitive, self-serving, and elitist as it was – such a revolutionary, indeed, democratic force. At every level of government, this new commercial class constantly battled the arbitrary behavior of princely authority. In doing so it helped inspire a new political and economic ideology, one which located the sole justification for government in the protections it provided for both person and property. As the great English political theorist, John Locke (1689/1823: 159) famously observed in giving voice to this new sentiment, "The great and chief end . . . of men uniting into commonwealth and putting themselves under government is the protection of property." In Locke's view, as of countless others, any government who failed its duty in this regard was illegitimate and unworthy of its citizen's support.

If the risks involved in long-distance trade acted as inspiration for new financial instrument and accounting methods, there were nevertheless a number of factors that limited this business domain to a fortunate few. Nowhere was this more evident than in trade with the East, the source of much sought after spices, silks, and cottons. In part, reason for the monopolization of the eastern trade by a comparative handful of traders is found in the winds. In the Mediterranean, winds favor easterly travel in the spring and westerly movement in late summer and autumn, effectively limiting medieval Italian shipping to one return voyage a year. In bypassing the perils of the Middle East, the ship captains of the early modern era faced even longer periods away from home. To reach the East from Portugal, Britain, or the Netherlands entailed sailing ships following the trade winds to South America, before catching the "Roaring Forties" to the Indian Ocean. Typically, it took an outward-bound ship at least 6 months simply to obtain the coastline of India. Such circumstances excluded most small operators from the eastern trade, and by the early seventeenth century this lucrative business was effectively the domain of two state-protected monopolies: the English East India Company (est. 1600) and the Dutch East India Company (est. 1602). Almost immediately, each of these public share companies effectively became a "state within a state," possessing its own armies, navies, and state bureaucracies and ruling over vast territories. Through military action the Dutch evicted the Portuguese from the East Indies (modern Indonesia), turning this fabled territory into a company fief. In India the English East India Company followed similar strategies, gaining military control of Bengal and a string of coastal ports. Such companies were, it needs to be emphasized, far removed from the modern firm, which operates in a market economy according to law. Yes, they did undertake the management functions of planning, organizing, leading, and controlling. But they never showed much affection for either market forces or law. Instead, their business model was built on exclusion of competition and a capacity for extreme violence. Even in the Atlantic trade, where there were fewer natural obstacles to large-scale commerce, any tendency toward free trade was curtailed by the "mercantilist" policies pursued by every European government during the seventeenth century. Such policies, which sought to create trade surpluses by limiting commerce to favored local monopolies, restricted the most profitable areas of trade to a small well-connected coterie. In the case of eighteenth-century France, where mercantilist policies were pursued with particular vigor, the nation's entire international trade "was monopolized by less than a dozen powerful merchants" (Braudel 1986/1990: 556).

In fostering trade in luxuries and high-value staples, the merchant of the medieval and early modern era was constantly forced to secure their supply chain through an active involvement in the production process. Nowhere was this tendency more evident than in textiles and cloth making, the industry which – as we have previously noted – served as the core business for medieval trade. The merchant's domination of high-value manufacture of woolen, cotton, and silk fabrics was, in part, driven by necessity. The medieval textile worker, be they an urban craftsman or a rural cottage outworker, lacked the financial wherewithal to bring together the raw materials, woven cloth, and dyes required for the finishing of quality textiles. Instead, it was the merchant-capitalist who typically coordinated production, providing the artisan or cottager with materials and picking up the completed product so as to move it along to the next production stage. Intervention of the merchant in the production process was also forced upon them by the constant changes in fashion. It was not only alteration in the length, cut, and color of fabrics that drove changes in fashion. Everywhere, the merchant's need to stay abreast of the local fashion and techniques made him an enemy of craft restriction, a battle in which the merchant-capitalist constantly sought to either circumvent the master craftsman by "putting-out" work to rural cottagers or enforcing a series of controls that effectively reduced him to the status of a wage laborer (Braudel 1979/1982: 317). As in other business domains, therefore, the merchant-capitalist's battle with guild restrictions made him an agent for innovation. We should not, however, exaggerate the effects of his actions in this area. For, in the medieval and early modern era, the textile sector was rarely large enough to generate the multipliers necessary for sustained industrial advancement. Nowhere was more evident than in northern and central Italy. By the mid-seventeenth century, as Fig. 4 demonstrates, this one-time hub for textile manufacturer had become an economic backwater, subject to a collapse in real wages.

The capacity of Western commerce to lead societies into economic dead ends and archaic forms of production – as well as in the direction of innovation and industrial advancement – is also evident in the new forms of commerce and trade that emerged in the Baltic and the Atlantic from the sixteenth century. A number of factors drove such trends. In the first instance, Western Europe was propelled to acquire high-value staples (grain, timber, coal, fish, silver) so as to offset growing domestic shortages. In the case of Portugal, the first Atlantic maritime power, its initial ventures into the unmapped stretches of the Atlantic were thus driven by a search for new fisheries rather than eastern spices. Such was the frenzy of this search that within a few decades they had "fished out the Atlantic islands and hunted the seal colonies there, and . . . down to the Cape of Good Hope, to the brink of extinction" (Jones 1987: 78). Similarly, in the North Sea, the Dutch laid the basis for their commercial success by exploiting new herring fisheries in the North Sea, displacing the Baltic cities of the old Hanseatic League as Europe's principal supplier of salted fish (North and Thomas 1973: 112). From the North Sea, the Dutch forced their way into the Baltic, entrenching themselves in a trade which – even after the capture of the East Indies – remained the key to their commercial prosperity. Evidence of this domination is found in the tolls imposed by Danish officials on ships entering and leaving the

Baltic. In every year between 1550 and 1650, a majority of such ships were Dutch. In some years the figure stood at 85% (Cipolla 1981: 271). The key to the Dutch success, which enabled it to transport grain and timber at a profit, was a new type of ship: the *fluyt*. Constructed with an eye to labor productivity – the handling of sails facilitated by a complex system of pulley and blocks – the *fluyt* could be sailed with far fewer hands than rival ships, allowing the Dutch to undercut any competitor (Cipolla 1981: 274–275). In using the *fluyt* to control the Baltic trade, the Dutch pursued the same basic strategy in the sixteenth century which the Italians had pioneered in the thirteenth century: they played on aristocratic vanity and gullibility. Whereas the Italians had extracted cash from French aristocrats in exchange for the latest fashion, the Dutch traded cheaply made beer, low-quality wine, shoddily made furniture, and colorful cloths with the aristocrats of Poland, Latvia, Lithuania, and Russia. In return the aristocracy of Central and Eastern Europe organized the felling of vast forest reserves and the growing of huge quantities of grain (principally rye) on new, commercialized estates. Every Polish river became chocked with immense rafts of wood destined for the Baltic ports (Braudel 1967/1974: 269). To secure labor for their estates, the aristocracy also initiated a process which reduced the peasantry of Eastern Europe to the status of chattel serfs. In Poland, new legal statutes in 1519 and 1520 allowed the enforcement of 1 day a week of compulsory labor on the local landlord's estates. By 1550 a peasant could be legally subject to 3 days a week of compulsory toil. In 1660 the Polish government raised the period allowed to 6 days, effectively making the peasant a full-time serf (Braudel 1979/1982: 267).

The tendency for Western commercial capitalism to create the most backward forms of labor exploitation on its hinterlands – even as it was creating financial and technological innovation in its home markets – became ever more apparent in the plantation economies of the Americas. Whereas the Baltic remained Western Europe's principal provider of time-honored commodities (i.e., grain and timber), the plantations of the Caribbean and the Americas serviced novel demands for sugar, coffee, and tobacco. Of these new products, the British colonies of Virginia and Maryland quickly gained an ascendancy in the production and export of tobacco, a product initially marketed for its beneficial effect on the lungs. By 1699–1701 these two colonies alone were sending £22,000,000 ($3.44 billion in current US dollars) of product back to London, where it was re-exported all over Europe. Eighty years earlier, Virginia and Maryland had exported just £20,000 ($3.1 million current US dollars) (Cipolla 1981: 235). Prior to the Industrial Revolution, however, when production of American-grown cotton became essential to the functioning of Lancashire's mills, it was sugar which provided the principal foundation for the plantation economy of the Americas. In 1773 the value of Britain's trade with the sugar island of Jamaica was worth five times that of all its North American colonies. Among France's overseas territories the greatest jewel was Guadeloupe, the French crown readily surrendering the frozen wastes of Canada at the end of the Seven Years' War in order to hang on to Guadeloupe's cane fields (Ferguson 2008: 72). In every locality this sweet, lucrative bounty fed an insatiable demand for slaves. In the Caribbean, where slavery was a comparative rarity prior to 1600, an estimated 450,000 African slaves were imported during the course of the seventeenth century.

Brazil imported half a million. Across the Americas as a whole an estimated 1,325,000 Africans arrived in chains during the seventeenth century, destined for a life of misery (Curtin 1969: 77).

If the sugar, coffee, and tobacco exports of the Americas during the seventeenth century were associated with both great wealth and incomparable misery, we should nevertheless not exaggerate either its scale or its impact on the wider world economy of the time. Prior to the nineteenth century – when the Industrial Revolution brought about by a shipping revolution and a new mass consumer market – the exports of the Americas remained a luxury trade, peripheral to the experiences of most Europeans. Even the sugar industry, the most plebeian of the American exports, catered to the tastes of a luxury market prior to 1750. As Sidney Mintz (1985: 148) noted in his study into the global sugar trade, it was only from 1750 that English workers began to add the occasional teaspoon of sugar or treacle to their cup of black tea. As late as 1850, it was still a rarity in most household pantries. Even the seventeenth-century slave trade remained a comparatively small-scale affair compared to the ensuing century, when an increased demand for cotton and sugar gave slavery a new lease of life. In a single decade, 1740–1750, British ships carried a record 200,000 slaves to the Americas, a figure that equated to almost half the total Caribbean trade during the previous century (Thomas, 1997: 264). The small-scale nature of the early modern world's maritime trade – when compared to that which characterized the post-1750 world – can also be ascertained by looking at the tonnage of the European shipping fleet. In the early seventeenth century, it is estimated, Europe's total carrying capacity amounted to no more than 600,000 to 700,000 tons (Braudel 1967/1974: 265). This equates to the capacity of just four modern Capex-class ships (standard dead weight, 170,000 tons), vessels which act as the work-horses of today's maritime trade (Polo 2012: 27). Even in 1789, when tonnage stood at a record 3.4 million tons, Europe's carrying capacity was derisory by modern standards, equating to 20 of today's Capex-class ships.

In the early modern era, as in the Middle Ages, the revolutionary characteristic of European commerce and trade is found not so much in what was exchanged as in the financial skills that were acquired along the way. During the medieval era, when Italian merchants first perfected the "bill of exchange," the finance industry retained something of a cottage character. Settlement of accounts occurred at widely spaced intervals, typically occurring at one or other of the European trade fairs. As the new Atlantic economy expanded during the sixteenth century, however, finance and banking become professionalized, making possible a continuous trade in an increasingly exotic range of financial instruments. Central to the success of the new financial centers of Antwerp and – following Antwerp's pillaging by unpaid Spanish troops in November 1576 – Genoa and Amsterdam was the creation of large credit markets that allowed small investors to buy long-dated bonds and annuities. The Genoese, in particular, enriched themselves by acting as bankers to the Spanish Crown. The scale of this business can be ascertained by the fact that in 1562 the Spanish Crown – supported by the revenues of Castile, Aragon, Catalonia, southern Italy, Milan, the Low Countries, and a vast influx of American silver – was spending over 25% of its annual budget on interest (North and Thomas 1973: 129). Amsterdam, where the world's first stock exchange was created in 1602 to trade shares in the Dutch East India Company, was even more successful in attracting a large pool of small investors, many of whom were drawn to the stock market's speculative riches like moths to a flame. The most beneficial effect of this growth in investment capital was a sharp fall in borrowing costs. Whereas previously the standard interest rate charged by lenders was 20%, by the 1600s Dutch lenders were only charging 3% (Pirenne 1925/1952: 111; North and Thomas 1973: 142).

As the bourses, stock exchange, and lending houses of Genoa, Amsterdam, London, and Paris grew in sophistication and importance, their relationship with Europe's princely powers became increasingly problematic. On one hand, merchants and financiers looked to government to ensure law and order and the protection of property, just as Europe's crowned leaders looked to the financial sector for loans. On the other hand, the mindset of the various kings and princelings was essentially feudal, directed as it was toward dynastic aggrandizement and the perpetuation of aristocratic privilege. Increasingly, moreover, Europe's crowned heads – seeking to buttress their own financial position – began to impose a whole series of taxes and restrictions which came to be seen as "feudal" but which were in fact of recent contrivance. Every royal administration in Western Europe sought to make money in the sixteenth and seventeenth century by selling monopoly rights and royal charters. In France the dyeing of cloth was subject to 317 legal provisions in the mid-1600s, each potentially subject to royal inspections and fines (North and Thomas 1973: 126). On the eve of the French Revolution, the transport of a load of timber potentially exposed an entrepreneur to 35 separate tariffs and duties, imposed at 21 separate checkpoints (Braudel 1986/1990: 491).

By 1750, it is evident, Europe stood at a crossroads in which many of the new forces of commerce and industry rubbed up against not only the restrictions of government but also the limitations imposed by the small size of markets and the continued poverty of the bulk of the population. In considering this conundrum, Marx and Engels (1848/1953: 35) argued in their *Communist Manifesto* that the restrictions imposed by the guild system and the feudal state turned the "bourgeoisie" into "a most revolutionary" political and social force. There is, however, no intrinsic reason why the state of affairs that existed throughout most of Europe and the Americas in 1750 necessarily led in the direction of a new industrial economy. In 1750, as in 1150, the commercial and financial sectors serviced small luxury niche markets. In doing so, merchants and bankers enriched themselves. Even where revolutions reduced both royal powers on commerce, there is no inherent reason why this should cause any fundamental alteration in methods of work and production. If we are looking for the "most revolutionary" forces in Europe in 1750 – measured in terms of their capacity to fundamentally alter the nature of management – we would certainly not find them among the sugar and tobacco merchants of Virginia or London. Rather we would find them among the builders of the Bridgeport Canal, which helped create the world's first mass market, and among the engineers who serviced the new steam engines pumping water from Britain's coal mines.

Conclusion

In assessing managerial and business practices, and associated systems of work and technology, one needs to constantly maintain a sense of perspective, to neither understate nor overstate the degree of advancement. Yes, it is true, as Burckhardt (1867/1954: 101) famously observed in his study of the Italian Renaissance, that the growth of commerce during the late medieval era was seminal to the emergence of a fundamentally new sort of society, one that emphasized "individuality" and "a development of free personality." During the Renaissance the glorious island city of Venice was, for a time, "the jewel-basket of the world." It was from Venice's Rialto, so Burckhardt (1867/1954: 51) recorded with only a slight degree of exaggeration, that "the business of the world" was transacted. As Europe's preeminent businesspeople, the Venetians had little room for superstition or religious dogma. When in the early seventeenth century the mathematician and experimental scientist, Galileo Galilei, opened up new vistas in commerce and astronomy with his telescopes, the Venetians defended him against all criticism. Galileo's near fatal mistake was to leave the safety of the Venetian lagoon to live in less commercially oriented communities. Evidence of the transformative effects of commerce on the medieval mind is found in unlikely places. For example, in his *Treatise on the Rule and Government of the City of Florence*, Girolamo Savonarola (1495/2006: 195) – the radical Dominican infamously associated with the "Bonfires of the Vanities" (i.e., the public burning of books, paintings, and personal luxuries) – argued that the religious and political reform would benefit Florence "because merchants and other rich men, hearing of this good government, will flock to the city." And, the inevitable consequence of this, Savonarola (1495/2006: 203) continued, would be that "everyone will be free . . . and everyone will find work." Yet, in Savonarola's Florence we also get a sense of profound doubt as to where the society was headed, a sense that the glittering commerce of Renaissance Italy was trapped in an economic dead end. Such concerns were well founded. By the 1500s, real wages in Florence and nearby Milan had begun a long, grinding process of decline. In the latter half of the eighteenth century, the real wage of unskilled building workers stood at just 56.5% of its sixteenth century peak (Broadberry and Gupta 2006: 7).

In the final analysis, the failure evident in not only Florence and Milan but in most Europe societies in the early modern era must be attributed to a failure of management. Certainly we can find plentiful evidence of business entities, large and small, carrying out the basic functions of management: planning, organizing, leading, and controlling. When, however, we extend our definition – as we have throughout this chapter – to include a wider criteria (attention to costs, firm specialization, gearing of production to mass markets, legal protection of property and individual liberty, free movement of capital and labor) a very different picture emerges. Despite advances in accounting it was still the case in the mid-eighteenth century that few businesses either understood or cared about their cost structure (Hoskin and Macve 1986: 112—13). The reason for this is found in the fact that the great bulk of industry and commerce was geared either to local markets, where there was little competition, or to long-distance trade in luxuries and high-value staples. Profits could be made in such markets even with high costs. Of the Hungarian and Polish magnates who sold grain into Western European markets, Braudel (1979/1982: 271–272) observed, "Everything was easy for them . . . They did not strive to reduce the cost of production . . .Whatever the state of the harvest, it was all profit to them." Lack of attention to costs stemmed, in very large part, from the fact that there were no mass markets. On this front we can only attribute a small part of the blame to feudal tolls, charges, and guild restrictions. The real problem was logistical. Land transport remained slow and prohibitively expensive. The tonnage of shipping available at any one time was miniscule by modern standards, the total capacity of the European fleet being easily dwarfed by a handful of modern bulk carriers. Logistic problems also curtailed the movement of capital and labor. Even in 1750, most people lived and died within walking distance of where they were born. Admittedly, the early modern era did witness major advances in terms of protection of property and individual liberty, at least in Northwestern Europe and North America. For most people, however, their freedom was in many ways purely nominal. Living in small and still isolated communities, a vast majority lived on the land, engaged in backbreaking toil. Economically and socially, their options were limited.

If there is one seminal conclusion to emerge from this chapter is that we need to extend our definition of "modern management" even further than we have previously. For, as this chapter has discussed previously on numerous times, pre-industrial societies are built on wood. This causes many adverse effects. Because capital goods (ships, plows, bridges, etc.) are built of wood rather than iron they are inherently fragile. Energy – whether for lighting, heating, or vehicular propulsion – is always in chronically short supply. Inevitably, due to the insatiable demand for timber, there comes a point when native forest reserves are all but consumed. Yes, it is true that feudal society made major advances in harnessing the power of nature in the form of water mills and windmills. From the High Middle Ages onward, however, there was little further advancement, creating a technological ceiling which even the Dutch proved incapable of breaking through. In the end, only England proved capable of breaking through the barriers that had constrained other societies. England's pioneering role owes much to its unique capacity to link new forms of energy (most particularly coal and steam) to new forms of managerial organization. And while it is the mechanization of cotton manufacture that is most commonly associated with the initial stages of the Industrial Revolution, its advances, in truth, were only possible due to earlier gains in coal mining. For the utilization of coal on a mass scale involved far more than simply the mining of another commodity. It entailed a managerial revolution on many fronts. Unlike most other industries, coal mining was capital intensive, requiring the mobilization of large pools of capital through extensive partnerships and share companies. Always a comparative low-value commodity, the profitable mining of coal necessitated a transport revolution or, to be more exact, a series of transport revolutions. Throughout the early modern era the bulk of England's shipping fleet was made of colliers, one commentator observing in the mid-1600s that coal transport was "the chiefest in employment of [British] seamen" (cited, Cipolla 1981: 290). Entrepreneurial and logistical skills obtained in this field transferred to other areas of shipping, laying the basis for Britain's maritime prowess. To efficiently move coal from pithead to ship, England's coal owners also pioneered the world's first (horse-drawn) tram lines. The creation of the world's first true internal mass market was another direct result of the English coal industry as, beginning in the 1750s, a series of canals began to crisscross the country, bringing cheap sources of energy to the towns of England's interior. Unlike other industries the English coal trade was also highly competitive. Writing of the period between 1625 and 1700, John Neff (1932b/1966: 75) observed that "evidence of cut-throat competition and glutted markets" was "especially striking." Savage competition also created modern patterns of labor relations as employers were forced to manage some of the largest workforces of the pre-modern era amid constant fluctuations in sales and prices. In terms of production, Britain's mine managers needed to learn increasingly complex operational skills. People and coal had to be mechanically raised and lowered at the pitheads. Water had to be pumped out. As we have previously noted, the latter problem led to the production and widespread use of the world's first form of steam power: the Newcomen steam engine. Coal mining, and the coal-derived coke that was one of its offshoots, not only made iron making cheaper and easier, the industry also, subsequently, acted as a principal customer for England's eighteenth century iron and steel foundries. In short, in the English coal industry we witness the creation for the first time of an industry that was the antithesis of pre-modern forms of management: an industry characterized by capital intensity, complex forms of ownership, the organization of work around revolutionary new technologies, high-degrees of competition, and the direction of production toward mass markets rather than luxury consumption.

Cross-References

▶ From Feudalism to Modernity, Part 2: The Revolution in Ideas, AD 450–1750
▶ Management in Antiquity: Part 1 – The Binds of Geography
▶ Management in Antiquity: Part 2 – Success and Failure in the Hellenic and Roman Worlds
▶ Transformation: The First Global Economy, 1750–1914
▶ What Is Management?
▶ Work and Society in the Orthodox East: Byzantium and Russia, AD 450–1861

References

Allen RC (2003) Progress and poverty in early modern Europe. Econ Hist Rev 56(3):403–443
Allen RC, Bassino J-P, Ma D, Moll-Murata C, van Zanden JL (2011) Wages, prices, and living standards in China, 1738-1925: in comparison with Europe, Japan, and India. Economic History Review 64(1):8–38
Anderson P (1974) Passages from antiquity to feudalism. New Left Books, London
Bloch M (1940/1962) Feudal society, 2nd edn. Routledge & Kegan Paul, London
Braudel F (1967/1974) Capitalism and material life, 1400–1800. Fontan/Collins, London

Braudel F (1979/1982) The wheels of commerce: civilization and capitalism, 15th–18th century, vol 2. Collins, London

Braudel F (1986/1990) The identity of France: people and production, vol 2, 2nd edn. Harper Torchbooks, New York

Braudel F (1987/1993) A history of civilizations. Penguin Books, Harmondsworth

Broadberry S, Gupta B (2006) The early modern great divergence: wages, prices and economic development in Europe and Asia, 1500–1800. Economic History Review 49(1):2–31

Burckhardt J (1867/1954) The civilization of the renaissance in Italy, 2nd edn. The Modern Library, New York

Cipolla CM (1981) Before the industrial revolution: European society and economy, 1000–1700, 2nd edn. Cambridge University Press, Cambridge

Cole AH, Crandall R (1964) The international scientific committee on price history. J Econ Hist 24(3):381–388

Curtin PD (1969) The Atlantic slave trade: a census. University of Wisconsin Press, Maddison

Davis RHC (1970) A history of medieval Europe, 2nd edn. Longman, London

de Ballaigue C (2018) The Islamic enlightenment: the modern struggle between faith and reason. Vintage, London

Delanty G (2019) Formations of European modernity: a historical and political sociology of Europe, 2nd edn. Palgrave Macmillan, Cham

Ferguson N (2008) Empire: how Britain made the modern world, 2nd edn. Penguin, London

Ferguson N (2011) Civilization: the west and the rest. Allen Lane, London

Fussell GE (1966) Ploughs and ploughing before 1800. Agric Hist 40(3):177–186

Greengrass M (2014) Christendom destroyed: Europe 1517–1648. Penguin Books, London

Hoskin KW, Macve RH (1986) Accounting and the examination: a genealogy of disciplinary power. Acc Organ Soc 11(2):105–136

Huntington SP (1996/2003) The clash of civilizations and the remaking of world order. Simon & Schuster, New York

Jones EL (1987) The European miracle: environments, economies and geopolitics in the history of Europe and Asia, 2nd edn. Cambridge University Press, Cambridge

Jones G (2017) Business history, the great divergence and the great convergence. Working paper 18-004. Harvard Business School, Cambridge, MA

Kieser A (1987) From asceticism to administration of wealth: medieval monasteries and the pitfalls of rationalization. Organ Stud 8(2):103–123

Li B, van Zanden JL (2012) Before the great divergence? Comparing the Yangzi delta and the Netherlands at the beginning of the nineteenth century. J Econ Hist 72(4):956–989

Locke J (1689/1823) Two treatises on government. Thomas Tegg, London. Republished by McMaster Archive of the History of Economic Thought. http://www.yorku.ca/comninel/courses/3025pdf/Locke.pdf

Marx K, Engels F (1848/1953) The communist manifesto. In: Marx K, Engels F (eds) Selected works, vol 1. Foreign languages Publishing Gouse, Moscow, USSR, pp 21–61

Mintz SW (1985) Sweetness and power: the place of sugar in modern history. Viking, New York

Morgan LH (1878) Ancient society. Henry Holt and Company, New York

North DC, Thomas RP (1970) An economic theory of the growth of the Western world. Economic History Review 23(1):1–17

North DC, Thomas RP (1973) The rise of the Western world: a new economic history. Cambridge University Press, London

Neff JU (1932a/1966) The rise of the British coal industry, vol 1. Frank Cass and Co., London

Neff JU (1932b/1966) The rise of the British coal industry, vol 2. Frank Cass and Co., London

Palma N and Reis J (2019) From convergence to divergence: Portuguese economic growth 1527-1850. Journal of Economic History 79(2):477–506

Pacioli L (1494/1994) Accounting books and records: the *summa de arithmetica, geometria, proportioni et proportionalita*. Pacioli Society, Seattle

Parain C (1941/1966) The evolution of agricultural technique. In: Postan MM (ed) The Cambridge economic history of Europe, vol 1. Cambridge University Press, Cambridge, pp 125–179

Parthasarathi P (1998) Rethinking wages and competitiveness in the eighteenth century: Britain and South India. Past Present 158(1):79–109

Phelps Brown EH, Hopkins SV (1956) Seven centuries of the prices of consumables, compared with builders' wage rates. Economica 23(92):296–314

Pirenne H (1925/1952) Medieval cities: their origins and the revival of trade. Princeton University Press, Princeton

Pirenne H (1936) Economic and social history of medieval Europe. Routledge & Kegan Paul, London

Pirenne H (1939) Mohammed and Charlemagne. Barnes & Noble, New York

Polo G (2012) On maritime transport costs, evolution, and forecast. Ship Sci Technol 5(10):1–31

Pomeranz K (2000) The great divergence: China, Europe, and the making of the modern world economy. Princeton University Press, Princeton

Rostow WW (1963) Leading sectors and the take-off. In: Rostow WW (ed) The economics of take-off into sustained growth. Macmillan, London, pp 1–21

Rousseau J-J (1762/1979) Emile: on education. Penguin Classics, Lonond

Said EW (1978/2003) Orientalism, 25th anniversary edition. Vintage Books, New York

Savonarola G (1495/2006) Treatise on the rule and government of the city of Florence. In: Boreilli A, Passaro MP (eds) Selected writings of Girolamo Savonarola: religion and politics, 1490–1498. Yale University Press, New Haven

Smith A (1759/2017) The theory of moral sentiments. Early modern texts. https://www.earlymoderntexts.com/assets/pdfs/smith1759.pdf. Accessed 12 Sept 2019

Stevens CE (1941/1966) Agriculture and rural life in the later Roman empire. In: Postan MM (ed) The Cambridge economic history of Europe, vol 1. Cambridge University Press, Cambridge, pp 92–124

Thomas H (1997) The slave trade: the history of the Atlantic slave trade 1440–1870. Picador, London

van Bavel JP, van Zanden JL (2004) The jump-start of the Holland economy during the late-medieval crisis, c.1350–c.1500. Econ Hist Rev 58(3):6503–6532

van Zanden JL (2002) The 'revolt of the early modernists' and the 'first modern economy': an assessment. Economic History Review 55(4):619–641

Voltaire (1734/2002) Letters on England. Electronic series publication. Pennsylvania State University, Hazleton

Weber M (1905/2003) The protestant ethic and the spirit of capitalism. Dover, New York

Weber M (1922/1927) General economic history. The Free Press, Glencoe

Wirtz P (2017) Governance of old religious orders: Benedictines and Dominicans. J Manag Hist 23(2):259–277

From Feudalism to Modernity, Part 2: The Revolution in Ideas, AD 450–1750

10

Bradley Bowden

Contents

Introduction	216
The Catholic Legacy: Work, Innovation, and Poverty, c.AD 450–c.1250	222
A Calculative Mentality? Western Europe at the Crossroads, c.1250–1600	227
Society and the Scientific Revolution, c.1600–c.1750	234
Conclusion	238
Cross-References	240
References	241

Abstract

This chapter explores the ideas and intellectual ethos that both advanced and retarded managerial innovation and endeavor between AD 450 and 1750. Many of the factors that advanced managerial ideas and practices during this period owed their origins to the medieval monasteries. Prominent among these were a love of learning and new institutions for study in the form of universities. The medieval monasteries also placed a high value on the dignity of work, fostering a "Calvinist" work ethic long before the Protestant Reformation. It was also the case that work and study were seen as intertwined rather than separate in the medieval monastery. If, however, an emphasis on learning and work advanced both management and society as a whole, it was also the case that some of the institutions responsible for progress also acted as retardants. Prior to the Reformation, the Catholic Church's claim to the only legitimate source

---

B. Bowden (✉)
Griffith Business School, Griffith University, Nathan, QLD, Australia
e-mail: b.bowden@griffith.edu.au

© The Author(s), under exclusive licence to Springer Nature Switzerland AG 2020
B. Bowden et al. (eds.), *The Palgrave Handbook of Management History*,
https://doi.org/10.1007/978-3-319-62114-2_102

of knowledge acted as a brake on new forms of inquiry. The late medieval enthusiasm for Aristotelian philosophy and science was another obstacle; not only did Aristotle draw a sharp distinction between "theoretical" and "empirical" thought. He also believed "theology" to be "the most divine science." Only with the Scientific Revolution of the seventeenth century were new secular forms of research and inquiry legitimated.

Keywords

Management · Catholicism · Monasteries · Calvin · Dante · Isaac Newton · Scientific revolution

Introduction

The period between the fall of the Western Roman Empire and the Industrial Revolution was one characterized by profound shifts in ideas, a shift which saw management increasingly embrace science as a transformative agent. By 1750, it is clear, a unique capacity to link scientific inquiry with other factors peculiar to the economies of northwest Europe and North America – individual liberty, the need to motivate legally free workforces, guaranteed protections for private property, attention to costs, the gearing of production to mass markets, and a newfound capacity to exploit almost limitless reserves of artificial energy in the form of coal – underpinned a profound and irreversible alteration in the human condition. For, as we noted in ▶ Chap. 9, "From Feudalism to Modernity, Part I: Management, Technology, and Work, AD 450–1750" the societies of the medieval and early modern worlds always remained – whatever their other achievements – economically backward affairs, always on the edge of starvation. In discussing this fundamental fact in our earlier chapter, we noted how a skilled building worker from the south of England suffered a lower living standard in 1750 than what his predecessor had experienced 250 years before. It is thus fitting to begin this chapter by returning to the condition of this typical worker to see how this worker fared in the years after 1750. As Fig. 1 indicates, which draws on the Phelps Brown and Hopkins (1956) real wage index, the initial effect of the Industrial Revolution was negative as English society was torn from its agricultural moorings amid rising food prices and a mass relocation of people to the cities. From 1800 onward, however, real wages began an inexorable rise, belying – for the first time in history – Braudel's (1963/1975: 725) observation that the "price of progress" was always "social oppression," a process in which, "Only the poor gained nothing, could hope for nothing."

If we accept the premise that any profound alteration in the material conditions of life requires a change in mental outlook, a consideration of Fig. 1 forces us in the direction of two key propositions. The first of these stems from the observation that the inability of feudal and early modern societies to break through a seemingly fixed economic ceiling suggests the pervasive presence of ideas that hindered

10 From Feudalism to Modernity, Part 2: The Revolution in Ideas, AD 450–1750

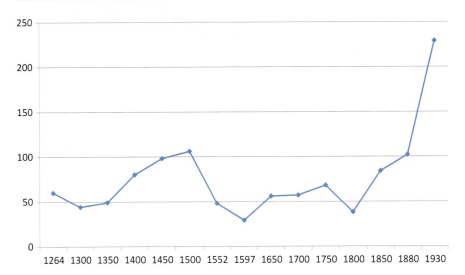

Fig. 1 Real wage of skilled building worker in Southern England, 1264–1930 (1447 = 100). (Source: Phelps Brown and Hopkins: "Seven centuries of ... builders' wage rates," Appendix B)

scientific inquiry and novel approaches to economic and managerial organization. The second proposition, which is necessarily cojoined to the first, is that the profound transformation that occurred after 1750 could only have occurred if the ideas and belief systems that retarded progress existed alongside ones that favored individual initiative, economic endeavor, and intellectual curiosity.

In exploring the factors that both retarded and advanced intellectual inquiry and scientific discovery, this chapter argues that the period between AD 450 and 1750 can be demarked into three broad epochs (c.AD 450–c.1250, c.1250–c.1600, c.160–c.1750), each of which saw an affirmation of some intellectual premises from the preceding period and a full or partial rejection of others.

The first of these epochs, which was to define Western Europe as a distinct civilization, fundamentally unlike either the societies of antiquity or those found elsewhere in the Old World, was clearly evident by AD 450 and on the wane by 1200. Unlike both preceding and ensuing periods of European history, the ideas which prevailed during this era – and which were literally held with religious force – were associated with a single institution: the Catholic Church. In an increasingly violent and unstable world, the Church and its various subsidiary institutions – most notably the monastic orders – were more than mere fonts of literacy. They also fostered a deeply held love of learning. Many of the Church's founding fathers (St John Chrysostom, St Augustine, St Benedict, Pope Gregory the Great) were educated in the secular schools of rhetoric and philosophy that continued to enrol would-be administrators and philosophers during the fifth and sixth centuries. As the French philosopher, Albert Camus (1935/2007: 62), observed in his study, *Christian Metaphysics and Neoplatonism*, much of Christianity's success is attributable to its ability to "express itself in understandable [Greek and Roman] formulas." The merger of Christian and Greek Neoplatonist thought was most pronounced in St Augustine's theological studies. Like Plato (c.380 BC/2003: 206), who believed that a just society could only be achieved through "the acquisition of knowledge," St Augustine (c.395/2010: 88) argued that, "knowledge is a higher and truer form of life …knowledge can never be evil." If, however, Catholic dogma during the so-called Dark Ages (c.AD 450–950) incorporated many of the philosophic understandings of the Late Empire, it also broke with Greek and Roman norms in ways that fostered new approaches to work and managerial organization. Nowhere was this rupture more evident than in attitudes to manual labor. Whereas in the Roman Empire any form of manual labor was perceived to be the degraded domain of slaves, the Christian theologians of the early Church considered physical work to be a form of spiritual fulfilment. As St Benedict (c.AD 516/1931: 22) expressed it in Chap. 48 of his famous Rule, would-be followers of Christ became true disciples when "they live by the work of their hands." Christian belief also differed from the norms that prevailed in antiquity in its emphasis on individual worth, regardless of material circumstances. As an early Church theologian, St John Chrysostom (c.AD 400/1984: 99–100) informed his congregation,

I do not despise anyone … he is a human being, the living creature for which God cares. Even if he is a slave, I may not despise him; I am not interested in his class, but his virtue.

If there were elements of Catholic faith that were supportive of new approaches to work, there were also dogmas that made the Church a long-term foe of commercial exchange and nascent forms of capitalism. Nowhere was this more apparent than in the Church's attitude to private wealth. St John Chrysostom (c.AD 398/1848: 382), who served as Archbishop of Constantinople at the dawn of the fifth century, warned his flock that private wealth was nothing more than a "vain shadow, dissolving smoke." In a more overt opposition to the possession of wealth, Pope Gregory the Great (c.AD 599/1959: 268), who laid the foundations for the medieval papacy, recorded how, on finding a deceased monk to be in possession of three gold pieces, he gave instruction to "cast his body into a grave dug in a manure pile." At the pulpit, churchgoers were constantly warned that the hoarding of wealth imperilled their immortal soul. This opposition to private wealth, it needs to be emphasized, does not mean that the Church's founding fathers were nascent socialists, opposed to all forms of social inequality. Nor was the Church, despite its constant emphasis on almsgiving, a champion of the poor in opposition to the powerful. In reflecting on the influence of St John Chrysostom, a theologian who embodied the Church's opposition to material wealth, Wendy Mayer (2009: 109) concludes, "If we are obliged to label him … it is more accurate to call him not a champion of the poor, but of poverty." Such observations are applicable to the medieval Church as a whole. Yes, it is true that the medieval monasteries were more than centers of learning and faith. They were also, as a biographer of St Benedict noted, "a great economic factor in the new Europe," places that disseminated the "fundamental arts of civilization" in the form of watermills and

10 From Feudalism to Modernity, Part 2: The Revolution in Ideas, AD 450–1750

efficient agricultural practices (McCann 1937: 100). It is also true, as Kieser (1987), Wirtz (2017), and others have pointed out, that over time, the commercial success of the monasteries – and the donations they received from an admiring public – tended to make them inordinately wealthy. Acquired monastic and church wealth, however, always flew in the face of the principles of faith that guided Catholic Christendom. Accordingly, material success continued to attract public approbation rather than praise. Dante Alighieri (c.1310/2012), for example, in his journey through hell, finds the souls of the "avarice" subject to eternal torment in an inner circle of the damned. Prominent among those these unfortunates are "popes" and "cardinals." "In that lot," Dante Alighieri (c.1310/2012: 31) observed, "avarice displays its worst."

The medieval Church's emphasis on poverty, manual labor, prudence, and almsgivings was, perhaps, well suited on the closed agricultural communities that characterized the European experience between AD 450 and 1250. However, by the time of Europe's thirteenth-century "Commercial Revolution" – associated with new forms of finance, banking, accounting, and a growth in long-distance trade – the dogmas of medieval faith were, to an ever-increasing extent, incompatible with the aspirations of the acquisitive merchant cities of Italy, the Low Countries, the Hanseatic League, and Southern Germany. Reflecting on this tension in his study of Renaissance Italy, Burckhardt (1867/1954: 148) observed that by 1300, there had "appeared a new civilization" which presented itself "as competitor with the whole culture of the Middle Ages, which was essentially clerical." At a popular level, the clearest expression of this "new civilization" was arguably found in Dante's *Divine Comedy*. Written in Italian rather than Latin, Dante's work was not only directed toward a secular audience; it also finds inspiration in the secular wisdom of antiquity. Dante's guide through hell and purgatory is not a Christian saint but rather the Roman poet, Virgil. On meeting Virgil for the first time, Dante acknowledges in glowing terms the inspirational effect of Virgil's writings on his own imagination, declaring "you are that Virgil . . . the light and glory of all poets . . . You are my teacher. You, my lord and law." Far more significant than Dante's musings, however, was the flowering of a unique offshoot of the medieval monastery, the university. Like the medieval monastery, the university was composed of novices and masters who dedicated their lives to learning rather than to the raising of families. Such was the enthusiasm for learning that many sacrificed any prospect of material advancement. As Compayré (1910: 266) recorded, "Great was the number of those who, destitute of all resources, joyfully braved privations, poverty, and the irksomeness of menial service, in order that they might penetrate at last into the sanctuary of knowledge." Despite sharing many commonalities with the medieval monastery, the universities of Paris, Bologna, Cracow, and elsewhere differed in that inquiries were increasing directed outward, at the problems of the secular world. From the outset, municipal authorities – anxious to foster the new centers of learning – guaranteed university staff freedom of speech and protection from persecution, guarantees that made the university "one of the great public forces of the Middle Ages" (Compayré 1910: 287). Within the new halls of learning, the most significant attempt to come to grips with the emerging commercial world was made by St Thomas Aquinas, a figure often described as the Father of Economics. Central to Aquinas' studies was his attempt to redefine or, to be more exact, *define* the concept of economic "value" in a system of market exchanges. Recognizing that the medieval understanding of a "just price" was rendered meaningless due to "the differences of supply," Aquinas (c.1270/1952: Q. 77, Article 2) concluded that, "the price of things saleable does not depend" on their physical nature but rather on their utility or "usefulness to man." Having come to this novel conclusion, St Thomas Aquinas (c.1270/1952: Q. 77, Article 4) proceeded to overturn Church dogma on usury (lending), arguing that money invested in long-distance trade and other ventures could justly claim a share of any profits because "the value of the thing [being traded] has changed with the change of place or time." The ethos of the new commercial world also found cogent expression in the work of another clerical scholar, the Franciscan friar, Luca Pacioli (1494/1994: preface, unpaged), who began his famed study of accounting by noting that a well-set out "accounting manual" was "much needed by businessmen" desirous of exercising "proper internal control" over their transactions.

In large part, the Renaissance (c.1250–c.1600) attempt to intellectually adapt to a growing market economy was framed in terms of the philosophy and principles of secular antiquity. Not only Dante but also Petrarch, Leonardo da Vinci, Michelangelo, and countless others sought, as Burckhardt (1867/1954: 148) noted with only slight exaggeration, "to think" and "to feel, as the ancients thought and felt." Such was the interest in Greek antiquity, Burckhardt (1867/1954: 376–377) continued, that by the 1400s, "All the writings of the Greek philosophers which we ourselves possess were . . . in everybody's hands."

Unfortunately, the attempt to construct a new intellectual edifice – capable of meeting the changing aspirations of an increasingly commercialized economy – brought with it pitfalls as well as promise. Nowhere were the retrograde effects of this tendency more apparent than in the medieval and early modern enthusiasm for Aristotelian philosophy. Although a master of logic, Aristotle's understandings of the natural sciences were profoundly misguided, as were those of his disciples, most particularly the astronomer, Ptolemy of Alexandria. Like Ptolemy (c.AD 160/1984), who used complex mathematical calculations to prove that the earth stood at the center of the universe, Aristotle (c.350 BC/1941: 712) drew a sharp distinction between "theoretical knowledge," or "truth," and "empirical" knowledge. In Aristotle's misguided opinion, "theoretical knowledge" must always give primacy to "the things that are always in the same state and suffer no change," a category within which Aristotle erroneously included "the heavenly bodies." Like Ptolemy (c.AD 160/1984: 35), who advised his readers that "theoretical" knowledge only dealt with "physics, mathematics and theology," Aristotle (c.350 BC/1941: 861) also argued that theology – what he called the "divine science" – was the highest form of knowledge because it "deals with the highest of things."

A number of factors combined to make Aristotelian philosophy a major impediment to economic and intellectual advancement. On the one hand, Aristotle's philosophy appealed to Catholic traditionalists due to its emphasis on an unchanging universe overseen by a divine being. On the other hand, the pseudoscience of

10 From Feudalism to Modernity, Part 2: The Revolution in Ideas, AD 450–1750

Aristotle and Ptolemy appealed to secular Renaissance scholars because it was rooted in the revered traditions of classical antiquity. It is therefore wrong to argue, as Delanty (2019: 111–112) does, that, "The Renaissance marked the end of the medieval age and the birth of modernity" and that the "Renaissance world" also "produced the Scientific Revolution." Instead, Western European culture in the time of the Renaissance found itself in a halfway house, looking backward rather than forward for intellectual inspiration. To break the Aristotelian straightjacket, with its backward-looking emphasis on antiquity and an unchanging universe, was to require a far more profound rupture than that which demarked the change of intellectual opinion in the thirteenth and fourteenth centuries.

In much of the historical literature, the pride of place in this final intellectual revolution – which laid the groundwork for the Industrial and Managerial Revolutions on the eighteenth and nineteenth centuries – is given to the Protestant Reformation in general and Calvinism in particular. Max Weber, in particular, most forcefully argued the supposed existence of a close and intimate connection between Calvinism and nascent capitalism. In Weber's (1922/1927: 367) opinion, the Calvinist "ethic" was seminal in capitalism's advance because it placed a value on the pursuit of wealth as "a God-given task" (also see Weber 1905/2003). Superficially appealing, Weber's thesis is nevertheless of dubious veracity. One is certainly hard put to establish a direct link between Protestantism and the Scientific Revolution of the seventeenth century. Nicolaus Copernicus, for example, who first challenged the Aristotelian understanding of the cosmos, was a wandering Catholic scholar who boasted a doctorate in Canon law. Galileo Galilei, whose use of telescopes in 1609 provided empirical support for the Copernican conception of the solar system, was also a pious Catholic. As for the effect of Calvinism in the realms of business and management, perhaps the best summation is that provided by R.H. Tawney (1926/1936: 132), who observed in his *Religion and the Rise of Capitalism* that, while Calvinism "had little pity for poverty," it also "distrusted wealth, as it distrusted all influences that distract . . . the soul."

If we are to understand the origins of the Scientific Revolution, and the ways in which it was harnessed by the subsequent Industrial and Managerial Revolutions, we need to look beyond the narrow confines of scientific research to enabling factors in the wider society. That these enabling factors - mechanical innovation, commercial and intellectual interchange, freedom of expression, and protection of property - were vital to scientific research was well recognized by Robert Hooke, whose studies in the realm of microbiology stand alongside those of Isaac Newton in physics in providing foundational principles for modern science. In describing how microscopes opened up "a new visible World to the understanding" – a world in which "every little particle" possessed "almost as great a variety of Creatures, as we were able to reckon up in the whole Universe" – Hooke (1665: preface, unpaged) paid tribute to the mechanics who had made his work possible through the development of "artificial instruments." In the dedication to his *Micrographia: Or Some Physiological Descriptions of Minute Bodies Made by Magnifying Glasses*, Hooke (1665: dedication, unpaged) also linked advances in "experimental learning" to the "calm prosperity" of seventeenth-century English society, a prosperity associated with "the improvement of manufactures and agriculture, the increase of commerce, and advantage of navigation." Significantly, Hooke looked not only backward to the factors that made his research possible; he also looked forward to the practical application of his endeavors. In doing so, Hooke (1665: preface, unpaged) indicated, he "not only hoped for Inventions to equalize" those of earlier generations. He also anticipated "multitudes" of applications "that may far exceed them." In Hooke, as with Newton, we can see not only an individual scientist but also a whole civilization at the cusp of two worlds. Hooke's discoveries were possible because he belonged to a society that, as Cipolla (1981: 182) observed, had "an irresistible taste for mechanical achievements," an outlook that had its roots in the ethos of medieval society with its emphasis on the dignity of work. Hooke's research had meaning because, as he was aware, he lived in a society intent on "the improvement of manufactures and agriculture."

The Catholic Legacy: Work, Innovation, and Poverty, c.AD 450–c.1250

In his *A History of Civilizations*, Braudel (1987/1993: 23) observed that by comparison with other cultures for whom religion remains seminal, "the West seems forgetful of its Christian sources." Yet, despite this, Braudel (1987/1993: 23) continues, "Ethical rules, attitudes to life and death, the concept of work, the value of effort ... all derive from it."

While there is merit in Braudel's observation, it is also the case that for more than a millennia, the ethos, culture, and modes of action in Western Europe were dominated by one peculiar form of Christianity: Catholicism. The Catholic Church, it must be emphasized, was never an unchanging monolith. Within the Church, the various monastic orders always enjoyed a semiautonomous existence. Papal control over its various national wings (i.e., France, Germany, etc.) waxed and waned. The mendicant or teaching orders that become an integral part of religious life in the High Middle Ages (i.e., Dominicans, Franciscans, Augustinians) only emerged during the course of the thirteenth century. Despite this organizational flux, the Church nevertheless remained constant in the values it embodied and the dogma it preached. Moreover, although Catholicism shared commonalities with other strands of Christianity (i.e., Arianism, Greek Orthodoxy, Nestorian dyophysitism, etc.), it also differed from them in being an historical product of a peculiar moment in Western European history, a period which saw the gradual eclipse of Roman traditions and institutions in the wake of the great Germanic *Volkerwanderung* of the fifth century. From this experience, three distinct strands or influences can be discerned.

The first of these strands, common to all Christian denominations, is found in the conditions of life that characterized Palestine during the time of the New Testament. By comparison with other parts of the Roman Empire (Italy, North

10 From Feudalism to Modernity, Part 2: The Revolution in Ideas, AD 450–1750

Africa, Syria), Palestine was comparatively poor, its citizens typically eking an existence from small-scale farming, herding, and fishing. As even the most cursory reading of the New Testament indicates, frugality – if not abject poverty – was the societal norm. The New Testament emphasis on thrift, self-denial, and assistance of one's neighbor is most pronounced in St Luke's *Acts of the Apostles*, which records the practices of the first Christian communities after the crucifixion. Among the "whole group of believers," Luke (c.AD 70/1985: 4: 32–35) stated:

> ... no one claimed private ownership of any possessions, as everything they owned was held in common ... None of their members was ever in want, as all those who owned land or houses would sell them, and bring the money from the sale of them to present to the apostles; it was then distributed to any who might be in need.

The asceticism of the early Christian communities also manifested itself in the prevalence of hermits and monks who sought to demonstrate their piety by retreating into caves, deserts, and mountaintops. In these locales, each of these ascetics seemed intent on outdoing the feats of John the Baptist, a figure who is described in the New Testament as wearing only a loincloth and "a garment made of camel-hair" while living on nothing but "locusts and wild honey" (St Mathew, c.AD 65/1985: 3: 4–5). Among the early Church theologian, the foremost advocate of frugality, even asceticism, was St John Chrysostom, whose study *On Wealth and Poverty* had a profound influence on both the Catholic and Orthodox versions of Christianity. To please God, Chrysostom (c.AD 400/1984: 76–77) warned, "it is absolutely necessary" to live "a laborious life, groaning with much toil and sweat." St John Chrysostom had a particular distrust of monetary wealth, believing such forms of prosperity were only legitimated when the wealthy freely lent of their money to the poor, a viewpoint that made Chrysostom – and subsequently the Catholic Church as a whole – a vigorous opponent of usury, i.e., the lending of money for profit. "For our money is the Lord's, however we may have gathered it," Chrysostom (c.AD 400/1984: 49–50) advised the faithful, adding: "This is why God allowed you to have more ... to distribute to those in need."

If the asceticism of the Catholic Church, and its abiding distrust of monetarized wealth, was rooted in the poverty of Palestine at the time of the New Testament, a second formative strand – which saw the Church come to an accommodation with the dominant, Neoplatonist philosophies of the Late Empire – came from the other end of the socioeconomic spectrum. For the new Christian faith could never have succeeded unless it appealed to elite opinion, speaking to the graduates of the secular schools of rhetoric and philosophy in terms which they understood. No one was more successful in mediating this process of accommodation than St Augustine. Indeed, it is arguable that the Catholic dogma that prevailed in Western Europe from the fifth century owed as much to St Augustine as it did to the New Testament. Evidence of St Augustine's profound effect on Western intellectual thought is found in the fact that even the revolutionary Protestant theologian, John Calvin, who repudiated most Catholic dogma, framed his thinking in an

Augustinian framework, declaring "I am teaching no novel doctrine, but what was long ago advanced by Augustine" (Calvin 1536/2014: 345). A North African scholar who, prior to his comparatively late conversion to Christianity, taught rhetoric in Milan, St Augustine's novel framing of Christian faith was laid out in three principal texts: *The Free Choice of the Will* (c.AD 395), *Confessions* (c.AD 400), and *The City of God* (c.AD 430). In the first of these works, and in Chap. X of *Confessions*, St Augustine argued philosophic premises that owed as much to Plato as they did to Christ. Like Plato, and unlike Aristotle, St Augustine (c.AD 400/2007: 153–157) believed that perception was based not on "the things themselves" but rather mental "images" generated by the objects of our senses. Like Plato, who believed that only study and knowledge brought one to truth, St Augustine (c.AD 395/2010: 73) argued, "it is altogether impossible to learn things evil." Like Plato (c.380 BC/2003: 236), who recorded that only an educated elite was capable of true knowledge, St Augustine (c.AD 395/2010: 141) wrote that "few men are capable of wisdom." Where St Augustine transcended Plato was in arguing that only God's grace allowed the student a full knowledge of truth. "For there is nothing so obscure and difficult that cannot, with God's help," St Augustine (c.AD 395/2010: 83) advised, "become perfectly easy clear and easy." Collectively, St Augustine's works not only legitimated the Church's sought-after place as the inheritor of antiquity's entire body of knowledge; it also made the Church the only portal through which knowledge could properly be acquired. St Augustine's insistence that the Church was the secular as well as spiritual successor of imperial Rome was reinforced in his final major work, *The City of God*, where he declared that the "most glorious society" was the "city of God's faithful," a transnational society of believers (St Augustine, c.AD 430/1945: 1).

Whereas St Augustine couched the second strand of Catholic faith in terms of reason, knowledge, and classical philosophy, the final strand – centered on spiritual mysticism and belief in a myriad of saints – was grounded in millennialism, a profound sense that the known material world was on the edge of destruction. By the sixth century, there was, admittedly, objective reason for fearing the end was nigh. Writing in the aftermath of the devastating Lombard invasions, Pope Gregory the Great (c.AD 559/1959: 186), for example, painted the bleakest of pictures, recording in his *Dialogues* how,

> *The population of Italy, which had grown vast, like a rich harvest of grain, was cut down to wither away. Cities were sacked, fortifications overthrown, churches burned, monasteries and cloisters destroyed. Farms were abandoned, and the countryside, uncultivated, became a wilderness. The land was no longer occupied by its owners, and wild beasts roamed the fields where so many people had once made their homes.*

In a land that had once boasted the likes of Cicero, Virgil, and Livy – and where people had previously placed their faith in Roman law – people now regularly claimed to walk alongside saints, risen from the dead. Societal belief in visions and saints, it needs to be emphasized, was more than mere folk lore. It was made an article of faith by the Papacy. In explaining the purposes of his *Dialogues*, for example, Pope Gregory the Great (c.AD 559/1959: vi) declared that, "He wanted them [the people] to realize that they were living in a land of saints and that great miracles were as numerous among the Fathers of Italy as they had been among the Fathers of the Desert." What brought the saints and other divine beings into the material world, Pope Gregory argued, was a merging of the spiritual and material worlds as the existence of the latter ebbed away. "For," Pope Gregory (c.AD 559/1959: 251) explained, "as the present world approaches its end, the world of eternity looms nearer, manifesting itself by ever clearer signs ... In this way the end of the world merges with the beginnings of eternal life."

In summing up the ethos of the Catholic Church, we can thus discern an emphasis on work but a hostility to monetarized wealth, sitting alongside a claim that the Church was not only the sole legitimate source of knowledge but also a portal to a world of saints and spirits. At one level, this ethos was not only outward looking but transnational, claiming the allegiance of people whatever their social status, gender, or ethnicity. In doing so, it created a common Western European culture of "Christendom" that did much to facilitate exchanges of not only ideas but also of goods, technologies, business practices, and people. Consequently, a traveler going about their business in Medieval Europe, "felt as much at home in Lübeck as in Paris, in London as in Bruges, in Cologne as in Burgos, Milan or Venice. Moral, religious and cultural values ...were the same everywhere" (Braudel 1987/1993: 315). At another level, however, the dogma espoused by the Church was not only inward looking but also inherently conservative, valuing the past rather than a problematic material future. Admittedly, there was always a gap between Church dogma and practice, a gap that was most pronounced in the Church's attitude toward wealth, where an all too obvious hypocrisy often prevailed. As we noted in our earlier ▶ Chap. 8, "Management in Antiquity: Part 2 – Success and Failure in the Hellenic and Roman Worlds," by the fourth century, the Church was "amongst the greatest" of "landlords," controlling swathes of countryside and armies of serfs (Stevens 1941/1966: 122). In medieval society, everyone, rich and poor alike, was forced to surrender 10% of their income to the Church. Among the construction projects of the medieval world, there was nothing to equal the great Gothic cathedrals. Yet, as we discussed in the introduction to this chapter, clerical displays of wealth almost always provoked condemnation rather than admiration precisely because they flew in the face of the Church's fundamental principles. The organizational result of this conflict between principle and practice was a sad cycle of reform and decay, in which new religious orders (Cistercians, Franciscans, etc.) were built on a promised return to foundational principles (i.e., poverty, self-denial, manual labor) only to suffer the same problems as their predecessors.

Nowhere was the tension between work and wealth, between spirituality and worldliness, more pronounced than in the Catholic monasteries, institutions where "the puritan work ethic created by the monks led to the accumulation of immense wealth" (Kieser 1987: 103). This tension was central not only to the fate of the Church but also the economic advancement of Western Europe as a whole. "Because of their rational organization," Kieser (1987: 113) maintains, "Benedictine monasteries attained more than their secular counterparts … not only in management, production, and architectural methods, but also in agricultural skills, e.g. the art of planning orchards and improving fruit trees through grafting, breeding of livestock, wine and beer-making." In the thirteenth century, it was the Cistercian monasteries, built around a return to St Benedict's original Rule, that moved to the fore, becoming European leaders in metal smelting, in glass production, and in the use of windmills (Kieser 1987: 118). Between the ninth and thirteenth centuries, moreover, it was the monasteries who were at the forefront of what has been called a "massive operation of internal [European] colonization" (Braudel 1986/1990: 138), bringing land that had reverted to forests and swamps back into cultivation. Belying the Church's patriarchal hierarchy, female monasteries figured prominently in this process of internal colonization, Graetzer and Rost (2015: 23) estimating that they made up almost 30% of the Catholic total. The organizational principles espoused by the monasteries also acted as an inspiration for the emerging state bureaucracies, "training bureaucrats and providing a model of dedicated service" (Wirtz 2017: 260). So significant were monasteries in the economic and managerial reconstruction of Western Europe that Braudel (1986/1990: 114) declared "the abbeys in their forest clearings" to be the most significant institutions of the age, far more important "than the palaces or villas of the kings."

Central to the success of the monastic movement was an emphasis on the nobility of manual labor and a disdain for a life of leisure, St Benedict's (c.516/1931: 22) famed Rule warning would-be monks that "Idleness is inimical to the soul." The Benedictine Rule, however, differed from earlier monastic movements in eschewing extreme acts of ascetic self-denial. In the Prologue to the Rule, St Benedict (c.516/1931: 2) advised readers that "the institution" which he had established would avoid practices that were either "harsh" or "burdensome." Accordingly, St Benedict (c.516/1931: 22) recommended that, "To weak and delicate brethren let there be assigned such suitable occupation and duties that they be neither overcome of idleness nor so oppressed by exhaustion through work that they be driven to flight." Rationality and thoughtful care also characterized the Benedictine relationship with the communities within which the monasteries were located, St Benedict's Rule (c.516/1931: 17, 24) requiring the provision of sustenance to local children, the poor, and any wandering traveler. The Benedictine Rule also required monasteries to act as centers of literacy and learning. In the winter months, between October and Easter, when there was little agricultural work to be done, monks were instructed to spend their spare time in reading and writing (St Benedict, c.516/1931: 22). Among the skills in which the Benedictine monasteries became master, none was arguably more significant for the future of Western civilization than their use of a revolutionary new form of manuscript, the Codex book. By locating bound pages within a solid, rectangular cover, the Codex "book" was not only more durable than papyrus scrolls; it also allowed the bringing together of the hitherto disparate sections of a textual source. Prior to the late fourth century, for example, there was no such thing as the "Bible" or the

"New Testament" as we understand it. The Christian enthusiasm for the new form of manuscript reproduction thus represented a turning point in not only European but human intellectual potential, bringing the written word before ever larger populations (Vessey 2007).

If the religiously inspired practices of the early medieval world provided a platform for subsequent economic and managerial advancement, the underlying societal ethos nevertheless remained distrustful of business endeavors undertaken for private monetary gain. Central to medieval economic practices was the concept of a socially acceptable "just price," the Church regarding as sinful any price fixed at a higher level. St Benedict (c.AD 516/1931: 25–26), for example, warned monks against "the evil of avarice . . . in the matter of the prices charged for the goods." Enforced by clerical rule within the monasteries, the concept of a "just price" also legitimated the restrictive behavior of the various craft guilds outside the cloistered walls. Although in theory the enforcement of a "just price" benefited the poor, in practice, it had the reverse effect, trapping society in an endless cycle of poverty through its restrictions on market mechanisms that may have favored innovation and competition. As the great Belgium historian, Henri Pirenne (1936: 186) observed, the long-term effect of guild regulation and the concept of a "just price" was "the destruction of all initiative. No one was permitted to harm others by methods which enabled him to produce more quickly and more cheaply than they. Technical progress took on the appearance of "disloyalty."

In the final analysis, the intellectual and institutional success of the Catholic Church during the medieval period rested on the fact that it spoke to a society in which abject poverty was the norm, a condition that the Church, instead of remedying, cloaked in spiritual legitimacy. Yes, it is true, that the Church constantly chided the rich, emphasizing the sanctity of almsgiving and warning against frivolous displays of prosperity. But the Church also cautioned the poor against complaint as to their social condition, St John Chrysostom (c.AD 400/1984: 39) counselling in his highly influential, *On Wealth and Poverty*, "what pardon [from God] will the poor have who grumble and complain because they beg for a living" when biblical figures had suffered even graver injustices. Acceptance of one's lot was, in short, the best course, rather than business or managerial efforts aimed at rectification.

A Calculative Mentality? Western Europe at the Crossroads, c.1250–1600

Writing of "the great [economic] take-off of the twelfth century," the accounting historians, Hoskin and Macve (1986: 109), argued that the High Middle Ages witnessed the emergence of "a new knowledge elite" possessed of a revolutionary "calculative" mentality. In their view, the primary drivers of this new mental outlook were "the nascent universities" which emerged out of Catholic Church's monastic system. By training both clerical and secular bureaucrats in new auditing and accounting techniques, the Foucauldian-inspired Hoskin and Macve (1986: 112) contend, universities permeated society with a new "discourse of control." Hoskin and Macve's contention that new accounting and auditing practices first emerged in the universities – before ultimately flowing through to the world of business – flies in the face of traditional wisdom. Burckhardt (1867/1954: 51, 57), for example, in his study of Renaissance Italy, indicated that it was Venice – the city "where the business of the world" was transacted – which had the preeminent "claim to be the birthplace of statistical science" and modern methods of accounting. Pirenne (1925/1952: 86) came to similar conclusions, noting that: "No scruple had any weight with the Venetians. Their religion was a religion of business men." Certainly, if we look to Pacioli's famed text on accounting, the evidence strongly suggests that the new calculative mentality flowed from the world of business to the university, rather than the other way around, Pacioli (1494/1994: 2) informing his readers that, "This book describes the accounting system used in Venice."

Whether the new "calculative mentality" flowed from the university system to business or (more likely) in the reverse direction, two things are nevertheless clear: first, that among a significant section of *elite* opinion the old clerical prohibitions on usury, finance, and other associated forms of commercial endeavor lost favor, and, second, that even as rational secularism gained favor among some, large swathes of the populace found themselves attracted to new Protestant forms of religious faith. What is less clear is the extent to which secularism and a "calculative mentality" pervaded the society as a whole, creating intellectual conditions more favorable to business and managerial innovation.

It is the *Divine Comedy*, in which Dante Alighieri is guided through the perils of hell and paradise by the Latin secular poet, Virgil, which perhaps best captures this tension between Renaissance religious faith and a newfound secular humanism. A striking indication of the ways in which long-distance commerce broadened the European mind is found in Dante's Alighieri (c.1310/2012: 19–20) description of a netherworld beyond the edges of hell, a place of "bright enameled green" and "verdant lawn" inhabited not only by the great poets of antiquity (Virgil, Homer, Ovid, Lucan). Also found among this illustrious company were the Muslim scholars Avicenna and Averroes and the warrior-sultan, Saladin. For previous generations, any goodwill toward such Muslim luminaries would have been unthinkable. At the same time, as we noted in the introduction to this chapter, Dante retained the Catholic distrust of moneymaking, placing the "avarice" in one of the inner circles of hell. The same tension between faith and the new secular world is also evident in the writings of Girolamo Savonarola (1452–1498), the Dominican friar who forged a democratic Florentine republic between 1494 and 1498 amid numerous "bonfires of the vanities" (i.e., public burnings of luxuries). Constantly in Savonarola we find an appeal to the benefits of business investment. Through "the government" of Florence "being a good one," Savonarola (1495/2006: 203) wrote in his *Treatise on the Rule and Government of the City of Florence*, "wealth will abound ... because God gives the greatest reward to those who govern their cities well." Prefiguring the work of Thomas Hobbes, John Locke, and Jean-Jacques Rousseau, Savonarola (1495/2006: 179) also called for the restraint of arbitrary power, declaring that "government is bad which forsakes the common good ... such a government is called tyranny." Yet, despite this embrace of constitutional principles, Savonarola also preached a message favoring frugality and asceticism that was little different to that previously advocated by St John Chrysostom. Although "it is not evil to have property and honours," Savonarola (1494a/2006: 145) warned his flock, unless they let "go of possessions," surrendering "them to the poor," they would "die like dogs." Such views, it must be emphasized, were not those of an inconsequential friar. Rather they were ones embraced, for a time, by a majority of Renaissance Florence's population.

In the university sector as well, we see a similar tussle between ideas associated with the new commercial forces and religious faith, the university becoming a pulpit for genuine debate, one observer noting the academic tendency "to talk about everything, discuss everything, intervene in everything" (Colville, cited Compayré 1910: 290).

Among the theologians who dominated intellectual life in the new universities, the most significant attempt to bring about an accommodation of Catholic faith with the new worlds of business and commerce was made, as we noted in our introduction, by St Thomas Aquinas (1225–1274), a Dominican friar who both studied and taught at the University of Paris. Although Aquinas published on a vast range of topics (theology, law, philosophy, science) – my copy of his *Summa Theologica* running to 9453 pages – it is his reflections on the relationship between markets, prices, value, and investment which had the most profound effect on the future directions of Western business and management. In undertaking these explorations in the midst of the "Commercial Revolution" of the thirteenth century, St Thomas Aquinas confronted two questions that were fundamental to the business communities of his time, namely:

1. "Whether it is lawful to sell a thing for more than its worth?" (St Thomas Aquinas, c.1270/1952, Q. 77, Article 1)
2. "Whether it is lawful to ask for any ... consideration for money lent?" (St Thomas Aquinas, c.1270/1952, Q. 78, Article 2)

In responding to the first of these questions – which the Church had previously answered with a resounding "no" – Aquinas quickly shifted the debate from theology and law to economic value, a disciplinary area which he effectively pioneered. In doing so, as we noted in the introduction to this chapter, Aquinas (c.1270/1952, Q. 77, Article 2) emphasized a revolutionary point: that in an economy built on market exchanges, the value of "salable (sic) commodities" will "be different in different places, on account of the differences of supply." From this insight, Aquinas drew an even more radical conclusion. The "value" of any good, Aquinas (c.1270/1952, Q. 77, Article 2, Article 4) recorded, reflected its utility or "usefulness," goods typically selling for a higher sum than their initial purchase price "either because he [the initial buyer] has bettered the thing, or because of the value of the thing has changed with the change of place or time." In other words, if one purchased grain when it was plentiful, stored it, and then sold it at a time when grain was scarce, one could justly, rather than sinfully, demand a higher price. If St Thomas Aquinas' responses to the first question noted above legitimated most forms of commercial trading, his response to the second question also had the practical effect of legitimating commercial lending, finance, and investment – activities hitherto regarded as crafts of the devil. For while Aquinas continued to regard the charging of interest on loans directed toward private consumption (i.e., giving a neighbor a short-term loan to buy food) to be usury, and thus sinful, he came to a different conclusion in the far more important realm of commercial or investment loans. For the person who "entrusts his money to a merchant or a craftsman so as to form a kind of society," Aquinas (c.1270/1952, Q. 78, Article 2) recorded:

> *... does not transfer the ownership of his money to them, for it remains his, so that at his risk the merchant speculates with it, or the craftsman used it for his craft, and consequently he may lawfully demand as something belonging to him, part of the profits derived from his money.*

In comparison with the economic reflections of St Thomas Aquinas, which were directly germane to the business problems of his time, the intellectual influence of another French-trained academic, John Calvin (1509–1564), is far more problematic. The difficulties in assessing Calvin's influence on managerial and management thought, it must be noted, are less attributable to Calvin himself than to the historical claims made on his behalf, in which Calvin is transformed from a deeply religious reformer into a herald of a new individualistic strain of capitalism. The association of Calvin, Calvinism, and capitalism is one that owes much to the so-called Weber-Tawney thesis. According to Weber (1922/1927: 367), the German sociologist, Calvinism not only legitimated a ruthless pursuit of wealth; it also excused a "ruthless exploitation" of workers in the pursuit of "eternal salvation." Similarly, for the English historian, Richard Tawney (1926/1936: 94), Calvin "accepted the main institutions of a commercial civilization, and supplied a creed to the classes which were to dominate the [capitalist] future." In fact, Calvin was only tangentially concerned with the problems of the business world. In Calvin's main body of work, the massive two-volume *Institutes of the Christian Religion*, there is no mention of either "usury" or "lending." Where he did venture into commentary on profane business affairs, his tone was cautious. In introducing his brief study *De Usuris (On Usury)*, for example, Calvin advises the reader, that "I have learnt by the example of others how perilous it is give a reply to the question [of usury]" (cited Wykes 2003: 42). Admittedly, his eventual tentative conclusion that "there is no witness of scripture by which all usury is totally forbidden" (cited Wykes 2003: 42) did have the *practical* effect of legitimating all forms of lending. This finding, however, hardly amounted to a ringing endorsement of capitalist lending practices. Its practical effects were, moreover, arguably less significant than St Thomas Aquinas' earlier endorsement of commercial lending and investment. Yes, it is true that Calvin's (1536/2014: 629) belief that God's "elect" received "unequivocal tokens" of their esteemed status from God – in the form of "strength," "fortitude," and "wealth" – no doubt gave his followers a sense that their material success reflected divine providence. This, however, was hardly a novel idea. Savonarola (1494b/2006: 156) expressed similar views, advising his followers that, "one who is in God's grace has the sign of being among His elect." St Augustine (c.395/2010: 235) also preached about the predestined grace of God's Elect even as he emphasized the centrality of human free will.

Although most of the claimed linkages between Calvinism and capitalism are built upon simplification and overstatement, it is nevertheless evident that Calvin's theological dogma had profound implications for the future of Western business and management. Unlike Martin Luther, who continued many of the institutional practices of Catholicism in his version of Protestantism (although not monasticism), Calvin and his supporters professed a version of Christianity shorn of its traditional bureaucratic and material forms. In Calvin's view, a "church" was simply a community of believers. Any "veneration" of "houses and buildings" was therefore "misplaced," given "that the Church may exist without visible form" (Calvin 1536/2014: 31–32). Despite the zeal with which Calvin approached his tasks, the Calvinist conception of a "Church" inevitably produced an expansion of secular institutions (courts, schools, charities) at the expense of religious ones. Nowhere was this shift more evident than in attitudes toward the sick, the widowed, and the poor. Whereas Catholic faith had always tied individual redemption to almsgiving and "good works," Calvin viewed such activities as meaningless for one's salvation. Instead, Calvin (1536/2014: 350) argued, those destined for eternal paradise "were elected before the creation of the world." If we are thus to sum up the positive implications for Calvinism, and Protestantism more generally, for business and management practices, we need to see it primarily in terms of a process of Schumpeterian "creative destruction." The schism that Calvin and other Protestant leaders created within Christendom permanently destroyed the Catholic Church's claim to be the sole legitimate source of knowledge. In doing so, they created space for not only freedom of religious conscious but also greater intellectual diversity. By shearing away the charitable and monastic institutions that were an integral part of Catholic Christendom, the new Protestant faiths also fostered a more individualistic orientation. Whether or not the Dutch trader of the sixteenth century was a more calculating and ruthless business operative than their Venetian counterpart must, however, remain a moot point.

If, in the economic analysis of St Thomas Aquinas and the theology of John Calvin, the new university system produced studies that had a profound effect on the future course of Western business endeavor, we should, nevertheless, not exaggerate the alteration in either the human condition or the overall intellectual climate. Prior to the invention of Gutenberg's printing press in 1452, there were few books. In Renaissance Italy, only 9% of the population was literate in 1500. The English literacy rate was even lower at 6% (Allen 2003: 415). Improvements in real wages owed more to the labor shortages induced by the winnowing of the Black Death (1347–1350) that to any gains in productive efficiency. Amid plagues, famines, and war, many retained a sense that the end of the world was nigh. Across Europe, population and economic growth stagnated.

According to Josiah Russell's estimates (1948: Table 7.2), the population of England in 1603 (3.78 million) was little different to that found in 1348 immediately prior to the plague's arrival (3.76 million). Of the rural experience that still shaped the lives of an overwhelming majority, Bloch (1940/1962: 72) observed, "wolves prowled in every wilderness ... behind all social experience there was a background of the primitive, of submission to uncontrollable forces, of unrelieved physical constraints."

In this still economically primitive world, it is hardly surprising that a medieval mind-set – which saw both the cosmos and the human condition in unchanging terms – coexisted alongside novel and even revolutionary understandings of new commercial world.

Often this coexistence of medieval and remarkably modern ideas existed within the same individual. Savonarola, as we have noted, embraced laws favoring business investment even as he burnt the priceless art treasures acquired through Florentine business success. The same Janus-like tendencies are also evident in St Thomas Aquinas, arguably the most brilliant mind of the late medieval period. While his understandings of economic value and utility justify his status as the Father of Economics, St Thomas Aquinas was also largely responsible for the late medieval and Renaissance enthusiasm for Aristotelian philosophy, an enthusiasm that hindered rather than enhanced intellectual and economic advancement.

Significantly, the late medieval embrace of Aristotelian philosophy represented a major intellectual rupture within Western Christendom, overturning the Augustinian marrying of Christianity and Neoplatonist ideas, a marrying which had been a seminal feature of the early Catholic Church. In terms of its understanding of the cosmos, this earlier Neoplatonist/Augustinian amalgam emphasized a more ephemeral and idealist view of heaven and earth than did its Aristotelian rival, St Augustine (c.AD 400/2007: 219) referring to the "formlessness of which heaven and earth were made." By contrast, Aristotelian philosophy had a far more definitive view of the cosmos due to Ptolemy of Alexandria's observations and calculations. Long lost, Ptolemy's *Almagest* began to again circulate in Europe following the translation in Spain of an Arabic copy, quickly surpassing "any scientific work except Euclid's *Elements*" in terms of its influence (Toomer 1984: 2). According to Ptolemy's (c.AD 160/1984) complex (and impressive) calculations, the universe comprised a series of spheres revolving around the earth, an inner sphere containing the sun and the planets, and an outer sphere containing the "fixed" stars. Admittedly, Ptolemy (c.AD 160/1984: 45) did consider the possibility that the heaven's observed motions were due to the earth's rotation, conceding that there was "nothing in the celestial phenomena which would count against the hypothesis." However, he immediately dismissed "such a notion" as "ridiculous" due to the fact that if the earth did revolve, it would have to do so at a speed which would cause it to constantly "outrun and overtake" the "clouds" (Ptolemy, c.AD 160/1984: 44).

Ptolemy's views on the cosmos became integral to late medieval and Renaissance understandings due to their becoming – along with other elements of Aristotelian philosophy and science – entrenched in Catholic dogma. In foolhardily pursuing this course of action – in which Catholic and Aristotelian credibility became

10 From Feudalism to Modernity, Part 2: The Revolution in Ideas, AD 450–1750

intertwined – the Church caused "many things," as St Thomas Aquinas (c.1270/ 1952, Q. 32, Article 4) recorded, to be "considered as heretical which were not formerly so considered." That this unfortunate situation prevailed, in which any would-be opponent of Aristotelian science was threatened with execution as a heretic, is in large part attributable to St Thomas Aquinas himself. Indeed, it is largely through Aquinas' commentaries that Aristotle's works – which also began arriving from Muslim Spain in the twelfth century – became a foundation stone of medieval and Renaissance thought, Aquinas (c.1270/1952, Q. 1, Article 1) beginning his *Summa Theologica* with the argument that it was Aristotle who "proved" that "theology" was "the divine science." Indeed, so heavily did Aquinas rely on Aristotle – his works being full of references to Aristotle as "the Philosopher" – that one leading theologian, Servais Pinckaers (1995: 168) has questioned whether Aquinas' work was primarily Aristotelian rather than Christian.

That clerically endorsed Aristotelian philosophy was a barrier to further scientific advance was demonstrated in the condemnation as heretical of Nicholas Copernicus pioneering study, *De Revolutionibus* (*On the Revolutions*), a study which placed the sun at the center of the solar system. Despite the iconic status enjoyed by this work today, its initial impact was almost nonexistent, Donald Kobe (1998: 190) observing that the intellectual climate "remained dominated by Aristotelian philosophy and the corresponding Ptolemaic astronomy." The muted response to the enunciation of the Copernican system of the cosmos reflected more than clerical opposition. It was also the case, as Kobe (1998: 190) noted, that there was simply "no reason to accept the Copernican theory." As Ptolemy had correctly concluded, any suggestion that the earth was not located at the center of the solar system flew in the face of the empirical observations of the time. Sixteenth-century Europe lacked the array of scientific instruments (telescopes, microscopes, accurate mechanical clocks, etc.) that became commonplace in the ensuing century. Nor was there a wide body of educated secular opinion interested in pursuing heretical scientific theses. Universities in Protestant as well as Catholic Europe were dominated by theologians, Martin Luther proving as hostile to Copernican ideas as any of his Catholic enemies (Kobe 1998: 194).

Despite the hostility with which Copernicus' *De Revolutionibus* was greeted, its publication nevertheless stands as a landmark event in human history, heralding not only a new way of looking at the cosmos but also new principles for research. For in the preface to his book, Copernicus (1541/2008: 4) suggested that every "philosopher" should "endeavor to seek the truth in all things, to the extent permitted to human reason by God." Having made "human reason" the effective judge of every problem, Copernicus (1541/2008: 5) then argued that belief should always be based on hypotheses supported by empirical evidence. "For if the hypotheses," Copernicus (1541/2008: 5) explained, are "not false, everything which follows" from the hypotheses "would be confirmed beyond doubt." In pursuing these principles, Copernicus himself made major errors. For while he correctly believed that the planets orbited the sun, Copernicus (1541/2008: 24) also erroneously believed that beyond planets, there existed a zone of "immovable stars." Such errors of fact are, however, inconsequential when compared to the research principles – based around the scientific testing of hypotheses – upon which they were based.

The strengths and limitations of the intellectual world of the European Renaissance are also indicated in another foundational text, Niccolo Machiavelli's *The Prince*, a work that revolutionized understandings of statecraft and political science. At many levels, Machiavelli's analysis seems to embody the modern, rational approach to political and economic affairs. Like his Florentine contemporary, Savonarola, Machiavelli displayed an unusual awareness of the importance of private business endeavor in societal success. As Machiavelli (1532/2011: 90) expressed it, kingdoms or republics would not prosper unless they reassured their subjects that they could "go calmly about their business . . . without worrying that if they increase their wealth they'll be in danger of having it taken away from them, or that if they start up a business they'll be punitively taxed." Yet, despite such insights, Machiavelli's understanding of power was essentially feudal, perceiving organized violence – rather than economic success – to be the hallmark feature of a successful state. For, in Machiavelli's (1532/2011: 57) opinion, "A ruler . . . must have no other aim or consideration, nor seek to develop any other vocation outside war, the organization of the army and military discipline." For the fractious societies of Renaissance Italy, this was the worst possible advice, contributing in some measure to the ruinous wars and internal conflicts that helped reduce Italy from the status of economic leader to laggard. Burckhardt (1867/1954: 390), in his study of Renaissance Italy, also seemed blind to the reasons behind the society's declining fortunes during the sixteenth and seventeenth century, attributing Italy's fall from grace to "foreign invasions and the Counter-Reformation." In fact, Italy, the wonder of Europe in the fifteenth century, lost its way primarily because it fell behind the societies of Northwest Europe in terms of technological, scientific, and managerial innovation. In consequence, as Robert Allen (2003: 412) records, "English and Dutch exports drove Italian producers out of business."

Society and the Scientific Revolution, c.1600–c.1750

In his greatest work, *Leviathan*, the English political philosopher, Thomas Hobbes (1651/2002: 40) drew, for the first time, a distinction between the natural and social sciences, or what he called "politics and civic philosophy." For Hobbes, it was a self-evident truth that advancement in one of these domains was conditional on progress in the other. It was also obvious to Hobbes that neither could advance unless there was a conducive environment for commerce, industry, innovation, and investment. Key to the creation of this conducive environment, Hobbes argued, was the legal guarantee of property rights and individual liberty, a guarantee that necessarily required a constitutional restraint of princely authority. For, Hobbes (1651/2002: 62) continued, without "such conditions there is no place for industry, because the fruit thereof is uncertain; and consequently no culture . . . no knowledge of the face of the earth; no account of time; no arts; no letters." And, without these attributes of industry and civilization, Hobbes (1651/ 2002: 62) famously concluded, human life was invariably "solitary, poor, nasty, brutish, and short."

It is the confluence of these factors – scientific progress, political protections of property and person, and advancement of industry and commerce – that distinguished the 1600–1750 era from the two previous periods discussed in this chapter. The collective result was a transformation of both the context in which scientific research occurred and in the resources available to inquiry and experimentation. This transformation was highlighted in the account of the visit by the English traveler, Arthur Young, to the Parisian household of Antoine and Anne-Marie Lavoisier in the late eighteenth century. In one part of the household, Young (1792/1909: 95) found the "splendid machine" in which the Lavoisiers, in a pioneering study, had measured the amount of oxygen consumed in the process of combustion. Elsewhere in the Lavoisier abode, Young (1792/1909: 95) found "an electrical apparatus" used for "electrical experiments."

The lauding of the Lavoisiers for their scientific curiosity is a pointer to the profound alteration in social attitudes that had occurred since the time of Copernicus. Nevertheless, despite this generalized interest in scientific experimentation – evident across Western Europe and North America – it was only in England that we witness a society where science informed managerial practice in an economically significant way. As Young discovered in his journey across France, the landlords and peasants of the French nation remained ignorant of the most recent advances in agricultural practices, and in patterns of crop rotation, that were commonplace across the Channel. In Northern France, a comparatively prosperous area, Young (1792/ 1909: 19) observed that, "the fields are scenes of pitiable management, as the houses are of misery." For the French philosopher, Voltaire, the contrast between the French and English countryside was also stark. Whereas France allowed smallpox to exact a heavy toll on its peasantry, England vaccinated its young (Voltaire 1734/2002: 35). Moreover, Voltaire (1734/2002: 33) added in amazement after visiting rural England for the first time: "The feet of the peasants" were "not bruised by wooden shoes; they eat white bread." The comparative backwardness of French society was something even the Lavoisiers were willing to concede, Anne-Marie Lavoisier advising Young of the "general [technological] inferiority" of France (Young 1792/1909: 95). Even the "splendid machine" with which the Lavoisiers carried out their experiments on the combustion of oxygen was English made, Young (1792/1909: 95) observing that, "It is well known that we [the English] have a considerable exportation of mathematical and other curious instruments to every part of Europe, and to France amongst the rest."

The experiences of the Lavoisiers, whose scientific experiments relied upon English technologies, highlight the fact that we cannot understand how new scientific ideas informed the Industrial Revolution without a comprehension of the profound alteration of opinion in the social sciences, an alteration that favored commerce, inquiry, and innovation.

In looking to the most significant works in political philosophy published between 1600 and 1750 – Hobbes' (1651/2002) *Leviathan*, John Locke's (1689/1823) *Two Treatises of Government*, Montesquieu's (1748/1989) *The Spirit of the Laws*, and David Hume's (1739/1896) *A Treatise on Human Nature* – only Hume concerned himself with markets and then only tangentially. New understandings in the field of economics – associated with Richard Cantillon's (1755/2010) *An Essay on Economic Theory*, Francois Quesnay's (1758) *Tableau Economique*, and Adam Smith's (1776/1999) *The Wealth of Nations* – lay in the future. It was not matters such as economic value, utility, the division of labor, managerial efficiency, or competition that primarily concerned Hobbes, Locke, Hume, and Montesquieu. Instead, it was a far more basic precondition for material advancement: security of person and property. Hobbes (1651/2002: 66), for example, in drawing up principles for a "covenant" between rulers and ruled, argued that "security" was key to ensuring the advancement of both "industry" and "knowledge." Whether such an outcome occurred through absolutist monarchy or democracy little concerned Hobbes. A generation later, John Locke (1689/1823: 159) similarly observed in his *Two Treatises of Government*, "The great and chief end . . . of men uniting into a commonwealth, and putting themselves under government, is the preservation of their property." In France, Montesquieu in his *The Spirit of the Laws* also believed that a system of "civil laws" – enforced by state apparatuses – was a precondition for industry. For without such protections, Montesquieu (1748/1989: 290–292) concluded, people would be "very few" and constantly "prey to their enemies." Into this debate about the appropriate frameworks for commercial and industrial advancement, Hume's (1739/1896) *A Treatise on Human Nature* represented a revolutionary departure. According to Hume, self-interest was society's primary glue. For, Hume (1739/1896: 273) reasoned, not only is it so that humanity is mainly "govern'd by [self] interest"; it is also the case that the benefit of upholding a system of market exchange is "palpable and evident, even to the most rude and uncultivated of the human race."

The emphasis placed by Hobbes, Locke, and Montesquieu (if not Hume) on the importance of the state's protective umbrella highlights the fact that the societies of the seventeenth century and even (to a lesser degree) the eighteenth century were not market economies as we understand them. For, as we noted in ▶ Chap. 9, "From Feudalism to Modernity, Part I: Management, Technology, and Work, AD 450–1750," the seventeenth and eighteenth centuries represented the heyday of "mercantilism," an era in which each European government sought to beggar their neighbor by restricting trade to ships flying their own national flag. Internal commerce and industry also favored firms boasting royal charters or monopolies. Nevertheless, within this web of government regulation, it is clear that England increasingly stood at the forefront not only in terms of political philosophy (Hobbes, Locke, Hume) but also in terms of a political and social climate that favored both commercial endeavor and scientific inquiry.

The importance of political and social climate for the nascent Scientific Revolution is highlighted in the very different receptions obtained by two studies published in the opening decade of the seventeenth century: Galileo Galilei's (1610/1989) *Sidereus Nuncius* (*The Starry Messenger*) and Francis Bacon's (1605/1902)

The Proficience and Advancement of Learning. In the former work, Galileo – the University of Padua mathematician who had previously demonstrated the commercial possibilities for the newly invented telescope – described the discoveries obtained when he turned his telescope to the heavens. In words of historic significance, Galileo (1610/1989: 5, 8) began his study by stating, "I discovered these stars unknown to all previous astronomers," adding:

> *Certainly it is a great thing to add to the countless multitude of fixed stars visible hitherto by natural means and expose to our eyes innumerable others never seen before, which exceed tenfold the number of old and known ones.*

Not content with simple empirical observation, Galileo proceeded to the destruction of the Aristotelian (and hence Catholic) understanding of the cosmos. In providing proof in support of "the Copernican system," Galileo (1610/1989: 58) informed his readers that, whereas the moon revolved around the earth, "both run through a great circle around the Sun." Safe while he lived among the merchants of the Venetian republic, Galileo erred in leaving its protection for Rome. Tried for heresy in 1633, Galileo lived out his life under house arrest.

If Galileo's work did much to overturn the Aristotelian/Ptolemaic understanding of the cosmos, it was Bacon's work which acted as a renunciation of the whole structure of Aristotelian thought. Arguing for research in both the natural and social sciences to be based on empirical observation rather than the writings of antiquity, Bacon (1605/1902: 61) argued that, "as water ascends no higher than the level of the first spring, so knowledge derived from Aristotle will at most rise no higher again than the knowledge of Aristotle." As to the scientific "usefulness" of Greek philosophy as a whole, Bacon (1605/1902: 11) declared it "puerile," "talkative" rather "than generative – as being fruitful in controversies, but barren in effects." Significantly, among the areas that Bacon (1605/1902: 480) indicated as a priority for research was the "Doctrine of Business; or books upon all kinds of civil employments, arts, trades, etc." In a subsequent book, *Novum Organum: True Suggestions for the Interpretation of Nature*, Bacon (1620/1902: 5) returned to the theme that research must be based on original observation rather than ancient dogma, declaring: "They who have presumed to dogmatize on nature ... in the professorial style, have inflicted the greatest injury on philosophy and learning." Raised to the peerage in 1618 as Baron Verulam, Bacon also served as England's attorney-general and Lord Chancellor, playing a seminal role in the founding of Newfoundland, Virginia, and the Carolinas. That Bacon, like Galileo, eventually fell foul of the law owed little to his ideas, for which he enjoyed contemporary esteem, but rather to a predilection for accepting money from those seeking the favor of the British crown. Politically disgraced, Lord Bacon was left to pursue his scholarly pursuits in considerable comfort.

The abandonment of Aristotelian dogma, and an embrace of the research principles advocated by Bacon, laid the groundwork for one of the most extraordinary periods of scientific advance in human history. Across the seventeenth century, discoveries came thick and fast: William Harvey's (1628/1928) publication on the circulation of blood (1628/1928); Robert Boyle's (1661) work on chemical structure; Hooke's (1665) research into single-called organisms; Isaac Newton's (1687/1968) study on gravity and planetary motion; and Antonie van Leeuwenhoek's (1676) development of the new field of microbiology. All of these works, it should be noted, came from the business-oriented societies of England (Harvey, Boyle, Hooke, Newton) and the Netherlands (van Leeuwenhoek). Nor was it the case that such scientific research was restricted to an educated few. Any work of significance typically found its way into the pages of The Royal Society's monthly journal, *Philosophical Transactions*. A perusal of the pages of the *Philosophical Transactions* highlights the extent to which scientific advance now informed managerial activities. In the April 1673 edition, for example, we find articles on the processing of cocoa, new techniques for hardening marble saws, shipbuilding advances in Virginia, and variations in animal coronary structure (Royal Society 1673a). In the ensuing issue, we read of Dutch microbiological studies, a new drug to curtail bleeding, novel metallurgical techniques, and animal respiratory behavior (Royal Society 1673b).

Among the works published across the course of the seventeenth century, Newton's (1687/1968) *The Mathematical Principles of Natural Philosophy* has deservedly won special recognition. As Dominiczak (2012: 655) recently observed, Newton's theories represented a final nail in the coffin for "Aristotelian mechanics," facilitating "the transformation of natural philosophy into science." For in his study, Newton (1687/1968: 19) did more than explain gravity and motion. Newton also spelt out in unequivocal terms both the problems of scientific research and the process of inquiry required in order to overcome those problems. As Newton (1687/1968: 17) explained it, the principal problem with research in the natural sciences is that we are dealing with motions, forces, and forms that "by no means come under the observation of our senses." "Yet," Newton (1687/1968: 19) added, using the study of motion as an example:

> ... the thing is not altogether desperate; for we have some arguments to guide us, partly from the apparent motions, which are the differences of the true motions; partly from the forces, which are the causes and effects of the true motions.

In other words, the connections between phenomena are often by no means obvious, and it is only through experimentation and thesis testing that we can distinguish the true cause of things. It was upon such principles – as applicable in the social sciences as the natural sciences – which the modern world of rational, inquiring managerial endeavor was to be built.

Conclusion

In his *Writing and Difference*, the French philosopher, Jacques Derrida (1967/2001: 48) stated that there is a "fundamental permanence" in the West's "logico-philo-sophical heritage ... Whatever the momentary break, if there was one ...this break and this alteration are late and secondary developments." As with many of

10 From Feudalism to Modernity, Part 2: The Revolution in Ideas, AD 450–1750

Derrida's observations, this claim is part fact, part fallacy. There are probably few who believe today, as Pope Gregory the Great (c.AD 559/1959: 199–200) evidently did, that the sick can be healed by bringing them before "the lifeless remains" of church martyrs or that "the dead" are "restored to life" through exposure to such mummified forms. Nor, one suspects, are there many business people who share the opinion of St Thomas Aquinas (c.1270/1952: Q. 77, Article 1) that a trader risks eternal damnation if they "have recourse to deceit in order to sell a thing." Across the vast stretch of time that this chapter has considered (i.e., c.AD 450–1750), we can nevertheless detect constants in terms of moral and intellectual values, in habits of thought. Three of these stand out as being particularly significant in informing modern managerial and business systems. First, there is not only a love of learning but also a unique societal determination to foster and protect institutions of learning. Initially manifest in the early medieval monasteries, in the High Middle Ages, this cultural imperative produced the flowering of a unique historical institution: the university. In the university, as Compayré (1910) observed, was found all "there was of good in monastic rules, the constant contact between many minds devoted to the same work . . .the advantages pertaining to intellectual association." To such benefits of the old monastic order, the university system adding another vital ingredient: intellectual liberty, a freedom to inquire and debate. A second constant, which also emerged out of the medieval monastic system, was an emphasis on the dignity of work. As McCann (1937: 100) argued, the "principle" that required a monk "to regard no honest labour as beneath him" was "of itself . . .a valuable contribution to human progress." Outside the cloisters of the monastery, as within, there emerged a cultural expectation that no matter what one's station in life, no matter how rich you were, you would work for a living. Across Europe as a whole, therefore, we can witness clear evidence of the "Protestant" or "Calvinist" work ethic of which Weber (1905/2003) spoke long before the Reformation. The third constant, which was again the product of medieval monasticism, was to approach one's daily work with an inquisitive rational mind, constantly seeking after greater efficiencies. Within the medieval monastery, there was an expectation that, whatever job you did, one would do it with the utmost thought and care, to be best of one's ability. The emphasis on efficiency also stemmed in part from the monastic marrying of learning and work, St Benedict's (c.516/1931: 22) famed Rule requiring monks "to be occupied, at fixed seasons, with manual work and again at fixed seasons with spiritual reading." Scholarship and work were intertwined, not separate activities.

If Western European advancement was built upon a number of intellectual constants, managerial and scientific progress also ultimately required ruptures, the overturning of many of the fundamental premises upon which the civilization was constructed. The first was the idea that the pathway to knowledge and truth was the monopoly of a single institution and its associated dogma. A characteristic feature of medieval society, in which the Catholic Church constantly threatened dissidents with arrest and execution as heretics, this tendency was also evident in the Protestant faiths which emerged in the sixteenth century. As Calvin (1536/2014: 350) informed his followers, "The origin of all good clearly appears ... to be from no other than God alone; for no propensity of the will to any thing (sic) good can be found." During the High Middle Ages and Renaissance, the retarding effects of religious belief were accentuated through its association with Aristotelian philosophy and science. Not only were Aristotelian principles made articles of faith by the Church; they also appealed to secular scholars' intent on reviving the wisdom of antiquity. The problems this produced were considerable. Aristotle (c.350 BC/1941: 712, 693), for example, believed that "theoretical knowledge" and "empirical knowledge," were distinct and separate. He also argued that theology was "the most divine science." Through its association with Ptolemy of Alexandria's theorems on astronomy, Aristotelian philosophy was also associated with a static understanding of the cosmos. Not until the publication of Newton's *The Mathematical Principles of Natural Philosophy* was the credibility of Aristotelian science finally destroyed, Newton (1687/1968: 17) noting that his own scientific conclusions "do strain the Sacred Writings." The third key rupture in the Western *episteme* that paved the way for the Industrial and Managerial Revolutions of the eighteenth and nineteenth centuries was a transformation in attitudes toward private property and wealth creation. The best way to characterize the ethos of the medieval world is to note that it was a "civilization of poverty," as both lived experience and philosophic ideal. In the opinion of St John Chrysostom (c.AD 398/1848: 136), a religious society was founded through necessity upon "the poor, the lame, the crippled, the infirm." Their suffering not only helped guarantee their own place in paradise. They also provided a pathway for the rich. For, in God's terrible judgement in the afterlife, the almsgiving of the rich would appear as a positive attribute in the divine ledger book of sins and good work. For St Benedict (c.516/1931: 17) as well, private property was an awful "vice," a sin which every successful monastery had to "cut off ... by the roots." Not until the seventeenth century were private property and wealth creation perceived by political and moral theorists as the necessary bedrock for societal economic and managerial success. As political thinkers such as Hobbes, Locke, Hume, Voltaire, and Montesquieu realized, the main beneficiary of laws in defense of private property were not the rich – who rarely needed them – but people of modest means, the craft worker, the laborer, and the small entrepreneur. And, without the industrious efforts of such people, no long-term social, economic, or managerial progress is possible.

Cross-References

▶ From Feudalism to Modernity, Part I: Management, Technology, and Work, AD 450–1750
▶ Management in Antiquity: Part 1 – The Binds of Geography
▶ Management in Antiquity: Part 2 – Success and Failure in the Hellenic and Roman Worlds
▶ What Is Management?
▶ Work and Society in the Orthodox East: Byzantium and Russia, AD 450–1861

References

Alighieri D (c.1310/2012) The divine comedy. Penguin Classics, London
Allen RC (2003) Progress and poverty in early modern Europe. Econ Hist Rev 56(3):403–443
Aristotle (c.350 BC/1941) Metaphysics. In: McKeon R (ed) The basic works of Aristotle. Random House, New York, pp 681–934
Bacon F (1605/1902) Advancement of learning. P.F. Collier & Son, New York
Bacon F (1620/1902) Novum organum: true suggestions for the interpretation of nature. P.F. Collier & Son, New York
Bloch M (1940/1962) Feudal society, 2nd edn. Routledge & Kegan Paul, London
Boyle R (1661) The sceptical chymist. J. Caldwell, London
Braudel F (1963/1975) The Mediterranean and the Mediterranean world in the age of Philip II, vol 2. Fontana Press, London
Braudel F (1986) The identity of France: people and production, vol 2, 2nd edn. Harper Torchbooks, New York
Braudel F (1987/1993) A history of civilizations. Penguin Books, London
Burckhardt J (1867/1954) The civilization of the renaissance in Italy, 2nd edn. The Modern Library, New York
Calvin J (1536/2014) Institutes of the Christian religion, vol 1. Project Gutenberg eBook. http://www.gutenberg.org/ebooks/45001
Camus A (1935/2007) Christian metaphysics and Neoplatonism. University of Missouri Press, Columbia
Cantillon R (1755/2010) An essay on economic theory. Ludwig von Mises Institute, Auburn
Cipolla C M (1981) Before the industrial revolution: European society and the economy, 1000 – 1700. 2nd edition. Cambridge University Press, Cambridge, UK.
Compayré G (1910) Abelard and the origin and early history of universities. Charles Scribner's Sons, New York
Copernicus N (1541/2008) De Revolutionibus (On the revolutions). http://www.geo.utexas.edu/courses/302d/Fall_2011/Full%20text%20-%20Nicholas%20Copernicus,%20_De%20Revolutionibus%20(On%20the%20Revolutions),_%201.pdf
de Montesquieu B (1748/1989) The spirit of the laws. Cambridge University Press, New York
Delanty G (2019) Formations of European modernity: a historical and political sociology of Europe, 2nd edn. Palgrave Macmillan, Cham
Derrida J (1967/2001) Writing and difference. Routledge Classics, London/New York
Dominiczak MH (2012) Science and culture in the 18th century: Isaac Newton. Clin Chem 58(3):655–656
Galilei G (1610/1989) Sidereus nuncius. University of Chicago Press, Chicago
Graetzer G, Rost K (2015) Structural effects of sex-ratios and power distribution on the survival rates of female monasteries. Paper presented to the Academy of Management Annual Meeting, Vancouver. https://www.researchgate.net/publication/291365800_Structural_Effects_of_Sex-Ratios_and_Power_Distribution_on_the_Survival_Rates_of_Female_Monasteries
Harvey W (1628) Exercitatio anatomica de motu cordis et sanguinis in animalibus: anatomical studies of the motion of the heart and blood. Charles C Thomas, Springfield
Hobbes T (1651/2002) Leviathan. Broadway Press, Peterborough
Hooke R (1665) Micrographia: or some physiological descriptions of minute bodies made by magnifying glasses. Royal College of Surgeons, London
Hoskin KW, Macve RH (1986) Accounting and the examination: a genealogy of disciplinary power. Acc Organ Soc 11(2):105–136
Hume D (1739/1896) A treatise on human nature, vol 2. Clarendon Press, Oxford
Kieser A (1987) From asceticism to administration of wealth: medieval monasteries and the pitfalls of rationalization. Organ Stud 8(2):103–123
Kobe DH (1998) Copernicus and Martin Luther: an encounter between science and religion. Am J Phys 66(3):190–196

Locke J (1689/1823) Two treatise on government. McMaster Archive of the History of Economic Thought, Toronto. https://socialsciences.mcmaster.ca/econ/ugcm/3ll3/locke/government.pdf

Machiavelli N (1532/2011) The prince. Penguin Classics, London

Mayer W (2009) John Chrysostom on poverty. In: Allen P, Bronwen N, Mayer W (eds) Preaching poverty in late antiquity. Evangelische Verlagsnstalt, Leipzig

McCann DJ (1937) Saint Benedict. Sheed and Ward, London

Newton I (1687) The mathematical principles of natural philosophy. Dawsons of Pall Mall, London

Pacioli L (1494/1994) Accounting books and records: the summa de arithmetica, geometria, proportioni et proportionalita. Pacioli Society, Seattle

Phelps Brown EH, Hopkins SV (1956) Seven centuries of the prices of consumables, compared with builders' wage rates. Economica 23(92):296–314

Pinckaers S (1995) The sources of Christian ethics. Catholic University of America Press, Washington, DC

Pirenne H (1925/1952) Medieval cities: their origins and the revival of trade. Princeton University Press, Princeton

Pirenne H (1936) Economic and social history of medieval Europe. Routledge & Kegan Paul, London

Plato (c.380 BC/2003) The republic. Penguin Classics, London

Ptolemy of Alexandria (c.AD 160/1984) Almagest. Duckworth, London

Quesnay F (1758) Tableau economique. https://www.sapili.org/livros/fr/mc00222x.pdf

Royal Society (1673a) Philos Trans 93:6007–6030

Royal Society (1673b) Philos Trans 94:6031–6050

Russell JC (1948) British medieval population. University of New Mexico Press, Albuquerque

Savonarola G (1494a) Aggeus: Sermon XII. In: Savonarola G, Boreilli A, Passaro MP (eds) Selected writings: religion and politics, 1490–1498. Yale University Press, New Haven, pp 139–150

Savonarola G (1494b) Aggeus: Sermon XIII. In: Savonarola G, Boreilli A, Passaro MP (eds) Selected writings: religion and politics, 1490–1498. Yale University Press, New Haven, pp 151–175

Savonarola G (1495/2006) Treatise on the rule and government of the city of Florence. In: Savonarola G, Boreilli A, Passaro MP (eds) Selected Writings: Religion and Politics, 1490–1498. Yale University Press, New Haven, pp 176–206

Smith A (1776/1999) An inquiry into the nature and causes of the wealth of nations. Penguin Classics, London

St Augustine (c.AD 430/1945) The city of God, vol. 1. Everyman's Library, London

St Augustine (c.AD 400/2007) Confessions. Barnes & Nobles Classics, New York

St Augustine (c.AD 395/2010) The free choice of the will. In: St Augustine, The teacher: The free choice of the will; grace and free will. Catholic University of America Press, Washington, DC

St Benedict (c.516/1931) The rule of St Benedict. A Pax Book, London

St Gregory the Great (c.AD 559/1959) Dialogues: the fathers of the church. Catholic University of America Press, Washington, DC

St John Chrysostom (c.AD 398/1848) The homilies of St John Chrysostom on the Gospel of St John. John Henry Parker, London

St John Chrysostom (c.AD 400/1984) On wealth and poverty. St Vladimir's Seminary Press, Crestwood

St Luke (c.AD 70/1985) Gospel. In: Warsbrough J (ed) New Jerusalem Bible. Darton, Longman & Todd, London, pp 1798–1846

St Mathew (c.AD 65/1985) Gospel. In: Warsbrough J (ed) New Jerusalem Bible. Darton, Longman & Todd, London, pp 1609–1654

St Thomas Aquinas (c.1270/1952) The summa theologica. Classic Christian Library. http://www.documentacatholicaomnia.eu/03d/1225-1274,_Thomas_Aquinas,_Summa_Theologiae_%5B1%5D,_EN.pdf

Stevens CE (1941/1966) Agriculture and rural life in the later Roman Empire. In: Postan MM (ed) The Cambridge economic history of Europe, vol 1. Cambridge University Press, pp 92–124

Tawney RH (1926/1936) Religion and the rise of capitalism. John Murray, London

Toomer CJ (1984) Introduction. In: Toomer CJ (ed) Ptolemy's Almagest. Duckworth, London

van Leeuwenhoek A (1676) Observation communicated to the publisher: concerning little animals by him observed. In: The Royal Society, Philosophical transactions, Royal Society, London. https://royalsocietypublishing.org/doi/pdf/10.1098/rstl.1677.0003

Vessey M (2007) Introduction. In: Vessey M (ed) St Augustine's confessions. Barnes & Noble Classics, New York

Voltaire (1734/2002) Letters on England. Pennsylvania State University Electronic Series Publication, Hazelton

Weber M (1905/2003) The protestant ethic and the spirit of capitalism. Dover, New York

Weber M (1922/1927) General economic history. The Free Press, Glencoe

Wirtz P (2017) Governance of old religious orders: Benedictines and Dominicans. J Manag Hist 23(2):259–277

Wykes M (2003) Devaluing the scholastics: Calvin's ethics of usury. Calvin Theol J 38(1):27–51

Young A (1792/1909) Travels in France: 1787, 1788 and 1789. George Bell and Sons, London

The Origins of Robust Supply Chain Management and Logistics in the Caribbean: Spanish Silver and Gold in the New World (1492–1700)

11

Oliver W. Aho and Robert A. Lloyd

Contents

Introduction	246
Evolution of the European Economy	247
The European Quest for Gold	248
Three Sources of Gold and Silver	249
Transportation via Treasure Fleet	250
Spanish Logistics and Supply Chain Management	252
Robust Supply Chain Practices	254
Leadership Commitment	255
Human Capital	256
Intra-organizational Relationship Magnitude	257
Risk Management	258
Node Criticality	260
Bargaining Power	261
Visibility	262
Network Complexity	263
Long-Distance Trade and the Development of Capitalism	263
New World Riches and the Impact on the Iberian Peninsula	266
Conclusion	266
References	267

W. Aho
Department of Economics, Management, and Project Management, Western Carolina University, Cullowhee, NC, USA
e-mail: waho@email.wcu.edu

R. Lloyd (✉)
Fort Hays State University, Hays, KS, USA
e-mail: ralloyd@fhsu.edu

© The Author(s), under exclusive licence to Springer Nature Switzerland AG 2020
B. Bowden et al. (eds.), *The Palgrave Handbook of Management History*,
https://doi.org/10.1007/978-3-319-62114-2_13

Abstract

The Spanish Empire had a head start on their European counterparts in establishing themselves in the Caribbean and South America. They discovered a surfeit of resources in newly explored regions of the Caribbean, including most notably, gold and silver. Collecting, processing, protecting, and transporting these riches from the Caribbean to Spain was a tremendous undertaking and required the Spaniards to adopt new practices in supply chain management and employ innovative logistical techniques. This chapter explores the history of the Spaniards in the Caribbean and northern South America and analyzes their practices in terms of our modern understanding of supply chain and logistics. This chapter begins with a historical context of Spanish exploration. We then describe the supply chain practices that begin by extracting gold from Peru, Colombia, and Ecuador, transporting to Panama, crossing the isthmus via mule train, and aggregating the gold in Cartagena and Havana prior to transportation to Spain.

Supply chain management has been conceptualized as "the planning and management of all activities involved in sourcing and procurement, conversion, and all logistics management activities. Importantly, it also includes coordination and collaboration with channel partners, which can be suppliers, intermediaries, third-party service providers, and customers" (CSCMP (2016) Council of supply chain management professionals. Available at: http://cscmp.org/about-us/supply-chain-management-definitions. Accessed 17 Nov 2016). Using this framework, we provide a case study of this time period that contextualizes the origins of supply chain management as employed by the Spaniards.

Keywords

Spanish gold and silver · Logistics and supply chain management · New World riches · Capitalism

Introduction

The Spanish exploration of the New World, the discovery of gold and silver, and the repatriation of these riches to Europe hastened the development of long-distance trade and dramatically altered the shape of capitalism in the known world. According to Peterson (1975), during the Spanish rule of the New World, an estimated $4 billion to $6 billion worth of precious metals and gems were transported to Spain, which represents five or more times the value a similar sum would have today. To support the extraction, refining, and safe transportation of this wealth to Spain, an ingenious system of planning, logistics, and supply chain management evolved. This chapter traces the roots of the European desire for metallic riches, which in turn prompted voyages to the unknown, and ultimately, the evolution of a new world economy. Long-term, the abundance mined from the New World did not prove beneficial to the economic development of the Iberian Peninsula (Pach 1968). Instead, profits from the Spanish treasure fleets were squandered on wars and the support of an economy dependent on goods imported from other countries. The correlation from events that took place over four centuries ago and today's global political and economic scenario is profound.

Evolution of the European Economy

Europe, at the dawn of the fifteenth century, was emerging from the ravages of the Black Death, a bubonic plague that killed 60% of its entire population (Beneductow 2005). The political, social, and economic system of feudalism, the strict hierarchy of rank where every person knew their place began to change as the century unfolded (Olsen-Raymer 2014). In addition to the clergy (cardinals, archbishops, bishops, abbots) and the aristocracy (descendants of the warlords who were owners of vast parcels of land), a new class of citizen evolved. Known as the bourgeoisie, these were the merchants, the shopkeepers, and the master-craftsmen.

Towns and large villages arose throughout Europe. Behind the strong walls and moats of these fortresses, medieval craft production developed. Textiles, furniture, furs, fruits, even the production of weapons furthered the advancement of commerce and trade (Engels 1957). The economy according to Braudel (1992) consisted of two gigantic spheres: production and consumption. However, a third world existed, the market, the place where the exchange of goods took place. Markets were typically held on fixed days. Commodities such as bread, cheese, meat, vegetables, fruit, fresh game, wool, hemp, flax and on and on – the production side – could be sold directly to the consumption side, the consumer via the market. Goods were bartered or sold, money exchanged hands, and credit was little used – capitalism in its rudimentary form.

From a macrostandpoint, the European economy was isolated from the rest of the world with the exception of the neighboring Muslim lands (Walton (1994). Political connections with far-off civilizations in the West, the Far East, and Africa south of the Sahara were nonexistent with only a minuscule amount of international trade conducted. The one striking exception to the absence of foreign commerce was the trade in spices. The Muslims, through their conquests, had control or influence over a wide array of territories where spices richly coveted for food preservation and flavoring were grown and harvested. Powerful Italian city-states including Venice, Florence, and Genoa, following the path of the Crusades, dominated the market for spices, trading with the Muslims through Levant, the ancient ports of the eastern Mediterranean (Ashtor 1975).

Trade in the European markets as well as what little international commerce took place had long utilized coins as a means of payment. Europeans coveted precious metals which could be fashioned into coins, the only stable and dependable form of currency at the time. Coins could be subdivided. Coins could be stored and did not deteriorate in value, provided there was faith in the quality of the metals used to form the currency. Gold and silver were comparatively rare, malleable which allowed them to be worked into handy shapes, and held an alluring appearance. Coins fashioned out of gold or silver could be exchanged for any commodity, at any place, at any time, and played a fundamental role in the development of European commerce (Walton 1994).

A phenomenon occurred in the second half of the fifteenth century that altered the course of history. As European merchants began to expand their reach into areas such as Africa and the Western Hemisphere, they discovered that with the exception of the Muslims who despite political and religious differences shared similar ideas about trade and money, the concept of using gold and silver which had intrinsic value and could be used for coinage was not unilateral. The imbalance between areas of the world with more advanced notions of commerce and a need for precious metals and areas which held large amounts of gold and silver but expressed scant interest in utilizing these resources for monetary purposes began to emerge (Walton 1994). Those who could take advantage of this contradictory situation stood to reap significant profits. The hunt for gold and silver began in earnest.

The European Quest for Gold

European thirst for gold and silver was heightened by the fall of the Christian city of Constantinople to the Ottoman Turks in 1453. The Turks subsequently held control of an important center of economic, political, and cultural influence. They also held sway over the Balkan silver mines of Serbia, Bosnia, and Kosovo. According to Erlichman (2010), the annual production of the Central European silver mines in the mid-fifteenth century had collapsed to fewer than 2.5 tons. The loss of the Balkan silver mines deprived the Italians of nine tons of silver. England's annual production of 65,000 lbs sterling in 1474 was half of its production in 1350. The Netherlands output of silver was down two-thirds. All of which meant a tightening of currencies and a slowdown in business activity. A sense of urgency for new sources of gold and silver prevailed.

Ironically, the smaller, less powerful, less affluent country of Portugal became the catalyst for a giant leap in the search for metallic riches, and ultimately, the evolution of capitalism. Vilar (1969) contended that Portugal, a small country, achieved more than countries much larger in population and resources due to its location at the crossroads of the Mediterranean, the Atlantic, and Africa. Prince Henry the Navigator, considered the father of Portuguese maritime expansion, jump-started his country's exploration of Africa. The Portuguese roamed far and wide around the west of Africa colonizing the Madeiras and the Azores, exploring as far south as the Ivory Coast, Niger, and Cameroon, searching for African gold, slaves, and a shorter route to the spice and silk markets of India and Malaysia. These activities captured the attention of competing countries. Portugal's exploration and commercial successes in West Africa had rendered the Spanish Kingdom of Castile to a lesser status on the Iberian Peninsula. The marriage of Fernando of Aragon and Isabel of Castile altered the dynamics of the region. The royal duo of Fernando and Isabel proved formidable, conquering the Muslim kingdom of Granada in 1491, unifying most of

Spain. The duo then turned their attention to beating the Portuguese to spice markets of South Asia (Erlichman 2010).

Christopher Columbus, a Genoese with a commercial and sailing background, in search of a more direct route to the spice markets of Asia, proposed a western route in sharp contrast to the Portuguese intent to head east. Columbus, having been turned down by the English and twice by the Portuguese, found a willing partner in the Spanish monarchs. To finance Columbus's first expedition, 1,600,000 maravedis, the equivalent of 14–16 kg of gold had to be found, with the hope that a sum exceeding that amount would come back. The Spanish monarchy provided 1,140,000 maravedis, Columbus paid an eighth of the costs, but it was the banker de Santangel who raised the capital (Vilar 1969). After a 10 week sail across the uncharted Atlantic, Columbus landed on an island in the Bahamas on October 12, 1492, thinking that he had located a chain of islands off the eastern coast of Japan (Erlichman 2010). According to Thomas (2003), some of the natives Columbus first encountered upon his landing had gold hanging around their necks and from holes pierced in their noses, instantly capturing the explorer's interest. Whether Columbus desired to recover the costs of the voyage or a quest for wealth, his hunger for gold was apparent, mentioning the subject in his diary more than 65 times (Vilar 1969).

The discovery of gold in the Caribbean islands spawned an unprecedented rush to search for New World riches. The next 50 years witnessed a gold cycle in the islands. The Spanish confiscated Indian gold used for ornamentation and forcibly subjugated natives in their search for gold in local vicinities. Death and infirmity of the indigenous population took place as the Spaniards moved from Santo Domingo to Puerto Rico, Cuba, and Hispaniola. Ultimately, the Spaniards began to spread elsewhere as the discovery of gold and silver in other Latin America countries ensued. While gold was the initial draw, as the decades of the sixteenth century unfolded, silver became so critical that gold comprised only 15% of the value of the riches being returned to Spain (Vilar 1969).

Three Sources of Gold and Silver

The viceroys of New Spain failed to discover the fabled *El Dorado* city of gold, even after sending search envoys as far north as Kansas and as far west as the Grand Canyon. However, the Spanish Empire's efforts in New Peru proved much more fruitful. Pizarro conquered the Incan empire in 1532 and the Spanish Empire acquired the Cerro Rico de Potosi silver mine. Some historians estimate that 85% of all silver extracted from the Andes came from this mine alone (Weatherford 2010).

Mining operations were run predominantly with the labor efforts of conquered Incans. Despite the widespread use of imported slaves from Africa as a labor source in other regions of the empire, Incan slaves were already acclimated to high altitudes. Spanish governors adapted the practice of *mit'a*, a labor law implemented by Incan predecessors requiring Incan youth to provide a given period of public service.

However, instead of the Incan practice of using this labor to build roads and public edifices, the Spanish employment of *mit'a* was used to mine silver (Thomas 2003). This practice quickly segued into full-scale forced labor referred to as *encomiendas*. In addition to the gold and silver mines that were discovered throughout Peru, Bolivia, Ecuador, and Colombia, the Vice Royalty of Peru also discovered several mercury mines, an integral component in the processing of silver. The proximity of mercury, most notably from the Huancavelica mine, afforded both cheaper processing because mercury did not have to be imported from foreign sources, and expedited exportation of the processed silver. The silver was transported to the coastal cities of Arica, Lima, and Callao in Peru where it was loaded on ships and sailed to Panama City. The silver was loaded onto mule trains and crossed the Isthmus of Panama to coastal cities of Nombre de Dios and Porto Bello to await transportation to Spain.

The Cerro Rico silver mountain was the first major mining acquisition for the Spanish Empire. A second major source of wealth was discovered in northern South America. In 1514, the coastal cities of Cartagena and Santa Marta were established as a base for exploration of the rivers and tributaries of the Andes Mountains. The rich gold deposits found there were extracted by the now-common *encomienda* enslavement practices, but also by the importation of African slave labor. These riches were taken to Cartagena to await transportation to Spain.

Finally, despite initial discoveries of small silver and gold deposits in Mexico in the early 1500s, the Vice Royalty of New Spain continued to search for larger collections of these metals. They discovered abundant deposits of silver most notably in Zacatecas and Guanajuato in Mexico in 1546. The silver extracted from these mines was carried by mule train to the coastal city of Veracruz to await transportation to Spain. Once the gold and silver were staged in Cartagena, Porto Bello, and Vera Cruz, they were transported via Spanish galleon to the port of Havana which served as a final staging area prior to shipment to Spain as illustrated in Fig. 1.

Transportation via Treasure Fleet

By 1520, the Spanish established a system of convoys whereby two fleets would depart from Seville, Spain, to retrieve the newly discovered gold and silver. The flotilla consisted of war galleons heavily laden with cannon, supply frigates, and merchant carracks, which purveyed the Caribbean colonies with manufactured and trade goods. Under this system, the fleet would sail to Caribbean whereby half the fleet would head south to Cartagena and Porto Bello, while the other half of the fleet would recover the silver and gold supply from Caribbean outposts, notably Vera Cruz. The fleet would then rendezvous in Havana in preparation for the return trip to Spain. To further protect their supply chain, the Spaniards augmented the fortifications and increased standard garrison sizes in these port cities which staged the gold and silver.

11 The Origins of Robust Supply Chain Management and Logistics in the...

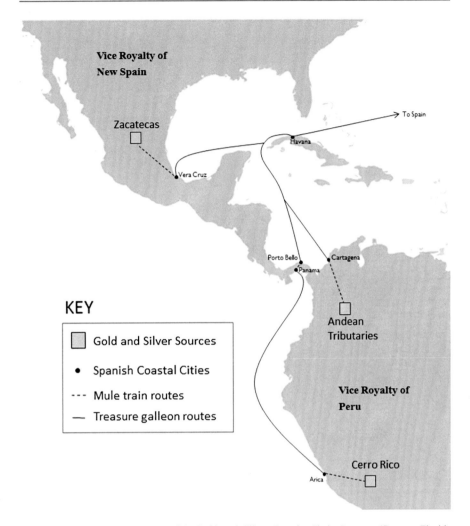

Fig. 1 Seventeenth Century Spanish Gold and Silver Supply Chain Routes. (Source: Florida Department of State. Retrieved from http://info.flheritage.com/galleon-trail/plateFleets.cfm)

The main production centers of Spanish gold and silver were too far inland to be susceptible to sacking. However, once the Spanish treasure galleons departed the staging docks of Cartagena, Porto Bello, and Vera Cruz, they were the target of attack at sea by a myriad of characters. Piracy, as the Spanish called it, consisted of all foreigners, mostly Protestant, who assaulted their assets (Thomas 2003). Despite the all-encompassing characterization of piracy by the Spanish, the constitution of these actors varied in both legitimacy and tactics. Piracy consisted initially of the French and English attempting to disrupt Spain's progress towards wealth. They achieved this by sacking cities, seizing ships, and funding settlements from which to base their operations. This exercise of legitimate force by established foreign navies eventually digressed into independent actors partaking in the attacks. Piracy by the mid-seventeenth century had become an independent endeavor. Privateers were nonmilitary contractors of Spain's enemies, buccaneers were ostensibly free-lance sea robbers and bandits, and freebooters were French pirates in the Antilles that attacked merchant and treasure ships alike prior to arriving in Spain. The attacks on Spanish ships were so pervasive throughout the Caribbean during this time period that scholars refer to the seventeenth century as the Golden Age of pirates.

Spanish Logistics and Supply Chain Management

To comprehend the scope of the Spaniards' extraction, processing, and movement of the immense amount of physical riches mined from the New World, we must put this into the context of modern day logistics and supply chain management. The concept of logistics, the movement of equipment and supplies, emerged from the military's support of troop activities in the field. Today, the Council of Supply Chain Management Professionals define logistics as "that part of the supply chain process that plans, implements, and controls the efficient, effective flow and storage of goods, services, and related information from the point-of-origin to the point of consumption in order to meet customers' requirements" (Enarsson 2009, p. 1). According to Rodrique (2012), the principle of continuous flow is at the heart of efficient use of logistics to support supply chain management as shown in Fig. 2.

By examining Rodrique's (2012) modern day logistic chain, we can visualize the Spaniards process of logistics management. First they extracted gold and silver from various New World sources. Then they processed the raw material and fabricated the silver into loaf-shaped bars that weighed about 70 lbs, wedges that weighed anywhere from 2 to 10 lbs, or smaller cakes that weighed a pound or so. Gold followed much the

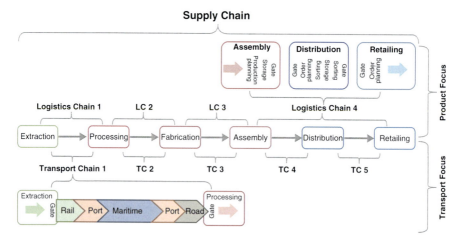

Fig. 2 The Scope of a Supply Chain, Logistics Chains and Transport Chains. (Source: Rodrique (2012), chapter 4, p. 5)

same process and was cast into similar shapes as silver but weighing only ounces rather than pounds (Peterson 1975). Following the processing and fabrication which took place at the various mining sites, the gold and silver was transported, typically by mule train, to assembly points in Vera Cruz, Mexico, Panama City, Panama, and Cartagena, Colombia. From these locations, Spanish ships made their way to Havana for final assembly and transport to Spain. To appreciate the scale of the Spanish logistics movement of riches to Spain, we need to consider the mode of maritime transportation. By the 1550s, the galleon had become the workhouse of the Spanish treasure fleet. Galleons were, on average, about 100 ft long, 30 ft wide and carried artillery plus supplies necessary to support a crew that could number as many as 200–300 men which included military personnel. Spanish galleons had a carrying capacity anywhere from 500 to 600 tons (Walton 1994), minute compared to today's modern cargo vessels where a medium size container ship is 700 ft in length and carries a load of 25,000 tons. To move the billions worth of riches to Spain, it is evident the Spaniards, against enormous challenges, focused efforts on achieving their version of a state of continuous logistics flow from the New World to Spain despite the fact that each voyage could take anywhere from 2 to 3 months, were comprised of 60 or more ships, and typically sailed in the spring to avoid the hurricane season.

The Spaniards modeled the logistics chain flow of extraction, processing, fabrication, assembly, distribution, and retailing centuries before the concept had been formulated. Lest there be confusion about the word retailing, the last step in the logistics flow process (Rodrique 2012), it is important to understand how the Spanish Crown's stake in New World riches evolved. Initially, the Spanish King demanded the bulk of the wealth confiscated from the Americas. However, it became evident that without proper incentive to navigate unchartered waters, bear harsh conditions, risk everything including life and limb, the proper development of the New World riches would languish and the full potential of exploiting this opportunity never achieved. The royal share was lowered and by 1500, the king's share was half, then reduced to a third, and in 1504 became a fifth. Where difficult mining conditions prevailed, the King's share could have been as low as a tenth (Peterson 1975). The larger share of New World abundance went to the merchants who financed the search for gold, silver, and other riches – the use of *variable or rolling capital*, money used in the production as defined by Braudel (1992). The regulation of trade between Spain and the New World was under the control of the Spanish House of Trade which was under the administration of the Council of the Indies and was responsible for formulating trade policies and procedures. So linked was the Merchant Guild of Seville to the House of Trade, members could be compelled to advance money to the crown to meet the financial needs of the state or finance fleets of treasure ships (Hamilton 1929). Figure 3 reveals in pesos the average annual imports of registered public and private treasure from the New World.

The value of this treasure to the Spanish Crown and the Merchants of Seville is best illustrated by the fact that "at the rate prevailing for un-skilled labor in Andalusia, Spain, the average annual receipts for 1591–95 would have paid for 21 ½ days' work of all the persons in the country employed for salaries and wages" (Hamilton 1929, p. 464).

Fig. 3 Average Annual Imports of Treasure in Pesos by Ten-Year Periods, (Source: Hamilton (1929), p. 464)

Period	Public	Private	Total
1503-1510	75,176.3	211,756.2	286,932.5
1511-1520	114,690.5	323,059.4	437,749.0
1521-1530	61,444.6	173,076.6	234,521.2
1531-1540	356,649.1	760,975.7	1,117,624.9
1541-1550	470,092.0	1,622,451.2	2,092,543.2
1551-1560	1,039,400.4	2,533,505.5	3,572,905.9
1561-1570	1,120,855.2	3,948,895.0	5,069,750.2
1571-1580	1,989,667.8	3,842,042.2	5,831,710.0
1581-1590	3,118,763.3	7,522,685.2	10,641,448.5
1591-1600	4,199,533.3	9,723,139.3	13,922,672.6
1601-1610	3,013,912.9	8,147,794.1	11,161,707.0
1611-1620	2,312,141.9	8,615,974.2	10,928,116.1
1621-1630	1,901,991.4	8,491,049.6	10,393,041.0
1631-1640	1,885,025.5	4,800,065.7	6,685,091.2
1641-1650	1,261,754.9	3,845,115.0	5,106,869.9
1651-1660	569,080.4	1,561,896.1	2,130,976.5

Robust Supply Chain Practices

The supply route the Spanish empire established during this time was unlike any others seen in history. The Romans had a network of roads to connect the farthest regions of their empire, but these were already well-established trade routes into a relatively known world (Grant 1991). Marco Polo's route to Asia was exploratory in nature and yielded relatively low trade volumes, and military conquests such as those undertaken by the Mongols and Alexander had a clear origin to front lines supply chain, but were subject to short term fluctuations in quantity and limited duration (Cole and Symes 2014). The Spanish transportation of precious metals from their newly established vice-royalties in Central and South America was truly the world's first supply chain that was maintained in consistent quantities over a sustained period of time (centuries) in an environment where the risks were unknown and extreme. Their success is remarkable by historical standards. Moreover, they changed the economy of Western Europe and established supply chain practices their European neighbors would emulate in their New World conquests.

Current knowledge of supply chain management is rooted in a mature stream of empirical and theoretical scholarship. The Spanish supply chain practices need to be contextualized in this contemporary understanding so that the fullness of their innovation can be brought to light. More specifically, in what ways does their supply chain conform to modern best practice? Many scholars argue that robustness is the defining characteristic of supply chain best practice (Kouvelis et al. 2006; Asbjornslett and Rausand 1999; Durach et al. 2015; Nair and Vidal 2011). Meepetchdee and Shah (2007) offer that robustness consists of "the extent to which the supply chain is able to carry out its functions despite some damages done to it" (p. 203). This characterization identifies resiliency in spite of setbacks as a key element in supply chain robustness. The Spanish Empire certainly persevered in spite of myriad detriments to their operation. The treasure fleet was successfully captured in 1628 and destroyed in 1656 and 1657. Maritime weather sunk the treasure fleet in 1622, 1715, 1733, and 1750. Pirates successfully sacked port cities of Nombre de Dios (1595), Campeche (1663), Panama (1671), Vera Cruz (1683), Cartagena (1683), Porto Bello (1739), and Havana (1748). These efforts emboldened pirates and foreign navies to continue their sally on the Spanish treasure fleet and compelled Spanish governors to further fortify their port redoubts. Despite these setbacks, the Spanish supply chain continued to function. Klibi et al. (2010) opine that a supply chain is robust if it can sustain value creation under all plausible future scenarios. The Spanish successfully imported more than 89 million pesos from American origin between 1503 and 1660, which equates to more than 500,000 pesos per annum (Hamilton 1929). Their sustainable value creation vis-à-vis the silver and gold routes demonstrates the robustness of their supply chain. Wieland and Wallenburg (2012) characterize robustness as the ability of a supply chain to resist change to its initial configuration. Hence, a consistency of purpose characterizes robustness. The Spanish supply chain advanced as nautical, shipbuilding, and navigational technology improved, and they used these advances to expand their armada of fleets and continue global navigation and exploration, notably in South America and Philippines. They fought wars with their English, French, and Dutch counterparts. They established their new colonies, expanded their population centers, and established new commercial trade routes. They never abandoned their efforts to continue gold and silver extraction during the era of these concomitant opportunities. The incentive to maintain their lucrative supply chain was clear. Their reliance (and dependency) on gold and silver to fund these expansive endeavors fueled their commitment to maintaining the supply chain. This consistency of purpose further characterizes their supply chain as a robust one.

The Spanish supply chain can be regarded ostensibly as the world's first robust supply chain because the results of their efforts reflect the resiliency, sustained value creation, and consistency of purpose that characterizes robustness. A comprehensive understanding of their supply chain requires a deeper exploration of the factors that contributed to this robustness. Durach et al. (2013) conducted a meta-analysis of robustness as a supply chain construct and identified eight antecedents. They found that the factors contributing to a robust supply chain include leadership commitment, reliable human capital, intra-organizational relationship magnitude, an aggressive orientation on risk management, node criticality, bargaining power, visibility, and network complexity. The Spanish supply chain is contextualized in light of these factors.

Leadership Commitment

A robust supply chain begins with unwavering commitment from organizational leadership. In the years prior to the discovery of these new resources, the Spanish monarchy ushered in what would become the most influential union the era would see – that of Ferdinand of Aragon and Isabella of Castile. Their impact on the

Spanish search for and production of silver and gold during this early period set the precedents that proceeding kings and queens would use to grow their presence in the new world. This royal couple was committed to the Spanish supply chain for myriad reasons. First, the Spanish empire was in the midst of vanquishing the last bastion of Muslim presence in Spain. Their victory at Granada (1492) was the last step in evicting Muslim presence after eight centuries of occupation. In the postbellum years of Granada, Isabel and Ferdinand took measures to establish and sustain a unified and independent Spanish identity (Thomas 2003). They funded more wars and conquests for expansion using the funds from the resources they extracted from their new vice-royalties. The Spanish fought in campaigns against Morocco (1497), Muslims (1499), Ottomans (1499), Italy (1499), Papal States (1508), Tainos in the Caribbean (1508, 1511), Algiers (1518), Aztecs (1519), Mayans (1523), Switzerland (1526), Incas (1531), France (1551), Protestants (1562), Philippines (1567), and the Eighty Years War that began in 1567. The constant need to supply front lines, billet soldiers, hire mercenaries, incentivize exploration, and compensate the ever-growing list of nobles, officers, and governors to rule the expanded territories left Spain unwavering in their search for more gold and silver. The leadership commitment to maintain the supply chain was stark, even after the Isabela and Ferdinand era had ended. Spanish powers continued to pour resources into maintenance and development of the supply chain because had they not, they would have lacked the financial means to engage their empirical conquests of foreign lands and defense of their own. Thomas (2003) suggests that the Spanish monarchs ostensibly bankrupted their country by using their treasure from the New World to fund an incessant series of wars. The gold and silver they extracted continued to depreciate in value by nature of the increase in supply. The commitment to war and the inflation collectively contributed to the bankruptcy of the monarch.

The depreciation of precious metals during this time meant they needed even more to maintain their level of warlike relationships with neighboring European powers and American exploration and conquest. Leadership commitment to the supply chain became absolute as a result of this dynamic.

Human Capital

Human capital is an essential element in establishing and maintaining a robust supply chain. The origins of the metals in mines required the Spanish to employ slave labor of conquered peoples. The encomiendas were forced labor practices whereby the Spanish used local native populations who were well acclimatized to the weather of the Mexican heat and the altitude of the Andes. In more accessible regions, the Spanish would also import African slaves to areas such as Northern Colombia. Human capital for gold and silver processing was accessible to the Spanish in the form localized slave labor.

Once the Spanish transported the gold and silver to coastal cities such as Cartagena, Puerto Bello, and Vera Cruz, the empire relied on the military chain of command to transport and protect the gold as they made it Havana and then to Spain.

The Spanish navies were financed by the treasures extracted from the Americas and represented a source of human capital integral to the supply chain.

In addition to production and transportation of the treasure from origin to destination, the Spanish treasury funded the production of supplementary inputs to the entire process. They paid for Spanish shipbuilders in port cities of Seville and Cadiz to produce the galleons, barques, sloops, and merchantman carracks needed to execute this maritime supply system. They had access to the goods produced by domestic Spanish labor which supplied their Caribbean and American outposts. They funded transportation of Spanish families across the Atlantic which were fundamental in the operation and localized expansion of their burgeoning colonies.

Finally, the Spanish nobility had a robust system of governorship under which the colonies would be administrated. They placed governors in each of their major hubs to oversee the welfare of not only their cities but their part in the Spanish supply chain. Part of this governorship required the human capital to populate the garrisons of the forts which guarded the harbors of towns like Cartagena, Cumana, Maricaibo, Havana, San Juan, and Santa Marta.

In short, the Spanish empire had the necessary human capital to execute their supply chain via forced local labor to produce the metal, Spanish navy to transport and protect the treasure, supporting industries to supply the inputs, and a series of Spanish administrators to govern the entire process.

Intra-organizational Relationship Magnitude

Intra-organizational relationship magnitude within a robust supply chain represents the degree to which the unique entities within the organization work cooperatively and communicate. The monarchical nature of power and reporting hierarchies allowed the Spanish empire to strengthen the intra-organizational relationship of their supply chain. Their intra-organization relationship was enhanced by both the accountability measures practiced at the time and the punishments for non-compliance. For example, Spain sent royal accountants to their royal outposts to ensure the proper distribution of goods and collection of tariffs. They ensured that treasuries were accounted for and that the king and queen received their agreed upon share of private expeditions, and the entirety of what they were owed from origin production. Ship captains were required to keep logs and bills of lading that were reviewed by the appropriate authorities at various stages in the process. These accountability measures contributed to intra-organizational relationship. A king or queen in Spain could reasonably account for their production and treasure from origin in the Americas, to coffers in Spain. What made these accountability measures so effective was the punishment for noncompliance. A royal accountant who identified mistreatment or misplacement of royal funds could identify and report a governor or official and subjugate them to deportation back to Spain. This was precisely the case with Columbus in 1500. He was sent home to Spain in chains where he defended his case with the Isabel and Ferdinand. The Spanish navy had severe punishments for mutiny and insubordination. These included death, flogging, and even relegation to Spanish penal colonies (Ortiz-Minaya 2014). The empire had demonstrated in the fifteenth and sixteenth century's vis-à-vis the Spanish Inquisition the ruthlessness and monarchial power that could use to enforce the rules. The combination of accountability and punishment for noncompliance contributed to the overall adhesiveness of the intra-organizational relationships.

Risk Management

A global supply chain faces a diverse set of risks due to disruptions, breakdowns, political factors, and disasters both natural and man-made, all of which complicate the process of assuring the safe passage of goods and making risk management challenging. Nowhere was this truer than what the Spanish faced while transporting riches from the New World to Spain. When looking at the Spanish risk management process through the lens of modern day risk management practices, we used the four categories of risk proposed by researchers (Manuj and Mentzer 2008; Christopher and Peck 2004) which were supply, demand, operational, and security. Figure 4 displays the interrelationship between the different types of risks.

For the Spanish, the risks were enormous to both the crown and the Merchants of Seville. By necessity, they became ingenious at developing risk mitigation strategies aimed at the primary challenges of the operational risk of inventory ownership; demand risk of competitor moves; and supply risks such as natural disasters, piracy, transit time variability, and confiscation by foreign adversaries.

The Spanish first line of risk management was to properly secure inventory ownership which was compounded by illegal smuggling, the stowage of gold and

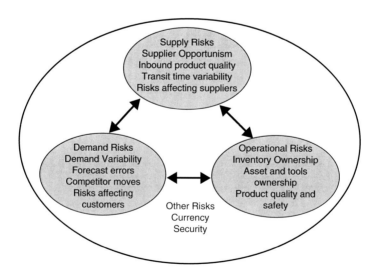

Fig. 4 Risks in Global Supply Chains. (Source: Manuj and Mentze (2008), p. 201)

silver aboard the Spanish ships. Responsibility for the safety of the gold and silver bullion lay with the *master de plata* (silver master) who was appointed by the Spanish Crown. This individual was chosen with great care and was obligated to post a bond of 25,000 ducats in silver with the Spanish officials. Multiple copies of the cargo manifest were developed as precautions against smuggling and to certify property ownership. Two were sent in ships other than the one carrying the treasure, one stayed behind, and one went with the actual ship carrying the gold and silver. These precautions were developed to expedite accounting should a disaster befall the ship or the entire fleet of ships (Peterson 1975). In theory, the cargo manifest should have listed each and every ounce of gold and silver going to Spain and had to be accredited as tax-paid. However, viewed by the Spanish officials, tax evasion and smuggling had grown so pervasive that The Law of 1580 was enacted stating any ship captain or officer caught in the act would have their bullion confiscated and be held liable in full to the ship owner. By 1593, the offense of smuggling was punishable by the loss of position for 4 years and should the offender prove to be an everyday seaman, they were consigned to the galleys for that amount of time. Those on the receiving end of unregistered bullion, often the Seville Merchants, would have their property seized by the Crown and banished from Spain and all Spanish territories. The Spanish Crown and the Seville Merchants in effect ran a monopoly and was determined to hang onto that monopoly at all costs.

The Spanish treasure fleets were subject to demand risks created by competitor's moves of piracy and confiscation by foreign adversaries. Barbour (1911) contended that the majority of those acting against Spain were privateers, in essence entrepreneurs seeking Spanish treasure through violent means while sailing under letters of marque or retribution, which gave them legal authorization to appropriate Spanish ships and the goods they carried. Spain's foreign competitors, the French, Dutch, and English, freely issued letters of marque in concerted efforts to capture a portion of the Spanish treasure being repatriated to Spain. While there were occasions of pirate buccaneers of fictional lore, they made up a small portion of the assaults committed in the Indies and Caribbean.

To combat these strategic adversarial moves, according to Walton (1994), the Council of the Indies in 1560s issued operational directives that governed the shipping of New World treasures to the mother country. These proclamations included extensive Spanish naval patrols in areas vulnerable to attack; primarily the Caribbean and the Atlantic waters off the coast of Spain; and initiating a system of regularly scheduled Spanish convoys that were heavily guarded. Large fleets including merchant ships and protective warships traveled in these convoys. Smaller craft accompanied the convoy to carry messages and scout surrounding waters (Walton 1994).

The Spanish had to contend with the supply risk of primitive navigation techniques and weather that impacted their continuous logistics flow. Maritime navigation in the fifteenth, sixteenth, and seventeenth century was archaic by today's standards. Seafarers had long possessed the ability to measure latitude, how far north or south they were from their home. However, determining their longitude –

their position east or west from a given point – was a challenge. The sailor could determine the local time by the position of the sun, but without a clock that had the ability to function despite corrosive elements and the rocking of a ship, it came down to a guess as to how long they had been traveling east or west (Schuler 2014). Despite, or perhaps because of these primitive navigation techniques, the treasure fleets developed the practice of departing for Spain from Havana, following the Gulf Stream north before turning east toward Spain. While the Spanish utilized enormous risk mitigation strategies to combat piracy and hostile action by foreign competitors, the most serious threat to the successful passage of the treasure ships was the weather. While weather conditions were generally better during the summer months, the warm waters of the Atlantic could spawn hurricanes. The Spanish lost ships to Caribbean storms in 1590, 1591, 1601, 1605, and 1614 (Walton 1994). Without the aid of modern day satellites, radar, GPS systems, and electronic depth finders to detect shoals and reefs, the best the Spanish could do was recognize through hard lessons, the time of the year that gave them the best chance of good weather and safe passage to the deep waters of the Atlantic. Should a weather related disaster or similar catastrophe occur, the Spanish Crown and the Seville Merchants utilized various contingency plans to mitigate the supply side risk of defaulting on the loans that financed the treasure fleets. Clauses were written into the loan contracts that allowed for the suspension of payments should a sizeable, unanticipated event occur and debt restructuring including the extension of the debt, alteration to the interest rate were common (Drelichman and Voth 2014).

Despite these risks and challenges, the Spanish Empire had a major impact on shaping the world economy. The European-style monetary system became the model in the western hemisphere. The treasure fleets first linked the continents together. The Spanish system was a success primarily because it met the needs of two forceful and influential factions: the Spanish Crown and the Merchants of Seville.

Node Criticality

There were three nodes, critical points where the Spanish logistics aspect of their supply chain system intersected. The first, node 1, were the main collection points of Vera Cruz, Panama, and Cartagena where the extracted and processed gold and silver was delivered from mines scattered throughout the Spanish America. The second, node 2, was the primary gathering point in Havana where shipments from node 1's were collected, stored, inventoried, and ultimately loaded onto ships bound for Spain. As characterized by Adenso-Diaz et al. (2012), critical nodes as shown in Fig. 5 are those that would cut the primary flow of the commodity if they were shut down. An argument could be made that a 3rd node could exist anywhere along the route of the Spanish treasure fleet once departed from Havana due to risks posed by weather, attack by privateers or pirates. The Spanish, however, took great care to control what they could control in the logistics flow of wealth from the New World to Spain.

11 The Origins of Robust Supply Chain Management and Logistics in the... 261

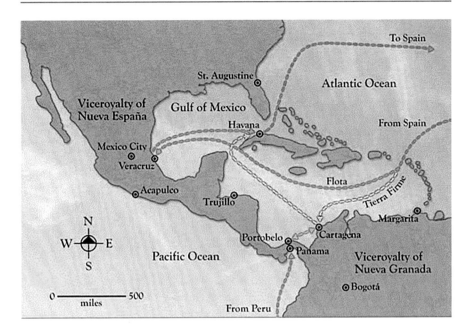

Fig. 5 Node Points: Spanish Supply Chain. (Source: Florida Department of State. Retrieved from http://info.flheritage.com/galleon-trail/plateFleets.cfm)

Bargaining Power

According to Campbell (1998), a significant goal of supply chain management is to reduce uncertainty and create optimum conditions for long-term continuity, factors important to those responsible for the movement of gold and silver from the New World to Spain. Due to the monopoly held by the Crown and the Seville Merchants, one might ask "What bargaining power?" But when viewed as the need for task interdependence by Spanish miners, processors, transporters, and sailors operating in a challenging environment, thousands of miles from home, the subject takes on a different perspective.

Thompson (1967) argued that three types of task interdependencies exist – pooled, sequential, and reciprocal. Pooled interdependencies occur when various parties do not need to coordinate their activities. An example would be a merchant and its suppliers. Once orders are placed, it matters only to the owner of the shop when supplies are delivered and little coordination between vendors is required. This is not the case when moving large quantities of metals across long distances fraught with uncertainty. Sequentially interdependent tasks arise when one participant's job must be finished in order for the next participant's job to begin, which necessitates arrangements and schedules. Thus was the movement of New World riches to Spain which required the coordination of sequentially interdependent tasks. Once the gold and silver was mined and processed, it required coordinated movement to the major gathering points of Mexico City, Vera Cruz, and Cartagena. Sequentially, the processed New World riches

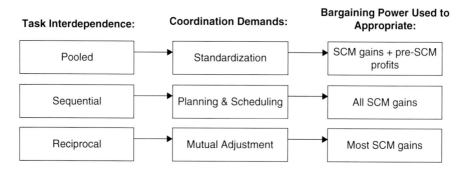

Fig. 6 Connection between task interdependence, needs for coordination, and bargaining power. (Adapted from Crook and Combs 2007, p. 549)

moved to Havana and then onto Spain. Each step of the process needed the prior step to be completed and required coordination of totally different tasks and ran on prearranged schedules. Reciprocal interdependence happens when organizations require the involvement of other people or units of operation (Thompson 1967). Reciprocal tasks most likely occurred where New World riches were mined and processed. The connection between task interdependence, needs for coordination, and bargaining power is shown in Fig. 6.

Crook and Combs (2007) pointed out that sequentially interdependent tasks require a heightened need for planning and the sequencing of events as one group's outputs becomes the next in line's inputs. It was in the best interests of all parties involved in the process of moving gold and silver to Spain to function together and deliver optimal performance under trying conditions. Bargaining power, defined by Bush (2016) as the ability or power to impact another, was likely minimal as long as the process flowed smoothly and supply chain management profits maximized. Every member of the logistics system, large or small, reaped profits and were controlled by the dual monopolies of the Spanish Crown and the Merchants of Seville.

Visibility

The scope of the Spanish global exploration, colonization, and exploitation of New World riches was breathtaking. Despite the limitations of navigation systems of the day and communication between the New World and Spain that relied totally on maritime travel, the factor of visibility played a role in the function of the Spanish supply chain management system. According to McCrea (2011), visibility in the logistics and supply chain process is when all parties, the shippers, the various business associates, and end users know where products are within the supply chain – from raw materials to the final destination. Modern day enterprise resource systems (ERP) integrates the shipper with the supplier and enables both parties with a click of a few computer keys to check on the status, location, and anticipated deliver of a particular order. This was not the case when it came to managing the process of moving gold and silver from the New World to Spain.

To understand the Spanish approach to managing the timing of the activities of mining, processing, overland transportation, and final shipment of gold and silver to Spain, it is useful to view this process through Vernon's (2008) definition of visibility in supply chain management as the *"identity, location and status of entities* transiting the supply chain, captured in timely *messages* about *events*, along with the *planned and actual dates/times for these events"* (p. 182). The entity in the Spanish movement of riches was the specific product (gold, silver). Identity was the system with which the Spanish coded the shipment components (Crowns portion, Saville Merchants portion). Location was where the product was in the process of movement from the mines to Spain. A visibility event was when a specific function within the process was completed and the next function began, i.e., movement from the mine and process site to the gathering site, overland movement to the primary shipment sites, and finally, onboard a ship headed to Spain. Planned and actual dates refer to when an event was to take place (Vernon 2008). In the 1560s the Council of the Indies decreed rules and regulations that stipulated procedures for the operation of the fleets between Spain and the New World. This edict required accelerated naval patrols in the critical areas of the Caribbean and the Atlantic waters off the shore of Spain, exposed areas where the treasure fleets initiated and completed their voyages and stipulated the timing of the sailing of two enormous convoys that departed from Spain each year filled with supplies and laden with New World riches on their return. Three factors were calculated into the timing of their sailing: (1) take advantage of the winds and currents, (2) bypass the steamy heat of the summer, and (3) attempt to sidestep the powerful storms, including hurricanes in the fall and winter which ultimately proved to be the most significant threat to the Spanish treasure fleet system (Walton 1994).

Network Complexity

Harland et al. (2003) concluded that as the complexity of the supply chain network increased, risk increased. As noted by Durach et al. (2015), two key factors add to an increase in network complexity: (1) the greater the number of nodes within the supply chain, (2) the supply chain tends to become ever more protracted and complex. In the case of moving New World riches to Spain, the Spanish were able to limit the number of nodes, but due to the sheer length of their supply chain and the challenges posed by primitive navigation devices, nonexistent communication systems, the constant threat of privateers, and unpredictable weather, the Spanish supply chain was complex. The overall success of the Spanish treasure fleets was a testament to Spanish ingenuity, courage, and planning.

Long-Distance Trade and the Development of Capitalism

Spanish activity in the New World, spawned by the discovery of gold and silver, marked a significant leap forward in the development of a global economy. For the general masses of the European population, commerce continued in its most basic form, the local market where merchants bartered their goods in exchange for other goods or exchanged their wares for money. Some international trade, the merchants of the Italian states, for example, might have purchased goods in their locale, re-sold them in Egypt, used the proceeds to acquire spices, peppers, and other highly desirable commodities, to be re-sold in Italy at a profit. This mechanism represents what Braudel (1992) called a trade zone or market. According to Cetina (2006), the evolution of international trade required the development of long supply chains and intermediaries, a business model quite different from central markets. This trading process passed through an expanding maze of import-export merchants, financiers, and commercial adventurers who were not producers but brokers who locate, purchase, and stock goods to resell at a later date to consumers and other traders at the end of a supply chain. As the global economy developed, trading networks dominated by powerful groups were established inside and outside Europe. Charter trading companies emerged including the East India Company and the Hudson's Bay Company who subsequently built far-reaching international trading domains that focused on trade rather than the production of goods (Gereffi 2005).

Boxer (1969) argued that true world trade came about when a maritime connection was established with the four great continents with silver as the catalyst. China became the predominant buyer of silver when they converted from a paper-money system to silver in the 1570s. Silver flowed to China via three trade routes: (1) across the Atlantic to Europe and on to Asia, (2) from Europe around the African Cape, and (3) Mexico to Manila, to China. On the production side, Spanish America produced over 150,000 tons of silver between 1500 and 1800, likely more than 80% of the world output. Conventional thinking was that the driving factor behind the flow of silver to China was the European's desire for Asian luxury goods such as silk and porcelain which created a trade deficit that had to be settled. Contrarily, Flynn and Giraldez (1995) contended that the switch of more than a quarter of the world's population to the use of silver as currency contributed to a situation where silver's value in China was double its value in other parts of the world and gave birth to world trade. Irrespective of the ultimate cause, world trade blossomed and can be measured as seen by the rapid growth of European cities located along the Atlantic seaboard. Between 1600 and 1750, 40% of urban growth in Europe took place in just 15 Atlantic port cities (de Vries 2007). Intercontinental trade grew from approximately 2500 tons in 1501, approaching 800,000 tons in 1795 as illustrated in Fig. 7.

Braudel (1992) wrote that long-distance trade was a significant factor in the evolution of merchant capitalism and that the import-export merchants were a category apart. The risks of long-distance trade were extraordinary, but outlandish profits based on the price differences between markets far apart were the rewards of success. Supply and demand were not factors and controlled solely by the merchant wholesaler. A striking example of extravagant profits was "a kilo of pepper, worth one or two grams of silver at the point of production in the Indies, would fetch 10–14 grams in Alexandria, 14–18 in Venice, and 20 to 30 in the consumer countries

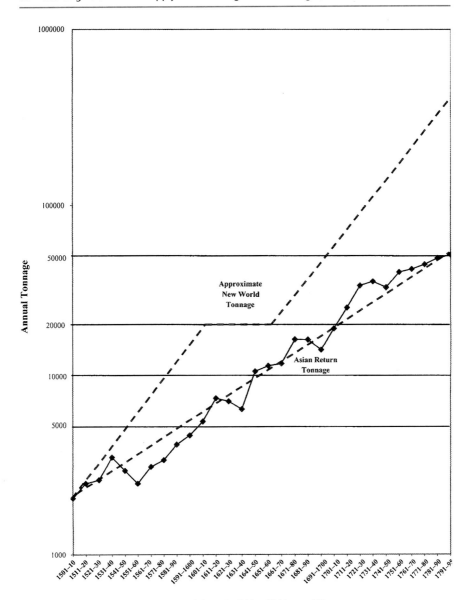

Fig. 7 Intercontinental trade. (Adapted from De Vries 2010, pg. 26)

of Europe" (Braudel 1992, p. 405). Sizeable profits were not the sole domain of luxury goods. Commodities including grain, wool, and manufactured cloth made their way through various trade routes and the contrast between the purchasing and selling prices was so great, that even factoring the cost of transport, the profits were sizeable. As noted by Braudel (1992), the preeminence of the import-export merchants and long-distance trading were crucial factors in the development of merchant capitalism and the establishment of the merchant bourgeoisie.

New World Riches and the Impact on the Iberian Peninsula

Vilches (2010) wrote that the flood of gold and silver from the New World created a serious problem, price inflation on the Iberian Peninsula. Money was no longer simply a medium of exchange with a fixed and intrinsic value. Gold and silver became a commodity that could change in value based on supply and demand. Several scenarios unfolded that proved consequential. First, as the New World Spanish colonies matured, they required textiles, paper, and other manufactured products. Spain could produce just a fraction of the goods required by their overseas conquests which meant Spanish merchants had to seek products produced outside of Spain for re-export to Spanish colonies. The result was reduced profits, Spanish silver now going to foreign markets, and tax revenues experiencing a sharp decline. Second, Spain's aggressive foreign policy required huge amounts of money sent abroad to support its fleets and expansionist plans. Third, less than productive uses of Spanish riches ensued including a series of seemingly unending foreign wars, state debt, and excessive bureaucracy, all of which began crippling the Spanish economy (Walton 1994).

By the end of the seventeenth century, Spain was in decline. The French, Dutch, and English had aggressively colonized the Americas and Spain was being outmaneuvered by her fierce rivals politically and economically. War, exodus to the colonies, and famine contributed to a Spanish population decline of two million in 1700 from the start of the quest for New World riches in the early 1500s. Poor political decisions by an administration run by lawyers, aristocrats more inclined to showcase their wealth, and former military officers proved inadequate in developing programs and economic policies capable of revitalizing the country. As the century wore on, the Spanish Crown continued in a series of wars that required borrowing massive money from foreign bankers. Finally, an ongoing series of suspension of loans and suspension of payments led to Spain's creditors to cease loaning money to the Spanish Crown.

Conclusion

The Atlantic trade spurred by the Spanish quest for gold and silver played a significant role in the development of a new global economy. According to Acemoglu et al. (2002), Atlantic trade delivered significant profits to a segment of European merchants, the bourgeoisie. With these profits, the bourgeoisie were able to increase their investments, expand their trading, and grow the economy. On a grander scale global trade began when the major continents of the world began the routine transfer of goods on more or less a continual basis (Flynn and Giraldez 1995). While these achievements were inevitable, they were hastened by the courageous and ingenious Spanish system of logistics and supply chain management. One can argue that the Spanish were also responsible for the demise of a significant portion of the indigenous native population as they institutionalized their processes of moving New World riches to Spain. Acknowledging this fact and leaving further exploration into this subject for another essay, one can visualize the dramatic changes that ensued post the rush for New World riches. The amount of foreign trade had become so immense that it became more and more challenging to clear international accounts. The discovery of gold in North America, the invention of ships made from metal and driven by coal-powered steam engines dramatically altered seaborne transportation. The emergence of alternate means of a money that included paper, letters of credit, the electronic transfer of funds and the United States bowing out of the promise to redeem its currency for gold were economic factors resulting from the long-ago Spanish quest for New World riches. This quest for riches compelled the Spanish Empire to adopt innovative supply chain practices, which reflect the basic framework of what modern scholars consider a robust supply chain.

References

Acemoglu D, Johnson S, Robinson J (2002) The rise of Europe: Atlantic trade, institutional change and economic growth. National Bureau of Economic Research, Cambridge, MA. Retrieved from https://www.nber.org/papers/w9378.pdf

Adenso-Diaz B, Mena C, Garcia-Carbajal S, Liechty M (2012) The impact of supply network characteristics on reliability *Supply Chain Management:* An Int J 17(3):263–276. Retrieved from https://www.researchgate.net/profile/Santiago_Carbajal/publication/233919540_The_Impact_of_Supply_Network_Characteristics_on_Reliability/links/0deec52a836aae9431000000/The-Impact-of-Supply-Network-Characteristics-on-Reliability.pdf

Asbjørnslett BE, Rausand M (1999) Assess the vulnerability of your production system. Prod Plan Control 10(3):219–229

Ashtor E (1975) Profits from trade with the Levant in the fifteenth century. Bull Sch Orient Afr Stud Univ Lond 38(2):250–275. Retrieved from https://www.jstor.org/stable/pdf/613212.pdf?casa_token=tM8HKJpOd5EAAAAA:CcbfKaDVaoRuin9dCsnTztcjWGCXxZekdfB39YGXwDV_uOLDGGJI0KKiH8E0sJ-91hjbWffd8IHMwkM6jDVNCwTbZsTFDa5-Q1V_2xnSzfCY90fRqw

Barbour V (1911) Privateers and pirates of the West Indies. Am Hist Rev 16(3):529–566. Retrieved from https://www.jstor.org/stable/pdf/1834836.pdf

Beneductow O (2005) The black death: the greatest catastrophe ever. Hist Today 55(3):42–49. Retrieved from https://www.historytoday.com/ole-j-benedictow/black-death-greatest-catastrophe-ever

Boxer CR (1969) The Portuguese Seaborne Empire – 1414 – 1825. Hutchinson, London

Braudel F (1992) The wheels of commerce. University of California Press, Berkley

Bush T (2016) What is bargaining power in business? PESTEL Analysis. Retrieved from https://pestleanalysis.com/bargaining-power-in-business/

Campbell A (1998) Cooperation in international value chains: comparing an exporter's supplier versus customer relationships. J Bus Ind Mark 13(1):22–39. Retrieved from https://www.emeraldinsight.com/doi/abs/10.1108/08858629810206197

Cetina KK (2006) The market. Theory Cult Soc 2(3):151–156. Retrieved from http://kops.uni-konstanz.de/bitstream/handle/123456789/11724/The_Market_2005.pdf?sequence=1&isAllowed=ycdentral markets

Christopher M, Peck H (2004) Building the resilient supply chain. Int J Logist Manag 15(2):1–13. Retrieved from https://dspace.lib.cranfield.ac.uk/bitstream/handle/1826/2666/Building_the_resilient_supply_chain-2003.pdf?sequence=3&isAllowed=y

Cole J, Symes C (2014) Western civilizations: their history & their culture, 18th edn. Norton and Co, London

Crook TR, Combs JG (2007) Sources and consequences of bargaining power in supply chains. J Oper Manag 25:546–555. Retrieved from https://pdfs.semanticscholar.org/20ad/6dc4772028553dad032be4153d3f6eed1b3f.pdf

CSCMP (2016) Council of supply chain management professionals. Available at: http://cscmp.org/about-us/supply-chain-management-definitions. Accessed 17 Nov 2016

de Vries J (2007) The limits of globalization in the early modern world. The Economic History Review 63(3):710–733. Retrieved from https://www.jstor.org/stable/40929823?seq=1#metadata_info_tab_contents

Drelichman M, Voth H (2014) Risk sharing with the monarch: contingent debt and excusable defaults in the age of Philip II. University of Zurich, Department of Economics, pp 1556–1598. Retrieved from https://www.econstor.eu/bitstream/10419/111205/1/econwp145.pdf

Durach CF, Wieland A, Machuca JAD (2015) Antecedents and dimensions of supply chain robustness: A systematic literature review. Int J Phys Distrib Logist Manag 45(1/2):118–137. Retrieved from https://openarchive.cbs.dk/bitstream/handle/10398/9123/Durach_et_al_2015_Antecedents_and_Dimensions_of_Supply_Chain_Robustness_postprint.pdf?sequence=3

Enarsson L (2009) What do we really mean by supply chain management? Supply Chain Logist Q. Retrieved from https://www.supplychainquarterly.com/topics/Logistics/scq200901book/

Engels F (1957) The decline of feudalism and the rise of the bourgeoisie. Mon Rev 445–454. Retrieved from https://www.marxistsfr.org/archive/marx/works/1884/decline/index.htm

Erlichman HJ (2010) Conquest, tribute, and trade. Prometheus Books, Amherst

Flynn DO, Giraldez A (1995) Born with a "silver spoon": the origin of world trade in 1571. J World Hist 6(2):201–221. Retrieved from https://www.jstor.org/stable/pdf/20078638.pdf?refreqid=excelsior%3A454abd482e435629dedd8f1c998f4ca0

Gereffi G (2005) The global economy: organization, governance, and development. In: Smelser NJ, Swedberg R (eds) The handbook of economic sociology. Princeton University Press, Princeton, p 161

Grant M (1991) The founders of the Western world: a history of Greece and Rome. Charles Scribner's Sons, New York

Hamilton EJ (1929) Imports of American gold and silver into Spain, 1503–1660. Q J Econ 43(3):436–472. Retrieved from https://www-jstor-org.proxy195.nclive.org/stable/pdf/1885920.pdf?refreqid=excelsior%3A9ea2de89d58c40afcedaf6fb9f217d76

Harland C, Brenchley R, Walker H (2003) Risk in supply networks. J Purch Supply Manag 9:51–62. Retrieved from http://citeseerx.ist.psu.edu/viewdoc/download?doi=10.1.1.471.2910&rep=rep1&type=pdf

Klibi W, Martel A, Guitouni A (2010) The design of robust value-creating supply chain networks: a critical review. Eur J Oper Res 203(2):283–293

Kouvelis P, Chambers C, Wang H (2006) Supply chain management research and production and operations management: review, trends, and opportunities. Prod Oper Manag 15(3):449–469

Manuj I, Mentzer JT (2008) Global supply chain risk management strategies. Int J Phys Distrib Logist Manag 38(3):192–223. Retrieved from https://search-proquest-com.proxy195.nclive.org/docview/232593322/fulltextPDF/4D08ADF1258A4169PQ/1?accountid=14968

McCrea B (2011) Supply chain logistics technology: defining visibility. Logist Manag. Retrieved from https://www.logisticsmgmt.com/article/supply_chain_and_logistics_technology_defining_visibility

Meepetchdee Y, Shah N (2007) Logistical network design with robustness and complexity consideration. Int J Phys Distrib Logist Manag 37(3):201–222

Nair A, Vidal JM (2011) Supply network topology and robustness against disruptions –an investigation using multi-agent model. Int J Prod Res 49(5):1391–1404

Olsen-Raymer G (2014) The Europeans – why they left and why it matters. Humboldt State University Department of History. Retrieved from http://users.humboldt.edu/ogayle/hist110/expl.html

Ortiz-Minaya R (2014) From plantation to prison: visual economies of slave resistance, criminal justice, and penal exile in the Spanish Caribbean 1820–1886. ProQuest Dissertations Publishing. Retrieved from https://search.proquest.com/openview/d731b34443decce2dd019e575ca0d170/1?pq-origsite=gscholar&cbl=18750&diss=y

Pach ZP (1968) The shifting of international trade routes in the 15th–17th centuries. Inst Hist Res Cent Humanit Hung Acad Sci 14(3/4):287–321. Retrieved from https://www.jstor.org/stable/pdf/42554829.pdf?casa_token=BzYZMRcj8hYAAAAA:_FoKt8pcPVcT05nO5IO9RKEsgUL9HYcW_cN_hRJSjR96wNCWUT_fvLAmedfMB71hVacH0vb-aVi3W76XhJGcoK8fJbKwKFspDzYpYa8YB5T7zTIi3w

Peterson M (1975) The funnel of gold. Little, Brown, & Company, Boston

Rodrique JP (2012) Supply chain management, logistics changes and the concept of friction. In: Hall PV, Hesse M (eds) Cities, regions and flow. Routledge, London, p 5

Schuler CJ (2014) Ships, clocks and starts: the birth of navigation. Here 360. Retrieved from https://360.here.com/2014/08/06/ships-clocks-stars-birth-navigation/

Thomas H (2003) Rivers of gold. Random House Publishing, New York

Thompson JD (1967) Organizations in action. McGraw-Hill, New York

Vernon F (2008) Supply chain visibility: lost in translation? *Supply Chain Manag* An Int J 13 (3):180–184. Retrieved from file:///C:\Users\Wayne\Downloads\Supply_chain_visibility_lost_%20(1).pdf

Vilar P (1969) A history of gold and money. Verso Books, London

Vilches E (2010) New world gold: cultural anxiety and monetary disorder in early modern Spain. University of Chicago Press, Chicago

Walton T (1994) The Spanish treasure fleets. Pineapple Press, Sarasota

Weatherford J (2010) Indian givers: how native Americans transformed the world, 2nd edn. Three Rivers, New York

Wieland A, Wallenburg CM (2012) Dealing with supply chain risks – linking risk management practices and strategies to performance. Int J Phys Distrib Logist Manag 42(10):887–905

Transformation: The First Global Economy, 1750–1914

12

Bradley Bowden

Contents

Introduction	272
Industrial or Managerial Revolution? Britain, 1750–1830	279
Conquering Time and Space: The Global Economy, 1830–1890	285
Alfred Chandler, Railroads, Management, and Markets	291
Management, Slavery, and Colonial Subjugation	295
New Economy, New Workers, New Problems	297
Conclusion	302
Cross-References	304
References	304

Abstract

In 1750, most of the world's population lived in conditions that were little changed from time immemorial. In the absence of mechanical cloth production, most people only owned one or two sets of clothes. The cost of all forms of land transport meant that the bulk of production was geared towards local markets. By 1914, however, a totally new world had been created. Across the globe, steam-powered ships and railroad locomotives brought people and goods from near and far. As a global market emerged, competition increased inexorably. In the final analysis, the new global economy was both the creation of new systems of management and the creator of modern management. Initially confined to textile production, a revolution in both technology and management cascaded through the economy. As competition increased, management became more attuned to costs. Managers also sought after increased productivity so as to maximize outputs from a minimum of inputs. Increases in production also led to a spike in real wages. Wage gains, however, were incapable to quelling a rising tide of labor

---

B. Bowden (✉)
Griffith Business School, Griffith University, Nathan, QLD, Australia
e-mail: b.bowden@griffith.edu.au

© The Author(s), under exclusive licence to Springer Nature Switzerland AG 2020
B. Bowden et al. (eds.), *The Palgrave Handbook of Management History*,
https://doi.org/10.1007/978-3-319-62114-2_25

271

unrest, revealing the "human problem" to be management's major unresolved difficulty.

Keywords

Globalization · Industrial revolution · Chandler · Taylor · Technological change · Real wages · Trade unions

Introduction

In 1920, John Maynard Keynes penned what is undoubtedly his most readable book, a work that was also in many ways his most profound: *The Economic Consequences of the Peace*. "Before 1870," Keynes (1920: 7) recalled, the population of Europe, "taken as a whole … was substantially self-subsistent." "After 1870," Keynes (1920: 7) continued, "an unprecedented situation" prevailed in which the fate of the European "Old World" became intertwined with the New World. In reflecting on this process of integration, Keynes (1920: 9) remembered how a London resident such as himself,

> … could order by telephone, sipping his morning tea in bed, the various products of the whole earth, in such quantity as he might see fit, and reasonably expect their early delivery upon his doorstep; he could at the same moment and by the same means adventure his wealth in the natural resources and new enterprises of any quarter of the world.

Although Keynes was clearly describing the circumstances that prevailed at the top of the British social hierarchy, he also believed that the new global economy opened up new opportunities for social mobility. Any person, Keynes (1920: 9) reflected, "of capacity or character at all exceeding the average" was capable of joining "the middle and upper classes, for whom life offered …conveniences, comforts and amenities beyond the compass of the richest and most powerful monarchs of other ages." In Keynes's estimation, the economic relationship between Europe and North America lay at the core of this global economy. Indeed, Keynes (1920: 20) noted, the "prosperity of Europe" was unimaginable without "the large exportable surplus of foodstuffs in America." Nor was the prosperity of the new world order conceivable in the absence North America's immigrant population, peoples of mainly European extraction who farmed the land and built "the railways and ships which were to make accessible to Europe food and raw products from distant sources" (Keynes 1920: 8).

In summation, Keynes's argument was that the modern world with its systems of management, business organization and commercial exchanges only began in the 1870s. By contrast, for the noted management historian, Sidney Pollard (1965: 1), "the genesis of modern industrial management" was found in the Industrial Revolution that occurred in Great Britain between 1760 and 1830. The association of modern forms of work and management with the Industrial Revolution is a common one. Adam Smith (1776/1999: Book 1, para. 5), in one of the opening paragraphs of

The Wealth of Nations, ascribed the "great increase of the quantity of work" to not only "the division of labour" but also to "the [recent] invention of a great number of machines which ... enable one man to do the work of many." Karl Marx and Frederick Engels also believed that by 1848, industrialization had fundamentally changed the human condition. The result, Marx and Engels (1848/1951: 36) argued, was, "Constant revolutionising of production, uninterrupted disturbances of all social conditions, everlasting uncertainty." If, however, Pollard, Marx, and others ascribe the origins of modern management and capitalism to the industrialization of Britain, Alfred Chandler famously argued a different position. In Chandler's (1977: 3) opinion, "as late as 1840 there were no middle managers in the United States." Nor was there evidence prior to the 1840s, in the United States or elsewhere, of the modern "multiunit business enterprise" (Chandler 1977: 49). The reason for the slow emergence of modern managerial and business forms of organization, Chandler (1977: 49, 78) believed, was largely "technological." Only with the coming of railroads and telegraphs did the world witness, for the first time, genuine mass markets that demanded greater levels of coordination, both internally within the firm and externally in firm-market relationships.

From the preceding paragraphs, we can discern three broad arguments:

1. That modern systems of management owed their origins to the Industrial Revolution in Britain (1760–1830).
2. That modern forms of management and business only emerged when new forms of transport and communication allowed for mass markets (1840–1880).
3. That the modern world of global capitalist exchanges was a product of a unique set of circumstances that prevailed between 1870 and 1914.

How can we balance these competing arguments which reflect the opinion of some of the greatest minds in economics (Smith, Marx, Keynes) and management and business history (Pollard, Chandler)?

A good place to start is to look at some key measures of economic and managerial progress. Throughout history, the basic requirements for human existence have always been the same: food, clothing, shelter, and heating (both for cooking and warmth). Of these, clothing was historically the most difficult to achieve. Producing a set of clothes from spun fibers was always an inherently time-consuming and expensive business. Throughout history, in consequence, most people only possessed one or two sets of clothes, creating an insatiable demand for second-hand clothes. In the Middle Ages, as we noted in our earlier ▶ Chap. 9, "From Feudalism to Modernity, Part I: Management, Technology, and Work, AD 450–1750," "Peasants were always clothed in rags ...During epidemics of plague ... people waited for others to die to take their clothes" (Cipolla 1981: 31–32). Given the demand for cloth, the consumption of wool, cotton, and flax fibers provides a gauge of a society's capacity to meet a basic need. Historically, Britain's manufactured exports, like those of neighboring Flanders, were largely associated with woolens. Even though cottons gained a preeminent position during the Industrial Revolution, the output of woolen mills also increased, forcing Britain to import wool from Spain and

Saxony (Germany). British wool imports, therefore, provide a measure of not only British textile production but also of the logistics chain created to service factory demand. With this in mind, a perusal of Fig. 1, which traces wool imports in millions of pounds between 1835 and 1906, highlights two things. First, by 1845, Spanish and German growers were being forced out of the market. Australasian (Australian and New Zealand) producers now dominated. Secondly, that post-1855 imports – and hence production – were of a different order of magnitude to anything seen before.

The same broad pattern is evident when we turn our attention, as we do in Fig. 2, to the quintessential industry of the Industrial Revolution: cotton textiles. As most business and management historians would be aware, the invention by Eli Whitney of the "cotton gin" – which quickly and easily separated cotton lint from seed – provided cotton growers and manufacturers with an unexpected boost. In the United States, which came to dominate world cotton production, exports grew from a mere 138,328 pounds in 1792 – the year before the introduction of the first cotton gin – to almost 17.8 million pounds in 1820 (Thomas 1997: 569). From this point onwards, American exports and European (largely British) cotton manufacture advanced hand-in-hand. Once more, therefore, production of a resource staple is a pointer to both the level of industrialization and the complexity of the global supply chains that supported manufacture. As Fig. 2 indicates, the increase in the United States cotton exports was extraordinary, the slave-based workforces of the American South underpinning the expansion of British manufacture. By the 1850s, as managerial efficiencies accumulated all along the logistics and manufacturing chain, the price of

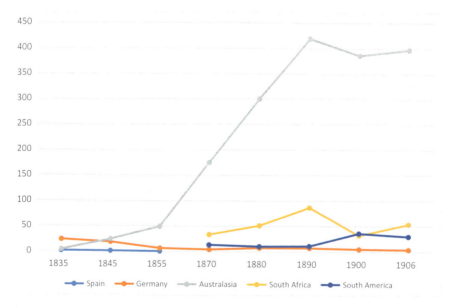

Fig. 1 British wool imports, 1835–1906 (in millions of lbs). (Sources: Clapham 1932/1967: 6; Ville 2005: Table 3; Knibbs 1909: 293)

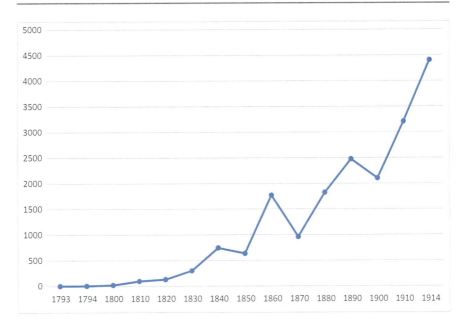

Fig. 2 The United States cotton exports, 1793–1914 (in millions of lbs). (Source: U.S. Department of Commerce 1975: Series U 274–294)

a piece of British cotton cloth fell to five shillings. In the 1780s, the same piece of cloth would have cost 40 shillings (McCloskey 1985: 59). It is, however, the process of post-1850 expansion that it most remarkable. As the United States cotton exports rose almost sevenfold between 1850 and 1914 – even as ever-increasing volumes of fiber were consumed by America's domestic factories – breathable and washable cottons came within the reach of the ordinary person for the first time (U.S. Department of Commerce 1975: Series U 274–294).

What explains the marked spike in the New World export of both woolen and cotton fiber after 1850? In brief, a revolution in shipping. Although wooden paddle steamers worked the Atlantic routes prior to the 1850s, they restricted their business to high-value passenger and mail services. By 1850, however, higher quality steel allowed for the construction of high-pressure "compound" (i.e., multiple cylinder) engines. Iron screw-propulsion also proved more efficient than side paddles. Greater production of iron and steel allowed for all-metal construction. The efficiency of the new technologies was demonstrated with the construction of the first iron ship using propellers instead of paddle wheels, the collier *James Bowes*. Undertaking its maiden voyage in June 1852, the ship hauled more coal in 5 days than two sailing ships could have carried in a month (Clapham 1932/1967: 71). By the mid-1860s, even though the tonnage of Britain's sailing ships outnumbered that of the nation's iron-bottomed ships by more than five to one, it was the latter that carried most cargo (Clapham 1932/1967: 71). The success of Britain's iron and steel ships rested, in the first instance, on a revolution in shipbuilding. Indeed, by 1870, shipbuilding represented the apex of Britain's industrial prowess, the typical shipyard employing 570 workers – far more than was the norm in either textiles or the iron and steel industry (Clapham 1932/1967: 116–117). The impact of this revolution in shipping on the all-important Atlantic routes – and by implication on routes connecting Europe with Asia and Oceania – can be ascertained by Fig. 3 which records the tonnage of ships calling in to the United States ports between 1790 and 1914. Once more, 1850 marks a fundamental turning point, the tonnage entering port growing by 221% across the decade. Interrupted by the Civil War, this spike in shipping – carrying migrants to the United States and grain, beef, and minerals to the Old World – continued until 1914 and beyond (U.S. Department of Commerce 1975: Series Q 506–517).

The revolution in shipping, which allowed for a massive expansion in the oceanic transport of people and produce, rested in the final analysis on a dramatic increase in iron and steel production, an increase that was only possible due a revolution in coal mining. As we noted previously in ▶ Chap. 9, "From Feudalism to Modernity, Part I: Management, Technology, and Work, AD 450–1750," much of the explanation as to why Britain was the initial pacesetter in the Industrial Revolution is found in its successful exploitation of its coal deposits. By 1700, as John Nef (1932/1966: 322) recorded, "The entire production of the rest of the world did not perhaps amount to much more than a sixth of that of Great Britain." From the 1830s, the extraordinary British achievement was matched by the United States, as coal production in both nations soared to unprecedented levels. As Fig. 4 indicates, which traces British coal output from 1560 and the United States production from 1820, an outwardly peculiar

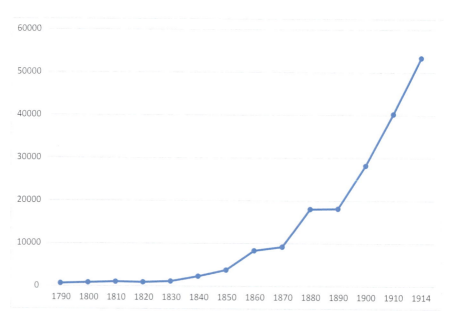

Fig. 3 Shipping tonnages at the United States ports, 1790–1914 (in thousands of tons). (Source: U.S. Department of Commerce 1975: Series Q 506–507)

12 Transformation: The First Global Economy, 1750–1914

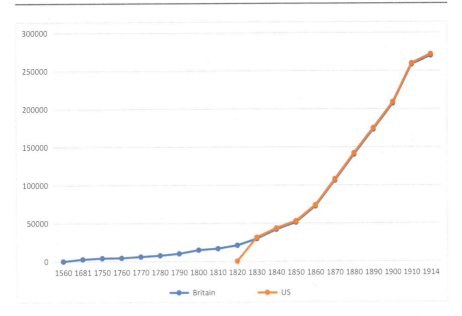

Fig. 4 British and the United States coal output, 1560–1914 (in thousands of tons)*. *British figures for period 1560–1914. The United States figures for period 1820–1914. (Sources: Pollard 1980: 216, 229; UK Department of Business, Energy & Industrial Strategy 2019; U.S. Department of Commerce 1975: Series M 93–103 and Series M 123–137)

feature of this expansion was the way in which British and the United States production rose in almost perfect tandem from 1830 to 1914. In 1860, for example, the United States production (73.9 million tons) shaded that of Britain (72 million tons) by the barest of margins. In 1914, on the eve of the First World War, a similar situation still prevailed, the United States output (271.9 million tons) exceeding that of Britain (270 million tons) by an inconsequential amount (Pollard 1980: 216, 229; UK Department of Business, Energy, and Industrial Strategy 2019; US Department of Commerce 1975: Series M 93–103, Series M 123–137). This unusual outcome is, however, suggestive of something more than historical coincidence. Rather it points to similar levels of demand, pursued with similar levels of managerial ingenuity, exploiting similar technological advantages.

In returning to the theoretical problem enunciated in our opening paragraph – i.e., was the first truly global economy a product of the Industrial Revolution (c.1750–1830) or of subsequent developments associated with revolutions in transport and communications? – we can conclude that Pollard, Chandler, Keynes, Smith, and Marx were all correct in emphasizing one *stage* of what was in effect a cascading series of interconnected revolutions. Initially, small technological improvements in textile manufacture caused entrepreneurs in Australia, New Zealand, and the United States to initiate managerial innovations that increased supply to the expanding factories. A growth in global logistics chains caused improvements in shipping. The growing importance of steam-powered ships and railroad locomotives in the logistics chain was, in turn, only possible due to gains in iron and steel production; additions that rested upon a massive increase in coal output.

At first glance, it appears possible to explain the "first global economy" simply through reference to market economics, proof that a market economy is inherently superior to all others in bringing forth innovation and in matching supply with demand. While there is truth in this supposition, it is nevertheless the case that – as Keynes, Chandler, and Marx emphasized –the new global (and even national) markets were as much a creation of this period of history as a creator. In the final analysis, the gains made between 1750 and 1914 were ones made by people: not impersonal market forces. Moreover, every significant advance required a managerial revolution. It is certainly folly to think of the transformation underway by 1750 in terms of "technological determinism," i.e., as a simple and inevitable flow-on from technological innovation. Nor is it correct to see the cascading series of revolutions that occurred between 1750 and 1914 as simply a product of steam power. For technological and managerial innovation manifested themselves in very different ways in different industries. The massive increase in Australasian wool exports that we identified in Fig. 1, for example, owed very little to steam power and much to a far more prosaic innovation: barbed wire. Realizing that in the benign Australian climate that sheep could be left overnight without protection, pastoral managers dispensed with shepherds, initiating instead a massive fencing project. In the then British colony of New South Wales alone, some 2.6 million kilometers (1.625 million miles) of fencing was built between the 1870s and the 1890s (Glover 2008: 32). Once completed, this fencing project eliminated the need for a significant pastoral workforce outside of the lambing and shearing seasons, when casual labor employed on piece rates was hired. As employment opportunities plummeted, the number of sheep soared, growing from 16.5 million in 1862 to 89.3 million in 1892 (Butlin 1964/1972: 67). This happy managerial outcome made the Australian pastoral sector the most efficient in the world. Despite employing a comparative handful of people, in 1886–1900 it was responsible for 12.8% of Australia's gross domestic product (GDP). By contrast, the agricultural and manufacturing sectors, each of which employed far more people than the pastoral industry, were responsible for only 5.8% and 11.8% of Australian GDP, respectively (Butlin 1964/1972). In shipping, as well, the gains evident in Fig. 3 would have been impossible without a profound transformation on shipboard patterns of management and work. For the addition of steam power and screw-propulsion required the creation of an entirely new job hierarchy built around technical rather than traditional maritime skills. In turn, this demanded new systems of training, supervision, motivation, and shipboard communication, as those working below deck came to outnumber those employed above deck [Note: Between 1980 and 1988, the author worked as a seafarer both above and below deck on Australia's last commercially operated steamer].

One of the problems associated with assessing the global economy between 1750 and 1914 is that we are dealing with not only economic and managerial relationships but also political and imperial relationships. In essence, the global economy during this period was primarily directed towards the needs of the industrial districts of the

Atlantic littoral, regions that sucked in foodstuffs and raw materials and spewed out an ever-increasing stream of manufactured products. In the economic relationships created by this pattern of demand and supply, it is a mistake to frame all our thinking in terms of dominance and subservience. Certainly, the wheat farmer on the United States prairies, and the woolgrower in Australia's continental interior, would have taken umbrage with any suggestion that they were subservient to the British wholesaler who purchased their annual output. In such circumstances, a better descriptor of the economic relationship would be interdependence. When we turn our attention to the placement of Africa, the Indian subcontinent and East Asia in the new global economy, however, we are dealing with societies that – if not subject to actual military occupation – were the victims of unequal and militarily imposed treaties. In the continental interiors of Australia and the Americas, and in Oceania, indigenous populations faced the destruction of their traditional ways of life even as many traded with local representatives of the new economic order. In reflecting upon this fact in his oft maligned, *The Clash of Civilizations and the Remaking of World Order*, Samuel Huntington (1996/2003: 51) made the pertinent observation that:

> The West won the world not by the superiority of its ideas or values or religion (to which few members of other civilizations were converted) but rather by its superiority in applying organized violence. Westerners often forget this fact; non-Westerners never do.

Yet, even if unequal, economic relationships between the West and the established societies of Africa and Asia offered the latter benefits as well as subjugation. In the wake of the European armies trailed administrators, railroad engineers, bridge builders, doctors, and teachers. In India, British conquerors built the subcontinent's first railroad in 1853. By century's end, the region boasted 38,400 km (24,000 miles) of track. "In the space of a generation," Ferguson (2008: 169–170) observes, the railroads "transformed Indian economic and social life: for the first time, thanks to the standard third-class fare of seven annas, long-distance travel became a possibility for millions of Indians."

What is clear is that, by the closing decades of the nineteenth century, there was barely a corner of the globe that was not – for better or worse – part of the new international economy.

Industrial or Managerial Revolution? Britain, 1750–1830

Discussion of Britain's Industrial Revolution immediately conjures up William Blake's (1808/1969: 481) image of "dark Satanic Mills" consuming "England's green and pleasant land." For William Wordsworth (1814/1853: 297), as well, the new industrial factory was the embodiment of evil, "the master idol" that demanded "perpetual sacrifices" of "Mothers and little children, boys and girls." In fact, the Industrial Revolution that occurred between 1750 and 1830 owed more to managerial innovation than it did to steam power, McCloskey (1985: 66) describing it as "an age of improvement" in which managers maximized the benefits obtained from a comparative "handful" of technological innovations. Even in cotton textiles, where mechanization advanced the most, only spinning witnessed the virtual elimination of hand-powered tools between 1750 and 1830. Other production process remained the preserve of traditional technologies. One survey, conducted in 1830, estimated the number of power looms in cotton weaving across England and Scotland at no more than 60,000. By contrast, there were still 240,000 handlooms in operation (Clapham 1926/1967: 143).

The idea that the new textile mills were reliant on an unscrupulous use of child labor is also a misnomer. Yes, it is true that the early mills did scour orphanages in search of labor, adults showing an initial reluctance to enter into factory life. As mechanization took hold, however, children were found ill-suited to factory work, where increases in productivity were associated with literacy and training. By 1851, only 30% of English and Welsh children between the ages of 10 and 14 worked. Of those who did, only 15.4% of males and 24.1% of females were found in factories. Among girls, a greater percentage (25.3%) worked in domestic service, an industry where long hours and the likelihood of abuse were arguably worse than in supervised factory work. For boys, agriculture – an industry with many assorted perils – was the principal employer, giving work to 34.6% of those aged between 10 and 14 who were in some form of employment (Kirby 2011: 122–124). Spared work, a majority of children increasingly enjoyed something unique in history: a childhood devoted to schooling. Unlike children, however, who were soon displaced from factory work, females retained a long-term presence in textile manufacture. In 1851, when the first reliable occupational census was conducted, the 272,000 female cotton workers easily outnumbered the industry's 255,000 males (Clapham 1932/1967: 24). For early Victorian England, this large female industrial workforce was a source of national shame, provoking royal commissions and protective legislation. These female workers were, however, arguably more beneficiaries of the Industrial Revolution than victims. As the great English labor historian, E.P. Thompson (1963: 452–453) noted, the "abundant opportunities for female employment ... gave women the status of wage-earners." In consequence, the "spinster," the "widow," and the "unmarried mother" were able to free themselves in large numbers from a reliance on male relatives.

On the demand side, the key driver behind the initial take-off of mechanized cotton manufacture was not domestic need but rather the circumstances that prevailed in the Atlantic slave trade. In this highly profitable trade, the principal item exchanged for slaves was textile fabric, Thomas (1997: 318) estimating that before 1750 some 85% of British textiles were exchanged for slaves. Even in the decades after 1750, when lower prices boosted domestic demand, some 40% of British fabric was destined for the "slave coast." Unfortunately for British merchants, who shipped a record 200,000 slaves between 1740 and 1750 (Thomas 1997: 264), the quality of British fabric was often poor, forcing the importation of highly colored (and expensive) Indian "calicos" that were reexported aboard British slavers. Unsurprisingly, textile producers in the hinterland behind Liverpool and the other north England slave ports saw in this circumstance an attractive business proposition: the substitution of expensive Indian cottons with locally made product.

Although England had long boasted a cotton industry alongside the much more significant wool trade, "the quality of the product was rather poor, and its quantity insignificant" (Mantoux 1961: 199). To boast production, Liverpool's merchants initially resorted to the same methods that characterized most "manufacturing" at the time: "putting-out" or outsourcing. This saw merchants purchase cotton and then outsource production to "weavers," who then oversaw a complex process of further outsourcing and collection. Under this system, virtually all the spinning of fabric, and weaving of cloth, was devolved to the household sector, where spinning and weaving provided a significant supplement to agriculture income. The problem with the "putting-out" system was that it allowed for neither innovation nor supervision, outcomes that ensured a continuation of low output and indifferent quality. Between the 1760s and 1810, however, a series of primitive inventions (Hargreaves's "spinning jenny," Arkwright's so-called "water frame," Compton's "spinning mule"), a medieval source of power (the water mill) and new systems of management overcame these problems, heralding the birth of what we think of as the Industrial Revolution.

Of the inventions that transformed textile production, the "spinning jenny" invented by James Hargreaves in 1764 was the most primitive. Consisting of little more than a wooden frame that was moved manually backwards and forwards, it nevertheless allowed a single worker to draw cotton fibers on to multiple spindles (Mantoux 1961: 216–218). A more significant "invention" was Richard Arkwright's so-called "water frame" – so-called because, although most models were eventually located in water mills, in the 1760s the first examples were powered by horses. Too large for manual operation, the "water frame" twisted multiple strands of fabric into "a much stronger thread than the most skilled spinner could have made with a spinning wheel" (Mantoux 1961: 216–218). Only when the new mechanism was transferred to the banks of the Derwent River in Derbyshire, and located within water mills, was its potential realized, Arkwright's own mill boasting thousands of spindles and 300 workers by 1799 (Mantoux 1961: 224). Like many entrepreneurs who enriched themselves in the Industrial Revolution, Arkwright appears to have been as much charlatan as genius. The plans for the invention that made him famous were, it appears, pilfered from others, namely, James Paul and John Wyatt, Arkwright himself having no previous "knowledge either of spinning or mechanics" (Mantoux 1961: 231). Arkwright's real skill was as an entrepreneur and manager rather than as an inventor, taking an existing idea, modifying it and bringing it into commercial operation. Like Paul and Wyatt, the inventor of the "spinning mule," Samuel Compton, gained little from his pioneering in 1779 of a device that "became the spinning machine *par excellence*" (Mantoux 1961: 237). Just as a mule supposedly exhibits the best attributes of a female horse and a male donkey, the "spinning mule" combined the best features of the "jenny" and the "water frame." Not only was the spinning speed of the "mule" incomparably superior it also exceeded the quality of home-based craft workers, enabling "British manufacturers to outdo the renowned skill of Indian workers and manufacture 'muslims' of incomparable delicacy" (Mantoux 1961: 238). None of this production, however, occurred in factories owned by Compton, who vainly pursued legal action against those who profited from his conception. So successful was the "spinning mule," however, that by 1812, Britain boasted up to five million operational spindles, worked across hundreds of factories (Mantoux 1961: 237–238).

Much of the success of the early spinning contraptions is attributable to the fact that their construction required little in the way of either capital or skill. Their attractiveness was also enhanced by the fact that they could be powered from a plentiful and inexpensive source of energy, i.e., running water. In 1788, almost three-quarters of England's 123 cotton mills were located along mountain streams in the Pennines (Lancashire, Yorkshire, Derbyshire, and Nottinghamshire). Of these, almost half were in southern Lancashire, adjacent to Liverpool's merchants and slave traders (Mantoux 1961: 248). Indeed, the very ease with which one could enter the industry soon proved a major problem for cotton manufacturers as a surge in output drove down prices and profits. It was in this competitive environment that another revolutionary invention, the Boulton and Watt steam engine, gained acceptance. Although the Newcomen steam engine had been used in the coal industry since 1712, the Boulton and Watt engine, manufactured at the Soho factory near Birmingham, differed in being small enough and cheap enough for generalized use. Admittedly, installation of steam engines incurred costs, both in terms of capital investment and running costs (i.e., coal), that were not suffered in water-powered mills. However, numerous cost advantages offset such expenses. As James Watt explained to a potential Scottish customer in 1784, his firm's engines were "certainly very applicable to the driving of cotton mills, in every case where the convenience of placing the mill in a town, or ready-built manufactory, will compensate for the expense of coals" (cited, Mantoux 1961: 334). The practicability of coal-fired steam engines was also enhanced by the completion of a system of canals across the English Midlands, the first such canal (the Bridgewater Canal) linking Manchester to Lancashire's coalfields in 1761. A second canal, the Birmingham Main Line, linked Birmingham with the coalfields of the English "Black Country," a spur line passing the door of Boulton and Watt's Soho engine factory. This boost to the fortunes of steam engine manufacture was due to more than fortunate happenchance. Prominent among the Birmingham Canal's private underwriters was Mathew Boulton, the Soho factory's senior financial partner. The new canal system did more, however, than bring coal within reach of England's industrial consumers. It also effectively created the world's first mass market, allowing factories a cheap means of accessing raw materials, wholesalers, retailers, and other end-users. Such was the extent of the English canal system by 1830 that visitors from continental Europe often ascribed the nation's economic success to its creation. In 1825, for example, a French traveler, Baron Charles Dupin (1825: 181), advised his readers how England's canals providing an indispensable linkage between "opulent ports; industrious towns; fertile plains; and inexhaustible mines."

The first stage of the revolution in textile manufacture, it must be emphasized, only related to the *spinning* of yarn. The *weaving* of cloth was still, in large part, done by hand. To avoid the well-known problems of outsourcing, which gave management little direct control over quality, managers often brought weavers within the newly constructed factories as well. This "solution," and indeed the new factory system as a whole, brought with it a host of new problems for management. Weavers, long used to an independent existence, soon became dissatisfied with a proletarian existence. Intense competition added to downward pressure on wages, Pollard (1965: 91) observing of the cotton industry, "It was an environment encouraging ruthlessness, not only towards one's competitors, but also towards one's employees." Despite the passage of the *Combination Act 1799*, which outlawed trade unionism, a flourishing of labor organizations occurred across the entire textile industry. In 1812, discontent manifested itself in the most extensive strike ever experienced in Britain to that time. As Sidney and Beatrice Webb (1902: 52) record in their *History of Trade Unionism*, "From Carlisle to Aberdeen every loom stopped, forty thousand weavers ceasing work simultaneously."

In many ways, the workforce's propensity to unionize and engage in strike action was the least of management's problems, not only in the textile industry but also across all the sectors characterized by automation (brewing, potteries, engineering, and mining). The problems faced by management during this period are best summarized by Pollard in the introduction to his classic study, *The Genesis of Modern Management*. Unlike "the builders of the pyramids," Pollard (1965: 7) corrected identified, the managers of the early industrial age had to relate production efforts "to costs," selling their output into highly competitive markets. To achieve this end, managers pioneered what we think of as "cost accounting," generating estimates of costs at each *stage* of the production process. "In the most advanced works," such as Boulton and Watts's Soho engineering work, "departmental accounts would attempt to keep the returns of departments separate, down to elaborate schemes for allocating overheads fairly and proportionately" (Pollard 1965: 222). Often these early attempts at cost accounting were crude, if not misleading. Such failings, however, reflected the historically unique circumstances in which managers found themselves. As Pollard (1965: 215) explained, in managerial cost accounting "there was no tradition, no body of doctrine, no literature worthy of the name." Despite these difficulties, Pollard (1965: 209) nevertheless argued that, "the development of accounting for industry ... was one of the two main responses of large firms to the problems of management in the Industrial Revolution."

The second key response of larger firms to the Industrial Revolution was the realization that they needed a class of skilled salaried managers who stood in an intermediary position between the firm's owners and shop-floor foremen and supervisors. As with cost accounting, the emergence of a class of professional managers was an historic novelty, regarded with suspicion by many of society's leading members. Writing at the dawn of the Industrial Revolution, Adam Smith, for example, correctly identified the emergence of a class of professional directors and managers as one of the seminal events of his time. Rather than seeing this new class as agents of a more productive society, however, Smith saw them as an impediment to progress, declaring that "being the managers of other people's money rather than their own, it cannot well be expected that they should watch over it with the same anxious vigilance [as] ... their own" (Smith 1776/1999: Book V, Chap. 1, Article 1, para. 18). As there were no business schools or colleges given over to the training of managers, most firms initially recruited managers internally, either through the delegation of family members or by promoting workers from the shop floor. Firms slowly realized, however, that although technical knowledge was a useful attribute in running a business, it was not as important as general managerial ability: a capacity to identify operational problems, recruit and motivate staff, match supply with demand, and look for innovations not enjoyed by competitors. Pollard (1965: 127) notes that Britain's "northern collieries" were probably the largest suppliers of managers to Britain's expanding factories and mills. As Nef (1932/1966: 322) had correctly identified, this industry experienced "capitalistic forms of industrial organization" at an earlier stage than any other sector. The industry also pioneered the use of steam power in 1712 with the introduction of the first Newcomen engines. Competition was also historically fiercer, and workforces larger, in coal mining than elsewhere. Strikes and nascent forms of trade unionism were also a common feature of the northern coalfields. All of these experiences, garnered in the hard life of the coalfields, were invaluable elsewhere.

The propensity of workers to engage in disruptive strikes points to another managerial response evoked by the Industrial Revolution: the need to recruit, supervise, and motivate a large class of mechanically minded workers, most of whom boasted skills that would have been unimaginable a generation earlier. Of all the attributes that managers had to inculcate in their workers, however, none was more vital than punctuality and awareness as to the passage of time, E.P. Thompson (1967: 85) arguing "that the contest over time" was seminal to the ultimate success of the Industrial Revolution. Unlike outsourced handicraft work, where it made little difference when a worker chose to commence the operation of their handloom or spinning wheel, a mechanized factory could not operate upon the basis of workers strolling in and out whenever they felt like it. In a world where only the wealthy owned watches the factory siren – announcing various warnings as to the start of the next shift, as well as the commencement and conclusion of meal beaks – became a defining characteristic of the new industrial towns and villages. Whereas people had previously only measured time through reference to the rising and setting of the sun, workers and managers now fought each other over the hours and even minutes of work. Campaigns for the 10-h day and, subsequently, the 8-h day, were a ubiquitous feature of every mechanized industry. Unscrupulous managers, for their part, manipulated the work clocks, one Scottish worker complaining: "The clocks at the factories were often put forward in the morning and back at night, and instead of being instruments for the measurement of time, they were used as cloaks of cheating and oppression" (cited Thompson 1967: 86). Often reduced to the level of petty mindedness, the managerial struggle to impose time discipline on their workforce was nevertheless vital to the very future of industrial civilization. For without control over time, no other form of managerial planning and control can have any meaning.

Profound as they were, the industrial and, more importantly, the managerial effects of the transformation that occurred in Britain between 1750 and 1830 were, as we have previously noted, largely confined to a minority of the workforce. Outside of textiles, engineering, potteries, coal mining, and brewing, "the applications of novel machinery and of steam power were only tentative" (Clapham 1926/1967: 156). As Figs. 1, 2, and 3 indicated, the effect of the initial stage of the Industrial Revolution on global supply chains was also comparatively modest. The highly profitable slave trade, which provided much of the custom for British textiles, remained geared towards the production of coffee, tobacco, and, above all, sugar, rather than cotton. Most cotton still arrived in Britain from India and Egypt. When the first eight bales of American cotton arrived at Liverpool's wharves in 1784, disbelieving customs officers seized it as contraband, not crediting Americans with the wherewithal needed to produce and export such fibers (Mantoux 1961: 201, Footnote 3). Even sugar, which remained the backbone of the planation economies of the Americas, remained a luxury item in the second half of the eighteenth century. Only with the post-1850 revolution in shipping did sugar became an item of everyday consumption. Whereas prior to 1850, Mintz (1985: 148–149) observed in his study of the global sugar trade, sugar "did not make a significant calorific contribution to English working-class diet," after 1850 it became the "most important addition to the British working-class diet." By 1900, sugar – consumed either with tea or in the form of confectionary, biscuits, cakes, and "puddings" – made up a sixth of the British working-class diet (Mintz 1985: 149).

Although British manufactured exports prior to 1830 were miniscule compared to what was to follow, they were not without their global effects. Nowhere was this more evident than in the trade with India. As Marx (1853/1951: 315) noted in his study of *British Rule in India*, "From immemorial times, Europe received the admirable textures of India," produced by "myriads of spinners and weavers," paying for these magnificent textiles with "precious metals." As we noted above, prior to Compton's invention of the "spinning mule," Europe was incapable of matching the high-quality yarn and fabric of Indian "calicos." By the 1820s, however, the boot was firmly on the other foot. Not only did Britain's manufactured product drive Indian textiles out of European markets, they also began the conquest of India's home market. Between 1818 and 1836, Marx (1853: 315) noted, British textile exports to India rose 5200-fold. By 1824, British was selling 1,000,000 yards of cloth (914,000 m) into the Indian market. Thirteen years later, this total had risen to 64,000,000 yards (58,521,600 m). The social consequences were devastating, Marx (1853/1951: 313), advising his readers that, "the misery inflicted by the British on Hindostan [India] is of an essentially different and infinitely more intensive kind than all Hindostan had to suffer before."

Conquering Time and Space: The Global Economy, 1830–1890

In arguably the most influential work in Australian business and management history, *The Tyranny of Distance*, Geoffrey Blainey (1966: 70) observed "that anyone circumnavigating the [Australian] continent in 1800" – more than a decade after initial European settlement – "would have seen, after sailing from Sydney, only smoke rising from aboriginals' fires in remote places." Thirty years later not much had changed, European settlement amounting to little more than a collection of "isolated ports," some "flourishing," others "gasping or dead." A number of these isolated ports (Brisbane, Newcastle, and Hobart) were convict settlements. Others were the temporary abode of whalers and sealers, busily engaged in the mass slaughter of local marine life. Not only were European settlements in Australia and New Zealand remote from each other, they were also a long way from the European heartlands. The first fleet of convict ships to arrive in Australia took more than 9 months to sail the route from England, arriving in Sydney in January 1788. By the early 1850s, when the discovery of gold brought a rush of immigrants to Australia, things had theoretically improved due to the arrival of American-designed (and often built) "clipper" ships on the Australasian route. "The American clipper," Blainey (1966: 70) noted with admiration, "was the consummation of centuries of shipbuilding, the most glamorous ship that ever went before the wind." Although famously associated with the transport of the "American 49ers," the gold-seekers who ventured to California in 1849 in search of riches, it was the Australian route that held the key to the economic success of the clippers (Blainey 1966: 183). Capable of covering 400 miles per day (644 km), the clippers dramatically reducing sailing times, one skipper (dubiously) claiming to have undertaken the voyage to Australia in 74 days (Blainey 1966: 191). Even on the clippers, however, the journey to the Antipodes was no idyllic cruise. Under the battering of the Southern Ocean, the condition of the clippers rapidly deteriorated. William O'Carroll (1862/1863: 430–431), an Irish immigrant, described the ship that carried him to Australia as "a wretched, crazy-looking hulk, miserably provisioned in every respect." Another immigrant recounted how, "Our skipper was an uneducated man, who treated all passengers like dogs . . . We had but sixteen sailors, three of whom were all more or less disabled. But for the passengers, the ship would never have been worked" (cited Jordan 1864: 926). Personal tragedies were all too common, one immigrant recounting how "a child of mine was one of the many that died aboard the ship . . . from absolute exhaustion produced by a want of sufficient food" (cited, Queensland Government 1863: 431).

Although the remoteness of Australia and New Zealand made voyages to these destinations particularly arduous, there were comparative few who even risked the perils of an Atlantic crossing before the 1850s. As Fig. 5 indicates, few people immigrated to the United States before 1850, when a record 369,980 people arrived in the American republic, many of them fleeing the great Irish "potato famine." This single-year total far exceeded the *combined* total recorded between the ending of the War of Independence (1783) and 1819, during which time a mere 250,000 immigrants dared the Atlantic crossing. Even in 1840, when 84,060 individuals made the journey, the level of immigration was only 22.7% of that recorded a decade later. Interrupted by the Civil War, immigration returned to, and then exceeded, its pre-conflict peaks after the ending of the hostilities. Between 1880 and 1900, some 450,000 new citizens typically landed each year (U.S. Department of Commerce 1975: Chap. C, 97). As we noted in the introduction, the key to the post-1850 transformation was a revolution in shipping, underpinned by a massive expansion in

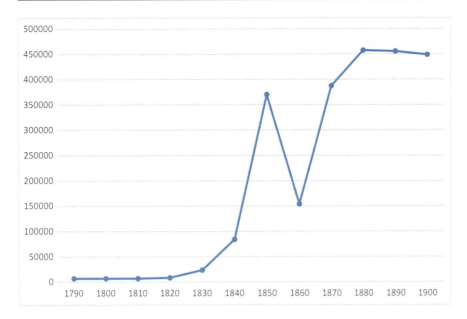

Fig. 5 Immigration to the United States, 1790–1900. (Source: U.S. Department of Commerce 1975: Series C 89–119)

iron and steel production and coal output. On the Atlantic route after 1830, first steam-powered paddle wheelers, and then iron-hulled screw-propulsion ships, rapidly displaced sail. Screw-propulsion ships were also sturdy enough to risk voyages in the Southern Ocean, a region where paddle steamers feared to go. In Australia, a flood of new arrivals made Melbourne the second city of the British Empire, the city's metropolitan area boasting a population of 387,000 by 1890. Thousands more lived in adjacent urban areas. In this sophisticated New World city, no more than wind-swept wilderness in 1830, some 2.7 million passengers commuted to work on the suburban rail network in 1890–1891. Millions of others commuted on the city's steam-powered cable cars (Speight 1892).

The creation, for the first time in human history, of a genuine global economy, characterized by the free movement of people and goods on an unprecedented scale, was the great novelty of the 1830–1890 period. As urban life became the norm across Western Europe and the eastern seaboard of the United States, so whole nations became utterly dependent on logistics chains that stretched around the globe. This dependency was most evident in wheat, the staple of the European diet. Writing of the role of the railroads in the post-1850 agricultural settlement of the New World, Walt Rostow (1963: 14) observed how, the "rising grain prices of the 1850s . . . made the massive laying of the rail lines attractive." Although there were local benchmark prices for grain – the Chicago wholesale price assuming a position of preeminence in the United States – the creation of a single global market made the London benchmark the ultimate arbiter of price. The good fortune of a wheat farmer in Manitoba (Canada), Victoria (Australia), or Minnesota (the United States) rested not

Fig. 6 Benchmark wheat prices: Chicago, London, and Victoria, 1871–1901 (historic US dollars). (Sources: *Victorian Statistical Register* 1871–1902; Wallace 1930)

only on their efforts, and the benevolence of local climate, but also on the global balance between supply and demand. Reflecting on the compression of global wheat prices in the latter half of the nineteenth century, the American economist and sociologist, Thorstein Veblen (1892: 82), in an article entitled *The Price of Wheat Since 1867*, identified 1882 as the "turning point" after which date prices were determined by "the aggregate volume of the world's crops."

As Fig. 6 indicates, in 1871, there was a significant price difference between what wheat wholesaled for in London when compared to either Chicago or Melbourne, then Australia's largest city. Whereas the London benchmark price averaged – when expressed in historic US dollars – $1.92, the benchmark price in Melbourne and the other port towns of Victoria averaged two-thirds of this ($1.27). In Chicago, the benchmark wheat price ($1.20) was 62.5% of the London wholesale price. This price differential made the growing, export, and transport of wheat and other grains (barley, corn, oats, etc.) a highly profitable affair. As railroad expansion brought an ever increasing acreage into production, however, the world grain market came to favor buyers rather than sellers. By 1901, the London benchmark ($0.81) had lost 58.2% of its 1871 value (Wallace 1930; Dunsdorfs 1956; Victorian Government 1882, 1902). As falling London prices rippled through the global market, the prices paid to New World farmers collapsed. By 1901, the Victorian and Chicago benchmark wheat prices were, respectively, a mere 46.4% and 40.1% of their 1871 levels.

The creation of a global market place, organized around revolutionary new technologies, created unprecedented levels of competition. At the heart of this global economy was something fundamentally new in the human experience: the *creation* of wealth through the *destruction* of economic *value*. In other words, the *value* of any given commodity (wheat, cloth, and oil) became constantly cheaper for the consumer due to increased supply, an outcome that left any producer utilizing constant inputs (labor, technology, and raw materials) with ever shrinking profits. In almost every area of life, a process of price deflation necessitated technological innovation, greater economies of scale through firm consolidation, and greater levels of managerial expertise. In textiles, the real purchase price for a meter of British factory-made cloth in 1860 was 13% of that charged in 1780 (McCloskey 1985: 60). In the oil industry – where the discovery of large reserves in western Pennsylvania in 1859 made kerosene lamps an affordable household item – the price of a Pennsylvania "barrel" (42 gallons or 159 litres) collapsed in the face of increased supply, falling from $12 in 1864 to $2.40 in 1866 (Chernow 1998/2004: 129). Not only was there a tendency for prices to fall, the same propensity was also evident in employment. In Britain, for example, the population in 1901 (37 million) was 76.2% higher than it had been in 1851 (21 million). As Figs. 1 and 2 indicated, the importation and manufacture of woolen and cotton fibers was vastly highly than it was earlier. Nevertheless, as Clapham (1932/1967: 29) indicated, the British textile industry employed fewer people (994,000) in 1901 than it did a half century before (1.1 million). The capacity to make more goods with fewer people caused Marx (1867/1954: 635–637) to identify an inevitable social cataclysm, in which increased productivity led to vast numbers of unemployed: what he referred to variously as "relative surplus-population" and "an industrial reserve army." What Marx failed to understand with this erroneous prediction was that technological and managerial innovation created entirely new industries: electricity, automobiles, and retail department stores. Such outcomes were not a mere by-product of industrial "take-off." They were a precondition for sustained growth in both production and employment. As Rostow (1963: 9) noted in his famed study of industrial "take-off," sustained economic growth in industrial societies always "requires the organization around new technology of new and vigorous management; new types of workers; new types of financing and marketing arrangements. It requires struggle ... against the constraints of the traditional society."

Falling prices across virtually every economic sector reflected more than simply increased supply. It reflected what Joseph Schumpeter (1950/1975: 84) described as a fundamentally new type of competition "which strikes not at the margins of the profits and the outputs of the existing firm but at their very foundations and their very lives." Famously describing this process as "creative destruction," Schumpeter (1950/1975: 84) argued that the new type of competition was not, primarily, caused by price differentials. Rather, it was characterized by the replacement of outdated forms of technology by more advanced manifestations, and by the displacement of old forms of firm organization by "the new type of organization (the largest-scale unit of control for instance)." In the period between 1830 and 1890, this process of "creative destruction" took many forms. In the British cotton-spinning industry, the first to experience mechanization, there were no technological transformations comparable to those which occurred in the pre-1830 period. Gains stemmed instead from "continuous minor improvements" as factory managers experimented with variations in machine parts and work practices (Clapham 1932/1967: 80). The collective effect of these incremental managerial improvements was profound. Whereas the average mill hand spun 3700 pounds of yard in 1859–1861, by 1880–1882, the typical textile worker was spinning 5500 pounds of yard – a 48.6% increase (Clapham 1932/1967: 81). A far more brutal example of "creative destruction" was provided by the United States oil industry, where John D. Rockefeller's Standard Oil Company gained a near monopoly of the production, refining, and transport of crude, allowing Rockefeller to buy cheap and sell dear. First, Rockefeller drove rival refiners out of business through a secret agreement with America's major railroad companies – the Pennsylvania, the New York Central, and the Erie. From 1871, Rockefeller received a discount price for the transport of his oil, allowing him to undercut his rivals. Rockefeller then destroyed the oil custom of his railway partners, constructing pipelines to the eastern seaboard from whence refined product was shipped to Europe (Chernow 1998/2004: 135, 219). Ruthlessly destroying all opposition, and corrupting the political process to obtain his personal ends, Rockefeller has understandably suffered poor press. Yet, it was largely due to his efforts that the oil industry made the strides it did between 1860 and 1890. As Chernow (1998/2004: 151) notes, "When Rockefeller took over competing refiners, he retained plants with up-to-date facilities and shuttered obsolete ones." Rockefeller not only conceptualized the idea of a network of oil pipelines, he also made it a reality.

Of all the industries that characterized the global economy of the mid-nineteenth century, none was more important – and more managerially complex – than the railroads. Everywhere, in both the Old World and the New, the railroads were at the center of economic advancement, assembling huge workforces and requiring a complexity of managerial organization unprecedented in human history. In the vast continental spaces of North America, Australia, Russia, Mexico, Argentina, and India, the railways assumed particular importance. Commenting upon nineteenth century American railway development, Stromquist (1987: 5) observed how the railroads "created the connecting sinews of a national market for American manufactured goods and an international market for the agricultural surplus of the West." A similar comment is applicable to virtually every other New World society. For the hundreds of thousands who entered into railway service, working life was shaped by where one stood in a complex job hierarchy. At the bottom of the pecking order was a host of semiskilled occupations that included navvies, porters, and freight handlers. At the top of the job hierarchy were the skilled craftsmen in the workshops and the engine drivers on the locomotives. Invariably, the railroads overshadowed other nineteenth century business organizations in terms of not only the size of their workforces but also in their level of capital investment. Of the mighty Pennsylvania Railroad, Chandler (1977: 204) noted that in 1891 it employed more than 110,000 workers, a number that exceeded the combined total of the United States defense forces and the postal service. In the Australian colony of Victoria – where the railroads were less important than in the geographically larger, pastorally oriented colonies of New South Wales and Queensland – the capital invested in state-owned railroads between 1886 and 1890 exceeded private sector investment in agriculture, the pastoral sector, mining, manufacturing, and non-residential construction, combined (Linge 1979: 210–211).

Alfred Chandler, Railroads, Management, and Markets

Nineteenth-century railroads have a special significance in business and management history due to their centrality to Alfred D Chandler, Jr's, schema: an analysis that provides a sweeping but well-researched explanation as to the rise of the modern world that has had a profound theoretical influence over the last half century. Initially spelt out in an article published in *Business History* in 1965, "The Railroads: Pioneers in Modern Corporate Management" – and then more fully in *The Visible Hand: The Managerial Revolution in American Business* and *Scale and Scope: The Dynamics of Industrial Capitalism* – Chandler (1965, 1977, 1990) argued a number of key propositions. First, he reasoned that it was the railroads rather than canals that were responsible for the world's first mass markets. It asserting this proposition, it should be noted, Chandler (1965, 1977, 1990) was well aware that by 1830 canals were already carrying significant volumes of bulk freight in not only Britain but also in the United States and most other Western European societies. Nevertheless, Chandler argued that canals were best suited for low-value bulk commodities (coal, grain, etc.) and ill-suited to either large-scale passenger movement or the haulage of high-value manufactured goods. Although the noted American economist, Robert Fogel (1962, 1964), mounted a case for the continued importance of canal systems during the "railroad age" – pointing to the fact that the United States canal freight tonnages were comparable to those of rail well into the nineteenth century – most historians accept Chandler's argument that railroads offered qualitative and quantitative advantages over canals. Unlike the canals of northern Europe and North America, railroads did not freeze over in winter. Unlike canals, they could also transverse the dry continental interiors of South Africa, the Ukraine, India, Australia, Argentina, and North America with relative ease. Above all, they "provided the fast, regular and dependable transportation and communication so essential to high-volume production and distribution" (Chandler 1977: 79). The railroads also made long-distance travel an inexpensive exercise. In France, for example, prior to the coming of the railways, it took up to 5 days to travel from Paris to the nearby Norman town of Caen. With the coming of the railroad, this journey could be comfortably completed in a few hours, regardless of the weather or the season (Braudel 1986/1990: 473). The railroads also facilitated the creation of entirely new industries. The movement of livestock by train, for example, allowed for high-volume meat-processing plants. In the vast spaces of the Argentine pampas, the American prairies and the Australian outback, railroads allowed commercial cattle-raising on an industrial scale. Refrigerated freight trains brought affordable meat supplies to the family table. Mail-order catalogues permitted even remote farming household a capacity to peruse and purchase the latest fashion, knowing that the sought-after item would be delivered within a short span of time.

If Chandler's argument that the railroads created the first mass markets has attracted broad agreement – Braudel (1986/1990: 467) noting with regard to the French situation that "before the coming of the railways, France was not really a national market" – his other propositions are more contentious. For whereas classical economics argued that it was market forces that determined the relationship between supply and demand in a capitalist economy, Chandler argued a fundamentally different proposition. On the opening page of *The Visible Hand: The Managerial Revolution in American Business*, Chandler (1977: 1) stated that although the "market" still generated *demand* for goods and services, the "modern business took over the functions of coordinating flows of goods and services through existing processes of production and distribution." At a subsequent point in *The Visible Hand*, Chandler (1977: 12) articulated his position in more unambivalent terms, arguing:

> The visible hand of management replaced the invisible hand of market forces when and where new technology and expanded markets permitted a historically unprecedented high volume and speed of materials through the process of production and distribution.

It is clear that Chandler's key thesis as to the relationship between management and markets was influenced by Oliver Williamson's (1976: 8–9) understandings of "transaction cost economics." This framework holds that the uncertainties of market exchanges create costs for a firm that are often higher than if they were internalized (i.e., it would be cheaper if the firm produced a good itself rather than purchasing it in the marketplace). Chandler's analysis, however, went much further than Williamson as he brought to the fore *the* most important issue in economics and management studies, namely the relationship between management and markets. In Chandler's view, *modern* management differed from *premodern* management precisely, because new technologies had created mass markets that exposed producers in one location to competition from more efficient firms located in distant locales. At the same time, Chandler believed, modern management also had far more tools at its disposal (improved communication, better understanding of consumer demand, and a greater understanding of costs) than previously, allowing it a proactive capacity to not only match supply to demand but also the ability to manipulate consumer perceptions and create new markets. Such explanations provide a more original insight into the *actual* workings of modern capitalism than what is typically found in economic textbooks, where most lend support to John Stuart Mills's (1848/1965: 795) premise that "every restriction" of competition "is an evil, and every extension of it ... is always an ultimate good." For large modern firms invariably seek to destroy rather than facilitate competition. The reasons for this are *not* those typically expounded by economists, who link reduced competition with monopolistic behavior and *higher* prices. Instead, the drive to reduce competition stems from the problems inherent in business operations where most costs are found in capital investments rather than in labor or variable costs. As became obvious in the railroads of the mid-to-late nineteenth century, a highly capitalized business typically gains little by curtailing production when selling at a loss. Most of its costs are fixed and thus incurred whether or not the business produces anything, meaning that some income is better than none. Accordingly, as the nineteenth century American economist, Arthur Hadley (1885: 40, 70–71) noted, "Whenever there is a large fixed investment, and large fixed charges, competition brings price down below cost of service .... Then we have bankruptcy, ruin to the investor." In such situations, the logic of production leads to continued output that flies in the face of the logic of the market, which calls for curtailment of production when supply matches demand. Invariably, problems of this sort are resolved not by the "market" but rather by proactive managerial initiative that manifests itself in a number of ways: firm mergers, selling cartels, reorienting production towards other markets, etc.

Chandler (1990: 253) also famously argued that the railroads of the nineteenth century were responsible for the "first managerial hierarchies with lower, middle, and top levels of management." Even in Britain, Chandler (1990: 253) suggested, management as we understand it (i.e., a class of professional managers organized in a hierarchy) only emerged through the demands imposed by the railroads. Previous factory manifestations were, in his opinion, less consequential. In the case of the United States, Chandler (1977: 3) argued, "as late as 1840 there were no middle managers." Only with the railroads did the nation first witness this social novelty, an innovation that was soon replicated in other industries. Where the United States differed from other nations, Chandler (1977, 1990) believed, was not in the "managerial hierarchies" that were common to all but rather in the pioneering of a new form of business organization: the "multiunit enterprise." With this organizational structure, "autonomous units" were given the capacity for strategic decision-making while garnering the financial, buying, and marketing resources of the entire organization. This could see a firm organized around geographical divisions (i.e., midwestern states, mountain states, etc.), functional divisions (i.e., freight haulage, passenger services, marketing, etc.), or a combination thereof. In Chandler's estimation, the reason behind the supposed American pioneering of the "multiunit enterprise" is found in "the geographical extent" of the American nation. Put simply, a geographically larger and more populous nation demanded the construction of a "far greater mileage . . . than in other industrial countries" (Chandler 1990: 53). This high American mileage, Chandler believed, entailed a complexity of managerial problems that was beyond the capacity of a single chain of command, necessitating a delegation of responsibility to semiautonomous units.

Although few business or management historians would disagree with Chandler's assessment that the railroads were central to the creation of a modern global economy, many would quibble with his suggestions that American managerial performance was inherently superior to that of all other nations, either within the railroads or without. Where Chandler saw in the railroads of nineteenth century America a story of efficiency and human progress, others (Kolko 1965; Berk 1994; Perrow 2003; White 2011) perceived a tale of rapacious greed, squandered resources, and the building ahead of a demand that, not infrequently, never arrived. Of the vast transcontinental railroads built across the United States from the 1860s onwards, White (2011: xxxvii–xxxviii) declares them "transformative failures" that "never paid for themselves."

Certainly, the claims by Chandler as to the managerial efficiency of America's nineteenth century railroads appear at first glance to be contradicted by the fact that many were constantly on the verge of bankruptcy. The business circumstances of the railroads west of the Mississippi River, which relied upon agricultural custom, was particularly precarious, one newspaper editor recording how "the [financial] condition of the railroads is deplorable in each Western state" (Robinson 1890: 23). Chandler explained away such difficulties in three ways. First, Chandler (1977: 134) suggested, financial difficulties primarily stemmed from competition, which produced not only negative attributes (bankruptcies) but also positive attributes (innovation and efficiency). Secondly, he pointed – as Adam Smith (1776/1999: Book V, Chap. 1, Article 1, para. 18) had done before him – to the fact that investors and managers had distinct and separate interest. Of America's railroad managers, Chandler (1977: 171) observed that, "They were willing to risk bankruptcy to assure the continuing, long-run flow of traffic across their tracks. Even if the investors lost their investments, the managers had their [rail] system." Finally, Chandler (1977: 126) noted that railroad freight rates were tied to the custom being carried, and that managers could only "charge what the traffic would bear." Accordingly, the haulage of low-value freight – while socially and economically beneficial – was often unprofitable.

While there is merit in all three of Chandler's explanations, there are also serious flaws in his thinking that highlight a common failing of management historians. Whereas economists typically overstate the importance of market forces and understate the proactive role of entrepreneurs and managers, the analysis made by management historians often suffers from the reverse problem, i.e., they overstate the proactive capacities of managers and understate the continuing importance of markets. As I (Bowden 2017: 301) argue elsewhere, the fundamental problem with Chandler's analysis stems from a lack of understanding of market forces. For when Chandler refers to "competition," he is referring to competition between railroads in meeting a *direct* demand (i.e., people want to ship their wheat by rail). However, when he is referring to charging "what the traffic would bear," he is referring to *derived* demand (i.e., a baker in London wants wheat from which they can make bread). The fundamental problem that New World railroads suffered from is that they were *always* at the mercy of far-distant sources of derived demand. By increasing mileage in virgin territory, and bringing land under the plough, they were creating not only new sources of revenue. They were also creating the mechanism for eventual global oversupply. This is evident in Fig. 7, which compares the per ton freight income received by the railroads of two Australian colonies – Queensland and Victoria – with that obtained in two American regions, namely, the Northern Plains (Minnesota, Nebraska, Iowa, Wyoming, Montana, and the Dakotas) and the South-West (Arkansas, Kansas, Colorado, Missouri, New Mexico, Oklahoma, and Texas). Given the fact that Australian railroads were state-owned monopolies, whereas those of the United States were private competitors, one would expect little similarity between Australia and American railroad rates during this period. However, as is self-evident, railroad rates in all four regions followed an almost identical pattern. Falling away sharply in the early 1880s, each suffered new lows in the mid-to-late 1890s. The immediate driver of this common pattern of railroad rate decline is found in Fig. 6 which records the secular decline in wheat prices that occurred after 1871. The ultimate determining factor was the new global economy that the railroads themselves did so much to create, bringing new competitive pressures into almost every part of the world.

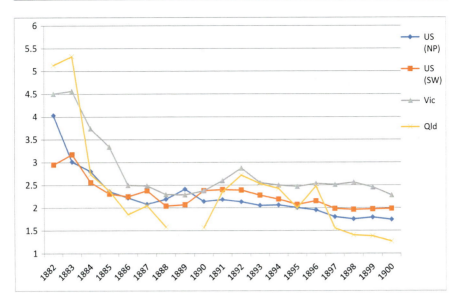

Fig. 7 Per ton freight income in US dollars: Victoria, Queensland, US Northern Plains, and US South-West, 1882–1900*. (Source: Bowden 2017). *No Queensland figures for 1889 due to change to financial year measurement)

Management, Slavery, and Colonial Subjugation

In the New World societies inhabited by people of predominately European ancestry (North America, Argentina, Australia, and New Zealand), the new global market offered both threats and opportunities. Things were, however more problematic in regions dominated by non-European workforces. Although slavery was abolished in the British Empire from 1834, slavery remained a fact of life in most of the plantation economies of the Caribbean and the Americas. Writing of the efforts to curtail the slave trade during the 1830s and 1840s, Thomas (1997: 750) observes of the situation in "the Cuban slave-powered economy" that anti-slavery campaigns had only "the slightest effect." The reason for the lack of progress in Cuba, Brazil, and elsewhere, Thomas (1997: 751) concluded, was simple: "The profits were too high to ignore." Of the situation that prevailed in the United States South in 1860, Byrer (2012: 528) observes that the region's 400,000 slave owners "possessed 93.1% of the South's agricultural wealth, having on average 13.9 times the wealth of non-slave owners." Those who had many slaves invariably fared better than those with comparatively few. The top 10% of slave owners, who held 44% of the region's slaves in shackles, boasted 40% of the South's agricultural wealth.

The continued existence of a slave economy well into the nineteenth century has continually caused problems for economic and management historians, just as it was a source of anxiety for the people of the time. In their recent *A New History of Management*, for example, Cummings et al. (2017: 62) argue that Adam Smith was a fervent opponent of slavery, arguing "radical," "anti-slavery" positions. To support this view, Cummings et al. (2017: 78) provide a quote from Book III, Chap. II of Adam Smith's *The Wealth of Nations*. In this chapter, Smith (1776/1999: Book III, Chap. II, para. 10) observed that, "The experience of all ages and nations, I believe, demonstrates that the work done by slaves, though it appears to cost only their maintenance, is in the end the dearest of any." In making these comments, however, Smith was discussing the transition from slavery to free labor in the early medieval world, the chapter being titled, "Of the Discouragement of Agriculture in the Ancient State of Europe after the Fall of the Roman Empire." This does *not* mean that he opposed legal interference in the system of slavery that existed in his own time, Smith believing that slaves were the legitimate private property of their owners. For in discussing slavery in North America, Smith (1776/1999: Book IV, Chap. VI, Part II) declared any action by a "magistrate" that "protects the slave, intermeddles in some measure in the private property of the master," and that "he dare not do this but with the greatest caution and circumspection." As is evident, Smith is loath to consider any action that "protects" a slave. There is no mention of freedom. The Marxist historian, Rob Bryer (2012), also adopts some convoluted theoretical positions in arguing that the slave plantations of the American South were not "capitalist." In Bryer's view, they could not be "capitalist" as they did not employ waged labor. Nor did the slave owners, in Bryer's opinion, demonstrate a sufficiently acquisitive and calculative capitalist mentality. To exclude the American South from the global capitalist economy of the nineteenth century, however, is difficult. American cotton was central to the success of the Industrial Revolution. Slave owners, moreover, profited inordinately from their participation in the system.

Were then the slave owners who grew cotton in the American South "managers" in the modern sense? It comes down to what we mean by the term "management." If we go by the standard textbook definition – that "management" amounts to "planning, organizing, leading and controlling" – then the answer must be "yes." However, from the very first chapter in this *Palgrave Handbook* (Chap. 2, "What I Management?"), I have argued in favor of a broader definition, associating "management" with attention to costs, competitive markets, legal protections of person and property, and the need to motivate legally free workforces. By this definition, the answer as to whether or not the slave economies of the Americas were examples of "modern management" must be "no." For in the end, the slave economies of the Americas – as with the enserfed workforces of Tsarist Russia – proved incompatible with a modern, capitalist system of management. That oceans of blood were shed during the American Civil War to bring about an end to slavery is proof that, in the final analysis, modern management and free-market capitalism are incompatible with systems of slavery and subjugation.

The problematic nature of the new global economy was also evident in the areas subject to colonial occupation in Africa and Asia. In the case of India, Ferguson (2008: 217) notes that between 1757 and 1914, the per capita Gross Domestic Product (GDP) of Britain went up by 347%. During the same period, in India – the crown jewel of the British Empire – per capita GDP grew by a mere 14%. This was no accident. Britain ruled India with British interests in mind, not Indian concerns. Nevertheless, as Ferguson (2008: 216) also highlights, a large share of Britain's accumulated wealth was invested in India. Whereas only 5% of Indian land was irrigated in the precolonial era, by the time the British left 40% of fields were irrigated. A coal industry was created from nothing, the industry producing 16 million tons per year by 1914. Indian life expectancy increased by 11 years due to immunization for smallpox and other diseases. British systems of management and language became the norm in Indian businesses. Whether the cost-benefit ratio worked in India's favor is a matter of subjective opinion. What is nevertheless clear is that by the close of the nineteenth century, India – like the rest of Asia – was an integrated component of the new global economy.

New Economy, New Workers, New Problems

In writing of the initial stages of Britain's Industrial Revolution, the labor historian, E.P. Thompson (1963: 217) declared it a "truly catastrophic experience." "For most people," Thompson (1963: 217–218) continued, "the crucial experience of the Industrial Revolution was felt in terms of changes in the nature and intensity of exploitation ... an intensification of two intolerable forms of relationship: those of economic exploitation and of political oppression." While any debate as to lived working-class experiences always engenders strong opinions, Thompson's emphasis on exploitation does an injustice to what is a complex question. In previous chapters, I have referred to the Phelps-Brown (1956) real wage index in relation to changing patterns of wealth across the centuries. In Fig. 8, we return to this index by looking at changes in the real wage of skilled building workers in southern England on a decade-by-decade basis across the 1750–1913 period. As is self-evident, it is certainly true that real wages did fall between 1750 and 1800. Only in 1830 did real wages for skilled building workers surpass those obtained in 1750. How much of the 1750–1800 decline is attributable to the Industrial Revolution is, however, unclear. It *is* likely that the social dislocation inaugurated by the Industrial Revolution caused *some* of the decline. It is also probable, however, that much of the decline was caused by the Napoleonic wars, and the stresses and strains caused by a generation of warfare. What is nevertheless clear is that from 1800 real wages began an unprecedented ascent. By 1900, real wages were 352.6% higher than they had been in 1800. Even Frederick Engels (1892/1951: 376), a fierce opponent of capitalism, acknowledges that by the early 1890s the economic position of skilled workers organized into "Trades' Unions" was "remarkably improved." Such workers, Engels (1892/1951: 376) added, "have succeeded in enforcing for themselves a relatively comfortable position."

Engels, in his reflections upon the state of working-class life in the early 1890s, worried about a loss of revolutionary zeal. Others, however, saw the opposite: a rising tide of worker militancy, organized into powerful trade unions that were distrustful of management. Writing of the British situation, Sidney and Beatrice Webb (1902: 452) estimated that in the 1890s, there were 20,000 part-time trade union officials serving as "Secretaries and Presidents of local Unions." "These men,"

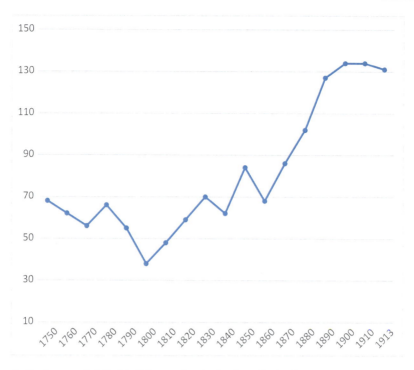

Fig. 8 Real wage of skilled building worker in Southern England, 1750–1913 (1447 = 100). (Source: Phelps Brown and Hopkins 1956: Appendix B)

the Webbs (1902: 452) argued, "were the backbone of the Trade Union world …Dependent for their livelihood on manual labour, they retain to the full the workman's sense of insecurity, privation, and thwarted aspirations." Everywhere, the Webbs (1902: xvii) noted, workers and their unions demanded acceptance "of the principle of Collective Bargaining," a principle premised on the belief that managers were unfit to unilaterally decide wages and working conditions. This distrust of management was not confined to Britain. Across all Western European societies and their New World offshoots (Canada, Australia, New Zealand, the United States, and South America), there was a profound sense that the rich had no intention of sharing either their wealth or their power with the new industrial working-class. Distrust of society's magnates – and employers more generally – found cogent expression in *The Iron Heel*, the novel penned by the American social activist, Jack London, in 1908. In this book, London (1908/1947: 135, 142) recalls a conversation with a member of the Philomath Club, comprised of "the most select" members of "Pacific Coast" society, in which London is supposedly advised:

> When you reach out your vaunted strong hands for our palaces and purpled ease, we will show you what strength is. In roar of shell and shrapnel and in whine of machine-guns will our answer be couched. We will grind your revolutionists down under our heel, and we shall walk

12 Transformation: The First Global Economy, 1750–1914

upon our faces. The world is ours, we are its lords, and ours it shall remain. As for the host of labor, it has been dirt since history began … And in dirt it shall remain.

In the United States, the period between 1890 and 1914 witnessed the most violent industrial strikes in the nation's history. In the Homestead steel strike of July–November 1892, at least 10 people were killed in armed clashes between striking workers and Pinkerton company guards employed by Carnegie Steel. In the United States railroads a rising tide of militancy culminated in a national stoppage in 1894, the so-called Pullman Boycott, Stromquist (1987: 24) describing the railroad disputes of the time as "the clarion call of a new class." Along the Rocky Mountains, members of the militant Western Federation of Miners clashed with company guards and local militias at Coeur d'Alenes, Cripple Creek, and Leadville, the union's president calling upon "every miner" to arm themselves with "a modern rifle and a supply of ammunition" (Haywood 1929: 65). From these western mining conflicts emerged the most militant union in the American experience, the Industrial Workers of the World (IWW), colloquially referred to as the "Wobblies." In the preamble to its constitution (cited Haywood 1929: 185), adopted in 1905, the IWW declared, "The working class and the employing class have nothing in common. There can be no peace as long as hunger and want are found among the millions of working people."

In Australia, as well, the 1890s saw the most significant strikes in the nation's history. In 1890, a maritime strike closed the waterfronts. Pastoral strikes followed in 1891 and 1894, curtailing production in the nation's preeminent industry for months at a time. In the course of the pastoral strike of 1891, Henry Lawson, arguably Australia's best loved poet, penned the following verses (cited Fitzpatrick 1944/1968: 123), published in a trade union newspaper,

> So we must fly a rebel flag,
> As others did before us,
> And we must sing a rebel song,
> And join the rebel chorus.
> We'll make the tyrants feel the sting
> Of those that they would throttle.
> They needn't say the fault is ours,
> If blood should stain the wattle.

In reflecting upon the great strikes of the 1890s, William Spence (1909: 111), the leader of Australia's largest mining and shearing unions, declared 1890 to be the "great turning point in the history of Australian Labor." It is also arguable that 1890 was the "great turning point" in Australian history more generally. As was the case in Britain and New Zealand, the union militancy of the 1890s gave strength to newly formed Labor parties. Committed to a social democratic program of social welfare, and government intervention in the economy, these Labor parties soon gained a mass following. In Australia, success came early with the election of the first federal Labor government in 1904. Across Europe, powerful new socialist and social democratic parties gained a mass following, Robert Michels (1911/2001: 165) referring to the

German Socialist Party of 1911 as a "gigantic and magnificently organized party." For private-sector managers, the emergence of an organized labor movement, embracing tens of millions of followers around the globe, created unprecedented problems in terms of workforce management. The new labor and social democratic movements also became, however, a significant and novel form of managerial organization in their own right. As Michels (1911/2001: 165) astutely observed in his famed study, *Political Parties: A Sociological Study of the Oligarchical Tendencies of Modern Democracy*, the "gigantic" new working-class parties invariably required "a no less gigantic apparatus of editors, secretaries, bookkeepers, and numerous other employees, whose sole task is to serve the colossal machine." Over time, thousands more professionalized workers – many recruited from the shop floor – found employment in unions associated with the various labor and social democratic parties. Even more found work as local, state, and federal politicians, or as bureaucrats associated with such political figures. The inevitable result of this, Michels (1911/2001: 229) was "a new dominant minority," a working-class oligarchy that progressively entrenched their own interests "in the name of socialism."

Among labor and management theorists the so-called "labor problem," which manifested itself in strikes, trade unionism and a political contest for control of the economy, produced two main responses in the pre-1914 period. The first of these, associated with Beatrice and Sidney Webb in Britain, and John Commons and the so-called Wisconsin School in the United States, called for an industrial compact between management and organized labor. In every sector of the economy, the Webbs (1897/1920: 279, 281) noted, the prime objective of the various unions was a "Common Rule" that would standardize wages and conditions across the entire industry. Such standardization, the Webbs (1897/1920: 716–718) believed, benefited both management and labor, forcing managers to do their "utmost to raise the level of efficiency so as to get the best possible return for the fixed conditions." In other words, labor regulation worked to enhance, rather than retard, productivity and workplace efficiency. In the United States, John Commons, in a book entitled *Trade Unionism and the Labor Problem*, argued a similar thesis. Industry-wide collective agreements, Commons (1905: 11) suggested, benefited the fair and honest employer by "taking wages out of competition," thereby depriving the unscrupulous employer of any unfair advantage.

Perhaps unsurprisingly, relatively few early twentieth century employers showed much interest in a compact with organized labor. Greater curiosity was shown in the ideas of a professional engineer and business consultant, Frederick Taylor, who published his *The Principles of Scientific Management* in 1911. As most readers would be aware, Taylor's views on "scientific management" have always garnered divided opinion, both within his lifetime and since. The premises from which Taylor operated, however, are perhaps best summed up by Edwin Locke (1982: 15), who observed that Taylor believed that conflict between management and organized labor could be avoided "as long as the [economic] pie were large enough." Because the pie was larger, workers could look forward to higher wages, even as employers secured higher profits. To achieve this desirable outcome, Taylor advocated five basic principles to improve workplace efficiency. The first of these, which is typically overlooked in most accounts of scientific management, emphasized the need for a "close, intimate, personal relationship" between management and the individual worker, a relationship in which the manager provided their workers with "the most friendly help" (Taylor 1911/ 1967: 26). Without such personal relationships, Taylor argued, all other prospective changes would almost certainly come to nought. The second reform that Taylor (1911/1967: 36) called for was for a revolution in managerial thought and practice, in which managers assumed "new burdens, new duties, and responsibilities never dreamed of in the past." Building on his call for a managerial revolution, Taylor articulated his best-known principle: that management had to instruct workers in the "one best method" of doing each and every work task (Taylor 1911/1967: 25). In doing so, Taylor (1911/1967: 21) argued in favor of his fourth key principle, whereby managers were advised to overcome "systematic soldiering" by employees, a silent conspiracy waged by workers so as to maintain control of the (slow) pace of work. Finally, Taylor (1911/1967: 32–33) linked increased worker productivity with a system of "special incentives" such as higher pay, reduced hours of work, and faster promotion.

By 1914, the industrializing societies of both the Old World and New World found themselves in a paradoxical situation. As Fig. 8 indicated, real wages had never been higher. A revolution in transport, associated with steam-powered ships and railroad locomotives, made transport to even fast distant locations an easy and comparatively inexpensive task. Children had largely disappeared from the workplace, their parents sending them off instead to long years of schooling. Clothing had become an inexpensive item in the household budget. Slavery and serfdom were distant memory. Yet, at the same time, evidence of social unrest and worker disquiet was all too obvious. Reflecting back on the years that immediately preceded World War I, George Dangerfield (1935: vii, 207) in his *The Strange Death of Liberal England*, recalled how "by the end of 1913 Liberal England was reduced to ashes," destroyed in part the industrial militancy of the "workers of England." Such was the level of worker discontent, Dangerfield (1935: 207) added, that militancy "might have reached a revolutionary conclusion" but for the intervention of war, when workers abandoned strike action to rally around the flag. The problems over which Dangerfield and others fretted pointed to a failure by management to resolve the "labor problem." For the fundamental failing of the pre-1914 solutions to the "labor problem," whether advocated by the Webbs, Commons, or Taylor, was to largely associate worker satisfaction with extrinsic rewards (i.e., money, shorter hours, and promotion). What was missing in such calculations was an understanding of what was lost in the transition to an industrial society. Yes, it is true: industrialization had delivered untold material benefits which few workers wished to throw away. But it also caused a loss of autonomy, a feeling that the individual worker was no longer the master of their own destiny. On the other side of the Great War, it was these concerns – relating to human dignity, emotion, and sense of worth – that was to increasingly preoccupy management, rather than traditional concerns relating to production and efficiency.

Conclusion

Often talk of historic "turning points" and "revolutionary change" turns out to be more literary hyperbole than an accurate reflection of lived reality. The period between 1750 and 1914 was, however, a time of truly revolutionary change on an unprecedented scale. In 1750, even in England, most people lived and died within sight of where they were born. If they lived away from the coast, where water transport allowed the importation of products from distant locations, they had to make do with goods made locally. Land transport was simply too slow, too expensive, and too risky to allow for significant internal markets. Among the vast bulk of the population, there was little understanding of time, beyond the rising and setting of the sun and the passing of the days. In the absence of clocks, and the accurate measurement of time, there could be little understanding of labor efficiency, i.e., the capacity to produce a good or service in a specified period. The absence of artificial lighting, other than smelly and expensive tallow candles, meant that work had to be curtailed at sunset. Hand spinning and weaving of cloth made clothing an expensive household item. Most people owned no more than two sets of clothes, one or both of which would typically be hand-me-downs. By the late nineteenth century, however, life was profoundly different at every level. Mechanization, railroads, steam-powered shipping, the ever-present factory clock and siren, and artificial lighting (kerosene lanterns, gas and electric lighting) transformed life across the world. Mass markets brought not only much cheaper goods within range of the typical household but they also brought competition, with all its transformative and destructive effects. Even in the remote villages of the Indian Punjab or the Ganges Valley, there was no escaping the new economic and managerial order. Across the subcontinent, railroads brought cheap British-made products into the local marketplace.

The new world order that emerged after 1750 was both the creation of a new system of management and the creator of modern management. In many areas, management built on past achievement. Double-entry book-keeping and efficient systems of accounting were a late medieval inheritance, the product of long-distance commerce. As Cipolla (1981: 180) noted, the post-1750 world also inherited from medieval Europe a mechanical "inventiveness," proving itself "extraordinarily receptive" to technologies imported from elsewhere. In England, moreover, the pre-1750 expansion of coal production allowed it to overcome the "main bottleneck of preindustrial communities ... the strictly limited supply of energy" (Cipolla 1981: 113). Across Western Europe, a long series of battles had gradually ensured the protection of private property. In the final analysis, however, all of these pre-1750 achievements only brought England, Europe, and subsequently the whole world to the cusp of a new economic and managerial order. The final step required innovation, risk taking, and a certain level of ruthlessness. As McCloskey (1985: 67) accurately noted, ultimately the "explanation of the [industrial] revolution must be sought in ... human effort and spirit, and in the luck of invention." Initially, in the first stage of the Industrial Revolution (1750–1830), innovation was largely confined to textile production. Technological and economic take-off in this sector of the economy, however, soon led to a cascading series of revolutions in logistics, transport, and agriculture that integrated the New World into the new systems of production and management. Along the way, management had to confront novel problems. In the new factories, shipyards, and steel works, the most difficult task was arguably that associated with the recruitment, training, and motivation of legally free workforces. Almost immediately, this new industrial workforce gained a fair measure of bargaining power. At the individual level, they could walk away, finding work in another factory or catching the train to a distant region. Collectively, they could and did form trade unions, threatening employers with widespread industrial stoppages. The growth of mass markets brought with it increased levels of competition, forcing managers to constantly improve and innovate. Competition also made an understanding of internal costs a necessity. Attentiveness to costs led to a focus on productivity, i.e., the maximization of outputs from a minimum of inputs. An emphasis on productivity caused management to be attentive to time-measurement as managers increasingly focused on the intensity of work and the efficiency of labor. Competition and high capital costs also forced firm specialization in its intended area of "comparative advantage." As real wages rose, and the number of middle-class managers and professionals grew, so too did pools of savings. By accessing these large pools of small individual savings, investors were able to engage in more capital-intensive activities. As Bryer (1991: 447) noted in reflecting upon investment in Britain's railroads, most of the money tapped for railroad expansion came not from "the very wealthy" but rather from "provincial merchants," "entrepreneurs," and the "middle-classes." After 1860, it was these capital-intensive activities – shipping, steelmaking, oil drilling and refining, and, above all, the railroads – that became the defining characteristic of the new global economy.

If the achievements of the 1750–1914 period are indubitable, there was nevertheless by the time of the First World War a deep sense of pessimism as to the future. Writing after the war, Keynes (1920: 217, 213) detected a decline in productivity that he feared was irreversible, warning his readers that, "The danger confronting us ... is the rapid depression of the standard of life of the European populations to a point which will mean actual starvation." Although Keynes clearly underestimated the managerial and entrepreneurial capacities of the new industrial societies, the problems he identified were, in part, attributable to managerial failings. Pre-1914 managers typically paid more attention to the *costs* of production than the *purpose* of production. As Chester Barnard (1938: 82) observed in his pioneering study, *The Functions of the Executive*, "efficiency" was meaningless without "effectiveness," an attribute which he defined as "the relevance of its purpose to the environmental situation." Even greater problems were evident with the so-called "labor problem," a difficultly that manifested itself after 1914 in armed revolution in Russia, Hungary, Germany, and Italy. This problem and these revolutions were proof that satisfaction of material needs was no guarantee of either employee happiness or social harmony. As Elton Mayo (1933: 165, 172) was to note in his *The Human Problem of an Industrial Civilization*, the "modern condition" often manifested itself in "social disorganization," "personal maladjustment," and a sense of "personal futility." The redress of this "human problem" was to become – and remain – the central problem of management in the post-1914 world.

Cross-References

▶ Conflicting Understandings of the Industrial Revolution and its Consequences: The founding Figures of British Management History
▶ What Is Management?
▶ Work and Society in the Orthodox East: Byzantium and Russia, AD 450–1861

References

Barnard C (1938) The functions of the executive. Harvard University Press, Cambridge, MA
Berk G (1994) Alternative tracks: the constitution of American industrial order. John Hopkins University Press, Baltimore
Blainey G (1966) The tyranny of distance. Sun Books, South Melbourne
Blake W (1808/1969) Milton. In: Keynes G (ed) Blake: complete writings. Oxford University Press, London, pp 480–535
Bowden B (2017) An exploration into the relationship between management and market forces: the railroads of Australia and the American West, 1880–1900. J Manag Hist 23(3):297–314
Braudel F (1986/1990) The identity of France: people and production, vol 2, 2nd edn. Harper Torchbooks, New York
Bryer RA (1991) Accounting for the 'railway mania' of 1845 – a great railway swindle. Acc Organ Soc 16(5/6):439–486
Bryer RA (2012) Americanism and financial accounting theory – part 1: was America born capitalist? Crit Perspect Account 23(7–8):511–555
Butlin NG (1964/1972) Investment in Australian economic development 1861–1900. Australian National University Press, Canberra
Chandler AD Jr (1965) The railroads: pioneers in modern corporate management. Bus Hist 39(1):16–40
Chandler AD Jr (1977) The visible hand: the managerial revolution in American business. Belknap Press, Cambridge, MA
Chandler AD Jr (1990) Scale and scope: the dynamics of industrial capitalism. Belknap Press, Cambridge, MA
Chernow R (1998/2004) Titan: the life of John D. Rockefeller, 2nd edn. Vintage Books, New York
Cipolla CM (1981) Before the industrial revolution: European society and economy, 1000–1700, 2nd edn. Cambridge University Press, Cambridge, UK
Clapham JH (1926/1967) Economic history of modern Britain: the early railway age 1820–1850. Cambridge University Press, Cambridge, UK
Clapham JH (1932/1967) Economic history of modern Britain: free trade and steel 1850–1886. Cambridge University Press, Cambridge, UK
Commons J (1905) Trade unionism and the labor problem. Augustus Kelley, New York
Cummings S, Bridgman T, Hassard J, Rowlinson M (2017) A new history of management. Cambridge University Press, Cambridge, UK
Dangerfield G (1935) The strange death of liberal England. Constable & Co., London
Dunsdorfs E (1956) The Australian wheat-growing industry 1788–1948. Melbourne University Press, Melbourne
Dupin C (1825) The commercial power of Great Britain. Charles Knight, London
Engels F (1892/1951) Preface of the 1892 edition: the condition of the working-class in England in 1844. In: Marx K, Engels F (eds) Selected works, vol 2. Foreign Languages Publishing House, Moscow, pp 368–380
Ferguson N (2008) Empire: how Britain made the modern world, 2nd edn. Penguin, London
Fitzpatrick B (1944/1968) A short history of the Australian labor movement, 2nd edn. Macmillan of Australia, South Melbourne

Fogel RW (1962) A quantitative approach to the study of railroads in American economic growth: a report on some preliminary findings. J Econ Hist 22(2):163–197

Fogel RW (1964) Railroads and American economic growth. John Hopkins University Press, Baltimore

Glover I (2008) Fence me in. Outback 62:28–45

Hadley AT (1885) Railroad transportation: its history and its laws. G P Putman's Sons, New York/London

Haywood WD (1929) Bill Haywood's book: the autobiography of William D. Haywood. International Publishers, New York

Huntington SP (1996/2003) The clash of civilizations and the remaking of world order. Simon & Schuster, New York

Jordan H (1864) Third annual report of the Queensland emigration commissioner. Queensland Government Gazette, Queensland Government Printer, Brisbane, pp 920–928

Keynes JM (1920) The economic consequences of the peace. Cambridge University Press, Cambridge, UK

Kirby P (2011) The transition to working life in eighteenth and nineteenth-century England and Wales. In: Lieten K, van Nederveen Meerkerk E (eds) Child labor's global past, 1650–2000. Peter Lang, Bern, pp 119–135

Knibbs CH (1909) Commonwealth of Australia yearbook, 1908. Commonwealth of Australia Printer, Melbourne

Kolko G (1965) Railroads and regulation 1877–1916. Princeton University Press, Princeton

Linge GJR (1979) Industrial awakening: geography of Australian manufacturing 1788 to 1890. Australian National University Press, Canberra

Locke EA (1982) The ideas of Frederick Winslow Taylor: an evaluation. Acad Manag Rev 7(1):14–24

London J (1908/1947) The iron heel. In: Foner PS (ed) Jack London: American rebel – a collection of his social writing. Citadel Press, New York, pp 133–221

Mantoux P (1961) The industrial revolution in the eighteenth century: the outline of the beginnings of the modern factory system in England. Jonathan Cape, London

Marx K (1853/1951) The British rule in India. In: Marx K, Engels F (eds) Selected works, vol 1. Foreign Languages Publishing House, Moscow, pp 312–318

Marx K (1867/1954) Capital, vol 1. Foreign Languages Publishing House, Moscow

Marx K, Engels F (1848/1951) The communist manifesto. In: Marx K, Engels F (eds) Selected works, vol 1. Foreign Languages Publishing House, Moscow, pp 32–61

Mayo E (1933) The human problem of an industrial civilization. Macmillan, New York

McCloskey D (1985) The industrial revolution 1780–1860: a survey. In: Mokyer J (ed) The economics of the industrial revolution. George Allen & Unwin, London, pp 53–74

Michels R (1911/2001) Political parties: a sociological study of the oligarchical tendencies of modern democracy. Batouche Books, Kitchener

Mills JS (1848/1965) Principles of political economy. Toronto University Press, Toronto

Mintz SW (1985) Sweetness and power: the place of sugar in modern history. Viking, New York

Nef JU (1932/1966) The rise of the British coal industry, vol 2. Frank Cass and Co., London

O'Carroll W (1862/1863) Letter to Ireland. In: Queensland Government (ed) Minutes of evidence of the select committee on the operation of the Queensland immigration laws. Queensland Government Gazette, Queensland Government Printer, Brisbane, pp 419–505

Perrow C (2003) Organizing America: wealth, power, and the origins of corporate capitalism. Princeton University Press, Princeton

Phelps Brown EH, Hopkins SV (1956) Seven centuries of the prices of consumables, compared with builders' wage rates. Economica 23(92):296–314

Pollard S (1965) The genesis of modern management: a study of the industrial revolution in Great Britain. Edward Arnold, London

Pollard S (1980) A new estimate of British coal production, 1750–1850. Econ Hist Rev 33 (2):212–235

Poor HV (1891) Manual of the railroads of the United States, 1891. V H Poor and H W Poor, New York

Queensland Government (1863) Minutes of evidence of the select committee on the operation of the Queensland immigration laws. Queensland Government Gazette, Queensland Government Printer, Brisbane, pp 419–505

Robinson HP (1890) Our railroads: the value and earnings of the railroads of the western states, 2nd edn. Northwestern Railroader, St. Paul

Rostow WW (1963) Leading sectors and the take-off. In: Rostow WW (ed) The economics of take-off into sustained growth. Macmillan/St Martin's Press, London/New York, pp 1–21

Schumpeter JA (1950/1975) Capitalism, socialism and democracy, 3rd edn. Harper Perennial, New York

Smith A (1776/1999) An inquiry into the nature and causes of the wealth of nations. Penguin Classics, London

Speight R (1892) Report of the Victorian railway commissioners, 1890–1891. Victorian parliamentary papers. Victorian Government Printer, Melbourne

Spence WG (1909) Industrial awakening. The Worker Trustees, Sydney/Melbourne

Stromquist S (1987) A generation of boomers: the pattern of railroad labor conflict in nineteenth-century America. University of Illinois Press, Urbana/Chicago

Taylor FW (1911/1967) The principles of scientific management. W. W. Norton & Co., New York

Thomas B (1985) Food supply in the United Kingdom during the industrial revolution. In: Mokyer J (ed) The economics of the industrial revolution. George Allen & Unwin, London, pp 137–150

Thomas H (1997) The slave trade: the history of the Atlantic slave trade 1440–1870. Picador, London

Thompson EP (1963) The making of the English working class. Penguin, Harmondsworth

Thompson EP (1967) Time, work-discipline, and industrial capitalism. Past Present 38(1):56–97

United Kingdom Department of Business, Energy & Industrial Strategy (2019) British coal data 1853–2018. United Kingdom Department of Business, Energy & Industrial Strategy. https://www.gov.uk/government/statistical-data-sets/historical-coal-data-coal-production-availability-and-consumption

United States Department of Commerce (1975) Historical statistics of the United States. Colonial times to 1970: bicentennial edition. U.S. Department of Commerce, Washington, DC

Veblen T (1892) The price of wheat since 1867. J Polit Econ 1(1):68–103

Victorian Government (1882) Statistical register of Victoria, 1881. Victorian Government Printer, Melbourne

Victorian Government (1902) Statistical register of Victoria, 1901. Victorian Government Printer, Melbourne

Ville S (2005) The relocation of the international market for Australian wool. Aust Econ Hist Rev 45(1):73–95

Wallace H (1930) Agricultural prices. University of Iowa Press, Des Moines

Webb S, Webb B (1897/1920) Industrial democracy. Seahams Divisional Labour Party, London

Webb S, Webb B (1902) History of trade unionism, 2nd edn. Longmans, Green and Co., London

White R (2011) The transcontinentals and the making of modern America. W. W. Norton & Co., New York

Williamson OE (1976) Markets and hierarchies: analysis and antitrust implications. Free Press, New York

Wordsworth (1814/1853) Excursion, 2nd edn. Edward Moxton, London

Part IV

The Foundations of Knowledge and Management: An Introduction

The Foundations of Knowledge and Management: An Introduction

13

Bradley Bowden and Kaylee Boccalatte

Contents

Problems of Economic Understanding 310
Problems of Epistemology 313
Cross-References 317
References 318

Abstract

As a discipline, management history has suffered from the fact that it has typically paid insufficient heed to economics, just as economics has suffered from paying insufficient heed to management and the mechanics of production. In recent years, management history has also divided over matters related to epistemology, the intellectual principles that guide our inquiries and understandings of the world. Accordingly, this Part of the Handbook has two aims. First, it explores the core theoretical principles that have informed economics through a study of classical economics, neo-classical economics, and Marxism. Second, it considers the origins of contemporary debates relating to positivism and postmodernism in the intellectual ferment of the eighteenth and early nineteenth centuries, a period that witnessed both epistemological understandings that supported the emergence of capitalism and modern management as well as philosophies deeply opposed to the advance of science, rationality, and industrialization.

B. Bowden (✉)
Griffith Business School, Griffith University, Nathan, QLD, Australia
e-mail: b.bowden@griffith.edu.au

K. Boccalatte
James Cook University, Douglas, QLD, Australia
e-mail: kaylee@btfarms.com.au

© The Author(s), under exclusive licence to Springer Nature Switzerland AG 2020
B. Bowden et al. (eds.), *The Palgrave Handbook of Management History*,
https://doi.org/10.1007/978-3-319-62114-2_110

Keywords

Empiricism · Idealism · Romanticism · Postmodernism · Foucault · Derrida · Nietzsche · Karl Popper · Immanuel Kant

Problems of Economic Understanding

In the general introduction to this *Palgrave Handbook of Management History*, we observed that, "Management history as a discipline is different from business and economic history in that it is primarily concerned with the supply side of the economic equation, with the nature of work, the ideas that guide it, and the economic wealth that is produced" (▶ Chap. 1, "Management History in the Modern World: An Overview" by Bowden). It is also noted that one of the weaknesses of management history is the lack of attention that is typically paid to economics, a failing that mirrors that found in economics, where economists typically pay insufficient heed to management, the problems of production, and what makes for an efficient and effective business. Where economic concepts are utilized in management and business history, they are often used in error. Alfred Chandler (1977: 1), for example, in the opening page of his famed study, *The Visible Hand: the Managerial Revolution in American Business*, spoke of "what Adam Smith referred to as the invisible hand of market forces." In fact, as we discuss in the chapter in this Part entitled, ▶ Chap. 15, "Economic Foundations: Adam Smith and the Classical School of Economics," Smith never spoke of "the invisible hand of the market." Instead, in his only reference to "an invisible hand" in *The Wealth of Nations*, Smith (1776: Book IV, Chap. 2, para. 9) associated the concept with self-interest and the economic pursuits of the individual businessperson, declaring that in directing "industry":

> ... in such a manner as its produce may be of the greatest value, he intends only his own gain, and he is in this, as in many other cases, led by an invisible hand to promote an end which was no part of his intention.

Spurious understandings of economics in general and Smith in particular also characterize Cummings et al's (2017) recent *A New History of Management*, where the authors fancifully claim that Smith was an enthusiast of neither capitalism nor the division of labor. Such conclusions are belied by Smith's (1776: Book 1, Chap. X, para. 53) observation that, "In opulent countries the market is generally so extensive that any one trade is sufficient to employ the whole labour and stock of those who occupy it." Only in "poor countries," Smith (1776: Book 1, Chap. X, para. 53) added, did one witness production methods built around anything other than the "division of labor."

Even if economics has played – and will continue to play – a secondary role in management history, it is nevertheless the case that the management historian invariably brings to their analysis an understanding of economics, be it implicit or explicit, spurious, or accurate. One of the primary purposes of this Part is therefore one of redressing misunderstandings of economics. To this end, this Part devotes chapters to both classical and neo-classical economics. In the first of these, we (▶ Chap. 15, "Economic Foundations: Adam Smith and the Classical School of Economics" by Bowden) discuss how the genius of Adam Smith lay in his capacity for synthesis rather than in original thought. His ideas on "self-interest" as the prime motive force in a capitalist society were derived from his close friend, David Hume. His concept of value was obtained from the French *physiocrat*, Richard Cantillon. Such was Smith's propensity to borrow unreferenced ideas from others that Murray Rothbard (2006: 435) declares him "a shameless plagiarist, acknowledging little or nothing and stealing large chunks . . . from Cantillon . . . he originated nothing that was true." Rothbard's condemnation was misplaced. Yes, Smith borrowed some of his central concepts from others without formal acknowledgement. Nevertheless, in synthesizing concepts derived from elsewhere, and adding insightful additions of his own, Smith deserves his status as the effective founder of modern economics. One of the key distinctions that Smith drew, and which still escapes the understanding of many, is the distinction between "wealth" and "capital." This distinction certainly eluded Thomas Piketty in his much cited but deeply flawed study, *Capital in the Twenty-First Century*. Throughout his study, Piketty (2012/2014) constantly conflated "wealth" and "capital," using the terms interchangeably. However, as Smith understood, "wealth" (i.e., consumables, jewellery, wine, etc.) is something that results from the combination of "labor" and "capital" (i.e., machinery, factory buildings, etc.). As such items of personal "wealth" typically have an "exchange" value but little if any "use" value. Accordingly, the productive capacity of a society ultimately rests on the "wealth" that it allocates to "capital" rather than the goods and services that it consumes at any given point in time.

In our second chapter on economic thought, we (▶ Chap. 16, "Neo-classical Thought: Alfred Marshall and Utilitarianism" by Boccalatte) explore how understandings of utility and value were transformed through the insights of Jeremy Bentham, David Ricardo, John Stuart Mill, and, above all, Alfred Marshall. Whereas Adam Smith primarily understood "utility" as a good's usefulness to a consumer, Jeremy Bentham (1781/2000), in his *An Introduction to the Principles of Morals and Legislation*, made "utility" the basis of a complex moral philosophy, one where individual choice is driven by an oscillating sense of pleasure and pain. Libertarian in its ethos, utilitarianism in Bentham's analysis always returns to individual choice, to the individual capacity to choose between pleasure and pain. By contrast, for Ricardo – as subsequently for Marx – the utility or value of a good was associated with the quantity of labor invested in its production. For his part, John Stuart Mill, in considering the problems of utility and value, found inspiration in both Bentham and Smith. In one of his later works, *Utilitarianism*, Mill (1861/2009) adopted an essentially hedonistic view of utilitarianism. More commonly, however, Mill spoke of utility in classical economic terms, adding little to the opinions previously advocated by Smith. It was the genius of Marshall, however, who fundamentally transformed not only our understandings of utility and value but also of economics more generally. As Marshall understood it, utility does not exist in isolation, just as production is incomprehensible apart from consumption. Instead, utility is influenced by price. In other words, a good's usefulness to me is indicated by the price that I am prepared to pay for it. For almost every good or service, there will thus come a point where the price at which it is sold exceeds its perceived utility, an outcome that curtails demand. Each good or service thus has what Marshall (1890/1997) called its "marginal utility," a want that increases or diminishes in accordance with price.

If classical and neo-classical are central to understandings of management in liberal, free market economies, it is also the case that these understandings have always encountered opposition: from "romantic" defenders of a bucolic existence, Marxists, non-Marxian socialists, anarchists, postmodernists. During the latter half of the nineteenth century and for most of the twentieth century, capitalism's principal opponent was Marxism. In our third chapter on economics, we (▶ Chap. 18, "The Marxist Opposition to Capitalism and Business" by Boccalatte) consider not only the nature of Karl Marx's ideas but also how these ideas emerged out of a now largely forgotten debate between a youthful Marx and the French socialist, Pierre-Joseph Proudhon. In responding to Proudhon's (1847/1888) *La Philosophie de la Misère* (*The Philosophy of Poverty*) – a work that argued that capitalism and its system of private property is based upon theft – Marx (1847/1955) penned a similarly (if sardonically) titled book, *La Misère de la Philosophie* (*The Poverty of Philosophy*). As we note, many of the core concepts that came to characterize Marxism – that labor is the sole source of wealth, that the capitalist acquires wealth by purloining the "surplus-value" of the waged laborer, that the ever-increasing use of machinery was furthering both the growth of a proletariat and an inevitable class conflict – were derived from Proudhon. Despite this acquisition, however, we suggest that it is wrong to depict Marx as a plagiarist. As with Smith, who derived his key ideas from Hume and Cantillon, Marx used his understandings to reach fundamentally different conclusions to Proudhon, synthesizing novel understandings of economics and politics. Whereas Proudhon's view of capitalism was uniformly hostile, Marx's understandings – as expressed in *Capital* – were more nuanced. Where Proudhon perceived the worker as the sole creator of value, Marx (1867/1954: 72–73) argued that capitalist production was always a collective endeavor with the "specific social character of each producer's" efforts only revealing "itself in the act of exchange." Accordingly, Marx (1867/1954: 146) continued, "The circulation of commodities is the starting-point of capital." In short, Marx – like Marshall – argued that the problems of capitalism and management can never be ascertained solely by looking to workplace circumstances. We also need to locate these problems within the wider context of the society that it serves. The tragedy of Marxism, of course, lay not only in its belief that the capitalist market could be replaced by a planned economy, but also in its understanding that history *always* revolved around class struggle. In every Marxist society, to a greater or lesser extent, this view of society manifested itself in woes far more grievous than a stultified market and a chronic mismatch between production and consumption. It also resulted in societies built upon denunciation, in which every failing is perceived to be the result of some real or imaginary enemy.

Problems of Epistemology

If the problems and achievements of management cannot be understood apart from economics, and the debates that economics has engendered, it is also the case that debates as to the nature of management are intertwined with different understandings of epistemology. Many now subscribe to Michel Foucault's (1976/1978: 100) view that, "it is in discourse that power and knowledge are joined together." Conversely, many "traditional" historians, positivist by inclination, ascribe to a "common sense" view of knowledge, sharing Thomas Hobbes's (1651/2002) learned opinion that, "science is the knowledge of consequences, and dependence of one fact upon another." Unfortunately, for the advocates of a "common sense" view of knowledge, one does not need to be a postmodernist to ascertain the flaws in their epistemological premises. As the great Austro-English philosopher, Karl Popper (1935/2002: 12) observed, "the most important and most problems of epistemology must remain completely invisible to those who confine themselves to analyzing ordinary or common-sense knowledge." For it is the nature of the human condition that our minds constantly deal in abstractions – management, freedom, productivity, marginal utility, use value, geometry, algebra – that are a creation of our minds, not the world. Historical processes are also in large part the product of social and economic institutions, of accumulated capital and physical resources. But they are also the result of human consciousness and will, of attempts to reshape the world anew. As an historian, there is thus no greater difficultly than in giving proper weight to these different motive forces, one grounded in the past (i.e., institutions, physical resources, culture, etc.) and the other in the present (i.e., human consciousness and will).

One of the unfortunate tendencies that mares contemporary management history is the tendency to embrace various epistemologies and methodologies without explaining either their origins or, more importantly, the *implications* for using the nominated approach *vis-à-vis* another. Accordingly, the first and second last chapters in this Part – (▶ Chap. 14, "Intellectual Enlightenment: The Epistemological Foundations of Business Endeavor" by Bowden) and (▶ Chap. 17, "Foundations: The Roots of Idealist and Romantic Opposition to Capitalism and Management" by Bowden) – speak to the origins of the intellectual debates that currently transfix management history: debates that see postmodernist understandings opposed to more "traditional" approaches grounded in positivism.

Through an exploration of the origins of the empiricist or positivist tradition, the first chapter in this Part – ▶ Chap. 14, "Intellectual Enlightenment: The Epistemological Foundations of Business Endeavor" – pays special heed to the foundational ideas of Hobbes, John Locke, David Hume and Edmund Burke. Among the exponents of the empiricist or positivist tradition, arguably none was more insightful then Hume. In his most significant work, *An Inquiry Concerning Human Understanding*, Hume outlined three key propositions. First, Hume (1748/1902: 25) began by noting that "human reason" deals with not only "matters of fact" but also with the "operation of thought, without dependence on what is anywhere existent in the universe." In explaining this distinction, Hume noted the common use of circles and triangles in geometry, even though "there were never a [pure] circle or triangle in nature." The second foundational principle that Hume expounded was one that emphasized the fundamentally skeptical and conservative nature of the intellectual tradition that Hume himself helped establish. Declaring, "our thought" is "confined within very narrow limits," Hume (1748/1902: 19, 30) concluded that we are incapable of determining "any single evident, or infer any cause or effect, without the assistance of observation and experience." Finally, and most controversially, Hume argued that the human mind is incapable of judging cause and effect relationships given the uniqueness of each historical experience. As a result, Hume (1748/1902: 36–37) advised his readers, the most we can ever infer is that from "causes which appear *similar* we can expect similar effects. This is the sum of all our experimental conclusions" [stress in original].

In reflecting upon Hume's arguments, the German philosopher, Immanuel Kant (1783/1902: 3–4), thoughtfully concluded that, "since the origin of metaphysics ... nothing has ever happened which was more decisive to its fate than the attack made upon it by David Hume." In turning to Hume's key argument – that human reason is incapable of determining cause and effect – Kant (1783/1902: 58–59) came to argue on a contrary proposition, that the "concept of cause ... is a pure concept of the understanding, which is totally disparate from all possible perception." Often derided as an idealist philosopher, Kant (1783/1902: 48–49) himself vigorously denied the charge, declaring: "My protestations ... against all charges of idealism is so valid and clear as even to seem superfluous ... My idealism concerns not the existence of things ... since it never came into my head to doubt it." In his most famed study, the *Critique of Pure Reason*, Kant (1787/2007: 348) continued his denial of charges of idealism with the declaration that "the real, or the material" exists in "space actually and independently of all fancy." Nevertheless, despite this denial, Kant continued to chart a fundamentally different path to Hume, establishing in the process a third intellectual tradition in between empiricism on the one hand and philosophical idealism on the other. For whereas Hume believed that reason and thought progressed from empirical observation, Kant (1787/2007: 137) argued the reverse, stating,

> All knowledge requires a concept, however obscure and imperfect that concept may be; and a concept is always, with regard to its form, something that is general and that can serve as a rule.

If Kant sought to weave a path between pure empiricism and pure idealism, in the course of the nineteenth century the various strands of idealist philosophy grew in strength, intermingling with the English "Romantic" tradition and eventually giving motive force to postmodernism is its disparate hues. Beginning our discussion of philosophic idealism in the first chapter in this Part (▶ Chap. 14, "Intellectual Enlightenment: The Epistemological Foundations of Business Endeavor"), we return to a discussion of German idealism and English Romanticism – and the ways in which they have informed postmodernist thought – in our penultimate ▶ Chap. 17, "Foundations: The Roots of Idealist and Romantic Opposition to Capitalism and Management."

13 The Foundations of Knowledge and Management: An Introduction

Although the linkages between philosophical idealism and the dominant figures in postmodernist thought – Jacques Derrida, Michel Foucault, Hayden White – are rarely discussed in the "critical management" literature, it is our contention that it is impossible to understand these dissident traditions apart from their origins in German idealism. Like Nietzsche, who declared that through acts of will it is always possible to break the "invisible spell" of societal mores (Nietzsche 1886/1989: 31, 27), Foucault (1966/1994: xx) believed that we can break free of the "fundamental codes" of "culture" through acts of will. This Foucauldian/Nietzschean emphasis on consciousness and will as transformative forces owes a clear debt to Schopenhauer's (1859/1969) *The World As Will and Representation*, a work that proclaimed that, "this world is, on the one side, entirely *representation*, just as, on the other, [it] is entirely will" [emphasis in original]. In turn, not only Schopenhauer but also Nietzsche, Foucault, Martin Heidegger, and Derrida derived core understandings from Friedrich Schelling's (1809/2006) *Philosophical Investigations into the Essence of Human Freedom*. In this, Schelling (1809/2006: 33) argued for the "complete freedom" of individual consciousness and will "above and outside of all nature." In his critique of modernity, Derrida also found inspiration in an intellectual lineage that stretched back through Heidegger, Edmund Husserl, Schopenhauer, and Schelling to Johann Fichte, arguably the true founder of German idealist thought. Like Derrida, who argued that language had "traces" of previous forms of existence of which the author is often unaware, Fichte (1799/1910: 7) argued, that "every existence" signals within it "another existence."

In exploring the intellectual roots of postmodernism and other idealist traditions hostile to capitalism and modern forms of management, our penultimate chapter also traces the way in which a critical tradition emerged through the cross-fertilization between German idealism and English "Romanticism." Like the English Romantics – who believed that the new factory cities cut humanity off from what Wordsworth (1802/1935: 296) described as "eternal Nature, and the great moving spirit of things" – Fichte (1799/1910: 11) declared that "Nature is one connected whole." Within this spiritually infused Nature, Fichte (1799/1910: 11) continued, one cannot "move a single grain of sand . . . without thereby . . . changing something throughout all parts of the immeasurable whole." Finding a resonance in the contemporary environmental movement, the English "Romantics" (William Blake, Samuel Coleridge, William Wordsworth, Percy Shelley, Mary Shelley, John Polidori, Lord Byron) also argued that the human spirit found "a better soil" in a "low and rustic life" than it did in an urban existence (Wordsworth 1800/2009: 142, 144). Far from offering humanity a way forward, William Blake (1808/1969: 481) famously argued in its epic poem on *Milton*, industrialization condemned ever-growing numbers to lives among "dark Satanic Mills."

The enduring value German idealist philosophy and English "Romantic" literature is found in its emphasis on human consciousness, spirit, and will as central elements in the historical experiences. Nevertheless, the depiction of a bucolic existence as one superior to that offered by an advancing modernity was a figment of largely aristocratic imaginations. For the overwhelming majority of the population in a preindustrial society the reality of daily life was one of filth, illiteracy, powerlessness, backbreaking toil, disease, and early death. As the French political theorist, Jean-Jacques Rousseau (1762/1979: 47) observed in reflecting upon life in eighteenth-century France, "Almost all of the first age is sickness and danger. Half the children born perish before their first year." Although there is a tendency to think of the Renaissance, the Reformation and the Age of European Discovery as an era of rising prosperity, in truth the conquest of empire and a one-sided trade with the non-European world did little to change the living conditions of people either within Europe or without. As Palma and Reis's (2019) recent study has shown, despite the benefit of empire the per capita incomes of most European societies in the mid-nineteenth century remained barely above the subsistence level. Accordingly, as Fig. 1 indicates – which records per capita income in so-called Geary-Khamis "international" United States dollars that adjust for inflation and national price variations – only in Britain do we witness a society able to break from of the misery and poverty that was the historic norm. In doing so, Britain provided the world with an economic and managerial model where the benefits soon far outweighed the long-term costs. If the English "Romantics" in particular provided an idealized image of preindustrial life that little corresponded to reality, it is also the case that – with the partial exception of Percy and Mary Shelley – both the English "Romantic" movement and German idealism tended to regard democracy and the advance of the common citizen with disdain. Of the English advocates of the popular vote, Byron (1820/2015: 353) declared them "a pack of blackguards ... who disgust me with their Cause ... I shall pause before I lend myself to the views of such ruffians." In a similar vein, William Wordsworth (1821/1978: 27–28) argued that only through "an

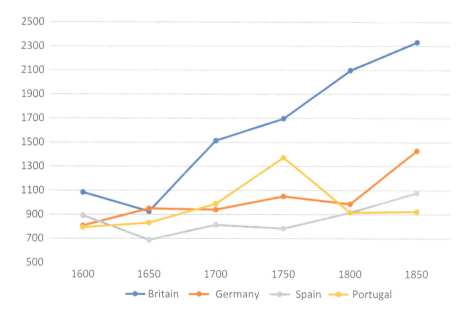

Fig. 1 Output per Capita in US Dollars (1990 value), 1600–1850 –England, Germany, Portugal and Spain. (Source: Palma and Reis, "From Convergence to Divergence," p. 500, Table 4)

armed Yeomanry" and a "Press properly curbed" was the maintenance of "order" possible. For Nietzsche (1874: 39–40) as well, "the popular masses and working classes" were "dangerous," "unintelligent," the "lowest clay and loam layers of society."

If those who seek inspiration in the intellectual traditions of German philosophic idealism and English "Romanticism" are misinformed if they think these traditions are democratic in ethos, it is also the case that one is misguided if one believes that these traditions are the basis for a sound epistemology, a set of principles that helps one explain the world. Yes, it is true, as Popper pointed out, that the empiricism of Hume was misguided in its rigid adherence to experience and observation as the touchstone of understanding. Nevertheless, as Popper (1935/2002: 280) accurately observed in *The Logic of Scientific Discovery,* "We do not stumble upon our experiences, nor do we let them flow over us like a stream. Rather, we have to 'make' our experiences ... every step is guided by theory." In other words, as Kant inferred, research begins with concepts and theses, with propositions that act as our guides, guides to whom we adhere or dispense with to the extent that their guidance is confirmed by evidence.

Central to the debates that currently divide management history, as it divides other disciplines, is the process of energy-intensive industrialization that commenced with the "Industrial Revolution." Few of us stop to think, however, of where the term "Industrial Revolution" came from – a term used neither by John Stuart Mill nor Karl Marx. Nor do we stop to consider why the Industrial Revolution is typically dated from 1760 to 1830, dates that correspond with the accession of George III and the death of George IV rather than any particular economic or technological transformation. The arbitrary nature of the dates and terminology associated with *the* Industrial Revolution are such that the Chicago-based John Nef (1943: 1) declared that, "There is scarcely a conception that rests on less secure foundations." In the final chapter of this section, therefore, we explore how the concept of the "Industrial Revolution" emerged from the posthumous publication of the lectures of Arnold Toynbee the elder (1884/1894), a work that gained renown as *Lectures on the Industrial Revolution of the eighteenth century in England.* From this starting point we (▶ Chap. 19, "Conflicting Understandings of the Industrial Revolution and Its Consequences: The Founding Figures of British Management History" by Bowden) explore in our final chapter, how the concept of *the* Industrial Revolution became a source of contestation among economic, labor and social historians – most notably John Nef, John Clapham, Arnold Toybee the younger, Sidney and Beatrice, E.P Thompson and Sidney Pollard – and how the discipline of management history arose in large part as a response to these debates.

Cross-References

▶ Conflicting Understandings of the Industrial Revolution and Its Consequences: The Founding Figures of British Management History

▶ Economic Foundations: Adam Smith and the Classical School of Economics

- ► Foundations: The Roots of Idealist and Romantic Opposition to Capitalism and Management
- ► Intellectual Enlightenment: The Epistemological Foundations of Business Endeavor
- ► Neo-classical Thought: Alfred Marshall and Utilitarianism
- ► The Marxist Opposition to Capitalism and Business

References

Bentham J (1781/2000) An introduction to the principles of morals and legislation. Batoche Books, Kitchener

Blake W (1808/1969) Milton. In: Keynes G (ed.) Blake: Complete Writings. Oxford University Press, Oxford

Byron L (1820/2015) Letter from Lord Byron to John Murray, 21 February 1820. In: Byron L (ed) Byron's letters and journals: a new selection (ed: Lansdown R). Oxford University Press, London, pp 351–353

Chandler AD Jr (1977) The visible hand: the managerial revolution in American business. Belknap Press, Cambridge, MA

Cummings S, Bridgman T, Hassard J, Rowlinson M (2017) A new history of management. Cambridge University Press, Cambridge, UK

Fichte JG (1799/1910) The vocation of man, 2nd edn. Open Court Publishing House, Chicago

Foucault M (1966/1994) The Order of Things. Vintage Books, New York

Foucault M (1976/1978) The history of sexuality – an introduction (trans: Hurley R). Pantheon Books, New York

Hobbes T (1651/2002) Leviathan. Broadway Press, Peterborough

Hume D (1748/1902) An inquiry concerning human understanding. In: Hume D (ed) Inquiries concerning the human understanding and concerning the principles of morals (ed: Selby-Bigge LA), 2nd edn. Clarendon Press, Oxford, pp 2–165

Kant I (1783/1902) Prolegomena (trans: Carus P). Open Court Publishing, Chicago/La Salle

Kant I (1787/2007) Critique of pure reason (trans: Weigelt M), 2nd edn. Penguin Classics, London

Marshall A (1890/1997) Principles of economics, 8th edn. Prometheus Books, New York

Marx K (1847/1955) The poverty of philosophy. Progress Publishers, Moscow, USSR

Marx K (1867/1954) Capital: a critical analysis of capitalist production, vol 1. Foreign Languages Publishing House, Moscow, USSR

Mill JS (1861/2009) Utilitarianism. Floating Press, Auckland

Nef JU (1943) The industrial revolution reconsidered. J Econ Hist 3(1):1–31

Nietzsche F (1874) On the use and abuse of history for life (trans: Hollingdale R). http://la.utexas.edu/users/hcleaver/330T/350kPEENietzscheAbuseTableAll.pdf

Nietzsche F (1886/1989) Beyond good and evil: prelude to a philosophy of the future (trans: Hollingdale R). Vintage Books, New York

Palma N, Reis J (2019) From convergence to divergence: Portuguese economic growth 1527–1850. J Econ Hist 79(2):477–506

Piketty T (2012/2014) Capital in the twenty-first century (trans: Goldhammer A). Belknap Press, Cambridge, MA

Popper K (1935/2002) The logic of scientific discovery. Routledge, London/New York

Proudhon P-J (1847/1888) The philosophy of poverty. McMaster University, Hamilton

Rothbard MN (2006) Economic thought before Adam Smith: an Austrian perspective on the history of economic thought, vol 1. Ludwig von Mises Institute, Auburn

Rousseau J-J (1762/1979) Emile: on education (trans: Bloom A). Penguin Classics, London

Schelling FWJ (1809/2006) Philosophical investigations into the essence of human freedom. State University of New York, Albany

Schopenhauer A (1859/1969) The world as will and representation, 3rd edn. Dover Publications, Dover

Smith A (1776/1999) An inquiry into the nature and causes of the wealth of nations. Penguin Classics, London

Toynbee A (1884/1894) Lectures on the industrial revolution of the 18th century in England. Longman, Green, London

Wordsworth W (1800/2009) Preface of 1800. In: Wordsworth W (ed) Prose Works of William Wordsworth (ed: Owen WJB, Smyser JW), vol 1. Humanities e-Book http://ebookcentral.proquest.com/lib/griffith/detail.action?docID=3306065

Wordsworth W (1802/1935) Letter to John Wilson June 1802. In: Wordsworth W (ed) The early letters of William and Dorothy Wordsworth 1787–1805 (ed: Selincourt E). Clarendon Press, Oxford, pp 292–298

Wordsworth W (1821/1978) Letter from William Wordsworth to Viscount Lowther, 9 February 1821. In: Wordsworth W (ed) The letters of William and Dorothy Wordsworth 1821–1828 (ed: Hill AG, Selincourt E), 2nd edn. Clarendon Press, Oxford, pp 27–29

Intellectual Enlightenment: The Epistemological Foundations of Business Endeavor

14

Bradley Bowden

Contents

Introduction 322
The Empiricist Tradition 326
The Idealist Tradition 334
Logic 339
Conclusion 342
References 343

Abstract

At first glance, the matters pertaining to research appear self-evidently simple. On the basis of evidence and testing, we draw conclusions that are amenable to further scrutiny. Complacency disappears, however, the moment we think seriously about the nature of evidence and human reasoning. If we are seeking for generalizable theories that help explain the human condition, how can we do this in ways that give weight to individual being, whereby humans interact with the world in idiosyncratic ways? Do we give primacy, as idealist philosophy would suggest, to individual consciousness? Or, alternatively, are we to be guided by observed experiences and evidence, as the empiricist or positivist tradition would have us do? Should we embrace both inductive logic and deductive logic or should we – as Karl Popper suggested – abjure the former and only rely on the latter? In seeking answers to these problems, this chapter argues in favor of a middle course. We should accept, as idealist philosophy contends, that our understandings are not generated directly through sensory perception and experience but rather through the play of experience on our imagination and reasoning. Conversely, we should reject the extreme skepticism of idealist thought,

---

B. Bowden (✉)
Griffith Business School, Griffith University, Nathan, QLD, Australia
e-mail: b.bowden@griffith.edu.au

© The Author(s), under exclusive licence to Springer Nature Switzerland AG 2020
B. Bowden et al. (eds.), *The Palgrave Handbook of Management History*,
https://doi.org/10.1007/978-3-319-62114-2_84

recognizing that there is an objective world independent of our fancy. We should also reject Popper's aversion to inductive logic so as to embrace all the conceptual tools at our disposal. For if deductive logic has great utility for testing theories, it is also the case that inductive logic is of particular benefit in generating new theses.

Keywords

Berkeley · Empiricism · Foucault · Hobbes · Hume · Idealism · Kant · Locke · Marx · Popper · Positivism · Postmodernism · Rousseau · Vico · Weber · White

Introduction

As first blush, the roots of modern business and managerial endeavor seem self-evident. They are located in the Industrial Revolution, when a combination of science, new technologies, and new managerial principles associated with the efficient use of resource inputs enabled modernizing economies to break earlier bonds. In explaining the "novel" features of modern "industrial management," Sidney Pollard (1965: 6), in his *The Genesis of Management,* accurately observed that British managers in the late eighteenth century differed from their predecessors in combining "different objectives and methods into one," methods associated with motivating legally free workforces in ways that enabled them to sell their output "competitively." Yet to get to this point, managers and their workers – and indeed the society at large – had to cross an intellectual divide that separated them from previous generations. On one side of this divide was a world that is now utterly alien to us, a world associated with hidebound beliefs, superstition, and deference to religious authority. On the other is the intellectual world that we take for granted, a world characterized by critical thinking, experiment, and a capacity to apply innovative ideas to practical problems. The difficulties involved in crossing this divide between the premodern and modern worlds are perhaps best indicated in the preface to the book within which in 1541 Nicolaus Copernicus enunciated his revolutionary theorem that the sun was at the center of the solar system. Fearing with considerable justification that his beliefs would see him condemned for heresy, Copernicus (1541/2008: 4–7) directed his preface to then Pope, Paul III, calling upon him to recognize rationality and reason as the touchstones for any debate: not long-accepted tradition. In doing so, Copernicus put forward two revolutionary maxims that effectively launched what we think of as the "scientific revolution." First, Copernicus (1541/2008: 4) suggested that every "philosopher" should "endeavor to seek the truth in all things, to the extent permitted to human reason by God." Having made "human reason" the effective judge of every problem, Copernicus (1541/2008: 5) then argued that belief should always be based on hypotheses supported by empirical evidence. "For if the hypotheses," Copernicus (1541/2008: 5) explained, are "not false, everything which follows" from the hypotheses "would be confirmed beyond doubt."

Although Copernicus crossed a perilous divide with his publication of *De Revolutionibus* (*On the Revolutions*) in 1541 – a divide so perilous that Copernicus sensibly protected himself from retribution by only publishing his study on his deathbed – generalized acceptance of critical inquiry had to wait to the long century (1650–1789) of the European Enlightenment, what the French referred to as *le siècle des Lumières* (century of light). What gave the Enlightenment its power and transformative effect was not so much its commonality of conclusions, for no such commonality emerged. Rather it was its willingness to subject all aspects of human existence – be it matters relating to science, religion, politics, or economics – to critical scrutiny. In seeking to explain the physical and social worlds, however, all the intellectual traditions that emerged from the Enlightenment confronted the same essential problem: How does one explain human outcomes in ways that identify causal relationships while allowing scope for the free exercise of human consciousness and will? In Britain, the founders of the empiricist tradition – Thomas Hobbes, John Locke, and David Hume – answered this question by giving primacy to the senses. As Hobbes (1651/2002: 3) explained it in his *Leviathan*, a study that effectively launched not only the empiricist tradition but also the Enlightenment's critical inquiries in general, "there is no conception in a man's mind that hath not at first, totally or by parts, been begotten upon the organs of sense...The cause of sense is the external body or object." In Hobbes's (1651/2002: 38) well-argued reasoning, "sense and memory" produced "knowledge of fact" upon which "science" could be built, which he defined as "the knowledge of consequences, and dependence of one fact upon another."

The problem with the empiricist tradition, in Hobbes's time as well as our own, is twofold. First, the senses can deceive, producing falsehoods in our imagination, telling us, for example, that the moon is of variable shape and that the earth stands still as the sun transverses the sky. A second and more fundamental problem relates to human consciousness and will, which is not an "external body or object" but rather something internal to each individual. As all of us can understand, it is this consciousness and will that enables humanity to shape the material world into images of its own creation. Recognition of the importance of consciousness and will led inevitably to an intellectual tradition diametrically opposed to empiricism: philosophic idealism. In giving vent to this tradition, the English cleric, George Berkeley (1710/1996: 36), proved its most radical and uncompromising exponent, arguing that with each of us, the *only* thing of which we can be certain is our own consciousness and existence, i.e., the world outside our consciousness may be nothing but illusion. In Berkeley's view, our sense of there being a material world – which imposes a clearer sense of being "real" than mere dreams or imaginings – is due solely to the fact that "ideas of sense are more strong, lively, and distinct than those of the imagination." Over time, the idealist tradition bifurcated into two distinct streams of thought. On the one hand, there were those, most notably Georg Hegel, who detected commonalities in the exercise of human consciousness and will; commonalities that Hegel (1837/1956: 36) argued reflected the existence of God's divine plan which "philosophy strives to comprehend." Opposed to this strand of idealist thought was a tradition which found its foremost exponent in Friedrich

Nietzsche and which held that human will was – or should be – the primary factor in all human endeavors. As Nietzsche (1883/1970: 137) explained it in *Thus Spoke Zarathustra*, everything stems from "the will itself, the will to power, the unexhausted, procreating life-will."

To complicate matters further, there emerged – in between the rival traditions of empiricist and idealist thought – a third tradition associated with the work of Immanuel Kant (1788/2002: 71) that self-consciously sought to bridge the "cognition that concerns the existence of things" (i.e., empiricism) and the "toughest skepticism (sic)" of idealist inquiry. Although often dismissed by his critics as merely a more sophisticated exponent of idealist thought – the noted management scholar, Edwin Locke (2002: ix), blaming Kant for the rise of postmodernism with the declaration that Kant "was the first philosopher to sever reason (consciousness) from reality" – Kant himself saw his efforts differently. As Kant (1788/2002: 71–73) explained it in his *Critique of Practical Reason*, we can only "deduce" causal relationships through the analysis of abstractions, abstractions that are, however, drawn from observations of the objective world. Accordingly, causal relationships are not self-evident but must instead emerge from the systematic scrutiny of evidence. In the view of Karl Popper (1935/2002: 23), it was through this realization that scientific conclusions stemmed from the testing of theories – not from direct observation – that Kant made his singular contribution to Western thought. Where Kant differed from Popper, and from the empiricist tradition more generally, was in giving primacy to logical induction – where one proceeds from observation of evidence to the generation of theories – over logical deduction (i.e., the testing of theories against evidence) (For Popper's rejection of inductive reasoning, see Karl Popper, *The Logic of Scientific Discovery*, 6). In justifying his preference for logical induction, Kant (1787/2007: 137) declared in his *Critique of Pure Reason* that "All knowledge requires a concept, however obscure and imperfect that concept may be; and a concept is always...something that is general and can serve as a rule."

For most of us, particularly those of us located within practice-oriented disciplines such as business and management, an exploration of the epistemological foundations of the intellectual traditions that inform that practice seems not only daunting but unnecessary. Instead of such endeavors, one suspects a general preference for the guidance offered by David Hume (1738a/1896: 288–289) in the final volume of his *Treatise on Human Nature*, where he advised that the best judge of the difference between fact and fiction was "common sense." There are, nevertheless, two reasons that make an understanding of the foundations of Western thought an imperative. First, a lack of understanding of epistemological foundations exposes one to constant bamboozlement by those who claim – often on the basis of limited and confused "understandings" – to possess such knowledge. Second, the epistemological principles that guide our thinking circumscribe the things that we believe are socially or managerially important and achievable. This is perhaps most evident in the empiricist tradition, which emerged in the first instance from the British struggles against arbitrary authority during the seventeenth and eighteenth centuries, experiences that produced an inherent conservatism as to both the tradition's ambitions and societal objectives. Restraint of arbitrary authority, whether imposed from above or below, was the shared concern of its founding figures. As John Locke (1689/1823: 193) observed in his *Two Treatises of Government*, "Wherever law ends, tyranny begins." It is this caution that makes empiricism, as Popper (1944a: 120) accurately observed, a natural foe of "social engineering" and an advocate instead of "piecemeal tinkering." Inherently cautious, empiricist traditions have always been suspicious of not only radical societal reforms but also of grand theorizing and elaborate conceptual framings. In expressing such caution in his *Leviathan*, Hobbes (1651/2002: 20) declared that those "seeking of truth" should always abstain from "absurd assertions," most particularly those involving "metaphors, tropes, and other rhetorical figures." Among idealist thinkers, those who give priority (as most do) to individual consciousness and will are also necessarily opposed to theoretical generalizations. Accordingly, those steeped in this tradition – as today's postmodernists are – are liable to endorse Michel Foucault's (1969/1972: 8–9, 11) view that the human experience is contingent by nature, characterized by "discontinuities" and a "living, fragile" existence. Conversely, if one is guided by the belief, as Hegel (1837/1956) was, that human consciousness and will are guided by shared commonalities – be they divine or otherwise – then one is prone to detect generalizable laws that explain organizational and societal outcomes. If one stays within an idealist framework, however, then the unifying commonalities must always be psychological or spiritual in nature. Despite such constraints, Hegel's (1837/1956) belief that history was leading toward a preordained high point also proved attractive to those outside the idealist traditions who shared more radical reforming visions. Karl Marx (1873/1954: 19–20), for example, in his afterword to the second German edition of *Capital*, freely acknowledged that his view that history had a preordained purpose was inspired by Hegel's writings, Marx merely substituting social class for God's will as the agent of change. Hegel was, Marx (1873/1954: 20) advised, the first to explain historical outcomes as "working in a comprehensive and conscious manner." Within both his own work and Hegel's, Marx (1873/1954: 20) continued, not only was every "historically developed social form" perceived as being "in fluid movement," in each case history was also seen as being directed toward an ultimate "crowning point."

If epistemological preferences have a profound influence on any given author's research directions and conclusions, so it is the case that a liking for logical deduction over logical induction (or the reverse) must also have weighty implications as to the nature of one's thinking and research. The key benefit of inductive logic, as Henri Poincare (1902/1905: xxi, 167) observed in his *La Science et L'hypothese* (*Science and Hypothesis*), is found not in any certainties that stem from its use but rather in the generation of hypotheses that can then be subject to scrutiny and experimentation. By contrast, as Popper (1935/2002: 25–26) explained, "the deductive [logic] method of testing cannot establish or justify the statements which are being tested." Instead, testing occurs through the scrutiny of subsidiary statements. What is left in abeyance in this process of logical deduction is how we generated our original thesis. As a general rule of thumb, the bigger the research problem we are confronting, the less amenable it is to logical deduction and empirical testing – an outcome that Max Weber (1904/1949: 56) recognized in his article, *Objectivity in Social Science and Social Policy* where he observed that "One thing is certain under all circumstances, namely, the more 'general' the problem involved...the less subject it is to a single unambiguous answer on the basis of the data of empirical sciences." This is particularly the case, Weber (1904/1949: 92) argued, with matters relating to culture, leadership, personal charisma, and the factors behind national and regional variation. In dealing with such problems, the best we can hope for, Weber concluded, is evidence that a hypothesis or outcome is "objectively possible" rather than being empirically verifiable.

In summary, understanding of epistemological debates is important primarily because we cannot proceed as researchers in any direction unless we first comprehend the principles that are informing – either consciously or unconsciously – our conceptual and methodological biases. For, as the English historian E.H. Carr (1961/2002: 18) expressed it, "facts...are like fish swimming about in a vast and sometimes inaccessible ocean." What one catches in this ocean is primarily determined by the part of the ocean one "chooses to fish in" and the type of fishing tackle one "chooses to use." Everything, in short, stems from conceptual framings. It is only such framings that give "facts" their meaning.

The Empiricist Tradition

If the emergence of the British empiricist tradition was a seminal feature of the European Enlightenment, it is nevertheless the case that this tradition – as with its rivals – owed much to the ancient Greeks. This debt is indicated by the fact that the first major work undertaken by Thomas Hobbes (1629/1839) – a pioneer for the emerging empiricist tradition – was a translation of Thucydides' *History of the Peloponnesian War*, the most sophisticated historical analysis handed down to us from the ancient world, undertaken by a soldier cum scholar described by Molesworth (1839: viii) as "the most politic historiographer that ever writ." There were, in particular, two aspects of Thucydides' work that had a profound influence on Hobbes and through him on us. First, Thucydides outlined an approach to the collection and assessment of evidence that still embodies the empiricist approach. Declaring a preference for "the plainest evidence," Thucydides (c.411 BC/1975: 47–48) also advised the readers of his *History of the Peloponnesian War* that in his "factual reporting," he relied as far as possible on "eye-witnesses whose reports I have checked with as much thoroughness as possible." In assessing the evidence of these primacy sources, moreover, Thucydides (c.411 BC/1975: 48) sought to set aside personal bias and "partiality" and to check different accounts of events so as to minimize the effects of misreporting that inevitably stem "from imperfect memories." Only through such cautious assessment, Thucydides (c.411 BC/1975: 48) concluded, was it possible to discover "the truth" in historical events, a conclusion which – in its abiding belief that there is an objective truth accessible to discerning inquiry – differs little from the much later opinion of the great British empiricist,

G.R. Elton (1967/1969: 74), who declared that we "will always be able to say: this once existed or took place, and there is therefore a truth to be discovered if only we can find it."

In addition to his stated approach toward evidence, the second commonality that Thucydides shares with the empiricist tradition that emerged from the European Enlightenment is a profoundly pessimistic view of human nature. From start to finish, the *History of the Peloponnesian War* is a cautionary tale as to the evils and miseries that stem from human ambition and the misuse of acquired power. Even though the war afflicted "unprecedented suffering" and "loss of life, Thucydides (c.411 BC/1975: 48) nevertheless concludes that similar events would transpire in the future...and in much the same ways...human nature being what it is." Although Thucydides (c.411 BC/1975: 145) cites with favor the principles of democracy – which saw the Athenian leader, Pericles, declare that with democracies "what counts" is "the actual ability" a person possesses "not membership of a particular class" – the democratic practices that he observed during the war proved anything but inspiring. Endorsing a series of populist leaders who favored aggressive military forays away from home and repression of dissident opinion at home, its failings eventually led to its replacement by a broad-based oligarchy based upon Athens's propertied classes. It was this regime, associated with the so-called Council of Five Thousand, that Thucydides (c.411 BC/1975: 598–599) declared to be "a better government than ever before...There was a reasonable and moderate blending of the few and the many."

The opinions that informed Thucydides' *History of the Peloponnesian War* – a suspicion of all forms of power and a concern for the protection of proprietary interests – were also a characteristic feature of the foundational texts of British empiricism. As John Locke (1689/1823: 159) concluded in his *Two Treatises of Government*, "The great and chief end...of men uniting into commonwealths, and putting themselves under government, is the preservation of their property." In Locke's (1689/1823: 192) assessment, "tyranny" could be exerted by democracies as well as monarchies, by "one or many." Previously, Hobbes (1651/2002) had also emphasized that in every society, the security of life and property overrode every other concern. Wherever people "live without other security than what their own strength and their own invention shall furnish them," Hobbes (1651/2002: 62) observed, "there is no place for industry," and without industry life is invariably "solitary, poor, nasty, short and brutish." Hume (1738a/1896: 252) also held to the opinion that it was "by society alone" that humanity's inherent "defects" were "compensated," leaving an organized society's citizens in every respect more happy, than "tis possible" in their "savage and solitary condition, ever to become."

If the seminal works of British empiricism shared with Thucydides a belief that societies needed to protect their members from the arbitrary actions of the many as well as the few, they also shared with him a liking for "the plainest evidence," built upon scrutiny of verifiable facts. As Hobbes (1651/2002: 5) explained it, proper understandings can only be based upon "experience," experiences that involve the direct use of one's senses. Accordingly, Hobbes (1651/2002: 30) believed that all knowledge stemmed from a "knowledge of fact," which in every case is "originally sense" (i.e., a sensory experience), and "ever after memory" (i.e., memories are differentiated from fantasy by being based on fact and sensory perception). Those who departed from reliance on plain, verifiable facts to create elaborate theories that were not grounded in evidence, Hobbes (1651/2002: 22) argued, merely produced *ignes fatue* (foolish fires) and "innumerable absurdities." The inherent conservatism that was to become a defining feature of British empiricism is also evident when Hobbes shifted his discussions from evidence to theory and causal explanations. In drawing for the first time a distinction between knowledge in the "natural sciences" and the social sciences he also noted that any causal explanation based upon evidence must always be "conditional" given that "No discourse whatsoever can end in absolute knowledge of fact, past or to come" (Hobbes 1651/2002: 30). Among empiricism's founding figures, David Hume was if anything even more scornful than Hobbes of the idea that generalizable laws could be discerned to explain the human condition. As Hume (1738a/1896: 288–89) advised his audience, "strict adherence to any general rules...are virtues that hold less of reason, than of bigotry and superstition." As most readers would be aware, the empiricist tradition has maintained this suspicion of generalizable laws across the centuries, Elton (1967/1969: 42) wishfully declaring in his *Practice of History* – a work that was a set text for most budding historians (including this author) in the latter decades of the twentieth century – that few "would probably nowadays fall victim to the search for laws."

Paradoxically, given their belief that it was humanity's flawed nature that demanded a system of societal constraints, the early empiricist thinkers (most particularly Hobbes and Locke) paid scant attention to the role of consciousness and emotion in determining organizational and economic outcomes. Among empiricist thinkers – be they British or French – only Hume made the study of emotion a central part of his work. Devoting the second volume of his *A Treatise on Human Nature* to "passions," Hume (1738a/1896: 240) accurately observed that – unlike reason – "'tis evident our passions" are "not susceptible" to rational "agreement or disagreement." Whereas Hobbes (1651/2002: 3) argued that all "conceptions" were created in the first instance by external bodies or objects, Hume (1738b/1896: 144) differentiated between "impressions of sensation" – which stemmed from external objects – and "reflective impressions," which he defined as "passions, and other emotions resembling them." Having identified "passions" as a key driver of human behavior, Hume (1738a/1896: 145) then drew a distinction between what he referred to as "calm passions" – associated with love, appreciation of beauty, humility, and care for others – and "violent" passions: greed, hatred, feelings of revenge, pride, etc. In any human society, Hume (1738b/1896: 146) argued, the latter was typically more important than the former due to the fact that "more violent" passions produced stronger sensory perceptions than "calm" ones.

Having identified "passions" as a central explanatory factor in human behavior, Hume was confronted with the difficult task of weaving an understanding of emotion into a framework that avoided a descent into idealist philosophy. Hume's solution to this problem – which was to have immeasurable and enduring significance for disciplines concerned with the study of business, economics, and management – was obtained through his identification of "self-interest" as humanity's preeminent emotion and concern. As Hume (1738b/1896: 266) expressed it, "Men being naturally selfish, or endow'd with a confin'd generosity, they are not easily induc'd to perform any action for the interest of strangers, except with a view to some reciprocal advantage." It was, Hume (1738b/1896: 267) further reflected, only as a result of "this self-interested" reasoning that "commerce...begins to take place, and to predominate in society." In other words, Hume identified in commonalities in human behavior caused by "self-interest", an explanation that incorporated passion and emotion into the compass of rational empirical inquiry. As we will discuss in the ensuing chapter, Hume's emphasis on self-interest and its role in stimulating commerce was subsequently taken up by Hume's close friend and fellow Scotsman, Adam Smith. Indeed, it was in "self-interest" that Smith (1776/1999: Book IV, Chap. 2, para. 9) identified in his *The Wealth of Nations* an "invisible hand" that guided economic exchanges and business organization rather than the "invisible hand of the market": a term which, contrary to popular opinion, he never actually used. In highlighting the role of "self-love" as the central factor in determining economic behaviour, Smith (1776/1999: Book I, Chap. 2, para. 2) concluded that "Nobody but a beggar chooses to depend chief upon the benevolence of his fellow-citizens...It is not from the benevolence of the butcher, the brewer, or the baker that we expect our dinner, but from their regard to their own interest."

In 1757 Hume's discussions of self-interest were taken up by Edmund Burke, arguably the greatest and most influential empiricist scholar, in an oft-overlooked study into the nature of both knowledge and social organization: *A Philosophical Inquiry into the Origin of our Ideas of the Sublime and the Beautiful*. Like Hume, Burke (1757/1823: 44) identified "self-preservation" as "the most powerful of all passions." However, like Hobbes and Locke – and unlike Hume and Smith – Burke saw the passions associated with self-preservation (fear, anger, retribution, envy) as essentially destructive. Fortunately, Burke (1757/1823: 46) argued, the negative effects of such passions were offset by another equally powerful human instinct: a primeval drive to intermingle and collaborate with other individuals as part of a wider "society." As he (Burke 1757/1823: 53) observed: "Good company, lively conversation, and the endearments of friendship, fill the mind with great pleasure." It was only through the effects of these social interactions, Burke (1757/1823: 46) concluded, that civilized existence differed from the life of "brutes." Caught between the destructive emotions associated with self-interest and the positive effects of social engagement, every human society's survival depended on its capacity to restrain negative behaviors while preserving the stabilizing effects of social institutions. This required, in Burke's considered opinion, a cautious, conservative intellectual approach that avoided overambitious theorizing and societal reforms. In seeking to understand the world around us, Burke (1757/1823: xi) observed, "The characteristics of nature are legible...but they are not plain enough to enable those who run, to read them. We must make use of a cautious…timorous method of proceeding." Accordingly, grand theorizing should be avoided and research conclusions limited to what could be verified by evidence. As Burke (1757/1823: xiii) expressed it, "A theory founded on experiment and not assumed, is always [only] good for as much as it explains. Our inability to push it indefinitely is no argument at all against it."

Burke's theses as to the nature of knowledge and societal organization found their fullest expression in his noted *Reflections on the Revolution in France*. First published in 1790 when the French Revolution was still in its infancy, Burke's pamphlet still stands as arguably the best-reasoned defense of constitutional government based on piecemeal reforms that allow for new economic and political interests while defending private property and social order. In Burke's (1790/2017: 34) opinion, politics and the organization of government were best regarded as an "empirical science" like any other, built upon careful and cautious adaptation and adjustment. Whenever societies abandoned this approach and relied instead on political abstractions (liberty, freedom, equality, etc.) as their guide – as the French had with the revolution of 1789 – then disaster, oppression, and tyranny must inevitably ensue (Burke 1790/2017: 3). In taking this stance, Burke was, it should be emphasized, *not* arguing for the perpetual entrenchment of the status quo. For, Burke argued, reaction and blind conservatism imperiled social stability as much as irrational revolutionary fervor. This was due to the fact, Burke (1790/2017: 11) concluded, that "A state with no means to make changes has no means to preserve itself. Without such means a state might even risk the loss of the part of its constitution that it most fervently wished to preserve." Outlining principles that subsequently came to be regarded as the intellectual cornerstones of modern systems of constitutional government, Burke (1790/2017: 11) argued that effective and enduring systems of government required the constant balancing of two competing imperatives: "conservation and correction." Without "conservation," a society risked anarchy and chaos. Without "correction," it risked stagnation and, eventually, revolution and upheaval.

In the era of the European Enlightenment, the intellectual and political caution embodied in the British empiricist tradition – to which Burke arguably provided its most fully developed expression – found a notable opponent in the French political philosopher, Jean-Jacques Rousseau. In the realm of political philosophy, Rousseau's critiques were unusual in that they shared with the empiricist thinkers such as Hobbes, Hume, and Burke a close interest in economic and social experience while eschewing the inherent conservatism of the empiricist tradition in favor of the abstract conclusions which Burke found so dangerous. On the one hand, therefore, Rousseau's work showed a detailed understanding of the lived experience of society's ordinary citizens to which British empiricist thinkers showed scant interest. Thus we are informed in Rousseau (1762b/1979: 47) *Emile* that the typical experience of common humanity was "sickness and danger" with half of all children perishing "before the first year." Like Hobbes, the founding father of British empiricism, Rousseau (1762b/1979: 239) also regarded Thucydides' work to be the embodiment of good scholarship, observing, "Thucydides is to my taste the true model...He reports the facts without judging them." Like Burke, Rousseau (1762b/1979: 460) also believed that it was only through agreed social convention and rules that stable societies could exist, noting that, "Each of us puts his goods, his life, and all his power in common under the supreme direction of the general will, and we as a body accept each member as a part indivisible from the whole." Alongside this hardheaded appreciation of human existence and social organization, however, Rousseau also gave vent to a dissident opinion as to the benefits of industrialization and Western economic progress. "By dint of gathering machines around us," Rousseau (1762b/1979: 176) suggested, humanity was losing its capacity for independent action and thought, an outcome that made the human products of modern society inherently inferior individuals when compared to the noble "Canadian savage." For, by contrast to their urbanized counterparts, those living closer to nature benefited from experiences that created not only stronger bodies but also greater "subtlety of mind" (Rousseau 1762b/1979: 176, 118). Rousseau's emphasis on the benefits of a "natural" existence also caused him to denounce the "reasoning of materialists" (i.e., empiricists such as Burke and Voltaire) as akin to that of the "deaf" in that they failed to give due attention to consciousness and "will" (Rousseau 1762b/1979: 176, 280).

Among Enlightenment thinkers, it was this romanticized view of human existence and human nature – which stood in stark contrast to the fundamentally pessimistic view of human nature that characterized British empiricism – that caused Rousseau to become the foremost advocate of social reorganization based on abstract understandings of freedom and liberty, Rousseau (1762a/1950: 1) famously beginning his best known work, *The Social Contract*, with the declaration that "Man is born free, and he is everywhere in chains." Although Rousseau's maxim inspired both the American Declaration of Independence and the French Declaration of the Rights of Man and the Citizen, it was his emphasis on freedom as an abstraction – rather than being the product of historical and constitutional circumstance as Burke suggested – that led Rousseau's thinking in the direction of dangerous generalizations and universal principles. Basing his thinking on the optimistic belief that "the people" as a whole "is never corrupted," Rousseau (1762a/1950: 18-19, 26) then deduced that the "general will," acting as "sovereign" through "the free vote of the people, 'is always right.'" From this point, Rousseau's radically democratic ideas led toward distinctly totalitarian conclusions. Not only did Rousseau (1762a/1950: 33) argue that the "sovereign," being "always right," must always be the "sole judge of what is important," it was also the case that "every malefactor, by attacking social rights, becomes a rebel, a traitor to his country." The totalitarian consequences of this line of thinking quickly became evident during the French revolutionary terror of 1793–1794, when passionate followers of Rousseau – each believing themselves to be the chosen agent of the "general will" – were found in the front ranks of both revolutionary leaders (notably, Maximilien Robespierre and Louis Antoine de St Just) and counterrevolutionary assassins (notably, Charlotte Corday).

If the violence of the French Revolution appeared to confirm the benefits of the methodological and conceptual caution advocated by the British empiricist tradition, it was also the case that adherents to this tradition typically produced research that had more than a passing resemblance to Thucydides' *History of the Peloponnesian War*. War, politics, the role of political and organizational leaders, and the fortunes of political parties were its forte. The empirical tradition also proved well-suited to the task of recording shifting intellectual trends and their political and organizational impact. Those informed by the empiricist tradition have also seen short-term "events" – associated with particular individuals or circumstances – as the appropriate focus of their research endeavors (see, e.g., Elton 1967/1969: 22). By contrast, the empiricist tradition has shown less interest in the effects of long-term changes in economics, demography, and culture; domains that demand the aggregation of individual actions into statistical series that shift explanation from the individual or group to more impersonal factors. It is the inherent tendency of those within the empiricist or positivist tradition to focus on defined historical or organizational events that has caused its critics the greatest concern. In dismissing the study of "events" as reflective of interest in mere "surface disturbances, crests of foam that the tides of history carry on their strong backs," the French historian, Fernand Braudel (1946/1975: 21) went on to condemn those within the empiricist tradition for living among "jumbled facts" and for inhabiting a "delusive fantasy" in which their research saw them intellectually "consorting with princes" and other leaders (Braudel, 1950/1980: 11). The perpetual problem with such studies, which Braudel (1950/1980: 11) argued were myopic in their focus, was that they perpetually described a world "torn from its context."

In the history of post-Enlightenment scholarship, Karl Popper occupies a unique dual place at the apex of the empiricist tradition and as a perceptive critic of its shortcomings. Like Burke, whose thinking was shaped in large part by his observations of the violence that ensued from the pursuit of abstract ideals in the French Revolution, Popper's viewpoints were molded by his abhorrence of Nazi Germany and Stalinist Russia during the 1930s and 1940s – nations where the pursuit of ideological objectives also caused social catastrophe. Like earlier empiricists, Popper (1944a: 120) also advocated "piecemeal tinkering" with societal institutions rather than revolutionary transformation. Similarly, Popper sat clearly within the intellectual legacy of Hobbes, Locke, and Burke in believing that knowledge and social action had to be built upon a careful scrutiny of empirical evidence. As Popper (1944b: 100) explained it, the "indispensable" basis for action required the prior detection and analysis of "all those facts" relevant to the problem. Like Hume, Popper (1944a, b) declared fierce opposition to those who claimed a capacity to detect historical laws that predict future outcomes, famously condemning such thinking as "historicism." Despite such areas of agreement, there were, nevertheless, two areas were Popper broke from earlier empiricist or (what he preferred to call) positivist thought. First and most significantly, Popper (1935/2002: 12; 1959, xxii) rejected the empiricist opposition to abstract "metaphysics" and theory as well as the traditional empiricist reliance on "common sense" as the ultimate judge in all things. Instead, he argued "that the most important and most problems of epistemology must remain completely invisible to those who confine themselves to analyzing ordinary or commonsense knowledge." Instead, Popper emphasized the importance of theory formation and testing. It was only on this basis that Popper correctly observed that new conceptual understandings could occur. As Popper (1935/2002: 280) observed in *The Logic of Scientific Discovery*, "We do not stumble upon our experiences, nor do we let them flow over us like a stream. Rather, we have to 'make' our experiences…every step is guided by theory." Popper's second key departure from traditional empiricist thinking is found in his rejection of inductive logic (i.e., the drawing of theses or generalizable laws from observation and evidence). In Popper's (1935/2002: 6, 25) view, the problems of "inductive logic" were "insurmountable" due to the fact that the conclusions drawn solely from this method of reasoning could never be definitively verified or disproved. The rationale behind Popper's reasoning can be discerned if, for example, we consider the statement that "Charismatic leaders have the capacity to inspire followers to take action without thought for material reward." The problem with such statements is that the relationship between evidence and thesis tends to be circular. In other words, we only look to studies of "charismatic" leaders for proof of the statements, which will of course confirm the statement. Conversely, if the evidence suggests that the leader cannot inspire without recourse to material rewards we do not reject the statement but instead conclude that the leader is "transactional" rather than "charismatic."

In rejecting "the method of induction," Popper (1935/2002: 11) conceded in his *The Logic of Scientific Discovery* that "it may be said, I deprive empirical science of what appears to be its most important characteristic." While Popper's conclusions have obtained something approaching semidivine status in academia that leads to uncritical acceptance of his maxims, there is nevertheless much truth in Popper's concession – a concession that points to a failing in not only his work but the empiricist tradition more widely. For the problem with relying solely on deductive logic and testing is that it is better suited to small matters (i.e., are consumers likely to spend more at Christmas time than at other times of the year) than bigger and more complex problems, a point which – as we noted in the introduction to this chapter – was well made by Max Weber in 1904. As anyone with a passing knowledge of Weber's work would be aware, Weber's solution to the methodological problem of applying inductive rather than deductive logic to research problems was to develop "ideal" types – typologies that captured none of the unique qualities of the particular individual or institution but which nevertheless revealed commonalities in how they related to the wider society. In dealing with the historical uniqueness of "charismatic" individuals, for example, Weber (1922/1978: 1113) found social meaning for this phenomenon in the fact that charismatic leadership is "the opposite, of bureaucracy…charisma is by nature not a continuous institution, but in its pure type the very opposite…In its pure form charisma is never a source of private income; it is neither utilized for the exchange of services nor is it exercised for pay." Such methodological solutions highlight the fact that research is not, as the empiricist tradition would like to believe, always amenable to definitive conclusions based on verifiable or refutable facts. More often than not the best we can hope to obtain in way of conclusions are mere probabilities or possibilities.

The Idealist Tradition

If the empiricist tradition has always made understanding of the objective world (i.e., the objects and beings that impact directly on our senses) its central focus, the idealist tradition has made the subjective world of consciousness, emotion, and individual being its primary concern – an emphasis which in the contemporary world has informed the burgeoning bodies of postmodernist thought.

As with the empiricist tradition, idealist philosophy and epistemology owe their foundational understandings to the ancient Greeks, among whom Plato's *The Republic* (c. 380 BC/2003) has proved particularly influential. Rather than understanding the world directly through our senses, Plato believed that we comprehend objective reality through the creation of abstract mental images in our imagination, and it is upon these images that we act. In drawing and then measuring the dimensions of a "circular" field, for example, we are dealing solely with abstractions – what Plato (c. 380 BC/2003: 232) called mental "forms" – that are an idealized substitution (or representation) for objective reality, it being the case that there are probably no "pure" circular shapes in nature. In other words, the concept of a "circle" does not exist naturally. It is a creation of our reason. Similarly, when a person walks into a room and sees a "bed" for example they do not create a separate mental category for that object. Rather it is perceived in its generalized "form," as simply another "bed." Only if there is a particular need (i.e., the person was intending to sleep in the bed), would the mind substitute more specific "forms" (i.e., "hard" bed, "soft" bed).

The key problem that Plato – and all subsequent idealist thinkers – faced was in ascertaining principles that enabled one to distinguish between mental "forms" that correspond to objective reality from those associated with mere illusions or fantasies. A key step in the process to true knowledge for Plato was therefore the discernment of the pathways through which one differentiated "truth" from what the Greeks called *eikasia* (illusion). In Plato's opinion, this could only be achieved by careful training, a process in which an educated elite obtained understandings that are beyond the capacity of ordinary folk. In *The Republic* (c. 380 BC/2003: 240–244), Plato explained the process of intellectual enlightenment through his famous "Simile of the Cave," which describes how prisoners chained underground come to mistake the shadows reflected on walls for reality. When one is freed and taken outside the cave, the escapee finds themselves "dazzled by the glare." Only through a painful period of adjustment does the escaped prisoner finally "grow accustomed to the light." Plato (c. 380 BC/2003: 234–238) also saw knowledge as involving a series of steps toward full enlightenment as minds were trained to distinguish not only reality from illusion but also proper knowledge from mere opinion or belief. The problem with this solution for distinguishing reality from illusion was twofold. First, although Plato held that training and education enabled an eventual discernment of "knowledge," he never outlined clear principles by which reality and illusion could be distinguished. On the contrary, Plato (c. 380 BC/2003: 239) held that "the real objects" of any "investigation" must always remain "invisible except to the eye of reason." Thus in trying to distinguish reality from illusion, we can *never* refer back to reality itself but only to mental abstract "forms" and "representations." As Plato

(c. 380 BC/2003: 239) explained it, "The whole procedure involves nothing in the visible world, but moves solely from form to form, and finishes with forms." The second problem with Plato's thinking is that it led toward not only intellectual elitism but also totalitarianism. Believing that only an elite could grasp "true reality" and thereby create a "just" world, Plato (c. 380 BC/2003: 236, 36, 248) also concluded that only this elite was fit to fill the role of "guardians of our state" for they alone were capable of understanding "the principles of good government."

In the medieval and early modern eras, with their emphasis on human spirit and individual being, idealist philosophy tended to be subsumed within the canons of religious thought. Even with the revival of secular strands of idealist philosophy, it remained the case that many of its proponents – most notably George Berkeley, Gottfried Leibniz, and Georg Hegel – sought to incorporate understandings of the divine into their thinking. However, where such thinkers differed from earlier scholastic traditions is that they relied solely on reason – rather than religious texts or authority – for their conclusions. Hegel (1837/1956: 30, 9), for example, while believing that God's hands shaped the course of history, also believed that "Reason is the Sovereign of the World," a fact that made human consciousness, spirit, and experience all subject to reasoned inquiry.

What unites all the strands of idealist philosophy is the belief that the interior world of consciousness and thought is far more important than the exterior world. This emphasis is found even in the work of Georg Hegel (1837/1956) who argued that freedom of spirit and consciousness could only be achieved through organized societies and states. In expressing the central idealist understanding, the French philosopher and mathematician, Rene Descartes (1641/1991: 1–31), concluded in his *Mediations on First Philosophy* that each human individual existed as "only a thinking thing." Not only was the human mind and thought different from the objective world in being "entirely indivisible," it was also the case that thought and emotion typically produced sharper images in the mind than direct sensory perceptions – an outcome that caused Descartes (1641/1991: 1–31; 1–19) to also consider the possibility that "all things" that relate to the external world "are nothing but dreams and chimeras." Consequently, it was therefore possible to either "persuade myself" that "nothing has ever existed" or a contrary position, i.e., the material world has and does exist (Descartes 1641/1991: 1–8).

In his *Critique of Pure Reason*, Immanuel Kant (1787/2007: 238–239) described Descartes' analysis as "problematic idealism" in that it subjected all evidence and all the sensations generated by our senses to the utmost skepticism – an approach Kant accepted as "a sound philosophic mode of thought" in that it questioned rather than categorically denied the nature of material existence. Subsequent to Descartes' conclusions, however, there emerged a far more radical and far-reaching form of idealist thought in the work of the English cleric, George Berkeley. Pushing idealist skepticism to its ultimate limits, Berkeley (1710/1996: 24), in his *Principles of Human Knowledge*, declared that the only thing we could be certain of was our own "ideas," ideas created by that "perceiving, active being" that "I call mind, spirit, soul, or myself." In consequence, "All things that exist, exist only in the mind, that is, they are purely nominal" (Berkeley 1710/1996: 38).

In the era of the European Enlightenment, other idealist philosophers came to conclusions which, although different from those of Berkeley, were also far removed from the principles that informed British empiricism and scientific inquiry more generally. In Germany, Gottfried Leibniz (1714/2017: 1–2, 7), for example, argued that all forms of existence are comprised of "monads," each sharing various levels of being and perception and each acting on other monads (forms of existence). As Leibniz (1714/2017: 11) explained, "basically there is the same thing in *all* living things and animals." Only in the human mind, however, did Leibniz believe that there existed an essence capable of both spiritual communication and abstract reasoning.

Where Berkeley and Leibniz advocated a form of idealism that was highly abstract and which held out little prospect that the human condition was amenable to understanding through generalizable laws, the nineteenth century German philosopher, Georg Hegel, held a contrary view. In Hegel's (1837/1956: 1, 5, 38) view, human history should be understood as "universal history" that sees humanity gradually advance from a primitive state toward increasing levels of intellectual and political "freedom." In Hegel's (1837/1956: 40–41) opinion, "freedom" does not exist in "nature" (i.e., in undeveloped economies and societies) but must instead be "sought out and won." In other words, the advance toward "freedom" is not something that individuals can achieve alone. Instead, it must be created through complex social organizations that provide systems of "constitutional" rights. As Hegel (1837/1956: 41) expressed it, "Society and the State are the very conditions in which Freedom is realized." In pursuing this search for "freedom," Hegel (1837/ 1956: 36) argued – in an understanding that distinguished his thinking from "materialist" thinkers such as Karl Marx – that human endeavors were unconsciously "carrying out" God's "plan." In other words, it was God's divine plan that was the glue that held human endeavors together, steering humanity toward ever more sophisticated forms of social organization and understandings. Accordingly, both individuals and societies were ultimately successful only to the extent that they fulfilled God's intention. Even history's "great" men – Alexander the Great, Luther, and Napoleon – were only successful to the extent that their actions corresponded, without their conscious knowledge – to "a concealed fount" that reflected the "universal" plan that God had decided upon before the beginning of time (Hegel 1837/1956: 30).

Hegel differed from other idealist thinkers not only in his belief that history was governed by "universal" principles but also in his approach to knowledge. Where other idealists were diametrically opposed to empiricist methodologies, questioning whether the material world was in fact real at all, Hegel embraced rational, empirical inquiry. Accordingly, Hegel (1837/1956: 2) argued that "legends," "ballads," and other forms of invented narrative needed to be put aside. Condemning those who put "subjective fantasies in the place of historical data," Hegel (1837/1956: 7, 10) went on to argue that researchers must always "proceed historically – empirically." Only through such rational inquiries was it possible to understand not only the process of history but also, ultimately, God's will. For,

Hegel (1837/1956: 11) concluded, "To him who looks upon the world rationally, the world in its turn presents a rational aspect."

Paradoxically, the significance of Hegel's brand of idealist thinking is found not in its contribution to idealist philosophy but also in the conceptual framework that it provided to the most materialist of all epistemologies: Marxism. For if one abandons the religious element that was at the core of Hegel's thinking, then the rest of it – the belief that history is a rational process, that it operates according to universal laws that can be ascertained through rational inquiry, and that research should proceed empirically through a careful scrutiny of evidence – can easily be transferred to a non-idealist framework. This is what Marx did, famously describing his work as "dialectical materialism," a step through which Marx (1873/1954: 19–20) "openly avowed" himself "the pupil of that mighty thinker" (i.e., Hegel). Praising Hegel for "being the first to present its [i.e., history's] general form of working in a comprehensive and conscious manner," Marx (1873/1954: 20) ruthlessly ransacked Hegel's postulations to suit his own revolutionary needs. Like Hegel, Marx (1873/1954: 20) saw humanity history advancing through a series of stages toward a "crowning point." Like Hegel, Marx (1873/1954: 20) believed this process was guided by a set of "universal" historical laws, Marx merely substituting economic forces for God's will. As with Hegel, Marx (1873/1954: 19) believed that careful rational inquiry enabled one to "trace out" the "inner connection" that guided humanity's economic and social development.

If Hegel's idealist thinking provided direct inspiration for Marxism, other forms of idealist philosophy provided conceptual frameworks which – in the course of the twentieth century – became part of the intellectual bedrock of postmodernism. Among these intellectual progenitors of postmodernism, there are two idealist philosophers who deserve special mention. The first of these is the Italian philosopher, Giambattista Vico, whose study, *The New Science*, provided inspiration for both Michel Foucault and – to an even greater degree – the American postmodernist, Hayden White. Completed in 1744, Vico's study paralleled Rousseau in arguing that the advance of civilization came at excessive cost to the human spirit. Prior to the numbing effects of civilisation, Vico (1744/1968: 118) ascertained that people possessed "vast imagination," an imagination that was "entirely immersed in the senses, buffeted by the passions." In this primeval state, humanity produced "sublime" poetic fables, of which Homer's the *Iliad* was "first in the order of merit" (Vico 1744/1968: 120). As civilization advanced, Vico (1744/1968: 128) argued, so "these vast imaginations shrank." All that was left were literary "tropes" and "metaphors" that provided a remnant existence of an older, more spiritual way of perceiving the world. Such "tropes" and "metaphors" were, therefore, not "ingenious inventions" of writers but were instead an inherited link to "the first poetic nations" (Vico 1744/1968: 131). By strengthening the role of "metaphor" in language we could, so Vico (1744/1968: 131) believed, recapture something of the "vast imagination" that civilization had stripped from us. In other words, what is important in research and writing is not things such as evidence, facts, and truth. Instead, what counts is the capacity of a given literature to inspire the spirit.

While Foucault (1969/1972: 158, 180) freely acknowledged the impact of Vico on his conceptualizations, it is through the work of Hayden White that Vico's thinking has had its most significant impact. All of Vico's key formulations were embraced by Hayden White, subsequently becoming a core component of the dominant strands of postmodernism in the Anglosphere (see, e.g., Durepos and Mills 2012). According to White (1973: x) and his intellectual heirs, the researcher who constructs a narrative should perceive their study not as a work of science but rather as "an essentially *poetic* act" [emphasis in original]. Moreover, as the purpose of such research is *primarily* inspirational, it must have as its main focus "felt needs and aspirations that are ultimately personal" (White 1973: 283), a suggestion that leads toward narratives built around personal experiences premised on racial, religious, sexual, and social identity. As, according to White (1998), fable and myth are the highest forms of representation, this not only justifies but necessitates academic "reconstructions" of a "fictive character." The benefit of this, White (1973: 371) concluded, is that it allows for the "erection" of an "illusionary world, outside the original world of pure power relationships," a world in which authors can initiate "a process in which the weak vies with the strong for the authority to determine how this second world will be characterized."

Vico's (and White's) emphasis on the capacity of a given literature to inspire – rather than its correspondence to what is factually real – found in the fullest expression in another idealist philosopher whose influence on postmodernism was to prove even more profound: Friedrich Nietzsche. Although we will return to a full discussion of Nietzsche later in this volume, it is nevertheless useful at this point to highlight both his main arguments and the ways in which they directly impinged on postmodernist canons. For what makes Nietzsche's thinking so significant – in addition to its influence on postmodernism – is its total and complete emphasis on individual will and consciousness to the exclusion of all else. Whereas previous idealist philosophers (Berkeley, Leibniz, Hegel) were influenced by religious belief, identifying human spirit with divine spirit, Nietzsche severed this nexus. As Nietzsche (1895/1990: 174–175) declared in *The Anti-Christ*, not only did his work recognize "no God," any religious reverence is condemned as "a crime against life." What counted instead was solely the capacity of ideas to inspire human will toward feats of purposeful endeavor through which they enforced their will over others. "Ultimately the point" of any writing was not whether it was based on falsehood and lies but rather "to what end a lie is told" (Nietzsche 1895/1990: 187). The idea that there are any economic or social laws, discernible to inquiry, was summarily dismissed by Nietzsche. To the extent that any "laws in history" were observable, these were declared to be "worth nothing" (Nietzsche 1874: 39). The "scientific person," who guided their research and actions on the basis of rational inquiry, was also discounted as a "chatterer," an "educated Philistine" (Nietzsche 1874: 42). Morality was also declared to be worthless, Nietzsche (1883/1970: 299) observing in *Thus Spoke Zarathustra* that "evil is man's best strength. Man must grow better and more evil." Having dismissed every concept and precept that prior philosophers had regarded as important – rationality, religion, historical purpose, discernible laws, evidence, and truth – Nietzsche left his readers with only one resource: their own consciousness and will. It was through this alone, Nietzsche argued, that human behavior and history were shaped.

Logic

When Copernicus published his *De Revolutionibus* in 1541, a publication that effectively launched the "scientific revolution," he was expressing insights gained from inductive logic. On the basis of observation of the inner planets and the stars, conducted without mechanical aids such as telescopes, Copernicus (1541/2008) concluded that existing explanations, which posited the earth at the center of the universe, were deficit and that observed behavior was better explained through a thesis that placed the sun at the center. In this Copernicus was only partially correct. For while he correctly believed that the planets orbited the sun, Copernicus (1541/2008: 24) also believed that beyond planets there existed a zone of "immovable stars." Not until the publication in 1610 of Galileo's *Sidereus Nuncius* (*The Starry Messenger*), based on physical observations conducted through a telescope, was the fallacy of Copernicus thesis regarding the behavior of stars revealed. In coming to his conclusions, however, based on the use of telescopes and deductive logic (i.e., the testing of a theory against evidence), Galileo benefited from having Copernicus's thesis as his point of departure – a thesis that was itself devised from empirical observation (i.e., inductive logic). Such outcomes suggest that inductive and deductive logic fulfill essentially complementary roles. But such outcomes also highlight the fundamentally different roles that inductive and deductive logic play in research. In essence, inductive logic leads toward the construction of theories based on generalizations from typically incomplete evidence – conclusions that are frequently found to be fully or partially fallacious by a wider examination of evidence. By contrast, deductive logic, by subjecting theses to empirical testing, plays an essentially constraining or limiting role, constantly revealing the limits of generalizable theories by emphasizing all of the contingent factors that are invariably associated with any set of causal relationships. It is this more cautious approach, better suited to "piecemeal tinkering," that caused Karl Popper to embrace deductive logic but abjure inductive logic, declaring that:

> . . .the study of society is fundamentally different from the study of nature. . .I do not believe in the 'method of generalisation', that is to say, that is to say, in the view that science begins with observations from which it derives its theories by some process of generalisation or induction. (Popper 1944a: 134–135)

The disputes over how we apply logic to the research problems before us are not unrelated to the other problem that we have highlighted in this chapter: How do we understand the world? In responding to this second question, it is easy to embrace a pure empiricist approach, accepting the view that we understand the world through a combination of sensory perception and the facility of "common sense." There is, however, also much merit in the idealist approach with its emphasis on consciousness and abstraction. As Plato (c. 380 BC/2003: 336–339) correctly pointed out almost two and a half thousand years ago, abstractions – or what he called "forms" or "representations" – are essential to our understandings. It is in the nature of the human condition that we constantly move from experience to generalization and theory, using concepts that have meaning for us but which do not exist in the world of direct sensory perception – concepts such as markets, supply, demand, freedom, efficiency, etc.

The basis of human knowledge, in business and management as in any other field, is thus dependent in the first instance on how we balance the conflicting merits of empiricist and idealist thought and of inductive and deductive logic. That this debate has been going on not only for centuries but for millennia indicates that there is no definitive answer to this problem. Each of us must find our own solution to this quandary. It is the author's opinion, however, that the best synthesization is found in the work of the German philosopher from the Age of Enlightenment, Immanuel Kant. Admittedly, despite Kant's preeminent place among the pantheon of philosophic thinkers, the utility of his work has been curtailed by his complex and opaque writing style, Kant (1787/2007: xviii) accurately observing in relation to his most important work, his *Critique of Pure Reason*, that "This work can never be made suitable for popular use."

Despite their complexity, Kant's theorems can arguably be reduced to a small number of propositions. A number of these – including the belief that we experience reality not as corporeal entities, as "things in themselves," but rather as "the mere play of representations" (Kant 1787/2007: 130–131); that understanding of the material world is generated through the effect of "sensible intuition" on the mind (Kant 1787/2007: 142–143); and that our "imagination" has the capacity to generate "representations" that do not exist in the real world, i.e., a perfect circle (Kant 1787/ 2007: 149) – differ little from theorems found in Plato's *The Republic*. With his other key understandings, however, Kant decisively broke with idealist canon, holding that reality "is something" and that, even if perceptions of it come to us as "only outer appearances," objective reality nevertheless exists "actually in time and space" (Kant 1787/2007: 283, 332, 348). In other words, the fact that I experience reality through images created in my imagination – images that may vary according to whether it is light or dark – does not mean it is any less real. Accordingly, Kant (1787/2007: 291) placed in the hands of human reason a capacity to judge the validity of the "concepts" generated by our senses and imagination. Thus, for example, if my senses – as an Australian living in the Southern Hemisphere – generate the concept in my understanding that the sun must always appear in the sky's northern quadrant, my reason can dismiss this concept on the basis of not only my travels to the Northern Hemisphere but also on the basis of what I have read about astronomy. In emphasizing the power of reason to distinguish between reality and "fancy," Kant (1787/2007: 212) also put forward his "law of causality," a law which was based on what he referred to as the "principle of succession in time." This held – in contradiction to Hobbes' law that the "knowledge of consequences" is based on understanding the "dependence of one *fact* upon another" (Hobbes 1651/ 2002: 38) – that laws explaining both the natural and social worlds can be ascertained by tracing the *sequence* of events. In other words, B can only explain the occurrence of A if it came before it. Collectively, Kant (1787/2007: xiv) argued, his formulations would allow humans a capacity to explain outcomes through the formulation of the various laws "which reason...seeks and requires." In other words, it is our reason that allows us to draw generalizations from experience, generalizations that become the basis for testable theories (Kant 1788/2002: 29).

In his *Logic of Discovery*, Popper (1935/2002: 38) also linked knowledge with theory rather than simply observed experience, accurately observing that "The empirical sciences are systems of theories," not mere collections of facts. Significantly, Popper (1935/2002: 29–31), in taking this stance, like Kant before him, decisively rejected a pure empiricist or positivist approach, noting that "facts" only obtain their meaning from the intellectual and social context within which they are placed. However, in attempting to strike a balance between the claims of empiricist epistemologies (with their emphasis on experience) and idealist philosophies (with their emphasis on human consciousness and will), Popper also – as we have noted on numerous occasions throughout this chapter – rejected the use of inductive logic. In taking this stance, it is evident that Popper was fearful that the continued embrace of inductive logic would lead people – as it had with Marxists – to sweeping generalizations and what he referred to as "historicism," i.e., the belief that societal outcomes are determined by historical factors that are beyond the scope of human choice. While Popper's reasoning is – given the time and place in which it occurred – understandable, it is also nevertheless unduly constraining on two counts. First, as noted previously, it restricts our capacity to come to generalizable conclusions (i.e., theories) on the basis of observed evidence. Second, it restricts the field of our inquiries.

Among those who have considered the epistemological foundations of our understandings, it is arguably Max Weber who most succinctly makes the case for a continued embrace of inductive logic alongside deductive logic. In countering the proposal that "the attempt to formulate laws" has "no scientific justification in the cultural sciences," Weber (1922/1978: 79, 87) declared that "the construction of a system of abstract and therefore purely formal propositions analogous to those of the exact natural sciences, is the only means of analysing and intellectually mastering the complexity of social life." Significantly, Weber did *not* believe that theoretical generalization allowed for universal laws that were applicable to all circumstances in time and place. Indeed, virtually all of Popper's subsequent objections to "historicisms" are evident in Weber's (1904/1949: 86) dismissal of what he referred to as "naturalistic dogma" (which he primarily associated with Marxism) – a term which Popper subsequently also used interchangeably with "historicism." However, unlike Popper, Weber concluded – accurately in this author's opinion – that we can only *begin* to make sense of the world through inductive logic, through generalizations based upon observations. The fact that we develop "ideal types" on the basis of such generalizations – i.e., a market economy, a liberal democracy, a charismatic leader, an efficient producer, etc. – does not necessarily entail a denial of individuality or of contingent circumstances. For, as Weber (1904/1949: 86) correctly concluded, "the unique individual character" of any phenomenon – be it human or organizational – is found in the degree to which it diverges from the average or the typical. We can, in short, only understand the particular in relation to the general.

Conclusion

In his *Critique Practical Reason,* Kant (1788/2002: 29, 43) noted that the key task of epistemology (i.e., the theory of knowledge) is to ascertain generalizable principles or "laws" that help us explain the human condition while at the same time allowing scope for the "autonomy of the will" (i.e., the capacity of individual or group action to reshape their environment). A seemingly easy task, the solution to his balancing act remains elusive. Broadly, opinion has divided along two lines. One fissure has seen empiricist or positivist thinkers, who emphasize the value of sensory perception and experience, aligned against idealist modes of thought which highlight the value of consciousness, individual will, and abstraction. Another divide sees proponents of inductive logic (Kant, Weber, etc.) argue along different lines to those who emphasize reliance on deductive logic (most notably, Karl Popper). For whose occupying one or other of the polar extremes in these epistemological debates, the issues at stake are typically portrayed in deceptively simple terms. In the opinion of Hobbes (1651/2002: 38), who effectively founded the modern empiricist tradition, "knowledge of fact" comes from "sense and memory," whereas "science" is based upon the "knowledge of consequences." To get from the former to the latter requires no more than an understanding of "the dependence of one fact upon another." Conversely, at the idealist pole, an extreme skepticism suggests that there is no objective reality at all and that all we can instead by sure of is – as Berkeley (1710/1996) argued – our own consciousness. In the contemporary world, this extreme idealist skepticism finds expression in the various strands of postmodernism. According to the prominent US postmodernist, Hayden White (1980: 10), for example, "the very distinction between real and imaginary events" is one that needs to be dismissed. Far from being something that reflects objectively real experiences, "history," according to White (2005: 333), "is a place of fantasy." Nor can we discern causal relationships. As Keith Jenkins (1997: 10) advised in a much cited study, "in postmodern terms, nothing connects."

As with many things, this chapter argues that the best solution when confronted with the epistemological divisions that characterize research endeavors is to follow a middle path. To restrict ourselves, as the unadulterated empiricist or positivist tradition would have us do, to the world of experience and sensory perception is to deny ourselves the full use of our imagination, of abstraction, and of theoretical exploration. As Popper (1959: xxii) indicated, the point of research is not simply to add fact upon fact but rather "to contribute to the advance of knowledge – scientific knowledge, that is." Such an objective can only be achieved if we embrace theory, which in turn means an embrace of abstract concepts and understandings. In embracing abstraction, however, there is no need to abandon the belief that abstraction and theory should be based or drawn from empirical evidence. Nor,

14 Intellectual Enlightenment: The Epistemological Foundations of... 343

in accepting the view that we perceive the world through "forms" or "representations" – caused by the play of sensory perceptions on our imagination – do we need to abandon belief in the existence of objectively real conditions and experiences, as idealist and postmodernist philosophy would have us do. For, as Kant (1787/2007: 283, 348) indicated, "Reality is something." Nor should we abandon, as Popper would have us do, the use of inductive logic for fear that it will lead into destructive and grandiose conclusions. For in exploring the human condition, we need all the tools that we can muster. As Poincare (1902/1905: 167) correctly noted, "Every generalisation is a hypothesis." If, as occurred with Copernicus theorems relating to the nature of the solar system, many of our hypotheses are proven by subsequent scrutiny and testing to be in error, then we should rejoice. For, as Poincare (1902/1905: 168) concluded, "If it is not verified, it is because there is something unexpected about it, because we are on the point of finding something unknown or new."

References

Berkeley G (1710/1996) The principles of human knowledge. In: Berkeley G, Robinson H (eds) Principles of human knowledge and three dialogues. Oxford University Press, Oxford, pp 1–96

Braudel F (1946/1975) The Mediterranean and the Mediterranean in the age of Philip II, vol 1. Harper Torchbooks, New York

Braudel F (1950/1980) The situation in history in 1950. In: Braudel F (ed) On history. Chicago University Press, Chicago, pp 6–22

Burke E (1757/1823) A philosophical inquiry into the origin of our ideas of the sublime and the beautiful. Thomas McLean, London. https://archive.org/details/philosophicalinq00burk. Accessed 1 Feb 2018

Burke E (1790/2017) Reflections on the revolution in France. Jonathan Bennett, Early Modern Texts. http://www.earlymoderntexts.com/assets/pdfs/burke1790part1.pdf. Accessed 30 Jan 2018

Copernicus (1541/2008) De Revolutionibus (On the revolutions). http://www.geo.utexas.edu/courses/302d/Fall_2011/Full%20text%20-%20Nicholas%20Copernicus,%20_De%20Revolutionibus%20(On%20the%20Revolutions),_%201.pdf. Accessed 30 Jan 2018

Descartes D (1641/1991) Meditations on first philosophy. Internet encyclopedia. http://selfpace.uconn.edu/class/percep/DescartesMeditations.pdf. Accessed 2 Feb 2018

Durepos GAT, Mills AJ (2012) Anti-history: theorizing the past, history, and historiography in management and organization studies. Information Age Publishing, Charlotte

Elton GR (1967/1969) The practice of history. Collins Fontana, Sydney

Foucault M (1969/1972) The archaeology of knowledge. Pantheon Books, New York

Hegel G (1837/1956) Lectures on the philosophy of history. Dover Publications, New York

Hobbes T (1629/1839) Translation of Thucydides' history of the Peloponnesian war. In: Hobbes T, Sir William Molesworth (eds) The English works of Thomas Hobbes, vol 8. Online Library of Liberty. http://oll.libertyfund.org/titles/thucydides-the-english-works-vol-viii-the-peloponnesian-war-part-i. Accessed 30 Jan 2018

Hobbes T (1651/2002) Leviathan. Broadway Press, Peterborough

Hume D (1738a) Treatise on human nature, vol 3. Clarendon Press, Oxford

Hume D (1738b) Treatise on human nature, vol 2. Clarendon Press, Oxford

Jenkins K (1997) Introduction: on being open about our closures. In: Jenkins K (ed) The postmodern history reader. Routledge, London/New York, pp 1–30

Kant I (1787/2007) Critique of pure reason. Penguin Classics, London

Kant I (1788/2002) Critique of practical reason. Hackett Publishing Company, Indianapolis

Leibniz GW (1714/2017) The principles of philosophy known as monadology. file://staff.ad. griffith.edu.au/ud/fr/s361170/Documents/Palgrave%20Macmillan%20book%20series/Founda tions/New%20Chap%201%20-%20F/leibniz1714b.pdf

Locke J (1689/1823) Two treatises of government. McMaster archive of the history of economic thought, Toronto. https://socialsciences.mcmaster.ca/econ/ugcm/3ll3/locke/government.pdf. Accessed 17 Jan 2018

Locke EA (2002) Preface: modernism, postmodernism, management and organization theory. Res Sociol Organ 21:ix–xi

Marx K (1873/1954) Afterword to the second German edition of the first volume of capital. In: Marx K (ed) Capital: a critical analysis of capitalist production, vol 1. Foreign Language Publishing House, Moscow, pp 12–20

Molesworth W (1839) Introduction. In: Hobbes T, Sir William Molesworth (eds) English works of Thomas Hobbs, vol. 8. Online Library of Liberty. http://oll.libertyfund.org/titles/hobbes-english-works-of-thomas-hobbes-11-vols. Accessed 30 Jan 2018

Nietzsche F (1874) On the use and abuse of history for life. http://la.utexas.edu/users/hcleaver/ 330T/350kPEENietzscheAbuseTableAll.pdf. Accessed 4 Feb 2018

Nietzsche F (1883/1970) Thus spoke Zarathustra. Penguin Books, London

Nietzsche F (1895/1990) The Anti-Christ. In: Nietzsche H (ed) Twilight of the idols/the Anti-Christ. Penguin Classics, London

Plato (c. 380BC/2003) The Republic. Penguin Classics, London

Poincare H (1902/1905) Science and hypothesis. Walter Scott Publishing, New York

Pollard S (1965) The genesis of modern management: a study of the industrial revolution in great Britain. Edward Arnold, London

Popper K (1935/2002) The logic of scientific discovery. Routledge, London/New York

Popper K (1944a) The poverty of historicism, II. Economica 11(43):119–137

Popper K (1944b) The poverty of historicism, I. Economica 11(42):86–103

Popper K (1959) Preface to the first English edition. In: Popper K (1935/2002) The logic of scientific discovery. Routledge, London/New York, pp xviii–xxvii

Rousseau JJ (1762a) Emile: on education. Penguin Classics, London

Rousseau JJ (1762b) The social contract. In: Cole CDH (ed) The social contract and discourses. Dent & Sons, London, pp 1–141

Smith A (1776/1999) An inquiry into the nature and causes of the wealth of nations. Penguin Classics, London

Thucydides (c.411 BC/1975) History of the Peloponnesian war. Penguin Classics, London

Vico V (1744/1968) The new science, 3rd edn. Cornell University Press, Ithaca

Weber M (1904/1949) Objectivity in social science and social policy. In: Weber M (ed) The methodology of the social sciences. The Free Press, Glencoe, pp 50–112

Weber M (1922/1978) Economy and society, vol 2. University of California Press, Berkeley

White H (1973) Metahistory: the historical imagination in nineteenth century Europe. John Hopkins University Press, Baltimore

White H (1980) The value of narrativity in the representation of reality. Crit Inq 7(1):5–27

White H (1998) The historical text as literary artefact. In: Fay B, Pomper P, Van RT (eds) History and theory: contemporary readings. Blackwell Publishers, Oxford, pp 15–33

White H (2005) The public relevance of historical studies: a reply to Dirk Moses. Hist Theory 44 (3):333–338

Economic Foundations: Adam Smith and the Classical School of Economics

15

Bradley Bowden

Contents

Introduction 346
Value and the Foundations of Classical Economics 350
Society and Markets 356
Conclusion 363
Cross-References 363
References 364

Abstract

Although economic debates remain central to our world, they are wrapped in myth and misunderstanding. Many believe that Adam Smith provided the basis for classical economics through his exposition of the principle that outcomes are best decided through "the invisible hand of the market." In truth, Smith never used the term, instead associating the concept of an "invisible hand" with self-interest. Smith's ideas about self-interest were, moreover, derived from David Hume. Many of his ideas about value were obtained from the earlier work of Richard Cantillon. This chapter nevertheless argues that understanding of the foundational principles of classical economics – concepts associated with production as well as markets and exchange – remains central to our time. There is particular utility in understanding the nature of economic value and how it is created. For what is most revolutionary about the modern world is not its mechanisms for distribution and exchange but its systems of production; systems underpinned by the division of labor, the utilization of fixed capital, and the self-interested pursuit of occupational and firm advantage.

B. Bowden (✉)
Griffith Business School, Griffith University, Nathan, QLD, Australia
e-mail: b.bowden@griffith.edu.au

© The Author(s), under exclusive licence to Springer Nature Switzerland AG 2020   345
B. Bowden et al. (eds.), *The Palgrave Handbook of Management History*,
https://doi.org/10.1007/978-3-319-62114-2_20

346   B. Bowden

Keywords

Cantillon · Chandler · division of labor · Engels · Foucault · Friedman · Hayek ·
Hobbes · Hume · Keynes · Locke · Lyotard · markets · Marshall · Marx · Mill ·
Picketty · postmodernism · Quesney · Ricardo · Smith · value · White

Introduction

As a creature of both the Industrial Revolution and the European Enlightenment
(1680–1789), the modern world has been characterized by the harnessing of rationality and science to the cause of material progress. In the realm of technology, steam
power – which found its first usage in 1715 in the shape of huge, cumbersome
machines designed to pump water from coal mines – was gradually adapted to a
variety of more revolutionary uses: powered factory machinery, steam-powered
railways and ships, heating, and power generation. In the wake of this initial
technological breakthrough, others followed: telegraph, radio, electricity, computerization, etc. Managers, in harnessing the power of new technologies and more
efficient forms of work organization, also sought accurate estimates for their costs
at each stage of the production process. Yet, for all the obvious emphasis on science
and rationality, many of the seminal intellectual influences in the Age of Enlightenment – Thomas Hobbes, John Locke, David Hume, the Baron de Montesquieu
(Charles de Secondat), Francois-Marie Arouet (Voltaire), and Adam Smith – were
as much concerned with human irrationality, violence, passion, and emotion as they
were with rationality. In his *Leviathan*, a foundational text of the Enlightenment,
Hobbes (1651/2002: 40) argued that it was only the enforced order of society that
protected humanity from its own vices; whenever this enforced order was absent
than humanity lived in a "brutish manner." In France, Montesquieu (1748/1989: 5), in
his *The Spirit of the Laws*, similarly reflected that society was comprised of inherently
flawed individuals, each "subject to ignorance and error . . . to a thousand passions."

In Scotland, Hume (1739/1896: 241) devoted the second volume of his *A
Treatise on Human Nature* to "passions," observing that – unlike reason – "'tis
evident our passions" are "not susceptible" to rational "agreement or disagreement." Where others, however, associated passions and emotion with human evils,
Hume argued a contrary position. Identifying "self-interest" as humanity's preeminent emotion and concern, Hume (1739/1896: 266) concluded that, "Men being
naturally selfish, or endow'd with a confin'd generosity, they are not easily induc'd
to perform any action for the interest of strangers, except with a view to some
reciprocal advantage." It was, Hume (1739/1896: 267) further reflected, only as a
result of "this self-interested" reasoning that "commerce . . .begins to take place,
and to predominate in society." It was, in other words, from what others recognized
as a vice (self-interest) that needed to be restrained, that Hume identified a positive
motive force for economic and business organization. Subsequently, and more
famously, the idea of organizing business endeavor on the basis of self-interest
rather than economic regulation was taken up by Hume's close friend, Adam
Smith. Whereas Smith is best – and wrongly known – for his maxim about "the

15 Economic Foundations: Adam Smith and the Classical School of Economics

invisible hand of the market" (a term he never used), in fact Smith associated the concept of "an invisible hand" (not "the invisible hand") with self-interest, declaring in *The Wealth of Nations* (1776: Book IV, Chap. 2, para. 9) that, in directing "industry":

> *... in such a manner as its produce may be of the greatest value, he intends only his own gain, and he is in this, as in many other cases, led by an invisible hand to promote an end which was no part of his intention.*

In emphasizing the importance of "self-love" in determining economic outcomes in the opening chapters of *The Wealth of Nations*, Smith (1776: Book I, Chap. 2, para. 2) concluded that, "Nobody but a beggar chooses to depend chief upon the benevolence of his fellow-citizens ... It is not from the benevolence of the butcher, the brewer, or the baker that we expect our dinner, but from their regard to their own interest."

If an emphasis on self-interest led to a growing belief that economic outcomes were best decided by freely chosen market exchanges rather than government oversight, another eighteenth-century interest of political economy focused on what was to prove an increasingly divisive debate: the organization and management of production. At first blush, the question that drove this debate – "How is value created?" – appears innocuous. It was, nevertheless, a question that was to tear societies apart over the course of the nineteenth and twentieth centuries. Whereas some primarily attributed the creation of value to capital and management, others – who identified with Karl Marx's critiques of capital – believed these economic agents occupied as an essentially parasitic place in the production process, expropriating the hard-wrought economic value created by labor.

Although it was Adam Smith's views on value that were to prove most influential, in this – as with his formulations on self-interest – Smith built his insights on the work of others. In this domain it was to be the French *physiocrat*, Richard Cantillon, who provided the decisive impetus. Described (Rothbard 2006: 345) as the real "father of modern economics," Cantillon's (1755/2010) seminal work, *An Essay on Economic Theory*, was written in 1730 but – due to French censorship laws – not published until 1755, 11 years before Smith's *The Wealth of Nations* hit the printing presses. While it was obvious to Cantillon that the most dynamic part of the French economy was associated with commerce and industry, he nevertheless concluded (Cantillon 1755/2010: 22) that, "Land is the source or matter from which all wealth is drawn." In coming to this essentially feudal conclusion, Cantillon's thinking was guided by two accurate observations. First, Cantillon (1755/2010: 22) noted, human endeavor merely transforms into more useful objects the natural produce of the land, produce that takes the form of both a living bounty – "grass, roots, grain, flax, cotton" – and inanimate "minerals." Without this initial bounty, no wealth is possible. Second, he observed, the "labor" that transforms the land's abundance is itself dependent upon the land for its sustenance. This meant, in turn, that a nation's economic capacity was ultimately determined by its agricultural capacity, Cantillon (1755/2010: 62) calculating that the worth of a common object was equal to "double the product of the land used to maintain ... the work of the cheapest peasant or laborer," i.e., if a worker made an object in 1 day than it would be worth the landed produce the person consumed over two. As a society's productive capacity was, Cantillon (1755/2010: 63) believed, constrained by labor availability, it logically followed that it was agricultural efficiency that was the key element in wealth and value creation. The more that could be produced from an acre of land, the greater the supply of labor available and – consequently – output, value, and wealth.

Despite his flawed conclusions, Cantillon laid the groundwork for all who followed in his wake by linking three key concepts: value, labor, and efficiency. Abandoning Cantillon's attempts to link these concepts with landed production, Smith (1776: Book I, Chap. VII, para. 4, 7) drew a distinction between what he called the "natural price," which was determined by actual costs of production, and "market" price, which could "either be above, or below, or exactly the same with its natural price." Emphasizing this same point, Alfred Marshall (1920: 291), in his *Principles of Economics*, declared that "the shorter the period we are considering," the greater is "the influence of demand on value; and the longer the period, the more important will be the influence of the cost of production on value." Believing (Smith 1776: Book I, Chap. V, para. 17) that labor – rather than the value of the land's output – was "the only universal, as well as only accurate measure of value, or the only standard by which we can compare the values of different commodities at all times, and at all places" (i.e., the more labor expended in producing a good, the more expensive it is vis-à-vis other goods), Smith also accurately concluded that increased societal wealth must stem from a greater volume of outputs from each given unit of labor. It was on this point that Smith (1776: Book I, Chap. I, para. 1) famously began *The Wealth of Nations* by observing, "The greatest improvement in the productive powers of labour, and the greater part of the skill, dexterity, and judgement with which it is anywhere directed, or applied, seem to have been the effects of the division of labour." Although it has been argued (Magnusson 2009: 2–3) that Smith's ideas are of limited utility as they stemmed from a "proto-industrialized" society and line of thinking based on handicraft production rather than technological innovation, in truth Smith's logic was revolutionary precisely because he was the first to grasp the transformative effect of investment in machinery and other forms of fixed capital. Emphasizing this point, Smith (1776: Book I, Chap. I, para. 5) argued in *The Wealth of Nations* that the "division of labor" had become the principal driver of increased productivity and wealth precisely because of its association with "the invention of a great number of machines which facilitate and abridge labour, and enable one man to do the work of many."

Whereas Smith and his intellectual heirs (David Ricardo, John Stuart Mill, Alfred Marshall, Friedrich Hayek, Milton Friedman) identified societal advance with self-interest, market exchanges, and labor and firm specialization, Karl Marx and his intellectual and political heirs had very different understandings of the relationships between value, output, and labor. Whereas Smith (1776: Book 1, Chap. 5, para. 6–12) saw labor as the only universal *measure* of value, and but one component in the *creation* of value – alongside "rent," the worth of the "stock" or capital consumed in production, and the "profit" which represented the employer's "deduction" for venturing their time and capital – Marx (1867/1954) saw labor as the *only* source of value. Everything

15 Economic Foundations: Adam Smith and the Classical School of Economics 349

else – profit, the money saved from the production process that was reinvested in more fixed capital, a business's administrative costs – came from the extraction of an unremunerated surplus from labor, what Marx referred to as "surplus value." Under "the miserable character of this appropriation," Marx and his communist colleague, Frederick Engels (1848/1951: 45–46), proclaimed in *The Communist Manifesto*, "the labourer lives merely to increase capital, and is allowed to live only in so far as the interest of the ruling class requires it." Where Smith (1776: Book 1, Chap. 5, para. 8–9) saw an economy operating on the self-interested cooperation of capital and labor – the latter constantly needing an employer "to advance them the materials of their work, and their wages and maintenance till it can be completed" – Marx and Engels (1848/1951: 61) perceived nothing but "hostile antagonism" between the classes. Where Smith and his intellectual heirs saw a society based on market exchange, Marx and Engels (1848/1951: 50) argued that society was best served by the centralization of all "production in the hands of the state."

If over time the Marxist intellectual challenge to industrial capitalism and its associated systems of management has waned, many of the criticisms that Marxists once made have been taken up by postmodernists of various hues. With the "generalized computerization of society," the French postmodernist, Jean-Francois Lyotard (1979/1986: 47, 51) argued in his *The Postmodern Condition*, the capitalist focus on "development" has become an ever more "dehumanizing process". In his subsequent *The Inhuman*, where Lyotard (1988/1991: 67, 6) again suggested that humanity's "enjoyment" of the present was being constantly sacrificed in the name of "efficiency" and "development." Lyotard's postmodernist colleague, Michel Foucault (1976/1978: 140–141), painted an even bleaker picture of "the development of capitalism," suggesting its advance was associated with an unprecedented exploitation of "bio-power" – human sexuality and psychological identity – that involved "the controlled insertion of bodies into the machinery of production and the adjustment of the phenomenon of population to economic process." The result of this, Foucault (1976/1978: 145) continued, was new systems of "micro-power" engaged in "infinitesimal surveillances, permanent controls, extremely meticulous orderings of space, indeterminate medical or psychological examinations." Today, announced hostility to any analysis that emphasizes "markets" and "efficiency" is endemic among even business-school academics. In a highly influential article, Peter Clark and Mick Rowlinson (2004: 337), for example, suggest that analysis that highlights the benefits of "markets" and "efficiency" necessarily "mitigates against both historical and ethical considerations."

Almost 300 years after Cantillon first penned his *An Essay on Economic Theory*, it is evident that the debates about value, labor, and the efficient use of resources are arguably even more divisive now that they were at the dawn of the Industrial Revolution. Understanding and resolution of these debates are, moreover, not mere academic exercise. Over the last century, societies have risen and fallen over these issues (i.e., the Soviet Union). Revolutions and civil wars have been fought over them. Economic progress has advanced and faltered. Debates about value, labor, and efficiency remain, in short, seminal to the human condition.

Value and the Foundations of Classical Economics

In exploring the foundations of classical economics and its continuing impact, it is useful to remind ourselves of the material and intellectual conditions that existed at the dawn of the Industrial Revolution. In France, Britain, and, to a lesser degree, Prussia – Europe's leading economies – the intellectual dynamism of an urban elite was self-evident. In visiting Paris before the Revolution, the English agronomist, Arthur Young (1792/1909: 95–96), chanced to visit the residence of Antoine and Marie-Anne Lavoisier, observing the scientific laboratories in which they completed experiments into chemical structure, the generation and use of electricity, and the creation of vacuums. Across Europe, the writings of George Berkeley, David Hume, Voltaire, Jean-Jacques Rousseau, Montesquieu, Rene Descartes, Immanuel Kant, and Johann Goethe were laying the foundations of modern philosophic and political thought. Underpinning intellectual advance was a rising tide of wealth. Along the Atlantic seaboard, the ports of Britain and France were flooded with the imported produce of the Americas (sugar, coffee, tobacco, and cotton), creating in both countries a large commercial bourgeoisie of merchants, financiers, and insurers. According to Fernand Braudel (1986/1991: 553), the profits enjoyed by this class were extraordinary; a successful sea voyage – which traded European goods for slaves in West Africa and slaves for plantation produce in the Americas – typically delivered profits of between 50 and 80 percent. The intellectual effect of this commercial dynamism was noted by Voltaire (1733/2002: 36) in his *Letters on England* where he recorded that, "A trading nation ... grasps at every discovery."

If the dynamism that Voltaire described was very real, it was nevertheless equally true that beyond the wealthy circles of commerce – and the intellectual salons of London, Paris, and Berlin that proved Voltaire's natural abode – there existed a world of mass misery. Before the Industrial Revolution and its manufactured demand for a literate workforce, few could read or write. Reflecting on this circumstance and the condition of Paris's intellectual elite, Arthur Young (1792/1909: 24) – who recorded his observations in a subsequently published journal – observed that, "This society does like other societies – they meet, converse, offer premiums, and publish nonsense. This is not of much consequence, for the people, instead of reading their memoirs, are not able to read at all." Outside Paris, Young (1792/1909: 18) discovered that "the fields are scenes of pitiable management, as the houses are of misery." Throughout the countryside, Young continued, "girls and women, are without shoes or stockings." Although serfdom was no longer a feature of the French landscape, the peasantry were still subject to the *corvee*, a system of forced labor that obliged rural folk to spend up to 40 days a year building roads, digging ditches, replacing walls, etc. If the British rural populace was spared such obligations, the revolution in the island nation's agriculture brought about by the "enclosure movement" (i.e., the fencing of formerly common and wasteland and its use for commercialized farming) was nevertheless associated with the displacement of millions from the land. The Catholic Irish and the crofters of the Scottish Highlands were hardest hit. In describing a typical experience, Marx (1867/1954: 420–21) recounts how between 1814 and 1820 the 15,000 "Gaels" who lived in Scotland's Sutherland district "were systematically hunted and rooted out. All their villages were destroyed and burnt, all their fields turned into pasture." Everywhere the threats of bankruptcy, personal ruination, violence, riot, and mass social explosion were not too far away. Even glittering careers ended in condemnation and tragedy. In reflecting upon his time at the Lavoisier household in Paris, for example, Young (1792/1909: 95) recounted how he "was glad to find this gentleman splendidly lodged, and with every appearance of a man of considerable fortune." Much of Lavoisier's "considerable fortune," however, came from his shares in the *Ferme Générale*, a company that bought the right to "farm" French taxes. When with the Revolution all the leading figures in the *Ferme Générale* were placed under arrest, Lavoisier lost not only his fortune but his head, guillotined in early 1794 at the age of 50.

Caught between a dynamic world of commerce on one side and a world of mass misery and violence on the other, the founding figures of classical economics were dealing with more than abstractions. Rather, they were seeking a set of principles that would benefit the many rather than the few, a sense of purpose that is perhaps best captured by Smith (1776: Book 1, Chap. I, para. 10) in the opening paragraphs of *The Wealth of Nations*, where he observed that through "the great multiplication of the productions of all the different arts," it was possible "in a well-governed society" to achieve "that universal opulence which extends itself to the lowest ranks of the people." What concerned them was not the possession of wealth and its consumption, but rather the processes through which value was created. Reflecting this fundamental distinction, the French eighteenth-century economist, Francois Quesnay (1766: 1), began his influential *Tableau Economique* by observing that, "*La nation est. réduite à trois classes de citoyens: la classe productive, la classe des propriétaires et la classe sterile*" ("The nation is reduced to three classes of citizens: the productive class, the class of owners and the sterile class"). Ten years later, Smith (1776: Book II, Chap. III para. 1), in *The Wealth of Nations*, drew a similar distinction between "productive" and "unproductive" labor noting that, "There is one sort of labour which adds to the value of the subject upon which it is bestowed: there is another which has no effect." Wages spent on "menial servants" attracted Smith's particular attention, Smith (1776: Book II, Chap. III, para. 1) observing that the labor of such individuals "does not fix or realize itself in any particular subject or vendible commodity. His services generally perish in the very instant of their performance." In addition to servants, Smith (1776: Book II, Chap. III, para. 2) also excluded from his list of "productive" labor both "important" and "frivolous professions," notably: "churchmen, lawyers, physicians, men of letters of all kinds; players, buffoons, musicians, opera-singers, [and] opera-dancers." Although John Stuart Mill (1848/2002: 74) subsequently decided to count as productive those "officers of government" engaged in "affording the protection" of society and industry (i.e., police, armed force, judges, prison guards, etc.), the distinction between productive and unproductive labor retained its importance. Mill (1848/2002: 100–101) was particularly scornful of money spent on government, declaring: "Whenever capital is withdrawn from production ... to be lent to the State and expended unproductively, that whole sum is withheld from the labouring classes." Marx also drew a sharp distinction between productive and unproductive labor.

In Marx's analysis, the transformative potential of any capitalist society rested primarily in the "proletariat," a group that included only those who produced a "surplus value" that added to a society's productive capacity. In Marx's (1867/1954: 477) view, even a "schoolmaster" who "works like a horse" to make a profit for their employer is unproductive in that they fail to produce surplus value. Accordingly, "That labourer alone is productive, who produces surplus-value for the capitalist, and thus works for the self-expansion of capital."

Although the foundational texts in economics were united in drawing a distinction between "productive" and "unproductive" labor, they differed in their estimations as to what constituted "productive" work. In France, the nation's economists and *physiocrats* tended to the view that only farmwork created real value. Quesney (1766: 2), for example, defined "La classe sterile" (the sterile class) as comprising "tous les citoyens occupés à d'autres services et à d'autres travaux que ceux de l'agriculture" (all the citizens engaged in work other than those of agriculture). As we noted in the introduction to this chapter, Quesney's view corresponded to the earlier analysis of Cantillon, who saw land as the sole "source or matter from which all wealth is drawn." Smith, by contrast, concerned as was with the wealth-multiplying effects of the division of labor, saw productive work and value creation in much wider terms. In his estimation (Smith, 1776: Book II, Chap. III, para. 4), economic value came "either from the ground, or from the hands of productive labourers." Perhaps even more significantly, Smith (1776: Book II, Chap. III, para. 4) drew a fundamental distinction between *how* a society's annual wealth is distributed between immediate consumption and savings or "capital" directed toward future production. It was upon the size of the latter, rather than the former, that Smith believed a society's wealth rested.

Smith's differentiation between "wealth" and productive "capital" is a fundamental distinction that still eludes many. In his much-read *Capital in the Twenty-First Century*, Thomas Piketty (2012/2014: 1), for example, opened his book by stating, "The distribution of wealth is one of today's most widely discussed and controversial issues." Piketty (2012/2014: 48) then, however, immediately proceeded to conflate "wealth" with "capital," defining "'national wealth' or 'national capital' as the total value of everything owned by the residents and government," a definition that counted the value of residential real estate, currency in bank deposits, artwork, and the like as "capital." Piketty's conflation of capital, wealth, and landed property – a viewpoint that his French predecessors, Quesney and Cantillon, would have endorsed – ignores the fact (which Smith understood) that businesses and societies have to constantly decide whether to allocate money toward consumption, which adds to the immediate material "wealth" of its citizens, and "saving," production geared toward capital goods, or other forms of investment, which adds to future productive capacity. Accordingly, in measuring "wealth," the most common current measure is gross domestic product, which is an estimate of the value of goods and services produced over a particular period of time. By this measure, it is a society's *productive capacity* that determines its wealth and the wealth of its citizens, not the society's store of gold, silver, diamonds, and monetary currency. Accordingly, a house or apartment will only figure in gross domestic product in the year in which it

15 Economic Foundations: Adam Smith and the Classical School of Economics

is constructed, further appearances being restricted to the value attached to repairs or additions incurred in future years. Using gross domestic product as a measure of wealth, a prosperous society that witnessed the destruction of all of its houses, but none of its capital investment, would be considered to be still well-to-do. By comparison, a society that suffered the loss of all its capital, but none of its houses, would be regarded as destitute.

In the eighteenth and nineteenth centuries, the divisions relating to the nature of productive labor were also reflected in differing perceptions of value. Although all political economists well understood that the *exchangeable* value of a commodity varied according to market circumstances (i.e., variance in supply and demand, seasonal variations, government-imposed restrictions and taxes, etc.), they had conflicting views as to what determined a good's "intrinsic" value or "natural" price.

As with many things in economics, it is Smith's formulations regarding value that are typically regarded as the discipline's foundational understandings, Smith (1776: Book I, Chap. IV, para. 13) famously drawing the distinction between "use" value and "exchange" value through the analogy of water and diamonds. "Nothing is more useful than water," Smith (1776: Book I, Chap. IV, para. 13) observed, "but it will purchase scarce anything; scarce anything can be had in exchange for it. A diamond, on the contrary, has scarce any value in use; but a very great quantity of other goods may frequently be had in exchange for it." Although unacknowledged, it is clear that Smith's famed analogy owes – as with other things – a considerable debt to Cantillon, who in his *An Essay on Economic Theory* (1755/2010: 54) reflected how:

> The price for taking a jug of water from the Seine River is nothing, because there is an immense supply, which does not dry up. However, in the streets of Paris, people give a sol [a low denomination silver coin] for it, which is the price, or measure, for the labor of the water carrier.

In extending this analogy, Cantillon (1755/2010: 54) was also the first to explore in a systematic fashion the factors that determined "the intrinsic value of a thing;" an exploration that reflected his realization that prices must ultimately reflect production costs rather than market factors, i.e., a good cannot be consistently sold below the cost of production. In Cantillon's (1755/2010: 54) estimation, the "intrinsic" value or price for any given commodity is determined by "the quantity of land and of labor entering into its production, having regard to the fertility or productivity of the land, and to the quality of the labor." Drawing a clear distinction for the first time between "intrinsic value" and "market" price, Cantillon (1755/2010: 55) noted that "it often happens" that goods "are not sold in the market" according to their "intrinsic" value due to variations in "the desires and moods of men." Nevertheless, Cantillon (1755/2010: 55) suggested, "in well-ordered societies, the market prices ... do not vary much from the intrinsic value."

Having provided solid foundations for subsequent theorization through his differentiation of use and exchange value, and of "intrinsic" and "market" prices, Cantillon then proceeded to make a number of errors. First, Cantillon (1755/2010: 55) wrongly believed that, "There is never variation in the intrinsic value of things," an estimation which, if true, would have ruled out the constant reduction in prices – and hence increased material wealth – that characterize modern market economies. Cantillon's second critical error, which was the cause of the first, was to believe that *all* economic value is ultimately determined by landed output (i.e., farm produce and minerals). In explaining his reasoning, Cantillon (1755/2010: 56) argued that as labor was the only element that factored in the creation of value other than land, "and as those who work must subsist on the production of the land, it seems that some par value or ratio between labor and production of the land might be found." As we noted in the introduction to this chapter, Cantillon (1755/2010: 62) calculated that the intrinsic value of a commodity was worth twice the value of the landed output consumed by the worker who made the object during the period of production, i.e., if I manufacture a chair over 2 days, then the chair is worth the landed output I consumed over 4 days.

Cantillon's conflation of "value" and "landed" output reflected not only the overwhelmingly rural nature of the French society within which Cantillon operated but also the slow progress of industrialization in France vis-à-vis Britain, a hesitancy that was to stymie not only France's economic advancement but also the intellectual, scientific, and technological ascendancy that France superficially appeared to have secured during the eighteenth century. In explaining France's inability to match the pace of Britain's industrial progress, Braudel (1986/1991) traces the root cause back to energy shortages. "The problem, not to say tragedy," Braudel (1986/1991: 523) concluded, "was that there were not enough French coalmines, and those there were proved difficult and costly to operate. The mining areas were far away from the consumers." Forced to rely on wood for heating and charcoal long after British consumers had switched to coal, France confronted immense difficulties when it sought to adopt steam-powered technologies. Consequently, when machinery was introduced into Paris's cotton-spinning industry in the early 1800s, the factories were forced to rely on horses – not steam engines – for their motive power. As late as 1857, barely a third of France's cotton mills were steam powered, most relying instead on age-old water-driven technologies (Braudel 1986/1991: 520–521).

If in Cantillon's hands, the concept of value, by being linked to landed production, was trapped within a static formulation. Smith's genius lays in creating from this a dynamic theory. To begin with, Smith (Book I, Chap. VII, para. 7) adopted Cantillon's differentiation between "market" prices and intrinsic value, or what Smith referred to as "natural price," which could "either be above, or below, or exactly the same" as its market price. In turning to the determining factors in a good's "natural price," however, Smith rejected Cantillon's association of value with landed output, choosing (Smith Book II, Chap. VII, para. 3–7) sensibly decided to calculate a good's "natural price" according to the *monetary* value of its cost; costs consolidated under three headings: rent, wages, and "stock" (fixed capital). When a good sold for an amount equal to these costs – what Smith (Book I, Chap. VII, para. 5) called its "prime cost" – Smith (Book I, Chap. VII, para. 4) concluded that it "then sold for what may be called its natural price." As the disciplines of cost and management accounting emerged during the nineteenth century, Smith's theorem laid the basis for what is referred to as the "costs attach" concept of value, i.e., the value of a good or service is the total sum of the costs expended in its creation. Significantly, Smith did not include the "profits" of the entrepreneur either as a "prime cost" or as an item in its "natural price," merely counting instead a sum equal to the replacement cost of the "stock" consumed by the production process. Moreover, in exploring how the self-interested drive for profits underpinned the expansion of economic activity, Smith (1776: Book I, Chap. X, Part 1, para. 26) observed that the profit motive was typically driven as much by irrational greed as rational calculation, noting how, "The chance of gain is by every man more or less over-valued, and the chance of loss is by most men under-valued." As a general rule, however, Smith (1776: Book I, Chap. X) associated the size of the profit obtained relative to the sum ventured to be dependent on two things: the degree of risk and the demand for the objects produced with the entrepreneur's capital. The biggest profits and the larger losses were, Smith (1776: Book I, Chap. X, para. 44) calculated, invariably associated with newly created industries where demand and costs were poorly understood. Inherently speculative in the first instance, any profits above the norm – so Smith (1776: Book I, Chap. X, para. 44) argued – were soon curtailed as "competition reduces them to the level of other trades."

Smith's understanding of value, adapted as they were from Cantillon, has permeated not only economics but also almost all aspects of management and public policy. Where Cantillon (1755/2010: 55) in expressing the view that "There is never variation in the intrinsic value of things" reflected an essentially feudal view of wealth – where *retaining* value is all important – those who followed in Smith's intellectual footsteps understood that increased societal wealth was associated with *reductions* in value, i.e., we can consume more objects as they become cheaper relative to our income. In comprehending the drivers of this simultaneous *reduction* in value and *creation* of wealth, it is critically important that we understand – as Smith evidently did – that we are *not* primarily talking about changes in "market" prices but rather falls in the "natural" prices of things. For whereas with regard to the former we are principally talking about short-term variations in price given *current* levels of production and demand, in relation to the latter we are paying regard to permanent falls in production prices due to improved technologies and/or systems of work. Among Smith's intellectual heirs, this point was best made by Alfred Marshall (1920: 314–315), who drew a distinction between not only "market prices" and "normal prices" (what Smith called "natural prices") but also "secular prices," the latter being determined by long-term changes in knowledge and/or productive capacity, i.e., computer prices have fallen precipitously due to the revolutionizing of silicon memory chips.

Among political economists, only Marx has put forward a far-reaching counter to the understandings of value that Smith pioneered. In essence, Marx took Smith's (1776: Book I, Chap. V, para. 17) formulation that labor is "the only accurate measure of value," to an extreme if logical conclusion: economic value *only* comes from the "surplus value" created by manual workers in agriculture, mining, and, above all, manufacturing. As Marx (1867/1954: 313) explained in *Capital*, "The directing motive, the end and aim of capitalist production, is to extract the greatest amount of surplus-value." For Marx, surplus value was the wealth created by a worker that exceeded the sum necessary for their bare family subsistence. To get around the contribution of machinery and other "stock," Marx (1867/1954: 57) declared that all "fixed capital" was "congealed" labor. According to this formula, if a worker labored for a month for a subsistence wage of $400 to produce a good whose "relative" value (i.e., its value measured in terms of either money or some other comparative form) was $1000, but in that month the machinery the worker used cost $200 (in terms of wear and tear and consumables such as oil), then the "surplus value" extracted from the worker is $400. By so reducing everything to labor costs, Marx created a theoretical model that was of greater use as a political weapon against capitalism than as a framework for understanding how a business operated. For in Marx's analysis, the key driver of capitalist expansion is the industrial working class, the proletariat: not the entrepreneur.

The fundamental problem with Marx's critique is that it focuses on the problem of value *creation*, just as Cantillon's model focused on the retention or permanence of value. What both frameworks willfully overlooked was that the key to capitalist production is – as noted above – the constant *reduction* in the value of the objects being produced. For what makes modern industrial capitalism such a revolutionary force is not the constant alteration in "market" prices but rather the continual declines in the underlying "natural" or "normal" price. As Schumpeter (1942/1975: 84) famously observed in his discussion of "creative destruction," what is most revolutionary about capitalist production is its constant destruction of inefficient and outmoded producers. Accordingly, for existing producers, the most deadly form of competition is not textbook "market" competition, Schumpeter (1942/1975: 84) argued, but rather the competition that fundamentally alters the nature of production; competition "which strikes not at the margins of profits . . . but at their foundations."

Society and Markets

Typically, discussion of classical economics revolves mainly – or even solely – around markets. As we noted in the introduction to this chapter, however, the foundational understandings of markets in classical economics rested on even more fundamental debates relating to the nature of value, the essential character of human nature, and the appropriate form for the "well-governed society" which Smith (1776: Book 1, Chap. I, para. 10) identified as a prerequisite for economic expansion.

Prior to Smith, it was universally believed that security rather than liberty was the essential precondition for material advancement. Thomas Hobbes (1651/2002: 66), for example, in drawing up principles for a "covenant" or "contract" between rulers and ruled, argued that "security" was the key societal factor in securing the advancement of both "industry" and "knowledge." Whether this was achieved through an absolutist monarchy or a democracy was of no great interest to Hobbes as long as government had the capacity to enforce its will. For Hobbes (1651/2002: 85) concluded, "covenants without the sword are but words." A generation later, John Locke (1689/1823: 159) similarly observed in his *Two Treatises of Government*,

"The great and chief end ... of men uniting into commonwealth, and putting themselves under government, is the preservation of their property;" property constantly threatened in nature by sentiments of "passion and revenge." In France, Montesquieu, in his *The Spirit of the Laws*, also believed that a system of "civil laws" – enforced by state apparatuses – was a precondition for industry. For without such protections, Montesquieu (1748/1989: 290–292) concluded, people would be "very few" and constantly "prey to their enemies." Voltaire (1756/1963: 246–247) similarly held to the opinion that without a "powerful" state guided by law – created through "favourable circumstances over many centuries" – humanity was condemned to a "brutish state," scarcely able to "provide for their own needs."

As we noted in the introduction to this chapter, the emphasis on a strong state, guided by "civil laws" that protected citizens from arbitrary actions – with by state officials or their fellow citizens – reflected a fundamentally pessimistic view of human nature. Where humanity is unprotected from its own vices through a system of "government," Hobbes (1651/2002: 62) famously observed, life is inevitably "solitary, poor, nasty, brutish, and short." The necessity for a strong state was, however, even shared by Jean-Jacques Rousseau (1762/1950: 1), who differed from most other Enlightenment thinkers in having a far more optimistic view of human nature and who memorably began his *Social Contract* with the statement that, "Man is born free, and he is everywhere in chains." However, Rousseau (1762/1950: 18–19) believed that complete freedom can only exist in a "natural" world inhabited by noble "savages" and subject to nature's laws. In exchanging this rustic life for civilized existence, Rousseau (1762/1950: 28–29) contended, all of society's members must submit to the "absolute power" of the state's "sovereign will." Within such a civil society, Rousseau (1762/1950: 27) argued, any "partial society" of distinct interests must be avoided so as to avoid both discord and actions contrary to the "general will."

Into this debate about the appropriate political and economic frameworks for commercial and industrial advancement, guided by near unanimity as to the benefit of regulation, David Hume's (1739/1896) *A Treatise on Human Nature* represented a revolutionary departure. Whereas others perceived societal organization stemming from the need to impose restraints on human instincts and passions, Hume argued that it was primarily self-interest – not enforced laws – that acted as a society's primary glue. For Hume (1739/1896: 273) reasoned, not only is it the case that humanity is mainly "govern'd by [self] interest," it is also the case that the benefit of upholding a system of mutual social and economic exchange is "palpable and evident, even to the most rude and uncultivated of the human race."

With Smith and *The Wealth of Nations*, Hume's argument that self-interest was the main societal glue was transformed into the central explanation for economic exchange, an explanation that marginalized the proper role of the state in a "well-governed society." What underpinned a "civilized society," Smith (Book I, Chap. II, para. 2) argued, was not force but rather the fact that each individual "stands at all times in need of ... co-operation and assistance." In seeking the "cooperation" of their fellow, citizens Smith (Book I, Chap. II, para. 2) continued, "it is in vain for him to expect it from their benevolence only. He will be more likely to prevail if he can interest their self-love in his favour, and show them that it is for their own advantage." In terms of economic functioning, it was this "self-love" that underpinned what Smith (Book I, Chap. II, para. 1) suggested was a natural "propensity of human nature," namely, "the propensity to truck, barter, and exchange one thing for another." In Smith's view, this innate propensity had two key positive effects. First, it encouraged individuals and firms to specialize in those activities in which they had a competitive advantage, knowing that they could then exchange the product of their labor; an outcome that entrenched the specialized division of labor that was essential to economic efficiency. Second, Smith (Book I, Chap. V, para. 4) believed that it was through the propensity for exchange and the resultant "higgling and bargaining of the market" that an economy was able to determine what goods and services were required for production without state-mandated directions. As Smith (Book I, Chap. VII, para. 9) lucidly explained it, whenever "the quantity of any commodity ... falls short of the effective demand," so there occurs an increase in the "market price," thereby bringing more supply into the market. Once this additional supply reaches the market, prices will then return to more or less their "natural" price as equilibrium is restored. Taken up with gusto by subsequent economic studies in the early nineteenth century, most notably by David Ricardo (1817/1969) and John Stuart Mill, belief in the efficacy of market competition became a cornerstone of classical economics, Mill (1848/2002: 795) recording in his *Principles of Political Economy* that "every restriction" of competition "is an evil, and every extension of it ... is always an ultimate good."

As readers would be aware, it is Smith's conceptualizations regarding markets – rather than his ideas relating to value, price, labor specialization, human nature, and the nature of productive labor – that have had the most enduring legacy; a legacy that is, however, wrapped in myth and misunderstanding. Even such a noted authority as Alfred D. Chandler, Jr. (1977: 1), began his most influential study, *The Visible Hand: The Managerial Revolution in American Business*, by wrongly attributing to Smith the maxim that economic outcomes are best determined by "the invisible hand of market forces." For while it is evident that Smith *did* believe that self-interested market exchanges provided the most efficient way of balancing supply and demand, it is also apparent that he well understood that the "invisible hand" of self-interest constantly impeded such exchanges. At every point, as Smith discussed repeatedly in *The Wealth of Nations*, people conspire to subvert market forces so as to secure private gain. Anyone who imagined, Smith observed (Book I, Chap. VIII, para. 13), "that masters rarely combine, is as ignorant of the world as of the subject. Masters are always and everywhere in a sort of tacit, but constant and uniform combination ... We seldom, indeed, hear of this combination, because it is the usual, and one may say, the natural state of things." Smith (Book I, Chap. X, Part II, para. 23) also observed how townsfolk, "being collected into one place" and able to "easily combine together," conspired against country residents, charging them more for city manufacturers than what was conscionable. In addition, the "greater part of corporation laws," Smith cynically reflected (Book I, Chap. X, Part II, para. 23), existed for the purpose of "restraining that free competition" which, if allowed, would contribute to a reduction in prices.

Although he did not reflect upon the matter, it is evident that the division of labor also hinders the "perfect liberty" of the market that Smith favored. As firms become increasingly capitalized, the entrance of new suppliers into any given market becomes an increasingly complex affair; an outcome that often leaves established market participants with an oligopolistic stranglehold. With the increasing size of markets and firms – and the commensurate growth in the complexity of financing arrangements, supply chains, and purchasing contracts – the simple market exchanges that Smith, Ricardo, and Mill regarded with favor also become increasingly problematic. As the Nobel prize-winning economist, Oliver Williamson (1976: 8–9), noted in outlining the principles of "transaction cost economics," the uncertainties and opportunism of market exchanges create costs for a firm that are often higher than those that would have been suffered if they had been internalized. By internalizing market functions, firms can not only avoid price gouging by suppliers, they can also mitigate the effects of variations in seasonal supply. In a similar vein, Chandler (1977: 1) famously argued in his *The Visible Hand* – a work that redefined not only the discipline of business history but also our understandings of the historic role of the business corporation – that over time "the modern business enterprise" increasingly took over "functions hitherto carried out by the market," most particularly those relating to distribution and the coordinated flow of goods and services. In Chandler's (1977: 1) estimation, this historical change not only made "managers the most influential group of economic decision makers" in modern society, it also heralded the displacement of free-market capitalism by new forms of economic organization associated with what he called "managerial capitalism."

The tendency over time for firms to displace free-market exchanges with intra-firm mechanisms is indicated in Fig. 1.1 which is based on a World Bank (2017: 61, SF2.1) analysis of US custom's records since the global financial crisis of 2007–2008. In the period between 2010 and 2014, which was the period for which the World Bank had the most complete results, it was found that the rate of "intra-firm" imports grew 55.9 percent faster than that for what it referred to as "arm's length" imports, i.e., conventional purchase and sale through market mechanisms. Even when it came to exports, the World Bank (2017: 61, SF2.1) found that the pace of "intra-firm" exchanges is growing significantly faster than that for direct market

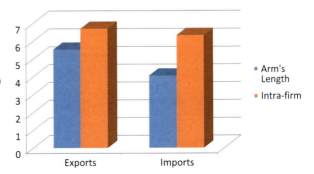

Fig. 1 Percentage growth in US "intra-firm" and "arm's length" trade, 2010–14 (Source: World Bank Group, *Global Economic Prospects, June 2017*, 61, Figure SF2.1)

dealings; a result that appears to reflect growing concern at the disruptive effects of changes in currency movements and other forms of trade and financial volatility.

In increasingly complex markets, where supply for a particular good or service is often dominated by a small number of firms, the idea that increased prices must necessarily lead to increased supply, and hence a return to lower prices, also proved problematic. As Keynes (1931: 393) noted in his critique of Friedrich Hayek's (1931) *Prices and Production* (which had defended the neoclassical belief in free markets), "a changing price-level merely *redistributes* purchasing power between those who are buying at the changed price-level and those who are selling." In other words, decreased supply and a higher price tend to increase the power of the seller rather than the buyer. It is, moreover, to the seller's benefit (if they have sufficient market control) to continue this situation, thereby recouping a higher return for the same costs of production, rather than in restoring price equilibrium through increased supply.

Chandler (1977: 1), in summing up the continuing role for markets in modern democratic societies, concluded that although the coordination of distribution and supply is increasingly done via intra-firm mechanism, it is nevertheless the case that the market remains "the generator of demand for goods and services." While there is considerable truth in this proposition, it is also an overly simplistic enunciation as to the relationship between managerial functions and market mechanisms. For while most of us, when we think of demand and supply, think of the direct provision of *consumer* demand, there is invariably an intermediate step between supply and demand: investment. For without investment, there can be no assured future supply. In looking at the place of investment in the economy, however, we are not primarily looking toward *current* demand as to *future* demand. In other words, firms invest to the extent to which they see future demand as being beyond the scope of the currently available resources. Despite this future focus, it is nevertheless also evident that "investment" creates its own current demand, not only for material goods but also for services and labor. In other words, "demand" comprises not only "consumer" demand but also the various forms of demand created by investment. Demand is also not, as classical economists assumed it was, totally elastic, able to consume to the fullest the fruits of industry and commerce. Rather, in the case of consumer demand at least, it is ultimately constrained – even where personal financial credit is obtainable – by income.

Now the economic constraints imposed by a society's deficient income have been long recognized. Arthur Young (1792/1909: 27), for example, in observing at first hand the condition of prerevolutionary France, concluded that the nation's principal economic failing was the "poverty" of the ordinary citizen; a poverty that struck "at the roots of national prosperity" by constraining the demand for goods and services. For Young (1792/1909: 27) accurately reflected, "a large consumption among the poor" is "of more consequence than among the rich." In classical economics, however, waged income is invariably counted as a business cost that is best reduced rather than as something that has a dual character: as both a business cost and a source of business demand and income. Accordingly, it is argued that any increase in wages must have a detrimental effect on profits and productive capacity. As David Ricardo (1817/1969: 76) expressed it in outlining his theory of a "wages fund" (i.e., the amount of money payable to wages at any given time is fixed and immutable and can only be temporarily increased at the expense of future economic capacity), higher wages "invariably affect the employers of labour by depriving them of their real profits." The problem with this still widely held view is that it fails to provide a mechanism to escape either a deflationary wage-price spiral (i.e., a situation where falling wages have an adverse effect on overall consumer demand) or the entrenched poverty that Young described in prerevolutionary France. It was on this point – rather than on the basis of a general hostility to classical economics – that John Maynard Keynes parted company with Smith and his intellectual successors. In Keynes (1936/1973: 293) view, the key to escaping a deflationary wage-price spiral and/or an entrenched deficit in demand is to focus not on consumer demand but rather on investment demand. By increasing investment, Keynes (1936/1973: 293) argued, an economy is able to not only increase its long-term capacity, it can also provide an immediate stimulus to wages, business activity, and demand. Although in his *The General Theory of Employment, Interest and Money* Keynes made few references to the role of government, it is nevertheless clear that he saw public policy as best fulfilling a role where it provided *incentives* and *mechanisms* that brought about increased *private-sector* activity. As Keynes (1936/1973: 129) explained in a famed, if somewhat flippant example:

> *If the Treasury were to fill old bottles with bank-notes, bury them at suitable depths in disused coal-mines ... and leave it to private enterprise on well-tried principles of **laissez-faire** to dig the notes up again (the right to do so being obtained, of course, by the tendering for leases of the note-bearing territory), there need be not more unemployment and ... the real income of the community, and its capital wealth also, would probably become a good deal greater.*

If there are evident deficiencies in the understandings of classical economics in relation to the operation of modern markets, this should nevertheless blind us to its continuing utility when it comes to not only the overall relationship between supply and demand but also its insights into value, the efficient use of labor, and the motive forces behind economic growth. The continuing relevance of classical economics to all aspects of business and management is perhaps best indicated in the assessment that Keynes – arguably the most perceptive critic of the genre – made in his *The General Theory of Employment, Interest and Money*. Pausing to highlight the continued veracity of the key insights that Smith first elucidated, Keynes (1936/1973: 379–380) argued that by allowing "the play" of the economic factors that Smith highlighted – "self-interest," "the exercise of personal choice," and the resultant "decentralization of decisions" – a society was ensuring not only economic "efficiency" but also "individualism." The lessons of the last 80 years provide confirmation of this assessment. For as the experiences of societies that have departed from the societal and economic model that both Smith and Keynes endorsed – a model built around choice, individual and business autonomy, critical inquiry, and innovation – mass tragedy has invariably ensued.

Whereas in the past the critics of classical economics, most particularly Marx and Keynes, were focused on the role of labor in the creation of value and on the importance of demand mechanisms in economic growth, the rise of postmodernism has been associated with critiques that challenge the very legitimacy of economics. With Michel Foucault (1976/1978: 7), the most influential of postmodern theorists, "the economic factor," the idea that business endeavor and wealth creation are core social objectives, is dismissed in favor of new "discourses," the initiation of challenges against power wherever it exists, the "overturning of global laws," and "the proclamation of a new day to come." Far from being a liberating force, modernity is depicted as entailing "new methods of power" and oppression, "methods that are employed on all levels and in forms that go beyond the state and its apparatus (Foucault 1976/1978: 89). Mere "obedience" is no longer enough. Instead, Foucault (1976/1978: 89) argued, a "normalization" of accepted values and power structures is demanded. In the work of the late Hayden White (1973: 1–2), arguably the most influential Foucauldian postmodernist in the English-speaking world, "the presumed superiority of modern, industrial society" is also dismissed as nothing but "a specifically Western prejudice." As we noted in the introduction to this chapter, hostility to economics is now endemic in business-school academia. In a much-cited article announcing the so-called historic turn in organizational studies, Clark and Rowlinson (2004: 337), for example, dismissed economic "models" as mere products of "a hierarchical set of fixed preferences." Postmodernists also announce hostility to the traditions of scientific inquiry upon which not only economics but Western intellectual endeavor in general has been built. Writing in *Business History*, Decker, Kipping, and Whadhwani (2015: 30–40) – where the former is co-editor – declare rejection of "the dominant science paradigm and its hypothesis-testing methodology." Elsewhere we are told by Novecivic, Jones, and Carraher (2015: 13) that management cannot be understood on the basis of "positivist factual truth-claims."

The postmodernist hostility to economic inquiry means that its critiques rarely if ever engage with those debates that were long central to Marxist and Social-Democratic intellectual traditions; traditions that asked a number of the same questions posed by Adam Smith and his successors, albeit in ways that led to different questions. In seeking answer to questions relating to the nature of economic value, for example, Marxists and Social-Democrats typically placed greater emphasis on the contribution of labor than capital. Similarly, in seeking answers to questions relating to productivity and wealth creation, Marxists and Social-Democrats tended to place greater emphasis on education and training than those schooled in the traditions of Adam Smith. What all shared, however, was that the worlds of work and wealth creation were not marginal issues for a society. Rather, they are the seminal concerns. As the global economy emerges from the Coivid-19 pandemic and its aftermath, it will be a global tragedy with devastating consequences if such issues are not once more given a central place.

Conclusion

It is unfortunate truth that even among management scholars and practitioners, a knowledge of the economic debates that have been seminal to humanity's progress over the last 250 years is becoming increasingly uncommon. One often hears people talk of Smith's "invisible hand of the market," even though Smith never used the term. When listening to exponents and opponents of "classical," "neoclassical," and "neoliberalism" talk about economics, we also find they are invariable referring to the veracity of "market" principles. Yet, as we have discussed, classical economics was always concerned with far more than markets. The nature of value, the components that contribute to its creation, the efficient organization and use of labor, and the calculation of profit were all central to its inquiries. Everyone who has followed in the footsteps of this intellectual tradition, including critics such as Karl Marx and John Maynard Keynes, has drawn on these conceptual tools to frame their thinking.

Typically, most researchers trace the foundations of classical economics back to Smith and *The Wealth of Nations*. As this chapter has indicated, such a course can only be undertaken with many caveats. For in estimating Smith's contribution to economics, as we have previously noted, Murray Rothbard (2006: 435) declares him to be "a shameless plagiarist, acknowledging little or nothing and stealing large chunks, for example, from Cantillon ... he originated nothing that was true." Certainly there is some truth to this point. Smith's understandings of "self-interest," which he saw as "an invisible hand" that guided human endeavor, were obtained from Hume. Smith's understandings of value were drawn in large part from Cantillon. Even the example he used in outlining the nature of "use value" (i.e., water) was an unacknowledged paraphrasing of Cantillon. The fact that Smith was as much a synthesizer of other people's ideas as an original exponent of his own concepts should not, however, cause us to devalue either his ideas or the foundational concepts of classical economics. What was particularly revolutionary about Smith's ideas was his linking of individual market choice, value, production, and the efficient use of labor through specialization and competitive advantage. Whereas Cantillon (1755/2010: 55), who believed that all value and wealth ultimately stemmed from the land, and perceived "intrinsic value" (i.e., the real economic value or worth of a commodity) as something that never varied, Smith demonstrated that wealth is created by *reducing* the value of things; an outcome that reflects the effects of machinery and specialization in causing objects to be produced with ever *less* labor. Accordingly, the foundational concepts of classical economists – by pointing to efficiencies in production as well as to the utility of market exchanges – proved no less revolutionary than the steam engine in underpinning material advancement. As such, they also remain central to our times.

Cross-References

▶ Chandler and the Visible Hand of Management
▶ Hayden White and His Influence
▶ Paul-Michel Foucault: Prophet and Paradox

References

Braudel F (1986/1991) The identity of France: people and production. Fontana Press, London

Cantillon R (1755/2010) An essay on economic theory. Ludwig von Mises Institute, Auburn

Chandler AD Jr (1977) The visible hand: the managerial revolution in American business. Belknap Press, Cambridge, MA

Clark P, Rowlinson M (2004) The treatment of history in organisation studies: towards an 'historic turn'? Bus Hist 46(3):331–352

de Montesquieu B (1748/1989) The spirit of the laws. Cambridge University Press, New York

Decker D, Kipping K, Whadwani RD (2015) New business histories! Plurality in business history research methods. Bus Hist 57(1):30–40

Foucault M (1969/1972) The archaeology of knowledge. Pantheon Books, New York

Foucault M (1976/1978) The history of sexuality – an introduction. Pantheon Books, New York

Hayek FA (1931) Prices and production. G. Routledge, London

Hobbes T (1651/2002) Leviathan. Broadway Press, Peterborough

Hume D (1739/1896) A treatise on human nature, vol 2. Clarendon Press, Oxford

Keynes JM (1931) The pure theory of money: a reply to Dr. Hayek. Economica 34:387–397

Keynes JM (1936/1973) The general theory of employment, interest and money. Macmillan, London

Locke J (1689/1823) Two treatise on government. McMaster Archive of the History of Economic Thought, Toronto. https://socialsciences.mcmaster.ca/econ/ugcm/3ll3/locke/government.pdf. Accessed 17 Jan 2018

Lyotard J-F (1979/1986) The postmodern condition: a report on knowledge. Manchester University Press, Manchester

Lyotard J-F (1988/1991) The inhuman. Stanford University Press, Stanford

Magnusson L (2009) Nation, state and the industrial revolution: the visible hand. Routledge, London

Marshall A (1920) Principles of economics. Macmillan Publishers, London

Marx K (1867/1954) Capital: a critical analysis of capitalist production, vol 1. Progress Publishers, Moscow

Marx K, Engels F (1848/1951) The communist manifesto. In: Marx K and Engels F, selected works, vol 1. Foreign Languages Publishing House, Moscow, pp 32–61

Mill JS (1848/2002) Principles of political economy. Prometheus Books, New York

Novecivic M, Jones JL, Carraher S (2015) Decentering Wren's evolution of management thought. In: PG ML, Mills AJ, Weatherbee TG (eds) The Routledge companion to management and organizational history. Routledge, London/New York, pp 11–30

Piketty T (2012/2014) Capital in the twenty-first century. Belknap Press, Cambridge, MA

Quesnay F (1766) Tableau economique. https://www.sapili.org/livros/fr/mc00222x.pdf. Accessed 16 Jan 2018

Ricardo D (1817/1969) The principles of political economy and taxation. Everyman's Library, London/New York

Rothbard MN (2006) Economic thought before Adam Smith: an Austrian perspective on the history of economic thought, vol 1. Ludwig von Mises Institute, Auburn

Rousseau JJ (1762/1950) The social contract. In: Rousseau JJ (ed Cole CDH) The social contract and discourses. Dent & Sons, London, pp 1–141

Schumpeter JA (1942/1975) Capitalism, socialism and democracy. Harper Perennial, New York

Smith A (1776/1999) An inquiry into the nature and causes of the wealth of nations. Penguin Classics, London

Voltaire (1733/2002) Letters on England. Pennsylvania State University Electronic Series Publication, Hazleton

Voltaire (1756/1963) Essay on the customs and spirit of nations. In: Voltaire (ed Brumfitt) The age of Louis XIV and other selected writings. Twayne Publishers, New York, pp 240–311

White H (1973) Metahistory: the historical imagination in nineteenth century Europe. John Hopkins University Press, Baltimore

Williamson OE (1976) Markets and hierarchies: analysis and antitrust implications. Free Press, New York

World Bank (2017) Global economic prospects, June 2017: a fragile recovery. World Bank Group, Washington, DC

Young A (1792/1909) Travels in France: 1787, 1788 and 1789. George Bell and Sons, London

Neo-Classical Thought: Alfred Marshall and Utilitarianism

16

Kaylee Boccalatte

Contents

Utility: From Bentham to Mill 371
Utility: Alfred Marshall and Neo-Classical Thought 376
Conclusion 382
Cross-References 384
References 384

Abstract

Few people have inspired a shift in economic thought. Alfred Marshall is one of the few. One hundred years following the publication of Marshall's seminal work, the *Principles of Economics*, his thoughts and ideas remain not only relevant to the theoretical inquiries of the modern age but of practical significance to today's managers. Central to Marshall's contribution to the foundations of modern management is his concept of utility. Utility throughout time has been described as many things by many people. Associated with morals, usefulness, and later correlating with human wants and desires, our understanding of utility underwent a marked transformation throughout the Classical and Neo-Classical eras. In order to appreciate the role Alfred Marshall played in the development of economic understanding therefore, it is necessary that we also examine how his Neo-Classical explanation of utility emerged from his classical predecessors. This chapter explores Alfred Marshall and Utilitarianism.

Keywords

Alfred marshall · Neo-classical economics · Utility · Utilitarianism · Classical economics · Jeremy bentham · David ricardo · John stuart mill

K. Boccalatte (✉)
James Cook University, Douglas, QLD, Australia
e-mail: kaylee@btfarms.com.au

© The Author(s), under exclusive licence to Springer Nature Switzerland AG 2020   367
B. Bowden et al. (eds.), *The Palgrave Handbook of Management History*,
https://doi.org/10.1007/978-3-319-62114-2_24

Few people have inspired a shift in economic thought. Alfred Marshall is one of the few. Uniting the concepts of supply *and* demand into a "modern" theory of value, Marshall has been described as a "supreme" authority "among the economists of the English-speaking world" (Davenport 1935/1965). This chapter explores the contribution Alfred Marshall and Utilitarianism – or as it is otherwise known, utility – made to the foundations of modern management. Utility throughout time has been described as many things by many people. Associated with morals, usefulness, and later correlating with human wants and desires, our understanding of utility underwent a marked transformation throughout the Classical and Neo-Classical eras. Notable, is the relationship between utility and value. Classical economists including David Ricardo and John Stuart Mill (in his later work) used the term utility to describe usefulness. If a good has use or satisfies some desire, it has utility. Goods that have utility consequently have value in exchange, a value that defines the power that good commands on the market. Marshall, however, later shifted the definition of utility associating it not with use value, but with exchange (Marshall 1890/1997).

Ricardo and Mill considered labor (or more specifically the cost of labor) as "the force determining the exchange value of goods," Marshall, on the other hand, did not (Marshall 1890/1997; Ricardo 1817/2001; Mill 1848/2004). Within the 1920 version (eighth and final edition) of Marshall's chief publication, the *Principles of Economics*, the Neo-Classical economist successfully argued that the exchange value of goods was influenced by the consumers "Desire or Want" for the good, or, in other words, the good's utility (Marshall 1890/1997; Davenport 1935/1965). According to Marshall, the "Desire for a commodity influences its value by influencing the eagerness of purchasers for it at a given value" (Marshall 1923/1929). The approach adopted by Marshall shifted the way one considers value to be created, enhanced, or diminished, for no longer are we focusing on the cost side of economics in the measurement of exchange value – the labor costs of producing the good – but rather both supply *and* demand. Although the labor and expenses embedded in the supply of a good provides a floor under the value for which management would aim to exchange their goods, supply costs do not determine utility. Nor do production costs directly influence the relative value a consumer is *willing* to exchange in order to acquire the good. Costs are but one factor influencing exchange value. Neo-Classical economists expand the scope of analysis to examine the role demand plays in influencing value. The Neo-Classical study of markets recognizes that exchanges are designed to optimize the want/satisfaction derived through "atomistic and individualistic" transactions (Reisman 1986/2011). For consumers, this want is found in maximizing utility, while for managers or capitalists, this want is found in the generation of profit (Reisman 1986/2011). Unlike Ricardo and Mill – who understood exchange value to be created through the goods "scarcity," the "quantity of labor," or "expense" embedded in a good (Ricardo 1817/2001; Mill 1848/2004) – Marshall acknowledged that where there exists no *want* for a good at any given time and place (e.g., "a house in a deserted mining village") (Marshall 1890/1997), despite the costs embedded (or sunk) in its supply, the item may have no value in exchange. In order to properly appreciate the influence Neo-Classical thought brought to the field of economic management, specifically, Alfred Marshall and

Utilitarianism, it is necessary that we understand how Neo-Classical economics emerged from its classical predecessors.

The classical economic period is delineated by three authors within this chapter: Jeremy Bentham, David Ricardo, and John Stuart Mill. While the Classical era comprised a range of authors, beginning with Adam Smith's publication of *The Wealth of Nations* in 1776 (Hollander 2016), in this chapter we examine how Bentham's founding concepts of utility and the late classical work of Ricardo and Mill – who are "traditionally" linked to Marshallian economics (Zamagni 2005; Colander 2000; Reisman 1986/2011) – informed and differed from Neo-Classical economics. Let us begin by outlining how management and the theory of value is discussed in classical economics. Jeremy Bentham, the author of *An Introduction to the Principles of Morals and Legislation*, began his book with a discussion of the principle of utility. Founded on the notion that utility is associated with the actions of people, conforming to Bentham's principle of utility required these actions to augment the "pleasure" (or "diminish" the "pain") of an agent (i.e., person, government), leaving that agent better off than they would otherwise have been (Bentham 1781/2000). While Bentham's work is founded on a moral philosophy, the ethical underpinnings found in his book are largely forgone in Ricardo's work and the later publications of Mill; within the third edition of Ricardo's book, *On the Principles of Political Economy and Taxation*, and Mill's *Principles of Political Economy*. Both authors principally focus on exploring the concept of value. Mill and Ricardo both embrace Smith's definition of value which has two different meanings: "Value in Use" and "Value in Exchange" (Ricardo 1817/2001; Smith 1776/1999; Mill and Laughlin 1885/2009). *Value in use* is defined as the goods utility – how useful or desirable the product is to a given person, while *value in exchange* refers to the purchasing power that product has on the market, or the quantity of other commodities for which it will exchange (Ricardo 1817/2001). Despite the importance of a good's value in use, it is a commodity's exchange value that is paramount in commercial transactions. According to Ricardo, "commodities derive their exchangeable value from ... their scarcity and ... the quantity of labour" embedded within them (Ricardo 1817/2001). Managing the quantity of labor required in production of the product is thus said to influence or "regulate" the exchange value (Ricardo 1817/2001). According to Ricardo's definition, we should see a correlation between the quantity of labor realized in a product, and its exchange value. Thus, if the quantity of labor increases, there should be a correlative increase in the power it commands over the market, a trend that continues in the opposite direction with every diminution in the quantity of labor (Ricardo 1817/2001).

Mill's understanding of exchange value is similarly founded on the contribution of labor. "Though we cannot create matter," Mill says, "we can cause" matter "to assume properties, by which" "it becomes useful" (Mill 1848/2004). It is labor, therefore, that creates utilities. Like Ricardo, Mill concedes to Smith's explanation that a good's value can be measured through two means: its value in use and its value exchange. In commercial markets, wherein commodities are exchanged for the purpose of generating benefits (e.g., profit), Mill recognizes that a product must "satisfy a desire, or serve a purpose" (have *use*) although it is the product's resulting "purchasing power" that defines the product's value in exchange (Mill 1848/2004).

In order to have exchange value a good must (a) have utility and (b) "some difficultly in attainment" (Mill 1848/2004). Where a good has utility and is able to be multiplied (i.e., reproduction is not limited), the exchange value gravitates toward the "labour and expense" invested in producing the product (Mill 1848/2004). Two commodities developed with the same value of labor (i.e., the same quantity of labor, with the same wages across the same time) will therefore, all things being equal, exchange for one another or, in other words, have the same exchange value (Mill 1848/2004). Any fluctuation in value is measured only in relation to the quantity of other things which it will exchange for at any given time (Mill 1848/2004). The inclusion of time into the discussion of exchange value is significant. For acknowledging the role time plays in changing market and comparative values, aids in explaining how, for example, a bottle of milk may exchange for half a loaf of bread today, but in 1 year, may exchange for two loaves of bread (e.g., supply of milk has severely declined). While money prices may rise (or decline) "generally," exchange values do not.

Alfred Marshall shifts the paradigm for measuring exchange value. No longer is exchange value measured by the labor costs involved in supplying the good, but rather, by the consumer's want for the good – the good's utility (Marshall 1890/1997). According to Marshall, utility defines the usefulness of a "thing" or the "total pleasure or other benefit" that thing will yield for a person (Marshall 1890/1997). While the value of utility *cannot* be measured directly, it *can* be measured indirectly, by examining the price (or money value) a given person is willing to exchange in order to satisfy their "Desire or Want" (Marshall 1890/1997). In other words, the utility of a given product to any given person cannot be measured by their "want" for the product – for an innumerable number of factors would need to be considered – but rather by the amount of money they are willing to forgo in order to satisfy their desire and acquire the product. Utility, therefore, is measured on an individual basis and cannot be measured "generally," for what a loaf of bread is worth to one person may be vastly different to what it is worth to another. However, as we will see throughout the body of this chapter, one can find a broad correlation between utility and value – for when the exchangeable value of a good (the sale price) decreases, this will commonly be followed by an increase in sales. In other words, the number of people satisfying their desire or want for the product by purchasing it. This correlation is in part the result of the increased "consumer surplus" gained by the buyer through a lower exchange price. Greater consumer surplus is gained with every increase in the difference between the price one would be "*willing* to pay rather than go without" [emphasis added] the good and the price one "*actually* does pay" [emphasis added] (Marshall 1890/1997). Marshall, like classical economists, acknowledges the significance of labor costs embedded in the ultimate cost of producing a commodity, for in commercial transactions where profit (or *surplus value*) is desired by an organization, production costs act as a floor under the sale price. Marshall, however, builds upon the classical theories to incorporate the importance of utility, namely, the consumes perceived want or desire for a product into the equation.

16 Neo-Classical Thought: Alfred Marshall and Utilitarianism

One hundred years after the publication of Alfred Marshall's seminal work, the *Principles of Economics*, his thoughts, and ideas remain not only relevant to the theoretical inquiries of the modern age but of practical significance to today's managers. Ultimately, management actions within a business are governed by the anticipation of profits (Besanko et al. 1996), optimizing the difference (i.e., *real* surplus value) between the costs of production and the sale price of their product (goods or services) over a given period of time. According to Neo-Classical economic thought, consumers are central to such transactions, for, in order to sell or exchange their products, management requires their product to have utility and thus, a level of consumer demand suitable to meet their income needs. Neo-Classical economics acknowledges the consumer's regulatory power over the level of demand for a business's product lines and/or service provisions, recognizing that the "ultimate regulator of demand is consumer demand" (Marshall 1890/1997). Acknowledgment of this power provides management with the ability to ensure their time and money is invested not only in the development or supply of products with utility but also in enhancing existing lines to increase the utility of (or the consumers "Desire or Want" for) the product. In order to appreciate the contribution Marshall's work made to the development and understanding of value and utility, it is necessary in the first instance to recognize how these concepts were known before his time. Classical economic theorists such as Mill and Riccardo, when addressing the question of how value is exchanged, focus much of their attention on the supply side of the equation, specifically the labor component embedded in the final product (Myint 1948; Ricardo 1817/2001; Mill 1848/2004). Neo-Classicalist Marshall, on the other hand, incorporates an analysis of the demand side, the consumer's perceived utility of a good. The significance of the transition from Classical economics to Neo-Classical economics, therefore, lies not in how each paradigm finds different answers to the same question but, rather, how the different paradigms ask different questions (De Vroey 1975). The purpose of this chapter is to examine Neo-classical thought: Alfred Marshall and Utilitarianism. Two key concepts lie central to this purpose: Value and Utility. In order to meet the objectives of this chapter, we examine not only Alfred Marshall's concept of utility but also how his Neo-Classical explanation of utility has emerged from his classical predecessors.

Utility: From Bentham to Mill

Utility appears at first instance to be a simple term, easily understood. However, upon tracing its history, it is clear that the definition has undergone a marked transformation between the Classical and Neo-Classical eras. While the early concept of utility can be traced back to the time of Epicurus (241–270 B.C.E.) (Mill 1863/2009; De Witt 1954), it is within Benthamite's 1718 version of *An Introduction to the Principles of Morals and Legislation* where we will commence our analysis within this chapter. A fundamental understanding of the classical framework – from Bentham to Mill – is essential to tracing the development of utility and how it is understood in Alfred Marshall's Neo-Classical form.

Founded on the notion that utility comes "under the governance of two sovereign masters, *pain* and *pleasure*" (Bentham 1781/2000), Bentham's hedonistic definition of utilitarianism provided the foundation for the current study of utility (Légé 2018; Jevons 1871). Associating the principle of utility with an intricate moral philosophy, Bentham asserts that each person's actions, thoughts, or words are balanced against two things: on one hand, "right and wrong," while on the other, their "causes and effects" (Bentham 1781/2000). In practice, *conforming* to the principle of utility is said to augment the pleasure or "happiness of the party whose interest is in question," a party which may be an individual or collective group (Bentham 1781/2000; Reisman 1986/2011). As such, the comparative value of alternative options must be examined and weighed to ensure that when making decisions related to utility, the option generating the greatest pleasure (along with the lowest pain) is adopted. Bentham proposes that it is possible to measure the outcome or potential degree of pleasure or pain any decision may give rise to (for an individual) through an analysis of six factors: *intensity, duration, certainty* (or uncertainty), *propinquity* (or remoteness), *fecundity,* and *purity* (Bentham 1781/2000). Utility is only said to be achieved when the pleasure – achieved through an "action" or through the properties – "in any object" (Bentham 1781/2000) – exceeds the pain. This does not mean that *pleasure* (e.g., happiness, advantage, or benefit) must be attained. It does, however, mean that the *pain* (e.g., "evil, unhappiness, or mischief") must be reduced or prevented in order to conform to the principle of utility (Bentham 1781/2000). For an individual, conforming to this principle may not only see, for example, the purchase of a good increase their pleasure at a greater degree than the pain that would be incurred by not purchasing it but more broadly, an improvement in their overall "happiness." While Bentham does not investigate how an individual's "happiness," "pleasure," or "utility" could be harnessed by management or enhanced (thus capitalized upon), he does assert that the term "pleasure" may also coincide with "profit" (which Bentham deems as a "distant pleasure") (Bentham 1781/2000). Bentham goes on to state that the "ordinary commercial motive of pecuniary interest" is "good" (Bentham 1781/2000) and from this, we can assume that *typically* business transactions, and by extension the actions of management, conform to the principle of utility. The rather broad nature of Bentham's definition of "pleasure" and "pain," however, gives rise to many questions. Not least of which is how does one measure *in practice* the cumulative benefits gained by the majority holding group, against an aggregate of the individual's pain incurred as the minority? For example, if the development of an aluminum production plant was approved to commercially benefit the state as a whole through its value in use, by generating jobs, increasing prosperity, and improving national wealth, it would conform to the principle of utility. However, how is it possible to measure the aggregate of *individual* pains of every member of the minority who may lose their house, develop illnesses, or die at an earlier age as a result, balanced against the benefits of the majority? David Ricardo, a friend of Bentham in his later life (Cremaschi 2004) supposed this type of comparison is not possible due to the inherently different desires (needs and wants) of individuals. He states "One set of necessaries and conveniences admits of no comparison with another set; value in use cannot be measured by any known standard; it is differently estimated by different persons" (Ricardo 1951/2004).

Utility to Ricardo and Mill principally means something *useful*. Irrespective of its contribution to the betterment of pleasure or the diminishment of pain, utility as defined by Riccardo is the "faculty, which certain things have of satisfying the various wants of mankind" (Ricardo 1951/2004). Riccardo goes on to explain that "we do not create objects: all we can do is to reproduce matter under another form – we can give it utility" (Ricardo 1951/2004). In simple terms, this means that even when goods are formed in nature, such as air, water, or salt, it is human labor either directly or indirectly (through the use of machinery) which is required to collect, gather, or acquire the good. Put another way, "we cannot create matter, we can cause it to assume properties, by which, from having been useless to us, to become useful" (Mill and Laughlin 1885/2009). As labor is, therefore, required to sustain all facets of life, be it collecting apples from the orchard, cutting lumber for homes, or building generating stations that power a network of electrical grids, labor is the key ingredient that transforms properties into utilities. As such, according to these political economists: labor is central to utility. However, if Mill and Ricardo are not aiming to measure "happiness," we must question if "utility" defined as something useful, can be measured. In order to achieve this objective, we must understand one overarching factor: the relationship between utility and value.

A commodity which is of use has utility and, by extension, value. While there are many services or intangible "goods" that may have use (e.g., music playing on an instrument), it is only the "material products" upon which it is possible to assign a value (Myint 1948; Malthus 1820/1836). According to Riccardo, an object's utility – its usefulness in "satisfying the various wants of mankind" – is "the foundation" of its value, not the "measure of value" (Mongiovi and Petri 1999/2014; Ricardo 1817/2010). Riccardo (along with Mill, Jevons, and Marshall) adopted Adam Smith's bipartite understanding of value which states that utilities have two easily distinguished values: *value in use* and *value in exchange* (Ricardo 1817/2001; Mill and Laughlin 1885/2009; Jevons 1871/2013; Marshall 1890/1997; Smith 1776/1999). "Value in use" is defined through a commodity's application to the owner or its value to a person for *use* or in other words an expression of that objects "utility" (Ricardo 1817/2001). For example, if one bakes a loaf of bread at home, "use value" defines the value of that loaf to the baker to use or consume themselves (not exchange). "Value in exchange," on the other hand, defines the value of a commodity in an exchange or, in other words, the power that loaf commands in trade (Ricardo 1817/2001). The exchange value of the home bread baked will be defined by what it can be exchanged for (e.g., one loaf in exchange for one fish) or alternatively, the price it will demand (e.g., one loaf in exchange for three dollars). There is, however, no correlation between a commodities value in use and value in exchange. A good which is necessary to sustain life such as "water or air" has a high *use value* (i.e., without *using* it, we die), yet may be worth little in exchange (Ricardo 1817/2001). For example, a business person aiming to sell "air" will typically find, that despite their commodity being essential to life, "air" will not command a high value in exchange. On the other hand, commodities such as diamonds, while providing little value in use, can exchange for very high quantity of other goods or a high price (Ricardo 1817/2001; Smith 1776/1999; Jevons 1871/2013). In commercial markets, organizations may produce utilities for their own use though integrated supply chains, or alternatively and perhaps more frequently, undertake the production of goods for the purpose of exchange.

According to Ricardo, it is the quantity of labor embedded in a product that regulates the exchangeable value of that product (Ricardo 1817/2001; Zamagni 2005). In simple terms, this means "how much of one shall be given in exchange for another" (Ricardo 1817/2001). While the availability (or "scarcity") of goods has a direct influence on the value of some products (e.g., "rare statues" or "scarce books") for those goods that *can* be increased "by human industry," it is the labor – or "human exertion" – embedded in that commodity, which determines exchange value (Ricardo 1817/2001; Zamagni 2005). For example, if building a 10-foot boat took 10 days and, all things being equal, it took 20 days to build a 20-foot boat, we could say that the 20-foot boat is worth twice that of the 10-foot boat in exchange. For according to Ricardo, "the exchangeable value of the commodity's production would be in proportion to the labour" (including that labor invested in tools and equipment used) "bestowed on their production" (Ricardo 1817/2001). By this rationale, increasing the "quantity of labour" ingrained within a good "must augment the value of that commodity," and every "diminution must lower it" (Ricardo 1817/2001). Ricardo's explanation of exchange value is a complex calculation of the total cost, measured by labor time, involved in bringing a good "to market" (Ricardo 1817/2001). At the heart of his explanation, however, it is not utility or price that determines the exchange value of goods but labor (Reisman 1986/2011).

Mill, like Ricardo, asserts that it is through labor alone that "natural objects" are transformed into useful articles, or *utilities* (Ricardo 1817/2001; Mill 1848/2004). Mill's early work, namely, within his book entitled *Utilitarianism*, took a hedonistic approach to the analysis of utility, one similar to that of his predecessor Bentham (Mill 1863/2009; Zamagni 2005). However, his later work in the *Principles of Political Economy* diverges from the central themes of pleasure and pain, adopting a stronger economic focus for the discussion of value and utility. Mill ascertained that the utility of a good – its ability to "satisfy a desire, or serve a purpose"– is found in its use value (Mill 1848/2004). Thereby in apparent agreeance with Marshall's take on utility many years later, Mill indicates that "a person will give, to possess a thing" a price which correlates with their desire to acquire it. Roscher who published a book by the same name *Principles of Political Economy*, 60 years after Mill, distinguishes between utility and use-value, stating "Utility is a quality of things themselves, in relation, it is true, to human wants. Value in use is a quality imputed to them, the result of man's thought, or of his view of them. Thus, for instance, in a beleagured [sic] city, the stores of food do not increase in utility, but their value in use does" (Roscher 1854/1882). Mill, however, does not make any such distinction, leading us to conclude that a good utility is measurable by its use value.

Mill similarly fails to expand on the analysis of use value or describe in depth its correlation (if any) with exchange value, other than to say that both the "Value in use" and "the utility of a thing ... in the estimation of a purchaser, is the extreme limit of its exchange value" (Mill 1848/2004). Instead, Mill focuses on measuring the exchange value of goods. He states that in measuring the value of articles – articles that are not scarce and can be indefinitely multiplied – supply and demand (i.e., consumer demand) measures only the "perturbations" in the exchangeable value of a commodity because "on the average, commodities exchange at ... their natural value," their cost of production (Mill 1848/2004). As labor, whether direct, indirect, or past, is "nearly the sole" necessary contributor to production costs – alongside "profits" (Mill 1848/2004) – the value of a commodity "depends principally on the quantity of labour required for their production" (Mill 1848/2004). Mills' concept of exchange value, therefore, correlates with Ricardo's. However, where Ricardo states it is the "quantity" of labor which determines the exchange value of a good, Mill acknowledges that it is not just the *quantity* of labor but the *value* of labor (typically measured by wages) that has been terminated in that commodity's production (Mill 1848/2004; Zamagni 2005). Any reduction in the value of labor invested in the production of a commodity (whether measured by time or wages) reduces the value of that product, namely, the power it commands over the market or the "quantity of other things which can be obtained in exchanged for it" (Mill 1848/2004). According to Mill, therefore, "If two things are made by the same quantity of labor, and that labor paid at the same rate, and if the wages of the laborer have to be advanced for the same space of time, and the nature of the employment does not require that there be a permanent difference in their rate of profit," then "these two things will, on the average, exchange for one another" (Mill 1848/2004). However, it cannot be said that these two things will exchange for each other at *any* given time. In order to illustrate this point, we will assign names to each of the "things," namely bread and milk. While today Ceteris Paribus, a loaf of bread may have the same exchange value as a carton of milk, if circumstances change (e.g., new machinery improves milk production rates), the value of labor embedded the milk will decrease, and so too will the product's exchange value. This means that the exchange value of milk has decreased and so too has its purchasing power in relation to all other goods (which have not undergone a reduction in exchange value) (Mill 1848/2004). In this circumstance, a loaf of bread does not have the same exchange value as a carton of milk, for milk's exchange value has decreased. Although it is unclear if Mill accounts for *all* labor costs in his explanation (e.g., labor embedded in machinery) as we will see below, such calculations are necessary for an accurate measure of exchange value (Mill 1848/2004). Adopting in part, a pragmatic approach to the analysis of the management process, Mill furthermore, acknowledges not only that the concept of value is relative (not absolute) and that the level of demand can contribute to the exchange value of a product. He also argues that without some form of profit (or some reward) embedded in "production costs," a capitalist can neither be inclined to invest in new capital nor continue to produce the commodity (Mill and Laughlin 1885/2009).

In considering the concept of production from a capitalist perspective, Mill examines the role labor plays in the development of a commodity. For, it is labor alone that can take a natural object (e.g., a seed) and through various motions transform that seed into another natural object (e.g., wheat), or into an "article fitted for some human use" (e.g., bread) (Mill 1848/2004). An understanding of value in a commercial society, wherein things are acquired by a "double exchange" (i.e., a purchase and a sale) is fundamental (Mill 1848/2004). Like Ricardo, Mill adopts a complex form of calculating the labor embedded in a commodity in order to calculate production costs, counting not only the direct labor (e.g., planting the seed) but the respective degrees of past labor (e.g., building the plough, tilling the ground) utilized in production of the commodity (Mill 1848/2004). For management, it is the effective coordination of input costs and output values that is of critical importance. Business objectives while varied and vast can typically be brought back to one central motive: to generate a "necessary price" in exchange for their goods (Mill 1848/2004). A price that includes the "wages of the labour" as well as "ordinary profit" (Mill 1848/2004; Zamagni 2005). Accurate calculation of production costs is therefore critical. Although organizations may produce a portion of goods for use (not exchange), it is through the portion produced for exchange that the firm must generate proceeds sufficient to cover the labor not only directly incurred through production but all the labor that came before, e.g., producing the machinery (Mill 1848/2004). It is the cumulative total of the labor costs embedded in producing a commodity therefore that dictate the cost of production or "natural value" of a product (Mill 1848/2004). Its exchange value, by contrast, is determined by the "quantity of other things for which" a good "will exchange," or, to put it another way, the "ratio of the quantity of one commodity to the quantity of some other commodity exchanged for it" (Mill 1848/2004; Jevons 1871). What both Mill and Ricardo fail to account for in their analysis of exchange value, however, is the influence of demand. For, if there are "two parties and two quantities to every exchange, there must be two equations" (Jevons 1871).

Utility: Alfred Marshall and Neo-Classical Thought

While the earlier political economists, John Stuart Mill and David Ricardo, identified labor as the primary factor influencing the exchange value of goods, Marshall surmised that equally important is the influence consumer wants or desires exert on value: the consumer's perceived *utility* of the good. Neo-Classical economics, therefore, depart from a labor-centered approach to measuring utility. Instead, the method adopted by Marshall acknowledges that while production costs are an important consideration in commercial transactions, they are not representative of utility. Rather it is the individuals "Desire or Want" for a commodity that is of greatest influence (Marshall 1890/1997). Although the first edition of Marshall's book, *Principles of Economics*, associates the term "pleasure" with utility (a term strongly associated with earlier economists such as Bentham and afterwards Jevons), by his later, and famed eighth edition, he has deterred from using this expression. Instead, he appears to adopt the concept provided by Henry Sidgwick, who, in his book entitled *The Principles of Political Economy*, states that "the Utility of material things" means "their capacity to satisfy men's needs and desires"

(Sidgwick 1883/1887; Marshall 1890/1997, 1890; Martinoia 2003). While the utility of a good cannot be measured directly, it *can* be measured indirectly through the price a person is willing to forgo to acquire it in exchange (Marshall 1890/1997). In other words, the measure of utility "is found in the price which a person is willing to pay for the fulfilment or satisfaction of" their "desire" (Marshall 1890/1997). The value (or utility) of any commodity to an individual is, hence, separate from though reflected in, the exchange price (Wright 2008). Organizational success does not, therefore, necessarily hinge on the firm's ability to produce utilities for a value equal or (preferably) less than the production costs. For in some situations, it is perhaps more important that management produce goods which have great enough utility (from the perspective of the consumer) that the price or monetary value a consumer is *willing* to forgo in exchange for acquiring the product (in order to satisfy a want or desire) is greater than the supply price.

Utility, according to Marshall is not an exact science. Like the tides, which can only be *estimated* in advance due to the relative unpredictability of weather, the wants of any one person, at any given time can only be *anticipated* ahead of time (Marshall 1890/1997). The inherently "various and uncertain" desires of individuals make attempts to anticipate human actions both "inexact and faulty" (Marshall 1890/1997). However, it is pertinent to acknowledge the reality of collective individualism. While each person is a free agent, free to make decisions as they see fit, as humans, they are at least in part creatures of habit (Krugman 2018). Such habit provides a degree of predictability which can be leveraged by management to increase demand, and encourage buyers to purchase more than was originally intended at the same price, or the same quantity at the higher price (Marshall 1890/1997). While we don't know exactly what an individual (e.g., John or Mary) is going to do, on average society *in general* will act in a predictable enough manner (Krugman 2018) that allows management to identify trends in consumer behavior when stimulated. For example, "every fall, however slight in the price of a commodity in general use, will, other things being equal, increase the total sales of it" (Marshall 1890/1997). People generally, therefore, "take advantages of opportunities," they "respond to incentives," they demand more when prices are low (Krugman 2018). Marshall's concept of utility provides management with an understanding of the important role demand plays in commercial transactions.

For humans, there is "a limit to each separate want" (Marshall 1890/1997). At some point, regardless of the incentives offered by management, an individual's desire for more of a good at a given time will cease. For as Jevons succinctly states "All our appetites are capable of *satisfaction* or *satiety* sooner or later, in fact, both these words mean, etymologically, that we have had *enough*, so that more is of no use to us" (Jevons 1871). The utility of a "thing" to any person can be measured indirectly by the price (i.e., "demand price") a person is willing to pay in order to satisfy their want or desire (Marshall 1890/1997). It cannot, however, be assumed that the same person will be willing to pay the same price for the same "thing" under any given conditions. According to the theory of marginal utility – i.e., *Grenznutzen*, a term coined by Friedrich Von Wieser (Ekelund 1970) – the desire for a commodity decreases as the "quantity already in use or possession" increases (Jevons 1871).

Consumer demand does not typically arise from the desire to purchase "aggregate quantities" of an item, but rather, "increments of quantities" (Marshall 1890/1997). Commercially, the "marginal" increments of a good, which a consumer is only just inclined to buy (i.e., their marginal purchase) are balanced against the perceived utility of that marginal purchase, i.e., its marginal utility (Marshall 1890/1997). If the consumer's want or desire for a product diminishes with every quantity they already possess, it follows therefore that the price that consumer is willing to exchange in order to *increment their quantity*, similarly decreases with every quantity already consumed. In other words, all things being equal, "the marginal utility of a thing" "diminishes steadily with every increase in" the consumers "supply of it" (Marshall 1890/1997). In order to illustrate this properly, we can consider the relationship between diminishing utility and price with reference to the purchase of work boots. How much a person is willing to pay in order to purchase work boots (the *demand price*) will likely be influenced by their current status (as boot owners). Assuming they don't currently own a set of boots, they might be happy to pay a few hundred dollars to get a good set, ones with ankle protection, comfort soles, and guaranteed durability. If they purchase their first set work boots how much would they be willing to pay to buy a second set of boots? They would probably pay far less for the second set then the first and they would likely pay even less again, to procure a third set. The law of diminishing marginal utility suggests that, all things being equal, a person will be willing to pay less for each successive item (i.e., work boots). In other words, the marginal demand price for the work boots diminishes (Marshall 1890/1997).

Utility does not exist in isolation. Instead, it is influenced by price. The relationship between price and utility is founded on various situational factors: (a) the elasticity of demand, (b) the utility of a commodity, and (c) the utility of money (Marshall 1890/1997, 1923/1929). While we have previously examined marginal utility – and how a person's want for a product decreases with each increase in the quantity in their possession – we have not yet examined the role price plays in the responsiveness of demand. Although Marshall cannot take credit for introducing the concept of price elasticity – for other including Mill had discussed it before him (Mill 1848/2004) – he was the first to "popularize" the analytical tool (Groenewegen 2007; Marshall 1890/1997). Price elasticity affects the consumer's response to changes in product pricing, when all else is equal. For a manager, wondering how to increase sales and profits – or what impact price changes will have on the consumer's demand – calculating the price elasticity of demand provides insight into a range of outcomes. For example, if the marginal demand for a good falls slowly, the price a person is willing to pay to increment their supply will similarly fall slowly. Thus, a small decrease in price will cause a comparatively large increase in purchases; in this case, the demand is *elastic* (Marshall 1890/1997). However, if marginal demand decreases quickly (the demand is *inelastic*), a small decrease in price will result in a comparatively small increase in purchases (Marshall 1890/1997). Conversely, small price *rises* where demand is elastic will cause a proportionally larger decrease in sales (which will decrease earnings) while in inelastic markets, a small price increase may only cause a small decrease in sales, and thus an overall increase in revenue. While these calculations appear to offer insight into the demand/price relationship, elasticity is ultimately the measure of one variable factor against another variable factor, looking at how one thing changes in response to another. In commercial markets, there are various other factors at play which influence the elasticity of demand. The availability of suitable alternatives, the commodity's difficulty in attainment (e.g., is it a rare item or mass produced), and the products necessity to life (e.g., is it medical assistance or a third handbag?) all influence demand and may require consideration in the calculation of price elasticity (Marshall 1890/1997). Nevertheless, understanding the "price elasticity of demand" equips management with a knowledge of how changes in price will affect demand in commercial markets when all else is equal.

Price, however, whether it be increased or decreased, when paid with money will be considered high or low by different people depending on their status of wealth. For, according to Marshall, "the effective value of money to each individual depends partly on the nature of" their "wants" (Marshall 1923/1929). Money has two purposes. Firstly to act as a *"medium of exchange,"* a "material thing" that can be transferred from person to person and with a value which "can be read at a glance" (Marshall 1923/1929) and secondly, as a *"standard of value,"* to "indicate the amount of general purchasing power" (Marshall 1923/1929). All things being equal, the less money a person has, the greater the utility a product must have in order to motivate a purchase. For, the greater utility *money* has to a person, the *less* they are willing (or able) to pay in order to satisfy their wants. Money has greater utility to those who have little to spare, for the more money one spends, the less money they retain and the less purchasing power remains under their control (Marshall 1890/1997). Comparatively, the more money a person has, the less utility *money* has to that person, and therefore, the higher the price they are willing to pay to satisfy their desire (Marshall 1890/1997). While utility can only be measured through the price an individual purchaser is willing to pay (Marshall 1890/1997), the predictable nature of groups of people allows economists to anticipate actions of the larger society. While individuals may act, want, and desire differently, when viewed collectively, their peculiarities become less important. For, according to Marshall, "in large markets, then – where rich and poor, old and young, men and women, persons of all varieties of tastes, temperaments and occupations are mingled together – the peculiarities in the wants of individuals will compensate one another in a comparatively regular graduation of total demand" (Marshall 1890/1997). As such, the demand for a product, all things being equal, can be expected to increase with a "fall in price" and diminish with a "rise in price" (Marshall 1890/1997).

Altering the price of goods is not the only method of enhancing demand. Improving a goods perceived utility may see people "buy more of it than" they "would before at the same price" or "buy as much of it as before at a higher price" (Marshall 1890/1997). When "voluntarily" exchanging "one thing for another," people typically expect "the latter to be of greater service" than "the former," or in other words, the value gained by what is *received* to be greater than that which is "given up" (Marshall 1919). Elevations in utility can be achieved through increasing the "consumer surplus" generated through a sale. Consumer surplus is the difference between what the consumer is *willing* to pay for an item and the price they *actually* pay (Marshall 1890/1997). From the consumers perspective, their surplus satisfaction stems from the difference between the satisfaction they garner through procuring a commodity and what they forgo in paying its price. Consumer surplus can be elevated in three fundamental ways: reducing cost, increasing utility, or some combination thereof. Firstly, this can be achieved, ceteris paribus, by management reducing the good's price, i.e., the price consumers *actually* pay for an item. As discussed earlier, price is central to demand. In many circumstances, the real "money costs of production" or "expenses of production" constitute the price floor under which a firm should not sell. As such, this price floor directly influences the consumer's demand for the good (Marshall 1890/1997). Reducing the expenses of production, therefore, all other things being equal, allows the firm to reduce the sale price of their goods, which in turn (if the law of demand prevails) increases the demand for their product (Marshall 1890/1997). While supply prices provide a price floor, they have no influence on the monetary amount a firm can expect to receive in exchange for their products. On the contrary, the consumer's perceived value of the product places a "roof" over the upper limit of the price at which the firm can reasonably expect to sell their goods. By increasing the consumer's perceived benefit of a product – the consumers "desire" and "want" for a good (the goods utility) – at a greater rate than which it costs to do so, the firm may in fact increase the surplus satisfaction gained through acquiring the product therefore, similarly increasing demand and ultimately profits (Marshall 1890/1997).

Is it necessary that the total "supply price" be offset at the point of sale? According to Marshall, the *total cost* of production must be paid in the long term. However, distinguishing between prime and supplementary costs allows management to ascertain which costs must be covered *immediately* by the sale price (short term) and those which can be recompensed over a *longer period* (long term) (Marshall 1890/1997). While business pricing should include an "allowance" for "earnings" (i.e., profits), distinguishing between prime and supplementary costs can be beneficial to management when aiming to determine the absolute "lowest price at which it will be worth … while to accept an order," most particularly in economic downturns or at times when competition is high (Marshall 1890/1997, 1919). Defined by their contribution to the development of a commodity, *prime* costs are those expenses that are directly incurred through the production of a commodity (i.e., materials and labor), while charges essential to a broader business operation such as overhead costs and the wages of managerial staff (indirect costs) are known as *supplementary or "general" costs* (Marshall 1890/1997, 1919). Drawing from Adam Smith's famous pin-maker example to illustrate the distinction, the fabrication of pins requires labor and equipment to undertake the sequential stages of production. These stages include the drawing out wire, straightening the wire, cutting the wire, creating a point in the wire, and so forth (Smith 1776/1999). The cost of the labor (paid per hour or per pin) and wire used in the production of the pins are *prime costs*. While the cost of (for example) salaried staff responsible for ensuring sufficient qualities and quantities of labor and wire are present each day, and the proportional cost of the equipment used by the workers are considered

16 Neo-Classical Thought: Alfred Marshall and Utilitarianism 381

supplementary costs. Although it may be simpler to calculate the prime costs embedded in the production of a good, it is vital for business sustainability that supplementary be determined and subsequently recompensed completely in the "long run" (Marshall 1890/1997). For, as Marshall states "the price at which it is just worth" "while to produce" commodities, even when trade is slack, is in practice generally a good deal above this prime cost" (Marshall 1890/1997).

A major factor in Marshall's theory of value is the role time plays in commercial markets. The passage of time brings with it various fundamental difficulties that influence demand prices, and by extension sales and consumption. Unavoidable changes in the market are evident in economics in five key areas: purchasing power, general prosperity, population shifts, the ability to delay purchases, and changing predilections (Marshall 1890/1997). The purchasing power of money – the measure of nominal value – varies over time whether in response to or in anticipation of certain events (e.g., inflation). This means that the quantity of goods that money can buy changes. While $3 may have purchased a loaf of bread last week, a change in the value of money (e.g., inflation) may see that $3 command enough power to purchase only half a loaf this week. Time can also change the general prosperity (and thus total purchasing power) of a nation. A decline in general purchasing power sees a correlative decline in prices, consumption and business profits (Marshall 1890/1997). For the less money people have under their command, the greater the utility of money to those people and the less they are willing or able to spend (Marshall 1890/1997). When consumers do buy, their ability to delay purchasing items can have a notable influence on consumption, and thus business profits (Marshall 1890/1997). When prices are high or money tight, there are many purchases that can be put off for a period of time, or until consumers are unable to delay the purchase any longer. Clothes, for example, often have a "great deal of reserve wear" (Marshall 1890/1997) meaning they can still be worn long after one would have ordinarily purchased replacements.

In acknowledging the influence of both supply and demand, Marshall adopted a characteristically pragmatic stance on value, stating that "whether variations in demand, or variations in cost of production, exert the stronger influences on value under competitive conditions in a given time, depends mainly on *the ease with which supply can alter its pace*" (Marshall 1919).

Changes in population, "fashions, and taste" – as well as "the discovery or improvement or cheapening" of goods (including substitute items) – are typically not of immediate concern to a manager, as there is often a lapse of time between the change occurring and its effect. However, such developments can have a detrimental effect on business revenue if not properly managed over the long term. For example,

> ... when a new tramway or suburban railway is opened, even those who live near the line do not get into the habit of making the most of its assistance at once; and a good deal more time elapses before many of those whose places of business are near one end of the line change their homes so as to live near the other end. Again, when petroleum first became plentiful few people were ready to use it freely; gradually petroleum and petroleum lamps have become familiar to all classes of society.

When most of us think of "demand" we tend to think of "direct" demand. However, consumer demand can be satisfied through direct and indirect means (Marshall 1890/1997). When a product satisfies a consumer's wants directly, that product is the consumer's *direct* demand. If a new brick house were to satisfy the consumer's needs, it is the house which is considered the consumer's direct demand. Satisfying the consumer's direct demand, however, is not possible without various factors of production each doing their part to produce the finished product. The demand for these factors of production, such as labor, tools, and equipment, is *"indirect"* and *"derived* from the direct demand" (Marshall 1890/1997). All direct demands are essentially broken up into a range of derived demands which are necessary for the production of the finished product. While the demand for each factor of production (e.g., the bricklayers) is indirect or derived (Marshall 1890/1997) when several demands are present "jointly" (e.g., labor, tools, and equipment), there is a "joint demand" for serviceable products (Marshall 1890/1997). In other words, there exists a "joint demand" for all the goods and services that combine to produce the ultimate product, which is the consumer's direct demand. Understanding the fundamental concepts of direct, indirect, derived, and joint demand gives greater significance to the relationships between different factors of supply and their corresponding influence on demand. Appropriate management of the costs of each factor of production is necessary for equilibrium to be reached between the supply price and demand price. For, as Marshall shows, each factor of production is connected, directly or indirectly, to a goods cost of production (Marshall 1890/1997). Hence, fluctuations in those costs (whether increasing or decreasing) will influence proportionally the value of the ultimate product. Without an understanding of the complex and shifting relationship of supply and demand, any managerial endeavor is ultimately doomed to fail.

Conclusion

The Classical to Neo-Classical eras were marked by a transformation in the theory of value. Considered to be the "leading economist" "in the world" at a time, Marshall's theory of value challenged the findings of orthodox economics, transforming the way value is defined and measured (Davenport 1935/1965). Rather than looking toward the relative labor costs and expenses embedded in the production of a commodity to define an exchange value, a feature characteristic of classical economists, Marshall acknowledged the influence of utility. His pragmatic approach to understanding value coincides with Jevons, who acknowledged that "value depends entirely upon utility" (Jevons 1871), or in other words, without utility, a product has no value in use or exchange. Utility is hence central to demand, and it is only upon acknowledging the influence of both supply *and* demand that an accurate understanding of value is attained (Colander 2000; Davenport 1935/1965). While Marshall transformed economic thought, he did not "revolutionize" his field. Economics, like industrial society, does not evolve in "kind" but rather in "degree"; therefore, Marshall's theory of value was "merely one stage of evolution" (Marshall, 1890/

16 Neo-Classical Thought: Alfred Marshall and Utilitarianism

1997, 1919). Marshall's contribution to management and economic history, consequently, cannot be fully appreciated without first an understating of how his Neo-Classical thoughts and ideas evolved from his Classical predecessors.

The Classical Economic period within this chapter is principally circumscribed by Bentham, Mill, and Ricardo. While Smith laid the foundations of political economy, it was Bentham that emphasized the contribution of utility. Bentham's founding concept of utility was morally inclined, correlating conformance with the ability to bring the greatest happiness to the greatest number of people. Bentham observed that a person's actions will typically be motivated by which outcome will increase their "pleasure" or minimize their "pain" (Bentham 1781/2000). While prima facie, Bentham's hedonistic understanding of utility seems incompatible with later economic explanations centered on *use* or *wants*, the ethical influences of people cannot be excluded from economic studies. For according to Marshall, "ethical forces" are necessary considerations in the science of economics, and past attempts at "excluding ethical considerations from economic decisions" have "not been successful" (Marshall 1890/1997). While Mill's early work reflected Bentham's ideals, in his later book *Principles of Political Economy*, as with Riccardo's *On the Principles of Political Economy and Taxation*, utility is defined simply as something useful. Within these later classical teachings of Ricardo and Mill, value was measured in exchange and comprised principally of the total labor and expenses embedded in a goods materialization (Mill 1848/2004; Ricardo 1817/2001).

Despite the use value or utility of a good being "absolutely essential" to exchange value, both Riccardo and Mill focused primarily on examining the supply side of the equation, failing to account for the role demand plays in trade (Ricardo 1817/2001; Mill 1848/2004). Their apparent exclusion of any detailed examination of the influence exerted by demand overlooks what Marshall in hindsight, regarded as "the more urgent" and the more difficult elements of economic science (Reisman 1986/2011). It was Ricardo's apparent belief that use value "cannot be measured" for "it is differently estimated by different persons" (Ricardo 1817/2010). However, according to Jevons "Ricardo 'regarded the natural laws of variation of utility as too obvious to require detailed explanation'" (Reisman 1986/2011). Adopting a "labour-embodied" approach, "value" was considered to be a measure of the total costs involved in producing a commodity and *not* "as a measure of the "intensity" of demand for the product" (Myint 1948). Although Ricardo acknowledges that demand *influences* price, he asserts that it is ultimately the cost of production that *defines* price. He states "supply follows close at" demands "heels" "and soon takes the power of regulating price," and "in regulating" price, price "is determined by cost of production" (Ricardo 1887). Mill, however, acknowledged that in a commercial society, goods must command a price in exchange which is sufficient not only to recompense the costs of production but furthermore, generate a rate of "ordinary profit" (Mill 1848/2004; Zamagni 2005). While Ricardo is credited as having "systemised the whole" – outlining theories related to various aspects of economics including value – Mill is recognized to have "expounded" the economic "branch of knowledge" by refining theoretical concepts (Jevons 1871).

Marshall's work attempts to synthesize these "old doctrines" with "new work" in order to present a "modern version" of economics (Marshall 1890/1997). Marshall's texts, notably *The Principles of Economics*, not only presents a more modern take on economics but does so in plain English, rendering his work "intelligible to the general public" (Colander 2000). For while Marshall (alike most economists) used mathematics to *understand* economics, he used English to *explain* economics (Krugman 2018; Marshall 1890/1997). Marshall's concept of utility shifted the way we think about a products value in exchange. By factoring in the consumers desire or want for the good – a demand side factor – the exchange value of a product became measurable (indirectly) by the price a consumer was willing to forgo in order to acquire the commodity (Marshall 1890/1997). Marshall's approach to understanding the theory of value diverges from the classically cost-focused analysis, measuring the labor and expenses involved in bringing the good to market, to emphasize the relationship between supply *and* demand. It was his apparent dedication to ensuring cohesion between "actual problems" and "theoretical problems" that reinforced his findings, and in part, contributed to his work, specifically *The Principles of Economics,* remaining relevant a century after its publication (Groenewegen 2007; Persky 1999; Colander 2000).

Cross-References

▶ Economic Foundations: Adam Smith and the Classical School of Economics
▶ The Marxist Opposition to Capitalism and Business

References

Bentham J (1781/2000) An introduction to the principles of morals and legislation. Batoche Books, Kitchener
Besanko D, Dranove D, Shanley M (1996) Economics of strategy. Wiley, New York
Colander D (2000) Complexity and the history of economic thought: perspectives on the history of economic thought: selected papers from the History of Economics Society conference, vol Book, Whole. Routledge, London
Cremaschi S (2004) Ricardo and the utilitarians. Eur J Hist Econ Thought 11(3):377–403. https://doi.org/10.1080/0967256042000246476
Davenport HJ (1935/1965) The economics of Alfred Marshall, vol Book, Whole. Cornell University Press, New York
De Vroey M (1975) The transition from classical to neoclassical economics: a scientific revolution. J Econ Issues 9(3):415–439. https://doi.org/10.1080/00213624.1975.11503296
De Witt NW (1954) Epicurus and his philosophy, vol Book, Whole. University of Minnesota Press, Minneapolis. https://doi.org/10.5749/j.cttts81p
Ekelund RB (1970) Power and utility: the normative economics of Friedrich Von Wieser. Rev Soc Econ 28(2):179–196. https://doi.org/10.1080/00346767000000030
Groenewegen P (2007) Alfred Marshall: economist 1842–1924, vol Book, Whole. Palgrave Macmillan, London. https://doi.org/10.1057/9780230593060
Hollander S (2016) Classical economics, vol Book, Whole. University of Toronto Press, Toronto
Jevons WS (1871) The theory of political economy. Macmillan, London/New York

Jevons WS (1871/2013) The theory of political economy, vol Book, Whole, 4th edn. Palgrave Macmillan, Houndmills/Basingstoke/Hampshire. https://doi.org/10.1057/9781137374158

Krugman P (2018) Economics and society. MasterClass, Online

Légé P (2018) History, utility and liberty: John Stuart Mill's critical examination of Auguste Comte. Eur J Hist Econ Thought 25(3):428–459. https://doi.org/10.1080/09672567.2018.1449877

Malthus TR (1820/1836) Principles of political economy. W. Pickering, London

Marshall A (1890) Principles of economics. Macmillan, London

Marshall A (1890/1997) Principles of economics. Great mind paperpack series (economics), 8th edn. Prometheus Books, New York

Marshall A (1919) Industry and trade, 2nd edn. Macmillan, St Martin's Street/London

Marshall A (1923/1929) Money credit & commerce. Macmillan, St. Martin's Street/London

Martinoia R (2003) That which is desired, which pleases, and which satisfies: utility according to Alfred Marshall. J Hist Econ Thought 25(3):349–364. https://doi.org/10.1080/1042771032000114764

Mill JS (1848/2004) Principles of political economy. Prometheus Books, Amherst/New York

Mill JS (1863/2009) Utilitarianism, vol Book, Whole. Floating Press, Auckland

Mill JS, Laughlin JL (1885/2009) Principles of political economy. D. Appleton And Company, New York

Mongiovi G, Petri F (1999/2014) Value, distribution and capital: essays in honour of Pierangelo Garegnani, vol Book, Whole. Routledge, New York

Myint H (1948) Theories of welfare economics. Longmans, Green and Co., Toronto

Persky J (1999) Marshall's neo-classical labor-values. J Hist Econ Thought 21(3):257–268. https://doi.org/10.1017/S1053837200004259

Reisman D (1986/2011) The economics of Alfred Marshall, vol Book, Whole. Routledge, New York/Abingdon. https://doi.org/10.4324/9780203813904

Ricardo D (1817/2001) On the principles of political economy and taxation, vol Book, Whole, 3rd edn. Batoche Books, Kitchner

Ricardo D (1817/2010) On the principles of political economy, and taxation. J. McCreery. Printer, Black Horse Court, London

Ricardo D (1887) Letters of David Ricardo to Thomas Robert Malthus 1810–1823. Clarendon Press, Oxford

Ricardo D (1951/2004) The works and correspondence of David Ricardo, vol I. Liberty Fund, Indianapolis

Roscher W (1854/1882) Principles of political economy, vol 1. Callaghan and Company, Chicago

Sidgwick H (1883/1887) The principles of politcal economy, 2nd edn. MacMillian, London

Smith A (1776/1999) The wealth of nations. Penguin Books Ltd, London

Wright I (2008) The emergence of the law of value in a dynamic simple commodity economy. Rev Polit Econ 20(3):367–391. https://doi.org/10.1080/09538250701661889

Zamagni ESaS (2005) An outline of the history of economic thought, vol Book, Whole, 2nd rev. and expand edn. Oxford University Press, New York/Oxford. https://doi.org/10.1093/0199279144.001.0001

Foundations: The Roots of Idealist and Romantic Opposition to Capitalism and Management

17

Bradley Bowden

Contents

Nature, Being, Consciousness, and Will 392
Evidence and Knowledge 398
Conclusion 404
Cross-References 406
References 406

Abstract

A seminal feature of the closing decades of the twentieth century was the emergence of new postmodernist traditions opposed to industrial capitalism and its associated managerial systems. Unlike Marxism, these new traditions are idealist in orientation, giving primacy to individual identity. In exploring the origins of these postmodernist traditions, this chapter argues that their epistemological roots are located within German philosophic idealism and English Romanticism. Like subsequent postmodernist canon, these traditions shared a hostility to industrialization, an emphasis on consciousness and will, and a belief that humanity's well-being rests on a harmonious relationship with nature. German idealism and English Romanticism also shared a distrust of empiricism or positivism, believing instead that evidence and knowledge are highly subjective. In assessing the influence of these traditions, this chapter suggests that their key assumptions – and of the postmodernist traditions that they helped inspire – are misguided. The pre-industrial, bucolic existence that they favored was a world of misery, filth, and illiteracy. An emphasis on consciousness and will frequently led to authoritarian conclusions. While rejecting positivist epistemological principles, this chapter also argues that the relativist assumptions of idealism,

---

B. Bowden (✉)
Griffith Business School, Griffith University, Nathan, QLD, Australia
e-mail: b.bowden@griffith.edu.au

© The Author(s), under exclusive licence to Springer Nature Switzerland AG 2020   387
B. Bowden et al. (eds.), *The Palgrave Handbook of Management History*,
https://doi.org/10.1007/978-3-319-62114-2_22

Romanticism, and postmodernism are in error. An objective world amenable to experimentation and inquiry does exist.

Keywords

Postmodernism · Epistemology · Philosophic idealism · Romanticism · Capitalism

The dominant narrative in the last quarter millennia of human history has been associated with a model of industrialization and urbanization that, once perfected in the North Atlantic littoral in the nineteenth century, gradually encompassed the entire globe. Industrial and financial capitalism has been the most constant, although not the universal, handmaiden of this advance. Even where capitalist, free-market models have been eschewed in greater or lesser degree – the Soviet Union, the People's Republic of China, North Korea, and Peronist Argentina – the inherent benefits of industrialization have been embraced rather than rejected. In all industrializing societies, capitalist or otherwise, the forms of management first pioneered in the factories of northern England in the late eighteenth and early nineteenth centuries have also been adopted with little if any hesitation. Everywhere, employment came under the direction of what Pollard (1965: 6–7) referred to as a "new class of managers," able to meld revolutionary technologies with new principles of work. Intellectually and culturally, the entrenchment of this managerial elite was universally associated with an embrace of science, rationality, and a belief in economic progress as an ultimate good. Where mass opposition to new societal and managerial models emerged, it was typically rooted in discontent with the distribution of the fruits of the new order. Marx and Engels, for example, the most vociferous opponents of industrial capitalism, readily endorsed the benefits of industrialization, declaring (1848/1951: 37) in their *The Communist Manifesto* that capitalism has produced "more colossal productive forces than have all preceding generations together." If, Marx (1853/1951: 323) later declared, entire peoples had to be dragged toward industrialization and "progress" through "blood and dirt, through misery and degradation," then so be it.

If, during the twentieth century, it was Marxism that provided inspiration for capitalism's most significant oppositional movements, it is also true that the intellectual demise of Marxism since the collapse of the Soviet Union has seen the emergence of very different oppositional forms; movements opposed to not just capitalism but also the industrial and managerial model which capitalism long fostered. Postmodernism in its various hues informs many of these new oppositional currents, Jacques Derrida (1993/2006: 106) declaring that "never have violence, inequality, exclusion, famine, and thus economic oppression affected so many human beings in the history of the earth and humanity." In Derrida's (1998: 2) opinion, the root cause of such perceived calamities is not simply capitalism but rather the whole canon of "Western morality," "Western philosophy," and "ethnocentric" understandings of language and thought. The late Hayden White (1973a: 1–2), arguably the most influential postmodernist thinker to emerge in the Anglosphere, similarly dismissed "the presumed superiority of modern, industrial society" as ethnocentric "Western prejudice." In such narratives, the central focus is not the matters that long concerned both capitalist managers and their Marxist foes – wealth, productivity, and employment – but rather the essence of the human spirit and intellectual liberation. This means, White (1998) explained, that research should be inspirational (rather than necessarily factual), focusing on "felt needs" that "are ultimately personal." Elsewhere, environmentalists argue that industrialization has not only defiled nature, it has disrupted the material and spiritual connections between humans and the natural world. In the view of a significant number (Lovelock 1995, 2009; Margulis 1998; Harding 2006), all living organisms exist in a myriad of interconnected ways with a natural world best perceived as living entity. Defile nature, and humanity suffers terrible consequences.

Arguably, the popular resonance of post-Marxist critiques of capitalism and management in large part reflects the fact that each draws on common traditions of thought that – although long condemned to minority status within our culture – have proved pervasive and enduring. In the Anglosphere, the roots of these oppositional traditions are most obvious in the English Romantic tradition (Blake, Coleridge, Wordsworth, Percy and Mary Shelley, Bryon, Carlyle). Central to this Romantic tradition is belief in what William Wordsworth (1802/1935: 296) described as "eternal Nature, and the great moving spirit of things" that connects humanity to the wellsprings of its spiritual existence. Material "existence," Samuel Coleridge (1817a: 47, 257) explained, is merely an outward manifestation of an "essence" that pervades all things. Without exception, those located within the Romantic tradition perceived industrialization not as a source of wealth and advancement but rather as an existential threat to humanity's spiritual survival. It was, William Blake (1808/1969: 481) famously observed in his epic poem on *Milton*, industrialization that caused increasing numbers to spend their lives among "dark Satanic Mills" rather than "England's green and pleasant land." For Lord Byron (1816a/1994: 99), as he declared in his *Song for the Luddites*, factory workers were justified in exchanging "the shuttle ... for the sword" in defense of their traditional artisan existence. The damaging effects of modernity are also associated in Romantic canon with inhuman monstrosities, the most vivid of which emerged from a night of storytelling amid the storms of Lake Geneva's foreshore in June 1816. From these lurid tales emerged monsters who have since occupied a permanent place in the Western imagination. The *vampyre* (vampire) owes its modern existence to Lord Byron (1816b/1817) and, more particularly, his physician and fellow author, John Polidori (1819). A creature of apparent wealth and sophistication at home in London's balls and dinner parties, Polidori's vampyre – like England's growing industrial world – feeds on the innocent blood of rural youth. If the vampyre/vampire – subsequently made famous by Bram Stoker's much later imitation – is evil lurking in civilized form, the other famed creation that emerged from the June 1816 night of storytelling, Mary Shelley's *Frankenstein*, is a none too subtle warning against the beguiling promises of science with their supposed capacity to "command the thunder of heaven" and "penetrate into the recesses of nature" (1818/2005: 49).

As the Industrial Revolution gathered pace, the concerns of the English Romantics with spiritual essence, and a spiritually infused nature, were shared by the leading exponents of German idealist philosophy, most notably Johann Fichte, Friedrich Schelling, and Arthur Schopenhauer. Like the English Romantics, this philosophic strand believed, as Fichte (1799/1910: 11) declared, that "Nature is one connected whole," a whole in which one cannot "move a single grain of sand from its place, without thereby ... changing something throughout all parts of the immeasurable whole." Even more than the English Romantics, German idealism was concerned with "inner being," or what Martin Heidegger (1927/1962) subsequently referred to as *Dasein*, understandings that were to profoundly influence Jacques Derrida and, through him, the post-structuralist strand of postmodernist thought. Unlike materialist-oriented thinkers (Adam Smith, Karl Marx, etc.), with their emphasis on the mechanics of production, German idealism made individual will the central force in human affairs, Schopenhauer (1859/1969: 272) declaring, "the will is not only free, but even almighty; from it comes not only its action, but also its world." Like the English Romantics, and the postmodernist schools of thought that they helped inspire, German idealist philosophers also held that all knowledge rested, as Fichte (1799/1910: 91) explained, on subjective "representation" rather than some objectively verifiable reality. Significantly, the commonalities apparent in English Romanticism and German idealism were not simply coincidental. Instead, they were the product of both a common examination of similar problems and a cross-fertilization of ideas, Coleridge (1817b: 103–104) declaring Friedrich Schelling to be not only "the founder of philosophy of nature" but also the "great and original genius" responsible for "the most important victories" in understanding the human spirit. In Schelling's (1799a / 2004: 196) schema, Nature was no mere collection of inanimate objects. Rather, it was an active force; a force comprised of a myriad of "actants" that gave Nature its essential, active essence.

In exploring the ways in which German idealist philosophy and the English Romantic tradition have informed critiques of management and industrial capitalism, this chapter argues two main theses. First, as this introduction has indicated, we argue that post-Marxist critiques of capitalism and management – most particularly postmodernism in all its variety – cannot be properly understood unless one comprehends their intellectual roots in German idealism and English Romantic thought. Second, it is argued that, although German idealism and English Romanticism can be seen as a corrective to a crude materialist emphasis on mechanical aspects of production (capital costs, variable costs, etc.), neither provides a useful basis for a critical understanding of the modern industrial world. The belief that nature has a spiritual essence that pervades all existence proved a philosophic and scientific dead end. For if one believes that nature has a spiritual essence – as did Coleridge, Wordsworth, Fichte, Schelling, and Georg Hegel – then one must necessarily abandon explanations drawn from the physical sciences, Schelling (1799a/2004: 201) condemning "empirical science" as "a mongrel idea" and "physics" as "nothing but a collection of facts." In the hands of Georg Hegel, a belief in all-pervasive historical spirit in nature also led in distinctly totalitarian directions, Hegel (1837/1956: 29–30) declaring that "World-Historical individuals" were those who unwittingly fulfilled the predestined purpose of the world's "inner Spirit." Although in postmodernist canon an emphasis on human consciousness and will is invariably linked to resistance to established power structures – Foucault (1976/1978: 95–96) suggesting that wherever power exists we also find alternative "discourses" that provide "swarm points" for resistance – this philosophical orientation can also lead to authoritarian conclusions. It would appear more than coincidental that both German idealism and English Romanticism culminated in the mid-nineteenth century in the idea that history is driven by "great men" and unadulterated power. For according to Thomas Carlyle (1840/2013: 21, 24), "the history of what man has accomplished in this world, is at bottom the history of Great Men," men whom "we ought to treat ... with an obedience that knows no bounds." In German idealist philosophy, Friedrich Nietzsche (1886/1989: 202) similarly argued in his *Beyond Good and Evil* that "the *fundamental principle of society* ... is *essentially* appropriation, injury, overpowering of what is alien and weaker; suppression, hardness [emphasis in original]." Certainly, it is a mistake to believe that the English Romantics were, any more than their German idealist counterparts, universal proponents of democracy and the interests of common humanity. In the wake of the Peterloo Massacre of 1819, brought about by a cavalry charge into unarmed protestors seeking an extended franchise, Lord Byron (1820a/2015: 353) wrote that he would have "happily passed" his "sword stick" through the leader of the protest and "then thrown myself on my Peers." Percy Shelley (1820/1920: 61) also declared the defense of private property to be the key "foundation" of political order, while Wordsworth's (1821a/1978: 26) response to campaigns for popular democracy was to call for an arming of "the Yeomanry" and a curbing of "the Press by vigilant prosecutions."

It is also the argument of this chapter that the theoretical relativism of both German idealism and English Romanticism with regard to evidence – which has become a defining feature of postmodernism in its various hues – is also misguided. For as the English historian, E.H. Carr (1961/2001: 21), noted: "It does not follow that, because a mountain appears to take on different shapes from different angles of vision, it has objectively either no shape at all or an infinity of shapes." To the extent that a philosophic idealist approach to evidence has utility, it is restricted to discussions of power and the realm of ideas (language, culture, epistemology), realms where postmodernism is now well established. Conversely, it has little utility in matters relating to economics and the mechanics of production, realms where postmodernism is conspicuous largely through absence.

The remainder of this chapter comprises two (lengthy) sections. In the first, we discuss understandings of nature, consciousness, and being in German idealism and English Romantic thought and the ways in which these traditions have influenced critiques of both capitalism and management. The second section considers the Romantic and idealist understandings of evidence and knowledge, understandings that currently inform postmodernist epistemologies. In this section, we will argue that although these schools were correct in believing that we perceive the world through intellectual representations, they were in error in typically denying the objective basis for such representations.

Nature, Being, Consciousness, and Will

Postmodernism as an idealist philosophy – or, to be more exact, a loosely interconnected collection of idealist philosophies – owes an immeasurable debt to German idealist thought. Derrida's (1967/2001: 60) core concept of "trace" – which suggests that past expressions of existence and being can be deconstructed from written texts – was drawn from Martin Heidegger and the earlier work of the French philosopher, Emmanuel Levinas, Derrida (1967/2001: 101) declaring the power of the latter's thoughts was such as to "make us tremble." In turn, Levinas (1957/1987: 103), who suggested in his *Meaning and Sense* that in written language a "trace" is like a face behind a mask in that "a mask presupposes a face," drew his ideas from the German idealist philosopher, Edmund Husserl, Levinas completing his PhD on Husserl's philosophy in 1930. Husserl's ideas were also seminal to Heidegger's thinking, the latter advising in the opening pages of his key work, *Being and Time*, that: "The following investigation would not have been possible if the ground had not been prepared by Edmund Husserl." According to Husserl (1913/1983: 35, 149–150), empirical research – with its emphasis on science and rationality – was a source of grave error, error caused by an unwillingness to recognize that "pure consciousness" was the true wellspring of human endeavors. In turn, both Husserl and Heidegger's ideas were informed by the philosophy of Arthur Schopenhauer, who declared in his *The World as Will and Representation* that all activity – whether human or natural – is guided by its inner "being or true essence," an essence that can only be ascertained through philosophical reflection, not empirical investigation. As a series of lectures given by Heidegger (1975/1985) clear, Heidegger's ideas were also profoundly influenced by Schelling's (1809/2006) *Philosophical Investigations into the Essence of Human Freedom*. In this, Schelling (1809/2006: 33) argued for the "complete freedom" of individual consciousness and will "above and outside of all nature." All of these interwoven strands of thought owe, moreover, a considerable debt to Johann Fichte, arguably the true founder of modern German idealist philosophy. For Fichte, as with the various strands of idealist philosophy that he helped spawn in greater or lesser degree, nothing is more important than the inner essence of being that pervades both individual consciousness and common bonds of existence. It being the case, Fichte (1799/1910: 7) argued that "every existence" signals within it "another existence," ideas that prefigure Derrida's (1967/2001: 254–255) central concept of *déférence* (difference), where the presence of one form of existence always exists alongside an absent existence.

The Foucauldian strand of postmodernism is also deeply rooted in German idealist thought. As Hayden White (1973b: 50) indicated in one of the first, and most insightful, studies of Foucault's work within the Anglosphere, Foucault's ideas represent "a continuation of a tradition ... which originates in Romanticism and which was taken up ... by Nietzsche in the last quarter of the nineteenth century." Like Nietzsche, who declared that through acts of will it is always possible to break the "invisible spell" of societal mores (Nietzsche 1886/1989: 31, 27), Foucault (1966/1994: xx) believed that we can break free of the "fundamental codes" of "culture" through acts of will. Like Nietzsche (1889a/1990) – who argued in his

Twilight of the Idols that all causal explanations (morality, economics, religion) should be rejected as "false causality," it being the case that only the exercise of will should guide behavior and explanations – Foucault rejected causal explanations (White 1973b). By leaving "causes to one side," Foucault (1966/1994: xiv, xviii) declared in *The Order of Things*, one is able to better focus on "transformations" that "shatter" and "destroy" existing understandings. In terms of intellectual heritage, this Foucauldian/Nietzschean emphasis on consciousness and will as transformative forces – and the commensurate dismissal of other factors – owes a clear debt to Schopenhauer's (1859/1969) *The World as Will and Representation*. Like Foucault and Nietzsche, Schopenhauer (1859/1969: 67–68) dismissed "the application of the law of causality" to human affairs. For the problem with the "law of causality," Schopenhauer (1859/1969: 99, 275) concluded that it can "never get at the inner nature of things," the inner sanctum where one finds "the will-in-itself, the inner content, the essence of the world." Nietzsche – and through him Foucault and the wider bodies of Foucauldian thought – also owes a debt to Schelling, who first identified human freedom with the ability to *choose* evil. Whereas previous philosophers had seen evil as something to be overcome, Schelling (1809/2006: 23–24) identified the capacity for *both* good and evil as the "most profound" issue "in the entire doctrine of freedom." Given that acts of will are the expression of human essence, Schelling (1809/2006: 36, 52) logically concluded that whoever lacks the will "to do evil, is also not fit for good." It was this total and utter emphasis on individual will and freedom, and its capacity to move beyond all imposed constraints, which became the defining hallmark of Nietzschean philosophy. When, therefore, Nietzsche (1883/1970: 299) indicated in *Thus Spoke Zarathustra* that "evil is man's best strength" and that "Man must grow better and more evil," he was asserting freedom of individuality beyond the constraints of the social world, rather than the evil per se.

Within the considerable body of postmodernist thought in business and management studies – and more particularly business and management history – ideas that have their roots in German idealism (Nietzsche, Heidegger, Husserl, Schopenhauer, Schelling) are today almost de rigueur. In *A New History of Management*, for example, the authors (Cummings et al. 2017: 40–41, 332) declare their intention to write a Foucauldian-inspired "counter-history" that will "overturn accepted continuities and discontinuities," thereby bringing about a "blurring of the boundaries with regard to what management could be." This "unsettling," we are informed, will "help us question and see alternatives" as to "how we live and evaluate our lives" (Cummings et al. 2017: 333). A new questioning can, in short, overturn material realities imposed by economics, occupational status, and educational attainment. Elsewhere, we are advised (Clark and Rowlinson 2004: 331, 341) that a "historic turn" in the way we research organizational studies can challenge the "efficiency principle" that shapes businesses' behavior, opening up in lieu "a view of history as flux, with continued crises, conflicts and dilemmas." Similarly, leading figures in management and organizational history (Booth et al. 2009: 89) inform us of the utility of "consciously fictive counterfactual narratives" in undermining existing "perceptions, beliefs, knowledge, values and so on." In like fashion an article co-authored by Roy Suddaby, the PDW Chair of the Management History Division, entitled "Craft, magic and the re-enchantment of the world," embraces a Nietzschean emphasis on will and "arationality," whereby "rhetoric" becomes "magical because it initiates action" (Suddaby et al. 2017: 294).

If there are clear linkages between concepts rooted in German idealist philosophy and current understandings in management history, it is also the case that the English Romantic tradition has had a powerful resonance. Although the youthful radicalism of many of the Romantic poets, most particularly Coleridge and Wordsworth, soon gave way to Tory conservatism, they nevertheless continued to underpin – as the great English labor historian, E.P. Thompson (1963: 945) remarked – "a resistance movement" opposed to the new industrial capitalism and "the enunciation of the Acquisitive Man." Like German idealist philosophers, those located within the Romantic tradition were concerned with fostering feeling, emotion, and spiritual being, not rationality and empirical understanding. As Coleridge (1817a: 47) put it, the purpose of literature should not be one of description but rather a spiritually uplifting journey of discovery into human essence "in its primary signification." For Wordsworth (1802/1935: 295–296) as well, the "great poet" was the one responsible for "new compositions of feeling" that proved "pure and permanent."

Universally, the English Romantics perceived the advance of industrialization and urbanization as a social and environmental blight. In Wordsworth's (1814/1853) *The Excursion*, the new industrial factories become places of demonic misery where humanity's body and soul are sacrificed for profit, it being observed in the case of one establishment that:

> . . . as they issue from the illuminated pile,
> A fresh band meets them, at the crowded door –
> . . . Mothers and little children, boys and girls,
> Enter, and each the wonted task resumes
> Within this temple, where is offered up
> To Gain, the master idol of the realm,
> Perpetual sacrifices.

In Blake's (1804/1969) epic poem, *Jerusalem*, the Satanic character of the new "looms" and "mills" is depicted in even starker terms, it being recorded that:

> . . . to those who enter into them they seem the only substances;
> . . . Scotland pours out his Sons to labour at the Furnaces,
> Wales gives his Daughters to the Looms; England nursing Mothers
> Gives to the Children of Albion . . .
> They compell (sic) the Poor to live upon a crust of bead
> . . . The living and the dead shall be ground in our rumbling Mills,

Lord Byron, in addressing the House of Lords (Parliament of United Kingdom 1812: 2), likewise vigorously condemned the new factories, observing that "machines" had "superseded the necessity of employing a number of workmen, who were left in consequence to starve." Similarly, for Percy Shelley (1820/1920: 11), "modern society" had become an all-consuming engine, "wearing away or breaking to pieces the wheels of which it is composed."

The Romantic hostility to industrialization manifested itself in two generalized responses, each of which has had an enduring legacy. First, in rejecting the emerging industrial world – which, other than for Blake, an engraver by trade whose poetry conveyed an intimate understanding of the lived experiences of factory life, was always something alien and spiritually distant – we find a Romanticization of bucolic life. In Wordsworth, this famously involved an embrace of those whom he (Wordsworth 1800/2009: 142, 144) described in the "Preface" to his (and Coleridge's) *Lyrical Ballads*, as those living a "low and rustic life," a lifestyle in which "the essential passions of the heart" inevitably "find a better soil." With Byron, nobility of soul is found among the peasantry of Switzerland, Italy, and Greece, one of his letters recording that he (Byron 1816c/2015: 233) could not adequately describe the impact of his acquaintance with shepherds of the Swiss mountains: a people "pure and unmixed – solitary – savage and patriarchal." Representation of the Swiss peasantry as living a life of freedom in harmony with nature also characterizes both Mary Shelley's short novel, *The Swiss Peasant*, and the poetry of her husband (Shelley 1816/1965: 231), who recorded in *Mont Blanc* how:

> The wilderness has a mysterious tongue . . .
> So solemn, so serene, that many may be
> . . . With Nature reconciled

The second enduring legacy of the Romantic tradition, following on, as an almost inevitable condition of the first, is the positing of a spiritual existence is nature that becomes the wellspring of the human spirit. To Wordsworth (1802/1935: 295–296), as we have noted in the introduction to this chapter, "human nature" can only achieve fulfillment when it is reconciled with "eternal Nature, and the great moving spirit of things." Similarly, Thomas Carlyle (1840/2013: 145) – in rejecting the utilitarian philosophy of Jeremy Bentham that underpinned the liberal, free-market ethos of Victorian England – warned that "he who discerns nothing but Mechanism in the Universe, has . . . missed the secret of the Universe altogether." Whereas for Carlyle (1840/2013: 91, 78), however, the operation of nature represented "the realised Thought of God," for Percy Shelley (1816/1965: 229), it was the "everlasting universe of things," and for Coleridge (1817a: 47, 255), it was spiritual "essence," "present at once in the whole and every part" of material existence. It is with Coleridge's *Biographia Literaria*, moreover, that we find the fullest expression of the concept that nature has a spiritual being, a *natura naturans* that provides "a bond between nature in the higher sense" and humanity's "soul" (Coleridge 1817a: 257). Although Coleridge (1817b: 102) indicates that he developed his ideas before his inquiries into German philosophy, they are nevertheless articulated within a German idealist framework. Fichte's philosophy is described by Coleridge (1817b: 101) as providing the "keystone of the arch" for his conceptualizations, while Schelling's *Philosophy of Nature* is declared a work of "original genius" (Coleridge 1817b: 103).

Like German idealist philosophy, where Schelling (1799a/2004: 201) lambasted "physics" and "empiricism" for studying the "body" of nature rather than its "soul," English Romanticism was associated with a distrust of science, rationality, industrial progress, and the new mechanics of management. As noted in the introduction, Mary Shelley's *Frankenstein* embodies this distrust in monstrous form. In a story that has seeped deep into the popular consciousness (albeit typically in cinematic rather than literary form), we follow Victor Frankenstein's slide into a spiritual abyss, an abyss caused by infatuation with scientific experimentation. Fostered by his chemistry lecturer, who informs Frankenstein that science has penetrated "into the recesses of nature, and shows how she works in her hiding places" (1818/2005: 49), this infatuation leads him beyond the bounds imposed by the natural world. Unlike Frankenstein himself, his monstrous creation at least has the wit to understand the significance of this transgression, reflecting "How, then, must I be hated, who am miserable beyond all living things" (1818/2005: 102). Within Romantic canon, we also find a near universal hostility directed toward the managers of the new industrial era, a class of people associated with exploitation rather than innovation. To Wordsworth's annoyance, this new class – having benefited from "the invention of machinery" that drove rural spinners and weavers out of existence (1835/1974: 223) – also despoiled his beloved Lake District, buying up "the ancient cottages" as holiday retreats. To Percy Shelley (1820/1920: 11, 42–43), the "new aristocracy" was essentially parasitic in nature, responsible for "the augmentation of misery," a process that left children, hitherto "at play before the cottage doors of their parents," as "lifeless and bloodless machines." In Polidori's (1819: xix–xx) *The Vampyre*, we see a similar parasitic monster, a "human bloodsucker" who feeds on "the young and the beautiful" but who is feted in London society. In academia today, one does not need to look far in business and management studies to find echoes of this questioning of managerial legitimacy. In *A New History of Management*, we are informed (Cummings et al. 2017: 177) that business organizations today are associated with "unprecedented economic, social and environmental crises," crises where a "critical questioning" will inevitably bring into doubt the "legitimacy" of "business schools," if not business itself. Elsewhere, we are advised (Clegg and Kornberger 2003: 60, 84) that modern organizations are "iron cages" and "psychic prisons," places where new "performance-management technologies" condemn workers and clients alike to prisonlike "panoptical arrangements" (Fourcade and Healy 2013: 559).

Present at the very birth of industrial capitalism and modern systems of management, it is evident that the English Romantic tradition cast both these revolutionary forces for change in a halo of illegitimacy that each has never fully escaped. If the Romantic critique lacked the institutional coherence of the subsequent Marxist denunciations of industrial capitalism, the fact that it appealed to consciousness, feeling, and emotion – rather than revolutionary violence – arguably added to its enduring presence in our culture.

In summing up the Romantic tradition's significance, E.P. Thompson (1963: 915) argued – in the final page of his *The Making of the English Working Class* – that the inability of "Romantic criticism" to ally itself with "social radicalism" was a "lost" moment in history, a failure that left all of us "among the losers," condemned to generations of inequality and suffering. This is a difficult conclusion for a management historian to support. Far from it being the case, as Wordsworth (1800/2009: 122, 124) advised, that a "low and rustic" life embodied the "beautiful and permanent forms of nature," for most a pre-industrial rural life involved an existence steeped in filth, illiteracy, and premature death. Coleridge (1817a: 32) was, among the English Romantics, highly unusual in recognizing this fact, dismissing Wordsworth discussions of rural life as fictive creations, creations that ignored the brutal labor of rural life that typically produced a population that was "selfish, sensually gross, and hard-hearted." Nor should we suppose that the opposition of those within the Romantic traditions to the advance of industrialization indicated farsighted concern for the plight of the poor. As a philosophic tradition, English Romanticism looked backward, not forward. Byron was, as Cochrane (2011: 15) has observed, only "a revolutionary" when "abroad." In England, he was "a conservative." As noted earlier, Byron was also an opponent of working-class campaigns for universal franchise. Of those fighting for such principles, Byron (1820b/2015: 356) wrote to a fellow peer, "our classical education should teach us to trample on such unredeemed dirt." Similarly, Percy Shelley (1820/1920: 82–83) regarded the industrial working class as morally abased, "sinking into a resemblance with the Hindoos." Wordsworth opposed property taxes to pay for the alleviation of the poor. The more you increase "the facilities of the poor being maintained at other people's expense," Wordsworth (1821b/1978: 39) complained, "the more poor you have." The conceptions of nature expounded by both English Romantics and German idealists were also profoundly misguided, the American physicist, Bernard Cohen (1948: 208), dismissing the "natural philosophy" that they espoused as "the lowest degradation of science," a "nightmare" that science only freed itself from with difficulty.

More fundamentally, the idea that we should abandon the modern industrial world and retreat to some "deep Vale" where there supposedly "abides a power and protection for the mind" (Wordsworth 1888: 31) is delusionary. Yes, it is true, as Blake (1808/1969: 481) recorded, that the new industrial factories appeared as "dark Satanic Mills" to people used to a rural existence and that the poor who worked within their walls initially did so "upon a crust of bread" (Blake 1804/1969: 656). Yes, it is true Byron, as (Parliament of United Kingdom 1812: 2) complained, that rural unemployment was the initial handmaiden of industrialization as "one man performed the work of many." It is, however, folly to believe that pre-industrial rural life was an idyllic world, where a mother was left to happily "rock the cradle of her peevish babe" (Wordsworth 1814/1853) and children to "play before the cottage door" (Shelley 1820/1920: 42). As Thompson's (1963: 320) own account of country weavers makes clear, poverty was their constant companion as family members worked without end, surviving on a diet of "oatmeal and potatoes" mixed "with old milk and treacle." The fact that the first generations to enter the new industrial factories suffered poverty is thus undoubtedly true but hardly historically unique. As Braudel (1946/1975: 725) noted, the "price of progress" has historically been "social oppression," in which only "the poor gained nothing." What is historically unique about the Industrial Revolution and its associated management systems is that by

1850 – two generations after its commencement – the poor had become major beneficiaries. As managers concerned with increased productivity quickly realized, the presence of children in a highly capitalized work environment was more of a hindrance than a help. Accordingly, child labor collapsed. By 1851 (Kirby 2011), only 30% of English and Welsh children worked. Of those who did, only 15.4% of males and 24.1% of females were found in factories. As the new industrial factories demanded literate workforces, attendance at school becomes the social norm, rather than the exception. For the great majority, in short, Romanticized hankering for a bucolic existence was something best left to poetry and literature.

Evidence and Knowledge

It is a peculiar if fundamental fact of research that debates about evidence and knowledge, and of the relationship between the two, is as contested today as they were in the ancient world. Thus we read in the pages of *Academy of Management Review* "that there is a 'literary' or 'fictive' element in all historical and scientific writing" and that "objectivist history" (i.e., one constructed around "facts") "is clearly inimical" to critical "reflexivity" (Rowlinson et al. 2014: 257, 254). Elsewhere, we are advised (Munslow 2015: 129) that we should profoundly question – if not reject – methodologies that are "realist, empiricist," that we should be "rhetorically reconfiguring the past" (Suddaby and Foster 2017: 31), and that useful business-related research can be based on "grounded fictionalism" (Foster et al. 2011: 109). Such approaches are deliberately subversive of established Western canon. For as Derrida (1998: 2) realized, by attacking the principles of language and epistemology upon which Western business endeavor is constructed, one is attacking its very foundations. There is thus much more than hyperbole to the claim by the Dutch postmodernist, Frank Ankersmit (1989: 142), that "The postmodernists' aim is to pull the carpet out from under the feet of science and modernism." If, however, we are to take such critiques seriously – rather than simply dismiss them out of hand as too many of their critics are wont to do (see, e.g., Gross et al. 1996; Windschuttle 2000) – then we need to first understand the origins of postmodernism and its roots in philosophic idealism. This, in turn, requires a comprehension of how German philosophic idealism and English Romanticism emerged in part as responses to British empiricism, a tradition intimately connected to the rise of industrial capitalism and its associated managerial systems.

In origin, the conflict between empiricism and philosophic idealism – and the fundamental principles at stake – can be traced back not centuries but millennia, the former finding its first cogent expression in Thucydides' *The History of the Peloponnesian War*, a work that has provided a guiding star for countless generations of historians. In Thucydides' (431 BCE/1954: 47–48) opinion, research should always be based on "the plainest of evidence," evidence based either on one's own observations or on "eye witnesses" whose accounts one "checked with as much thoroughness as possible." Although Thucydides' formulation did much to inform the empiricist or positivist tradition that emerged in Britain from the mid-seventeenth

17 Foundations: The Roots of Idealist and Romantic Opposition to...

century, in the ancient world it was not shared by the higher minds of Greek philosophy, most particularly Plato and Aristotle. For Plato (380 BCE/2003: 239–248), as he indicated in *The Republic*, it was evident that we do not perceive the world directly but rather through mental "representations," perceptions that we make sense of by giving them generalized mental "forms" which become the basis for reasoned thought. Thus, we categorize certain shapes as geometric "circles" even though it is probable that no perfect "circles" exist in nature. The problem for Plato, as for subsequent philosophers, was to distinguish not only between "representations" that are real from those that are based on illusion (*eikasia*) but also – in terms of the conclusions that we draw from evidence – between "knowledge" and unfounded "belief." To get around these difficulties, Plato chose to regard understanding as a series of hierarchical steps, a solution that caused him to conclude that only a trained elite was capable of comprehending "true reality." In confronting the same issues, Aristotle (c.330a BCE/1941: 689–670, 712–713) distinguished between "practical" and "empirical knowledge" on one hand (i.e., medicine, carpentry, etc.) and "natural science" and "theoretical knowledge" on the other. For Aristotle (c.330a BCE/1941: 712, 860–861) however, such "empirical knowledge" can never do more than provide a basis for "action" by what he called "practical" and "productive science" (i.e., engineering). Conversely, "truth" and "natural science" – which Aristotle (c.330a/1941: 861) associated solely with theoretical physics, mathematics, and theology – can only involve understanding of the inner "essence" of things that "suffer no change," a category within which he fallaciously included "the heavenly bodies" (Aristotle c.330a/1941: 859).

In the ancient world, the most significant attempt to reconcile conflicting views on evidence and knowledge was found in Book X of St. Augustine's (c.400/2007) *Confessions*, one of the most significant (if overlooked) works of Western philosophy that subsequently underpinned much of the thinking of both Immanuel Kant and (to a lesser degree) German idealist philosophy. Like Plato, and unlike Aristotle, St. Augustine (c.400/2007: 153–157) believed that perception was based not on "the things themselves" but rather mental "images" generated by the objects of our senses. Similarly, he held that we "intuit" within ourselves concepts that do not exist in the natural world, i.e., mathematical representations. Where St. Augustine (c.400/2007: 152) differed from Plato was in giving a primacy to the natural "reason" of human beings "to judge the evidence which the senses report."

Long dormant, the problematic nature of the relationship between evidence and knowledge was again brought to the fore in arguably the greatest "debate" in the history of ideas, waged between David Hume (1739b/1896, 1748/1902) – the most original thinker that British empiricism has produced – and Immanuel Kant (1783/1902, 1787/2001), a central figure in German philosophy. This "debate" – the term used advisedly as Hume died in 1776, prior to Kant's refutation of his conclusions – was inspired by Hume's (1748/1902) *An Enquiry Concerning Human Understanding*, which was a popularization of his earlier (1739a/1896) three-volume *A Treatise of Human Nature*. Such were the originality of Hume's insights, Kant (1783/1902: 7) declared, that they proved to be "the very thing" which interrupted him from his "dogmatic slumber," giving his own "investigations" a "new direction."

The revolutionary nature of Hume's insights stemmed from two key theses. First, in giving absolute primacy to physical evidence and experience, Hume (1748/1902: 36) argued that it is impossible to establish through either reason or experimentation any "law of causality." To the extent that we can draw cause-effect relationships, Hume (1748/1902: 43) added, these result from "the effects of custom" – what we generally think of common sense based on long experience – "not of reasoning." Seen from this perspective, everything in history becomes particular. Subsequently, several centuries after Hume, when G.R. Elton (1967/1969: 42) declared in his much read *The Practice of History*, that "[f]ew practicing historians would probably nowadays fall victim to the search for laws," he was therefore not making a new observation. Rather, he was restating what had become a bedrock principle of the British empiricist tradition within which he was located, a tradition that caused Elton (1967/1969: 74) to conclude that "history ... will always be able to say: this once existed or took place, and there is therefore truth to be discovered."

If the first of Hume's key theses made verifiable evidence and experience the central component, his second insight – that human behavior is driven primarily by "passions" and emotion – stands in at least partial contradiction to his first. Devoting the second volume of his *A Treatise of Human Nature* to "passions," Hume (1739b/1896: 241) accurately observed that – unlike reason – "'tis evident our passions" are "not susceptible" to rational "agreement or disagreement." Having identified "passions" as a central explanatory factor in human behavior, however, Hume confronted the problem of how to best weave an understanding of emotion into an avowedly empiricist framework. Hume's (by no means perfect) solution to this problem – which was to have immeasurable significance for disciplines such as economics and management – was obtained through his identification of "self-interest" as humanity's preeminent emotion. As Hume (1739b/1896: 266) expressed it, "Men being naturally selfish ... they are not easily induc'd to perform any action for the interest of strangers, except with a view to some reciprocal advantage."

Immanuel Kant, in countering Hume's treatises in ways that had profound significance for Western research – Popper (1934/2002: 23) observing that Kant was "the first to realize that the objectivity of scientific statements is closely connected with the construction of theories" –studiously ignored Hume's insights into the role of "passions," focusing instead of how we can understand causal relationships. Like Plato and St. Augustine – and unlike Aristotle, Hume, and the wider empiricist tradition – Kant (1783/1902, 1787/2001) argued that we perceive the material world indirectly through mental "representations," representations that can often deceive (i.e., the apparently fixed nature of the "heavenly bodies"). Like St. Augustine – and unlike subsequent exponents of both German idealism and postmodernism – Kant (1787/2001: 348) also believed that the objects of our "representations" *do* have an independent existence, "actually and independently of all fancy." Significantly, Kant (1783/1902: 43) vociferously rejected charges that he was himself a philosophic idealist – charges that grew ever louder after his death – declaring in his *Prolegomena* that "My idealism concerns not the existence of things ... since it never came into my head to doubt it, but it concerns" only the ways in which "things" are represented in our "imagination." Where Kant differed from his predecessors was in making the *testing* of concepts drawn from observation the central plank in his "law of causality." Kant, in coming to this solution to the problem of establishing causal links, effectively outlined principles for research using inductive logic, albeit in ways that avoided the express use of the term.

If Kant believed that, in finding an (imperfect) solution to what he (Kant 1783/1902: 7) referred to as "Hume's problem" – i.e., we can never by reasoned analysis determine causal relationships – it was nevertheless the case that the emergent German idealist traditions quickly honed in on the two obvious weak points in Kant's theorizing. First, in highlighting matters relating to being, consciousness, and will, German idealist thinkers – most notably Fichte, Schelling, Schopenhauer, Hegel, and Nietzsche – picked up the core aspect of Hume's philosophy that Kant had largely ignored: the role of passions, emotion, and feeling. The second problem that German idealism identified in Kant's thinking was the relationship between evidence and knowledge, an area where Kant (1783/1902, 1787/2001) in truth advanced epistemology little further than St. Augustine (c.400/2007), both relying on the powers of reason to distinguish between objective reality and illusion. Indeed, despite the complexity of Kant's thinking, his conclusions in relation to evidence were closer to Hume than subsequent idealist philosophers. As Kant (1783/1902: 102) concluded in his *Prolegomena* "there is something real without us which not only corresponds, but must correspond, to our external perceptions ... This means that there is something empirical, i.e. some phenomenon in space without us." Inherently logical, this is nevertheless a point whose veracity we can never be sure of. It is theoretically possible that the external world is all illusion. In pursuing this exact point, German idealist philosophy established its raison d'être. Within a few years of Kant's articulations, a far more subjective view of evidence found voice in Johann Fichte. Outlining positions that became de rigueur in German idealist philosophy, Fichte declared "that all reality ... is solely provided through imagination" (Fichte 1794/1889: 187) and "that what thou assumes to a consciousness of the object is nothing but a consciousness of thine own supposition of an object" (Fichte 1799/1910: 62). Now, it is true that similar, radical idealist positions were argued long before Fichte. Emphasizing the primacy of consciousness over sensory perception, René Descartes (1641/1991: 149–150) had declared in his *Meditations on First Philosophy* that it is equally possible to "persuade myself" that either "nothing has ever existed" or the reverse. Even more radically, the English cleric, George Berkeley (1710/1996: 24), concluded that all "things that exist, exist on in the mind, that is, they are purely nominal." Where German idealist philosophy differed from these earlier studies was in its establishment of a whole *school* of thought, a school that linked a subjective and relativist view of evidence with consciousness and will.

Although German idealism is universally characterized by an emphasis on consciousness and a distrust of "empirical" evidence and "experimental science" after Fichte it nevertheless bifurcated into two broad streams, albeit ones characterized by fluid rather than rigid borders. The first of these – exemplified in the work of Schelling and Hegel – believed that the "essence" that pervades all things reflects a deist being, a divine force that was to Schelling (1809/2006: 10) the "invisible driving force" in nature, and to Hegel (1837/1956: 36) a "God" whose "plan" determines "the History of the World." The second stream, which is seminal to understanding postmodernist critiques of capitalism and management, is best exemplified in the work of Schopenhauer and, subsequently, Nietzsche, Husserl, and Heidegger, a stream that tied understanding and knowledge to *individual* consciousness and will. In rejecting what he referred to as Kant's "realistic dogma," Schopenhauer (1859/1969: 15) demanded that we "absolutely deny to the dogmatist the reality of the external world . . .The whole world of objects is and remains representation, and is for this reason wholly and forever conditioned by the subject."

It does not take much imagination to see how Schopenhauer's ideas – which were seminal in Nietzsche's philosophy – flowed through Nietzsche, Husserl, and Heidegger to Foucault. Whereas for Schopenhauer (1859/1969: 275) it was "the will to live" that gave "the individual" the power to overcome all else, "even at the sight of death," for Nietzsche (1883/1970: 137) it was "the will itself, the will to power, the unexhausted, procreating life-will." Similarly, for Foucault (1976/1978: 94), power is, primarily, "not an institution" or "a structure" but rather something that is "immanent" and "internalized." For Heidegger (1927/1962: 61), it was also the case that knowledge and "knowing" are primarily due to inner "being," what he referred to as *Dasein* or "Being-in-itself." With Schopenhauer, representation, knowledge, and will are also interwoven in a single whole with speech and language, the claim being that "this world is, on the one side, entirely *representation*" and, on the other, "entirely will" (Schopenhauer 1859/1969: 4). Again, one does not need much imagination to see how such ideas have flowed through to recent postmodernist critiques. For Nietzsche (1874: 28), also drawing on Schopenhauer, what is important in representation is its relationship to an active will, it being the case that "great things never succeed without some delusion." Similarly, for Foucault (1966/1994: 305) – who (wrongly) declared Nietzsche to be "the first to connect the philosophical task with a radical reflection upon language" – representations of language are primarily mechanisms through which "codes of cultures" are enforced – and disrupted (Foucault 1966/1994: xx–xxi).

If the roots of postmodernist canon in German philosophic idealism are self-evident, we should not neglect the debt that this canon owes to English Romanticism. Again, it is not hard to find evidence of this connection, the late Hayden White (1973b: 50) accurately noting (as we have previously indicated) that Foucault's ideas were part of a tradition "which originates in Romanticism": a tradition united by "a common antipathy" to Enlightenment "rationalism." It is, however, through the influence of White himself that we find the principal mechanism through which the shared conceptions of the Romantic tradition – with its hostility to industrialization and a belief in the poetic imagination – enter into postmodernist canon. Described by Rowlinson et al. (2014: 251) as "a leader philosopher of history" whose approach "embodies the kind of history that we mean," White's own intellectual roots in Romantic opposition to industrial capitalism are indubitable. As White (1982: 12) – reflecting on his own conceptions – noted on one occasion, "Romanticism represented the last attempt in the West to generate a visionary politics on the basis of a sublime conception of the historical process." Like

Coleridge (1817b: 164), for whom literature should always act as a source of inspiration for humanity's "philosophic consciousness," for White (1973b: ix–x), any "historic work" must first and foremost be a "poetical act." Like Blake (1799/1980: 10), for whom "this world is all one continued vision of fancy or imagination," for White, "History's subject matter is a place of fantasy" (White 2005: 333), a place where the borders between the "truthful" and the "purely imaginary" are dissolved (White 1966: 130). As with Percy Shelley (1820/1920: 111), for whom the supposed "capabilities for happiness" created by the Industrial Revolution merely ensured an "augmentation of misery," for White (1973b: 2), "modern, industrial society" merely provided for the spiritual degradation of Western society and an associated intellectual subservience by other "cultures and civilizations." White also owed a very significant intellectual debt to the eighteenth-century Italian philosopher, Giambattista Vico (1744/1968: 186), for whom the use of metaphorical imagery in any narrative account was recommended as a means of recapturing the "vast imagination" that had been lost with the advance of civilization and urbanization.

As with German philosophic idealism, whose creed has gained contemporary expression in management and business history via Nietzsche, Derrida, and Foucault, one does not need to look far to see the influence of White and, through him, the Romantic poetic tradition. In assessing the state of organizational and management history, Munslow (2015: 132) places White at the top of his "list" of historical thinkers, declaring his ideas as seminal to the "epistemological insurgency" against "empirical-analytical-representationalist historying." In discussing the critical principles upon which management history should be based, Jacques and Durepos (2015: 96) also assign "White's theory" a primary place in their thinking, a theory which they argue opens up "the emancipatory potential of our discipline in the present and future." Similarly, Durepos and Mills (2012: 84–86), in outlining their conceptions of "ANTi-History," declare that their own "insights" draw on White's "elementary thoughts," thoughts which they argue have been seminal in shifting "historiography" away from "a focus on *truth* [emphasis in original]" toward an understanding of the "socially constructed nature" of historical writing. Elsewhere, the feminist historians, Ann Curthoys and Ann McGrath (2009: ix) declare that "the work of Hayden White" is the "[m]ost influential" force in recent historiography, demonstrating that historical writing is (supposedly) built around "creativity and textuality" rather than any claim to factual accuracy.

One does not need to regard postmodernism with totally antipathy to comprehend the problems that stem from grounding historical research – most particularly in business and management history – in subjective understandings of consciousness, will, and the poetic.

Not only can such an emphasis lead to a lack of thought being given to the material conditions of existence, it also often leads to sweeping epistemological generalizations being made without due consideration as to the implications that necessarily follows when one grounds one's ideas on such premises. If we are to "return to basics" in order to better comprehend our collective intellectual premises, a good place to start is the eighteenth-century "debate" waged between Hume and Kant. For Hume (1748/1902: 19, 30), as for the generations of positivist scholars who followed in his wake, "our thoughts" are always "confined within very narrow limits," limits that cause us to err whenever we move beyond "observation" and "experience." Accordingly, we will always search "in vain" for the "general causes" of things, given that experience restricts our observations to matters particular. Among positivist scholars, the legacy of Hume's dictates is seen in an emphasis on "verifiable" evidence, "facts," and a distrust of grand theorizing, attributes that make positivists natural foes of postmodernism in its various hues, even though (paradoxically) both schools of thought share a common distrust of generalizable "laws." Accordingly, positivist scholars typically seek to "refute" postmodernist-informed methodologies by pointing to factual errors in the latter, Tyson and Oldroyd (2017, 13), for example, finding most objectionable the willingness of "critical accounting" researchers to "wilfully distort or omit key factual information" so as to bolster "a moral stance." The problems with such positivist "refutations" are manifold. As Plato, St. Augustine, Kant, and others long appreciated, we only make sense of our "observations" through conceptual representations and generalizations. Typically, moreover, our conceptual generalizations either do not correspond to the objective world (i.e., the improbability of perfect "circles" existing in nature), or they only have meaning within a wider scaffolding (i.e., something is "high" only in comparison to something else). To complicate matters further, many of the conceptualizations that frame our thinking – democracy, freedom, emancipation, profit – do not have a material existence. How then to make sense of the world without embracing the philosophic relativism of idealist thought or postmodernism? The answer to this question, we suggest, is the necessarily imperfect path suggested by Kant, Popper, E.H. Carr, and others, whereby we start from concepts, concepts that we continually seek to find evidence for in the world of material existence. Now, it must be admitted, as Berkeley (1710/1996: 24) once asserted, that it is possible that the material world is only illusionary spirit and that all "things that exist, exist only in the mind." If, however, it remains the common experience of humanity that our generalized conceptualizations are continually supported by the "observation" and "experience" that Hume held so dear, then we can also logically endorse Kant's (1787/2001: 348) conclusion that there is in all probability a "material" world "actually and independently of all fancy." And if we accept these propositions, then there is no need to heed the siren calls of postmodernism, philosophic idealism, or Romanticism, each of which in their own ways asserted a subjective and "relativist" view of evidence.

Conclusion

For most of the twentieth century, the principal foe of Western capitalism and management was Marxism. For all the bloodshed that the Marxist challenge entailed, however, it was nevertheless the case that Marxism shared much common ground with its capitalist enemies. In terms of social purpose, Marxism shared the view that industrialization was to humanity's benefit. In terms of ideas, Marxism was a materialist philosophy. Like the exponents of classical economics (Smith, Mill, Marshall), Marxists believed in the verifiable nature of evidence. There were always, however, intellectual currents that shared few if any of the assumptions of either classical economics or Marxism. Of enduring significance among these alternative intellectual traditions were German philosophic idealism and English Romanticisms, each of which placed the human imagination, consciousness, and will at the center of their thinking, attributes which have since become a defining feature of the various forms of postmodernism. Like Jacques Derrida (1967/2001), who believed that within language every expression of being occurs alongside an absent existence, German idealism concluded that "every existence" signals "another existence" (Fichte 1799/1910: 7). Like Hayden White (2005: 333), who believed that history "is a place of fantasy," English Romanticism concluded that the world that we inhabit is primarily one of "imagination" (Blake 1799/1980: 10) and that historical writing should be based on the understanding that a "vein of poetry exists" at the "heart" of humanity (Carlyle 1840/2013: 79–80). Like Foucault (1976/1978: 100), who wrote that "power and knowledge are joined together," Coleridge (1817b: 114) recorded that "Knowledge is power." Similarly, in German idealism, we find the belief that "knowledge" represents assertion of "will" by one party over others (Schopenhauer 1859/1969: 337). Also pervading the canon of both German idealism and English Romanticism is the view that industrialization initiated an unprecedented "augmentation of misery" (Shelley 1820/1920: 11), a world of "dark Satanic mills" (Blake 1808/1969: 481) that reduced all within its grip to the status of "herd animals" (Nietzsche 1889a/1990: 130).

Within contemporary business and management history, the understandings that underpinned German idealism and English Romanticism now provide foundations for "critical" and postmodernist perspectives hostile to industrial capitalism and its associated systems of managerial endeavor. Thus we are advised that postmodernists consider "modernist criteria of truth or falsity" as irrelevant in "assessing how the past is re-presented" and that there is a fundamental social "truth" in the "fictive" (Munslow 2015: 139). Hostility to the whole structure of modern industrial society also provides a bond between contemporary postmodernist belief and earlier idealist and Romantic critiques. Accordingly, we are informed that "modernism" is an "utter failure" (Durepos 2015: 161); that "Truth and knowledge . . . are weapons by which a society manages itself" (McKinlay and Starkey 1998: 1); and that current managerial models are complicit in "unprecedented economic, social and environmental crises" (Cummings et al. 2017: 177).

As idealist philosophies, German philosophic idealism and English Romanticism have all benefited from the fact that appeals to imagination, individual consciousness, and the "poetic" are inherently more beguiling than explanations grounded in economics and the base nature of material existence. It has also been the contention of this chapter that postmodernism has benefited from the inherent difficulties that empiricist or positivist epistemologies have in countering the "relativism" of those who stand as heirs to the intellectual traditions of German idealism and/or English Romanticism. As we have noted, the apparent solidity of many positivist defenses crumbles when confronted with the fact that many of concepts central to our understanding do not exist in physical form (profit, freedom, etc.) and that even things do only have meaning when located in a wider intellectual scaffolding.

If the appeals of philosophic idealism, Romanticism, and postmodernism are indubitable, it is nevertheless the case that the underlying premises of these traditions are misguided. In terms of epistemology, it is far more likely that the material world does exist, as Kant (1783/1902: 102) observed, "as something real without us" than the reverse (i.e., the perceived world is a figment of our imagination). Once we accept this premise, then we can continually test our concepts and generalizations against evidence, i.e., that if my employees attend work every day, my output will be higher than if they do not. The association of modern capitalism and management with a universal "augmentation of misery" is also misguided. Rather than it being the case that "never have violence, inequality, exclusion . . .affected so many human being in the history of the earth" (Derrida 1993/2006: 106), capitalism and management have been associated with the advance of democracy and literacy and rising living standards. As the labor historian, E.P. Thompson (1963: 452), noted, industrial capitalism also opened up unprecedented opportunities for women as "independent wage earners," free from "dependence" on male relatives. Similarly, demand for child labor quickly collapsed in every industrializing nation as managers focused on productivity as the primary source of economic gain. It is also a mistake to associate philosophic idealism, with its emphasis on consciousness and will, as inherently democratic and emancipatory. On the contrary, a prioritization of individual will have a tendency to lead its exponents in anti-democratic directions. It is thus hardly surprising that most Romantic and idealist thinkers regarded common humanity with undisguised disdain, dismissing such citizenry as "unredeemed dirt" (Byron 1820b/2015: 356) and "the lowest clay and loam" (Nietzsche 1874: 39). Yes, it is true that Romantic literature and idealist philosophy make us think about individuality and our relationship with the natural world. Their words remain, as intended, spiritually uplifting across the space of centuries. They are, however, poor guides for either practical action or research.

Cross-References

▶ Intellectual Enlightenment: The Epistemological Foundations of Business Endeavor
▶ Economic Foundations: Adam Smith and the Classical School of Economics
▶ The Intellectual Origins of Postmodernism

References

Ankersmit F (1989) Historiography and postmodernism. Hist Theory 28(2):137–153
Aristotle (c.330a BCE/1941) Metaphysics. In: McKeon R (ed) The basic works of Aristotle. Random House, New York, pp 681–934
Aristotle (c.330b BCE/1941) Categoriae. In: McKeon R (ed) The basic works of Aristotle. Random House, New York, pp 3–37
Berkeley G (1710/1996) The principles of human knowledge. In: Berkeley G, Robinson H (eds) Principles of human knowledge and three dialogues. Oxford University Press, Oxford, pp 1–96

Blake W (1799/1980) Letter to Dr Trusler. In: Keynes G (ed) The letters of William Blake. Clarendon Press, Oxford, UK, pp 8–10

Blake W (1804/1969) Jerusalem. In: Keynes G (ed) Blake: complete writings. Oxford University Press, London, pp 620–747

Blake W (1808/1969) Milton. In: Keynes G (ed) Blake: complete writings. Oxford University Press, London, pp 480–535

Booth C, Rowlinson M, Clark P, Delahaye A, Proctor S (2009) Scenarios and counterfactuals as modal narratives. Futures 41:87–95

Braudel F (1946/1975) The Mediterranean and the Mediterranean world in the age of Phillip II, vol 2. Harper Torchbooks, New York

Byron GG (1816a/1994) Song for the Luddites. In: Byron GG (ed) The works of Lord Byron. Wordsworth Poetry Library, Ware, p 99

Byron L (1816b/1817) A fragment. In: Mazeppa. Murray John, London, pp 49–56

Byron GG (1816c/2015) Letter to Augusta Leigh 19 September 1816. In: Lansdown R (ed) Byrons letters and journals. Oxford University Press, London, pp 232–234

Byron GG (1820a/2015) Letter to John Murray 21 February 1820. In: Lansdown R (ed) Byrons letters and journals. Oxford University Press, London, pp 355–357

Byron GG (1820b/2015) Letter to John Cam Hobhouse 22 April 1820. In: Lansdown R (ed) Byrons letters and journals. Oxford University Press, London, pp 351–353

Carlyle T (1840/2013) On heroes hero-worship and the heroic in history. Yale University Press, New Haven

Carr EH (1961/2001) What is history? Palgrave Macmillan, London

Clark P, Rowlinson M (2004) The treatment of history in organisation studies: towards an historic turn. Bus Hist 46(3):331–352

Clegg SR, Kornberger M (2003) Modernism, postmodernism, management and organization theory. Res Sociol Organ 21:57–88

Cochrane P (2011) Byrons romantic politics: the problem of metahistory. Cambridge Scholars Publishing, Newcastle

Cohen B (1948) Science servant of man. Little Brown, Boston

Coleridge ST (1817a) Biographia Literaria: biographical sketches of my life and opinions, vol 2. Best Fenner, London

Coleridge ST (1817b) Biographia Literaria: biographical sketches of my life and opinions, vol 1. Best Fenner, London

Cummings S, Bridgman T, Hassard J, Rowlinson M (2017) A new history of management. Cambridge University Press, Cambridge, UK

Curthoys A, McGrath A (2009) Introduction. In: Curthoys A, McGrath A (eds) Writing histories: imagination and narration. Monash University Press, Melbourne

Derrida J (1967/2001) Writing and difference. Routledge Classics, London/New York

Derrida J (1993/2006) Spectres of Marx: the state of the debt, the work of mourning and the new international. Routledge Classics, London/New York

Derrida J (1998) Interview. In: Ben-Naftali M (ed) An interview with professor Jacques Derrida 8 January. Shoah Resource Centre, Jerusalem. https://www.yadvashem.org/odot_pdf/Microsoft %20Word%20-%203851.pdf. Accessed 9 Nov 2018

Descartes R (1641/1991) Meditations of first philosophy. In: Haldane E, Ross GR (eds) The philosophical works of Descartes, vol 1. Cambridge University Press, Cambridge, UK, pp 131–199

Durepos G (2015) Anti-history: toward a modern histories. In: McLaren PG, Mills AJ, Weatherbee TG (eds) The Routledge companion to management and organizational history. Routledge, London/New York, pp 153–180

Durepos G, Mills AJ (2012) Anti-history: theorizing the past and historiography in management and organization studies. Information Age Publishing, Charlotte

Elton GR (1967/1969) The practice of history. Collins Fontana, Sydney

Fichte JG (1794/1889) The science of knowledge. Trübner & Co, London

Fichte JG (1799/1910) The vocation of man, 2nd edn. Open Court Publishing House, Chicago

Foster WM, Suddaby R, Minkus A, Wiebe E (2011) History as social memory assets: the example of Tim Hortons. Manag Organ Hist 6(1):101–120

Foucault M (1966/1994) The order of things. Vintage Books, New York

Foucault M (1976/1978) The history of sexuality – an introduction. Pantheon, New York

Fourcade M, Healy K (2013) Classification situations: life-chances in the neoliberal era. Acc Organ Soc 38(8):559–572

Gross PR, Levitt N, Lewis MW (eds) (1996) The flight from science and reason. New York Academy of Sciences, New York

Harding S (2006) Animate earth: science, intuition and Gaia. Green Books, Totnes

Hegel G (1837/1956) Philosophy of history. Dover, New York

Heidegger M (1927/1962) Being and time. Blackwell, London

Heidegger M (1975/1985) Schellings treatise on the essence of human freedom. University of Ohio Press, Athens

Hume D (1739a/1896) A Treatise of Human Nature, 3 vols. Clarendon Press, Oxford

Hume D (1739b/1896) A Treatise of Human Nature, vol 2. Clarendon Press, Oxford

Hume D (1748/1902) An inquiry concerning human understanding. In: Hume D, Selby-Bigge LA (eds) Inquiries concerning the human understanding and concerning the principles of morals, 2nd edn. Clarendon Press, Oxford, pp 2–165

Husserl E (1913/1983) Ideas pertaining to a pure phenomenology and the phenomenological philosophy. Martinus Nijhoff Publishers, The Hague

Jacques R, Durepos G (2015) A history of management histories: does the story of our past and the way we tell it matter? In: McLaren PG, Mills AJ, Weatherbee TG (eds) The Routledge companion to management and organizational history. Routledge, London/New York, pp 96–111

Kant I (1783/1902) Prolegomena. Open Court Publishing House, Chicago

Kant I (1787/2001) Critique of pure reason. Penguin Classics, London

Kirby P (2011) The transition to working life in eighteenth and nineteenth-century England and Wales. In:Lieten K, van Nederveeen Meerkerk E (eds) Child labour's global past, 1650–2000, Peter Land, Bern, pp 119–136

Levinas E (1957/1987) Meaning and sense. In: Levinas E (ed) Collected philosophical papers. Martinus Nijhoff Publishers, Dordrecht, pp 75–108

Lovelock J (1995) The ages of Gaia: a biography of our living earth, 2nd edn. Oxford University Press, Oxford, UK

Lovelock J (2009) The vanishing face of Gaia: a final warning. Basic Books, New York

Margulis L (1998) The symbolic planet. Phoenix Press, London

Marx K (1853/1951) The future results of British rule in India. In: Marx K, Engels F (eds) Selected works, vol 1. Foreign Languages Publishing Press, Moscow, pp 319–326

Marx K, Engels F (1848/1951) The communist manifesto. In: Marx K, Engels F (eds) Selected works, vol 1. Foreign Languages Publishing Press, Moscow, pp 21–61

McKinlay A, Starkey K (1998) Managing Foucault: Foucault, management and organization theory. In: McKinlay A, Starkey K (eds) Foucault management and organization theory. Sage, London, pp 1–13

Munslow A (2015) Managing the past. In: McLaren PG, Mills AJ, Weatherbee TG (eds) The Routledge companion to management and organizational history. Routledge, London/New York, pp 129–142

Nietzsche F (1874) On the use and abuse of history for life. http://la.utexas.edu/users/hcleaver/330T/350kPEENietzscheAbuseTableAll.pdf. Accessed 16 Nov 2018

Nietzsche F (1883/1970) Thus spoke Zarathustra. Penguin Books, London

Nietzsche F (1886/1989) Beyond good and evil: prelude to a philosophy of the future new. Vintage Books, New York

Nietzsche F (1889a/1990) Twilight of the idols. In: Nietzsche F (ed) Twilight of the idols/the Anti-Christ. Penguin Classics, London, pp 1–125

Nietzsche F (1889b/1990) The Anti-Christ. In: Nietzsche F, Hollingdale RJ (eds) Twilight of the idols/the Anti-Christ. Penguin Classics, London, pp 126–228

Novecivic MN, Jones JL, Carraher S (2015) Decentering Wrens evolution of management thought. In: McLaren PG, Mills AJ, Weatherbee TG (eds) The Routledge companion to management and organizational history. Routledge, London/New York, pp 2–30

Parliament of United Kingdom (1812) House of Lords Hansard 21: 27 February. https://hansard.parliament.uk/lords/1812-02-27/debates/5dd001a5-1479-4b68-99bd-fed25fd2722d/LordsChamber. Accessed 13 Nov 2018

Plato (380 BCE/2003) The republic. Penguin Classics, London

Pollard S (1965) The genesis of modern management: a study of the industrial revolution in Great Britain. Edward Arnold, London

Polidori JW (1819) The vampyre. Sherwood Neely & Jones, London

Popper K (1934/2002) The logic of scientific discovery. Routledge Classics, London/New York

Rowlinson M, Hassard J, Decker S (2014) Research histories for organizational history: a dialogue between historical theory and organization theory. Acad Manag Rev 39(3):250–274

Schelling FWJ (1799a/2004) Introduction to the outline of a system of the philosophy of nature. In: Schelling FWJ (ed) First outline of a system of the philosophy of nature. State University of New York Press, Albany, pp 193–232

Schelling FWJ (1799b/2004) First outline of a system of the philosophy of nature. State University of New York Press, Albany

Schelling FWJ (1809/2006) Philosophical investigations into the essence of human freedom. State University of New York Press, Albany

Schopenhauer A (1859/1969) The world as will and representation, 3rd edn. Dover, Dover

Shelley PB (1816/1965) Mont Blanc. In: Ingpen R, Peck WE (eds) The complete works of Percy Bysshe Shelley, revised edition, vol 1. Gordian Press, New York, pp 229–233

Shelley M (1818/2005) Frankenstein or the modern Prometheus. Penguin Classics, London

Shelley P (1820/1920) A philosophical view of reform. Oxford University Press, London

St. Augustine (c.400/2007) Confessions. Barnes & Noble Classics, New York

Suddaby R, Foster WM (2017) Guest editorial: history and organizational change. J Manag 43(1):19–38

Suddaby R, Ganzin M, Minkus A (2017) Craft, magic and the re-enchantment of the world. Eur Manag J 35(4):285–296

Thompson EP (1963) The making of the English working class. Penguin, Handsworth

Thucydides (431 BCE/1954) The history of the Peloponnesian War. Penguin Classics, Handsworth

Tyson TN, Oldroyd D (2017) The debate between postmodernism and historiography: an accounting historians manifesto. Account Hist 22(1):29–43

Vico G (1744/1968) The new science, 3rd edn. Cornell University Press, Ithaca

White H (1966) The burden of history. Hist Theory 5(2):111–134

White H (1973a) Metahistory: the historical imagination in nineteenth century Europe. John Hopkins University, Baltimore/Atlanta

White H (1973b) Foucault decoded: notes from underground. Hist Theory 12(1):23–54

White H (1982) The politics of historical interpretation: disciplines and de-sublimation. Crit Inq 89(1):112–137

White H (1998) The historical text as literary artefact. In: Fay B, Pomper P, Van TT (eds) History and theory: contemporary readings. Blackwell, Oxford, UK, pp 15–33

White H (2005) The public relevance of historical studies: a reply to Dirk Moses. Hist Theory 44(3):333–338

Windschuttle K (2000) The killing of history: how literary critics and social theorists are murdering our past. Encounter Books, San Francisco

Wordsworth W (1800/2009) Preface of 1800. In: Owen WJB, Smyser JW (eds) Prose works of William Wordsworth, vol 1. Humanities e-Book. http://ebookcentral.proquest.com/lib/griffith/detail.action?docID=3306065. Accessed 13 Nov 2018

Wordsworth W (1802/1935) Letter to John Wilson June 1802. In: Selincourt E (ed) The early letters of William and Dorothy Wordsworth 1787–1805. Clarendon Press, Oxford, pp 292–298

Wordsworth W (1814/1853) Excursion, second edition, Edward Moxon, London.

Wordsworth W (1821a/1978) Letter to Viscount Lowther 7 February 1821. In: Hill AG, Selincourt E (eds) The letters of William and Dorothy Wordsworth 1821–1828, 2nd edn. Clarendon Press, Oxford, UK, pp 25–26

Wordsworth W (1821b/1978) Letter to Viscount Lowther 26 February 1821. In: Hill AG, Selincourt E (eds) The letters of William and Dorothy Wordsworth 1821–1828, 2nd edn. Clarendon Press, Oxford, UK, pp 38–40

Wordsworth W (1835/1974) A guide through the district of the lakes. In: Owen WJB, Smyser JW (eds) Prose works of William Wordsworth, vol 2. Clarendon Press, Oxford, UK, pp 151–253

Wordsworth W (1888) The recluse. Macmillan, London

The Marxist Opposition to Capitalism and Business

18

Kaylee Boccalatte

Contents

Introduction	412
Marxism Begins: Proudhon and Marx	415
Marx the Revolutionary: Communist Manifesto, Wage-Labour and Capital, and the British Rule in India	419
Marx the Economist: Capital	423
Implications for Management History: Reflections	426
Conclusion	429
Cross-References	431
References	432

Abstract

Marxism is a political ideology synonymous with worker exploitation and capitalist oppression. Marxist thoughts and ideas occupy a prominent place in management history. Regarded as one of the most influential authors of the "nineteenth century," Karl Marx's work was seen as a beacon of light for the "exploited" "proletariat." Motivated by the evident disparity between the "poverty" and "sickness" of the working class and the "triumph" of capitalists, Marx was uncompromising in his resolve to explain the class struggle brought about by private enterprise. While conceding the economic progress made possible through capitalism improved the social conditions for some, Marx believed that the consequence of this progress, the perpetual cycle of degradation and misery experienced by an exploited working class, was not an acceptable price to pay. Whether Marx's theories are supported or opposed, they have had a lasting influence on the minds and actions of those living within a capitalist society. Altering the "nature and direction" of "social science," Karl Marx's collective

---

K. Boccalatte (✉)
James Cook University, Douglas, QLD, Australia
e-mail: kaylee@btfarms.com.au

© The Author(s), under exclusive licence to Springer Nature Switzerland AG 2020
B. Bowden et al. (eds.), *The Palgrave Handbook of Management History*,
https://doi.org/10.1007/978-3-319-62114-2_105

works have endured as one of "the most powerful" forces "permanently transforming the ways in which" people "act and think." Within this chapter, we trace the development of Marxism from Marx's first public work *The Poverty of Philosophy*, written in response to the work of socialist Pierre-Joseph Proudhon, through to the first volume of Marx's *Capital*. This chapter examines the Marxist opposition to capitalism and business.

Keywords

Marx · Proudhon · Capitalism · Exploitation · Surplus value · Adam Smith · Division of labor · India

Introduction

Marxism is a political ideology synonymous with worker exploitation and capitalist oppression. Marxist thoughts and ideas occupy a prominent place in management history. Regarded as one of the most influential authors of the "nineteenth century," Karl Marx's work was seen as a beacon of light for the "exploited" "proletariat" (Marx 1867/2013; Marx and Engels 1848/2012; Berlin 1939/2013). Described in his early years as "the greatest" "genuine philosopher" alive, Marx was credited to be a living combination of the better parts of "Rousseau, Voltaire, Holbach, Lessing, Heine, and Hegel" and his publication *Capital*, "the bible of the working class" (Marx 1867/2013). Marx set out to distinguish his work from those who had come before him. He believed his philosophical predecessors had "only *interpreted* the world, in various ways," whereas he believed "the point" was "to *change* it" (Marx 1867/2013). Motivated by the evident disparity between the "poverty" and "sickness" of the working class and the "triumph" of capitalists, Marx was uncompromising in his resolve to explain the class struggle brought about by private enterprise (Berlin 1939/2013).

Whether Marx's theories are supported or opposed, they have had a lasting influence on the minds and actions of those living within a capitalist society (Berlin 1939/2013). Altering the "nature and direction" of "social science," Marx's work looked at the same problem of political economy differently to his predecessors (e.g., Adam Smith, David Ricardo) by examining the concept of capitalism from an alternative angle – that of the laborer (Berlin 1939/2013). While the scope of his examination did not extend far beyond those factors influencing the capitalist/laborer relationship, Marx's work shifted the way capitalism was perceived. While conceding the economic progress made possible through capitalism improved the social conditions for some (as Proudhon did), Marx believed that the consequence of this progress, the perpetual cycle of degradation and misery experienced by an exploited working class, was not an acceptable price to pay (Berlin 1939/2013; Proudhon 1847/1888). As a result, Marx devoted much of his working life to liberating the proletariat, the underclass of his time, both actively by inciting revolution and passively by educating society on the state of political economy. His contribution to societies understanding of how value is created and distributed in a capitalist society was significant. Karl Marx's collective works have endured as one of "the most powerful" forces "permanently transforming the ways in which" people "act and think" (Berlin 1939/2013). The significance of Marx's work lies in his different investigation of and reaction to the social and political consequences of "the evolution and structure of capitalist society" (Berlin 1939/2013). This chapter examines the Marxist opposition to capitalism and business.

Marxism commenced unceremoniously. Marx's first public work was a paper written in response to the work of socialist Pierre-Joseph Proudhon (Proudhon and McKay 2011). Proudhon was a popular socialist in France during the mid-nineteenth century and Marx's "main theoretical competitor within the socialist movement" (Proudhon and McKay 2011). Significant to Marx's ties with Proudhon was the conflict that existed between the two, a conflict rumored to have started with Marx's publication of *La Misère de la Philosophie* (or *The Poverty of Philosophy*). Written in response to Proudhon's the *La Philosophie de la Misère* or in English, *The Philosophy of Poverty*, Marx widely condemns Proudhon, inciting a feud between the Proudhonists and Marxists that would span years (Hoffman 1967). Central to the ongoing dispute is the origin of Marx's concepts such as surplus value and class conflict (Hoffman 1967). Supporters of Proudhon claim that Marx plundered various ideas from Proudhon, later restating or advancing them without acknowledging Proudhon's role in first, "propounding and proving" their legitimacy (Proudhon and McKay 2011). Despite questions surrounding the originality of Marx's economic theories, there is no doubt that the way in which Marx later developed and presented his ideas was his own (Tucker 1888). Although Marx was one of Proudhon's "harshest critics" he went on to name in various later texts, including *The Communist Manifesto* and *Capital* indicating that despite conflicts of opinion, Proudhon had left a lasting influence on him (Marx 1867/2013; Marx and Engels 1848/2012; Proudhon and McKay 2011). *The Poverty of Philosophy* was Marx's first major work and therefore provides insight into the origins of his doctrine, which ultimately became Marxism (Proudhon and McKay 2011). In order to understand Marxist thought therefore, it is necessary that we trace the development of his ideas back to their roots, roots which are irrefutably entwined with Proudhon. Marx, however, was not merely a man of words but a man inspiring action.

Marx's and Engel's publication of the *Communist Manifesto* aimed to ignite a fire in the hearts of proletariats. Distributed in Paris "shortly before the insurrection of June 1848," the *Communist Manifesto* was not recognized for its social and political significance until after the French Revolution of 1848 had been defeated (Marx and Engels 1848/2012). Going on to become one of the most widely distributed political pamphlets in the world, the Manifesto not only stands to end class divisions, private ownership, and the bourgeois rule but bring about a world united through public ownership (Marx and Engels 1848/2012). Recognizing, however, that the average working-class person – those who would ultimately partake in a proletarian revolution – had little knowledge or understanding of the economic foundations on which the bourgeois rule was built, Marx published a series of articles within a radical newspaper, the *Neue Rheinische Zeitung* (of which he later became "its chief editor")

(Marx 1849/2010; Berlin 1939/2013; Wheen 1999). Within these articles, subsequently republished as *Wage Labour and Capital* (Marx 1849/2010), Marx explained in simple terms, the fundamental elements of the economic situation at the time. He educated the public on how the capitalist class formed and maintained its power, giving each reader the ability to make an informed decision as to the merits (and drawbacks) of capitalism (Marx 1849/2010). No Marx publication, however, better illustrates the depth and scope of change capitalism brings to a previously "uncivilised" (by English standards at the time) society, than *The British Rule in India*, and *The Future Results of British Rule in India* (Marx 1951a, b). Writing on the conquering of India, Marx outlines how the British transformed the nature of the Indian society. No longer were the Indians living under a despotic regime, operating a "social division of labor, without production of commodities." For, under the rule of British bourgeoises, they became internally united by capitalist trade (Marx 1867/1887, 1951a, b. Capitalism, however, is akin to a double-edged blade, providing both benefits and drawbacks. Therefore, despite the bourgeoise, within "one hundred years," having "created more massive and more colossal productive forces than have all preceding generations together"; despite the "improvement" in "instruments of production" and the "immensely facilitated means of communication" drawing "even the most barbarian, nations into civilisation"; and despite the progressive developments occurring in response to the bourgeois rule, Marx saw the system as too productive, too powerful, and too narrow (Marx and Engels 1848/2012). Marx believed that "whatever could be defined as progressive in terms of the human conquest of nature had been achieved at the price of the increasing exploitation and degradation of the real producers – the working masses" (Berlin 1939/2013). Consequently, Marx believed the capitalist system needed to be overthrown in favor of Communism.

Central to capitalism is labor: the "alienated" workers "without whom" the system "would fail" (Marx 1867/2013). Living under a capitalist regime, wherein the class divisions between bourgeois and proletariat continue to expand, Marx was determined to thoroughly investigate the inherent inequality and exploitation brought forth by the system. By the late 1950s, Marx had fully developed his "criticism of political economy" (Marx 1849/2010). With methodical diligence, Marx constructed his foremost economic publication outlining the capitalist mode of production, *Das Kapital: Kritik der politischen Oekonomie* or as it is known in English, *Capital*. Acknowledging the work of classical economics including Adam Smith and his "general theory of value," which David Ricardo later revised and formalized, Marx's "theory of value" "in its fundamentals" was described as "a necessary sequel to the teaching of Smith and Ricardo" (Marx 1867/1887). Central to Marx's contribution to the study of economics is his study of labor value (Wolff and Resnick 2012; Berlin 1939/2013; Marx 1849/2010). Specifically, it is claimed that Marx was the first to "examine critically" the "two-fold" nature of labor within commodities; that labor has both a use value and an exchange value (Marx 1867/1887; Carey 2019). The value of labor, as understood by Marx, lies at the foundation of the bourgeoise's appropriation of surplus value and is thus central to the worker's plight under capitalist's rule. For it is through the value creating quality of labor-

18 The Marxist Opposition to Capitalism and Business 415

power where the capitalist extracts surplus value, a value which is transformed into capital and revenue (Marx 1867/1887). According to Marx, wealth is created when the "value of the elements consumed in production" – a value including raw materials, wear and tear of any equipment used during production, and labor power – is lower than the value of the product (Marx 1867/2013). The difference between the commodities two values (i.e., the value advanced in production and the value of the commodity in exchange) is surplus value, or, in other words, the capitalist's profit (Marx 1867/1887).

Marx's work is fundamentally different from those who came before him. Writing at a time in history which saw the movement from feudal rule to a free, capitalist economy, he not only bore witness to changing work relationships but advances in machinery, transportation, and communication which fostered significant improvements the means of production and distribution (Marx 1849/2010; Marx and Engels 1848/2012; Marx 1867/1887; Ackers and Payne 1998; Marx 1951a). Marx also bore witness to the birth of a new, capitalist society and through this, the emergence of wage-labor, capital, private property, and a new form of class distinction: the proletariat and bourgeoisie. Examining Marx and his contribution to the history of management is the central purpose of this chapter. While it is not possible to explore all of Marx's work, concepts, and ideas within this chapter, in large part due to the scope and depth of his writings, every effort will be made to do justice to those which are included and pertain to discussions as they are narrowly constructed. Prior to commenting on Marx's contribution to the history of management, it is necessary that we begin with an examination of Marxism's first public work, *The Poverty of Philosophy* and trace the development of Marxist concepts through select works, before concluding with the first volume of Marx's *Capital*.

Marxism Begins: Proudhon and Marx

The first "public work on Marxism" was *The Poverty of Philosophy*, a book entitled as a mimicry to Pierre-Joseph Proudhon's publication *The Philosophy of Poverty* (Proudhon and McKay 2011). Marx appears to have undertaken considerable effort to not only refute the work of his former acquaintance but disparage Proudhon's stance as "one of the leading socialist thinkers in France" of his time (McKay 2017). In the opening sentences of his book, Marx says:

> M. Proudhon has the misfortune of being peculiarly misunderstood in Europe. In France, he has the right to be a bad economist, because he is reputed to be a good German philosopher. In Germany, he has the right to be a bad philosopher, because he is reputed to be one of the ablest French economists. Being both German and economist at the same time, we desire to protest against this double error. (Marx 1847/1955)

Significantly, it is Proudhon's work which has been credited as the "originator" or "the stimulus responsible" for several of Marx's concepts including "surplus value," "materialism," and the "class struggle" (Hoffman 1967). However, claims of "plagiarism" or that Proudhon was the father of such concepts, according to Hoffman, attribute "unwarranted importance" to him, or more broadly, any single person (Hoffman 1967). While the "similarities in" both Marx and Proudhon "texts" indicate "that they probably learned much from each other" Hoffman says, "the differences between the two men were too great for them to influence each other significantly" (Hoffman 1967). It is, however, "fair to say" that if Marx had "appropriated" a number of "themes" from Proudhon, he did later develop these in greater depth (Proudhon and McKay 2011). Despite the disputes that exist between the Proudhonists and Marxists, it is undeniable that of some elements contained within Marx's later work (e.g., *Capital*, published 20 years after *The Philosophy of Poverty*) bears a marked resemblance to those first discussed by Proudhon (Proudhon and McKay 2011). Regardless of which side of the debate one stands, the interaction between Proudhon and Marx contributed to the development of Marxist ideology, an ideology which remains prevalent in the modern study of political science. In order to thoroughly examine Marxism therefore, it is necessary this chapter commence with a brief overview of Proudhon's work in *The Philosophy of Poverty* and Marx's response.

Capitalisms core purpose has always been the same: profits. The processes by which it is understood profits are achieved – and how they are measured – have undergone a marked transformation throughout the years. However, central to enduring understandings is the concept of value. Adam Smith "discovered the division of labor" and in turn, the force which produces "value": labor (Proudhon 1847/1888). Ricardo refined the theories of exchange value saying, "excepting those" things "which cannot be increased by human industry" (e.g., "rare statues") "labor time … is really the foundation of the exchangeable value all things" (Ricardo 1817/2001). However, during Proudhon's time (the mid-1800s), capitalism's defining characteristic was not the division of labor, nor was it labor time. Rather, it was wage-labor (Proudhon 1847/1888; McKay 2017). According to Proudhon, wage-"labor measured by time," is central to the creation of "surplus" or "excess" within a capitalist economy (Proudhon 1847/1888).

According to Proudhon, wage-labor emerged in response to the "employment of machinery," "the most powerful machine" being, "the workshop" (McKay 2017; Proudhon 1847/1888). A workshop organizes labor into "permanent" groups with a "specific purpose," working towards a united objective (Proudhon and McKay 2011). For the employer, organized workshops provide a means of controlling labor and therefore, "produce more steadily" and "more abundantly," with "less cost" (Proudhon 1847/1888). The ability to reduce production costs allows the capitalist to sell their goods at lower prices which increases sales and generates greater profit in return (Proudhon 1847/1888). The emergence of "the workshop," with increased productive capacities and access to greater capital, monopolized market share and reduced the ability for certain persons to "sell" their "products" of labor "directly" to the public (i.e., the cordwainer selling their shoes) (Proudhon 1847/1888). Unable to compete "against a power so superior" (i.e., the workshop), "isolated labor" in consequence came to work under a "master" which reduced their "rank" from "artisan to that of common workman" (Proudhon 1847/1888). Despite the employee being guaranteed a "perpetual market" for their labor, "steady work" for "a fixed price, and security" through this arrangement, their labor (and subsequent produce of) becomes the property of the "purchaser or middle-man" (i.e., the employer) (Proudhon 1847/1888). The resulting "master"–"labor" relationship is consequently marked by an inherent "institutional inequality" (McKay 2017; Proudhon 1847/1888), an inequality exacerbated by the laborer's loss of autonomy, authority, and status within the workplace. According to Proudhon, "Machinery plays the leading role in industry, man is secondary," for the "workshop" is designed to serve "exclusively the interests of" "the wealthiest class," not that of the labor working within, he thus lays the foundation of class conflict (Proudhon 1847/1888).

Proudhon "understood that wage-labor results in the exploitation of labor," exploitation that occurs at the point of production (McKay 2017). Marx, however, in his response *The Poverty of Philosophy*, had developed the "thesis" that "exploitation" was linked to "exchange" or the sale of goods (i.e., not labor) (McKay 2017; Moore 1993). Therefore, where Proudhon's solution to rectify the widespread exploitation was to reunite workers with the means of production they use," Marx's was "ending exchange" as it existed within a capitalist market (McKay 2017; Moore 1993). Marx states:

> "Economic categories are only the theoretical expressions, the abstractions of the social relations of production" and that "Social relations are closely bound up with productive forces. In acquiring new productive forces men change their mode of production; and in changing their mode of production, in changing the way of earning their living, they change all their social relations." (Marx 1847/1955)

According to Moore, when "one mode of production" is changed and "replaced by another," all "relations of production are changed" (Moore 1993). If therefore, the capitalist "mode of production" is "exchange," it follows that eliminating "capitalist exploitation," which occurs through exchange, is possible only by "ending exchange" (Moore 1993). For both Marx and Proudhon, despite their differing views on the point at which surplus is generated, labor is critical to capitalism.

Labour is the sole source of wealth, for, it is through labor alone, where the goods of nature are combined, altered, and transformed into "elements of wealth" in a "proportion" that will "give the greatest amount of well-being" (Proudhon 1847/1888). Proudhon, however, did not believe that labor had measurable value (Proudhon 1847/1888). He states labor has value, not "as merchandise itself" but through the value of its *potential*, thus labor only "becomes a reality through its product" (Proudhon 1847/1888). Proudhon believed, therefore, that it is more accurate to say "the daily product of this man's labor is worth five francs" and *not* that the "man's labor is worth five francs per day" (Proudhon 1847/1888). In other words, he believed that is was the resultant commodity (which becomes capital) that held value, and that labor was simply means of producing that capital. Of this Marx states:

> "All M. Proudhon's arguments are limited to this: labor is not bought as an immediate object of consumption. No, it is bought as an instrument of production, as a machine would be bought. As a commodity, labor has no value and does not produce. M. Proudhon might just

as well have said that there is no such thing as a commodity, since every commodity is obtained merely for some utilitarian purpose, and never as a commodity in itself." (Marx 1847/1955)

Marx counters that "labor, inasmuch as it is bought and sold, is a commodity like any other commodity" (Marx 1847/1955). As Marx's work matured, however, this view changed. Within *Capital,* he states "The purchaser of labor-power consumes it by setting the seller of it to work. By working, the latter becomes actually, what before he only was potentially, labor-power in action, a laborer" (Marx 1867/1887). According to Oakley, Marx later developed the idea propounded by Proudhon in his "concept of *labor power*" that "*as a commodity* labor produces nothing and it exists independently of and prior to the exercise of its potential to produce value as *active labor*" (Oakley 1981/2004; Proudhon and McKay 2011). On this topic of labor value, Marx goes on to say:

> In measuring the value of commodities by labor, M. Proudhon vaguely glimpses the impossibility of excluding labor from this same measure, in so far as labor has a value, as labor is a commodity. He has a misgiving that it is turning the wage minimum into the natural and normal price of immediate labor, that it is accepting the existing state of society. So, to get away from this fatal consequence, he faces about and asserts that labor is not a commodity, that it cannot have value. He forgets that he himself has taken the value of labor as a measure, he forgets that his whole system rests on labor as a commodity, on labor which is bartered, bought, sold, exchanged for produce, etc., on labor, in fact, which is an immediate source of income for the worker. He forgets everything. (Marx 1847/1955)

Marx's response, claimed McKay, "did not" at this point in time "understand the difference between wage-labor (selling your labor)" evident within capitalism "and commodity-exchange (selling the product of your labor)" (McKay 2017; Proudhon and McKay 2011). The examination of wage-labor within this chapter, however, has not yet considered one critical aspect, a "universally and absolutely true" principle: that "all labor should leave an excess" (Proudhon 1847/1888).

Perhaps one of the more significant outcomes of Proudhon's work (in relation to Marx) is the concept of surplus. A surplus of value is, in other words, profit (Proudhon 1847/1888). In order to construct an accurate understanding of Proudhon's theory of surplus value, it is necessary that we restate two key concepts that have been addressed within this chapter. First, labor does not have value, products have value. Labour is used to create products and thus create value. Second, wage-laborers have sold their labor and the rights to the commodities they produce to their employer. This means that in exchange for a wage, laborers work for the benefit of their master. Proudhon, "recognising that the worker was hired by a capitalist who then appropriates their produce in return for a less than equivalent amount of wages" and, ultimately, "located surplus value" in production (Proudhon and McKay 2011). According to McKay, Proudhon states in volume two of his, *The Philosophy of Poverty*:

> I have proven, in dealing with value, that every labor must leave a surplus; so that in supposing the consumption of the laborer to be always the same, his labor should create, on top of his subsistence, a capital always greater. Under the regime of property, the surplus of

labor, essentially collective, passes entirely [...] to the proprietor: now, between that disguised appropriation and the fraudulent usurpation of a communal good, where is the difference? The consequence of that usurpation is that the worker, whose share of the collective product is constantly confiscated by the entrepreneur, is always on his uppers, while the capitalist is always in profit [...] political economy, that upholds and advocates that regime, is the theory of theft. (McKay 2017)

Labourers therefore, employed by a "master," must, during the course of their work, create value, either individually or collectively that exceeds their income (required for subsistence). This surplus value is appropriated by the capitalists (i.e., the employer) and considered "profit." Proudhon discusses the "collective man" or "collective force" within the context of surplus value to ensure *collective* value is considered (in addition to individual) for "collective endeavours produced an additional value," a value "unjustly appropriated by the capitalist" (Proudhon and McKay 2011). For while a single laborer may produce ten pins per day (to use Smith's example (Smith 1776/1999)) and receive $20 pay, ten laborers working together "uniting or combining their forces" may produce 4,000 pins in a day (Proudhon and McKay 2011). Therefore, the capitalists, while only increasing their labor costs tenfold ($20 × 10 workers), receive a production increase of over 400-fold. This exploitative practice of "expropriating" the laborers "surplus" can only be rectified, according to Proudhon, by paying each laborer not in wages but an amount "equivalent" to the "service rendered" (Proudhon and McKay 2011).

Marx's response to Proudhon's discussion on surplus value is largely critical of Proudhon's explanation and his mathematical calculations. Discussions on the concept of surplus or excess are largely tied to criticisms rather than the fundamental notion that as owners of the product of wage-labor, capitalists extract "excess" or "surplus" value through the production process (Proudhon 1847/1888). Marx's later theories of surplus, however, as will be discussed in the following section of this chapter, do bear marked similarities to the concept provided by Proudhon. For example, within *Capital*, Marx states that the "labor-process" undertaken in order to produce value has two characteristics: "First, the laborer works under the control of the capitalist to whom his labor belongs," and second, "the product is the property of the capitalist and not that of the laborer, its immediate producer" (Marx 1867/1887). He then goes on to say that capitalists aim to create "surplus-value" by producing a "commodity whose value shall be greater than the sum of the values of the commodities" (i.e., "the means of production and labor-power") "used in its production" (Marx 1867/1887).

Marx the Revolutionary: Communist Manifesto, Wage-Labour and Capital, and the British Rule in India

From condemning to commanding, Marx's work (aided by Engels) in the *Communist Manifesto* cemented his name in the history books (Marx and Engels 1848/ 2012). In 1848, the "history of all hitherto existing society" was a "history of class struggles" (Marx and Engels 1848/2012). The bourgeoisie and proletariat were at one point aligned in their objectives: fighting alongside one another in overthrowing the European feudal order of 1848 (Marx 1849/2010; Marx and Engels 1848/1969b). However, the alliance between the bourgeoisie and proletariat was short lived (Marx 1849/2010; Marx and Engels 1848/1969b). Divided by class, by interest, and by condition, the bourgeois and the proletariat soon after found themselves opposed in their "first great battle": the "Parisian insurrection of June 1848" (Marx 1849/2010). Ultimately defeated by the bourgeois, the proletariat's uprising, at least for a time, ceased (Marx 1849/2010). Generating traction in the wake of these political revolutions, Marx's and Engel's *Communist Manifesto* became one of the most widely spread political pamphlets of its era (Marx and Engels 1848/2012; Marx and Engels 1848/1969b). Aiming to create a history of their own design, Marx and Engels within the *Communist Manifesto*, called for the Proletariats of "all countries" to "unite" in common aim: to forcibly "overthrow" "all existing social conditions" (Marx and Engels 1848/2012). At the center of these aims was the "dissolution of modern bourgeois property" (Marx and Engels 1848/2012). The *Communist Manifesto* was developed in response to the rising class inequality and the poor conditions experienced by the working-class proletariat as a result of industrialization (Marx and Engels 1848/2012). Founded on a "single, unconscionable freedom – Free Trade," "modern industry" with machinery and workshops (i.e., organized labor) was, unlike the preceding feudal system, underpinned by wage-labor (Marx and Engels 1848/2012). Characterized by free competition, the bourgeois advanced technological means of production to levels previously unimagined (Berlin 1939/ 2013; Marx and Engels 1848/1969b). Development of "machinery," "steam-navigation, railways" and "electric telegraphs" paved the way for significant improvements in "productive forces" (Marx and Engels 1848/1969b). Within the "modern industry," however, workers were no longer *giving up* a portion of the produce of their labor power, as was the case with serfs under the feudal system (Marx and Engels 1848/1969a). For, proletariats, working under the bourgeois were paid (i.e., they *receive*), not a portion of their produce (i.e., the resultant capital) but a wage (Marx and Engels 1848/1969a). In other words, the proletariats were, as workers, reduced to selling "themselves" (i.e., their time) "piecemeal," as a commodity in order to live (Marx and Engels 1848/2012). While the ruling class, the bourgeois, were unable to "exist without constantly revolutionising the instruments of production," the working class, dependent on the bourgeois, were unable to maintain a standard of life defined by their skill or personal initiative (Marx and Engels 1848/2012; Berlin 1939/2013). Rather, the proletarians lived only "so far as the interest of the ruling class" required it (Marx and Engels 1848/2012).

Alleviating the condition of the proletariat was the central purpose of the Communist movement. According to Marx and Engels, achieving a Communist rule required the abolishing "private property," and the "right of personally acquiring property" as a reward for laboring (Marx and Engels 1848/2012). For, the fundamental condition giving rise to the bourgeois is the "formation and augmentation of capital," a condition only advanced through wage-labor (Marx and Engels 1848/2012). Eliminating the ability for labor power to transform into capital or the ability for "individual property" (e.g., labor power) to transform into "bourgeois property" (i.e., capital), therefore, eliminates "individuality" and gives rise to "common property" (Marx and Engels 1848/2012). The Manifesto, however, calls for more than just the abolition of private property. In fighting the "battle of democracy," social reform required centralization of a national bank, as well as communication and transport system; income tax reforms; more equal opportunities for securing work and greater parity of between the populations of town and country; publicly funded education; and an end to child labor (Marx and Engels 1848/2012). Each objective contributing to the overarching aim of dissolving "class distinctions" and establishing a public system of production (Marx and Engels 1848/2012). Within the *Manifesto,* however, Marx and Engels are not simply calling for the people of Britain to revolt but for the people of "all countries" with a bourgeois rule to rise up (Marx and Engels 1848/2012). Marx believed that the failed French revolution of 1948, was in part, attributed directly to the "leaders" "thinking that they would be able to consummate a proletarian revolution within the national walls of France, side by side with the remaining bourgeois nations" (Spagnoli 2010). The *Manifesto,* therefore, not only provides a road map of objectives vital to achieving the communist cause. It also acts as a call to action for *all* those in *all* countries supporting a "Communistic revolution" (Marx and Engels 1848/2012). Marx and Engels, within the Manifesto, did not aim to merely understand proletariat exploitation, they aimed to change it. Emphasizing the need for unity among the working class to achieve their desired "ends," Marx and Engels conclude the famed *Communist Manifesto* exclaiming, "Working men of all countries, Unite!" (Marx and Engels 1848/2012).

Recognizing the "ignorance and confusion" surrounding the working class's understanding of "political economy," in April 1849, Marx began to publish a series of news articles (earlier written as lectures) within the radical newspaper *Neue Rheinische Zeitung* (Marx 1849/2010; Berlin 1939/2013). Ultimately becoming what is today known as *"Wage Labour and Capital,"* these articles provided a means of educating the general public on the "history and principles of economic development" (Marx 1849/2010; Berlin 1939/2013). Within these articles, Marx explains economic relations and outlines key characteristics of the capitalist class and how it formed (Marx 1849/2010). Targeting the workers who could ultimately partake in the proletariat revolution, Marx aimed to explain the economic conditions of the time "as simply and popularly as possible" (Marx 1849/2010). Commencing with a discussion on wages, Marx states that wages are paid by the capitalist, to the worker, in exchange for a "certain period of work or for a certain amount of work" (Marx 1849/2010). It is not, however, the workers "labor" that is being bought (by the capitalist) and sold (by the laborer), but it is *labor-power* (Marx 1849/2010). Distinguishing between labor and labor-power, Engels explains that labor cannot be purchased, it must be performed. Therefore, it is not labor that is exchanged but labor-power (Marx 1849/2010). It becomes evident at this point that Marx's conclusion in *The Poverty of Philosophy,* that "labor, inasmuch as it is bought and sold, is a commodity like any other commodity," is incorrect (Marx 1847/1955). For, it is labor power which is a commodity, like any other commodity that can be bought and sold (e.g., sugar) (Marx 1849/2010). He goes on to say, however, that labor power is a unique commodity, for unlike others, (e.g., sugar) labor-power adds to the product during production a "greater value than it previously possessed" (Marx 1849/2010). Workers therefore, do not only produce products. They also produce capital: "values which serve anew to command" their "work and to create by means of it new values" (Marx 1849/2010). Within the "relation of capital and wage-labor," Marx states, "the interests of capitals and the interests of wage-labor are diametrically opposed" (Marx 1849/2010). Herein lies the root cause of conflict between the bourgeois and proletariat.

Despite existing within a "free market," workers are bound to laboring under a bourgeois rule. Perhaps, to illustrate the scope of the English bourgeois control and how their influence can shape a country, Marx wrote *The British Rule in India*, followed by *The Future Results of British Rule in India* (Marx 1951a, b). A country with inhabitants divided by religion, tribe, and caste, with no centralization, India was almost "predestined" to be a "prey of conquest" according to Marx (Marx 1951b). With his papers, Marx describes, "Indian society" as having "no history at all, at least no known history" (Marx 1951b). "What we call its history," Marx says "is but the history of the successive intruders who founded their empires on the passive basis of that unresisting and unchanging society" (Marx 1951b). The British, while not the first to "intrude" upon India, were the first to conquer it (Marx 1951b; Hegel 1899/2004). In conquering the land, the English had a "double mission" to fulfil: "one destructive, the other regenerating." They had to annihilate the "old Asiatic society" and then lay the "material foundations of Western society in Asia" (Marx 1951b). Britain's means of colonizing India was, therefore, to first destroy the "Hindoo civilisation … by breaking up the native communities, by uprooting the native industry, and by levelling all that was great and elevated in the native society" (Marx 1951b). A vicious and barbaric undertaking in its own right, the destruction effected by the English found some reprieve. While India's "village communities" prior to colonization appeared "idyllic" and "inoffensive," under the surface their primitive culture was built on a foundation of "Oriental despotism" (Marx 1951a). The isolated communities, Marx said, with deeply ingrained religious beliefs "restrained the human mind within the smallest possible compass," "enslaving it beneath traditional rules, depriving it of all grandeur and historical energies" (Marx 1951a; Kumar 1992). Condemning, therefore, the means by which the bourgeois had overtaken the country and its people, Marx, reminds us that, "we must not forget that these little communities" before the English "were contaminated by distinctions of caste and be slavery, that they subjugate man to external circumstances instead of elevating man to be the sovereign of circumstances, that they transformed a self-developing social state into never changing natural destiny" (Marx 1951a).

Introduced to Western civilization and capitalism, the lives of Indians were forever changed. In colonizing India, Britain first established "political unity" (Marx 1951b). A unity that was "strengthened" by European's "electric telegraph," the "free press" and organization of a "native army" allowing the country, for the first time, to effectively fight off pending intruders (Marx 1951b). Private property emerged as a form of income (benefiting the British and former users) and education systems were established for the "Indian natives" (Marx 1951b). It was the introduction of machinery, however, that would cause the greatest change to Indian society. While steam power "brought India into regular and rapid communication with Europe" through the ports, it was the proposed "combination of railways and steam vessels" which would "annex" India to the "Western World" (Marx 1951b). Breaching the limitations imposed on exchange by the isolation of native "villages" and, where they existed, their "impracticable clay roads," the ability to transport via railway would expand irrigation and through it, farming land (increasing the countries yield) in addition to expanding the distribution range of supplies to include the isolated, the hungry, and the ill (Marx 1951b). Implantation of a rail network, however, would give rise to the need to improve the productive capacities of the county to a level which would "sustain the railway," at which point the rule of capital would be undeniable (Marx 1951b). India's culture, its purpose, and its people's way of life would be forever redirected toward the capitalistic objective of the English bourgeoisie. India's introduction to Western civilization through "Modern industry" (e.g., electric telegraph, steam) demonstrates the transformative power of a capitalist rule. And like the English proletarians, the Indian's will not "reap the fruits" of this capitalist system until one of two events transpire: (a) the English bourgeoisie have been overthrown by the "industrial proletariat" of Britain or (b) an uprising of "Hindoos" within the country wins power (Marx 1951b).

Marx the Economist: Capital

Expanding his fight against the bourgeois, Marx increasingly embraced economics as a tool of war. Capitalism in practice, according to Marx, is system of exploitation. Founded on class division, an underclass of people and a higher class – the working class laborers and the capitalists – capitalism was a system that saw the "majority" (i.e., proletariat) "work for the benefit" "of others" – their "oppressors" (i.e., the bourgeois) (Berlin 1939/2013). While the proletariat were the laborers physically expending their time and effort into the development of products and *creating* a surplus value, it was not they who received the produce of their labor but rather, the purchaser of their labor-power, the capitalist. As owners of the product created by the proletariat's labor-power, it is the capitalist who ultimately acquires any "surplus value" created by the proletariat in the subsequent exchange of the commodity in the "market" (Marx 1867/2013). It is the capitalist's seizure of this surplus value, created by the labor of the proletariat, that is the root cause of class conflict and the exploitation of workers. While Marx was not the first to discover the existence of a "surplus value," he is credited to be the first to have developed the concept (Tucker 1888).

In developing his concept of "surplus value," Marx's work represents a progression of classical economic thinking. Earlier political economists, including Ricardo, have examined the "notions of profits and rents" (i.e., the "surplus"). However, they did not investigate further its "origin and nature, or of the laws that regulate the subsequent distribution of its value" (Marx 1867/1887). Marx believed that what was lacking in the theories of earlier economists was a historical perspective

(Berlin 1939/2013). They assumed that "although social conditions may change, the laws that govern them do not" (Berlin 1939/2013). However, according to Marx, the characteristics of society, and thus "economic life," change in relation to the epoch being reviewed. Therefore one needs to identify the characteristics unique to the era under review (Berlin 1939/2013). For Marx, identifying the characteristics specific to the capitalist era (within a historical context), allowed him to create a "new system of concepts and definitions" relevant to the modern world (his modern world) (Berlin 1939/2013). One of these was the labor theory of value. Derived from classical economists including Locke, Smith, and Ricardo, Marx's labor theory of value was founded on the principle that the relative value of a commodity can be measured by the relative labor costs embedded in its production (Berlin 1939/2013; Wheen 1999; Davenport 1935/1965). Smith and Ricardo's concepts of value similarly posited that the value of a commodity was equal to the labor hours necessary to produce that commodity (Smith 1776/1999; Ricardo 1817/2001; Jevons 1871). While Ricardo noted that there were some commodities (e.g., "rare statues and pictures") "determined by their scarcity alone," for the remainder, he believed as Smith did, in an existing correlation between a commodities value and the labor embedded in its production (Ricardo 1817/2001). Marx, it appears uses a similar foundation for determining value. Providing an example of two commodities, "corn and iron," Marx highlights that at some proportion, these two commodities will have equal value (e.g., "1 quarter corn = c cwt. Iron") (Marx 1867/1887). He goes on to say "What does this equation tell us? It tells us that in two different things – in 1 quarter of corn and x cwt. of iron, there exists in equal quantities something common to both. The two things must therefore be equal to a third, which in itself is neither the one nor the other. Each of them, so far as it is exchange value, must therefore be reducible to this third" (Marx 1867/1887). For Marx, this third is labor, or more specifically, the commodity of labor-power (Marx 1867/1887; Prychitko 2002). As Marx had identified, labor was not a commodity, it was worker's *labor power* that was a commodity.

Value plays a central role in the capitalist economy. Like many political economists who came before him (e.g., Smith, Mill, Jevons, Ricardo, and Marshall), Marx recognized that value is defined by two characteristics: *use value* and *exchange value* (Ricardo 1817/2001; Mill and Laughlin 1885/2009; Jevons 1871/2013; Marshall 1890/1997; Smith 1776/1999; Marx 1867/2013). Marx, however, expanding on the classical definitions, claims to be the first to "point out and examine" this "two-fold nature of the labor contained in commodities" (i.e., use value and exchange value) (Marx 1867/2013). Marx's examination did not find, as Marshall's later did, that the exchangeable value of a good is relative (Marshall 1890/1997; Marx 1867/2013). For Marx, a commodity's exchange value is not "accidental" but rather is representative of the value of "human labor in the abstract" embedded in the materialization of the relevant quantities of goods (Marx 1867/2013). It is the "quantity of" homogeneous "labor expended on and materialised in" the "production" of a commodity that determines the commodities value in exchange (Marx 1867/2013). In other words, if 20 loaves of bread have the same value as one kilo of beef, it follows (according to Marx) that it must take the same value of "homogenous human labor" to produce the relevant quantities of both goods (Marx 1867/2013). It is the prefix "homogeneous" that is critical to Marx calculation of labor. For the value of goods do *not* increase in correlation with the *actual* quantity of labor hours embedded in a commodity. Thus, a good produced by idle or unskilled labor (i.e., more labor hours) does not have a greater value in exchange than the same product which is produced by efficient and skilled staff. For, according to Marx, the "value" of human labor congealed in a product is determined by an overarching system centered on theoretical calculations rather than actual. It is thus not the measure of *actual* labor time given to the manifestation of a good therefore that determines a commodities exchange value but the cumulation of what Marx terms, "the amount of labor socially necessary" "for its production" (Marx 1867/2013). This "labor time socially necessary" is measured by the time required to "produce an article under normal conditions of production," "with the average degree of skill and intensity prevalent at the time" (Marx 1867/2013). It is the fundamental concept of value formation that frames Marx's concepts of labor exploitation and the capitalist's capture of surplus value (Carey 2019; Cohen 1979).

Central to Marx's opposition to the capitalistic system is the extraction of surplus value from laborers. Surplus value is created in a capitalist economy when the "value of the product" is greater than the value of its constituent parts (i.e., "the means of production and labor power") (Marx 1867/2013). Capturing of surplus value, otherwise termed appropriating "unpaid labor," is a socially accepted process described as a "pervasive system of exploitation" (Carey 2019; Marx and Engels 1848/2012). The value of a new commodity is comprised of two component parts: constant capital and variable capital. The constant capital consumed in the development of a new commodity does not undergo any "quantitative alteration of value" (Marx 1867/1887) in ceasing to be a standalone exchange value and becoming an ingredient in a new commodity's value. The value of constant capital (e.g., raw materials, tools, and equipment) is "preserved" and transfers proportionally to the product thus is unable to be enhanced (Marx 1867/2013). *Variable capital* on the other hand – namely the value of labor power – "undergoes a metempsychosis" (Marx 1867/1887). As Marx discusses, labor power, unlike other commodities, has a unique ability not only to "preserve" its value but add "greater value than it previously possessed" to a commodity during production (Marx 1849/2010, 1867/2013). In the production process, labor "both reproduces the equivalent of its own value and also produces an excess, a surplus value" (Marx 1867/2013). It is this greater or "surplus" value added by the labor-power during production that is subsequently appropriated by the capitalist (Marx 1867/2013). While the *creation* of surplus value occurs during the production process, it is only upon exchange or sale of the commodity where it is seized in a monetary form by the capitalist (Marx 1867/2013).

In pursuit of accumulating capital, the bourgeois employ new ways to increase productivity. With the production of goods separated from demand, the capitalist, according to Marx, "Fanatically bent on making value expand itself" and thus "ruthlessly forces the human race to produce for production's sake" (Marx 1867/1887; Mandel 1967/1971). Capitalism thus has a contradictory characteristic. On the one hand, it aims to "reduce the labor time necessary for the production of each commodity," while on the other, "it sets up labor time as the only measure and source of wealth" (Mandel 1967/1971). Developments in mechanical devices within workplaces had a marked effect. Not only did machines improve the productivity of the workplace, enhancing output, they simultaneously decreased the labor time necessary for the production of commodities and thus, lowered the price of labor – the only means of sustenance for the proletariat (Mandel 1967/1971). Market competition, Marx identifies, brings another dynamic to the modern workplace (Berlin 1939/2013). For, the accumulation of capital is a twofold process. Not only do capitalists need to create surplus value within their production process, they must subsequently actualize this surplus through the exchange of the commodity (i.e., the sale of their good to consumers) (Marx 1867/1887). The growing production of goods, and "continual competition" between competing enterprises, sees capitalists compete for the consumer's business on the basis of price (Berlin 1939/2013). This sees capitalists decrease the wages of labor (i.e., a component of production cost) and "increase the working hours" of employees in an effort to reduce unit costs (Berlin 1939/2013). Improvements in the means and modes of production thus do not in the classic Marxist perspective directly benefit laborers in terms of their capacity to sustain themselves on their wage, an outcome that supposedly brings to light the enormous disparity between the conditions of the working class and that of the bourgeois.

Implications for Management History: Reflections

The study of management history would be incomplete without acknowledging the Marxist influence. For, as Berlin states, "Even if all" of the Marxist doctrines "specific conclusions were proved false, its importance in creating a wholly new attitude to social and historical questions, and so opening a new avenue of human knowledge, would be unimpaired" (Berlin 1939/2013).

Within Marx's work, capitalism centers on the relationship between two parties, the proletariat and the bourgeois. The bourgeois is defined as "the class of modern capitalists, owners of the means of social production and employers of wage labor" (Marx and Engels 1848/1969b). While the proletariats are "the class of modern wage laborers who, having no means of production of their own, are reduced to selling their labor power in order to live" (Marx and Engels 1848/1969b). Capitalism, therefore, centers on the relationship between the *owners* of production and the wage-labors who work for them. How then does management fit in? For Marx, the separation between management and owner, discussed in Vol. III of his book *Capital*, has no bearing on the fundamental nature of capitalist exploitation (Duménil and Lévy 2018). Marx acknowledges the existence of this third party in the capitalist mode of production saying, "Stock companies in general – developed with the credit system – have an increasing tendency to separate this work of management as a function from the ownership of capital, be it self-owned or borrowed" (Marx 1894). Marx then goes on to dismiss any notion that the involvement of management – an intermediary between the capitalist and worker – would disrupt the production process as it would occur under a capitalist. He states, the "manager who has no title whatever to the capital … performs all the real functions pertaining to the functioning capitalist as such, only the functionary remains and the capitalist disappears as superfluous from the production process" (Marx 1894). Management, therefore, replaces the capitalist in the workplace, performing the necessary duties as a "functioning capitalist" and thus influences no change on the fundamental system of appropriating surplus from wage-labor, that is capitalism (Marx 1894; Duménil and Lévy 2018). For as Marx says, "profit, hence surplus-value" is divided into two "individualised parts," "interest and profit" (Marx 1894). The "interest" is paid to the owner of capital, while the "profit" is "due to" the person "performing" the "capitalist" "function," the "functioning capitalist" (i.e., the manager) (Marx 1894). As such, the "division" between capitalist and management "alters nothing in the nature, origin, and way of existence of surplus value." (Marx 1894)

While Marx examines a real-world conflict, that between bourgeois and proletariat, he positions this conflict within a range of theoretical propositions (Adler 2011). Adopting a simplistic view of the capitalist function, Marx never really explored the reality of a workplace producing commodities. Growing up in a middle-class family (bourgeois), going on to become a student and then journalist, (in addition to writing and publishing) it does not appear that Marx had any significant experience as a wage-laborer (as defined by Marx) or with production processes (McKay 2017; Marx 1867/2013; Berlin 1939/2013). Discussion on workplace practices, therefore, could not stem from great practical experience. Accordingly, Marx's later concept of surplus value rests upon many suppositions. A "commodity" is a good produced for the purpose of exchange. Thus in order for production of the good to be undertaken by a capitalist, they must in the first instance "presuppose" that (a) the good will have an exchange value, (b) that the good's value in exchange will exceed its cost of production, and (c) that the good will have use value to the buyer equal to its exchange value (Marx 1867/2013; Adler 2011). If all three of these presupposed factors eventuate, there will, according to Marx, be a surplus of value created during production and realized during an exchange. However, what Marx does address, but fails to explore in any great depth, is what influence does a failure of *actualizing* surplus value (i.e., the exchange value does *not* exceed the cost of production) impose on a capitalist?

In examining this, we must first understand that Marx acknowledged this conundrum. He outlines that the transaction exchanging the produce of "labor power" (i.e., the product of labor power) is in no way linked to the transaction of purchasing labor-power (Marx 1849/2010). In other words, for the capitalist, two entirely independent transactions occur in the accumulation and realization of "surplus value" or profit. First, is the purchase of labor-power, (i.e., the capitalist engages a laborer to perform work) and in exchange for their labor-power pays a price to the laborer (i.e., wages). Second, as the owner of the product of the labors labor-power (e.g., a chandelier), the capitalist sells the commodity (i.e., the chandelier) to a buyer in exchange for a price. Marx asks, if, during the first transaction wherein the worker's labor power produced a product (e.g., a chandelier) worth \$500, does this mean that the "laborers wages are a share of" (Marx 1849/2010) the value of the product created? Marx says, "By no means" (Marx 1849/2010). He states, "it is possible that the employer found no purchasers" for the product (e.g., a chandelier), or even in sale, the employer may "not get even the amount of the wages" embedded in its production (Marx 1849/2010). He says that it is only upon "Realisation of the surplus-value" where the capitalist is refunded for "the value that was advanced" in the commodities production (Marx 1867/1887). The purchase of labor power is for the capitalist, therefore, an independent transaction. The labor utilized in production of the product (i.e., chandelier) "has no more share in the product" than do the tools used in its production (Marx 1849/2010). According to Marx, "the value of a commodity is, in itself, of no interest to the capitalist. What alone interests him, is the surplus-value that dwells in it, and is realisable by sale" (Marx 1867/1887). This is a significant point of interest for a capitalist, or at least the "functioning capitalist." For, at a practical level, surplus value must not simply be created, it must be *realized* (i.e., it must find demand – or buyers *willing* to purchase the good for the price asked) in order for profit to be made (Marx 1867/1887).

Having engineered a critical and somewhat mechanistic view of capitalism's impersonal production processes, when examining capitalism, Marx saw misery and suffering. The rise of "modern industry," which saw "steam and machinery" revolutionize "industrial production," forged a new means and modes of production (Marx 1867/1887), the effects of which were Marx's primary concern. It was not the invention of machinery but rather the capitalist's *adoption* of machinery to improve productive capacities and decrease production costs that were the cause of Marx's concern (Smith 2012; Marx 1867/1887). Advancing machinery revolutionized the workshop. Despite the division of labor giving rise to the "greatest improvement in the productive powers of labor," Marx saw it destroying many "handicraft" operations: enterprises which gave out under the increasingly lower-priced machinery-produced items. As smaller businesses went to the wall, so Marx depicted a further centralization of capital in the hand of the minority (Marx 1867/1887; Smith 1776/1999). Enforcing "uniformity, order, and economy," modern industries also "turned out cheaper and better commodities." It was also the case that "huge workshops" enabled an "elaborate division of labor," widely decreasing the autonomy of a labors work (Marx 1867/1887; Marx and Engels 1848/1969b). It was not only workshops, however, that changed in response to the introduction of modern machinery. An "international division of labor" arose, seeing various parts of the world adopt the mechanical devices and begin engaging a specific form of industry most suited to their location (Marx 1867/1887). India, under the British rule, for example, produced cotton while Australia was "converted into a colony for growing wool" (Marx 1867/1887). Invariably, the produce of these outlying regions was exchanged internationally (Marx 1867/1887). Marx saw that it was the bourgeoisie who owned these capital assets and thus the "means of social production" (Mandel 1967/1971; Marx and Engels 1848/2012). As a result, Marx saw the proletariat's were wholly dependent on the bourgeois to purchase their labor-power (Smith 1776/2007; Marx 1867/2013). Living "only so long as they find work," the proletariat could only secure work if they utilized their labor power to increase the "capital" of the bourgeois

(Marx and Engels 1848/2012). For Marx, modern machinery facilitated the ongoing exploitation of the working class, by the bourgeois (Marx 1867/1887).

Capitalism, while founded on capital accumulation and class explication, was regarded by Marx as "historically progressive" (Bookchin 1973). Class division was not a characteristic unique to Marx's time (Marx and Engels 1848/2012). For all recorded history therefore, "mankind had been divided into exploiter and exploited." History *is*, therefore, class struggle (Berlin 1939/2013; Marx and Engels 1848/2012). What was fundamentally different during Marx's time, however, was freedom. Free markets and free people. Following the defeat of the feudal reign, the workforce became fundamentally different from those of the past. For workers, no longer slaves beholden to a master or serfs bound to a feudal lord (Marx and Engels 1848/1969b) were free to choose and change their occupation or place of work. In India, villages were liberated from the castes and slavery imposed under a despotic rule and provided with education, communication and transportation, capabilities previously unattainable (Marx 1951a, b). Under capitalism, a new working relationship had emerged. In a free market, labor power became a commodity that could be bought and sold. The ability to buy and sell freely, a condition born of industrial progress, brought with it progressive improvements in the "means of production and exchange" (Mandel 1967/1971; Marx and Engels 1848/1969b). Competition among the bourgeois gave rise to new technologies, new forms of communication and exchange (i.e., steam vessels and railway), improving the productive capacities of work and the ability to distribute the produce of labor more widely and across the globe (Marx and Engels 1848/1969b; Marx 1867/1887). Despite the ensuing "crises of overproduction" pushing society into a "state of momentary barbarism," there was a marked improvement in society's general condition and public wealth as a result of modern industry (Marx and Engels 1848/1969b; Marx 1867/1887; Mandel 1967/ 1971). The progression witnessed through free trade, machinery, and organized labor is thus attributable to the bourgeoise.

Conclusion

Marx's dynamic view of the capitalist regime is economically centered, focusing on interpersonal forces, namely, technology and division of labor driving its success. Free competition between the bourgeoise, coupled with rapid improvements in mechanical devices and the organization of labor, saw productive capacities increase and commodity prices plummet (Berlin 1939/2013; Marx and Engels 1848/1969b). Unable to compete with the low prices of "machine labor," many of those producing by hand were driven out of business and unto wage-laboring jobs (Marx and Engels 1848/1969b). Despite the capitalist mode of production "revolutionising" countries knowing no former progress, such industrial progression was marked by an "inefficient" system of political economy (Marx and Engels 1848/1969b). This inefficiency saw the "overt ill-treatment of workers, unfair contracts, poor conditions, wage theft, and open disdain for the dignity and independence of the working class amongst much of the wealthy elite" (Marx 1867/2013; Carey 2019). Identifying the oppressed nature of the proletariat, Marx dedicated his life to the working class, with the aim of overthrowing the bourgeois rule and creating a communist economy of shared public wealth. Envisioning a society in which competition was abolished and replaced "with association," under the rule of communism, no person would have "the power to subjugate the labor of other by means of" "appropriation" (Marx and Engels 1848/2012). Under a communist rule, "people who produced the surplus would also receive it and decide how to utilize it: collectively as a community" (Wolff and Resnick 2012).

Commencing his journey to Marxism, Marx's thoughts were developing during his "answer" to Proudhon in *The Poverty of Philosophy*. While his publication heavily criticizes the work of Proudhon and many of his concepts, there is no denying that certain elements of Marx's later works exhibit some fundamental similarities to Proudhon's work within *The Philosophy of Poverty* (Hoffman 1967; Proudhon and McKay 2011). Evident similarities in the origin of theories, however, do not deduct from the credit owed to Marx's for later *developing* the theories related to these concepts, including that of surplus value and class conflict (Hoffman 1967; Tucker 1888). Although Marx's work, his ideas, and his concepts advanced over time, evident during his earliest publicly published work, and spanning his career, is his belief that there exists a "struggle between the proletarian class and the bourgeois class" (Marx 1847/1955). Having identified the oppressed class of his time, the proletariat, Marx dedicated his life to their liberation (Berlin 1939/2013). He was determined to *change* the world.

Recognizing that a proletariat uprising is the mechanism through which he could drive social change, Marx calls the "working men of all countries" to "Unite!" (Haworth 2004; Marx and Engels 1848/2012). Critical of the capitalist economic system, Marx and Engels publication of the *Communist Manifesto* outlines the rise and conditions maintaining the modern world of capitalism (Marx and Engels 1848/2012). Opposing the exploitative practices characteristic of the system, and providing an outline of Communist objectives that would abolish the bourgeois rule and provide liberation to the proletariat, the *Communist Manifesto* went on to become "the most influential political pamphlet of all time" (Marx and Engels 1848/2012; Wheen 1999). Later identifying the lack of understanding surrounding the nature of the social conditions of the time, Marx endeavored to explain capitalism within a series of easy to read newspaper articles that would become *Wage Labour and Capital* (Marx 1849/2010). Despite never completing the series, what endured was a structured explanation of many of the key factors upon which private enterprise was founded and maintained. Directed at an audience of the working class – the exploited proletariat – Marx's work within these articles spanned from those common elements of the corporate structure known to many (e.g., wages), through to topics more economically focused, e.g., *Effect of Capitalist Competition on the Capitalist Class the Middle Class and the Working Class*) (Marx 1849/2010). Explaining the influence of the bourgeois from a different angle, the publications of *The British Rule in India* and *The Future Results of British Rule in India* give an understanding as to the power held by the bourgeois class (Marx 1951a, b). According to Berlin, "Misery is the complex result of ignorance." Marx therefore, in educating the public, expanding their knowledge and awareness of the issues central to capitalism and how to overcome them, supposedly provided hope (Berlin 1939/2013).

Moving his work toward the field of economic science, Marx published a "treatise on economic science" (Berlin 1939/2013). Marx's publication *Capital* failed to receive much in the way of positive reviews for a lengthy period following its publication. However, the content of its pages – reviewed, deciphered, criticized, and praised by many throughout its time – went on to become Marx's "major work" (Wheen 1999; Amin 2018). Laying bare the structure of capitalism, Marx reveals the "pervasive system of explication" upon which it is built (Carey 2019). Capitalism centers around the exchange of private property – the proletariat who "have only their labor to exchange" and the bourgeois who "exclusively" possess the means of production (Mandel 1967/1971; Marx and Engels 1848/1969b). Significant to the exchange of private property is the emergence of a surplus value created by labor. This surplus value is expropriated by the capitalist within the exchange of private property, an act which forms the root cause of exploitation and capital accumulation (Amin 2018). While earlier classical economists such as Smith and Ricardo were aware that in a capitalist economy, value was added during exchanges, they had not examined how this value was added. Marx's "discovery of the secret of surplus value" filled this void in knowledge (Carey 2019).

The discipline of management history owes in large part a shift in thinking, a shift in *how* social and economic questions are asked, to Marx (Berlin 1939/2013). Societal evolution is necessary. One stage in life is replaced by another, more advanced stages necessarily succeed the former (Spagnoli 2010). Advancement, however, does not come freely, for as history shows, there is always a class division, or as Marx and Engels state an "oppressor and an oppressed" (Marx and Engels 1848/2012). The capitalist mode of production, emergent from Feudal reign, saw free trade, free people, and free competition facilitate advancements in the means and modes of production previously unseen (Marx and Engels 1848/2012). Negatively, however, it was built upon an imbalance of power between the capitalist and laborer and thus founded on exploitation (Spagnoli 2010; Marx 1867/1887). Marxism helped "shape modern political thought" and the way society views capitalism (Haworth 2004). Marx gave voice to the proletariat. Alleviating the trials and tribulations of primitive culture, yet sentencing the masses to sustenance by work, capitalism for the Marxist is both a savior and a curse.

Cross-References

▶ Economic Foundations: Adam Smith and the Classical School of Economics
▶ Foundations: The Roots of Idealist and Romantic Opposition to Capitalism and Management
▶ Indian Management (?): A Modernization Experiment
▶ Neo-classical Thought: Alfred Marshall and Utilitarianism
▶ What Is Management?

References

Ackers P, Payne J (1998) British trade unions and social partnership: rhetoric, reality and strategy. Int J Hum Resour Manag 9(3):529–550. https://doi.org/10.1080/095851998341062

Adler PS (2011) Marxist philosophy and organization studies: Marxist contributions to the understanding of some important organizational forms. vol 32. Emerald Group Publishing Limited, pp 123–153. https://doi.org/10.1108/S0733-558X(2011)0000032007

Amin S (2018) The communist manifesto, 170 years later. Socioloski pregled 52(2):430–452. https://doi.org/10.5937/socpreg52-16323

Berlin I (1939/2013) Karl Marx, 5th edn. Princeton University Press, Princeton

Bookchin M (1973) Listen. Marxist! Clone 7

Carey S (2019) Exploitation and Marx's theory of surplus value. Guardian (Sydney) 1893:4

Cohen GA (1979) The labor theory of value and the concept of exploitation. Philos Public Aff 8(4):338–360

Davenport HJ (1935/1965) The economics of Alfred Marshall, vol Book, Whole. Cornell University Press [u.a.], New York

Duménil G, Lévy D (2018) Managerial capitalism: ownership, management and the coming new mode of production, vol Book, Whole. Pluto Press, London

Haworth A (2004) Understanding the political philosophers: from ancient to modern times. Routledge, New York

Hegel GWF (1899/2004) The philosophy of history. Dover Publications, Inc., Mineola

Hoffman R (1967) Marx and Proudhon: a reappraisal of their relationship. Historian 29(3):409–430

Jevons WS (1871) The theory of political economy. Macmillan and Co., London/New York

Jevons WS (1871/2013) The theory of political economy. vol Book, Whole, 4. Palgrave Macmillan, Houndmills, Basingstoke. https://doi.org/10.1057/9781137374158

Kumar A (1992) Marx and engels on india. Indian J Polit Sci 53(4):493–504

Mandel E (1971) The formation of the economic thought of Karl Marx 1843 to Capital. Verso

Marshall A (1890/1997) Principles of economics. Great mind Paperpack series (economics), 8th edn. Prometheus Books, New York

Marx K (1867/1887) Capital: a critique of political economy, vol 1. Book One: the process of production of capital. Progress Publishers, Moscow

Marx K (1894) Interest and profit of Enterprise. Capital, vol III part V division of profit into interest and profit of Enterprise. Interest-Bearing Capital

Marx K (1951a) The British rule in India. In: Karl Marx and Frederick Engels: selected works, vol 1. Foreign Languages Publishing House, Moscow

Marx K (1951b) The future results of British rule in India. In: Karl Marx and Frederick Engels: selected works, vol 1. Foreign Languages Publishing House, Moscow

Marx K (1847/1955) The poverty of philosophy. Progress Publishers

Marx K (1849/2010) Wage labor and capital. Neue Rheinische Zeitung

Marx K (1867/2013) Capital. Wordsworth Editions Limited, Hertfordshire

Marx K, Engels F (1848/1969a) Draft of a communist confession of faith. Manifesto of the communist party. Progress Publishers, Moscow

Marx K, Engels F (1969b) Manifesto of the communist party. Progress Publishers, Moscow

Marx K, Engels F (1848/2012) The communist manifesto. vol Book, Whole. Yale University Press, New Haven

McKay I (2017) Proudhon's constituted value and the myth of labor notes. Anarchist Studies 25(1):32–67

Mill JS, Laughlin JL (1885/2009) Principles of political economy. D. Appleton and Company, New York

Moore S (1993) Marx versus markets. The Pennsylvania State University Press, University Park, Pennsylvania

Oakley A (1981/2004) Marx's critique of political economy. Routledge & Kegan Paul, Abingdon

Proudhon P-J (1847/1888) The philosophy of poverty. McMaster University, Hamilton

Proudhon PJ, McKay I (2011) Property is theft! A Peirre-Joseph proudhoon anthology. AK Press, Oakland

Prychitko DL (2002) Marxism. The concise encyclopedia of economics. Library of Economics and Liberty

Ricardo D (1817/2001) On the principles of political economy and taxation, vol Book, Whole, 3rd edn. Batoche Books, Kitchner

Smith A (1776/1999) The wealth of nations. Penguin Books Ltd, London

Smith A (1776/2007) An inquiry into the nature and causes of the wealth of nations. Metalibri, Melbourne

Smith K (2012) A guide to Marx's capital, vols. I–III. vol Book, Whole. Anthem Press, London \New York

Spagnoli F (2010) The neo-communist manifesto, vol Book, Whole. Algora Pub, New York

Tucker BR (1888) State socialism and anarchism: How far they agree, and wherein they differ. Liberty 5.16(120)

Wheen F (1999) Karl Marx. HarperCollins Publishers Ltd., London

Wolff RD, Resnick SA (2012) Contending economic theories: neoclassical, Keynesian, and Marxian, vol Book, Whole. MIT Press, Cambridge, MA

Conflicting Understandings of the Industrial Revolution and Its Consequences: The Founding Figures of British Management History

19

Bradley Bowden

Contents

Introduction 436
"To Serve as Galley Slaves": The Toynbees and Tawney on the Industrial Revolution
and Its Consequences 441
"Learning and Public Life": The Contrary Intellectual Contribution of John Nef and John
Clapham 447
Capitalism and Management: Exploitation or Opportunity? The Intellectual Contribution
of Webbs and E.P. Thompson 455
Sidney Pollard and the Origins of "Modern" Management 462
Conclusion 467
References 469

Abstract

The Industrial Revolution is a seminal event in the emergence of modern systems of management. It is also central to the British tradition of management history. Accordingly, this chapter is concerned not with the ideas about management that emerged in Britain during the nineteenth century, but rather with the emergence of the discipline of management history in Britain. If the very concept of the Industrial Revolution is primarily due to the posthumous publication of the lectures of Arnold Toynbee the elder (1852–1883), shifting understandings about the nature of British management have been built around profound disagreements as to the causes, duration, and effects of the Industrial Revolution. In the opinion of the American historian, John Nef, the importance of the Industrial Revolution of the eighteenth and nineteenth centuries is altogether overstated, Nef arguing that the success of nineteenth-century British managers is attributable

---

B. Bowden (✉)
Griffith Business School, Griffith University, Nathan, QLD, Australia
e-mail: b.bowden@griffith.edu.au

© The Author(s), under exclusive licence to Springer Nature Switzerland AG 2020   435
B. Bowden et al. (eds.), *The Palgrave Handbook of Management History*,
https://doi.org/10.1007/978-3-319-62114-2_114

to an earlier industrial relation in the sixteenth and seventeenth century. For some, such as E.P. Thompson, R.H. Tawney, and both Arnold Toynbee the elder and Arnold Toynbee the younger (1889–1975), the managerial order created by the Industrial Revolution was economically advantageous but socially retrograde. For others, notably John Clapham, Sidney and Beatrice Webb and, above all, Sidney Pollard, the Industrial Revolution was a socially liberating force. Only by understanding these debates can we comprehend the seminal ideas that have informed management history in Britain.

Keywords

Industrial revolution · Alfred chandler · The Webbs · Arnold toynbee · E.P. Thompson · Inequality · Real wages · Sidney pollard

---

Introduction

Management as an academic discipline and applied practice has long boasted a US flavor. In terms of management theory, there are few who have exerted a greater influence than citizens of the American republic (i.e., Frederick Taylor, Chester Barnard, Frank and Lillian Gilbreth, George Homans, Douglas McGregor, Peter Drucker, etc.) or citizens from elsewhere who plied their trade in the United States (i.e., Elton Mayo, Kurt Lewin). Among business historians, no one has been more influential than Alfred D. Chandler. In management history, the preeminent academic body, the Management History Division (MHD) of the Academy of Management, is not only a US institution, its leading office-bearers have until recently also traditionally been American. Of the people who have served as editor in chief of the re-established *Journal of Management History*, two (Patrick Murphy and Sean Carraher) have been American. The exceptions, David Lamond and myself, served as Chairs of the MHD, as did Murphy and Carraher.

If management history has long been a US-oriented discipline, it nevertheless remains the case that management's origins will always be associated in the popular and, indeed, the scholastic mind, with the British Industrial Revolution. In enunciating what has become well-established opinion, Arnold Toynbee (1976/1978, p. 565), for example, recorded that, "until the Industrial Revolution, the use of machinery ... was still rare. It now became normal." Yet, despite its central importance to the modern world, few of us stop to think where the concept of the "Industrial Revolution" came from. Nor do we tend to reflect on why this epoch-shaping event is typically dated between 1760 and 1830, dates that correspond to the accession of George III and the death of George IV rather than to any profound technological or managerial change. Among those who lived through what we think of as the Industrial Revolution, there was certainly an appreciation that they were witnessing transformative economic and social experiences. However, few if any understood this experience as an "Industrial Revolution" with clear start and finish dates. In their *Communist Manifesto*, written in 1848, Karl Marx and Frederick

Engels (1848/1951, p. 36), for example, spoke not of an "Industrial Revolution" but rather of a "constant revolutionizing of production." To the extent that they put a date on this new economic order, Marx and Engels (1848/1951, p. 37) spoke of a bourgeois "rule of scarce one hundred years" (i.e., since c.1730). One also searches in vain within John Stuart Mill's (1848/2004) *Principles of Political Economy* for any discussion of the "Industrial Revolution" and its transformative effects. Rather than pondering the exact circumstances that created the new industrialized world economy, Marx, Engels, and Mill more or less took its existence for granted, being more concerned with its *effects* than its *origins*. Yet, as we shall discuss, the intellectual provenance of the "Industrial Revolution" is neither assured nor unquestioned, the American historian, John Nef (1943, p. 1) declaring, "There is scarcely a conception that rests on less secure foundations."

A decidedly British phenomenon, the concept of an "Industrial Revolution," owes a debt primarily to British historians. Such accounts have typically – although, as we shall note, not universally – portrayed the Industrial Revolution as economically progressive but spiritually retrograde. E.P. Thompson (1963/1968, p. 217), for example, described it as a "truly catastrophic" event for English working people, in which they supposedly found themselves "subjected simultaneously to two intolerable forms of relationship: those of economic exploitation and of political oppression." By contrast, for John Clapham (1926/1967, p. 567), the "family income" enjoyed by industrial workers in the 1830s was "not too hopelessly inadequate." In terms of living conditions, Clapham (1926/1967, p. 39) observed a tendency to conflate the "worst" housing conditions of the Industrial Revolution with the "average." While the conditions of the worst were, Clapham (1926/1967, p. 39) continued, "impossible to exaggerate," it was nevertheless the case that, "In London and out of it, the skilled man, like the Durham miner, generally had a tolerable house or section of a house, and tolerable furniture."

The purpose of this chapter is to comprehend how understandings of what has become known as the "Industrial Revolution" emerged and evolved around a number of "British" historians between the 1880s and the 1970s, scholars who constantly engaged with previously published studies in this peculiar field, supporting some arguments and contradicting others. It needs to be understood that this chapter is *not* concerned with the genealogy of managerial ideas during the Industrial Revolution (i.e., Owen, Babbage, Ure, etc.). This aspect of management's history is well covered by my co-editor, Jeff Muldoon (▶ Chap. 20, "Certain Victory, Uncertain Time: The Limitations of Nineteenth-Century Management Thought"), in his chapter in Part 5 (*The Classic Age of Management Thought*) of this *Palgrave Handbook*. Rather, we are looking at the way in which the *discipline* of management history emerged from debates about both the nature of the Industrial Revolution and the fundamental features of "modern management." It should also be noted that some of the historians that we consider "British" were "British" only by intellectual orientation or immigration, rather than by birth. John Nef (1890–1988), for example, was not only Chicago-born he also spent almost his entire career at the University of Chicago. Nef's long career was directed, however, toward mainly British lines of inquiry, where he argued in favor of the transformative significance of an "early Industrial Revolution" between 1540 and 1640. Sidney Pollard (1925–1998), a management historian who, unlike Nef, did believe that *the* Industrial Revolution of the eighteenth and nineteenth centuries was a socially as well as economically progressive experience was an Austrian Jew, who anglicized his birth name (Siegfried Pollak) when he fled to Britain in 1938 to escape the Nazis.

Of the other historians whose ideas we highlight – Arnold Toynbee (1852–1883), John Clapham (1873–1946), R.H. Tawney (1880–1962), Arnold Toynbee (1889–1975), Beatrice Webb (1858–1943), Sidney Webb (1859–1947), and E.P. Thompson (1924–1993) – the reader faces evident confusion in our consideration of two Arnold Toynbees, the younger being the nephew of the first. Although the second Toynbee was not yet born when the first died at the age of 30, both were intellectually rooted in the reforming ethos of Victorian England, shocked by the contrast between the poverty and wealth around them. For both the older and younger Toynbee, as for Tawney and Thompson, the social consequences of the Industrial Revolution were altogether malevolent. As the older Toynbee (1884a/1894, p. 94) – who was largely responsible for the delineation of the Industrial Revolution as a unique historical event – expressed it, "The problem of pauperism" manifested itself "in its most terrible forms between 1795 and 1834." Prefiguring the subsequent rise of the environmental movement with its concerns as to climate change, the younger Toynbee (1976/1978, p. 17, 21) also believed that the Industrial Revolution led to a "wrecking" of the "biosphere," a process in which "demonic" greed and lust for material riches supposedly threatens to "liquidate" the entire planet. By contrast, Clapham and the Webbs viewed the effects of the Industrial Revolution more positively. The stance of Beatrice and Sidney Webb, the intellectual driving forces behind the British Fabian Society, is particularly significant. Whereas Thompson and other British socialists subsequently suggested that the Industrial Revolution led to a profound alienation of British workers from capitalist society, the Webbs argued that all most workers ever wanted was a greater share in capitalism's riches. Writing of the "New Model" unions that emerged during the 1850s, Sidney and Beatrice Webb (1894/1902, p. 223) accurately noted that their policy "was restricted to securing for every workmen those terms which the best employers were willing voluntarily to grant." In other words, they merely wanted less enlightened employers to grant the same wages and conditions as were already conceded by their "fair-minded" competitors. It was Pollard, however, who presented the most positive – if also most nuanced – account of the managers who shaped the Industrial Revolution. Yes, Pollard (1965, p. 258) agreed, the Industrial Revolution *did* take on the form of a "real class battle," a conflict in which managers struggled to transform an amorphous collection of ex-farmers and artisans into "the industrial proletariat of the large factories and mines." In waging this "battle," however, managers quickly discovered that the most important managerial attributes were "personal qualities," the "social skills" that allowed for the maintenance of "discipline without undue friction or severity" (Pollard 1965, p. 253). For, Pollard (1965, pp. 6–7) argued, the most significant characteristic "of the new capitalism" that emerged from the

Industrial Revolution, "underlying its ultimate power to create a more civilized society," was that it always dealt with legally free workers, ever capable of abandoning their post with all the attendant problems of staff turnover which that created for management.

Before turning to a discussion of the studies that have informed our understanding of Britain's Industrial Revolution, it must be conceded that the title chosen for this chapter, "The Founding Figures of British Management History," is in many ways a misnomer. Of those whom we consider, only Pollard would have regarded himself as a "management historian," a novel discipline that he himself did much to establish. Nef and Clapham would have considered themselves economic historians, a discipline that was also in its infancy when they wrote their seminal works. As for the Webbs, they are widely recognized as founding figures for yet another disciple: industrial relations. E.P. Thompson is arguably the most important labor historian who ever put pen to paper. The Toynbees, and R.H. Tawney, undoubtedly saw themselves simply as "historians." Despite this disciplinary diversity, however, all of the historians that we consider devoted their minds to the same basic problems. What was the Industrial Revolution? To what did it owe its origins? Were its effects positive or negative? Yes, it is true, that other scholars – Eric Hobsbawm, G.D.H. Cole, G.R. Porter, and William Cunningham – also sought answers to these questions. By tracing the debates and disagreements of the historians central to this chapter (the Toynbees, Tawney, the Webbs, Nef, Clapham, Thompson, Pollard), however, we can nevertheless comprehend how defining understandings as to the nature of "modern management" emerged from the historiography of the Industrial Revolution.

Finally, before proceeding, it is only fitting that I advise the reader as to my own prejudices and assessments as to the debates that we consider in this chapter. First, there is merit in Nef's (1932a, b, 1934, 1937, 1943) argument that *the* Industrial Revolution was only possible due to the achievements of an earlier English "Industrial Revolution" in the sixteenth and seventeenth centuries. As the subsequent research by Braudel (1986/1990), Cipolla (1981), and Allen (2011) has recognized, Nef's most important contribution is found in his demonstration of the significance of England's early exploitation of its coal reserves. In highlighting this point in his two-volume *The Rise of the British Coal Industry*, Nef (1932a, p. 322) recorded, "There was no parallel on the Continent for the remarkable growth in coal mining which occurred in Great Britain between 1550 and 1700 ... the coal industry provided a fertile field for the growth in capitalistic forms of industrial organization." Endorsing Nef's fundamental argument – that modern forms of industrial management are premised on the transition to a high-productivity, energy-intensive economy – Robert Allen (2011, p. 380) similarly concludes in his study, "Why the Industrial Revolution was British," that all:

> ... of the things that raised productivity in the nineteenth century depended on two things – the steam engine and cheap iron. Both of these ... were closely related to coal. The steam engine was invented to drain coal mines, and it burnt coal. Cheap iron required the substitution of coke for charcoal ... the railroad ... was [also] a spin-off of the coal industry.

If Nef was correct in pointing to the Industrial Revolution's prehistory in the sixteenth and seventeenth century, there is also value in his suggestion that *the* Industrial Revolution should be dated from 1790 rather than the conventional date of 1760. For, despite the advances that had occurred in ironmaking from the time of the Middle Ages, England in the early eighteenth century remained an economy built on wood rather than iron. Indeed, in the opening decade of eighteenth century, England's annual production of cast-iron amounted to a miniscule 25,000 tons per annum, a tonnage that was little different to that produced a century earlier. In Nef's estimation (1943, p. 240), it was only with the perfection of new smelting methods in 1780 – techniques trialed with mixed success between 1710 and 1750 – that a decisive "turning point" was reached. Once more, Nef's pioneering research has been endorsed by subsequent studies. As Fig. 1 indicates, which annual cast-iron output on a decade-by-decade basis as collated by Philip Riden (1977), English production moved forward in fits and starts between 1710 and 1790 as iron-makers experimented with new techniques which – when perfected – led to unprecedented increases in the 1790s.

Where this author differs from Nef is not in his assessment of the *technological* innovations that underpinned the Industrial Revolution of the eighteenth and nineteenth centuries, but rather in his underemphasis of the *managerial* advances that turned technological potential into profitable economic reality. For, as is the norm among economic historians, Nef paid much attention to the *economic* factors of production but little heed to the *human* factors. A similar failing, albeit one manifested in a different guise, is also evident in the discussions of the two Toynbees and Tawney, each of whom expressed much concern for the spiritual well-being of workers without the benefit of much discussion as to the lived experience of these workers in either the workplace or the home. In this latter regard, the work of Pollard and Thompson and, to a lesser degree that of Clapham and the Webbs, is much

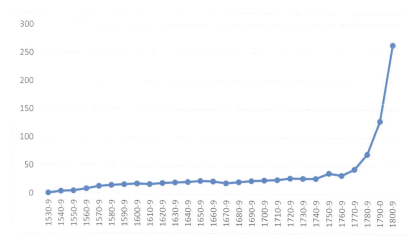

Fig. 1 Annual English cast-iron production, by decade, 1530–1539 to 1810–19 (in thousands of tons). (Source: Riden, "The Output of the British Iron Industry before 1860," pp. 443, 448, 455)

superior to that of Nef, the Toynbees, and Tawney. In the case of Thompson, a general hostility to capitalism and management existed alongside some of the most penetrating and profound insights into the problems experienced by managers during the Industrial Revolution. Nowhere is Thompson's understanding of the problems of management more evident than in his oft overlooked study, "Time, Work-discipline, and Industrial Capitalism." In this study, Thompson (1967, p. 61) makes the pertinent point that only with the Industrial Revolution and the widespread use of clocks does work-time become a measurable commodity, causing employees to "experience a distinction between their employer's time and their 'own' time." Despite Thompson's profound insights into the transformed nature of work in the Industrial Revolution, it is Pollard who best captures the central importance of the human factors in managerial travails and successes during this historic period. Of all the problems that Pollard identifies, none was arguably more significant than the creation of an entirely new social class of professional managers. As Pollard (1965, p. 104) accurately noted, "The concept of a 'manager', not even very clear today, had no fixed meaning at the time [of the Industrial Revolution], nor had related terms such as 'supervisor' and 'superintendent'." It was, however, only through the creation of a new class of professional managers – people attentive to markets, costs, recruitment, staff motivation, and retention, the technical problems of production – that the technological potential of the Industrial Revolution was realized.

"To Serve as Galley Slaves": The Toynbees and Tawney on the Industrial Revolution and Its Consequences

In concluding his final study into the Industrial Revolution and its consequences, published posthumously, the younger Arnold Toynbee (1976/1978, p. 578) argued that the uninterrupted advance of industrial civilization during the nineteenth and twentieth centuries had produced "increased productivity" at a terrible "spiritual price," causing workers "to serve as galley-slaves" at the behest of "the conveyor-belt and the assembly-line." In taking this stance, the younger Toynbee was not only following in his uncle's critical footsteps; he was also articulating the ethos of the Victorian middle class, a social cohort that Toynbee (1947a/1976, p. 29; Toynbee 1976/1978, p. 577) always considered to be the most significant force for social reform in the new industrial world. For, like all the historians that we are considering, other than Pollard and Thompson, the younger Toynbee was part of a generation that came of age before the First World War. Indeed, Toynbee (1947b/1976, pp. 15–16) noted in reflecting upon his own upbringing that, "my education was more old-fashioned than my mother's had been," his studies "at Oxford" based "almost entirely on the Greek and Roman classics." Convinced as to the moral superiority of the educated English middle class to which he belonged, Toynbee (1976/1978, p. 268) believed that the hope of humanity rested on the university-educated *intelligentsia* that imbibed its reforming values. It was "this Western middle-class – this tiny minority," Toynbee (1947a/1976) argued, which was the most important social force in the modern world, acting as "the leaven" that "leavened" the less well-educated "lump" of humanity. This moral evangelizing is arguably even more evident in the studies of the older Toynbee (1884a/1894, p. 58), who declared that his research into the Industrial Revolution was driven by a need to "lay bare the injustices to which the humbler classes of the community have been exposed." R.H. Tawney, similarly born and raised in the values of Victorian England, also declared himself part of "a generation disillusioned with free competition, and disposed to demand some criterion of social expediency more cogent than the verdict of the market." In his best-selling book, *Equality*, Tawney poured scorn on the idea – argued by John Maynard Keynes in *The Economic Consequences of the Peace* – that any person "of capacity or character at all exceeding the average" was capable of joining "the middle and upper classes" (Keynes 1920, p. 9). In enunciating what he called his "Tadpole" principle, Tawney (1929/1964, p. 105) declared the acclaimed social mobility of capitalism to be a thinly disguised fraud. For, among tadpoles, Tawney (1929/1964, p. 105) cynically observed, the fact that some "will one day shed their tails ... hop nimbly on to dry land, and croak addresses to their former friends on the virtues by which tadpoles of character and capacity can rise to be frogs," changes nothing for the great mass condemned to "live and die as tadpoles."

Typically, the intellectual reputation of a scholar rests on the words that they write. There are two notable exceptions to this rule: the Swiss linguist, Ferdinand de Saussure, whose ideas profoundly influenced Jacques Derrida and other postmodernist theorists, and the older Toynbee, a scholar whose intellectual frameworks defined "classical" understandings of the Industrial Revolution. In both cases, their claim to fame rests on the efforts of their former students, who reassembled and published their lectures from notes and shared memories. Of the written legacy of Toynbee the elder, his widow, Charlotte Toynbee (1884b/1894, p. xxix), recorded that, "nothing was left by my husband in a form intended for publication ...he neither wrote his lectures or addresses before delivering them, nor used any notes in speaking." Given Toynbee's preference for talking over writing, the enduring influence of his ideas is largely attributable to two of his former students at Oxford's Balliol College, W.J. Ashley and Bolton King. Working with a number of Toynbee's other former students, Ashley and King unselfishly acted as the unacknowledged editors for Toynbee's famed study, *Lectures on the Industrial Revolution of the 18th century in England* (see Toynbee 1884b/1894, p. xxxi, for a discussion of Ashley and King's role).

Although as Nef (1943, p. 2) observes, the term "Industrial Revolution" had been occasionally bandied about prior to Toynbee's lectures, its most common usage was found among the French, puzzled and curious as the strange events occurring on the other side of the channel. Central to Toynbee's defining depiction of the circumstances surrounding the Industrial Revolution was the belief that 1760 represented a total rupture in the human experience, an historical dividing line that separated an agrarian and artisan past from a mechanized future. Prior "to 1760," Toynbee (1884a/1894, p. 32, 38) advised his students, "none of the great mechanical inventions had been introduced," while in much of the countryside, "the agrarian system of the middle ages still existed in full force." From the outset, Toynbee (1884a/1894, p. 31) made it clear that his study was as much concerned with "proper limits of

Government interference" in a capitalist economy as with the "Industrial Revolution," *per se*. For, in Toynbee's analysis (1884a/1894, p. 86) the social problems of the new industrial society stemmed as much from "competition" and the "brute struggle" that saw "the weak . . . trampled underfoot," as from life in the new factories. Enunciating opinions that have since become commonplace, Toynbee (1884a/1894, p. 84) argued that the Industrial Revolution produced a "disastrous and terrible" decline in real wages that existed, "side by side," with "a great increase of wealth." The "result of free competition," Toynbee (1884a/1894, p. 84) continued, was also "seen in an enormous increase of pauperism," the "rapid alienation" of one social class from another," and "the degradation of a large body of producers."

In many ways, it was the social and educational "degradation" of the lower classes that most concerned Toynbee, a concern that was to be subsequently reflected in the writings of both his nephew and Tawney. For, in its "degraded" state, the industrial proletariat was, Toynbee (1884a/1894, p. 114) argued, incapable of moving "towards that purer and higher condition of society for which we alone care to strive." Accordingly, any State-directed interventions in the economy had to redress more than the poverty and social dislocation that Toynbee identified as inevitable consequences of the Industrial Revolution. Instead, the working class had to be provided with "better education and better amusements," so that workers and their families could better appreciate middle-class values based upon "moral restraints." For the younger Toynbee (1976/1978, p. 568), as well, the hope of humanity lay not in the industrial proletariat in whom Marx, Engels, and other socialists invested their aspirations, but rather in the middle class, most particularly the educated professionals "enlisted or created by governments to serve these governments' purposes." Due to their key position in the State bureaucracy, the younger Toynbee (1976/1978, p. 569) argued, the professional *intelligentsia* could guide not only the lower classes beneath it but also government itself, implementing an "independent line" directed toward "an increase in Man's spiritual potentiality." Similarly, for Tawney (1922/1938, p. 280), a church-going, self-declared Christian socialist, the fundamental problem with industrial capitalism was found in an abandonment of ethics as guiding societal principles in favor of "the idolatry of wealth."

Many of the propositions put forward by the older Toynbee – and subsequently pursued with vigor by the younger Toynbee, Tawney, and a host of social theorists and reformers – were neither novel nor profound. Toynbee's accounts of working-class poverty are inferior to those found in Engels' classic study, *The Condition of the Working Class in England*, a work in which Engels (1845/2010, p. 41) directly linked the condition of the "destitute millions" to the "property-holding, merchant class" who "systematically plundered" the created wealth of the nation. As a critique of industrial capitalism, Toynbee's *Lectures on the Industrial Revolution of the 18th century in England* hardly bares comparison to Karl Marx's (1867/1954) *Capital*, a work published 17 years before the collation of Toynbee's lectures. His account of the process of British industrialization is inferior to that found in G.R. Porter's (1836/1970) *The Progress of the Nation*, a book published long before Toynbee was born. Toynbee's discussions of the mechanics of management were inferior to those undertaken in Charles Babbage's (1832/1846) *On the Economy of Machinery and*

Manufactures, another work that was published before Toynbee was born. Admittedly, Toynbee did critically analyze Adam Smith's well-known condemnation of professional managers, in which Smith (1776/1937, Book V, Chap. 1, Article 1, para. 18) declared that wherever such people are employed, their activities lead not to greater efficiencies but rather to waste and mismanagement. In countering this assertion, Toynbee argued two proposals, neither of which were particularly profound. First, Toynbee (1884a/1894, p. 75) suggested that managers could be motivated to work more efficiently and honestly, "by giving them a share in the results of the enterprise they direct." Secondly, Toynbee (1884a/1894, p. 75) made the hardly original observation "that a big company" can typically employ better managers than their smaller competitors because they "can buy the best brains."

Weak as Toynbee's account of management and the Industrial Revolution was in many individual areas, its just claim for originality is found in its linking of Britain's social problems with a specific historical event (i.e., the Industrial Revolution) and to solutions that eschewed both free market economics and socialism. Unlike Adam Smith, David Ricardo, and John Stuart Mill, Toynbee (1884a/1894, p. 87) argued that "competition" was "neither good nor evil in itself" but rather an elemental force that "has to be checked ...studied and controlled." Unlike Marx, Engels, and the other socialists of his time, Toynbee (1884a/1894, p. 151) rejected any "Communistic solution," preferring instead a middle-class controlled program of municipal reform, directed toward improved education, housing, and consumer cooperatives. As such, Toynbee's lectures were a manifesto for a reform-minded professional middle class, a group of people that put much greater faith in the State and their own supposed intellectual brilliance than they did in either markets or private-sector entrepreneurs. In the course of the late nineteenth and early twentieth centuries, such sentiments obtained ever-increasing levels of support within the British Liberal Party and, more particularly, the Labour Party.

Matters relating to culture and spirit, and the ways in which culture and moral behavior were supposedly degraded by the effects of industrial work and – more particularly – competition, were central to the studies of Tawney and the two Toynbees. In describing what he felt were the profound failings of studies undertaken by "economists," the older Toynbee (1884a/1894, p. 28) complained that the worker was regarded "simply as a money-making animal," an analytic approach that disregarded "the influence of custom," the cultural practices and values that working people had long held dear. For the younger Toynbee (1947a/1976, p. 34), as well, the problem with studies that emphasized economic efficiencies and "technological innovations" was that they ignored the "moral ugliness" that advanced side by side with industrialization. It was, however, Tawney's most influential work, *Religion and the Rise of Capitalism*, that provided the best researched, most insightful, and, arguably, the most misguided assessment of the presumed link between culture, capitalism, and management. The published product of a series of lectures that Tawney delivered at King's College, London, in March–April 1922, Tawney explored the same problem that Max Weber considered in his *The Protestant Ethic and the Spirit of Capitalism*, namely, the relationship between religious belief and economic and managerial success. In Weber's study, however – which was originally published in two parts (in German) in 1904–1905 but which only appeared in English translation after the completion of Tawney's work – both Protestantism and capitalism were perceived far more positively than they were in *Religion and the Rise of Capitalism*. In Weber's opinion, there was a clear and economically beneficial link between Protestantism – most particularly Calvinism – and individual and organizational success. In every Western European society, Weber (1905/1958, p. 40) argued, Protestants revealed "a special tendency to develop economic rationalism which cannot be observed to the same extent among Catholics." Among Protestants, Weber (1905/1958, p. 43) continued, Calvinists demonstrated "an extraordinary capitalistic business sense … combined … with the most intensive forms of piety which penetrates and dominates their whole lives." Together, Weber (1905/1958, p. 43) concluded, these attributes made "the Calvinist diaspora the seedbed of capitalistic economy."

By comparison with Weber's famed study, Tawney's *Religion and the Rise of Capitalism* is superior in terms of research and historical accuracy although not, it is arguable, analytic insight and justifiable conclusions. In terms of religious beliefs, Tawney (1922/1938, p. 139) correctly pours scorn on the idea that John Calvin and his immediate followers were admirers of capitalism, observing that Calvinism in its original form "distrusted wealth, as it distrusted all influences that distract the aim or relax the fibres of the soul." Tawney (1922/1938, pp. 92–93) also dismissed the idea that Catholics were unusual in lacking a "commercial spirit," noting that in the early modern world, "it was predominately Catholic cities which were the commercial capitals of Europe, and catholic bankers who were its leading financiers." Rather than it being the case that Calvinism helped create a new capitalist spirt, Tawney (1922/1938, p. 226) suggested the reverse was true. In other words, a capitalist spirit at odds with John Calvin's original preaching captured Calvinism. From such accurate historical observations, however, Tawney proceeded to some dubious conclusions. First and most significantly, Tawney (1922/1938, p. 271) argued that the intertwining of Protestantism and the new capitalist spirit was destructive "of ethical values," weaving "a perilous" emphasis on "pecuniary gain …into the very tissue of modern civilization." The result, Tawney (1922/1938, p. 280) added, was "the negation of any system of thought or morals which can …be described as Christian." That, in fact, the advance of capitalism was associated with political liberty, democracy, legal protection of both person and property, an extension of the franchise and mass literacy, is not acknowledged. Instead, Tawney harked back to a golden medieval age of dubious provenance, a world in which the Church regarded usury and other forms of lending and commercial activity as the domain of the morally bankrupt. Even though he acknowledged that attempts to restrain capitalist practices proved "impracticable" in the end, Tawney (1922/1938, p. 73) nevertheless held to the opinion that there was a "nobility" to medieval "moralizing" of "economic life." In short, one was supposedly better off in a society where the Inquisition suppressed dissident views than in a world where markets dictate economic outcomes.

If both the older Toynbee and Tawney regarded capitalism and its economic agents as morally bereft, the younger Tawney's condemnations arguably have the greatest resonance in today's world, a society increasingly fixated by environmental and climate concerns. Central to Toynbee's final work, *Mankind and Mother Earth*, is the belief that humanity, "by making the Industrial Revolution," had created "a threat that had no precedent," its industrialized behavior placing the planet's "biosphere" in danger (Toynbee 1976/1978, p. 566). Whereas before "the Industrial Revolution," human activity "had devastated patches of the biosphere," in the wake of the Industrial Revolution forests were cut down "faster than they could be replaced" (Toynbee 1976/1978, p. 566). By placing unprecedented demands "on non-replaceable natural resources," humanity faced an inevitable economic and environmental tipping point, in which the needs of a growing population outstripped available food and energy stocks (Toynbee 1976/1978, p. 566). It is interesting to note that the younger Toynbee's environmental concerns – which existed side by side with the moral repugnance of capitalism that he shared with both his uncle and Tawney – predated concerns about "global warming" and "climate change." It is also interesting to note that, as with most predictions of inevitable catastrophe in human history, all of the environmental concerns that worried Toynbee – a reduction in the forests, an exhaustion of mineral deposits, and an imminent food shortfall – have been contradicted by subsequent events. As Fig. 2 indicates – which traces changes in world population, crop production, livestock production, and total food production between 1961 and 2014, as well as changes in forest cover since 1991 – food production has grown in recent decades at a far faster rate than the increase in world population. Significantly, this increase has had little effect on the percentage of the world's landmass under forest, which has remained almost constant at approximately

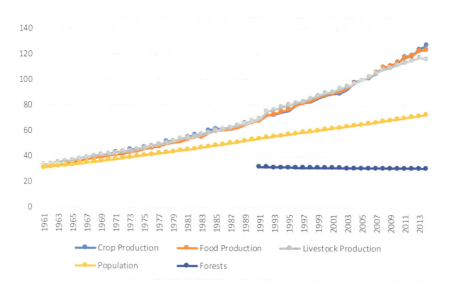

Fig. 2 Increase in world population and crop, food, and livestock production, 1961–2014 (2004–2006 output is index of 100). (Source: Calculated from World Bank, On-line Database: Indicators – Agricultural and Rural Development)

31%. Nor should we conclude that the mammoth increase in food output is only a First World phenomenon. Thus, whereas total world crop output grew by 392.7% between 1961 and 2014, the volume of production in the poorest and most indebted nations (found mainly in Africa) expanded by 421.3% (World Bank 2017). Human and managerial ingenuity, largely exercised in the free market societies that Toynbee condemned, have belied his expressed concerns.

"Learning and Public Life": The Contrary Intellectual Contribution of John Nef and John Clapham

A largely forgotten figure today, in 1941 John Nef was arguably the leading American economic historian of his generation. In the preceding decade, his articles in the British-based *Economic History Review*, as well as in his two-volume *The Rise of the British Coal Industry*, had punctured many of the assumptions that had prevailed since the publication of Toynbee's *Lectures on the Industrial Revolution of the 18th century in England*. Given his preeminent status, it is therefore not surprising that was chosen to deliver the keynote at the inaugural conference of the (American) Economic History Association in 1940, an address subsequently published in the first issue of the *Journal of Economic History*. In this address, Nef (1941, p. 5) made the pertinent observation that "learning and public life are locked together in a vicious circle," each informing and subverting the other in the contestation of ideas and policies. In this contestation, research only became meaningful when it managed "to guide the public on the basic and recurring issues of human existence." In order to meet this public obligation, Nef (1943, p. 4) reflected in a subsequent article, "The Industrial Revolution Reconsidered," it was "not enough" for the historian "to be in possession of a vast quantity of materials on some special aspect of history in some special period." Rather, historical research only becomes meaningful to the extent that specific historical events are comprehended in relation "to history as a whole." From Nef's perspective, there was no matter of greater historical and public importance than that relating to an understanding of the causes and effects of what we think of as the Industrial Revolution. In considering these issues, Nef consistently argued two propositions, both of which flew in the face of accepted wisdom. First, Nef (1943, p. 8) argued that "the conventional idea of the industrial revolution" had "interposed itself like a dense fog," blinding historians and the public alike to the fact that any economic and managerial transformation is only successful when it draws on established intellectual, technological, and institutionalized traditions. As noted in the introduction to this chapter, Nef believed that English industrial and economic success in *the* Industrial Revolution was only possible due to the effects of an earlier Industrial Revolution between 1540 and 1640. This was a period, Nef (1943, p. 11) successfully argued, when "the English nation," hitherto a European backwater, struck out "in new directions, economically, socially, philosophically, and artistically; directions different from those undertaken by most of the Continental peoples." Nef's second proposition – which shared commonalities with that of the two Toynbees and

Tawney – was that English society was a better place at the dawn of the (second) Industrial Revolution than at the end, identifying an "increasingly disharmony between very rapid industrial progress and the eighteenth-century civilization which made it possible." What Nef (1943, p. 27) admired most in eighteenth-century English society – a world he believed was destroyed by the very process of industrialization that it had fostered – were the norms of its aristocratic elite, values built around "ordered balance," "good taste," and a sense of moral and political restraint.

If Nef shared commonalities with the Toynbees and Tawney in his distrust of the social values of the new industrial world, on virtually every other point he was in profound disagreement. Whereas the older Toynbee (1884/1894, p. 84) associated the (second) Industrial Revolution with a "disastrous and terrible" fall in real wages – with the younger Toynbee (1976/1978, p. 564) similarly arguing that with the Industrial Revolution, factory workers "were barely able to subsist on their wages" – Nef argued a contrary position. Drawing on the work of the Australian economist, Colin Clark (1940), Nef concluded that as early as 1700, the "average" English citizen was enjoying unprecedented wealth, boasting a higher "command of economic goods" that obtained by the typical Italian, Russian, or Japanese citizen in the 1920s and 1930s (Nef 1943, p. 12). Even where wages did fall relative to food prices in the sixteenth century, Nef believed such costs were offset by new and cheaper consumables that stemmed from the "first" Industrial Revolution. In the mid- to late 1500s, for example, new techniques for making "small beer" (i.e., low-alcohol beer) brought a new source of "daily nourishment" into the household, at a time when drinking polluted water from wells and rivers risked disease and death (Nef 1937, p. 168). Implicit in Nef's analysis is the belief that that it is not industrialization that leads to an economic crunch where population outruns available resources, but rather the reverse: a failure to industrialize. For, as Nef (1937, p. 178) noted, pre-industrial societies boast little metal for ploughshares, hoes, axes, and other tools, an outcome that inevitably results in low levels of agricultural productivity.

On every one of the above points, recent research has endorsed Nef's findings. As Allen (2011, p. 364) notes, in the 1500s and 1600s it was only the commercial, industrializing societies of England, Belgium, and the Netherlands that avoided a "Malthusian" check, in which "real wages moved inversely to the population." By 1700, Allen's (2011, p. 362) research indicates real wages in London were probably the highest in the world, a finding that confirms Nef's earlier suspicion. Nef's belief that the "first" Industrial Revolution of the late sixteenth and early seventeenth century set England on a path to generalized prosperity that differentiated it from pre-industrial societies is also confirmed by the recent research of Broadberry and Gupta (2006). This is indicated in Fig. 3, which draws on Broadberry and Gupta's (2006, p. 6) collation of the daily grain wage – i.e., how many kilograms of wheat could a person buy if they spent all their wage on wheat or another grain equivalent – of unskilled workers in Southern England, Florence and Milan (treated together), and India between 1550–1599 and 1800–1849. Whereas real wages c.1600 were roughly the same in Southern England, Florence/Milan, and India – English wages

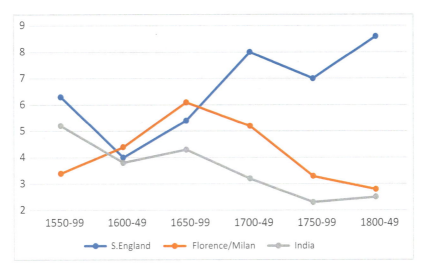

Fig. 3 Daily grain wage (kilograms of wheat) of unskilled workers, Southern England, Florence/Milan, and India, 1550–1599 to 1800–1849. (Source: Broadberry and Gupta 2006, p. 6)

having fallen during the sixteenth century in the face of rising population – from c.1600 the economic condition of the unskilled English worker began to diverge from that found elsewhere. While unskilled workers in Florence and Milan also enjoyed increased real wages in the early seventeenth century, this period of benign conditions proved short-lived, an outcome that suggests that there was something fundamentally different to English circumstances. Yes, it is true that there *was* a decline in English real wages in the late 1700s. However, this decline needs to be understood in the context of generally rising real wages. It is also probable that the short-lived dip in English real wages owed as much to the Napoleonic wars as it did to the social dislocation wrought by the Industrial Revolution.

In seeking explanation as to why from c.1600 the economic and managerial trajectory of England diverged from that of other societies, Nef paid greatest heed to England's shift "from a wood-burning to a coal-burning economy" (Nef 1934, p. 24). In doing so, Nef undoubtedly made his important intellectual contribution to what has become management history, highlighting the profound differences that differentiate pre-modern and modern forms of management. Whereas the younger Toynbee (1976/1978, pp. 565–566) associated the destruction of forests with industrialization, Nef's research highlighted the fact that the most destructive pressure on forests comes from population expansion in pre-industrial societies. For, while it is true, as Toynbee (1976/1978, p. 565) pointed out, that wind power and water power are "clean" and "inexhaustible," they are also unreliable. Streams run dry or freeze over. The wind stops blowing. Moreover, although medieval water mills could drive machinery, they could not be used for heating, cooking, firing bricks and pottery, roasting grains, and fermenting beer and in smelting metal. In the absence of coal, or of the peat reserves exploited by the Dutch in the early modern era, pre-industrial societies invariably place unsustainable demands on their forests; woodlands exploited not only for heating, cooking, and smelting but also for the construction of ships, bridges, workplaces, and homes. In China c.1100, for example, the use of wood-based charcoal in the manufacture of cast-iron placed such heavy demands on the forests that the Chinese rice region was turned into "a great clear-felled zone" (Jones 1987, p. 4). In Elizabethan England, when the English coal industry was still in its infancy, similar outcomes were apparent, Nef (1937, p. 180) recording that, "In county after county trees were felled in such profusion . . . that lands once thick with forests could be converted into runs for sheep and cattle." As forests were depleted, the cost of wood became prohibitive. Between 1510 and 1640, Nef (1937, p. 180) ascertained, the price of firewood rose 11-fold. During the same period, the cost of high-quality wood, used in naval ship construction, rose 15-fold. So expensive did wood become that by 1650 its price came to comprise around half of the costs involved in constructing a building or ship, far outweighing labor or capital costs (Nef 1937:179). Having stretched forest reserves to breaking point, England avoided a profound economic and demographic crisis only by exploiting the nation's cheap and plentiful coal reserves, Nef (1932a, pp. 19–20) estimating that England's coal production rose from a minuscule 200,000 tons per annum in 1560 to almost 3 million tons in 1681. By 1790, an incredible 10 million tons was mined annually. Increasingly, it was this transition to a coal-based, energy-intensive economy that differentiated England from other European societies. In comparing circumstances in England around 1710 with its great continental rival, France, Nef (1943, p. 18) observed that, "Compared with the high mounds besides the collieries in Durham and Northumberland . . . the piles of coal besides the chief French pits resembled anthills."

The rise of a large-scale commercial coal industry profoundly altered the conditions in which English managers operated as the effects of cheap coal rippled through the economy. As mines became larger and deeper, working beneath the water table, flooding became a problem. This demanded large-scale capital investment in pumps and machinery, driving out the small operator and turning the industry into a domain dominated by enterprises "conducted on scale which would have seemed incredible" to those born a generation or two earlier (Nef 1934, p. 10). The size of the coal mining workforces also had no precedent in English history, turning the coalfields of Durham and Northumberland into labor relations training schools. As Pollard (1965, p. 127) subsequently noted, in the (second) Industrial Revolution of the eighteenth and nineteenth centuries, it was the nation's "northern collieries" that were probably the largest suppliers of managers to Britain's expanding factories and mills. The English discovery of coke (i.e., a burnt residue of coal) as a substitute for charcoal also allowed for large-scale enterprises in a host of energy-intensive industries. For although, as we noted in our introduction, the use of coke in iron- and steelmaking was not perfected until the late eighteenth century, it soon became essential to the competitive advantage of English glassmakers, brickmakers, brewers, and potteries. Accordingly, Nef (1934, p. 22) estimated, by 1640 England boasted "hundreds of new, capitalistically owned enterprises," employing tens of thousands of high-wage workers.

In making his case for the importance of the "first" Industrial Revolution, it soon became apparent that Nef exaggerated the size of many sixteenth and seventeenth businesses, Pollard (1965, p. 273, n. 7) subsequently referring to "the many doubtful methods by which Nef succeeds in enlarging the scale of early industrial enterprises." Nevertheless, Nef's assumption that it was England's substitution of an economy based on wood for one built around coal that best explains its role as an industrial pioneer *is* one that has been confirmed by subsequent research. Fernand Braudel (1986/1990, p. 521, 523), in reflecting upon France's inability to follow the English industrial and managerial lead in the eighteenth and nineteenth centuries observed that, "The problem, not to say tragedy, was that there were not enough French coalmines, and those there were proved difficult and costly to operate." Similarly, Cipolla (1981, p. 246), writing of the "timber crisis" that curtailed economic growth in Italy, records that in Genoa, the price of wood used in ship building rose 12-fold between 1463 and 1468. Across the Lombard plains of northern Italy, only 9% of the region's woodlands survived in 1555, an outcome that caused Cipolla to conclude that, "The main bottleneck of preindustrial societies was the strictly limited supply of energy." Through its early use of coal, England not only avoided this energy crunch; it also laid the platform for something unique in human history: industries that boasted an international cost advantage despite suffering high-wage costs. The reason for this unusual outcome, Allen (2011) notes, was that England was able to offset high costs in one area (i.e., wages) with low costs in another (i.e., energy). Indeed, Allen (2011) argues, it was the combination of high-wage costs and low-energy costs, which drove England in the direction of energy and capital-intensive production methods in lieu of labor-intensive techniques. Although, according to Allen's (2011, p. 364) calculations, the disparity between high-wage costs and low-energy costs made the problems of production and management in London profoundly different to those found in virtually any continental European center; this disparity was even more marked in the English coal towns: Newcastle, Sheffield, Birmingham, etc. For even though wages in these towns were marginally lower than in London, coal prices were far less. As a result, the incentive to industrialize was far higher in these coal towns than it was in London, a fact subsequently reflected in the geography of English industrialization.

Given Nef's association of industrialization with cheaper energy, higher wages, larger business entities, and economic growth, his disquiet with the results of the (second) Industrial Revolution appears odd at first glance. Nef was certainly unconcerned by changes in wage levels or social inequality. In his opinion, rising wages offset any adverse effects stemming from social inequality. He was also unconcerned by the effects of the transition to an energy-intensive economy on the environment, for the use of coal protected rather than depleted forest reserves. Rather, as a US citizen with a special fondness for Great Britain, Nef feared the rise of totalitarianism, which by the 1930s was all too obvious in Italy, Germany, Spain, Portugal, and the Soviet Union. For, in Nef's (1943, p. 13, 30) opinion, the great economic strength of such societies was manifest in evil, in "the concentration camp and the firing squad." Writing in the 1930s and early 1940s, Nef's fears were well founded. In today's world, a number of authoritarian societies – China, North Korea, etc. –

still use the powers unleashed by industrialization for the purposes of surveillance and the State control of dissidents. However, if there is one lesson of the twentieth century, it is that democratic, free market societies survive and prosper, whereas ultimately totalitarian societies do not.

In many ways, the career and intellectual interests of Sir John Clapham mirrored those of his contemporary, John Nef. A one-time President of the (British) Economic History Society, Michael Postan (1946, p. 56) said of him at his death that he embodied "the intellectual and moral virtues of the Victorian middle classes at their best – a head which was shrewd and cool, an outlook which was wholly unsentimental and a rule of life disciplined to the point of being hard." Even more than Nef, Clapham – whose contribution to economic, labor, and management history largely rests on his three-volume study, *An Economic History of Modern Britain* – was a firm believer that the Industrial Revolution profoundly altered the human condition for the better. "That the industrial revolution, with the attendant changes in agriculture and transport," Clapham (1926/1967, p. 54) reflected, "rendered the maintenance of a rapidly growing British population possible, without resort to the cabin-and-potato standard of life, is beyond question." For all the sanitary and overcrowding problems of Britain's industrial towns and cities, Clapham (1926/1967) nevertheless accurately noted that they were safer and healthier than any other large urban centers in the human experience. The British population rose sharply, Clapham (1926/1967, p. 55) observed, not because – as Thomas Malthus (1798), John Stuart Mill (1848), and the elder Toynbee (1884/1894) had assumed – of working class immorality and a high birth rate, but rather because the death rate fell, most particularly for the newborn. Among the factors contributing to longevity were immunization against smallpox, improvements in obstetrics, the disappearance of scurvy due to improved food supplies, and better urban drainage. The ready availability of cheap, washable cottons – in lieu of the soiled woollen clothes that were the historic norm – also contributed to a marked improvement in personal hygiene (Clapham 1926/1967, p. 55). "London might be honey-combed with cesspools and rank with city graveyards," Clapham (1926/1967, pp. 55–56) thoughtfully concluded, "but it was better to be born a Londoner than a Parisian, better to be born a Londoner of 1820 than a Londoner of 1760." Clapham (1926/1967, p. 52) also dismissed as a misnomer the view that British working class of the Industrial Revolution was sunk in ignorance and moral degradation. In doing so, he cited a French visitor to Scotland who reported, "In all the workshops and manufactories that I visited, I found the workmen well informed, appreciating with sagacity the practice of their trade, and judging rationally of the power of their tools and the efficacy of their machinery" (Dupin 1825, p. 52).

Like Nef, Clapham (1926/1967, p. 15) also noted the positive effect of industrialization on the area of land under tree cover. Under relentless pressure from Britain's pre-industrial population, Britain was by the eighteenth century virtually devoid of woodland, left with nothing other than "sandy waste heath, fenland, rough mountain pasture." From the 1780s, however, under the auspices of a newly established forestry commission, a process of systematic reafforestation commenced. By the 1820s, Clapham (1926/1967, p. 12) recorded, in areas long devoid of tree cover, the land was "sprinkled over with wood – coppice screen and clump of pine or larch or spruce."

If Clapham's research bares resemblance to Nef's in terms of macro-level conclusions, it differed in providing a far more nuanced and detailed picture of the process of British industrialization. Indeed, by paying far greater heed to the social consequences of industrialization, and to patterns of managerial organization, Clapham charted a fundamentally new course that placed management and workplace relations at the fore – rather than economic factors of production. This research direction, it appears, was not one much favored by other British economic historians. In the obituary to Clapham published in *The Economic History Review*, for example, the journal's editor, Michael Postan (1946, p. 58), declared Clapham's "third volume of the *Economic History of Modern Britain* is better than his first two." Presumably, what Postan did not like about Clapham's work was what he described as Clapham's propensity for "weed-killing" and for being "rooted too deeply in facts" (Postan 1946, p. 57). However, this attention to detail arguably made him Britain's first true "management historian." For Clapham was someone who looked beyond generalities about technology and steam power to explore circumstances at the firm level. In perusing the pages of Clapham's three-volume *Economic History of Modern Britain*, what stands out is how industrialization was continually advanced by innovations – typically involving a modest variation of past practices – at the firm level, adaptations that were then quickly seized upon by competitors. In Clapham's (1926/1967, p. 426) first volume, covering the period between 1820 and 1850, we thus read how in 1831 the small Scottish Calder ironworks ascertained that high-grade coal could be used in ironmaking without the need for coking. This discovery favored new firms over old-established rivals who had invested in now dated technology, a fact that led to a 20-year supremacy of Scottish iron smelters at the expense of their Welsh and English rivals. Similarly, in Clapham's second volume (1932/1967, p. 129) of his *Economic History of Modern Britain*, covering the period 1850–1886, we are taken through the process of subcontracting involved in English ship building in the 1870s. Elsewhere, Clapham (1926/1967, 1932/1967, 1938/1951) explores almost every aspect of agricultural, commercial, and industrial life: labor relations, home life, finance, technological change, transport, and communications.

Constantly, Clapham emphasizes the comparatively modest contribution of steam power and technology to economic growth during the first half century of the Industrial Revolution and, conversely, the importance of managerial endeavor and organization. As late as the mid-1830s, Clapham (1926/1967, p. 442) ascertained, the motive capacity of Britain's entire stock of steam engines amounted to a feeble 30,000 horsepower, almost all of which was found in three locations: Lancashire, Cheshire, and Glasgow. Although the vaunted cotton industry employed more workers than any other manufacturing sector, comparatively few employees were nevertheless found within the confines of a cotton mill. In 1830, Clapham (1926/1967, p. 54) calculated, the "cotton-mill population of Great Britain . . . was perhaps one-eighteenth of the total population." Most British workers continued to work for small businesses and entrepreneurs, the "average" firm employing only 5.5 workers according to the British census of 1851 (Clapham 1926/1967, p. 70). London in particular was "the home of small businesses," Clapham (1926/1967, p. 68, 70) observing that in 1831, it "had no thousand-man businesses to keep up the average and plenty of craftsman-shops to keep it down." Where large-scale, industrialized businesses were established they were invariably on or adjacent to active coalfields. For nothing, Clapham (1926/1967, p. 42) reflected, was "more essential" to the viability of a large industrial enterprise or town than "a supply of coal at reasonable prices."

Where Clapham's analysis profoundly differed from those who had previously reflected on the Industrial Revolution – the elder Toynbee, Tawney, the Webbs, and Nef – was in effectively dating its commencement not from the 1760s (as per Toynbee) or the 1790s (as per Nef) but rather from the 1830s and the advent of the railroads. Reflective of this emphasis is the subtitle, *The Early Railway Age 1820–1850*, to the first volume of Clapham's three-volume book on industrialization. Yes, Clapham recognized, the advent of the railways depended on the *preexistence* of a whole series of preconditions: steam power, large-scale coal and iron production, a skilled engineering workforce, and large pools of private savings eager for new sources of investment. Nevertheless, in Clapham's estimation, it was the railroad and the steamship that profoundly altered the human condition, destroying local market monopolies and shattering the pre-industrial sense of space and time. Although English railroad developers anticipated that the bulk of their revenues would come from freight, it soon became apparent that passenger transport was more valuable, comprising 64% of gross railroad revenue in 1845 (Clapham 1926/1967, p. 400). Whereas, previously, most people lived and died within sight of where they were born, the coming of the railroad transformed people's physical and intellectual horizons. Far more than the mechanization of textile production, the backward and forward linkages created by the railroads profoundly altered economic and managerial relations, creating the largest and most capital-intensive private-sector organizations in the human experience. "At once effect and cause," Clapham (1926/1967, p. 425) noted, "railway development coincided with a development of metallurgy and mining quite without precedent." In every field of metal production, engineering, and mining, the needs of the railroads drove large-scale increases in production. In 1847–1848 alone, British railroads placed orders for 400,000 tons of iron running rails (Clapham 1926/1967, p. 428). Locomotives and rolling stock also placed huge demands on iron smelters, as did a booming export trade. Not only British railroads relied on the output of the nation's smelters and iron works. In France and the United States during the 1840s, all of the iron rails laid down were British made (Clapham 1926/1967, p. 427).

In essence, Clapham's thesis as to the central importance of the railroads in the process of industrialization closely resembles that subsequently – and more famously – argued by Alfred D Chandler, Jr. In Chandler's (1965, 1977) estimation, as with Clapham, the modern industrial world was first and foremost a product of the railroads. As Chandler (1977, pp. 79–80) expressed it, not only were the railroads "the pioneers in the management of modern business enterprise"; they were also "essential to high-volume production and distribution – the hallmark of the large modern manufacturing or marketing enterprises." Given the marked similarities between Clapham and Chandler's research, one would suspect that Chandler owed an intellectual debt to Clapham. This, however, does not appear to be the case. There is not a single reference to Clapham in either Chandler's (1965) original article on American railroads ("The Railroads: Pioneers in Modern Corporate Management") or Chandler's (1977) famed study, *The Visible Hand: The Managerial Revolution in American Business*. What explains Chandler's apparent ignorance of Clapham's work, given its close resemblance to his own? Part of the problem lies in the fact that, unlike Nef, Clapham rarely published in mainstream journals after World War I, a fact evident from the "Bibliography of Sir John Clapham's Work" appended to Postan's (1946, pp. 58–59) obituary piece. Instead, it appears, his massive three-volume *Economic History of Modern Britain* – and his (Clapham 1944/1966) two-volume study, *The Bank of England: A History* – consumed most of his time. Until their republication by Cambridge University Press in the mid-1960s, it would also appear that the readership of these books – originally published in the midst of economic depression and war – was small. The size of Clapham's books also probably deterred would-be readers. The first volume of his *Economic History of Modern Britain* goes to 623 pages. Volumes 2 and 3 comprise 554 pages and 577 pages, respectively. The greatest strength of Clapham's research – his capacity to explore in depth a variety of interrelated issues (labor relations, technology, firm size, managerial organization, technology, etc.) – was also a weakness. For, unlike Chandler's great study, *The Visible Hand*, where the theme and argument were relentlessly pursued, Clapham's books were – as Postan (1946, p. 57) remarked – "rooted too deeply in fact." One is easily drowned in the detail.

If Clapham's American readership appears to have been small, his work nevertheless remains seminal to our understanding of the Industrial Revolution and the transformative role that management played in this process of economic transformation. Certainly, one cannot fully understand the defining works in labor history by E.P. Thompson, and in management history by Sidney Pollard, without comprehending the ways in which they framed their arguments for and against Clapham. For if Chandler did not read Clapham, Thompson and Pollard certainly did.

Capitalism and Management: Exploitation or Opportunity? The Intellectual Contribution of Webbs and E.P. Thompson

Among historians who came of age in the 1970s and 1980s, as I did, arguably no work was more influential in the fields of social history and labor history than E.P. Thompson's *The Making of the English Working Class*. A Marxist – who abandoned his membership of the Communist Party after the Soviet invasion of Hungary in 1956 – Thompson's defining work provided a fundamentally different way at looking at the Industrial Revolution, and, indeed, history as a whole. Rather than writing history in terms of dominant intellectual currents, economics, finance, or politics, Thompson aspired to write a history "from below," from the point of the view of the supposed victims rather than the victors of the Industrial Revolution. In his brilliantly written six-page preface to *The Making of the English Working Class* – the only section of the book that one suspects most readers ever peruse in full – Thompson (1963/1968, p. 13) proclaimed, "I am seeking to rescue the poor stockinger, the Luddite cropper, the 'obsolete' hand-loom weaver, the 'utopian' artisan . . . from the enormous condescension of posterity." For Thompson, unlike Marx and Engels, the "working class" was not primarily the results of economics, but rather a cultural creation, the product of shared values and experiences. Accordingly, the English working class was, Thompson (1963/1968, p. 9) declared in the opening paragraph of his book, "present at its own creation." Rejecting the view that there were a multitude of "working classes" (domestic servants, farm laborers, factory workers, etc.), Thompson (1963/1968, p. 12) argued in favor of a single "English working class," who "came to feel an identity of interests as between themselves and as against their rulers and employers." Rather than highlighting the reforming instincts of the middle class, as the Toynbees and Tawney had done, Thompson argued that the British Industrial Revolution was a catastrophic experience for working people, imposed relentlessly and remorselessly. "The process of industrialization is necessarily painful," Thompson (1963/1968, p. 486) reflected, "But it was carried through with exceptional violence in Britain . . .Its ideology was that of the masters alone." Constantly detecting an undercurrent of revolution in English society, Thompson (1963/1968, p. 898) fancifully concluded that by "the autumn of 1831 . . . Britain was within an ace of a revolution." Although this revolt never eventuated, Thompson nevertheless argued that the Industrial Revolution created a host of "social evils" – workplace degradation, inequality, and power imbalances – "which we have yet to cure."

In many ways, Thompson's classic study suffered from the same strengths and weaknesses as Clapham's earlier three-volume *Economic History of Modern Britain*, a tendency to be drown the reader in detail. My Penguin copy of the 1968 edition, which differed from the initial print run only through the edition of a short "postscript," runs to 958 pages. Now, it is true that the political and social purpose of what is an aggressively Marxist analysis is self-evident in *The Making of The English Working Class*. As one early reviewer observed, "Mr. Thompson sticks very close to his theme" (Best 1965, p. 271). Nevertheless, its *intellectual* goal (i.e., the research opinions that it seeks to challenge and refute) is by no means readily apparent to the lay reader. Indeed, in my Penguin copy of *The Making of The English Working Class*, this is only articulated on pages 213–214, where Thompson (1963/1968, pp. 213–214) declares his work to be a "challenge" to "a new anti-catastrophic" historiography on the Industrial Revolution, an "orthodoxy" that emerged as a repudiation of the earlier "catastrophic" analysis of Marx and Arnold Toynbee. In taking aim of this "anti-catastrophic" viewpoint, Thompson (1963/1968, p. 214) lists "Sir John Clapham" in the first rank "among its most notable exponents." Thompson (1963/1968, pp. 226–227) took particular aim at Clapham's well-articulated argument that the Industrial Revolution – at least by the 1830s – was associated with a marked improvement in working-class living standards. Arguing in favor of the reverse proposition, Thompson (1963/1968, pp. 228–229) recorded that, "The condition of the majority was bad in 1790; it remained bad in 1830 ...even in the mid-40s the plight of very large groups of workers remains desperate."

Undoubtedly, this "catastrophic" view of the Industrial Revolution, and its associated systems of capitalism and management, does much to explain the enduring success of *The Making of The English Working Class*, a viewpoint that Thompson weaves into virtually every section of his book. The fact that few of Thompson's readers are probably familiar with the work of Clapham – or with the critical reviews (i.e., Best 1965; Chambers 1966) that emerged in the wake of the publication of *The Making of The English Working Class* – also no doubt adds to the continued prevalence of the "catastrophic" image of the Industrial Revolution. Alan McKinlay (2006, p. 95), for example, in an influential article in *Management & Organizational History*, declares the period of the Industrial Revolution to be "monstrous," associated as it was with "mechanization and the subjugation of labor." Now, of course, one *could* argue that the Industrial Revolution was associated with "subjugation" even though living standards rose. This was not, however, the path that Thompson chose to follow.

In retrospect, Thompson's decision to associate the Industrial Revolution with labor subjugation *and* falling living standards appears more than a little odd. For by the late 1950s, as we have noted in previous chapters, the findings of the International Scientific Committee on Price History – which ascertained the relationship between prices and wages since the early medieval period – were making their way into print. In Britain, the most significant result of this research was the so-called Phelps Brown and Hopkins Index, which traced the real wage of English building workers, both skilled and unskilled, between the thirteenth and twentieth centuries. While this Phelps Brown and Hopkins (1956) Index did identify the dip in real wages already noted in Fig. 3, it also identified 1800 as a fundamental turning point for real wages in Britain. After this date, as Fig. 4 indicates, living conditions for

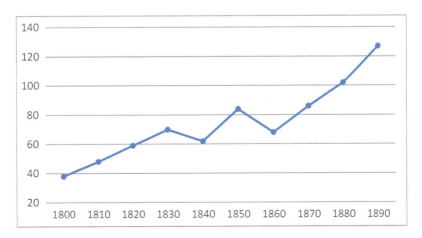

Fig. 4 Real wage of skilled building worker, Southern England, 1800–1880 (1447 = 100). (Source: Phelps Brown and Hopkins: "Seven centuries of ... builders' wage rates," Appendix B)

English workers were characterized by steady improvement, culminating in a level of mass prosperity without precedent in the human experience. It soon became apparent to Thompson himself that his arguments in favor of falling living standards were indefensible. In the "postscript" appended to the second edition of *The Making of The English Working Class*, Thompson (1963/1968, p. 917) chose to beat a retreat, declaring his chapter on "Standards and Experience" to be "clearly inadequate." Thompson (1963/1968, p. 917) also advised readers, in a confusing turn of phrase, to read instead "those economic historians whose assumptions are, in this chapter, under criticism." Presumably, this statement should be read as an acceptance as to the basic accuracy of John Clapham's earlier research, given that it was against Clapham that Thompson primarily directed his attacks. The problem with this concession – which was probably read by few people and understood by even fewer – is that Thompson's "catastrophic" viewpoint was not confined to a single chapter. Rather, it pervaded his whole book. A number of Thompson's other core assumptions are also without much merit. Of Thompson's constant identification of revolutionary tendencies among Britain's workers, Chambers (1966, p. 184) declares it "a really remarkable flight of fancy" as "there was not revolution to stop." Geoffrey Best (1965, p. 276) also declares Thompson's capacity to find a single united working class in industrializing England to be figment of the imagination.

Given the evident problems in Thompson's famed study, what makes it a foundation text for anyone attempting to understand management history? First and foremost – far more than Clapham or, indeed, any scholar before or since – Thompson forces the "human factor" constantly to the fore. Thompson constantly takes us into the workplaces and homes of English workers, some of whom enjoyed comparative prosperity and others undoubted misery. We get to know not only employers but also workers and their family members by name, to sit with them in their cottages and understand the detail of their work. For example, of the "heavy manual occupations at the base of industrial society" that were dominated by Irish immigrants (i.e., canal and railroad construction, tunneling, wharf laboring), Thompson (1963/1968, p. 473) observed that their work "required a spendthrift expense of pure physical energy … which belongs to pre-industrial labourrhythms." In the case of the handloom weavers of "the Pennine uplands" whose historic mode of existence was being destroyed by the new industrial factories, we read how they lived on a diet composed almost entirely of "oatmeal and potatoes," supplemented with "old milk and treacle" (Thompson 1963/1968, p. 320). For all his Marxist sympathies, Thompson also showed an acute sense of the problems faced by managers. More often than not, Thompson willingly conceded, managerial demands for workplace discipline profoundly altered worker behavior for the better. Between 1780 and 1830, Thompson (1963/1968, p. 451) concluded, "The 'average' English working man became more disciplined, more subject to the productive tempo of the 'clock', more reserved and methodical, less violent and less spontaneous." Nowhere is this sympathy for the problems of management more apparent than in his article, "Time, Work-discipline, and Industrial Capitalism." As Thompson (1967, pp. 70–71) correctly noted, "accurate and representative time-budgets" – and hence any sense of workplace efficiency and cost-benefit ratios – are virtually impossible in pre-industrial situations. There are simply too many variables. Bad weather, the shortage of one or more input of production, illness to a household member, drunkenness, and the slow pace of a particular worker in the production process all worked to destroy any sense of predictability. The absence of watches and clocks also meant that most worked to the natural rhythms of the day, rather than to any sense of predetermined start and finish points. In Thompson's estimation, a viewpoint with which this author concurs, no managerial task was more important to the future of industrial society than the effort to internalize a sense of time and work discipline among workers. Through a host of initiatives – "the division of labour; the supervision of labour; fines; bells and clocks; money incentives" – a new approach to work was forged, centered on "a new time-discipline" (Thompson 1967, p. 90). Thompson (1963, pp. 452–453 was also unusual in identifying the ways in which the new industrial capitalism opened up unprecedented opportunities for women as "independent wage-earners," free from "dependence" on male relatives. "Even the unmarried mother," hitherto a virtual social outcast, found in factory employment "an independence unknown before."

Arguably, the greatness of Thompson's work, for all its obvious flaws and inaccuracies, is found in his recognition that the Industrial Revolution was built around "paradoxes," in which – even by his estimates – the opportunities often outweighed the social disadvantages (Thompson 1963/1968, p. 453). This sense of paradox, of industrial capitalism's opportunities outweighing its exploitative tendencies, is even more apparent in the work of Beatrice and Sidney Webb. It is also the case that, even though Beatrice Webb (d.1943) and Sidney Webb (d.1947) both died long before *The Making of The English Working Class* was published, their work is in many ways more "modern" than Thompson's studies. It constantly speaks to contemporary concerns such as productivity, the enhancement of workplace skills, female participation in the workforce, and a fostering of cooperative relationships between workers and employers.

Although the Webbs are typically associated with collective bargaining and trade unions, their concerns were in truth far more catholic. The starting point for the Webbs – as expressed in the "Preface" to the original edition of *The History of Trade Unionism* – was that in a "democratic State," social and economic interests only become meaningful to the extent that they are expressed institutionally, in "the course of continuous organizations" (Webb and Webb 1894/1902, p. xxvii). The primary significance of trade unions was thus found in the fact that they were "a State within our State," speaking on behalf of a special interest group that represented a large section of the population. In granting trade unions an important role, the Webbs were, however, never uncritical supporters. Unlike Thompson, who was at best equivocal in his attitude toward the productivity-enhancing activities of management, the Webbs were enthusiasts for productivity maximization and workplace efficiency. Trade unions only succeeded – and only played a socially beneficial role, the Webbs argued in the Preface to the 1902 edition of *The History of Trade Unionism* – when they associated the interests of their members with "the utmost possible stimulus to speed and productivity" (Webb and Webb 1902, p. xix).

Conversely, they argued, any union "struggle against … maximising productivity … must necessarily fail" (Webb and Webb 1902, p. xviii). Like Adam Smith (1776/1937, Book I, Chap. VIII, para. 13), who argued against artificial restrictions on the supply of workers, the Webbs "unreservedly condemned" any union attempt to protect one class of worker by excluding others or by artificially inflating the number to be employed (Webb and Webb 1897/1920, p. 810). Such restrictive practices, the Webbs declared, were "hostile to the welfare of the community as a whole" (Webb and Webb 1897/1920, p. 810). The Webbs also strongly supported managerial prerogative when it came to recruitment and promotion, advising their readers that, "It is clear that the efficiency of industry is best promoted by every situation being filled by the best available candidate" (Webb and Webb 1897/1920, p. 717). No doubt to the chagrin of the union leaders with whom they rubbed shoulders, the Webbs were also deeply suspicious of union-endorsed apprenticeship schemes, supporting them when they genuinely served the needs of industry and opposing them when they sought to artificially restrict entry into a trade or occupation (Webb and Webb 1897/1920, pp. 456–457, 478). In general, the Webbs believed that the apprenticeship system long supported by unions was "Undemocratic in its scope, unscientific in its education methods, and fundamentally unsound in its financial aspects" (Webb and Webb 1897/1920, p. 481). The Webbs were also fervent opponents of trade union attempts to restrict female employment, devoting a whole section of their classic study, *Industrial Democracy* to "The Exclusion of Women."

Critical rather than uncritical supporters of trade unionism, the Webbs nevertheless argued that trade unionism was a *potentially* progressive force for two reasons. First, they argued, the educated trade union leader – more than the individual employer – dealt with the most fundamental problems of an industrial society in that they had to consider matters from the point of view of an entire occupation or industry, rather than from the narrow viewpoint of the individual firm. For the problem "in each trade," the Webbs declared, was how "to adjust all the technical conditions of the contract of service, so as to combine the utmost possible productivity, and the greatest possible improvement in processes, with the maintenance and progressive improvement of the manual worker's "standard of life" (Webb and Webb 1902, p. xi). In other words, the Webbs supported unions where they supported productivity and living standards and castigated them when they did not. The second socially progressively role that the Webbs associated with trade unionism was in the enforcement of a "Common Rule," which acted to take "wages out of competition" by setting wage rates, worker hours, and "prescribed conditions of Sanitation and Safety" that were common to all in any given industry (Webb and Webb 1897/1920, p, 716). In their well-reasoned estimation, not only workers and trade unions benefited from the enforcement of a "Common Rule." So too did the reputable employer, intent on paying his or her employees fairly for a fair day's work, who was protected from undercutting by unscrupulous rivals. The Webbs also believed that a "Common Rule" worked to the benefit of the overall society by forcing employers to focus on more productive work practices rather than lower labor costs. As Sidney and Beatrice Webb (1897/1920, pp. 716–717) explained it,

> If the employer cannot go below a minimum rate, and is unable to degrade the other conditions of employment down to the lowest level … he is economically impelled to do his utmost to raise the level of efficiency so as to get the best possible return for the fixed conditions.

For management historians, the work of the Webbs deserves a special place in our discipline due to the ways in which they perceived employment, management, living standards, worker and employer interests, productivity, and training as an integrated whole. The "human factor" was for them always at the forefront of their attention, prefiguring the subsequent work of the US "human relations movement" (i.e., Elton May, George Homans, etc.). As such, their work has a contemporary resonance that exceeds that of any of the other scholars we have considered so far. Certainly, in my own research, whenever I come to consider some employment or labor relations issue, I invariably thumb my way through my well-worn copies of *Industrial Democracy* and *The History of Trade Unionism* before putting pen to paper. For whatever problem I am considering, it is likely that the Webbs have already written on it. Despite their deep and genuine interest in productivity and efficiency, however, the Webbs were at heart – like the Toynbees and Tawney – well-meaning Victorian moralists, intent on raising workers from their perceived poverty and degradation. Thus, we read in the "Introduction to the 1920 Edition" of *Industrial Democracy*, that the Webbs believed that, "the gravest" social evil "in the opening decades of the twentieth century is the lack of physical vigour, moral self-control, and technical skill of the town-bred, manual-working boy" (Webb and Webb 1920, p. xii). This problem primarily stemmed, the Webbs continued, from the fact that "hundreds of thousands of youths" were "taken on by employers to do the unskilled and undisciplined work," paid "comparatively high wages," but "taught no trade" (Webb and Webb 1920, p. xii). Devoid of any sense of long-term purpose or career, such workers invariably became, in the Webbs opinion, a source of "hooliganism," "constant delinquency," and "physical degeneracy" (Webb and Webb 1920, p. xii).

Invariably, the Webbs saw the ultimate solution to nearly every workplace, managerial and social problem in regulation, imposed either through collective bargaining or, preferably, under the auspices of State control. Among the controls advocated in *Industrial Democracy* were compulsory vocational education at the employer's expense, compulsory conciliation and arbitration of industrial disputes, a minimum wage, and the exclusion of "boy-labour where economically inefficient" (Webb and Webb 1920, p. xiii, xv; Webb and Webb 1897/1920, p. 453, 484, 790).

While any one of the above recommendations has arguable merit, a willingness to put one's faith in government and State control at the expense of entrepreneurship has often led in unfortunate directions. The Webbs – whose early research remains core to our understandings of work and employment – provide proof of this maxim. After being lionized by the Stalinist regime during a visit to the Soviet Union in 1932, the Webbs published two accounts of their visit, a two-volume book that ran to 1,200 pages, *Soviet Communism*, and a shorter, 30-page pamphlet, *Is Soviet Communism a New Civilisation?* (Webb and Webb 1935, 1936). Neither did them much credit. As with many visitors to the Soviet Union, the Webbs chose to see and record only those aspects of communism that coincided with their pre-existing beliefs and prejudices. Thus, we read how, "The highly organised trade unions of the USSR ... are not only whole-heartedly in favour of increasing the productivity ...but are also constantly pressing for the adoption of more and more labour-saving inventions" (Webb and Webb 1936, p. 8). Elsewhere, we read how "the habit of able-bodied persons living without work has become disgraceful" (Webb and Webb 1936, p. 7). In terms of the overall ethos of Soviet society, the Webbs reported that: "Husbands and wives, parents and children, teachers and scholars ... managers and factory operates ... live in an atmosphere of social equality" (Webb and Webb 1936, p. 11). In short, the Webbs claimed to detect almost everything that they had advocated in *Industrial Democracy*, although – in truth – two vital ingredients were missing, namely, democracy and managerial prerogative to direct production efforts toward market needs. Yes, it is true that Stalinist Russia did create a "new civilization," although it hardly resembled the one depicted by Sidney and Beatrice Webb. Instead, the reality of working life in the new Soviet "civilization" is well captured in Karl Schlögel's description of work on the Moscow-Volga canal between 1932 and 1938. "Working conditions were unimaginably harsh," Schlögel (2008/2012, pp. 283–284) records, "Everything hinged on finishing the canal in the shortest possible time ... Workers went without lunch ...They stood in water and swampy ground and were unable to warm themselves or dry their clothes." Perhaps there was in this a "Common Rule," a uniformity of working conditions such as that which the Webbs had advocated in *Industrial Democracy*. It was, however, a "Common Rue" set at the level of totalitarian barbarism.

Sidney Pollard and the Origins of "Modern" Management

The genius of Pollard primarily rests in the fact that he gave much thought to definitions before blundering forth, as many do in either amassing a huge data set or in coming to some grandiose conclusion. This proclivity to pay much attention to definitions is evident in Pollard's thoughts on the two most significant questions in management history. What is modern management? What was the Industrial Revolution? To the first question, as I, a critical disciple of Pollard, have also argued consistently in this *Palgrave Handbook*, Pollard (1965, pp. 6–7) drew a clear distinction between "modern management" and pre-modern management – and, by implication, that found in modern totalitarian societies – in that modern management had the following distinguishing characteristics:

- Managers had "to control" large workforces, "but without powers of compulsion: indeed, the absence of legal enforcement of unfree work was not only one of the marked characteristics of the new capitalism, but one of its seminal ideas."
- Managers "had not only to show absolute results in terms of certain products of their efforts, but to relate them to costs, and to sell them competitively."

19 Conflicting Understandings of the Industrial Revolution and Its... 463

- Managers had to combine capital-intensive production "with labour," transforming both "into instruments of production embodying the latest achievements of a changing technology."
- Managers "had to transform ... much of the rest of their environment, in the process of creating their industrial capitalism."

As to the nature of the Industrial Revolution, Pollard argued it was first and foremost a "managerial revolution" rather than a "technological revolution" and that modern management was both the creation and the creator of the Industrial Revolution. For the defining hallmark of the Industrial Revolution, Pollard (1965, p. 102) argued was not so much technological change as:

> ... improvements in organization ...involving better layout of factory space, division of labour, design of the product with the process of production in mind, interchangeability of parts, control of raw material stocking and supply.

Where Pollard differed from both Clapham and Chandler – both of whom associated the emergence of the modern managerial world with the advent of the railroads in the 1830s and 1840s – was in following the convention established by Toynbee the elder and dating the Industrial Revolution to the years between 1760 and 1830. Of little obvious importance, this difference in dates has profound significance for our understanding of both management and the Industrial Revolution. For – unlike the pre-1830 period – large firms, extremely high levels of capital intensity, and a need to draw on external sources of finance characterized the post-1830 era. By comparison, comparatively primitive machines that could be purchased and operated by entrepreneurs boasting little in the way of either capital or technical knowhow characterized the earlier period, most particularly the decisive years between 1760 and 1810. As Pollard (1989, p. 92) explained it, "In the early days of industrialization, the sums required for fixed capital in Britain were small, and could usually be raised locally or ploughed back by the firms themselves." In such circumstances, a firm's survival typically depended on superior managerial skills rather than the possession of a Boulton and Watt steam engine.

Certainly, for most successful firms in the early Industrial Revolution, ingenuity in the organization of work was typically more important than any productivity enhancement that resulted from new technologies. A case in point is found in the methods by which Josiah Wedgewood's revolutionized the English pottery industry, transforming it from a sector dominated by "small workshop-units" catering "for a narrow luxury demand" into the dominant force in the global market (Pollard 1965, p. 98). Yes, it was true, Pollard (1965, p. 98) conceded, that Wedgewood operated two steam engines at his pottery works "before the first Lancashire cotton mill had ordered one." Nevertheless, Pollard (1965, p. 99) concluded, the key to success was "a far reaching division of labour." In essence, Wedgewood targeted two distinct markets, a small luxury market catered for by "craftsmen of a high order" and a mass market that sold its wares on the reputation of the former. It was around this second production category, upon which the bulk of Wedgewood's fortune was built, that the "division of labour" was pursued to the fullest. For this type of work, painted decoration was undertaken not by skilled craft workers but by newly recruited women, who transferred printed designs onto unglazed surfaces prior to firing. Even in the famed Soho engineering works in Birmingham – which made the Boulton and Watt steam engines that powered early factories – Pollard (1965, p. 81) noted that the key to the firm's success was not so much its utilization of its own steam engines as the "organizational advantages" that followed from the division of labor.

Among the industries central to the success of the Industrial Revolution – mining, smelting, engineering, civil construction, and textiles – Pollard argued that the highly mechanized process of cotton spinning was atypical in a number of regards. For, Pollard (1965, p. 90) observed, the fact that entrepreneurs and managers in the cotton mills organized production around machines, more or less common to all, created unusual problems as well as benefits. Standardized machinery meant that "organization and management techniques could be copied without thinking," an outcome that also meant there was "much less scope for individual design, skill or new solutions to new problems." In turn, the inability of most cotton producers – other than those in a few specialized areas such as lacemaking – to distinguish themselves from their rivals through superior methods resulted in high levels of competition around a range of standardized products. This did much to ensure the cotton mills status as the ugly face of the Industrial Revolution. "It was an environment," Pollard (1965, p. 91) reflected, that encouraged "ruthlessness, not only to one's competitors, but also to one's employees." Where enlightened employer attitudes prevailed, such as at Robert Owen's famed experiment at New Lanark – an experiment whose ultimate failure is well covered in ▶ Chap. 20, "Certain Victory, Uncertain Time: The Limitations of Nineteenth-Century Management Thought" by Muldoon's – better working conditions were conceded not because the business concerned necessarily believed a more progressive attitude would be more profitable. Rather, the reverse typically applied, i.e., a business was more generous because it already enjoyed unusual profits. As Pollard (1965, p. 246) noted of Owen's operation at New Lanark, it boasted "a monopolistic position at the fine end of the spinning industry," a circumstance that ensured "exceptionally high" profits no matter what labor relations policy was pursued.

It is certainly wrong to assume that all circumstances in the Industrial Revolution led in the direction of similar labor relation outcomes or that the employment circumstances that prevailed in the cotton mills were applicable elsewhere. For, as Pollard (1963) discussed in an article entitled, "Factory Discipline in the Industrial Revolution," in the cotton mills the only real concern was with discipline and vigilance in carrying out a narrow range of routinized jobs, many of which were performed by children and adolescents. In consequence, labor relations in the cotton mills revolved around fines, dismissals, and even corporal punishment (Pollard 1963, p. 263). Such managerial behavior would have been suicidal in industries such as engineering and metallurgy, built around skilled workers. At the Soho engineering works, Pollard (1963, p. 261) records, whenever the temperamental inventor, James Watt, demanded the sacking of a skilled worker, the manager, Mathew Boulton, "quietly moved them elsewhere until the storm had blown over."

In emphasizing the atypical nature of cotton manufacture, Pollard – like Nef and Clapham before him – downplayed its overall significance in the Industrial Revolution, emphasizing instead the importance of mining, smelting, and engineering. Primarily concerned as he was with the emergence of a new class of professional managers, Pollard (1965, p. 127) believed the largest, most technically qualified reservoir of managerial expertise – a group without whose skills the Industrial Revolution is almost inconceivable – were the "coal viewers," the independent consultants who provided advice to owners as to the safe and profitable operation of their mines. Recruited out of coal mining to work in a host of new mechanized industries, the "coal viewers" rubbed shoulders with another important group of technically trained professionals: the civil engineer. Of the managerial circumstances of civil engineers in the 1770s, Pollard (1965, p. 130) observed that, "Those of any standing were supervising several works at the same time." As a new class of professional managers slowly emerged during the late eighteenth and early nineteenth centuries, a defining characteristic of the new vocation was the pioneering of what we think of as "cost accounting." "In the most advanced works," such as Boulton and Watts's Soho engineering work, "departmental accounts would attempt to keep the returns of departments separate, down to elaborate schemes for allocating overheads fairly and proportionately" (Pollard 1965, p. 222). Although estimates of costs were typically led astray by the difficulties in accounting for various "overheads" (i.e., capital depreciation, administrative costs, etc.), the significance of these efforts cannot be underestimated. For mindfulness as to costs, and the need to sell competitively into constantly evolving markets, was, ultimately, the *raison d'être* of the new class of professional managers.

As a management historian – rather than a business or economic historian – Pollard was, as is the norm in our discipline, more concerned about the supply side of the economic equation than the demand side. This differentiated his ideas from those of Clapham and Chandler, both of whom put a greater emphasis on the ways in which the railroads and steam-powered shipping created new mass consumer markets after 1830. For Pollard, the most important driver "from the side of demand" was not the consumer, but rather the supply side needs of other industries. Consequently, for Pollard (1958, p. 217) – unlike the Toynbees, Marx, Nef, Clapham, and Chandler – the key event in the Industrial Revolution, around which everything else turned, was "the emergence of an engineering industry," capable of creating and maintaining "the new equipment and the motors or engines needed by the first industries to be mechanised." From this central and indispensable core, Pollard (1958, p. 217) identified a ripple effect that fueled industrial take-off as the engineering industry fostered increased coal and iron production, improved transport, and enhanced managerial and employee skills.

In arguing his case for "the unique features of the transformation which began in Britain about 1760," Pollard (1958, p. 215) poured scorn on what he considered the unfortunate tendency "to describe every major technical innovation as yet another 'industrial revolution'." In making this comment, Pollard clearly had John Nef mainly in mind. However, he was evidently also unsympathetic to the view, advocated by Clapham and (subsequently) Chandler that the most significant change in managerial and human circumstances occurred after 1830 with the advent of the railways, telegraphs, and steam-powered shipping. Significantly, unlike all the other authors that we have considered in this chapter, Pollard was also little concerned with changes in real wages *during* the Industrial Revolution. For Pollard (1958, p. 221), "the substantial rise in real wages after about 1850" was an inevitable result of the new industrial, free-market capitalism, an economic order whose ascent would have been impossible without "forced savings" at the expense of labor during the 1760–1830 period. That many suffered was unfortunate but necessary, Pollard (1958, p. 221) concluding that,

> ... those who battled for a larger share for the workers ... were battling against the flood tide of a victorious economic development which needed, for a critical period, the greatest amount of output, and the lowest level of personal consumption, which could be imposed on the population.

How to assess Pollard's intellectual contribution, which stands in opposition to the other authors we have considered on a whole series of points, yet which nevertheless provides a theoretical bedrock for the subsequent development of management history? Pollard is certainly correct in emphasizing that the Industrial Revolution between 1760 and 1830 was unique by comparison with anything that had gone before it. Yes, it is true that the large-scale exploitation of coal during the early "Industrial Revolution" of the sixteenth and seventeenth centuries – and the transition from a wood-burning to a coal-burning economy – provided a *precondition* for the Industrial Revolution of the eighteenth and nineteenth centuries, setting England on a fundamentally different course to that of any other European society. However, we should not exaggerate either the scale or the nature of the "early" Industrial Revolution. For, while the exploitation of coal fueled the expansion of a range of industries (brickmaking, brewing, glassmaking, etc.), the performance of work still revolved around largely unaided manual labor. To the extent that mechanical means were utilized, they relied on either animal power or unreliable water and wind power. If we can conclude, nevertheless, that Pollard probably understated the importance of the "earlier" Industrial Revolution in emphasizing the uniqueness of the subsequent Industrial Revolution, his tendency to downplay post-1830 developments is less defensible. For, as his study, *Britain's Prime and Britain's Decline: The British Economy 1870–1914*, makes clear, Pollard saw the changes that characterized Britain during the latter half of the nineteenth century in largely negative terms, as a squandering of the hard-fought gains of the Industrial Revolution by "a small financial and commercial elite" (Pollard 1989, p. 259). Yet, as Clapman and Chandler emphasized, the movement to a different form of industrial capitalism – characterized by large firms, highly capitalized industries, and patterns of investment that only large financial institutions made possible – can also be seen as an inevitable result of the forces unleashed between 1760 and 1830. In consequence, as I have argued in ▶ Chap. 12, "Transformation: The First Global Economy, 1750–1914", the "Industrial Revolution" is best understood as a series of cascading revolutions, which had their pre-history in the "early" English "Industrial Revolution" of the sixteenth and seventeenth centuries and which produced a fundamentally different society and economy after 1750.

In assessing Sidney Pollard's intellectual contribution, we must conclude that his most profound insight was his realization that the success of free-market industrial capitalism rests primarily on people rather than machines, and on the managers who organize production and exchange rather than impersonal economic forces. Accordingly, the (second) Industrial Revolution of the late eighteenth and early nineteenth centuries – which in truth boasted comparatively few machines and very little in the way of mechanized horsepower – is best conceived as a "managerial revolution" rather than anything else. If those steeped in the "catastrophic" accounts of the Toynbees, Tawney, and Thompson no doubt believe that Pollard erred in paying sufficient heed to the oppression of the poor, we can only note that oppression of the poor has been common to all societies. As Braudel (1963/1975, p. 725) observed, prior to the Industrial Revolution, "The price of progress" was always "social oppression," a process in which, "Only the poor gained nothing, could hope for nothing." With the Industrial Revolution, however, the poor could genuinely hope for a better life, and, invariably, if not immediately than within a generation, those hopes began to be fulfilled as ever-greater numbers enjoyed a material plenty that was unimaginable to the peoples of pre-industrial societies.

Conclusion

In his study, *Memory, History, and Forgetting*, the French philosopher, Paul Ricoeur (2000/2004, p. 412), in countering the ideas of the American postmodernist, Hayden White, observed that "no one can make it to be that" the past "should not have been." In other words, the experiences of the past are not imaginings belonging to some mythical dreamtime, but actual occurrences that helped shape the present. The past is thus an ontologically real phenomenon, a process whereby real lived experiences create the present. Yet, it is also true that we can never experience the distant past directly through experience. Instead, we understand it through interpretation and historical reconstruction, a process that gives rise to intellectual debates and, ultimately, to academic disciplines that hold dear certain principles, methodologies, and understandings.

In management history, most particularly in Great Britain, the discipline largely owes its origins to the debates and controversies associated with the Industrial Revolution, debates that brought forth – as we have previously noted – two key questions. What was the Industrial Revolution? What is modern management? Ironically, defining understandings that still dominate much of the public consciousness are largely attributable to an Oxford scholar, Arnold Toynbee the elder, who died at the age of 30 without publishing a word of note. His ideas reconstructed from the lecture notes of some of his former students; it is to Toynbee (1884a/1894) that we owe the very concept of the "Industrial Revolution" as a unique historical event that occurred in Britain between 1760 and 1830. In Toynbee's estimation, the Industrial Revolution was not only a transformative event, it was also a catastrophic experience for most of the population, bursting with unexpected fury on a largely pre-industrial society. "The effects of the

Industrial Revolution," Toynbee (1884a/1894, p. 93) proclaimed, "prove that free competition may produce wealth without producing wellbeing. We all know the horrors that ensued in England before it was restrained by legislation and [trade union] combination." This "catastrophic" understanding of the Industrial Revolution, pioneered by Toynbee the elder, gave birth to a large and arguably still dominant historiography, boasting among its proponents three historians to whom we have paid special heed: R.H. Tawney, Toynbee the younger, and E.P. Thompson. For Tawney (1922/1938, p. 266), as for the first Toynbee, the Industrial Revolution was not only a source of suffering and inequality; it was also the product of a profound cultural shift, an alteration that saw Protestant religious beliefs and a "ruthless materialism" welded together in a dominant ideology "prepared to sacrifice every other consideration to their economic ambitions." In the opinion of Toynbee the younger (1976/1978, p. 564, 566), the industrialized world's propensity to burn coal, a "non-replaceable natural resource," instead of wood that could be "regenerated," posed dire threats to woodlands and the environment more generally. Among labor and social historians, the "catastrophic" historiography of the Industrial Revolution was reinforced by E.P. Thompson's *The Making of the English Working Class*, a work that depicted a "distinguished popular culture" at constant war with "the exploitative and oppressive relationships intrinsic to industrial capitalism."

On almost every point of substance, the "catastrophic" historiography of the Industrial Revolution has been in error. While it is true, as Toynbee the elder observed, that the Industrial Revolution of the late eighteenth and early nineteenth centuries *did* represent a profound transformation in the human condition its arrival was hardly unannounced. As the work of John Nef (1932a, b, 1934, 1937, 1941, 1943) demonstrated, due to an "early Industrial Revolution" between 1540 and 1640, England differed from other societies in making a transition from a wood-burning economy to a coal-burning society; a development that made pre-industrial Britain a leader in a range of energy-intensive industries. Contrary to the beliefs of the younger Toynbee (1947a/1976, 1976/1978), the burning of coal protected rather than diminished woodland and other nature reserves, leading to a gradual reafforestation of Britain. The work of John Clapham (1926/1967, 1932/1967) also exposed as myth the view that the Industrial Revolution caused a catastrophic fall in popular living standards, a point eventually (and begrudgingly) conceded by E.P. Thompson (1963/1968, p. 916). The idea that the English "working class" was united in their opposition to "industrial capitalism" was also shown to be a misnomer by Sidney and Beatrice Webb (1897/1920, 1902), who demonstrated that most workers and trade union members wanted to share in the benefits of capitalism, not overthrow it. In like fashion, Sidney Pollard (1958, 1963, 1965, 1989) revealed as spurious the understanding that the Industrial Revolution revolved around revolutionary new technologies, introduced *en masse* into the textile industry. In truth, as Pollard demonstrated, the "Industrial Revolution" was really a "managerial revolution," boasting the use of comparatively few machines.

If the "catastrophic" historiography of the Industrial Revolution was largely in error, it is nevertheless the case that the emergence of the discipline of management history in Britain can only be understood in terms of the fundamental debate that this historiography produced. In doing so, it shifted the debate from a focus on machines to the "human factor," causing a fundamental reappraisal as to the nature of "modern management" and its role as a transformative economic and social agent. If we look beyond the standard definitions of "management" (planning, organizing, leading, controlling), we can also ascertain some additional defining characteristics in addition to those put forward by Pollard (1965, pp. 6–7) and which we enumerated at the beginning of our previous section, entitled "Sidney Pollard and the Origins of Modern Management." For "modern management" differs from pre-modern forms of management not only in dealing with legally free workforces, and in using capital-intensive production methods to sell into competitive markets, but also in having the following attributes: that it operates within a system of legal protections for person and property, that it exploits energy-intensive production systems in which manual labor is replaced in large measure by artificial forms of energy, that is metal dependent in that it requires smelted metals for durable capital goods and consumables, and that it results in material abundance and standards of living unimaginable in pre-industrial societies.

References

Allen RC (2011) Why the industrial revolution was British: commerce, induced invention and the scientific revolution. Econ Hist Rev 64(2):357–384
Babbage C (1832/1846) On the economy of machinery and manufactures, 3rd edn. John Murray, London
Best G (1965) Review: the making of the English working class. Hist J 8(2):271–281
Braudel F (1963/1975) The Mediterranean and the Mediterranean world in the age of Philip II, vol 2. Fontana Press, London
Braudel F (1986/1990) The identity of France: people and production, vol 2, 2nd edn. Harper Torchbooks, New York
Broadberry S, Gupta B (2006) The early modern great divergence. Econ Hist Rev 49(1):2–31
Chambers JD (1966) Review: the making of the English working class. History 51(172):183–188
Chandler AD Jr (1965) The railroads: pioneers in modern corporate management. Bus Hist 39(1):16–40
Chandler AD Jr (1977) The visible hand: the managerial revolution in American business. Belknap Press, Cambridge, MA
Cipolla CM (1981) Before the industrial revolution: European society and economy, 1000–1700, 2nd edn. Cambridge University Press, Cambridge, UK
Clapham JH (1926/1967) Economic history of modern Britain: the early railway age 1820–1850. Cambridge University Press, Cambridge, UK
Clapham JH (1932/1967) Economic history of modern Britain: free trade and steel 1850–1886. Cambridge University Press, Cambridge, UK
Clapham JH (1938/1951) Economic history of modern Britain: machines and national rivalries 1887–1914. Cambridge University Press, Cambridge, UK
Clapham JH (1944/1966) The Bank of England: a history, 2 vols. Cambridge University Press, Cambridge, UK
Clark C (1940) The conditions of economic progress. Macmillan, London
Dupin C (1825) The commercial power of Great Britain, 1 vol. Charles Knight, London

Engels F (1845/2010) The condition of the working class in England. https://www.marxists.org/archive/marx/works/download/pdf/condition-working-class-england.pdf

Jones EL (1987) The European miracle: environments, economies, and geopolitics in the history of Europe and Asia, 2nd edn. Cambridge University Press, Cambridge, UK

Keynes JM (1920) The economic consequences of the peace. Cambridge University Press, Cambridge, UK

Malthus TR (1798) An essay on the principle of population and its effects on the future improvement of society. J. Johnson, London

Marx K (1867/1954) Capital, vol 1. Foreign Languages Publishing House, Moscow

Marx K, Engels F (1848/1951) The communist manifesto. In: Marx K, Engels F (eds) Selected works, vol 1. Foreign Languages Publishing House, Moscow, pp 32–61

McKinlay A (2006) Managing Foucault: genealogies of management. Manag Organ Hist 1(1):87–100

Mill JS (1848/2004) Principles of political economy. Prometheus Books, London

Nef JU (1932a) The rise of the British coal industry, vol 1. Frank Cass, London

Nef JU (1932b) The rise of the British coal industry, vol 2. Frank Cass, London

Nef JU (1934) Prices and industrial capitalism in Germany, France and England 1540–1640. Econ Hist Rev 7(2):155–185

Nef JU (1937) The progress of technology and the growth of large-scale industry in Great Britain 1540–1640. Econ Hist Rev 5(1):3–34

Nef JU (1941) The responsibility of economic historians. J Econ Hist 1(1):1–8

Nef JU (1943) The industrial revolution reconsidered. J Econ Hist 3(1):1–31

Phelps Brown EH, Hopkins SV (1956) Seven centuries of the prices of consumables, compared with builders' wage rates. Economica 23(92):296–314

Pollard S (1958) Investment, consumption and the industrial revolution. Econ Hist Rev 11(2):215–226

Pollard S (1963) Factory discipline in the industrial revolution. Econ Hist Rev 16(2):254–271

Pollard S (1965) The genesis of modern management: a study of the industrial revolution in Great Britain. Edward Arnold, London

Pollard S (1989) Britain's prime and Britain's decline: the British economy 1870–1914. Edward Arnold, London

Porter GR (1836/1970) The progress of the nation. Augustus M. Kelley, New York

Postan MM (1946) Obituary notices: Sir John Clapham. Econ Hist Rev 16(1):56–59

Ricoeur P (2000/2004) Memory, history, and forgetting. University of Chicago Press, Chicago

Riden P (1977) The output of the British iron industry before 1870. Econ Hist Rev 30(3):442–459

Schlögel K (2008/2012) Moscow 1937. Polity Press, Cambridge, UK

Smith (1776/1937) An inquiry into the nature and causes of the wealth of nations. Modern Library, New York

Tawney RH (1922/1938) Religion and the rise of capitalism. Penguin, Harmondsworth

Tawney RH (1929/1964) Equality, 4th edn. Unwin Books, London

Thompson EP (1963/1968) The making of the English working class, 2nd edn. Penguin, Harmondsworth

Thompson EP (1967) Time, work-discipline, and industrial capitalism. Past Present 38(1):56–97

Toynbee A (1884a/1894) Lectures on the industrial revolution of the 18th century in England. Longman, Green and Co., London

Toynbee CM (1884b/1894) Prefatory note. In: Toynbee A (ed) Lectures on the industrial revolution of the 18th century in England. Longman, Green and Co., London, pp xxix–xxxi

Toynbee A (1947a) The present point in history. In: Toynbee A (ed) Civilization on trial and the world and the West. New American Library, New York, pp 26–36

Toynbee A (1947b) My view of history. In: Toynbee A (ed) Civilization on trial and the world and the West. New American Library, New York, pp 15–25

Toynbee A (1976/1978) Mankind and mother earth. Granada Publishing, London

Webb S, Webb B (1894/1902) Preface to the 1894 edition. In: Webb S, Webb B (eds) The history of trade unionism. Longmans, Green and Co., London, pp vii–xxxiv

Webb S, Webb B (1897/1920) Industrial democracy. Seaham's Divisional Labour Party, London

Webb S, Webb B (1902) The history of trade unionism, 2nd edn. Longmans, Green and Co., London

Webb S, Webb B (1920) Introduction to the 1920 Edition. In: Industrial democracy. Seahams Divisional Labour Party, London, pp vi–xvii

Webb S, Webb B (1935) Is soviet communism a new civilisation? The Left Review, London

Webb S, Webb B (1936) Soviet communism, 2 vols. Longmans, Green & Co., London.

Weber M (1905/1958) The Protestant ethic and the spirt of capitalism. Charles Scribner's Sons, New York

World Bank (2017) On-line database: indicators – agricultural and rural development. https://data.worldbank.org/topic/agriculture-and-rural-development?view=chart. Accessed 8 Nov 2017

Part V

The Classic Age of Management Thought (Mid-Nineteenth Century Until 1939)

Certain Victory, Uncertain Time: The Limitations of Nineteenth-Century Management Thought

20

Jeffrey Muldoon

Contents

Introduction 476
Robert Owen: Radical Reactionary 477
Owen's Ideas and Biography 478
Owen's Contribution 481
Owen's Failure 481
Babbage and Ure: The Cyborgs 482
Henri Fayol: The General 488
Conclusion 494
Cross-references 495
References 495

Abstract

The purpose of this chapter is to explore the beginnings of modern management by tracing the development of nineteenth-century management thought in Europe. I examine the lives of Owen, Babbage, Ure, and Fayol, noting both their contributions and the limitations of their thought in their historical context. My contention was that management did not really emerge as a distinct field of study until the time of Taylor. Namely that the industrial world was too new and thought to be a fad that limited the intellectual development of management. In addition, Ure and Babbage were polymaths, devoted to fields which limited their management contributions. Fayol was compared with Taylor, which limited his appeal, even though both men wrote about different aspects. Although there are themes of modern management in the work of Owen and others, various issues prevented them (either the limitations of their thought or other circumstances) from being the prime mover.

J. Muldoon (✉)
Emporia State University, Emporia, KS, USA
e-mail: jmuldoon@emporia.edu

© The Author(s), under exclusive licence to Springer Nature Switzerland AG 2020
B. Bowden et al. (eds.), *The Palgrave Handbook of Management History*,
https://doi.org/10.1007/978-3-319-62114-2_26

475

Keywords

Robert Owen · Charles Babbage · Andrew Ure · Henri Fayol · Management

Introduction

In 1886, Henry Towne, an American engineer, delivered a famous speech arguing for the need for management as a distinct field of study. Frederick Winslow Taylor would begin the process of management development – creating, according to Drucker, what would become America's most notable contribution to the world, besides the Federalist papers. The development of the division of labor supported by management provided escape from subsistence production. Prior to the twentieth century, most humans lived in conditions similar to the Stone Age. Starvation and depravation affected most people. The average life was short, working life brutish, and afflictions common (the quote from Hobbes [2002] was "poor, nasty, brutish, and short"). Abraham Lincoln lost three sons to early death – for conditions treatable today. Until the development of the steam engine, information moved as quickly as the quickest horse. Napoleon and Wellington received information at the same speed as Alexander the Great and Caesar did. Most people never left the area in which they were born. Sons mostly took on the professions of their fathers. Life was cheap.

Management created the economic conditions to alter this course, to create a new, modern world through encouraging the specialization of labor, costs reduction, increasing wealth, consumption, and wages. Management also allowed for the new developments, such as machines and steam engines, to improve. The telegraph allowed information to be sent quickly between different places. Lincoln did not have wait months, as did James Madison did, to know the success of his armies in the field. The development of canals, railroads, and roads lead to the development of massive markets in the United States and Great Britain due to the reduction of transportation costs. No wonder, when Samuel Morse sent the first message over the telegraph, it was "What God Hath Wrought." Morse's generation believed that the millennium was at hand (Howe 2007).

Yet, these developments caused as many problems as they solved. The commodification of labor meant that work was no longer done at home, necessitating new techniques to manage workers. Peasants moved from their native homelands to cities to find work. Tradition and religion were slowly washed away in the tide of progress. The question of coordination and management issues created the "Labor question" – how to manage this new class of laborers. There was the whiff of revolution in the air; France, Germany, Britain, Austria, and Russia faced revolt, destruction of property, and even rebellion. The United States fought a brutal and destructive Civil War.

To explore nineteenth-century management thought and the European contribution to the history of management, I have selected four thinkers, whose influence is continued to be felt to this day. The first is Robert Owen, one of the first socialists and promoters of social science as a solution to the problems of the industrial world.

Owen had a focus on human resource development. The next two thinkers are Charles Babbage and Andrew Ure, whose focus on machinery makes them some of the first scholars to examine operations. Owen, Babbage, and Ure, were targets of scorn in Marx's Kapital. Finally, Henri Fayol moved management beyond the shop floor to the boardroom, confirming his position as the father of strategic management.

There were many solutions to the problems caused by industrialization. Some, such as Robert Owen, wanted to take the best elements of the past and the best modern elements to create a new society. Others, such as Charles Babbage and Andrew Ure, loved the development of machines and hoped that the resulting increase of knowledge would lead to a general uplift of humanity. Henri Fayol, the most practical, sought to develop a theory of management that would provide managers with tools needed to manage labor relations. Each of these approaches had great promise, but management as a field did not emerge until the progressive era in the United States, with Frederick Winslow Taylor as the leader. The purpose of this chapter is to explore the strengths, limits, and contradictions of various nineteenth-century management thinkers. The contention is that the need for management was too new and that many people believed industry was a passing fancy. Each of these men, for one reason or another, found it difficult to gain support. However, each, in their own way, paved a way for future management research.

Robert Owen: Radical Reactionary

Robert Owen is a paradoxical historical figure. For some, such as G.D.H. Cole (1925), Owen is an idealistic figure attempting to create a harmonious society from the social wreckage of the industrial age. For others, such as Joshua Muravchik (2002), Owen was a wild eyed maniac, whose ill-begotten dreams inspired the ravaged twentieth century. Some view Owen as a nonpolitical figure who used social persuasion to transform society; others as the ultimate political operator. Many commentators see him as someone who fought the good fight against capitalism, religion, and status; others see him as a crank who practiced spiritualism and defended the paternalistic system of the South. He was an inspiration and target of scorn for Marx and Engels. He was a narcissist who deeply cared about humanity. He was a skeptic who attacked Christianity, but whose ideas flourished in a Christian culture. He was the industrialist who coined the term socialism. To some, he was a greatly respected figure, to others a figure of scorn. Most of his critics admire his intelligence and integrity. His admirers denounce his paternalism and his courting of elites.

These diverging viewpoints indicate the complex character of the man. Owen simply was a figure that had the ability to produce strong emotions. Owen's principal contribution was the development of socialism and the use of social science for managing society (Claeys 1986, 1987, 1989). He anticipated that the emerging capitalistic movement, the introduction of machines and scientific knowledge, would reorder society. Therefore, the old superstitions and institutions of society would disappear and it would be up to management to create cooperation – a belief shared by Elton Mayo. Yet unlike the incremental Mayo, Owen wanted to give birth to a new society and new man (Iggers 1959).

Owen's Ideas and Biography

Robert Owen was born in 1771 in Newtown, Montgomeryshire, Wales, to an ironmonger and small business owner. He was the sixth of seven children. Despite his family's wealth, he received only 2 years of education from 5 to 7 whereby he tutored the younger students for 2 years. At ten, his parents put him on the coach to London with forty schillings in his pocket. Owen worked a number of jobs moving up the managerial pyramid (Davis and O'Hagan 2010). When Owen was 21, Peter Drinkwater gave Owen the chance to manage 500 employees at his mill. After 2 years with Drinkwater, he found partners and started his new company, the Chorlton Twist Mills. Owen (Donnachie 2000) left Drinkwater because he was not interested in marriage with Drinkwater's daughter.

On a trip to Scotland, he met and fell in love with Ann Caroline Dale, the daughter of David Dale, a wealthy mill owner. To aid in the courtship of his ladylove, he offered to purchase Dale's mills at New Lanark. He noted two primary issues with contemporary management thought. The first was that very little attention was given to workers in comparison to machines. The second was that he was unable to find enough talented and sober workers who would not steal from the company or destroy property (Unwin 1922). When he went to New Lanark, he found that of the approximately 1800 employees, about 500 employees were indentured children, ages 5–10, who the company provided food, shelter, and clothing in exchange for work (Pollard 1963, 1964).

Therefore, he decided to make some various reforms. Owen not just managed the workplace; he managed nearly every aspect of their life, like other factory owners. In comparison with other factory owners, the conditions under which Owen's workforce labored and lived were much more humane. His company store provided better goods just above wholesale prices. He added a second floor to each home, stressed cleanliness, regulated alcohol purchases, and educated workers (Harrison 1967). He accomplished these goals without using either religion or harsh punishments. Contrary to many expectations, the workers became sober, cleaner, healthier, and more productive, profits soared as a result (Doheny 1991; Dutton and King 1982). Another explanation for Owen's success could be that Owens had a quasi-monopolistic position in lace-making. Yet, despite annual returns of 15 percent with about 5 percent of investment paid in dividends, his partners remained nervous. Accordingly, he found a new set of investors, including the noted philosopher Jeremy Bentham (Muravchik 2002; Wren and Bedeian 2018). Mostly, Owens greatest contribution was, as E.P. Thompson (1963) noted (p. 884), that "Owenism was the first of the great social doctrines to grip the imagination of the masses in this period, which commenced with an acceptance of the enlarger productive powers of steam and the mill."

After the end of the Napoleonic Wars, the widespread unemployment, rioting, and social upheaval convinced Owen to propose the development of village models based on New Lanark (Browne 1936). These villages would consist of 1200 people settled on 1200–1500 acres. The inhabitants would live in one single square building with a common room for the kitchen and other social gatherings. Parents would raise children until the age of 3, then they would be raised jointly by the community (Harrison 1969). Owen's ideal location was the United States because there was plenty of land. The other reason was religious – an irony in that Owen was a skeptic. The United States was in the throes of the Second Great Awakening, a period in which many American people, even President Adams, believed would usher in a period of plenty and peace called millennialism (Howe 2007). Millennialism was a fusion of the Enlightenment and the cosmos of biblical prophecy; one foot in the world of steam engines and the other in the Bible. Owen's Christian wife pointed out to him the overlap between his views and the Bible. He soon took to quoting scripture (Browne 1936).

Arriving in the United States, he lectured up and down the East coast, gaining attention from the most prominent religious leaders. He purchased land from a religious sect called the Rappites. About 800 people flocked to the new community, but they were mostly intellectuals and thinkers lacking needed skills (Van Cleave 1951). There were also problems with not having enough materials to build the homes. The fields and gardens had been neglected and there were hogs all over the place. Mostly, the community could not agree upon anything. Rather than opening a new world, New Harmony ended with a whimper. The community survived but in a different form than Owen's vision – at the expense of most of his fortune (Farrell 1938).

Owen returned to England where he found a friendlier welcoming then when he had left to start New Harmony. The repeal of the Combination Acts of 1824 allowed for the development of unions, and soon there was a burgeoning union movement called the Owenite movement (Claerys 1987). He continued to stress his beliefs toward socialism, setting up labor exchange where people could exchange labor time for labor notes. The movement gained momentum with middle class joining because of the Reform Bill of 1832. The outcome of this was the Grand National Consolidated Trade Union, a gigantic union that spanned the country with 500,000 members (Muravchik 2002), but the movement broke down fighting. Owen died in 1858 still a respected executive, but one who various communitarian endeavors had failed (Muravchik 2002).

Owen was both a rationalist and a romantic, a mix of the eighteenth and nineteenth century. His Enlightenment beliefs were deism, reason, associationism, and rationality. Ignorance and superstition caused most problems; science was the solution (Harrison 1967, 1969). Owen was also a romantic. The Romantic Movement stressed that nature could be conquered especially by the individualistic genius, which Owen, with great justification, believed himself to be. Technology and progress would create an abundance through the conquest of nature. Owen's romanticism and amazing ascent from poverty to wealth and admiration activated his narcissism (Harrison 1969).

His political beliefs, a combination of both rationalism and utopianism, have confounded historians over the years. E.P. Thompson (1963) noted that Owen did not care, place much thought in, or action in the nature of politics. Preferring, as his biographer G.D.H. Cole noted, economic determinism over politics as a focal point of change in society. He was also involved in various reforms in Parliament, despite his dislike for political expediency. He spent time trying to gain patronage from the intellectually gifted and politically powerful in both the United States and Great Britain. Both of which suggests pragmatism. As Claeys (1987, 1989) argues, Owen was a Tory, if we define Toryism as the politics of the unpolitical. Owen was also a radical, noting reform would fail as institutions were inert. Revolution would come from example, not violence. The Luddite movement shifted his views to voluntary reform through communitarianism. Some actually thought he had gone crazy. Owen's interest in the United States was his belief that institutions in the United States were more plastic (Bestor 1970). Owen encouraged factory owners to do the same as he did, settling upon the complete overhaul of society, eliminating almost everything that made British and American societies unique: free labor, division of labor, and capitalism (Calhoun 1993; Cole 1925).

Likewise, Owen's opinions on slavery have confounded scholars for many years scholars who have puzzled over his defence of slavery. Also causing puzzlement is the contradiction between Owen's enlightenment values and his views on slavery. Yet, contemporary observers noted similarities between Owen's and the slave system, such as Robert Wedderburn, a child from a slave mother. Owen articulated a paternalistic system similar to that of the slave owners, seeking to create protective structures from market forces. Slave owners compared their system of labor to the Northern version of free labor and noted that they provided slaves with cradle to grave protection (Foner 1970). Like many other free market critics, he admired the South as a legitimate alternative, believing slaves happier (Genovese 1976). However, Owen failed to recognize the brutal nature of slavery (Muravchik 2002; Stampp 1956; Taylor 2013). You might compare his ideas with Smith's, who seemed to have no objection to slavery in the Americas, observing, in *Wealth of Nations*, "we must not, however, upon that account, imagine that they are worse fed, or that their consumption of articles which might be subjected to moderate duties, is less than that even of the lower ranks of people in England." This happy outcome, Smith concluded, resulted from the fact that it was in "the interest of their master that they should be fed well and kept in good heart" so as to maximize their output (Smith 1937).

Owen's admiring of the paternalistic South reveals the greatest contradiction of Owen's thought. Despite Owen's radicalism, he was a reactionary. Just as Owen was creating a socialistic and communitarian society, other societies in the rural United States were becoming capitalistic, abandoning communitarianism (Sellers 1991). For instance, the community of Sugar Creek started out communitarian, but the values of the community dramatically changed, becoming more capitalistic and stressing private property, encouraged by economic development (Faragher 1986). Owen wanted to eliminate all this by going with, what some historians believed was, an updated version of the poor house or, at best, a modernized version of a rural community (Claeys 1987).

Owen's Contribution

Owen made several notable contributions. Firstly, Owen anticipated the work of Stanley Milgram and Philip Zimbardo. Much like Milgram and Zimbardo, he downplayed traits, free-will, and stressed that circumstances could lead to behavior. Owen rejected the Christian thought of original sin. Instead, he believed that no two human beings are born alike due to the large number of variables genetically and through circumstance, creating infinite diversity. Therefore, situations, not genetics or inborn depravity, drove behaviors (Morton 1962). For example, if we place people in a positive environment, we should note that they would behave positively (Calhoun 1993; Browne 1936). Unlike Milgram and Zimbardo, he focused on positive aspects rather than negative (Harrison 1969). A principle difference between their ideas was the time period in which these men conducted their research (an Owenite idea). Owen wrote his during an optimistic time; Milgram and Zimbardo in a ravaged century. Owen, much like later management thinkers Mayo, Fayol, Herzberg, and Pfeffer, saw the workplace as a place of socialization and enjoyment. Owen was also a developer of human resource development, stressing education and moral improvement of his workers (Ashcraft 1993). However, there were several issues with Owen's work. One, Owen's ideas were primitive, moralistic, atheoretical, and inconsistent. Second, Harrison had difficulty with the idea that character is formed "for him and not by him," noting that Owen treated this slogan as if it were the great truth of the ages. Third, Harrison observed that a great many people did not treat Owen's social science as a relevant science due to Owen's moralizing.

Owen's Failure

Owen did not lead a revolution in management thought. He contributed, but most of his ideas withered and died. He faltered for four reasons. Firstly, he focused on issues that were not related to management. He attacked religion, the authenticity of the bible, and traditional gender roles and supported birth control, and taking children from parents – positions that would have won him few converts in nineteenth-century America (Thies 2000; Muravchik 2002). Secondly, he was too radical (Claeys 1987, 1989). Although workers in Great Britain were able to reach some class consensus and opposition, the picture in the United States was very different. Craftsmen wanted to be paid (Bestor 1970). Owen was unable to get enough skilled laborers to be interested in his work. Many of his followers were free riders. They were too interested in gaining acceptance into the new market economy (Howe 2007). People were unwilling to ignore money incentives. In fact, the contract that created the community did not define property rights, creating even more problems

(Bestor 1970). Even more telling, New Harmonians were unwilling to surrender their social status and promote true equality. Thirdly, planning was poor (Thies 2000). There was little anticipation for the demand for housing nor was there little planning for farming. Thomas Peers had to prod the overseeing committee to deploy at least 3 or 4 plows. Yet it should be noted, as Hatcher does, that Owen ran his business differently than he did his community by providing both wages and benefits (Hatcher 2013; Claeys 1989).

Another reason the community failed was Owen's narcissistic personality (Humphreys et al. 2016). It would be natural to assume that his narcissism prevented him from exercising sufficient leadership to hold the community together. Humphrey and his coauthors suggested that narcissists demonstrate high (as did Owens) paternalism. Although Owen held hope in humanity, in general, he had a poor opinion of his follower's abilities – an astounding viewpoint given the level of learning of many of the people in New Harmony. Owen took credit for what worked and blamed others for what did not. What is fairly remarkable is that Edmund Wilson (1940) falsely argued Owen tended to give recognition for success to workers rather than himself.

Owen's narcissism was a factor – but the founder of the Shakers, Mother Ann Lee, believed that she was the second coming of Jesus. Of the 50 or so backwoods utopias, most of them were religious in orientation. The success rate of these communities was low. Those utopias that succeeded tended to be religious in orientation, allowed for private property, and had anarchic governance (Thies 2000). New Harmony flunked each of those qualifications. Joshua Muravchik (2002) noted the largest reason for the failure of New Harmony was that social influences would produce a new man. Yet to produce socialism, people needed to be raised under the new social system. But if people were products of the old system how could they get to socialism? The direct failure of New Harmony was that socialists understood that the transformation of society had to come through political, and even revolutionary, action if it was to be successful (Feuer 1966).

Babbage and Ure: The Cyborgs

Charles Babbage (1791–1871) and Andrew Ure (1778–1857) had a differing viewpoint of society than Owen. Each understood that the world had changed. Industry was not a passing fancy. They believed in reason as the basis of authority. In addition, they constructed a place from which they could make out the "lineaments" of the factory system, downplaying politics. Yet the differences were stark. Owen, a radical reactionary, sought communitarianism as a solution. Babbage and Ure, as futurists, sought to use machines to transform workers into rational beings. Babbage and Ure did not articulate a full vision of management – focusing more on the use of machines only (Kumar 1984; Zimmerman 1997).

Charles Babbage, the preeminent polymath of his time, was a successful mathematician, management theorist, inventor, and statistician (Stigler 1991). The modern computer has its genesis in the work of Babbage. His work had a profound influence on Frederick Winslow Taylor. However, Babbage was considered a crackpot, as his works were so complex that no one understood them. Frustrated, Babbage died a bitter man, hating humanity in general, Englishman in particular, and organ grinders most of all. Charles Babbage was born in London as the son of a banker. He matriculated at Cambridge University's Trinity College, studying mathematics, although such was the standard of his knowledge that he gained little new insights from his studies (Becher 1995). Instead, becoming friends with John Herschel and George Peacock, he embarked on a mission to improve the standard and usefulness of British mathematics (Moseley 1964). Soon after graduation, Babbage won acceptance to the Royal Society. Subsequently, scholars would separate Babbage's work on computer and management, something Babbage would have disagreed with. Babbage was interested in decision-making. As Ashforth (1996) noted, Babbage and Herschel also sought to transform society by breaking the alliance between religion and state and replacing it with rationality. Like the radical political philosopher Thomas Paine, who provided inspiration to Babbage and Herschel, both believed that all men could be engineers. In doing so, humanity would be better equipped to handle the various demands brought on by the new factory system and changes in the economy (Rosenbloom 1964; Wren and Bedeian 2018).

To aid in his goals, Babbage sought an efficient, universal, and visible mental technology by means of universities. However, Babbage worked in a system where the scholarly community resembled a country club. Unlike the more technically oriented universities that were to emerge in continental Europe, most particularly Germany, Britain's colleges and universities continued to emphasize skills (languages, history, etc.) that benefited the gentleman and the colonial administrator rather than the entrepreneur. Accordingly, Babbage and friends looked at the factory as a place where they could develop their new ideas. Both Babbage and Herschel were bedazzled through division of labor due to its efficiency and rigor, which placed unprecedented demands on machine tool shops turning into innovative places. So, he turned his attention to manufacturing and the development of his analytical machine, the first general computer. The analytic machine could be used to input data and used a binary system similar to George Boole's. Basically, the analytical machine had the workings of the modern computer (Ashworth 1996; Moseley 1964).

Two issues haunted his work. Firstly, there was social and cognitive distance between designers, machinists, and draughtsmen. The input cards existed for his machine but little else. Babbage, therefore, had to develop complex programming to deal with matters such as polynomials, iterative formulas, Gaussian elimination, and Bernoulli numbers. He lacked a team of programmers and it appeared that only his friend Countess Ada Lovelace understood the analytical machine. There were no existing technologies and programmers to service the machine. There were also the questions of whether the machine would overheat and on the difficultly of removing the punch cards (Wren and Bedeian 2018).

To understand what tasks his machine would need to undertake, Babbage turned his research to manufacturing, publishing his classic book on operations management called *On the Economy of Machinery and Manufactures* (1832). In fact, it was a continuation of his interest in improving and developing machines. Babbage analyzed the economic principles of manufacturing, tools and machines, expenses, and operations. He also made notable contributions to the economic benefits of specialization, statistics, and price differentials. Babbage not only endorsed the division of labor, he also took the concept further than others, arguing that there was no need for a worker to have any more skills other than those directly related to his or her specific task. By minimizing training and maximizing each worker's capacity to complete a single task, a factory could combine such efforts in ways that would produce something much cheaper and quicker than could be achieved by an artisan. He also developed techniques of observations that would become standard place for later efficiency experts (Wren and Bedeian 2018).

Convinced of the productive benefits of the new factory system, Babbage also served as a spokesperson for the new industrial order. He pleaded with the Chartists to understand the benefits of the machines and stressed mutuality of interests between workers and managers. Babbage did recognize that the machine would potentially increase the power of capital over labor, leading to the creation of unwholesome working conditions and long hours. Yet, he opposed any attempt to stop the use of the machine, believing that in its scientific value as well as its role as a public good. He also rejected the use of trade unions on pragmatic grounds since the unions would drive locations, encouraging the relocation of factories and more automation. He did recognize the role of unions in terms of administrative grounds. Rosenbloom (1964) noted that Babbage had come across the primary problem within business – the contradiction between advances in technology versus the rights of workers. Is this so? That is how it appears, but the argument is that the need for productivity drove hours down just as the wealth of output increases real income. By 1850, as Hugh Cunningham (2011: p. 68) observes, management was "seeing the advantages in an intensive rather than an extensive use of labour … In this kind of environment children were more of a hindrance than a help." Babbage's solution was to offer a bonus plan to align interests. However, he also recognized that the increase size and scope of factories would limit the ability of workers' efforts to lead towards the success of the firm.

Babbage died a frustrated man. Although he had been nominated for various honors including knighthood and a Baronetcy, he also had the reputation for eccentricity and public fraud. He also, along with other management thinkers, was attacked for making workers tied to the machines. In some ways, the newness of his viewpoints and his vast arrogance did him in. Babbage had a flair of narcissism in him – he wrote the Duke of Wellington – himself the champion of the aristocracy – that his machines were his to dispose as he saw fit since they more sacred than hereditary and acquired property. However, there was no denying his brilliance. Marx recognized that Babbage made a notable contribution in that he recognized the crucial role of machinery and division of labor in increasing productivity. Babbage was able to capture the interests of the engineering managers and sought automated systems that allow for cheaper employment (Becher 1995; Wilkes 2002).

Why did Babbage's innovations not take root during his lifetime? A reason could be Babbage himself, who definitely demonstrated various eccentric behaviors that probably would have appeared odd to many people. After all, this was the same man, perhaps facetiously, who formed a group that sought to free its members from an asylum. It does not take much imagination to understand that people would have a difficult time accepting the seriousness of a man obsessed with the evils of organ grinders. Babbage proved a poor developer of followers. Unlike the latter Taylor and Mayo, Babbage did not leave a school of followers that would continue his work beyond his death nor did he seem able to curry favor among the most powerful members of society. True, Babbage did make connections, but despite his relationship with Sir Robert Peel, seemed to lack influential patrons. He was too early an adopter in computing. There was a distinct lack of parts, trained personnel, and support from society.

Andrew Ure was another polymath and, as Farrar (1973) noted, a major target in Marx's *Das Kapital* (Kumar 1984). He was also a doctor, scholar, chemist, scriptural geologist (i.e., used geology to research the Bible), and leading business theorist. Ure was born in Glasgow in 1778 to a cheese-monger. He earned his medical doctorate from Glasgow University. After a brief stint as an army medical doctor in 1804, he took a position at the Andersonian Institution, where he replaced the eminent chemist George Birkbeck. He stayed until 1839. During his time as a lecturer, he gained renown as an academic interested in innovation. Yet, he had a poor reputation in the scientific community. The great chemist, John Dalton, the founder of modern atomic theory, noted that Ure did not understand the difference between pure ether and the mixture sold by druggists that was a combination of ether and alcohol. Yet after the Napoleonic Wars, Ure sought to build an international reputation and toured France to absorb their science (Edwards 2001; Kumar 1984).

Much like Babbage, Ure came to management through his scientific accomplishments. The Andersonian institution was designed to educate the artisan class, unlike Oxford and Cambridge. From this college, the first classes of salaried managers were soon hired. Ure's most notable contribution to management thought was his 1835 book entitled *The Philosophy of Manufactures; or, An Exposition of the Scientific, Moral, and Commercial Economy of the Factory System of Great Britain*. The book had three general aims: to extol the great importance of manufacturing to countries against agrarian interests, denounce workingmen in forming groups, and persuade people about the humanitarian benefits of the factory system. Ure's principal focus revolved around the discipline and organization that Ure believed machines imposed on workers. As such, Ure's book did not attempt to define management by outlining, in a systematic way, the tasks and procedures that the new discipline would entail (Caton 1985). His analysis centered on machine imposed control. It did not describe a pure management system. Ure also defended the new factory system, noting that workers lived in better conditions, had more food, and were healthier than artisans had been in the past. He also noted that the factory system meant better working conditions than the previous handicraft system, where both irregularity of work and long hours of toil were the norm. In terms of the charge that factories had both child and female laborers, he noted, correctly, that the previous domestic system had employed both children and females (Wren and Bedeian 2018).

There were several notable issues with his book on manufacturing. Firstly, he was prone to exaggeration and character assassination, at several points calling his opponents atheists and whores. He also damaged his arguments through poor analysis. As Farrar (1973) noted, it was sufficient to state the factory workers were healthier – but he undermines his argument when he noted that the principal health problem was overconsumption of bacon. What he failed to note was the prime difference between the domestic system and the factory system that workers were now managed by nonfamily members, a difficult transition. However, Ure did imply that factory owners did owe workers decent conditions, schools, clean air, and decent housing. Whiting (1964) noted that there were early strains of the Human Relations in Ure's work.

Despite these issues, Ure had a clearer understanding of industrialization than did Adam Smith (Caton 1985). Writing in 1776, at the very dawn of the Industrial Revolution, Smith appreciated the benefits of the division of labor and the growing importance of fixed capital as a business cost. However, Smith understandably – given the time of his writing – failed to fully appreciate the revolutionary potential of new steam-powered machines. Nor did he properly appreciate the transformative role that management was to have in the post-1776 world, observing in *The Wealth of Nations* that "being the managers of other people's money rather than their own, it cannot well be expected that they should watch over it with the same anxious vigilance [as] . . . their own." "Negligence and profusion," he added, "must always apply" in such circumstances (Smith 1937).

What were the contributions of Ure and Babbage to management thought? Daniel Wren has praised them over the years in his various works, noting the primary contributions of both men, especially Babbage. Since the time of Marx, writers found key differences. Yet, there were key similarities as well. First, they recognized that machines were here to stay. This was not a common viewpoint at the time. Many people in Great Britain believed that the factory was merely a temporary intruder to the old industrial order. Consequently, as Zimmerman (1997) noted, Babbage and Ure's work could be seen as part of a concerted attempt to validate the new factory system. Indeed, they were among the writers who changed the meaning of the word factory, which had meant warehouse or production center, to a factory within a production system. Both understood what the factory would mean for labor – something that neither Smith nor Ricardo really developed. Babbage and Ure also sought to defend the factory system from various challenges. Agricultural life was hard, but based on tradition rather than the externally imposed control and discipline associated with factory life and the mill clock (Edwards 2001). There was little description or reason as to why the new order was needed. Babbage and Ure defended division of labor and the use of machines (Farrar 1973). Unlike Owen, who wanted to save man from the machine, Ure and Babbage sought to save the machine from man.

The problem with their thought was that it was not a true management philosophy – even if there are elements of management philosophy in their writing. It was also an inhumane philosophy to adjust men to machines. Ure and Babbage, unlike Taylor and Mayo, did not seek to train and develop managers to handle social problems. Rather they believed that machines can control and discipline men. Their work also degraded the worker who long had control over his own tools and knowledge (Zimmerman 1997). The machine created value, so as Ure argued, capitalists should gain the value, since they owned the machines. Babbage agreed with Ure noting that machines controlled the floor (Wren and Bedeian 2018).

A primary difference between Babbage and Ure was over the role of specialization and division of labor. Ure, unlike Babbage, did not have the wide range of experience in factories, so he argued that division of labor was obsolete because factory productivity was due to machines. Babbage defended specialization of labor. Ure also disagreed with Babbage's views over the evolution of human thought – arguing that society was better through the administration of enlightened factory owners rather than (an implicit attack on Babbage) academics who base their decisions on outdated statistics. Ure also believed that the factory system would lead to better jobs, better conditions, and more productivity and would not lead to an accumulation of power that may damage workers. Babbage had a dissenting view and sought incentives to align interests. Ure doubted radical improvements to workers conditions they were simply a fact; Babbage believed in improvement. Babbage sought to make workers think like engineers; Ure saw them as docile and machine like (Rosenbloom 1964).

The limits of their thought could be summarized as follows. Ure believed that machines were the basis of capitalism – rather than division and commodification of labor or the market. His Frankenstein-like experiments on human cadavers indicated that humans could be fine-tuned with scientific methods. Ure also believed in the inherent good of the factory system – he was called the "Pandar of the Factory" by Marx, and scholars have called his viewpoints Panglossian. Babbage saw society as an evolutionary process that neither man nor machine could control. He understood that the machine produced tedium. Rather than the machine controlling labor completely, methods of management, such as bonuses, were needed to ensure compliance. Yet, unlike Frederick Winslow Taylor, both did not understand the need for an overall management philosophy, preferring a technological focus. They missed Taylor's key insight; capitalists control machines, but labor controls itself. The ability of machines to control men was limited, greatly over-estimating the ability of machines to monitor workers. Workers can destroy machines; they can misuse and abuse them; and the ability for machines to monitor worker misconduct was limited. After all, if a machine is damaged or destroyed, could a manager know which worker destroyed it? The major takeaway was that workers needed to be trained, educated, and compensated. Unlike Ure and Babbage, Taylor developed an integrative system of management. He also had a wide array of followers who were able to carry his research beyond his death. Unlike Ure, Babbage did provide the basics of Taylor – but he did not develop a true philosophy of industry. Both understood the need for a new mental framework, but did not provide it. They focused more on machines (Edwards 2001; Kumar 1984; Rosenbloom 1964).

Henri Fayol: The General

Unlike Owen, Babbage, and Ure, who came from Great Britain, Henri Fayol lived his life in France when it shifted from monarchy to republic to empire and back to republic. France, during his lifetime, witnessed crushing defeats (i.e., Sedan) to notable victories (i.e., First Battle of Marne). Similarly, during Fayol's lifetime, France's once unchallenged position, as continental Europe's preeminent economic power, was increasingly eroded by the rapid advance of science and industry in a unified Germany. Like Owen, Babbage, and Ure, Fayol never received the recognition that was his due during his lifetime. His own son supported the work of Taylor over his father. In fact, Fayol only started to receive major attention in 1949 when his book *General and Industrial Management* was translated into English. Previously, when people wished to read his work, it had to come through the British consultant Lyndall Urwick, who went so far as to say that Fayol did not write about management, but rather administration (Parker and Ritson 2011). Even worse, Fayol's ideas have been misunderstood and his work was viewed in light of Taylor's work, ignoring the obvious merit of Fayol's analysis. Consequentially, Fayol is one of those scholars who is widely known, but not necessarily widely read. Few really understand or even knew what his arguments were, tending to rally against the straw man version of his argument. However, every student of management, from the introductory class to college professors, has encountered, at one time or another, Fayol's ideas (Parker and Ritson 2005a, b).

Henri Fayol (1841–1925) was born to a noncommissioned engineer officer who was named superintendent of works to build the Galata Bridge in Istanbul, a bridge that remains an iconic landmark across the famed Golden Horn. However, despite his father's intelligence, skill, and ability, he was never able to reach a rank that was his due. This disappointment was a major part of the motivation that caused Fayol to become an engineer, business executive, and management theorist. Fayol also sought to create, based on these experiences, a philosophy to assist in France's recover from its disastrous defeat in the Franco-Prussian War. The war provided an impetus to change: leading to the separation of church and state in education, greater labor unrest, and increased focus on technical skills. Yet, it was also true that the emergence of the Third Republic provided a greater sense of stability than what had existed during the revolutionary period, the Bourbon restoration, and the Napoleons. His father recognized that his son needed an education. Fayol graduated from the École Nationale Supérieure des Mines in 1861 majoring in mining rather than metallurgy. He started working at the "Compagnie de Commentry-Fourchambault-Decazeville" as an intern, rising to director in 1865 and then managing director in 1888. By the time Fayol took over the firm, however, it was a faltering company (Wren and Bedeian 2018). Indeed, he was initially appointed to sell off the struggling company. Instead, however, he turned the company around by selling off failing mines and acquiring new mines that had both coal and iron deposits. He also built a business line around smelting iron to raw steel. By the time he retired, the company was one of the largest and strongest in Europe despite the destruction of several mines during the German invasion of France. He made money for the shareholders and provided a higher standard of living for his workers. Whether the advancement of the company was due to his managerial acumen, the end of the Long Depression (a period of slow global growth and depressed prices that lasted from 1873 until the late 1890s), the increase of value of iron ore, or some combination thereof, scholars, even his defenders, remain uncertain. However, Fayol had an excellent reputation as managing director, earning many laurels (Wren 2001).

These accomplishments came to him despite, not because of, his technical training. Fayol recognized soon after he became a manager that he lacked the skills to handle the industrial scope of the company. Consequently, he began writing down observations of managerial issues and solutions. For example, he noticed that work had stopped for a day due to a horse breaking aleg. The livery stable-keeper lacked the authority to purchase a new horse even though he was responsible for the horse. Fayol recognized that authority and responsibility should go hand in hand (Reid 1995). He also recognized that in order to increase motivation, jobs needed to be redesigned to make them less monotonous. He also saw the need to give workers more responsibility to make the job more meaningful and impactful. Fayol was a pioneer in identifying the social and organizational benefits from work teams. In addition, Fayol recognized that — although technical skills were important to firm success – managerial ability was even more important. In fact, as one rose throughout the organization, need for managerial skills increased; an outcome that was also evident as small family firms were replaced by large-scale enterprises. He recognized the need for management theory and this need was all the more acute because the future belonged to managers (Pryor and Taneja 2010; Voxted 2017; Wren and Bedeian 2018).

What were Fayol's contributions to management thought? His first notable contribution was the recognition that there were six important skills for successfully running a business: administrative skills, technical skills, marketing skills, financial abilities, safety abilities, and accounting abilities. Fayol's conception of management, as a distinct field from technical skills, was an important contribution. Wren (2001) noted that firms, such as Andre Citoroen, which promoted technical skills at the expense of managerial skills, performed poorly – proving Fayol's point. He also identified that there were five functions of management: planning, organizing, commanding, coordinating, and controlling. The principle focus was on organizing. Fayol understood the need for human resource management and that workers were the company's main productive resource. In the first chapter of most principles of management textbooks, Fayol's functions are still taught (Voxted 2017). He was also prescient in that he saw how workers, rather than being a cost to be minimized, could be the most important asset to the firm, anticipating the development of strategic human resource management nearly 80 years later. Fayol's most ambitious contribution was the 14 principles of management – ambitious since (to borrow Clemenceau's comment on Wilson's 14 points) the Lord almighty only had Ten Commandments. The 14 principles consisted of the following: division of work, authority, and responsibility, discipline, unity of command, unity of direction, subordination, remuneration, centralization, scalar chain, order, equity, stability of tenure, initiative, and esprit de corps. Promoting team spirit will build harmony and unity within the organization (Reid 1995).

These ideas were notable for several reasons. Firstly, they formed that basis for a normative theory of management serving as a development point for later theorizing. Secondly, it was an overall philosophy of management – one that could be used to describe management from top-level managers on down. This is particularly important since it provides coordination for specialized activities. Finally, since the theory discusses how managers should deploy resources it forms a basis of what would become strategic management. Fayol also anticipated several trends including behavioral and transformative leadership, agency, contingency and systems management, and the knowledge-based view of the firm (Parker and Ritson 2005a, b; Spatig 2009).

Did Fayol really produce a theory of management? Fayol's (1949) definition of theory "was [the] collection of principles, rules, methods, and procedures tried and checked by general experience." If this definition of theory was correct, then Fayol did create a theory. Fayol's formulations were certainly a comprehensive philosophy of management that could be used in a wide variety of contexts besides military and industrial. But he fell short of theory as we properly define the term. The modern statement of theory is a statement that explains why and makes a prediction on various phenomena. Importantly, the "why" statement is one that usually emerges from a body of knowledge and which has some generalizability (Bacharach 1989).

Did Fayol explain and make predictions? In my view, he did not. This is especially true since his conclusions can lead to alternative explanations that may be equally valid. Firstly, it is unclear whether his practices actually saved his company. There are other explanations for the company's growth including improved economic conditions. Secondly, his account of the horse – in which he claimed that workers were unable to address issues with the horse due to a lack of authority – could be due to hazing rather than poor administration. After all, it is not uncommon for workers to make it difficult for first time managers. Thirdly, he was unclear with his use of terms, making it difficult to develop his constructs. The fact that his thoughts were translated into a different language (English) exacerbates this problem. Based on this definition of theory, we can perhaps conclude that Fayol used the term theory to gain legitimacy. In fact, Fayol admitted as such – since there was no theory of management, how could it be taught in schools. Fayol provided a useful vocabulary and structure of terms, which allowed for subsequent theoretical development. In short, he did what George Homans did in the *Human Group*, take a bunch of observations, name them, and provide a conceptual scheme that had practical use (Homans 1984).

Fayol left an extraordinary record as he defined managerial actions and skill. More so than even Taylor, he truly defined managerial endeavors, and unlike Taylor, he focused more on the principles of organization and coordination. Taylor, despite his writings on incentives and training, remained very much an engineer with a primary focus on the plant floor and an inability to see over the plant floor. Fayol transcended the plant floor and saw the overall picture of the organization. From this perspective, Fayol, and not Taylor, could be seen as the most influential management thinker in history since his was an overall management theory. Maybe even more than Taylor's, Fayol's theories have stood the test of time – many of his ideas are still found in the introductory books, and his other ideas, such as esprit de corps, are the basis of a great many ideas in management. Fayol could be seen as the father of strategic management, as many of his ideas formed the basis of that field (Fells 2000).

Yet, Fayol seems to be underrated. In Bedeian and Wren's (2001) list of influential management texts, Fayol's *General and Industrial Management* is ranked 16th; a high ranking to be sure, but one that probably underestimates the influence his book had. Heames and Breland (2010), in their list, rank him fifth: also, arguably an underestimation. There are several important explanations for Fayol's comparatively modest ranking. Firstly, Fayol wrote in French – and did his work primarily in France – at a time when Great Britain, the United States, and Germany were the world's dominant commercial powers. In addition, Germany had become the major place for learning as universities worldwide adopted the German scientific model, a model that emphasized technical and applied skills. Had Henri been a Henry or Heinrich, his work would have arguably received more recognition. The First World War also prevented his work from receiving a large audience as wartime demands were placed. Finally, Fayol did not leave a cadre of followers to carry his work beyond his grave.

Part of the problem with the criticisms related to Fayol is that they often have little to do with what Fayol wrote and more to do with the interpretation that Gulick and Urwick gave to his writings. By contrast, few people read Fayol – they mostly hear about him from other scholars or viewed him through the prism of Taylor's work. In addition, academic scholars often dislike the practical orientation of his work. For instance, Herbert Simon attacked his theory for being based on observation – noting that, despite his success as a manager, there is no reason to believe that his propositions would stand up to analysis (Smith and Boyns 2005). Simon similarly doubted that any principles of management can be discerned, arguing that the importance of experience was not an important indicator of theory development. In contradiction, others – such as Ralph C. Davis, Harold Koontz, and Wren (1995) – have responded by suggesting that Simon underestimated the value of practical experience and practicality (Parker and Ritson 2005a, b).

Another charge that has been labeled against Fayol was the idea that he advocated universal principles that could not be empirically supported. This is a common criticism that has been labeled against Fayol over the years. Brunsson (2008), for example, argues that whether you view management as contingent or universal depends upon what perspective of the organization you view from, noting that Taylor was a contingency thinker since he understood the firm from the ground up and Fayol was a universalist since he viewed downward. Brunsson goes further to argue that universalist assumptions and normative theory have created various fads in management thought, ignoring the complexity of thought. Fayol's thinking was, in short, too ambitious (Brunsson 2008). In noting such criticism, Wren noted that although some criticized the work of Fayol as being simplistic; there were others who found it useful. In reality, they are both. What Fayol did was to provide a rudimentary understanding and vocabulary to management when none had really existed, filling a much needed vacuum. Of course, it would appear simplistic in comparison with latter works. Just as we have moved beyond Adam Smith and have provided more specificity to his framework, so we have with Fayol. His work was based on his successful experiences providing a greater sense of legitimacy than theorizing based on abstract ideas (Wren 1995). Perhaps the reason why managers struggle is less to do with the body of knowledge we have acquired and more on the idea that we do not actually teach that body of knowledge. We no longer research things that offer practical advice. In treatments, such as Gabor's work, the Carnegie school is praised as they made management more scientific. Yet, that could also be considered a curse – stripping management from a practical footing (Miller 2007).

Contrary to many of his critics, Fayol was in truth not a universalist. Instead, Fayol wrote his ideas with the view that they be applied in a flexible fashion, accepting that they would not have the same validity in all circumstances. For instance, Fayol would oppose such modern ideas such as "zero tolerance" punishments (i.e., a punishment should be applied for a particular action no matter what the circumstances), noting that we should consider the circumstance and purpose (Schimmoeller 2012). He also understood that the type of skills required vary according to both a manager's position in the organization and the size of the company. He is obviously innocent of the charge of universalism. Of course, the historical debate over contingency versus universal principles ignores the issue as to whether a firm has a choice to be different or not. There is a tremendous amount of literature in the institutional and resource dependence areas that firms do not have control over their internal processes and will appear to be similar due to mimicry. The adoption of Affirmative Action plans would be an example of this outcome.

Some modern management scholars have challenged Fayol's idea that management has five core functions. Prominent among these critics are Fred Luthans, Fred Mintzberg, and John Kotter. Each notes that managers were unlikely or unable to perform such tasks, or, to some extent, were too simplistic in scope to have meaningful applications. Luthans, Mintzberg, and Kotter were also critical and believed that Fayol had developed his ideas through normative theorizing rather than observation, contradicting previous generation of scholars, who believed the opposite. Brunsson argues that empirical studies indicate that management is a mishmash of far from orderly activities. This is, however, not the case. As Wren (1990), Fells (2000), and Lamond (2004) have demonstrated, management activities tend to be very similar and there is a distinct overlap between the ideas of Fayol and his critics. Lamond went further, finding that Fayol's functions are what managers wish to do, and Mintzberg what they actually do.

One problem in estimating Fayol's original contribution is that Fayol and Taylor are often compared to each other. Some scholars, such as Wren and Bedeian (2018), have argued that Fayol and Taylor were complements to each other. Berdayes (2002) suggests that Fayol and Taylor were fellow travelers agreeing on the need for hierarchical division of labor, the use of incentives, and emphasis on work processes. George (1972) noted that Taylor wanted to change management from the shop room floor; Fayol from the boardroom. Other scholars, such as Donald Reid (1995), have argued that they were competitors. Still, others, such as Voxted (2017), Brunsson (2008), and Parker and Riston (2005a), dismiss the question entirely. In fact, Parker and Riston argue that Fayol has become a fellow traveler of Taylor even though the two men wrote in very different contexts about very different issues. Pryor and

Taneja (2010) reduce Fayolism to an offshoot of Taylorism. Yet, it is also ahistorical to dismiss the comparison since contemporaries, such as de Freminville (and Fayol), made it. However, such a division of competitor and complement is an unwarranted dichotomy as they could be both.

We have noted where Fayol and Taylor agreed and where they complemented each other. How did they differ? Taylor viewed things as a mechanical engineer. Accordingly, he believed that inefficiency was due to variance from a correctly designed and performed norm. Accordingly, Taylor sought to eliminate variance by standardization of material and performance, a focus that reflected the fact that he came from the shop floor. Fayol, whose background was from mines, did not worry much about standardization. Due to the physical isolation of men work, there was little direct supervision of workers in mines. Rather, what he sought was ingenuity, adaptability, and productivity of the workers. Taylor believed that managers should be technical experts who could perform the tasks better than their subordinates could. Fayol disagreed – if you have many bosses based on skill, how can you coordinate? Instead, Fayol envisioned an organization of experts who benefitted from a general management education. Although scholars have argued that Fayol was authoritarian and paternalistic, he also sought ways to undercut manager's domination by clearly stating what he expected from managers (Brunsson 2008).

Fayol and Taylor also differed on compensation issues. The standard textbook views Taylor and Fayol as believing in monetary incentives and romantic rationalists. Taylor was a rationalist who stressed extrinsic benefits, such as pay. In contrast, Fayol placed tremendous emphasis on building loyalty and an affective connection to workers. There was little in Taylor's writings on how a firm should compete and ownership issues. Fayol's work was focused on the orderly integration and arrangement of the organization. In fact, Fayol's work could be used to implement Porter's generic strategies. Fayol also understood that there were problems between principals and agents. He understood that the board was too tied to the market, too interested in creating profits, and that profit was a primitive means of judging corporate performance – anticipating Agency Theory (Parker and Ritson 2005a, b; Reid 1995).

Was Fayol more influential than Taylor? Probably not due to the factors above, but the largest reason was that Taylor changed the field from one of random observations to one based on the scientific method of testing, hypotheses, and replication. More than anyone, Taylor demonstrated that management should be taught and developed as a science, rather than a humanity, such as history. Taylor's use of science was something that fit the zeitgeist that placed an emphasis on science, objectivity, and replication. Taylor made the study of management into a legitimate field of research. Even today, when there is debate over whether his ideas work or not, we still use Taylor's methods of science to research issues. This could not be said for Fayol's ideas. Based on this contribution, Taylor truly "made" management; not in the sense that he was original or he created a field where none existed, but he made management a legitimate field of study (Drucker 1974).

Fayol's contribution was important as well, but different. Brunsson (2008) argues that the principal benefit from Taylor was that his was a top down approach and that the true success of management was organization efficiency. Yet Fayol understood that this viewpoint ignores the fact of how firms could compete if everyone is efficient – such an approach would reduce the economic benefits of owning a firm. Although Fayol did not use the term effectiveness, he understood that organizations must have a united mission to direct efforts towards a common goal. Fayol understood that the goal could vary from firm to firm, and so would the management forms they would take. How firms achieve the common goal is what makes firms survive. They also create diversity. In fact, a vast amount of literature expresses the need for firms to be different whether it is in pricing, resources, or simple location. In other words, the principles of management Fayol made are universal, but how they are implemented will be dependent on situations, a point that Fayol recognized. Taylor's inability to see above the plant floor obscured this vision. This is not to take away the brilliance or contribution of Taylor's views, but Fayol extended management to the firm level while Taylor addressed the primary problem of the early twentieth century, namely labor. Taylor sought to use science to achieve cooperation. The great powers were primarily concerned with ensuring production both for imperial reasons and restive workers (Kennedy 1980). Fayol anticipated strategy, but strategic concerns did not emerge until after the Second World War (Brunsson 2008).

Conclusion

Owen, Babbage, Ure, and Fayol made many contributions. Owen produced elements of what would become human resources and organizational behavior, focusing on worker training, incentives, and job design. Owen also anticipated the modern idea of work-family spillover. Babbage produced the beginnings of scientific management. Both Ure and Babbage produced the forerunner to operations management and Fayol, strategic management. Yet they did not produce a legitimate and influential approach. Owen focused on other areas, often at the expense of his writing on management. In addition, his major management project, New Harmony, was doomed to failure. Likewise, Babbage lacked the personal skills, temperament, and devotion to management to make a lasting contribution. If one looks closely, Babbage did provide a system similar to that of Taylor – but this system was in a morass of other ideas, which were considered crackpot. History has a long list of crackpots like Babbage, who did not get their due because of the newness of their ideas. It also has an even longer list of people who were just crackpots. We take Babbage seriously because with hindsight, we know he was correct. But can you really take someone, like Babbage, seriously if you were a contemporary? Andrew Ure was not a true management thinker – he placed more concern on what became operations. Finally, Fayol stressed issues that were not in vogue. Another issue that held these men back was the fact that management was not considered necessary until later in the industrial revolution. Factories were just a passing fancy. In the United States, where Taylor worked, there was an understanding that management was needed to handle the vast new underclass that was being created. Likewise, a new middle class could become managers. Taylor found a fertile and interested country for his ideas.

Cross-references

▶ Economic Foundations: Adam Smith and the Classical School of Economics
▶ Intellectual Enlightenment: The Epistemological Foundations of Business Endeavor
▶ Neo-classical Thought: Alfred Marshall and Utilitarianism

References

Ashcraft R (1993) Liberal political theory and working-class radicalism in nineteenth-century England. Polit Theory 21(2):249–272

Ashworth WJ (1996) Memory, efficiency, and symbolic analysis: Charles Babbage, John Herschel, and the industrial mind. Isis 87(4):629–653

Bacharach SB (1989) Organizational theories: some criteria for evaluation. Acad Manag Rev 14 (4):496–515

Becher HW (1995) Radicals, whigs and conservatives: the middle and lower classes in the analytical revolution at Cambridge in the age of aristocracy. Br J Hist Sci 28(4):405–426

Bedeian AG, Wren DA (2001) Most influential management books of the 20th century. Organ Dyn 29(3):221–225

Berdayes V (2002) Traditional management theory as panoptic discourse: language and the constitution of somatic flows. Cult Organ 8(1):35–49

Bestor A (1950, 2nd edn 1970) Backwoods utopias. University of Pennsylvania Press, Philadelphia

Browne CA (1936) Some relations of the New Harmony movement to the history of science in America. Sci Mon 42(6):483–497

Brunsson KH (2008) Some effects of Fayolism. Int Stud Manag Organ 38(1):30–47

Calhoun C (1993) "New social movements" of the early nineteenth century. Soc Sci Hist 17 (3):385–427

Caton H (1985) The preindustrial economics of Adam Smith. J Econ Hist 45(4):833–853

Claeys G (1986) Individualism, "Socialism," and "Social science": further notes on a process of conceptual formation, 1800–1850. J Hist Ideas 47(1):81–93

Claeys G (1987) Machinery, money and the millennium: from moral economy to socialism 1815–1860. Princeton University Press, Princeton

Claeys G (1989) Citizens and saints. Politics and anti-politics in early British socialism. Cambridge University Press, Cambridge

Cole GDH (1925) Life of Robert Owen. Ernest Benn Limited, London

Cunningham H (2011) Child labour's global past 1650–2000. In: Lieten K, van Nederveen Meerkerk E (eds) Child labour's global past, 1650–2000. Peter Lang, Bern, p 68

Davis RA, O'Hagan FJ (2010) Robert Owen. Continuum Press, London

Doheny J (1991) Bureaucracy and the education of the poor in nineteenth century Britain. Br J Educ Stud 39(3):325–339

Donnachie I (2000) Robert Owen: Owen of New Lanark and New Harmony. Tuckwell Press, East Linton

Drucker P (1974) Management: tasks, responsibilities, practices. Harper & Row, New York

Dutton HI, King JE (1982) The limits of paternalism: the cotton tyrants of North Lancashire, 1836–54. Soc Hist 7(1):59–74

Edwards S (2001) Factory and fantasy in Andrew Ure. J Des Hist 14(1):17–33

Faragher JM (1986) Sugar Creek: life on the Illinois prairie. Yale University Press, London

Farrar WV (1973) Andrew Ure, FRS, and the philosophy of manufactures. Notes Rec R Soc Lond 27(2):299–324

Farrell EL (1938) The new harmony experiment, an origin of progressive education. Peabody J Educ 15(6):357–361

Fayol H (1949) General and industrial management (trans: Storrs C). Pitman & Sons, London

Fells MJ (2000) Fayol stands the test of time. J Manag Hist 6(8):345–360

Feuer LS (1966) The influence of the American communist colonies on Engels and Marx. West Polit Q 19(3):456–474

Foner E (1970) Free soil, free labor, free men: the ideology of the Republican party before the Civil War. Oxford University Press, New York

Genovese E (1976) Roll, Jordan, roll: the world the slaves made. Knopf, New York

George CS Jr (1972) The history of management thought, 2nd edn. Prentice-Hall, Englewood Cliffs

Harrison JF (1967) "The steam engine of the new moral world": Owenism and education, 1817–1829. J Br Stud 6(2):76–98

Harrison JFC (1969) Robert Owen and the Owenites in Britain and America: quest for the new moral world. Routledge, London

Hatcher T (2013) Robert Owen: a historiographic study of a pioneer of human resource development. Eur J Train Dev 37(4):414–431

Heames JT, Breland JW (2010) Management pioneer contributors: 30-year review. J Manag Hist 16 (4):427–436

Homans GC (1984) Coming to my senses. Transaction, New Brunswick

Howe DW (2007) What hath god wrought: the transformation of America, 1815–1848. Oxford University Press, New York

Humphreys JH, Novicevic MM, Hayek M, Gibson JW, Pane Haden SS, Williams WA Jr (2016) Disharmony in New Harmony: insights from the narcissistic leadership of Robert Owen. J Manag Hist 22(2):146–170

Iggers GG (1959) Further remarks about early uses of the term "social science". J Hist Ideas 20 (3):433–436

Kennedy DM (1980) Over here. Oxford University Press, Oxford

Kumar M (1984) Karl Marx, Andrew Ure and the question of managerial control. Soc Sci 12 (9):63–69

Lamond D (2004) A matter of style: reconciling Henri and Henry. Manag Decis 42(2):330–356

Miller D (2007) Paradigm prison, or in praise of atheoretic research. Strateg Organ 5(2):177–184

Morton AL (1962) The life and ideas of Robert Owen. Lawrence & Wishart, London

Moseley M (1964) Irascible genius, the life of Charles Babbage. Henry Regnery, Chicago

Muravchik J (2002) Heaven on earth: the rise and fall of socialism. Encounter Books, New York

Parker LD, Ritson P (2005a) Fads, stereotypes and management gurus: Fayol and Follett today. Manag Decis 43(10):1335–1357

Parker LD, Ritson PA (2005b) Revisiting Fayol: anticipating contemporary management. Br J Manag 16(3):175–194

Parker LD, Ritson P (2011) Rage, rage against the dying of the light: Lyndall Urwick's scientific management. J Manag Hist 17(4):379–398

Pollard S (1963) Factory discipline in the industrial revolution. Econ Hist Rev 16(2):254–271

Pollard S (1964) The factory village in the industrial revolution. Engl Hist Rev 79(312):513–531

Pryor MG, Taneja S (2010) Henri Fayol, practitioner and theoretician–revered and reviled. J Manag Hist 16(4):489–503

Reid D (1995) Fayol: from experience to theory. J Manag Hist 1(3):21–36

Rosenbloom RS (1964) Men and machines: some 19th-century analyses of mechanization. Technol Cult 5(4):489–511

Schimmoeller L (2012) Henri Fayol and zero tolerance policies. Rev Manag Comp Int 13(1):30

Sellers C (1991) The market revolution. Oxford University Press, New York

Smith A (1937) An inquiry into the nature and causes of the wealth of nations. Modern Library, New York

Smith I, Boyns T (2005) British management theory and practice: the impact of Fayol. Manag Decis 43(10):1317–1334

Spatig L (2009) Rediscovering Fayol: parallels to behavioralist management and transformational leadership. Proceedings of the Northeast Business & Economics Association. Marist College School of Management

Stampp K (1956) Peculiar institution: slavery in the ante-bellum south. Knopf, New York

Stigler GJ (1991) Charles Babbage (1791+200=1991). J Econ Lit 29(3):1149–1152

Taylor A (2013) The internal enemy: slavery and war in Virginia, 1772–1832. W. W. Norton, New York

Thies CF (2000) The success of American communes. South Econ J 67(1):186–199

Thompson EP (1963) The making of the English working class. Victor Gollancz, London

Unwin G (1922) The transition to the factory system (continued). Engl Hist Rev 37(147):383–397

Van Cleave HJ (1951) The New Harmony venture and its relation to natural science. Bios 22 (4):263–275

Voxted S (2017) 100 years of Henri Fayol. Manag Rev 28(2):256–274

Whiting RJ (1964) Historical search in human relations. Acad Manag J 7(1):45–53

Wilkes MV (2002) Charles Babbage and his world. Notes Rec 56(3):353–365

Wilson E (1940) To the Finland station: a study in the writing and acting of history. Doubleday, Garden City

Wren DA (1990) Was Henri Fayol a real manager? In: Academy of management proceedings, vol 1. Academy of Management, Chicago, pp 138–142

Wren DA (1995) Henri Fayol: learning from experience. J Manag Hist 1(3):5–12

Wren DA (2001) Henri Fayol as strategist: a nineteenth century corporate turnaround. Manag Decis 39(6):475–487

Wren DA, Bedeian AG (2018) The evolution of management thought, 7th edn. Wiley, New York

Zimmerman A (1997) The ideology of the machine and the spirit of the factory: Remarx on Babbage and Ure. Cult Crit 37:5–29

Taylor Made Management

21

Jeffrey Muldoon

Contents

Introduction 500
Taylor's Contribution 501
Taylor's Relationship to Progressivism 502
Taylor's Role 506
Criticisms 507
Taylor and Unions 510
Taylor and Peasant Culture 513
Conclusion: Flawed Giant 515
Cross-references 517
References 517

Abstract

The purpose of this chapter is to examine the life and career of Frederick Winslow Taylor, father of scientific management. This chapter discusses both how Taylor's actions, as well as the environment within the United States, nurtured the rise of scientific management. The contention is that America's progressive era, as well as the transformation of knowledge, allowed for management to become a field of study. Taylor's work is discussed, as well as a discussion of the criticisms that have been levelled at Taylor. In addition, the chapter provides a discussion of how scientific management clashed with peasant work culture.

Keywords

Frederick Winslow Taylor · Scientific management · Progressive Era · Taylorism

---

J. Muldoon (✉)
Emporia State University, Emporia, KS, USA
e-mail: jmuldoon@emporia.edu

© The Author(s), under exclusive licence to Springer Nature Switzerland AG 2020   499
B. Bowden et al. (eds.), *The Palgrave Handbook of Management History*,
https://doi.org/10.1007/978-3-319-62114-2_27

Introduction

Frederick Winslow Taylor's life could be a plot from a bad movie. The son of the Quaker aristocracy, he abandoned Exeter and Harvard to work in a factory. He was a champion athlete, brilliant inventor, and an aggressive advocate for work improvement. He had the ability to inspire great, often contradictory, emotions from people. In death, Taylor was esteemed in some circles as the successor to James Watt; in others, he was attacked as a mountebank. Taylor desired and sought to create order, to a point where he created his own rules for the games he played as a child. Taylor sought order in industry as well, producing ideas that changed the world, but at a cost to the worker who surrendered freedom for slightly higher wages and slightly fewer hours. Taylor's writing sounded reasonable, but in practice, by his hand and others, they were anything but. He inspired love from the manager, hatred from the intellectual, distrust from the worker, and frustration from the capitalist. His ideas could be complex and subtle, or so basic that he could have been a caricature created by Marx, Weber, or Freud. Taylor could be considered the savior of modern civilization from the scourge of Bolshevism and Nazism; others saw him as a shill for the powerful elite, who used "science" to place the worker in chains. John Dos Passos, Upton Sinclair, and Charlie Chaplin attacked him. Edwin Locke and Peter Drucker defended him. Kyle Bruce and Chris Nyland have argued that scientific management has been demonized; Andrea Gabor, James Hoopes, and Matthew Stewart see Taylor as a demon that needs to be exorcised (Kaingel 1997; Copley 1923).

Despite his mixed reputation, Taylor remains the most influential and respected figure in management. For better or worse, management is a distinct field due to Taylor's actions legitimizing the field as separate from sociology, psychology, economics, and engineering. Taylor made management, not in the sense that he coined the term or even that he was the first to post a theory of management, but he provided the field with legitimacy. When Owen, Babbage, and Ure did their work, they did not have a concept of what a manager does – their focus was on the specialization of labor and the machine. Taylor wanted to develop tools for managers so they could better administrate the new industrial order. The importance of Taylor's actions came at the time that modern professions began to emerge, eclipsing the older ones such as artisans and the clergy. Modern professions, such as psychologist, sociologist, and manager, were the result of the progressive era.

For this reason, Taylor remains (more than a hundred years after his death) the preeminent management thinker. His principle book, the *Principles of Scientific Management*, remains a classic in the field, and he remains the most written about scholar in the preeminent *Journal of Management History* (Bedeian and Wren 2001; Schwarz 2015). Whenever a scholar theorizes or tests models, they are living in the shadow of Taylor. Management is considered a social science, not a humanity, due to the influence of Taylor. We are all Taylorists because we accept his general idea that work should be scientifically studied. Yet, management scholars and others, have pointed out that Taylor was not original, he was a liar, a plagiarizer, and an autocrat. He also provided management with the image of the clueless consultant, who sells fads based on voodoo statistics (Stewart 2009). His defenders challenge these accusations by pointing out the timelessness of his vision and that he was correct. Despite being an autocrat, he was someone who wished to better the lives of workers (Wren and Hay 1977; Heames and Breland 2010). Some of his critics come from the management field, but mostly they come from history, industrial relations, and the arts.

This chapter will discuss some general observations about Taylor. Firstly, his contribution to the field of management will be discussed. Secondly, Taylor's relationship with the Progressive era will be explained and why management emerged as a distinct field of study. The explanation was that finally, conditions enabling management to emerge were present. Thirdly, the various criticisms labeled at Taylor will be discussed and most of them are found to be overheated. Fourthly, his complication with both unionized and non-unionized labor will be addressed to understand why they opposed him as vehemently as they did.

Taylor's Contribution

Edwin Locke (1982), arguably Taylor's most able defender, once argued that it was not that Taylor's vision was correct at the time but appears to be correct for all time. In fact, according to Payne (2006) and coauthors, we can see Taylor's development on the following elements of modern management: job analysis, job design, selection, motivation, incentive systems, job performance criteria, performance appraisal, employee attitudes, group processes, human factors, and organizational change and development. Payne overestimates the role that Taylor had in forming attitudes and group processes. Those elements were really developed by Elton Mayo, although Taylor did have these elements within his work (Cooper 1962). If Taylor had founded just one of those managerial processes, that would have been an amazing contribution, but for him to develop each of them, basic mainstays of modern human resource management, is a remarkable feat indeed. Taylor also researched fatigue and scholars have viewed him as one of the intellectual godfathers to goal-setting theory, one of the most validated management theories. Taylor left such a dominant imprint on management that other management figures, such as Mayo, Fayol, Follett, Barnard, and Munsterberg, are seen through the prism of Taylor's work (Bendix and Fisher 1949; Cooper 1962; Locke 1982; Parker and Ritson 2005; Payne et al. 2006; Taneja et al. 2011). In fact, no scholars really refuted him; they merely expanded his work into new areas.

Daniel Wren (2005) also argues that Taylor was the major push of the second phase of the industrial revolution. To Wren, the first phase marked the development of large firms; technological advances were the major concern. In fact, we can see references to this idea in the work of Babbage and Ure, who seemed more concerned with machines then with management as a distinct idea. Taylor, in the second phase, realized that technical skill was necessary but was an insufficient condition to ensure the proper functioning of work. He noted that production was about one-third of what it should be because of opportunistic behavior by workers caused by the arbitrary nature of management. He called this behavior soldiering. He argued that it happened for two reasons, the natural tendency for people to shirk work and to protect themselves from an arbitrary and coercive management. Workers had been badly trained as well, developing work heuristics based on tradition. When Taylor was a manager, he attempted to fine workers, but he found it troublesome, due to worker retaliation. He had to find another way.

Taylor prized knowledge and science over experience and tradition – this was arguably his greatest contribution. His other contributions stem from this. Taylor decided to set the rate in a scientific way so that workers could understand that their wage was not set on a whim. Furthermore, Taylor broke down each act into its smallest parts and performed the act with a stopwatch to determine the most effective way to work the system. Taylor also broke each job down into individual components, i.e., the smallest parts, and then reconstructed them as they should be done. Furthermore, he made note that all tools, machines, and methods should be standardized. In addition, Taylor was willing to pay workers for extra production when a lesser man would have used coercion. Taylor used incentives on a day-to-day basis, so the workers could be further engaged. When Taylor developed the notion of first class work, he did so with the idea that workers should produce as much as they are physically and mentally capable. Those who were not physically or mentally capable had different options in the plant. Taylor developed a task management system that allowed more work to occur but allowed for breaking up the supervisor's work so that he could function within a discrete area (Boddewyn 1961). Taylor believed that managers would become better, more suited to analyzing their specific area of expertise with authority derived from knowledge and skill, not position or power (Locke 1982).

Taylor's greatest contribution to society was that he brought the unskilled and immigrant to the marketplace (Wren 2005). David Montgomery (1979) noted that Taylorism deskilled labor, but he also noted that many immigrants did not have new skills to lose. Taylor's rationalization of work reduced training time, allowing unskilled workers to find gainful employment and higher wages. Although workers had witnessed a 15% increase in pay from 1873 to 1893 (during the Long Depression), this increase was not equally divided, as only skilled laborers really benefitted. The creation of scientific management was a boon to the unskilled. Taylorism meant that there was not an unskilled, radical immigrant labor pool that could have potentially caused a revolt. Taylor's work, as well as welfare capitalism and the emergence of popular culture, created a sense of belonging. Along with Ford, Taylor created a new world that lifted the laboring classes to middle class life, with every worker owning a home and a radio. According to Drucker, Taylorism helped create the amazing industrial complex in the United States that enabled it, despite a great percentage of its experienced workers being away in the military, to outproduce the rest of the world during the World War II.

Taylor's Relationship to Progressivism

Peter Drucker (1954) has argued that it was scientific management that slayed Karl Marx. He does not provide enough explanation for this occurrence. William H. Knowles (1952) pointed out that a principle problem was the lack of knowledge on what was a fair day's work and a fair day's pay. The price mechanism failed to establish the proper rate, because employment is a continuing transaction, rather than a spot transaction. The development of additional incentives and its relationship to the work movement was needed. Accordingly, Taylor needed to scientifically determine a structure through time studies and wage systems that would be based on an unarguable system of laws to produce cooperation. After all, no one argues whether the sun will come up in the morning. Scholars have also pointed out that Marx did not consider the growth of free labor unions and protective legislation – part of the Taylorist coalition (Bruce and Nyland 2001; Nyland 1995, 1998, 2000).

Knowles's explains how Taylor was able to create a new order. It does not answer the question of why and where. After all, what made Taylor and his world different from the world of Babbage? This question, and others, can be answered by considering Taylor's relationship to the burgeoning progressive movement in the United States. The progressive movement has long frustrated scholars (Filene 1970). Lawyers, social workers, clergy, doctors, businessmen, intellectuals, academics, and the old elite and new professional middle classes have all been concerned, at one point or another, as part of the progressive movement. There were great divisions between followers of Woodrow Wilson, who wanted regulated competition, and Theodore Roosevelt, who wanted regulated monopoly (Cooper 1983). There were progressives who were concerned with the inner city, some with the rural community, some wanted to regulate the economy, and others, morality (Kloppenberg 1986; Kolko 1963; McGerr 2003). There were progressives who wanted to Americanize immigrants and still others who wished to build a multicultural society. At one point, historians grew fed up with the whole process declaring that the progressive movement was dead (Filene 1970).

What is important is to understand the overlap of progressive visions rather than its differences. The progressive movement, despite its many faces, had a deep concern to bring order to chaos and affirm certain values in the face of radicalism (Keller 1992, 1998). "As the network of relations affecting men's lives each year became more tangled and more distended," wrote Robert Wiebe, "Americans in a basic sense no longer knew who or what they were. The setting had altered beyond their power to understand it, and within an alien context they had lost themselves" (Wiebe 1967, pp. 42–43). The purpose of progressivism was to provide a sense of social control that would limit one group taking advantage of another. The breaking away of small town America, the interconnection of America by train and telegraph, and the emergence of new immigrant groups forced Americans to develop methods of regulating both a new economy and society. The principal concern was that business was a corrupting force in politics and economically disruptive (McCormick 1981). The concern over workers was the idea that wages would decline to the point of starvation due to the presence of machines.

The purpose of this new progressivism was the use of both knowledge and power to restrain unwarranted individual behavior for the greater good. The vanguard of this new movement was various professions that emerged, including management. Taylor's version of management is best described as purposeful social action to promote rationalization for the corporate world, just as social work was to do so for home life. The appeal of science, the emergence of objective laws, and expert planning would produce submission, on the part of workers and employers, by eliminating arbitrary decisions and rejecting idleness. Samuel Haber (1964, 1991) argues that the success of scientific management was due to its ability to combine notions of scientific efficiency with personnel virtues of hard work and material improvement. The new educational system brought over through the German University, as well as the corporate training that Taylor urged, meant that managers would emerge as a class (Larson 1979; Rodgers 1998). In addition, the Morill Act created schooling for engineers that enabled a profession that would be closely aligned with management. It should not be a surprise that a great many managers were engineers, including Taylor. As James Kloppenberg (1986) noted, the attractiveness of bureaucracy and rationalization was based on bureaucracy's claim to science. The fact that Taylorism had a basis in the scientific method also made it attractive. Taylor recognized that the development of scientific management could play a role, besides that of work life, in both social life and government (Tarr 2001). In fact, after Taylor's death, some of his associates, such as Lillian Gilbreth, would undertake this vision by designing the modern kitchen under the principles of scientific management. The alignment of scientific management with the progressive movement was a boon for Taylor.

Aiding management in its emergence as a social science was the joint emergence of sociology and psychology as distinct fields of research (Turner and Turner 1990). Although sociology had been around for a number of years (there were pre-Civil War references to it), it found itself as a natural ally to management; an alliance that did not continue into the Hawthorne years (Muldoon 2017). Prior to the 1930s, sociology was primarily concerned with the field of social work, rather than a distinct science directed toward construction of theory and objective research. The purpose of sociology was to develop effective techniques that could help manage the lower class by providing them with examples of middle class behavior. Michael Katz (1996) noted that social workers and management often criticized the poor for exhibiting certain behaviors, such as drunkenness, and sought methods of control. Additionally, as Sanford Elwitt (1988) noted, the emergence of strikes after 1877 forged an alliance between social workers and management as a means of improving worker morals. William Howe Tolman was a social reformer who worked with Taylor. Tolman believed that sociology should not just reform but should create a sense of interdependence between capital and labor.

Taylorism played a role in the efficiency movement (Bruce and Nyland 2001). The efficiency movement meant different things to different people. The national efficiency movement in Great Britain was a national cross-party movement that was dedicated to promote efficiency due to the inability of the British Empire's military to deal with the Boer commandos (Searle 1971). The purpose of the efficiency movement was less a move towards democracy but more to shame the British elite into reforming the system. And so, the British were not swept away due to the changing international scene caused by the emergence of Germany and the United States. Besides reforming the British military, the British efficiency movement sought to reform British society by improving human capital through better education, political reform, and better nourishment. The United States efficiency movement was dedicated to the purpose of increasing consumption by lowering prices (Nelson 1980). Scientific management fit into this movement since, like control, regulation, and mastery, the scientific movement suggested that rationalization could tame the marketplace (Haber 1964, 1991; Rodgers 1998; Wiebe 1967).

There were several connections between Taylor and the burgeoning progressive movement. One of the most prominent connections was the relationship between Taylor and the famous attorney, later Supreme Court justice, Louis Brandeis (Urofsky 1971). Brandeis was a crusading attorney from Massachusetts, who had started out as a corporate attorney, and after making his fortune, switched his interests to the public good. Brandeis had come across scientific management during the famous Interstate Commerce case, when he opposed the increase of rates on the part of railroads (Martin 1971). Looking for an advantage, Brandeis recalled some of the exciting research on scientific management, from Taylor's *Shop Management*, as well as articles written by Harrington Emerson. Brandeis recognized that if he could attack the railroads lack of efficiency, he could win the case. So, Emerson invited Brandeis, along with Gantt, Carl G. Barth, and Frank Gilbreth, to a meeting at Gantt's house. They decided that they would name the overall efficiency system by the title of scientific management (Aldrich 2010). Brandeis's arguments helped block the rate increase. Kraines (1960) noted that this case and Brandeis's embrace of scientific management helped to launch his career.

Taylor was highly esteemed by Thorstein Veblen (Diggins 1978). Veblen saw Taylorism as the means to tame business by promoting a system to replace profits with the notion of efficiency based on scientific ends. Walter Lippmann agreed with Veblen in the belief that, through the use of science, management could be tamed. The opposite occurred – both efficiency and profit would be the goals of management. As John Patrick Diggins noted, Veblen, Lincoln Steffens, and Hebert Croly failed to understand the role between managerial rule and the process of rationalization. There was little recognition in Veblen that the process of managerial control could be extended to all aspects of life. Max Weber understood the limits of Taylorism. To Weber, the rationalization could lead to a prevalent form of control in industrial life and that all aspects of life could be consumed by administrative domination, reducing human interactions into impersonal rules (Diggins 1978, 1996).

Another important reason why scientific management became an accepted part of work was a transformation of knowledge. The transformation of knowledge that occurred from 1870 to 1920 broke barriers between different ideas, such as empiricism, idealism, laissez-faire, and socialism. Creating, what Kloppenberg (1986) called, a middle way. The idea that truth was not the subject of eternity was something that clearly occurred to Taylor, who was both an empiricist and an idealist. Taylor had an understanding that management should control the means of production, including equipment and the plant. He also argued that, in some circumstances, management should control knowledge of the work process. Previously, workers controlled both tools and knowledge. Scientific management would deprive both elements to workers under the policy of standardization. However, Taylor was unconcerned, arguing that although management controlled the means of production, workers controlled themselves. Taylor developed this idea by recognizing that coercion was an ineffective stimulus in gaining cooperation and production. Empiricism avoids the need for workers to control the means of production and provides a block against managerial aggression through the discovery of the laws of work (Wagner-Tsukamoto 2007).

Taylor's Role

Rather than delving into the unproductive questions as to whether Taylor was original or not, it is more productive to answer the question why was Taylor so influential. Andrew Hargadon (2003) argued that innovations are not the result of creative genius nor were they created in secrecy, rather innovations are a combination of elements that forms the basis of a new system. These are ideas passed through a network of likeminded individuals. It is true that Charles Babbage used a stopwatch to observe workers and that Taylor had probably read about this research when he was a student at the Stevens Institute of Technology. Yet, it was Taylor that used the stopwatch to improve performance. The difference was that Taylor recognized that there was a benefit to efficiency in a manner that Babbage did not (Wren and Bedeian 2018).

This innovation was passed along a research network (Burt 2004). Another advantage that Taylor had over Babbage was that the United States had a network of managers and engineers who were willing to work and expand on Taylor's initial ideas. An example of this would be Frank Gilbreth creating motion study or Carl Barth producing the slide rule. Dean (1997a, b) pointed out that Gilbreth served Taylor well over the controversy of the fundamentals of management in *America Magazine*. Problems with the lack of business education would remain an issue for Great Britain well into the 1960s. However, the United States had an educational system that produced managers and a support network that could provide consistent training. Taylor understood this and spread his ideas far and wide, even lecturing at the Harvard Business School without a fee. Yet, it is also important to note that Taylor was the major innovator because he was the nexus of the network, often bridging a wide group of scholars (Rogers 1962).

Unlike Owen, Ure, and Babbage, Taylor was a monomaniac obsessed with management. The other three men had different interests, sometimes widely different. As Peter Drucker has noted, usually it is a monomaniac who makes significant contributions to society (Wrege and Greenwood 1991). Taylor was a change agent. He recognized that management needed to change. Through the use of his social network, Taylor and his associates passed information and created a standardized system with some exceptions. Taylor also had the ability to make clients understand the need to change. He rooted his idea, in the deep need of the United States, to produce a sense of order from the chaotic nature of post-Civil War industrial life. Taylor also made connections with various opinion leaders, either major industrialists or future Supreme Court justices. If he had avoided his blind spot towards unions, and cultivated their leaders, as his disciples had done, he could have spread the use of scientific management much more easily. In this case, his obsession against unions prevented him from recognizing an important truth – unions wished to eliminate arbitrary management as much as he did.

This led to Taylor's other important contribution to management thought – the legitimacy of the manager as a distinct class. James Burnham (1941) once argued that the emergence of the manager as a distinct class was proof that the future did not belong to Marx. It was the manager, who had the ability to control and plan, and would guide the future rather than owners. This could not have happened without Taylor, who provided management with a sense of legitimacy. Mark Suchman (1995) argued that legitimacy was "a generalized perception or assumption that the actions of an entity are desirable, proper, appropriate within some socially constructed system of norms, values, beliefs, and definitions." Before Taylor, there was neither a systematic approach nor a basic understanding of management. Through his linking to elements of the Progressive Era and changes in thought, Taylor made management a respectable profession. That he also piggybacked on engineering made this feat easier. Despite the previous developments of the nineteenth century, Henry Towne (in 1886) could still proclaim the need for a management theory. Prior to Taylor, management was not legitimate because no one was certain what it precisely stood for (Tarr 2001).

Criticisms

As Locke pointed out, it was not just that Taylor was correct in his time; it appears that he may be correct for all time. Yet it seems more profitable, and more interesting to demonstrate what Taylor got wrong since it reveals the limits of both the man and, by extension, scientific management. Taylor has been challenged on several grounds: lack of originality, ethical violations, and autocratic nature of work (Gabor 2000). Taylor has been challenged for the unethical and sensationalistic nature of his work. In fact, the charge that Taylor was a showman who often made his work more simplistic and productive is a common one. Even Wren and Bedeian (2018), who are sober defenders of Taylor, noted (based on an analysis by Carl Barth) that Taylor overstated production. For his critics, Taylor's failures (real or imagined) seem to be fertile grounds for criticism. James Hoopes (2003, p. 33) states that "Taylor often made up facts to place himself, and his work, in the best possible light, including tall tales of his work." Going even further, Hoopes argues that Taylor was a "self-righteous hypocrite," who showed a lack of consciousness, while at the same time holding others to high moral standards. Taylor was a man so hated that he was forced to have an armed guard take him home at night, or so the story goes. Another scholar noted that Taylor was a cliché that only Freud could have dreamed about (Lears 1997). Taylor has been accused of cheating at baseball and golf. His moral failing as a husband was noted by the fact that his wife seemed to get much healthier when he died (Gabor 2000). He frequently clashed with both workers and plant owners and had a distinct and almost unrivaled ability to make enemies. It seems that the only people he had apparent warmth towards were his children.

Taylor, simply stated, was not original. He did not claim to be the first person to study work. There were others, in the past or concurrently, that were using science to aid industrial labor. Donald Etz (1964) sees the systematic study in the work of the Qin legalist scholar, Han Fei Tzu. Han Fei argued that the basis of leadership was on laws rather than moral authority or personnel competence. The legalist school placed emphasis on standard laws rather than moral persuasion or Confucian ritual. During Taylor's lifetime, Wilkinson (1965) conducted research on work. This theme of multiple discoveries is a common one in social sciences, so common that we have a name for it, Stigler's conjecture – there is nothing new under the sun. Yet Wren (2005) and others have noted that Taylor was the first to take measurements with the purpose of studying work. For reasons mentioned above, Taylor's contributions changed management.

His most notable critic was the late management historian Charles D. Wrege, who chased Taylor with a ferocity and tenacity greater than Javert tracking down Jean Valjean. Wrege's initial paper on Taylor is a detailed analysis of the famous pig iron experiment conducted at Bethlehem Steel in 1899. Wrege and Perroni were able to track down the famous Schmidt, who was a worker named Henry Knoll, an immigrant, who was building his own house, a structure that stood until 1960. Knoll worked as many days under Taylor's system as he did otherwise. In addition, Knoll was not selected at random, seemed to have a boundless amount of energy, and was a sample size of one. Wrege and Perroni demonstrated that Taylor's story account varied from one telling to the next. More serious was the accusation from Wrege and Stotka (1978) that Taylor plagiarized the Fundamentals of Management from Morris Cooke. Wrege and Perroni (1974) argued (p. 26) that scholars should "think to look at the idol early enough in the game to discover that it had feet of clay before it was hoisted onto a pedestal." One could conclude that Dr. Wrege was not a fan!

What does one make of these accusations? To start, despite the claims of Dos Passos, Taylor did not cheat at baseball (Taylor and Bedeian 2008). The "pig tale" accusation is overblown. Hough and White (2001, pp. 590–591) argue that Taylor told the iron story to illustrate that even the most menial tasks can be standardized.

> Nothing was more basic than handling pig; no special knowledge, skills, or tools were required. The work was easily described to all audiences and served as an example to management that even basic processes are inefficient but could be substantially improved through systematic examination and standardization. For workers, the object lesson was that by following the instructions provided by management, rather than depending on "do your best" methods, those individuals suited to a particular class of work would earn higher wages.

Knolle was not a victim, but a willing participant who wished to earn extra money. Using analysis from courtroom testimony, they concluded that Taylor was basically honest. Taylor was not publishing an academic paper but was relaying the story using memory devices that make a connection with previous knowledge. Memory is a fickle outcome. The historian Arthur M. Schlesinger, Jr. (2000) observed that people often create memories about important events due to memory failure and attribution. Martha Banta (1993) makes a note that Taylor's stories served as a way of passing the principles of scientific management through a narrative device. These stories were less a scientific paper and more of an explanation of the principles of scientific management. The stories provided management with an understanding that they could produce more at less cost; for workers, they provided a way to get involved in management's experiments. These stories were used by Taylor's followers into the 1930s as a means of spreading the gospel of efficiency. Taylor was selling his ideas, not delivering a scientific paper.

The charge of plagiarism is a serious one, but Wrege and Stotka (1978) overplay their hand. It is true that the *Principles of Scientific Management* was written in part by Morris Cooke. But it is also true, as Edwin Locke (1982) points out, that Cooke wrote the book based on lectures that Taylor had given. Therefore, it would appear that Taylor had plagiarized based on Cooke plagiarizing from Taylor! The reality is that both men wrote the manuscript, but it was mostly Taylor's ideas, with Cooke as a contributor. Taylor also published his book with Cooke's knowledge and consent, even offering to provide royalties to Cooke. Hough and White (2001) point out that it was Taylor's ideas and published under Taylor's name. Taylor was the author in the "true sense" in that he assumed responsibility and the book was published using his authority (Hough and White 2001).

Taylor's critics have often come from the literary world, as he has been a target of writers such as Upton Sinclair, John Dos Passos, and the movie director Charles Chaplin. This is a testimony to his wide-ranging influence but also his rebelling against some of the norms of the literary and philosophical world. The principle reason for this criticism comes from the concept that Taylor's ideas reduced work to materialism since it eliminated other benefits of work replacing benefits with a pecuniary and market driven system. This criticism came from the Victorian repudiation of habit since it dims the mind. In that vein, Senator Henry Cabot Lodge preferred artisanship over scientific management due to his connection to the Italian Renaissance. Joseph M. Thomas argues that one of the reasons why late Victorians opposed scientific management was based on the notion of habit. Jackson Lears (1997) goes forward noting that the reason why many academics support scientific management was that they were not under its jurisdiction. Yet, it is also important to note that the movie *Modern Times* was not the only depiction of scientific management on screen. Buster Keaton, Chaplin's competitor, in his movie *One Week*, demonstrates the exciting and inspiring nature of work (Thomas 1993).

Taylor tended to focus on the most menial tasks with the dimmest of workers. "Schmidt," an ethnic and social stereotype created by Taylor, is not just a story device; it is also emblematic of a man with a deep bias against the lesser type (Klaw 1979). There are numerous disparaging remarks about Italians, Hungarians, and African Americans throughout his work (Taylor 1947). This attitude was typical of the middle class reformer when interacting with the poor and destitute. Aditya Simha and David J. Lemak (2010) argue that what is harsh today may not be harsh in the past. This attitude ignores that a vast many people from similar backgrounds lacked class and ethnic bias. It would be inconceivable to imagine that Mary Parker Follett would write such biased viewpoints. Although these stories did have the ability to undermine Taylor's conceptions of cooperation with the worker, as he often referred to workers as "apes" and "cows."

Taylor and Unions

Taylor's views of unions are more complex than scholars have initially thought. The traditional response was that Taylor was anti-union. While this was true in certain aspects, it was not in others. Locke was the first to note Taylor's complex position on unions, noting that under scientific management, unions would not be necessary since it addressed most of the workers' concerns, namely, the arbitrary nature of employment. Scholars, such as Wren and Bedeian (2018), Locke (1982), Bruce (Bruce and Nyland 2001), and Nyland (1998, 2000), have placed the blame on the worker for not understanding Taylorism. To their credit, Bruce and Nyland demonstrate the relationship between Taylorism and unions could have been fruitful – but not with Taylor himself.

Presumably, we base the assumption of misunderstanding on the fact that Taylor was correct on monetary pay and the systematic study of work. There has been little understanding of the peasant work culture that Taylorism destroyed. One of the common criticisms made against the Hawthorne studies was the skepticism that members of the American upper-middle class could really understand workers (Bruce and Nyland 2011; Muldoon 2017). After all, what could T.N. Whitehead, son of a Cambridge Don, understand about the worker's experience? Later oral histories would verify that this viewpoint was true. This point has not been previously made about Taylor's ideas.

In some ways, Taylor was the best friend possible for labor workers. Through his techniques, millions of workers were able to become part of the market process, whereas before they would have lacked the skills. Yet his heavy-handed nature prevented the spread of scientific management in his lifetime. George Claeys (1987, 1989) noted that workers had an easy time adjusting to life in the factory. E. P. Thompson (1963) would argue the reason for this is that workers kept their own culture, which had a different set of values than the one imposed by management. In fact, workers were neither lazy nor docile. If they soldiered, it was because there were reasons to do so – namely, as a counter strike against management.

There is a principal issue with scholars who study what Taylor said and what he did. In writing, Taylor had the ability to seem reasonable; in practice, he was very inflexible. There is little consideration of other viewpoints – a lack of empathy that has pervaded defenses of Taylor. One of the reasons why both Herbert Croly and John Dewey took issue with Taylorism was that it did not allow for democracy, going so far as to argue that scientific management was oppressive since there was no worker voice (Kloppenberg 1986). Both felt that for scientific management to work there must be a voice for workers. Others noted that scientific management was a violation of volunteerism and democracy due to its rigid standards of laws (Wagner-Tsukamoto 2008).

Taylor was naive. He shared the same ends as did most employers: he opposed trade-unions, set standards to deal with only individual workers, found ways to increase production, and opposed collective bargaining. Yet, there was considerable disagreement regarding the means of achieving these ends. Taylor believed that science should be the absolute authority, not understanding that, in the workplace, science could not create absolute laws of gravity. In addition, the implementation of scientific management required large costs with unknown outcomes. Finally, Taylor clearly understood the opportunism of workers, but not managers. He assumed that science would provide management with a full program for industrial life. As Reinard Bendix (1956) noted, management could embrace some, but not all, aspects of the program. Taylor ignored what Bendix pointed out. For example, managers could embrace piecework and the bonus system, but they could ignore the functional foreman and time and motion studies. The net result could dramatically shift power to management, causing a rapid decline. David Montgomery (1987) noted both Taylor and Bill Haywood understood that work was in the hands of the worker, in that workers often had superior intelligence than managers. In fact, some craftsmen had the ability to hire and fire their own helpers. Taylor sought to undermine what little protection workers had (Bell 1956; Montgomery 1987).

At first, Taylorism seemed to hurt, rather than benefit, workers. As Montgomery (1987) noted, the use of piecework in some industries resulted in employees only being paid when there was work to be done. Under the old system, when there was little work employees were still paid as they would produce extra parts. As Reinard Bendix (1956) has noted, Taylor was not on the side of labor – he was on the side of management. His goals reflected the goals of management. However, his conflict with management occurred because they would not uphold the results of his experiments and would not pay workers. The flaw of the piecework system was that it placed the costs of inefficiency on the worker. When there was a lack of coordination between departments, workers could be waiting until they received the parts they needed. When they did not produce, they were not paid. It was also not uncommon for management to use women and men against each other when they jointly determined piecework plans. For example, in a Bridgeport plant, women would often ignore the ceiling on the day's output, often producing more when the men would. This caused serious problems. The notion of pay was also influenced by the social structures in which workers found themselves in. Young female workers would often produce enough to get paid for what their families needed and not more. The solution to this problem was to determine what the family needed and then deduct that from what was paid to the worker. Yet not all employers would make this distinction.

The relationship between Taylor and labor could be seen through the prism of the relationship between Taylorism and the leader of the most powerful union, Samuel Gompers of the American Federation of Labor. Samuel Gompers was not a radical labor leader. Gompers understood that the United States presented a different situation, as did continental Europe. So he rejected Marxian notions of radical confrontation. Rather he sought cooperation with management. Gompers hated socialism and made common cause with the conservative Republican leader Mark Hanna. He sought to create labor based on class, political, and economic power by making labor demands pragmatic and achievable. Union leaders did not want control of the means of production; they simply wanted their share of the cut. Gompers sought to make agreements with management to produce a standardization of practices across an industry. He did not seek strikes or boycotts as a solution, since they seemed to have little impact. Gompers seeking to use agreements was keeping with the mood of his times that harmony should replace disorder. Gompers also sought to maintain prerogatives for labor in that he opposed the immigration of unskilled workers (Kaufman 1973; Livesay 1978; Mandel 1963).

Yet, Gompers and Taylor were enemies instead of collaborators. Taylor regarded labor leaders as misleaders and Gompers as the greatest misleader of them all. For his part, Gompers regarded Taylorism as a hoax with the single purpose of getting workers to work as fast as possible. Gompers believed that the notion of systematic soldiering was a myth as well. He argued that a worker's reputation as a man, pride in his work, fear of losing a job, and hunger were sufficient motivators. For his part, Gompers did not understand that workers could band together and protect themselves from the incursion of management. Another issue that Gompers and other labor leaders had was that scientific management had a direct impact on skilled labor, often by deskilling jobs. The technical skills workers possessed shifted from the workers minds to the organization of the factory. Gompers opposed that workers only received a 40% increase in wages when production went up 400%. Gompers did not seek to gain all 400% of efforts, he understood that management had played a role in production increasing, but he could not understand why workers received such a small portion of the increase. Gompers also opposed Taylorism because he sought the preservation of unions, noting that among the supporters of scientific management, only Brandeis was a friend of labor. He was wrong in this regard. Morris Cooke was also a friend of labor, but he understood that scientific management could be used to attack unions (Kaufman 1973; Livesay 1978; Mandel 1963; Nadworny 1955).

However, Gompers views on the issue changed. The entrance of the United States in to the War created an even greater zeal for cooperation and unity, downplaying the need for class struggle. As Mandel noted, Gompers had little to say on how to promote cooperation, but he did have a suggestion, namely, the use of scientific management, to eliminate waste and inefficiency. The Commission on Industrial Relations held hearings on the subject in 1914. Labor leaders noted that, at the time, labor's opposition to scientific management would disappear if they were invited to cooperate. Taylor sought cooperation, but he wished cooperation between individual workers and management, not workers as a group. He did not seek to cooperate with labor as a group, largely because he believed that it would treat all workers the same. The new generation of industrial engineers, taking up scientific management after Taylor died, understood that cooperation was needed to remove obstacles. Morris Cooke and Robert G. Valentine became collaborators with Gompers during the war. Gompers even offered his support and cooperation to Taylor at the time of the Hoxie report, but Taylor refused (Kaufman 1973; Livesay 1978; Mandel 1963; Nadworny 1955).

The issue was not with Taylorism, but with Taylor himself. Many officials, including the chair of the congressional committee assigned to investigate scientific management, found Taylor to be most unreasonable. In fact, Taylor stated that he, and he alone, was the sole determiner of what was and was not scientific management. The largest issue that Taylor did not understand was that labor unions did not trust management. In some ways, Taylor fed this distrust by noting that management's decisions, in the past, had been arbitrary and unjust. Taylor believed that science would be the solution to the problem. What he could not understand, was that without union collaboration, unions would be distrustful of scientific management. Harold Livesay (1978) pointed out that Cooke and others believed that engineers would not be tempted to act in the interest of management because of the standards of the field. Robert K. Merton (1947) was not so sure about this idea. Agreements and contracts are created because there is distrust between parties about intentions and the ability to adhere to the arrangement. In a world of perfect trust, there would be no need for agreements because both parties would trust one another to carry out their promise. Taylor did not have an issue with labor unions, but he had an issue with labor unions primary function – collective bargaining (Nigro 1986). How could Taylor support unions at the same time as disagreeing with their primary function? This would be like saying that you are fine with scrambled eggs, but you dislike the egg part.

Unions defended seniority on the basis of collective agreement, revealing that they preferred negotiated contracts to legislated or discovered rules. Collective bargaining was what unions regarded as cooperation. If they were going to surrender control over work, they needed additional protection through collective bargaining. This was their version of cooperation. When Taylor stated he viewed collective bargaining as antithetical to scientific management, he was basically saying to unions that he did not believe in cooperation. No wonder they regarded him as a liar (Nigro 1986).

Taylor and Peasant Culture

Most scholars have based their research on the relationship between Taylorism and workers on traditional labor history. This approach is flawed because it ignores the fact that most workers were non-unionized, with a distinct culture that was opposed to Taylor's notions of maximizing utility. Many modern scholars believe that maximizing utility is an automatic feature of the society – when in fact, it is not. The assumption made by many was that the Protestant work ethic emphasized the value of achievement. However, as Herbert Gutman (1973) noted, the Protestant work ethic was merely one of the ethical and cultural models that existed among workers. Taylor made the same mistake himself, being unaware that economic benefit is not the sole reason why people work and, in some cases, in traditional societies, it is not a major reason. Most workers drawn into the factories maintained a belief system that was the product of a preindustrial and rural/village in orientation. Workers bring more than themselves to the workplace. They also bring their culture. This type of ethos played little emphasis on economic gain and property rights and more emphasis on cooperation and enjoyment from work (Gutman 1973; Locke 1982).

The notion that workers should work hard all week was not a commonly held viewpoint. In fact, in times of celebration (such as a wedding), workers would take many days off. As E.P. Thompson (1963) noted, the workplace was a combination of intense labor and bouts of idleness. The common picture was that workers did not take breaks until scientific management. This could be further from the truth. Montgomery notes that idle time could be up to 70% of the work experience. From this perspective, rather than providing breaks, scientific management actually made the workers work more! Employers were aware of these issues and often did not demand a full day's work. The notion of specialization created anxiety among workers. They even opposed specialization when it brought higher pay, preferring the variety that came from work. Other workers were driven by wages with a lack of care for safety. They wanted higher wages because the sooner they were paid, the quicker they could go back to their homeland, even if the conditions were unsafe. Their conflict with Taylorism was that they were not paid enough. Daniel Nelson (1980) noted that Taylorism provided a better deal than did the previous way of working, but David Montgomery (1987) also noted that Nelson and others ignore the heavy price of industrialization.

It took a long period of time for workers to establish a class consciousness. There is no reason to expect, as demonstrated by studies, that workers would automatically desire higher wages. In fact, economic desires are often a self-fulfilling prophecy. Gutman (1973, p. 541) noted "that American working class was continually altered in its composition by infusions, from within and without the nation, of peasants, farmers, skilled artisans, and casual day laborers who brought into industrial society ways of work and other habits and values not associated with industrial necessities and the industrial ethos." In fact, it was not until the 1930s, when popular culture emerged, that a consistent set of values came to the working class, creating a common class consciousness when all we had before was a mass of competing ethnic groups. One of the reasons why industrial/organizational psychology became a major field was to make the workers able to function in a factory setting. The Second War would speed this process up. Once it did, the roots of scientific management were able to take hold thanks to the collaboration between management and labor.

One of the reasons why union leaders wished to collectively bargain was to ensure that workers did not suffer from arbitrary treatment (Gutman 1973). Both unionized and non-unionized workers determined where to set production levels. They often found pride in their work. The craftsmen included positions (such as mule spinner, brick layers, iron workers, boil makers, and miners) that were often considered to be simple jobs manned by the most unskilled of workers. It is important to note that often labor had to struggle to keep pace with management. Their control over work was by no means assured. Compounding this problem was that the face of the factory changed as more and more immigrants brought with them new attitudes and values that were often in opposition to management. Workers often stated manly virtues, which featured dignity, egalitarianism, responsibility values, as a means of demanding respect and often glared back at the boss. Some workers would not work if they were being observed. Doing more at work was considered hoggish and at the expense of their brothers. Work control was based upon technical, as well as ethical, aspects of work. Taylorism threatened both. Union rules codified these basic workplace values. As time moved on, strikes became less about wages and more about enforcing unions rules and recognition.

Taylor's movement was not just a push to standardize work – it was also a response to uproot the practices that had protected labor. The movement also sought to discredit labor practices and, by extension, workers knowledge. Taylor stated that even the best mechanic could not understand what scientific management was. Taylor's comments about soldiering on were a shot against worker culture. His statement about the "first-class man" would have sounded, to the worker, like someone who was attempting to better himself at the expense of his brothers. This attitude would have been more acceptable to craftsmen, but less acceptable to the majority of workers (Gutman 1973).

In his testimony to congress, Taylor boasted that scientific management would eliminate the vast amount of knowledge and experience from workers. Many workers were against Taylorism because they would lose prestige and importance. Often times, workers were required to work more under scientific management due to the glut of workers. Taylor's belief that he could discern the laws of work was an act of hubris. When hubris is present, its sibling, nemesis, is soon to follow. One of the aspects of rationalization is attempting to gain the consent of others in the system. Failure to do so will create more conflict. Taylor's inability to see this issue helped to create conflict between labor and management, where none had to be. The problem, as Bruce Kaufman noted, was not that scientific management was not sound in theory, but its implementation was flawed. It was flawed because managers could be opportunists, a fact that labor well understood. Labor unions wanted a voice to negotiate arrangements, something that scientific management did not allow. Management also disliked the intrusion of experts onto their prerogative. Industrial and human relations were not just a correction of the old laissez-faire system but also engineered designed management. Taylor's defenders argue, with considerable justification that not all jobs would be specialized. What Taylor intended was to match worker's abilities to the job – unskilled workers would do unskilled jobs and skilled workers, skilled jobs. Yet the general lack of distrust on the part of labor caused them to misunderstand Taylor's point. Taylor himself did not help this problem by referring to workers as apes and cows (Gutman 1973; Nigro 1986).

Conclusion: Flawed Giant

Frederick Winslow Taylor was an idealistic empiricist. The contradiction between these two ideas was reconciled during the Progressive Era, but not in Taylor's mind. Despite his obvious intelligence, experience, and education, or because of, Taylor was unable to remove himself from the plant floor, unable to see the clay feet of scientists. He remained more concerned with worker opportunism than he did management, believing that management's problem was based on knowledge. Taylorism was based on a major assumption, one that remained from the old industrial order that workers (and management) pursue self-interest and attempt to maximize prosperity. This assumption is untrue – even people at the time understood that both parties can fail to cooperate, even when it was in their best interest. As we have seen from the work of both Gutman and Montgomery, there was a vast gulf between Taylor and immigrant workers. The ease at which they settled into the factory system versus the difficultly they had settling into Taylorism suggests that the fault lay with Taylorism. It has been repeated both in the United States, Great Britain, and elsewhere, that Taylorism and the worker culture had an enormous gulf, one that Taylor was unwilling and unable to bridge due to his idealistic nature (Whitston 1997).

As Bendix and others pointed out, the scientific management movement dovetailed with the open shop movement to undermine the nascent union movement. Both combined to change the image and working conditions of both labor and management. Bendix (1956) noted that scientific management encountered problems from both labor and management. The principle problem was that employers could take or leave scientific management as they saw fit. Despite the attempts of Taylor to control his innovation, other adapters were free to use it as they saw fit. Accordingly, this freedom could be potentially abused by various employers. Labor had to resort to either clandestine resistance or use the political realm. Management attacked labor because labor attacked the celebrated myth of good judgment and the superior ability of management. Labor attacked management for the simple reason that management invaded the work zone and made it appear that there was little in the way of actual cooperation. It is highly doubtful that a modern consultant would be able to have as much leeway as Taylor desired. Nor could Taylor control his intellectual property rights due to the ability of corporations to reverse engineer scientific management. With little safeguards on management, as well as the erosion of previous safeguards, unions could find themselves at the mercy of management. If stripped of their ability to collectively bargain, they would be at the mercy of owners. Therefore, under pure Taylorism, there was little incentive for workers to adopt scientific management (Kreis 1995). As Kipping (1997) noted, scientific management was popularized due to its spread by the government, which workers had trust in.

Scholars blame the failure of labor to understand the process. In truth, the mistake was on the part of managers and later scholars to understand peasant work culture. A great part of the research involving worker resistance has come to focus on union resistance to scientific management, ignoring the fact that most workers were not unionized. Nor did they understand the vast conflict between Taylor's rationalism and the peasant work culture. When people go on benders for days at a time, how could pay be the most important motivator? This idea of maximizing utility, a common mind-set in our time, did not exist for all time. It was, as Daniel Bell (1956) argues, the result of management thinkers rationalizing the work place, as they did with other aspects of life. Scientific management eliminated the peasant work culture. Several examples of the New Labor History in this paper illustrate this issue.

Yet, despite his lack of understanding of peasant culture, Taylor was a progressive and a modernizer. Because of Taylor's pioneering work, the working class became middle class – with property, ownership, and consumerism becoming common behaviors. Bruce and Nyland's notable contribution is to place Taylorism within the larger progressive and liberal atmosphere of thought. It was not clear to many that

Taylor would be listed as a progressive. Many of the classic works on progressivism do not list Taylor or scientific management as a notable contribution despite Taylorism's clear response to addressing social concerns through the presence of a scientifically trained middle class. Scientific management is often forgotten in most approaches of the progressive age. Neither historians nor most social scientists consider scientific management an important subject – since it was perceived as not being related to politics or social uplift, only to the base pursuit of profit. Where scholars have followed scientific management, they have done so up to the end of the progressive age. Samuel Haber (1964), for instance, assumes that scientific management ended with the progressive era after the World War. He was correct in a way; scientific management became simply management (Merkle 1980; Tipple 1970). Management scholars are aware of the benefits of scientific management and this could explain why management holds Taylor is such high esteem whereas other fields do not.

Sadly, Taylor's system failed to discover any hard and fast truths. Taylor made two assumptions. Firstly, scientific laws could be found at work. Despite a century of workplace studies, predictions remain poor as to the practical benefits of research. If this is the case, his failure to understand worker protection becomes all the worse. The lack of collective bargaining limited the appeal of his program. Taylor did not recognize, at least at the time of his death, the value of collective bargaining and unionization as a means of rationalization. Secondly, he also failed to understand that what he valued and what the worker valued were different things. Taylor's assumption that workers were utilitarian was a false one. What Taylor failed to recognize was that many times what appears to be science was merely a set unchecked assumption. Like many social scientists, Taylor believed that he had scientifically created a set of laws, but he merely was a prisoner of his own heuristics (Kreis 1995).

Cross-references

▶ Organizational Psychology and the Rise of Human Resource Management

References

Aldrich M (2010) On the track of efficiency: scientific management comes to railroad shops, 1900–1930. Bus Hist Rev 84(3):501–526
Banta M (1993) Taylored lives. University of Chicago Press, Chicago
Bedeian AG, Wren DA (2001) Most influential management books of the 20th century. Organ Dyn 29(3):221–225
Bell D (1956) Work and its discontents. Beacon Press, Boston
Bendix R (1956) Work and authority in industry: ideologies of management in the course of industrialization. Wiley, New York
Bendix R, Fisher LH (1949) The perspectives of Elton Mayo. Rev Econ Stat 31(4):312–319
Boddewyn J (1961) Frederick Winslow Taylor revisited. J Acad Manag 4(2):100
Bruce K, Nyland C (2001) Scientific management, institutionalism, and business stabilization: 1903–1923. J Econ Issues 35(4):955–978

Bruce K, Nyland C (2011) Elton Mayo and the deification of human relations. Organ Stud 32(3):383–405

Burnham J (1941) The managerial revolution: what is happening in the world. John Day Company, New York

Burt RS (2004) Structural holes and good ideas. Am J Sociol 110(2):349–399

Claeys G (1987) Machinery, money and the millennium: from moral economy to socialism 1815–1860. Princeton University Press, Princeton

Claeys G (1989) Citizens and saints. Politics and anti-politics in early British socialism. Cambridge University Press, New York

Cooper WH (1962) The comparative administrative philosophies of Frederick W. Taylor and Elton Mayo. Unpublished doctoral dissertation, University of Pennsylvania

Cooper JM (1983) The warrior and the priest: Woodrow Wilson and Theodore Roosevelt. Belknap, Cambridge

Copley FB (1923) Frederick W. Taylor, father of scientific management. Harper & Brothers Publishers, New York

Dean CC (1997a) The principles of scientific management by Fred Taylor: exposures in print beyond the private printing. J Manag Hist 3(1):4–17

Dean CC (1997b) Primer of scientific management by Frank B. Gilbreth: a response to publication of Taylor's principles in the American magazine. J Manag Hist 3(1):31–41

Diggins JP (1978) The bard of savagery: Thorstein Veblen and modern social theory. Seabury Press, New York

Diggins JP (1996) Max Weber: politics and the spirit of tragedy. Basic Books, New York

Drucker P (1954) The practice of management. Harper & Brothers Publishers, New York

Elwitt S (1988) Social science, social reform and sociology. Past Present 121:209–214

Etz DV (1964) Han Fei Tzu: management pioneer. Public Adm Rev 24(1):36–38

Filene PG (1970) An obituary for "the progressive movement". Am Q 22(1):20–34

Gabor A (2000) The capitalist philosophers. Times Business, New York

Gutman HG (1973) Work, culture, and society in industrializing America, 1815–1919. Am Hist Rev 78(3):531–588

Haber S (1964) Efficiency and uplift: scientific management in the Progressive Era, 1890–1920. University of Chicago Press, Chicago

Haber S (1991) The quest for authority and honor in the American professions, 1750–1900. University of Chicago Press, Chicago

Hargadon A (2003) How breakthroughs happen: the surprising truth about how companies innovate. Harvard University Press, Cambridge, MA

Heames JT, Breland JW (2010) Management pioneer contributors: 30-year review. J Manag Hist 16(4):427–436

Hoopes J (2003) False prophets: the gurus who created modern management and why their ideas are bad for business today. Basic Books, New York

Hough JR, White MA (2001) Using stories to create change: the object lesson of Frederick Taylor's "pig-tale". J Manag 27(5):585–601

Kanigel R (1997) The one best way: Frederick Winslow Taylor and the enigma of efficiency. Little, Brown and Company, London

Katz MB (1996) In the shadow of the poorhouse: a social history of welfare in America, 2nd edn. Basic Books, New York

Kaufman SB (1973) Samuel Gompers and the origins of the American Federation of Labor. Greenwood Press, West Port

Keller M (1992) Regulating a new economy: public policy and economic change in America, 1900–1933. Harvard University Press, Cambridge MA

Keller M (1998) Regulating a new society: public policy and social change in America, 1900–1933. Harvard University Press, Cambridge, MA

Kipping M (1997) Consultancies, institutions and the diffusion of Taylorism in Britain, Germany and France, 1920s to 1950s. Bus Hist 39(4):67–83

Klaw S (1979) Frederick Winslow Taylor: the messiah of time and motion. Am Herit 30(5): 26–39

Kloppenberg JT (1986) Uncertain victory: social democracy and progressivism in European and American thought, 1870–1920. Oxford University Press, New York

Knowles WH (1952) Economics of industrial engineering. Ind Labor Relat Rev 5(2):209–220

Kolko G (1963) The triumph of conservatism: a reinterpretation of American history, 1900–1916. The Free Press, New York

Kraines O (1960) Brandeis' philosophy of scientific management. West Polit Q 13(1):191–201

Kreis S (1995) Early experiments in British scientific management: the health of Munitions Workers' Committee, 1915–1920. J Manag Hist 1(2):65–78

Larson MS (1979) The rise of professionalism. University of California Press, Berkeley

Lauer Schachter H (2016) Frederick Winslow Taylor, Henry Hallowell Farquhar, and the dilemma of relating management education to organizational practice. J Manag Hist 22(2):199–213

Lears J (1997) Man the machine. New Repub 217(9):25–32

Livesay HC (1978) Samuel Gompers and organized labor in America. Little, Brown and Company, Boston

Locke EA (1982) The ideas of Frederick W. Taylor: an evaluation. Acad Manag Rev 7(1):14–24

Mandel B (1963) Samuel Gompers: a biography. Penguin Group, New York

Martin A (1971) Enterprise denied: the origins of the decline of American railroads, 1897–1917. Columbia University Press, New York

McCormick RL (1981) The discovery that business corrupts politics: a reappraisal of the origins of progressivism. Am Hist Rev 86(2):247–274

McGerr M (2003) A fierce discontent: the rise and fall of the progressive movement in America, 1870–1920. Oxford University Press

Merkle JA (1980) Management and ideology: the legacy of the international scientific management movement. University of California Press, Berkeley

Merton RK (1947) The machine, the worker, and the engineer. Science 105(2717):79–84

Montgomery D (1979) Worker's control in America. Cambridge University Press, New York

Montgomery D (1987) The fall of the house of labor: the workplace, the state, and American labor activism, 1865–1925. Press Syndicate of the University of Cambridge, New York

Muldoon J (2017) The Hawthorne studies: an analysis of critical perspectives 1936–1958. J Manag Hist 23(1):74–94

Nadworny M (1955) Scientific management and the unions 1900–1932: a historical analysis. Harvard University Press, Cambridge, MA

Nelson D (1980) Frederick W. Taylor and the rise of scientific management. University of Wisconsin Press, Madison

Nigro LG (1986) Scientific management: seniority and productivity in the public sector. Public Productivity Rev 10(1):73–80

Nyland C (1995) Taylorism and hours of work. J Manag Hist 1:8–25

Nyland C (1998) Taylorism and the mutual gains strategy. Ind Relat 37:519–542

Nyland C (2000) A contemporary account of scientific management as applied to women's work with a comment by Frederick W. Taylor. J Manag His 6:248–271

Parker LD, Ritson P (2005) Fads, stereotypes and management gurus: Fayol and Follett today. Manag Decis 43(10):1335–1357

Payne SC, Youngcourt SS, Watrous KM (2006) Portrayals of FW Taylor across textbooks. J Manag Hist 12(4):385–407

Rodgers DT (1998) Atlantic crossings: social politics in a progressive age. Harvard University Press, Cambridge, MA

Rogers EM (1962) Diffusion of innovations, 1st edn. Free Press of Glencoe, New York

Schlesinger AMJ (2000) A life in the twentieth century. Houghton Mifflin, Boston

Schwarz C (2015) A review of management history from 2010–2014 utilizing a thematic analysis approach. J Manag Hist 21(4):494–504

Searle GR (1971) The quest for national efficiency: a study in British politics and political thought, 1899–1914. Basil Blackwell, Oxford

Simha A, Lemak DJ (2010) The value of original source readings in management education: the case of Frederick Winslow Taylor. J Manag Hist 16(2):233–252

Stewart M (2009) The management myth: debunking the modern philosophy of business. Norton, New York

Suchman MC (1995) Managing legitimacy: strategic and institutional approaches. Acad Manag Rev 20(3):571–610

Taneja S, Pryor MG, Toombs LA (2011) Frederick W. Taylor's scientific management principles: relevance and validity. J Appl Manag Entrep 16(3):60

Tarr GA (2001) Laboratories of democracy? Brandeis, federalism, and scientific management. Publius 31(1):37–46

Taylor FW (1947) Scientific management (comprising shop management, the principles of scientific management, and testimony before the special house committee). Harper & Brothers Publishers, New York

Taylor SG, Bedeian AG (2008) The Fred Taylor baseball myth: a son goes to bat for his father. J Manag Hist 14(3):294–298

Thomas JM (1993) Figures of habit in William James. N Engl Q 66(1):3–26

Thompson EP (1963) The making of the English working class. Victor Gollancz, London

Tipple J (1970) The capitalist revolution: a history of American social thought. Pegasus, New York

Turner SP, Turner JH (1990) The impossible science: an institutional analysis of American sociology. SAGE library of social research. SAGE, Newbury Park

Urofsky MI (1971) A mind of one piece: Brandeis and American reform. Scribner, New York

Wagner-Tsukamoto S (2007) An institutional economic reconstruction of scientific management: on the lost theoretical logic of Taylorism. Acad Manag Rev 32(1):105–117

Wagner-Tsukamoto S (2008) Scientific management revisited: did Taylorism fail because of a too positive image of human nature? J Manag Hist 14(4):348–372

Whitston K (1997) Worker resistance and Taylorism in Britain. Int Rev Soc Hist 42(1):1–24

Wiebe R (1967) The search for order, 1877–1920. Macmillian, New York

Wilkinson NB, du Pont L (1965) In anticipation of Frederick W. Taylor: a study of work by Lammot du Pont, 1872. Technol Cult 6(2):208–221

Wrege CD, Greenwood RG (1991) Frederick W. Taylor, the father of scientific management: myth and reality. Irwin Professional Pub, New York

Wrege CD, Perroni AG (1974) Taylor's pig-tale: a historical analysis of Frederick W. Taylor's pig-iron experiments. Acad Manag J 17(1):6–27

Wrege CD, Stotka AM (1978) Cooke creates a classic: the story behind F. W. Taylor's principles of scientific management. Acad Manag Rev 3:736–749

Wren DA (2005) The history of management thought, 5th edn. Wiley, New York

Wren DA, Hay RD (1977) Management historians and business historians: differing perceptions of pioneer contributions. Acad Manag J 20(3):470–476

Wren DA, Bedeian AG (2018) The evolution of management thought, 7th edn. Wiley, New York: John Wiley & Sons

Henry Ford and His Legacy: An American Prometheus

22

Jeffrey Muldoon

Contents

Biography 523
Jacksonian Viewpoint and Ideology 526
Management Thought and Contributions 528
Five-Dollar Day 528
Sociological Department and Savings Plan 530
African American Employees 530
Unions and Politics 531
Relationship with Taylorism 532
Corporate Governance 535
Management Talent 536
Limitations 536
Conclusion 541
Cross-References 542
References 542

Abstract

The purpose of this chapter is to discuss the complicated life and history of Henry Ford. While Ford was an engineering genius, his ignorance of politics, incomplete management philosophy and drive to be independent nearly destroyed his legacy. His life, career, management style, relationships with Alfred Sloan and Taylorism are discussed.

Keywords

Henry Ford · Fordism · Alfred Sloan

J. Muldoon (✉)
Emporia State University, Emporia, KS, USA
e-mail: jmuldoon@emporia.edu

© The Author(s), under exclusive licence to Springer Nature Switzerland AG 2020   521
B. Bowden et al. (eds.), *The Palgrave Handbook of Management History*,
https://doi.org/10.1007/978-3-319-62114-2_28

Many figures in management history are shrouded by paradox. This theme is most true of Henry Ford: hero and villain, visionary and reactionary, defender and scourge of the worker, genius engineer and inept manager, the anti-Semite whose factories helped to destroy Nazi Germany, a deep internationalist whose rhetoric provided support for isolationism, and a pacifist who was a war profiteer. Ford was the richest man on earth whose corporation did not turn a profit for 15 years. Ford proved the statement that if you live long enough, you will become a villain. Had Ford died in 1918, soon after his Senate defeat, he would have been seen as a prophet and a martyr (Lewis 1976). Yet he lived on, facing a world that no longer supported him and one that he did not support. That Ford remained a hero is a testimony of his previous greatness and his ability at public relations (Watts 2005). Despite his faults, Ford is still considered the greatest business leader in history (McCormick and Folsom 2003).

Ford continues to cast a deep shadow on business practices. Even more than Frederick Winslow Taylor, Ford was the creator of the modern world. David Halberstam (1979) wrote, "yet, though he shared the principles, yearnings, and prejudices of his countrymen, he vastly altered their world. What he wrought reconstituted the nature of work and began a profound change in the relationship of man to his job." Ford left such a deep impression that Aldous Huxley's classic work, *Brave New World*, has divided the world into Pre-Ford and After-Ford history. Ford was both a genius and an ignoramus. His vision gave birth to the modern world, continuing the transportation revolution of the nineteenth century into a complete transformation of the modern world. Yet despite his genius, Ford was completely ignorant and unsure of how the United States became a nation. However, Ford also had a deep respect for history. He may not have known who murdered President Lincoln in Ford's theater, but he certainly would have owned and persevered the theater box for future generations (Lacey 1986).

That Ford should be included in a book about management thinkers is something of an irony as, according to Peter Drucker (1954), Ford sought to eliminate the need for management. Once again, this irony is apropos. Ford's life was a combination of triumph and tragedy caused by the inherent paradox of his own values. Although Ford is seen by most as a man of the future, leading the world into the modern industrial era, he remained, at the same time, someone who yearned for the small-town, agrarian simplicity that the advent of cars ended. If we are to place this paradox in terms of American tradition, we would state that Ford had elements of the Whig and Jacksonian traditions in his intellectual prevue. The Whig tradition, as exemplified by such luminaries as Presidents John Quincy Adams and Abraham Lincoln, stressed knowledge, science, and technological development. Its emphasis was on the future (Howe 2007). The Jacksonian tradition (named after President Andrew Jackson) focused on self-reliance and independence as its primary focus (Meyers 1957).

The son of a farmer and an advocate for rural America, Ford found himself very much in the Jacksonian tradition of self-reliance and independence (Kline and Pinch 1996). Much of Ford's program stressed above-market wages, shorter working days, consumerism, to design cheaper products, both from an economic and ideological perspective, and to provide workers with independence (Lacey 1986). Ford's desire to maintain independence – whether from investors, managers, banks, or the federal government – was the hallmark of his management thought and actions (Nye 1979). Despite his fabulous wealth, Ford remained the son of a farmer (Gelderman 1981).

Ford attempted, in vain, to save rural America (Wik 1962, 1964). However, his own efforts furthered its destruction as Ford's strategy led to the growth of the suburb. Ford also was a Whig; although the son of a farmer, he was trained as a mechanical engineer, one of the positions that made the new world possible (Howe 2007). Whigs stressed technological and transportation improvements to unite the country to ensure the proper development of society. They stressed hierarchy and moral improvement of society. Even some of the odious elements of his paternalism, such as his dislike for alcohol and his monitoring and education of employees, have its roots in the nineteenth century. Robert Owen would have found much to admire in his actions. The Whigs strived for economic consolidation, trade, and, unlike Jacksonians, did not fear integration or large wealth. Like Ford, the Whigs were great believers in technological advancement. The Whigs also stood for order and rationalization of processes (Howe 2007). Such processes meant centralization of authority and power. Ford was not a small businessman; he owned one of the largest companies on Earth. Yet he ran his corporation the way you would run a small business where cronyism, owner whims, and paternalism dominate (Jardim 1970). His actions were often indicative of one who wished to maintain control over his company – something that becomes more difficult with increased size and the stakeholders that follow that size. As McCraw and Tedlow (1997) noted, this tension created a great and unresolved paradox in Ford's mind and actions.

The purpose of this chapter is to examine the career, life, and context of Henry Ford to understand his contribution to management thought. The first part of the chapter goes through Ford's background, the foundation of Ford, its epic growth, and the idealistic ignorance of Ford. The second part focuses on Ford's management philosophy, the sociology department, wage policy, and Ford's relationship with scientific management. The third part of the chapter focuses on the sad decline of Ford and the Ford Motor Company, with special emphasis on his anti-management philosophy and his competition with Alfred Sloan and General Motors.

Biography

Henry Ford was born in 1863 to an Irish-born farmer named William Ford, whose family had fled Ireland to escape from the potato famine of 1846–1848. Ford immigrated to America in the belief that he would be able to find work and own property – noting that in America, you were an owner and not a renter (Halberstam 1979). William Ford had natural ability as a carpenter, making enough money through work and saving to buy a farm. Despite his son's numerous accomplishments – and the immeasurable wealth that he would one day collect – Henry would remain, in his heart (like William), an agrarian – believing in the simple world of the small town. Like many agrarians, Henry Ford disliked banks, believing that it was idle money (Lacey 1986). Once, when one of the children of his friend boasted about his savings, Ford responded he would have been better off purchasing tools and making something. Ford maintained this attitude all of his life, focusing on creation, work, and thrift, rather than leisure – the man who made the modern world remained hopelessly stuck on the virtues of the nineteenth century (Gelderman 1981).

Yet despite his love of the country, Ford hated farming, initially disappointing his father, who wanted his son to take over the farm (Nevins and Hill 1954). Ford also hated school, believing that learning was not an end in and of itself, but rather believed that learning should be hands on and technical. He despaired learning about moral lessons from the school reader, even if he would deploy these lessons later in his life and in the lives of his workers. This gap in his education continued as he got older, explaining why he was an ignoramus on a wide variety of issues and facts. Ford's true love and talent was for machines, for which he showed both a true aptitude and passion. Ford could take a machine, separate the parts, put it together, and make it run better. In just his early teens, he built a machine that allowed his father to open the gate to the farm without leaving his wagon and demonstrated that he had a natural ability as a watch repairman. At 17, Ford left the farm, walking half a day to Detroit – a journey that changed the world.

Detroit was just then becoming a major industrial city, featuring 10 railroads, machinist shops, and foundries. It was an ideal spot for a talented, hard-working mechanic. Indeed, the country was going through the industrial revolution, and there were plenty of opportunities for the talented. Ford soon found work at James Flower & Brothers and then later the Detroit Dry Dock, where he secured work as a machinist (Brinkley 2003a, b). He also worked at the McGill Jewelry Store, cleaning and repairing watches. It was there that he had his first idea about making a watch so cheap that everyone could purchase one. While the technical aspects appealed to him, marketing the watches did not. Ford's disinterest in understanding markets would later haunt him in the future. While Ford had been trained as a mechanic, the only business training, practical or otherwise, was his learning about basic bookkeeping.

His father wanted Ford to return to the farm, and so he did, getting 80 acres from his father. His time on the farm convinced him that his passion and future was for machines (Lacey 1986). He attempted to build a steam-powered tractor, but he recognized that future lay with the internal-combustion engine, and so he sought to build a "horse-less carriage." First, he felt that he needed more training in electricity, so he got a job Detroit Edison. Soon he built his first car and sold it for $200. He soon convinced William Murphy, a lumber merchant, to start his first company, Detroit Automobile Company. The company was successful, but the investors did not share his enthusiasm for building a car that the working class could use. So in 1900, the company was dissolved. In 1903, Ford started a new company that still bears his name today (Nevins and Hill 1954).

Ford needed capital to start the company, so he began to sell stock in his enterprise to investors. Despite the initial early success of the company, his investors doubted the over strategy of the company, in particular Alexander Malcomson. According to David Halberstam (1979):

Malcomson, like Ford's prior backers, argued that fancy cars costing $2,275 to $4,775 were what would sell. At the time, nearly half the cars being sold in America fell into this category; a decade later, largely because of Ford, those cars would represent only 2 percent of the market. Malcomson wanted a car for the rich; Ford, one for the multitude. Though the early models were successful—the company sold an amazing total of 1,700 cars in its first 15 months—it was the coming of the Model T in 1908 that sent Ford's career rocketing. It was the car that Henry Ford had always wanted to build because it was the car that he had always wanted to drive—simple, durable, absolutely without frills, one that the farmer could use and, more important, afford. He was an agrarian populist, and his own people were farmers, simple people; if he could make their lives easier, it would give him pleasure. He planned to have a car whose engine was detachable so the farmer could also use it to saw wood, pump water, and run farm machinery.

The investors made vast fortunes. James Couzens, future US Senator, invested $2400 and, when he sold his shares back to Ford in 1919, received $29 million (Lacey 1986).

The Model T was, arguably, the most successful product ever released (Brinkley 2003a, b). More than 15 million were launched from 1908 until 1927. The shutdown of the Model T was considered a watershed moment in automobile history. In fact, Brinkley (2003a, b) selected the car as the most important automobile of the twentieth century. It was designed to handle country and dirt roads better than cars that were more expensive. It was tough, durable, reliable, inexpensive, and painted black. Ford selected the color black not because he liked the color per se but because black paint dried quicker than other colors (Drucker 1954; McCraw and Tedlow 1997). Nor was it, contrary to popular mythology, the only color the car ever came in, as the universal application of black paint was not implemented until 1914. Previously, buyers of the Model T had the option of gray, green, blue, and red.

Once Ford had created the general model, he started on the process of making the cars cheaper and quicker to produce than anything else in the automobile industry (Brinkley 2003a, b). To do so, he hired the best efficiency experts, moved the location of his plant, and based on the suggestion of Walter Flanders, moved production into an assembly line – with the sole purpose of increasing production to staggering amounts (Halberstam 1979). Before the development of the assembly line, it had taken roughly 13 h to produce a chassis. After the development of the assembly line, it would take about five and a half hours to produce a chassis. By 1914, after Ford had added a conveyor belt to move items along the line – giving the "assembly line" its classic image – the time it took for a chassis to be produced was reduced even further, to only 93 min (Batchelor 1994).

Given the reductions in production time, the number of Model Ts produced went from 13,840 in 1909 to 260,720 in 1913, and finally to 2 million in 1925. When the Model T was first produced, the company's cash balance was $2 million; when it ended, it was $673 million. Ford outproduced the rest of the automobile industry. As Halberstam (1979) wrote:

In 1913 the Ford Motor Company, with 13,000 employees, produced 260,720 cars; the other 299 American auto companies, with 66,350 employees, produced only 286,770. Cutting his price as his production soared, he saw his share of the market surge—9.4 percent in 1908,

20.3 in 1911, 39.6 in 1913, and with the full benefits of his mechanization, 48 percent in 1914.

Ford Motor Company was, to use an entrepreneurship term, a gazelle, one of the rare companies that can experience growth rates that exponential (Wren and Greenwood 1998).

Ford selected to use what later came to be known as Porter's generic strategy of cost leadership (Porter 1980). The development of the assembly line system and the specialization of labor and coordination of business activities meant that Ford could produce the least expensive car and a durable one at that. The fact that Ford was able to produce such a good car, one that fit the roads at the time, was another source of competitive advantage. Other companies could not compete. Ford also recognized that he gained market share by slashing prices on his cars. In 1909, the average profit was $220.11; in 1913, the average profit was $99.34. Ford recognized that if he reduced prices, the more he could sell. The price of the Model T went from $780 in 1909 to $350 in 1914, and at that price, Ford sold 730,041 cars (Nevins and Hill 1954). Ford was aided by the discovery of oil in Spindletop, Texas (Halberstam 1979). The net result was that the price of gasoline was drastically reduced, making the internal-combustion engine utilized by the automobile even cheaper to use. Ford also benefited from being in the United States where the vastness of the national territory had long created problems with regard to internal population movement. By contrast, automobile production in Great Britain was initially curtailed by the so-called the red flag law, whereby under the *Locomotive Act 1865* internally powered vehicles were required to have a crew of three, one of whom carried a red flag to warn other road users; a law that was not repealed until 1896 (McCraw and Tedlow 1997).

Jacksonian Viewpoint and Ideology

The Jacksonian movement was a vast political and social movement led by President Andrew Jackson (President, 1829–1837) as a response to the growing market and transportation revolution then occurring in the United States. Like other political movements, there were various debates among those who considered themselves to be Jacksonians (Sellers 1991). Nevertheless, there was overlap among those who identified with the Jacksonian ideology. According to Marvin Meyers (1957: pg. 6),

> Jacksonian spokesmen drew upon an exhaustive repertory of the moral plots which might engage the political attention of nineteenth-century Americans: equality against privilege, liberty against domination; honest work against idle exploit; natural dignity against factitious superiority; patriotic conservatism against alien innovation; progress against dead precedent.

Above all, Jacksonians disliked institutions, such as banks, that prevented them from exercising their freedom to pursue their own interests while avoiding complex legal and economic arrangements. They preferred producers to bankers, social arrangements to public arrangements, and sought to make democratic that which had been the domain of the wealthy. They sought the American dream on individualistic terms (Feller 1995).

Many believed Jackson to be a tyrant (Howe 2007). So a second political party formed as a response to Jackson, called the Whigs, named after the British political party. Like the Jacksonians, the Whigs had a futuristic mindset and vision of American Greatness. Unlike the Jacksonians, the Whigs stressed modernity, the development of social and economic arrangements that would allow for unity in the national political life. For example, the Whigs stressed the development of a strong banking and transportation system as a means of producing higher degrees of growth throughout the nation. In addition, they sought an education system that would train a professional class. In some ways, as Robert Wiebe (1967) noted, the progressive era was, in part, driven by Whig notions of rationalization, unity, and order becoming the standard. Big business would now be regulated by the government; its executives would be professionally trained; ownership and management would be separate.

Ford was an admirer of Jackson, even visiting Jackson's home, the Hermitage (Nye 1979). Much like Jackson, Ford hated unearned profits and investments. Rather Ford sought to invest his profits back into his business and reduce the costs of his cars. Much like Jackson, he believed that once laws and economic relations were established, economics should be left in private hands rather than entrusted to the government (Nye 1979). Ford sought an enlightened industrial leadership, largely a political one dedicated to "spreading the benefits of production." Ford hated both capitalism and socialism, since it placed nonproducers in charge of the economy. He hoped that his system would provide the benefits of both capitalism and socialism through the enlightened administrative elite (Nye 1979). Although Ford hated welfare, the Ford Motor Company's Sociology Department (established in 1913) provided a broad range of welfare benefits, causing Ford to be regarded by many as the founding father of welfare capitalism (Brandes 1976).

Yet there was a vast contradiction between Ford's dreams and his overall goals. Namely, that Jacksonians would have viewed Ford's corporation with a degree of suspicion due to its size. Progressive era thinkers, such as Woodrow Wilson and Louis Brandeis, feared the accumulation of capital, especially its threat to politics, and sought to break up large corporations (Cooper 1983). Others, such as Theodore Roosevelt, sought to regulate monopoly. The United States shifted toward Roosevelt's view. No longer did business have a free hand; increasingly the business executive would have to work under government regulation (Cooper 1983). Ford's transportation revolution played a similar role in that it allowed for greater connectivity. Rather than a series of loosely connected regions, better transportation connected the country, making bureaucracy possible (Wiebe 1967). Finally, Ford's desire for an administrative elite would have meant increased education and training. Each of these elements would have encouraged greater rationalization. Ford sought solutions to a world that no longer existed. The United States had become a rationalized country where managers, rather than entrepreneurs, were the guiding light – a framework that would last until the 1970s (Patterson 1997).

Management Thought and Contributions

Ford's contribution to management thought was transforming workers into consumers, as Nye (1979) states, "sustaining prosperity between capital and labor." Ford's contribution to management was severalfold. The first and most important contribution is found in his establishment system that came to be known as "Fordism," and which was characterized by cheap, mass-produced goods and labor forces sufficiently well-paid to afford the fruits of their labor. Fordism had three distinct elements to it. Firstly, products needed to be standardized – made by a combination of machine and unskilled labor. Secondly, the assembly line would feature unskilled workers working in specialized jobs. The assembly line was, mostly notably, the most impressive feature of Ford's genius. The historian Douglas Brinkley (2003a, b) argued that Ford was a more notable contributor than Taylor since the assembly line made efficiency practical rather than theoretical. Taylor's biographer, Robert Kanigel (1997), agrees arguing that Taylor would have been incapable of producing such a process. Thirdly, the employees would be paid a living wage with the idea that they should purchase from the corporation. Ford's fourth contribution to management was the development of the sociology department to aid in the Americanization and training of workers. Ford's fifth contribution was the development of welfare capitalism (Brandes 1976).

Five-Dollar Day

The "Five-dollar day" was perhaps the most distinguishing feature of Ford's managerial contribution (Meyer 1981). It is also still referred to as a distinct contribution by the Ford Motor Company. The Five-dollar day is usually mentioned by Ford's defenders when his attitudes toward labor are mentioned. The Five-dollar day is one of the most discussed and analyzed events in business history (Nevins and Hill 1957). The reason was that the Five-dollar day greatly raised wages for the employees – the great majority of employees had only been making $2.34 a day. There are numerous arguments for why Ford raised wages. Nevins and Hill (1954) view this as an idealistic step on the part of a man trying to do the right thing for workers. Meyer (1981) views it as a form of social control to block attempts of collective action on the part of the worker. Lacey (1986) views it as an attempt to purchase the good faith of workers to overcome their turnover concerns. In addition, it could be seen as an attempt to make investors happy, who were growing concerned over issues related to turnover, which was rampant. Nye viewed it as an attempt by Ford to destroy socialism by promoting a more egalitarian form of capitalism. Ford claimed it was part of a process in which he gained improved marketing. Raff and Summers (1987), two economists, note that marketing was a potential explanation for Ford's decision-making.

Raff (1988) argues that there is little evidence to suggest that there was anything gained from offering above-market wages. The market itself was low skilled; people were still willing to work at the company. Raff wrote:

"But I have found no evidence whatsoever that the company had any difficulty filling vacancies (actual or prospective). There are no traces that the company advertised for help." He also argued that there was little cost in training new to hire workers. Adverse selection in labor is the idea that workers possess characteristics that prevent them from performing on the ideas that are known to them, but unknown to the worker. Raff based on Meyer argued that this was not the case: Division of labor [had] been carried on to such a point that an overwhelming majority of the jobs consist of a very few simple operations. In most cases a complete mastery of the movements does not take more than five to ten minutes. All the training that a man receives in connection with his job consists of one or two demonstrations by the foreman, or the workman who has been doing that job. After these demonstrations he is considered to be a fully qualified "production."

Moral hazard, the idea that some workers may not work hard or ignore their duties, was also dismissed, because monitoring had been improved. Raff argues that there is little evidence of poor or incomplete work.

Raff's (1988) opinion was that the Five-dollar day was a rent-sharing arrangement between the company and labor to prevent collective action on the part of employees. While it would have been possible to contend with a single employee, if whole groups of employees caused problems with the firm, the firm would be unable to handle the rebellion:

The profits were bigger the more efficiently all these machines were used, the more intensively all fixed and quasi-fixed factors were exploited. Collective action which interfered with this was a direct threat to the rents. The company's means of dealing with shirkers (or anyone who wanted to interfere with centrally determined pace and coordination), however effective for isolated individuals, would have been much less efficient in dealing with groups.

Likewise, Ford understood that the employees came from cultures where peasant norms and values were very different and so they would be more likely to question authority.

Raff and Summers (1987) offer a slightly different viewpoint. They argue that Ford did experience above-average returns from a higher wage: They experienced queues in waiting for jobs and had a better selection of employees. All of which suggest that Ford did pay efficiency wages. There are several reasons why increases in wages lead to an increase in production. Firstly, Ford recognized that there was a serious morale problem at the plant. He also recognized that monitoring employees could be very costly and detrimental to the working conditions. So he decided to head it off by providing higher wages. Nevins and Hill (1954) pointed out that Ford had seen employees become more productive when wages were increased when he visited a plant in England. Raff and Summers (1987) also concede that increased morale may have been a source of an increase in production based on wages. Finally, Ford and the company understood that not every employee would be able to handle the working conditions (Meyer 1981). Therefore, Ford was willing to pay those that would work within the system and create a boost in production. Mostly, as Meyer notes, the Five-dollar day was an attempt to provide a great sense of rationalization over the workforce – educating immigrant workers on the need to work wages.

Sociological Department and Savings Plan

The Sociological Department is another notable managerial contribution by Ford (Nevins and Hill 1957). It has confounded many historians over the years as to its real purpose. It is also the most conversational element of the Ford program. Brinkley (2003a, b) noted that the home life of the employee should not have been the business of the corporation. Yet as we have noted in the previous chapter on Owen, there was a deep interest in the home life of employees during the eighteenth and nineteenth century. Headed by the Rev. Samuel S. Marquis, the purpose of the sociology department was to educate workers and their families on the proper use of money, the development of adequate moral behaviors, and to provide English language lessons for new immigrants. They also sought to Americanize immigrants by teaching them how to save, keep flies off food, and general cleanliness. The Ford sociology department, in other words, performed actions similar to social workers in the United States and elsewhere (Katz 1996). It was also in accordance with Ford's wishes that people should be independent or rather Ford was teaching them to be independent by developing a sense of thrift. The other side of the sociological department was nefarious. Its purpose was to spy on workers and their families to make sure that they were not wasting their salaries. This was a strange viewpoint, but it fitted Ford's image of himself as a village chieftain (Jardim 1970).

The employee savings plan was yet another example of Ford's managerial philosophy. According to Nevins and Hill (1957), investment certificates were available in dominations of $100 to employees. These certificates were comparable to nonpreferred stock and were available to any employee who stayed on payroll. The certificates yielded 6% interest and dividends. The certificates were non-negotiable and nonassignable. In addition, the employee could only use one third of his salary on them. Despite the limitations, the savings were popular, and they were designed to aid employees when there was a downturn in the economy.

African American Employees

Ford was willing to hire anyone – except women and Jews (Lacey 1986). He believed that women should work at raising children, keeping home, and running the house. His hatred of Jews will be discussed later in this chapter. Yet he was willing to hire anyone else. Although in our time we would regard these opinions as retrograde, they were surprisingly enlightened for the time-period. Ford was especially keen on hiring African American employees. In fact, a great many African Americans moved to Detroit with the understanding that they would find employment from Ford. The type of African American worker whom Ford sought to hire were young men, unmarried, but in search of long-term employment so they could get married. In fact, work at the Ford Motor Company was seen, along with the Pullman Company, as regarded as one of the best jobs that a member of the African American community could aspire to. Not only were they attractive, failure to get a job at Ford usually meant that the applicant had to leave Detroit and – almost certainly – delay marriage. More remarkable was that Ford actually paid the same wage to African Americas as he did whites – a most unusual policy (Maloney and Whatley 1995).

But there were limits to Ford's largesse. Like everything else he did in his career, there were usually strings attached. Ford did not believe in charity. He also sought to turn a situation to his advantage. African Americans did not have other employment options available to them. Ford understood this. Yet given his job design, he had serious turnover problems. One solution to these problems was to have African Americans work in foundries, the hottest, most dangerous place to work in the corporation (Foote et al. 2003). White males did not have these issues – they could leave Ford easily and find employment elsewhere. Ford also encouraged racial divisions through his use of the police service for preventing unionization. One of the reasons why the United States struggled with forming strong labor groups had been the racism of the American workers. Ford used this idea to his advantage, sowing discord between white and African American workers (Brueggemann 2000).

Unions and Politics

Ford's relationship to labor was a highly complex and, at times, contradictory one. Ford was, at his heart, a deeply paternalistic man who viewed himself as a chief of the village. Ford's reputation as being hostile to labor was one that was justifiably born out of his resistance to unionization at the Ford Motor Company during the 1930s (Kennedy 1999). The picture of a beaten and bloody Walter Reuther – the long-term leader of the United Automobile Workers who was beaten to near pulp along with a number of aides outside Ford's Rouge plant in Many 1937 – recalls some of the harrowing photographs that were (and could have been taken) in Nazi Germany or Soviet Russia (Lichtenstein 1995). Ford hated unions. The reason again was simple. They were a threat to Ford's independence. His position against unions was strengthened through his relationship with Harry Bennett, the head of Ford security. Bennett played on Ford's worst fears, suggesting that union members may try to assassinate and kidnap him (Lacey 1986). Even before Ford's battles with the United Automobile Workers – when Ford maintained a reputation as a generous and benevolent manager, he was notable for the control he sought to exert over his workers' private lives – firing them for drinking or smoking.

Ford was no ordinary ogre to workers. Ford dramatically raised wages with the Five-dollar day. He pushed for the 8-h work day. He allowed for weekends off. In addition, he provided his workers with financial services, social services, and education, enabling them to move into the middle class. At the start of the Great Depression, Ford raised wages, at the behest of President Hoover, to $7 a day. Many of the services that Ford offered his workers were key objectives of the American labor movement. Brandes (1976) noted that American unionists wanted aspects of welfare capitalism in their bargaining and political activities rather than taking more control of the workplace. Gordon (1992) noted that the later union movement merely federalized what management had promised workers in the 1920s.

Ford provided these services, in part, not out of altruism but because he wished to avoid unions. There were multiple ways to deal with the so-called labor question. The first was to have unions, capitalistic in nature or radical. Worker representation plans like the ones the Rockefellers proposed was a potential solution (Bruce and Nyland 2011). Ford was part of what has been called as the welfare capitalism movement. The welfare capitalist movement was designed to overcome the labor problem. In fact, from a modern eye it offered similar benefits that modern corporations currently run, including retirement benefits, life insurance, bonus and profit-sharing, educational, and recreational activities. According to David Kennedy (1999), the real purpose of these plans was to maintain corporate control over labor, by proposing programs that the federal government might offer. Kennedy also notes that these plans were often poor substitutes to entitled government programs and collective bargaining. The Great Depression mostly ended these programs due to the corporations' inability to maintain them (Cohen 1990). Eventually even Ford abandoned their programs.

Ford also had real difficulty with the National Recovery Administration (NRA), which was President Franklin Roosevelt's first attempt to deal with the Depression (Gordon 1992). The purpose of the NRA was to end the deflationary wage-price spiral in which the United States found itself through a combination of price controls, strengthened trade union rights and government, and government infrastructure projects (Kennedy 1999). Ultimately, it sought to eliminate wasteful competition between corporations, as well as unneeded conflict between labor and capital (Brinkley 1995). Widely regarded as a failure both at the time and subsequently, the NRA suffered from hostility from business as well as the fact that its planned scope exceeded the government's legal powers (Skocpol and Finegold 1982). Despite being courted by President Roosevelt and NRA Director, General Hugh Johnson, Ford was a notable opponent of the NRA, joining in the legal actions undertaken to curtail its activities. According to Sidney Fine (1958) – Ford agreed with many of the policies of the NRA but hated the fact that the government forced these policies on him. Yet it is also important to recognize that Ford did not oppose Hoover's policies in the 1920s, when Hoover was Commerce Secretary (Hawley 1974). Much like the NRA, Hoover sought to control prices and production by forming voluntary trade associations that would stabilize and monitor the market place (Hawley 1978). Ford supported this program because it was volunteered based and one where the worker had a choice. The shift to mandatory controls – even that as a large producer Ford had some control over – was why Ford opposed unions and government actions. These viewpoints were increasing out of vogue in the progressive era and completely out of vogue in the New Deal.

Relationship with Taylorism

What is the relationship between Taylorism and Fordism? To some commentators, there was little difference between the two concepts. For instance, David Halberstam (1979) wrote, modern ideas about production, particularly those of Frederick Winslow Taylor, the first authority on scientific industrial management. Taylor had promised to bring an absolute rationality to the industrial process. The idea was to break each function down into much smaller units so that each could be mechanized and speeded up and eventually flow into a straight-line production of little pieces becoming steadily larger.

Peter Drucker (1954) went even further, writing that even if Ford had never even heard of Taylor, he was the greatest disciple of Taylorism. In fact, this viewpoint does have considerable evidence behind it. Firstly, much like Taylorism, Fordism was intentionally concerned with both the rationalization and efficiency of work, suggesting that they had common goals. The purpose of both was to control worker responses and find ways to make the process cheaper. Secondly, the other overlap between the two was recognition of monetary compensation and highly specialized, low-skilled jobs. Thirdly, both viewpoints greatly angered the literati and intellectuals at the time, as it provided a sense of standardization and control of expression. Hughes (1990) noted that Weimar Germany saw Taylor (scientific management) and Ford (assembly line) as joint forces producing something uniquely American and could together unlock the secrets of production. Doray (1988) viewed them as a madness that infected the worker in tandem. In his view, Taylorism alienated the worker; Fordism tied them to machines.

Others, such as Daniel Wren (2009) and Frank Gilbreth, disagree with the above assertion. Wren argues that Fordism and Taylorism are distinct constructs from each other. Although they shared some aspects of scientific management, such as specialization and division of labor, they were different. For example, Wren notes that one of the outstanding features of Taylorism was its outstanding level of cost accounting. This was something that Ford lacked knowledge of. In fact, the cost accounting framework would be adopted by General Motors, who had a connection to Taylorism through its DuPont investors. Secondly, the use of the conveyor belt and assembly line system was an aspect that Taylorism did not feature. Scientific management tended to place emphasis on human labor, and less on machines. In fact, the first automobile company to devote its energies to scientific management was Franklin Motor Company, advised by Carl Barth and George Babcock, but once Fordism had taken root, scientific management's sway over the automobile industry languished. Finally, Frank Gilbreth noted that the job design in Ford was poor. Daniel Nelson (1970) felt that Ford was not a company that utilized scientific management. In fact, some scholars have argued that attacks on scientific management mostly should have been directed more at Ford.

At the time of Toyota's ascent to the top of the automobile industry, Fordism and Taylorism were seen as one entity in industrialization noted Jürgens et al. (1993). They viewed both Fordism and Taylorism as rationalizing business activities to increase efficiency as the primary goal of industrial life. They noted that modern industry combined two separate concepts. From Taylorism, industrial life separated "thinking from doing" reducing work into a series of repetitive tasks, led by managers who make decisions that had little basis in the actual running of the business. Fordism produced standardization as its primary focus, with human behaviors and products produced in a similar fashion. Both reduced work motivation to mere financial rewards, separating both social and intrinsic motivation. Jürgens and coauthors compare the Ford-regulatory model with the new model of Toyotism, which featured different types of motivations, teamwork, and more democratic decision-making.

My viewpoint is similar to Wren's, but for different reasons. Wren is correct in that the behaviors, testing, job design, and managerial accounting between scientific management and Fordism is stark and quite different. Taylor did not propose anything similar to an assembly line. Ford would have used a conveyor belt rather than a first-class man to haul pig iron, believing that it was both cheaper and more efficient. Although there was experimentation and analysis in designing the assembly line, I am not sure Taylor would have had a high opinion of Ford's corporate design. Taylor would have been horrified by Ford's accounting department – where the main goal was to dodge taxes and confuse the government (Halberstam 1979). Yet if we examine the processes, both produced rationalization of work – namely that it was designed to produce efficiently, quickly, and homogenously. Although there were different mechanisms, the goal was similar – rationalization of work.

There were two key differences between Fordism and Taylorism. The first is that Ford recognized that if we could have mass production, we could also have mass consumption (Brinkley 2003a, b). Accordingly, Ford provided higher wages to overcome turnover, but also to provide workers with a financial ability to purchase from the company. Ford also sought ways to provide credit and other services to ensure that his workers had the ability to become productive members of society. His high wages provided a vast expansion to those who wished to buy a car – his workers were his customers. His decision to provide the Five-dollar day was as a way to market the company, suggesting that use of corporate social responsibility of marketing well before the current interest in it. Ford also regarded this movement as a form of business rather than altruism.

The second difference was that Fordism had the idea and the need to provide socialization to workers (Nevins and Hill 1957; Gelderman 1981). Taylor produced the notion that workers should be trained through standardized processes; Ford stressed the other part of training, namely socialization. Ford was the pioneer of the socialization aspect of training. A tremendous amount of training these days considers the role of socialization – which entails work norms, how to interact at work, and legal/ethical responsibilities. In Ford's case, it was the Americanization of workers. Just as Taylor had to contend with, Ford had to deal with a vastly different working population due to the consistent influx of new immigrants, changing the working culture. Therefore, what Ford sought to do was to Americanize them by providing English classes and opportunities to socialize, in order to prepare them for modern industrial life and a work culture that was very different from the peasant work culture. This was part of the reason why Ford took an interest in his workers. It fit a progressive era pattern of managing the social life of the immigrant.

Corporate Governance

Ford hated bankers and the art of finance. He did not understand the value of stockholders and the oversight that came from corporate governance. Halberstam (1979) stated Ford hated that stockholders got wealthy on the company's expense but provided little aid in return. There is much wisdom to this statement, but I would go further: stockholders interfered with Ford's independence in running the company. Simply put, the Ford Motor Company was his as he saw fit to run it, regardless of what others thought. The "others" included his own son, family members, and longtime executives. Ford wanted to use money to expand the company, trying new and various experiments. At one board meeting, Ford told his right-hand man, Harry Bennett, that there was little reason for them to stay; they would simply do what they wished (Nevins and Hill 1962). When the Dodge brothers sued over dividends, Ford fought them tooth and nail (McCraw and Tedlow 1997). During the case, Ford called profits immoral, noting that a company should be run so that profits were spent on the business. He lost the case and created a resolve to free himself from control at the earliest possible moment.

In 1919, Ford gathered the needed funds to make the Ford Motor Company a family-owned affair (McCraw and Tedlow 1997). This Quixotic adventure was undertaken at the time when the Ford Motor Company should have been investing in a replacement for the Model T and/or developing new car models to diversify his business. Rather than plowing his profits back into the company, Ford used his capital to purchase the investors' stock which, other than the Dodge brothers, had mostly been on his side. Unfortunately, Ford had selected an unpropitious time for his buy-back. A post-war depression had started. Ford was short of the needed funds. Accordingly, he put the financial squeeze on his dealers, forcing them to pay a higher rate to the company (Lacey 1986). This was at the time when Sloan had taken over General Motors and was moving against him. Ford also began losing his senior executives. The loss of one in particular, William Knudsen, was particularly detrimental to the company. Knudsen was a production genius who had successfully guided the company's production during the First World War. Yet Ford believed that Knudsen was getting too important, exercising too much authority, and becoming too close to Ford's talented son, Edsel, the latter being seen by Ford as a combination of heir and usurper. Knudsen, tired of being humiliated, left the company, taking a pay cut in the process, and joined General Motors. Many of other outstanding Ford executives also left the company (McCraw and Tedlow 1997).

The lack of proper oversight was dangerous for the company, since there were few checks and balances on Ford's behavior. More troubling was that this occurred during a time when Ford was starting to lose mental control, becoming ever more paranoid, cynical, and narcissistic (Lacey 1986). Had shareholders remained in place, they could have made sure that the company remained profitable. Perhaps, they would have forced Ford to make necessary changes, such as abandoning the Model T, or adding another production line. When Edsel recommended developing credit lines to help people purchase Ford cars, shareholders may have forced Ford to accept it.

Shareholders also would have checked the profitability of the company. When Arjay Miller joined the company, he attempted to find out what the profits were per month. Instead, he found an elaborate system, dedicated to calculating the amount of paper used per month. When Miller asked for the figures, the accounting department said they are what we make them – to which Miller realized he was in never-never land. The only oversight at Ford came from Edsel, who was abused by his father, and Harry Bennett, Ford's chief goon. Only after Edsel had died, in part due to the stress his father put him through, did Ford's wife (and Edsel's mother) begin wresting the company from the old man (Halberstam 1979).

Management Talent

Halberstam (1979) noted that Ford did not have friends and saw them as a limitation to be avoided. Yet such a statement cannot be squared with the fact that Ford often kept people in power because he found them useful or, more likely, they appealed to his prejudices (Brinkley 2003a, b). Ford had something worse than friends. He had lackeys and flunkies. A comparison with Alfred Sloan would allow us to see the difference. Sloan did not have friendships with his managers; they were simply employees who were hired to do a job, based on their merit (Farber 2002). Sloan sought relationships outside the firm. Ford sought talented workers. Indeed, in the early days of the company, Ford had a wide range of talented executives and engineers who were attracted to the company because of its progressive nature. Yet as the company became successful, Ford's narcissism was activated. He sought executives who would tell him what he wanted to hear. He also hated it when his managers used their autonomy to make changes. When Ford visited Europe in 1912, his executives made modifications to the Model T, turning it into a smoother riding vehicle, hoping to surprise him with this new development. Ford was not amused and stopped the changes (Brinkley 2003a, b). Ford drove away much of his company's talent, as many grew tired of dealing with this unpredictable man. One of Ford's long-term executives, Bennett, was a thug, who stole from the company, bullied workers, and played on Ford's worst fears. Again, there was little managerial oversight or checks on Ford's increasing irrational behavior.

Limitations

I find Ford's inclusion in a text on management thought to be interesting. Although Ford has a high esteem among business and management historians, he did not leave a management philosophy, and in some ways, disdained a management approach. Unlike Sloan's careful and well-planned managerial charts – where duties, authorities, and responsibilities were clear – Ford's had little organization and the responsibility was always with him (Drucker 1954). Ford actually would appoint two different people to a similar position, provide them with same duties, and sit back while the two managers struggled over authority. Ford also punished executives who demonstrated too much authority and independence. He even bullied his only legitimate son, Edsel, when he showed a streak of independence. Peter Drucker (1954) noted that the principle issue that manager's face is not managing workers, but managing managers – namely handling the relationships with managers above and below. The major reason for this is that each manager plays a role in the organization of the company and without coordination between these various managers, the organization cannot produce.

Drucker went further – he argued that Ford tried to manage without managers. Drucker concedes that there could be other reasons, such as senility. I would argue that Ford's narcissism and mental decline contributed to this decision. Ford simply did not want to lose control of the organization, and if the price was disharmony within the organization, then that was the price he was willing to pay. Ford did not just have his police force spy on his workers. He also had them spy on his own executives. Those executives that showed any independence were forced out. One of the reasons why, according to Drucker, Harry Bennett was able to emerge as a supreme power within the company was that he was Ford's creature. Bennett lacked the standing and experience to be an executive on his own. So he could not betray Ford. But once Ford was out of power, so was Bennett.

Ford wanted lackeys, executors of his will, but not managers, investors, or government oversight (Brinkley 2003a, b). He ran his company with complete authority. This accomplishment is unlike any in the modern world, where, even in a market economy, there is oversight of managerial activities. The one department where management was allowed to function within Ford was the sales department. Ford was also willing to pay a high amount of money for engineers, but not for managers. Unlike engineers, they were too much of a threat to his power. Ford's preference for engineers over managers reflected his focus on technical and operation issues rather than managerial issues such as organization, coordination, and strategy. Although he selected a cost-leadership strategy, Ford ignored that his company could use other approaches and offer other products. Drucker (1954) noted that Ford recognized that he could provide colors other than black – but to do so, would threaten the uniformity of his product. But Drucker went further – Ford, despite his adoption of mass production, continued to maintain that uniformity of the product was needed for mass production, an old-fashioned view. What Ford failed to realize – mostly because he did not have an adequate training in management – was that what matters was standardization of parts. Drucker wrote "it (mass production) does not rest on uniform products. It rests on uniform parts which can be massed-assembled into a large variety of different products."

Sloan understood this idea. Yet it was a basic management idea. What Sloan further recognized was that one could go further than just achieving symmetry with different parts, rather than different products. Sloan recognized that vertical integration could reduce transaction costs between various divisions. Ford recognized something similar in his vast Rouge River plant, a vast edifice constructed between 1917 and 1928. At this integrated industrial complex, steel was made in house, allowing for a car to be produced 21 days after the raw material had arrived. But his organization and accounting procedures were too crude to really take advantage of this. Sloan recognized that a company could offer multiple products in the same field. For example, as people aged, they could move from say a Buick all the way up to a Cadillac (McCraw and Tedlow 1997).

Sloan would emerge as the greatest challenge that Ford would face, and one that he was not equal to. Sloan represented in some ways a shift in the American experience. Educated, connected, a technocrat, Sloan represented the shift to a formal system of management where the purpose of management was to coordinate among various divisions within the corporation. In addition, Sloan did not own the business – he was an employee who had the backing of the DuPont family. Sloan was an administrative genius who would provide the organization and coordination that General Motors had lacked under its previous head, Billy Durant (Farber 2002). Durant was a corporate buccaneer, a promoter, an acquirer of corporations, and general visionary. Durant's vision was to build a corporation that sold a wide variety of cars to different customers. Unfortunately, for General Motors, Durant was not an administrator. When the DuPonts took over the company, there were no standard accounting procedures, no way of telling whether a division lost or gained money. The corporation lacked direction.

Concerned with their investment, the DuPonts decided to oust Durant from the company. They sought to provide better organization to the company. They selected Sloan in part because of his previous success at the Hyatt Roller Bearing company and his background in engineering which, at that point, was held in high esteem and considered to be a font of knowledge on how to manage corporations. The DuPonts were also interested in the corporation because they believed that while Ford controlled the market, his share could be reduced.

Sloan was almost the exact opposite of Ford. Whereas Ford wanted recognition from the press and courted them (Farber 2002), Sloan was reserved, preferring to operate in the shadows. Ford sought to dominate his firm – pitting managers against each other, so that decisions remained solely in his domain. Sloan hired the best possible managers, including several former Ford executives, including William Knudsen, inventor Charles Kettering, financial expert Donaldson Brown, and Charles E. Wilson. Neither Ford nor Sloan really had friends – Ford's best friend was Thomas Edison, Sloan's was Walter Chrysler. But whereas Sloan kept his executives at a distance, Ford sought flunkies, such as Harry Bennett. There were also differences in how they handled dealers. Ford could control his flunkies, but the flunkies could lie and manipulate Ford. Ford bullied his dealers, often forcing them to pay for cars where there was no major market. By contrast, Sloan kept this dealer's confidence, using them as a resource and fountain of information.

Accordingly, the story of Sloan and Ford is one of a competition, whereby a manager is pitted against an entrepreneur. Sloan was not an entrepreneur. He did not start General Motors. Nor, according to Peter Drucker (1946), did he seek innovation. Sloan was a genius at creating a command and control structure that allowed for the use of divisions to produce different products for different customers. His concern was on the process, not the product. If one understood that process, it could be manipulated, changed, and diversified to fit different customers' needs and desires. Sloan was bound by his shareholders, and they stood as a check on his behavior. Ford was an entrepreneur who bucked tradition and conventional wisdom in that he understood that average people wanted items deemed luxurious and found a way to produce them. Ford did not understand that a corporation needed to do many things. He simply did not understand the command and control nature of the cooperation.

Sloan also recognized that no one could compete against Ford's prices (McCraw and Tedlow 1997). Ford's value chain was too efficient to be defeated. Where Ford could be, and was, defeated was if a competitor could offer a different product, one that had more variety. Through such a strategy, General Motors could gain market share relative to Ford. Sloan understood that as a market matures it goes from a period in which only a few people can afford to purchase the product to one where mass consumption is possible. The next phase would be when a dominant company emerges, one that competes primarily on price, efficiency, and branded products. Yet this phase is transitory. Firms often learn how to reduce price. Ford's system could not provide a long-term competitive advantage because it could be copied by competitors. In fact, several of his production executives left the firm, taking their knowledge with them. The next phase focuses on brand differentiation, brand loyalty, and diverse products. Ford failed this test.

Another problem with Ford, and why the lack of oversight caused so many problems, was that Ford suffered from a narcissistic personality. Although it is admittedly difficult to assess historical figures psychologically, the process of psychobiography has gained widespread acceptance in the historical profession – management history being no exception. For example, several scholars have provided added insight on both Taylor and Robert Owen over the years. A narcissistic personality is a personality characteristic where the person has an exalted sense of themselves, they believe that they have more worth and value than others, they often have a difficult time accepting criticism, and are typically prone to manipulation through over-laudatory compliments (Paulhus and Williams 2002). Narcissists are also prone to be angry when they are opposed. Narcissists are also predisposed to see themselves as saviors. Narcissists are often prone to paranoia and often greatly overstate their level of expertise. In addition, narcissism could be activated as a trait, the more success a person has the more that narcissistic tendencies in his/her personality are likely to become pronounced.

Ford demonstrated many aspects of narcissism. A man that could boast that he created the modern age indicated a tremendous amount of self-worth. He hated sharing recognition with others and surrendering his independence. When the workers rejected his largesse, he responded, through his agents, with extreme violence. The Model T was sacrosanct to Ford. No one could make changes to it – as if the car had been created by God. He disliked it when managers showed initiative. Ford wanted his executives to be executors of his will. Ford seemed to prefer to use the word "I" often when describing his behaviors. He also left several books on his beliefs and a biography. He purchased his boyhood home and preserved it as a museum. Finally, he was paranoid – believing that bankers and Jews were out to ruin the world. Although I proposed that Ford had developed a Jacksonian outlook, political beliefs are influenced by personality. A belief that would encourage impendence would be attractive to someone who was narcissistic.

This explains, in part, the most bizarre episode in a life of bizarre episodes – namely Ford's hatred of Jews. At the time Sloan was building a juggernaut to assault

Ford, Ford seemed more concerned with imaginary Jewish conspiracies. Ford's attack on Jews was the most weird, disgusting, worthless, and venal endeavor that he ever took on. What is remarkable was that Ford had worked with Jews before, especially during his quixotic campaign to end the First World War (Kraft 1978). Although anti-Semitism was a common element in the United States at the time, made worse by the war, Ford's championship of the cause provided the movement with a real dose of legitimacy. After all, Ford was considered the equal of Moses at the time. Ford's work was largely published in the *Dearborn Independent*, a paper owned and financed by Ford himself.

Ford's message found an audience (Lee 1980). That the paper did not make money was of little concern. Ford was more interested in being the voice for rural America than he was in turning a profit. The damage done by Ford was enormous. Simply put, he not only provided support to one of the most evil movements of the twentieth century, his message also provided intellectual support of the Nazi regime. This is not to suggest that Ford caused the Holocaust. But he did provide, according to various Nazis, an intellectual justification. Late in his life, when Ford saw the first pictures of the Nazi Death Camps and beheld the final fruits of anti-Semitism, his guilt and loathing for his actions brought on his final stroke, rendering him for his last few years more paranoid than he had been.

Ford's anti-Semitic comments are arguably the most baffling and detrimental of his actions in terms of the effect on the reputational status of not only Ford but his company. Ford began to focus on anti-Semitism soon after the First World War, writing frequently about Jewish conspiracies in his personal newspaper, the *Dearborn Independent*. The collection of his works was evidently published under the title the *International Jew*, perhaps, with the exception of Mein Kampf, the most anti-Semitic publication of the twentieth century. Apparently, Ford found the Tsarist forgery, the *Protocols of the Elders of Zion*, to be accurate, as he legitimately believed that there was a Jewish conspiracy to take over the world. Mostly, Ford blamed the war on international bankers (a code for Jews) and sought to limit their influence in society (Baldwin 2001).

Why would a man as brilliant as Ford believe and write such nonsense? Conspiracy theories are often believed by the uneducated. Despite Ford's genius and brilliance as an engineer, he was widely ignorant of basic facts of history, politics, and social science (Lacey 1986). For example, Ford did not even know how the United States came into being. Ford's greatest admirers, those who pushed him into a career in politics, felt that he could not serve as government executive, since he was ignorant about many things – but he could make an effective senator. In addition, the attacks on Ford, often personal, slowly turned him into a cynical person. His defeat in the 1918 Michigan Senatorial contest, through the use of illegal money, also played a role in his increasingly erratic behavior. After the war, Ford was surrounded by men of poor character. His secretary, Ernest Liebold, was not only anti-Semitic but encouraged Ford to publish his ideas. Finally, Ford had personality characteristics of someone who would believe in conspiracies, including paranoia, narcissism, and Machiavellianism. While Ford was spewing nonsense, Alfred Sloan was creating strategies to overtake Ford.

Scholars have often argued that Ford lost his effectiveness as an executive. The Roosevelt administration was so concerned with the poor management of Ford that they discussed several options to deal with the problem, including nationalization or providing funds to Studebaker to purchase the company. However, Ford retained the ability to produce machines quickly and cheaply. What Ford lost was the tempo and rhythm of society. The world of 1943 was a much different one from when Ford had been born in 1863. But how to mass produce remained, more or less, the same. During the Second World War, Ford built an impressive production facility at Willow Run (nicknamed the Run). The Run was so impressive and such as tribute to American know-how, that Ford's head Charles Sorenson boasted that if the Japanese and Germans saw it, they would commit suicide. The Run produced 8500 B-24 bombers, the symbol of American military and economic might. By 1944, a B-24 bomber was produced every 63 min. What Henry Kaiser was to ship-building, Ford was to airplanes (Kennedy 1999).

Ford's shift to the mass production of weapons provided the executives with many hurdles. Ford, for instance, took to hiring midgets, to inspect the inside of the plane. Yet there were other problems for workers, such as housing, healthcare, working conditions, and other social issues. Ford and his executives claimed that what workers did off the job was none of their concern. This statement seemed to endear little positive feelings from workers and politicians, who remembered some of the worst aspects of the sociology division. Compounding problems was the death of Ford's son, Edsel, one of the two voices of reason at the company (the other being Charles Sorenson). The amazing production at Willow Creek could not have been possible without the aid of former Ford and General Motors executive and head of war production, William Knudsen (O'Neill 1993). The bulk of production praise went to executives such as Henry Kaiser, who were more in tune with government action, union membership, and worker welfare. Ford's attitude cost him his only legitimate son, Edsel, whose long-running battles with his father and his cronies finally took his life. Ford died 5 years later, after turning over the company to his grandson, Henry Ford II. Henry Ford II led the turn-around that saved the company, moving Ford from its position as the United States' fifth largest automobile company to a permanent second behind General Motors.

Conclusion

Ford left a complex legacy befitting his complex character. He was, as David Halberstam claims, a genius mechanic, a semi-genius in business, but a crackpot offering semi-literate responses on issues. The world had become more complex and more integrated than ever during Ford's life. The establishment of a cult of celebrity, based on the international media – and with Ford being a celebrity – meant that his opinions would be spread everywhere, much to the determinant of his reputation. Ford's narcissism did not help his ability to overcome his ignorance. Ford's attitude toward power suggests a man who would no longer be dictated to, regardless of the foolishness of his ideas, or the power of his opponents. Ford would be free – even at the expense of his reputation and wallet. The last few years at Ford under his rule could be described as a country under a crazy ruler – with the populace hoping that the ruler dies, hoping the son will be king.

Ford's desire to be independent, which resulted from his Jacksonian beliefs, was another major hindrance to his functioning in the modern world. From 1880 until around 1920, the United States witnessed a breaking down of barriers, amid an integration of communities that helped destroy the old America that had stressed frugality, independence, and moralism. According to Robert Wiebe (1967: 132),

> ... they had enough insight into their lives to recognize the old ways and old values would no longer suffice. Often confused, they were still the ones with the determination to fight these confusions and mark a new route into the modern world.

This new class wanted rationalization, bureaucracy, and administration – concepts that would have been foreign just several years ago. The development of an educated middle class and the use of roads and railroad meant the end of the old order that Ford had stood for. Bold decision-making and entrepreneurship were downplayed in this new order. The bureaucracy would intervene in the relationship between workers and managers; now law, rather than promise, was the way of the land. Part of the irony was that Fordism was one of the concepts that brought in this new order. Ford's successes had made his old world impossible.

Yet despite this, his bigotry and his heavy handedness, Ford remained a popular person with the average American, especially the rural community. Even if Ford was no longer viewed as Moses, he still remained a respectful figure to the average worker. The reason was simple; Ford was an American Prometheus – instead of fire, Ford stole mobility from the wealthy. Intellectuals and the wealthy hated him for that. Yet the average American remained grateful to Ford because he allowed for the average person to be able to commute to and from work, go and visit relatives, and go away for a day trip. From this perspective, Ford was the greatest friend the worker ever had. Unfortunately, Ford refused to see neither the limits of his vision nor how his success ended the old world. He was truly bound like Prometheus, but instead of iron chains, the chains were delusion, ignorance, and paranoia. But the people loved him.

Cross-References

▶ Taylor Made Management
▶ The Age of Strategy: From Drucker and Design to Planning and Porter

References

Baldwin N (2001) Henry Ford and the Jews: the mass production of hate. Public Affairs, New York
Batchelor R (1994) Henry Ford: mass production, modernism and design. Manchester University Press, Manchester/New York

Brandes SD (1976) American welfare capitalism, 1880–1940. University of Chicago Press, Chicago

Brinkley A (1995) The end of reform. Knopf, New York

Brinkley D (2003a) Prime mover. Am Herit 54(3):44–53

Brinkley DG (2003b) Wheels for the world: Henry Ford, his company, and a century of progress. Penguin Books, New York

Bruce K, Nyland C (2011) Elton Mayo and the deification of human relations. Organ Stud 32 (3):383–405. https://doi.org/10.1177/0170840610397478

Brueggemann J (2000) The power and collapse of paternalism: the Ford Motor Company and black workers, 1937–194. Soc Probl 47(2):220–240

Cohen L (1990) Making a new deal: Industrial workers in Chicago, 1919–1939. New York: Cambridge University Press

Cooper JM Jr (1983) The warrior and the priest. Harvard University Press, Cambridge, MA

Doray B (1988) From Taylorism to Fordism: a rational madness. Free Association Books, London

Drucker PF (1946) Concept of the corporation. New York: The John Day Company

Drucker PF (1954) The practice of management. Harper and Row, New York

Farber D (2002) Sloan rules: Alfred P. Sloan and the triumph of general motors. The University of Chicago Press, Chicago

Feller D (1995) The Jacksonian promise America, 1815 to 1840. Johns Hopkins Press, Baltimore

Fine S (1958) The Ford Motor Company and the NRA. Bus Hist Rev 32(4):353–385

Foote CL, Whatley WC, Wright G (2003) Arbitraging a discriminatory labor market: black workers at the Ford Motor Company, 1918–1947. J Labor Econ 21(3):493–532

Gelderman C (1981) Henry Ford: the wayward capitalist. Dial Press, New York

Gordon C (1992) New deals: business, labor, and politics in America, 1920–1935. Cambridge: Cambridge University Press

Halberstam D (1979) Citizen Ford. Am Herit 1986 37(6):49–64. Interpretive essay. http://www.americanheritage.com/content/citizen-ford

Hawley EW (1974) Herbert Hoover, the commerce secretariat, and the vision of an "associative state," 1921–1928. J Am Hist 61:116–140

Hawley EW (1978) The discovery and study of a "corporate liberalism". Bus Hist Rev 52(3):309–320

Howe DW (2007) What hath god wrought: the transformation of America, 1815–1848. Oxford University Press, New York

Hughes TP (1990) American genesis: a history of the American genius for invention. Penguin Books, New York

Jardim A (1970) The first Henry Ford: a study in personality and business leadership. Massachusetts Institute of Technology Press, Cambridge, MA

Jürgens U, Malsch T, Dohse K (1993) Breaking from Taylorism: changing forms of work in the automobile industry. Cambridge University Press, New York

Kanigel R (1997) The one best way: Frederick Winslow Taylor and the enigma of efficiency. Little Brown, London

Katz MB (1996) In the shadow of the poorhouse. Basic Books, New York

Kennedy DM (1999) Freedom from fear: the American people in depression and war 1929–1945, vol 9. Oxford University Press, New York

Kline R, Pinch T (1996) Users as agents of technological change: the social construction of the automobile in the rural United States. Technol Cult 37(4):763–795

Kraft BS (1978) The peace ship: Henry Ford's pacifist adventure in the first world war. Macmillan, New York

Lacey R (1986) Ford: the men and the machine little. Brown, Boston

Lee A (1980) Henry Ford and the Jews. Rowman & Littlefield Publishers, Inc. New York:Stein and Day

Lewis DI (1976) The public image of Henry Ford: an American folk hero and his company. Wayne State University Press, Detroit

Lichtenstein N (1995) The most dangerous man in Detroit: Walter Reuther and the fate of American labor. Basic Books, New York

Maloney TN, Whatley WC (1995) Making the effort: the contours of racial discrimination in Detroit's labor markets, 1920–1940. J Econ Hist 55(3):465–493

McCormick B, Folsom BW (2003) A survey of business historians on America's greatest entrepreneurs. Bus Hist Rev 77(4):703–716

McCraw TK, Tedlow TS (1997) In McCraw edited Creating modern capitalism: how entrepreneurs, companies, and countries triumphed in three industrial revolutions. Cambridge, Harvard University Press

Meyer S (1981) The five dollar day: labor management and social control in the Ford Motor Company, 1908–1921. State University of New York Press, Albany

Meyers M (1957) The Jacksonian persuasion: politics and belief. Stanford University Press, Stanford

Nelson D (1970) Frederick W. Taylor and the rise of scientific management. MIT Press, Madison

Nevins A, Hill FE (1954) Ford: the times, the man, the company. Charles Scribners' Sons, New York

Nevins A, Hill FE (1957) Ford: expansion and challenge, 1915–1933. Charles Scribners' Sons, New York

Nevins A, Hill FE (1962) Ford: decline and rebirth, 1933–1962. Charles Scribners' sons, New York

Nye DE (1979) Henry ford: "ignorant idealist". Kennikat, Washington, DC

O'Neill W (1993) A democracy at war: America's fight at home and abroad in World War II. Free Press, New York

Patterson JT (1997) Grand expectations. New York, NY: Oxford University Press

Paulhus DL, Williams KM (2002) The dark triad of personality: narcissism, Machiavellianism, and psychopathy. J Res Pers 36(6):556–563

Porter ME (1980) Competitive strategy. Free Press, New York

Raff DM (1988) Wage determination theory and the five-dollar day at Ford. J Econ Hist 48(2):387–399

Raff DM, Summers LH (1987) Did Henry Ford pay efficiency wages? J Labor Econ 5(4, Part 2): S57–S86

Sellers C (1991) The market revolution: Jacksonian America, 1815–1846. Oxford University Press, New York

Skocpol T, Finegold K (1982) State capacity and economic intervention in the early new deal. Polit Sci Q 97(2):255–278

Watts S (2005) The people's tycoon: Henry Ford and the American century. Knopf, New York

Wiebe (1967) The search for order, 1877–1920. Hill and Wang, New York

Wik RM (1962) Henry Ford's science and technology for rural America. Technol Cult 3 (3):247–258

Wik RM (1964) Henry Ford's tractors and American agriculture. Agric Hist 38(2):79–86

Wren DA (2009) The evolution of management thought (5th ed.). New York: Wiley

Wren DA, Greenwood RG (1998) Management innovators the people and ideas that have shaped modern business. Oxford University Press, New York

Spontaneity Is the Spice of Management: Elton Mayo's Hunt for Cooperation

23

Jeffrey Muldoon

Contents

Mayo's "Findings"	548
The Vital Center Does Not Hold	550
The Great Depression	551
The Good War	553
An Inchoate Movement	556
Elton Mayo: The Manager as Therapist	558
Conclusion	560
Cross-References	562
References	562

Abstract

This chapter covers the career of Elton Mayo and the impact of the Hawthorne studies upon the field of management. The first section of the chapter discusses Mayo's contribution to the management literature. This section argues that Mayo's best elements – his empathy and charisma – have not survived, but he leads a great legacy, as a scholar, for his influence in the field. The second section of the chapter covers the role of the Great Depression and World War II on Mayo's work. The third section compares Mayo's work to his major competitors – Whiting Williams and Henry S. Dennison. The final section compares Taylor to Mayo, arguing that they were complements rather than competitors.

Keywords

Mayo · Hawthorne and Human Relations

J. Muldoon (✉)
Emporia State University, Emporia, KS, USA
e-mail: jmuldoon@emporia.edu

© The Author(s), under exclusive licence to Springer Nature Switzerland AG 2020   545
B. Bowden et al. (eds.), *The Palgrave Handbook of Management History*,
https://doi.org/10.1007/978-3-319-62114-2_29

The Hawthorne studies, a series of experiments carried out at Western Electric's large assembly and manufacturing plant in Illinois between 1925 and 1932, have an iconic status in management literature. Yet our understanding of what happened remains shrouded in controversy. Although the studies extended over many years, only one part is typically remembered – a study of female assemblers taken off the shop floor and exposed to a variety of experiences that supposedly demonstrated the importance of intrinsic, socially-based rewards in work performance. Revolutionary in its conclusions, which shifted attention away from monetary rewards, the work of Elton Mayo and the Hawthorne studies loom large over management research.

Perhaps no study has created as much controversy and praise as Hawthorne. There is a long list of books and articles published that have attempted to unearth the mysteries of Hawthorne. Only Frederick Winslow Taylor has attracted as much attention. What is more notable is that there is little consensus among scholars regarding the study. I (Muldoon 2012) view the studies as a positive step in management thought. While Kyle Bruce (2006) views them as a step backward, H. M. Parsons (1974) and Alex Carey (1967) view the studies as worthless and wasteful. George Homans (1984) and Talcott Parsons (1940) believed that they were important in the development of theory. Some scholars have praised the studies' originality; other scholars have attacked its lack of originality. Management, psychology, and sociology each have a different perspective on the studies. The original criticisms of Mayo's work were overwhelmingly sociological in nature, suggesting that different disciplines have different standards and values. Which was also happened, even with individual researchers, perspectives change over time. For example, in 1947, Daniel Bell (Bell 1947) believed that the studies were a step toward fascism with a docile worker; in 1973 (Bell 1973) he argued that Mayo had a prime insight that the majority of socializing occurs at work.

When Hawthorne is attacked, Mayo faces a greater brunt of the criticism. Henry A. Landsberger (1958) defended the Hawthorne studies by suggesting that Mayo's work was illegitimate compared with the scientific rigor of *Management and the Worker*. This statement is like saying *Hamlet* is a good play except for the lead character. Mayo's arguments and influences clearly affect the works associated with the study. Other scholars have attacked the uncredentialed and unlettered Mayo. Still more scholars, including Kyle Bruce, Chris Nyland (2011), and Michael Rose (1975), have argued that the Hawthorne studies were a form of fascism. Other scholars, such as Morris Viteles, Peter Drucker, and the left-wing political activist Stuart Chase, have praised Mayo's ideas as a defense against fascism. Some of his critics, such as Reinhard Bendix, (1956) have noted Mayo's contributions to management ideology. His defenders, such as Homans (1984), Chase (1946), Drucker (1946), have noted Mayo's shortcomings as both as scholar and a man.

Mayo's reputation has been comparatively low since his death. In life, Mayo was praised as a social scientist in league with Thorstein Veblen and John Dewey (Smith 1998). Now, Mayo is, by a growing number, seen to be a mountebank who took management down an unneeded path. In 1977, Mayo was ranked fourth among all management thinkers (Wren and Hay 1977). In 2010, he was ranked 11th, a precipitous slide (Heames and Breland 2010). Despite the Hawthorne studies connection to launching organizational behavior as a distinct field of study, the studies are also ranked comparatively low. Even with the, now proven, importance of attitudes and relationships, scholars still attack Mayo's work and the findings of the study. Little research has traced the actual influence of the studies to understand its great influence on the fields of sociology, psychology, and management. In fact, the old suggestion that human relations replaced an undemocratic and inhumane scientific management has come under attack.

There is a tremendous amount of research attempting to unearth what happened at Hawthorne – such an approach is chimerical. Scholars often bring their own baggage when researching Hawthorne (present author included). Edwin Locke and Gary Latham (1984) argue that the increase in production is due to goal-setting. Peach and Wren (1991) argue that monetary incentives matter the most. H. M. Parsons (1974) argues for the role of behavioral management. Some scholars have researched the data, others the context of the plant, still others have written about the various figures in the study, some scholars have conducted oral histories. The stream of these studies has shed light on the fact that we do not know what happened. Wren and Bedeian (2018) conclude that it is impossible to know what happened at Hawthorne. The net result of these varying views is that scholars have devoted too much attention to what happened at the plant. A tremendous amount of hand wringing would have been avoided if scholars paid closer attention to the arguments by Homans (1949a), Roethlisberger (1977), Sonnenfeld (1985), and even Mayo (1945), who stated that the studies proved nothing. Their importance was to develop new approaches in examining management thought.

Scholars have begun to research the context of the studies but ignore the wider academic, social, and political context of which the studies occur. I do not claim any final statement about Hawthorne. I merely write to explain several important issues related to the Hawthorne studies. Firstly, I make a point that a combination of the Great Depression, World War II, and its aftermath played a key role in making the Hawthorne experiments the dominate study in Human Relations. Secondly, I seek to explain why the studies dominated literature, in comparison to other contenders, such as Whiting Williams and Henry Dennison. Thirdly, I would like to note the complex relationship between Taylorism and Mayoism. My contention here was less that Mayoism contradicted Taylorism, but instead addressed certain limitations that Scientific Management suffered from, as well as building on its developments. Hopefully, each objective will shed light on what the Hawthorne studies meant for management and their continuing importance to the field.

The combination of these points is the following: Mayo stressed noneconomic incentives at a time when both workers and managers believed that the Great Depression was now a permanent feature of industrial life. The second point was that the Great Depression ended welfare capitalism, creating a new approach in industrial relationships. The third point is that while Mayo was successful in spreading the word to business leaders in the 1930s, the academic spread of human relations was limited by the fact that there were few academic jobs and journals to maintain the research. In addition, competing frameworks had some of the same baggage as did the Hawthorne studies, but lacked the academic support led by Mayo's associates. Finally, we make an important note about the relationship between Mayoism and Taylorism noting the complementary relationship between both ideas.

Mayo's "Findings"

Elton Mayo left a complex legacy (Gillespie 1991; Trahair 1984). For the historian, he left some slim, underdeveloped books. He did not leave a theory. Nor did he research or conceive the Hawthorne studies. The Hawthorne studies did not prove anything. Both William Foote Whyte (1956) and George Homans (1949a) argued that Mayo's findings were only the genesis of research. Others had a similar view, like Kornhauser (1934), who argued that Mayo's (1933) book provides more questions than answers. Park (1934) and Powell (1957) suggest that the work was more exploratory and the purpose of the work was to develop new approaches. Rogers (1946) argues that the work's major focus on groups was a contribution, but was more developmental than a final statement. The best of Elton Mayo was his charm, wit, and empathy – he had, what *Fortune* (1956) called, a high voltage personality. Time eroded these strengths – few, if any, people alive today had any major dealings with Mayo. What is left is his turgid prose in his short, underdeveloped books and the recorded memories of his disciples. Figures, such as Taylor (scientific management), Fayol (the fourteen principles of management), Chester Barnard (zone of indifference), and Herbert Simon (bounded rationality), each left a defined concept. What did Mayo leave? It is not as clear.

Compounding the problem was that Mayo distorted and even lied about his background, failing to correct people who believed he had a medical degree. Mayo did not address his critics, was imprecise in writing, failed to acknowledge the work of others, and appeared conservative in his politics. Scholars, including Ellen O'Connor (1999a, b), Bruce and Nyland (2011), and Richard Gillespie (1991) have all argued that the Hawthorne studies were less science and more advocacy. Scholars have challenged Mayo's arguments over his opinions on unions, the originality of his ideas, and the roles of groups, attitudes, and social motivations in the workplace (Muldoon 2017). His most persistent and ablest critic, Bruce, pointed out that Mayo was more concerned with providing businessmen with the ammunition to fight off unions and coddling favors with the Rockefellers than true science.

Mayo's accomplishment was as a codifier as well as an advocate. Mostly, what Mayo did was to focus on what scholars knew (that social relationships motivate) and to direct that knowledge in discovering how, where, and when social relationships matter. He also advocated for the need for industrial research to understand cooperation. With the chaos of the postwar years reigning, people began to hear his ideas and sought more complete understandings of work. He did not launch a theory, but launched a school of scholars who would refine his work. Whyte notes one of the first textbooks in industrial relations was Burleigh Gardner and Moore's (1945) book *Human Relations in History*, where the primary focus was on the Hawthorne studies. Stone (1952), Bell (1947), Moore (1947), Whyte (1956), Homans (1949a), Chase

(1946), Powell (1957), Drucker (1946), Parsons (1940), Hart (1943), Parsons and Barber (1948), and others have suggested the primary propulsion to study social relationships within the organization came from Mayo's monomaniac, obsessive appeals to do so. These men were contemporaries, students, critics, and competitors of Mayo, but were experts in their own fields at the time. Some, such as Wilbert Moore and Bell, decried Mayo's influence, but they understood that it was nevertheless vast.

Therefore, Mayo's contribution was to place focus squarely on researching worker relationships. Most of the research that commenced in analyzing worker relationships had roots in Mayo, either copying his methods or trying to improve them. Some scholars criticized the political implications, but scholars on the left sought to use some of the Mayo's methods to recreate the Hawthorne studies under a different context. Mayo also demonstrated that pay was only one element in terms of work motivation. Perhaps, he went too far to suggest that pay was not that important, but he suggested that social and intrinsic elements could be important as well. Mayo created a general structure where Whyte and other scholars would discover that workers do not necessarily care about pay in absolute terms; they care deeply about it in relative terms (Muldoon 2012). Subsequent work on both equity theory and justice would demonstrate this issue more clearly to the point where Cropanzano and Mitchell (2005) have suggested that justice is where social and economics influences dovetail. Scholars also discovered that piece-rate systems could lead to other problems within the work group as collaboration diminishes. Furthermore, in knowledge-based jobs, the primary emphasis on collaboration and overly strenuous competition can diminish information exchange. In fact, different types of pay systems can cause major problems within plants.

C.W. M. Hart (1943, 1949) pointed out that one of the major implications of the study was that people are not consistent in their thoughts about work. Hart went further, arguing that the combination of social sciences that Hawthorne represented could push towards more practical and interesting research. The studies of Hawthorne indicate that the total situation at work – mind, body, social system, talents, motivations, and desires – plays a key role in performance. Today we would suggest that person-job and person-organization fit are extremely important. The Hawthorne studies were key indicators of these. One can also see elements of situation – personality interactions within the workers. Namely, situations can influence behaviors or tap into negative feelings. Mayo did not use personality theory, but instead used the work of Janet and Freud to illustrate the issues of frustration and alienation in modern work life.

Mayo is a founding father of human resource development. Much like Robert Owen, Mayo was concerned with the worker's total situation, viewing them as more of a total person, and less like raw material. Both men sought managerial interventions to make workers better: Owen through education and Mayo through socialization. Owen and Mayo saw better management had a social impact. As Drucker (1946) noted, one of the principle problems with traditional management was that it viewed people as raw materials, while Mayo saw them as people. Homans could similarly claim that industrial sociology owed its seminal understandings of human-work interaction to

Mayo, whose work changed the nature of management research by shifting the emphasis to work groups and away from technology or task. Homans (1949a, b) points out that Mayo viewed the Hawthorne studies as a potential first step towards laying the basis of organizational behavior.

Mayo's principle idea was that trust existed in primitive society due to rituals, ceremonies, and other social arrangements and provided the necessary underpinnings for cooperation in work-based activities. The shift to modern society destroyed these arrangements. Yet despite the shift, Mayo understood that behavior was not wholly rational, but often driven by sentiments. Accordingly, the way to understand people was to address "the whole situation," meaning that we should examine both intrinsic and extrinsic elements at work. Roethlisberger noted that in every group, workers form their own rituals and routines that ensure cooperation within the group.

Drucker noted that it was Elton Mayo and his group that made the primary contribution to management thought as he contributed the principles and methods of industrial research. Mayo provided a rudimentary conceptual scheme, as well as vocabulary, with his discussions of sentiments, understanding of nonlogical thinking, and the role of social factors. Later work would, sometimes by his students and protégés, refine and expand Mayo's general scheme. The most notable contribution was a rebuffing of economic determinism, which had been the major intellectual explanation for behaviors since the time of Marx. By deemphasizing economic motivations and stressing other human elements, such as social relationships, Mayo made a notable contribution. Such an approach would have been a popular undertaking in both political science and history at the time. The inability of the Great Depression to crush American capitalism indicated that economic factors alone could not predict behavior (Brinton 1948; Drucker 1946).

The Vital Center Does Not Hold

"The world over, we are greatly in need of an administrative elite who can assess and handle the concrete difficulties of human collaboration," Elton Mayo wrote in 1933. In 1945, he argued that society had failed to develop means of collaboration. Based on the destruction from the wars, Mayo had a pessimistic view of from future of humanity. His critics, such as Daniel Bell and others, also looked to the future with a fearful eye. The argument laid forth in this section is that Elton Mayo worked in a period of social and political upheaval when people sought means to promote cooperation; the failure of other management and political solutions provided an opening for human relations. Mayo grimly noted that churches, social groups, and families no longer held sway. He argued for the development and training of a new elite to handle society's issues and others agreed. The changes to industrial life brought on by the Great Depression and World War II aided Mayo in selling his view (Brinkley 1998). This process is discussed in this chapter.

The Great Depression

The Great Depression was the major economic event of the twentieth century (Kennedy 1999). Its impact on management has not received major study. Likewise, scholars have provided scant commentary of the importance of World War II on management thought. This is not to say that scholars have not addressed either issue, but have not adequately provided enough of a context for both events. In other fields, such as psychology and sociology, there have been studies to document the role the war played in shaping those fields. Likewise, we have documentation of how the war dramatically changed and shaped modern liberalism. Some scholars, such as Albert G. Mills (Foster et al. 2014; Williams and Mills 2017) and others, have begun to fill in the gap. For the purposes of this chapter, to understand the importance of both events would reveal the intellectual importance of the Hawthorne studies.

The Great Depression is the most researched economic event in history. Despite various attempts by the Roosevelt administration, it seemed that the economic conditions were not going to improve. Comments from academics, politicians, and common people support this point. Lizabeth Cohen (1990) wrote:

> During the 1930s American industrial workers sought to overcome the miseries and frustrations that long had plagued their lives neither through anticapitalist and extra-governmental revolutionary uprisings nor through perpetuation of the status quo of welfare capitalism but rather through their growing investment in two institutions they felt would make capitalism more moral and fair – an activist welfare state concerned with equalizing wealth and privilege and a national union movement of factory workers committed to keeping a check on self-interested employers. (pp. 365)

She does not suggest that workers believed that a growth period could occur, therefore increasing the financial pie. They wanted capitalism to be fairer in distributing the benefits, a very different perspective than Taylorism, which assumed a growing bounty (Cohen 1990; Kennedy 1999; Leuchtenburg 1995; Hamby 2004). Amity Shales (2007) gets this point right; the American people believed that the economy was permanently broken. Mostly Americans took the Great Depression as one would a major natural disaster – it simply happened.

If this were true, it would explain the crucial point regarding the Hawthorne studies – namely, if wages could no longer be paid, if economic incentives were limited, how do we motive workers? Taylorism assumed a consistently growing economy. In fact, its defenders, then and now, have pointed out the explicit purpose of creating plenty. However, it appeared that the era of the growing economy had ended. If so, what other elements could blend society together? The common response was government intervention. In fact, many intellectuals looked toward fascist Italy or Soviet Russia as a potential guide. Others looked toward the government to create stability. The initial New Deal response was to eliminate competition between labor and capital through the National Recovery Act, which set wages, production, and working conditions. This model was based on the War Industries Board from World War I (Kennedy 1999).

John Hassard (2012) has suggested that the Hawthorne studies were unneeded, citing the presence of welfare-capitalism at the Hawthorne plant. Hassard argued:

> The Hawthorne plant, which officially opened in 1907, soon developed a reputation within American industry as a champion of 'welfare capitalism' or the practice of businesses providing welfare-like services to employees. Under welfare capitalism, companies would typically offer workers higher pay and superior non-monetary compensation (such as health care, housing, and pensions, plus possibly social clubs, sports facilities, and in-house training) than available from other firms in the industry.

Richard Gillespie (1991) has agreed, arguing that the Hawthorne track team, formed in 1927, was the very flower of welfare capitalism, predating Mayo's work. The purpose of welfare capitalism, as Lizbeth Cohen (pg. 161) has proposed, was that "the enlightened corporation, not the labor union or the state, would spearhead the creation of a more benign industrial society." However, Cohen also noted, welfare capitalism died in the Great Depression, since companies (even a monopoly like the phone company) did not have the funds for it anymore.

Based on these two issues, we could draw a number of important conclusions. Mayo would have liked some aspects of welfare capitalism; it caused interaction between workers and management. People work to consumption is the old saw. However, what could make workers work, when incentives do not exist and consumption is impossible? Welfare capitalism all but died by 1933 when Mayo was arguing for attempts to discover spontaneity at work, and was dead in 1945, when he argued for more efforts to understand cooperation.

Rather than seeking government involvement, Mayo sought another benefit to this approach – it would provide laborers with a greater sense of connection to society, which would eliminate radical tendencies. Mayo's work frequently cited and sought inspiration from the work of anthropologists Radcliffe-Brown and Malinowski. In fact, when he tutored his great student George Homans (1984), most of his classes were interested in anthropological work on primitive societies, which Mayo believed had the clues to offer guidance in how to promote a better society. Mayo did not come up with a solution, noting in 1945 that modern sociology and psychology failed to provide a response. He merely noted that the Hawthorne research could lead to an explanation. His suggestion was that the use of rituals could be a solution, which received some confirmation with Roy's Banana Time (Roy 1959) article that indicated that "times and themes" can create a sense of unity. Mayo, during the 1930s, tried to sell his ideas to a wide array of business leaders. He did receive funding – but mostly his ideas were too under developed to be really applied.

Mayo's suggestions found intellectual conformation. Crane Brinton (1948) argued that what Mayo and his colleagues had done was to demonstrate that when economic conditions are clearly measurable, people still want to feel the sense of sharing, satisfaction of the ego, and emotional satisfaction. Brinton also notes, when referring to industrializing England, that economic values do not necessarily correspond to upheaval. Kornhauser (1934) and Elliott (1934) viewed Mayo's work as an attempt to develop answers to the widespread social disorganization, presumably caused by the war. Parsons (1940) motivation of economic activities argued that the institutionalization of self-interest had been one of the distinguishing characteristics of modern life. Yet, modern management techniques were needed. Parks praised the interdisciplinary work of the studies as a means of addressing various contemporary social issues.

The Good War

Mills and coauthors have demonstrated that the Hawthorne studies did not receive notice in the textbooks until after World War II. My own work (Muldoon 2012, 2017) has found that many of the articles, especially criticisms, did not occur until after 1946, with Bell's article in *Commentary* serving as a jumping point for criticism. The largest explanation for this occurrence was that the economic hardship of the depression limited the spread of the Hawthorne studies' message (Blum 1976. O'Neill 1993; Kennedy 1999). Sociology, psychology, and economics each faced hardships. There were few journals launched, few jobs, and fewer books. World War II also limited the degree to which books could be published owing to restrictions on the usage of paper. Therefore, it was not until after World War II and its aftermath that the Hawthorne studies received their due from scholars. Part of this reason was that, as *Fortune* (1946) magazine noted, Mayo's ideas and the research he inspired were just beginning to bear fruit.

The other significance of World War II to the Hawthorne studies has to do with the labor market. The war had dramatically changed the relationship between labor and capital. Labor's prewar desires had been nationalized by the War Labor Board. Unions had provided a guarantee not to strike. Unemployment had been all but eliminated. Wages did not rise, but neither did prices, due to price controls. Consumption was limited due to the war. People had money but consumer goods were rare. Instead, companies provided healthcare and other benefits to attract workers. Therefore, there was little economic reason for workers to strike. There were little social reasons as well. There was a strong sense of patriotism. Workers were encouraged to believe that they had a part to play in the war. People who were able to work and chose not to were considered slackers. Even the most radical elements of the American society supported the war. In fact, as Eric Foner has noted, World War II was the only war in history that did not have a major protest movement. Labor unions had moved to a position of accommodation with capital under the aegis of the New Deal broker state. The spirit of Gompers had won over unions, forsaking anything similar to the Industrial Workers of the World. Accordingly, labor unions agreed not to strike (Blum 1976; Kennedy 1999; O'Neill 1993).

Yet in both the war and its aftermath, a wide variety of union confrontations with management and the government were seen despite organized labor's promise not to strike that were unprecedented in the United States. Mining leader, John L. Lewis, continued striking during the war. Future President Harry S. Truman, a friend of labor, wanted Lewis shot for treason, claiming that the only reason why this did not occur was that President Franklin Roosevelt lacked guts (Kennedt 1999). For his part, Roosevelt felt that Lewis was the most dangerous man in the country. In addition, *Stars and Stripes*, the Army's official newspaper, attacked labor leaders who struck during the war. Although labor leaders were able to gain some concessions, the loss in reputation, confidence, and political support was, in the words of historian David Kennedy, "immeasurable" (Kennedy 1999: 643). Unions seemed unable to control labor. In 1944, there were 4956 labor stoppages alone. In 1945, there were 4750, and in 1946, there were 4985. These were shocking to the nation (Blum 1976; Kennedy 1999; O'Neill 1993). There was industrial upheaval in Europe and Great Britain as well.

These strikes occurred despite the fact that they were often illegal, wildcat strikes not endorsed by unions. These strikes had issues beyond simple pay; they were often the result of racial difficulties as well as issues with various managers. These wildcat strikes were, in essence, spontaneous actions done by labor against the approval and agreement of either the union or the government. James R. Zetka (1992) has noted that the close collaboration of working together actually provided workers with sufficient trust with other workers that encouraged strikes. Workers also violated the contracts that unions signed with management. The Mayo group noted that humanistic management prevented the wildcat strikes. Jerome Scott and George Homans researched a wildcat strike in Detroit, finding that the actions of one manager, who had developed a sense of trust with workers, prevented the wildcat strike. Scott and Homans, argued for the need for cooperation, the need to study human skills, having discussions with labor about issues, are perhaps the clearest statements on Mayoism. In essence, social interaction with management to encourage trust between workers and management was Mayo's major suggestion.

Mostly, Mayoism was a modification to the notion of rationalization, in that there would always be spontaneous actions since behavior had nonlogical antecedents. The notion was to develop better social skills to replace bureaucratic responses. The flowering of social sciences during the war could provide administrators with the tools needed to manage society. The use of collective bargaining – although still important – was viewed as a necessary but insufficient condition to ensure peace. The idea that workers can have spontaneous behaviors – beyond that of the work contract – meant that there was a need for new techniques to promote cooperation.

A series of articles published after the war hailed the development of new social sciences in aiding cooperation. In addition, several new human relations programs were founded after the war and many of them had connections to Mayo. D. N. Chester (1946) notes that Mayo attempted to address the major concerns of industrial life. The impact of the war could be seen in Kimball's review, where he noted the need to examine the development of social skills. In an article on the war and its relationship with sociology, Parsons and Barber (1948) noted that universities turned to other social issues, including education, race relations, public opinion, crime, alienation, social work, and anthropology with the purpose of promoting cooperation and integration.

One of the major new approaches was industrial sociology. The most notable success was the establishment of a department at the University of Chicago, with W. Lloyd Warmer and Burleigh Gardner as key figures. Both Warner and Gardner had a connection with the Hawthorne studies and Elton Mayo. They took up Mayo's criticism that the university needed to be the focal point of research and training for the administrator. Bladden (1948), who was a critic of Mayo, found himself a director of an industrial relations department a year after the war. Many social scientists were produced by the war providing a supply, while the problems of peace providing the demand (Kimball 1946; Parsons and Barber 1948).

Accordingly, Mayo's work saw acknowledgment in the press in a major way. *Fortune* (1946) magazine was one of the first to recognize the merit of Mayo's work. The unsigned article, as was the practice at the time, noted several important facets of the work. Firstly, *Fortune* noted that Mayo discovered one of the primary elements of behavior in the Hawthorne studies that social factors helped determine production. People did not wish to produce too much, which itself was an element of the peasant work culture that Taylor had only partially exorcised. Secondly, *Fortune* magazine argued that Mayo's ideas were a challenge to the notions held by both Adam Smith and Karl Marx that economics was the principle driver of behavior. *Fortune* magazine also noted that Mayo's ideas went beyond collective bargaining, attempting to seek spontaneous cooperation between various groups within society. In terms of Mayo's attitudes towards unions, *Fortune* found several interesting aspects. Union leader Clinton Golden felt that the work of the Hawthorne studies, especially its emphasis on the informal group, was a step in explaining how unions came to be. Golden went further by noting that unionization merely made these informal arrangements more permanent. Golden also pointed out that some of the social aspects that workers desired could not be explained with collective bargaining. As anyone who has worked a tedious job would understand, social relationships can make the job far more rewarding.

Drucker also pointed out that one of the principle attentions has been on the divide between labor and capital. For the system to work, there must be a reduction in conflict. Drucker asked why did conflict occur? Drucker notes that the principle conflict between labor and management is objective work conditions not someone's villainy. Few people bought into the image of the fat-cat owner or the lazy worker (Drucker 1946). Locke (1982) once noted that the principle contention between management and labor was over monetary wages. Yet, Drucker demonstrated that wage rates are rarely the cause of the problem – the problem is the overwhelming lack of trust that occurs between labor and management. This distrust is the primary driver of labor contention. Drucker notes that managerial unfairness, as well as arbitrary work elements, is the primary causes of dissatisfaction.

Drucker argued that collective bargaining does not substitute for trust. Since contracts are incomplete and enforcement mechanisms are costly, management often attempts to challenge the union on even the most benign matters (Drucker 1946; Locke 1982). Drucker also pointed out that there would be nothing as potentially dangerous as splitting up workers and separating them socially, arguing that workers seek acceptance and validation from their peers. He noted that two different plants – one in Dayton, where workers could compete and socialize with one another, and another at Indianapolis, where workers could not, had a distinct difference in production. Dayton was more productive (Drucker 1946).

An Inchoate Movement

The anti-Hawthorne movement had a high level of reliability, but it is unclear whether other scholars could form a legitimate alternative to the Hawthorne research. The reason is that the Hawthorne studies were a research study that had elements in sociology, political science, anthropology, management, and economics. Each of these fields has different research ends and means, funding, and different levels of legitimacy. The 1930s saw the development and hope that there would be an integrated social science. Robert Lynd, Mayo, and others were calling for science to develop more applied solutions. Talcott Parsons and George Homans would take this a step further by developing theories that explained a wide variety of human behaviors through the lens of sociology, psychology, and economics. C.W.M. Hart (1943) and others praised the Hawthorne studies for attempting to bend the boundaries between fields (Muldoon 2012; Muldoon 2017).

Yet this new science did not emerge. The fields had too many different assumptions and ends. For example, scholars criticize Mayo's work for attempting to improve production and morale. Yet, both of those ends are completely legitimate variables in management and psychology. It would be difficult to publish a paper in organizational behavior that did not have performance, or some variable similar to morale, as a criterion of research. This difference placed an impossible divide between critics and the Mayo group. Mayo's sociological critics talked past the Human Relations writers; Mayo and Roethlisberger did not respond; Homans talked past the critics. There was little conceptual overlap of work-related phenomena research. Psychologists ignored unions; economists placed emphasis on unions; sociology both ignored and placed emphasis on unions. The best reason why would be to follow the money. Sociology received money from unions, and psychology and management from business (Muldoon 2017).

My contention is that the major contenders for the father of human relations, Whiting Williams and Henry S. Denison, would also fail some, if not all, of the criticisms labeled on the Hawthorne studies. I found that there are generally about six major criticisms of the Hawthorne studies listed in the literature between 1936 and 1958. Contrary to Landsberger, the majority of the criticisms came from sociology and reflected the ongoing debates within the sociology literature. I also state that Bell's famous criticism was the focal point of launching the anti-Hawthorne movement. In this section, I would like to dwell on Williams and Denison as competitors to Hawthorne.

Whiting Williams was an early sociologist who conducted research on workplace behaviors during the 1910s and 1920s. He discovered many of the same "findings" that the Hawthorne studies did. Williams found that workers were motivated by feelings, worth (even managers), social relationships, social comparison based on pay, and the need for social interactions on the part of the worker. He also noted that workers sought union membership due to ineffective and arbitrary management. He discovered most of what would become Human Relations. Henry S. Denison, an executive and member of the Taylor Society, made similar findings, by stressing nonfinancial rewards, job enlargement, and social interactions, noting their role in increasing production. Wren and Bedeian note that one of the reasons why Human Relations commences with Hawthorne was that the Hawthorne studies had more of a scientific element (Bruce 2015; Wren 1987).

Yet the work of Williams and Denison would flunk several of the same criticisms leveled at the Hawthorne studies. For instance, sociology scholars would have had issue with the fact that job performance and cooperation were still dominant themes in the work of Williams and Dennison. Performance and cooperation would have been regarded not as objective criteria, but desired outcomes. In addition, scholars would have attacked Williams and Dennison (the same way as the Hawthorne studies) as observations collected at random, rather than a systematic study or experiment. Some radical scholars, such as C. Wright Mills and Daniel Bell, would have attacked Denison and Williams since they both supported maintaining, while reforming current structures of power, rather than overthrowing them. In addition, radical scholars would have challenged the idea that Dennison and Williams, men of privilege, would have really understood workers – a criticism that was placed on the Mayo group. Williams's type of research, undercover, was increasingly losing its influence over the field to survey and experiment.

Finally, the 1940s saw the emergence of theory within the field of sociology as a means to gain respect and legitimacy. Accordingly, several papers at the 1946 meeting of the American Sociological Society addressed the need for theory as well as scholars publishing work on how to theorize. This approach was hegemonic within the field, touching on the most prestigious schools in sociology, Harvard and Columbia. Theory, it is important to note, is hypotheses deduced from a set of propositions that are logically true called covering laws (Homans 1984).

This is different than theorizing based on observation. This was a stunning turn for the field, which up to the 1930s, had been devoted to practical research on social issues. Moore, one the drivers of theory, stated plainly that Mayo "is ignorant of the role of theory in social research" and that he instead "advocates amassing observations, apparently at random." Moore argued that this approach caused the misnaming of variables and confused hypotheses. I believe that both Williams and Denison flunk this test as well. I see little theory in Williams, as noted at the time; he provided interesting insight but with little explanation. Denison was considered, as Bruce notes, a theorist but one who was practical in orientation that developed observations inductively. As I note in my work on Homans and Fayol, this approach would have been considered illegitimate in the logical positivist 1940s and 1950s.

There is nothing new under the sun. Henri Fayol described the Hawthorne findings before Williams and Denison. St. Benedict predated Fayol. Roethlisberger suggested that Mayo was an update of the Gospel of St. Luke. Hawthorne, despite its problems, was perceived to have better methods, as well as stimulating scholars to research boundaries. It is not just knowledge, but also the methods we use to discover knowledge. The reason for multiple discoveries is often that a researcher made a fatal flaw, such as when Copernicus developed the heliocentric model. Galileo and Kepler were the ones who made it work.

Alternatively, Denison and Williams did not leave behind a generation of scholars to replicate and refine the original work. Alternatively, they worked, when their research was not in vogue. As I have noted, the Hawthorne studies combined better methods, explanations, and inspirations than the work that followed. Hilda Weiss Parker (1958) could claim that, until Mayo's work, there was little systematic and experimental research conducted in relationships at work. Williams work was reviewed, but scholars had some issues with the methods and insights. I have found not a single review of Denison's work in JSTOR. However, Mayo's work directly inspired subsequent research. My 2012 article has a long list of studies that were inspired by Mayo and this is merely a sample.

Mayo's work was disseminated at a time when scholars were attempting to move past bureaucracy to develop means of trust. The other reason why the Hawthorne studies became the dominate field was the human and social capital that Mayo reproduced. He legitimized the business school at Harvard, launched the careers of the two most cited sociologists of the 1960s (Parsons and Homans), and launched work centers at Chicago and Cornell. Elton Mayo inspired the political scientist Harold Laswell. Even Mayo's arch critic, Daniel Bell, noted that the emergence of industrial research at the university was because of Mayo. Put simply, Mayo inspired a generation of scholars to refute, expand, or explain his findings, or develop theory based on his findings. Mostly, the Hawthorne studies were the most significant contribution in that it forced the study of workplace behaviors as a distinct field separate from the worker and community (Trahair 1984).

Elton Mayo: The Manager as Therapist

Scholars have placed Mayo and Taylor as a match pair fighting over the nature of industrial life. These two men are in opposition to each other because Burleigh Gardner and Stuart Chase sought to separate the work of both men. In addition, as Bruce noted, the Taylor society held less than promising views of the Hawthorne studies. Depending on your perspective, it is the scientifically valid Taylor versus the unscientific Mayo or the inhuman Taylor versus the humanist Mayo. Other scholars, such as Edwin Locke (1982), J. Boddewyn (1961), and Daniel Wren (2005), have noted that Taylor preceded Mayo. We should see the Hawthorne studies as both an attempt at an applied social science and answering the limitations of scientific management. Mayo and Taylor should not be viewed as competitors rather as complements. Along with Stephen Warring (1994), I view modern organizational behavior to have elements of both Mayo and Taylor.

Lyndall Urwick (1937, 1943, 1944) attempted to combine both viewpoints into a new management theory. Mayo addressed the Taylor society; Roethelisberger praised Taylor. Powell (1957) sees Taylor as the genesis of the human relations movement, noting that Mayo considers issues of social organization, but that Taylor also had a simplistic understanding of social and psychological issues. It should be noted that this was the case, as we will discuss later. Powell also noted that Williams produced some of the most important work; he developed shrewd insights about plant life. Yet, Powell also notes that it was Mayo who built on the work of Powell in expanding the role of worker social behavior at work. Time magazine noted:

The seeds of this change were sewn by two great pioneers whose names are scarcely known – Frederick Winslow Taylor, a one-time day laborer, and Elton Mayo, an Australian immigrant turned Harvard sociologist. Their work did not seem related but it was. Taylor, who died in 1915, was the father of scientific management; he increased industrial production by rationalizing it. Mayo, who died in 1949, was the father of industrial human relations; he increased production by humanizing it.

Bendix and Fisher (1949) noted that in the future we should see them as "not unrelated." Wren and Bedeian have argued that they should be seen as complements.

William Hawley Cooper (1962) delivered the most sustained analysis of the relationship between Hawthorne and Taylor. He argued that they both focused on different aspects of the job. Taylor was, according to Cooper, (pg. 23) a form-perceiving manager,

> aware of his surroundings in terms of shape, structure, and orderly arrangement. His perceptions are analogous to those of a builder who takes a disorderly mass of raw material and converts it into a recognized useful order, or to a scientist who looks at the seeming chaos in nature and either defines or creates an orderly pattern, or to an artist who sets down on canvas an arrangement of patterns that he hopes are meaningful.

Mayo viewing tasks and procedures as a process-receiving manager might as one who views life as transitory and lacking set form.

Mostly, to use contemporary terms, Taylor was concerned with economic exchange, where the terms of the exchange are discussed beforehand, where everyone has distinct roles and remuneration is known beforehand. Taylor sought to increase trust through scientifically determining both work and pay conditions. Yet, Taylor ignores that a great amount of meaning is determined through social interaction and that not all aspects of work could be broken down. Mayo's recognition was that in an earlier, preindustrial society, people clearly understood their obligations because roles were socialized through rituals, which in turn allowed for trust and spontaneous cooperation to ensue. Mayo recognized that the new order, one based primarily on economic benefit, had washed away this old society, creating a new society where acquisition was the primary obligation, ignoring other social issues. This created a lack of trust and cooperation. Mayo was more concerned with what makes spontaneous cooperation possible. Social outings, encouraged by management, are not, by definition, spontaneous.

The notion of cooperation is one of the principle driving factors behind the development of both scientific management and the advent of the human relations movement. William H. Knowles (1952) argues that the term "cooperation" is one dependent on the field. For example, economics focuses on the ability of the market to ensure cooperation between various partners who use prices to coordinate between buyer and supplier. Yet, anticipating transaction cost economics, Knowles's perspective breaks down in the face of larger collectives. After all, most transactions are nonmarket. The price mechanism often sets a bare minimum of cooperation, namely, what a worker could do without losing his job. From the manager's perspective, the maximum amount of effort sought would increase the speed of production without facilitating a strike. Compounding this problem is the issues raised by Karl Marx, who pointed out the paradox – that capitalism's growth was based on the growth of cooperation. Cooperation would be based on division of labor, which would require the need for a directing authority and that this directing authority would extract as much production on an increasingly dependent workforce. Therefore, a new system of coordination was needed to aid in exchange. Marx's solution was dictatorship of the proletariat and control means of production. Taylor sought to use science and financial incentives to solve the problem; Mayo sought to use social ties.

As Wagner-Tsukamoto (2007) noted, Taylorism was mostly concerned with the ability of managers to handle issues of opportunism on the part of workers. Taylor saw the solution to opportunism as both science and incentive, ignoring the fact that a great many parts of work are, as Mayo noted, spontaneous. In a system that is rationalized, where every arrangement is determined by job design and job performance is quantified, there is little in the way of actual trust and discretion. Thus, there is very little need for actual management, since everything is determined by function. Taylorism was incomplete because it could not understand that trust can be a solution to work problems. Many organizations have shifted away from the hierarchical model of performance to a model based on social exchange relationships. The reason is that, once again, we have recognized that there are certain behaviors that could not be preprogrammed. A usual job description contains some, but not all, of the tasks required by the company, as companies often use the open phrase "as determined by the supervisor." How could management ensure completion of those tasks, especially for behaviors that are informal and unrewarded (Organ et al. 2006).

Mayo understood that group interactions were a common part of the job. He was correct that groups could allow soldiering. The difference was that Mayo understood that financial incentives were not the basis of cooperation, because the manager/scientists could not conceive of every element at work. Nor could government structures and rules ensure compliance. Human relations seemed to become more popular in the years after World War II as a means of dealing with wildcat strikes, of which there were many, despite the "no strike" promises offered by management. Mayo was also correct that no amount of money could eliminate the need for social interactions. Although he overstated his case greatly, even his greatest critic, Daniel Bell, recognized the majority of social relationships come from work. Certain studies performed during the 1950s, such as Roy's Banana Time, confirm this general idea. Mayo's belief was that modern social scientists should create rituals as a means of ensuring cooperation. To summarize, Mayo added the social element to Taylorism, creating a system of both formal and informal inducements to create trust and effort.

Conclusion

Elton Mayo left a great record. Even Bell, his most notable critic, both in his 1947 article and his later work, recognized that Mayo had developed a new approach in recognizing the importance of studying workplace behaviors, as well as the importance of the manager to society. Again, this is not to say that Mayo was original. I find myself in agreement with Drucker that Mayo was a true scholar in that he was a codifier and an originator. I wrote (Muldoon 2012):

> Hawthorne's second contribution was that it provided researchers with a more focused analysis of workers' interactions within the organization, such as the social interaction between workers and supervisors. Contemporaries understood that the work of the Hawthorne researchers was not only more rigorous than the work of Williams, but also provided new paths and understandings for future research. Whether the contribution was providing the concept of the man in the middle or exploring the dynamics of social influence on production (Whyte 1956), scholars noted that the Hawthorne studies provided a new and significant break from the work of Williams and other contemporaries. Summed up this idea when he conceded that the original and pioneering effort of industrial sociology was *What's on the Worker's Mind*. He also noted, however, that Mayo's group made the most influential contribution because it focused attention squarely on the internal organization so that it became the dominant concern of industrial sociology. The general conclusion from both Mayo and Williams was that workers' motivation was a combination of both monetary and non-monetary benefits. (Parsons 1940; Rogers 1946)

It was not that Mayo was original, nor did he develop a theory, nor did found a school – his disciples had rigorous arguments between them. He did not produce an applied solution to the labor question nor did he endorse any propose solutions. In fact, he argued that there were no known solutions. What Mayo did was to demonstrate the complexity of modern work life and the need to take the attitudes, feelings, and other motivations of workers seriously. He codified the other findings of the 1920s.

Modern organizational behavior bares his imprint directly. Due to Mayo's efforts, we demonstrated that work motivation has intrinsic and social elements in addition to monetary benefits. We have demonstrated that job satisfaction, organizational commitment, and morale are important outcomes to job performance and that managers should pay attention to them. We know that work stress and injury is related to relationships and attitudes, as well as working conditions. There is vast literature on the need for managers to develop relationships with workers that create spontaneous behaviors and cooperation. We also have demonstrated, through transaction cost economics, that not every work condition can be known beforehand nor can we effectively monitor workers. This rich legacy was due to the Hawthorne studies and Elton Mayo. Mayo may not have been a deep and rigorous thinker, but he understood the big picture of the modern world better than anyone, including Taylor (Whyte 1987).

The failures of welfare capitalism and pure unionism to produce a cooperative society have been noted during Mayo's time. In fact, the importance of supervisor/subordinate relationships within the organization is intensified in the current business environment due to the presence of reorganization, downsizing, and layoffs. All of which limit the social rewards and potential satisfaction individuals derive from the organization, making it necessary for these individuals to seek satisfaction elsewhere. Supervisor/subordinate dyads enable both parties to gain satisfaction, thus encouraging them to exchange resources that aid the organization.

Consequently, supervisors are encouraged to create quality relationships with their subordinates as a means of ensuring the proper functioning of the organization (Cappelli et al. 1997; Organ 1988; Rousseau 1998).

If Mayo did not matter, why do we spend so much time looking at measures related to job satisfaction and commitment? If spontaneous behaviors and relationships beyond economic exchange were not important, why is there vast literature on social exchange? Mayo's contemporary and historical critics fail to answer those questions. The profession owes them a great deal however, since they force us to examine why Mayo emerged and the intellectual context of the research. Part of the problem, as Landsberger suggested, should be placed directly on the shoulders of Mayo. Mayo did not have the ability to define his interests precisely and was too ambitious in his endeavors. Had he simply suggested that he was looking at spontaneous behaviors, in conjunction with programmed behaviors, he would have made his contributions more clear. In addition, had he engaged the scholarship literature or his critics, his contribution would have been more obvious. This combination means that Mayo's legacy contains unneeded complexity. Like Taylor, Mayo suffered a lack of empathy or understanding with his critics – repeating his mantra "let the heathen rage." His unwillingness to engage meant that Mayo only produced more heathens (Smith 1998).

Cross-References

▶ Organizational Psychology and the Rise of Human Resource Management
▶ Taylor Made Management

References

Bell D (1947) Adjusting men to machines. Commentary 3:79–88
Bell, D. (1973). The coming of post-industrial society. New York: Basic.
Bell D (1976) The cultural contradictions of capitalism. Basic Books, New York
Bendix R (1956) Work and authority in industry: ideologies of management in the course of industrialization. Wiley, New York
Bendix R, Fisher LH (1949) The perspectives of Elton Mayo. Rev Econ Stat 31(4):312–319
Blum JM (1976) V was for victory. Harcourt Brace Janocvich, Boston
Boddewyn J (1961) Frederick Winslow Taylor revisited. J Acad Manag 4(2):100–107
Brinkley A (1998) Liberalism and its discontents. Harvard University Press, Cambridge, MA
Brinton C (1948) The manipulation of economic unrest. J Econ Hist 8(S1):21–31
Bruce K (2006) Henry S. Dennison, Elton Mayo, and the human relations historiography. Manag Organ Hist 1(2):177–199
Bruce K (2015) Activist manager: the enduring contribution of Henry S. Dennison to management and organization studies. J Manag Hist 21(2):143–171
Bruce K, Nyland C (2011) Elton Mayo and the deification of human relations. Organ Stud 32(3):383–405
Cappelli P, Bassi L, Katz H, Knoke D, Osterman P (1997) Change at work. Oxford University Press, New York
Carey A (1967) The Hawthorne studies as radical criticism. Am Sociol Rev 32(3):403–416
Chase S (1946) Calling all social scientists. Nation Mag 162:538–540

Chester DN (1946) Book review of "the social problems of an industrial civilization." Econ J 56(222):288–290

Cohen L (1990) Making a new deal: industrial workers in Chicago. Cambridge University Press, New York, pp 1919–1939

Cooper WH (1962) The comparative administrative philosophies of Frederick W Taylor and Elton Mayo. Unpublished doctoral dissertation, University of Pennsylvania

Cropanzano R, Mitchell MS (2005) Social exchange theory: an interdisciplinary review. J Manag 31:874–900

Drucker PF (1946) For industrial peace. Harper's Weekly 193:385–395

Elliott M (1934) Book review of human problems of an industrial civilization. Am Econ Rev 24(2):322–323

Fortune (1946) The fruitful errors of Elton Mayo. Fortune 34:181–186

Foster J, Mills AJ, Weatherbee TG (2014) The new deal, history, and management & organization studies: constructing disciplinary actors and theories. J Manag Hist 20(2):179–199

Gardner BB, Moore DG (1945) Human relations in industry. Richard D. Irwin, Chicago

Gillespie R (1991) Manufacturing knowledge: a history of the Hawthorne experiments. Cambridge University Press, Cambridge

Hamby AA (2004) For the survival of democracy. Free Press, New York

Hart CWM (1943) The Hawthorne experiments. Can J Econ Polit Sci 9(2):150–163

Hart CWM (1949) Industrial relations research and social theory. Canadian Journal of Economics and Political Science/Revue canadienne de economiques et science politique, 15(1):53–73

Hassard JS (2012) Rethinking the Hawthorne studies: the western electric research in its social, political, and historical context. Hum Relat 65(11):1431–1461

Heames JT, Breland JW (2010) Management pioneer contributors: 30-year review. J Manag Hist 16(4):427–436

Homans GC (1949a) The perspectives of Elton Mayo: some corrections. Rev Econ Stat 31(4):319–321

Homans GC (1949b) The strategy of industrial sociology. Am J Sociol 54(4):330–337

Homans GC (1984) Coming to my senses: the autobiography of a social scientist. Transaction Books, New Brunswick

Kennedy DM (1999) Freedom from fear: the American people in depression and war, vol 9. Oxford University Press, New York, pp 1929–1945

Kimball DS (1946) Book review of the social problems of an industrial civilization. Ann Am Acad Polit Soc Sci 245(1):206–207

Knowles WH (1952) Economics of industrial engineering. Ind Labor Relat Rev 5(2):209–220

Kornhauser AW (1934) Book review of the human problems of an industrial civilization. Ann Am Acad Polit Soc Sci 172:171–171

Landsberger HA (1958) Hawthorne revisited: management and the worker: its critics and developments in human relations in industry. Cornell University Press, Ithaca

Leuchtenburg WE (1995) The FDR years. Columbia University Press, New York

Locke EA (1982) The ideas of Frederick W. Taylor: an evaluation. Acad Manag Rev 7(1):14–24

Locke EA, Latham GP (1984) Goal setting: a motivational technique that works! Prentice Hall, Englewood Cliffs

Mayo E (1933) The human problems of an industrial civilization. Macmillan, New York

Mayo E (1945) The social problems of an industrial civilization. Harvard University Press, Cambridge

Moore WE (1947) Book review. Am Sociol Rev 12(1):123–124

Muldoon J (2012) The Hawthorne legacy: a reassessment of the impact of the Hawthorne studies on management scholarship, 1930–1958. J Manag Hist 18(1):105–119

Muldoon J (2017) The Hawthorne studies: an analysis of critical perspectives, 1936–1958. J Manag Hist 23(1):74–94

O'Connor ES (1999a) The politics of management thought: a case study of the Harvard Business School and the human relations school. Acad Manag Rev 24(1):117–131

O'Connor E (1999b) Minding the workers: the meaning of 'human' and 'human relations' in Elton Mayo. Organization 62:223–246

O'Neill W (1993) A democracy at war: America's fight at home and abroad in World War II. Free Press, New York

Organ DW (1988) Organizational citizenship behavior: the good soldier syndrome. Lexington Books, Lexington

Organ DW, Podsakoff PM, MacKenzie SB (2006) Organizational citizenship behavior: its nature, antecedents, and consequences. Sage, Thousand Oaks

Park RE (1934) Industrial fatigue and group morale. Am J Sociol 40(3):349–356

Parker HW (1958) Industrial relations, manipulative or democratic?. Am J Econ Sociol 18(1):25–33

Parsons T (1940) The motivation of economic activities. Can J Econ Polit Sci 6(2):187–202

Parsons HM (1974) What happened at Hawthorne? Science 10:259–282

Parsons T, Barber B (1948) Sociology, 1941–1946. Am J Sociol 53(4):245–257

Peach EB, Wren DA (1991) Pay for performance from antiquity to the 1950s. J Organ Behav Manag 12(1):5–26

Powell DSF (1957) Recent trends in industrial sociology. Am Cathol Sociol Rev 18(3):194–204

Roethlisberger FJ (1977) The elusive phenomena. Harvard University Press, Cambridge

Rogers M (1946) Problems of human relations in industry. Sociometry 9(4):350–371

Rose M (1975) Industrial behaviour: theoretical development since Taylor. Allen Lane, London

Rousseau DM (1998) LMX meets the psychological contract: looking inside the black box of leader member exchange. In: Dansereau F, Yammarino FJ (eds) Leadership: the multiple level approaches. JAI Press, Greenwich, pp 149–154

Roy D (1959) Banana time: job satisfaction and informal interaction. Hum Organ 18(4):158–168

Shales A (2007) The forgotten man: a new history of the great depression. HarperCollins, New York

Smith JH (1998) The enduring legacy of Elton Mayo. Hum Relat 51(3):221–249

Sonnenfeld JA (1985) Shedding light on the Hawthorne studies. J Occup Behav 6:110–130

Stone RC (1952) Conflicting approaches to the study of workers. Soc Forces 31(2):117–124

Trahair RCS (1984) The humanist temper. Transaction Books, New Brunswick

Urwick LF (1937) The function of administration. In: Gulick L, Urwick LF (eds) Papers on the science of administration, Institute of Public Administration. Columbia University, New York, pp 115–130

Urwick LF (1943) Administration in theory and practice. Br Manag Rev 8:37–59

Urwick LF (1944) The elements of administration. Harper & Row, New York

Wagner-Tsukamoto S (2007) An institutional economic reconstruction of scientific management: on the lost theoretical logic of Taylorism. Acad Manag Rev 32(1):105–117

Warring S (1994) Taylorism transformed, Reissue edition. The University of North Carolina Press, Chapel Hill

Whyte WF (1956) Problems of industrial sociology. Soc Probl 4(2):148–160

Whyte WF (1987) From human relations to organizational behavior: reflections on the changing scene. Ind Labor Relat Rev 40(4):487–500

Williams, Mills AJ (2017) Frances Perkins: gender, context and history in the neglect of a management theorist. J Manag Hist 23(1):32–50

Wren DA (1987) The white collar hobo. Iowa State University Press, Ames

Wren DA (2005) The history of management thought, 5th edn. Wiley, Hoboken

Wren DA, Hay RD (1977) Management historians and business historians: differing perceptions of pioneer contributions. Acad Manag J 20(3):470–476

Zetka JR Jr (1992) Work organization and wildcat strikes in the US automobile industry, 1946 to 1963. Am Sociol Rev 57:214–226

Organizational Psychology and the Rise of Human Resource Management

24

Jeffrey Muldoon

Contents

Introduction 565
The Rise of Psychology 566
Great Apart, Better Together: The Gilbreths 570
Munsterberg, Scott, and Van Dyke 573
World War I 576
Human Relations: Barnard and Follett 578
Welfare Capitalism and the New Deal 584
Conclusion 587
References 587

Abstract

The purpose of this chapter is to explain the development of both human resource management and psychology. The major contention of this chapter is that both human resource management and psychology were created to supplement, but not supplant, Taylorism by providing a better understanding of social motives and tests to scientifically select workers.

Keywords

I/O psychology · Human resource management · Welfare capitalism · Human relations

---

J. Muldoon (✉)
Emporia State University, Emporia, KS, USA
e-mail: jmuldoon@emporia.edu

© The Author(s), under exclusive licence to Springer Nature Switzerland AG 2020   565
B. Bowden et al. (eds.), *The Palgrave Handbook of Management History*,
https://doi.org/10.1007/978-3-319-62114-2_30

Introduction

In the previous chapter on Taylorism, I argued that Taylorism could be seen as an attempt to rationalize worker behavior based on new developments in knowledge, the rise of science, and a sense of idealism that knowledge transforms working and social conditions. In this chapter, I argue that the emergence of Taylorism leads to the emergence of human resource (HR) management. That is to say, the early proponents of human resource management recognized, like Taylor, the importance of workers in terms of production. Unlike Taylor, they recognized that Taylorism had underplayed social motivations and so sought ways to understand social influences. Like Taylor, early HR proponents recognized that workers had different skills and aptitudes, but unlike Taylor, they began to develop techniques to scientifically select workers based on mental abilities. Much like Taylor, early HR advocates also recognized the need for higher wages based on performance, but unlike Taylor, they also recognized the need for social interactions at work. In essence, they were on the other side of the progressive movement – one focused on the individual in society, rather than technical skill. They were competitors to and complements to Taylorism.

The development of HR took place in Germany, with the emergence of scientific psychology as a field of study in the nineteenth century, and continues to cast a shadow on contemporary psychology and management (Robinson 1995). Psychology was brought to the United States by émigré Germans (like Hugo Munsterberg) and American students (like Walter Dill Scott; Benjamin 2007). HR was adopted by Americans, such as Frank and Lillian Gilbreth, who wished to provide psychological techniques to better understand the workers' mental processes. The nascent field of human resource management was encouraged and legitimized by the United States experience of World War I (Kennedy 1980). Human resource management was both a progressive action and a conservative compromise to prevent radical solutions to industrial problems. Mostly, it was a modernist-inspired reform that occurred to improve social and working conditions by raising workers from their premodern, peasant work culture to the new modernist culture of plenty. Human resource management can be seen as a progressive reform attempt to address ongoing social problems. It also occurred because philosophers debated the relationship between individual and society, realism and idealism, and agency and determination.

The Rise of Psychology

While psychology has been studied for centuries but as a subset of philosophy (Boeree 2018), scholars did not believe it could be a science until the last 200 years (Benjafield 2010). This view was held by philosophers such as Immanuel Kant. General historical psychology studies, both popular and academic, start with the classical philosophers stretching from antiquity up to the nineteenth century, when psychology began to emerge as a distinct field. In fact, most of the psychologists who set the general models of psychology (with the exception of B. F. Skinner) were born in the nineteenth century (Robinson 1995). Many of the early professional and academic psychologists had backgrounds in philosophy or medicine, which continued up to the career of Elton Mayo (Robinson 1995; Traihair 1984). Several important developments of the nineteenth century allowed for psychology to become a distinct field apart from philosophy.

The birth of psychology occurred in Germany and would spread to the United States during the period of 1870–1940 (Benjamin 2007; Benjafield 2010). Many of the concepts of human resource management would develop in Europe, but the greatest application would be in the United States. There are several drivers to this, but the largest was that reformers understood that American exceptionalism, the idea of a nation of small farms and providers (Lincoln's America), died during the Civil War (White 2017). The Civil War, and other events, aided in the interconnection of America through communication and transportation, and the emergence of bureaucracy provided the challenge to the Old America of small farms and businesses (Wiebe 1967). In addition, the proclamation of the end of the frontier by the federal government provided further ammunition for reformers that American exceptionalism had run its course. According to Daniel Rodgers (1998), America entered into an asymmetrical relationship with Europe to solve social problems. As Rodgers and others noted, America's contribution was Fordism – my contention was that American thinkers took European ideas and used them to create human resource management.

This genesis started with a rejection of the Kantian philosophy of science. Like many scholars of his generation, Kant believed that Newtonian models held the secret to science and that any true science should be based on Newton's work (Benjafield 2010). For Kant, this meant that science should be based upon mathematical models (Mischel 1967). Kant, however, did not believe psychology could ever become a science, like physics, and should be held as a philosophy (Benjafield 2007). His reasoning is that the processes of the mind were organized temporarily, unlike the physical world, which is organized spatially. Kant believed that the processes of the mind could not be studied mathematically as they changed too quickly. However, Kant also recognized that the progress of science could change commonly held nostrums.

German scholars of subsequent generations could challenge Kant's arguments. What Green et al. (2001) called the "transformation of psychology" occurred due to scholars understanding that psychology could be studied through mathematics and then through experimentation. J. F. Herbart, who took Kant's position at the University of Konigsberg, was one of the first to recognize that ideas could facilitate each other the same way that physical forces could. These forces could also vary, like physical forces, in their intensity. Therefore, if ideas mirrored physical forces, then they could be studied mathematically. G. T. Fechner built on these ideas by developing an approach to psychology that could be considered truly scientific (Benjafield 2007). Fechner developed psychophysics which held that we could develop a mathematically precise relationship between "stimulation and sensation that could be tested through experimental data" (80). In addition, Fechner understood that outside forces can influence the mind – basically the relationship between stimulation and recognition.

Another important contribution to emerging psychology was the work of Charles Darwin, the father of evolution (Benjafield 2007). The concept of evolution rebutted the medieval world ideas of the time which argued that God had organized the world into hierarchies and those hierarchies were immutable. Darwin observed that species can evolve and change. Darwin preached the concept of natural selection and survival of the fittest which stated that the worthy would be more likely to pass their genetics onward to the next generation (Benjafield 2007). Darwin's concept meant that humanity was not bound by God's limits, but could evolve and change. Darwin's concepts meant that humans could be studied and modified to fit the needs of society (Goldman 1952).

Another important outcome of psychology's emergence as a science was the development of laboratory psychology. If psychology could be reduced to mathematical terms, then it could be studied like other sciences (Robinson 1995; Benjamin 2007). The origin of this type of study occurred in Germany, which was at the forefront of laboratory research (Benjamin 2007). Wilhelm Wundt led this movement and would become the founder of modern psychology. The reason why scholars have provided him with this honor is due to the fact that Wundt melded philosophy with physiology through the use of "that enduring motif" of modern psychology, the laboratory (Capshew 1992). Wundt's laboratory psychology sought to understand how elements of the conscious experiences could lend themselves to mental aggregates that could be studied. Wundt also influenced and mentored many psychologists including G. Stanley Hall, James McKeen Cattell, Walter Dill Scott, and Hugo Munsterberg, who holds the title of the first applied psychologist.

Wundt's contemporary and rival was William James, the Harvard psychologist and philosopher, who created the first psychology lab in 1874. Whereas James's lab was one of demonstration, Wundt's was one of research (Benjafield 2010). Yet James made three contributions to psychology. The first one was the concept of habit in that people perform activities that are consistent, distinct, and similar that emerge from adaptation to the environment. James, along with his contemporary John Dewey, argued that thought must lead to action. Second, James further developed Kant's idea of understanding (e.g., demonstrating that experience was a condition of knowledge) by arguing that knowledge interacts with the environment rather than just being a reflection of it (Kloppenberg 1986). Third, James, the father of pragmatism, forced scholars to consider the practical implications of actions – which is that knowledge should be tested to be verified (Gutek 2014).

Another important development of the nineteenth century and early twentieth century was the transformation of knowledge that recognized a midpoint between idealism and empiricism. Much like Taylor's work, which held that work could be quantified, scholars of what Kloppenberg called the via *media* developed ways to enable psychology to be studied. These scholars were Wilhelm Dilthey, Thomas Hill Green, Henry Sidgwick, Alfred Fouillée, William James, and John Dewey. Firstly, they rejected the idea that humans were bound by invisible forces that constrained and defined human interaction. The previous generation believed, like Abraham

Lincoln, that they were controlled by events (Donald 1995). However, the post-Civil War generation believed that people had agency. As Kloppenberg noted these intellectuals "revealed that freedom is an irreducible part of immediate experience that neither science nor metaphysics can challenge or explain away" (412). This meant that individuals could be melded and reformed. It also meant that people were not a singular group bound by original conditions. Yet they also recognized that people were connected by history and society through a web of relationships and circumstances; an "idea that social relations are a fundamental part of individual life altered the meaning of individuality by excluding the possibility of prosocial or nonsocial experience on which so much earlier political theory relied" (412). This meant that individuals could be studied as groups because society existed rather than everyone being a distinct individual.

One of the questions was the influence of outside forces on individuals. James was distressed by the deterministic nature of Wundt's psychology, and his exposure to it placed him in a malaise that lasted for a period of 5 years (Kloppenberg 1986). Their argument was over Darwinian concepts. Wundt believed that human behavior was determined by its environment and was not changeable. Yet James was able to resolve this issue by reading poetry of Wordsworth, who, according to Kloppenberg (1986), convinced him that free will was not an illusion. James took it a step further – noting that free will and determinism was a false dichotomy. Individuals are free to choose, but they are also defined and constrained by outside forces. In fact, adaption to those outside forces is a concept that people were able to survive. This concept became what Eric Goldman (1952) called "reform Darwinism," in that the use of knowledge and science can liberate individuals from their current status as there is no natural law that stated they had to be that way forever.

Goldman's concept of "reform Darwinism" and via *media* could refer to the idea of government reform, and, in fact, both are cornerstones of modern liberalism and social democracy (Kloppenberg 1986). However, both concepts could refer to the application of social science at solving society's problems. Indeed, the modern fields of social work, psychology, sociology, and management all have their genesis during this time period. Part of the reformers problem was to maintain the benefits of the new world of machination and factory while reducing some of the worst examples associated with it. For this reason, a multitude of scientists sought to solve problems through reform. Compassion for the poor, driven in part by Christian morality, secular humanism, and modern science, motivated reformers (Link and McCormack 1983). Their target was the working class, whose conditions made them a prime place for testing new concepts. The concept of intersubjectivity, that is, humans discover their true selves in interactions with others, would underline much of the concept of human resource management. Workplace reform has been given a short shift in traditional studies of the progressive movement. Yet the modernization of work could be seen as providing similar problems as reforming the working class. According to Bruce Kaufman (2008), the emergence of human resource management took place because workers needed skill development and training and socialization to the new work environment and businesses needed scientifically developed selection techniques in order to select workers. In other words, it reflected the reform instincts of the progressive movement. As I mentioned before, management could be seen as providing modernization to the workplace, in order to overcome the pre-modern nature of work habits.

Great Apart, Better Together: The Gilbreths

Frank and Lillian Gilbreth made tremendous contributions to the field of management over the course of their careers. The timeline of their contributions was incomparable. From the 1890s until the early 1970s, both Frank and Lillian, sometimes together, sometimes apart, made significant and far-reaching contributions to fields as disparate as construction, sports, office work, healthcare, and the modern kitchen. It was a testimony to their greatness that in Wren and Hay's (1977) evaluation of management thinkers, Frank is placed third and Lillian, fifth. Although they faired more poorly in Heames and Breland's (2010) reconsideration, both Gilbreths still cast a large shadow upon the field of management. Frank achieved greatness before Lillian and Lillian, after Frank died. But they worked better together. Their contribution was to combine efficiency engineering with humanism – in essence helping our modern understanding of human resource management (Mousa and Lemak 2009) and modern production, such as the Toyota system (Towill 2010). In fact, the timelessness of their viewpoints is why scholars still recommend Gilbreths' work to improve ongoing work and social problems, such as healthcare (Towill 2009). Their guiding light was efficiency both at work and at home (Bedeian and Taylor 2009), a common refrain in the Progressive Era (Haber 1964). Perhaps the reason why they were attracted to each other was that they shared the same goals and a recognition that they could accomplish more together than they could apart. In many ways, they were like another couple at the time, Sidney and Beatrice Webb, in that they had the spirit of reform coursing through their lives (Himmelfarb 1991).

Frank Bunker Gilbreth (1868–1924) was born to a New England family, whose roots traced back to the Colonial times (Gibson et al. 2016b). Frank was the third child born to a prosperous hardware store owner and his wife. Frank learned the Yankee principles of thrift and hard work from his parents. His father died from pneumonia when Frank was 3, and Frank's mother either mismanaged the inheritance, or more likely, it was stolen from them by Frank's paternal relatives (Lancaster 2004). This devastated the family, forcing Frank's mother to open a boarding house in Boston. Yet there was a benefit to this; Frank and his sisters were able to attend some of the best public schools in the country (Yost 1949). However, Frank was a poor and indifferent student – but he excelled in mechanical, science, and math classes (Gibson et al. 2016a, b). Frank also demonstrated an ability in drawing and writing – which, according to Gibson et al., would be a major benefit to him when he later became a consultant. Frank's grades improved enough to the point where he was able to gain admission to the Massachusetts Institute of Technology. However, Frank made the decision to turn down college to work in construction.

Gilbreth's mechanical skills and choice of a career were not unusual; building tradesman was often paid higher than other professions. Gilbreth advanced rapidly, learning every part of the construction job, designing his own techniques, and building scaffolds, and within 5 years was a superintendent of the company and, 10 years after he started, the chief superintendent of the company (Wren and Bedeian 2018). Gilbreth's attention was peaked when he noticed that Tom Bowler, the "star bricklayer," taught Gilbreth three different ways to place bricks. This encouraged Gilbreth to understand that there could be an optimal way to work, and he took steps to find that way. He also realized that proper supervision, training, and incentives would allow men to work and produce more. Unlike Taylor, Gilbreth joined the American Federation of Labor and sought to have a strong relationship with organized labor (Gibson et al. 2016a, b). Lillian would also agree with Gilbreth and against Taylor about workers motivations and needs (Graham 2000).

When Gilbreth failed to make partner in the construction firm, he started his own firm which quickly became a success. Gilbreth already owned patents on the Gilbreth Waterproof Cellar which prevented leaks during construction, Vertical Scaffold which allowed for bricks to be moved, and a concrete mixer whose sales were very helpful during the early years of his company. Due to his innovations, he was able to dramatically reduce prices. According to Gibson et al. (2016a, b), Gilbreth's company built factories, power plants, and canals where his "cost plus fixed sum" bidding system, albeit controversial, provided him with a competitive edge against the competition (as well as numerous court appearances). His success made him very famous, and he had an office in London, where he consulted with the British admiralty (Wren and Bedeian 2018).

In 1903, Frank Gilbreth met Lillian Moller Gilbreth (1878–1972) who would become his wife, academic partner, one of the first industrial/organizational psychologists, and the first lady of management (Wren and Bedeian 2009). Lillian was the 2nd of 11 children born to middle-class German-American parents. Lillian had been homeschooled for several years until she started first grade at the age of 9, making her older, better educated, and shyer than her classmates. Her parents opposed sending Lillian to college, but due to the influence of her aunt, Lillian was able to convince her parents to attend college, but only at the University of California at Berkeley (Gibson et al. 2015). For her masters, Lillian went to Columbia University to study English. Unfortunately for Lillian, the professor she wished to study with would not take female students or even allow them in his class. Fortunately for management, Lillian took a course under Edward Thorndike, who developed in Lillian a passion for psychology (Gibson et al. 2015).

Fate intervened when Lillian fell ill, having to leave Columbia to complete her master's degree at Berkeley. Lillian's drive for a career was due in part in her belief that she was unattractive and had little to offer the opposite sex. Her career goal was to become a college dean. When the "shy" Lillian met the "ball of energy" Frank Gilbreth (Gibson et al. 2015), Frank provided Lillian with a confidence that she did not have before; her decision to focus on management was due to her marriage – although her prior experience with Thorndike played a role as well. For Frank, she provided a new dimension to management – psychology. Lillian would complete the equivalent of two doctorates (Wren and Bedeian 2018). Her work at Berkeley would become *The Psychology of Management*, one of the first books on industrial and organizational psychology (Gibson et al. 2015). But she was denied her degree due to a residency requirement. However, she completed her dissertation at Brown University with her dissertation on eliminating waste in teaching.

The combination of both psychology and production efficiency produced a cutting-edge version of management – in some ways similar, but even more advanced than some of the recent techniques devoted to quality (Mousa and Lemak 2009). Frank Gilbreth understood, more than even Taylor, that the implementation of scientific management would be more difficult than Taylor thought. Lillian provided the psychology background that would strengthen the relationship between scientific management and psychology. While both Frank and Lillian were concerned with waste in industry, they also took a broader societal perspective on the nature of waste and inefficiency in all aspects of life (Graham 2000).

To summarize, the contributions of the Gilbreths are as follows: according to Krenn (2011), the Gilbreths' book, *The Fatigue Study*, combined the study of scientific management's concerns with the physical aspects of work with the psychological aspects of work. According to Gibson et al. (2015), the most notable contribution of the Gilbreths was that:

> While supportive of Taylorism, Lillian and Frank believed that it lacked a human element, which Lillian was able to introduce based on her academic training in psychology and understanding of scientific management. Her methods included capitalizing on individual skills and satisfactions by using psychology to develop the work experience, and this was the basis of her thesis "The Psychology of Management." Lillian brought the training, insight and understanding to move the human aspect of the scientific management effort forward by recognizing that workers need to feel included in the decision making, be interested in their work by applying relevant skills and have a sense of job security. She acknowledged that satisfaction varies among people and championed the idea that workers should be treated fairly.

Accordingly, they expanded on Taylor's notions of training to include considering the satisfaction of workers.

The Gilbreths had a complicated relationship with Taylorism. Both Gilbreths were disciples, peers, and rivals of Taylor (Nadworny 1957). They agreed with Taylor for the need to develop of a science of work to promote efficiency in order to reduce waste and increase production (Dean 1997). They also admired many aspects of Taylorism – but they sought to develop and further the structure. While Taylor recognized the need for a mental revolution, the Gilbreths took steps, through Lillian's psychological background, to help make that mental revolution happen (Gibson et al. 2015). Gilbreth also believed that motion study was superior to time study as a means of increasing production. For his part, Taylor supported some aspects of the Gilbreths' work, but he also doubted that Frank Gilbreth would spend the time needed – according to Taylor 4–5 years – to fully implement Taylorism. Also, Taylor believed that Frank Gilbreth cut corners and hurt their relationship with one of their clients (Wren and Bedeian 2018). Although a public reconciliation happened between the Gilbreths and the Taylor Society, they remained adversaries.

Munsterberg, Scott, and Van Dyke

Other scholars recognized the importance of psychology to the field of work (Van De Water 1997). The pre-World War I era saw a blossoming of psychology research on applied questions. The shift of psychology was now from the laboratory to the factory, school, household, and even the mud and trenches of World War I (Benjamin 2007). The branch of psychology that worked with management is industrial-organizational psychology (I-O), which is the psychological study of work. The relationship between management and psychology continues to this day. Psychologists regularly published in such high-quality journals as the *Academy of Management Review* and the *Journal of Management*; management scholars publish in the *Journal of Applied Psychology* and *Personnel Psychology*. Some top management scholars, such as Edwin Locke, hold degrees in psychology.

There are three psychologists who can lay claim as the first I-O psychologist: Hugo Munsterberg, Walter Dill Scott, and Walter Bingham Van Dyke (Van De Water 1997; Benjamin 2007). Each man combined scientific rigor with entrepreneurial activity (Van De Water 1997). As Van De Water (1997, p. 487) noted:

> Applied psychologists' self-promotion in a wide variety of media targeted the general public, government, business people, and skeptics in the academic community. These applied practitioners soon established themselves as professionals by means of new journals, independent membership organizations, educational institutions, and even private companies offering psychological services. This combination of internal and external forces helped transfer industrial psychology from a few individuals' visions into larger, self-perpetuating institutions.

Their goal was correcting Taylorism. Taylor had promised management a mental revolution and a solution to societal unrest (Nelson 1980, 1995). Unions complained that scientific management eliminated the need for collective bargaining and that some of their findings were less than scientific (Nadworny 1955). I-O psychology replaced many aspects of Taylorism with a more thorough understanding of human motivation and better testing (Van De Water 1997). Yet it was also true that psychology absorbed most of the traits of scientific management, including the preoccupation with efficiency (Baritz 1960).

Hugo Munsterberg was an academic star, whose light once shone brightly in the academic firmament, but his reputation is now a burnt-out husk. At one time, Munsterberg's opinion was sought by companies, politicians, professors, and reformers, but when he died, he was the most hated man in America (Hale 1980; Keller 1979). Benjamin (2000) noted that in Munsterberg's papers, there are four full folders of hate mail. Yet despite this, Munsterberg is the leading candidate for the title of the father of industrial/organizational psychology (Landy 1992). For most of his career, Munsterberg was recognized as a preeminent psychologist. His fame and renown was such that Harvard spent several years courting him. Munsterberg provided comments on many aspects of life whether it was jury selection, vocational guidance, educational matters, and even film (Spillmann and Spillmann 1993; Porfeli 2009). Yet his own value as a scientist was consistently undermined through a combination of his own arrogance as well as his pro-German stance around the time of World War I (Landy 1992). Munsterberg lost some of his professional standing due to feuds with Wilhelm Wundt and William James (Landy 1992; Spillmann and Spillmann 1993; Benjamin 1997).

His pro-German stance during World War I won him little credit from his contemporaries. Munsterberg was aggressive, arrogant, and imperious. Munsterberg was frequently known to attack colleagues in print – not by name, but by implication, a practice unknown to American psychologists at the time (Benjamin 1997, 2000). Professionally, Munsterberg did not present his ideas in a scientific manner; he often used testimonials. Landy (1992) summarized the attitude of the next generation of scholars:

> Burtt recalled that Munsterberg was an idea man and excellent in experimental design and instrumentation but not very good at statistics. This description is confirmed by others (Hale 1980). It was this weak empirical base that most likely led to the less-than-positive views of the next generation of industrial-organizational (I-O) psychologists as represented by Viteles, Kornhauser, and others (e.g., Viteles 1932).

Despite being recognized as the top psychologist at the time of his death, his reputation was in complete tatters 3 years after he died (Landy 1992). By 1919, less than 3 years after his death, there was hardly any reference to any of his more than ten books and dozens of articles in basic and applied psychology. Landy's own review of citations from the *Journal of Applied Psychology* bears this out. If Lewin died in the midst of things, Munsterberg died at the end of things. In fact, his death saved him from prison, a fate that many dissenters of war suffered (Kennedy 1980).

Yet Munsterberg's contributions to management were many and varied. Munsterberg commented on a wide variety of topics including juries, hypnosis, African Americans, and Christian Science, but it was to the psychological side of management where Munsterberg made his most dynamic contributions (Spillmann and Spillmann 1993; Benjamin 2000). Munsterberg was forced to go into applied psychology and industry due to his feud with James (Van De Water 1997). Munsterberg's prime focus was on work sample testing and aptitude testing. He was one of the first to introduce the concept of validation to work samples – seeking to make sure that his tests accurately reflected both measure and theory. Munsterberg developed tests with content and construct orientated validity. For some jobs, his tests were holistic; for others, they were detailed and complex. Unlike one of his rivals, James McKeen Cattell, Munsterberg would change his tests to reflect the needs of his clients (Van De Water 1997). Through the use of these tests, Munsterberg gained a sense of renown that helped to replace some of the luster of his failed position at Harvard (Landy 1992).

Munsterberg's great challenger to the title of "father of I-O psychology" is Walter Dill Scott, who many in America believe is the real father (Vinchur and Koppes 2007; Benjamin 2007). Much like Munsterberg, Scott was both an entrepreneur and a student of Wundt. Unlike Munsterberg, Scott was a skilled politician, who would become a University President at Northwestern and would win a Distinguished

Service Medal. Scott did make several contributions to management, but he is primarily known as the expert in the field of advertising, where he developed the notion that consumers are irrational and prone to manipulation through suggestion (Kuna 1976). For example, for a food advertisement, the consumer should be able to taste the food; for a piano, they should hear the music. Scott also devoted his interests to I-O psychology and personnel management in particular. In 1903, Scott published, according to Ludy T. Benjamin (2007), the first book on I-O psychology, which was a compilation of his work on advertising. Scott's (1910) book on personnel management was one of the first works on the subject. According to Lynch (1968), Scott's concern was with the motivation and selection of workers, topics he believed were given scant research and attention previously. Scott argued that one of the principle concepts that managers should create should be loyalty. But Scott reasoned, unlike Taylorism, that loyalty needed more than fair wages and good working conditions. Anticipating Mayo, the human relations movement, and work on social exchange, Scott argued that managers should take a personal interest in their workers. Scott's greatest contribution to psychology would be his work for the United States, where he helped to mobilize three million men, in what would become the world's most powerful army. He was the one psychologist recognized by his government for his war efforts (Von Mayrhauser 1989).

Walter Van Dyke Bingham (Vinchur and Koppes 2007) was another psychologist who made important contributions to I-O psychology. Much like Scott, Bingham was an empire builder. He served as head of the Division of Applied Psychology at the Carnegie Institute of Technology, where he recruited Scott and others. According to Van De Water (1997, p. 490):

> Under Bingham's direction, the Applied Psychology Division at Carnegie Tech soon offered graduate degrees and drew corporate support for an additional Bureau of Salesmanship Research. This cooperative business-college venture was headed by Walter Dill Scott in 1916, making him the first to bear the label professor of applied psychology in the United States. Overall, the founding of Carnegie Tech opened the commercial sector as a source of funds for psychology research and spawned a new generation of students specializing in industrial psychology.

Bingham's primary contribution was to help develop aptitude testing for both business and the military, becoming one of the creators of the alpha and beta test (McGuire 1994). The emergence of the *Journal of Applied Psychology* illustrated the development of this field of study.

One last psychologist who warrants consideration as the first I-O psychologist was Morris Viteles, who was a University of Pennsylvania psychologist (Viteles 1967). Viteles was considered to be one of the prime and early examples of the practitioner-scholar model (Knopes 2014). Viteles's work with the Yellow Taxi Company is considered to be a classic in the field (Mahoney 2014). Viteles asked one of the prime questions of modern life: Who is a better driver, men or women? Viteles and his coauthor Helen Gardner found that both men and women believe that their sex is the better driver. But what Viteles and Gardner found (Mahoney 2014, p. 102) was that differences in driving ability were the result of "training, experience, and exposure to hazards may differ between men and women." Viteles's prime work would be his book on *Industrial Psychology* (1932). According to Mills (2012a, b, p. 41):

> Beginning almost immediately after its publication and continuing for some time, Viteles's text was considered to be the new bible in the field of industrial psychology explicitly discussing important issues that had been neglected by previous texts. For instance, he covered leadership, dissected training, and thoroughly highlighted the zeitgeist into which industrial psychology had emerged, including social and economic issues, which led in part to the concern with efficiency. Nevertheless, Viteles makes explicit in the text that he considered industrial psychology to have an equal responsibility toward the well-being and betterment of workers as it does toward efficiency. This outlook is reinforced by Viteles's later interest in humanistic psychological principles and their potential industrial applications.

Viteles followed this contribution with his 1953 *Motivation and Morale*, which talked about developments in motivation research and added the organizational side to I-O psychology.

World War I

World War I and its aftermath changed the world. In fact, it would be fair to say, the war ushered out the premodern world and produced the modern one. It was not the first modern war (the American Civil War holds that claim), nor was it entirely removed from the nineteenth century. World War I was a carnage on a scale never seen before – a vision of total war, whereby the populations of nations were targets as much soldiers in the field, where the war could be won or lost as much in the factory, farm, or home, as it could on the battlefield due to the requirements of modern warfare. The demands of creating modern armies almost from scratch, including training and development, astounded even the most astute observers. When Lord Kitchener stated that the war would last 3 years and require huge new armies, people felt he was crazy. Only after several years did people realize how wise he was, but only after a generation of men were killed. Some scholars have noted that if both the Central Powers and the Allies recognized the loss of life and treasure, they probably would not have fought in the first place.

According to David Kennedy (1980, vii), the War was "crucial for an understanding of modern American history." Many aspects of the New Deal, the war effort of World War II, and the birth of popular culture have its genesis during World War I. The war also provided America with an opportunity to claim world power, but America "had neither the skills, nor the wisdom, nor the compulsion of interest, to play that role as productively as Great Britain had played her part in the nineteenth century" (Kennedy 1980, p. 346). For academics, the war, as do all wars, provided ample opportunities and fertile testing grounds for social scientists (Kennedy 1980; Stagner 1981). John Dewey and the New Republic crowed that the war "provided an opportunity pregnant with 'social possibilities'" (Kennedy 1980, pp. 49–50). But the reverse was also true; to academics like Munsterberg, the historian Charles Beard, and the economist Scott Nearing, who produced "doubt-breeding complexities" (Kennedy 1980, p. 58), the war meant the end of their careers.

The demands of this war provided the field of psychology, just like scientific management, with many opportunities to prove its worth (Stagner 1981; Van De Water 1997). The war placed many demands that psychology could meet. One of those demands was for the need to train and develop soldiers, sailors, pilots, and workers. Other demands included handling soldiers, problems with shell shock, propaganda, trying to sell the war, and the need for sacrifice by soldiers. Many psychologists, like Walter Dill Scott and other entrepreneurial orientated scholars, jumped into the fray with great enthusiasm (Van De Water 1997). One of the principle outcomes of the war was that it provided social scientists with a real-life laboratory to test out various principles and theories. One of the reasons why the United States could be seen as an innovator on many of these issues was because it had 3 years to observe what worked and what did not in terms of building a military. In addition, American industry and universities had plenty of scholars ready to apply new ideas (Schaffer 1991).

The psychologists of other countries were not as readily deployed as American psychologists. For instance, in Great Britain, most of the psychologists (Myers, Rivers, McDougall, and Brown) worked in hospitals with shell-shocked patients, whose symptoms confounded neurologists (Shepard 2015). One of those psychologists was a young Elton Mayo (Traihair 1984). The irony was that Charles Spearman, the father of intelligence theory, spent most of his war guarding a depot in the north of England. According to Shepard, one of the reasons why psychologists were not deployed was that many of them had connections to Germany as students and felt tension between their allegiance to the Crown and their past. In Germany, Wundt and other academics signed a declaration refuting charges of barbarism. In addition, German psychologists provided aptitude tests to fliers, applied fatigue research to munitions workers, and educated the German population on diet restrictions. In France, most of the research was devoted to industrial work. Both Germany and France, despite their traditions, did not have any research as comprehensive as the United States in support of the war.

The United States noted that the British had lost a generation of its most skilled and talented during the first few years of the war. To put it bluntly, the British lost a generation of leaders in the mud of Flanders Fields (Kennedy 1980). The United States desired to avoid this outcome and so sought out ways to prevent its best and brightest from being cannon fodder. This elitist approach to society was par the course for many in the Progressive Era and should not surprise anyone (McGerr 2003). The theory that provided the answer to this problem was general mental ability. Charles Darwin's cousin Francis Galton noted that it was possible for offspring to pick up the traits of their parents (Boeree 2018). One of those traits, Galton believed, was mental ability – noting that (not surprising from a scion of a great science family) genius was hereditary. This idea was further advanced by Charles Spearman who proposed that a common factor, which he called g for general factor, was the driver of all activities regarding intelligence. Spearman based his ideas on the correlation between various mental activities that tended to be similar (Boeree 2018). Spearman's notion of g remains one of the major concepts in intelligence testing. Despite its high levels of prediction, it remains very controversial as it implies that there is a natural elite (Boeree 2018). Yet scholars, such as Lewis Terman and Alfred Binet (fathers of the Stanford-Binet IQ test), developed a test that measured intelligence (Benjamin 2007).

Whether this intelligence test captured the elusive g factor is one of debate. The problem was that despite the years of research, psychologists had only a rudimentary understanding of intelligence and little understanding of emotional stability (Benjafield 2007). According to Mayrhauser (1989), the test captured the loose definition of intelligence of the test makers. One of the questions on the alpha test was "Who was the author of *The Raven*?" (Kevles 1968). These are the types of questions that a college educated person would know, but not necessarily someone with a fourth-grade education. Compounding problems, Robert M. Yerkes's motives were more scientific than practical (Mayrhauser 1989). Worse than that, Yerkes's system would have required recruits to be interviewed for 10 min each (Van De Water 1997). This would have meant that the US military would have spent more time testing in this country than overseas fighting the Kaiser.

What is not up for debate is that many American psychologists recognized psychology's role in the war. Wars provide social scientists with real-world opportunities to apply and test various theories. Wars also provide professions with opportunities to create higher degrees of legitimacy. The net result was that many people at the time believed that the tests worked, even if both the military and psychologists overstated the predictions (Samelson 1977). Despite its prewar promise, psychology did not have an endowed laboratory, it did not attract the most able of researchers, and professors had low salaries and few opportunities to publish (Benjamin 2007). The War changed this (Schaffer 1991).

Human Relations: Barnard and Follett

The human relations movement also made a substantial addition to the burgeoning human resources movement. The contribution of the Mayo group was discussed in the previous chapter. In this section, I will discuss the contributions that both Mary Parker Follett and Chester Barnard made. Much like psychology, human relations focus was on the individual in a collective – more specifically, what makes cooperation possible. Both Follett and Barnard were connected to Harvard University through their undergraduate experience (Wren and Bedeian 2018). Follett was a social worker and an independent scholar who made many notable contributions to both political science, social thought, and management (Tonn 2003). Her work focused on the concept of conflict resolution and the need to create situations that produce winners on both sides. Barnard, an executive, focused on what makes cooperation possible and the difficulty of maintaining cooperation within an organization. Barnard's ideas would produce many positive concepts in management (Mahoney 2002). Follett did not receive her due until recently, but she has since been recognized for her role in producing better leadership outcomes that added a spiritual side to management (Phipps 2011). Both scholars are grouped together when discussed due to the similarity of their viewpoints, namely, individuals working together based on cooperation (Wren and Bedeian 2018). Their work illustrates two common viewpoints: people are revealed in their interactions with others, and bureaucracy alone cannot ensure agreement – fully illustrating the intellectual condition of the time period (Kloppenberg 1986).

Mary Parker Follett (1868–1933) was a Harvard-trained social worker, political philosopher, and management thinker who made numerous contributions to several fields (Tonn 2003). She has been called the "mother of scientific management," and some have called her the "mother of management" (Gibson et al. 2013). Even though Follett was initially ignored, she is now one of the important scholars of the field and a subject of books and articles (Schwarz 2015). As Wren and Bedeian (2018) have noted, although Follett did her work during the period of scientific management, she belonged mostly to the human relations movement. However, Follett's ideas about participation and creating a democratic society were very much germane to the Progressive Era, making her a contemporary of Taylor (Mattson 1998). In fact, many of her ideas, such as those on voluntary collectivism, would form parts of the liberal mood in 1918 (Kennedy 1980). One of the salient features to the progressive movement was to seek idealistic approaches to conflict resolution through community involvement and engagement (Mattson 1998). Although not the principle difference between the progressives and the later New Deal Liberals, progressives sought to change society through moral and social improvement, while the New Deal, being less idealistic, sought to use police power of the government to serve as a referee between business and labor (Hostadter 1956). This difference explained why many progressives had a difficult time supporting the New Deal (Graham 1967).

Follett was born to a wealthy but dysfunctional family. Her father was an alcoholic; her mother was sick and "incompetent, demanding, and alien to her needs" (Tonn 2003, p. 16). Follett mostly had to raise her brother due to the inability of her parents to do so. Academics became her method of escape. She encountered and impressed some of the best and brightest minds in both America and Great Britain when she was a student, including Albert Bushnell Hart, perhaps the greatest American historian of his generation (Gibson et al. 2013). She quickly validated the high opinion of her mentors. Her Radcliffe thesis on *the Speaker of the House* is, despite its publication over a century ago, the definitive statement of work on the subject (Wren and Bedeian 2018). However, the scope of her book was radically different than her later work in that it praised consolidation of power at the expense of the community (Mattson 1998). Although she was originally interested in becoming an academic, that route was largely closed due to her gender (Mattson 1998). Therefore, she became a social worker. Social work was one of the popular callings for people who were interested in promoting the welfare of the poor. Like many of her generation, including a great many women, such as Jane Addams, the way to promote social and moral improvement was through social work (Mattson 1998).

During her time as a social worker, Follett recognized the idea for community spaces as a means of producing cooperation and support. These experiences changed her life – making her recognize the benefit that collective social centers could heal the community and promote welfare. "In these largely volunteer organizations, operating with little or no authority, she realized that there was a need to rethink previously held concepts of authority, organization, leadership, and conflict resolution" (Wren 2005, p. 302). The combination of these events made her think of issues from a democratic perspective, different than her previous work. What Follett came to recognize was that power and authority should not be based on class or position, but on knowledge and facts, which she called the "law of the situation." In addition, Follett recognized that individuals received their character through their interaction with others – a recognition of the idea of intersubjectivity – which is a different approach than rejection of the self for the benefit of the community (Wren and Bedeian 2018). Follett's work as an example of the via *media* philosophers, focusing on the interaction between group and individual (Verstegen and Rutherford 2000). Therefore, the solution to both work and social problems is integration – a new way of looking at issues that would promote a new sense of unity (Armstrong 2002).

Gibson and coauthors note the influence of the German Idealist School of Philosophy, especially Fichte, on Follett's work. They also note Follett's embrace of Hegelian thought – especially the thesis, antithesis, and synthesis – which formed the basis of circular response (Gibson et al. 2013). Gestalt psychology influenced her beliefs in that it examined the human mind and behavior as whole (Cherry 2011). Yet Follett maintained her connection to empiricism and pragmatism through her idea of "interpenetration" in that it occurred during social meetings, whereby ideas are discussed and processed that both preserved and transformed them into a new unity (Mattson 1998). This approach would also promote pluralism and unity at the same time due to its basis on both idealism and empiricism. Unlike idealists, Follett did not believe in universal standards like justice or freedoms – the ends were too complex to promote an idealist approach. Yet she was an idealist in that she believed in integration and discussion (Mattson 1998). Her work also mirrored the work of Oliver Sheldon (Damart and Adam-Ledunois 2017).

In terms of business ideas, Follett anticipated many current ideas. Firstly, Pireto and Phipps (2014, p. 271) view her as an early example of a social entrepreneur because of her belief that work should have a "greater meaning" and "should serve a greater purpose." Follett's ideas about emergent leadership and group processes have been well documented over the years (Gibson et al. 2013). Her recognition that people could receive social benefits from work anticipated some of the findings of the Hawthorne studies and Mayo's suggestions. Her ideas of multiple groups working together for a common goal were suggestive of the concepts related to the stakeholder view of the firm (Schilling 2000). McLarney and Shelley Rhyno (1999) view her works as adding to strategic management – similar to, but also different from, the works of Henry Mintzberg. Follett's ideas were not just ahead of their time; they were also timeless.

Yet there were many downsides to the work of Mary Parker Follett, most of which is papered over by her legion of admirers in management. The idea of using a group to develop unity does have several drawbacks. Firstly, Follett's idea of socialization did not allow the concept of apathy to reign (Mattson 1998). Applied to work, many people just show up for pay – nothing more and seek their social fulfillment elsewhere. Secondly, people cannot always create unity; in fact, there are certain aspects where discord would always happen (Mattson 1998). At the end of the day, labor and management have a divide that cannot be totally bridged. Even Mayo, who was as much of an idealist as Follett, had the same skepticism of bureaucracy and recognized that unity could not always be achieved (Homans 1949). Finally, the biggest issue was that democratic participation and coercive voluntarism can lead to the destruction of dissent (Capozzola 2008). Follett's participation could be seen as forced by the mob or the elite. One of the reasons why Munsterberg was silenced was because citizens sought unity of participation. Follett wrote that the group could produce "the only rights" that a person would have. As Capozzola (2008) wrote, Follett talked a lot about groups but not about mobs.

Chester Barnard (1886–1961) attended Harvard University (but did not graduate due to his lack of a laboratory science) and concentrated in economics. Barnard was a Massachusetts farm boy who did well, a scholarship student who paid his way through Harvard by running a dance band and selling pianos. After college, Barnard got a job at the American Telephone and Telegraph Company, rising to President of the New Jersey Bell company in 1927. During the course of his lifetime, he held many positions of influence, including directing the relief system of New Jersey during the Depression, serving as President of the United Service Organizations, working with David E. Lilienthal regarding nuclear power, serving as President for the Rockefeller Foundation, and serving as an advisor to President Franklin Roosevelt. For his efforts, Barnard won the Presidential Merit Award (Wren and Bedeian 2018).

Yet his greatest contribution was as a management thinker. Barnard, befitting a self-made man, was also a self-made scholar. Running a company that is a monopoly should leave one with a lot of downtime. Barnard filled it by reading the works of Pareto, Follett, Lewin, Max Weber, and Alfred North Whitehead (Wren and Bedeian 2018). His level of erudition impressed Harvard's imperious Lawrence J. Henderson, a biochemist, nascent management scholar, and advisor to President Lowell. Henderson had a deep respect and admiration for Pareto – viewing him as an antidote to socialism (Homans 1984). So Henderson formed the famous Harvard Pareto circle – which included a who's who of social scientists and intellectuals, including Talcott Parsons, Crane Brinton, George Homans, and Bernard DeVoto (Keller 1984). Barnard made a deep impression on Henderson with his knowledge of Pareto and based on that was invited to give the Lowell lectures, a series of lectures given by the Lowell Institute, which included some of the top scholars at the time: Arthur M. Schlesinger Jr., Joseph Schumpeter, and Elton Mayo.

Although Barnard did not publish much, what he did publish had a remarkable and lasting impact. In fact, his major work, *The Functions of the Executive*, was based on his Lowell lectures. His book *The Functions of the Executive*, is poorly written, jargon loaded, according to Paul DiMaggio (1995); featured large sections that were quaint and vacuous; and carried a whiff of elitism (Dunphy and Hoopes 2002). Although these criticisms are true, Barnard's book is also insightful, powerful, original, and passionate about management. It is also ethical (Strother 1976). Its passion has inspired scholars, students, and practitioners for 80 years, despite some calls that it is outdated. In short, it was the work of genius. Joseph Mahoney (2002, p. 160) sums it up best:

> I observe that Barnard's teachings uniquely inspire many students at all educational levels. Barnard's teachings breathe life into the discipline of management and infuse a feeling of renewed idealism in the typical undergraduate, a feeling of a renewed responsibility in the modern executive, and a sense of the importance of management in many current doctoral students.

The power of the book was that it would directly influence three distinct trends in the literature: the institutional school, the Carnegie school, and Human Relations (Mahoney 2002). It also influences the field of transaction cost economics, upper echelons, political approaches, and social exchange theory. It is little wonder why the book is considered to be the second most influential book published in management in the twentieth century. Andrews, Simon, Mahoney, Parrow, Mayo, Roethlisberger, Homans, Williamsons, Parsons, and Selznick have praised and/or were influenced by it (Singleton 2013). Its most direct influence was on Herbert Simon who used it to create a distinct viewpoint called the Barnard-Simon legacy (Mitchell and Scott 1988).

A whole book can be and has been written about Barnard's work (Wolf 1973, 1974; Scott 1992). For the purpose of this chapter, we will focus on one aspect. Much like Follett, Barnard was concerned with gaining cooperation from workers which, to him, was the point of the organization. Organizations are able to function because they are able to gain resources from its members. When an organization can no longer gain resources from its members, it will die. Barnard noted that, with the exception of the Catholic Church, all organizations die (Barnard 1938). The reason why they fail is that the effectiveness (goal attainment) and efficiency (cost reduction) are comprised due to a lack of cooperation (Barnard 1938). Barnard noted that the basis of the formal organization is cooperation, "formal organization is that kind of cooperation among men that is conscious, deliberate, purposeful," and that "successful cooperation in or by formal organizations is the abnormal, not the normal, condition." The reason why organizations failed at gaining cooperation was that too much attention was placed on government and religious organizations (Wren and Bedeian 2018).

Attention had been given to gaining cooperation from individual workers, but little attention was provided to gaining cooperation from groups of workers. Fayol had provided some template with his notions of purpose and esprit de corps, but his work had yet to be translated. Furthermore, while Fayol provided a language and vocabulary of management, Barnard would start developing a true science of management, providing an outline for the Carnegie School, especially the work of Herbert Simon. Barnard provided an understanding of what executives needed to do: establish and maintain a system of communication, secure essential services from other members, formulate organizational purposes and objectives, manage people, and make sure they do their jobs. One of the principal differences between Fayol and

Barnard was that Barnard's ideas supported his nature of cooperation and had more of a theoretical understanding. It was perhaps, for this reason, why Simon thought highly of Barnard, but little of Fayol.

Barnard sought to gain cooperation through various types of inducements. As Wren and Bedeian noted, Barnard understood that the "intensity and timing of willingness" to cooperate would wax and wane due to whether or not the worker was experiencing satisfaction or dissatisfaction. Therefore, various inducements, both material (financial) and immaterial (prestige, socialization), were needed to promote cooperation in the group. In words that would be similar to social exchange theorists, especially people using Homans's original theory, inducements were needed to offset the costs of being a member of the group (Homans 1958, 1961). In addition to the inducements, a common purpose is needed to unify the group, not the individual member's purpose, but something that could unite the group as a whole (Barnard 1938). This purpose should be supported through the use of incentives as well. Anticipating much of agency and expectancy theory, members needed to understand the mission of the organization, be able to achieve the organization goals, and have incentives to reduce individual desires.

Perhaps the most important part of Barnard's contribution has been the concept of the zone of indifference. The zone of indifference is important because it provides a limitation on the level of authority that managers possess over subordinates. It builds on ideas of Taylorism. One of the basic concepts behind Taylor's philosophy was the basic need for workers to accept management's role in determining pace and output. Barnard discussed under what conditions workers would be willing to accept management's prerogative. Much like later scholars who worked in transaction cost economics, such as Oliver Williamson and William Ouchi, Barnard understood that factors emerge within the organization that protect workers from management control and oversight (Mahoney 2002). There is a line from Barnard to Simon to Williamson and Ouchi regarding the difficult nature of managerial oversight. But Barnard also recognized something important – that the way to gain worker cooperation was to make them indifferent to managerial commands (Wren and Bedeian 2018). Once indifferent, the natural tendency for people to carry out orders will take them the rest of the way. This was an important observation.

One last important observation needs to be made about Barnard's work and, by extension, the work of the Human Relations scholars. There have been criticisms over the years, mentioned by various scholars, that the work of the human relations scholars has downplayed the role and importance of monetary reasons for production and by work (Locke 1982). Barnard has not escaped this criticism. James Hoopes (2002) has taken aim at Barnard by noting that Barnard let ideology get the better of him. Hoopes (2002, p. 1017) wrote about Barnard's respect and courtesy to resolve the riot, that this idea was an "undeniably important contribution to management knowledge," but that Barnard "underestimated older techniques" including power and money to resolve problems. These attitudes ignore what was one of the key insights gathered from the human relations movement, namely, the idea that monetary issues sometimes have little to do with monetary issues (Drucker 1946). At the heart, the problem is a lack of trust between both sides. Unions struck during World War II – when their aims had been socialized by the government, when everyone was employed, and when wages and perks were high – simply because they did not trust management (Kennedy 1999). Scholars have also confirmed Barnard's arguments in that interpersonal skills are key when handling a difficult issue (Greenberg 1993).

Welfare Capitalism and the New Deal

The labor question had dominated American/British/Commonwealth thought over the period from 1880 to 1945. Unionized and coordinated labor meant strikes, destruction, and war between labor and capital. Robber barons, such as Henry Clay Frick, lived in fear of assassination by radical labor leaders. Frick's would-be assassin received 21 years, in a quick trial, but only served 14. This did little to solve concerns on the part of management. Even those leaders who were considered benevolent faced various strikes and issues (Brandes 1976). Turnover was high as was destruction of property (Tone 1997). The number of police businesses employed in Pennsylvania was more than the state police, by a factor of 20 to 1. Business built fortresses, armed police, built armored cars, and employed criminals to keep workers in line. Murder and violence were not uncommon at the workplace. Between 1880 and 1900, 23,000 strikes occurred, or a new strike every 3 days (Brandes 1976). These strikes tended to be short and brief – real working-class solidarity was something that would not come until the future.

Despite the increasing wealth of the country, many reformers, businessmen, and politicians were deeply concerned that the new technocratic structure would not weld with the US traditions of small government and liberalism. Despite this new technocratic, the United States still remained, during the Gilded Age, a series of isolated communities (Wiebe 1967). One of the legacies of the Civil War was a creation of a unified nation, but this would take time and energy (White 2017). As Robert Wiebe wrote (1967, pp. 42–43), "Americans in a basic sense no longer knew who or what they were. The setting had altered beyond their power to understand it, and within an alien context they had lost themselves." Labor remained too ethnically and ideologically divided to launch a socialist movement (Weinsetein 1967). Likewise, increasing immigration meant that workers would maintain old world rivalries that would limit opportunities for collective action. Yet the middle class, despite its doubts and anxieties, launched a series of reforms to promote rationalization of American life.

Businessmen were one of the leaders of this new reform movement (Wiebe 1988). One of their prime contributions to this was called welfare work or, as it is more commonly known, welfare capitalism. Welfare capitalism was a series of programs that businesses took to reform the workplace (Brandes 1976). Companies provided housing, sports and social opportunities, health and welfare benefits, cooking classes, newspapers/magazines, and language and education classes. Workers at the National Cash Register Company could play tennis, golf, or baseball in the company park. Welfare capitalism also witnessed wage incentive plans, benefit programs, and offered stock ownership in the company and profit-sharing. US Steel had 19 pools in which workers could swim. The Hawthorne plant had its own pageant which did not end until the 1980s. The educational systems were vast. The Colorado Fuel and Iron Company provided teachers for its schools. Some companies offered high wages and sought to turn their workers into consumers. IBM, Kodak, and especially Ford were considered high points of ethical capitalism.

Scholars have remained divided as to what the business leaders' motivations were in offering welfare capitalism programs. Irving Bernstein, one of the first historians to cover the question, argued that managers did so to prevent a unionized workforce. For Bernstein, welfare capitalism was the velvet glove that hid the iron fist. Subsequent scholars attacked this assertion noting the benefits of the system. Stuart Brandes argued that managers offered these programs due to the fact that they were a better alternative to police forces and that managers' primary concern was profit. Andrea Tone argues that it was the basic paternalism of managers and capitalism who wanted to protect workers and their families – noting, based on the work of Theda Skocpol (1992), that much of the early welfare state was designed to protect mothers and children. Business revisionists, such as Allan Nevins and Ernest Hill, have argued that welfare capitalism provided real benefits to workers.

The real questions are as follows: Did welfare capitalism work? Why did it emerge? Why did it end? As to whether welfare capitalism worked, the answers remain unknown (Brandes 1976). The polling evidence suggest that workers were lukewarm about welfare capitalism, preferring that they be paid a bonus or extra wages. Yet the labor violence that marked much of the industrial period all but ended in the 1920s (Meyer 1981; Kennedy 1999). This is suggested by the rise of conservative politics by both the Democrats and Republicans. The workers were relatively happy during this period. Scholars have been debating the economy of the 1920s since the era of Keynes, but there still seems to be a consensus, that at least for a short period, the economy of the 1920s was sound (Kennedy 1999). It is difficult to claim that workers were desperate – especially with the emergence of the telephone, radio, movies, and modern sports. Turnover, especially at Ford, declined (Meyer 1981).

Brandes notes that the examination of welfare capitalism has ignored what became known as the "organizational synthesis." Scholars, such as Robert Wiebe and Louis Galambos, have argued that the most salient factor of post-Civil War America was the emergence of modern bureaucratic organizations. Yet the emergence of large government and organized labor, unlike the modern corporation, was delayed due to several factors. Namely, the US government remained federalized – meaning that there were vast differences between states on questions related to welfare and labor. Not until the New Deal, and especially World War II, did questions of labor and welfare become federalized. Labor had a difficult time uniting on any particular issue. According to Lizabeth Cohen (1990, p. 6), "isolated in local neighborhoods and fragmented by ethnicity and race workers proved incapable of mounting the unified action necessary for success." This meant that Italian workers would hold their Polish and Hungarian counterparts with a sense of deep skepticism and hostility; and vice versa. In addition, Samuel Gompers sought to only unionize skilled labor, rather than unskilled labor. Finally, radical reformers, such as Bill Heyward, head of the International Workers of the World, were probably too radical for most workers who dreamed about earning wealth and remained wedded to conservative social views. As Cohen wrote (1990, p. 43), a "successful...strike in the future would require a work force more capable of coordinating on a national level and more unified ethnically and racially."

Therefore, welfare capitalism was the best solution, perhaps the only solution, which could meet the varying demands placed on society. It was a compromise, one that reflected American concerns about both labor and consolidation of power and one that reflected both a concern for legitimate worker issues and maintained the respect for businessmen and private enterprise. It also reflected general concerns over paternalism that impacted American leaders during the time period – whether it was reflected in "Americanizing" immigrants, protecting widows with legitimate children, or searching for ways to improve morals in society. The system also had the benefit in that it allowed workers to have a limited amount of empowerment that enabled them to gain limited positive outcomes (Meyer 1981).

That is the real irony of welfare capitalism. It did succeed in socializing workers and Americanizing them. It is also succeeding in convincing workers that they had the right to certain outcomes such as bonus work, overtime, and social benefits. Workers were willing to abide by the structure as long as they were paid (Meyer 1981). When the Depression hit, welfare capitalism ended, and workers unionized on an enormous scale. Welfare capitalism also produced Americanization that allowed for workers to unionize and take collective action. Its own successes fueled its eventual demise. As Cohen (1990, p. 211) wrote, "ethnic provincialism was breaking down at the workplace, as it was in the real world." These attitudes would be aided by the rise of the radio and consumerism (especially in the 1930s), the Catholic Church, and the emergence of Prohibition, which greatly offended ethnic America. Rather than being seen as an enlightened company, workers viewed Hawthorne with a hostile eye.

Yet welfare capitalism did not die. The politics of the New Era (1920s) still remained a template for business and worker relationships. In many ways, the New Deal solidified these relationships into collective bargaining, rather than cooperation like Mary Parker Follett and Elton Mayo would have preferred. Yet workers still looked to their companies, rather than the government, as a source of welfare. The American experience during World War II furthered these relationships. Due to war-imposed price controls, American companies had to institute healthcare plans to gain workers to deal with labor shortages. This was unlike the model in Western Europe. Great Britain, the country America is usually compared to, saw the emergence of the welfare state that included a national healthcare system. The American attempt to create a similar model went down to ignominious defeat. Today, US corporations offer healthcare, social opportunities, education (especially in terms of healthcare), and stock options. Welfare capitalism did not die – it merely was transformed.

Conclusion

Arthur Bedeian argued for the study of history to improve management's present and future. He argued that professional maturity is a gift. Despite the strength of his arguments, and his high position in management, scholars have not heard his message. Management scholars should be attuned to his message. As we can see from this chapter, the early days of human resource management still continue to play a deep role. Some scholars, taking what is called the historic turn of the firm, have argued that management is preoccupied with the period of 1880–1940 (Cummings et al. 2017). These same scholars, despite the aptness of their observation, do not pursue the question as to why so much attention is paid to this time period. When they do, they argue that scholars have linked management's roots to Taylorism, ignoring uncomfortable truths, such as the role of management in slavery. However, as we can see, there are two reasons why management starts during this period. One was the emergence of psychology, based on the transformation of knowledge that inspired the progressive and social democratic movement. While management was embraced by business as a solution, it should not lessen its progressive nature. Management matched with other elements of progressivism in that it sought protection of private property and basic protection of the weak. Both management and progressivism had paternalism and democracy at its roots. The second reason is that we continue to talk about these issues in modern business. As was noted before, the Gilbreths' ideas formed the basis of Toyota's work culture; Scott's ideas of respect of the relationship between management to worker formed the basis of leader member exchange; and Barnard's notions of honesty and respect formed the basis of justice. The early iteration of human resource management still provides the basis for today's practice. In conclusion, management was a modernist attempt to promote economic and social well-being that emerged at the same time as did other social sciences.

References

Armstrong HD (2002) Mary P. Follett: conflict resolution through integration. Peace Res 34(2):101–116

Baritz L (1960) The servants of power Middletown. Wesleyan University Press, Middletown

Barnard (1938) Functions of the executive. Harvard University Press, Cambridge, MA

Bedeian AG, Taylor SG (2009) The Übermensch meets the "One Best Way" Barbara S. Burks, the Gilbreth family, and the eugenics movement. J Manag Hist 15(2):216–221

Benjafield (2010) A history of psychology, 3rd edn. Oxford University Press, New York

Benjamin LT (1997) The origin of psychological species: history of the beginnings of American Psychological Association divisions. Am Psychol 52:725–732

Benjamin LT (2007) A brief history of modern psychology. Wiley-Blackwell, New York

Benjamin LT Jr (2000) Hugo Münsterberg: portrait of an applied psychologist. Portraits Pioneers Psychol 4:113–129

Boeree (2018) History of psychology. CreateSpace Independent Publishing Platform, Scotts Valley

Brandes SD (1976) American welfare capitalism, 1880–1940. University of Chicago Press, Chicago

Capozzola (2008) Uncle Sam wants you: World War I and the making of the modern American citizen. Oxford University Press, New York

Capshew JH (1992) Psychologists on site: a reconnaissance of the historiography of the laboratory. Am Psychol 47(2):132

Cherry K (2011) What is gestalt psychology? About.com.psychology. http://psychology.about.com/od/schoolsofthought/f/gestalt_faq.htm. Accessed 26 Oct 2011

Cohen L (1990) Making a new deal: Industrial workers in Chicago, 1919–1939. New York, NY: Cambridge University Press

Cummings S, Bridgman T, Hassard J, Rowlinson M (2017) A new history of management. Cambridge: Cambridge University Press

Damart S, Adam-Ledunois S (2017) Management as an integrating activity: a comparative textual analysis of the work of Mary Parker Follett and Oliver Sheldon. J Manag Hist 23(4):452–470

Dean CC (1997) Primer of scientific management by Frank B. Gilbreth: a response to publication of Taylor's principles in the American magazine. J Manag Hist 3(1):31–41

DiMaggio PJ (1995) Comments on What theory is not. Administrative science quarterly, 40 (3):391–397

Donald DH (1995) Lincoln. New York. Simon and Schuster

Drucker PF (1946) For industrial peace. Harper's Wkly 193:385–395

Dunphy SM, Hoopes J (2002) Chester Barnard: member of the "élite"? Manag Decis 40(10):1024–1028

Gibson JW, Chen W, Henry E, Humphreys J, Lian Y (2013) Examining the work of Mary Parker Follett through the lens of critical biography. J Manag Hist 19(4):441–458

Gibson JW, Clayton RW, Deem J, Einstein JE, Henry EL (2015) Viewing the work of Lillian M. Gilbreth through the lens of critical biography. J Manag Hist 21(3):288–308

Gibson JW, Clayton, Deem J, Einstein JE, Humphreys JH (2016a) Applying a critical biography perspective to the work of Frank Gilbreth. J Manag Hist 22(4):413–436

Gibson JW, Deem J, Einstein JE, Humphreys JH (2016b) Applying a critical biography perspective to the work of Frank Gilbreth. J Manag Hist 22(4):413–436

Goldman EF (1952) Rendezvous with destiny: a history of modern American reform. Knopf, New York

Graham OL (1967) An encore for reform: The old progressives and the New Deal. Oxford University Press, USA. New York

Graham L (2000) Lillian Gilbreth and the mental revolution at Macy's 1925–1928. J Manag Hist 6(7):285–305

Green CD, Shore M, Teo T (2001) The transformation of psychology: the influences of 19th-century natural science, technology, and philosophy. American Psychological Association, Washington, DC. https://doi.org/10.1037/10416-000

Greenberg J (1993) Stealing in the name of justice: informational and interpersonal moderators of theft reactions to underpayment inequity. Organ Behav Hum Decis Process 54(1):81–103

Gutek G (2014) Philosophical, ideological, and theoretical perspectives on education. Pearson, New York

Haber S (1964) Efficiency and uplift: scientific management in the progressive era, 1890–1920. University of Chicago Press, Chicago

Hale M Jr (1980) Human science and social order. Hugo Münsterberg and the origins of applied psychology. Temple University Press, Philadelphia

Himmelfarb G (1991) Poverty and compassion: the moral imagination of the late Victorians. Knopf, New York

Homans GC (1949) The perspectives of Elton Mayo: some corrections. Rev Econ Stat 31:319–321

Homans GC (1958) Social behaviour as exchange. American Journal of Sociology, 63(6):597–606

Homans GC (1961) Social behaviour: Its elementary forms. New York, NY: Harcourt, Brace & World

Homans GC (1984) Coming to my senses: The autobiography of a social scientist. New Brunswick, N.J.: Transaction Books

Hoopes J (2002) Managing a riot: Chester Barnard and social unrest. Manag Decis 40(10): 1013–1023

Hostatder (1956) The age of reform. Knopf, New York

Kaufman BE (2008) Managing the human factor: The early years of human resource management in american industry. Cornell University Press. Ithaca, NY

Keller P (1979) States of belonging: German-American intellectuals and the first World War. Harvard University Press, Cambridge, MA

Keller (1984) The Harvard "Pareto Circle" and the historical development of organization theory. J Manag 10(2):193–204

Kennedy DM (1980) Over here: the first world war and American society. Oxford University Press, New York

Kennedy DM (1999) Freedom from fear: The American people in depression and war, 1929–1945. New York, NY: Oxford University Press

Kevles DJ (1968) Testing the Army's intelligence: Psychologists and the military in World War I. Journal of American History, 55(3):565–581

Kloppenberg JT (1986) Uncertain victory: social democracy and progressivism in European and American thought, 1870–1920. Oxford University Press, New York

Knopes LL (ed) (2014) Historical perspectives in industrial and organizational psychology. Lawrence Erlbaum Associates, Mahwah

Krenn M (2011) From scientific management to homemaking: Lillian M. Gilbreth's contributions to the development of management thought. Manag Organ Hist 6(2):145–161

Kuna DP (1976) The concept of suggestion in the early history of advertising psychology. J Hist Behav Sci 12(4):347–353

Lancaster J (2004) Making time. Northwestern University Press, Boston

Landy FJ (1992) Hugo Münsterberg: victim or visionary? J Appl Psychol 77(6):787

Link AS, McCormack RL (1983) Progressivism. Harlan Davidson, Wheeling

Locke EA (1982) The ideas of Frederick W. Taylor: an evaluation. Acad Manag Rev 7(1):14–24

Lynch EC (1968) Walter Dill Scott: pioneer industrial psychologist. Bus Hist Rev 42(2):149–170

Mahoney JT (2002) The relevance of Chester I. Barnard's teachings to contemporary management education: communicating the aesthetics of management. Int J Organ Theory Behav 5(1–2): 159–172

Mahoney B (2014) Who's gonna drive you home tonight? Looking back at Viteles' work with yellow cab. Soc Ind Organ Psychol 50(2):100–103. 4p. Database: Academic Search Complet

Mattson (1998) Creating a democratic public: the struggle for urban participatory democracy during the Progressive Era Kevin Mattson. Pennsylvania State Press, University Park

McGerr (2003) A fierce discontent: the rise and fall of the progressive movement in America, 1870–1920. Oxford University Press, New York

McGuire F (1994) Army alpha and beta tests of intelligence. In: Sternberg RJ (ed) Encyclopedia of human intelligence. Macmillan, New York, pp 125–129

McLarney C, Rhyno S (1999) Mary Parker Follett: visionary leadership and strategic management. Women Manag Rev 14(7):292–304

Meyer S (1981) The five dollar day: labor management and social control in the Ford Motor Company, 1908–1921. State University of New York Press, Albany

Mills MJ (2012a) The beginnings of industrial psychology: the life and work of Morris Viteles. Soc Ind Organ Psychol 49(3):39–44

Mills MJ (2012b) TIP Ind Organ Psychol 49(3):39–44. Database: Academic

Mischel T (1967) Kant and the possibility of a science of psychology. Monist 51:599–622

Mitchell TR, Scott WG (1988) The Barnard-Simon contribution: a vanished legacy. Public Adm Q 1071:348–368

Mousa FT, Lemak DJ (2009) The Gilbreths' quality system stands the test of time. J Manag Hist 15(2):198–215

Nadworny MJ (1955) Scientific management and the unions: 1900–1932. Harvard University Press, Cambridge, MA

Nadworny M (1957) Frederick Taylor and Frank Gilbreth: competition in scientific management. Bus Hist Rev 31:23–34

Nelson DA (1980) Frederick W. Taylor and the rise of scientific management. University of Wisconsin Press, Madison

Nelson DA (1995) Managers and workers: origins of the twentieth-century factory system in the United States 1880–1920. University of Wisconsin Press, Madison

Phipps ST (2011) Mary, Mary, quite contrary: in a male-dominated field, women contributed by bringing a touch of spirituality to early management theory and practice. J Manag Hist 17(3):270–281

Porfeli EJ (2009) Hugo Münsterberg and the origins of vocational guidance. Career Dev Q 57(3): 225–236

Prieto LC, Phipps STA (2014) Capitalism in question: Hill, Addams and Follett as early social entrepreneurship advocates. J Manag Hist 20(3):266–277

Robinson (1995) An intellectual history of psychology. The University of Wisconsin Press, Madison

Rodgers DT (1998) Atlantic crossings: social politics in a progressive age. Harvard University Press, Cambridge, MA

Samelson F (1977) World War I intelligence testing and the development of psychology. J Hist Behav Sci 13(3):274–282

Schaffer R (1991) America in the Great War: the rise of the war welfare state. Oxford University Press, New York

Schilling MA (2000) Decades ahead of her time: advancing stakeholder theory through the ideas of Mary Parker Follett. J Manag Hist 6(5):224–242

Schwarz C (2015) A review of management history from 2010–2014 utilizing a thematic analysis approach. J Manag Hist 21(4):494–504

Scott WD (1910) Increasing human efficiency in business. Macmillan, New York

Scott WG (1992) Chester I. Barnard and the guardians of the managerial state. University Press of Kansas, Lawrence

Shepard (2015) https://thepsychologist.bps.org.uk/volume-28/november-2015/psychology-and-great-war-1914-1918

Singleton LG (2013) Exploring early academic responses to functions of the executive. J Manag Hist 19(4):492–511

Skocpol T (1992) Protecting soldiers and mothers. Harvard University Press, Cambridge, MA

Spillmann J, Spillmann L (1993) The rise and fall of Hugo Münsterberg. J Hist Behav Sci 29(4):322–338

Stagner R (1981) Training and experiences of some distinguished industrial psychologists. Am Psychol 36:497–505

Strother G (1976) The moral codes of executives: a Watergate-inspired look at Barnard's theory of executive responsibility. Acad Manag Rev 1(2):13–22

Thompson Heames J, Breland JW (2010) Management pioneer contributors: 30-year review. J Manag Hist 16(4):427–436

Tone A (1997) The business of benevolence: industrial paternalism in progressive America. Cornell University Press, Ithaca

Tonn JC (2003) Mary P. Follett: creating democracy, transforming management. Yale University Press, New Haven

Towill DR (2009) Frank Gilbreth and health care delivery method study driven learning. Int J Health Care Qual Assur 22(4):417–440

Towill DR (2010) Industrial engineering the Toyota production system. J Manag Hist 16(3): 327–345

Traihair RCS (1984) The humanist temper. Transaction Books, New Brunswick

Van De Water TJ (1997) Psychology's entrepreneurs and the marketing of industrial psychology. J Appl Psychol 82(4):486

Verstegen RL, Rutherford MA (2000) Mary Parker Follett: individualist or collectivist? Or both? J Manag Hist 6(5):207–223

Vinchur AJ, Koppes LL (2007) Early contributors to the science and practice of industrial psychology. Historical perspectives in industrial and organizational psychology, 37–58

Viteles MS (1932) Industrial psychology. Norton, New York

Viteles MS (1967) In: Boring EG, Lindzey G (eds) A history of psychology in autobiography, vol 5. Appleton-Century-Crofts, New York, pp 415–449

Von Mayrhauser RT (1989) Making intelligence functional: Walter Dill Scott and applied psychological testing in World War I. J Hist Behav Sci 25(1):60–72

Weinsetein (1967) The corporate idea in the liberal state, 1900–1918. Beacon Press, Boston

White R (2017) And the republic for which it stands. The United States during Reconstruction and the Gilded Age, 1865–1869. Oxford University Press, New York

Wiebe RH (1967) The search for order, 1877–1920. Hill and Wang, New York

Wolf WB (1973) Conversations with Chester I. Barnard, New York State School of Industrial and Labor Relations. Cornell University, Ithaca

Wolf WB (1974) The basic Barnard: an introduction to Chester I. Barnard and his theories of organization and management, New York State School of Industrial and Labor Relations. Cornell University, Ithaca

Wren DA (2005) The history of management thought. Wiley, Hoboken

Wren DA, Bedeian AG (2009) The evolution of management thought, 6th edn. Wiley, New York

Wren DA, Bedeian AG (2018) The history of management thought, 7th edn. Wiley, Hoboken

Wren DA, Hay RD (1977) Management historians and business historians: differing perceptions of pioneer contributors. Acad Manag J 20(3):470–476

Yost E (1949) Frank and Lillian Gilbreth: partners for life. Rutgers University Press, New Brunswick

To the Tavistock Institute: British Management in the Early Twentieth Century

25

Jeffrey Muldoon

Contents

Introduction	594
British Management 1870 to 1940: A Snapshot	596
The Establishment	599
Education and Culture	600
Raging Against the Dying Light: Lyndall Urwick	605
Taylorism, Fordism, and Human Relations in Great Britain	605
To Tavistock and Modern British Management	608
Conclusions	609
Lessons	611
References	612

Abstract

The purpose of this chapter is to discuss management in Great Britain from the late nineteenth to early twentieth century. The principle question that this chapter is asking is why, despite the large lead in the first industrial revolution, did the British fail to develop a theory of management. Emphasis is provided to both British corporate structure, culture, and educational system. The second question the chapter asks is how the British interacted with American management concepts. The final question is what lessons do the British example provides for modern America. The contention of the paper is that the inability to develop management helped to accelerate British their decline. What can the British experience teach us?

J. Muldoon (✉)
Emporia State University, Emporia, KS, USA
e-mail: jmuldoon@emporia.edu

© The Author(s), under exclusive licence to Springer Nature Switzerland AG 2020   593
B. Bowden et al. (eds.), *The Palgrave Handbook of Management History*,
https://doi.org/10.1007/978-3-319-62114-2_31

594   J. Muldoon

Keywords

British management; Great Britain · Lyndall Urwick · Eric Trist

Introduction

At Waterloo, astride his horse, Copenhagen, the Duke of Wellington, defeated the world's conqueror, Napoleon, settling the Napoleonic Wars and making Great Britain the undisputed power in the world (Cannadine 2017). Wellington had not just beaten Napoleon; he ended the largest threat to the British Empire, France, and had settled the "European problem" for all time. Despite the cost, loss of the American colonies, and the War of 1812, Britain bravely stood up to Napoleon, at times alone, in a process producing numerous heroes and creating the largest empire in history. They had the largest economy, the largest navy, and an excellent army. They were the world's creditor and, in the following years, would create miracles and advancements in science, literature, business, and the arts. Their largest contribution was the scientific and business advance, the Industrial Revolution, which lifted humanity from depravation. All the more remarkable was that the British Isles is a small island, not much larger than the states of New York, Pennsylvania, and Ohio combined, with a population smaller than France, Russia, and the Germany states separately. The nineteenth century was truly the British century, and greater heights were to be expected.

Yet the twentieth century would not be Britain's. Rudyard Kipling's poem "Recessional" turned out to be true, rather than just a warning – Britain's power was, like Nineveh and Tyre, one of the past. In fact, the twentieth century could be dubbed the anti-British century, as Britain lost an empire and its position in finance and industry, its military battered, and became, for lack of a better term, a client state of the United States (Barnett 1972). In fact, the United States had so little fear of Britain as a great power that the United States provided Britain with nuclear weapons. This could be a testimony to the "special relationship," but others, such as Corelli Barnett, have scoffed at this explanation (Barnett 1982). This collapse of British power has had many explanations: the costly and destructive wars with Germany, culture, lack of industrial investment, lack of a strong state, overextension, and geography.

Although there is a tremendous amount of truth to the explanations above, one particular issue has been ignored: the lack of British support for management. Management, not natural resources, is the path to wealth, comfort, and power (Chandler 1977). As discussed in the chapter on nineteenth-century management, the British had elements of a systematic management approach from the time of Robert Owen – it never developed managers to the degree needed for industry support. This would consist of both middle managers and entrepreneurial managers (Chandler 1990; Coleman 1973). In fact, British businessmen, with the exception of those in finance, were more concerned with becoming gentlemen and landed gentry than they were in becoming world titans (Wiener 1981). John D. Rockefeller's overriding motivation was to become the wealthiest man and greatest oil baron in the world, Marcus Samuel, the lord mayor of London. This lack of development can be blamed on numerous factors, including culture and education.

This image belies the picture of British industry being ingenious and innovative. The British developed the airplane, the dreadnaught, jet engines, and radar. Rolls Royce produced the world's finest engines. Marcus Samuel built the world's first oil tanker, *the Murex*. Without these innovations, the free world would have collapsed to either Imperial or Nazi Germany. The best chance that Hitler had at winning the war, according to the John Lukacs, was the "duel" between Hitler and Churchill (Lukacs 1991). Although Hitler seemed to have the best weapons, this perception was false as British planes and radar made the difference. Barnett, one of the critics of British war planning, actually argued that this reality is true. But he also noted, as historians such Arthur Herman (2013) and William O'Neill (1993) have pointed out, that without American aid, the war would have been lost. The British lacked the production capabilities and food supplies to endure. True, the British had excellent weapons – they just did not have enough. My contention is that British management never developed the mass production capacities needed due to culture, education, and the class system.

This chapter is written against the back drop of British decline and the inability to craft management having modern elements. Modern management in the United States was based on expertise, knowledge, enterprise, and size (Chandler 1977, 1990). The United States produced companies, such as the successors of Standard Oil, General Motors, General Electric, Ford, and Boeing, which would become symbols of the twentieth-century capitalism. Through various business schools and the emergence of salaried managers, the United States was fully able to take advantages of modern industrialization in a way that other countries could not (Herman 2013). The British did not develop a modern notion of management, preferring premodern notions of smaller, family knit corporations (Chandler 1990; Wilson and Thomson 2006). As several scholars have pointed out, the British focus was on different issues than just pure economic efficiency, as the Americans were (Thomas 1978). Rather, the British focus was on social responsibility and ethics, arguing that management should be more qualitative than quantitative. It was not until later in the twentieth century that British management became modern.

I seek to discuss several topics in this chapter: the comparative lack of management development and education, how the "public school culture" shaped these ideals, how the lack of management stalled British production and caused capital to flee elsewhere, the attempts of the British to adopt scientific management, the emergence of the "ethical" British management, and the work of Lyndall Urwick, concluding with the emergence of the Tavistock Institute and lessons for America. My contention is that the British embrace of "ethical" management combined aspects of premodernity and modernity that limited the growth of industry, as well as limiting the industrial and military power of Great Britain. My contention is that the United States faces a similar choice in that we are combining modernity and postmodernity that could threaten America's current economic and military might.

British Management 1870 to 1940: A Snapshot

There have been several major works on British management written over the years (Child 2011; Thomas 1978; Wilson and Thomson 2006). Through these works, a picture of British management in which certain crucial characteristics emerge. Firstly, as Sidney Pollard (1965) argues, by 1850, the British owner-manager model had become dominant and generated an unwillingness to hire and promote salaried managers, in the process creating many family owned and controlled businesses. These family owned businesses produced a different set of agency problems, namely, the pressure to aid family members (Bendickson et al. 2016a, b). Rather than increase wealth, family owners/managers sought to provide for the family, even those that could be considered "bad" children (Barnett 1972). Therefore, family owned businesses had little pressure to improve in the market since, as family owned firms, they were immune to shareholder pressure to modernize. In fact, given the levels of intermarriage between owners of firms, market stabilization occurred through personal relationships (Chandler 1990). Families still made money selling in Britain and the Imperial markets. The business class felt no need to produce the type of wealth of the Rockefellers and other robber barons.

Secondly, the British Empire created another set of problems (Heffer 2017; Searle 2004). Given the lack of management, the British had a difficult time competing on the international scene, producing a trade deficit (Searle 2004). The trade deficit was an ongoing issue for Great Britain regarding visible goods. However, the picture on invisible goods was quite different. Financial resources, such as investments and insurance, in addition to the merchant fleet, made the difference and put the British in the black. That being said, while London was enriched, whether this wealth spread throughout the country remains a question (Wiener 1981). In fact, this different level of prosperity caused some social and economic problems (Heffer 2017; Searle 2004). Furthermore, British dependencies, domains, and territories helped their industry. India was a great benefit to the Lancaster textile market. The white settlements, such as Australia, Canada, Cape Colony, Natal, and New Zealand, played a crucial role in terms of supporting British industry. Therefore, the Empire also provided a safety net for Great Britain, which sought to use their Empire as a trade zone, in what Joseph Chamberlain would call "imperial" preference (Searle 2004). This provided a soft market place for British companies, which insulated them for greater competition (Searle 2004).

Thirdly, British industries remained consistently small, even in industries where they should have vertically integrated, such as steel and automobile (Chandler 1990). There was not a British analogue for US Steel, General Motors, or Ford. Also, the British were unwilling to move industries from where they had settled (Coleman 1987; Wilson and Thomson 2006). Part of the problem was that British invested abroad. From an Imperial standpoint, they invested in the wrong country; Britain's potential rival, the United States, was the major source of British investment (Searle 2004). The vast amount of economic growth the United States experienced after the Civil War would not have been possible without British capital.

Fourthly, British industries remained small due to a lack of investment. For this reason, in the large capital-intensive industries, such as Dunlop, glass (Pilkington), explosives (Nobel), and chemicals (Courtaulds), growth was financed from retained earnings, rather than private equity. The reason why capital was spent elsewhere was the divide between the industrial north and Banking London (Wiener 1981). The division between finance and industry promoted a deep divide in the capitalistic class. British banks did not support the type of innovation needed due to the failure of the City of Glasgow Bank. London banks were no longer willing to support long-term national projects. The net result, according to W. P. Kennedy, was that the system emerged to maintain the gains of the first industrial revolution, creating a sustainable rather than a profit maximizing culture (Kennedy 1976). Businessmen drifted to finance, rather than production. Finance was more respected. The American system was the opposite of the British. Its industrial heroes were figures such as Henry Ford rather than bankers such J. P. Morgan. The British equivalent, William Morris, was scorned (Wiener 1981).

Fifthly, another reason why the British did not have to develop the size and scope of American business had a great deal to do with the size and density of the British population and the size of Great Britain (Chandler 1990). With a smaller country and a more dense population than America, the British did not feel the pressure to create corporate structures that could handle business across a continent. The shift of Great Britain to an industrial state was accomplished more easily than in the United States. For example, the British railroad industry became very efficient in hauling freight. Yet the continental size of the United States forced challenges in the United States that required innovative solutions. For example, while department stores developed along similar lines in Great Britain and the United States, there was no equivalent to Sears or Montgomery Ward, both of which were mail houses designed to reach the far flung farmer.

Sixthly, the manager was not esteemed or desired. Managers were considered not much more than clerks, whose status during the nineteenth century was declining (Wilson and Thomson 2006). Although the manager's relative power increased due to the emergence of the railroads, they were still considered servants, rather than members of an important profession. In addition, there were managers hired based on their technical ability, but there were too few to create a profession. Management's associate field, engineering, was not in high demand (Barnett 1986). Wilson and Thomson (2006) point to four factors that limited the development of professional management. First, contemporary ideas about proprietorial rights; second, since managers worked on the floor, they had low social status; third, there was little in the way of training; and fourth, the externalization of many functions. Another major difference between the British and the United States was that the British capitalistic class consisted of gentlemen – owners (and their sons) and players who were salaried managers. According to Donald Coleman (1973), the goal of the players was to become gentlemen, rather than becoming a distinct class. The education and training was very different. The gentlemen went to Oxbridge; the players were trained on the job.

Gentlemen did not compete. The mentality of competition seemed to be ignored by British elite and managers. One could see some of the early elements of Mayoism in the work of some of the British management thinkers. One such thinker, R. B. Haldane, held the belief that competition was dangerous; it promoted destruction and could drive companies out of business and lower wages (Thomans 1978; Wiener 1981). When Germany began to surpass Great Britain around 1900, many British commentators felt that it was due to the unfair business practices that the Germans employed (Bell 1996). Such an attitude is to be expected in that the British believed that managerial ability was inherited and bred. Nepotism dominated hiring as salaried managers were not trusted (Casson 1997).

These factors lead Chandler (1990) to conclude that the British failed to make the essential threefold investment in manufacturing, marketing, and management. When large investments were made, they were sufficient to produce economies of scale, but not to fully utilize them. Given the small levels of investment compared to the United States, different organizational structures emerged. The British had a greater focus on family owned and run, rather than publicly owned and run business. This notable limitation prevented the British from developing further capabilities. Given the low levels of investment, the British focused more on industry cooperation from marriage between different families in the same industry. Yet despite this merger, corporate units still maintained businesses as discrete operations with little rationalization. Rather than possessing market capitalism, the British had what Chandler referred to as personal capitalism. Business was performed on the basis of personal, rather than market or institutional arrangements. The owner/manager kept a stronger hand in the implementation of strategy since they had direct contact with workers and first-line and middle managers.

Therefore, British businesses offered a smaller line of products and had higher degrees of backward integration than did American firms (Chandler 1990). For the most part, British firms focused on branded and packaged goods, such as candies, where they had an excellent reputation (Coleman 1987). Nevertheless, with the exception of Guinness, most businesses did not have modern notions of control. The crucial factor in mass production was control. Ford's system would not have worked in Britain. His British equivalent, William Morris, lacked control systems. These patterns were strengthened by what Wilson and Thomson call the path-dependent nature of British industry. Namely, the lack of major upheaval meant the patterns set in the first phase of the industrial revolution remained fixed. The ruling families had little reason to adopt to new structures and ways of doing things. Pollard argues that the British devoted their time and energy into fields in which they had an early start (Pollard 1965, 1989). Furthermore, British managers lacked the ability to be entrepreneurial (Landes 1969). Some of the most prominent British businessmen, such as Cadbury and Rowntree, came from the chocolate industry, a source of enjoyment but hardly a source of innovation.

The Establishment

The British subjects who crafted the first British Empire in the seventeenth and eighteenth centuries were men (and women) who were cold and calculating, with a tough-minded focus on the outcomes, whether it was power or profit (Barnett 1972). Perhaps the best example of this trend was Churchill's great ancestor, John Churchill, the First Duke of Marlborough (Holmes 2008). Churchill emerged from poverty due to his connection to his patron, James, the Duke of York, fated to be the infamous James II. Churchill served as a soldier, then a general, and was one of the commanders who crushed the Monmouth Rebellion. However, Marlborough soon turned on his King and benefactor, defecting to William and Mary. Marlborough kept up a deep correspondence with the deposed king, as well as the Kings in Hanover, in terms of making sure that he was on favorable side. In addition, his wife Sarah used her relationship with Queen Anne to maintain her husband's grasp on power. Marlborough's behavior was very typical: aggressive, opportunistic, and profit seeking. According to Barnett, it was this attitude that laid the foundations for British supremacy.

Yet during the Georgian period, there was an increased discussion of high-mindedness that began to pervade politics (Barnett 1972). Some early examples of this would be Edmund Burke and Pitt the Elder's denunciation of the war on the American colonies. It would receive further sentiment during the Napoleonic Wars. After Waterloo, both Whig and Tory went out of their way to praise Wellington, until Wellington was attacked for returning paintings that Napoleon's forces had stolen (Muir 2014). The first source of this high-mindedness was Romanticism, which was discussed in the chapter on Owen. These attitudes were also reinforced by Methodism and other evangelical sects, which had entered into the Church of England (Barnett 1972). What developed was a viewpoint that believed in brotherly love, rather than business or profit. These viewpoints were also strengthened by the involvement of Prince Albert, who sought to improve welfare.

These viewpoints were strengthened in public schools, which sought less to educate but more to develop "Christian gentlemen" (Barnett 1972). One of the primary goals of these public schools was to produce administrators, generals, and politicians to handle Britain's large empire and the demands that empire imposed on the country. This style imposed a stifling atmosphere that required conformity, obedience, and submission to authority. Every aspect of student life was regulated – for rebels, such as Winston Churchill, punishment and potential exclusion from fellow students would follow. These views intermingled with aristocrats, such as Churchill (grandson of a Duke) and the middle class as well, taming the arriviste qualities (Roberts 2018).

Education and Culture

The education system was a major part of the problem. There was no national education system (Barnett 1972), and it lacked a coherent bridge between school and college. Brits usually stopped education around elementary school – despite the fact that America had made education compulsory in the North before the Civil War (Howe 2007; McPherson 1988). The British system failed the working classes, who remained ignorant due to a lack of education and the lower middle classes, who usually entered into employment at the local government level, abandoning trade jobs or college in general, where they could rise (Barnett 1972). In my opinion, the picture that George Orwell drew in 1984 of an ignorant working class and frustrated lower middle class has its realities in the England Orwell grew up in.

Job training, the hallmark of Taylorism, was nonexistent, as the British preferred practical men who learned on the job (Barnett 1972). Likewise, there was comparatively little in the way of scientific education in Great Britain, preferring the craftwork of the "practical" man of the first industrial revolution. Increasingly, the work of production was shifting from the practical man to the scientific man in the United States. This occurred in Great Britain as well. Although it was a practical man, Henry Bessemer, that made modern steel production possible, it was based on the metallurgist Robert Mushet's advice. Before 1884, there was no university department in metallurgy, and biochemistry fared just as poorly. Yet the British remained skeptical of new engineering techniques such as Taylorism. When a Yorkshire iron maker received a copy of the Principles of Scientific Management from Taylor, he responded by sending a book by the Latin poet Horace (Barnett 1972).

Human resources provided another major problem at both worker and manager positions. In terms of the worker, despite the picture drawn by middle-class intellectuals, the working class remained largely uneducated, radical, and had a high distrust of management (Thompson 1963). The other prevalent characteristic was the pressure to conform (Hoggart 1957). Rather than viewing themselves as poorer than the middle class, they considered themselves apart – distinct (Thompson 1963). Attempts to climb out or produce more were deemed as unnecessary – the only interaction with management was to fight over payments. At home, as Hoggart (1957) noted, incompetent home management created improvident spending and poor food selection. Despite the fact families would often struggle for food, there was always enough money for beer, cigarettes, and the occasional bet. The lack of desire to rise was very different than in the United States, where workers consistently strove to rise, often lacking a strong working class spirit.

Education for the upper class probably was worse; it trained its students in the classics to produce gentlemen, rather than the science of application (Barnett 1972). The education system produced, according to Barnett, a ruling class of essay writers, rather than problem solvers. The principle drive of college education was to prepare character, not to train students either for careers in science or other subjects, such as foreign languages or history. Greek was a requirement at Cambridge until 1919 and at Oxford until 1920. The role of Greek was so strong at Cambridge that they lost a chance for a program in naval architecture when the donor found out that students would have to take ancient Greek. Compounding the problem was the high degree of institutional isomorphism in the British education system. The "red brick" institutions, created in part to challenge the dominance of Oxbridge, adopted some of the classical core of their rivals. Part of this was due to the fact, as new institutions, they had to conform to certain practices dictated by London University's external examination policy.

These problems were not common in America. The American University model was radically different. Despite the dominance of the Ivy League, there were consistent movements to modernize universities. The Americans were an early adopter of the German University model, stressing research and technical training (Novick 1988). Johns Hopkins, Stanford, and the New University of Chicago were founded on the premise of the German model and the production of doctorates. The Morrill Act produced land grant institutions throughout the land (McPherson 1988). The time period saw the emergence of technical schools such as the Massachusetts Institute of Technology (MIT) and the California Institute of Technology (Cal Tech). Charles W. Eliot created the elective system and helped to build the Harvard Business School which, at one point, sought to hire Taylor. Woodrow Wilson, although an opponent of the German system, sought to move Princeton from a Presbyterian institution filled with potential ministers and the sons of affluence, to a meritocratic institution, where excellence in education was stressed.

The picture of the American working environment was completely different. Firstly, America never had any experience with a powerful landed gentry – even during the revolution (Genovese 1974; Wood 1992). To be sure, plantation owners had large business concerns, but comparatively speaking, they were poorer and less influential than their British counterparts. In addition, although landowners dominated the South, they were not the major entrepreneurs of the North. Also, America had a tradition of education – even the very poor in the frontier could read, and illiteracy was looked down upon (McPherson 1988). American working class participated in political culture and then later mass culture. American middle classes also used business to promote middle-class values. One of the business methods was welfare capitalism, a massive series of education, training, and social techniques that were designed to promote middle-class values and Americanization. Those who strove to improve were regarded positively – even on the frontier. Abraham Lincoln gained as much respect for his self-education and becoming a lawyer as he did for his wrestling ability.

Mostly, the difference between America and Britain was political and cultural. Both the North and South had voting for white males, regardless of property, before the Civil War. This meant that the working class had a deep connection to the system, a belief that they could rise above poverty and become President. Many of the founding fathers and the succeeding generations came from poverty-stricken backgrounds. Andrew Jackson, Abraham Lincoln, and Andrew Johnson all came from backgrounds of great poverty and all became President. It was not until Ramsay McDonald that the British had someone from a true working class or poor background. American business, educational system, and political leadership came from diverse backgrounds. Politically, the focus of America was the creation or protection of markets. In fact, until the New Deal, political movements sought to free markets or create them (Brinkley 1995, 1998). And even the New Deal sought to create new markets throughout the South and Midwest (Brinkley Brinkley 1995, 1998).

The historian Martin Wiener's work (1981) on English culture remains one of the most influential and controversial works on England. The book was a response to and an influence on the Thatcher government. Keith Joseph claimed it was the bible of the Thatcher government. The book has left a deep mark on some works; influences can be seen with Alfred Chandler, Barnett, and Sidney Pollard, and it has also been widely criticized by Noel Annan and David Edgerton. The purpose of the book was to provide an overview of British culture during the time period where the British went from the top economy to about 14th overall, a major decline. In essence, what Wiener seeks to provide is an explanation for what Barnett called the "English disease." The explanation that Wiener provides is cultural, one of the difficult things that an intellectual historian can make. Wiener's contention is that the British underplayed economic development, showing a focus more on social issues. Wiener does not provide statistics of industry, but he does cite examples of culture and statements on business from politicians and intellectuals.

Wiener noted that economic explanations for British decline do not explain the full process. His explanation is that the British have never felt comfortable with progress. There has been a deep romantic attachment to the English countryside, one that is reflected in various types of work literature. He goes further and argues that this approach is mostly British in character. Attachment to a bucolic existence at the expense of economic progress was also notably absent in other British colonies such as Canada, Australia, and New Zealand. Britain's most successful colony, the United States, never exhibited those beliefs. In fact, despite the American dream of the yeoman farmer, the capitalistic and acquisitive nature of the American yeoman and worker was apparent from the start, to the point where even political movements, such as the Jacksonian Democrats were, in the words of Richard Hofstadter, incipient capitalists (Hofstadter 1948). For American politicians, Democrat and Republican, liberal and conservative, the primary drive, until recently, was production for the purpose of acquisition. America is a nation of consumers. Whereas the British mentality, expressed by Sir Stafford Cripps and others, was against materialism.

Part of the English problem was that unlike America, their emergence from premodern to modernity was accomplished peacefully. America's was accomplished in a violent civil war, which destroyed not only the slaveholding class but also the old divided United States (White 2017). The industry's need to produce ended the vision of the small laboring class, forcing size upon American corporations. Great Britain saw tremendous transformation with very little violence, comparatively speaking. In fact, the new industrialized order grew without any marked detrimental effect on the old land owning system, which remained dominant politically, socially, and economically. In fact, the English land owners were more powerful and influential than the Prussian Junkers in Bismarck's Germany (Wiener 1981). In addition, the old aristocracy was more willing to accept industrialists than the Germans. The short timeframe of industrialization in Germany had less time to accept the new class. The net result was that there was no bourgeois overthrow of the old order – there was no equivalent to Abraham Lincoln. What the British bourgeois faced was a strong, insular, and richer aristocracy. This aristocracy was capitalist, but according to Wiener, they were rentier capitalistic, not entrepreneurial.

What made the Industrial Revolution happen? One of the principle arguments was that it was the transformation of culture that started in Europe and eventually spread over the world. This shift in culture placed an emphasis on what Deidre McCloskey (2006, 2010) referred to as "Bourgeois Virtue." Where the more the bourgeois were valued, the more likely the country was to embrace capitalism. The shift came from institutions and culture-respecting self-improvement. Take Lincoln, he was widely respected and admired – held up as the greatest American, because he raised himself from a log cabin to the White House. Even his political campaign highlighted his rise. I imagine if he were British, some would have dubbed him an upstart.

The question was, which model of capitalism would dominate, rentier or bourgeois? The answer was that new middle classes and the new wealthy would be absorbed into the old aristocracy. Even outsiders, such as the Jewish Marcus Samuel, could be raised to a peerage. In Samuel's case, he became the Viscount Bearsted, and his goal was to become Lord Mayor of London. Other industrialists found themselves embraced by the establishment and indoctrinated into the religious and social outlook of the old. This is what Wiener would dub as "the gentrification of the industrialist."

David Edgerton (1991, 1996, 2005) has launched a small cottage industry critical of the work of Wiener, Barnett, Chandler, and Pollard. Edgerton notes that the British industry did not decline as much as critics have noted. The British did not get surpassed as an economic power per capita by its rivals (Germany, France, Italy, and Japan) until the 1960s. The concept of relative decline fails to note that the British were far more productive and wealthy at a later date. He attacked the notion that innovation is the source of technological growth. He also notes the British developed the airplane and other technical marvels in a welfare/warfare state. The entrepreneurial failure listed by Landes (1969) and others were rational responses to economic conditions. To suggest otherwise, ignores historical conditions. The British also had an education system much more in tune with science and technology. In fact, Britain could be seen as a technological innovator, whose inventions have been used by other countries.

Edgerton (2005) goes further noting that critics of British policy, such as Wiener and Barnett, often cite evidence out of context. In fact, he goes so far as to call their work anti-historical. He noted that Wiener demonstrated no interest in British industry or the British industrial spirit. His focus was on the anti-industrial spirit within the country. Of course, Wiener (1981) also noted that Britain's most similar rival, the United States, never had such an anti-industrial spirit. The American elite were much weaker making the system more open to industrial change. In fact, there was an argument that the antibusiness movement from the Progressives was an attempt of old elite (from families like the Roosevelts) to curtail the new elite. Yet Barnett's basic point that the "audit of war" revealed British weakness is supported by the fact that the British were willing to accept bad terms with the Americans to maintain the flow of war weapons into the country. Britain's initial response to the Morgenthau's plan to transform Germany into a pastoral state was muted because Britain had to beg for a loan (Kennedy 1999).

Furthermore, Edgerton's criticism ignored the common problem: Why did a country that had so many prime mover advantages fritter them away? Furthermore, why did a country that created so many brilliant concepts not enjoy a higher status in the world economy? Edgerton is right to be skeptical that innovation is not a direct cause of national wealth because it ignores a major problem – management. Management is the pathway in which innovations are implemented, proper innovation is selected, and innovations become efficient. Management and its social networks are the process through which innovation is spread. Edgerton does not mention management and the expertise that management could bring to handling problems. The British had many consultants, but it seemed that there was not a business school or trade networks to spread ideas and train new managers.

The British military production does reveal tremendous strength. As Barnett noted, British industry produced 100,000 planes by June 1944, with 10,000 of them being heavy bombers. They also produced 135,000 artillery pieces, 21,000 antiaircraft, 25,000 tanks, 900,000 wheeled vehicles, and 4 million machine guns. This was despite the needed dispersal of factories due to constant bombing and the vast reorganization socially and industrially that the bombings caused. This remarkable performance was a testament to the British collective spirit caused by the war, as well as the ingenuity and bravery of the British people. However, Barnett also argues that such a remarkable portrait hides the real truth, namely, that British production remained higher than average cost and lower than average production than its main rivals: United States, Germany, and the Soviet Union (Barnett 1986, p. 88). Even British airplanes required parts from many countries. This is revealed in their problems producing tanks – the fact that the British navy had to import steel from Germany. In fact, in the production of pig iron, Britain had been overtaken by Belgium by 1908, a country that was not considered to be a rival of British production (Barnett 1972).

In conclusion, Edgerton makes several important points in his writing. Namely, the British were able to create technological wonders. However, despite his arguments, I remain unconvinced. The British created many technological wonders to be sure, but they simply did not produce enough. Churchill, despite his issues with his mother's country and the pride in his father's, understood that British survival needed American weapons of war. As Arthur Herman (2013, p. 2) noted,

American business produced two-thirds of all Allied military equipment used in World War II. That included 86,000 tanks, 2.5 million trucks and a half million jeeps, 286,000 warplanes, 8,800 naval vessels, 5,600 merchant ships, 434 million tons of steel, 2.6 million machine guns, and 41 billion rounds of ammunition—not to mention the greatest superbomber of the war, the B-29, and the atomic bomb.

This production occurred despite the conflict between businessmen and New Dealers, despite the eroding of America's industrial might during the Great

Depression, and despite American industry's poor performance during the First World War. The Americans provided the British with one-third of their planes. The Soviet Union's advance would not have been possible without American trucks. These wonders occurred due to American management and entrepreneurship. Although the British had the ability to create better engines, radar, and jet planes, they lacked the ability to produce them in sufficient qualities to make the difference. British innovation and American management were unbeatable.

Raging Against the Dying Light: Lyndall Urwick

Lyndall Urwick warrants his own section in this chapter. Urwick was one of the top management consultants of the twentieth century; a prolific writer, whose work covered about 60 years. Awarded many honors – and one of the preeminent champions of management theory of the twentieth century – Urwick was an early proponent of Follet and Fayol, recognizing their brilliance before many of their contemporaries. The downside was that Urwick did not devote as much time to the nuances of the work he drew upon for his ideas. As Parker and Ritson (2011) note (which I think is very charitable):

> Urwick's legacy included a lifetime campaign to reconcile scientific management with succeeding schools of thought, today's management literature stereotyping of some of his contemporary thinkers, and a contribution to management literature's predilection for the labelling of theories and principles.

Despite such criticisms, Urwick sought to combine schools of management thought into a universal theory of management, becoming, with the exception of Fayol, the preeminent classicist of the twentieth century. Urwick was also successful in building an extensive informal scholarly network which, over time, took on a more formal, international hue. Intellectually, as an officer in World War II, Urwick was introduced to the concepts of scientific management when he was recovering from injury. It was his embrace of Taylor, however, that created significant problems for him, problems that were especially damaging since Taylor's writings were held, at the time, in low regard.

Taylorism, Fordism, and Human Relations in Great Britain

The Americans developed many concepts in management, and these concepts were spread across the globe. How the British received them was driven by their culture. The 1870s were a time when the British mentality toward business really began to shift. Previously, the British philosophy regarding management was based on the entrepreneurial spirit and the concepts of self-help and laissez-faire. Shifts in British industry began to emerge post 1870. There were some concepts of incentive-based pay to quail worker protests. There was also a shift to altruism driven by Christian ethics. As John Child (2011, p. 34) writes,

> Thus by the 1890s, some employers were prepared to treat wage levels not as given by the market but as a variable, which could be manipulated to increase worker co-operation. Piece-rate systems came into operation particularly in engineering and railway workshops. Many of the top British industrialists came from a Christian, especially Quaker background.

This led many British thinkers to embrace concepts related to social responsibility. The British began to pioneer concepts related to industrial welfare, some of which correspond to later welfare capitalism.

Child takes a differing viewpoint arguing that British managers felt this impulse less due to altruism and more to deal with diminishing worker radicalism. Child (2011, p. 37) notes:

> Industrial welfare may also be distinguished according to whether it was designed to close the enterprise to trade unions or whether a more open-minded policy was adopted. Welfare that was little more than an arbitrary dispensation of favours could lead to the worst aspects of paternalism when, as with some railway companies, it represented an attempt to suppress unionism.

Child does note that some humanistic managers, such as Seebohm Roundtree, did recognize that workers could be placed in a difficult circumstance – namely, having to choose between their relationship with their employers and their fellow workers. One particular issue was that many of the elites believed that the well-off had a responsibility to take care of the less well-off. These beliefs would color how the British would respond to American concepts.

Taylorism had an interesting relationship with British thought. Firstly, the British recognized parts of the Taylor system, as it had many elements that were a rehash of Babbage's work. But what was new was that Taylor had created a system of management. It also provided the British with a system that could reduce poverty and reject the laissez-faire. However, the reception was muted and complex. According to Child (2011, p. 38):

> Scientific management involved a search for optimum principles of industrial operation and a conscious endeavor to inject a new philosophy of relationships in industry. Yet, on the other hand, it lacked that sympathetic view of workers and their representative organizations upon which Quaker employers particularly insisted.

British criticisms anticipated those of the human relations movement about 20 years beforehand. The net result was that there was little application of Taylorism before the First World War.

The extent to which the British adopted Taylorism is complex. The traditional narrative is that the British were indifferent toward the adoption of Taylorism (Littler 1982; Locke 1984). However, Littler and Locke's primary focus was on the years 1911 and 1912, during a period of labor unrest. Whitson (1997) concludes,

> A review of the leading British engineering journals in the early twentieth century reveals that Taylorism received a fair amount of attention, and much of it positive. By the beginning of the First World War, the majority of trade journals were echoing Taylor's demands for a new type of management.

The primary drive for the adoption of scientific management was consultants, although working managers were certainly aware of scientific management (Brech et al. 2010). However, British employers were hesitatant in adopting Taylorism due to the fact that they were small in size and continued to use batch production. Worker resistance was not the problem, and even employers began to embrace scientific management. Thanks to the work of consultants, like Lyndall Urwick, as well as the government, the British began to embrace the concepts of scientific management after the war.

The British seemed to have more difficulty embracing Fordism (Wiener 1981). The idea of mass production and consumption was something that the British began to really adopt in the 1950s, about 30 years after the Americans (Campbell 1987; Wiener 1981). One particular issue was that British society preferred batch work rather than mass production – aesthetics over materialism. Fordism with its emphasis on vast production and employee consumption would not have found a place in Great Britain during the 1920s. Coleman (1987) and Pollard (1989) argue that the British devoted their time and energy to business fields in which they had an early start. Some of the most prominent British businessmen, such as Cadbury and Rowntree, came from the chocolate industry. These industries did not require the integration or productive capacity as did the automobile.

The reception of human relations to the British Isles was one of great complexity (Thomas 1978). The British anticipated human relations by about 10 years according to Harris. However, one could see the elements of human relations early on in the writings of Quaker businessmen before the turn of the century. According to Child, the practical implications of human relations were not new to the British. However, the theoretical implications, such as social satisfaction, spontaneous cooperation, and informal organization, were very interesting to British management thinkers. The most influential human relations author was not Mayo, but T. N. Whitehead, whether this was due to his research being more in depth at the later stages or his famous last name, we could not be sure. Above all, Mayo's concept that managers had a social mission, fit into the British management mindset articulated before the war. However, despite this, the legitimacy of Mayo's work did not receive recognition until the next decade.

The British, like the Americans, used some of the spirit of the human relations movement to counsel workers. British managers also recognized that economic incentives did not cover all of work motivation. The British and Mayo also had a deep level of idealism in their work. But it was more in Britain that this idealism encouraged scientific work. Mayo's student and ablest defender noted, George Homans in his defense of Mayo, that Mayo's ideas were demonstrated through research, downplaying the role of ethics. The ethical criticism of Mayo would not come from psychology or business, but mostly from sociologists (Muldoon 2017).

There were also significant differences between the countries on human relations (Thomas 1978). British concerns over human relations had roots in Christian values and ethics. The United States' concern was over scientific transformation of work, and Mayo's political ideology was also attractive since he wanted to reduce destructive conflict between labor and management. The second issue is that of unions. Mayo pretty much ignored them; Whitehead argued that they served only a social role, ignoring collective bargaining. British management ignored the role of unions, but increasingly after the First World War, the British did pay increased attention to the economic and social benefits of unions. Harris notes that the difference could be that unions were not considered in the Hawthorne studies due to the lack of unions in the United States at the time. Many of the unions, prior to the New Deal, tended to be company unions.

One of the impediments to the British accepting management was the idea that they should trust democracy rather than the expert. The British view is that there is no viewpoint, nor theory, that could be made without exception. According to Rosamund Thomas (1978), the British preferred a practical person, trained in history and classics, rather than a manager trained in formalistic ways, like scientific management or human relations. If management is art and science, then the British preferred to focus on the art rather than science. The outcome was different. The outcome of American management was on greater production with greater efficiency and science. The purpose of work research was to scientifically discover the means of production and how to influence the human aspect at work. Taylor and his disciples, the early psychologists, and the Mayo group were all devoted, to lesser and greater degrees, toward scientific research. The British response was different – although they had elements in scientific research (certainly engineers were interested) – ethics were as important as efficiency. In addition, since ethics are valued and, according to them, cannot be scientifically researched, efficiency should be qualitative as well as quantitative.

To Tavistock and Modern British Management

The Second World War ended the old Britain. Common suffering and depravation created a sense of unity that had previously been absent in the country (Leff 1991). The cry from the British people was "never again" would the British suffer such destruction, loss, and poverty. This rallying cry produced a "New Jerusalem," a massive welfare state that would provide coverage from cradle to grave. This new attitude provided a major focus on industrial research and would help to create a modern management (Garrity et al. 2018). The war had "audited" the British economy, revealing deep weaknesses. This created a push for the development of research tanks, such as Tavistock, and would move industrial research into the university.

Like other postwar British arrangements, the Tavistock Institute had its genesis during the war, when a group of very talented psychologists, psychiatrists, and anthropologists banded together to work on the war Trist and Murray (1990).

They called themselves the Tavistock group, due to their connection to the Tavistock clinic. The clinic itself had its genesis after World War I, when British psychologists researched battle fatigue and other issues that people suffered due to the war. The British also faced vast problems during the war due to the demands of having to promptly build a large army. The Tavistock group consulted on the following issues: selection and training of army officers, training of pilots, handling the repatriation of the prisoners of war, and methods to gain roles of acceptance. After the war, the Tavistock group was formed based on their experiences during the war and a grant from the Rockefeller Institute. In addition, Tavistock formed a new journal, *Human Relations*, with a partnership with the Lewin research group, which was located at the University of Michigan. The damage done to the British economy – the devaluation of the pound, the lack of capital, and the nationalization of various industries – meant that there were opportunities for management scholars.

Another example of an important British contribution came from a surprising source, a classist named Joan Woodward (Garrity et al. 2018). Woodward recognized the abundant opportunities that were available for industrial research and switched to management from classics. Her brilliance and ability as a classist provided the nascent field of industrial research with an important boost in prestige; it is likely that her work was published by Oxford due to her reputation as a classical scholar. Woodward was able to make this contribution because of new government and industry support, as well as the weakness of British sociology. The contribution was the basis of contingency management, namely, that universal theories do not hold. One particular contingency was Woodward's focus on technology. This insight has received increased attention in recent years as Apple, Google, and Amazon are changing business processes. Woodward's influence during her lifetime was very high as she directly influenced Lawrence and Lorsch, Burns and Stalker, and Perrow, who were other scholars that played a role in the creation of contingency management.

Conclusions

Was Britain really a cultural, management, and entrepreneurial cripple as suggested by Landes, Barnett, and Wiener? Or was it a technically advanced nation as suggested by Edgerton? The reality is more complex than either of those extreme positions. The type of intellectual history deployed by Wiener and Barnett is inherently difficult to assess due to the sweeping statements deployed. Mostly, intellectual history focuses less on the grand narrative and more on the particulars. The explanation is that the aggregation of a sweeping thought necessarily ignores some of the particulars in the details. In this case, they ignore outcomes, such as the development of the airplane and the other technical marvels, in which British industry acted as a pioneer. If the British were as weak and feeble as claimed, they would have folded to the onslaught of the Nazis, no matter how brave their people. For despite British's supposed problem in moving into new industries, British industry in the 1940s was still a world leader in the aviation field, an industry that they largely developed and promoted. The planes, both bombers and fighters which Britain produced in World War II, were exceptional and may have been the best of the war. Barnett concedes that this was the case, noting the strength the Hurricane, the Spitfire, the Lancaster Bomber, and the quality of the Rolls Royce engines. The success of these planes helped to ensure the eventual defeat of Nazi Germany and remain, to this day, symbols of great national pride.

However, Barnett, ever the critic, noted that the aircraft industry was the result of government involvement, not spontaneous cooperation (unlike the American aircraft industry). With the exception of the jet engine, the aircraft manufacture required foreign innovations and equipment. Moreover, it is suggested the industrial problems that characterized other industries were reproduced in aviation, causing significant managerial and production failings. The lack of logistical control and economies of scale produced bottlenecks of production. The greatest problem was efficiency – the British required more workers to produce their aircraft, and much of the production was batch, rather than mass produced. If the British industry was as competent and powerful as Edgerton suggests, they would not have gone hat in hand to the Americans during both World Wars, especially the Second. Without American production, produced by American management, the war, despite the economic advantages held by the allies, may have been lost. Even the communist Joseph Stalin, who rarely had a good word about capitalists, stated that American production won the war.

The reason is simple: as Peter Drucker and historians have pointed out, Americans developed a concept of management that provided them with an advantage. True, American managers had a greater population and a larger economy to draw upon, but they were also more efficient in production. In just 4 short years, the Americans went from having a military on par with Belgium to being the largest and best equipped military on earth, boasting the second largest army, the largest navy and air force, and having sole possession of the atomic bomb. While other nations were broke, Americans had even more and better weapons on the drawing board, ready to be launched. Other nations, by contrast, suffered privations nearly unmanageable. The Eastern Front was a kill zone, whereby one out of every six people who lived between Germany and Moscow died. In Britain, consumers were forced to use acorns for coffee. In the United States, however, there was always plenty of food – despite the price controls and lack of consumer goods. The primary reason for this is simple: Americans had embraced the modernity of management.

The reasons behind Britain's comparative managerial failure, as mentioned in this chapter, are the following. Firstly, British culture played a key role in retarding the growth of an entrepreneurial capitalist class. Secondly, the pervasiveness and enduring effect of this culture remained manifest due to its embodiment in the educational system, both in terms of the "public" (i.e., nondenominational but private) secondary schools and the dominance of the Oxbridge model in tertiary education. Thirdly, the British elite lacked intellectual diversity. While they accepted outsiders such as Marcus Samuel, it was on their rules. Fourthly, the working class had the mentality of a working class, viewing entrepreneurial endeavor and associated social advancement with disdain. By contrast, the American working class were incipient capitalists. Finally, the British elite remained at heart wedded to ideas associated with the old landed aristocracy, a class whose political and social influence endured beyond the Industrial Revolution.

Lessons

Currently, the postwar consensus of the United States is gradually weakening. The emergence of Trump and Sanders as leaders, confirmed or de facto, of the Republican and Democratic parties indicates that the factors that once held Americans together are weakening. Like Britain before it, the United States' once unchallenged supremacy as a military and economic power appears to be waning. New powers, most particularly China, loom as industrial and (potentially) military rivals.

The British example can provide some insights that help explain America's current quandary. The British are not perfect examples; they were a net exporter of capital and people. Historically, the United States has been a net importer of both, a role that certainly characterizes its current economic and demographic situation. However, the real question right now is whether the United States can continue its role as the dominant economic power or will it be overtaken by other countries. This question has been posed many times before. Some in the 1930s looked to the Soviet Union, Fascist Italy, and Nazi Germany. In the 1980s, it was Soviet Union and Japan. In the 1990s, we heard about Europe and the challenge of the European Union. Today it is China. In fact, many commentators are noting that China will overtake the United States, if it has not already. There is a ticking bomb with US debt. Any attempt at austerity is beaten down at the polls. Much like the British in 1900, we are completely blind to the challenges of the new world. We do not produce enough tradesmen, or enough engineers, while producing too many individuals with Liberal Arts degrees. Increasingly, college graduates, especially from private schools, believe that they have been sold a bill of goods.

From a management standpoint, the United States is also facing problems that mirror that of the early twentieth-century Britain in terms of its elite, legal, and corporate structure. Much like those individuals who put together the British Empire, American businessmen and leaders were ruthless and aggressive in expanding their interests. Yet as the British pursued and developed modernity, they remained premodern, sentimental, and emotionally attached to the old England. Whereas British producers should have been more aggressive in educating and training workers, expanding companies, and adding productive capacity, they preferred to muddle through, focusing on ethical considerations, rather than questions of profit and economic efficiency. It was therefore not without reason, that the British, despite some interest, did not adopt Taylorism and regarded Fordism with complete disdain. The pursuit of ethics, instead of economic growth, ended in economic and social disaster.

However, the attitude today is very different; rather than being calculating, it has become more emotional, resistant to discuss certain topics. For example, try publishing a skeptical paper regarding global warming or diversity in a major journal? Imagine questioning the costs that could be incurred by switching to a green technology – even before that technology is ready to be used. The discussion of facts, science, and evidence has taken a backseat to wish and emotion. The United States is rapidly embracing a postmodernist mindset and the inherent danger that such as mindset can imply. Most decisions seem to be based on wishes and emotions rather than a full consideration of the facts. Given some of the scandals in the research world – both in management and environmental science – greater skepticism of results needs to be commonplace. But we treat debatable issues like a mantra.

Likewise, what made American leadership so remarkable was the diversity of background and opinions. To combat Nazi Germany and Imperial Japan, the Harvard-educated patrician Franklin Roosevelt made common cause with businessmen, as did Henry J. Kaiser and William Knudsen, both of whom came from poorer backgrounds. Knudsen was skeptical about the ability of government to mobilize a democracy at war. Today, we have increased background in racial and gender matters to the benefit of the nation. However, this comes at a great cost, in that education and the media do not encourage free debate and discussion, but go so far to name what is correct and right for society. In addition, one of the principle issues that managers implicitly face is that, due to the decline of social groups, church memberships, and neighborhoods, is socialization. As Elton Mayo once recognized the majority of socialization occurs outside of work. Given the pressure to conform, it makes sense that indoctrination can work. We are producing a generation that has high levels of conformity and a lack of critical thinking.

References

Barnett C (1972) The collapse of British power. William Morrow and Company, New York
Barnett C (1982, 16 March) Long-term consequences of Trident sale. The Times 11
Barnett C (1986) The audit of war. MacMillan, London
Bell PMH (1996) France and Britain, 1900–1940: entente and estrangement. Longman, New York
Bendickson J, Muldoon J, Liguori E, Davis PE (2016a) Agency theory: the times, they are a-changin. Manag Decis 54(1):174–193
Bendickson J, Muldoon J, Liguori EW, Davis PE (2016b) Agency theory: background and epistemology. J Manag Hist 22(4):437–449
Brech E, Thomson A, Wilson JF, Urwick L (2010) Management pioneer: a biography. Oxford University Press, New York
Brinkley A (1995) The end of reform. Knopf, New York
Brinkley A (1998) Liberalism and its discontents. Harvard University Press, Cambridge, MA
Campbell J (1987) Nye Bevan and the mirage of British socialism. Weidenfeld & Nicolson, London
Cannadine D (2017) Victorious century: the United Kingdom 1800–1906. Viking, New York
Casson M (1997) Information and Organization: A New Perspective on The Theory of the Firm. Oxford University Press, Oxford
Chandler AD (1990) Scale and scope: the dynamics of industrial capitalism. The Belknap Press of Harvard University Press, Cambridge, MA

Chandler AD Jr (1977) The visible hand: the managerial revolution in American business. The Belknap Press of Harvard University Press, Cambridge, MA

Child J (2011) British management thought (Routledge revivals). Routledge, Abingdon

Coleman DC (1973) Gentlemen and players 1. Econ Hist Rev 26(1):92–98

Coleman DC (1987) Failings and achievements: some British businesses, 1910–80. Bus Hist 29(4):1–17

Edgerton D (1991) England and the aeroplane: an essay on a militant and technological nation. Science, technology and medicine in modern history. Macmillan, London

Edgerton D (1996) Science, technology and the British industrial 'decline' 1870–1970. Cambridge University Press, Cambridge. ISBN 978-0-521-57778-6

Edgerton D (2005) Warfare state: Britain 1920–1970. Cambridge University Press, Cambridge. ISBN 978-0-521-67231-3

Garrity C, Liguori EW, Muldoon J (2018) Woodward's aegis: a critical biography of Joan Woodward. J Manag Hist 24(4):457–475

Genovese ED (1976) Roll, Jordan, Roll: the world the Slaves Made, 1974. Alfred A. Knopf, New York

Heffer S (2017) The age of decadence. Penguin Random House, New York

Herman AS (2013, July 2). Freedom's forge: How American business produced victory in World War II. Random House Trade Paperbacks, New York, Reprint edition

Hofstatder R (1948) The American political tradition and the men who made it. A. A. Knopf, New York

Hoggart R (1957) The uses of literacy: aspects of working class life. Chatto and Windus, London

Holmes R (2008) Marlborough: England's fragile genius. HarperCollins, New York

Howe DW (2007) What hath God wrought: the transformation of America, 1815–1848. Oxford University Press, New York

Kennedy WP (1976) Institutional response to economic growth: capital markets in Britain to 1914. In: Management strategy and business development. Palgrave Macmillan, London, pp 151–183

Kennedy DM (1999) Freedom from fear: the American people in depression and war, 1929–1945, vol 9. Oxford University Press, New York

Landes DS (1969) The unbound prometheus: technological change and industrial development in Western Europe from 1750 to the present. Press Syndicate of the University of Cambridge, Cambridge/New York

Leff MH (1991) The politics of sacrifice on the American home front in World War II. J Am Hist 77(4):1296–1318

Littler CR (1982) The development of the labour process in capitalist societies. Heinemann, London, p 226

Locke R (1984) The end of practical man: entrepreneurship and higher education. Jai Press, London, 9

Lukacs J (1991) The duel: 10 May–31 July 1940: the eighty-day struggle between Churchill and Hitler. Ticknor & Fields, New York

McCloskey D (2006) The bourgeois virtues : ethics for an age of commerce. University of Chicago Press, Chicago

McCloskey D (2010) Bourgeois dignity: why economics can't explain the modern world. University of Chicago Press, Chicago. https://en.wikipedia.org/wiki/Bourgeois_Dignity

McPherson JM (1988) Battle cry of freedom: the Civil War era. Oxford University Press, New York

Muir R (2014) Wellington: Waterloo and the fortunes of peace 1814–1852. Yale, New Haven

Muldoon J (2017) The Hawthorne studies: an analysis of critical perspectives, 1936–1958. Journal of Management History 23(1):74–94

Novick P (1988) That Noble Dream: The "Objectivity Question" and the American Historical Profession. Cambridge University Press

O'Neill W (1993) A democracy at war: America's fight at home and abroad in World War II. Free Press, New York

Parker LD, Ritson P (2011) Rage, rage against the dying of the light: Lyndall Urwick's scientific management. J Manag Hist 17(4):379–398

Pollard S (1965) The genesis of modern management: a study of the industrial revolution in Great Britain. Harvard University Press, Cambridge

Pollard S (1989) Britain's prime and Britain's decline: the British economy, 1870–1914. Edward Arnold, London

Roberts A (2018) Churchill: Walking with Destiny. Viking. New York

Searle GR (2004) A new England?: peace and war 1886–1918. Oxford University Press, New York

Thomas R (1978) The British philosophy of management. Longman, London

Thompson EP (1963) The making of the English working class. Victor Gollancz, London

Trist EL, Murray H (1990) The social engagement of social science: a Tavistock anthology: the socio-ecological perspective (Tavistock anthology). University of Pennsylvania, Philadelphia

White R (2017) The republic for which it stands: the United States during reconstruction and the Gilded Age, 1865–1896. Oxford University Press, New York

Whitson K (1997) The reception of scientific management by British engineers, 1890–1940. Bus Hist Rev 71:207–229

Wiener MJ (1981) English culture and the decline of the industrial spirit 1850–1980. Cambridge University Press, Cambridge

Wilson JF, Thomson A (2006) The making of modern management: British management in the historical perspective. Oxford UP, Oxford

Wood GS (1992) The Radicalism of the American Revolution, Alfred A. Knopf (New York)

Kurt Lewin: Organizational Change

26

Jeffrey Muldoon

Contents

Biography 617
Lewin's Contribution to Management 620
Lewin and Other Management Thinkers 625
Criticism 627
Conclusion 630
Cross-References 630
References 631

Abstract

I cover the life, career, and contributions of the German-born and trained psychologist Kurt Lewin, whose primary contribution to management thought was describing the process of organizational change. I argue that Lewin, despite the time in which he lived, was a deeply committed idealist and democrat. I argue that these values permeated his work. The merits and weaknesses of his work are discussed.

Keywords

Lewin · Organizational change · Taylor · Mayo

Kurt Lewin was a natural-born democrat both in his private and professional life (Marrow 1969). Democracy was an article of faith and scientific fact to Lewin. He believed that democratic societies would, in the end, overcome autocratic societies.

J. Muldoon (✉)
Emporia State University, Emporia, KS, USA
e-mail: jmuldoon@emporia.edu

© The Author(s), under exclusive licence to Springer Nature Switzerland AG 2020
B. Bowden et al. (eds.), *The Palgrave Handbook of Management History*,
https://doi.org/10.1007/978-3-319-62114-2_32

615

This was not a popular viewpoint during his lifetime. His native Germany elected Adolf Hitler as Chancellor in 1933 despite his avowed totalitarian views. Even in the United States and Great Britain, there were those who no longer believed in democracy – preferring various types of authoritarian arrangements (fascism, communism, etc.). Lewin was born in 1890 at a time where humanities' hope in progress remained high; he died in 1947, after 30 years of bloodshed and destruction with the potential of more to come. Yet, despite the bloodshed (even within his own family), Lewin still believed in democracy (Lewin 1992).

Lewin never stopped believing that man was inherently good (Bargal et al. 1992). The idea that people can change their attitudes based on interventions indicates that prejudice and hatred were less the products of man's depravity but rather the circumstances that man found himself in. This was another bold belief since Lewin's native Germany had gone from a constitutional monarchy to a totalitarian society. Many of his contemporaries, such as Reinhold Niebuhr, Hannah Ardent, and Daniel Bell, were convinced of man's rotten core (Brinkley 1998). Even professed liberals, like Arthur M. Schlesinger, Jr., felt the need to temper their liberalism with a more hard edged, skeptical view of human nature (Schlesinger 2000). Yet Lewin, despite his family loses in the Holocaust, believed that, through science, man would overcome the limitations of hatred and prejudice. Much like Frederick Winslow Taylor and Andrew Ure, Lewin was an optimist (Burnes and Bargal 2017).

After his death, Lewin was recognized as eminent a psychologist as Sigmund Freund – a bit of an overstatement to be sure – but he was still ranked 18th most influential psychologist of the twentieth century (Marrow 1969; Haggbloom et al. 2002). A remarkable feat is Lewin was consistently an outsider during his life – a Jew in Germany and a German Jewish refugee in America – among professors he was viewed as too practical, and among businessmen, he was considered to be too theoretical (Lewin 1992). Even his academic appointments in the United States were marginal – he was not in the psychology department at Cornell, but home economics – at the University of Iowa, he was at the childhood welfare department. Yet he was still able to attract a legion of top flight graduate students everywhere he went (Weisbord 2004).

Despite his career struggles, Lewin had a tremendous faith in science, not just science in terms of traditional science, such as chemistry and physics, but also psychology, then a field that was just an offshoot of philosophy. Yet there was little belief in psychology that issues such as emotions, attitudes, and other latent variables could be researched – making scholars doubt that rigor of the field. Lewin changed that perception – leaving contributions in a wide variety of fields from his home in social psychology to child psychology to leadership studies and management (Lewin 1992). Lewin was not only a theorist, but he was also an empiricist – validating his theories through painstaking research in laboratory experiments. His contributions in management have focused on organization and development. Lewin receives a high, but not universal, level of praise. Despite his works being published over 70 years ago, Lewin still casts a vast shadow on his work on how to initiate change, even with the criticisms that occurred over the years. Lewin's work and name are known to even undergraduate students. Yet some scholars have not regarded him highly. For instance, in his 1974 work on management, Peter Drucker does not mention Lewin (Drucker 1973). This should not be taken as a deep dig at Lewin personally. Management scholars have had a difficult time demonstrating who is and who is not considered a management scholar (Muldoon et al. 2018). Scholars, such as Lewin, who wrote from a different field sometimes do not receive the recognition they are warranted. Yet despite the silence from Drucker and others, most management scholars acknowledge the deep debt the field has toward Lewin. As Hendry (1996: 624) wrote:

> Scratch any account of creating and managing change and the idea that change is a three-stage process which necessarily begins with a process of unfreezing will not be far below the surface.

In fact, some scholars such as Burnes (2004a, b) argue that we should revisit Lewin's ideas again to improve the ethical performance of management.

The purpose of this chapter is to examine the contribution of Kurt Lewin to management thought. The chapter is divided into four sections. The first section is a brief biography of Lewin where it covers his early life and career to his emergence as a notable social psychologist. The second section will examine the various contributions that Lewin made to management. Like Burnes, we argue that the three-step approach is complementary. The third section of the paper covers Lewin's relationship with other management thinkers, including Chris Argyris, Frederick Taylor, and Elton Mayo. The fourth section of the paper covers the various criticisms that have been leveled on the work of Lewin.

Biography

Kurt Lewin was born in 1890 in the Prussia province of Posen – now part of Poland – to Leopold and Recha Lewin. The village in which Lewin grew up was part of a very hierarchical society with aristocrats on top and Jews, like the Lewin family, at the bottom. As Miriam Lewin (1992) wrote "no Jew could become an officer in the military, obtain a position in the social service, or own a farm." Yet the Lewin family was well-regarded within the Jewish community and was relatively well-off. The family owned a store and a family farm (although the farm was legally under a Christian's name). Lewin was also blessed in that both parents stressed education. Leopold spoke Polish, Yiddish, and German and possessed a high school education. Lewin got his democratic notions from his family and from his surrounding environment. His family may have been a top Jewish family, but they were still considered second class citizens. Lewin was not pretentious in his dealings with people – this was a trait that he picked up from his father. From both of his parents, Lewin also developed a sympathetic understanding of the downtrodden. These traits would enable him to become an excellent mentor to his students (Marrow 1969).

When Lewin was 15, the family moved to Berlin so the children could receive a better education. Lewin was trained in the classics: mathematics, history, natural science, Latin, Greek, and French. Lewin received good grades and started at the University of Freiburg to study medicine. He later transferred to the University of Munich. It was at Munich where Lewin took his first class in psychology. Lewin then transferred to the University of Berlin, where he continued his courses in medicine until he realized he hated dissection. He then switched to philosophy (which was then part of philosophy) taking a wide range of courses. One of the primary intellectual influences of Lewin was the work of Immanuel Kant, one of the fathers of German idealism (Lewin 1992). Kant differed from other idealist philosophers, however, in emphasizing how social change can be enacted through the use of one's reason. As he indicated in his 1784 study, *What is Enlightenment?*, Kant (1784: 1) believed that the first toward social enlightenment begins with personal enlightenment and the freeing of one's self from "self-incurred tutelage." This framework would become a major intellectual influence on Lewin, encouraging him that hatred and prejudice could be overcome through science and education.

Lewin's primary professor (and future dissertation advisor) was Carl Stumpf, one of the leading figures in psychology. In the department, Stumpf hired three stars of psychology: Max Wertheimer, Karl Koffka, and Wolfgang Kohler. Stumpf also supported Gestalt psychology; his students Koffka and Kohler were the founding fathers. Gestalt psychology sought to research how perceptions emerge in chaos. The basis of this research was gained through laboratory analysis – to make psychology distinct from philosophy. Lewin and his professors were determined to demonstrate that research topics, such as group dynamics and social climate were compatible with scientific inquiry used in the natural sciences (Lewin 1977). Miriam Lewin (1992) noted that although American psychologists shared the same ends as Lewin did, there was a difference. For an American scholar, a commitment to rigor was only superficial; for Lewin it was a driving orientation to explore the inner logic of psychology.

Lewin wrote his dissertation under the direction of Stumpf, but it was a distant relationship, at best. He did not talk about his dissertation with Stumpf until the day of the defense. As Lewin and others have noted, this was not the behavior he would display when he became an advisor. In fact, he was the opposite. He was dynamic, engaged with his students, and in the process attracted many students, both in Germany and then later in the United States. Among his students were Bluma Zeigarnik, Jerome Frank, Donald Adams, Anitra Karsten, Ronald Lippett, Leon Festinger, Alfred Morrow, and John Thibaut (Marrow 1969; Weisbord 2004). Many of his doctoral students would become leaders in psychology. Festinger would become one of the preeminent social psychologists of his time. Lewin also directly influence Chris Argyris, who, although he was not a student of Lewin, was someone who was deeply influenced. Lewin convinced Eric Trist to abandon English Literature to become a psychologist. His conversation with Trist was so stimulating that Lewin needed to be forced onto his departing train. He also influenced Philip Zimbardo and Stanley Milgram.

The primary guiding virtue for Lewin was tolerance, whether it was another's opinion or their personal limitations. Lewin did not demand intellectual conformity from his students. During his famous study on leadership, one of his assistants,

Ralph White, made a mistake when providing directions. According to Wolf (1996):

> This was something between Kurt and Lippitt [Ron Lippitt]. The plan was to have two styles of leadership – democratic and autocratic – and they set up the experiment for these two styles. Ralph White is a very quiet man – in many ways the opposite of Lippitt. Lippitt came from Boy Scouts and from group work with youngsters, and was really tremendously helpful. I don't think Kurt could ever have done those experiments without him. Ralph White was supposed to be the democratic leader. Ralph is very quiet, and I don't think he ever had much experience with kids. When his group was discussed, Ronald Lippitt said 'that isn't democratic leadership. That is laissez-faire.' This was the typical way of Kurt's working with graduate students. He didn't throw anything out just because it wasn't planned that way. Kurt said 'okay, we'll make a third group. A laissez-faire group.'

The only thing that Lewin was not tolerant of was totalitarian beliefs or destructive behaviors. Lewin, however, was not a radical. He rejected Marxism because he believed that it did not have an empirical basis. Instead, he sought to reform society by developing better techniques. Lewin's attitude toward Marxism was similar to many American intellectuals at the time. Yet many of his comemporaires embraced destructive ideologies during the tumultuous events of the early twentieth century. Lewin himself lived through dark times, including combat experience in World War I, where he was wounded and a brother lost. Returning to university after recovering from his wounds, Lewin found refuge in his work, becoming more convinced for the need for science to promote solutions to societal problems. Lewin continued to work during the horrors of the war and also contributed a paper to Stumpf's 70th birthday. After the war, Lewin continued his career at Berlin Psychological Institute. In 1922, Lewin became a lecturer, a marginal position where he was paid by how many students he taught (Lewin 1992). Yet despite his heavy teaching loads, he remained a productive and insightful scholar. The rise to power of Hitler, however, threatened even that tenuous foothold in academia. Unlike many other Germans (whether Jewish or not), Lewin quickly grasped the unique evil of Hitler. Hitler soon imposed his anti-Semitic views on society (Evans 2003). The doctor who had delivered Lewin's children was very hesitant to deliver his next child as Hitler banned Jews from attending university (Lewin 1992). Lewin did not want to teach at a university where his children could not attend. He decamped to the home economics department at Cornell, thanks to the efforts of Ethel Warring. After a few years, Lewin left for the University of Iowa, where Lewin may have been at his happiest. Lewin created an agricultural-based community like the one he had grown up in. He attracted a wide range of brilliant students and visiting colleagues, such as Margaret Mead. Lewin loved to hold informal picnics where people could sing, play, and talk about psychology. It was during this time that Lewin was perhaps his most productive as well (Marrow 1969).

The Second World War and its resulting destruction provided a further incentive for Lewin to look to democratic solutions for societal problems. His study of leadership, conducted with White and Lippett (Lewin et al. 1939), convinced him that the "interdependence of fate" rather than similarity was key to fighting prejudice. This viewpoint enabled him to come to two major conclusions. The first one, according to his daughter, was that the Jewish community needed to act as one, regardless of their differences in class, nationality, or religious outlook. The second conclusion was that proper leadership and experience can enable individuals to overcome bias and prejudice. However, all was not well in Lewin's world, the Holocaust consuming some of his family members, including his mother, and effectively destroying the German Jewish community.

Lewin left Iowa after he formed the "Research Center for Group Dynamics," a group at the cutting edge of action research which linked advanced theoretical academic research to social solutions (Weisbord 2004). During this time, Lewin was committed to doing both industrial research as well as research on prejudice. He also produced some very original research and published in the first editions of *Human Relations*, work which would stand as his major contribution to management. Lewin died in 1947 at the age of only 57, in the midst of things, overworked by his research agenda as well as his role as director for the "Research Center." Lewin left a major legacy and his influence continues to shine to this day. Very little research conducted these days is as practical as Lewin's work (Burnes 2009a). Today, management scholars wonder how much impact and relevance we have in management. The answer to this question is not much. If management wishes to remain a respected field, it must devote more energy to solving practical problems – in other words, take up Lewin's standard.

Lewin's Contribution to Management

Lewin left a deep impression on the field of management despite the fact that he was a social psychologist and not from the management field. He was almost the only early German psychologists who had an interest in management. Miriam Lewin (Papanek 1973) stated that Lewin made the following contributions:

> 1. the concepts of field theory, 2. action research (the interweaving of laboratory experiment, systematic research in the field, and client service), 3. the study of group dynamics, and 4. aspects of sensitivity training techniques. His ideas appear today in discussions of productivity, management by participation, job enrichment, organizational development, organizational stress, and organizational change.

William Wolf (1973) viewed Lewin's most significant contributions to be tracking the process of organization change and helping to develop some rudimentary understanding of open systems. Wolf also stated that Lewin had a direct influence on the work of Chester Barnard. Miriam Lewin stated that Lewin's biggest contribution was in the development group dynamics (Papanek 1973). Yet it is Lewin's refreezing/freezing framework that is still widely cited and influential. Even though we may have moved past Lewin's work, it still remains something that scholars need to grapple with. However, like Burnes, I would suggest that the unfreezing framework is an outcome of Lewin's other ideas such as leadership and force field analysis. The next section of this chapter will document Lewin's work, the various recent studies influenced by it, and his relationship to other management thinkers.

Lewin's greatest contribution to management was his unfreezing/refreezing framework. However, we must consider, as did many of the people who knew, that there was great similarity to his work. Each of his theories was designed to produce some change, to create a more diverse, less discriminating society. As Lewin's widow wrote:

> Kurt Lewin was so constantly and predominantly preoccupied with the task of advancing the conceptual representation of the social-psychological world, and at the same time he was so filled with the urgent desire to use his theoretical insight for the building of a better world, that it is difficult to decide which of these two sources of motivation flowed with greater energy or vigour. (Lewin 1948b)

As Burnes (2004b, 2009a) has written, Lewin was a humanitarian who believed that using social science to reduce social conflict would produce a better world. Burnes (2009) agrees with both Lewin and his wife in noting the overall thematic coherence of Lewin's work, a coherence that saw each theme reinforce each other to produce relevant change within the group, organization, or society (Burnes and Bargal 2017).

In many minds, Lewin's contribution to management thought is forever associated with force field analysis. Force field analysis is an attempt to understand behavior by understanding the total forces that influence a behavior through the use of maps to understand the interaction and complexity of the forces behind the behavior (Lewin 1943). Lewin noted that status quo is maintained through an interplay between these forces. The key to understanding behaviors would be the relationship between the person and the environment in which they find themselves. For example, if a person is currently a smoker, whether they maintain or stop smoking will be an interplay between driving forces and restraining forces (Weisbrod 2004). A driving force that would stop a person from smoking could potentially be the cost of smoking, fear of cancer, or social pressure. The driving forces are those forces that would encourage a person to stop smoking. Yet these forces would face restraining forces, which would encourage the person to continue the current practice. Habit, for instance, would be a restraining force that would encourage people to continue smoking.

Lewin's work on force field analysis provides an early example that change will come only slowly due to the restraining forces within the organization. As Burnes (2004, pg. 982) has written:

> forces would need to be diminished or strengthened in order to bring about change. In the main, Lewin saw behavioural change as a slow process; however, he did recognize that under circumstances, such as a personal, organizational or societal crisis, the various forces in the field can shift quickly and radically.

The principal takeaway from force field analysis is that behavior is a function between the person and the environment or $B = f(P, E)$ (Sansone et al. 2003). An individual may have certain desires and wishes, but they can be constrained or encouraged by environmental factors. Another important consideration is that people do not make decisions on just past outcomes, but current desires as well. Often, routines are created and maintained due to the fact that the need for change is insufficiently enforced. Force field analysis remains arguably the most poorly understood part of Lewin's work. Nevertheless, several organizational change theorists have considered this approach in their work.

Group dynamics is another major contribution Lewin made to management (Lewin 1947). One of its basic referents is Lewin's equation about behavior. Several scholars (including Allport & Burnes) have noted that Lewin was one of the first scholars to write about group dynamics. According to Lewin, what determines a group is the interdependence of fate, namely, the idea that people in the group will share the same outcome. This idea explains why the difference in status or personality does not matter, a conceptualization that reflects Lewin's personal past as a Jewish refugee from Germany, where Jews were hunted down and murdered regardless of education or past service to the nation. As Kippenberger (1998a, b) noted, Lewin's interest in groups was also underpinned by his desire to understand the forces that cause groups to behave in a particular direction. Lewin went further in arguing that there was little point in attempting to change individual behavior. If behavior needs to be changed, it needs to occur at the group level. Scholars today are somewhat more skeptical of Lewin's analysis (Burnes 2009a). Oftentimes, the reason why a group exhibits similar behavior is that the people who are attracted to the group are often very similar. For example, if we take a personality score of accountants, we would probably discern similarities, namely, attention to detail and order. The interdependence here would not be of fate or outcome but similar interests, desires, and wants. Nevertheless, applied to change within an organization, we need to consider the roles that groups play.

Lewin recognized that while he had the basics, he needed more thorough and practical measures to lead to meaningful change. Two notable outcomes of Lewin's practical approach would become action theory and the three-step change approach (also called the unfreezing/refreezing framework). What is particularly noteworthy is that Lewin developed these ideas to answer the needs of various organizations that were seeking his help. This first approach is action theory. According to Burnes (2004: 983), action theory is designed to answer two major needs:

> Firstly, it emphasizes that change requires action, and is directed at achieving this. Secondly, it recognizes that successful action is based on analyzing the situation correctly, identifying all the possible alternative solutions and choosing the one most appropriate to the situation at hand.

The primary need to change is driven by the person's inner recognition that change is needed. Without this desire, the restraining forces maintain their hold over the individual. A key aspect of this change process reflects Lewin's Gestalt psychology background, which emphasized how we should make the person consider the totality of the situation.

This idea that we should consider the total role of change is one of the reasons why Lewin and others claimed that if we wish to change organization, we must understand the entirety of the situation. In this framework – which emphasizes both social forces and the interplay of groups – we see that action research is based on Lewin's complete ideas (Weisbord 2004). Lewin also understood that routines and patterns have value because they encourage group norms. Therefore, if we wish to enforce change, we need to consider changing routines and patterns. The major thrust of action research is learning. Often referred to as Lewin's spiral, Lewin's model is a course of planning, learning, and fact-finding. Lewin's work in action research was initially conducted with the Italian and Jewish street gangs in American cities to reduce their violence. Action research was later adopted by the British Tavistock Institute to aid with the nationalization of mines in that country (Weisbord 2004). Lewin recognized that for change to become permanent, the intervention is needed to support the permanence so that it was not a fleeting thing.

Force field analysis, action research, and group dynamics lead up to Lewin's greatest management accomplishment – the unfreezing/refreezing framework (Lewin 1947). There are two important considerations about this framework (Weisbord 2004). Firstly, Lewin meant to use it as a complement to his previous work. Secondly, he developed this framework for organizations that were not just business in nature, i.e., community organizations, government departments, etc. The unfreezing, change intervention, and freezing framework have their basics in force field analysis. Attitudes and behaviors are either changed or kept through the interplay of various forces that an individual faces. Force field analysis has its connection to group dynamics in that it considers how group interplay can influence a person's behavior and adoption of change. It also has its connection to action research in that it considers the totality of the situation.

The first step of the process is the unfreezing phase. Lewin recognized that for people to embrace change, they must begin to challenge the status quo. This status quo is kept at near equilibrium due to an interaction of forces on the individual. If there is to be change, there must be an action to disrupt the equilibrium. In essence, to use the analogy of freezing, at the first step, values and beliefs have been frozen by a series of forces. How an unfreezing takes place can come in multiple ways due to each situation having a distinct interplay of forces. Oftentimes, emotional appeals can produce fear or pride that can lead people to change the status quo. When either politicians or managers seek something different, there is an emotional appeal as part of getting other people to consider new things. When in 1947 Harry S. Truman launched America's involvement in European affairs to contain the Soviet Union, it had been recommended to him that he scare the American people (Hamby 1995).

Lewin recognized that unfreezing was not an end in and of itself. Once people are open to change, there must be change intervention to change behaviors and attitudes. At best unfreezing can get people to consider change. During a change intervention phase, learning new behaviors should take place. This phase of change considers the notions of training, explanation, and championing of new behaviors. Recent suggestions, regarding change intervention, are the need to establish small wins or minor victories to encourage adoption of new roles by making the task seem less daunting (Wieck 1984). During this phase of the process, people understand that change is occurring but remain uncertain what the final step will be. The final phase of change is refreezing which is to arrange these new behaviors and attitudes in a new equilibrium. In another words, it is to make sure that people within the organization truly adopt the new ideas. In the words of Burnes:

> .... degree, congruent with the rest of the behaviour, personality and environment of the learner or it will simply lead to a new round of disconfirmation (Schein 1996). This is why Lewin saw successful change as a group activity, because unless group norms and routines are also transformed, changes to individual behaviour will not be sustained.

In other words, when producing change within an organization, the people directing it must be careful not to stop the change intervention too soon. Rather they need to produce force fields to maintain these new ideas. This explains why, according to Lewin, change is very difficult to perform (Weisbord 2004). Thus, Lewin performed two distinct approaches to change. The first was to provide, through force field analysis and group dynamics, an explanation as to why values remain secure. Once we understand the forces that keep beliefs and behaviors steady, we can then break the forces that hold. This occurs through action research and its idea of education. Lewin also suggested that we need to create new forces to sustain the new beliefs.

Although not directly related to his work on change, Lewin's work on leadership, along with Lippett and White (1943), warrants consideration in this chapter for the reason that leadership is an important part of organizational change. Lewin and his co-authors argued that there are three types of leadership. The first is authoritarian leadership where the leader determines policy and sets tasks. This leader uses hostility and coercion to ensure individual cooperation. This type of leadership is not desirable becomes it causes discord and anguish in members in the group. Members often attack fellow members when the leader is not there. The second type is laissez-faire leadership whereby the leader does not provide any information and support. This type of leadership is also associated with poor outcomes. In the third type, democratic leadership, the leader creates an environment allows for choice and determination on the part of people in the group to make decisions. In addition, leaders show concern for members within the group as well as provide explanations as to why they are performing certain behaviors. In democratic leadership, we see higher performance, greater acceptance of leader's direction, and less destructive behavior.

I would argue that during the three-step approach to organizational change, it is a democratic leadership style in action. Namely, the leader in the three-step approach provides direction, explanations for why the change is occurring, gets feedback for the subordinates, and allows for both the leader and follower to work together to promote the change. This type of leadership style typically reduces the fields that impede the need to change, impediments that include politics, obstruction, and a lack of understanding. Over the years, scholars have reaffirmed such findings in relation to the important role of democratic leadership in both change and politics within the organization, thereby confirming the important role of leadership in organizational change.

Lewin and Other Management Thinkers

One of Lewin's first published articles was a criticism of Frederick Winslow Taylor. The criticism was so harsh that Marvin Weisbrod (2004) viewed Lewin as Taylor's antithesis. Lewin criticized Taylorism for not having much appreciation of intrinsic motivation. Lewin believed that job design that created boredom and reduced learning opportunities was one that denied the "life value" of work. Such designs diminished, rather than enabled, human aspirations. Weisbrod noted that, unlike Taylor – where the focus was on industrial engineers making decisions – Lewin sought real partnership between workers and managers in an environment where shared decisions were made in relation to conditions at work. Although Taylor did concede that workers and management should share decisions, it was often the reverse. Lewin was one of the first to recognize what we crave job satisfaction and psychological empowerment.

Several scholars, including Weisbrod, have argued that Lewin was a more democratic and enlightened version of Taylor. It should be noted, however, that democratic values are themselves normative and do not always fit. In fact, shared governance need not be democratic but should merely consider voices. Taylor was not a dictator (Nyland 1998). Rather, he believed that science should be the guide to behavior rather than democracy or dictatorship. Taylor noted that much of what workers and managers knew was based on faulty information. Therefore, a radical orientation of perspective was required of both workers and managers. Taylor also stressed that there should be a partnership between management and the worker. At his core, Taylor wanted to free workers from the tyranny of poor management (Locke 1982). Taylor also understood social motivation. Lewin's contribution was similar to Mayo encouraging scholars to consider social motivations in depth.

Elton Mayo and Kurt Lewin both deserve consideration as important figures in the forming of organizational behavior. There is a strong tendency in the literature to view Elton Mayo as the father of organizational behavior, but such a statement is ahistorical. Moreover, Mayo's work and Lewin's work should both be considered as providers of foundational concepts in organizational behavior. Both men researched roughly similar issues: attitudes, satisfactions, social motivations, and leadership activities (Minor 2002). Mayo's primary insight involved the recognition that the shift to the modern industrial order meant that there was a need to research how to create and maintain spontaneous cooperation (Homans 1949). Future research was needed to make this contribution for Mayo. Lewin's work was, by contrast, clearer and more precise. Lewin was a scholar in a way that the intuitive Mayo could not hope to be. Lewin was also theoretically stronger than Mayo, whose work had a ring of advocacy to it. Lewin hit the right mixture between advocacy and research rigor.

Both Wolf and Minor suggest that it was Lewin who provided the field with real scientific rigor. Minor (2002) goes even further, portraying Lewin up as a paragon of scientific rigor when compared with Mayo, the advocate. Consequently, Minor and Weisbrod are compelled to ask the question: why did Lewin receive little note in the literature as opposed to Mayo? Minor proposes several potential explanations: anti-Semitism and Lewin's liberal views. These explanations fail to consider actual facts.

Firstly, Daniel Bell (1947), who was Jewish, stated that research in organizational behavior (or work-life) commenced with Elton Mayo, but Lewin's research was also recognized. Secondly, Mayo's work was considered conservative and in many of the fields, such as sociology, liberalism reigned. Many sociologists admired Hawthorne and sought something similar but with liberal leanings in their own work (Muldoon 2017). Arguably, the secret of Mayo's success lay in the fact that he codified what people already knew and encouraged scholars to develop understanding as to what made spontaneous cooperation possible at work. Mayo had a cadre of researchers and theorists – including George Homans and Talcott Parsons – seeking to refine the studies or explain them theoretically (Smith 1998). Lewin did have followers, but he did not insist they follow his lead. Nor did he focus his entire research efforts on work life. Mayo, as was Taylor, was a mono-manic in that he focused in on one thing at a time.

There is one clear point of difference between the two men. Mayo was a conservative of an unusual sort. At Harvard, Mayo consorted with some of the most conservative, and even reactionary, members of the faculty, including President A. Lawrence Lowell, Lawrence Henderson, and George Homans (Traihair 1984). When he lived in Australia, he opposed both the election of Labor government and the marked extension of trade union power that occurred during the first two decades of the twentieth century. Mayo was also not unadulterated enthusiast for either the New Deal or attempts to nationalize industries. According to J.H. Smith, Mayo expressed viewpoints that were libertarian in nature – a viewpoint out of step with the professoriate. Mayo viewed the utilitarian viewpoint of the new modern world with skepticism, believing that the primitive world, through ritual, created adaptive societies based on systems of cooperation that looked beyond economic or material gain. For Lewin (and Taylor), the modern world allowed for the development of new ideas and knowledge that could overcome the prejudices and tyrannies of the past. Unlike Mayo, the modern world, despite its horrors, was a place of opportunity for Lewin – where education can be a light.

Chris Argyris (1997) is another scholar that Lewin influenced. Argyris was not, however, a formal student of Lewin. Rather, Argyris met with him during his time as an undergraduate at Clark University. Despite this limited interaction, Lewin would have a deeply profound influence on Argyris, an influence only exceeded by that of Argyris's only mentor, William F. Whyte. According to Argyris, Lewin's influence over his thinking mainly related to the nature of theory. As Argyris wrote:

> I believe that scholars are free to generate any theory about action research that they choose to develop. I also believe that they are not free not to make explicit what they believe are the features of sound theory, Lewin did say, in effect, that there was nothing as practical as sound theory. He defined the properties of any sound theory. I will make some of these properties explicit and illustrate their implications for scholarly consulting.

Argyris provided more functionality to the nature of learning. According to Finger and Asún (2001), "unlike Dewey's, Lewin's or Kolb's learning cycle, where one had, so to speak, to make a mistake and reflect upon it – that is, learn by trial and error – it is now possible thanks to Argyris and Schön's conceptualization, to learn by simply reflecting critically upon the theory-in-action."

Two social psychologists, Stanley Milgram and Philip Zimbardo, were also influenced by Kurt Lewin (Zimbardo 2016). Whereas Lewin sought to understand what factors encourage people to become more democratic and ethical, Milgram and Zimbardo researched circumstances that cause people to operate on an undemocratic and/or unethical basis. Zimbardo's study of prisons provided an overview that in prison circumstances both guards and prisoners adopt the roles that are assigned to them. Therefore, prisons are bad places, not because of the people involved but the circumstances involved. Although Zimbardo noted that his work carried on Lewin's understandings of behavior, the reality was that both Milgram and Zimbardo demonstrated that there are circumstances that cause a person to act in ways that eliminate the previous self. An interesting difference between Lewin and Zimbardo/Milgram is that Lewin, despite being persecuted and seeing members of his family murdered, remained optimistic about humanity. By contrast, Zimbardo/Milgram, members of the American meritocracy, and in a much more democratic and humane country (although far from perfect), had grave doubts about humanity's good nature.

Criticism

Like other prominent scholars, Lewin's work has come under attack by others over the years. The most serious charge labeled against Lewin is that his research is too simplistic to have real value for scholars and practitioners (Burnes 2004). Lewin's approach to change can be placed within the classical school of management, a school which believes that there are only a handful of goals that really matter to business (namely, profit-making) and that managers can plan and determine what types of techniques and interventions they wish to use. In addition, managers possess complete information and have clarity of goals. Lewin's work does share assumptions with classical management, albeit imperfectly. Lewin nevertheless understood, unlike others in the school, that workers can block and overcome managerial dictates. Lewin's framework was, moreover, for all organizations: not just for-profit corporations. Yet the same idealistic vein of information and rationality flows from Lewin's work. Lewin's force field analysis assumes that all forces can be considered as well as their direct proportion to each other. There is also an assumption that individuals can change their viewpoint – all they need is additional information and aid from others. Few scholars in strategy or organizational behavior believe these assumptions today (Whittington 2001).

Some of the major challenges to Lewin have come from evolutionary economics and the processual school of management (Whittington 2001). Both of these schools of thought have consistently challenged the underlying assumptions of the three-step process. Economists have long believed that managerial action is less important than environmental fit. Usually industries go through set patterns of change. A new industry is discovered, various companies enter into the field, there is fierce competition, and then in the end, there are only a few surviving companies. Only fit companies will survive. Evolutionary economists believe that there is little managers can do to anticipate where the next change in the market will occur. Therefore, there is little a manager can do in the face of industry evolution. Managers can only control some part of the information in the market – prices and resources vary and fluctuate at random. Some companies become so large that they could actually pick the market they wish to function in. Nevertheless, such companies are rare. A company that sold buggy whips would have gone out of business when the car became popular – there was little they could do in the face of this new technology. They lacked the expertise and resources to compete in the new market. Once buggy whip manufactures realized that the car was here to stay, there were on their way to obsolesce. Chester Barnard (1938), although not traditional considered an evolutionist, recognized that all firms will eventually die. Barnard recognized that forces in the firm, the zone of indifference, make it difficult for change to occur. The constant turnover in companies that make the Dow Jones composite bears this out.

Andrew Pettigrew, the father of the processional school of management (Pettigrew 1987, 1997), has been a noted critic of Lewin's work. The processual school of management does not focus on a single outcome such as profit sharing. Nor does it believe that managers' actions are predetermined. Instead, it highlights how any given managerial action can have multiple outcomes, outcomes that often only make sense afterward. The assumptions that Pettigrew employs come from the Carnegie school (Whittington 2001), which states that individuals are bounded rational – meaning that they lack perfect information. Behaviors tend to become entrenched within the company because routines and standard operating procedures are often resistant to change due to political forces within the company. In fact, strategy creation is often a process managers use to reduce the uncertainty the company faces – akin to ducking under the desk when a nuclear bomb attack occurs. It provides a sense of control – but it does not really work. In fact, some companies actually come up with the solution and then search for the problem – a very different viewpoint to that of Lewin.

Despite such criticisms, we can conclude that Lewin's work was neither simplistic nor wrong; rather it was incomplete. Lewin's work is on firm ground when it examines the ways in which the various forces aligned within an organization can use politics or other techniques to resist managerial leadership within an organization. Lewin was correct when he asserted that certain types of change can be planned and then implemented. For instance, when a firm decides to implement a new recommendation from the government, it would use techniques similar to those that Lewin recommended. Yet Lewin's views are also incomplete. It seems that there are types of change that cannot be planned or prepared for. When they occur, there is little managers can do to prevent the destruction of their firm. Lewin's framework suggests that change is a one-time moment; dynamic capabilities literature suggests change cannot be a one-time moment to the evolutionary nature of the market, which makes continuous change a necessity (Teece et al. 1997). However, this criticism needs to be tempered with the work of Burnes (2004), who argued that Lewin's work can lead to continuous change. Rather, firms should align their recourse to be consistently learning and absorbing new information.

Lewin's famous thesis is that behavior is a function that results from the individual interacting with the environment or $B = f(P, E)$. One of the most famous criticisms was issued by Benjamin Schneider (1987), who argued that environments were a function of people behaving in them or $E = f\{P, B\}$. Schneider's framework would become known as the attraction-selection-attrition model. Schneider argues that people are attracted to organizations based on a convergence of needs, selected by the organization based on perceived similarity, and those who do not fit well leave the organization. Schneider's basic point is that some people are hardwired to act a particular way. Interventions to change people's dispositions are limited. If an organization wishes to change, the implication is that it must bring in new workers and ideas. People are bigoted, sometimes not because of their environment or education or experience, but because they are, at root, the people that they are. The ASA model also suggests that people are more likely to be attracted to people who are similar to them. The idea of "shared experience" often fails in comparison with ethnic differences, belief systems, and personality differences. Research conducted both in management and elsewhere indicates that trust is something that emerges from institutions. Countries and groups characterized by high levels of diversity often have serious problems with trust. This indicates the world is more provincial and divided than Lewin thought.

Yet recent work theorizing in personality research indicates that people and their environment interact with each other. This theory, called trait activation theory, argues that task, social, and organizational cues can activate or, in certain aspects, deactivate traits (Tett and Burnett 2003). For example, scholars found that Machiavellianism, a personality trait that focuses on obtaining outcomes – either ethically or otherwise – was activated under abusive supervision (Greenbaum et al. 2017). Tett and Guterman (2000) found that personality traits would be activated if they found relevant cues. Kamdar and Van Dyne found that strong social exchange relationships can eliminate personality traits, such as conscientiousness and agreeableness. Likewise, some negative traits, such as neuroticism, can be overcome through positive relationships. It is possible, applying this framework to organizational change, that some personality types (conscientiousness and agreeableness) will be activated during a period of organizational change. This suggests a move back to some Lewinian concepts rather than the attraction-selection-attrition framework. Even such ardent personality researchers as Barrick and Mount propose that situational and personality interaction is perhaps more important than simple personality in the workforce.

One point needs to be made on Lewin's work versus the work that is conducted today. It is true that Lewin's work was simplistic in comparison of what has come to be. But his work still shines a deep light on a wide variety of topics in change management. The reverse could be claimed today as well: management research is too abstract and abstruse to provide managers with anything meaningful to properly run businesses. What advice we do offer is often basic knowledge, common sense, trivial, or legally suspect. We recommend that managers select on intelligence without really considering that such advice is legally circumspect. The field of management has lost its impact on practitioners.

It is surprising given Lewin's degree of fame and influence and that he has received little in the way of criticism. This finding bears an interesting comparison with Henry

Ford, Elton Mayo, Frederick Winslow Taylor, and Robert Owen, whose reputations appear to often wax and wane in historical circumstances. Lewin is still well considered even if he is not given full credit for his work. Several explanations for this research finding are as follows: one, Lewin was an exceptional man and scholar, whose rigor and pleasantness avoided negative feelings, and the second explanation is that Lewin's students helped to maintain his legacy. Nevertheless, Lewin still made certain mistakes that warrant examination in the little of recent research.

Conclusion

Lewin left a deep and lasting record on the field of management and psychology. He worked at a time when scholars were not bounded by profession nor blind to the problems of society. Despite the destruction of the old order, it was still possible for someone born during this time to remain confident about the ability of science, especially social science, to provide a new path for a better society. Yet Lewin's faith in both knowledge and humanity was a remarkable flame, one that was not extinguished by war, genocide, hatred, or economic depression. During Lewin's life, the fields of psychology, sociology, or management were launched and gained respect in the academic world, as well as business and government. No longer would bureaucrats and executives make decisions blindly, they would do so based on knowledge, verified through experiments.

Lewin was not just a passive observer to these events but an active participant in the development of knowledge. His accomplishments as a researcher and teacher developed new fields and redefined old ones. That Lewin did these accomplishments as an outsider, one with marginal appointments, and as a Jew at a time of extreme anti-Semitism, was a major accomplishment. It is right that Lewin's work is still read and taught today, both to undergraduates and faculty. Few scholars of this time period still continue to be more than a ceremonial cite, with Chester Barnard and Mary Parker Follett as most auspicious company.

Yet there was a deep sense of idealism in Lewin's writings that bordered on naivety. Some men, regardless of education or societal inducements, would continue antisocial behaviors. Lewin's Germany, despite having a highly educated populace, sunk into a barbarism not seen since the Middle Ages. Likewise, some people, regardless of the information provided, good intentions, or necessity, will not embrace change until the bitter end. Furthermore, change, especially in corporations, is often a signal that the corporation is in decline and will fall regardless of managerial actions. People are not as honest or rational than Lewin seemed to believe.

Cross-References

► Henry Ford and His Legacy: An American Prometheus
► Spontaneity Is the Spice of Management: Elton Mayo's Hunt for Cooperation
► Taylor Made Management

References

Argyris C (1997) Kurt Lewin award lecture, 1997 field theory as a basis for scholarly consulting. J Soc Issues 53(4):811–827

Bargal D, Gold M, Lewin M (1992) Introduction: the heritage of Kurt Lewin. J Soc Issues 48(2):3–13

Barnard CI (1938) The functions of the executive. Harvard University Press, Cambridge, MA

Brinkley A (1998) Liberalism and its discontents. Harvard University Press, Cambridge, MA

Burnes B (2004a) Kurt Lewin and complexity theories: back to the future? J Chang Manag 4 (4):309–325

Burnes B (2004b) Kurt Lewin and the planned approach to change: a re-appraisal. J Manag Stud 41(6):977–1002

Burnes B (2009a) Reflections: ethics and organizational change–Time for a return to Lewinian values. J Chang Manag 9(4):359–381

Burnes B, Bargal D (2017) Kurt Lewin: 70 years on. J Chang Manag 17(2):91–100

Drucker (1973) Management: tasks, responsibilities, practices. Harper & Row, New York

Evans RJ (2003) The coming of the Third Reich. Allen Lane, London, p 2003

Finger M, Asún JM (2001) Adult education at the crossroads: learning our way out. NIACE, Leicester

Greenbaum RL, Hill A, Mawritz MB, Quade MJ (2017) Employee Machiavellianism to unethical behavior: the role of abusive supervision as a trait activator. J Manag 43(2):585–609

Haggbloom SJ, Warnick JE, Jones VK, Yarbrough GL, Russell TM, Borecky CM, McGahhey R et al (2002) The 100 most eminent psychologists of the 20th century. Rev Gen Psychol 6(2):139–152

Hamby A (1995) A man of the people. Oxford University Press, New York

Hendry C (1996) Understanding and creating whole organizational change through learning theory. Hum Relat 49(5):621–641

Homans GC (1949) The perspectives of Elton Mayo: some corrections. Rev Econ Stat 31(4): 319–321

http://infed.org/mobi/kurt-lewin-groups-experiential-learning-and-action-research/

Kippenberger T (1998a) Planned change: kurt lewin's legacy', 77M? Antidote 3(4):10–12

Kippenberger T (1998b) Managed learning: elaborating on lewin's model. Antidote 3(4):13

Lewin K, Lippitt R, White RK (1939) Patterns of aggressive behavior in experimentally created social climates. J Soc Psychol 10:271–301

Lewin K (1943) Defining the "field at a given time". Psychol Rev 50:292–310

Lewin K (1947) Frontiers in group dynamics: concept, method and reality in social science; social equilibria and social change. Hum Relat 1(1):5–41

Lewin GW (1948b) Preface. In: Lewin GW (ed) Resolving social conflict. Harper & Row, London, pp xv–xviii

Lewin MA (1977) Kurt Lewin's view of social psychology: the crisis of 1977 and the crisis of 1927. Personal Soc Psychol Bull 3(2):159–172

Lewin M (1992) The impact of Kurt Lewin's life on the place of social issues in his work. J Soc Issues 48(2):15–29

Locke EA (1982) The ideas of Frederick W. Taylor: an evaluation. Acad Manag Rev 7(1):14–24

Marrow AJ (1969) The practical theorist: the life and work of Kurt Lewin. Basic Books, New York

Miner JB (2002) Organizational behavior: foundations, theories and analysis. Oxford University Press, New York

Muldoon J (2017) The Hawthorne studies: an analysis of critical perspectives 1936–1958. J Manag Hist 23(1):74–94

Muldoon J, Liguori EW, Bendickson J, Bauman A (2018) Revisiting perspectives on George Homans: correcting misconceptions. J Manag Hist 24(1):57–75

Nyland C (1998) Taylorism and the mutual gains strategy. Ind Relat 37:519–542

Papanek ML (1973) Kurt Lewin and his contributions to modern management theory. In: Academy of management proceedings, vol 1. Academy of Management, Briarcliff Manor, pp 317–322.10510

Pettigrew AM (1987) Context and action in the transformation of the firm. J Manag Stud 24(6):649–670

Pettigrew AM (1997) What is a processual analysis. Scand J Manag 13(1997):4

Sansone C, Morf CC, Panter AT (2003) The Sage handbook of methods in social psychology. Sage, Thousand Oak, CA

Schneider B (1987) The people make the place. Pers Psychol 40(3):437–453

Schlesinger AMJ (2000) A life in the twentieth century. Houghton Mifflin, Boston

Smith JH (1998) The enduring legacy of Elton Mayo. Hum Relat 51(3):221–249

Teece D, Pisano G, Shuen A (1997) Dynamic capabilities and strategic management. Strateg Manag J 18(7):509–533

Tett RP, Burnett DD (2003) A personality trait-based interactionist model of job performance. J Appl Psychol 88(3):500

Tett RP, Guterman HA (2000) Situation trait relevance, trait expression, and cross-situational consistency: testing a principle of trait activation. J Res Pers 34(4):397–423

Trahair RCS (1984) The humanist temper. Transaction Books, New Brunswick

Weick KE (1984) Small wins: redefining the scale of social problems. Am Psychol 39(1):40

Weisbord MR (2004) Productive workplaces revisited: dignity, meaning and community in the 21st century. Jossey-Bass/Wiley, San Francisco

Whittington R (2001) What is strategy — and does it matter? 2nd edn. Intl, London

Wolf WB (1973) The impact of Kurt Lewin on management thought. In: Academy of management proceedings, vol 1973(1). Academy of Management, Briarcliff Manor, pp 322–325

Wolf WB (1996) Reflections on the history of management thought. J Manag Hist 2(2):4–10

Zimbardo PG (2016) Carrying on Kurt Lewin's legacy in many current domains Lewin award 2015. J Soc Issues 72(4):828–838

Part VI

Postmodernism

Postmodernism: An Introduction

27

Bradley Bowden

Contents

On the Ignorance of Postmodernism's Origins and Principles 636
Postmodernism and the Nature of Freedom 640
Cross-References 642
References 642

Abstract

This section of The Palgrave Handbook of Management History explores the origins of postmodernism as well as the seminal understandings of Paul-Michel Foucault, Jacques Derrida, and Hayden White. In doing so, this section highlights the marked differences in the thinking of these three philosophers, differences that are all too often overlooked by critical management historians. In the final analysis, this chapter argues, the fundamental differences between postmodernist and non-postmodernist historians revolve more around different understandings of freedom rather than different epistemologies. As disciples of Friedrich Nietzsche, Martin Heidegger, or Benedetto Croce, all three postmodernist philosophers that we consider advocated a complete freedom of individual will and being. In considering this call for absolute freedom, this chapter echoes Albert Camus's belief that absolute freedom is always tyrannical, just as absolute virtue is always homicidal.

Keywords

Postmodernism · Foucault · Derrida · Hayden White · Nietzsche · Camus · Heidegger · Historic turn

---

B. Bowden (✉)
Griffith Business School, Griffith University, Nathan, QLD, Australia
e-mail: b.bowden@griffith.edu.au

© The Author(s), under exclusive licence to Springer Nature Switzerland AG 2020 635
B. Bowden et al. (eds.), *The Palgrave Handbook of Management History*,
https://doi.org/10.1007/978-3-319-62114-2_118

On the Ignorance of Postmodernism's Origins and Principles

Postmodernism, rather than Marxism, is today the dominant ideology of the left, both within academia and without. Invariably, postmodernism in its contemporary iteration is not only rebellious of established authority. It is also aggressively secular. In the book that made his popular reputation, *Metahistory*, Hayden White (1973a: 331) declared that through a rewriting of history, one can bring about "new forms of community in which men might be . . . freed of the restrictions placed upon them by national states and churches." Such opinion, however, belies postmodernism's existentialist origins amid the coffee houses and bars along the Boulevard Saint-Germain during the 1940s, a time when French intellectuals and students became enamored of the German idealist philosophy of Friedrich Nietzsche, Edmund Husserl, and, above all, Martin Heidegger. In reflecting upon subsequent developments, Jacques Derrida (1987/1989: 3–4) lamented in *Of Spirit: Heidegger and the Question* how the central concept of a transcendental "spirit," which had occupied "a major and obvious place in his [Heidegger's] line of thought, should have been disinherited . . . No one wants anything to do with it anymore." Despite this disinheritance, none of the dominant strands of postmodernism – whether they owe a debt to Michel Foucault, Derrida, or even Hayden White – are fully comprehensible unless we understand their roots in German and, to a lesser degree, Italian philosophic idealism. Desirous of countering modern concepts of science and rationality without recourse to traditional Christian philosophy, idealist philosophy placed emphasis on matters relating to consciousness, individual being, and psychic freedom rather than material concerns such as economics, organizational efficiency, or profitable business endeavor.

Postmodernism's concern with matters relating to consciousness, individual being, and transcendental spirit is most obvious in the work of Derrida. Like Heidegger (1926/1962: 162), who believed that the essence of being, what he called *Dasein*, is "expressed in language," Derrida (1967a/1976: 65–66) believed that language contained within itself various "traces," the "psychic" imprints of "lived experience." Even within the nominally secular and even anti-religious philosophy of Foucault and White, however, the underlying foundations rest on philosophical concerns about consciousness and being. Like Nietzsche (1885/1990: 35), who advocated a "life-advancing, life-preserving, species preserving" freeing of the individual from all restraints, in which the individual is "beyond good and evil," Foucault (1966/1994: 330, 328) called for each individual to embrace the "unique" and "precarious existence of life," a world of thought and freedom in which "no morality is possible." If we turn to White, who drew inspiration from the Italian idealist philosopher and one-time fascist supporter, Benedetto Croce, a similar emphasis on individual consciousness and being is apparent. Like Croce (1915/1921: 66–67, 141), who believed that a "philosophy of history" should be "transcendental" – embracing the "particular" and "special" nature of each individual and each historical "event" – White (1973a: 371) called for the creation of "an *illusionary* world, outside the original word of pure power relationships." In this imagined world, where historical outcomes are "mediated by a uniquely human facility, consciousness," White (1973a: 371) argued that "the weak" are able to "vie with the strong for the authority to determine how this second world will be characterized."

If the various strands of postmodernism share a common emphasis on individual consciousness, being, and freedom, there are nevertheless profound theoretical differences within the genre, differences to which erstwhile disciples of Foucault, Derrida, and White all too often show a blissful ignorance, combining concepts in ways akin to mixing water and oil. Foucault, for example, regarded Derrida precepts with ill-disguised contempt. Derrida was, Foucault (1972/2006: 573) declared, "the most decisive representative, in its waning light" of a discredited "pedagogy" built around "the invention of voices behind the text," a charlatan who spuriously taught "the student that there is nothing outside the text." Derrida for his part was equally dismissive of Foucault's work. In critiquing Foucault's *Madness and Civilization*, for example, Derrida (1967b/2001: 49) accurately noted that "everything transpires as if Foucault knew what 'madness' means ... The same kind of questions could be posed concerning the truth that runs through the book." There were also profound differences between the intellectual principles of Foucault and White. In terms of evidence, Foucault (1976/1978: 100, 13) advised his readers – even as he proclaimed that "it is in discourse that power and knowledge are joined together" – that research should start "from historical facts that serve as guidelines." By contrast, White declared that "Facts belong to speech, language and discourse, not to the real world" (cited Domanska 2008: 5). Indeed, in White's historiography the boundaries between the "real" and "imaginary" were ones that the historian needs to dissolve, rather than highlight. As White (2014: 47) expressed it in *The Practical Past*: "Fantasies of alien cultures in outer space and theories of parallel or antithetical universes" can be as "real" as a carefully constructed historical narrative.

When one turns one's attention from the foundational texts of postmodernism to what passes for postmodernist scholarship in management history, one all too often witnesses an abysmal ignorance as to the basic principles of the theoretical frameworks that are cited or to the differences between one body of postmodernist thought and another. Even worse is the tendency to cite some supposed expert(s), without discussing in any detail either the actual ideas of the erstwhile expert or the source of their postmodernist-informed ideas. Despite claims to "critical" scholarship, it is also the case that – all too often – any attempt at critical appraisal is abandoned, thereby allowing for the furtherance of confused postmodernist understandings to ever-wider audiences. In the case of Hayden White, for example – a self-declared postmodernist whom Rowlinson et al. (2014: 151) describe as "a leading philosopher of history" – I know of no "critical studies" academic in management history, business history, or organizational history who has discussed the two major controversies that beset White and his supporters. The first of these controversies, involving the existence of the Holocaust as either a factual or an imaginary event, saw Berel Lang (1995: 89) ask whether "historical narratives ... are unfettered by anything more than the historian's imagination." In responding to this line of argument, White's close supporter, Hans Kellner (1998: 237), reiterated White's longtime argument that historical narratives are *always* the imagined creation of the historian and that, accordingly, the Holocaust was simply a rhetorical term, "an imaginative creation, like all historical events." In returning to debates about the Holocaust in *The Practical Past*, White (2014: 28–29) confronted the question as to whether the Holocaust was "true" by declaring, "this question ... is of secondary importance to discourses making reference to the real world ... cast in a mode other than that of simple declaration." If White's response to the Holocaust debate was hardly one of model clarity, he also never responded effectively to Dirk Moses's (2005) criticism that White and his supporters, in declaring history to "fictive" and "mythical," were blind to the ways in which mythical accounts of history justified "unspeakable atrocities" committed by "ethnic groups and nationalizing states." In response to this accusation, White (2005: 333) merely restated his core belief that "History's subject matter, that is, the past, is a problematic object of study ... It is a place of fantasy."

The propensity to advocate postmodernist (mis)understandings through reference to some nominal "expert," without discussing the underlying ideas that inform them, is unfortunately evident on almost every front in management history. In a guest editorial in the *Journal of Management History*, entitled "Nurturing the historic turn: 'history as theory' versus 'history as method,'" Durepos and Van Lent (2019) constantly advanced postmodernist understandings. There were, however, no references to either Foucault or Derrida. The sole reference to Hayden White revolved around the statement that "stories" are "constructed around 'traces' of the past, which are the raw materials of the historian's discourse rather than the events themselves." Now, the concept of the "trace" – the idea that we look within a *pre-existing* text to find transcendental evidence of *previous* experience – *was* seminal to the work of Derrida (1967b/2001: 97–192) who, as he made clear in *Writing and Difference*, derived the concept from both Heidegger and Emmanuel Levinas. It was *not* a seminal feature of White's work, which emphasized instead a contrary position: that "history" is the imagined creation of the historian, whereas the past is "the realm of the dead" (White 2005: 333). Instead of citing foundational postmodernist texts, Durepos and Van Lent (2019) – as is now almost the norm among "critical" management historians – hold up as an exemplar the so-called "historic turn," an article penned by Clark and Rowlinson in 2004 under the title, "The treatment of history in organisation studies: Towards an 'historic turn'?". In advocating the "historic turn," Durepos and Van Lent (2019: 431) enthusiastically proclaim that it has "spawned a significant body of work that explores the usage of historically grounded research in the study of organizations."

What are the core premises of the so-called historic turn that currently acts as the touchstone for postmodernist-informed "critical" theory in management history? A superficial reading of Durepos and Van Lent, and like-minded articles, could easily lead one to believe that the so-called historic turn advocates a return to historical basics and to thesis testing and a careful scrutiny of historical evidence. A perusal of Clark and Rowlinson's article, however, reveals that this is far from being the case. Rather than embracing conventional understandings of history, Clark and Rowlinson called for their dismantlement. "The historic turn," Clark and Rowlinson (2004: 331) advised, "is part of a wider transformation that is alluded to in terms such as the 'discursive turn', deconstruction and post-modernism." Clark and Rowlinson (2004: 331) also declared that the "historic turn" involves "a turn to . . . historical theories of interpretation that recognize the inherent ambiguity of the term 'history' itself." If Clark and Rowlinson's article at least makes clear that an embrace of "post-modern" understandings is advocated, the reader is nevertheless left in the dark as to the underlying "post-modern" theories that are being embraced. Despite advising the reader that the "historic turn" is part of a "transformation" that includes textual "deconstruction," the article is devoid of references to Derrida, Levinas, or Roland Barthes, the central figures in "deconstructionist" theory. Despite advocating an "embrace" of "discursive" understandings, the article is bereft of direct references to Foucault. Instead, readers are pointed in the direction of an earlier article by Rowlinson and Carter (2002), entitled "Foucault and History in Organization Studies." In terms of the overall theoretical underpinnings of their article, Clark and Rowlinson (2004: 331, 347, endnote 2) primarily rely upon a book chapter by Brian Fay, published in 1998 under the title, "The Linguistic Turn and Beyond in Contemporary Theory of History." Only when we turn to Fay's chapter do we finally ascertain the theoretical underpinnings of the so-called historic turn. Associating the publication of White's *Metahistory* with a decisive "shift in the theory of philosophy of history," Fay (1998: 2) declared that with White's work "the topics of narration and representation replaced [theoretical] law and explanation as burning issues of the theory and philosophy of history." This shift, Fay (1998: 2) continued, brought "the poetics of history . . . to the fore" (i.e., history as poetic imagining).

As we note in our subsequent chapter, "Hayden White and His Influence," it is White rather than Foucault who is – despite the constant propensity to conflate postmodernist theories from diverse sources – arguably the dominant influence among critical management/postmodernist historians. Like White (1973a: 1–2), who argued in favor of "the fictive character of historical reconstruction," Rowlinson, Hassard, and Decker (2014: 257) declare "that there is a 'literary' or 'fictive' element in all historical . . . and scientific writing." Like White (1966: 115), who declared "that the historical consciousness must be obliterated," the late Alun Munslow (2015: 136) advised readers of *The Routledge Companion to Management and Organizational History* that "Meanings are fictively constructed. There are no lessons in the past." Like White (1968: 48), who believed that the historical narrative resembles the historical novel in being built upon metaphor and multiple interpretations, Jacques and Durepos (2015: 99) declare that "Our goal is to demonstrate that every story we could possibly tell is contestable." Despite the academic popularity of White's "liberation historiography" (Paul 2011), its proponents invariably resist the temptation to explain why they adopted this perspective over another or their opinion as to its all too obvious flaws. For, if as Jacques and Durepos (2015: 99) suggest "every story we could possibly tell is contestable," this means – as Lang (1995: 89) accurately observed – that the judgment as to whether or not a person existed "five minutes ago depends entirely on what historians . . . say about them."

If "critical" management historians are loath to acknowledge any opinion that is critical of their chosen intellectual mentor and guide, there is also a tendency to hop from one perspective to another while ignoring the problems this necessarily entails. In their article in *Academy of Management Review*, co-written with Stephanie Decker in 2014, Michael Rowlinson and John Hassard, for example, point to White as an exemplar (Rowlinson et al. 2014: 231). Three years later, in *A New History of Management*, Rowlinson and Hassard signed on to a rewriting of management history from a "Foucauldian" perspective (Cummings et al. 2017: 35). Now, to jump from White to Foucault is no mean feat. White believed that "history" is what it is imagined to be. By contrast, Foucault (1971/1984) argued that history is a contemporary discourse, a fusion of power and knowledge, within which each discourse boasts a unique genealogy. In other words, history in Foucault's opinion was not something that simply stems from the historian's imagination. Instead, it is something that emerges from the external world, from established social structures and the discourses that support them.

Despite the evident reluctance of Cummings et al. and other like-minded Foucauldians to admit the existence of flaws within their perspective, the weaknesses in Foucault's thinking have long been obvious to people who cannot be regarded – by any stretch of the imagination – as "conventional" or "traditional" historians or philosophers. The French existentialist philosopher, Jean-Paul Sartre (1966/1971: 110), for example, declared Foucault's work a "denial of history," accurately noting that – while Foucault provided an explanation as to how a dominant discourse existed in the present – he failed to explain "how each thought" or discourse is superseded, as people and cultures move from one set of beliefs to another. The result, Sartre (1966/1971: 110) concluded, was that Foucault replaced history as "cinema," a process of continuous historical events and motions, "with a magic lantern, movement by a succession of immobilities." As a Foucauldian-inspired historian, one might of course find reasons to counter Sartre's critique. Nevertheless, one surely should at least acknowledge its existence. This, however, is not what Cummings et al. (2017) chose to do in their "new" history of management.

Postmodernism and the Nature of Freedom

The postmodernist debate is central to our times in part because it speaks to the oldest debates in the human experience, disputes that revolve around the nature of freedom and the extent to which historical outcomes can be explained through reference to either the institutional character of a society or, alternatively, the free will of the individuals who comprise it.

Despite their many differences and flaws, Foucault, Derrida, and White were not only idealist philosophers; they also followed in the footsteps of Nietzsche, Heidegger, and Croce in arguing in favor of an untrammeled individualism. In the opinion of Derrida (1967a/1976: 10), the source of oppression resided deep within Western culture, in "phonetic writing, the medium of the great metaphysical, scientific, technical, and economic adventure of the West." Advocating a "Romantic" conception of history, White (1968: 52, 55) argued that the "individual" is almost always "the victim" rather than "the beneficiary" of society and that established "social institutions, ideas, and values" needed to be perceived as "bastions against the free expression of nature and individual human will." Foucault, for his part, focused on a wide array of oppressive social forces – *epistemes* and the "fundamental codes of a culture" (Foucault 1966/1994: xx), the ways in which "power and knowledge are joined together" through "discourse" (Foucault 1976/1978: 94), the "disciplinary" society with its "infinitesimal surveillances, permanent controls, extremely meticulous orderings of space" (Foucault 1975/1991: 308). In his first book, *Madness and Civilization: A History of Insanity in the Age of Reason*, Foucault (1961/1965: 9) also argued that through "reason's subjugation of non-reason," people have come to "communicate and recognize each other through the merciless language of non-madness," suppressing in the process "the lyricism of protest." Also supposedly lost was an appreciation of "desire and murder, of cruelty and the longing to suffer" (Foucault 1961/1965: 221). In *Madness and Civilization*, Foucault (1961/1965: 221) found special meaning in the writings of the Marquis de Sade, arguing that through de Sade's "words of unreason ...man discovers a truth he has forgotten." For, Foucault (1961/1965: 221) added, "Sadism ...is a massive cultural fact."

In the final analysis, the postmodernist quest is not dismissible due to either its internal contradictions or literary obtuseness. Nor are its epistemological positions, based as they are on a long tradition of European idealist thought, the key issue. Rather, postmodernism's validity stands and falls on its understanding of freedom, the belief that individuals become free when they are no longer constrained by institutional rules or cultural mores. Summing up Foucault's understanding of freedom, White (1973b: 50) accurately noted that "Foucault represents a continuation of a tradition of historical thought which originates in Romanticism and which was taken up ... by Nietzsche in the last quarter of the nineteenth century." A similar comment was applicable to White himself and, to a lesser degree, Derrida. In considering the nature of freedom in *The Rebel*, the French existentialist philosopher, Albert Camus (1951/1978: 26, 47), concurred with White's assessment that Romanticism represented a fundamental rupture in Western thought, transforming rebellion from a physical act into a "metaphysical" quest for freedom, a quest that has "shaped the history of our times." Camus's study also prefigured Foucault in identifying the Marquis de Sade as the preeminent exponent of both metaphysical rebellion and total freedom. Declaring de Sade to be "the first theoretician of absolute rebellion," a person who was "centuries ahead of his time," Camus (1951/1978: 36, 46–47) argues the value of his thought lays in his revelation of the logical consequences of "the demand for total freedom," i.e., an unrestrained capacity for evil, a license to destroy whatever one wants. For, invariably, as Nietzsche understood, complete freedom of the individual involves empowering the strong over the weak, a world in which any would-be de Sade is free to perpetrate barbarities without fear of censure or restraint. This association of postmodernism with the ideas of de Sade may, at first glance, appear unwarranted. However, it was not only Camus who drew the connection between the demand for metaphysical freedom and de Sade. It was also, as we have just noted, central to Foucault's first book. Foucault, like de Sade, could see where the logic of his argument took him. He did not recoil from it.

If Foucault, like Nietzsche before him, never shied away from the logical consequences of his call for unrestrained freedom, Camus (1951/1978: 296–297) drew different conclusions in perusing the same textual positions, arguing that absolute freedom is always tyrannical, just as "pure and unadulterated virtue" is always "homicidal." At the end of the day, these are not idle issues. In embracing Derrida, Foucault, and White, postmodernist management historians are advocating an understanding of freedom that stands without acknowledged restraints. For the reader, the key question before them as they consider the chapters in this section must therefore be: Is this a conception of freedom that I also share?

Cross-References

▶ Foundations: The Roots of Idealist and Romantic Opposition to Capitalism and Management
▶ Hayden White and His Influence
▶ Jacques Derrida: Cosmopolitan Critic
▶ Management History in the Modern World: An Overview
▶ Paul-Michel Foucault: Prophet and Paradox
▶ The Intellectual Origins of Postmodernism

References

Camus A, Bower A (trans) (1951/1978) The rebel. Alfred A Knopf, New York
Clark P, Rowlinson M (2004) The treatment of history in organisation studies: towards an 'historic turn'? Bus Hist 46(3):3331–3352
Croce B, Ainslie D (trans) (1915/1921) Theory and history of historiography. George G Harrap & Co., London
Cummings S, Bridgman T, Hassard J, Rowlinson M (2017) A new history of management. Cambridge University Press, Cambridge, UK
Derrida J, Spivak G (trans) (1967a/1976) Of grammatology. John Hopkins University Press, Baltimore
Derrida J (1967b/2001) Writing and difference. Routledge and Kegan Paul, London and New York
Derrida J, Bennington G, Bowlby R (trans) (1987/1989) Of spirit: Heidegger and the question. University of Chicago Press, Chicago and London
Domanska E (2008) A conversation with Hayden White. Rethink Hist 12(1):3–21
Durepos G, Van Lent W (2019) Guest editorial: nurturing the historic turn: 'history as theory' versus 'history as method'. J Manag Hist 25(4):429–443
Fay B (1998) The linguistic turn and beyond in contemporary theory of history. In: Fay B, Pomper P, Van RT (eds) History and theory: contemporary readings. Blackwell Publishers, Oxford, pp 1–12
Foucault M, Howard R (trans) (1961/1965) Madness and civilization: a history of insanity in the age of reason. Pantheon Books, New York
Foucault M (1966/1994) The order of things: an archaeology of the human sciences. Vintage Books, New York

Foucault M (1971/1984) Nietzsche, genealogy, history. In: Rabinow P (ed) The Foucault reader. Penguin, Harmondsworth, pp 76–100

Foucault M (1972/2006) Appendix II – my body, this paper, this fire. In: Foucault M (trans: Murphy J and Khalfa J), History of madness, 2nd edn. Routledge, London, appendix II, pp 550–574

Foucault M, Sheridan A (trans) (1975/1991) Discipline and punish: the birth of the prison. Vintage Books, New York

Foucault M, Hurley R (trans) (1976/1978) The history of sexuality – an introduction. Pantheon Books, New York

Heidegger M, Macquarie J, Robinson E (trans) (1926/1962) Being and time. Blackwell Publishing, London, UK

Jacques R, Durepos G (2015) A history of management histories: does the story of our past and the way we tell it matter. In: McLaren PG, Mills AJ, Weatherbee TG (eds) The Routledge companion to management and organizational history. Routledge, London and New York, pp 96–111

Kellner H (1998) "Never again" is now. In: Fay B, Pomper P, Van RT (eds) History and theory: contemporary readings. Blackwell Publishers, Oxford, pp 225–244

Lang B (1995) Is it possible to misrepresent the Holocaust? Hist Theory 34(1):84–89

Moses D (2005) Hayden White, traumatic nationalism, and the public role of history. Hist Theory 44(3):311–332

Munslow A (2015) Management the past. In: McLaren PG, Mills AJ, Weatherbee TG (eds) The Routledge companion to management and organizational history. Routledge, London and New York, pp 129–142

Nietzsche F, Hollingdale RJ (trans) (1885/1990) Beyond good and evil: prelude to a philosophy of the future. Penguin Books, London

Paul H (2011) Hayden White: the historical imagination. Polity, Cambridge, UK

Rowlinson M, Carter C (2002) Foucault and history in organization studies. Organization 9(4):527–547

Rowlinson M, Hassard J, Decker S (2014) Research strategies for organizational history: a dialogue between historical theory and organization theory. Acad Manag Rev 39(3):250–274

Sartre J-P, D'Amico R (trans) (1966/1971) An interview: replies to structuralism. Telos 9(1):110–116

White H (1966) The burden of history. Hist Theory 5(2):111–134

White HV (1968) Romanticism, historicism, and realism: toward a period concept for early 19th century intellectual history. In: White HV (ed) The uses of history: essays in intellectual and social history presented to William H Bossenbrook. Wayne State University, Detroit, pp 15–58

White H (1973a) Metahistory: the historical imagination in nineteenth-century Europe. John Hopkins University Press, Baltimore/London

White H (1973b) Foucault decoded: notes from underground. Hist Theory 12(1):23–54

White H (2005) The public relevance of historical studies: a reply to Dirk Moses. Hist Theory 44(3):333–338

White H (2014) The practical past. Northwestern University Press, Evanston

The Intellectual Origins of Postmodernism

28

Bradley Bowden

Contents

Introduction	646
Language and Knowledge: From Plato to Derrida	650
Power and Discourse: From Nietzsche to Foucault and White	655
Modernity and Postmodernism: From Rousseau to Lyotard	660
Conclusion	664
Cross-References	666
References	666

Abstract

Postmodernism is today one of the most powerful intellectual and social forces in Western society. Within postmodernist canon there is, however, considerable division. Jacques Derrida and his intellectual heirs among "deconstructionists" believe that texts can be reinterpreted to give voice to the excluded; a view that Michel Foucault viewed with disdain, arguing instead that knowledge comes from the "discourses" of various social groups. Given these fundamental divisions, what gives postmodernism both an internal unity and intellectual strength is the long traditions of critical thought that it draws upon. Some of these relate to the nature of knowledge. Others traditions of thought – most notably those associated with Friedrich Nietzsche – give a primacy to spirit, consciousness, and individual will over matters relating to material progress. Postmodernism also draws on a deep suspicion of the process of mechanization and industrialization that was heralded by the Industrial Revolution. The purpose of this introductory chapter,

B. Bowden (✉)
Griffith Business School, Griffith University, Nathan, QLD, Australia
e-mail: b.bowden@griffith.edu.au

© The Author(s), under exclusive licence to Springer Nature Switzerland AG 2020
B. Bowden et al. (eds.), *The Palgrave Handbook of Management History*,
https://doi.org/10.1007/978-3-319-62114-2_77

therefore, is one of tracing the diverse strands of thought that gave rise to postmodernism; an analysis that necessitates an estimation of the inherent strengths and weaknesses of the intellectual traditions that inform postmodernism.

Keywords

Postmodernism · Foucault · Derrida · Heidegger · White · Vico · Barthes · Levinas · Nietzsche · Plato · Saussure · Albert Mills · Rowlinson · Berkeley · Descartes · Lyotard · Rousseau · Taylor · Mayo

Introduction

Postmodernism is today one of the most powerful intellectual and social forces in Western society. In a world where the collectivist institutions of the past – churches, trade unions, consumer and producer cooperatives, class-based political parties – have lost social sway, the postmodernist focus on matters relating to identity, consciousness, and local manifestations of power has indubitable appeal. For those who take inspiration from Michel Foucault (1976/1978: 145), modern industrial societies are viewed as places of entrenched oppression: an oppression imposed through systems of "micro-power" that are found in each and every social circumstance, whether they be in the home, the school, or the workplace. Viewed from this perspective, social and political inequalities are maintained – and resisted – through the creation of "discourses," it being the case that in discourse "power and knowledge are joined together" (Foucault 1976/1978: 100). For those who take inspiration from Foucault's one-time student and long-term critic, Jacques Derrida (1967/2001: 251, 284–285), inequalities of power and understanding are embedded in the very structure of language; an outcome that demands a re-reading and reinterpretation of every text so as to rescue the voices of those who have been excluded from earlier tellings. Arguing along a different track, the work of Paul Ricoeur (2004: 448) – Derrida's one-time academic supervisor – informs us that our understandings of the past are typically the product of "manipulated memory" and "the ideologizing of memory." What unites these and other postmodernist critiques is their focus on the ways in which our understanding of "truth" and objective "reality" are all supposedly based – either in full or in part – on images, texts, and/or discourses that reflect the vested concerns of self-interested individuals and groups. By contesting these accounts we are, in the opinion of postmodernist canon, engaging in acts of resistance against "repression" and the "infinitesimal surveillances" that entrenches inequality (Derrida 1967/2001: 285; Foucault 1976/1978: 145).

Much of the appeal of postmodernism is found in the universality of its message. Oppression is everywhere. Oppression is primarily based on the control of knowledge, not on courts and police forces. Thus we are informed "facts" are "never innocent." They always serve some particular interest (Munslow 1997: 8). Accordingly, the de-legitimization of established authority must begin with the de-legitimization of established knowledge. As the Dutch postmodernist, Frank

28 The Intellectual Origins of Postmodernism

Ankersmit (1989: 142), explained, "The postmodernist's aim ... is to pull the carpet out from under the feet of science and modernity." Rooted in philosophic idealism, postmodernism's starting point is not the objective world that we deal with in every waking second of our existence but rather with self, with how I represent that external world in my imagination, and how that representation is necessarily different from that suggested by other individuals and groups. This emphasis on self, and the contested status of knowledge and representation, also does much to explain the popularity of postmodernism in domains such as media and cultural studies; domains where accounts of reality are increasingly conveyed through individual Facebook and twitter accounts rather than through established media outlets.

As readers would no doubt be aware the appeal of postmodernism is not restricted to media and cultural studies. Rather, its adherents are found in every nook and cranny of academia. In most university business departments, there will be at least a sprinkling of postmodernists. Postmodernist-inclined thinkers also control an increasing number of academic journals. The journal *Management & Organizational History* was co-founded (and edited until 2013) by the prominent Foucauldian postmodernist, Michael Rowlinson. Currently, Rowlinson serves as Associate Editor of *Organization Studies*. At *Business History*, the preeminent journal in the field, Stephanie Decker, a frequent co-author with Rowlinson, is Associate Editor. At the *Academy of Management Review,* one of the most prestigious journals within academia, Roy Suddaby – whose critiques of business "rhetoric" have proved most influential – served as Editor from 2011 to 2014, having previously served as Associate Editor from 2008 to 2011. Postmodernist influence is also evidenced by a growing number of books that are redefining understandings of management and organizations. Prominent among these are: *Organizations in Time: History, Theory, and Methods* (published in 2013, and edited by Marcelo Bucheli and Daniel Whadwhani), *The Routledge Companion of* Management *and Organizational History* (2015 – edited by Patricia McLaren, Albert Mills, and Terrance Weatherbee), *ANTi-History* (2012 – authored by Gabrielle Durepos and Albert Mills), and *A New History of Management* (2017 – authored by Stephen Cummings, Todd Bridgman, John Hassard, and Michael Rowlinson).

Among both adherents and critics of postmodernism the commonalities that characterize its intellectual canons – that all knowledge is inherently subjective and amenable to multiple interpretations, that power and authority rest on the acceptance of particular viewpoints and interpretations, that language and/or discourse can be weapons of both oppression and resistance – cause many to assume that postmodernism represents a single, coherent body of thought. Accordingly, many combine conceptualizations that are diametrically opposed: a tendency that this author witnesses continually in his capacity as Editor-in-Chief of the *Journal of Management History*. There is a particular tendency to conflate ideas drawn from Foucault – most notably those relating to social "discourse" – with those inspired by Derrida, most significantly Derrida's contention that language always contains "traces" of those that the author/s chose to exclude from their narratives. In truth, Foucault and Derrida came to view each other's ideas with increasing scorn. In his *Writing and Difference*, for example, Derrida readily dismissed Foucault's claims that he could ascertain the stance of the insane, the mad, and other marginalized groups. In a review that eviscerated Foucault's (1965) *Madness and Civilization*, Derrida (1967/2001: 40, 49) declared that the "maddest aspect" of Foucault's "project" was his claimed ability to write as if he "knew what 'madness' means." Foucault's claimed ability to ascertain the generalized understandings of social groups also caused Derrida (1967/2001: 66–67) to condemn Foucault's work for its "structuralist" and "totalitarian" tendencies. For his part, Foucault (1972a/2001: 573) regarded with incredulity Derrida's claim that he could ascertain "traces" of past existence in through a reinterpretation of texts. Such claims, Foucault (1972a/2001: 573) asserted, revealed Derrida to be "the most decisive representative, in its waning light," of a "pedagogy that teaches the student that there is nothing outside the text"; a pedagogy that allowed the researcher to engage in a spurious "invention of voices behind the text."

The bitter denunciations of each other's work by Derrida and Foucault reflect much more than a clash of egos. They reflect fundamentally different understandings as to how human being's comprehend their world. For Foucault, knowledge – be it *epistemes* that reflect shared understandings of an historical epoch or discourses that define particular groups – are *always* the creation of *groups*. As Foucault (1969/1972: 73–74) indicated in his *The Archaeology of Knowledge*, understandings reside within the "discourse itself," rather than in an assortment of individuals. Accordingly, intellectual and social conflict always manifests itself in a struggle for dominance by competing discourses; a struggle in which the competing groups talk about "the same things," place themselves "at the same level" and oppose one another "on the same battlefield" (Foucault 1969/1972: 126). For Derrida, by contrast, there was, as he famously declared in his, *On Grammatology*, "*Il n'y a pas de hors texte*" (there is nothing outside the text). What counts is not the social group but rather existence, individual "essence," "unconscious experience," "psychic" imprint; expressions of being that always left "traces" in writing that allowed the discerning reader to ascertain the relationship between "psyche, society, the world" (Derrida 1967/2001: 255, 185).

Foucault and Derrida's profoundly different understandings of knowledge and power – and of the purposes of academic inquiry – are indicative of how the thinking of each was shaped by fundamentally different philosophic influences. In the case of Foucault, his concern with how power and social behavior are shaped by competing discourses betrays the particular influence of the nineteenth century German philosopher, Friedrich Nietzsche (1895/1990: 187), who declared that, "Ultimately the point is to what end a lie is told." By contrast, the intellectual roots of Derrida's work – which sought to overturn the whole Western heritage of language and thought, or what Derrida (1967/1976: 10–11) referred to as the "de-construction" of the "logocentrism" and "phoncentrism" of the Western intellectual tradition – were very different. In countering the view that all languages have a defined structure that is embedded within a particular linguistic group, Derrida consciously sought to overturn the "structuralist" understandings of the early twentieth century Swiss linguist, Ferdinand de Saussure, drawing in the process on the work of Roland Barthes. A French semiotician, Barthes denounced the concept of the "author" as peculiarly "modern," fatally influenced "by English empiricism, French rationalism,

28 The Intellectual Origins of Postmodernism

and the personal faith of the Reformation" (Bathes 1984/1986: 49). Derrida's most radical arguments – which were associated with the view that discerning readers could detect traces of past existence within texts – were moreover taken in a largely unaltered form from the earlier work of Emmanuel Levinas and Martin Heidegger. Other postmodernist thinkers have been guided by even more idiosyncratic idealist schools of thought. Hayden White, for example, whose influence has rivalled Foucault in the English-speaking world, built his intellectual career around the work of the early twentieth century historian, Benedetto Croce (1915/1921) and the eighteenth century Italian philosopher, Giambattista Vico (1744/1968: 120), who argued that the advance of rationality and industrialized societies was associated with the loss of the "sublime" feelings and poetic thinking of pre-modern societies. To recapture this lost spirituality, Vico (1744/1968: 129–131) recommended organizing writing on poetic lines whereby plots were prefigured around literary "tropes," most particularly metaphor, metonymy, synecdoche, and irony; a suggestion that became a cornerstone of the postmodernist narratives of White (1976) and his imitators (see, for example, Curthoys and McGrath 2009).

To understand postmodernism we must, given its multiple intellectual influences, first examine the various strands of idealist philosophies that emerged during the long century of the European Enlightenment; a period of intellectual fervor that began in the middle decades of the seventeenth century and ended in the conflicts of the French Revolution. Yet, before we can even undertake this task, we must push the timelines for our analysis even further back, to the ancient Greeks and Plato. For in the opinion of Vico, Heidegger, and Derrida, the problems of the modern world stem not simply from the Industrial Revolution but from the ancient Greeks when, according to Heidegger (1926/1962: 9), an emphasis on "Scientific research" created a schism in human thinking, emphasizing reason at the expense of existential being. In endorsing "the revolution against reason," Derrida (1967/2001: 42) also found fault with the commitment of the ancient Greeks to phonetic writing. The problem, Derrida (1967/1976: 43) argued – as did Heidegger (1926/1962) before him – was that phonetic writing unnecessarily restricted the human imagination, thereby curtailing expressions of existence and being.

Through an exploration of the intellectual roots of postmodernism, it becomes manifest that postmodernist canon is opposed not only to modernity and inequalities of power and authority but to reason itself, to the very underpinnings of Western thought. In examining this commonality within the diverse and often conflicting postmodernist perspectives, this chapter undertakes three main tasks, each equating to a section within its text. In our first section, we trace the epistemological origins of the hostility of the post-structuralist school of postmodernism – associated with Heidegger, Levinas, Barth, and Derrida – to the very structure of Western language and thought. By contrast, our second section explores how the influence of Nietzsche and Vico affected the work of Foucault and White, and through their writings, the postmodernist understandings of discourse and the use of narrative writing. Finally, we explore how postmodernism – although an idealist school of thought – has taken up earlier objections to the advance of industrialization and modernity from outside idealist philosophy; a critical tradition within which the ideas of Jean-Jacques Rousseau remain preeminent.

Language and Knowledge: From Plato to Derrida

Hostility to the Western tradition of reasoned inquiry has long been a characteristic feature of the critical philosophic tradition that informs postmodernist thought. In his seminal study, *Time and Being*, Heidegger (1926/1962: 9), for example, argued that the root of humanity's problems – which he traced back to the suppression of existential being or what he referred to as *Dasein* – stemmed from the Western embrace of the Greek "concept of the *logos*," whereby "reason" became the dominant factor in "discourse." Almost two centuries before Vico (1744/1968: 118) emphasized similar themes in his *The New Science*. By building our language and understandings around "abstractions" that are "refined by the art of writing," Vico (1744/1968: 118) suggested, "civilized minds" had become emotionally and spiritually dulled, "detached from the senses." Reflecting his placement within this tradition of hostility to rationality and science, Derrida (1967/2001: 278) likewise argued that Western societies had been heading down the wrong intellectual and spiritual path "at least since Plato."

At one level, the hostility of Derrida and his intellectual predecessors to the ancient Greeks in general and Plato in particular is paradoxical, given that it was in Plato's *The Republic* that a convincing argument emerged for the first time in favor of the view that we do not experience the world directly through the senses – as empiricist thinkers suggest – but rather through idealized representations in our imagination, or what Plato (c. 380 BC/2003: 336–339) referred to as "forms"; a terminology and understanding that has become a characteristic feature of postmodernism. As with current-day postmodernists who espouse an extreme skepticism of the idea that there is any such thing as objective "truth," Plato (c. 380 BC/2003: 345) highlighted the inherent unreliability of the mental "forms" created in our imagination by the senses, declaring that their "representation deals with something at third remove from truth." Where, however, postmodernists have used the fact that we understand the world through idealized representations (i.e., we categorize all beds as "beds," whatever their shape and degree of softness) to deny the possibility of verifiable truth, Plato argued a diametrically opposed position to which none in the postmodernist tradition would concur. For Plato's ultimate sin, from a postmodernist perspective, was his (Plato, c. 380 BC/2003: 205) belief that through the exercise of our reason we could ascertain "true reality" from the representations or forms conveyed in our imagination. This happy outcome, Plato (c. 380 BC/2003: 239) argued, stemmed from the fact that the human mind primarily deals with abstractions that are "invisible except to the eye of reason." Indeed, many of the concepts that inform our thinking – the geometrical forms relating to circles and triangles, political concepts such as democracy, and economic concepts such as value – do not exist in the material world. In thinking about such abstractions, Plato (c. 380 BC/2003: 239) convincingly argued, "The whole procedure involves nothing in the visible world, but moves solely from form to form, and finishes with form." In other words, although objective reality does exist it is given meaning by the categories into which we organize our thoughts.

28 The Intellectual Origins of Postmodernism

If no postmodernist of any hue would endorse Plato's views about knowledge, it is also the case that those we think of as "poststructuralists"– most notably Derrida – have been equally opposed to Plato's thesis that language is primarily associated with verbal speech; speech which written text can never do more than provide an imperfect representation. On this front, it was Plato's *Phaedrus* that caused most ire; a work in which Plato (c. 370 BC/1972: 159) dismissed "written discourse" as being no more than "a kind of image" of "living speech." The problem with even well-written discourse, Plato (c. 370 BC/1972: 158) argued, is that it represents a dead form of language and thought, for "they go on telling you just the same thing forever." In his *Phaedrus*, Plato (c. 370 BC/1972: 124, 160) also provoked subsequent postmodernist hostility by arguing in favor of a "dialectical method" based upon a highly structured form of language; a structure that allowed the "scientific practitioner" to demonstrate a pathway towards "truth" through a careful delineation of the linkages between evidence and proof.

In the opening decade of the twentieth century the emphasis that Plato had placed on the importance of linguistic structure and verbal speech found powerful expression in de Saussure's (1915/1974) *Course in General Linguistics*, a study that provided the corner stone for the new discipline of semiotics. Like Plato, de Saussure (1915/1974: 27) believed that the act of speaking – what de Saussure referred to as *parole* – is the embodiment of "language" in its most dynamic state. By contrast, written text is an historical laggard, often recording archaic forms of language that no longer resemble spoken pronunciation (i.e., knight, receipt, etc.). Where de Saussure differed from Plato was in his emphasis on the deeply embedded structure of language. For in de Saussure's (1915/1974: 15, 8, 71–73) estimation, "language is a social institution," a "system" that is always "homogenous" in both "nature and application." Accordingly, once a linguistic "sign" is established (i.e., a feline animal is described as a "cat"), then it is beyond the capacity of an individual to change that meaning (de Saussure 1915/1974: 69).

From the outset the postmodernist tradition that is generally referred to as "post-structuralism" or "literary de-constructionism" has had the "structuralism" of de Saussure firmly in its sights. In doing so, post-structuralist adherents (and their intellectual predecessors such as Heidegger) have argued three fundamental points: that texts can (and should) be interpreted in ways different to that intended by the author; that written language is inherently superior to spoken words; that the scrutiny of texts can reveal "traces" of those voices previously excluded from the historical record.

In support of the first of these points – that texts can be interpreted in ways different from that intended by the author/s – poststructuralists argue that language, far from being "homogenous" as de Saussure believed, is in fact heterogeneous with every combination of words being subject to multiple interpretations. Among post-structuralists, the French semiologist, Roland Barthes, is arguably the best is making the case that there is often more than one meaning in language. Echoing themes that became a mainstay of Derrida's work, Barthes (1966/1987: 33) argued that the "first writing" of every work should be subject to "a second writing" by the reader. Through such a course, Barthes (1966/1987: 33) continued, new understandings of language could "threaten the power of power," "democratizing" the "literary state" with its "strict code" of agreed meanings. In another theme that became commonplace among postmodernists, Barthes (1984/1986: 49) argued that the "author" and their stated opinions should be excluded from textual interpretation so as to allow a new "plural meaning."

In its most radical iteration the post-structuralist emphasis on multiple linguistic interpretations causes them to deny any necessary connection between written words and linguistic "signs" (i.e., the use of written or verbal "signifiers" that designate an object that is "signified"). In this, poststructuralists such as Derrida went far beyond de Saussure's (1915/1974: 67) observation that there is no universally fixed connection between verbal *sounds* and the object being "signified," it being the case, for example, that the French and English language use different words – "cat" and "chat" – to describe the same feline animal. For while de Saussure (1915/1974: 69) accepted that different *linguistic groups* use a variety of terms for the same object, he also observed that within a given culture or group there was little variety, it being the case that "the individual does not have the power to change a sign in any way once it has become established in the linguistic community." By contrast, Derrida (1967/2001: 13) declared – in a formulation that become the second cornerstone of post-structuralist thought – that "language is born" only when it "is written" and is thus "deceased as a sign-signal." In other words, written text should not only be perceived as having an independent existence separate from speech, it is also the case that this written form of language is inherently *superior* to verbal expression. According to Derrida (1967/2001: 285) – and hence subsequent post-structuralist exponents – what made writing so valuable is that enables us to fully explore the "vigilance" and "censorship" that are a natural but largely unconscious feature of social exchanges. For although the author/s may not be aware of the intricate patterns of oppression that characterize human existence, it nevertheless remains the case that they unconsciously embed the underlying structure of their society's oppressive mechanisms in their writing, it being the case that, "Writing is unthinkable without repression" (Derrida 1967/2001: 285).

If Derrida and subsequent poststructuralists lifted the idea that writing texts are capable of many different interpretations from Barthes, so it is the case that the key concept of "trace" was obtained from Emmanuel Levinas: an author who derived his understanding from Heidegger, who was in turn influenced by another German idealist philosopher, Edmund Husserl (see, Derrida 1967/2001: 97–192). According to Husserl (1913/1983: 35, 149–150) the fundamental failings of human understanding stemmed from a reliance on the "misunderstandings and prejudices" of empirical research; prejudices that led to the constant "excluding" of the "pure consciousness" that was the true well-spring of all human endeavors. In developing this emphasis on consciousness and exclusion, Heidegger (1926/1962: 29, 35) argued that every attempt to reveal one aspect of existence or a phenomenon – a word which he noted came from Greek verb "to show itself" – entailed the "covering-up" of other manifestations of existence. From these formulations, Levinas enunciated the idea that "traces" of past existence could be ascertained in language. As Levinas (1957/1987: 102) – who had completed his PhD on the work of Edmund Husserl in 1930 – explained it in his *Meaning and Sense*, "trace" is like a face behind a mask. We always know a face must be behind a mask as "a mask presupposes a face." Building on this analogy, Levinas (1957/1987: 103) developed formulations that prefigured those of Derrida, suggesting that detection of "traces" allowed researchers to ascertain "an immemorial past," and even "perhaps eternity" (i.e., there is no limit to the meanings that one can detect hidden within texts). Grasping Levinas's concept of "trace," Derrida (1967/2001: 66) in turn used the concept to underpin his argument that a textual presence always prefigures "difference," or to be more exact, "déférence" (from the French, "déférer"). According to this formulation, textual presence exists alongside a referred absence; an absence that can be ascertained by the reader undertaking the "second writing" that Barthes recommend. As each individual reader can theoretically discern a very different understanding within a text to that of their fellow readers, the application of the concepts of "trace" and "déférence" means that any given written passage is subject to a myriad of alternative explanations.

The arguments made by Derrida, Barthes, Levinas, and their intellectual heirs have attracted both intellectual brickbats and bouquets. In 1996, Mario Bunge (1996: 97), a Canadian philosopher, dismissed the deconstructionist references to "Being" and "trace" as "gobbledygook" and "unrecyclable rubbish." More than 30 years earlier, Raymond Picard (cited Barthes 1987: 29), a doyen of the French literary establishment, declared Barthes and his colleagues in the "New Criticism" movement to be "intellectually empty, verbally sophisticated" imposters who owed their success solely to intellectual "snobbery," wherein being incomprehensible was seen as a virtue. The fact that such criticisms were made 30 years apart, and could be made with equal force today, is an indicator of the longevity of the literary "post-structuralism" or "deconstructionism" that Derrida and Barthes initiated in the 1950s. Perhaps the most enduring legacy of this school of postmodernist thought is found in a changed research focus among broad swathes of the Western intelligentsia; a shift that has seen *reinterpretation* of texts and other signs (i.e., American Civil War monuments, statues commemorating New World "discoverers," visual art, etc.) gain increasing primacy. In postmodernist theory, this profound shift is described as "horizontality" – rather than "verticality" – of interest (Ankersmit 1989: 145–146). In other words, one no longer needs to – or should – look downwards (or outwards) at the objective reality of the world; a focus that leads to "primary sources" (e.g., statistics on employment, consumption, company profits, etc.). Instead, one should look sideways, at what has already been written or physically recorded by others. The reason for this, as the Dutch postmodernist, Frank Ankersmit (1990: 281), explains, is that, "Texts are all we have and we can only compare texts with texts." In short, nothing exists before it is recorded in some form of "writing." So-called reliable primary sources are, in this line of thinking, mere manifestations of past and present structures of power and inequality.

Superficially attractive and capable – as events have proved – of mass appeal, the fundamental failing of the post-structuralist/deconstructionist strand of postmodernist theory is found in the artificial rupture that it creates between objective reality and the written record. This failing is evident in the theorem of Ankersmit cited in the previous paragraph, where it is asserted that "we can only compare texts with texts." For the assumption here – which is characteristic of this strand of postmodernism – is that "texts" only exist in the form of deliberately created records, i.e., archives, diaries, journals, newspaper articles, and the like. In these *particular* forms of written evidence there is merit – as historians and others have recognized for generations – in the argument that one needs to very aware, as the "amodernist" authors Durepos and Mills (2012: 39) note, of "the role played by the interests of knowledge creators." There is, however, a very *different* type of written evidence that allows us to compare texts with material reality, instead of matching texts against texts; a type of evidence that was *never* designed for the purpose of shaping present or future interpretations of the world. This type of evidence – which includes production figures, sales, payments to employees and suppliers, shipping volumes, school attendance, hospital admissions, etc. – typically comes, moreover, at a significant cost to its producer. A wheat farmer, for example, is not likely to regularly book and pay for the use of railroad freight wagons simply for the purpose of manipulating future images as to the success of their business venture.

It is by constantly cross-referencing textual records against statistical evidence of material outputs that we can – most particularly in business and management – break out of the circularity of research to which adherents of post-structuralism/deconstructionism are condemned. By pursuing a "verticality" rather than a "horizontality" of research, in which we constantly look outwards or upwards to the material world that sustains our existence, we can also avoid the gross errors of fact that are an all too common hallmark of postmodernist research. Evidence of this postmodernist predilection for getting their facts wrong is readily found in the recent *A New History of Management*, where the authors (Cummings et al. 2017: 179) endorse the statement that, "millions of people are now facing radically reduced living conditions because of the actions of a few," as evidence of failed corporate behaviors. In truth, corporate behavior and private enterprise have in recent decades rescued hundreds of millions, if not billions from poverty and suffering. As the World Bank's (2017a) record of global food production indicates, since 1961 the world's food output has risen at almost twice the pace of population growth with the most rapid increases occurring in the developing world. Since 1991, global Gross Domestic Product per capita (measured in terms of purchasing power parity) has increased by more than 50%. In the United States, the Euro zone, and across the world as a whole, the level of per capita income has never been higher than it is today (World Bank 2017b). The level of extreme global poverty has also fallen precipitously. Whereas 42.1% of the world's population lived in extreme poverty in 1981, in 2013 only 10.2% experienced such a state of misery (World Bank 2017c). In the developing world, as the most recent report of the United Nation's Secretary-General, Antonio Guterres (2017: 23), makes clear, literacy and attendance at school – rather than endless toil – are now the norm for preadolescents. Even in sub-Saharan Africa, historically a laggard, 80% of children were attending school in 2015. In short, far from it being the case – as the authors (Cummings et al. 2017: 179, 177 of *A New*

28 The Intellectual Origins of Postmodernism

History of Management) constantly assert throughout their book – that modern management is associated with "reduced living conditions," "unprecedented crises," and a myopic "narrow focus," in truth it is the case that managerial endeavor has been associated with the delivery of increased wealth and opportunity to unprecedented numbers.

Power and Discourse: From Nietzsche to Foucault and White

Among postmodernism's founding figures Foucault was the most structurally-inclined, his early work being described by Gibson Burrell (1998: 17) – himself a postmodernist – as "quasi-structuralist." In making this observation as to the early work of Foucault, Burrell clearly had in mind Foucault's discussions of language and culture in *The Order of Things*; a work in which Foucault (1966/1994: xx) claimed to have discovered the key to the "fundamental codes" of culture. It is, however, Foucault's constant concern with power and uses – which is apparent in his first major work, *Madness and Civilization*, as it is in this latter works – that provides the clearest proof of "structuralist" influences on his thinking. Of particular influence was his early mentor and life-long friend, Louis Althusser, the French Marxist who in the early 1950s persuaded Foucault to join the French Communist Party (he soon left). It is certainly the case that many of Althusser's understandings – that capitalism exerted its power mainly through its command of ideas; that authority and resistance existed alongside each other in the various institutions of power; that in asserting dissident ideas an intellectual is engaged in transformative struggle – appear in various guises in the work of not only Foucault but also Jean-Francois Lyotard and other postmodernists (see, Althusser 1970/1977, for a concise summary of his work). Similarly, a central theme of the "mature" Foucault (1976/1978: 100), "that knowledge and power are joined together," would not sit out of place in any of Althusser's later works.

Given the similarities between Foucault's work and that of not only Althusser but also the so-called Frankfurt School of neo-Marxism (Herbert Marcuse, Jürgen Habermas, Max Horkheimer, Theodor Adorno) – similarities that often cause critics to wrongly dismiss postmodernism as just another form of Marxism – what explains Foucault's profound and continuing influence? Arguably, the key factor in Foucault's enduring influence – obtained despite the often sloppy nature of his empirical research, and his typically convoluted and opaque writing style – is found in his willingness to see power and oppression in terms that went far beyond the Marxist class-based approach. Instead, the concept of exclusion is made the center point for Foucault's analysis. According to Foucault, exclusion was, moreover, largely based on unwritten cultural and social mores rather than class or work-based relations; mores that oppressed women, racial, and religious minorities, homosexuals, and the mad as well as those possessed of a generally nonconformist orientation. Everywhere, Foucault (1975/1991: 308; 1976/1978: 145) suggested, modernity had created a humanity surrounded by "institutions of repression, rejection, exclusion, marginalization"; institutions that subject all those whose behaviour runs counter to society's "power of normalization" to "infinitesimal surveillances, permanent controls, extremely meticulous orderings of space." In contrast to Marxists, Foucault (1976/1978: 92–94) linked oppressive "power" *not* to "a general system" but instead to a myriad of manifestations where oppressive power is "everywhere," "exercised from innumerable points." In all such circumstances, oppression – be it physical or psychological – is grounded in the discourses that legitimize power and compel obedience. This means, Foucault (1976/1978: 85) continued, that, "All the modes of domination, submission, and subjugation are ultimately reduced to the effect of obedience." This Orwellian conclusion also means that disobedience can only manifest itself in significant form if it too is grounded in discourse. Fortunately, Foucault (1976/1978: 95–96) would have readers believe, points of resistance – and alternative discourses – are also found "everywhere," producing "swarm points" that traverse "social stratifications," "fracturing unities."

In one of the earliest reflections in the English-speaking world upon Foucault's work, Hayden White (1973: 50), who was himself to become one of the dominant postmodernist theorists, observed that Foucault's work represented "a continuation" of the romantic and idealist opposition to modernization that found its fullest expression in the work of "Nietzsche in the last quarter of the nineteenth century." To the novice reader, however, the connection between Foucault's later work, marked by calls for resistance to all forms of micro-power, and Nietzsche is by no means obvious. This is, after all, a philosopher whose disdain for common humanity was all-pervasive, declaring variously that "liberal institutions" only benefit "the herd animal" (Nietzsche 1889/1990: 103); that we should not "write history from the standpoint of the masses" who are "the lowest clay and loam layers of society" (Nietzsche 1874: 39); "that evil is man's best strength. Men must grow better and more evil" (Nietzsche 1883/1970: 39). There are, nevertheless, three aspects of Nietzsche's work that make him not only postmodernism's natural progenitor but also a key figure in Western philosophy more generally. First, prior to Nietzsche, idealist philosophy – which gave primacy to matters relating to consciousness and spirit rather than material circumstance – was invariably espoused by those with a religious bent. George Berkeley, for example, who articulated the most radical and far-reaching form of idealist philosophy in his *Principles of Human Knowledge* – in which he declared that the only thing we could be certain of was our own "ideas" created by what we "call mind, spirit, soul" (Berkeley 1710/1996: 24) – was a Bishop in the episcopalian Church of Ireland. Georg Hegel (1837/1962: 36), a dominant figure in German idealist thought, believed that "the History of the World" was subject to God's divine plan; a plan that "philosophy strives to comprehend." With Nietzsche, however, these religious underpinnings are decisively rejected. Not only was Nietzsche's thinking utterly secular, it also regarded all forms of religion – but most particularly Christianity – with complete hostility. "From the start," Nietzsche (1886/1989: 60–61) wrote in *Beyond Good and Evil*, "the Christian faith" has entailed "a sacrifice of all freedom, all pride, all self-confidence of the spirit; at the same time, enslavement and self-mockery."

Having cut idealist philosophy from its religious moorings, Nietzsche also differed from his idealist forebears in approaching matters relating to evidence, proof, truth, and the like with studied indifference rather than the thoughtful skepticism that had characterized the work of Berkeley (1710/1996) and Descartes (1641/1991). In Nietzsche's view, what counted in research was not whether an argument was based on fact or illusion but rather how it can be used as a spur to action. For "all great things," Nietzsche (1874: 28) observed, "never succeed without some delusion." As most readers would be aware, the Nietzschean disregard for the borders that separate fact and fancy is now one of the characteristic features of postmodernism. "Truth and knowledge, from the Foucauldian perspective" – so Mckinlay and Starkey (1998: 1) advise – are not objective categories but are instead merely the "weapons by which a society manages itself." More recently, the authors of one of the lead articles in *The Routledge Companion to Management and Organizational History*, similarly announced their rejection of "positivist factual truth-claims" (Novecivic et al. 2015: 13). Elsewhere, in the *Academy of Management Review* – one of the most prestigious in management academia – we are informed that, "Objectivist history" (i.e., one guided by facts) "is clearly inimical to the kind of reflexivity that would be required to counter the impositionist objection" (i.e., one based on factual evidence) "to narrative" that has a "literary" or "fictive" emphasis (Rowlinson et al. 2014: 254).

The third and arguably most significant Nietzschean contribution to postmodernism – and indeed to philosophical and political thought more generally – is found in its unrivalled emphasis on individual will, consciousness, and identity. In Nietzsche's (1889/1990: 59–60) view, the only factor of note in any human endeavor – be it politics, economics, or war – is the individual human will. Every other explanation represents "a false causality"; a falsehood that seeks to not only deny the power of individual will but also constrain it. Accordingly, there is nothing more important, Nietzsche (1883/1970: 62) argued that "the Self" which, if unencumbered by morality and other societal restrictions, "subdues, conquers, destroys" all before it. Among the many evils that Nietzsche (1895/1990: 127) saw as imposing unnecessary constrains on the individual, "will to power" was the idea of "progress," which he condemned as "a modern idea," a "false idea." Due to the stultifying effects of industrialization, urbanization, and "higher education," Nietzsche concluded (1889/1990: 105, 67) the mass of the population across the "entire West" had been stripped of their spiritual freedom, being "weakened" and reduced to the status of "sickly beasts." Only by rejecting all of the institutional constraints of modern society – democracy, religion, morality, liberalism – could the individual "will to power" be revived (Nietzsche 1889/1990: 75, 103; 1883/1970: 137).

As with his studied disregard for the concept of truth, Nietzsche's hostility to societal restraints on individual being and will has become central to postmodernist canon. Like Nietzsche, Foucault (1976/1978: 140) in the first volume of his *The History of Sexuality*, also linked the advance of industrialization and modernization with "an explosion of numerous and diverse techniques for achieving the subjugation of bodies and the control of populations." Like Nietzsche, Foucault (1976/1978: 143) associated the West's material progress with a curtailment of identity and spirit.

Whereas for "millennia" the human "living animal" had voluntarily come together in "a political existence," it was now the case that the mechanism of political power placed "existence as a living being in question." Central to these new mechanisms of control was what Foucault (1976/1978: 141) referred to as the harnessing of "bio-power" (i.e., the manipulation and control of sexuality and psychic identity) and its "controlled insertion" into "the machinery of production." Such mechanisms of oppression, so Foucault would have us believe, effected the rich at least as much as the poor. Indeed, Foucault (1976/1978: 120) argued, it was "the economically privileged and politically dominant class" which first suffered the effects of the new "rigorous techniques" for control of being and identity.

Although there is no gainsaying the fact that Foucault was by the early 1970s a clear and obvious disciple of Nietzsche, it is also evident that his embrace of Nietzschean principles was restricted by his ingrained "quasi-structuralist" modes of thought. Whereas Nietzsche regarded any commitment to truth and evidence with disdain, Foucault espoused contradictory positions. On the one hand, he argued that "knowledge" and understanding emerged not from experience, from an objective and verifiable reality, but from "discursive formations" that expressed the views and prejudices of particular social groups (Foucault 1969/1972: 32–33). Conversely, he also argued in favor of "starting from historical facts" (Foucault 1976/1978: 13). That the latter view was not an idle slip is indicated by his bitter – and detailed – refutation of Derrida's "deconstructionist" approach in 1972. In this repudiation, Foucault (1972b/2001: 575–576) rejected with scorn the idea that "all knowledge" and "all rational discourse" had to be reinterpreted through a philosophic lens. Instead, Foucault (1972b/2001: 576–577) emphasized how his research, through a long series of careful empirical investigations, had demonstrated that there are always "conditions and rules for the formation of knowledge"; rules to which "any philosophical discourse is subject." Seen from a Nietzschean perspective, the problem with this view is that it accepted as an inevitable part of the human condition the restraints that Nietzsche saw as crippling for the individual "will to power."

If Foucault's "quasi-structuralist" intellectual baggage restricted his embrace of Nietzsche's precepts, such restrictions did not impede Hayden White, whose 1973 study *Metahistory* can claim a level of influence within postmodernist canon that rivals anything penned by Foucault himself. Writing in 1989, Ankersmit (1989: 142) declared White's *Metahistory* to be "the most revolutionary book in the history of philosophy over the past twenty-five years." Almost a decade later, Brian Fay (1998: 1) declared that through White's understandings "an entire generation of historians was educated to theory and metatheory in a way no previous generation was." Similarly, in 2012 the critical management theorists, Gabrielle Durepos and Albert Mills (2012: 84), declared that – although Foucault "broadly influenced cultural theorists" – White was profoundly responsible for "redirecting scholars from a focus on *truth* toward a postmodernist emphasis on the socially constructed nature of the *historical* form."

Unlike the contradictory positions espoused by Foucault, White's Nietzschean break from the idea of verifiable truth was to become a consistent theme in his work. In his most influential study, *Metahistory*, for example, White (1976:

372–373) declared that the objective in any narrative should be to dissolve "the authority of all the inherited ways of conceiving." Consequently, he continued, "Historical representation becomes once more all story, no plot, no explanation, no ideological implication at all – that is to say, 'myth.'" The only problem, White (1980: 10) argued in a subsequent study, comes when one treats "real events" as if they had some objective truth. Instead, we need to dismiss the idea that there is a "distinction between real and imaginary events." Accordingly, we need to think of the "real" as simply "referents" in a discourse, something that is "spoken about" but not allowed to dominate the story (White 1980: 8). By pursuing this path, White (2005: 333) later advised, "history"– and by implication other social sciences – can be transformed into "a place of fantasy" where any outcome is possible. If forced to choose between two competing discourses, we are, therefore, best guided not by which of the two is more accurate but rather by "ethical" or "moral" judgments (White 1973: 26, xii). By creating this morally superior "illusionary world," White (1973: 371) urged authors to initiate "a process in which the weak vie with the strong for the authority to determine how this second [illusionary] world will be characterized."

If White and his intellectual heirs among today's postmodernists clearly owe a debt to Nietzsche the key to White's success lay in marrying a Neitzschean conceptual framework with a narrative style that self-consciously reflects the influence of the eighteenth century idealist philosopher, Giambattista Vico. As we noted in the introduction to this chapter, Vico (1744/1968: 120) argued that prior to the numbing effects of civilization, people possessed "vast imagination"; an imagination that was "entirely immersed in the senses, buffeted by the passions." In this primeval state, humanity produced "sublime" poetic fables, of which Homer's the *Iliad* was "first in the order of merit." As civilization advanced, Vico (1744/1968: 128) argued, all that was left were literary "tropes" and "metaphors" that provided a remnant existence of an older, more spiritual way of perceiving the world. Such "tropes" and "metaphors" were, therefore, not "ingenious inventions" of writers but were instead an inherited link to "the first poetic nations" (Vico 1744/1968: 131). By strengthening the role of "metaphor" in language we could, so Vico (1744/1968: 118) believed, recapture something of the "vast imagination" that civilization had stripped from us.

All of Vico's conceptualizations were embraced by White, subsequently becoming part of the postmodernist mainstream. According to White (1973: x), the researcher who constructs a narrative should perceive their study not as a work of science but rather as "an essentially *poetic* act" [emphasis in original]. Further, as the purpose of such research is *primarily* inspirational, it must have as its main focus "felt needs and aspirations that are ultimately personal" (White 1973: 283); a suggestion that leads towards narratives built around personal experiences premised on racial, religious, sexual, and social identity. White's concepts were also notable in contributing to a postmodernist displacement of the "Scientific Attitude" with the so-called Rhetorical Attitude; or what Alvesson and Kärreman (2000:144–145) refer to as "grounded fictionalism." Associated with what is variously referred to as the "linguistic" or "discursive" turn in the social sciences, the "Rhetorical Attitude" perceives all knowledge as essentially ideology, mere devices for both maintaining and challenging power.

The idea that there is no objective reality appears to have merit as long as one deals with abstractions. It collapses when one is faced with matters of indisputable fact such as the Holocaust of World War II that saw millions die in Nazi death camps. The problems that such historical events cause for the historical relativism of White was demonstrated when one of his adherents, Hans Kellner (1994: 140), published an article in *History and Theory* that concluded that the Holocaust, "like all historical events ...was an imaginative creation," that events at Babi Yar (a Ukrainian gully where thousands of Jews were executed) and Wannsee (the site where Nazi officials decided upon the "Final Solution") had no meaning until "they were imaginatively constituted." Though certain individuals may have witnessed horrors, Kellner (1994: 132) continued, "no one witnessed the Holocaust" as this concept was only a post-event literary imposition. In responding to Kellner's points, White (1994: 52) side-stepped the epistemological issues raised, arguing that the Holocaust was a problem of "modernism" and that "the best way to represent the Holocaust and the experience of it may well be a kind of 'intransitive writing'" (i.e., writing that does not have a direct object). In taking the stance he did, however, Kellner was – as he correctly observed – operating in accord with well-established postmodernist principles. If one was to make a "special" case for accepting accounts of the Holocaust as objective, Kellner (1994: 139) noted, then why would researchers not extend exception to all other historical occurrences?

Modernity and Postmodernism: From Rousseau to Lyotard

Although the term "postmodernism" has become associated with a whole body of knowledge that is critical of modernity, in its original meaning – as articulated by Jean-François Lyotard (1986) in *The Postmodern Condition* – the term referred to humanity's current condition. In this study, and in his subsequent *The Inhuman* (Lyotard 1991), Lyotard associated postmodernity with transformations that exacerbated detrimental trends that had been initiated by the launch of the Industrial Revolution in the eighteenth century. With the mechanization and "computerization" of virtually every aspect of employment and work, Lyotard (1986: 63, 51) argued, the mass of the workforce had become subject to a regime of "terror," ruled by "technocrats" who oversaw a "dehumanizing process" in which those who cannot speak the idioms of science are economically excluded. With the "generalized computerization of society," moreover, even previously autonomous "institutions of higher learning" (Lyotard 1991: 5) found themselves within the maw of an oppressive "performativity principle." Although, Lyotard (1986: 47) argued, capitalism had historically legitimized itself by promising liberation "through science and technology," this process is accentuated in the postmodern condition as ever increasing "efficiency" provides a "self-legitimizing" circularity; a process in which the successful achievement of improved efficiency only encourages a greater emphasis on efficiency.

28 The Intellectual Origins of Postmodernism

Part of reasons for the success of postmodernism and its depiction of the process of modernization as one of human degradation is that it resonates with a long tradition of literature and thought: a tradition that can be traced back through Nietzsche, the English Romantic movement and others to the dawn of the Industrial Revolution. Many of those images evoked by this tradition still maintain their hold over our imagination. As readers would be well aware, Mary Shelley's *Frankenstein*, although first published in 1818, remains a Hollywood favorite. In this tale of warning the young Swiss scientist, Victor Frankenstein, falls under the thrall of science's promise after his chemistry lecturer declares that "modern" scientists had obtained the key that enabled them to "penetrate into the recesses of nature, and show how she works in her hiding-places ... They have acquired new and almost unlimited powers; they can command the thunder of heaven, mimic the earthquake" (Shelley 1818/2005: 49). If we move further back in time to the opening decades of the Industrial Revolution, William Blake's (1796: 12) *Songs of Innocence and Experience*, first published in 1794, confronts us with the image of dark Satanic mills and of "thousands of [chimney] sweepers ... all of them locked up in coffins of black."

In the long tradition of literary and philosophic opposition to the process of modernization from which postmodernism draws sustenance it is arguably the case that the most powerful critiques stem from the work of the pre-revolutionary French political philosopher, Jean-Jacques Rousseau. Although Rousseau (1762/1950: 1) is best known for the opening words of his *The Social Contract*, where he observed that, "Man is born free, and he is everywhere in chains" from the beginning to end of his career he also remained a powerful opponent of modernization with its cities, factories, and new modes of work. In his early *A Discourse on the Arts and Sciences*, Rousseau (1750/1950: 146, 172) cast scorn on the view that the "miracles" of science and associated technological progress added "to our happiness." Five years later, in *A Discourse on the Origin of Inequality*, Rousseau (1755/1950: 215–216) argued that a "natural state" – whereby humanity lived a "rustic" life where people "were satisfied with clothes made of the skins of animals" – was "altogether the very best man could experience." By contrast, Rousseau regarded the increased urbanization that industrialization entailed with a mixture of disdain and horror. "Cities are the abyss of the human species," Rousseau (1762/1979: 59) declared in his greatest work, *Emile*, where he added that, "Men are not made to be crowded into anthills ... The more they come together, the more they are corrupted." Rousseau also regarded the expanded use of new technologies and machines with particular concern, observing (Rousseau 1762/1979: 176–177) that, "By dint of gathering machines around us" that were ever "more ingenious" so it is that "the cruder and more maladroit our organs become."

Among all of the developments which Rousseau observed in association with the nascent industrialization of his times, it was, however, the division of labor that caused him greatest concern. "Do you not see that in working" a laborer "exclusively for one station," Rousseau (1762/1979: 194) asked his readers, that "you are making him useless for any other," If employers and society continued down this path with regard to the division of labor, Rousseau (1762/1979: 194) prophetically warned, society would find itself "in a state of crisis" and an "age of revolutions."

As is self-evident, not only was it the case that Rousseau's warnings with regard to the increased division of labor fell on deaf ears, so it was that this mode of work organization became the cornerstone of industrial and managerial advance, Adam Smith (1776/1999: Book 1, Chap. 1, para. 1) famously opening *The Wealth of Nations* with the observation that: "The greatest improvement in the productive powers of labour ... seem to have been [caused by] the effects of the division of labour." With Frederick Taylor and his famed (or infamous depending on your viewpoint) *The Principles of Scientific Management*, conceptualizations relating to the division of labor were incorporated into an integrated system of management around Taylor's (1911/1967: 25) maxim that – for each task – management had to decide upon and implement the "one best method" For many in business and management, Taylor's precept opened the door to increased prosperity and shorter hours of work, the noted manager researcher, Peter Drucker (1955/1968: 337) declaring "scientific management" to be one of "the most lasting contributions that America has made to Western thought." For at least equal numbers, however, the division of labor and increased managerial control of the work process has been perceived in Rousseau-like terms. Elton Mayo (1933: 165, 172), for example, widely regarded as the founding figure of the discipline of human resource management, warned that the "modern condition" often manifested itself in "social disorganization," "personal maladjustment," and a sense of "personal futility." Similarly, in a work subtitled *The Degradation of Work in the Twentieth Century*, Harry Braverman (1974: 120–121) – in effectively gave birth to the subdiscipline of "labor process theory" – declared that "Modern management," having "come into being" with Frederick Taylor and his "principles of scientific management," worked to reduce individuals "to the level of general and undifferentiated labor power."

Given the long history of concern that the embrace of the division of labor and workplace efficiency as primary goals is leading society – as Rousseau warned – into "an abyss," a perpetual "state of crisis," so it is that many postmodernists in management and organization studies boast previous academic careers in "labor process theory"; figures who include Mick Rowlinson (co-founder of the journal, *Management & Organizational History*), Rowlinson's frequent co-author, John Hassard, Stewart Clegg and Gibson Burrell (see, for example, Rowlinson 2015: 70–80). Accordingly, what we see in their work is a merging of the Rousseau/Braverman hostility to the division of labor with a Nietzschean/Foucauldian/Lyotardian belief that retrograde developments in the realm of work correspond to an increase in oppressive societal arrangements more generally. As Clegg (1998: 36) explained, "control via discipline first develops not in the factory, but in the various state institutions. Capitalists masters adopt it from prison masters, from beadles, and superintendents of asylums." For Rowlinson and Carter (2002: 540), the detrimental effects of the system of disciplinary control are found not just in the performance of workplace tasks but also in the "boring and shitty bureaucratic organizations" in which most of use spend our active lives. In the view of Burrell (1997: 139), the Nazi concentrations are just but an extreme if logical extension of the deeply embedded systems of disciplinary control that characterize our world. In consequence, Burrell (1998: 21) subsequently continued, "the despotic character of the disciplinary mode of domination is built into the heart, the essence of contemporary society and affects the body of the individual, of whatever class, at the minutest level."

There is no doubt, as the postmodernist theorists in management and organizational studies assert, that power and disciplinary control are an integral part of modern life, just as they were in previous epochs. It is also indubitably the case that many of these manifestations are objectionable to any right-thinking person. What is generally overlooked in the postmodernist depictions of disciplinary power and oppression, however, is the fact that repressive arrangements are very poor substitutes for the societal and workplace cooperation that is the true bedrock of our industrial world. Even if we turn to Frederick Taylor's (1911/1967: 26) *The Principles of Scientific Management*, a work which arguably puts the most forceful case for the "division of labor," it is evident that Taylor saw employee-management cooperation as laying at the heart of any system of productivity improvements, observing that, "close, intimate, personal cooperation between management and the man is of the essence of modern scientific or task management." It would also appear no accident that the successful advance of firms and societies since the dawn of the Industrial Revolution has been associated not only with market-based economies but also a flourishing of democracy, an extension of individual rights and freedoms, and the legislation of a whole system of employee protections in terms of bargaining rights, health and safety, working conditions, and the like. Conversely, those societies that have sought to entrench economic expansion through systems of totalitarian control and various forms of unfree labor – Nazi Germany, Franco's Spain, the Soviet Union – have proven ignoble failures. In short, rather than it being the case that disciplinary control is the key factor in our world, it is the reverse that appears to apply: the organizations and societies that boast the greatest degree of success are those able to garner the active cooperation and engagement of their citizens and employees.

If we need to be wary of accepting the view that disciplinary control and oppression are the distinguishing features of our time, we should also avoid unduly romanticizing the pre-industrial world which Rousseau held in such high regard. Admittedly, part of the greatness of Rousseau as a thinker is that in defending a "rustic" existence he freely acknowledged the costs that this entailed. Accepting sickness and premature death as a natural condition of existence, Rousseau argued against the use of science and medicine to mitigate the effects of disease. "Medicine," by offering succor to the weak, also merely revealed itself – in Rousseau's (1762/1979: 54) opinion – as "an art more pernicious to men than all the ills it can cure." It was, moreover, a crime against society to provide an education to "a sickly and ill-considered child," as money spent on such an individual would merely result in "doubling society's loss" (Rousseau 1762/1979: 53). Rousseau, in other words, clearly understands what life in a pre-industrial society entailed. It was, as Thomas Hobbes (1651/2002: 62) in England famously observed, "solitary, poor, nasty, brutish, and short." This is the world that technology, science, the division of labor, and managerial endeavor have rescued us from.

Conclusion

Much of the success of postmodernism can be attributed to the fact that it draws on deep intellectual roots; intellectual roots which have long expressed disquiet at the processes of modernization and industrialization. Moreover, in its most radical "poststructuralist" or "de-constructionist" form – associated with Emmanuel Levinas, Roland Barthes, and Jacques Derrida – postmodernism challenges not only the legitimacy of modern industrial society but also the entire fabric of Western language and thought. In terms of language, it takes umbrage with the idea, espoused since Plato's *Phaedrus*, that written language is a mere shadow or representation of verbal speech. Hostility is also announced to the precepts of the Swiss linguist, de Saussure (1915/1974: 15), who argued that for a linguistic group (i.e., English speakers, French speakers) language is a "social institution," bound by rules that individuals cannot readily disregard. In rejecting such views for being embodiments of the "phonocentric" and "logocentric" traditions of Western thought, post-structuralists – drawing on the idealist philosophies of Edmund Husserl (1913/1983) and Martin Heidegger (1926/1962) – argue that Western language and thought have been based around a process of exclusion. In writing, however, so it is asserted (Heidegger 1926/1962: 29; Levinas 1957/1987: 103; Derrida 1967/2001: 66), "traces" can be detected of lost voices; voices that represent the remnant existence of those consciously or unconsciously excluded from the historical record. By contrast, Michel Foucault was not interested in the supposed presence of historical remnants within written texts. Indeed, he rejected the whole "deconstructionist" mode of thinking espoused by Derrida and his co-thinkers. In his (Foucault 1972b/2001: 569) view, the so-called discovery of remnant "traces" in written texts amounted to nothing more than a spurious "invention of voices behind the text."

In contrast to Derrida, what Foucault was interested in was the relationship between power and knowledge *in the present*. For Foucault (1969/1972: 24), not only was it the case that power and knowledge were expressed through *epistemes* (i.e., the ideas that pervade a whole society or epoch) and/or discourse (i.e., the ideas shared by a group and which give it its social and political integrity and legitimacy), these manifestations had to always be understood "as and when" they occur. What needs to be emphasized at this point is that for Foucault the key focus is *not* – as it is with Derrida – text or the individual subject. Rather, it is the *discourse*, the set of *rules* for language and knowledge through which individuals obtain their intellectual frameworks and understandings. In other words, Foucault is *not* interested in textual deconstruction (as Derrida was) but rather with larger social "discourses." This means, for example, that a Foucauldian analysis of the "discourses" that I am involved in as a business academic and management historian would primarily concern itself with the common understandings and concerns that shape debates in those disciplines, i.e., profit, efficiency, organizational structure, business strategy.

As Foucault's thinking evolved so it was that his interest increasingly shifted towards how power manifested itself in "micro-forms," in the myriad of oppressions and systems of inequality that supposedly characterize our lives. In this, Foucault – as with Hayden White and much of the wider body of postmodernist thought – increasingly drew inspiration from the idealist philosophy of Friedrich Nietzsche; a philosopher who advocated an overriding concern with individuality, with "Self" and with what he referred to as the individual "will to power" (Nietzsche 1883/1970: 137). Such was Nietzsche's concern with individual will and self that he readily abandoned all and any commitment to the ideas of truth, morality, objectivity, and impartiality. What counted was not whether something was true or not but the purpose for which the information or narrative was used; or, as he (Nietzsche 1895/1990: 187), bluntly put it, "to what end a lie is told." As we have explored in the latter half of this introductory chapter, this emphasis on the purpose to which a narrative is told – and a willingness to embrace the "fictive" to support an argument – became a defining characteristic of the work of White and his intellectual heirs.

Postmodernism is, therefore, not a single strand of thought. It is, instead, made up of competing and often contradictory lines of thinking, each of which draws on different bodies of idealist philosophy. There are, however, three things that not only give unity to postmodernism but which do much to explain its success. First, postmodernism – in its various strands – places issues relating to exclusion at the center of its analysis. For Derrida and deconstructionists, the battle against exclusion involves the rescue of lost voices from language. For Foucault (1976/1978: 94), it involves confronting inequalities of power wherever they manifest themselves; a task that necessarily entails the manufacture of competing discourses. The second understanding that unites postmodernism is the idea that research and inquiry entails a "horizontality" of focus. In other words, one is not interested in finding some new fact or piece of information. Instead, one is primarily interested in exposing how existing texts and/or discourses entrench inequality and oppression. For there is no such thing as an objective fact. Instead, facts obtain the meaning from either textual interpretation (the deconstructionist view) or from discourse (the Foucauldian view). The third unifying element is a deep hostility to mechanization and industrialization; a hostility that can be traced back through Nietzsche to Jean-Jacques Rousseau. For Derrida (1967/1976: 85), the need to purge language of its "logocentric" inheritance is necessitated by the fact that this language now embodies the "oppression" of the "technical and scientific economy." Similarly, for Foucault (1976/1978: 89) the advance of modern industrial society was utterly retrograde, bringing with it "new mechanisms of power" that "are employed on all levels and in forms that go beyond the state and its apparatus, reaching down into every aspect of individual existence."

If the unity of postmodernist thought around a set of core principles, and the fact that those principles draw on a long intellectual heritage, does much to explain its success, it is nevertheless this author's view that all of its core understandings are flawed. Yes, exclusion and inequality still characterize our world. Yet it is also true, as we have emphasized on a number of occasions throughout this chapter that societal and organizational success since the dawn of the Industrial Revolution has been associated with engagement rather than exclusion. A literate population emerged in lieu of an illiterate one because the new factories and trading companies could not survive and grow without an educated workforce. For the first time, the mass of the female population had realistic opportunities for advancement outside the household hearth. In economies across the globe today, the percentage of females in paid employment is at an historic peak. Discrimination on the basis of religion or race is outlawed. A man of color has served as President of the world's most economically and politically significant nation. In every Western economy, workers are guaranteed fundamental rights in terms of their employment; rights that include the ability to form unions, to bargain, to obtain an enforceable minimum wage for the labor. To ignore such historic gains, to ignore the importance of engagement in our businesses and societies, is to willfully overlook the most fundamental feature of our world. To assume that all knowledge is mere discourse and textual invention is also only possible through willful oversight. Yes, there is a whole body of evidence that is "secondary" in that it indicates a particular perspective to the exclusion of others; evidence that includes business and labor archives, newpapers, journals, and the like. There is, however, a second type of evidence that is grounded in objective material conditions of existence; evidence that records, as we have previously noted, production and employment figures, hospital admissions, births and deaths, etc. If our "secondary" sources of evidence – most particularly in business and management – are to have credence than there should be a correspondence between this type of evidence and the latter. It is also the case that modernization and industrialization have entailed far more benefits than costs. No longer is it the case, as Rousseau (1762/1979: 47) observed in the mid-eighteenth century, that, "Half the children born perish before the first year." Nor is it the case, as Hobbes (1651/2002: 62) observed in the mid-seventeenth century, that life is any more "solitary, poor, nasty, brutish, and short." Fortunately, despite postmodernist objections to the perceived oppressions and exclusions of our world, such experiences are now increasingly a thing of distant memory.

Cross-References

▶ Debates within Management History
▶ Intellectual Enlightenment: The Epistemological Foundations of Business Endeavor
▶ What Is Management?

References

Althusser L (1970/1977) Ideology and ideological state apparatus. Louis Althusser L, Lenin and philosophy and other essays. New Left Books, London, pp 85–136
Alvesson M, Kärreman D (2000) Taking the linguistic turn in organizational research. J Appl Behav Sci 36(2):136–158
Ankersmit FR (1989) Historiography and postmodernism. Hist Theory 28(2):137–153
Ankersmit FR (1990) Reply to professor Zagorin. Hist Theory 29(3):137–153
Barthes R (1966/1987) Criticism and truth. University of Minnesota Press, Minneapolis
Barthes R (1984/1986) The rustle of language. Basil Blackwell, Oxford, UK
Berkeley G (1710/1996) The principles of human knowledge. In: Berkeley G, Robinson H (eds) Principles of human knowledge and three dialogues. Oxford University Press, Oxford, UK, pp 1–96

Blake W (1796) Songs of innocence and experience. British Library Online. https://www.bl.uk/works/songs-of-innocence-and-experience#. Accessed 22 Feb 2018

Braverman H (1974) Labor and monopoly capital: the degradation of work in the twentieth century. Monthly Review Press, New York

Bucheli M, Whadwhani D (eds) (2013) Organizations in time: history, theory and methods. Oxford University Press, Oxford

Bunge M (1996) In praise of intolerance to charlatanism in academia. In: Gross PR, Levitt N, Lewis MW (eds) The flight from science and reason. New York Academy of Sciences, New York, pp 96–115

Burrell G (1997) Pandemonium: towards a retro-organization theory. Sage, London

Burrell G (1998) Modernism, postmodernism and organizational analysis: the contribution of Michael Foucault. In: McKinlay A, Starkey K (eds) Foucault and organizational theory. Sage, London, pp 14–28

Clegg S (1998) Foucault, power and organization. In: McKinlay A, Starkey K (eds) Foucault and organizational theory. Sage, London, pp 14–28

Croce B (1915/1921) Theory and history of historiography (trans. Ainslie D). George G Harrap & Co., London

Cummings S, Bridgman T, Hassard J, Rowlinson M (2017) A new history of management. Cambridge University Press, Cambridge, UK

Curthoys A, McGrath A (2009) Introduction. In: Curthoys A, McGrath A (eds) Writing histories: imagination and narration. Monash University ePress, Melbourne, pp. 8–16.

de Saussure F (1915/1974) Course in general linguistics. Fontana Collins, New York

Derrida J (1967/1976) Of grammatology. John Hopkins University Press, Baltimore

Derrida J (1967/2001) Writing and difference. Routledge and Kegan Paul, London/New York

Descartes D (1641/1991) Meditations on first philosophy. Internet encyclopaedia. http://selfpace.uconn.edu/class/percep/DescartesMeditations.pdf. Accessed 2 Feb 2018

Drucker P (1955/1968) The practice of management. Pan Books, London

Durepos GAT, Mills AJ (2012) ANTi-history: theorizing the past, history, and historiography in management and organization studies. Information Age Publishing, Charlotte

Fay B (1998) The linguistic turn and beyond in contemporary theory of history. In: Fay B, Pomper P, Van RT (eds) History and theory: contemporary readings. Blackwell Publishers, Oxford, pp 1–12

Foucault M (1965) Madness and civilization: a history of insanity in the age of reason. Pantheon Books, New York

Foucault M (1966/1994) The order of things: an archaeology of the human sciences. Vintage Books, New York

Foucault M (1969/1972) The archaeology of knowledge. Pantheon Books, New York

Foucault M (1972a/2001) Reply to Derrida . . . from Paideia. In: Foucault M (ed) History of madness, 2nd edn. Routledge, London, appendix II, pp 575–590

Foucault M (1972b/2001) My body, this paper, this fire. In: Foucault M (ed) History of madness, 2nd edn. Routledge, London, appendix II, pp 550–574

Foucault M (1975/1991) Discipline and punish: the birth of the prison. Vintage Books, New York

Foucault M (1976/1978) The history of sexuality – an introduction. Pantheon Books, New York

Guterres A (2017) Report of the Secretary-General on the work of the organization, 2017. United Nations, New York

Heidegger M (1926/1962) Being and time. Blackwell Publishing, London

Hegel G (1837/1962) Philosophy of history. Dover Publications, New York

Hobbes T (1651/2002) Leviathan. Broadway Press, Peterborough

Husserl E (1913/1983) Ideas pertaining to a pure phenomenology and to the phenomenological philosophy. Martinus Nijhoff Publishers, The Hague

Kellner H (1994) "Never again" is "now". Hist Theory 33(2):127–144

Levinas E (1957/1987) Meaning and sense. In: Levinas E (ed) Collected philosophical papers. Martinus Nijhoff Publishers, Dordrecht, pp 75–108

Levinas E (1987) Collected philosophical papers. Martinus Nijhoff Publishers, Dordrecht

Lyotard J-F (1986) The postmodern condition: a report on knowledge. Manchester University Press, Manchester

Lyotard J-F (1991) The inhuman. Stanford University Press, Stanford

Mayo E (1933) The human problems of an industrial civilization. The Macmillan Company, New York

Mckinlay A, Starkey K (1998) Managing Foucault: Foucault, management and organization theory. In: Mckinlay A, Starkey K (eds) Foucault, management and organization theory. Sage, London, pp 1–13

McLaren PG, Mills AG, Weatherbee T (eds) (2015) The Routledge companion to management and organizational history. Routledge, London/New York

Munslow A (1997) Deconstructing history, 2nd edn. Routledge, Abington

Nietzsche F (1874) On the use and abuse of history for life. http://la.utexas.edu/users/hcleaver/330T/350kPEENietzscheAbuseTableAll.pdf. Accessed 21 Feb 2018

Nietzsche F (1883/1970) Thus spoke Zarathustra. Penguin Books, London

Nietzsche F (1886/1989) Beyond good and evil: prelude to a philosophy of the future. Vintage Books, New York

Nietzsche F (1889/1990) Twilight of the idols. In: Nietzsche H (ed) Twilight of the idols/the anti-Christ. Penguin Classics, London, p 1

Nietzsche F (1895/1990) The anti-Christ. In: Nietzsche H (ed) Twilight of the idols/the anti-Christ. Penguin Classics, London

Novecivic MM, Jones JL, Carraher S (2015) Decentering Wren's evolution of management thought. In: McLaren PG, Mills AJ, Weatherbee T (eds) The Routledge companion to management and organizational history. Routledge, London/New York, pp 11–30

Plato (c. 370 BC/1972) Phaedrus. Cambridge University Press, Cambridge, UK

Plato (c. 380 BC/2003) The Republic. Penguin Classics, London

Ricoeur P (2004) Memory, history and forgetting. University of Chicago Press, Chicago

Rousseau J-J (1750/1950) A discourse on the arts and sciences. In: Rousseau J-J, Cole CDH (eds) The social contract and discourses. Dent & Sons, London, pp 143–174

Rousseau J-J (1755/1950) A discourse on the origin of inequality. In: Rousseau J-J, Cole CDH (eds) The social contract and discourses. Dent & Sons, London, pp 175–182

Rousseau J-J (1762/1950) The social contract. In: Rousseau J-J, Cole CDH (eds) The social contract and discourses. Dent & Sons, London, pp 1–141

Rousseau J-J (1762/1979) Emile: on education. Penguin Classics, London

Rowlinson M (2015) Revisiting the historic turn: a personal reflection. In: McLaren PG, Mills AJ, Weatherbee T (eds) The Routledge companion to management and organizational history. Routledge, London/New York, pp 70–80

Rowlinson M, Carter C (2002) Foucault and history in organization studies. Organization 9(4):527–547

Rowlinson M, Hassard J, Decker S (2014) Research strategies for organizational history: a dialogue between historical theory and organization theory. Acad Manage Rev 39(3):250–274

Shelley M (1818/2005) Frankenstein, or the modern Prometheus. Penguin Classics, London

Smith A (1776/1999) The wealth of nations. Penguin Classics, London

Taylor FW (1911/1967) The principles of scientific management. W.W. Norton, New York

Vico G (1744/1968) The new science. Third edition of 1744. Cornell University Press, Ithaca

White H (1973) Foucault decoded: notes from underground. Hist Theory 12(1):23–54

White H (1976) Metahistory: the historical imagination in nineteenth century Europe. John Hopkins University Press, Baltimore

White W (1980) The value of narrativity in the representation of reality. Crit Inq 7(1):5–27

White W (1994) Historical emplotment and the problem of truth. In: Friedlander S (ed) Probing the limits of representation. Cambridge University Press, Cambridge, UK, pp 37–53

White W (2005) The public relevance of historical studies: a reply to Dirk Moses. Hist Theory 44(3):333–338

World Bank (2017a) On-line database: indicators – agricultural and rural development. https://data.worldbank.org/topic/agriculture-and-rural-development?view=chart. Accessed 8 Nov 2017

World Bank (2017b) On-line database: world development indicators. https://data.worldbank.org/indicator/NY.GDP.PCAP.PP.KD?year_high_desc=tru. Accessed 29 Nov 2017

World Bank (2017c) On-line database: indicators – agricultural and rural development. https://data.worldbank.org/indicator/SI.POV.DDAY?end=2016&start=1981&view=chart. Accessed 8 Nov 2017

Paul-Michel Foucault: Prophet and Paradox 29

Bradley Bowden

Contents

Introduction 672
Foucault (1945–1970) 677
Foucault (1970–1978) 682
Foucault (1978–1984) 687
Conclusion 692
Cross-References 694
References 694

Abstract

Paul-Michel Foucault, better known simply as Michel Foucault, is arguably the dominant intellectual influence in Western academia, if not Western society more generally. A prophet to many, Foucault's life and work were characterized by an almost endless series of paradoxes. Claiming to speak on behalf of the marginalized and excluded members of the society, Foucault boasted a privileged existence. Graduating from France's most prestigious high school, the Lycée Henri-IV, Foucault spent almost his entire life within France's elite cultural and educational institutions. A long-time disciple of Nietzsche, Foucault nevertheless emphasized the conditions that constrain freedom rather the capacity of the will to overcome obstacles. A historian by inclination and practice, Foucault became, as Hayden White observed, "an anti-historical historian," a scholar who argued that the "will to truth" was a source of oppression. In exploring the paradoxes of Foucault's life and work, this chapter traces the development of Foucault's ideas from his entry into the Lycée Henri-IV in 1945 until his death from AIDS in 1984.

B. Bowden (✉)
Griffith Business School, Griffith University, Nathan, QLD, Australia
e-mail: b.bowden@griffith.edu.au

© The Author(s), under exclusive licence to Springer Nature Switzerland AG 2020   671
B. Bowden et al. (eds.), *The Palgrave Handbook of Management History*,
https://doi.org/10.1007/978-3-319-62114-2_78

Keywords

Foucault · Derrida · Postmodernism · Hayden White · Sartre · Camus · Existentialism · Neo-liberalism

Introduction

Paul-Michel Foucault, better known simply as Michel Foucault, is arguably the dominant intellectual influence in Western academia, if not Western society more generally.

Foucault's core understandings – that knowledge is socially constructed, that oppressive power "is exercised from innumerable points" (Foucault 1976/1978: 94), that power is exercised culturally through "procedures of exclusion" (Foucault 1970/ 1981: 52), that social order is primarily maintained by the "fundamental codes of a culture" (Foucault 1966/1994: xx), and that "it is in discourse that power and knowledge are joined together" (Foucault 1976/1978: 100) – have a deep resonance, influencing the understandings of power and personal identity of countless millions. In the discipline of management history, Cummings et al. (2017: 36–40, 333) declare that by utilizing Foucault's ideas we can create "a new, deeper history of manage-ment" and a "history that promotes big questions ... new thinking and liberating actions." Elsewhere we read that Foucault's work is key to understanding "the disciplinary mode of domination ... built into the heart, the essence of contemporary society" (Burrell 1998: 21).

A prophet to many, Foucault's life and work were characterized by an almost endless series of paradoxes. Claiming to speak on behalf of the marginalized and excluded members of society, Foucault boasted a privileged existence. A member from birth of France's *haute bourgeoisie* and the son of a prominent surgeon, Foucault followed an educational path to which few French citizens could aspire. After studying at the elite Lycée Henri-IV adjacent to the Pantheon in 1945, Foucault immediately progressed to the nation's most prestigious higher educational institu-tion school, the École Normale Supérieure. Yet, despite this privileged French education experience, Foucault constantly advised his friends that he felt uncom-fortable living in France (Rabinow 2015: 8). A product of elite educational institu-tions, Foucault's ideas also fitted into the milieu of his times. However, despite emerging from the idealist and existentialist philosophical climate of postwar Paris – and sharing a lifelong fascination with the German philosophic idealism of Edmund Husserl, Martin Heidegger, and, above all, Friedrich Nietzsche – Foucault rejected the humanist premises of Jean-Paul Sartre. Whereas Sartre (1943/1956: 30) argued in his *Being and Nothingness* that "the essence of [a] human being is suspended" in their "freedom" and that "freedom is impossible to distinguish from the being of 'human reality'," Foucault depicted the human condition as one of constant subjugation (Poster 1975: 334–335). Widely seen as central to an emergent "post-modernist" intellectual tradition, Foucault regarded others in this tradition with ill-disguised contempt. Of Jacques Derrida, Foucault (1972a/2006: 573) said that he was "the most decisive representative, in its waning light" of a discredited "pedagogy" built around "the invention of voices behind the text." As a historian, Foucault (1976/1978: 13) argued at times in "starting from historical facts that serve as guidelines for research." More frequently, Foucault advocated a Nietzschean view of history, calling for the dismantling of accepted understandings in order to bring about the "liberation of man" (Foucault 1971/1984: 88). As Hayden White (1973: 26) expressed it, Foucault was "an anti-historical historian" who wrote his version of "'history' in order to destroy it, as a discipline, as a mode of consciousness."

Like Nietzsche before him, Foucault (1966/1994: 328) rejected the idea of a guiding moral code, declaring that "For modern thought, no morality is possible." On meeting Foucault for the first time in 1971, the American linguist and social activist, Noam Chomsky, said of him, "I'd never met anyone who was so totally amoral . . .It's as if he was from a different species" (cited, Miller 1993: 201, 203). Associating sexuality "with the mechanisms of power" (Foucault 1976/1978: 147), Foucault (1977/1988: 204) also advocated greater acceptance of sexual relationships between adults and children "who consent," noting, "There are children who throw themselves at an adult at the age of ten."

A contradictory and polarizing figure, Foucault's line of reasoning, and his modes of research, frustrated even his ardent supporters. In reflecting on Foucault's (1961/1965) *Madness and Civilization: A History of Insanity in the Age of Reason* – an abridged version of his doctoral thesis and the first of Foucault's studies to be translated into English – Hayden White (1973: 38) concluded that it was "a rambling discourse" constructed from "a very limited body of data." In considering Foucault's entire lifework, Peter Miller (1993) noted that "Foucault left behind no synoptic critique of society, no system of ethics, no comprehensive theory of power, not even (current impressions to the contrary) a generally useful historical method." Among management historians, Michael Rowlinson and Chris Carter note Foucault's universal tendency to ignore other viewpoints in his work. "Reading Foucault's histories," Rowlinson and Carter (2002: 534) recorded, "one could be forgiven for thinking that his is the only interpretation, since it pretends not [to] be an interpretation."

If flaws in Foucault's work were apparent even to his supporters, his many critics – opponents found among the ranks of both postmodernist and more traditional scholars – were even more willing to point to his flaws. In the opinion of the Marxist historian, Perry Anderson (1998: 120), Foucault's intellectual frameworks hindered rather than advanced understandings of inequality by "overstretching" the concept of power to the point where it became almost meaningless. The result, Anderson (1998: 120) suggested, was "the banalization of power." In terms of historical methodology, Richard Evans (1997: 200) argued that Foucault and his disciples legitimated an intrusion of the author into the historical text "to such a degree that in some cases their presence all but obliterates the historical subject." Arguably the most devastating critique of Foucault's work – and the one that caused him the greatest personal angst – was that levelled by Jacques Derrida in a Sorbonne conference paper, entitled "The Cogito and the History of Madness," subsequently republished in Derrida's *Writing and Difference.* In critiquing Foucault's *Madness and Civilization*, Derrida (1967/2001: 49) accurately noted that:

> ... everything transpires as if Foucault knew what 'madness' means. Everything transpires as if ... an assured and rigorous precomprehension of the concept of madness ... were possible and assured ... The same kind of questions could be posed concerning the truth that runs through the book.

Not content with these insightful comments, Derrida (1967/2001: 69–70) went on to advise Foucault that his approach posited "a totalitarian and historicist style which eludes meaning and the origin of meaning."

It is certainly easy to find flaws in Foucault's work. Foucault was himself critical of some of his own key work. Of the best-selling book that first brought him to public attention – *The Order of Things* – Foucault lamented that it was "the most difficult, the most tiresome book I ever wrote" (cited, Miller 1993: 158). When, after a long delay, Foucault (1972a/2006 and 1972b/2006) responded to Derrida's criticism of *Madness and Civilization*, he largely skirted around the points that Derrida had made, engaging instead in a cutting attack of Derrida's own work. There is, however, one commonly made charge against Foucault that is misplaced, namely, the accusation that Foucault was inconsistent in his thinking, and that he "refused to retain one position for longer than the period between his last book and the next" (Burrell 1998: 15.), and that his "work was characterised by constant shifts, reversals ... and inconsistencies" (Grey 1994: 6; also see Caillat 2015: 16). In discussing Foucault's work, there is thus an almost universal tendency to talk about Foucault's "archaeological" approach or period (i.e., the ideas associated with *The Order of Things*), his "genealogical" approach or period (i.e., the ideas associated with *The Archaeology of Knowledge*), and his focus on "governmentality" (i.e., the lectures on governmentality given to the College of France) – as if each of these approaches or periods represented a fundamental rupture in Foucault's thinking. While there is no doubt that Foucault – like most researchers – shifted the *focus* of his research across his career, the tendency to compartmentalize Foucault's work does him a disservice, disguising rather than elucidating the fundamental cohesion of his work across the decades.

In one of the first and most insightful English language critiques of Foucault's works, Hayden White (1973: 47–48) made the pertinent point that Foucault did "have both a system of explanation and a theory of the transformation of reason and science, or consciousness, whether he knows it or will admit it or not." Like his existentialist and postmodernist contemporaries – Sartre, Albert Camus, Roland Barthes, Derrida – Foucault spent a significant part of his youth living under Nazi occupation, a time when much of the French population willingly threw in their lot with the totalitarian Vichy regime. In responding to these experiences, Foucault – like his existentialist and postmodernist contemporaries – was primarily concerned with the essence of individual freedom and the conditions that restricted its free and untrammeled existence. Accordingly, the issues that concerned both classical economics (i.e., Adam Smith, David Ricardo, John Stuart Mill) and Marxism – the organization of production, the efficient managerial allocation of resources, the creation of wealth, and the global nature of capitalism – were secondary or inconsequential issues for Foucault, as they were for his existentialist and postmodernist contemporaries. In exploring the individual and physic essence of human freedom, Foucault – like his existentialist and postmodernist contemporaries – was primarily guided by German philosophical idealism. Like Sartre and Derrida, Foucault found inspiration in Martin Heidegger. Reflecting on his years as a student at the Lycée Henri-IV and the École Normale Supérieure, Foucault recalled that Heidegger was for him "the essential philosopher … My entire philosophical development was determined by my reading of Heidegger" (cited, Miller 1993: 46).

Sharing many commonalities with his existentialist contemporaries, Foucault differed from them in two important regards. First, after a summer reading the works of Nietzsche in 1953, Foucault became a lifelong Nietzschean, sharing Nietzsche's belief that it is individual human will – what Nietzsche called the "will to power" – that is the decisive force in history and politics. Like Nietzsche, Foucault also came to believe that whatever empowered the individual will was good and whatever restrained it was bad. The second fundamental point where Foucault differed from Sartre and likeminded French existentialists was in seeing oppression, rather than freedom, as the common human experience; oppression enforced primarily through cultural norms and shared understandings of the past and present. As Foucault (1972c/2006: 544) explained it in an appendix to a revised edition of his study of madness, the human condition "does not begin with freedom, but with the limits and the line that cannot be crossed." Over time, Foucault shifted his focus from one supposed manifestation of physic and personal oppression to another. In *Madness and Civilization*, Foucault (1961/1965: 293) argued that "Western culture" was fundamentally retrograde in repressing accounts of "the agony" of the Marquis de Sade's victims. For, Foucault (1961/1965: 293) asks, "what desire can be contrary to nature" that "was given to man by nature itself?" Subsequently, Foucault focused on different manifestations of power and oppression – *epistemes* and the "fundamental codes of a culture" (Foucault 1966/1994: xx); "language" and "discourse" (Foucault 1976/1978: 94); the "disciplinary" society with its "infinitesimal surveillances, permanent controls, extremely meticulous orderings of space" (Foucault 1975/1991: 308); and "biopolitics" and the emergence of "a society 'with a sexuality'" (Foucault 1976/1978: 147). Nevertheless, throughout this shifting research agenda, the fundamental premise remained the same: individual freedom is trapped within oppressive cultural and epistemological norms.

A constant advocate of revolt at every level, Foucault is the personification of "The Rebel," as identified by arguably the greatest of the French existentialist thinkers, Albert Camus. Like Foucault, Camus (1951/1978: 18–19) associated rebellion with individual identity, with "the passionate affirmation" of the innermost "part" of one's "being." Where Camus differed from not only Foucault but virtually all of his existentialist contemporaries, however, was in seeing the inherent dangers of every act of rebellion, the manifest tendency of the rebel to become an intolerant exponent of their own views at their expense of others. Writing at a time when Foucault was only a recent graduate of the École Normale Supérieure, Camus was already concerned by the ascent of the perpetual rebel, the "nihilist" who claimed to oppose every form of power and oppression while remorselessly advancing their own agenda and interests. "Methods of thought which claim to give the lead to our world in the name of revolution have become, in reality," Camus (1951/1978: 246–247) lamented, "ideologies of consent and not of rebellion ... The contemporary revolution that claims to deny every value is already, in itself, a standard of judging values." Camus (1951/1978: 177) also noted the unfortunate tendency of twentieth-century rebels to use the state as an instrument of their own interests, noting that "All modern revolutions have ended in a reinforcement of the power of the State." Throughout his career, Foucault – like most of his subsequent disciples – showed a strange blindness to the authoritarian tendencies of the various rebel movements he supported. In the late 1960s and early 1970s, this blindness manifested itself in sympathy for Maoism and the Cultural Revolution, Foucault declaring in a television interview that the victory of "the proletariat" would "quite" possibly result in "a violent, dictatorial, and even bloody power. I can't see what objection one could make to this" (cited, Miller 1993: 203). Nowhere, however, was Foucault's foolhardy embrace of revolutionary movements more evident than in his attitude toward the Iranian Revolution of 1979, a revolt that Foucault covered for the Italian newspaper, *Corriere della Sera*. Where others soon identified the potential for a totalitarian Islamic state, Foucault (1979a/1988: 216, 218) perceived only "beauty," "an expression of public right," "of living the Islamic religion as a revolutionary force."

The blindness of Foucault to the totalitarian tendencies of many of the rebel causes he espoused, points to the fundamental failing in Foucauldian thinking. By assuming that oppression, rather than freedom, is the universal human condition, Foucault – unlike Thomas Hobbes, John Locke, Edmund Burke, Montesquieu, Sartre – paid little heed to the circumstances that support freedom and democracy. Yes, it is true that Foucault (1976/1978: 94) highlighted resistance to societal power, arguing that wherever "there is power, there is resistance." But resistance is not freedom. Resistance to established forms of power can come, moreover, from murderous totalitarian forces as well as from well-meaning democrats: think of the Nazis in Germany during the 1920s and 1930s, the Bolsheviks in Russia in 1917, or the ayatollahs in Iran in 1978–1979. If we thus turn our minds from oppression to freedom, and the conditions of freedom, we can make a number of pertinent observations. The first, and the one most easily overlooked, is that there has never been an enduring democracy – based on the political and social freedom of all members of the society – in any pre-industrial economy. Yes, ancient Athens pioneered not only the idea but also the practice of democracy. However, as we noted in our earlier ► Chap. 7, "Management in Antiquity: Part 1 – The Binds of Geography," Athens was also not only a slave society but an imperial tyranny. The wealth, education, and leisure that made the Athenian democracy possible rested on the slave-operated silver mines at Laurion and the tribute forcibly exacted from the Delian League. If democracy and social participation are to be made available to all members of the society, it is necessary, therefore, that the society boasts sufficient wealth to allow the ordinary citizen the leisure, the education, and the informed capacity to engage in the political process, free of the tutelage of any slave master, feudal lord or authoritarian state. For, in the final analysis, democracy and social freedom are mass phenomena, only possible when the society possesses the capacity to liberate the mass of humanity from everyday drudgery. The second pertinent point to make in reflecting upon the preconditions for freedom is that no democracy has persisted in a noncapitalist society, devoid of both the wealth-producing effect of capitalism and the diffusion of wealth and power that is its inevitable handmaiden. This is not to say that all capitalist societies are democracies. Franco's Spain, fascist Italy, and Nazi Germany were capitalist economies that were overtaken by totalitarianism. That capitalist societies *can* fall prey to totalitarianism points, however, to another failing in Foucault's understanding of power: the need for a system of checks and balances. If we look to the most successful democratic societies – Britain, Canada, Australia, New Zealand, the United States, the Scandinavian countries, the Netherlands, and Belgium – it is interesting to note how many are constitutional monarchies, societies where elected politicians are denied presidential power. Indeed, of the countries I just listed, only the United States is a republic. To be truly effective, however, checks and balances need to extend beyond politics into the very fabric of the society in the form of market competition, legal protection of person and property, freedom of movement, and the freedom of workers to choose both their occupation and employer.

If we think of the underpinnings of freedom of which Foucault seemed blissfully unaware – competition, legal protection of person and property, freedom of movement, and the capacity to choose one's employer – these are *all* attributes that I have constantly identified as defining characteristics of "modern management" throughout *The Palgrave Handbook of Management History*. For not only does modern management create the wealth that allows society's humbler members the education and leisure to participate in the political process, it also differs from management systems in both pre-industrial and totalitarian societies in being premised on the principles of freedom and respect for the individual. Yes, it is true that "modern management" is hierarchical. But its scope is not unlimited, unlike the situation that prevailed in either Stalinist Russia or Nazi Germany. Moreover, it has to constantly recruit and motivate legally free workers as a condition of its very existence. In a modern, liberal democratic society, it is thus the case that "modern management" underpins freedom rather than the system of universal oppression that Foucault perceived.

Foucault (1945–1970)

The intellectual principles that defined Foucault cannot be understood apart from the cultural and political milieu of wartime and postwar France. Unlike English-speaking nations, the French during the period of German occupation (May 1940–August 1944) suffered not only national humiliation but also a complex relationship with their occupier. While only a minority were active supporters of the pro-German Vichy regime, virtually all had to come to some sort of accommodation with the occupier. This produced among the French intellectuals who came of age during the war and its immediate aftermath a profound questioning of the nature of freedom and human existence, a questioning that occurred in an environment where things

German were manifest on every front. In this environment of German totalitarianism, the intellectual embrace of German philosophical idealism seems paradoxical. Interest in the ideas of Martin Heidegger, the disgraced philosopher who had been one of the Third Reich's most fervent intellectual supporters, appears particularly strange. There was, however, even before the war, an intellectual interest in the idealist philosophies of Husserl and Heidegger among French intellectuals opposed to fascist and totalitarian ideologies. In the late 1920s, for example, Emmanuel Levinas – a French intellectual of Jewish-Lithuanian extraction whose ideas were to profoundly influence Derrida – studied under both Husserl and Heidegger in Germany before completing his doctoral thesis on Husserl in 1930. Of this thesis, Derrida (1967/2001: 104) observed in a paper entitled, "Violence and Metaphysics: An Essay on the Thought of Emmanuel Levinas," subsequently published in *Writing and Difference*, that its insights into the work of Husserl and Heidegger brought a transformative "light" to French philosophy.

Already a legitimate source of anti-totalitarian thought prior to World War II, the philosophy of Husserl and, more particularly, Heidegger found its fullest expression in Sartre's wartime book, *Being and Nothingness* – a title which was a deliberate play on Heidegger's principal work, *Being and Time*. Whereas Heidegger (1927/1962: 161, 2919) argued that the "existentialist" essence of being or *Dasein* was the "foundation for the primordial phenomenon of truth," Sartre associated the essence of individual being with not only a search for truth but also a primordial struggle for freedom. As Sartre (1943/1956: 591) expressed it, outside of "the notions of freedom" any understandings of human existence "lose all meaning."

Sartre's humanist interpretation of Heidegger, with its emphasis on freedom and resistance as the essence of being, was clearly either an accidental or wilful misinterpretation of Heidegger's more elemental views of what he referred to as *Dasein* or "Being-in-the-world," a point that Heidegger made in repudiating Sartre's interpretation (Miller 1993: 47). Nevertheless, Sartre's work popularized not only "existentialism" but also the works of Heidegger for a whole generation whose ties to traditional beliefs were torn from their moorings by the war. As Mark Poster (1975: 73) observed, "Ex-Vichyites, youngsters from the bourgeoisie . . . the outcasts of society – these motley followers of existentialism found in the new doctrine justifications for their despair."

In coming to study in 1945 at the prestigious Lycée Henri-IV – located in close vicinity to both the Pantheon and the Sorbonne – Foucault found himself at the epicenter of the Parisian fascination with existentialism and German philosophic idealism. The "unofficial world headquarters of existentialism" was also only a few hundred meters away at the Café de Flore on the Boulevard Saint-Germain. Among his teachers at the Lycée Henri-IV, the Hegelian philosopher, Jean Hyppolite, was a noted admirer of Heidegger (Miller 1993: 40). On graduating from the Lycée Henri-IV, Foucault also came under the influence of the Marxist, Louis Althusser, who began work as a tutor at the elite École Normale Supérieure in 1948. Becoming a lifelong friend of Althusser, Foucault was persuaded to join the French Communist Party in 1950, remaining a member until 1953. Although Foucault formally broke from communism in 1953, the influence of Althusser's peculiar brand of "structural" Marxism can nevertheless be detected in Foucault's subsequent work. Like the mature Foucault, Althusser was vehemently opposed to the humanist version of both existentialism and Marxism then popular in France, arguing that by the time Marx wrote *Capital* he had abandoned the Hegelian philosophy and humanism of his youth. Like the mature Foucault, Althusser (1968/2001) also came to believe that the authority of capitalism and the modern state was primarily maintained by ideology and culture and what he called the "Ideological State Apparatus" (i.e., schools, churches, cultural institutions). Like the mature Foucault (1966/1994: xxi), who argued in *The Order of Things* that "the existence of order" is maintained by "the ordering codes" of culture, knowledge, and grammar, Althusser (1968/2001: 125) similarly believed that ruling "ideologies" were "realized" not only in "institutions" but also in the "rituals and practices" which they established.

Although Foucault's research was arguably always characterized by an underlay of Althusser's structural Marxism – Derrida (1967/2001: 69) correctly pointing to the "structuralist" underpinnings of Foucault's first significant work, *Madness and Civilization* – the masculine, proletarian world of French communism was inherently ill-suited to Foucault, a person who never hid his homosexuality. The bookish son of a well-to-do provincial surgeon from Poitiers, Foucault never spent much time in the mundane jobs that characterized the life of the typical French citizen during the 1950s. Instead, after graduating from the École Normale Supérieure, Foucault drifted between research and teaching posts before beginning his doctoral studies into mental illness, studying patients at the Hôpital de la Salpêtrière.

Amid the turmoil and dislocation of France in the 1950s – a time when France found itself in savage colonial wars in Indochina and Algeria – it is perhaps unsurprising that Foucault would find his intellectual lodestar in another troubled and bookish soul, Friedrich Nietzsche. Where Marx had placed the proletariat and the impersonal forces of economics at the center of his analysis, Nietzsche, more than any author before or since, made individual identity and the power of the human will the center of concern. In Nietzsche's (1889/1990: 97) opinion, it is delusion to think that "man" and mankind had any meaning outside "the individual." It was not economics or political institutions that were important in understanding human affairs, Nietzsche (1883/1970: 62) stated in *Thus Spoke Zarathustra*, but rather the "self," which "subdues, conquers, destroys." To reach their full potential, to transcend their current ordinariness and become a totally new expression of individual will, "the Superman," Nietzsche (1883/1970: 215; 1887/1989: 40–41) argued that the individual needed to embrace their primordial and irrational "inner core," allowing "the animal," "the beast of prey . . .to get out again." When it came to the writing of history, Nietzsche (1874: 26, 12) expressed hostility in his *On the Use and Abuse of History for Life* to history as a fact, arguing that an uninspiring, fact-based account "cripples the active man." Instead, Nietzsche (1874: 26) proclaimed, history only becomes a useful source of inspiration for the will to power when it was turned "into art work," providing "a purely artistic picture" that arouses the primeval "instincts."

A lifelong convert to Nietzschean philosophy following a summer reading his work during an Italian holiday in 1953, Foucault's (1966/1994: 322) admiration for Nietzsche was manifest in *The Order of Things*, where he recorded that "Nietzsche's thought . . .has for us for us, such a disturbing power," bringing with it "the Promise-Threat" that modern "man" – by an embrace of his primal instincts – could "be replaced by the superman."

If a Nietzschean world view informed Foucault's thinking from an early stage, his ideas were hidden from view during the 1950s. Instead, Foucault continued to follow an unsettled if privileged existence, moving between a series of diplomatic and teaching posts in Sweden, Poland, and Germany while working on his doctoral thesis on madness. Published in 1961 as *Histoire de la Folie* as part of the French doctoral submission process, Foucault's study has typically been perceived as a study written from the point of the outcast, the marginalized, and the psychologically impaired, people whose eccentricities were no longer tolerated in what Foucault called Europe's "classical Age" (i.e., c. 1400–c. 1750). Whereas Foucault (1961/1965: 10) claimed the "mad" had been an accepted part of medieval society, they now found themselves subject to what Althusser called the Ideological State Apparatus (i.e., hospitals, medical specialists, legal controls) as "madness" was constituted "as a mental illness." In emphasizing this, the most obvious argument contained within Foucault's doctoral thesis, José Barchilon (1961/1965: 7–8) advised the reader in the introduction to the abridged English translation of the thesis that Foucault had dispelled "the myth of mental illness," re-establishing "folly and unreason in their rightful place as a complex, human – too human – phenomena."

In truth, Foucault's study of madness was built more around a concern for the plight of the "sane" than the "mad," the work being underpinned by the Nietzschean belief that "modern man" had become a shadow of his former "self" in embracing rationality at the expense of irrationality, trading a trust in one's primeval instincts in favor of a belief in science. As a result of "reason's subjugation of non-reason," Foucault (1961/1965: 9) argued, people have come to "communicate and recognize each other through the merciless language of non-madness," suppressing "the lyricism of protest." In doing so, Foucault (1961/1965: 12) added, humanity had lost powerful insights into "the secret powers of the world," creating "a world without images, without positive character." Also lost was an appreciation of "the strange contradiction of human appetites: the complicity of desire and murder, of cruelty and the longing to suffer, of sovereignty and slavery" (Foucault 1961/1965: 221). Whereas others had found in the writings of the Marquis de Sade – an incorrigible rapist and sadist – evidence of insanity, Foucault (1961/1965: 221) claimed that "Sadism . . .is a massive cultural fact" and that through de Sade's "words of unreason . . .man discovers a truth he has forgotten." Only by embracing the views and behaviors of those dismissed as mad, Foucault (1961/1965: 293) concluded, was humanity capable of "rediscovering the secret of unreason's nothingness."

Foucault (1972c/2006: 542), in writing an appendix to the second edition of his study of insanity, published as *History of Madness*, recorded that the key to understanding any society was found in "the relationship of the culture to the very thing that it excludes." While societal prohibitions on "forbidden acts," including acts of "madness," were "familiar" to most, Foucault (1972c/2006: 544) continued, less "understood" were "the organization of prohibitions in language," in the ways we both understand the world and communicate our understandings to others. It was to this supposed problem that Foucault devoted his attentions during the 1960s, his efforts finding expression in arguably his two most significant works, *The Order of Things* and *The Archaeology of Knowledge*. In pursuing these endeavors, Foucault boasted a more academically secure if still unstable personal situation. Commuting once a week from his Paris residence to a full-time position at the University of Clermont-Ferrand between 1960 and 1966, in 1966, Foucault accepted a position at the University of Tunis, returning to Paris when – in an act of inexplicable madness – the Gaullist government appointed him Head of the Department of Philosophy at an experimental campus at Vincennes. Even before the new campus formally opened its doors, in January 1969 Foucault joined an occupation of the rector's office by Maoist-aligned students, throwing bricks at the police from a rooftop vantage point. Never destined to end well, the certifications for Foucault's degree program were officially withdrawn after one of his staff, Judith Miller, began handing out degrees to passing strangers along with the observation that "the university is a figment of capitalist society" (cited, Miller 1993: 180).

In pursuing studies of language, Foucault was in part pursuing the latest Parisian intellectual fashion, where a revived interest in the "structural" analysis of the turn-of-the-century Swiss philologist, Ferdinand de Saussure (1915/1974), sparked a debate in which Claude Levi-Strauss, Derrida, and Roland Barthes were prominent. Through his study, *Mythologies*, Barthes, in particular, proved the "oracle of the hour" (Miller 1993: 133). Drawing on his experiences of Japanese society, where nonverbal cues are an important aspect of language, Barthes (1957/1972: 115) argued that in art and literature, in particular, the depiction of one concept or object often masks a far more fundamental understanding. Foucault, although boasting no formal training in linguistics, pursued the themes which Barthes had developed with a remorseless vigor in *The Order of Things*. By looking at the "vocabularies," "syntaxes," and the language "sounds" of various "civilizations and peoples," rather than simply "the words they spoke," Foucault (1966/1994: 87) suggested, we can "open up a whole historical field that had not existed in previous periods." Moreover, Foucault (1966/1994: 86) famously argued, "Knowledge and language are rigorously interwoven. They share, in representation, the same origin and the same functional principle; they support one another; complement one another." In "any given period," Foucault (1966/1994: 158, xxi) continued, "the totality of experience" in any "field of knowledge" was delineated by "a priori" understandings shared within what Foucault referred to as the "episteme," "the codes of language, perception, and practice" that act as both the foundation and constraint of all knowledge. Grandiosely, Foucault (1966/1994: xxi, xx) also claimed that by adopting his approach the reader would come to understand that the "codes of culture" that currently prevail "are perhaps not the only possible ones or the best ones." In his subsequent, and more accessible study, *The Archaeology of Knowledge*, Foucault (1969/1972: 8–9) also expounded a more overtly Nietzschean perspective, arguing that historical accounts that depict patterns of order, "of convergence and culmination," were merely a misleading "discourse" that denied a supposed human capacity to reshape the past as well as the present. Rather than depicting a pattern of order, Foucault (1969/1972: 8–9, 25) argued in favor of the "notion of discontinuity" as "both an instrument and an object of research," a notion that would supposedly allow the history of the past to be "known, forgotten, transformed, utterly erased."

To the typical lay reader, *The Order of Things* and *The Archaeology of Knowledge* appear *primarily* to be studies of language, knowledge, and the maintenance of cultural norms. As Jean-Paul Sartre and the rest of the French literary establishment well understood, however, behind this apparent focus was a full-throated attack on Sartre's existential humanism. For, Foucault (1966/1994: 385–386) argued in *The Order of Things*, the current human condition – and the very concept of "man" – is entirely the creation of the "modern *episteme*" with its humanist values, "a recent invention" that is doomed to perish along with the *episteme* that created it. Although what would follow on from supposed "disappearance of man" is left hanging in Foucault's (1966/1994: 386) account, the clear inference is that the humanist "man" will be replaced by the Nietzschean "Superman," a person of remorseless energy, will, and irrational power. In an interview originally published in *L'Arc* in 1966, and subsequently republished in the English-language *Telos*, Sartre (1966/1971: 110) responded with a devastating attack on Foucault's work, dismissing him as a populist chaser of linguistic fashion devoid of "true original thought." Nowhere, Sartre (1966/1971: 110) accurately observed, did Foucault address the most important questions about knowledge and its creation, namely, the relationship between ideas and the material conditions of life and the ways in which humans progress from belief in one set of ideas to a diametrically different opinion. Instead, Sartre (1966/1971: 110) cynically noted, Foucault merely provided the populace "with a magic lantern" in which "movement" was more apparent than real, occurring as it did "by a succession of immobilities."

As I (Bowden 2018: 149) have argued elsewhere, Foucault's published studies in the 1960s also suffered from conclusions that went both too far and not far enough. Foucault (1966/1994: xxiii) goes too far by arguing that it is only through changes in language and knowledge that "man enters . . .for the first time, the field of Western knowledge," assertions which ignore events such as the American War of Independence, the French Revolution, and the British Industrial Revolution. Conversely, Foucault goes not far enough by beginning his analysis with what he calls the "Classical Age." As Derrida (1967/2001: 6, 12–13) accurately noted, any study that starts around 1500 ignores the previous "twenty centuries" of Western thought, traditions whose philosophical and philological foundations can be traced back to the ancient Greeks.

Foucault (1970–1978)

Contrary to a popular opinion, Foucault was the perpetual insider rather than the eternal outcast. Almost his entire life was spent within the comfortable milieu of the French cultural and political elite. From the time of his entry into the Lycée

Henri-IV in 1945, his career involved a steady advancement through the corridors of some of the most prestigious French institutions. Even before the publication of his best-selling *The Order of Things*, he was already a senior academic, serving on an official commission appointed by the then Gaullist government into the reform of higher education. Even his 2-year sojourn to the University of Tunis was hardly unusual for French academia, where long-standing ties with North Africa were commonplace. Both Camus and Derrida, for example, were Algerian-born. In terms of career progression, Foucault's appointment in 1970 to the prestigious College of France brought him to the pinnacle of success. Despite his impressive record of career advancement, however, Foucault was always an odd fit for many of the institutions that willingly opened their doors to him. Admitted to the École Normale Supérieure, he was detested by his fellow students. As an exponent of language and linguistics, he might have achieved popular success, but his lack of study and training in these domains meant that he was never going to compete with the likes of Sartre, Barthes, and Derrida in the salons and seminars of the Parisian literary and philosophical elite.

If Foucault's life prior to 1968 was that of a somewhat uncomfortable insider, the student-worker uprising that shook the French nation to its core in May 1968 transformed Foucault's place in the world. Spontaneous in nature, and driven by opposition rather than by objectives, the protests of '68 embodied the Nietzschean angst and will to power which Foucault had proclaimed in *The Order of Things*. As a graduate of the French Communist Party, Foucault was, moreover, hardly a political novice, blind to the potential opportunities that the uprising offered for the Nietzschean dissident. Another profound shift in the Western political and cultural landscape – involving a shift from traditional class-based politics to one's centered on personal identity and sexuality – was also heralded by the so-called Stonewall riots in New York in June–July 1969, a disturbance that followed on from a police raid on a gay bar in Greenwich Village. In the months and years that followed, across the United States and the wider Western world, an increasingly vocal gay rights movement wove a potent new strand into identity politics, a social movement already given substance by campaigns for women's liberation and civil rights for racial minorities.

In the post-'68 environment, the logic of a pivot toward issues of identity, sexuality, and power could hardly have escaped Foucault. In his inaugural lecture to the College of France, delivered on 2 December 1970 and entitled "The Order of Discourse," Foucault laid out a research agenda that linked his previous studies of knowledge and discourse with sexuality and politics. Building on his earlier research, Foucault (1970/1981: 55) advised his audience that power and wealth were grounded on "the three great systems of exclusion which forge discourse," namely "forbidden speech," "madness" and "the will to truth." Arguing a Nietzschean position, Foucault (1970/1981: 54, 61) argued that the obsession with "truth" was a recent innovation and that what was defined as true was merely that which ascribed to "the rules of discursive 'policing'" laid down by various academic disciplines. To break out these exclusionary constraints, Foucault postulated two historical methodologies that were to define not only his research but also that of the wider Foucauldian tradition that gained an ever-increasing academic following.

First, Foucault (1970/1981: 70) informed his listeners of the benefits of a "critical approach" in which one begins with current "forms of exclusion," before tracing their origins and the interests which they served. Second, Foucault (1970/1981: 70) expounded on the merits of the "genealogical" approach that he had explored at length in *The Archaeology of Knowledge*, in which one traced how "discourses" came to be accepted as true, interweaving knowledge and power. Although told in a far more direct, succinct, and comprehensible form than was the Foucauldian norm, none of this was particularly new. What was new was his focus on sexuality, politics, and power, Foucault arguing that not only were the grids of cultural and linguistic control at their "tightest' in these domains, it was also at these sites that resistance was most powerfully manifest (Foucault 1970/1981: 52).

Flagged in his December 1970 lecture to the College of France, Foucault's newfound interest in biopolitics – on the ways in which sexuality, discourse, and disciplinary control are interwoven – found its fullest expression in two books published in the mid-1970s, *Discipline and Punish* and *The History of Sexuality: An Introduction*, the latter boasting a title markedly different to the French original: *La Volonté de Savoir* (The Will to Know).

Having acted in the early 1970s as the spokesperson for the Prison Information Group – in reality a front for an ultraleft Maoist group, *Gauche Proletarienne*, to which Foucault's long-term partner, Daniel Defert, secretly belonged (Miller 1993: 186–187) – Foucault and his close circle of friends were soon congratulating themselves on the impact of *Discipline and Punish*. As one, Arlette Farge (2015: 33) later recalled, "With *Discipline and Punish*, Foucault totally blew apart everything that had been said about prisons and the system of power." Certainly the imagery that Foucault conveyed in *Discipline and Punish* was disquieting. Within the Panopticon – and by implication the "disciplinary society" that was its natural outcome – every person finds themselves powerless, "alone, perfectly individualized and constantly visible," forced to modify their behavior in order to placate their all-seeing supervisors (Foucault 1975/1991: 5). The inevitable end result of a world modeled on the Panopticon, we are led to believe, is remorseless "normalizing power," a society where the "judges" of normality "are present everywhere. We are in the society of the teacher-judge, the doctor-judge, the educator-judge" (Foucault 1975/1991: 304). Of all the concepts conveyed across his career, certainly none was more powerful than that of the "Panopticon," both (supposedly) as an actual 12-sided prison and a model for a "disciplinary society" where the individual is subject to perpetual surveillance and control. In reflecting on the state of management and organizational theory at the end of the twentieth century, McKinlay and Starkey (1998: 3, 5), for example, noted how the concept of the Panopticon and "disciplinary power" – which they declared to be "the central theme of Foucault's work" – had transformed the field. No longer was it possible, McKinlay and Starkey (1998: 5) continued, to regard managerial systems as merely the product of necessity. Instead, we need to understand them as Foucault did, as a "complex of power/knowledge" that embody material and physic oppression.

Foucault's depiction of a society where everyone is exposed to supervision and control on every front was reinforced in his *The History of Sexuality*. The very condition of modernity, Foucault (1976/1978: 89, 94) proclaimed, rested on "new mechanisms of power" that "took charge" of every aspect of "existence," including individuals "as living bodies," exposing them to power "exercised from innumerable points." Whereas society had previously forbidden certain sexual activities – homosexuality, sadism, etc. – it now engaged in the "medicalization of the sexually peculiar" (Foucault 1976/1978: 44). Such normalizing forms of control, Foucault warned, were not incidental to modern society but instead revealed its true, remorseless totalitarian nature. For, Foucault (1976/1978: 140–141) continued, modern industrial capitalism marked "the beginning of an era of 'bio-power' . . . [that] was without question an indispensable element in the development of capitalism: the latter would not have been possible without the controlled insertion of bodies into the machinery of production." This was achieved, Foucault (1976/1978: 145) concluded, by a system of micro-power that involved "infinitesimal surveillances" and "indeterminate medical or psychological examinations." Accordingly, we have become:

> . . . a society 'with a sexuality': the mechanisms of power are addressed to the body, to what cases us to proliferate, to what reinforces the species, its stamina, its ability to dominate, or its capacity for being used. (Foucault 1976/1978: 147)

There was no doubt that *Discipline and Punish* and *The History of Sexuality* captured the rebellious spirit of his times, appealing to a new literary market: the university-educated professional with career aspirations who was little concerned with the bread-and-butter concerns of the old blue-collar proletariat. Moving from a rebellious university existence to the humdrum of the office and the classroom – worlds dominated by older, more conservative workers and supervisors – this new professional class typically shared a generalized hostility to the exercise of power, perceiving evidence of discrimination on the basis of race, gender, and sexual orientation on every front. Education and increased prosperity also made the philosophically framed writings of Foucault and his ilk a "cultural *produit deluxe*," a top-shelf literary product whose possession allowed one to demonstrate one's educational superiority (Lamont 1987: 593–594). In crafting both *Discipline and Punish* and *The History of Sexuality*, Foucault and his supporters also constantly claimed that they were rooted in fact, in thorough archival research. In *The History of Sexuality*, for example, Foucault (1976/1978: 13) claimed that he was "starting from historical facts that serve as guidelines for research." As for the writing of *Discipline and Punish*, his student and colleague, Arlette Farge (2015: 31) reported that "I often saw him in the archives, though historians criticized him for not having researched and interpreted archival material. His interest in the archives was greater than any other historian's." Across the years, others have made similar defenses of Foucault's work, Rowlinson and Carter (2002: 530) lamenting that "few of Foucault's acolytes in organization studies have followed him into the archives."

Far from being based on thorough archival research and a deep understanding of his topics, Foucault's *Discipline and Punish* and *The History of Sexuality* in fact followed a now well-established modus operandi: an opportunistic exploitation of a topic of popular interest, a willingness to enter into a field in which he had little in the way of either training or expertise, sweeping generalizations, clever literary imagery, a propensity to stretch evidence beyond its normal bounds, and an implicit claim to be an agent of resistance and transformative change. Of *Discipline and Punish*, Miller (1993: 235) observes, "Despite the apparent erudition of the work, it was based on a relatively small number of archival sources." The Panopticon – the 12-sided penitentiary that Foucault declared was a model example of the new "disciplinary society"– never existed. Instead, the concept was derived from some obscure letters and reflections written by the English economist, Jeremy Bentham. Not only did Bentham never publicly campaign for his model prison, it was a project of which the world remained largely ignorant until Foucault made it the centerpiece of his analysis (Božovič 1995).

One of the features of Foucault's work that most angered more conventional scholars was the paucity of references and sources that characterized his publications. A ploy that allowed him to circumvent the fact that he boasted little expertise in many of the fields in which he ventured (linguistics, prison reform, sexuality, etc.), the practice also no doubt added to the popular appeal of his studies, sparing the lay reader a mass of tiresome references. Foucault's essay, "Nietzsche, Genealogy, History," is thus unusual in providing us with a well-referenced insight into the inspiration for Foucault's work in the early 1970s. Of the 55 references to a literary source, 54 cite Nietzsche. Similarly, the "genealogical" approach to history which he advocates is pure Nietzsche, Foucault (1971/1984: 88) advising the reader that "History becomes 'effective' to the degree that it introduces discontinuity into our very being …It will uproot its traditional foundations and relentlessly disrupt its pretended continuity." Like Nietzsche, Foucault argued that the purpose of historical writing is *not* one of recording a more-or-less accurate account of past events, but rather one of tracing how historical *understandings* have emerged from past accounts. Where such past accounts depict some pattern of order and explanation rooted in economics, political necessity, or underlying social trends – as is normally the case – than their intellectual foundations need to be destroyed at their "roots," thereby allowing the "liberation of man by presenting him with other origins than those in which he prefers to see himself" (Foucault 1971/1984: 96).

A clear disciple of Nietzsche in 1971, Foucault subsequently sought to escape from Nietzsche's shadow, desirous of portraying himself as a creative philosopher in his own right. Accordingly, in an interview in 1983, published in *Telos*, Foucault continually downplayed the influence of Nietzsche on his thinking. "The only rather extravagant homage I have rendered Nietzsche," Foucault (1983/1988: 31–32) declared – apparently forgetful of his essay, "Nietzsche, Genealogy, History" – "was to call the first volume of my *The History of Sexuality* "The Will to Knowledge." When pressed on the matter, Foucault (1983/1988: 33) coyly stated, "I do not want to get into this argument for the very simple reason that it is years since I have read Nietzsche." Like Paul denying knowledge of Christ on three occasions on the eve of the crucifixion, Foucault's denial of Nietzsche has an air of pathos to it. Yet there is also a sense that Foucault's attempt to distance himself from Nietzsche reflects an awareness that his emphasis on a "disciplinary society," and a world modeled on the Panopticon, made him in many ways a reverse Nietzschean, someone who paid greater heed to the controls that individuals are subjected to rather than their capacity for freedom. For what made Nietzsche's work a call for individual freedom was his constant emphasis on the "Will to Power," the belief that through an exercise of will every obstacle can be overcome. Yes, it is true that the mature Foucault's work *did* continue to emphasize resistance to sources of power and authority. In his *The History of Sexuality*, for example, Foucault (1976/1978: 94) proclaimed that "Where there is power, there is resistance." However, it is also true that the emphasis on social and cultural control, the power of the "disciplinary society," became more rather than less pronounced in Foucault's work during the 1970s. In part, the increasingly pessimistic tone of Foucault's work no doubt reflects the fading promise of the student and worker rebellions that had characterized Western societies in the late 1960s. More fundamentally, however, it pointed to the fact that Foucault himself had no alternative social and economic model to offer his readers. As a result, by distancing himself from Nietzsche, Foucault also distanced himself from the emphasis on human will and freedom that was Nietzsche's seminal contribution to Western philosophy.

Foucault (1978–1984)

The increasingly pessimistic overtones to the mature Foucault's work were highlighted in 1978, when he abruptly announced in his College of France lectures that he would be shifting the focus of attention from "biopolitics" to "governmentality." In explaining the rationale for this shift, Foucault (1979b/2008: 2) subsequently declared, "I wanted to study the art of governing, that is to say … I wanted to study government's consciousness of itself" and how "governing was conceptualized both within and outside government." Extending his discussions to what he referred to as "neo-liberalism," Foucault's ideas on "governmentality" were to profoundly influence disciplines such as management, organizational studies, and accounting. In assessing the transformative impact of Foucault's ideas on the discipline of accounting between 1976 and 2015, Christine Cooper (2015: 15), for example, emphasized how his ideas on "neo-liberalism" had become central to disciplinary understanding of power, government, and the social effect of accounting (also see McKinlay and Starkey 1998; Armstrong 1994, 2015; Clark and Rowlinson 2004, for similar assessments). Influential as Foucault's ideas on governmentality and "neo-liberalism" were, they were also arguably the source of more misunderstanding and confusion than any other area of Foucault's work.

Of all Foucault's writings, it is Foucault's later writings on governmentality and "neo-liberalism" that provide the most apparent comfort for conservative thinkers. In articulating this opinion in the neoconservative journal, *Jacobin*, in December 2015, David Zamora (2015), for example, recorded:

> Foucault was highly attracted to economic liberalism: he saw in it the possibility of a form of governmentality that was much less normative and authoritarian than the socialist and

communist left, which he saw as totally obsolete. He especially saw in neoliberalism a "much less bureaucratic" and "much less disciplinarian" form of politics than that offered by the postwar welfare state.

Zamora's analysis arguably understates Foucault's concerns as to the power of the state, whose power he now placed at the center of his analysis. Like an invasive virus, it advances its interests through self-serving policies while constantly adapting itself to accord with the historical context within which it operated. Whereas other economic historians saw the "mercantilist" policies of eighteenth-century Europe as driven by commercial, fiscal, and trade imperatives, Foucault (1979b/2008: 5) perceived "the state" out to "enrich itself through monetary accumulation." As Foucault himself well-realized, the inherent problem with this model of an all-powerful state was in explaining the autonomy of markets, market competition, and, hence, capitalism and the social classes associated with it. In other words, how does one explain the transformation of what Foucault (1979b/2008: 5, 46–47) called the mercantilist "police state" of the eighteenth century into a society of market "liberalism" in the nineteenth and twentieth centuries? To get around this quandary, Foucault (1979b/2008: 17) argued that the secret to the extension of state power – and the key to "the art of government" in the modern world – was found in the deliberate "self-limitation of governmental practice." Although Foucault (1979c/2008: 44) claimed that the modern state was still only concerned with "its own growth, wealth, population, and power," he also suggested that the process of "self-limitation" demanded "a complex interplay between individual and collective interests, between social utility and economic profit, between the equilibrium of the market and the regime of public authorities." One would think that the realization that democratic societies are built around a plurality of interests would lead one to conclude that the end result was a weakening of the power of the state as its policies and directions were fought over by competing social forces. This is not, however, the conclusion that Foucault came to. Instead, he argued the exact opposite, claiming that it was "precisely" through the interplay of diverse interests with the state "that government can get a hold on everything that exists for it in the form of individuals, actions, words, wealth, resources, property, rights, and so forth" (Foucault 1979b/2008: 45).

It is arguable that Foucault's peculiar understanding of markets, capitalism, and state power could only have emerged in societies such as France, where – as Fernand Braudel (1986/1991: 666) observed – capitalism "took a long time to penetrate French society ... France was never consumed by the necessary passion for the capitalist models, by that unbridled thirst for profits without which the capitalist engine cannot get started." The factors behind the success of Britain's Industrial Revolution – the ingenuity of the small entrepreneur, the willingness of the Lancashire mill owner to invest in revolutionary new steam technologies, a new found awareness of costs – are all beyond the explanatory capacity of Foucault's ideas on the state and governmentality. For, as Joseph Schumpeter (1950/1975: 124) accurately observed, the key to "the Rise of Capitalism" was not state power but rather the reverse, the creation of "social space for a new class that stood upon individual achievement," a class of people always distrustful of the state and its agencies. Even in France, however, the veracity of Foucault's model is dubious in the extreme. If the French state had shown the "self-limiting" rationality which Foucault believed it possessed, it would have avoided the French Revolution. Indeed, far from limiting its regulatory footprint so as to allow "the equilibrium of the market," the French state dramatically increased the number of "feudal" imposts during the eighteenth century, Braudel (1986/1991: 491) noting that in 1788 – the year before the Revolution – a load of timber transported across France would have been subject to 35 different tariffs and customs duties, imposed at 21 different locations. Rather than demonstrating proof of a supposed "new rationality" of "governmental practice" (Foucault 1979b/2008: 15), such suicidal economic behavior lends credence to the well-known maxim about the French Bourbons that they "learned nothing and forgot nothing."

Confusion and misrepresentation of Foucault's ideas are most evident in discussions of "neo-liberalism" by his erstwhile supporters. In discussing the utility of Foucault's understanding of "neo-liberalism" for accounting research, Christine Cooper (2015: 15), for example, refers to it as "marketization," a process associated with the victory of the market in which "All conduct is economic conduct." Such views, associating Foucault's understanding of "neo-liberalism" with the "neo-liberalism" of Margaret Thatcher, Ronald Reagan, and the neoclassical economics of the Anglosphere during the 1980s, are profoundly in error.

To comprehend Foucault's ideas on "neo-liberalism," we need to first understand the context within which they were written. In terms of Foucault's enunciation of his views on "neo-liberalism," these were principally outlined in a series of lectures to the College of France between late January 1979 and late March 1979. At the time of these lectures, which would have presumably been prepared in the preceding year, Margaret Thatcher was not yet elected; her term in office began in May 1979. Ronald Reagan's election was more than 18 months away. Accordingly, the societal interest in "neo-liberalism" as we understand them was hardly a matter of either political or philosophical concern in 1978–1979.

Constantly, in discussing "neo-liberalism," Foucault informed his audience at the College of France that his concern was with the state and political power rather than markets. Thus, on 14 February 1979, Foucault (1979d/2008: 131–132) advised his listeners that:

> Neo-liberalism is not Adam Smith; neo-liberalism is not market society . . . Neo-liberalism should not therefore be identified with laissez-faire, but rather with permanent vigilance, activity, and intervention.

Neo-liberalism was thus, in Foucault's (1979d/2008: 133) estimation, the polar opposite of "contemporary American anarcho-capitalism," involving as it did a "government [that] is active, vigilant, and intervening."

Rather than identifying the emergence of "neo-liberalism" with the English-speaking world, Foucault associated its origins with postwar Germany. Declaring that modern societies are characterized by the "gradual, piecemeal, but continuous take-over by the state," Foucault (1979e/2008: 76, 80) dated "neo-liberalism" from

April 1948 when West Germany relaxed wartime controls in order to foster economic growth. In explaining the significance of this shift, Foucault (1979e/2008: 85–86, 83) argued that the actions of the German state were a classic example of a rational "self-limiting" state that builds its own power by allowing a substantial measure "of economic freedom," thereby fostering economic growth that acts as "a legitimizing foundation of the state." Arguing that "neo-liberalism" was rooted in "German Christian Democracy," Foucault (1979f/2008: 185–186, 192) also suggested that the success of the German model – based on "economic freedom" within the confines of a supervisory state – saw it gradually adopted by other states, including those of France and the United States.

In referencing Foucault's ideas on "neo-liberalism," *both* neoconservatives and opponents of the Thatcherite-Reagan process of economic deregulation take too much solace from Foucault's writings. "Neo-liberalism" as Foucault understood it was premised on a dominant state apparatus, powerful trade unions, joint oversight of firms by management-union works councils, and a Christian democratic emphasis on social welfare. Despite this, it is also nevertheless the case that neoconservatives can justly take more comfort in Foucault's views in 1978–1980 than can proponents of socialism or even Keynesianism. In a lecture to the College of France on 31 January 1979, for example, Foucault (1979e/2008: 85–86) advised his audience that in "the practice of economic freedom" the modern state "rediscovers" its "real foundation." Foucault (1979e/2008: 81) also informed his listeners that "a state which violates the basic freedoms, the essential rights of citizens, is no longer representative of its citizens." This is a formula that closely resembles that outlined by Jean-Jacques Rousseau (1762/1950: 58) in *The Social Contract*, where he argued that the state is legitimated through the fact it is an agent of "the general will." If it fails to serve the needs of the "general will," then it loses its legitimacy.

A significant shift in Foucault's thinking is also heralded by what he came to regard as the essential precondition for economic success in modern societies, namely, an investment in "human capital." Pointing to the extraordinary success of the Western and Japanese economies in the postwar period, Foucault (1979g/2008: 232) concluded that these achievements could not be ascribed to the "variables of classical analysis," but were instead the result of "cultural and educational policies." Conversely, the postcolonial "failure of Third World economies" was attributable, in Foucault's (1979g/2008: 232) estimation, primarily to an "insufficient investment in human capital." Foucault also famously associated "human capital" with a new manifestation of "homo economicus," whereby the worker brings "his own capital" (i.e., his or her educational attributes, motivation, social skills, etc.) to the employment contract. In commenting on Foucault's usage of this terminology, Cooper (2015: 15) associated it with yet another manifestation of "disciplinary" power, whereby the "neo-liberal conception" of "entrepreneurs of the self" caused humans to "lose their standing as being simply valuable as *humans*" [emphasis in original]. While there *is* a hint of this interpretation in Foucault's wording, Cooper's interpretation is nevertheless misguided. Far from associating "entrepreneurs of the self" with manifestations of oppression, Foucault was linking it to a more educationally rounded worker, one who had a far more dynamic and important role in the creation of wealth than did earlier generations of workers.

If we were to summarize Foucault's understanding of governmentality, the state, and "neo-liberalism," it is evident that his *primary* concern was still with oppressive manifestations of power, which in the late 1970s he increasingly associated with a "self-limiting" state. In the German form of "neo-liberalism," however, he saw hopeful signs, associated with "economic freedom" and a greater enrichment of "human capital."

The changed emphasis in Foucault's discussions of the relationship between the state, the markets, and the individuals was no doubt a reflection of a number of things. Expert in detecting the winds of shifting intellectual fashion, Foucault's more considered discussion of markets and economic growth reflected in part the climate of the times as the postwar economic boom lost steam during the 1970s amid recession and the so-called Middle Eastern "oil shock." More fundamentally, we can detect in Foucault's lectures an increasingly libertarian tone in which his liberal ideas on sexuality and personal identity are reflected in his ideas on economics. Constantly, in his lectures before the College of France, we see evidence of Foucault's (1979c/2008: 42, 22; 1979b/2008: 22) interest in the relationship between "liberalism" and "freedom and of law," and between "liberalism" and economic "liberty" and "freedoms." It is hard not to associate this shift with the ever-increasing amounts of time that Foucault was spending not only as a visiting professor at the University of California, Berkeley, but also as a patron of the gay bathhouses and sadomasochist bars of San Francisco's Folsom Street. Reflecting on "the wide-open, almost giddy social whirl of the leather scene in San Francisco," Foucault informed a colleague that the new "way of life" that he had discovered was "extraordinary" and "unbelievable. These men live for casual sex and drugs. Incredible! There are no such places in France" (cited, Miller 1993: 261). Nowhere on earth was there a more libertarian culture than that constantly inhabited by Foucault in the late 1970s and early 1980s.

For the discipline of management history, there are no more important topics than those touched on by Foucault in 1978–1979, issues relating to freedom, human capital, employee motivation, markets, and the role of the state in a liberal, capitalist society. By 1981, however, Foucault had lost interest in these seminal issues, focusing instead on "subjectivity and truth" and the ways in which a self-centered "care for oneself" had supposedly characterized antiquity during "the long summer of Hellenistic and Roman thought" (Foucault 1982a/2005: 2, 9). Given Foucault's personal circumstances, which saw him constantly travelling between Paris and San Francisco's gay bars and bathhouses, a renewed focus on personal identity and sexuality was hardly surprising. In addition to Foucault's lectures to the College of France, his renewed interest in these themes also manifested itself in the completion in 1984 of two new volumes in his *The History of Sexuality*, namely, *The Use of Pleasure: Volume 2 of the History of Sexuality* and *The Care of the Self: Volume 3 of the History of Sexuality* (Foucault 1984a/1985, 1984b/1986). Increasingly, however, Foucault's lectures were as much concerned with death as with life. In a lecture given on 24 March 1982, Foucault (1982b/2005: 478) solemnly advised his audience that "death is, of course, not just a possible event; it is a necessary event," one that "many occur at any time, at any moment." Rather than treating death "as the supreme misfortune," Foucault (1982b/2005: 478) continued, we should embrace it, treating it as "a privileged exercise." Tragically, such words suggested someone preparing for their own imminent demise. So it transpired, Foucault dying from AIDS on 25 June 1984 at Paris's Hôpital de la Salpêtrière, the very one in which he had studied mental illness as part of his doctoral studies (Miller 1993: 24).

Conclusion

From the ruins of war and German occupation, postwar France profoundly influenced not only Western philosophy but also the whole intellectual climate of the West through the work of Jean-Paul Sartre, Albert Camus, Louis Althusser, Jean-Francois Lyotard, Jacques Derrida, Roland Barthes, Paul-Michel Foucault, and countless others. For all their differences, the unifying thread to this body of work was a quest for freedom, circumstances that would allow individual being the fullest expression of its capabilities. Paradoxically, however, in the course of this quest, all of these French intellectuals – with the partial exception of Camus – sought inspiration in nineteenth- and early twentieth-century German thought. Althusser looked to Marx. Sartre's work on existentialism was informed by Heidegger. Derrida derived many of his key ideas, directly or indirectly, from Husserl. Foucault, even though he downplayed the link late in his career, was a disciple of Nietzsche. In speaking to issues of human existence and freedom, the ideas of all these French intellectuals clearly found a global resonance. Yet, in exploring the nature of power, oppression, and freedom, all of these French thinkers spoke to a Western society that had never been freer or more prosperous, a world where not only democracy but also civil and social rights for women, gays, and people of color advanced at an unprecedented rate. This points to a circumstance where, for many, pondering over matters of personal identity were more important than the problems of subsistence and economic growth that had concerned previous generations.

Among France's postwar intellectuals, Foucault was more successful than any other in speaking to the concerns of his time. In doing so, Foucault expounded an essentially Nietzschean world view, one little interested with the mechanics of production and economics but much concerned with the limits that the society placed on the individual. His doctoral thesis, published in the English-speaking world as *Madness and Civilization: A History of Insanity in the Age of Reason*, spoke not only to the plight of the eccentric, the outcast, and the marginalized. It also argued – as Nietzsche had done – that "reason's subjugation of non-reason" in the modern world had resulted in a diminishment of human essence, which had supposedly thrived in the mysticism, violence, and irrationality of the pre-modern world (Foucault 1961/1965: 9, 221). Always able to adapt the focus of his research in accordance with shifts in intellectual fashion, in the mid-to-late 1960s Foucault (1966/1994: xx, 86–87) published on the importance of language and of the relationship between conformism, "the fundamental codes of a culture," *epistemes* of knowledge, and the ways in which knowledge, language, and power "are rigorously interwoven." In the mid-1970s, in *Discipline and Punish* and *The History of Sexuality: An Introduction*, Foucault took up themes that spoke to the fears and aspirations of a new, rebellious generation. Modern society, Foucault (1975/1991) warned in *Discipline and Punish*, was modeled on the Panopticon, a mythical 12-sided prison where the supervisory sources of power and authority were able to direct their "normalizing" gaze into every corner of existence. Similarly, in *The History of Sexuality*, Foucault (1976/1978: 140, 145) advised his readers that we have entered "an era of 'bio-power'" that embraced "the entire political technology of life." In writing about historical method in his essay, "Nietzsche, Genealogy, History," Foucault (1971/1984: 54, 61) suggested – as did Nietzsche – that what was held to be historically true was merely a social construct, one maintained by "the rules of discursive 'policing'." In the late 1970s, Foucault made the power of the state and "governmentality" the central focus of interest, identifying its power and oppressive authority with a new "regime of truth" in which the "liberal" state entrenched its power through an exercise "of governmental reason" that co-opted various social and economic interests (Foucault 1979b/2008: 1).

If Foucault's research career was characterized by a measure of opportunism – Jean-Paul Sartre (1966/1971: 110) declaring that "Foucault gives the people what they needed" – there was nevertheless a fundamental consistency to his work. In Foucault's estimation, power is exercised by obtaining the consent – or rather the "normalization" – of the individual, a process secured by the socialized acceptance of the "codes of culture," and of the dominant and dominating *epistemes* and discourses. In the final analysis, this social, cultural, and linguistic mechanism of control is perceived to be historical in nature, supposedly built around an agreed understanding of how the society came to be constructed around values and beliefs which the society holds as "true." Accordingly, for Foucault – as with Nietzsche – the path to freedom lies in overturning accepted understandings of history and substituting a new, liberating vision of the past, present, and future.

In assessing Foucault's work, Sartre (1966/1971: 110) accurately noted that it was built around "the denial of history," not only as it was recorded but also as it had historically transpired. This Nietzschean rejection of history confronts us with the same issues that transfixed France's famed generation of postwar intellectuals: the nature of freedom, the truth, and the historical experience. These are complex problems that Foucault invariably solved in a Nietzschean fashion. For Foucault's – as with Nietzsche – historical experience and historical discourse are one and the same thing. In other words, if we change a society's historical discourse – what it holds to be true – we change history. This is a profoundly mistaken view. For history is manifest not only in written words and theoretical imaginings but also in an institutional inheritance: machines, managerial expertise, political institutions, institutionalized social relationships, and competing interests. We can change our imaginings of the past and still be trapped in the past's institutional and material legacy. At the time of writing (early 2020), for example, the people of Hong Kong are engaged in a battle for political and economic freedom.

This battle, in part, involves the Hong Kong people freeing themselves from concocted Chinese Communist Party imaginings of the past. However, to simply invent a new "liberating" history in a Nietzschean/Foucauldian fashion does everyone a disservice. For Hong Kong, even if it was free of communism, would still face many perils, all of them rooted in the historical experience: a conservative Confucian intellectual tradition, a political tradition of Western legal rights constructed without the democratic institutions and practices that underpin these rights elsewhere, an economy heavily dependent upon their powerful neighbor/ruler. None of these problems can be imagined away. Rather they need to be fully understood if they are to be transcended.

If the Foucauldian intellectual tradition is a hindrance rather than a help in overcoming the legacies of the past, it manifests even bigger problems in its understandings of freedom. Libertarian in ethos, Foucault's body of work – like that of Nietzsche – opposed authority on every front. But, as Albert Camus (1951/1978: 159) asked in considering the nature of individual freedom, "is a world without laws a free world?" In Camus's (1951/1978: 287) considered opinion, the experience of history reveals the answer to this fundamental question, namely, that "Absolute freedom is the right of the strongest to dominate." The greatness of Nietzsche's work is found in the fact that he never shied away from this obvious conclusion, identifying absolute freedom with the "superman," a remorseless and amoral individual free of all restraints. Inevitably, this is the end that the Nietzschean and Foucauldian dreams and imaginings lead toward.

Cross-References

▶ Foundations: The Roots of Idealist and Romantic Opposition to Capitalism and Management
▶ Management History in the Modern World: An Overview
▶ Management in Antiquity: Part 1 – the Binds of Geography
▶ The Intellectual Origins of Postmodernism
▶ What Is Management?

References

Althusser L (1968/2001) Ideology and ideological state apparatus. In: Althusser L (ed) Lenin and philosophy and other essays (trans: Brewster B). Monthly Review Press, New York, pp 85–136
Anderson P (1998) The origins of postmodernity. Verso, London/New York
Armstrong P (1994) The influence of Michel Foucault on accounting research. Crit Perspect Account 5(1):25–55
Armstrong P (2015) The discourse of Michel Foucault: a sociological encounter. Crit Perspect Account 27(1):29–42
Barchilon J (1961/1965) Introduction. In: Foucault M (ed) Madness and civilization: a history of insanity in the age of reason (trans: Howard R (1961/1965)). Pantheon Books, New York, pp 5–8

Barthes R (1957/1972) Mythologies. Hill and Wang, New York

Bowden B (2018) Work, wealth and postmodernism: the intellectual conflict at the heart of business endeavour. Palgrave Macmillan, Cham

Božovič M (1995) Introduction. In: Božovič M (ed) Jeremy Bentham: the panopticon writings. Verso, London/New York, pp 1–28

Braudel F (trans: Reynolds S) (1986/1991) The identity of France: people and production. Fontana Press, London

Burrell G (1998) Modernism, postmodernism and organizational analysis: the contribution of Michael Foucault. In: McKinlay A, Starkey K (eds) Foucault and organizational theory. Sage, London, pp 14–28

Caillat F (2015) Introduction. In: Caillat F (ed) Foucault against himself. Arsenal Pulp Press, Vancouver, pp 13–23

Camus A (1951/1978) The rebel: an essay on man in revolt (trans: Bover A). Alfred A Knopf, New York.

Clark P, Rowlinson M (2004) The treatment of history in organisation studies: towards an 'historic turn'? Bus Hist 46(3):3331–3352

Cooper C (2015) Entrepreneurs of the self: the development of management control since 1976. Acc Organ Soc 47(1):14–24

Cummings S, Bridgman T, Hassard J, Rowlinson M (2017) A new history of management. Cambridge University Press, Cambridge, UK

de Saussure F (eds: Bally C, Sechehays A) (1915/1974) Course in general linguistics. Fontana Collins, New York

Derrida J (1967/2001) Writing and difference. Routledge and Kegan Paul, London/New York

Evans RJ (1997) In defence of history. Granta Books, London

Farge A (2015) On the perception of the intolerable. In: Caillat F (ed) Foucault against himself. Arsenal Pulp Press, Vancouver, pp 25–54

Foucault M (trans: Howard R) (1961/1965) Madness and civilization: a history of insanity in the age of reason. Pantheon Books, New York

Foucault M (1966/1994) The order of things: an archaeology of the human sciences. Vintage Books, New York

Foucault M (1969/1972) The archaeology of knowledge. Pantheon Books, New York

Foucault M (1970/1981) The order of discourse: inaugural lecture at the College of France. In: Young R (ed) Untying the text: a post-structuralist reader. Routledge & Kegan Paul, Boston, pp 48–78

Foucault M (1971/1984) Nietzsche, genealogy, history. In: Rabinow P (ed) The Foucault reader. Penguin, Harmondsworth, pp 76–100

Foucault M (1972a/2006) Appendix II – My body, this paper, this fire. In: Foucault M (ed) History of madness, 2nd edn (trans: Murphy J, Khalfa J). Routledge, London, Appendix II, pp 550–574

Foucault M (1972b/2006) Appendix III: Reply to Derrida ... from paideia. In: Foucault M (ed) History of madness, 2nd edn (trans: Murphy J, Khalfa J). Routledge, London, pp 575–590

Foucault M (1972c/2006) Appendix 1: Madness, the absence of an oeuvre. In: Foucault M (ed) History of madness, 2nd edn (trans: Murphy J, Khalfa J). Routledge, London, Appendix II, pp 541–549

Foucault M (trans: Murphy J, Khalfa J) (1972d/2006) History of madness, 2nd edn. Routledge, London

Foucault M (trans: Sheridan A) (1975/1991) Discipline and punish: the birth of the prison. Vintage Books, New York

Foucault M (trans: Hurley R) (1976/1978) The history of sexuality – an introduction. Pantheon Books, New York

Foucault M (1977/1988) Confinement, psychiatry, prison: a dialogue with David Cooper, Jean-Pierre Faye, Marie-Odile Faye and Marine Zecca. In: Kritzman LD (ed) Michel Foucault: politics, philosophy, culture – interviews and other writings, 1977–1984. Routledge, London/New York, pp 178–210

Foucault M (1979a/1988) Iran: the spirit of a world without spirit. In: Kritzman LD (ed) Michel Foucault: politics, philosophy, culture – interviews and other writings, 1977–1984 (trans: Sheridan A). Routledge, London/New York, pp 211–224

Foucault M (trans: Burchell G) (1979b/2008) Lecture, 10 January 1979. In: Foucault M (ed) The birth of biopolitics: lectures at the College of France, 1978–79 (ed: Senellart M). Palgrave Macmillan, London/New York, pp 1–25

Foucault M (trans: Burchell G) (1979c/2008) Lecture, 17 January 1979. In: Foucault M (ed) The birth of biopolitics: lectures at the College of France, 1978–79 (ed: Senellart M). Palgrave Macmillan, London/New York, pp 27–50

Foucault M (trans: Burchell G) (1979d/2008) Lecture, 14 February 1979. In: Foucault M (ed) The birth of biopolitics: lectures at the College of France, 1978–79 (ed: Senellart M). Palgrave Macmillan, London/New York, pp 129–157

Foucault M (trans: Burchell G) (1979e/2008) Lecture, 31 January 1979. In: Foucault M (ed) The birth of biopolitics: lectures at the College of France, 1978–79 (ed: Senellart M). Palgrave Macmillan, London/New York, pp 76–95

Foucault M (trans: Burchell G) (1979f/2008) Lecture, 7 March 1979. In: Foucault M (ed) The birth of biopolitics: lectures at the College of France, 1978–79 (ed: Senellart M). Palgrave Macmillan, London/New York, pp 185–213

Foucault M (trans: Burchell G) (1979g/2008) Lecture, 14 March 1979. In: Foucault M (ed) The birth of biopolitics: lectures at the College of France, 1978–79 (ed: Senellart M). Palgrave Macmillan, London/New York, pp 215–235

Foucault M (trans: Burchell G) (1982a/2005) Lecture, 6 January 1982: first hour. In: Foucault M (ed) The Hermeneutics of the subject: lectures at the College de France, 1981–82 (ed: Gros F). Picador, New York, pp 1–24

Foucault M (trans: Burchell G) (1982b/2005) Lecture, 24 March January 1982: second hour. In: Foucault M (ed) The Hermeneutics of the subject: lectures at the College de France, 1981–82 (ed: Gros F). Picador, New York, pp 477–489

Foucault M (1983/1988) Critical theory/intellectual history: an interview with Gérard Roulet. In: Kritzman LD (ed) Michel Foucault: politics, philosophy, culture – interviews and other writings, 1977–1984. Routledge, London/New York, pp 17–46

Foucault M (trans: Hurley R) (1984a/1985) The care of the self: volume 3 of the history of sexuality. Random House, New York

Foucault M (trans: Hurley R) (1984b/1986) The use of pleasure: volume 2 of the history of sexuality. Random House, New York

Grey C (1994) Debating Foucault: a critical reply to Neimark. Crit Perspect Account 5(1):5–24

Heidegger M (1927/1962) Being and Time. Blackwell Publishing, London

Lamont M (1987) How to become a dominant French philosopher: the case of Jacques Derrida. Am J Sociol 93(3):584–622

McKinlay A, Starkey K (1998) Managing Foucault: Foucault, management and organization theory. In: McKinlay A, Starkey K (eds) Foucault, management and organization theory. Sage, London, pp 1–13

Miller J (1993) The passion of Michel Foucault. Simon & Schuster, New York

Nietzsche F (trans: Hollingdale R) (1874) On the use and abuse of history for life. http://la.utexas.edu/users/hcleaver/330T/350kPEENietzscheAbuseTableAll.pdf

Nietzsche F (trans: Hollingdale R) (1883/1970) Thus spoke Zarathustra. Penguin Books, London

Nietzsche F (1887/1989) On the genealogy of morals. In: Nietzsche F (ed) On the genealogy of morals/Ecco Homo (trans Hollingdale R). Vintage Books, New York, pp 24–163

Nietzsche F (1889/1990) Twilight of the idols. In: Nietzsche F (ed) Twilight of the idols/the anti-Christ penguin classics (trans: Hollingdale R). London, pp 1–125

Poster M (1975) Existential Marxism in postwar France: from Sartre to Althusser. Princeton University Press, Princeton

Rabinow P (2015) Foreword. In: Caillat F (ed) Foucault against himself. Arsenal Pulp Press, Vancouver, pp 7–12

Rousseau J-J (trans: Cole CDH) (1762/1950) The social contract. In: Rousseau J-J (ed) The social contract and discourses (ed: Cole CDH). J.M. Dent and Sons, London, pp 1–141

Rowlinson R, Carter C (2002) Foucault and history in organization studies. Organization 9(4):527–547

Sartre J-P (trans: Barnes H) (1943/1956) Being and nothingness. Routledge, London

Sartre J-P (trans: D'Amico R) (1966/1971) An interview: replies to structuralism. Telos 9(1):110–116

Schumpeter JA (1950/1975) Capitalism, socialism and democracy. Harper Perennial, New York

White H (1973) Foucault decoded: notes from underground. Hist Theory 12(1):23–54

Zamora D (2015) Can we criticize Foucault? Jacobin, 10 December. https://www.jacobinmag.com/2014/12/foucault-interview/

Jacques Derrida: Cosmopolitan Critic

30

Bradley Bowden

Contents

Introduction	700
Derrida's Formative Concepts: Spirit, Knowledge and Language	705
Critiquing the Western Intellectual Heritage, 1967–1980	710
Derrida, 1981–2004: Political and Social Critic	714
Conclusion	717
Cross-References	719
References	719

Abstract

The product of a glorious flowering of post-war French intellectual thought, Derrida's ideas were an "assemblage," constructed from a unique synthesis of the work of Friedrich Nietzsche, Edmund Husserl, Martin Heidegger, Ferdinand de Saussure, and Emmanuel Levinas. As such, they spoke to the key issues in the human experience: knowledge, individual identity, consciousness, language, and freedom. In exploring these themes in the late 1960s and early 1970s, Derrida proclaimed an uncompromising message. The entire structure of Western language, based upon "four thousand years of linear writing," was responsible for a deeply entrenched system of psychic and physical "oppression," a system of tyranny that manifested itself in a "technical and scientific economy" that paid little heed to the spiritual well-being of its members. Calling for a "Nietzschean demolition" of the Western logos, Derrida advocated a far-reaching "deconstruction" of the whole structure of Western language and thought. In practice, however, Derrida's far-reaching objectives have proved difficult to achieve, "deconstructionism" typically manifesting itself simply as a device for literary or textual criticism. In exploring the strengths and weaknesses of Derrida's

---

B. Bowden (✉)
Griffith Business School, Griffith University, Nathan, QLD, Australia
e-mail: b.bowden@griffith.edu.au

© The Author(s), under exclusive licence to Springer Nature Switzerland AG 2020
B. Bowden et al. (eds.), *The Palgrave Handbook of Management History*,
https://doi.org/10.1007/978-3-319-62114-2_79

theoretical frameworks, this chapter traces Derrida career and intellectual development from the submission of his thesis on Edmund Husserl in 1954 until his death from pancreatic cancer in 2004.

Keywords

Derrida · Foucault · Heidegger · Husserl · Deconstructionism · Post-structuralism · Postmodernism · Linguistic turn · Sartre · Camus

---

Introduction

Jacques Derrida stands alongside Michel Foucault as a commanding giant of twentieth-century postmodernist thought. In many ways, the lives and intellectual progress of these two men moved in parallel. Both studied at France's most prestigious educational institution, the École Normale Supérieure, Derrida meeting Foucault on his first day as a student. As students, both were fed on the same diet of German-dominated idealist philosophy: Georg Hegel, Edmund Husserl, Martin Heidegger, and Friedrich Nietzsche. Studying in a Parisian intellectual climate where the existentialist philosophy of Jean-Paul Sartre and Albert Camus was predominant, both men eventually rebelled against existentialism's undercurrent of humanism. Products of France's elite cultural and educational institutions, both became perpetual insiders, enjoying appointments to a series of prestigious positions. Of the two, Derrida arguably boasted the more conventional and meritorious career. After graduation, Derrida obtained a scholarship to study at Harvard. Between 1964 and 1984, he taught at his old *alma mater*, the École Normale Supérieure. In 1981, the French government appointed him as a Director of the College International de Philosophie, responsible for the standing of the French nation in terms of its philosophic reputation (Lamont 1987: 599). His intellectual standing assured, Derrida found permanent employment in 1986 at the University of California, Irvine, teaching there until his death from pancreatic cancer in 2004.

Across his well-rewarded career, Derrida – like Foucault – proved a relentless critique of modernity and the whole structure of Western thought. Whereas a Nietzschean interest in power underpinned Foucault's critiques, Derrida focused his attention on the interrelationship between knowledge and language, declaring in the introduction to the book that first won him international attention, *Speech and Phenomena*, that in any "theory of knowledge ... First we must deal with the problem of language" (Derrida 1967a/1973: 7, 10). From this standpoint, Derrida (1967b/2001: 47) launched an assault on what he called "the fundamental permanence of the logico-philosophical heritage" (i.e., the Western intellectual tradition), associating it with "nothing but the most original and powerful ethnocentricism" (Derrida 1967c/1976: 3). Once ensconced in California, his criticisms became more overtly political, Derrida (1993a/2006: 106) arguing in *Spectres of Marx* – a book based on a series of Derrida's American lectures from 1993 – that "never have violence, inequality, exclusion, and thus economic oppression affected so many human beings in the history of earth and humanity."

If the careers of Derrida and Foucault often seemed to march in unison, there were also notable differences. Unlike Foucault, a member from birth of France's *haute bourgeoisie* (Miller 1993: 39), Derrida (2003a/2008: 31) described himself as "a sort of child in the margins of Europe, a child of the Mediterranean." Born into a family of Algerian Jews, Derrida and his family experienced persecution due to their religious faith. During World War II, the anti-Semitic policies of the pro-German Vichy regime caused Derrida to be excluded from his secular school in Algiers, studying instead at a Jewish religious school. After Algerian independence, the anti-Semitic policies of the Arab regime stripped Derrida's family of their citizenship, forcing Derrida's parents to flee to France. In reflecting on Derrida's youth, David Mikics (2009: 11) concludes that he was from "the beginning ... an intellectual outsider, a rebel." This is overstatement. Like his Algerian-born and raised contemporary, Albert Camus, Derrida grew up in a society that regarded itself as French. Algeria itself was regarded as part of metropolitan France rather than an overseas territory, as much a part of France as Normandy or Brittany. As Derrida (2003a/2008: 32–33) himself recalled, even though he "lived on the edge of an Arab neighbourhood," the language of Arab majority "was unknown ... to me." Once the Vichy regime was evicted in November 1942, Algiers also became – as Derrida (2003a/2008: 32) remembered – the "French literary capital in exile," a society characterized by "a cultural effervescence, the presence of writers, a proliferation of journals." Arriving in European France at the age of 19, Derrida gained entry to a peculiar French institution, the *hypokhâgne*, a boarding school that prepared students for the entrance examinations to the École Normale Supérieure, a place where his diligent studies made him part of a cultural elite (Mikics 2009: 23). Rather than it being the case that Derrida's background made him an "outsider," it is more accurate to say that his experiences caused him to feel himself a cosmopolitan member of a "universal civilization," a "Western culture" that included the Middle East, the Maghreb, and Islam among its constitutive elements (Derrida 2003b/2008: 39). As Mustapha Chérif (2003/2008: 103) expressed it at his funeral, Derrida lived a life faithful "to more than one identity, as a Frenchman, as an Algerian, as a Jew, as a citizen of the world."

Cosmopolitan in his origins, Derrida's comparatively humble background – his father was a wine and spirit salesman – also appears to have made him a more diligent student than Foucault, who throughout his life showed a constant propensity to move into new areas where he boasted little in the way of training or expertise: language, prison reform, sexuality, and forms of government. Completing his mandatory thesis at the École Normale Supérieure on the philosophy of Edmund Husserl in 1954, Derrida developed an encyclopedic understanding of Western philosophy in general and German idealist philosophy in particular. Clearly annoyed by Foucault's willingness to pontificate on matters where he had limited understanding, in the 1960s Derrida could not resist opportunities to show his superior knowledge vis-à-vis his better known contemporary. In a Sorbonne conference paper delivered in 1963, entitled "The Cogito and the History of Madness," subsequently republished in *Writing and Difference,* Derrida carried out a devastating evisceration of Foucault's (1961/1965) *Madness and Civilization*, a work based on Foucault's thesis. In doing so, Derrida (1967b/2001: 45) accused Foucault of a multitude of "methodological" and "philosophical" errors. In 1968, another attack followed, this time aimed at Foucault's (1966/1994) *The Order of Things*, the best-selling book that made Foucault an intellectual celebrity. Although Derrida avoided mentioning Foucault by name on this occasion, the title of the paper, "The Ends of Man," left the reader in little doubt as to the intended target. Any confusion as to intended target was also alleviated by a quote from Foucault's book that stood at the commencement of Derrida's (1968a/1982: 111) paper, in which Foucault is cited as saying "man is an invention of recent date. And one perhaps nearing its end." In condemning "such and such an author" (i.e., Foucault), Derrida (1968a/1982: 119) noted a propensity to "read . . . a text poorly, or simply not at all," while at the same time laying claim "to great ingenuousness" and a supposed capacity to have "surpassed or overturned" previous intellectual understandings.

Boasting an encyclopedic understanding of philosophy and a penetrating mind, Derrida was arguably at his best in critiquing or "deconstructing" the work of other authors. In his comprehension of the strengths and weaknesses of the work of Hegel, Husserl, Heidegger, Ferdinand de Saussure, and Emmanuel Levinas, Derrida was arguably unsurpassed. His deep understanding of the some of the most complex and difficult works of idealist philosophy and language also enabled Derrida to construct a unique, inherently complex theoretical framework. As Derrida (1968b/1973: 130) himself explained in his famed study on "Differance," initially presented to the French Philosophic Society in January 1968, his core theoretical framework drew on many sources. From Levinas, Derrida obtained the concept of "trace," the idea that one concept or phrase contains evidence of something fundamentally different. From Heidegger, Derrida derived his understanding of "Being," the primordial essence of existence that is supposedly repressed by the experience of modernity. Husserl, with his belief that knowledge rests on a "transcendental consciousness" was central to Derrida's understanding of knowledge. The Swiss linguist, de Saussure, provided Derrida with his understandings as to structure and differences in language.

In essence, Derrida's claim to theoretical originality rested on one complex (and dubious) construct: a construct summed up in the word "differance" [spelt with an "a" rather than an "e"] or to be more exact, the French word "déférence."

Drawn from the verb "déférer," a word that technically translates into English as "to defer," the concept of *differance* as applied by Derrida involved a number of interrelated understandings. As Derrida (1968b/1973: 160, 149) expressed it, *differance* is supposedly produced by the "marriage between speech and Being," and is thus "inseparable" from the "concept of trace." In turn, "the trace" is a "psychic imprint" (Derrida 1976c/1976: 66), a "ultratranscendental concept of life" that is spiritually alive but which "cannot reside in the world but only in language, in the transcendental disquietude of language" (Derrida 1967a/ 1973: 14–15). Much simplified, and translated into ordinary English, what Derrida is saying is that language *always* contains evidence – behind the accepted meanings of the words – of a repressed essence, a partially excluded and hidden identity. Thus, for example, when we consider one phrase, i.e., American Independence – a "signifier" in linguistic terminology – what is conventionally being conveyed in terms of meaning – what is linguistically "signified" is the inaugural struggle for American independence and freedom, c.1776. Derrida, however, would have us believe that behind this "signifier" there lurk not only different meanings – i.e., Native American dispossession, the exclusion of adherents to Britain, the entrenchment of slavery in the American South – but also a variety of "psychic imprints," in which language maintains "transcendental life" as "the archives" of consciousness (Derrida 1967a/1973: 15). Significantly, in looking at the ways in which "traces," "psychic imprints," are given existence through language, Derrida (1967c/1976: 14) argued for the primacy of written language over verbal speech, suggesting that "there is no linguistic sign before writing." Indeed, Derrida argued, because verbal speech disappears into the ether the moment it is spoken – and because the physical experience of the past is irretrievable – it is only through the "privileged" status of writing that the spiritual essence of the past survives. Accordingly, as Derrida (1967c/1976: 158), famously concluded in *Of Grammatology*, "*Il n'y a pas de hors texte*" ("there is nothing outside the text").

On the basis of his insights into language and knowledge, Derrida (1967c/1976: 10, 86) grandiosely claimed that not only could one "deconstruct" a given text, one could also – and should also – participate in the deconstruction of the entire Western intellectual tradition; a process that necessarily entailed the "de-sedimentation" of "four thousand years of linear writing." Indeed, Derrida (1968b/1973: 135) warned, to attempt "deconstruction" using conventional methodologies risked not only one's own intellectual contamination, it would also lead to one "ceaselessly confirming, consolidating" the existing structures of language and knowledge rather than undermining them "in a discontinuous and irruptive fashion." What was at stake in this intellectual battle, Derrida (1967c/1976: 86) had one believe, was the very essence of human freedom and being; a psychic freedom suppressed by the terrible "technical and scientific economy" that Western language, thinking and rationality had produced.

Inherently complex, Derrida's deconstructionist methodology has been embraced – in general principle – by wide swathes of Western academia. In a book entitled *Deconstructing History*, the late British historian, Alun Munslow (1997: 3) proclaimed that, "The deconstructionist consciousness" defines history as "the study not of change over time" but, rather, as "the study of the information produced by historians"; a formulae that echoed Derrida's view that "there is nothing outside the text." In a similar vein, the Dutch postmodernist, Frank Ankersmit (1989: 145) noted that, "in the postmodernist view, evidence does not point towards the *past* but different *interpretations* of the past" [emphasis in original]. Summing up the situation that prevailed in Britain in 1992, Raphael Samuel (1992: 220–221) – in an article sub-titled "Fact-grubbers and Mind-readers" – lamented how, with "the deconstructivist turn," history had come to be widely seen "not as a record of the past, more or less faithful to the facts … but as an invention, or fiction."

If Derrida's deconstructionist approach found favor among many, it also attracted a host of detractors. Prominent among those who regarded Derrida's proposed methodology as an elaborate theoretical hoax was Michel Foucault. In an appendix to *History of Madness* – an expanded and modified version of the earlier *Madness and Civilization* – Foucault (1972/2006: 573) dismissed Derrida's approach as a "well-determined little pedagogy . . .which teaches the student that there is nothing outside the text." As a result, Foucault (1972/2006: 573) continued, historians were reduced to a spurious "invention of voices behind the text," avoiding in the process the far more productive task of "situating discursive practices in the field of transformation where they are carried out." Newton Garver, whose translation of *Speech and Phenomena* first brought Derrida's work to the English-speaking world, also worried about the implications of Derrida's thinking. By "attacking the whole tradition in which language is conceived as founded on logic rather than on rhetoric," Garver (1973: xiii, xxvii) bemoaned in his Preface to *Speech and Phenomena*, Derrida "may be enticing us along a path to nowhere." Many traditional historians were even more dismissive of Derrida's formulations, Chris Lorenz (1998: 356) advising his readers that, "Anyone who applies Derrida's '*Il n'y a pas de hors texte*' to the writing of history ceases to be of interest to the historian *qua* historian."

Arguably the greatest problem with Derrida's deconstructionist framework is the fact that it is nigh impossible of application in anything like its originally articulated form. In this Derrida's intellectual influence suffered by comparison with Foucault. As Derrida well-understood, Foucault's concepts were typically based on dubious theoretical interpretations and a thin body of reading. Theoretically weak, Foucault's ideas on discourse, power, and governmentality were nevertheless creative, more easily digested, and more easily applied. By comparison, those who apply a Derrida-informed deconstructionist approach – most particularly in history – rarely pay much heed to the philosophical underpinnings of Derrida's work; underpinnings associated with highly abstract views on "Being," "trace," "difference" and "psychic imprint." Instead, the "deconstructionist" historian has typically done little more than reference Derrida while carrying out a fairly conventional work of literary criticism, where one pays greater heed to a study's philosophical and political underpinnings than to the "facts" it outlines. Such problems are evident in Derrida's own attempt to engage in a "radical deconstruction of the distinction between war and terrorism" in the wake of the 9/11 attacks on New York and Washington. In an analysis that borders on the banal, Derrida (2003c: 86–87) constantly downplays the significance of the "event" with the repeated observation "that we do not know what we are talking about." For, Derrida (2003c: 89) claimed, the "event," "the so-called "thing" (i.e., 9/11), is more an "impression" than a fact, a creation of an "information apparatus," an "organizing information machine." On the other hand, Derrida (2003c: 110, 121) pays much attention to the "incredibly destructive computer technologies" associated with "an age of so-called globalization," an epoch that saw the Islamic world "dispossessed of the so-called natural riches of the world." Whether one agrees with the thrust of this analysis or not, there was nothing in it that was philosophically profound. Similar themed articles could easily be read in the popular press.

In exploring Derrida's ideas in depth, this chapter must necessarily also consider the ideas that shaped his thinking, underpinnings that are theoretically complex in nature. Accordingly, in tracing the shifts in Derrida's understandings we begin the section entitled, "Derrida's Formative Concepts: Spirit, Knowledge and Language" of this chapter with a consideration of Edmund Husserl's ideas on knowledge, and the shifting relationship of Derrida's own epistemological positions vis-à-vis Husserl. In doing so, this section also traces how Derrida's ideas were subject to profound alteration during the late 1950s and early 1960s as the French intellectual world became transfixed by debates about language associated with de Saussure. In the ensuing section "Critiquing the Western Intellectual Heritage, 1967–1980," we explore how in the 1960s and early 1970s Derrida constructed his own perspective by amalgamating understandings from Husserl, de Saussure, Heidegger, Levinas, and Roland Barthes. In the chapter's final section, we explore the ideas articulated by Derrida in his later years after moving to the United States, a period when Derrida adopted theoretical and political positions that were characterized by both a greater clarity of language and shallowness of thought.

Derrida's Formative Concepts: Spirit, Knowledge and Language

In a lecture delivered in March 1987, and subsequently published as *Of Spirit: Heidegger and the Question*, Derrida (1987/1989: 3–4) lamented the fact the concept of transcendental "spirit," which had occupied "a major and obvious place in his [Heidegger's] line of thought, should have been disinherited ...No one wants anything to do with it any more ... no one ever speaks of spirit." A similar comment could be made in relation to all of the German idealist thinkers who influenced Derrida. In an increasingly secular world to explain human knowledge, individual behavior and historical events through reference to a divine or spiritual being would be seen by most, I suspect, as ludicrous, harking back to an age of superstition out of keeping with a modern world premised on science and rationality. It was, however, the embrace of science and rationality – and a corresponding neglect of matters relating to the soul, the spirit, feeling and emotion – that most concerned German idealist thinkers from Johann Fichte to Heidegger. Accordingly, if we to understand the underpinnings of not only German idealism but also Derrida's thinking, we need to understand these frameworks in terms of their own essential purpose: to explain the human condition in terms of Enlightenment intellectual principles that avoided traditional Christian theology while giving a central place to consciousness, spirit, and a pervasive transcendental essence or being.

In attempting to explain both the place of humanity in the world and the importance of individual consciousness, Fichte – who arguably laid the foundations for all subsequent German idealist thinkers and, hence, Derrida – postulated that an all-pervasive spirit, which he called "Nature," gave motive force to every expression of physical existence. As Fichte (1799/1910: 11, 7) expressed it, "When I contemplate all things as one whole, one Nature, there is but one power ... for Nature is one connected whole ... Every part contains the whole, for *only* through the whole is each part of what it is" [emphasis in original]. If Fichte's ideas of an all-pervasive spirit profoundly influenced all subsequent German idealist philosophy, we can nevertheless discern two distinct substrands within it: one emphasizing the ways in which the "Spirit" supposedly guided the whole historical process and the other concerned with the centrality of spiritual essence to individual consciousness, will and freedom. Among those who emphasized the essential unity of the historical process, none was more significant than Georg Hegel (1837/1956: 25) who argued in his *Philosophy of History* that individual actions – and indeed those of entire nations – are merely "the means and instruments of a higher and broader purpose of which they know nothing," but "which they realize unconsciously." Significantly, during the time that Derrida and Foucault were students at the École Normale Supérieure, interest in Hegel's thought was at its peak. Both studied under the leading Hegelian philosopher, Jean Hyppolite. In a Preface written in 1990 to mark the publication of the dissertation he completed at the École Normale Supérieure, Derrida (1990/2003: xiv) also singled Hyppolite out for his formative influence, noting how in 1954 Hyppolite had read and commented upon his thesis "with his normal solicitude"; a comment that points to a close and influential relationship.

If Hegelianism was a significant element in both French existentialist and Marxist philosophy in Paris during the early 1950s, even more important was the second substrand of German idealist thought, a tradition that emphasized the overriding importance of individual consciousness and spirit. As Martin Heidegger (1975/1985) noted in a series of lectures subsequently published as *Schelling's Treatise on the Essence of Human Freedom*, the writings of Friedrich Schelling were most significant in establishing this tradition, profoundly influencing not only Heidegger himself but also Nietzsche and Husserl. For Schelling (1799a/2004, 1799b/2004, 1809/2006), as for those who followed in his footsteps, empiricism with its attention to facts and material reality was a curse, hindering rather than assisting understanding. As Schelling (1799a/2004: 201) explained, "experimental science" is nothing but "a mongrel idea," and "physics …nothing but a collection of facts." Both mistake the outward manifestations of spirit for its inner purposeful essence. In the case of human consciousness, Schelling (1809/2006: 10) argued in his *Philosophical Investigations into the Essence of Human Freedom*, an inner spirit (*triesfeder*) provided every human with their "unconscious and invisible driving force," a force that – if left unfettered – impelled the individual towards both "freedom" and a "striving for knowledge." For Arthur Schopenhauer, whose ideas profoundly shaped the thinking of Nietzsche, it was also the case that "knowledge" stemmed primarily from an inner spirit. The "knowledge of cause and effect, as the universal condition of understanding," Schopenhauer (1859/1969: 19, 124) argued, stems not from experience and inquiry but rather from within, as an "a priori" construct of consciousness; a consciousness that is in turn a product of an inner "being or true essence."

As a student at the École Normale Supérieure in the early 1950s, Derrida operated in an environment where German idealist understandings as to consciousness, being, and knowledge were predominant. In undertaking his dissertation for his Diploma of Advanced Studies, it is thus not surprising that Derrida turned his attention to Edmund Husserl, a secular Jew born in the modern-day Czech Republic who served

30 Jacques Derrida: Cosmopolitan Critic

as Professor of Philosophy at the University of Freiburg between 1916 and 1928. In this role, Husserl directly influenced not only Emmanuel Levinas, a French philosopher and linguist who completed his doctoral thesis on Husserl in 1930 – and whose concept of the "trace" was seminal to Derrida's mature work – but also Heidegger, who served as Husserl's understudy in the early 1920s. Such was the influence of Husserl on Heidegger's thinking that in completing his seminal work, *Being and Time*, Heidegger (1927/1962: 38) recorded that, "The following investigation would not have been possible if the ground had not been prepared by Edmund Husserl." Derrida's interest in Husserl was also facilitated by the Sorbonne's Maurice de Gandillac, who not only acted as Derrida's supervisor but who also, along with a Fr. Van Breda, organized access to Husserl's unpublished papers, held at Louvain in Belgium (Derrida 1990/2003: xiv). Derrida's lecturer in Hegelian thought, Jean Hyppolite, also helped bring about the publication of Derrida's (1962/1978) translation of Edmund Husserl's *Origin of Geometry*, a translation that represented Derrida's first venture into the world of book publishing.

In many ways, Husserl was an unlikely idealist philosopher, Derrida (1954/2003: 16) accurately describing him in his thesis as "a disappointed mathematician." Completing his PhD in mathematics at the University of Vienna in 1883, Husserl's transition from rationalist mathematician to idealist philosopher involved a circuitous exploration in to the nature of knowledge, triggered by the early twentieth-century revolution in mathematics and physics (Garver 1973: xii). This caused Husserl to ponder the nature of knowledge and the human capacity for abstract mathematical thought. In pondering these fundamental questions, Husserl initially found himself – as Derrida (1954/2003: 9–10) explained – torn between two different explanations: one founded on psychology which associated knowledge with learned experience and the other premised on Kantian philosophy, which associated abstract mathematics and conceptual understandings with "a priori" capacities. After considering these discordant positions, Husserl came to articulate ever-more idealist positions, eventually arguing in favor of what he called a "phenomenological philosophy." In doing so, Husserl (1913/1983: 35, 149–150) claimed that empirical research – with its emphasis on science and rationality – was a source of error; error caused by an unwillingness to recognize that "pure consciousness" was the true wellspring of knowledge.

By undertaking his thesis on Husserl, Derrida found himself considering the most fundamental philosophical debates as to the nature of knowledge; a not inconsiderable task for a student who was still only 24 years old when he submitted his thesis. In exploring Husserl's answers to these debates, Derrida (1954/2003: xix–xxii) asked an even more fundamental question than that explored by Husserl himself, namely: If a pure, transcendental conscious is the source of all knowledge, then what is the "genesis" or source of this transcendental consciousness? Posed at the start of his intellectual career, the search for an answer to this question was to remain central to Derrida's life work.

As a work of philosophy, Derrida's thesis is significant more for the questions he asked – and for the depth of knowledge that he diligently acquired – than for any far-reaching conclusions. What is nevertheless obvious in Derrida's theoretical conclusions is a belief that Husserl had understated rather than overstated the importance of a spiritually-inspired transcendental consciousness, the youthful Derrida (1954/2003: 173) arguing in favor of the displacement of "scientific objectivism" as a basis of knowledge by what he called "a transcendental subjectivism." Notable by its absence in Derrida's thesis is any discussion of language, or of the relationship between language and knowledge. The contrast between Derrida's thesis and the views that he articulated in his first major book, *Speech and Phenomena*, is therefore marked. In this latter work, Derrida (1967a/1973: 10) commenced his study with the claim that in any discussion of knowledge we must, "First . . . deal with the problem of language." Derrida (1967a/1973: 18) also now chose to lambast Husserl for his ignorance as to the difference between a linguist "signifier" and what is "signified."

In choosing to make his stand on the basis of language, Derrida was hardly showing great originality. By the late 1950s, as we have previously discussed in our (▶ Chap. 29, "Paul-Michel Foucault: Prophet and Paradox" by Bowden) chapter on Michel Foucault, interest in language and the ideas of de Saussure was almost universal in French intellectual circles. Through his study, *Mythologies*, Barthes, in particular, proved the "oracle of the hour" (Miller 1993: 133). Drawing on his experiences of Japanese society, where nonverbal cues are an important aspect of language, Barthes (1957/1972: 115) argued that in art and literature, in particular, the depiction of one concept or object often masks a far more fundamental understanding. Even in his newfound criticism of Husserl, Derrida was hardly original. As Derrida (1967a/1973: 18) himself conceded in *Speech and Phenomena*, "Everyone knows" that Husserl made "no distinction" between linguist signs, between what is signified and the signifier.

To understand the subsequent direction of Derrida's work, it is therefore necessary for us to first consider the understandings of language that were circulating in France during the late 1950s; beliefs built around concepts articulated by de Saussure prior to World War I.

Born in 1859, Saussure represented a type of academic that was once common but which is now rare: the well-trained and original scholar who conveys his research through teaching rather than publication. On his death in 1913, the intellectual legacy of de Saussure, who had written nothing of note during his career, was rescued by his former students, who pieced together their lecture notes so as to publish a *Course in General Linguistics* under de Saussure's name. In this, de Saussure (1915/1974: 15) is recalled as saying that although "speech" and the act of speaking (*parole*) are individual and "heterogeneous," it is nevertheless only through language as a "social institution" that meaning is established. Accordingly, individuals can vary through their speech but not language, which is historically constructed and bound by rigid rules of grammar and meaning. Contradicting classical understandings such as those recorded by Plato (c.370 BC/1972) in his *Phaedrus*, de Saussure also prioritized written language over spoken speech, noting that although the pronunciation of words varies over time, written language rarely suffers change. In the case of a Shakespeare play, for example, a modern performance would enunciate the words very differently to the pronunciation of

Elizabethan England. Nevertheless, the written words – and the meaning of those words – have remained constant across half a millennia. In emphasizing the ways in which written language gives a deep historical structure to knowledge and social interaction, de Saussure noted that one of the peculiarities of phonetic-based languages is that they do not reference concepts directly. Instead, they designate sounds. Not only was the association between sounds and concepts an indirect one, de Saussure (1915/1974: 113) observed, it was also inherently "arbitrary" in nature. Even in the same language a wide variety of sound combinations (and hence words) can be used to describe the same thing. In English, for example, I can describe someone I like as a "friend," "buddy," "mate," or "chum." To distinguish between the thing being described and the combination of sounds used to describe it, de Saussure described the former as what is "signified" and the latter as the "signifier." Thus, if we are describing a "cat" then the cat is what is "signified," and the terms used to describe a cat (cat, tabby, kitten, and moggy) are the "signifiers."

In his analysis of language, de Saussure came to two key conclusions that were of fundamental importance for the mature Derrida. First, as we have noted above, he argued that written language has a deep, historical structure that makes it "a social institution." Second, the inherently arbitrary association of sounds and concepts means that "language" is founded upon difference: differences in the organization of sounds; differences in the association of sounds and words; differences in emphasis; and difference in the placement of letters, words, and phrases. Indeed, de Saussure (1915/1974: 120) determined, "in language there are only differences . . . A linguistic system is a series of differences of sound combined with a series of differences of ideas."

Derrida, in reframing de Saussure's conclusions – and his own conceptual framework – articulated three core propositions. First, in the paper delivered at the Sorbonne in 1963 as a broadside against Foucault, "Cognito and the History of Madness," Derrida (1967b/2001: 47) argued – building upon de Saussure's idea of deep historical structure – that Western thought was based upon a "logico-philo-sophical heritage," a tradition of language, thought, and reasoning that stretched back in an unbroken chain to ancient Greek philosophy. By failing to recognize the cohesion and permanence of this tradition of thought, Derrida (1967b/2001: 46–48) suggested, Foucault had made a fundamental error. Moreover, Derrida (1967b/ 2001: 66–67) continued, in not appreciating the deep structure of Western thought and language – and the need to attack it at its roots – Foucault's work revealed itself as "structuralist," plagued by "a totalitarian and historicist style." Derrida's second, and even more significant argument, was built upon de Saussure's emphasis on linguistic difference. Emphasizing de Saussure's point that within a "system of language, there are only differences," Derrida (1968a/1973: 140) constructed his key concept of "déférence" or "differance" [spelt with an "a"]. As Derrida subsequently (1968a/1973: 14) argued, "differance" maintained not only "the difference that preserves language," it also preserved "memory" and, with it, the essence of spiritual being (Derrida 1967b/2001: 253–255). In articulating his concept of "differance," Derrida controversially argued that language, knowledge, meaning, memory, and the essence of being needed to be freed from the constraining structures of language. By "erasing" the very distinction between "signifier" and what is "signified," Derrida (1967b/2001: 354) believed that we can bring about a profound spiritual and intellectual awakening, dissolving "the opposition between the sensible and the intelligible." In expounding upon his concept of "differance," Derrida (1968b/1973: 149) linked it with the concept of a linguistic and spiritual "trace," advising attendees to a Paris conference in 1968 that, "The concept of trace" is "inseparable from the concept of differance." In part, Derrida's concept of trace was derived from Emmanuel Levinas (1957/1987: 103), who suggested in his *Meaning and Sense* that in written language a "trace" is like a face behind a mask, in that "a mask presupposes a face." In other words, behind one construction of words and their associated meaning there lurks "traces" of other meanings, of which the author themselves may be unaware. In becoming a critic rather than a critical disciple of Husserl, Derrida (1968b/1973: 152–153) – as he recounted in his 1968 paper – also drew inspiration for his own peculiar understanding of "trace" from the work of Nietzsche, Sigmund Freud, and, above all, Heidegger. In weaving Heidegger's concept of *Dasein* or primordial Being into his concept of "trace," Derrida made his understanding of language and "deconstruction" far more that a form of literary criticism. Instead, he argued that linguistic "trace" represented within language a "living present... a primordial and incessant synthesis that is constantly led back upon itself."

Inherently complex and of dubious veracity, the core concepts which Derrida was to expound from the late 1960s onwards – the oppressive nature of the Western "logico-philosophical heritage," "déférence"/"differance," and a primordial understanding of "trace" – were not only theoretically original, they were also grounded in a deep understanding of linguistic theory and German idealist philosophy.

Critiquing the Western Intellectual Heritage, 1967–1980

A relatively unknown intellectual figure in the mid-1960s, Derrida found fame in 1967 when three books: *Speech and Phenomena, Of Grammatology*, and *Writing and Difference* were published within months of each other. Finding favor among French readers, each of these works was also soon published in other languages as well, most notably English. In 1972, another three books appeared: *Positions* (Derrida 1972a/1981), *Dissemination* (Derrida 1972b/2004) and, most significantly, *Margins of Philosophy* (Derrida 1972c/1982). His works in popular demand, by the early 1970s Derrida was producing books at the rate of almost one a year. As Derrida's popular reputation soared his interest in the traditional norms of French academia and philosophy – and, correspondingly, the regard for Derrida within French philosophy departments – suffered a marked decline. Whereas between 1963 and 1967 Derrida had published between three and five articles per year in French philosophical journals, between 1978 and 1984 he published one, the solitary article appearing in 1984. During the same period, Derrida published only three articles in philosophy journals outside of France. By contrast, he published 25 articles in journals given over to literary criticism. Of these publications, 17 were associated with United States outlets (Lamont 1987: 604).

There has always been a paradoxical element to Derrida's popular success. Not only did Derrida deal with inherently complex philosophical matters, he also made his discussions of philosophy far more complex than they needed to be. As Newton Garver (1973: xxvi), one of the two translators of *Speech and Phenomena* noted, Derrida's work was "full of metaphors," of "unrestrained literary extravagance ... of florid language that sometimes leaves one mystified as to Derrida's intent." Cynically, the American sociologist, Michele Lamont (1987: 595) contends that is Derrida's very literary complexity that was key to his success as "deconstructionism" became "a cultural *produit deluxe,*" a luxury intellectual item "barely accessible even to the highly educated."

While there is no doubt an element of truth in Lamont's claim, obscurity of literary style by itself can hardly explain Derrida's remarkable success. Instead, his appeal must be primarily attributed to both the nature and timing of his message. Derrida's paper, "The Ends of Man" – which took aim at not only Foucault but the whole structure of Western politics, philosophy, and language – was delivered in Paris in the midst of the student-worker uprising of May 1968. To this youthful, educated, and rebellious cohort – disillusioned as it was with authority in general (including Marxism) – Derrida delivered an uncompromising message. In his May 1968 paper, for example, Derrida (1968a/1982: 114) declared that Western "freedom" was an illusion, a mere "image or appearance," capable of deceiving only the "naïve" and those who were "purposely blind." In the books published in the preceding year – most particularly *Of Grammatology* and *Writing and Difference* – Derrida advocated a similar position. The entire structure of Western language, based upon "four thousand years of linear writing," was responsible for a deeply entrenched system of psychic and physical "oppression," a system of tyranny that manifested itself in a "technical and scientific economy" that paid little heed to the spiritual well-being of its members (Derrida 1967c/1976: 86). Culturally imperialist, the "logocentrism" of the West – built around an overriding belief in rationality and science – was also, Derrida (1967c/1976: 3) declared, premised on "ethnocentrism," remorselessly "imposing itself" on non-Western societies.

In *Of Grammatology*, Derrida (1967c/1976: 3, 10) – like Schelling before him – also took aim at the "concept of science" and "the great metaphysical, scientific, technical and economic adventure of the West." Given that "the very idea of science was born in a certain epoch of [phonetic] writing," Derrida (1967c/1976: 27) continued, the principles of scientific inquiry had to be deconstructed and reconceptualized along with all the other intellectual and linguistic manifestations of the "logos." In carrying out this "deconstruction," Derrida (1967c/1976: 24, 43) proclaimed that it would necessarily entail a process of "subversion" of "the greatest totality," one which challenged "the concept of the *episteme* and logocentric metaphysics," of "writing" and "all the Western modes of analysis." While any reader of Derrida's work at this time might be confused as to the exact means through which this "deconstruction" of the entire structure of Western thought and language could be achieved, no one could doubt Derrida's far-reaching intent.

It was not only all the manifestations of the "logos" that were the target of Derrida's intellectual assault in the late 1960s and early 1970s. Derrida also targeted his existentialist and Marxist compatriots, finding particular offense in the existentialist humanism that Sartre had espoused during the 1940s and 1950s. Intellectually, this existential humanism, Derrida (1968b/1973: 115) accurately noted, was founded upon a mistranslation of Heidegger's concept of *Dasein*, a term which Sartre had translated in his most influential book, *Being and Nothingness*, as "human-reality." Declaring this translation to be "monstrous," Derrida (1968b/1973: 115, 134) lamented how French existentialism had led intellectual society away from a proper understanding of "the Heideggerian destruction of metaphysical humanism"; an understanding that placed consciousness, spirit and a primordial essence of being at the center of epistemology.

In taking aim at the whole structure of Western language and thought, Derrida made written language his chosen field of battle, famously declaring – as we noted in our introduction – that, "*Il n'y a pas de hors texte*" ("there is nothing outside the text"). In doing so, Derrida, (1967c/1976: 144–145) in his *Of Grammatology*, associated his comprehensions of "differance" and "trace" with the "concept of the supplement." According to Derrida's (1967c/1976: 144) estimation, any "representative image" in language "harbours within itself two significations whose cohabitation is as strange as it is necessary." Within language, Derrida (1967c/1976: 144) added, "The supplement adds itself, it is a surplus, a plenitude enriching another plenitude, the fullest measure of presence." Translated into ordinary English, the "concept of the supplement" points to multiple meanings within text. In applying his own understanding of the "supplement" to a deconstruction of Jean-Jacques Rousseau's *Essay on the Origin of Language* – one of Rousseau's more obscure texts that was never published in his lifetime – Derrida found hidden meanings that were previously undiscernible. In explaining his remarkable success, Derrida (1976c/1976: 246) advised the reader that Rousseau, "says what he does not wish to say, describes what he does not wish to conclude." In other words, Derrida could detect a meaning fundamentally different from that which Rousseau had consciously intended. Significantly, Derrida (1967c/1976: 246) claimed that, "Rousseau is not alone in being caught in the graphic of supplementary. All meaning and therefore all discourse is caught there." In following through this logic to its conclusion, Derrida suggested that every reader could – and should – follow his example in searching for supplementary or alternative meanings within texts. Accordingly, Derrida (1967c/1976: 159) concluded, all "our reading must be intrinsic and remain within the text."

In dismissing Derrida's ideas of "deconstruction," "Being," and "trace as "gobbledygook" and "unrecyclable rubbish," the Canadian philosopher, Mario Bunge (1996: 97), no doubt summed up the attitude of many. Such perfunctory dismissals, however, cannot disguise the extraordinary impact of Derrida's seminal ideas from the late 1960s and early 1970s, ideas that underpinned the so-called linguist turn in the social sciences (Fay 1998).

Deconstructionism's enduring legacy is found in a changed research focus among broad swathes of the Western intelligentsia; a shift that has seen *reinterpretation* of texts and other signs (i.e., American Civil War monuments, statues commemorating New World "discoverers," theatrical plays, visual art, etc.) gain increasing primacy. The reason for this, as Ankersmit (1990: 281), explained in a deliberate echo of Derrida, is that, "Texts are all we have and we can only compare texts with texts." In short, nothing exists before it is recorded in some form of "writing." So-called reliable primary sources are, in this line of thinking, mere manifestations of past and present structures of power and inequality. Indeed, as Derrida (1967b/2001: 284–285) concluded in *Writing and Difference*, such records are supposedly based on constant "censorship," the continued "vigilance" of the powerful "over perception."

Amid the brickbats and bouquets that Derrida's deconstructionist notions have attracted arguably the most balanced and insightful was that made by Newton Garver in the preface to Derrida's first significant book, *Speech and Phenomena*. In his analysis, Garver (1973: xii) made the accurate observation that, historically, post-Enlightenment philosophy had discussed knowledge without reference to language. Even more significantly, Garver (1973: ix) observed, since the Middle Ages the whole tradition of Western thought – where it did focus on language – paid much greater heed to grammar and logic than to rhetoric. Typically, logic was perceived as a pathway to rationality, science, and an accurate understanding of the world, whereas rhetoric was a matter of mere style. What Derrida's critiques sought to achieve, Garver (1973: xii) continued, was to undermine "the whole tradition in which language is conceived as founded on logic rather than rhetoric." In other words, Derrida sought to make language more an agent for social and intellectual transformation rather than of understanding.

The idea that rhetoric as an agent of change should predominant in the writing of history has arguably never been stronger than it is at the present. In the field of management history – as I pointed out in my earlier study, *Work, Wealth and Postmodernism* – this is reflected in the historical methodologies advocated by what I have called the "Rhetorical School," a school of thought principally associated with Roy Suddaby (currently the Program Chair of the Management History Division of the Academy of Management) and his various co-authors and collaborators: William (Bill) Foster, Royston Greenwood, Alison Minkus, Diego Coraila, and Max Ganzin (see Bowden 2018: 220–230, for a summary of this literature). Thus we are informed by Suddaby and Greenwood (2005: 41), in an article entitled "Rhetoric Strategies for Resistance," that: "Rhetorical strategies are the deliberate use of persuasive language to legitimate or resist innovation." Like Derrida before them, those that emphasize the power of "rhetoric" believe that history is not objectively real but is instead "highly malleable and open to revision" (Suddaby and Foster 2017: 31). Viewed from the point of view of the Rhetorical School, it therefore follows that managerial authority can be dismantled through alternative "rhetorics" of resistance (Suddaby and Greenwood 2005: 41). According to Suddaby (2016: 54–55), we also need to free ourselves from "the objective elements of history of truth" as these constrain "what can and cannot be done in the social-symbolic realm"; a formulae that would no doubt have won Derrida's approval.

Derrida, 1981–2004: Political and Social Critic

Derrida's intellectual reputation largely rests on the books he published between 1967 and 1972, works that drew on the idealist philosophies that characterized postwar France. In these works, Derrida rarely concerned himself with contemporary debates about politics or social affairs. Instead, his focus of study was the entire "logico-philosophical heritage" of Western culture. Implicit in Derrida's work in the late 1960s and early 1970s is the belief that any contemporary campaigns for social or political change merely scratch the surface, given that the fundamental problem of society is found in the psychic repression and ethnocentrism that is supposedly intrinsic to the whole structure of Western language and thought.

Hitherto directed towards an elite philosophical market, in the 1980s and 1990s a profound shift characterized the style and direction of Derrida's work, if not its underlying philosophical and epistemological principles. Increasingly, Derrida spoke directly to the perceived problems of contemporary society, addressing such matters as inequality, anti-Semitism, terrorism, totalitarian tendencies in modern societies, and even illegal drug use. In doing so, the form and style of Derrida's work also changed. Whereas Derrida's three seminal studies from 1967 – *Speech and Phenomena*, *Of Grammatology* and *Writing and Difference* – were philosophically abstract and linguistically convoluted works of considerable length, Derrida's publications from the mid-1980s onwards largely fell into two categories: academic articles directed towards American literary criticism and collected works built around short essays, lectures, and interviews. Prominent among this latter category were: *Of Spirit: Heidegger and the Question* (Derrida 1987/1989), *Points: Interviews, 1974–1994* (Derrida 1992a/1995), *Spectres of Marx* (Derrida 1993a/2006), the Shoah Research Centre's *An Interview with Professor Jacques Derrida* (Derrida 1998), *Islam and the West: A Conversation with Jacques Derrida* (Derrida 2003d/2008), *Paper Machine* (Derrida 2002/2005), and the edited interviews in *Philosophy in a Time of Terror: Dialogues with Jürgen Habermas and Jacques Derrida* (Borradori 2003).

It is easy to attribute the shift in Derrida's work to his relocation to the University of California, Irvine, in 1986. However, it is perhaps more accurate to conclude that Derrida's physical relocation was an *effect* of the changed style in Derrida's work and in the audience to whom it was directed. In French intellectual circles, as Lamont (1987: 601) noted, interest in Derrida's deconstructionist theories "decreased significantly after a 1972–73 boom." By comparison, in the United States, most particularly in the field of critical literature, fascination with Derrida's theories increased exponentially. As we have previously noted, it was also the case that after 1968 Derrida virtually ceased publishing in French philosophical journals. In other words, the primary audience for Derrida's work after 1980 was no longer the cultural elite of France but rather the American market.

In terms of intellectual themes, Derrida's later work was built around two key arguments. First, he now drew a direct link between twentieth-century totalitarianism and the Western world's cultural and linguistic heritage. In *Of Spirit: Heidegger and the Question*, for example, Derrida (1987/1989: 109–110) made a causal connection

30 Jacques Derrida: Cosmopolitan Critic

715

between "Nazism" and Western "culture," arguing that the rise of Nazism was only made possible due to the sheltering "silence" of "political regimes, economic structures, religious or academic institutions." The second theme that came to characterize Derrida's work was the argument that modern Western societies were lurching towards new forms of totalitarianism that involved frequent but unrecorded "quasi-instantaneous mass murders" and "incredibly destructive computer technologies" (Derrida 2003c: 89, 110). Everywhere, Derrida (1993a/2006: 15) claimed to experience "a troubling effect of '*déjà vu*', and even of a certain '*toujours déjà vu*'" (repeatedly seen before), in which contemporary circumstances reminded him of the slide towards fascism that he experienced during his childhood. In an interview with Israel's Shoah (Holocaust) Research Centre in 1998, Derrida (1998: 2) went on to argue that any supposed advantages of "Western rationality" were "called into question" by the Nazi-induced Holocaust and death camps of World War II; events that "the Western metaphysics of Europe" made "possible," or at least did not make "impossible."

Increasingly, Derrida's pronunciations were directed not towards the philosophical and linguistic underpinnings of Western society but rather towards denunciations of what he perceived to be a catastrophic present. In summing up his views on modernity in a series of interviews published as *Philosophy in a Time of Terror*, Derrida (2003c: 121) asserted that "the disparities between human societies, the social and economic inequalities, have probably never been greater and more spectacular." In a new globalized economy built around "computer technologies" and "technoeconomic power," Derrida (2003c: 110, 121) also found evidence of systematic global inequalities in patterns of internet access, noting that whereas "in 1999 half of all American households" had internet access, across the globe "less than 5 percent of humanity" enjoyed this benefit. In an article originally published in the journal, *Differences: A Journal of Feminist Cultural Studies*, Derrida also engaged in a deconstruction of the official narrative around illegal drug use. Associating drug use with systems of pleasure and play, Derrida (1993b/1995: 236. 230) called for an "effective and transforming questioning" of drug enforcement laws, advising his readers that, "Natural law dictates that each of us be left the freedom to do as we will with our desire, our soul, and our body; as well as with that stuff known as 'drugs'." In many ways, Derrida (1993b/1995: 234) continued, the taking of illegal drugs was no different to common practices of writing. "Writing is irresponsibility itself," Derrida (1993b/1995: 234) claimed, "the orphanage of a wandering and playful sign. Writing is not only a drug, it is a game, *paideia*, and a bad game if it is no longer ruled by a concern for philosophic truth."

In his new role as a global Jeremiah of impending doom, Derrida also increasingly drew upon a Marxist viewpoint that he had spurned in his youth. "Upon rereading the [Communist] *Manifesto* and a few other great works of Marx," Derrida (1993a/2006: 13, 14) advised the readers of *Spectres of Marx*,

> I said to myself that I know of few texts in the philosophic tradition, perhaps none, whose lessons seemed more urgent today ... No text seems as lucid concerning the way in which the political is becoming worldwide ... And few texts have shed so much light on law,

international law, and nationalism ... There will be no future without this. Not without Marx, without the memory and the inheritance of Marx.

In their opposition to the contemporary "politico-hegemony" of capitalism, Derrida (1993a/2006: 15, 67) continued, he and like-minded colleagues were thus "heirs of Marxism, even before wanting or refusing to be."

It is easy to find fault with Derrida's messianic predictions which associated humanity's future with famine, privation and oppression. For, far from being associated with a slide into an economic and social abyss, the closing decades of the twentieth-century and the opening decades of the twenty-first century were associated with unprecedented improvements in the circumstances of the world's poorest people. As the United Nations Secretary-General, Antonio Guterres (2017: 23) noted in his 2017 Secretary-General's Report, the percentage of the global population experiencing malnourishment fell to an historic low of 11% in 2014–2015. Between 2000 and 2016, the percentage of the world's population estimated to be living in poverty also halved (Guterres 2017: 10–11). Derrida's belief that internet usage was a preserve of wealthy nations, and the source of a new global system of inequality, was also misplaced. In mid-2019, more than half the world's internet users – an incredible 2.3 billion people – were found in Asia. There were also far more Internet users in Africa (522.8 million) and Latin America and the Caribbean (453.7 million) than there were in North America (327 million). In Latin America and the Caribbean, and in the Middle East, the percentage of the population who boasted access to the internet was close of 70%. Even in Africa, the continent with the lowest level of access, 39.6% of the population were using the Internet in 2019 (Internet World Stats 2019). Everywhere, increased Internet access made the position of authoritarian and totalitarian regimes more difficult, providing the global population access to a wider range of views and – as the recent experiences in Hong Kong have demonstrated – an organizing platform for rebellion.

If the individual predictions of Derrida were often faulty a more fundamental problem is found in his fundamental premise that Western language and thought is inherently oppressive, a constant breeding ground for totalitarianism. For, far from it being the case that totalitarianism is the natural condition of Western societies, the reverse applies. In virtually every Western society, democracy is well-established. Where totalitarianism threats have emerged they have been fiercely resisted, often at great human and material cost. Nor has science provided the threat to the human spirit that Schelling, Husserl, Heidegger and Derrida believed it to be. Across the globe, science and improved technology has entailed higher levels of education, improved leisure opportunities, better health conditions and greater economic opportunities for ever increasing numbers. In 2015, in virtually every Western society, more than a quarter of the adult population boasted a university degree (Bowden 2018: 282). Thus, when those who find inspiration in Derrida, whether directly or indirectly, end up declaring that the "postmodernist's aim ... is to pull the carpet out from under the feet of science and modernism" (Ankersmit 1989: 142), they are declaring opposition not only to the sins of modernity but also to the circumstances that make its immeasurable benefits possible. Admittedly, Derrida (2003b/2008: 42–

30 Jacques Derrida: Cosmopolitan Critic

43), in one of his last recorded interviews, *did* declare himself a supporter of democracy with the observation that, "To exist in a democracy is to agree to be challenged ... A democracy is a social organization in which every citizen has the right to say everything, the right to criticize." What Derrida did not explain, however, is how this praiseworthy democratic outcome emerged from the "logico-philosophical heritage" that he spent his life condemning.

Conclusion

In his translator's introduction to arguably Derrida's most important book, *Writing and Difference*, Alan Bass (1977/2001: xv) warned would-be readers that, "Derrida is difficult to read." In reflecting on Derrida's writing style, Newton Garver (1973: xxvi) made a similar observation, advising his readers that, "I would not expect them to read the present work without frequent discomfort and occasional dismay." The inherent difficulty involved in reading Derrida's seminal texts – and the fact that these studies typically dealt with some of the most complex matters in idealist philosophy – impede explanation of Derrida's extraordinary popular success, the latter decades of his career being built around the sale of books (typically in English translation) rather than the esteem he was held in philosophic circles. Nor was Derrida himself ever able to clearly designate the principles upon which the "deconstruction" of a text should be based. In attempting to explain his principles in an interview conducted late in his career, for example, Derrida (1992b/1995: 216) confusingly declared, "All texts are different. One must try never to measure them 'on the same scale'. And never to read them 'with the same eye'. Each text calls for, so to speak, another 'eye'."

How then to explain Derrida's appeal? In essence, Derrida – like Foucault and Hayden White – benefited from the timing of his message, one which spoke of knowledge and "the dream of emancipation" (Derrida 1967b/2001: 33) at a time when a rebellious, university-educated youth found itself alienated from the traditional norms and structures of society. For, as we have noted in this chapter, no one made a more sweeping critique of modernity than Derrida. Whereas Jean-Francois Lyotard (1979/1991: 47) spoke of "a generalized computerization of society," and Foucault wrote of constraining discourses and *epistemes*, Derrida associated oppression with the entire "logico-philosophical heritage" of Western language and thought. If there was any hope for human emancipation, Derrida (1967b/2001: 32) proclaimed in *Writing and Difference*, then this could only be built upon a prior emancipation from language. For, in Derrida's estimation, everywhere that the "ethnocentric" structures of Western language and thought advanced the inevitable consequence was psychic oppression and a repression of individual essence and Being. Through reference to his concept of "déférence" or "differance" [with an "a"], Derrida also claimed an ability to facilitate not only linguistic difference but also the essence of individual difference. Derrida also contended that written language contained "traces" and "residues" of a full range of experiences of which the author themselves may not have been fully consciously aware. Collectively, Derrida

(1967c/1976: 19) boasted in *On Grammatology*, the adoption of his principles would allow the groundwork for "the Nietzschean demolition" of the whole structure of Western *logos* (knowledge and understanding).

The product of a glorious flowering of post-war French intellectual thought, Derrida's ideas were inevitably – as he himself conceded in his paper on "Differance" in 1968 (Derrida 1968b/1973: 130–131) – an "assemblage," constructed from a unique synthesis of the work of Friedrich Nietzsche, Edmund Husserl, Martin Heidegger, Ferdinand de Saussure, and Emmanuel Levinas. As such, they spoke to the key issues in the human experience: knowledge, individual identity, consciousness, language, and freedom. Boasting the very best education that France could provide as well as a penetrating mind, Derrida was arguably at his best in raising questions rather than in providing answers, in critiquing the positions of others rather than in creating an intellectual model capable of being easily understood and applied by others. Yes, it is true, that modern academic practices of literary or textual "deconstruction" owe a clear debt to Derrida. Such practices are, however, a pale shadow of the claims made by Derrida on behalf of his theoretical framework in the late 1960s and early 1970s, a period that saw Derrida (1971/1973: 329) grandiosely declare that,

> Deconstruction does not consist in passing from one concept to another, but in overturning and displacing a conceptual order, as well as the nonconceptual order with which the conceptual order is articulated.

Having associated his work with unachievable intellectual outcomes, Derrida found himself in the position that Newton Garver (1973: xxvii), the translator of *Speech and Phenomena*, feared his work was heading in 1973, "along a path to nowhere." Certainly, none of Derrida's later work were characterized by the philosophic depth or originality of those published between 1967 and 1972. More fundamentally, Derrida's entire body of work pales by comparison with the leading figures of French humanist existentialism, most notable Jean-Paul Sartre and Albert Camus; figures who differed from Derrida in making the nature and conditions of freedom the center of their concerns. Whereas Derrida perceived psychic oppression in every aspect of the Western experience, Sartre (1943/1956: 30) argued in his *Being and Nothingness* that "the essence of [a] human being is suspended" in their "freedom," and that "freedom is impossible to distinguish from the being of 'human reality'." Whereas Derrida argued that a full and total "emancipation" requires the freeing of the individual consciousness from all the constraints imposed by Western language and its "logico-philosophical heritage," Camus 1951/1978: 291) observed in *The Rebel* that, "Absolute freedom mocks at justice," allowing the strong to overpower the weak. Accordingly, Camus (1951/1978: 290) concluded, "There is no justice in society without natural or civil rights as its basis. There are no rights without expression of those rights." In Camus's (1951/1978: 225) estimation, the very success of Western democracies rested on what he called "the law of moderation," a unique capacity to respect individual rights within a context of checks and balances. This is an understanding that Derrida never appears to have understood.

Cross-References

▶ Foundations: The Roots of Idealist and Romantic Opposition to Capitalism and Management
▶ Management History in the Modern World: An Overview
▶ Paul-Michel Foucault: Prophet and Paradox
▶ The Intellectual Origins of Postmodernism
▶ What Is Management?

References

Ankersmit FR (1989) Historiography and postmodernism. Hist Theory 28(2):137–153
Ankersmit FR (1990) Reply to professor Zagorin. Hist theory 29(3):263–274
Barthes R (1957/1972) Mythologies. Hill and Wang, New York
Bass A (1977/2001) Translator's introduction. In: Derrida J (ed) Writing and difference (trans: Bass A). Routledge Classics, London/New York, pp ix–xxiii
Borradori G (ed) (2003) Philosophy in a time of terror: dialogues with Jürgen Habermas and Jacques Derrida. University of Chicago Press, Chicago/London
Bowden B (2018) Work, wealth and postmodernism: the intellectual conflict at the heart of business endeavour. Cham, Switzerland
Bunge M (1996) In praise of intolerance to charlatanism in academia. In: Gross PR, Levitt N, Lewis MW (eds) The flight from science and reason. New York Academy of Sciences, New York, pp 96–115
Camus A (1951/1978) The rebel: an essay on man in revolt (trans: Bower A). Alfred A. Knopf, New York
Chérif M (2003/2008) Afterword: from the southern shores, adieu to Derrida. In: Derrida J (ed) Islam and the West: a conversation with Jacques Derrida (ed: Chérif M). University of Chicago Press, Chicago, pp 95–103
de Saussure F (1915/1974) Course in general linguistics (ed: Bally C, Sechehays A). Fontana Collins, New York
Derrida J (1954/2003) The problems of genesis in Husserl's philosophy (trans: Hobson M). University of Chicago Press, Chicago/London
Derrida J (1962/1978) Edmund Husserl's origin of geometry: an introduction (trans: Leavey JP). Northwestern University Press, Evanston
Derrida J (1967a/1973) Speech and phenomena. In: Derrida J (ed) Speech and phenomena and other essay's on Husserl's theory of signs (ed: Allison DB, Garver N and trans: Garver N). Northwestern University Press, Evanston, pp 1–128
Derrida J (1967b/2001) Writing and difference (trans: Bass A). Routledge and Kegan Paul, London/New York
Derrida J (1967c/1976) Of grammatology (trans: Spivak G). John Hopkins University Press, Baltimore
Derrida J (1968a/1982) The ends of man. In: Derrida J (ed) Margins of philosophy (ed and trans: Bass A). University of Chicago Press, Chicago/London, pp 111–136
Derrida J (1968b/1973) Difference. In: Derrida J (ed) Speech and phenomena and other essay's on Husserl's theory of signs (ed: Allison DB, Garver N and trans: Garver N). Northwestern University Press, Evanston, pp 129–160
Derrida J (1971/1973) Signature, event, context. In: Derrida J (ed) Speech and phenomena and other essay's on Husserl's theory of signs (ed: Allison DB, Garver N and trans: Garver N). Northwestern University Press, Evanston, pp 307–330
Derrida J (1972a/1981) Positions (trans: Bass A). University of Chicago Press, Chicago/London

Derrida J (1972b/1981) Dissemination (trans: Johnson B). Continuum, London

Derrida J (1972c/1981) Margins of philosophy (trans: Bass A). University of Chicago Press, Chicago/London

Derrida J (1987/1989) Of spirit: Heidegger and the question (trans: Bennington G, Rowley R). University of Chicago Press, Chicago/London

Derrida J (1990/2003) Preface. In: Derrida J (ed) The problems of genesis in Husserl's philosophy (trans: Hobson M). University of Chicago Press, Chicago/London, pp xiii–xvi

Derrida J (1992a/1995) Points: interviews, 1974–1994 (ed: Weber E). Stanford University Press, Stanford

Derrida J (1992b/1995) Is there a philosophical language? In: Derrida J (ed) (1992a/1995) Points: interviews, 1974–1994 (ed and trans: Weber E). Stanford University Press, Stanford, pp 216–227

Derrida J (1993a/2006) Specters of Marx: the state of the debt, the work of mourning and the new international (trans: Kamuf P). Routledge Classics, New York/London

Derrida J (1993b/1995) The rhetoric of drugs. In: Derrida J (ed) Points: interviews, 1974–1994 (ed: Weber E and trans: Israel M). Stanford University Press, Stanford, pp 228–254

Derrida J (1998) An interview with Professor Jacques Derrida (ed: Ben-Naftali M), 8 Jan. Shoah Resource Centre, Jerusalem

Derrida J (2002/2005) Paper machine (trans: Bowlby R). Stanford University Press, Stanford

Derrida J (2003a/2008) To have lived, and to remember, as an Algerian. In: Derrida J (ed) Islam and the West: a conversation with Jacques Derrida (ed: Chérif M and trans: Fagan TL). University of Chicago Press, Chicago, pp 29–35

Derrida J (2003b/2008) East-West: unity and difference. In: Derrida J (ed) Islam and the West: a conversation with Jacques Derrida (ed: Chérif M and trans: Fagan TL). University of Chicago Press, Chicago, pp 37–45

Derrida D (2003c) Autoimmunity: real and symbolic suicides – a dialogue with Jacque Derrida. In: Borradori G (ed) Philosophy in a time of terror: dialogues with Jürgen Habermas and Jacques Derrida (trans: Brault P-A, Naas M). University of Chicago Press, Chicago/London, pp 85–136

Derrida J (2003d) Islam and the West: a conversation with Jacques Derrida (ed: Chérif M). University of Chicago Press, Chicago

Fay B (1998) The linguistic turn and beyond in contemporary theory of history. In: Fay B, Pomper P, Van RT (eds) History and theory: contemporary readings. Blackwell Publishers, Oxford, pp 1–12

Fichte J (1799/1910) The vocation of man, 2nd edn (trans: Smith W). Open Court Publishing, Chicago

Foucault M (1961/1965) Madness and civilization: a history of insanity in the age of reason (trans: Howard R). Pantheon Books, New York

Foucault M (1966/1994) The order of things: an archaeology of the human sciences. Vintage Books, New York

Foucault M (1972/2006) Appendix II – my body, this paper, this fire. In: Foucault M (ed) History of madness (trans: Murphy J, Khalfa J), 2nd edn. Routledge, London, pp 550–574

Garver N (1973) Preface. In: Derrida J (ed) Speech and phenomena and other essay's on Husserl's theory of signs (ed: Allison DB, Garver N). Northwestern University Press, Evanston, pp ix–xxix

Guterres G (2017) Report of the secretary-general on the work of the organization, 2017. United Nations, New York

Hegel G (1837/1956) Philosophy of history (trans: Sibree J). Dover Publications, New York

Heidegger M (1927/1962) Being and time (trans: Macquarie J, Robinson E). Blackwell Publishing, London, UK

Heidegger M (1975/1985) Schelling's treatise on the essence of human freedom (trans: Stambaugh J). University of Ohio Press, Athens

Husserl E (1913/1983) Ideas pertaining to a pure phenomenology and the phenomenological philosophy (trans: Rojcewicz R, Schuwer A). Martinus Nijhoff Publishers, The Hague

Internet World Stats (2019) Internet usage statistics: the internet big picture – world internet users and 219 populations stats. Mimwatts Marketing Group. https://www.internetworldstats.com/stats.htm

Lamont M (1987) How to become a domain French philosopher: the case of Jacques Derrida. Am J Philos 93(3):584–622

Levinas E (1957/1987) Meaning and sense. In: Levinas E (ed) Collected philosophical papers (ed and trans: Lingis A). Martinus Nijhoff Publishers, Dordrecht, pp 75–108

Lorenz C (1998) Historical knowledge and historical reality: a plea for "internal realism". In: Fay B, Pomper P, Van RT (eds) History and theory: contemporary readings. Blackwell Publishers, Oxford, pp 342–376

Lyotard J-F (1979/1991) The postmodern condition (trans: Bennington G). Stanford University Press, Stanford

Mikics D (2009) Who was Jacques Derrida? An intellectual biography. Yale University Press, New Haven

Miller J (1993) The passion of Michel Foucault. Simon & Schuster, New York, NY

Munslow A (1997) Deconstructing history, 2nd edn. Routledge, Abington

Plato (c.370 BC/1972) Phaedrus (trans: Hackforth R). Cambridge University Press, Cambridge, UK

Samuel R (1992) Reading the signs II: fact-grubbers and mind-readers. Hist Work J 33(1):220–251

Sartre J-P (1943/1956) Being and nothingness (trans: Barnes H). Routledge, London

Schelling FWJ (1799a/2004) Introduction to the outline of a system of the philosophy of nature. In: Schelling FWJ (ed) First outline of a system of the philosophy of nature (trans: Petersen KR). State University of New York Press, Albany, pp 193–232

Schelling FWJ (1799b/2004) First outline of a system of the philosophy of nature (trans: Petersen KR). State University of New York Press, Albany

Schelling FWJ (1809/2006) Philosophical investigations into the essence of human freedom (trans: Love J, Schmidt J). State University of New York, Albany

Schopenhauer A (1859/1969) The world as will and representation, 3rd edn. Dover Publications, Dover

Suddaby R (2016) Toward a historical consciousness: following the historic turn in management thought. M@n@gement 19(1):46–60

Suddaby, Foster WM (2017) Guest editorial: history and organizational change. J Manag 43(1):19–38

Suddaby R, Greenwood R (2005) Rhetoric strategies for resistance. Adm Sci Q 50(1):35–67

Hayden White and His Influence

31

Bradley Bowden

Contents

Introduction	724
Hayden White, 1946–1973	728
Hayden White, 1973–2018	732
Hayden White's Influence in Management History	738
Conclusion	741
Cross-References	743
References	743

Abstract

A figure who courted controversy, White's profound influence on the discipline of management history is acknowledged by friend and foe alike. Like Foucault and Derrida, White made the interrelationship between language and knowledge the key to his unique brand of historiography, declaring that there is always a "fictive character" to "historical reconstruction." In consequence, "history" was for White "a place of fantasy . . . all story, no plot, no explanation, no ideological implication at all – that is to say, 'myth'." For White, historians do not "record" history. Rather they "do" history, creating a new, imaginary world. In exploring the life and ideas of Hayden White from the time of his entry into Detroit's Wayne State University in the late 1940s, this chapter observes that although White's ideas were similar to those of French postmodernists, he came to his conclusions via an independent path. In blurring the lines between history and myth, however, White continually confronted difficulty in debates as to whether historical events such as the Holocaust were "historically" real or simply matters of historical representations.

B. Bowden (✉)
Griffith Business School, Griffith University, Nathan, QLD, Australia
e-mail: b.bowden@griffith.edu.au

© The Author(s), under exclusive licence to Springer Nature Switzerland AG 2020
B. Bowden et al. (eds.), *The Palgrave Handbook of Management History*,
https://doi.org/10.1007/978-3-319-62114-2_81

723

Keywords

Derrida · Foucault · Postmodernism · Linguistic turn · Croce · Vico

Introduction

The son of a Detroit automobile worker who obtained a veteran's scholarship to Wayne State University after the briefest of stints in the navy during World War II, the late Hayden White (1968a: 10) described the city of his youth as a "cultural and social wasteland." Yet, within this metaphorical wasteland, a student at Wayne State University only had to wander a few hundred meters to find themselves amidst the artistic splendors of one of the world's greatest art galleries, the Detroit Institute of Art. Within its walls any visitor, then as now, was exposed to a wondrous reconfiguration of reality in the works of Pieter Bruegel the Elder, Albrecht Dürer, Henri Matisse, Pablo Picasso, and an almost countless array of Renaissance and Impressionist masters. Even if a visitor was blind to the institute's art collection, no one could ignore the reconfiguration of Detroit's working experience captured on the wall panels of the gallery's forecourt, the work of the Mexican communist, Diego Rivera. It is thus not entirely surprising that White came to embody a form of history that blurred the distinction between the historical narrative and literature, between the "factual" and the "fictive." Indeed, for White (2005a: 333), history's "subject matter, that is, the past," was "a place of fantasy," an intellectual world where myth and the historical narrative were inseparable.

A figure who courted controversy, White's profound influence on the discipline of management history is acknowledged by friend and foe alike. Writing in the late 1980s, the Dutch postmodernist Frank Ankersmit (1989: 183) declared White's *Metahistory* "the most revolutionary book in the philosophy of history" written in "the previous twenty-five years." In a similar vein, the Australian feminist historians, Ann Curthoys and Ann McGrath (2009: ix), hailed White for redefining "historical writing as writing, as a form of creativity and textuality." Even declared opponents, such as the English Marxist Alex Callinicos (1995: 51), concede that "White's work is undoubtedly the decisive influence on contemporary discussions of history as narrative." Among postmodernist-inclined or "critical" management historians, it is Hayden White – rather than Foucault – that has arguably been most influential in shaping a new dissident tradition within the discipline. In their recent chapter in the *Routledge Companion of Management and Organizational History*, Jacques and Durepos (2015: 96), for example, point to "White's theory of emplotment" as a model in terms of "how facts and traces get ordered into a story form." In an article in *Academy of Management Review*, Rowlinson et al. (2014: 251) similarly point to White in delineating "the kind of history we mean." In the opinion of the late Alun Munslow (2015: 129, 136) as well, White redefined the nature of "historical work," convincing many that "history" can never be more than "a prose discourse" in which meanings "are fictively constructed."

At first glance White's appeal appears paradoxical. In large part, White's reputation rests on a single book, *Metahistory*, published in 1973. His other major works – *Tropics of Discourse* (White 1978/1985), *The Content of the Form* (White 1987), and *The Practical Past* (White 2014) – are, for all intents and purposes, collections of short essays. It is also fair to say that none of his major works are an easy read. Of his best-selling *Metahistory*, White himself conceded:

> ... it's an intimidatingly long book. It's very tiresome and repetitive. Most people who read it read some of the introduction and maybe read around a bit. But no one reads it through. (Cited, McLemee 2018: 4)

White's claim to theoretical originality is also threadbare. As White himself willingly acknowledged, his main theoretical claims – that historical "facts" are manufactured by the historian, that the primary purpose of history should be one of inspiration rather than historical accuracy, and that the modern focus on science and rationality has come at a great cost to the human spirit – were drawn from Benedetto Croce, Giambattista Vico, and, to a lesser degree, Friedrich Nietzsche. White's understanding of language, and of the relationship between mythical representations and historical narrative, owed a debt to the French linguist and philosopher, Roland Barthes (Domanska 2008: 3–4; Paul 2011: 91). His argument that any historical narrative was inevitably organized around different "tropes" (i.e., metaphor, metonymy, synecdoche, irony) was obtained from Vico and Kenneth Burke's essay, "Four Master Tropes" (McLemee 2018: 3). Principally concerned with the history of ideas, White's interests were almost solely directed toward Western European philosophy and literature. His most notable study, *Metahistory*, for example, involved a consideration of the ideas of eight (dead white male) European and historians (Hegel, Michelet, Ranke, Tocqueville, Burckhardt, Marx, Nietzsche, Croce). Not surprisingly, this led to complaints by other "critical" historians that White's work was irredeemably "Eurocentric" (Waldman 1981: 785, 789). While the ancestry of White's theoretical conceptions is found in Italian idealist thought, with his key theoretical texts – "The Abiding Relevance of Croce's Idea of History" (White 1963) and "The Burden of History" (White 1966) – predating the major published works of both Jacques Derrida and Michel Foucault, it is nevertheless the case that White's ideas are not dissimilar to those of Foucault. Both believed that a "discourse" or "historical narrative" could never be "objective," given that any discourse or narrative is a social construction, supposedly serving the interests of certain individuals or groups at the expense of others. Highlighting the parallels between his own work and that of Foucault in one of the first English-language critiques of Foucault's ideas, White (1973a) observed that "Foucault represents a continuation of a tradition of historical thought which originates in Romanticism and which was taken up ... by Nietzsche in the last quarter of the nineteenth century." As White well understood, an identical comment could be made about his own work.

What explains White's extraordinary appeal among "critically" inclined historians? Why is it that so many historians choose to draw on White's conceptualizations rather than Foucault's, given that the latter had not only greater public recognition but also a much wider repertoire, exploring themes as diverse as madness, sexuality, prison reform, philosophy, and governmentality?

Arguably the principal attraction of White's work is found in his constant exposition of what his biographer, Herman Paul (2011: Chap. 2), refers to as a "liberation historiography," the belief that the historian should act as the moral guardian of individual freedom. In summing up his lifelong agenda in an interview with Ewa Domanska in 2008, White declared himself in favor of "progressive history," a genre he defined as:

> ... born of a concern for the future, the future of one's own family, of one's own community, of the human species, of the earth and nature, a history that goes to the past in order to find intimations ... that might be useful for dealing with these concerns. (Cited Domanska 2008: 18)

Whereas Foucault (1975/1991, 1977/1988) depicted the modern human condition as one trapped within the confines of a "disciplinary society," White advocated an essentially anarchistic – or what he would have called "romantic" – view of the world, in which all social institutions are regarded as oppressive. In summing up this "romantic" viewpoint in one of his earliest studies, White (1968b: 52, 55) declared that "the individual is *always* the victim, never the beneficiary, of society," adding that "Romanticism ... regards social institutions, ideas, and values as barriers to overcome" [emphasis in original]. In urging historians to be flagbearers in a universal opposition to authority, White also no doubt won favor by portraying historical writing not as a mundane craft bound to follow the "facts" but rather as "a poetic process" (White 1978/1985: 125), a practice that called for the dissolution of "the very distinction between real and imaginary events" in the cause of human liberation (White 1980: 10).

Associating his type of history with a "poetic" style and a morally virtuous purpose, White depicted more traditional historians as not only epistemologically misguided but also as enemies of freedom, the agents of an oppressive modernity. "What we postmodernists are against," White (2005b: 152) declared late in his career, "is a professional historiography, in service to state apparatuses that have turned against their own citizens, with its epistemically (sic) pinched, ideologically sterile, and superannuated notions of objectivity." Thus, in declaring oneself an adherent of White's methodologies and conceptualizations, one not only associates oneself with a "poetic" style of history but also with a morally virtuous "progressive" cause, a cause that sees one aligned against the dead hand of social reaction as well as outmoded historiographical traditions. Any disciple of White is also granted a license to dissolve accepted meanings in favor of a "liberation historiography." Munslow (2015: 140), for example, in taking inspiration from White, dismissed the practice and profession of management as a mere intellectual construct, arguing that "managers" do not "exist outside (their) discourse."

In White's methodology, the historical process is one constructed around the "event" and the meaning that historians and the wider society ascribe to individual "events" (i.e., the French Revolution, the 9/11 terror attacks). In considering any individual "event," White (2014: 46) argued in *The Practical Past* that the key issue is not whether or not the event actually happened but rather "the nature of the event, its relative novelty, the scope and intensity of its impact, and . . . what it reveals about the society in which it took place." If White had stopped his analysis at this point, there would have been few points of fundamental difference between his understandings of history and those elucidated by earlier generations of historians. Georg Hegel (1837/1956: 11), for example, in his *Philosophy of History*, observed that evidence "is by no means passive," taking meaning from the conceptual "categories" that the historian brings with them. Similarly, E.H. Carr (1961/2001: 18) in his *What Is History?* – a book that was standard fare when I was an undergraduate – advised erstwhile historians that, "By and large, the historian will get the kind of facts that he [or she] wants."

For better or worse, White did not stop his description of the historian's task by noting that the history is built upon interpretation, by weaving "facts' into an explanatory narrative. Instead, White enunciated principles that made him a prophet for some and a pariah for others. "The real" world, White (2005b: 147) proclaimed, consists "of everything that can be truthfully said about its actuality plus everything that can be truthfully said about what it could *possibly* be" [emphasis in original]. White also suggested that history only became "practical" or socially useful when it acted as an agent for "progressive' change. This necessarily entailed, White (2014: 8) advised in *The Practical Past*, a process of historical writing in which "the imagination, intuition, passion, and, yes, even prejudice" are "permitted to take precedence over considerations of veracity, perspicuity, 'plain' speech, and common sense." In abandoning "common sense," White (2014: 47) also concluded that, "Fantasies of alien cultures in outer space and theories of parallel or antithetical universes" are as "real" as a carefully constructed historical narrative if they "reflect the wish, hope, or fear" of a future fundamentally different to the present.

In giving "fantasies" an equal place alongside – or, rather, within – "history," White relegated "facts" to a secondary status, declaring: "Facts belong to speech, language and discourse, not to the real world" (cited Domanska 2008: 5). In short, the value of history is found in its capacity to inspire "progressive" social action.

White's understanding of "facts" and "history" was very different to that enunciated by the French historian, Marc Bloch, who wrote *The Historian's Craft* on scraps of paper while acting as a resistance leader in occupied France during World War II. Arrested, tortured, and, ultimately, executed by the Gestapo, Bloch (1944/1954: 83) observed, while standing on the edge of the grave, that "we have no right to make any assertion which cannot be verified." Yes, it is true that "facts" can be discovered, forgotten, contradicted, and interpreted in many different ways. But, contrary to what White and his intellectual followers have argued, the work of the historian is *not* built around the collection of facts so much as in the testing of hypotheses. Facts are only useful to the extent that they facilitate the verification or rejection of our arguments or theses. In this, the historian's task not only resembles that of the natural scientist but also the carpenter, the architect, and the bridge builder, all of whom are constantly testing theses against verifiable evidence (i.e., will this form of construction result in a stronger or weaker bridge?). In other words, in history – as in other disciplines – intellectual and social progress is obtained by confronting verifiable evidence, not by imagining a world of fantasy.

In exploring Hayden White and his influence, the body of this chapter will comprise three sections, namely, the idealist antecedents to White's historical understandings and his key publications prior to the release of *Metahistory* in 1973; the work of the "mature" Hayden White between the late 1970s and his death in 2018; and, finally, the ways in which White's work has profoundly influenced management history over the last two decades.

Hayden White, 1946–1973

Born in Martin, Tennessee in 1928, Hayden spent his childhood moving backward and forward between his ancestral home and Detroit, where his father obtained work during the Great Depression on a car assembly line. Boasting a humble background, White's personal circumstances were profoundly altered when he enlisted in the navy during the closing months of World War II. Once demobilized, he entered into a bachelor's program in history at Wayne State University with the benefit of a veteran's scholarship. For the rest of his long life, White never again left the hallowed halls of academia. On graduating from Wayne State in 1951, White completed a master's degree at the University of Michigan in 1952, before undertaking doctoral studies on the medieval papacy between 1952 and 1956. During his doctoral studies, White also benefited from a 3-year Fulbright Fellowship (1953–1956), a boon that funded an Italian residence. Having obtained his PhD, White then revisited Italy for another 2-year stint (1961–1962), courtesy of a Social Science Research Council Fellowship (Paul 2008: 78, 2011: 28). Returning to a position at the University of Rochester, White subsequently worked at the University of California, Los Angeles, before going back to Connecticut to take up at a position at Middleton's Wesleyan University. Coming to prominence with the publication of *Metahistory* while at the Wesleyan University, White also benefited from working alongside Richard Vann, the long-term editor of the critically inclined journal, *History and Theory*. His reputation established, White was in 1978 appointed director of the newly established History of Consciousness Department at the University of California, Santa Cruz, retaining a connection with the department for the remainder of his life (Rappaport 2018).

A perusal of White's first significant publication, "The Abiding Relevance of Croce's Idea of History," indicates that by the early 1960s the ideas that White was to articulate over the next half century were already well-formed. From the article's opening paragraph, White (1963: 109) outlined a theme that he returned to constantly in the ensuing decades, declaring: "The social theorist who does not realize that legendary modes of thought will inevitably intrude themselves into his narratives is either epistemologically naïve or is concerned solely with trivial questions." Elsewhere in the article, White (1963: 109, 111, 116, 118) outlined other intellectual positions that were to remain a constant feature of his work: that "Myth, fable and legend loom large in the social thought of our time," that history was only

31 Hayden White and His Influence

729

meaningful when it acted as "a history of human liberty," and that "when properly narrated, history becomes the equal in transforming power to tragic poetry."

Evidently, two factors profoundly influenced the thinking of the youthful White. The first of these, as White himself recounted, was a professor of history at Wayne State University, William H. Bossenbrook. Such was White's affection for Bossenbrook that in 1968 he edited a collection of papers by Bossenbrook's former students, which was then published by Wayne State under the title, *The Uses of History: Essays in Intellectual and Social History presented to William H Bossenbrook*. In the preface to this collection, White (1968b: 10, 9) recorded how Bossenbrook had the "power to endow ideas with the palpability of perceivable objects," adding: "Once exposed to Bossenbrook, it was impossible not to consider scholarship as a career . . . it was equally unthinkable not to try to teach and write in ways comfortable to what we thought he would approve of." If Bossenbrook was clearly decisive in instilling an interest in intellectual history in White, it is nevertheless also evident that he provided the mature White with few if any of his understandings of philosophy or history. As White's biographer notes, "the graduate student who in 1955 completed his thesis on the papal schism of 1130 did not resemble the White of *Metahistory* or *Tropics of Discourse*" (Paul 2008: 93). The causal factor behind the profound rupture in White's conceptualizations – turning him from a conventional historian interested in medieval history into a critic of mainstream historiography – was his sojourns in Italy (1953–1955, 1961–1962), where he befriended Carlo Antoni, a disciple of Benedetto Croce and a leading exponent of Italian philosophic idealism. Although White subsequently – as the pages of *Metahistory* make clear – showed a deep interest in German philosophic idealism, White nevertheless differed from postmodernist contemporaries such as Foucault and Derrida in making Croce and Giambattista Vico his primary touchstones rather than Nietzsche and Heidegger.

To understand the genealogy of White's understanding of history, it is therefore necessary that we first consider the idealist philosophy of both Giambattista Vico (1688–1744) and Benedetto Croce (1866–1952).

In his emphasis on history as poetry, and in "emploting" historical narratives in terms of tropes and metaphors, White owes a particular debt to Vico and his principal work, *The New Science*. Completed in 1744, Vico's work prefigured German idealist philosophers such as Johann Fichte, Friedrich Schelling, Arthur Schopenhauer, and Nietzsche in arguing that the advance of Western civilization came at excessive cost to the human spirit. Prior to the numbing effects of civilization, Vico (1744/1968: 118) believed, people possessed "vast imagination," an imagination that was "entirely immersed in the senses, buffeted by the passions." As civilization advanced, Vico (1744/1968: 128) argued, so "these vast imaginations shrank." All that was left were literary "tropes," "metaphors" that provided a remnant existence of an older, more spiritual way of perceiving the world. In Vico's (1744/1968: 131) view, "irony" was of particular use in interpreting the modern world as it is "fashioned in falsehood," thereby allowing for a greater reflection on societal falsehood.

The themes that Vico developed became a constant feature of White's work. In an article originally published in the journal, *Clio*, in 1974, for example, White (1974/

1985: 91) advised readers that "The historical narrative does not *image* the things it indicates; it *calls* to *mind* images ...in the same way metaphor does ...Properly understood, histories ... out to be read as symbolic structures, extended metaphors." Such comments, I suggest, only become fully meaningful if we locate them in the intellectual context that inspired them.

As an extended discussion in *Metahistory* made clear, White's (1973b: 415–422) opinion of Vico largely mirrored that of Croce, accepting Vico's emphasis on the "poetic" while rejecting his fundamentally pessimistic view of the human condition, supposedly trapped within the spiritually numbing advances of civilization. By contrast, White's embrace of Croce was enthusiastic. Indeed, in summing up Croce's contribution to historiography a youthful White highlighted features of Croce's work that were to subsequently become hallmarks of his own work. "All of Croce's historical works," White (1963: 121–122) accurately noted, were "more properly ... moral tracts than 'pure' scholarship," his "conception of liberty" revolving around the "rejection" of any institutionalized solution and a corresponding embrace of an individuality freed of restraints. Admittedly, in embracing Croce, White (1963: 110) realized he was associating his own work with a politically tainted product, given Croce's active support for Mussolini and fascism in the early 1920s. Indeed, White (1963: 110) lamented, "Croce's reputation has fallen as low as it is ever likely to fall, both in Italy and abroad." Fortunately for White, however, the fascist associations of Croce no more damaged his own reputation than did Derrida's framing of his work in concepts derived from the Nazi-inclined Heidegger.

Certainly, if we look to Croce's understandings – and most particularly his *Theory and History of Historiography* – we can ascertain almost all of the viewpoints that historians later came to associate with White. Like the mature White, Croce (1915/1921: 19, 12) believed that "history is principally an act of thought," an intellectual construct of the historian. As the experiences of the past are irreparably lost, any historical reconstruction has to be based on "documents" that are – whatever their claimed provenance – nothing more than "narratives," recorded by some past interest group (Croce 1915/1921: 21, 23). Accordingly, Croce (1915/1921: 75, 69) argued – prefiguring White's subsequent enunciations – "facts really do not exist," it being the case that what we think of as "facts are no longer facts ... but images." Like the mature White, Croce (1915/1921: 55–57) also repudiated the idea that we can explain historical outcomes through reference to any "universal law." Instead, Croce (1915/1921: 141) declared – as White was wont to do – that "history is always *particular* and always *special*," the product of individual thought and action. Indeed, Croce (1915/1921: 107) suggested, history can never properly be more than "the history of the individual." Consequently, any attempt to explain the "true cause" of events apart from the individual is fatally misguided. In short, for Croce – as, subsequently, for White – history as a lived experience is intensely personal, something that we can never comprehend outside of our own subjective consciousness. History as narrative, by contrast, is a construct of the historian, only fulfilling a useful role when it acts as a source of individual inspiration.

Having in 1963 outlined the principal source of his newfound understandings of history, White completed a more ambitious analysis 3 years later with the publication of "The Burden of History" in the journal, *History and Theory*. Outlining arguments

31 Hayden White and His Influence

731

identical to those found in Croce's *Theory and History of Historiography*, White (1966: 112) condemned "history" for acting as "the conservative discipline *par excellence*," distracting the populace from a necessary process of moral and social renewal based around the unrestrained powers of the individual. Calling for "the destruction of the conventional historian's conception of history," White (1966: 114, 127) advocated in its place a "surrealist, expressionistic, or existentialist historiography." In doing so, White (1966: 131, 130) ridiculed conventional historians for their obsession as to "the facts," arguing that the historian had to behave "like the artist," ordering their historical narrative around metaphors and "the purely imaginary." White also dismissed the idea that historians needed to base their work around verifiable theses, discarding those that proved unsatisfactory and adopting new ones in the light of the evidence. Instead, White (1966: 131) argued that the historian should advance metaphor by metaphor, abandoning the metaphor upon which one started in favor of "another, richer, and more inclusive metaphor." In doing so, White declared that historians had to reject concern for the past in order to embrace a transformative present. As White (1966: 123) expressed it, "only be disenthralling human intelligence from the sense of history" will humanity "be able to confront creatively the problems of the present." In other words, historians had to stop being chroniclers of the past so as to become prophets of the future. In doing so, White (1966: 133) concluded, the historian was bound by "a moral charge to free men from the burden of history," demonstrating to the citizenry "that their present condition" was the result "of specifically human choices." Change our choices, and we change past, present, and future. Or so White would have us believe.

The principles that White enunciated in "The Burden of History" were ones that, in broad brush, he remained loyal to for the rest of his life. In terms of the style of history he was proposing and its relationship with other genres, however, a more detailed picture was provided in the collection of essays that White edited for his former history lecturer from Wayne State, William Bossenbrook. Within this collection, in a chapter entitled "Romanticism, Historicism, and Realism," White argued two main propositions. First, he claimed that there was no fundamental difference between historical narratives and the "romantic" or "realist" literature of novelists such as Walter Scott, Honoré de Balzac, and Stendhal. They, White (1968b: 49) recorded, "address similar publics, use the same literary genres . . .and employ similar stylist devices." In other words, according to White, Walter Scott's novel, *Rob Roy*, should be seen in the same light as a conventional narrative history of life in the Scottish Highlands at the time of the Jacobite rising of 1745. This is an argument that has some merit, even if White overstates his case. In my chapter on pre-revolutionary Russia in this *Palgrave Handbook of Management History*, for example, I (▶ Chap. 49, "Work and Society in the Orthodox East: Byzantium and Russia, AD 450–1861") repeatedly refer to the novels of Leo Tolstoy, Ivan Turgenev, and Fyodor Dostoyevsky so as to describe not only the intellectual climate of Tsarist Russia but also, more importantly, the lived conditions of the Russian peasantry during the nineteenth century. While giving credence to these accounts, however, I do *not* treat them – as White would have us do – in the same way as I would a historical account, built upon documentary sources such as diaries, tax records, and contemporary descriptions of observed reality. For while Tolstoy's account of farm management in *Anna Karenina* is undoubtedly *based* upon observed experiences, I nevertheless understand that it is a work of fiction, recording the lives of imaginary rather than historical entities and beings.

If his suggestion that there is more than a passing resemblance between historical narrative and the historical novel has merit, White's other main argument in the collection of essays in honor of Bossenbrook – that conventional history, what he referred to as "historicism," is inferior to both literary "realism" and "romanticism" – is more controversial. Exploring a theme that he returned to constantly over his career, White contended that the professionalization of history (i.e., "historicism") was a peculiar and unfortunate attribute of post-Enlightenment Europe, largely attributable to the German theorists, Hegel and Leopold van Ranke. In White's estimation, "historicists" (i.e., professional historians) suffer from two irredeemable faults. First, White (1968b: 53) lamented, "like Vico, the historicist" believes that humanity is "condemned to society in the same way that they are condemned to history." In other words, "historicists" depict individuals not as free agents but as products of their society. The "historicists" second sin, related to the first, is found in the assumption that a study of "social institutions" is of greater value than inspirational narratives that emphasize "free expression" and "individual will" (White 1968b: 55–56). By contrast, White (1968b: 54) also suggested "realist" and "romantic" accounts were of use precisely because they contradicted the core assumptions of the "historicist," pointing to the inherently oppressive nature of all social institutions. Accordingly, as "historians" we are better advised to adopt a "romantic" perspective that inspires Nietzschean-like assertions of human will than an "historicist" approach bound by mundane facts about social institutions.

By 1968, it is evident all of the arguments and theoretical positions that were to characterize White's work – that conventional forms of history need to be demolished, that historical narratives should aspire to be works of literature capable of inspiring transformative change, and that history is better organized on the basis of metaphor rather than of fact – were already fully developed. What was missing from his theoretical positions was not so much a lack of internal cohesion as the absence of a mass readership for his ideas.

Hayden White, 1973–2018

In an editorial introduction penned in 1998, Brian Fay (1998: 2) dated "the so-called linguistic turn" in history from the publication of White's *Metahistory* in 1973. With this work, Fay (1998: 1) proclaimed, "an entire generation of historians was educated to theory and metatheory in a way no previous generation was." As a result, Fay (1998: 2) continued, "the topics of narration and representation replaced ... explanation" as "the central concern" of new age historians. In a separate assessment, Richard Vann (1998: 22), the editor of *History and Theory* and White's colleague at the Wesleyan University, declared that "The publication in 1973 of

Hayden White's *Metahistory* ... marked a decisive turn in philosophical thinking about history."

In essence, White's *Metahistory* is two books. The larger part, comprising chapters 2–10 (pp. 81–425), is an extended literature review that begins with Hegel and ends with Croce, White's philosophical hero. The second and much shorter part – covering the preface (pp. 9–12), the introduction, and chapter 1 (pp. 13–80) – represents an expansion of the theoretical and stylistic points that White had previously outlined in "The Burden of History" and "Romanticism, Historicism, and Realism." In summing up the larger part of *Metahistory*, Paul (2011: 60–61) accurately describes it as an account of "good guys and bad guys," of "heroes and villains." Heading up the list of villains are Hegel and, more particularly, Ranke. In comparing Ranke's professional histories unfavorably to Walter Scott's "novels of romance," White (1973b: 163, 174) declares that "repudiation of Romanticism was the basis of Ranke's realistic historiography," a failing that made Ranke – and, by implication, all other conventional historians – an inherently "conservative" ideologue, supposedly opposed to "new forms of community in which men might be ... freed of the restrictions placed upon." Among the "heroes" of *Metahistory*, Nietzsche is much lauded, given pride of place behind Croce. "In historical thought," White (1973b: 331) recorded, "Friedrich Nietzsche marked a turning point, for he ...denied the reality of any such thing as a historical process." In doing so, White (1973b: 332, 371) continued, Nietzsche not only destroyed "belief in a historical past"; he also created "a second *illusionary* world," a world "in which the weak vie with the strong for the authority to determine how this second world will be characterized."

As White himself understood, typically few readers of *Metahistory* get passed the preface (4 pages) and the introduction (42 pages). For those who do, White's summation of nineteenth-century philosophical positions is dubious in the extreme. As the German critic, Patrick Bahners observed, virtually every point that White made at one place in his book is contradicted by a statement provided elsewhere (cited Paul 2011:7). At times, his assessments can only be regarded as willful distortion. Nietzsche, for example, was never an advocate for the "weak." His concern, instead, was with the "strong," declaring at various times that "men are not equal" (Nietzsche 1883/1970: 124), that the "working classes ...are unintelligent," that mass of humanity represents "the lowest clay and loam layers of society" (Nietzsche 1874: 39–40), and that the advance of civilization has fatally weakened "the 'blond beast' that existed among Teutonic society prior to Christianity" (Nietzsche 1889/1990: 67).

If White's intellectual reputation rests on the introductory and concluding sections of *Metahistory* rather than the main body of the book, it is also fair to say that even these sections are – preface and conclusion aside – characterized by a convoluted literary style and complex arguments. In terms of substantive argument, White reiterated three main points. First and most importantly, White (1973b: 433) argued that by liberating humanity from the bonds of a historical past constructed around explanatory laws (i.e., economics, politics, religion, etc.), "we are free to conceive 'history' as we please, just as we are free to make of it what we will." In other words, both the historical past and the lived present can be what we imagine and will them to be. In pursuing this extreme voluntarist position, White (1973b: 1–2) advanced his second key argument: that the "character of historical representation" is inherently "fictive" and that it is *always* more a product of literary imagination than historical "fact." Upon this intellectual platform, White (1973b: 434) progressed to his third main proposition: that the historian should direct their efforts toward the liberation of the creative imagination," a process that necessarily entailed the historian's "own moral and aesthetic aspirations" – constructed around "a poetic and moral level of awareness" – taking precedence over other considerations.

While the propositions that White advanced in *Metahistory* represented a radical attack on established historical conventions, his ideas were nevertheless hardly original. As White's own book made clear, identical positions had previously been advocated by both Nietzsche and Croce. What was original about White's book was not so much his idealist and voluntarist understanding of history and its uses but rather the stylistic and literary suggestions that he put forward in order to achieve what Paul (2011) refers to as his "liberation historiography."

In making literary style rather than the collation of verifiable evidence the central task of the historian, White (1973b: x) identified "three kinds of strategy that can be used by historians to gain ...'explanatory effect'.'" In staking out an "ideological" position, White (1973b: x) declared that historians inevitably ascribe to "the tactics" of either anarchism, conservatism, radicalism, or liberalism. "For arguments," White suggested, "there are modes of Formism, Organicism, Mechanism and Contextualism." Far more significant that these two "strategies," however, was the "archetype" in which narratives were "emploted." On this front, White (1973b: x) detected four modes of "emplotment," these being "Romance, Comedy, Tragedy, and Satire." In other words, in "emploting" their account, the historian needed to think of their story as if it was a Shakespearean play, rather than as a traditional factual narrative. Beyond these three strategies, White (1973b: x) claimed to detect something even more profound about the way history is written, advising the reader that he "had been forced to postulate a deep level of consciousness on which a historical thinker chooses conceptual strategies." Declaring that he was following "a tradition of interpretation ...recently developed by Vico, [and unnamed] modern linguists, and literary theorists," White (1973b: x) opted to "call these types of prefiguration by the names of the four tropes of poetic language: Metaphor, Metonymy, Synecdoche, and Irony."

White's complex formulations inevitably raise two issues: one relating to attribution and the other to meaning. In terms of attribution, the preface of *Metahistory* is devoid of references. The conclusion to *Metahistory* is similarly unreferenced. Even the introduction and Chap. 1 of *Metahistory*, where White expands upon the literary concepts outlined in the preface, are lightly referenced. To the extent that he does provide references, White (1973b: 7–8) attributes his ideas on "emplotment" primarily to the Canadian literary critic, Northrop Frye. In later years, however, White indicated that his understandings of language and meaning were heavily influenced by the French linguist and philosopher, Roland Barthes (Domanska 2008). Certainly, it is hard to believe that White was unaware of the debate about language and power that transfixed French existentialist and postmodernist circles in the 1960s, given that his article on Foucault ("Foucault Decoded") was published prior to the publication of *Metahistory*. Indeed, as Miller (1993: 133) observes in his study of Foucault, by the late 1950s Barthes was "the oracle of the hour." Through his study, *Mythologies*, in particular, Barthes led the way in emphasizing the overlap between accepted knowledge and mythical understandings, themes that were central to White's arguments in *Metahistory*.

If the "genealogy" of the literary principles outlined in *Metahistory* are by no means clear, the understanding that erstwhile historians take away from a perusal of White's arguments is also unclear. If, for example, we turn to the work of highly accomplished academics who declared themselves followers of White – Frank Ankersmit, Keith Jenkins, Brian Fay, and Alun Munslow – there is little evidence that they paid much heed to White's ideas on historical narrative as "organicism," "synecdoche," and "satire." Instead, what critical or postmodernist historians have embraced in White's work is his more *general* epistemological principles: that "facts" are a literary artifact, that "history" is a "fictive" construct of the historian, and that history is only useful when it is part of a "liberation historiography." Certainly these are the themes that appear constantly in postmodernist histories. If we look to Ankersmit (1989: 144, 153, 145), for example, we read that "Style, not content, is the issue," that historical narratives need to bring about "ethical and aesthetic contemplation," and that "historical work" needs to be understood as "art." Similarly, in the writings of Munslow (2015: 136, 134, 135), we read that "Meanings are fictively constructed," that historical narratives "create" reality, and that "History is a substitution for the past." In a similar vein, Jenkins (2008: 67, 68, 70) informs us that "arguments are never true or false," that "history" is necessarily "rhetorical," and that through "countless readings" of the past the present can be "democratized." The lack of historical interest in White's ideas about literary "emplotment" is also suggested by White's own behavior in the years that followed the publication of *Metahistory*. Increasingly he turned his back on history as his ideas on literary emplotment found greater favor among literary theorists. As his onetime colleague, Richard Vann (1998: 148) recorded, "White became much less of a presence in historical circles, regularly preferring to attend Modern Language Association conventions rather than those of the American Historical Association."

For White, 1973 was notable not only for the publication of *Metahistory* but also of his article, "Foucault Decoded." In what remains one of the best assessments of Foucault's work, White readily identified the weaknesses in the French philosopher's work. Of Foucault's *History of Madness*, White (1973a: 38) accurately observed that it was "a rambling discourse," based upon "a very limited body of data." White (1973a: 31) also accurately summed up Foucault's relationship with causal explanations, noting that Foucault rejected "*all* causal explanations, of whatever sort" [emphasis in original]. Despite – or, because of – such problems, White (1973a: 26) also recognized in Foucault a kindred spirit, "an anti-historian historian," someone who wrote history "in order to destroy it." White (1973a: 50) also declared that "Foucault represents a continuation of a tradition of historical thought which originates in Romanticism and which was taken up . . . by Nietzsche in the last quarter of the nineteenth century." In associating Foucault with Nietzsche and romanticism, White was issuing his strongest possible endorsement, aligning his own assault on modernity with that of Foucault. At the same time, however, White took the opportunity to distinguish his own work *from* that of Foucault, spending several pages on discussions of Vico, "tropes," "synecdoche," and "metonymy," the meanings of which probably escaped the typical reader.

Intellectually, if not in terms of job progression, 1973 arguably represented White's career peak. In large part, White's subsequent publications represented merely a reiteration of points already made in "The Burden of History," *Metahistory*, and "Foucault Decoded." White's subsequent books – *Tropics of Discourse* (1978), *The Content of the Form* (1987), and *The Practical Past* (2014) – were also, as we have previously noted, essentially collections of short essays. In this White was undoubtedly playing to his own literary strengths, which belied his claims to poetic style and romantic beauty. For as his biographer, Herman Paul (2011: 7), notes, White's "favorite genre" was "not the monograph" – which suffered from reader "inaccessibility" – but the "essay" that lent itself to a "25-page outburst of creativity."

To the extent that White pursued new historical themes after 1973, it was typically in response to attacks on his work as White's understanding of "facts," "truth," and the "fictive" became mired in two major polemical debate.

The first and most significant of these controversies involved understandings of the Holocaust, a massacre of millions of innocents that belied White's (1973b: 1– 2) belief in "the fictive character of historical reconstruction." In an article entitled "Is it Possible to Misrepresent the Holocaust" – initially published in *History and Theory* and republished in the edited collection, *History and Theory: Contemporary Readings*, before reappearing in an expanded book form as *Holocaust Representation: Art within the Limits of History* – Berel Lang (1995, 1998, 2000) made a devastating assault on the relativism of White's historical genre. Putting the matter bluntly, Lang (1995: 89) declared that the issue of the Holocaust allowed the historian little wriggle room: Did they accept its factual existence or not? Extending his assault to the wider issue as to whether or not "historical narratives ... are unfettered by anything more than the historian's imagination," Lang (1995: 89) made the pertinent point that "Most people ... would be reluctant to concede that whether they existed five minutes ago depends entirely on what historians ... say about them." Even prior to Lang's attack, the issue of the Holocaust caused White professional grief as Carlo Ginzburg – a professor of Italian studies at the University of California, Los Angeles – used a conference on the Holocaust in 1990 to imply that White harbored proto-fascist ideas (Paul 2011: 121). In responding to the issues raised by the Holocaust, White's long-term colleague and supporter, Hans Kellner, chose to defend the indefensible. In Kellner's (1998: 237) belief, the Holocaust was simply a rhetorical term, "an imaginative creation, like all historical events." Yes, Kellner (1998: 237) conceded, various individuals were murdered at places like Babi Yar. But, "no one witnessed the Holocaust," which was instead "imaginatively constituted." For his part, White beat a somewhat confused retreat, attempting to defend his lifelong positions on the rhetorically constructed nature of the historical narrative while conceding a factual existence to the Holocaust, a position that long-term supporters such as Kellner (accurately) perceived as a failure of nerve. In devoting an entire chapter of *The Practical Past* (Chap. 2) to debates about the Holocaust, White (2014: 28–29) confronted the question as to whether the Holocaust was "true" by declaring, "this question … is of secondary importance to discourses making reference to the real world … cast in a mode other than that of simple declaration." From this muddled viewpoint, White (2014: 38) concluded that,

> My suggestion has been that we cannot establish on the basis of any strictly factual account whether the Holocaust was a new event, a new kind of event, or … an event peculiar to our modernity.

Understandably, this "solution" to the debate as to the factual truth of the Holocaust appealed to neither friend nor foe.

Whereas the controversy involving the Holocaust revolved around matters of fact, the second polemic that White found himself enmeshed in was a dispute over myth and its uses. In an article entitled "Hayden White, Traumatic Nationalism, and the Public Role of History," the Australian-based academic, Dirk Moses (2005: 312–313), acknowledged White "as a harbinger of postmodern literary theory, even its 'patron saint', while at the same time lambasting him for being blind as to the adverse impact of his ideas. As Moses (2005: 314) correctly surmised, "White thinks that national or ethnic mythologies are a legitimate use of the past insofar as they an answer to the burden of history." The problem, Moses noted, was that mythology was used by various ethnic groups to justify their historical standing vis-à-vis other religious or political communities. Pointing to recent experiences in Eastern Europe, Africa, and the Middle East, Moses (2005: 314–315) noted the "unspeakable atrocities" committed by "ethnic groups and nationalizing states in thrall to traumatic memories" and myths. White's response to this intellectual assault was in many ways even more unconvincing than that made in relation to the Holocaust controversy. In a reply to Moses published in *History and Theory*, White (2005a: 333) simply observed that "we have different notions about the nature of historical discourse and the uses to which historical knowledge can properly be put." Having made this all too obvious point, White (2005a: 333) then simply proceeded to restate his well-established belief that "history is a place of fantasy," unlike the past, which he dismissed as "the realm of the dead."

In many ways, Moses's denunciation of White's ideas on history and mythology was unwarranted, a case of a critical historian being more virtuous than the virtuous White. Hayden White can hardly be blamed for the savage civil wars that occurred in the Balkans and the Middle East during the opening years of the twenty-first century. It is, after all, highly unlikely that many members of the Kurdish *Peshmerga* or the Kosovo Liberation Front were inspired to take up arms by their reading of *Meta-history*. There is, nevertheless, more than a grain of truth in Moses's critique of White's work. As Lang (1995: 85) noted, there is little to be gained by those who take activist positions in historical discourse and metaphysical debates "burying their heads in the sand" when people take unfortunate conclusions from the messages that are conveyed. For, as White himself constantly emphasized, it is through understandings of history that cultures obtain their sense of identity. If these are based on myth, on "fantasy," rather than a sense of reality, it is more likely that adverse consequences will follow rather than any beneficial outcome.

Hayden White's Influence in Management History

Among historians, Hayden White remains a deeply divisive figure. The strength of these divisions is indicated in a tale recounted by Roy Suddaby, a former editor of *Academy of Management Review* and current program chair of the Management History Division (MHD) of the Academy of Management. During his time as *Academy of Management Review* editor, Suddaby remembers how he made the "naïve error" of favorably citing Hayden White before an American business historians' conference. "The crowd seethed" to such an extent, Suddaby (2016: 47) recalls, that he feared the use of "pitchforks." That so many people would be irate at mention of White's name points to the continued opposition to his ideas among "traditional" historians. Conversely, the fact that the editor of *Academy of Management Review* – arguably the most prestigious journal in management academia – would sing White's praises highlights the continuing influence of his ideas.

As someone who served as an executive member of the MHD between 2013 and 2018, and who has also had the privilege of being the editor in chief of the *Journal of Management History* since 2015, it is evident to me that White's influence within management history has never been higher than it is today.

The extraordinary reach of White's formulations is evidenced in the 2014 article by Rowlinson et al. (2014: 151, 157) in *Academy of Management Review* entitled "Research strategies for organizational history." This article not only begins by acknowledging White as "a leading philosopher of history," it also declares acceptance of his view "that there is a "literary" or "fictive" element in all historical . . . and scientific writing." In a subsequent article in *Academy of Management Review*, entitled "What is Organizational History? Toward a Creative Synthesis of History and Organization Studies," Godfrey et al. (2016: 599) echo similar themes, declaring "history" to be "a malleable substance that actors mould and shape to justify their actions." In his *History of History*, the influential British historian and founding coeditor of *Rethinking History*, Alun Munslow (2012: 8), also declared history to be "a *fictive* construction . . . *the construction of the historian*" [emphasis in the original]. In her review of recent debates in management and organizational history, the *amodernist* historian Gabrielle Durepos (2015: 153) ranks White alongside Foucault in terms of his importance in shaping "the modern versus postmodern debate by contributing to the development of postmodern historiography." In the inaugural editorial of *Management & Organizational History*, Charles Booth and Michael Rowlinson (2006: 10) also ranked White alongside Foucault in terms of the "philosophy of history and historical theorists" that they saw their newly established journal engaging with. White's concepts have also been seminal to the growing postmodernist displacement of the "scientific attitude" by the so-called "rhetorical attitude" or what Alvesson and Kärreman (2000: 144–145) refer to as "grounded fictionalism." Associated with the "linguistic" or "discursive" turn in the social sciences, the "Rhetorical Attitude" perceives all knowledge as essentially ideology, mere devices for both maintaining and challenging power (see, e.g., Suddaby and Greenwood 2005).

What explains the steady advance of postmodernist ideas, inspired in large part by Hayden White, within management history? In part, I suggest, this advance can be explained by the fact that the long-dominant traditions within management history – and within the MHD in particular – were always vulnerable targets. As I (▶ Chap. 1, "Management History in the Modern World: An Overview") indicate in the general introduction to this *Palgrave Handbook of Management History*, the MHD what I refer to as the George-Wren-Greenwood-Bedeian tradition; a school of thought that was positivist in orientation, supportive of free market capitalism in terms of ideology and dedicated to understanding the impact of changing patterns of management thought (George 1968/1972; Wren and Bedeian 1972/2017). Within this tradition, Dan Wren (University of Oklahoma) and Art Bedeian (Louisiana State University), were particularly influential. Concerned with sound scholarship and the rigorous training of their many students of management history, Wren and Bedeian – and their legion of graduates – paid much heed to intellectual history but little attention to abstract matters relating to ontology, epistemology and philosophy. Accordingly, when the postmodernist challenge arrived at the MHD's door, those located within the George-Wren-Greenwood-Bedeian tradition were ill-prepared for a defense. Some of Wren and Bedeian's former students defected, finding the "critical" abstractions of Foucault and White to their liking. Prominent among these defectors were Milorad Novicevic and Shawn Carraher, both former MHD chairs. In a co-authored study entitled "Decentering Wren's *Evolution of Management Thought*," both participated in a repudiation of the dominant George-Wren-Greenwood-Bedeian tradition, declaring that "our decentered examination of Wren's *Evolution of Management Thought* posits that this book should be viewed as a historical platform, rather than as a foundation of historical knowledge" (Novecivic et al. 2015: 27). Among those who steeped in the George-Wren-Greenwood-Bedeian tradition, only my fellow editor, Jeffrey Muldoon, has bothered to undertake the serious study of postmodernist ideas and principles that is a prerequisite for any counter-attack (see Muldoon 2019).

As with most postmodernists, White was wont to depict industrial capitalism and its associated systems of management as nothing but a catastrophe, a blight from which the typical citizen of the world gained nothing, could hope for nothing. In an interview in 2012, for example, White declared that:

> For me, the "history" of the world, or global history, is the story of the rise and expansion of an economic system which, in its very development, functions as a cancer on the human and earthly corpus which it purports to nourish by producing "wealth" out of "nothing." The exposure of this cancer is an ethical duty for any scholar. I would hope that historians would see their profession in this way. (Cited Sklokin 2012)

Like the reality of the Holocaust, White's comments on the achievements of capitalism and management cannot resolved through reference to one or more texts, a process that typically ends in a circle of claim and counterclaim. Rather, it is best considered by looking to evidence not intended as a "narrative discourse" of the past. As we discussed in previous chapters, a particularly useful source in this regard are the long-term records on European consumer prices and wages collated by the International Scientific Committee on Price History. Established in 1929, this committee created an extensive European database, recording the real wage of building workers, both skilled and unskilled, between the thirteenth and twentieth centuries (Cole and Crandall 1964). Of the studies that have emerged from this database, of particular utility is the so-called Phelps Brown and Hopkins (1956: 306) index, which traced the real wage of a skilled building worker from Southern England, measured against a basket of consumables. As is evident in Fig. 1 – which summarizes the results of this index for the period 1264 to 1930 (1447 representing 100 in the index) – it is evident that the only sustained improvement in living standards prior to the Industrial Revolution was associated with the Black Death, the bubonic plague outbreak of the fourteenth century that left survivors with a surfeit of arable land. With the managerial and technological revolutions of the eighteenth and nineteenth centuries, however, the living circumstances of the typical worker was fundamentally transformed for the better. Nor was it the case that these economic advances came, as White (1968b: 52, 55) suggested, at the expense of the individual, of freedom and free expression. Rather the reverse was true. Everywhere, the Western form of liberal, industrial capitalism was associated with increased literacy, democracy, the protection of children, and increased opportunities for society's female members. In short, whereas White (2005a: 333) associated the "liberation historiography" that he advocated with "history" as "a place of fantasy," a management historian can justly point to real achievements and a fundamental transformation in the human condition.

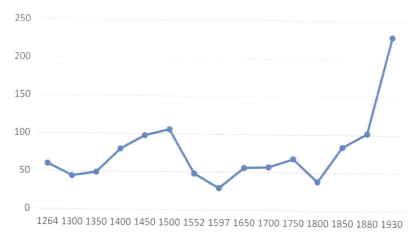

Fig. 1 Real wage of skilled building worker in Southern England, 1264–1930 (1447 = 100). (Source: Phelps Brown and Hopkins: "Seven centuries of ... builders' wage rates," Appendix B)

Conclusion

Hayden White enjoyed a fortunate life. Hailing from a Detroit working-class family, White joined the navy too late to see combat service in World War II but early enough to qualify for a postwar veteran's scholarship to university. Inspired to study medieval history while at Detroit's Wayne State University, White's doctoral studies at the University of Michigan benefited from a Fulbright fellowship that funded a long period of study in Italy. Falling under the influence of Carlo Antoni – a disciple of the Italian idealist philosopher and onetime fascist supporter, Benedetto Croce – White became expert in ideas that appeared novel in an American context. Having adopted the esoteric philosophical principles of Croce, with their emphasis on individualism and extreme voluntarism, White's ideas found unexpected favor with a mass audience during the late 1960s and early 1970s, a time when a disgruntled but highly educated younger generation felt alienated from society's dominant ideologies and institutions. As such, White's career paralleled that of publicly better known French postmodernists such as Foucault and Derrida but was nevertheless distinct from them. Whereas Foucault, Derrida, and the other French postmodernists invariably looked to German philosophical idealism for inspiration, White came to his conclusions by a separate and independent route.

Like Foucault and, more particularly, Derrida, White made the interrelationship between language and knowledge the key to his unique brand of historiography, (in)famously declaring that there is always a "fictive character" to "historical reconstruction" (White 1973b: 1–2). For White, history was "a place of fantasy" and "historical representation … all story, no plot, no explanation, no ideological implication at all – that is to say, 'myth'" (White 2005a: 372–373). As such, historians do not "record" history. Rather they "do" history, creating a new, imaginary world. In doing so, White (1973b: xii) advised in *Metahistory*, a historian needed to give "aesthetic and moral" concerns a greater weight than matters relating to evidence. Drawing on Giambattista Vico and Roland Barthes, White (2005b: 147) also argued that greater meaning was to be had from narratives that inspired the imagination that in those that boasted a spurious claim to "objectivity." For, White (2005b: 147) continued, the "real" should be perceived as far more than "the true," embracing in addition "the possible or imaginable." Like Foucault and, more particularly, Derrida, White (1968b: 55) regarded not just industrial capitalism but the entire social structure of the West as a blight, condemning "social institutions, ideas, and values as barriers to be overcome, bastions against the free expression of nature and individual human will."

Like Foucault and Derrida, White's work was Eurocentric in nature. Yes, it is true, White (1973b: 2) condemned as "a specifically Western prejudice … the presumed superiority of modern, industrial society" vis-à-vis other societies. Nevertheless, White's intellectual framework is one that only has meaning within a Eurocentric culture. It not only draws on complex traditions of Western idealist thought, it also primarily speaks to a highly educated Western intelligentsia with its talk of the "fictive" and literary "emplotment" around metaphor and literary tropes such as metonymy and synecdoche. As Waldman (1981: 791) accurately noted, the "distinctions" that White made between "historical and fictional narrative" were also ones that drew "from essentially Eurocentric research." It is also the case that if White had of published *Metahistory* in 2020 rather than 1973 he would have received brickbats rather than bouquets, condemned for an excessive interest in the philosophies of 8 dead, white males.

Much lauded, White's historiography, and the genre of historical narrative that it inspired, suffers from three interrelated problems. First, as we noted in the previous section, White treated all evidence as if it were narrative, a textual discourse on the past. Across a publishing career of more than half a century, White never paid any great heed to those sources of evidence that are – or should be – the lifeblood of a management historian: production output, transportation records, tax accounts, census figures, labor participation, and employment data. White's second failing, related to the first, is found in his myopic understanding of history. For White, history revolved around the "event," the specific historical experience that is supposedly the product of individual acts of consciousness and will. Given the supposedly unique nature of every event, White's methodology rules out any understanding of history as a product of decades and even centuries of accretion, in which each generation builds upon – and is shaped – by the effort of those who came before. As White (2006: 29) expressed it late in his career, "the knowledge with which history provides us is so situation-specific as to be irrelevant to later times and places." This is a very different – and much narrower – view of history than that advocated by the French historian, Fernand Braudel (1946/1975: 21), who dismissed "the history of events" as "surface disturbances, crests of foam that the tides of history carry on their strong back." Like it or not, we are all products of our history, a past that both empowers and limits the goals and aspirations of our own time. Together, White's myopic understanding of history and evidence resulted in a third failing: he never evinced much appreciation of the material achievements of the society that allowed him such a fortunate life. Instead, White increasingly advocated a Marxist condemnation of capitalism even as the Marxist societies of Europe crumbled into ruin, declaring in 2012:

> I view history or rather the course of socio-political development in the West from Rome to the present from a Marxist perspective, and my criticism of the historical profession in modern times stems from my conviction that it is part of the Superstructure of a Base dominated by the Capitalist mode of production. (Cited Sklokin 2012)

Finding little to commend in his own society, White instead found favor in the circumstances of Chinese communism, observing: "In my recent visits to China I was much struck by the ways in which Chinese intellectuals, including historians and social scientists, were trying to combine Maoist with Confucianist principles for the creation of a socially and political responsible knowledge" (cited Sklokin 2012). Such praise for a totalitarian regime, where dissent continues to be brutally suppressed, did White no credit.

In short, if we look to the stated goals of Hayden White's work, we are struck by the gulf between goals and the means of achieving those goals. Constantly, White spoke of broadening the historical imagination while advocating a myopic view of the historical process. Across his long career, he constantly spoke of individual freedom and will while showing a strange reluctance to condemn the very real threats to freedom from totalitarian societies. Declaring himself an opponent of European ethnocentric, White's whole genre was itself deeply ethnocentric. None of these intellectual contradictions, however, denied him a fortunate life.

Cross-References

▶ Foundations: The Roots of Idealist and Romantic Opposition to Capitalism and Management
▶ Management History in the Modern World: An Overview
▶ Paul-Michel Foucault: Prophet and Paradox
▶ The Intellectual Origins of Postmodernism
▶ What Is Management?

References

Alvesson M, Kärreman D (2000) Taking the linguistic turn in organizational research. J Appl Behav Sci 36(2):136–158
Ankersmit FR (1989) Historiography and postmodernism. Hist Theory 28(2):137–153
Barthes R (1957/1972) Mythologies. Hill and Wang, New York
Bloch M (1944/1954) The historian's craft (trans: Putan P). Manchester University Press, Manchester
Booth C, Rowlinson M (2006) Management and organizational history: prospects. Manag Organ Hist 1(1):5–30
Braudel F (1946/1975) Preface to the first edition (trans: Reynolds S). In: Braudel F (ed) The Mediterranean and the Mediterranean world in the age of Philip II. Harper Torchbooks, New York, pp 17–22
Callinicos A (1995) Theories and narratives: reflections on the philosophy of history. Polity Press, Cambridge
Carr EH (1961/2001) What is history? Palgrave Macmillan, Basingstoke
Cole AH, Crandall R (1964) The international scientific committee on price history. J Econ Hist 24(3):381–388
Croce B (1915/1921) Theory and history of historiography (trans: Ainslie D). George G Harrap & Co., London
Curthoys A, McGrath A (2009) Introduction. In: Curthoys A, Mc Grath A (eds) Writing histories: imagination and narration. Monash University ePress, Melbourne, pp viii–xvi
Domanska E (2008) A conversation with Hayden White. Rethink Hist 12(1):3–21
Durepos G (2015) ANTi-history: toward a modern histories. In: McLaren PG, Mills AJ, Weatherbee TG (eds) The Routledge companion to management and organizational history. Routledge, London/New York, pp 153–180
Fay B (1998) The linguistic turn and beyond in contemporary theory of history. In: Fay B, Pomper P, Van RT (eds) History and theory: contemporary readings. Blackwell Publishers, Oxford, pp 1–12
Foucault M (1975/1991) Discipline and punish: the birth of the prison (trans: Sheridan A). Vintage Books, New York
Foucault M (1977/1988) Confinement, psychiatry, prison: a dialogue with David Cooper, Jean-Pierre Faye, Marie-Odile Faye and Marine Zecca. In: Kritzman LD (ed) Michel Foucault:

politics, philosophy, culture – interviews and other writings, 1977–1984. Routledge, London/New York, pp 178–210

George (1968/1972) The history of management thought. Prentice Hall, Englewood Cliffs

Godfrey PC, Hassard J, O'Connor ES, Rowlinson M, Ruef M (2016) What is organizational history? Toward a creative synthesis of history and organization studies. Acad Manag Rev 41(4):590–608

Hegel G (1837/1954) Philosophy of history. Dover Publications, New York

Jacques R, Durepos G (2015) A history of management histories: does the story of our past and the way we tell it matter. In: McLaren PG, Mills AJ, Weatherbee TG (eds) The Routledge companion to management and organizational history. Routledge, London/New York, pp 96–111

Jenkins K (2008) "Nobody does it better": radical history and Hayden White. Rethink Hist 12(1):59–75

Kellner H (1998) "Never again" is now. In: Fay B, Pomper P, Van RT (eds) History and theory: contemporary readings. Blackwell Publishers, Oxford, pp 225–244

Lang B (1995) Is it possible to misrepresent the holocaust? Hist Theory 34(1):84–89

Lang B (1998) Is it possible to misrepresent the holocaust? In: Fay B, Pomper P, Van RT (eds) History and theory: contemporary readings. Blackwell Publishers, Oxford, pp 245–250

Lang B (2000) Holocaust representation: art within the limits of history. John Hopkins University Press, Baltimore/London

McLemee S (2018) Essay on the death of Hayden White. Inside Higher Ed. https://www.insidehighered.com/print/views/2018/03/09/essay-death-hayden-white

Miller J (1993) The passion of Michel Foucault. Simon & Schuster, New York

Moses D (2005) Hayden White, traumatic nationalism, and the public role of history. Hist Theory 44(3):311–332

Muldoon J (2019) Stubborn things: evidence, postmodernism and the craft of history. J Manag Hist 25(1):125–136

Munslow A (2012) History of history. Routledge, London/New York

Munslow A (2015) Management the past. In: McLaren PG, Mills AJ, Weatherbee TG (eds) The Routledge companion to management and organizational history. Routledge, London/New York, pp 129–142

Nietzsche F (1889/1990) Twilight of the idols. In: F Nietzsche (trans: Hollingdale R) Twilight of the Idols/The Anti-Christ Penguin Classics, London, pp. 1–125

Nietzsche F (1874) On the use and abuse of history for life (trans: Hollingdale R). http://la.utexas.edu/users/hcleaver/330T/350kPEENietzscheAbuseTableAll.pdf

Nietzsche F (1883/1970) Thus spoke Zarathustra (trans: Hollingdale R). Penguin Books, London

Novecivic MM, Jones JL, Carraher S (2015) Decentering Wren's *Evolution of Management Thought*. In: McLaren PG, Mills AJ, Weatherbee TG (eds) The Routledge companion to management and organizational history. Routledge, London/New York, pp 11–30

Paul H (2008) A Weberian medievalist: Hayden White in the 1950s. Rethink Hist 12(1):75–102

Paul H (2011) Hayden White: the historical imagination. Polity, Cambridge

Phelps Brown EH, Hopkins SV (1956) Seven centuries of the prices of consumables, compared with builders' wage rates. Economica 23(92):296–314

Rappaport S (2018) Influential historian Hayden White dies at 89. News centre: University of California, Santa Cruz. https://news.ucsc.edu/2018/03/hayden-white-news-obit.html

Rowlinson M, Hassard J, Decker S (2014) Research strategies for organizational history: a dialogue between historical theory and organization theory. Acad Manag Rev 39(3):250–274

Sklokin V (2012) It is no so much a paradigm shift as a total breakdown: a conversation with Prof. Hayden White. Historians. http://www.historians.in.ua/index.php/en/intervyu/258-it-is-not-so-much-a-paradigm-shift-as-a-total-breakdown-a-conversation-with-prof-hayden-white

Suddaby R (2016) Toward a historical consciousness: following the historic turn in management thought. M@n@gement 19(1):46–60

Suddaby R, Greenwood R (2005) Rhetoric strategies for resistance. Adm Sci Q 50(1):35–67

Van RT (1998) The reception of Hayden White. Hist Theory 37(2):143–161

Vico G (1744/1968) The new science (trans: Bergin TG, Fisch MH). Third. Cornell University Press, New York

Waldman M (1981) The "otherwise noteworthy year 711": a reply to Hayden White. Crit Inq 7(4):784–792

White HV (1963) The abiding relevance of Croce's idea of history. J Mod Hist 35(2):109–124

White H (1966) The burden of history. Hist Theory 5(2):111–134

White HV (1968a) Preface. In: White HV (ed) The uses of history: essays in intellectual and social history presented to William H Bossenbrook. Wayne State University, Detroit, pp 9–13

White HV (1968b) Romanticism, historicism, and realism: toward a period concept for early 19th century intellectual history. In: White HV (ed) The uses of history: essays in intellectual and social history presented to William H Bossenbrook. Wayne State University, Detroit, pp 15–58

White H (1973a) Foucault decoded: notes from underground. Hist Theory 12(1):23–54

White H (1973b) Metahistory: the historical imagination in nineteenth-century Europe. John Hopkins University Press, Baltimore/London

White H (1974/1985) Historical text as literary artefact. In: White H (ed) Tropics of discourse: essays in cultural criticism. John Hopkins University Press, Baltimore/London, pp 81–100

White H (1978/1985) Tropics of discourse: essays in cultural criticism. John Hopkins University Press, Baltimore/London

White H (1980) The value of narrativity in the representation of reality. Crit Inq 7(1):5–27

White H (1987) The content of the form: narrative discourse and historical representation. John Hopkins University Press, Baltimore/London

White H (2005a) The public relevance of historical studies: a reply to Dirk Moses. Hist Theory 44(3):333–338

White H (2005b) Introduction: historical fiction, fictional history, and historically reality. Rethink Hist 9(2–3):147–157

White H (2006) Historical discourse and literary writing. In: Korhonen K (ed) Tropes for the past: Hayden White and the history/literature debate. Rodopi, Amsterdam/New York, pp 25–33

White H (2014) The practical past. Northwestern University Press, Evanston

Wren DA, Bedeian AG (1972/2017) The evolution of management thought. Wiley, New York